D0221437

Calculus Volume 1

SENIOR CONTRIBUTING AUTHORS
EDWIN "JED" HERMAN, UNIVERSITY OF WISCONSIN-STEVENS POINT
GILBERT STRANG, MASSACHUSETTS INSTITUTE OF TECHNOLOGY

OpenStax
Rice University
6100 Main Street MS-375
Houston, Texas 77005

To learn more about OpenStax, visit https://openstax.org.
Individual print copies and bulk orders can be purchased through our website.

PRINT BOOK ISBN-10	**1-938168-02-X**
PRINT BOOK ISBN-13	**978-1-938168-02-4**
PDF VERSION ISBN-10	**1-947172-13-1**
PDF VERSION ISBN-13	**978-1-947172-13-5**
Revision Number	**C1-2016-003(03/18)-MJ**
Original Publication Year	**2016**

Printed in Indiana, USA

OpenStax

OpenStax provides free, peer-reviewed, openly licensed textbooks for introductory college and Advanced Placement® courses and low-cost, personalized courseware that helps students learn. A nonprofit ed tech initiative based at Rice University, we're committed to helping students access the tools they need to complete their courses and meet their educational goals.

Rice University

OpenStax, OpenStax CNX, and OpenStax Tutor are initiatives of Rice University. As a leading research university with a distinctive commitment to undergraduate education, Rice University aspires to path-breaking research, unsurpassed teaching, and contributions to the betterment of our world. It seeks to fulfill this mission by cultivating a diverse community of learning and discovery that produces leaders across the spectrum of human endeavor.

Foundation Support

OpenStax is grateful for the tremendous support of our sponsors. Without their strong engagement, the goal of free access to high-quality textbooks would remain just a dream.

Laura and John Arnold Foundation (LJAF) actively seeks opportunities to invest in organizations and thought leaders that have a sincere interest in implementing fundamental changes that not only yield immediate gains, but also repair broken systems for future generations. LJAF currently focuses its strategic investments on education, criminal justice, research integrity, and public accountability.

The William and Flora Hewlett Foundation has been making grants since 1967 to help solve social and environmental problems at home and around the world. The Foundation concentrates its resources on activities in education, the environment, global development and population, performing arts, and philanthropy, and makes grants to support disadvantaged communities in the San Francisco Bay Area.

Calvin K. Kazanjian was the founder and president of Peter Paul (Almond Joy), Inc. He firmly believed that the more people understood about basic economics the happier and more prosperous they would be. Accordingly, he established the Calvin K. Kazanjian Economics Foundation Inc, in 1949 as a philanthropic, nonpolitical educational organization to support efforts that enhanced economic understanding.

Guided by the belief that every life has equal value, the Bill & Melinda Gates Foundation works to help all people lead healthy, productive lives. In developing countries, it focuses on improving people's health with vaccines and other life-saving tools and giving them the chance to lift themselves out of hunger and extreme poverty. In the United States, it seeks to significantly improve education so that all young people have the opportunity to reach their full potential. Based in Seattle, Washington, the foundation is led by CEO Jeff Raikes and Co-chair William H. Gates Sr., under the direction of Bill and Melinda Gates and Warren Buffett.

The Maxfield Foundation supports projects with potential for high impact in science, education, sustainability, and other areas of social importance.

Our mission at The Michelson 20MM Foundation is to grow access and success by eliminating unnecessary hurdles to affordability. We support the creation, sharing, and proliferation of more effective, more affordable educational content by leveraging disruptive technologies, open educational resources, and new models for collaboration between for-profit, nonprofit, and public entities.

The Bill and Stephanie Sick Fund supports innovative projects in the areas of Education, Art, Science and Engineering.

Table of Contents

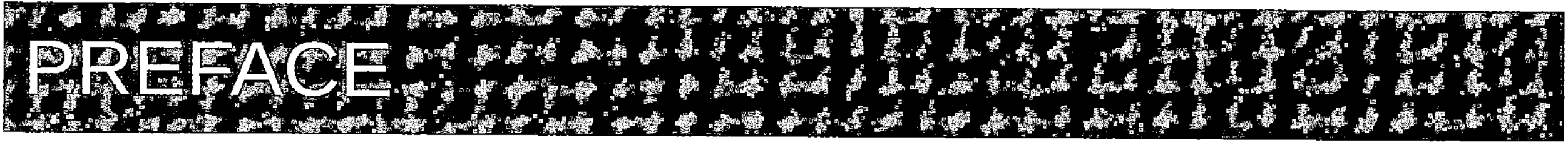

Welcome to *Calculus Volume 1*, an OpenStax resource. This textbook was written to increase student access to high-quality learning materials, maintaining highest standards of academic rigor at little to no cost.

About OpenStax

OpenStax is a nonprofit based at Rice University, and it's our mission to improve student access to education. Our first openly licensed college textbook was published in 2012, and our library has since scaled to over 25 books for college and AP® courses used by hundreds of thousands of students. OpenStax Tutor, our low-cost personalized learning tool, is being used in college courses throughout the country. Through our partnerships with philanthropic foundations and our alliance with other educational resource organizations, OpenStax is breaking down the most common barriers to learning and empowering students and instructors to succeed.

About OpenStax's resources

Customization

Calculus Volume 1 is licensed under a Creative Commons Attribution 4.0 International (CC BY) license, which means that you can distribute, remix, and build upon the content, as long as you provide attribution to OpenStax and its content contributors.

Because our books are openly licensed, you are free to use the entire book or pick and choose the sections that are most relevant to the needs of your course. Feel free to remix the content by assigning your students certain chapters and sections in your syllabus, in the order that you prefer. You can even provide a direct link in your syllabus to the sections in the web view of your book.

Instructors also have the option of creating a customized version of their OpenStax book. The custom version can be made available to students in low-cost print or digital form through their campus bookstore. Visit your book page on OpenStax.org for more information.

Errata

All OpenStax textbooks undergo a rigorous review process. However, like any professional-grade textbook, errors sometimes occur. Since our books are web based, we can make updates periodically when deemed pedagogically necessary. If you have a correction to suggest, submit it through the link on your book page on OpenStax.org. Subject matter experts review all errata suggestions. OpenStax is committed to remaining transparent about all updates, so you will also find a list of past errata changes on your book page on OpenStax.org.

Format

You can access this textbook for free in web view or PDF through OpenStax.org, and for a low cost in print.

About *Calculus Volume 1*

Calculus is designed for the typical two- or three-semester general calculus course, incorporating innovative features to enhance student learning. The book guides students through the core concepts of calculus and helps them understand how those concepts apply to their lives and the world around them. Due to the comprehensive nature of the material, we are offering the book in three volumes for flexibility and efficiency. Volume 1 covers functions, limits, derivatives, and integration.

Coverage and scope

Our *Calculus Volume 1* textbook adheres to the scope and sequence of most general calculus courses nationwide. We have worked to make calculus interesting and accessible to students while maintaining the mathematical rigor inherent in the subject. With this objective in mind, the content of the three volumes of *Calculus* have been developed and arranged to provide a logical progression from fundamental to more advanced concepts, building upon what students have already learned and emphasizing connections between topics and between theory and applications. The goal of each section is to enable students not just to recognize concepts, but work with them in ways that will be useful in later courses and future careers. The organization and pedagogical features were developed and vetted with feedback from mathematics educators dedicated to the project.

Volume 1

Chapter 1: Functions and Graphs

Chapter 2: Limits

Chapter 3: Derivatives

Chapter 4: Applications of Derivatives

Chapter 5: Integration

Chapter 6: Applications of Integration

Volume 2

Chapter 1: Integration

Chapter 2: Applications of Integration

Chapter 3: Techniques of Integration

Chapter 4: Introduction to Differential Equations

Chapter 5: Sequences and Series

Chapter 6: Power Series

Chapter 7: Parametric Equations and Polar Coordinates

Volume 3

Chapter 1: Parametric Equations and Polar Coordinates

Chapter 2: Vectors in Space

Chapter 3: Vector-Valued Functions

Chapter 4: Differentiation of Functions of Several Variables

Chapter 5: Multiple Integration

Chapter 6: Vector Calculus

Chapter 7: Second-Order Differential Equations

Pedagogical foundation

Throughout *Calculus Volume 1* you will find examples and exercises that present classical ideas and techniques as well as modern applications and methods. Derivations and explanations are based on years of classroom experience on the part of long-time calculus professors, striving for a balance of clarity and rigor that has proven successful with their students. Motivational applications cover important topics in probability, biology, ecology, business, and economics, as well as areas of physics, chemistry, engineering, and computer science. **Student Projects** in each chapter give students opportunities to explore interesting sidelights in pure and applied mathematics, from determining a safe distance between the grandstand and the track at a Formula One racetrack, to calculating the center of mass of the Grand Canyon Skywalk or the terminal speed of a skydiver. **Chapter Opening Applications** pose problems that are solved later in the chapter, using the ideas covered in that chapter. Problems include the hydraulic force against the Hoover Dam, and the comparison of relative intensity of two earthquakes. **Definitions, Rules,** and **Theorems** are highlighted throughout the text, including over 60 **Proofs** of theorems.

Assessments that reinforce key concepts

In-chapter **Examples** walk students through problems by posing a question, stepping out a solution, and then asking students to practice the skill with a "Checkpoint" question. The book also includes assessments at the end of each chapter so students can apply what they've learned through practice problems. Many exercises are marked with a **[T]** to indicate they are suitable for solution by technology, including calculators or Computer Algebra Systems (CAS). Answers for selected exercises are available in the **Answer Key** at the back of the book. The book also includes assessments at the end of each chapter so students can apply what they've learned through practice problems.

Early or late transcendentals

Calculus Volume 1 is designed to accommodate both Early and Late Transcendental approaches to calculus. Exponential and logarithmic functions are introduced informally in Chapter 1 and presented in more rigorous terms in Chapter 6. Differentiation and integration of these functions is covered in Chapters 3–5 for instructors who want to include them with other types of functions. These discussions, however, are in separate sections that can be skipped for instructors who prefer to wait until the integral definitions are given before teaching the calculus derivations of exponentials and logarithms.

Comprehensive art program

Our art program is designed to enhance students' understanding of concepts through clear and effective illustrations, diagrams, and photographs.

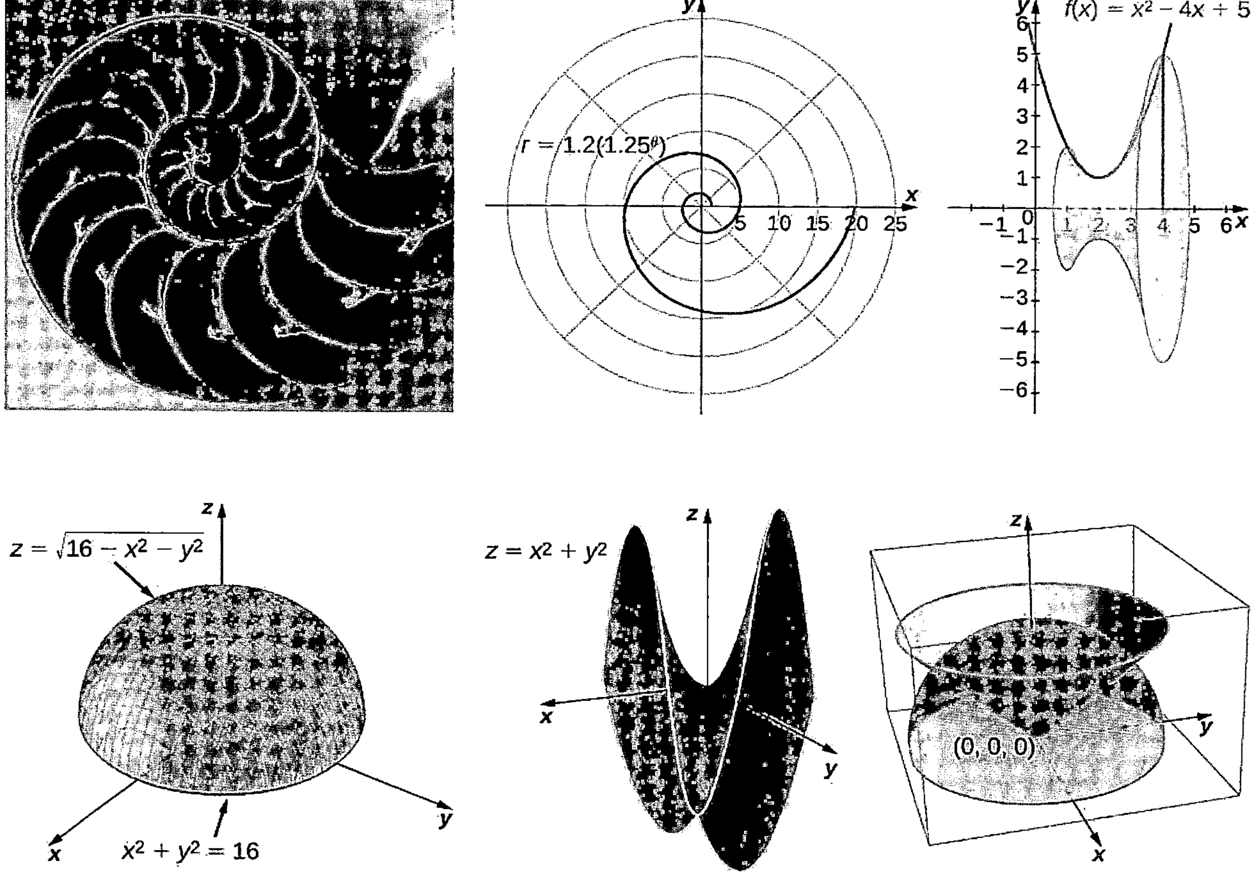

Additional resources

Student and instructor resources

We've compiled additional resources for both students and instructors, including Getting Started Guides, an instructor solution manual, and PowerPoint slides. Instructor resources require a verified instructor account, which can be requested on your OpenStax.org log-in. Take advantage of these resources to supplement your OpenStax book.

Community Hubs

OpenStax partners with the Institute for the Study of Knowledge Management in Education (ISKME) to offer Community Hubs on OER Commons – a platform for instructors to share community-created resources that support OpenStax books, free of charge. Through our Community Hubs, instructors can upload their own materials or download resources to use in their own courses, including additional ancillaries, teaching material, multimedia, and relevant course content. We encourage instructors to join the hubs for the subjects most relevant to your teaching and research as an opportunity both to enrich your courses and to engage with other faculty.

?To reach the Community Hubs, visit **www.oercommons.org/hubs/OpenStax**.

Partner resources

OpenStax Partners are our allies in the mission to make high-quality learning materials affordable and accessible to students and instructors everywhere. Their tools integrate seamlessly with our OpenStax titles at a low cost. To access the partner resources for your text, visit your book page on OpenStax.org.

About the authors

Senior contributing authors

Gilbert Strang, Massachusetts Institute of Technology

Dr. Strang received his PhD from UCLA in 1959 and has been teaching mathematics at MIT ever since. His Calculus online textbook is one of eleven that he has published and is the basis from which our final product has been derived and updated for today's student. Strang is a decorated mathematician and past Rhodes Scholar at Oxford University.

Edwin "Jed" Herman, University of Wisconsin-Stevens Point
Dr. Herman earned a BS in Mathematics from Harvey Mudd College in 1985, an MA in Mathematics from UCLA in 1987, and a PhD in Mathematics from the University of Oregon in 1997. He is currently a Professor at the University of Wisconsin-Stevens Point. He has more than 20 years of experience teaching college mathematics, is a student research mentor, is experienced in course development/design, and is also an avid board game designer and player.

Contributing authors

Catherine Abbott, Keuka College
Nicoleta Virginia Bila, Fayetteville State University
Sheri J. Boyd, Rollins College
Joyati Debnath, Winona State University
Valeree Falduto, Palm Beach State College
Joseph Lakey, New Mexico State University
Julie Levandosky, Framingham State University
David McCune, William Jewell College
Michelle Merriweather, Bronxville High School
Kirsten R. Messer, Colorado State University - Pueblo
Alfred K. Mulzet, Florida State College at Jacksonville
William Radulovich (retired), Florida State College at Jacksonville
Erica M. Rutter, Arizona State University
David Smith, University of the Virgin Islands
Elaine A. Terry, Saint Joseph's University
David Torain, Hampton University

Reviewers

Marwan A. Abu-Sawwa, Florida State College at Jacksonville
Kenneth J. Bernard, Virginia State University
John Beyers, University of Maryland
Charles Buehrle, Franklin & Marshall College
Matthew Cathey, Wofford College
Michael Cohen, Hofstra University
William DeSalazar, Broward County School System
Murray Eisenberg, University of Massachusetts Amherst
Kristyanna Erickson, Cecil College
Tiernan Fogarty, Oregon Institute of Technology
David French, Tidewater Community College
Marilyn Gloyer, Virginia Commonwealth University
Shawna Haider, Salt Lake Community College
Lance Hemlow, Raritan Valley Community College
Jerry Jared, The Blue Ridge School
Peter Jipsen, Chapman University
David Johnson, Lehigh University
M.R. Khadivi, Jackson State University
Robert J. Krueger, Concordia University
Tor A. Kwembe, Jackson State University
Jean-Marie Magnier, Springfield Technical Community College
Cheryl Chute Miller, SUNY Potsdam
Bagisa Mukherjee, Penn State University, Worthington Scranton Campus
Kasso Okoudjou, University of Maryland College Park
Peter Olszewski, Penn State Erie, The Behrend College
Steven Purtee, Valencia College
Alice Ramos, Bethel College
Doug Shaw, University of Northern Iowa
Hussain Elalaoui-Talibi, Tuskegee University
Jeffrey Taub, Maine Maritime Academy
William Thistleton, SUNY Polytechnic Institute

A. David Trubatch, Montclair State University
Carmen Wright, Jackson State University
Zhenbu Zhang, Jackson State University

1 | FUNCTIONS AND GRAPHS

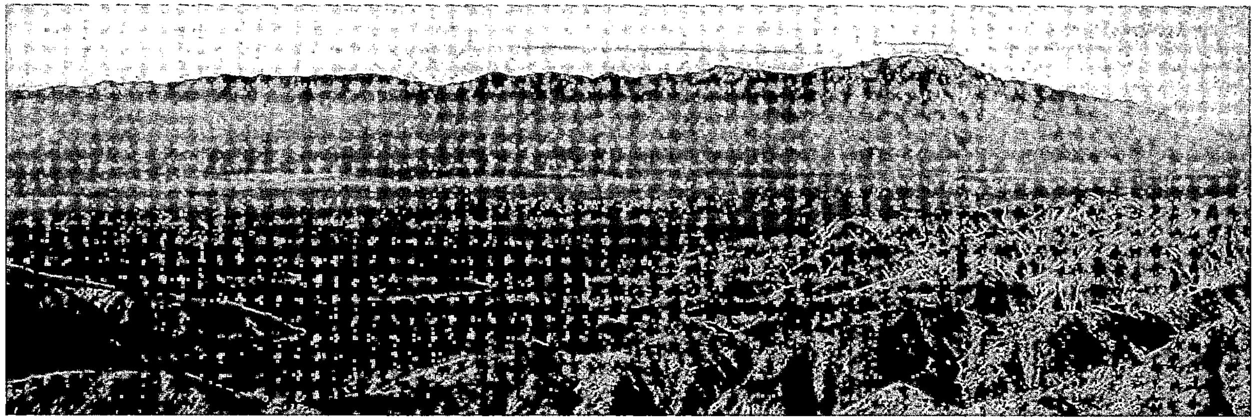

Figure 1.1 A portion of the San Andreas Fault in California. Major faults like this are the sites of most of the strongest earthquakes ever recorded. (credit: modification of work by Robb Hannawacker, NPS)

Chapter Outline

Introduction

In the past few years, major earthquakes have occurred in several countries around the world. In January 2010, an earthquake of magnitude 7.3 hit Haiti. A magnitude 9 earthquake shook northeastern Japan in March 2011. In April 2014, an 8.2-magnitude earthquake struck off the coast of northern Chile. What do these numbers mean? In particular, how does a magnitude 9 earthquake compare with an earthquake of magnitude 8.2? Or 7.3? Later in this chapter, we show how logarithmic functions are used to compare the relative intensity of two earthquakes based on the magnitude of each earthquake (see **Example 1.39**).

Calculus is the mathematics that describes changes in functions. In this chapter, we review all the functions necessary to study calculus. We define polynomial, rational, trigonometric, exponential, and logarithmic functions. We review how to evaluate these functions, and we show the properties of their graphs. We provide examples of equations with terms involving these functions and illustrate the algebraic techniques necessary to solve them. In short, this chapter provides the foundation for the material to come. It is essential to be familiar and comfortable with these ideas before proceeding to the formal introduction of calculus in the next chapter.

1.1 | Review of Functions

Learning Objectives

1.1.1 Use functional notation to evaluate a function.
1.1.2 Determine the domain and range of a function.
1.1.3 Draw the graph of a function.
1.1.4 Find the zeros of a function.
1.1.5 Recognize a function from a table of values.
1.1.6 Make new functions from two or more given functions.
1.1.7 Describe the symmetry properties of a function.

In this section, we provide a formal definition of a function and examine several ways in which functions are represented—namely, through tables, formulas, and graphs. We study formal notation and terms related to functions. We also define composition of functions and symmetry properties. Most of this material will be a review for you, but it serves as a handy reference to remind you of some of the algebraic techniques useful for working with functions.

Functions

Given two sets A and $B,$ a set with elements that are ordered pairs $(x, y),$ where x is an element of A and y is an element of $B,$ is a relation from A to $B.$ A relation from A to B defines a relationship between those two sets. A function is a special type of relation in which each element of the first set is related to exactly one element of the second set. The element of the first set is called the *input*; the element of the second set is called the *output*. Functions are used all the time in mathematics to describe relationships between two sets. For any function, when we know the input, the output is determined, so we say that the output is a function of the input. For example, the area of a square is determined by its side length, so we say that the area (the output) is a function of its side length (the input). The velocity of a ball thrown in the air can be described as a function of the amount of time the ball is in the air. The cost of mailing a package is a function of the weight of the package. Since functions have so many uses, it is important to have precise definitions and terminology to study them.

Definition

A **function** f consists of a set of inputs, a set of outputs, and a rule for assigning each input to exactly one output. The set of inputs is called the **domain** of the function. The set of outputs is called the **range** of the function.

For example, consider the function $f,$ where the domain is the set of all real numbers and the rule is to square the input. Then, the input $x=3$ is assigned to the output $3^2=9.$ Since every nonnegative real number has a real-value square root, every nonnegative number is an element of the range of this function. Since there is no real number with a square that is negative, the negative real numbers are not elements of the range. We conclude that the range is the set of nonnegative real numbers.

For a general function f with domain $D,$ we often use x to denote the input and y to denote the output associated with $x.$ When doing so, we refer to x as the **independent variable** and y as the **dependent variable**, because it depends on $x.$ Using function notation, we write $y=f(x),$ and we read this equation as "y equals f of $x.$" For the squaring function described earlier, we write $f(x)=x^2.$

The concept of a function can be visualized using **Figure 1.2**, **Figure 1.3**, and **Figure 1.4**.

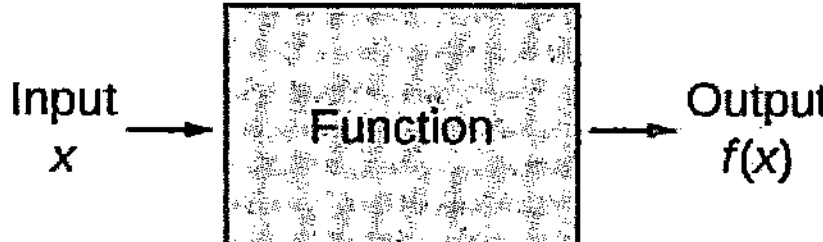

Figure 1.2 A function can be visualized as an input/output device.

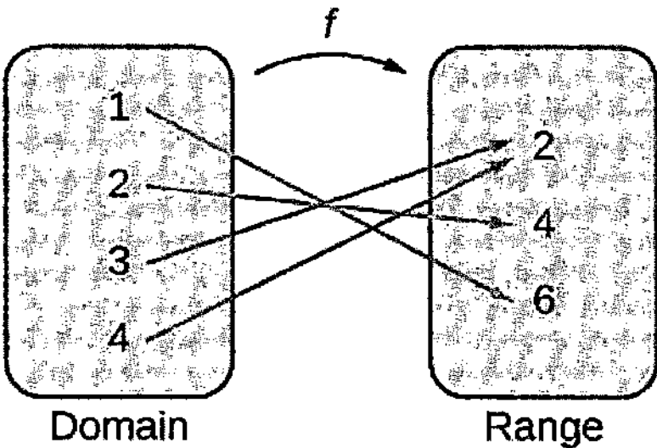

Figure 1.3 A function maps every element in the domain to exactly one element in the range. Although each input can be sent to only one output, two different inputs can be sent to the same output.

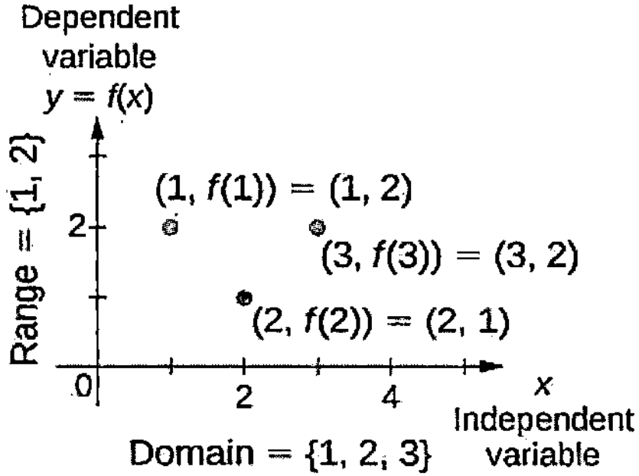

Figure 1.4 In this case, a graph of a function f has a domain of $\{1, 2, 3\}$ and a range of $\{1, 2\}$. The independent variable is x and the dependent variable is y.

Visit this **applet link (http://www.openstaxcollege.org/l/grapherrors)** to see more about graphs of functions.

We can also visualize a function by plotting points (x, y) in the coordinate plane where $y = f(x)$. The **graph of a function** is the set of all these points. For example, consider the function f, where the domain is the set $D = \{1, 2, 3\}$ and the rule is $f(x) = 3 - x$. In **Figure 1.5**, we plot a graph of this function.

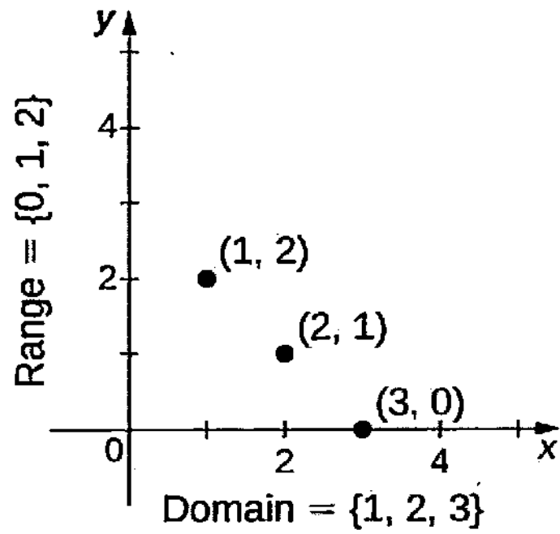

Figure 1.5 Here we see a graph of the function f with domain $\{1, 2, 3\}$ and rule $f(x) = 3 - x$. The graph consists of the points $(x, f(x))$ for all x in the domain.

Every function has a domain. However, sometimes a function is described by an equation, as in $f(x) = x^2$, with no specific domain given. In this case, the domain is taken to be the set of all real numbers x for which $f(x)$ is a real number. For example, since any real number can be squared, if no other domain is specified, we consider the domain of $f(x) = x^2$ to be the set of all real numbers. On the other hand, the square root function $f(x) = \sqrt{x}$ only gives a real output if x is nonnegative. Therefore, the domain of the function $f(x) = \sqrt{x}$ is the set of nonnegative real numbers, sometimes called the *natural domain.*

For the functions $f(x) = x^2$ and $f(x) = \sqrt{x}$, the domains are sets with an infinite number of elements. Clearly we cannot list all these elements. When describing a set with an infinite number of elements, it is often helpful to use set-builder or interval notation. When using set-builder notation to describe a subset of all real numbers, denoted $\mathbb{R}$, we write

$$\{x|x \text{ has some property}\}.$$

We read this as the set of real numbers x such that x has some property. For example, if we were interested in the set of real numbers that are greater than one but less than five, we could denote this set using set-builder notation by writing

$$\{x|1 < x < 5\}.$$

A set such as this, which contains all numbers greater than a and less than b, can also be denoted using the interval notation (a, b). Therefore,

$$(1, 5) = \{x|1 < x < 5\}.$$

The numbers 1 and 5 are called the *endpoints* of this set. If we want to consider the set that includes the endpoints, we would denote this set by writing

$$[1, 5] = \{x|1 \le x \le 5\}.$$

We can use similar notation if we want to include one of the endpoints, but not the other. To denote the set of nonnegative real numbers, we would use the set-builder notation

$$\{x|0 \le x\}.$$

The smallest number in this set is zero, but this set does not have a largest number. Using interval notation, we would use the symbol ∞, which refers to positive infinity, and we would write the set as

$$[0, \infty) = \{x|0 \le x\}.$$

It is important to note that ∞ is not a real number. It is used symbolically here to indicate that this set includes all real numbers greater than or equal to zero. Similarly, if we wanted to describe the set of all nonpositive numbers, we could write

$$(-\infty, 0] = \{x|x \le 0\}.$$

Here, the notation $-\infty$ refers to negative infinity, and it indicates that we are including all numbers less than or equal to zero, no matter how small. The set

$$(-\infty,\ \infty) = \{x|x \text{ is any real number}\}$$

refers to the set of all real numbers.

Some functions are defined using different equations for different parts of their domain. These types of functions are known as *piecewise-defined functions*. For example, suppose we want to define a function f with a domain that is the set of all real numbers such that $f(x) = 3x + 1$ for $x \geq 2$ and $f(x) = x^2$ for $x < 2$. We denote this function by writing

$$f(x) = \begin{cases} 3x + 1 & x \geq 2 \\ x^2 & x < 2 \end{cases}.$$

When evaluating this function for an input x, the equation to use depends on whether $x \geq 2$ or $x < 2$. For example, since $5 > 2$, we use the fact that $f(x) = 3x + 1$ for $x \geq 2$ and see that $f(5) = 3(5) + 1 = 16$. On the other hand, for $x = -1$, we use the fact that $f(x) = x^2$ for $x < 2$ and see that $f(-1) = 1$.

Example 1.1

Evaluating Functions

For the function $f(x) = 3x^2 + 2x - 1$, evaluate

a. $f(-2)$

b. $f(\sqrt{2})$

c. $f(a + h)$

Solution

Substitute the given value for *x* in the formula for $f(x)$.

a. $f(-2) = 3(-2)^2 + 2(-2) - 1 = 12 - 4 - 1 = 7$

b. $f(\sqrt{2}) = 3(\sqrt{2})^2 + 2\sqrt{2} - 1 = 6 + 2\sqrt{2} - 1 = 5 + 2\sqrt{2}$

c. $$\begin{aligned} f(a + h) = 3(a + h)^2 + 2(a + h) - 1 &= 3\left(a^2 + 2ah + h^2\right) + 2a + 2h - 1 \\ &= 3a^2 + 6ah + 3h^2 + 2a + 2h - 1 \end{aligned}$$

1.1 For $f(x) = x^2 - 3x + 5$, evaluate $f(1)$ and $f(a + h)$.

Example 1.2

Finding Domain and Range

For each of the following functions, determine the i. domain and ii. range.

a. $f(x) = (x - 4)^2 + 5$

b. $f(x) = \sqrt{3x + 2} - 1$

c. $f(x) = \dfrac{3}{x - 2}$

Solution

a. Consider $f(x) = (x - 4)^2 + 5$.

   i. Since $f(x) = (x - 4)^2 + 5$ is a real number for any real number x, the domain of f is the interval $(-\infty, \infty)$.

   ii. Since $(x - 4)^2 \geq 0$, we know $f(x) = (x - 4)^2 + 5 \geq 5$. Therefore, the range must be a subset of $\{y|y \geq 5\}$. To show that every element in this set is in the range, we need to show that for a given y in that set, there is a real number x such that $f(x) = (x - 4)^2 + 5 = y$. Solving this equation for x, we see that we need x such that

$$(x - 4)^2 = y - 5.$$

   This equation is satisfied as long as there exists a real number x such that

$$x - 4 = \pm\sqrt{y - 5}.$$

   Since $y \geq 5$, the square root is well-defined. We conclude that for $x = 4 \pm \sqrt{y - 5}$, $f(x) = y$, and therefore the range is $\{y|y \geq 5\}$.

b. Consider $f(x) = \sqrt{3x + 2} - 1$.

   i. To find the domain of f, we need the expression $3x + 2 \geq 0$. Solving this inequality, we conclude that the domain is $\{x|x \geq -2/3\}$.

   ii. To find the range of f, we note that since $\sqrt{3x + 2} \geq 0$, $f(x) = \sqrt{3x + 2} - 1 \geq -1$. Therefore, the range of f must be a subset of the set $\{y|y \geq -1\}$. To show that every element in this set is in the range of f, we need to show that for all y in this set, there exists a real number x in the domain such that $f(x) = y$. Let $y \geq -1$. Then, $f(x) = y$ if and only if

$$\sqrt{3x + 2} - 1 = y.$$

   Solving this equation for x, we see that x must solve the equation

$$\sqrt{3x + 2} = y + 1.$$

   Since $y \geq -1$, such an x could exist. Squaring both sides of this equation, we have $3x + 2 = (y + 1)^2$.
   Therefore, we need

$$3x = (y + 1)^2 - 2,$$

which implies

$$x = \frac{1}{3}(y+1)^2 - \frac{2}{3}.$$

We just need to verify that x is in the domain of f. Since the domain of f consists of all real numbers greater than or equal to $-2/3$, and

$$\frac{1}{3}(y+1)^2 - \frac{2}{3} \geq -\frac{2}{3},$$

there does exist an x in the domain of f. We conclude that the range of f is $\{y|y \geq -1\}$.

c. Consider $f(x) = 3/(x-2)$.

i. Since $3/(x-2)$ is defined when the denominator is nonzero, the domain is $\{x|x \neq 2\}$.

ii. To find the range of f, we need to find the values of y such that there exists a real number x in the domain with the property that

$$\frac{3}{x-2} = y.$$

Solving this equation for x, we find that

$$x = \frac{3}{y} + 2.$$

Therefore, as long as $y \neq 0$, there exists a real number x in the domain such that $f(x) = y$. Thus, the range is $\{y|y \neq 0\}$.

1.2 Find the domain and range for $f(x) = \sqrt{4-2x} + 5$.

Representing Functions

Typically, a function is represented using one or more of the following tools:

- A table
- A graph
- A formula

We can identify a function in each form, but we can also use them together. For instance, we can plot on a graph the values from a table or create a table from a formula.

Tables

Functions described using a **table of values** arise frequently in real-world applications. Consider the following simple example. We can describe temperature on a given day as a function of time of day. Suppose we record the temperature every hour for a 24-hour period starting at midnight. We let our input variable x be the time after midnight, measured in hours, and the output variable y be the temperature x hours after midnight, measured in degrees Fahrenheit. We record our data in **Table 1.1**.

Hours after Midnight	Temperature $(°F)$	Hours after Midnight	Temperature $(°F)$
0	58	12	84
1	54	13	85
2	53	14	85
3	52	15	83
4	52	16	82
5	55	17	80
6	60	18	77
7	64	19	74
8	72	20	69
9	75	21	65
10	78	22	60
11	80	23	58

Table 1.1 Temperature as a Function of Time of Day

We can see from the table that temperature is a function of time, and the temperature decreases, then increases, and then decreases again. However, we cannot get a clear picture of the behavior of the function without graphing it.

Graphs

Given a function f described by a table, we can provide a visual picture of the function in the form of a graph. Graphing the temperatures listed in **Table 1.1** can give us a better idea of their fluctuation throughout the day. **Figure 1.6** shows the plot of the temperature function.

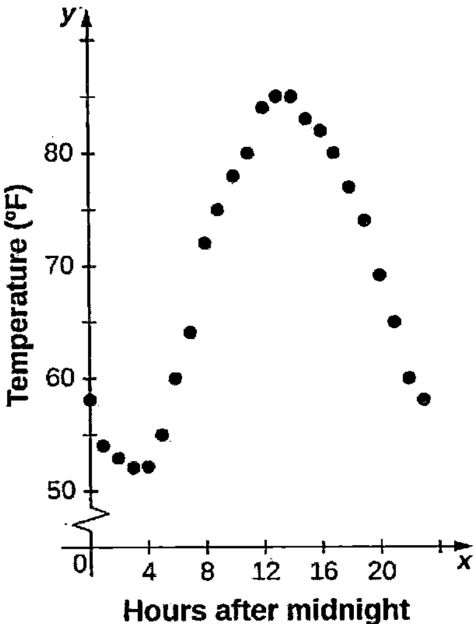

Figure 1.6 The graph of the data from **Table 1.1** shows temperature as a function of time.

From the points plotted on the graph in **Figure 1.6**, we can visualize the general shape of the graph. It is often useful to connect the dots in the graph, which represent the data from the table. In this example, although we cannot make any definitive conclusion regarding what the temperature was at any time for which the temperature was not recorded, given the number of data points collected and the pattern in these points, it is reasonable to suspect that the temperatures at other times followed a similar pattern, as we can see in **Figure 1.7**.

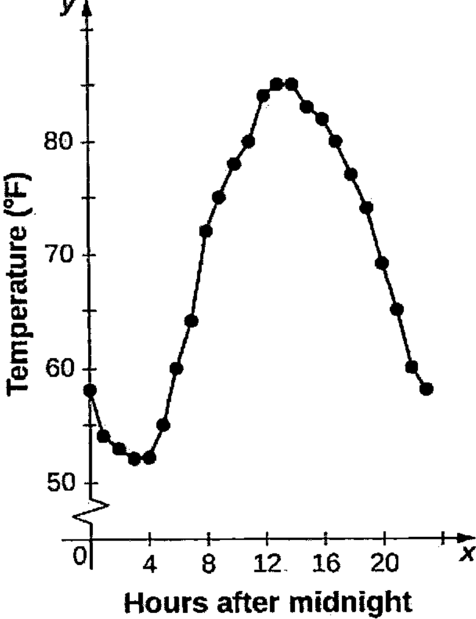

Figure 1.7 Connecting the dots in **Figure 1.6** shows the general pattern of the data.

Algebraic Formulas

Sometimes we are not given the values of a function in table form, rather we are given the values in an explicit formula. Formulas arise in many applications. For example, the area of a circle of radius r is given by the formula $A(r) = \pi r^2$. When an object is thrown upward from the ground with an initial velocity v_0 ft/s, its height above the ground from the time it is thrown until it hits the ground is given by the formula $s(t) = -16t^2 + v_0 t$. When P dollars are invested in an account at an annual interest rate r compounded continuously, the amount of money after t years is given by the formula $A(t) = Pe^{rt}$. Algebraic formulas are important tools to calculate function values. Often we also represent these functions visually in graph form.

Given an algebraic formula for a function f, the graph of f is the set of points $(x, f(x))$, where x is in the domain of f and $f(x)$ is in the range. To graph a function given by a formula, it is helpful to begin by using the formula to create a table of inputs and outputs. If the domain of f consists of an infinite number of values, we cannot list all of them, but because listing some of the inputs and outputs can be very useful, it is often a good way to begin.

When creating a table of inputs and outputs, we typically check to determine whether zero is an output. Those values of x where $f(x) = 0$ are called the **zeros of a function**. For example, the zeros of $f(x) = x^2 - 4$ are $x = \pm 2$. The zeros determine where the graph of f intersects the x-axis, which gives us more information about the shape of the graph of the function. The graph of a function may never intersect the x-axis, or it may intersect multiple (or even infinitely many) times.

Another point of interest is the y-intercept, if it exists. The y-intercept is given by $(0, f(0))$.

Since a function has exactly one output for each input, the graph of a function can have, at most, one y-intercept. If $x = 0$ is in the domain of a function f, then f has exactly one y-intercept. If $x = 0$ is not in the domain of f, then f has no y-intercept. Similarly, for any real number c, if c is in the domain of f, there is exactly one output $f(c)$, and the line $x = c$ intersects the graph of f exactly once. On the other hand, if c is not in the domain of f, $f(c)$ is not defined and the line $x = c$ does not intersect the graph of f. This property is summarized in the **vertical line test**.

Rule: Vertical Line Test

Given a function f, every vertical line that may be drawn intersects the graph of f no more than once. If any vertical line intersects a set of points more than once, the set of points does not represent a function.

We can use this test to determine whether a set of plotted points represents the graph of a function (**Figure 1.8**).

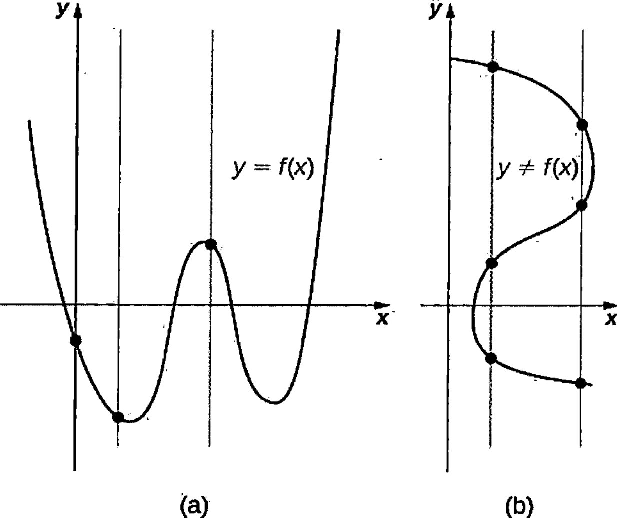

Figure 1.8 (a) The set of plotted points represents the graph of a function because every vertical line intersects the set of points, at most, once. (b) The set of plotted points does not represent the graph of a function because some vertical lines intersect the set of points more than once.

Example 1.3

Finding Zeros and y-Intercepts of a Function

Consider the function $f(x) = -4x + 2$.

a. Find all zeros of f.

b. Find the y-intercept (if any).

c. Sketch a graph of f.

Solution

a. To find the zeros, solve $f(x) = -4x + 2 = 0$. We discover that f has one zero at $x = 1/2$.

b. The y-intercept is given by $(0, f(0)) = (0, 2)$.

c. Given that f is a linear function of the form $f(x) = mx + b$ that passes through the points $(1/2, 0)$ and $(0, 2)$, we can sketch the graph of f (**Figure 1.9**).

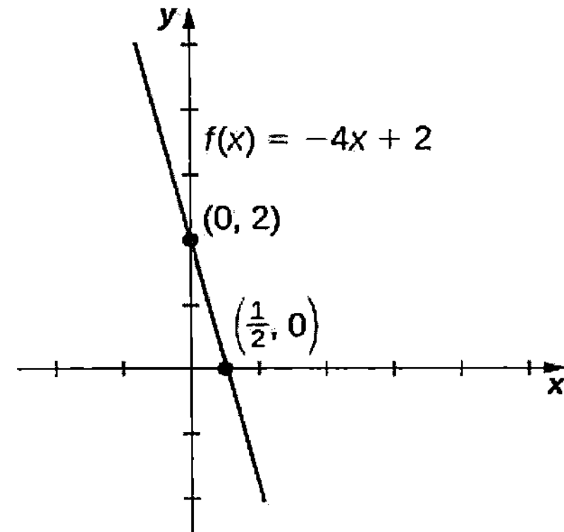

Figure 1.9 The function $f(x) = -4x + 2$ is a line with x-intercept $(1/2, 0)$ and y-intercept $(0, 2)$.

Example 1.4

Using Zeros and y-Intercepts to Sketch a Graph

Consider the function $f(x) = \sqrt{x+3} + 1$.

a. Find all zeros of f.

b. Find the y-intercept (if any).

c. Sketch a graph of f.

Solution

a. To find the zeros, solve $\sqrt{x+3} + 1 = 0$. This equation implies $\sqrt{x+3} = -1$. Since $\sqrt{x+3} \geq 0$ for all

x, this equation has no solutions, and therefore f has no zeros.

b. The y-intercept is given by $(0, f(0)) = (0, \sqrt{3} + 1)$.

c. To graph this function, we make a table of values. Since we need $x + 3 \geq 0$, we need to choose values of $x \geq -3$. We choose values that make the square-root function easy to evaluate.

x	-3	-2	1
$f(x)$	1	2	3

Table 1.2

Making use of the table and knowing that, since the function is a square root, the graph of f should be similar to the graph of $y = \sqrt{x}$, we sketch the graph (**Figure 1.10**).

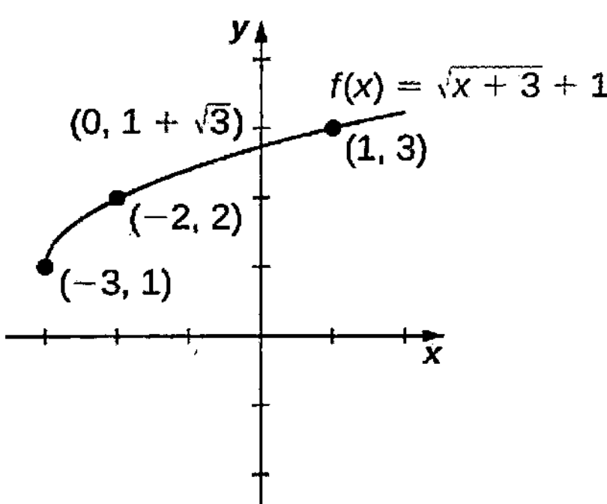

Figure 1.10 The graph of $f(x) = \sqrt{x + 3} + 1$ has a y-intercept but no x-intercepts.

1.3 Find the zeros of $f(x) = x^3 - 5x^2 + 6x$.

Example 1.5

Finding the Height of a Free-Falling Object

If a ball is dropped from a height of 100 ft, its height s at time t is given by the function $s(t) = -16t^2 + 100$, where s is measured in feet and t is measured in seconds. The domain is restricted to the interval $[0, c]$, where $t = 0$ is the time when the ball is dropped and $t = c$ is the time when the ball hits the ground.

a. Create a table showing the height $s(t)$ when $t = 0,\ 0.5,\ 1,\ 1.5,\ 2$, and 2.5. Using the data from the table, determine the domain for this function. That is, find the time c when the ball hits the ground.

b. Sketch a graph of s.

Solution

a.

t	0	0.5	1	1.5	2	2.5
$s(t)$	100	96	84	64	36	0

Table 1.3
Height s as a Function of Time t

Since the ball hits the ground when $t = 2.5$, the domain of this function is the interval $[0, 2.5]$.

b.

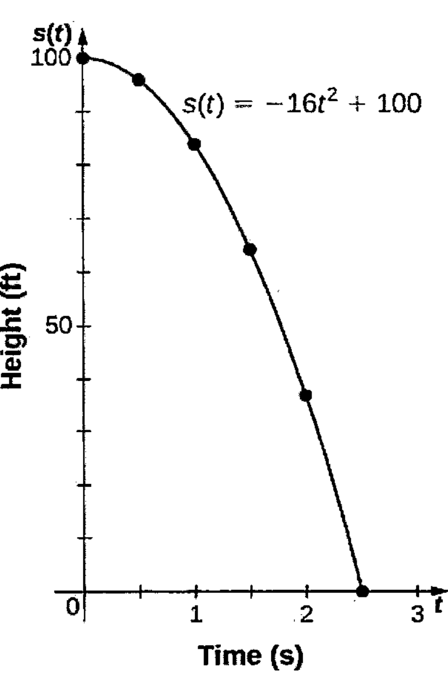

Note that for this function and the function $f(x) = -4x + 2$ graphed in **Figure 1.9**, the values of $f(x)$ are getting smaller as x is getting larger. A function with this property is said to be decreasing. On the other hand, for the function $f(x) = \sqrt{x + 3} + 1$ graphed in **Figure 1.10**, the values of $f(x)$ are getting larger as the values of x are getting larger. A function with this property is said to be increasing. It is important to note, however, that a function can be increasing on some interval or intervals and decreasing over a different interval or intervals. For example, using our temperature function in **Figure 1.6**, we can see that the function is decreasing on the interval $(0, 4)$, increasing on the interval $(4, 14)$, and then decreasing on the interval $(14, 23)$. We make the idea of a function increasing or decreasing over a particular interval more precise in the next definition.

Definition

We say that a function f is **increasing on the interval I** if for all $x_1, x_2 \in I$,

$$f(x_1) \le f(x_2) \text{ when } x_1 < x_2.$$

We say f is strictly increasing on the interval I if for all $x_1, x_2 \in I$,

$$f(x_1) < f(x_2) \text{ when } x_1 < x_2.$$

We say that a function f is **decreasing on the interval I** if for all $x_1, x_2 \in I,$

$$f(x_1) \geq f(x_2) \text{ if } x_1 < x_2.$$

We say that a function f is strictly decreasing on the interval I if for all $x_1, x_2 \in I,$

$$f(x_1) > f(x_2) \text{ if } x_1 < x_2.$$

For example, the function $f(x) = 3x$ is increasing on the interval $(-\infty, \infty)$ because $3x_1 < 3x_2$ whenever $x_1 < x_2$. On the other hand, the function $f(x) = -x^3$ is decreasing on the interval $(-\infty, \infty)$ because $-x_1^3 > -x_2^3$ whenever $x_1 < x_2$ (**Figure 1.11**).

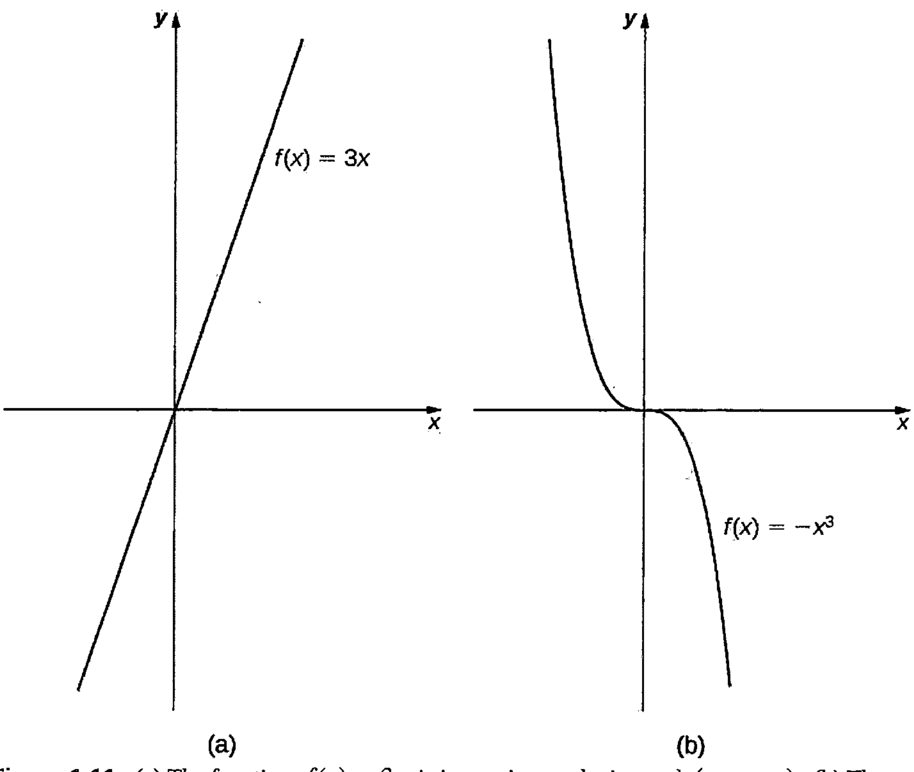

Figure 1.11 (a) The function $f(x) = 3x$ is increasing on the interval $(-\infty, \infty)$. (b) The function $f(x) = -x^3$ is decreasing on the interval $(-\infty, \infty)$.

Combining Functions

Now that we have reviewed the basic characteristics of functions, we can see what happens to these properties when we combine functions in different ways, using basic mathematical operations to create new functions. For example, if the cost for a company to manufacture x items is described by the function $C(x)$ and the revenue created by the sale of x items is described by the function $R(x)$, then the profit on the manufacture and sale of x items is defined as $P(x) = R(x) - C(x)$. Using the difference between two functions, we created a new function.

Alternatively, we can create a new function by composing two functions. For example, given the functions $f(x) = x^2$ and $g(x) = 3x + 1$, the composite function $f \circ g$ is defined such that

$$(f \circ g)(x) = f(g(x)) = (g(x))^2 = (3x + 1)^2.$$

The composite function $g \circ f$ is defined such that

$$(g \circ f)(x) = g(f(x)) = 3f(x) + 1 = 3x^2 + 1.$$

Note that these two new functions are different from each other.

Combining Functions with Mathematical Operators

To combine functions using mathematical operators, we simply write the functions with the operator and simplify. Given two functions f and g, we can define four new functions:

$$(f + g)(x) = f(x) + g(x) \qquad \textit{Sum}$$
$$(f - g)(x) = f(x) - g(x) \qquad \textit{Difference}$$
$$(f \cdot g)(x) = f(x)g(x) \qquad \textit{Product}$$
$$\left(\frac{f}{g}\right)(x) = \frac{f(x)}{g(x)} \text{ for } g(x) \neq 0 \qquad \textit{Quotient}$$

Example 1.6

Combining Functions Using Mathematical Operations

Given the functions $f(x) = 2x - 3$ and $g(x) = x^2 - 1$, find each of the following functions and state its domain.

a. $(f + g)(x)$

b. $(f - g)(x)$

c. $(f \cdot g)(x)$

d. $\left(\frac{f}{g}\right)(x)$

Solution

a. $(f + g)(x) = (2x - 3) + (x^2 - 1) = x^2 + 2x - 4$. The domain of this function is the interval $(-\infty, \infty)$.

b. $(f - g)(x) = (2x - 3) - (x^2 - 1) = -x^2 + 2x - 2$. The domain of this function is the interval $(-\infty, \infty)$.

c. $(f \cdot g)(x) = (2x - 3)(x^2 - 1) = 2x^3 - 3x^2 - 2x + 3$. The domain of this function is the interval $(-\infty, \infty)$.

d. $\left(\frac{f}{g}\right)(x) = \frac{2x - 3}{x^2 - 1}$. The domain of this function is $\{x | x \neq \pm 1\}$.

1.4 For $f(x) = x^2 + 3$ and $g(x) = 2x - 5$, find $(f/g)(x)$ and state its domain.

Function Composition

When we compose functions, we take a function of a function. For example, suppose the temperature T on a given day is described as a function of time t (measured in hours after midnight) as in **Table 1.1**. Suppose the cost C, to heat or cool a building for 1 hour, can be described as a function of the temperature T. Combining these two functions, we can describe the cost of heating or cooling a building as a function of time by evaluating $C(T(t))$. We have defined a new function, denoted $C \circ T$, which is defined such that $(C \circ T)(t) = C(T(t))$ for all t in the domain of T. This new function is called a composite function. We note that since cost is a function of temperature and temperature is a function of time, it makes sense to define this new function $(C \circ T)(t)$. It does not make sense to consider $(T \circ C)(t)$, because temperature is not a function of cost.

Definition

Consider the function f with domain A and range B, and the function g with domain D and range E. If B is a subset of D, then the **composite function** $(g \circ f)(x)$ is the function with domain A such that

$$(g \circ f)(x) = g(f(x)). \tag{1.1}$$

A composite function $g \circ f$ can be viewed in two steps. First, the function f maps each input x in the domain of f to its output $f(x)$ in the range of f. Second, since the range of f is a subset of the domain of g, the output $f(x)$ is an element in the domain of g, and therefore it is mapped to an output $g(f(x))$ in the range of g. In **Figure 1.12**, we see a visual image of a composite function.

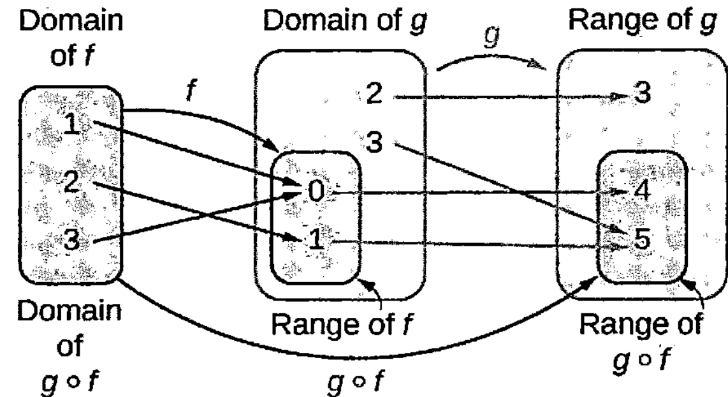

Figure 1.12 For the composite function $g \circ f$, we have $(g \circ f)(1) = 4$, $(g \circ f)(2) = 5$, and $(g \circ f)(3) = 4$.

Example 1.7

Compositions of Functions Defined by Formulas

Consider the functions $f(x) = x^2 + 1$ and $g(x) = 1/x$.

a. Find $(g \circ f)(x)$ and state its domain and range.

b. Evaluate $(g \circ f)(4)$, $(g \circ f)(-1/2)$.

c. Find $(f \circ g)(x)$ and state its domain and range.

d. Evaluate $(f \circ g)(4)$, $(f \circ g)(-1/2)$.

Solution

a. We can find the formula for $(g \circ f)(x)$ in two different ways. We could write

$$(g \circ f)(x) = g(f(x)) = g(x^2 + 1) = \frac{1}{x^2 + 1}.$$

Alternatively, we could write

$$(g \circ f)(x) = g(f(x)) = \frac{1}{f(x)} = \frac{1}{x^2 + 1}.$$

Since $x^2 + 1 \neq 0$ for all real numbers x, the domain of $(g \circ f)(x)$ is the set of all real numbers. Since $0 < 1/(x^2 + 1) \leq 1$, the range is, at most, the interval $(0, 1]$. To show that the range is this entire interval, we let $y = 1/(x^2 + 1)$ and solve this equation for x to show that for all y in the interval $(0, 1]$, there exists a real number x such that $y = 1/(x^2 + 1)$. Solving this equation for x, we see that $x^2 + 1 = 1/y$, which implies that

$$x = \pm\sqrt{\frac{1}{y} - 1}.$$

If y is in the interval $(0, 1]$, the expression under the radical is nonnegative, and therefore there exists a real number x such that $1/(x^2 + 1) = y$. We conclude that the range of $g \circ f$ is the interval $(0, 1]$.

b. $(g \circ f)(4) = g(f(4)) = g(4^2 + 1) = g(17) = \frac{1}{17}$

$(g \circ f)\left(-\frac{1}{2}\right) = g\left(f\left(-\frac{1}{2}\right)\right) = g\left(\left(-\frac{1}{2}\right)^2 + 1\right) = g\left(\frac{5}{4}\right) = \frac{4}{5}$

c. We can find a formula for $(f \circ g)(x)$ in two ways. First, we could write

$$(f \circ g)(x) = f(g(x)) = f\left(\frac{1}{x}\right) = \left(\frac{1}{x}\right)^2 + 1.$$

Alternatively, we could write

$$(f \circ g)(x) = f(g(x)) = (g(x))^2 + 1 = \left(\frac{1}{x}\right)^2 + 1.$$

The domain of $f \circ g$ is the set of all real numbers x such that $x \neq 0$. To find the range of f, we need to find all values y for which there exists a real number $x \neq 0$ such that

$$\left(\frac{1}{x}\right)^2 + 1 = y.$$

Solving this equation for x, we see that we need x to satisfy

$$\left(\frac{1}{x}\right)^2 = y - 1,$$

which simplifies to

$$\frac{1}{x} = \pm\sqrt{y - 1}.$$

Finally, we obtain

$$x = \pm \frac{1}{\sqrt{y-1}}.$$

Since $1/\sqrt{y-1}$ is a real number if and only if $y > 1$, the range of f is the set $\{y | y \geq 1\}$.

d. $(f \circ g)(4) = f(g(4)) = f\left(\frac{1}{4}\right) = \left(\frac{1}{4}\right)^2 + 1 = \frac{17}{16}$

$(f \circ g)\left(-\frac{1}{2}\right) = f\left(g\left(-\frac{1}{2}\right)\right) = f(-2) = (-2)^2 + 1 = 5$

In **Example 1.7**, we can see that $(f \circ g)(x) \neq (g \circ f)(x)$. This tells us, in general terms, that the order in which we compose functions matters.

1.5 Let $f(x) = 2 - 5x$. Let $g(x) = \sqrt{x}$. Find $(f \circ g)(x)$.

Example 1.8

Composition of Functions Defined by Tables

Consider the functions f and g described by **Table 1.4** and **Table 1.5**.

x	−3	−2	−1	0	1	2	3	4
$f(x)$	0	4	2	4	−2	0	−2	4

Table 1.4

x	−4	−2	0	2	4
$g(x)$	1	0	3	0	5

Table 1.5

a. Evaluate $(g \circ f)(3)$, $(g \circ f)(0)$.

b. State the domain and range of $(g \circ f)(x)$.

c. Evaluate $(f \circ f)(3)$, $(f \circ f)(1)$.

d. State the domain and range of $(f \circ f)(x)$.

Solution

a. $(g \circ f)(3) = g(f(3)) = g(-2) = 0$
$(g \circ f)(0) = g(4) = 5$

b. The domain of $g \circ f$ is the set $\{-3, -2, -1, 0, 1, 2, 3, 4\}$. Since the range of f is the set $\{-2, 0, 2, 4\}$, the range of $g \circ f$ is the set $\{0, 3, 5\}$.

c. $(f \circ f)(3) = f(f(3)) = f(-2) = 4$
$(f \circ f)(1) = f(f(1)) = f(-2) = 4$

d. The domain of $f \circ f$ is the set $\{-3, -2, -1, 0, 1, 2, 3, 4\}$. Since the range of f is the set $\{-2, 0, 2, 4\}$, the range of $f \circ f$ is the set $\{0, 4\}$.

Example 1.9

Application Involving a Composite Function

A store is advertising a sale of 20% off all merchandise. Caroline has a coupon that entitles her to an additional 15% off any item, including sale merchandise. If Caroline decides to purchase an item with an original price of x dollars, how much will she end up paying if she applies her coupon to the sale price? Solve this problem by using a composite function.

Solution

Since the sale price is 20% off the original price, if an item is x dollars, its sale price is given by $f(x) = 0.80x$. Since the coupon entitles an individual to 15% off the price of any item, if an item is y dollars, the price, after applying the coupon, is given by $g(y) = 0.85y$. Therefore, if the price is originally x dollars, its sale price will be $f(x) = 0.80x$ and then its final price after the coupon will be $g(f(x)) = 0.85(0.80x) = 0.68x$.

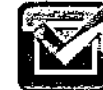

1.6 If items are on sale for 10% off their original price, and a customer has a coupon for an additional 30% off, what will be the final price for an item that is originally x dollars, after applying the coupon to the sale price?

Symmetry of Functions

The graphs of certain functions have symmetry properties that help us understand the function and the shape of its graph. For example, consider the function $f(x) = x^4 - 2x^2 - 3$ shown in **Figure 1.13**(a). If we take the part of the curve that lies to the right of the y-axis and flip it over the y-axis, it lays exactly on top of the curve to the left of the y-axis. In this case, we say the function has **symmetry about the y-axis**. On the other hand, consider the function $f(x) = x^3 - 4x$ shown in **Figure 1.13**(b). If we take the graph and rotate it $180°$ about the origin, the new graph will look exactly the same. In this case, we say the function has **symmetry about the origin**.

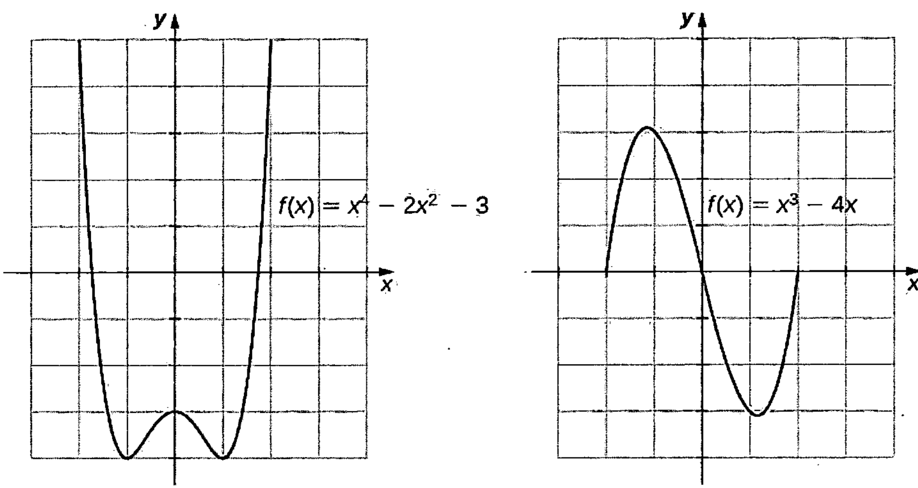

Figure 1.13 (a) A graph that is symmetric about the y-axis. (b) A graph that is symmetric about the origin.

If we are given the graph of a function, it is easy to see whether the graph has one of these symmetry properties. But without a graph, how can we determine algebraically whether a function f has symmetry? Looking at **Figure 1.14** again, we see that since f is symmetric about the y-axis, if the point (x, y) is on the graph, the point $(-x, y)$ is on the graph. In other words, $f(-x) = f(x)$. If a function f has this property, we say f is an even function, which has symmetry about the y-axis. For example, $f(x) = x^2$ is even because

$$f(-x) = (-x)^2 = x^2 = f(x).$$

In contrast, looking at **Figure 1.14** again, if a function f is symmetric about the origin, then whenever the point (x, y) is on the graph, the point $(-x, -y)$ is also on the graph. In other words, $f(-x) = -f(x)$. If f has this property, we say f is an odd function, which has symmetry about the origin. For example, $f(x) = x^3$ is odd because

$$f(-x) = (-x)^3 = -x^3 = -f(x).$$

Definition

If $f(x) = f(-x)$ for all x in the domain of f, then f is an **even function**. An even function is symmetric about the y-axis.

If $f(-x) = -f(x)$ for all x in the domain of f, then f is an **odd function**. An odd function is symmetric about the origin.

Example 1.10

Even and Odd Functions

Determine whether each of the following functions is even, odd, or neither.

a. $f(x) = -5x^4 + 7x^2 - 2$

b. $f(x) = 2x^5 - 4x + 5$

c. $f(x) = \frac{3x}{x^2 + 1}$

Solution

To determine whether a function is even or odd, we evaluate $f(-x)$ and compare it to $f(x)$ and $-f(x)$.

a. $f(-x) = -5(-x)^4 + 7(-x)^2 - 2 = -5x^4 + 7x^2 - 2 = f(x)$. Therefore, f is even.

b. $f(-x) = 2(-x)^5 - 4(-x) + 5 = -2x^5 + 4x + 5$. Now, $f(-x) \neq f(x)$. Furthermore, noting that $-f(x) = -2x^5 + 4x - 5$, we see that $f(-x) \neq -f(x)$. Therefore, f is neither even nor odd.

c. $f(-x) = 3(-x)/((-x)^2 + 1\} = -3x/(x^2 + 1) = -[3x/(x^2 + 1)] = -f(x)$. Therefore, f is odd.

1.7 Determine whether $f(x) = 4x^3 - 5x$ is even, odd, or neither.

One symmetric function that arises frequently is the **absolute value function**, written as $|x|$. The absolute value function is defined as

$$f(x) = \begin{cases} -x, & x < 0 \\ x, & x \geq 0 \end{cases}. \tag{1.2}$$

Some students describe this function by stating that it "makes everything positive." By the definition of the absolute value function, we see that if $x < 0$, then $|x| = -x > 0$, and if $x > 0$, then $|x| = x > 0$. However, for $x = 0$, $|x| = 0$. Therefore, it is more accurate to say that for all nonzero inputs, the output is positive, but if $x = 0$, the output $|x| = 0$. We conclude that the range of the absolute value function is $\{y|y \geq 0\}$. In **Figure 1.14**, we see that the absolute value function is symmetric about the y-axis and is therefore an even function.

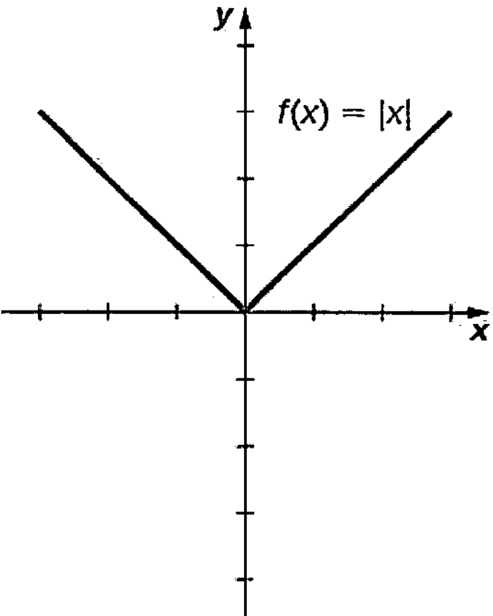

Figure 1.14 The graph of $f(x) = |x|$ is symmetric about the y-axis.

Example 1.11

Working with the Absolute Value Function

Find the domain and range of the function $f(x) = 2|x - 3| + 4$.

Solution

Since the absolute value function is defined for all real numbers, the domain of this function is $(-\infty, \infty)$. Since $|x - 3| \geq 0$ for all x, the function $f(x) = 2|x - 3| + 4 \geq 4$. Therefore, the range is, at most, the set $\{y|y \geq 4\}$. To see that the range is, in fact, this whole set, we need to show that for $y \geq 4$ there exists a real number x such that

$$2|x - 3| + 4 = y.$$

A real number x satisfies this equation as long as

$$|x - 3| = \frac{1}{2}(y - 4).$$

Since $y \geq 4$, we know $y - 4 \geq 0$, and thus the right-hand side of the equation is nonnegative, so it is possible that there is a solution. Furthermore,

$$|x - 3| = \begin{cases} -(x - 3) & \text{if } x < 3 \\ x - 3 & \text{if } x \geq 3 \end{cases}.$$

Therefore, we see there are two solutions:

$$x = \pm\frac{1}{2}(y - 4) + 3.$$

The range of this function is $\{y|y \geq 4\}$.

1.8 For the function $f(x) = |x + 2| - 4$, find the domain and range.

1.1 EXERCISES

For the following exercises, (a) determine the domain and the range of each relation, and (b) state whether the relation is a function.

1.

x	y	x	y
−3	9	1	1
−2	4	2	4
−1	1	3	9
0	0		

2.

x	y	x	y
−3	−2	1	1
−2	−8	2	8
−1	−1	3	−2
0	0		

3.

x	y	x	y
1	−3	1	1
2	−2	2	2
3	−1	3	3
0	0		

4.

x	y	x	y
1	1	5	1
2	1	6	1
3	1	7	1
4	1		

5.

x	y	x	y
3	3	15	1
5	2	21	2
8	1	33	3
10	0		

6.

x	y	x	y
−7	11	1	−2
−2	5	3	4
−2	1	6	11
0	−1		

For the following exercises, find the values for each function, if they exist, then simplify.

a. $f(0)$ b. $f(1)$ c. $f(3)$ d. $f(-x)$ e. $f(a)$ f. $f(a+h)$

7. $f(x) = 5x - 2$

8. $f(x) = 4x^2 - 3x + 1$

9. $f(x) = \frac{2}{x}$

10. $f(x) = |x - 7| + 8$

11. $f(x) = \sqrt{6x + 5}$

12. $f(x) = \frac{x - 2}{3x + 7}$

13. $f(x) = 9$

For the following exercises, find the domain, range, and all zeros/intercepts, if any, of the functions.

14. $f(x) = \frac{x}{x^2 - 16}$

15. $g(x) = \sqrt{8x - 1}$

16. $h(x) = \frac{3}{x^2 + 4}$

17. $f(x) = -1 + \sqrt{x + 2}$

18. $f(x) = \frac{1}{\sqrt{x - 9}}$

19. $g(x) = \frac{3}{x - 4}$

20. $f(x) = 4|x + 5|$

21. $g(x) = \sqrt{\frac{7}{x - 5}}$

For the following exercises, set up a table to sketch the graph of each function using the following values: $x = -3, -2, -1, 0, 1, 2, 3$.

22. $f(x) = x^2 + 1$

x	y	x	y
−3	10	1	2
−2	5	2	5
−1	2	3	10
0	1		

23. $f(x) = 3x - 6$

x	y	x	y
−3	−15	1	−3
−2	−12	2	0
−1	−9	3	3
0	−6		

24. $f(x) = \frac{1}{2}x + 1$

x	y	x	y
−3	$-\frac{1}{2}$	1	$\frac{3}{2}$
−2	0	2	2
−1	$\frac{1}{2}$	3	$\frac{5}{2}$
0	1		

25. $f(x) = 2|x|$

x	y	x	y
−3	6	1	2
−2	4	2	4
−1	2	3	6
0	0		

26. $f(x) = -x^2$

x	y	x	y
−3	−9	1	−1
−2	−4	2	−4
−1	−1	3	−9
0	0		

27. $f(x) = x^3$

x	y	x	y
−3	−27	1	1
−2	−8	2	8
−1	−1	3	27
0	0		

For the following exercises, use the vertical line test to determine whether each of the given graphs represents a function. **Assume that a graph continues at both ends if it extends beyond the given grid.** If the graph represents a function, then determine the following for each graph:

a. Domain and range
b. x-intercept, if any (estimate where necessary)
c. y-Intercept, if any (estimate where necessary)
d. The intervals for which the function is increasing
e. The intervals for which the function is decreasing
f. The intervals for which the function is constant
g. Symmetry about any axis and/or the origin
h. Whether the function is even, odd, or neither

28.

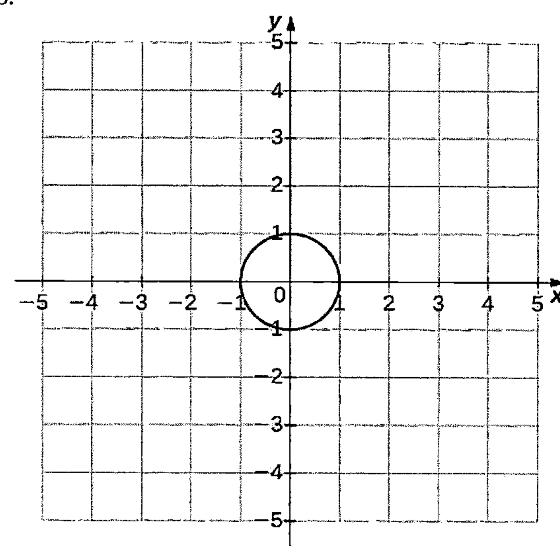

29.

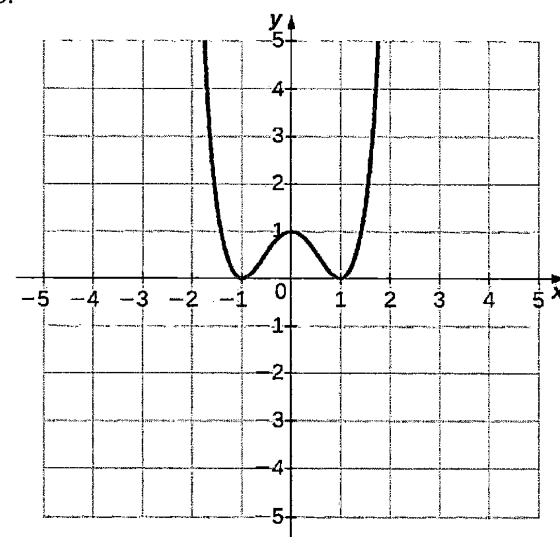

30.

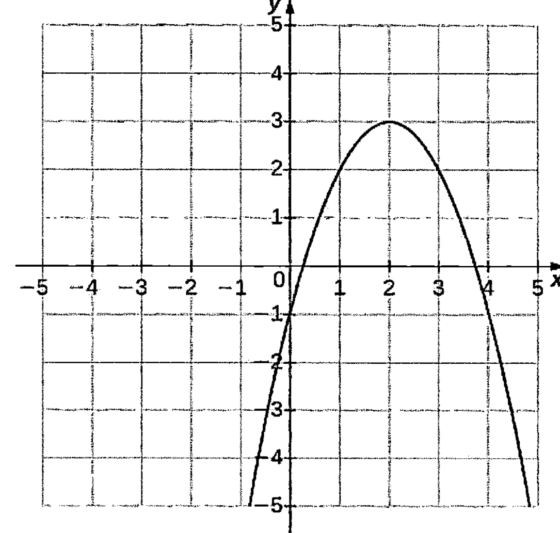

31.

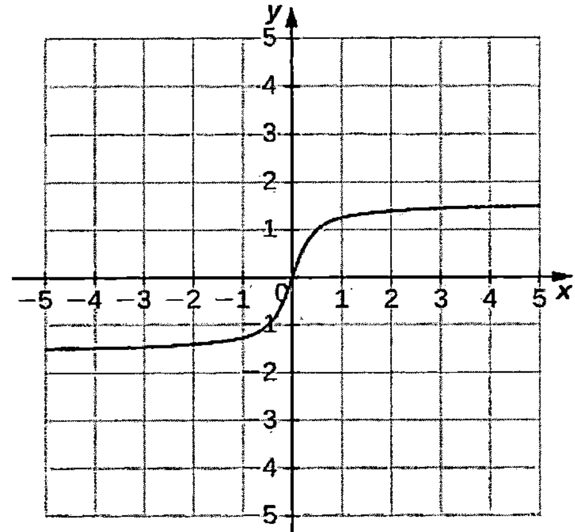

32.

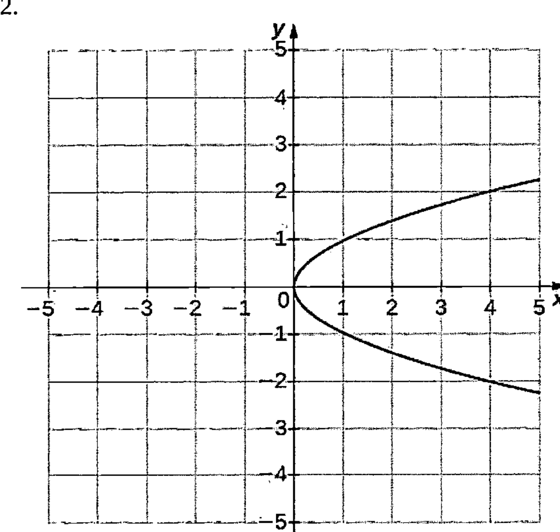

33.

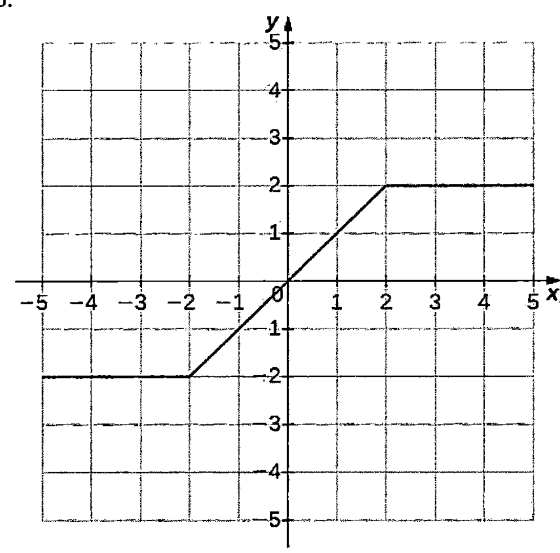

34.

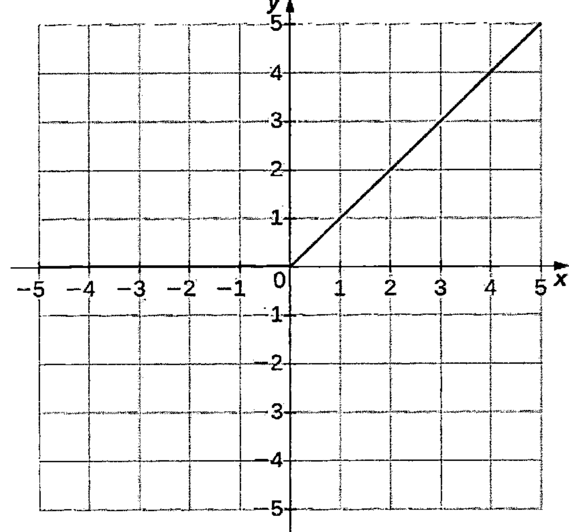

35.

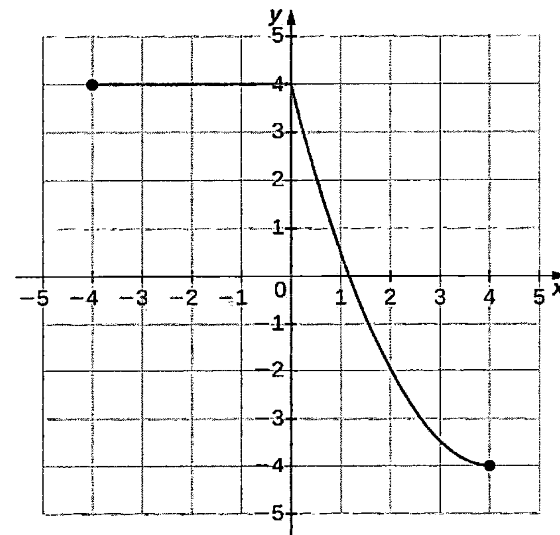

For the following exercises, for each pair of functions, find a. $f+g$ b. $f-g$ c. $f\cdot g$ d. f/g. Determine the domain of each of these new functions.

36. $f(x)=3x+4,\ g(x)=x-2$

37. $f(x)=x-8,\ g(x)=5x^2$

38. $f(x)=3x^2+4x+1,\ g(x)=x+1$

39. $f(x)=9-x^2,\ g(x)=x^2-2x-3$

40. $f(x)=\sqrt{x},\ g(x)=x-2$

41. $f(x)=6+\frac{1}{x},\ g(x)=\frac{1}{x}$

For the following exercises, for each pair of functions, find

a. $(f \circ g)(x)$ and b. $(g \circ f)(x)$ Simplify the results. Find the domain of each of the results.

42. $f(x) = 3x,\ g(x) = x + 5$

43. $f(x) = x + 4,\ g(x) = 4x - 1$

44. $f(x) = 2x + 4,\ g(x) = x^2 - 2$

45. $f(x) = x^2 + 7,\ g(x) = x^2 - 3$

46. $f(x) = \sqrt{x},\ g(x) = x + 9$

47. $f(x) = \frac{3}{2x + 1},\ g(x) = \frac{2}{x}$

48. $f(x) = |x + 1|,\ g(x) = x^2 + x - 4$

49. The table below lists the NBA championship winners for the years 2001 to 2012.

Year	Winner
2001	LA Lakers
2002	LA Lakers
2003	San Antonio Spurs
2004	Detroit Pistons
2005	San Antonio Spurs
2006	Miami Heat
2007	San Antonio Spurs
2008	Boston Celtics
2009	LA Lakers
2010	LA Lakers
2011	Dallas Mavericks
2012	Miami Heat

a. Consider the relation in which the domain values are the years 2001 to 2012 and the range is the corresponding winner. Is this relation a function? Explain why or why not.
b. Consider the relation where the domain values are the winners and the range is the corresponding years. Is this relation a function? Explain why or why not.

50. **[T]** The area A of a square depends on the length of the side s.

a. Write a function $A(s)$ for the area of a square.
b. Find and interpret $A(6.5)$.
c. Find the exact and the two-significant-digit approximation to the length of the sides of a square with area 56 square units.

51. **[T]** The volume of a cube depends on the length of the sides s.

a. Write a function $V(s)$ for the area of a square.

b. Find and interpret $V(11.8)$.

52. **[T]** A rental car company rents cars for a flat fee of \$20 and an hourly charge of \$10.25. Therefore, the total cost C to rent a car is a function of the hours t the car is rented plus the flat fee.

a. Write the formula for the function that models this situation.

b. Find the total cost to rent a car for 2 days and 7 hours.

c. Determine how long the car was rented if the bill is \$432.73.

53. **[T]** A vehicle has a 20-gal tank and gets 15 mpg. The number of miles N that can be driven depends on the amount of gas x in the tank.

a. Write a formula that models this situation.

b. Determine the number of miles the vehicle can travel on (i) a full tank of gas and (ii) 3/4 of a tank of gas.

c. Determine the domain and range of the function.

d. Determine how many times the driver had to stop for gas if she has driven a total of 578 mi.

54. **[T]** The volume V of a sphere depends on the length of its radius as $V = (4/3)\pi r^3$. Because Earth is not a perfect sphere, we can use the *mean radius* when measuring from the center to its surface. The mean radius is the average distance from the physical center to the surface, based on a large number of samples. Find the volume of Earth with mean radius 6.371×10^6 m.

55. **[T]** A certain bacterium grows in culture in a circular region. The radius of the circle, measured in centimeters, is given by $r(t) = 6 - \left[5/\left(t^2 + 1\right)\right]$, where t is time measured in hours since a circle of a 1-cm radius of the bacterium was put into the culture.

a. Express the area of the bacteria as a function of time.

b. Find the exact and approximate area of the bacterial culture in 3 hours.

c. Express the circumference of the bacteria as a function of time.

d. Find the exact and approximate circumference of the bacteria in 3 hours.

56. **[T]** An American tourist visits Paris and must convert U.S. dollars to Euros, which can be done using the function $E(x) = 0.79x$, where x is the number of U.S. dollars and $E(x)$ is the equivalent number of Euros. Since conversion rates fluctuate, when the tourist returns to the United States 2 weeks later, the conversion from Euros to U.S. dollars is $D(x) = 1.245x$, where x is the number of Euros and $D(x)$ is the equivalent number of U.S. dollars.

a. Find the composite function that converts directly from U.S. dollars to U.S. dollars via Euros. Did this tourist lose value in the conversion process?

b. Use (a) to determine how many U.S. dollars the tourist would get back at the end of her trip if she converted an extra \$200 when she arrived in Paris.

57. **[T]** The manager at a skateboard shop pays his workers a monthly salary S of \$750 plus a commission of \$8.50 for each skateboard they sell.

a. Write a function $y = S(x)$ that models a worker's monthly salary based on the number of skateboards x he or she sells.

b. Find the approximate monthly salary when a worker sells 25, 40, or 55 skateboards.

c. Use the INTERSECT feature on a graphing calculator to determine the number of skateboards that must be sold for a worker to earn a monthly income of \$1400. (*Hint*: Find the intersection of the function and the line $y = 1400$.)

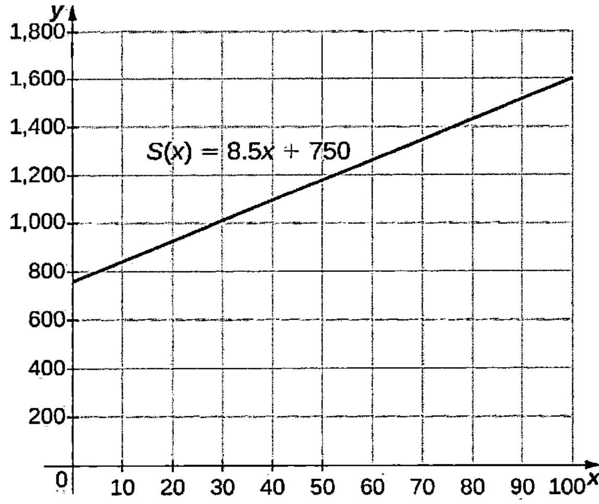

58. **[T]** Use a graphing calculator to graph the half-circle $y = \sqrt{25 - (x - 4)^2}$. Then, use the INTERCEPT feature to find the value of both the x- and y-intercepts.

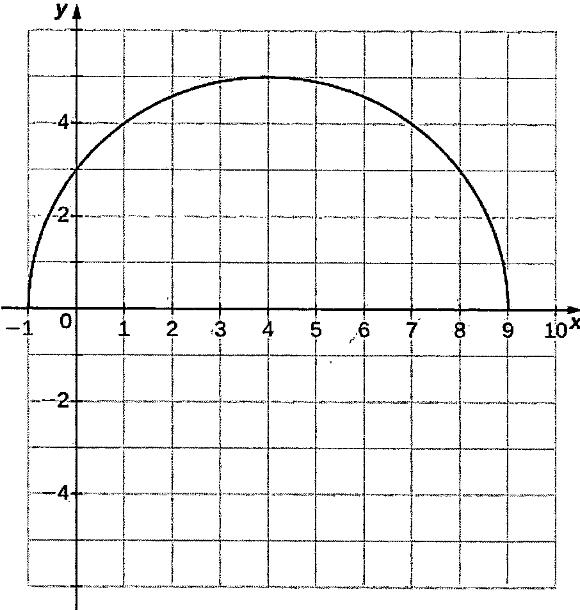

1.2 | Basic Classes of Functions

Learning Objectives

1.2.1 Calculate the slope of a linear function and interpret its meaning.
1.2.2 Recognize the degree of a polynomial.
1.2.3 Find the roots of a quadratic polynomial.
1.2.4 Describe the graphs of basic odd and even polynomial functions.
1.2.5 Identify a rational function.
1.2.6 Describe the graphs of power and root functions.
1.2.7 Explain the difference between algebraic and transcendental functions.
1.2.8 Graph a piecewise-defined function.
1.2.9 Sketch the graph of a function that has been shifted, stretched, or reflected from its initial graph position.

We have studied the general characteristics of functions, so now let's examine some specific classes of functions. We begin by reviewing the basic properties of linear and quadratic functions, and then generalize to include higher-degree polynomials. By combining root functions with polynomials, we can define general algebraic functions and distinguish them from the transcendental functions we examine later in this chapter. We finish the section with examples of piecewise-defined functions and take a look at how to sketch the graph of a function that has been shifted, stretched, or reflected from its initial form.

Linear Functions and Slope

The easiest type of function to consider is a **linear function**. Linear functions have the form $f(x) = ax + b,$ where a and b are constants. In **Figure 1.15**, we see examples of linear functions when a is positive, negative, and zero. Note that if $a > 0,$ the graph of the line rises as x increases. In other words, $f(x) = ax + b$ is increasing on $(-\infty, \infty)$. If $a < 0,$ the graph of the line falls as x increases. In this case, $f(x) = ax + b$ is decreasing on $(-\infty, \infty)$. If $a = 0,$ the line is horizontal.

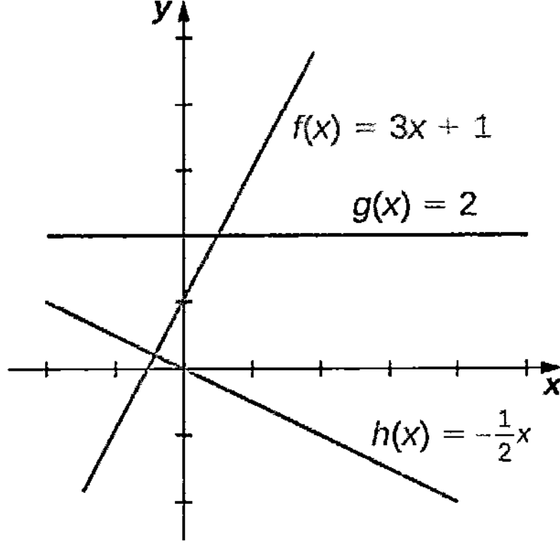

Figure 1.15 These linear functions are increasing or decreasing on (∞, ∞) and one function is a horizontal line.

As suggested by **Figure 1.15**, the graph of any linear function is a line. One of the distinguishing features of a line is its slope. The **slope** is the change in y for each unit change in x. The slope measures both the steepness and the direction of a line. If the slope is positive, the line points upward when moving from left to right. If the slope is negative, the line points downward when moving from left to right. If the slope is zero, the line is horizontal. To calculate the slope of a line, we need to determine the ratio of the change in y versus the change in x. To do so, we choose any two points (x_1, y_1) and (x_2, y_2) on the line and calculate $\frac{y_2 - y_1}{x_2 - x_1}$. In **Figure 1.16**, we see this ratio is independent of the points chosen.

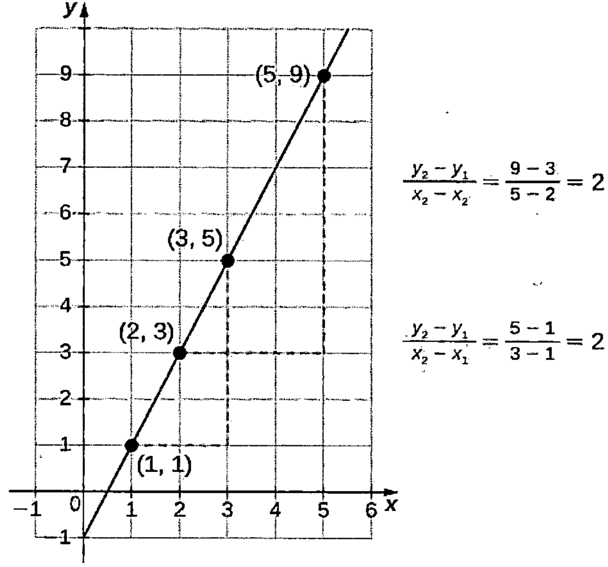

Figure 1.16 For any linear function, the slope $(y_2 - y_1)/(x_2 - x_1)$ is independent of the choice of points (x_1, y_1) and (x_2, y_2) on the line.

Definition

Consider line L passing through points (x_1, y_1) and (x_2, y_2). Let $\Delta y = y_2 - y_1$ and $\Delta x = x_2 - x_1$ denote the changes in y and x, respectively. The **slope** of the line is

$$m = \frac{y_2 - y_1}{x_2 - x_1} = \frac{\Delta y}{\Delta x}. \tag{1.3}$$

We now examine the relationship between slope and the formula for a linear function. Consider the linear function given by the formula $f(x) = ax + b$. As discussed earlier, we know the graph of a linear function is given by a line. We can use our definition of slope to calculate the slope of this line. As shown, we can determine the slope by calculating $(y_2 - y_1)/(x_2 - x_1)$ for any points (x_1, y_1) and (x_2, y_2) on the line. Evaluating the function f at $x = 0$, we see that $(0, b)$ is a point on this line. Evaluating this function at $x = 1$, we see that $(1, a + b)$ is also a point on this line. Therefore, the slope of this line is

$$\frac{(a + b) - b}{1 - 0} = a.$$

We have shown that the coefficient a is the slope of the line. We can conclude that the formula $f(x) = ax + b$ describes a line with slope a. Furthermore, because this line intersects the y-axis at the point $(0, b)$, we see that the y-intercept for this linear function is $(0, b)$. We conclude that the formula $f(x) = ax + b$ tells us the slope, a, and the y-intercept, $(0, b)$, for this line. Since we often use the symbol m to denote the slope of a line, we can write

$$f(x) = mx + b$$

to denote the **slope-intercept form** of a linear function.

Sometimes it is convenient to express a linear function in different ways. For example, suppose the graph of a linear function passes through the point (x_1, y_1) and the slope of the line is m. Since any other point $(x, f(x))$ on the graph of f must satisfy the equation

$$m = \frac{f(x) - y_1}{x - x_1},$$

this linear function can be expressed by writing

$$f(x) - y_1 = m(x - x_1).$$

We call this equation the **point-slope equation** for that linear function.

Since every nonvertical line is the graph of a linear function, the points on a nonvertical line can be described using the slope-intercept or point-slope equations. However, a vertical line does not represent the graph of a function and cannot be expressed in either of these forms. Instead, a vertical line is described by the equation $x = k$ for some constant k. Since neither the slope-intercept form nor the point-slope form allows for vertical lines, we use the notation

$$ax + by = c,$$

where a, b are both not zero, to denote the **standard form of a line**.

Definition

Consider a line passing through the point (x_1, y_1) with slope m. The equation

$$y - y_1 = m(x - x_1) \tag{1.4}$$

is the **point-slope equation** for that line.

Consider a line with slope m and y-intercept $(0, b)$. The equation

$$y = mx + b \tag{1.5}$$

is an equation for that line in **slope-intercept form**.

The **standard form of a line** is given by the equation

$$ax + by = c, \tag{1.6}$$

where a and b are both not zero. This form is more general because it allows for a vertical line, $x = k$.

Example 1.12

Finding the Slope and Equations of Lines

Consider the line passing through the points $(11, -4)$ and $(-4, 5)$, as shown in **Figure 1.17**.

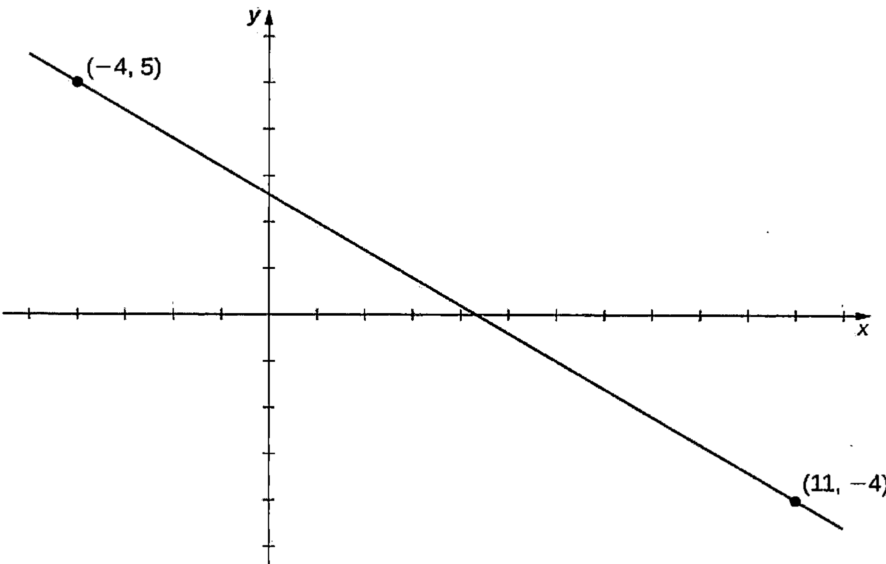

Figure 1.17 Finding the equation of a linear function with a graph that is a line between two given points.

a. Find the slope of the line.

b. Find an equation for this linear function in point-slope form.

c. Find an equation for this linear function in slope-intercept form.

Solution

a. The slope of the line is

$$m = \frac{y_2 - y_1}{x_2 - x_1} = \frac{5 - (-4)}{-4 - 11} = -\frac{9}{15} = -\frac{3}{5}.$$

b. To find an equation for the linear function in point-slope form, use the slope $m = -3/5$ and choose any point on the line. If we choose the point $(11, -4)$, we get the equation

$$f(x) + 4 = -\frac{3}{5}(x - 11).$$

c. To find an equation for the linear function in slope-intercept form, solve the equation in part b. for $f(x)$. When we do this, we get the equation

$$f(x) = -\frac{3}{5}x + \frac{13}{5}.$$

1.9 Consider the line passing through points $(-3, 2)$ and $(1, 4)$. Find the slope of the line.

Find an equation of that line in point-slope form. Find an equation of that line in slope-intercept form.

Example 1.13

A Linear Distance Function

Jessica leaves her house at 5:50 a.m. and goes for a 9-mile run. She returns to her house at 7:08 a.m. Answer the following questions, assuming Jessica runs at a constant pace.

a. Describe the distance D (in miles) Jessica runs as a linear function of her run time t (in minutes).

b. Sketch a graph of D.

c. Interpret the meaning of the slope.

Solution

a. At time $t = 0$, Jessica is at her house, so $D(0) = 0$. At time $t = 78$ minutes, Jessica has finished running 9 mi, so $D(78) = 9$. The slope of the linear function is

$$m = \frac{9 - 0}{78 - 0} = \frac{3}{26}.$$

The y-intercept is $(0, 0)$, so the equation for this linear function is

$$D(t) = \frac{3}{26}t.$$

b. To graph D, use the fact that the graph passes through the origin and has slope $m = 3/26$.

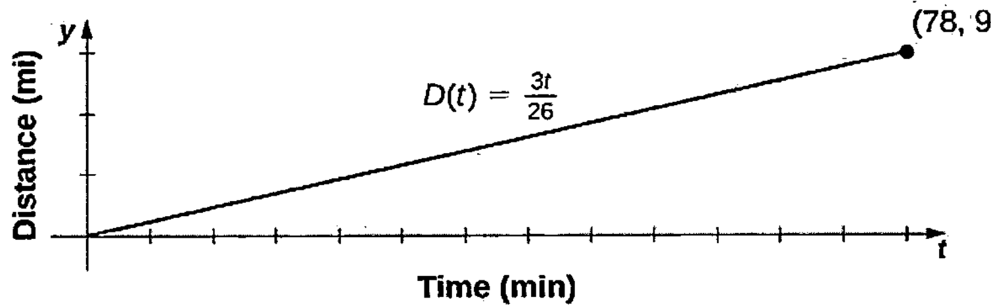

c. The slope $m = 3/26 \approx 0.115$ describes the distance (in miles) Jessica runs per minute, or her average velocity.

Polynomials

A linear function is a special type of a more general class of functions: polynomials. A **polynomial function** is any function that can be written in the form

$$f(x) = a_n x^n + a_{n-1} x^{n-1} + \ldots + a_1 x + a_0 \tag{1.7}$$

for some integer $n \geq 0$ and constants $a_n, a_{n-1}, \ldots, a_0$, where $a_n \neq 0$. In the case when $n = 0$, we allow for $a_0 = 0$; if $a_0 = 0$, the function $f(x) = 0$ is called the *zero function*. The value n is called the **degree** of the polynomial; the constant a_n is called the *leading coefficient*. A linear function of the form $f(x) = mx + b$ is a polynomial of degree 1 if $m \neq 0$ and degree 0 if $m = 0$. A polynomial of degree 0 is also called a *constant function*. A polynomial function of degree 2 is called a **quadratic function**. In particular, a quadratic function has the form $f(x) = ax^2 + bx + c$, where $a \neq 0$. A polynomial function of degree 3 is called a **cubic function**.

Power Functions

Some polynomial functions are power functions. A **power function** is any function of the form $f(x) = ax^b$, where a and b are any real numbers. The exponent in a power function can be any real number, but here we consider the case when the exponent is a positive integer. (We consider other cases later.) If the exponent is a positive integer, then $f(x) = ax^n$ is a polynomial. If n is even, then $f(x) = ax^n$ is an even function because $f(-x) = a(-x)^n = ax^n$ if n is even. If n is odd, then $f(x) = ax^n$ is an odd function because $f(-x) = a(-x)^n = -ax^n$ if n is odd (**Figure 1.18**).

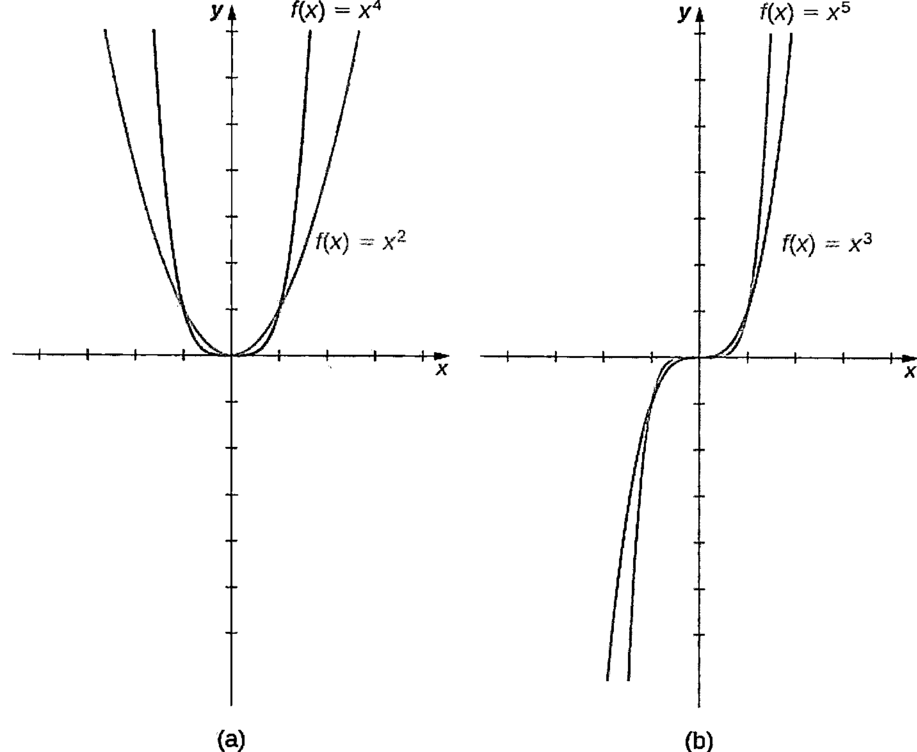

Figure 1.18 (a) For any even integer n, $f(x) = ax^n$ is an even function. (b) For any odd integer n, $f(x) = ax^n$ is an odd function.

Behavior at Infinity

To determine the behavior of a function f as the inputs approach infinity, we look at the values $f(x)$ as the inputs, x, become larger. For some functions, the values of $f(x)$ approach a finite number. For example, for the function $f(x) = 2 + 1/x$, the values $1/x$ become closer and closer to zero for all values of x as they get larger and larger. For this function, we say "$f(x)$ approaches two as x goes to infinity," and we write $f(x) \to 2$ as $x \to \infty$. The line $y = 2$ is a horizontal asymptote for the function $f(x) = 2 + 1/x$ because the graph of the function gets closer to the line as x gets larger.

For other functions, the values $f(x)$ may not approach a finite number but instead may become larger for all values of x as they get larger. In that case, we say "$f(x)$ approaches infinity as x approaches infinity," and we write $f(x) \to \infty$ as $x \to \infty$. For example, for the function $f(x) = 3x^2$, the outputs $f(x)$ become larger as the inputs x get larger. We can conclude that the function $f(x) = 3x^2$ approaches infinity as x approaches infinity, and we write $3x^2 \to \infty$ as $x \to \infty$. The behavior as $x \to -\infty$ and the meaning of $f(x) \to -\infty$ as $x \to \infty$ or $x \to -\infty$ can be defined similarly. We can describe what happens to the values of $f(x)$ as $x \to \infty$ and as $x \to -\infty$ as the *end behavior* of the function.

To understand the end behavior for polynomial functions, we can focus on quadratic and cubic functions. The behavior for higher-degree polynomials can be analyzed similarly. Consider a quadratic function $f(x) = ax^2 + bx + c$. If $a > 0$, the values $f(x) \to \infty$ as $x \to \pm\infty$. If $a < 0$, the values $f(x) \to -\infty$ as $x \to \pm\infty$. Since the graph of a quadratic function is a parabola, the parabola opens upward if $a > 0$; the parabola opens downward if $a < 0$. (See **Figure 1.19**(a).)

Now consider a cubic function $f(x) = ax^3 + bx^2 + cx + d$. If $a > 0$, then $f(x) \to \infty$ as $x \to \infty$ and $f(x) \to -\infty$ as $x \to -\infty$. If $a < 0$, then $f(x) \to -\infty$ as $x \to \infty$ and $f(x) \to \infty$ as $x \to -\infty$. As we can see from both of these graphs, the leading term of the polynomial determines the end behavior. (See **Figure 1.19**(b).)

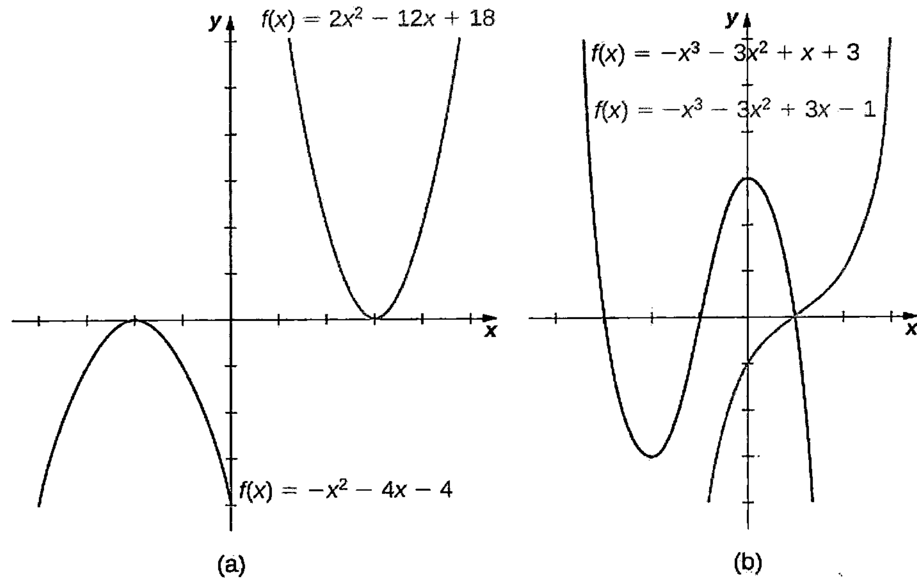

Figure 1.19 (a) For a quadratic function, if the leading coefficient $a > 0$, the parabola opens upward. If $a < 0$, the parabola opens downward. (b) For a cubic function f, if the leading coefficient $a > 0$, the values $f(x) \to \infty$ as $x \to \infty$ and the values $f(x) \to -\infty$ as $x \to -\infty$. If the leading coefficient $a < 0$, the opposite is true.

Zeros of Polynomial Functions

Another characteristic of the graph of a polynomial function is where it intersects the x-axis. To determine where a function f intersects the x-axis, we need to solve the equation $f(x) = 0$ for .n the case of the linear function $f(x) = mx + b$, the x-intercept is given by solving the equation $mx + b = 0$. In this case, we see that the x-intercept is given by $(-b/m,\ 0)$. In the case of a quadratic function, finding the x-intercept(s) requires finding the zeros of a quadratic equation: $ax^2 + bx + c = 0$. In some cases, it is easy to factor the polynomial $ax^2 + bx + c$ to find the zeros. If not, we make use of the quadratic formula.

Rule: The Quadratic Formula

Consider the quadratic equation

$$ax^2 + bx + c = 0,$$

where $a \neq 0$. The solutions of this equation are given by the quadratic formula

$$x = \frac{-b \pm \sqrt{b^2 - 4ac}}{2a}. \tag{1.8}$$

If the discriminant $b^2 - 4ac > 0$, this formula tells us there are two real numbers that satisfy the quadratic equation. If $b^2 - 4ac = 0$, this formula tells us there is only one solution, and it is a real number. If $b^2 - 4ac < 0$, no real numbers satisfy the quadratic equation.

In the case of higher-degree polynomials, it may be more complicated to determine where the graph intersects the x-axis. In some instances, it is possible to find the x-intercepts by factoring the polynomial to find its zeros. In other cases, it is impossible to calculate the exact values of the x-intercepts. However, as we see later in the text, in cases such as this, we can use analytical tools to approximate (to a very high degree) where the x-intercepts are located. Here we focus on the graphs of polynomials for which we can calculate their zeros explicitly.

Example 1.14

Graphing Polynomial Functions

For the following functions a. and b., i. describe the behavior of $f(x)$ as $x \to \pm\infty$, ii. find all zeros of f, and iii. sketch a graph of f.

a. $f(x) = -2x^2 + 4x - 1$

b. $f(x) = x^3 - 3x^2 - 4x$

Solution

a. The function $f(x) = -2x^2 + 4x - 1$ is a quadratic function.

i. Because $a = -2 < 0$, as $x \to \pm\infty$, $f(x) \to -\infty$.

ii. To find the zeros of f, use the quadratic formula. The zeros are

$$x = \frac{-4 \pm \sqrt{4^2 - 4(-2)(-1)}}{2(-2)} = \frac{-4 \pm \sqrt{8}}{-4} = \frac{-4 \pm 2\sqrt{2}}{-4} = \frac{2 \pm \sqrt{2}}{2}.$$

iii. To sketch the graph of f, use the information from your previous answers and combine it with the fact that the graph is a parabola opening downward.

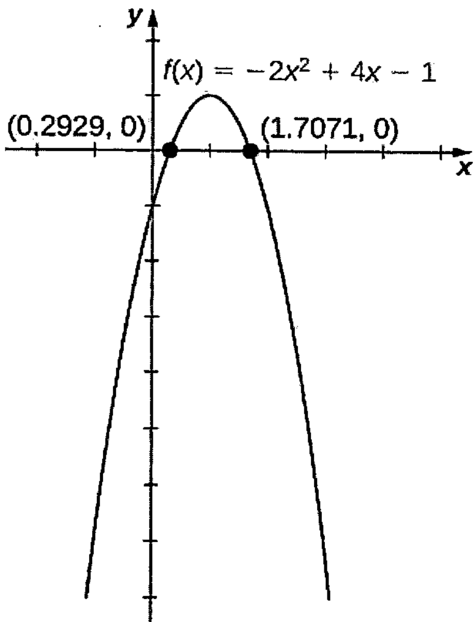

b. The function $f(x) = x^3 - 3x^2 - 4x$ is a cubic function.

i. Because $a = 1 > 0$, as $x \to \infty$, $f(x) \to \infty$. As $x \to -\infty$, $f(x) \to -\infty$.

ii. To find the zeros of f, we need to factor the polynomial. First, when we factor x out of all the terms, we find

$$f(x) = x(x^2 - 3x - 4).$$

Then, when we factor the quadratic function $x^2 - 3x - 4$, we find

$$f(x) = x(x - 4)(x + 1).$$

Therefore, the zeros of f are $x = 0,\ 4,\ -1.$

iii. Combining the results from parts i. and ii., draw a rough sketch of f.

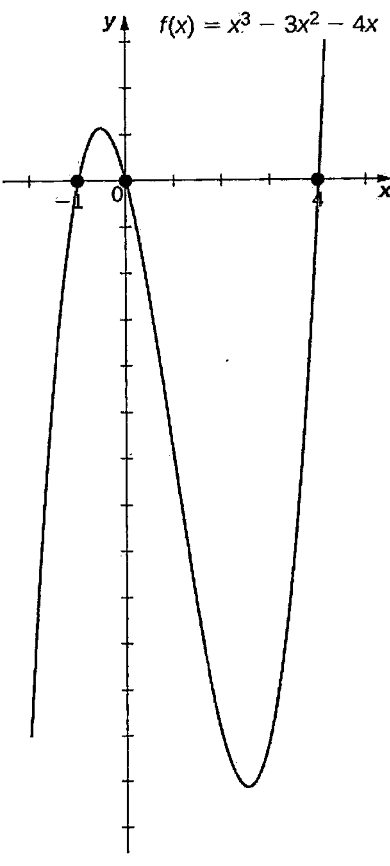

1.10 Consider the quadratic function $f(x) = 3x^2 - 6x + 2$. Find the zeros of f. Does the parabola open upward or downward?

Mathematical Models

A large variety of real-world situations can be described using **mathematical models**. A mathematical model is a method of simulating real-life situations with mathematical equations. Physicists, engineers, economists, and other researchers develop models by combining observation with quantitative data to develop equations, functions, graphs, and other mathematical tools to describe the behavior of various systems accurately. Models are useful because they help predict future outcomes. Examples of mathematical models include the study of population dynamics, investigations of weather patterns, and predictions of product sales.

As an example, let's consider a mathematical model that a company could use to describe its revenue for the sale of a particular item. The amount of revenue R a company receives for the sale of n items sold at a price of p dollars per item is described by the equation $R = p \cdot n$. The company is interested in how the sales change as the price of the item changes. Suppose the data in **Table 1.6** show the number of units a company sells as a function of the price per item.

p	6	8	10	12	14
n	19.4	18.5	16.2	13.8	12.2

Table 1.6 Number of Units Sold n (in Thousands) as a Function of Price per Unit p (in Dollars)

In **Figure 1.20**, we see the graph the number of units sold (in thousands) as a function of price (in dollars). We note from the shape of the graph that the number of units sold is likely a linear function of price per item, and the data can be closely approximated by the linear function $n = -1.04p + 26$ for $0 \leq p \leq 25$, where n predicts the number of units sold in thousands. Using this linear function, the revenue (in thousands of dollars) can be estimated by the quadratic function

$$R(p) = p \cdot (-1.04p + 26) = -1.04p^2 + 26p$$

for $0 \leq p \leq 25$. In **Example 1.15**, we use this quadratic function to predict the amount of revenue the company receives depending on the price the company charges per item. Note that we cannot conclude definitively the actual number of units sold for values of p, for which no data are collected. However, given the other data values and the graph shown, it seems reasonable that the number of units sold (in thousands) if the price charged is p dollars may be close to the values predicted by the linear function $n = -1.04p + 26$.

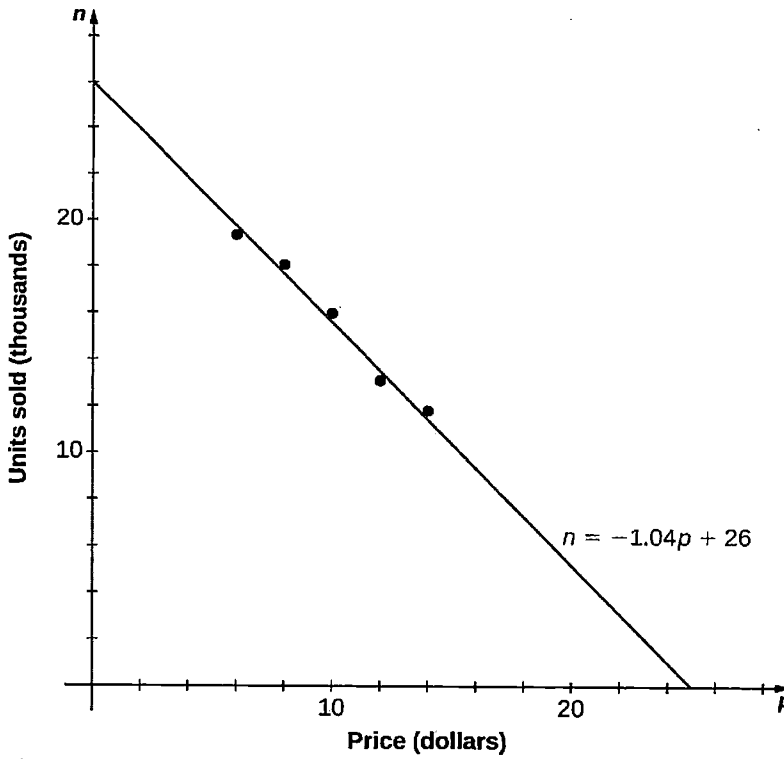

Figure 1.20 The data collected for the number of items sold as a function of price is roughly linear. We use the linear function $n = -1.04p + 26$ to estimate this function.

Example 1.15

Maximizing Revenue

A company is interested in predicting the amount of revenue it will receive depending on the price it charges for a particular item. Using the data from **Table 1.6**, the company arrives at the following quadratic function to model revenue R as a function of price per item p:

$$R(p) = p \cdot (-1.04p + 26) = -1.04p^2 + 26p$$

for $0 \leq p \leq 25$.

a. Predict the revenue if the company sells the item at a price of $p = \$5$ and $p = \$17$.

b. Find the zeros of this function and interpret the meaning of the zeros.

c. Sketch a graph of R.

d. Use the graph to determine the value of p that maximizes revenue. Find the maximum revenue.

Solution

a. Evaluating the revenue function at $p = 5$ and $p = 17$, we can conclude that

$$R(5) = -1.04(5)^2 + 26(5) = 104, \text{ so revenue } = \$104{,}000;$$
$$R(17) = -1.04(17)^2 + 26(17) = 141.44, \text{ so revenue } = \$144{,}440.$$

b. The zeros of this function can be found by solving the equation $-1.04p^2 + 26p = 0$. When we factor the quadratic expression, we get $p(-1.04p + 26) = 0$. The solutions to this equation are given by $p = 0, 25$. For these values of p, the revenue is zero. When $p = \$0$, the revenue is zero because the company is giving away its merchandise for free. When $p = \$25$, the revenue is zero because the price is too high, and no one will buy any items.

c. Knowing the fact that the function is quadratic, we also know the graph is a parabola. Since the leading coefficient is negative, the parabola opens downward. One property of parabolas is that they are symmetric about the axis, so since the zeros are at $p = 0$ and $p = 25$, the parabola must be symmetric about the line halfway between them, or $p = 12.5$.

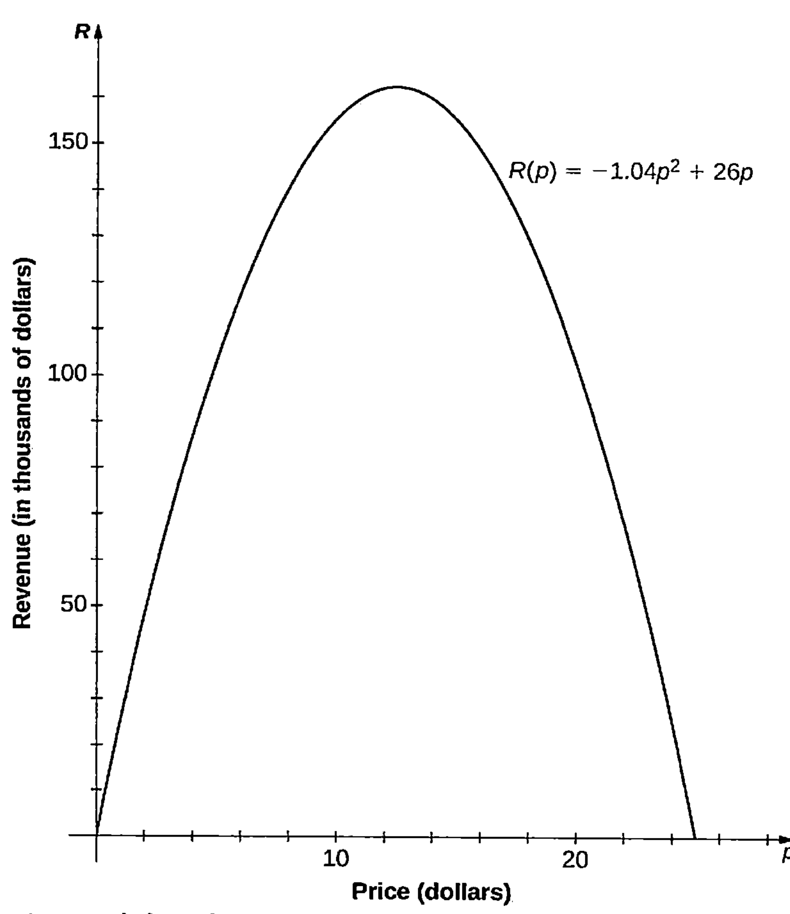

d. The function is a parabola with zeros at $p = 0$ and $p = 25,$ and it is symmetric about the line $p = 12.5,$ so the maximum revenue occurs at a price of $p = \$12.50$ per item. At that price, the revenue is $R(p) = -1.04(12.5)^2 + 26(12.5) = \$162,\ 500.$

Algebraic Functions

By allowing for quotients and fractional powers in polynomial functions, we create a larger class of functions. An **algebraic function** is one that involves addition, subtraction, multiplication, division, rational powers, and roots. Two types of algebraic functions are rational functions and root functions.

Just as rational numbers are quotients of integers, rational functions are quotients of polynomials. In particular, a **rational function** is any function of the form $f(x) = p(x)/q(x),$ where $p(x)$ and $q(x)$ are polynomials. For example,

$$f(x) = \frac{3x - 1}{5x + 2} \qquad \text{and} \qquad g(x) = \frac{4}{x^2 + 1}$$

are rational functions. A **root function** is a power function of the form $f(x) = x^{1/n},$ where n is a positive integer greater than one. For example, $f(x) = x^{1/2} = \sqrt{x}$ is the square-root function and $g(x) = x^{1/3} = \sqrt[3]{x}$ is the cube-root function. By allowing for compositions of root functions and rational functions, we can create other algebraic functions. For example, $f(x) = \sqrt{4 - x^2}$ is an algebraic function.

Example 1.16

Finding Domain and Range for Algebraic Functions

For each of the following functions, find the domain and range.

a. $f(x) = \dfrac{3x-1}{5x+2}$

b. $f(x) = \sqrt{4-x^2}$

Solution

a. It is not possible to divide by zero, so the domain is the set of real numbers x such that $x \neq -2/5$. To find the range, we need to find the values y for which there exists a real number x such that

$$y = \frac{3x-1}{5x+2}.$$

When we multiply both sides of this equation by $5x+2$, we see that x must satisfy the equation

$$5xy + 2y = 3x - 1.$$

From this equation, we can see that x must satisfy

$$2y + 1 = x(3 - 5y).$$

If $y = 3/5$, this equation has no solution. On the other hand, as long as $y \neq 3/5$,

$$x = \frac{2y+1}{3-5y}$$

satisfies this equation. We can conclude that the range of f is $\{y|y \neq 3/5\}$.

b. To find the domain of f, we need $4 - x^2 \geq 0$. When we factor, we write $4 - x^2 = (2-x)(2+x) \geq 0$. This inequality holds if and only if both terms are positive or both terms are negative. For both terms to be positive, we need to find x such that

$$2 - x \geq 0 \quad \text{and} \quad 2 + x \geq 0.$$

These two inequalities reduce to $2 \geq x$ and $x \geq -2$. Therefore, the set $\{x| -2 \leq x \leq 2\}$ must be part of the domain. For both terms to be negative, we need

$$2 - x \leq 0 \quad \text{and} \quad 2 + x \geq 0.$$

These two inequalities also reduce to $2 \leq x$ and $x \geq -2$. There are no values of x that satisfy both of these inequalities. Thus, we can conclude the domain of this function is $\{x| -2 \leq x \leq 2\}$.

If $-2 \leq x \leq 2$, then $0 \leq 4 - x^2 \leq 4$. Therefore, $0 \leq \sqrt{4-x^2} \leq 2$, and the range of f is $\{y|0 \leq y \leq 2\}$.

1.11 Find the domain and range for the function $f(x) = (5x+2)/(2x-1)$.

The root functions $f(x) = x^{1/n}$ have defining characteristics depending on whether n is odd or even. For all even integers $n \geq 2,$ the domain of $f(x) = x^{1/n}$ is the interval $[0, \infty).$ For all odd integers $n \geq 1,$ the domain of $f(x) = x^{1/n}$ is the set of all real numbers. Since $x^{1/n} = (-x)^{1/n}$ for odd integers $n,$ $f(x) = x^{1/n}$ is an odd function if n is odd. See the graphs of root functions for different values of n in **Figure 1.21**.

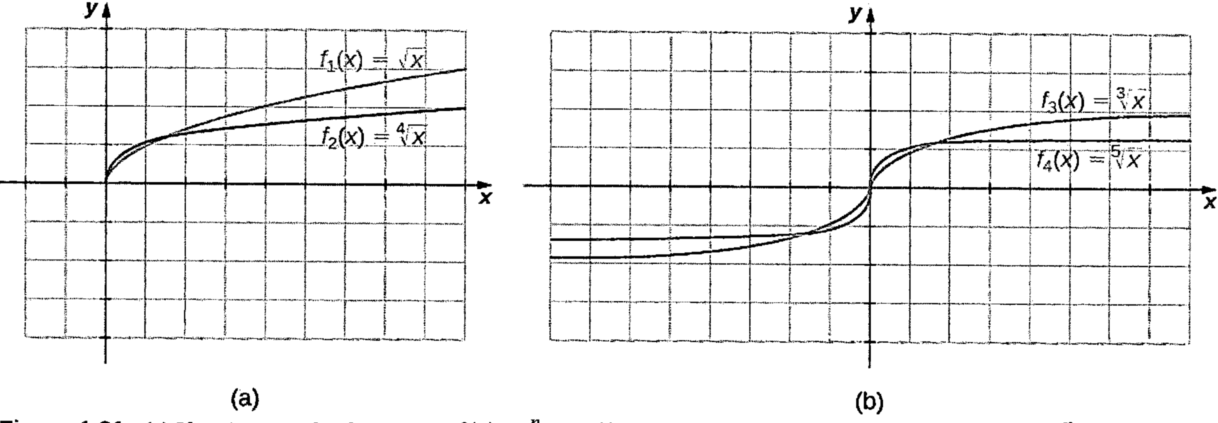

Figure 1.21 (a) If n is even, the domain of $f(x) = \sqrt[n]{x}$ is $[0, \infty)$. (b) If n is odd, the domain of $f(x) = \sqrt[n]{x}$ is $(-\infty, \infty)$ and the function $f(x) = \sqrt[n]{x}$ is an odd function.

Example 1.17

Finding Domains for Algebraic Functions

For each of the following functions, determine the domain of the function.

a. $f(x) = \dfrac{3}{x^2 - 1}$

b. $f(x) = \dfrac{2x + 5}{3x^2 + 4}$

c. $f(x) = \sqrt{4 - 3x}$

d. $f(x) = \sqrt[3]{2x - 1}$

Solution

a. You cannot divide by zero, so the domain is the set of values x such that $x^2 - 1 \neq 0.$ Therefore, the domain is $\{x | x \neq \pm 1\}.$

b. You need to determine the values of x for which the denominator is zero. Since $3x^2 + 4 \geq 4$ for all real numbers $x,$ the denominator is never zero. Therefore, the domain is $(-\infty, \infty).$

c. Since the square root of a negative number is not a real number, the domain is the set of values x for which $4 - 3x \geq 0.$ Therefore, the domain is $\{x | x \leq 4/3\}.$

d. The cube root is defined for all real numbers, so the domain is the interval $(-\infty, \infty).$

1.12 Find the domain for each of the following functions: $f(x) = (5 - 2x)/(x^2 + 2)$ and $g(x) = \sqrt{5x - 1}$.

Transcendental Functions

Thus far, we have discussed algebraic functions. Some functions, however, cannot be described by basic algebraic operations. These functions are known as **transcendental functions** because they are said to "transcend," or go beyond, algebra. The most common transcendental functions are trigonometric, exponential, and logarithmic functions. A *trigonometric function* relates the ratios of two sides of a right triangle. They are $\sin x$, $\cos x$, $\tan x$, $\cot x$, $\sec x$, and $\csc x$. (We discuss trigonometric functions later in the chapter.) An exponential function is a function of the form $f(x) = b^x$, where the base $b > 0, b \neq 1$. A **logarithmic function** is a function of the form $f(x) = \log_b(x)$ for some constant $b > 0, b \neq 1$, where $\log_b(x) = y$ if and only if $b^y = x$. (We also discuss exponential and logarithmic functions later in the chapter.)

Example 1.18

Classifying Algebraic and Transcendental Functions

Classify each of the following functions, a. through c., as algebraic or transcendental.

a. $f(x) = \dfrac{\sqrt{x^3 + 1}}{4x + 2}$

b. $f(x) = 2^{x^2}$

c. $f(x) = \sin(2x)$

Solution

a. Since this function involves basic algebraic operations only, it is an algebraic function.

b. This function cannot be written as a formula that involves only basic algebraic operations, so it is transcendental. (Note that algebraic functions can only have powers that are rational numbers.)

c. As in part b., this function cannot be written using a formula involving basic algebraic operations only; therefore, this function is transcendental.

1.13 Is $f(x) = x/2$ an algebraic or a transcendental function?

Piecewise-Defined Functions

Sometimes a function is defined by different formulas on different parts of its domain. A function with this property is known as a **piecewise-defined function**. The absolute value function is an example of a piecewise-defined function because the formula changes with the sign of x:

$$f(x) = \begin{cases} -x, & x < 0 \\ x, & x \geq 0 \end{cases}.$$

Other piecewise-defined functions may be represented by completely different formulas, depending on the part of the domain in which a point falls. To graph a piecewise-defined function, we graph each part of the function in its respective domain, on the same coordinate system. If the formula for a function is different for $x < a$ and $x > a$, we need to pay special attention to what happens at $x = a$ when we graph the function. Sometimes the graph needs to include an open or closed circle to indicate the value of the function at $x = a$. We examine this in the next example.

Example 1.19

Graphing a Piecewise-Defined Function

Sketch a graph of the following piecewise-defined function:

$$f(x) = \begin{cases} x+3, & x < 1 \\ (x-2)^2, & x \geq 1 \end{cases}.$$

Solution

Graph the linear function $y = x + 3$ on the interval $(-\infty, 1)$ and graph the quadratic function $y = (x-2)^2$ on the interval $[1, \infty)$. Since the value of the function at $x = 1$ is given by the formula $f(x) = (x-2)^2$, we see that $f(1) = 1$. To indicate this on the graph, we draw a closed circle at the point $(1, 1)$. The value of the function is given by $f(x) = x + 2$ for all $x < 1$, but not at $x = 1$. To indicate this on the graph, we draw an open circle at $(1, 4)$.

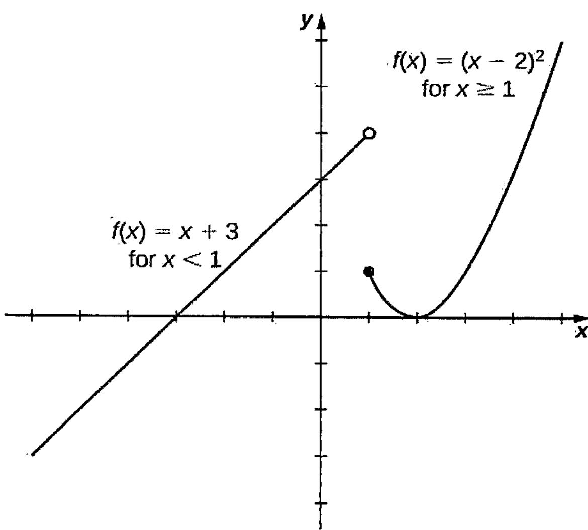

Figure 1.22 This piecewise-defined function is linear for $x < 1$ and quadratic for $x \geq 1$.

 **1.14** Sketch a graph of the function

$$f(x) = \begin{cases} 2-x, & x \leq 2 \\ x+2, & x > 2 \end{cases}.$$

Example 1.20

Parking Fees Described by a Piecewise-Defined Function

In a big city, drivers are charged variable rates for parking in a parking garage. They are charged \$10 for the first hour or any part of the first hour and an additional \$2 for each hour or part thereof up to a maximum of \$30 for the day. The parking garage is open from 6 a.m. to 12 midnight.

a. Write a piecewise-defined function that describes the cost C to park in the parking garage as a function of hours parked x.

b. Sketch a graph of this function $C(x)$.

Solution

a. Since the parking garage is open 18 hours each day, the domain for this function is $\{x|0 < x \le 18\}$. The cost to park a car at this parking garage can be described piecewise by the function

$$C(x) = \begin{cases} 10, & 0 < x \le 1 \\ 12, & 1 < x \le 2 \\ 14, & 2 < x \le 3 \\ 16, & 3 < x \le 4 \\ & \vdots \\ 30, & 10 < x \le 18 \end{cases}.$$

b. The graph of the function consists of several horizontal line segments.

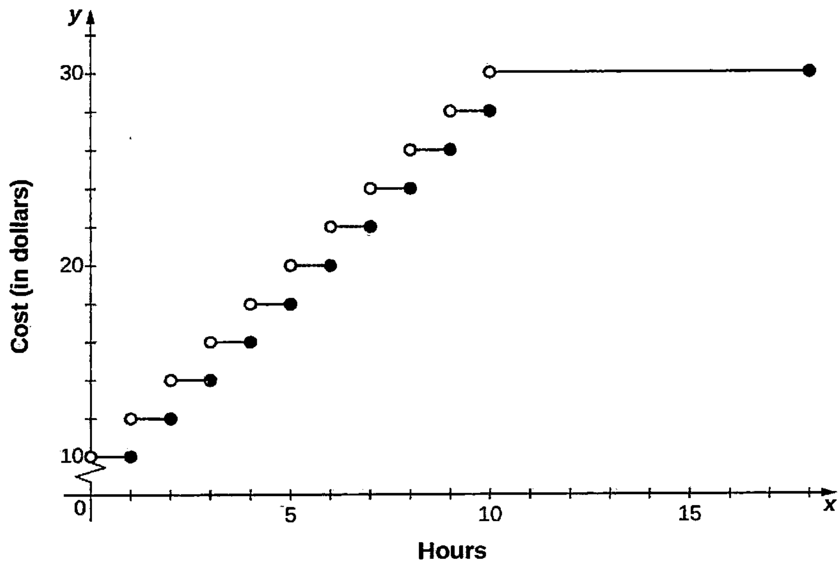

1.15 The cost of mailing a letter is a function of the weight of the letter. Suppose the cost of mailing a letter is 49¢ for the first ounce and 21¢ for each additional ounce. Write a piecewise-defined function describing the cost C as a function of the weight x for $0 < x \le 3,$ where C is measured in cents and x is measured in ounces.

Transformations of Functions

We have seen several cases in which we have added, subtracted, or multiplied constants to form variations of simple functions. In the previous example, for instance, we subtracted 2 from the argument of the function $y = x^2$ to get the function $f(x) = (x - 2)^2$. This subtraction represents a shift of the function $y = x^2$ two units to the right. A shift, horizontally or vertically, is a type of **transformation of a function.** Other transformations include horizontal and vertical scalings, and reflections about the axes.

A vertical shift of a function occurs if we add or subtract the same constant to each output y. For $c > 0,$ the graph of

$f(x) + c$ is a shift of the graph of $f(x)$ up c units, whereas the graph of $f(x) - c$ is a shift of the graph of $f(x)$ down c units. For example, the graph of the function $f(x) = x^3 + 4$ is the graph of $y = x^3$ shifted up 4 units; the graph of the function $f(x) = x^3 - 4$ is the graph of $y = x^3$ shifted down 4 units (**Figure 1.23**).

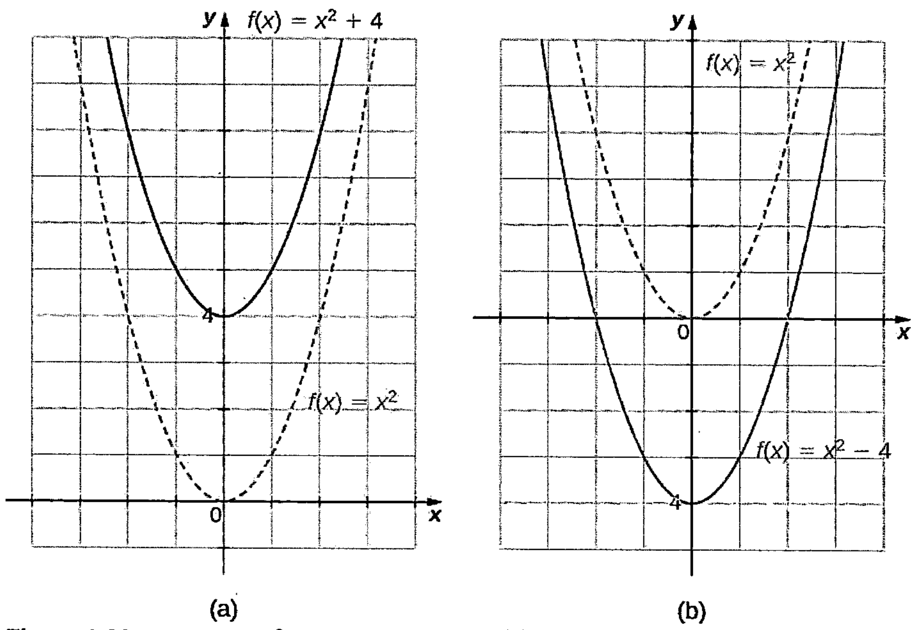

Figure 1.23 (a) For $c > 0$, the graph of $y = f(x) + c$ is a vertical shift up c units of the graph of $y = f(x)$. (b) For $c > 0$, the graph of $y = f(x) - c$ is a vertical shift down c units of the graph of $y = f(x)$.

A horizontal shift of a function occurs if we add or subtract the same constant to each input x. For $c > 0$, the graph of $f(x + c)$ is a shift of the graph of $f(x)$ to the left c units; the graph of $f(x - c)$ is a shift of the graph of $f(x)$ to the right c units. Why does the graph shift left when adding a constant and shift right when subtracting a constant? To answer this question, let's look at an example.

Consider the function $f(x) = |x + 3|$ and evaluate this function at $x - 3$. Since $f(x - 3) = |x|$ and $x - 3 < x$, the graph of $f(x) = |x + 3|$ is the graph of $y = |x|$ shifted left 3 units. Similarly, the graph of $f(x) = |x - 3|$ is the graph of $y = |x|$ shifted right 3 units (**Figure 1.24**).

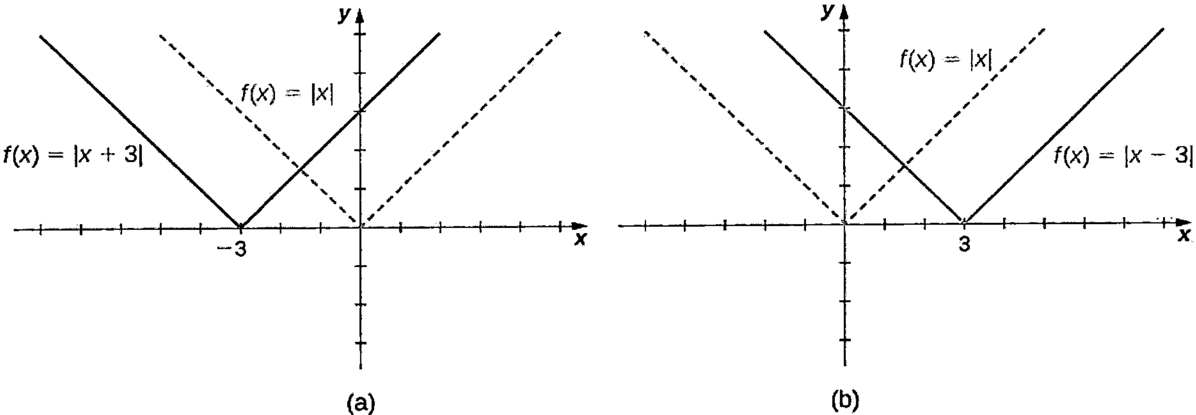

Figure 1.24 (a) For $c > 0,$ the graph of $y = f(x + c)$ is a horizontal shift left c units of the graph of $y = f(x).$ (b) For $c > 0,$ the graph of $y = f(x - c)$ is a horizontal shift right c units of the graph of $y = f(x).$

A vertical scaling of a graph occurs if we multiply all outputs y of a function by the same positive constant. For $c > 0,$ the graph of the function $cf(x)$ is the graph of $f(x)$ scaled vertically by a factor of $c.$ If $c > 1,$ the values of the outputs for the function $cf(x)$ are larger than the values of the outputs for the function $f(x);$ therefore, the graph has been stretched vertically. If $0 < c < 1,$ then the outputs of the function $cf(x)$ are smaller, so the graph has been compressed. For example, the graph of the function $f(x) = 3x^2$ is the graph of $y = x^2$ stretched vertically by a factor of 3, whereas the graph of $f(x) = x^2/3$ is the graph of $y = x^2$ compressed vertically by a factor of 3 (**Figure 1.25**).

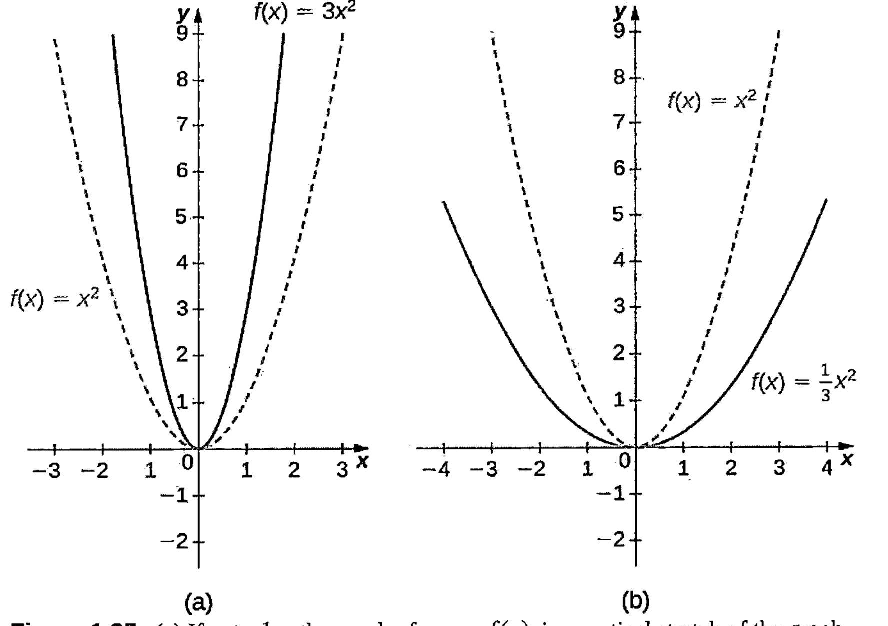

Figure 1.25 (a) If $c > 1,$ the graph of $y = cf(x)$ is a vertical stretch of the graph of $y = f(x).$ (b) If $0 < c < 1,$ the graph of $y = cf(x)$ is a vertical compression of the graph of $y = f(x).$

The horizontal scaling of a function occurs if we multiply the inputs x by the same positive constant. For $c > 0,$ the graph of the function $f(cx)$ is the graph of $f(x)$ scaled horizontally by a factor of $c.$ If $c > 1,$ the graph of $f(cx)$ is the graph of $f(x)$ compressed horizontally. If $0 < c < 1,$ the graph of $f(cx)$ is the graph of $f(x)$ stretched horizontally. For example, consider the function $f(x) = \sqrt{2x}$ and evaluate f at $x/2$. Since $f(x/2) = \sqrt{x}$, the graph of $f(x) = \sqrt{2x}$ is the graph of $y = \sqrt{x}$ compressed horizontally. The graph of $y = \sqrt{x/2}$ is a horizontal stretch of the graph of $y = \sqrt{x}$ (**Figure 1.26**).

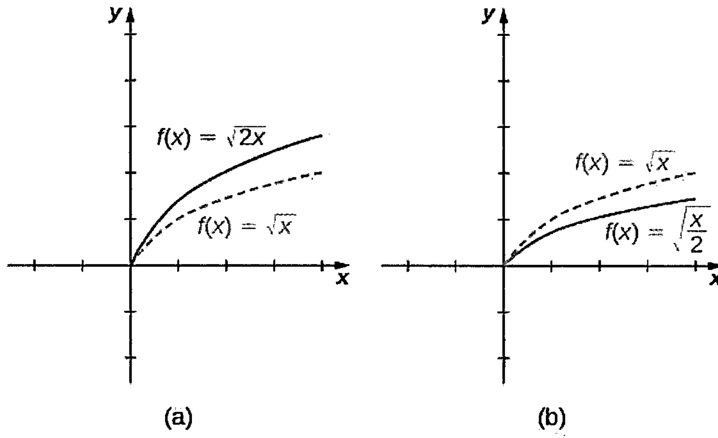

Figure 1.26 (a) If $c > 1$, the graph of $y = f(cx)$ is a horizontal compression of the graph of $y = f(x)$. (b) If $0 < c < 1$, the graph of $y = f(cx)$ is a horizontal stretch of the graph of $y = f(x)$.

We have explored what happens to the graph of a function f when we multiply f by a constant $c > 0$ to get a new function $cf(x)$. We have also discussed what happens to the graph of a function f when we multiply the independent variable x by $c > 0$ to get a new function $f(cx)$. However, we have not addressed what happens to the graph of the function if the constant c is negative. If we have a constant $c < 0$, we can write c as a positive number multiplied by -1; but, what kind of transformation do we get when we multiply the function or its argument by -1? When we multiply all the outputs by -1, we get a reflection about the x-axis. When we multiply all inputs by -1, we get a reflection about the y-axis. For example, the graph of $f(x) = -(x^3 + 1)$ is the graph of $y = (x^3 + 1)$ reflected about the x-axis. The graph of $f(x) = (-x)^3 + 1$ is the graph of $y = x^3 + 1$ reflected about the y-axis (**Figure 1.27**).

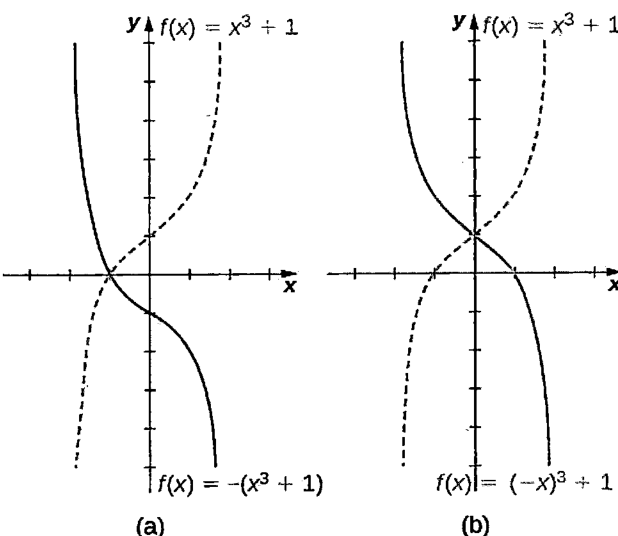

Figure 1.27 (a) The graph of $y = -f(x)$ is the graph of $y = f(x)$ reflected about the x -axis. (b) The graph of $y = f(-x)$ is the graph of $y = f(x)$ reflected about the y -axis.

If the graph of a function consists of more than one transformation of another graph, it is important to transform the graph in the correct order. Given a function $f(x)$, the graph of the related function $y = cf(a(x + b)) + d$ can be obtained from the graph of $y = f(x)$ by performing the transformations in the following order.

1. Horizontal shift of the graph of $y = f(x)$. If $b > 0$, shift left. If $b < 0$, shift right.
2. Horizontal scaling of the graph of $y = f(x + b)$ by a factor of $|a|$. If $a < 0$, reflect the graph about the y -axis.
3. Vertical scaling of the graph of $y = f(a(x + b))$ by a factor of $|c|$. If $c < 0$, reflect the graph about the x -axis.
4. Vertical shift of the graph of $y = cf(a(x + b))$. If $d > 0$, shift up. If $d < 0$, shift down.

We can summarize the different transformations and their related effects on the graph of a function in the following table.

Transformation of $f(c > 0)$	Effect on the graph of f
$f(x) + c$	Vertical shift up c units
$f(x) - c$	Vertical shift down c units
$f(x + c)$	Shift left by c units
$f(x - c)$	Shift right by c units
$cf(x)$	Vertical stretch if $c > 1$; vertical compression if $0 < c < 1$
$f(cx)$	Horizontal stretch if $0 < c < 1$; horizontal compression if $c > 1$
$-f(x)$	Reflection about the x-axis
$f(-x)$	Reflection about the y-axis

Table 1.7 Transformations of Functions

Example 1.21

Transforming a Function

For each of the following functions, a. and b., sketch a graph by using a sequence of transformations of a well-known function.

a. $f(x) = -|x + 2| - 3$

b. $f(x) = 3\sqrt{-x} + 1$

Solution

a. Starting with the graph of $y = |x|$, shift 2 units to the left, reflect about the x-axis, and then shift down 3 units.

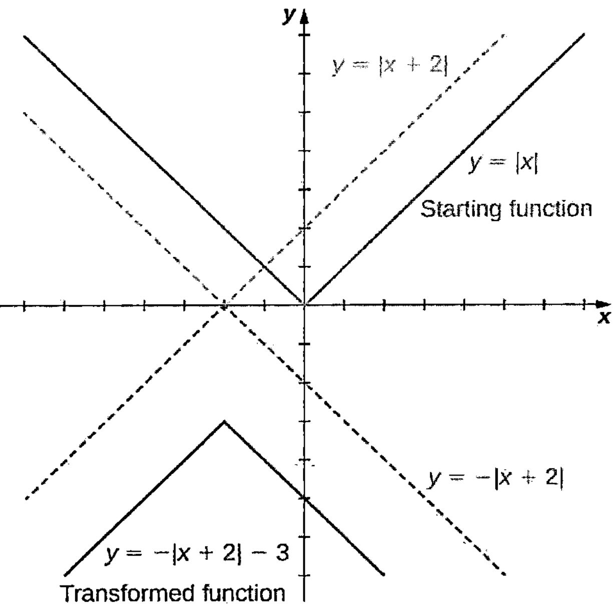

Figure 1.28 The function $f(x) = -|x+2| - 3$ can be viewed as a sequence of three transformations of the function $y = |x|$.

b. Starting with the graph of $y = \sqrt{x}$, reflect about the y-axis, stretch the graph vertically by a factor of 3, and move up 1 unit.

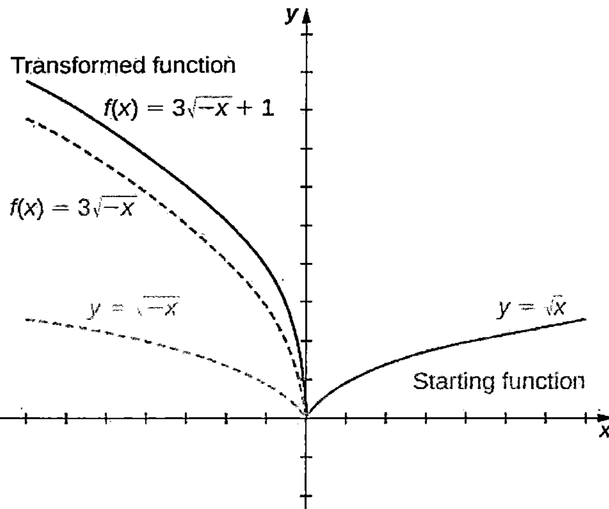

Figure 1.29 The function $f(x) = 3\sqrt{-x} + 1$ can be viewed as a sequence of three transformations of the function $y = \sqrt{x}$.

1.16 Describe how the function $f(x) = -(x+1)^2 - 4$ can be graphed using the graph of $y = x^2$ and a sequence of transformations.

1.2 EXERCISES

For the following exercises, for each pair of points, a. find the slope of the line passing through the points and b. indicate whether the line is increasing, decreasing, horizontal, or vertical.

59. $(-2, 4)$ and $(1, 1)$

60. $(-1, 4)$ and $(3, -1)$

61. $(3, 5)$ and $(-1, 2)$

62. $(6, 4)$ and $(4, -3)$

63. $(2, 3)$ and $(5, 7)$

64. $(1, 9)$ and $(-8, 5)$

65. $(2, 4)$ and $(1, 4)$

66. $(1, 4)$ and $(1, 0)$

For the following exercises, write the equation of the line satisfying the given conditions in slope-intercept form.

67. Slope $= -6,$ passes through $(1, 3)$

68. Slope $= 3,$ passes through $(-3, 2)$

69. Slope $= \frac{1}{3},$ passes through $(0, 4)$

70. Slope $= \frac{2}{5},$ x-intercept $= 8$

71. Passing through $(2, 1)$ and $(-2, -1)$

72. Passing through $(-3, 7)$ and $(1, 2)$

73. x-intercept $= 5$ and y-intercept $= -3$

74. x-intercept $= -6$ and y-intercept $= 9$

For the following exercises, for each linear equation, a. give the slope m and y-intercept b, if any, and b. graph the line.

75. $y = 2x - 3$

76. $y = -\frac{1}{7}x + 1$

77. $f(x) = -6x$

78. $f(x) = -5x + 4$

79. $4y + 24 = 0$

80. $8x - 4 = 0$

81. $2x + 3y = 6$

82. $6x - 5y + 15 = 0$

For the following exercises, for each polynomial, a. find the degree; b. find the zeros, if any; c. find the y-intercept(s), if any; d. use the leading coefficient to determine the graph's end behavior; and e. determine algebraically whether the polynomial is even, odd, or neither.

83. $f(x) = 2x^2 - 3x - 5$

84. $f(x) = -3x^2 + 6x$

85. $f(x) = \frac{1}{2}x^2 - 1$

86. $f(x) = x^3 + 3x^2 - x - 3$

87. $f(x) = 3x - x^3$

For the following exercises, use the graph of $f(x) = x^2$ to graph each transformed function g.

88. $g(x) = x^2 - 1$

89. $g(x) = (x + 3)^2 + 1$

For the following exercises, use the graph of $f(x) = \sqrt{x}$ to graph each transformed function g.

90. $g(x) = \sqrt{x + 2}$

91. $g(x) = -\sqrt{x} - 1$

For the following exercises, use the graph of $y = f(x)$ to graph each transformed function g.

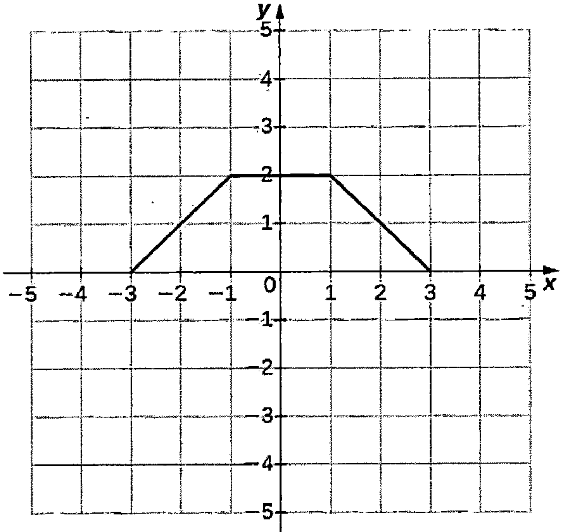

92. $g(x) = f(x) + 1$

93. $g(x) = f(x - 1) + 2$

For the following exercises, for each of the piecewise-defined functions, a. evaluate at the given values of the independent variable and b. sketch the graph.

94. $f(x) = \begin{cases} 4x + 3, \ x \le 0 \\ -x + 1, \ x > 0 \end{cases}$; $f(-3)$; $f(0)$; $f(2)$

95. $f(x) = \begin{cases} x^2 - 3, \ x < 0 \\ 4x - 3, \ x \ge 0 \end{cases}$; $f(-4)$; $f(0)$; $f(2)$

96. $h(x) = \begin{cases} x + 1, \ x \le 5 \\ 4, \ x > 5 \end{cases}$; $h(0)$; $h(\pi)$; $h(5)$

97. $g(x) = \begin{cases} \frac{3}{x - 2}, \ x \ne 2 \\ 4, \ x = 2 \end{cases}$; $g(0)$; $g(-4)$; $g(2)$

For the following exercises, determine whether the statement is *true or false*. Explain why.

98. $f(x) = (4x + 1)/(7x - 2)$ is a transcendental function.

99. $g(x) = \sqrt[3]{x}$ is an odd root function

100. A logarithmic function is an algebraic function.

101. A function of the form $f(x) = x^b$, where b is a real valued constant, is an exponential function.

102. The domain of an even root function is all real numbers.

103. **[T]** A company purchases some computer equipment for \$20,500. At the end of a 3-year period, the value of the equipment has decreased linearly to \$12,300.

a. Find a function $y = V(t)$ that determines the value V of the equipment at the end of t years.
b. Find and interpret the meaning of the x- and y-intercepts for this situation.
c. What is the value of the equipment at the end of 5 years?
d. When will the value of the equipment be \$3000?

104. **[T]** Total online shopping during the Christmas holidays has increased dramatically during the past 5 years. In 2012 $(t = 0)$, total online holiday sales were \$42.3 billion, whereas in 2013 they were \$48.1 billion.

a. Find a linear function S that estimates the total online holiday sales in the year t.
b. Interpret the slope of the graph of S.
c. Use part a. to predict the year when online shopping during Christmas will reach \$60 billion.

105. **[T]** A family bakery makes cupcakes and sells them at local outdoor festivals. For a music festival, there is a fixed cost of \$125 to set up a cupcake stand. The owner estimates that it costs \$0.75 to make each cupcake. The owner is interested in determining the total cost C as a function of number of cupcakes made.

a. Find a linear function that relates cost C to x, the number of cupcakes made.
b. Find the cost to bake 160 cupcakes.
c. If the owner sells the cupcakes for \$1.50 apiece, how many cupcakes does she need to sell to start making profit? (*Hint*: Use the INTERSECTION function on a calculator to find this number.)

106. **[T]** A house purchased for \$250,000 is expected to be worth twice its purchase price in 18 years.

a. Find a linear function that models the price P of the house versus the number of years t since the original purchase.
b. Interpret the slope of the graph of P.
c. Find the price of the house 15 years from when it was originally purchased.

107. **[T]** A car was purchased for \$26,000. The value of the car depreciates by \$1500 per year.

a. Find a linear function that models the value V of the car after t years.
b. Find and interpret $V(4)$.

108. **[T]** A condominium in an upscale part of the city was purchased for \$432,000. In 35 years it is worth \$60,500. Find the rate of depreciation.

109. **[T]** The total cost C (in thousands of dollars) to produce a certain item is modeled by the function $C(x) = 10.50x + 28{,}500$, where x is the number of items produced. Determine the cost to produce 175 items.

110. **[T]** A professor asks her class to report the amount of time t they spent writing two assignments. Most students report that it takes them about 45 minutes to type a four-page assignment and about 1.5 hours to type a nine-page assignment.

a. Find the linear function $y = N(t)$ that models this situation, where N is the number of pages typed and t is the time in minutes.
b. Use part a. to determine how many pages can be typed in 2 hours.
c. Use part a. to determine how long it takes to type a 20-page assignment.

111. **[T]** The output (as a percent of total capacity) of nuclear power plants in the United States can be modeled by the function $P(t) = 1.8576t + 68.052$, where t is time in years and $t = 0$ corresponds to the beginning of 2000. Use the model to predict the percentage output in 2015.

112. **[T]** The admissions office at a public university estimates that 65% of the students offered admission to the class of 2019 will actually enroll.

a. Find the linear function $y = N(x)$, where N is the number of students that actually enroll and x is the number of all students offered admission to the class of 2019.
b. If the university wants the 2019 freshman class size to be 1350, determine how many students should be admitted.

1.3 | Trigonometric Functions

Learning Objectives

1.3.1 Convert angle measures between degrees and radians.
1.3.2 Recognize the triangular and circular definitions of the basic trigonometric functions.
1.3.3 Write the basic trigonometric identities.
1.3.4 Identify the graphs and periods of the trigonometric functions.
1.3.5 Describe the shift of a sine or cosine graph from the equation of the function.

Trigonometric functions are used to model many phenomena, including sound waves, vibrations of strings, alternating electrical current, and the motion of pendulums. In fact, almost any repetitive, or cyclical, motion can be modeled by some combination of trigonometric functions. In this section, we define the six basic trigonometric functions and look at some of the main identities involving these functions.

Radian Measure

To use trigonometric functions, we first must understand how to measure the angles. Although we can use both radians and degrees, **radians** are a more natural measurement because they are related directly to the unit circle, a circle with radius 1. The radian measure of an angle is defined as follows. Given an angle $\theta,$ let s be the length of the corresponding arc on the unit circle (**Figure 1.30**). We say the angle corresponding to the arc of length 1 has radian measure 1.

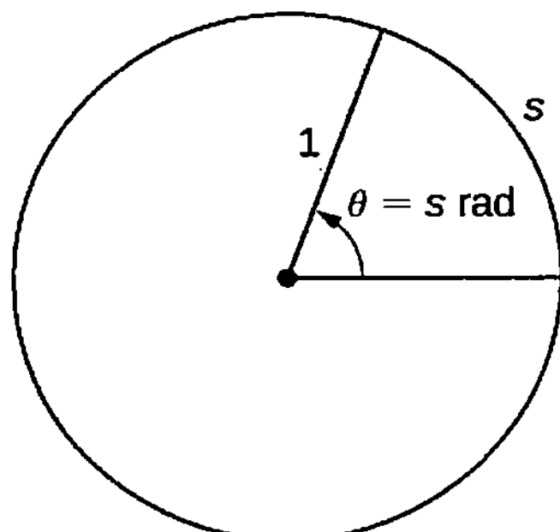

Figure 1.30 The radian measure of an angle θ is the arc length s of the associated arc on the unit circle.

Since an angle of $360°$ corresponds to the circumference of a circle, or an arc of length $2\pi,$ we conclude that an angle with a degree measure of $360°$ has a radian measure of $2\pi.$ Similarly, we see that $180°$ is equivalent to π radians. **Table 1.8** shows the relationship between common degree and radian values.

Degrees	Radians	Degrees	Radians
0	0	120	$2\pi/3$
30	$\pi/6$	135	$3\pi/4$
45	$\pi/4$	150	$5\pi/6$
60	$\pi/3$	180	π
90	$\pi/2$		

Table 1.8 Common Angles Expressed in Degrees and Radians

Example 1.22

Converting between Radians and Degrees

a. Express $225°$ using radians.

b. Express $5\pi/3$ rad using degrees.

Solution

Use the fact that $180°$ is equivalent to π radians as a conversion factor: $1 = \frac{\pi \text{rad}}{180°} = \frac{180°}{\pi \text{rad}}$.

a. $225° = 225° \cdot \frac{\pi}{180°} = \frac{5\pi}{4}$ rad

b. $\frac{5\pi}{3}$ rad $= \frac{5\pi}{3} \cdot \frac{180°}{\pi} = 300°$

1.17 Express $210°$ using radians. Express $11\pi/6$ rad using degrees.

The Six Basic Trigonometric Functions

Trigonometric functions allow us to use angle measures, in radians or degrees, to find the coordinates of a point on any circle—not only on a unit circle—or to find an angle given a point on a circle. They also define the relationship among the sides and angles of a triangle.

To define the trigonometric functions, first consider the unit circle centered at the origin and a point $P = (x, y)$ on the unit circle. Let θ be an angle with an initial side that lies along the positive x-axis and with a terminal side that is the line segment OP. An angle in this position is said to be in *standard position* (**Figure 1.31**). We can then define the values of the six trigonometric functions for θ in terms of the coordinates x and y.

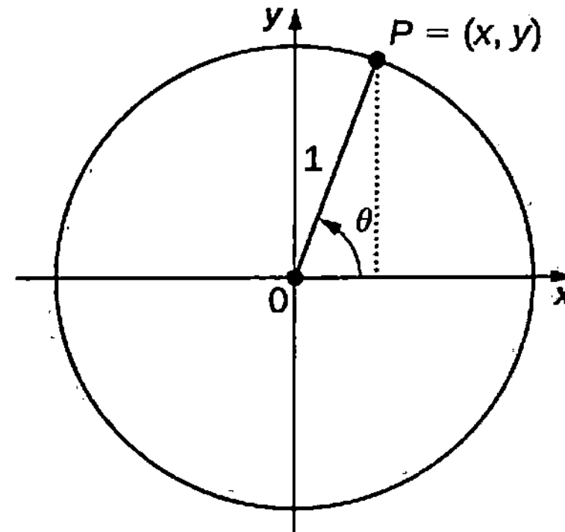

Figure 1.31 The angle θ is in standard position. The values of the trigonometric functions for θ are defined in terms of the coordinates x and y.

Definition

Let $P=(x, y)$ be a point on the unit circle centered at the origin O. Let θ be an angle with an initial side along the positive x-axis and a terminal side given by the line segment OP. The **trigonometric functions** are then defined as

$$\begin{aligned} \sin\theta &= y & \csc\theta &= \frac{1}{y} \\ \cos\theta &= x & \sec\theta &= \frac{1}{x} \\ \tan\theta &= \frac{y}{x} & \cot\theta &= \frac{x}{y} \end{aligned} \tag{1.9}$$

If $x=0$, $\sec\theta$ and $\tan\theta$ are undefined. If $y=0$, then $\cot\theta$ and $\csc\theta$ are undefined.

We can see that for a point $P=(x, y)$ on a circle of radius r with a corresponding angle θ, the coordinates x and y satisfy

$$\begin{aligned} \cos\theta &= \frac{x}{r} \\ x &= r\cos\theta \\ \sin\theta &= \frac{y}{r} \\ y &= r\sin\theta. \end{aligned}$$

The values of the other trigonometric functions can be expressed in terms of x, y, and r (**Figure 1.32**).

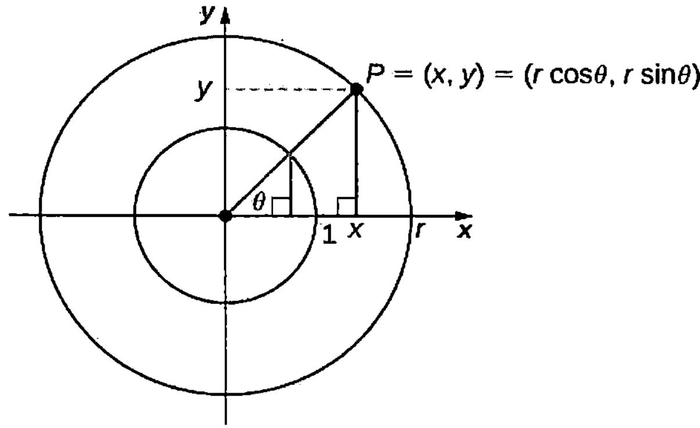

Figure 1.32 For a point $P = (x,\ y)$ on a circle of radius r, the coordinates x and y satisfy $x = r\cos\theta$ and $y = r\sin\theta$.

Table 1.9 shows the values of sine and cosine at the major angles in the first quadrant. From this table, we can determine the values of sine and cosine at the corresponding angles in the other quadrants. The values of the other trigonometric functions are calculated easily from the values of $\sin\theta$ and $\cos\theta$.

θ	$\sin\theta$	$\cos\theta$
0	0	1
$\frac{\pi}{6}$	$\frac{1}{2}$	$\frac{\sqrt{3}}{2}$
$\frac{\pi}{4}$	$\frac{\sqrt{2}}{2}$	$\frac{\sqrt{2}}{2}$
$\frac{\pi}{3}$	$\frac{\sqrt{3}}{2}$	$\frac{1}{2}$
$\frac{\pi}{2}$	1	0

Table 1.9 Values of $\sin\theta$ and $\cos\theta$ at Major Angles θ in the First Quadrant

Example 1.23

Evaluating Trigonometric Functions

Evaluate each of the following expressions.

a. $\sin\left(\frac{2\pi}{3}\right)$

b. $\cos\left(-\frac{5\pi}{6}\right)$

c. $\tan\left(\frac{15\pi}{4}\right)$

Solution

a. On the unit circle, the angle $\theta = \frac{2\pi}{3}$ corresponds to the point $\left(-\frac{1}{2}, \frac{\sqrt{3}}{2}\right)$. Therefore, $\sin\left(\frac{2\pi}{3}\right) = y = \frac{\sqrt{3}}{2}$.

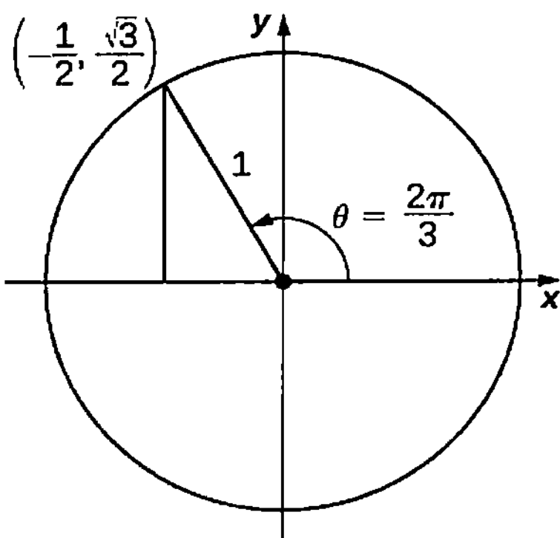

b. An angle $\theta = -\frac{5\pi}{6}$ corresponds to a revolution in the negative direction, as shown. Therefore, $\cos\left(-\frac{5\pi}{6}\right) = x = -\frac{\sqrt{3}}{2}$.

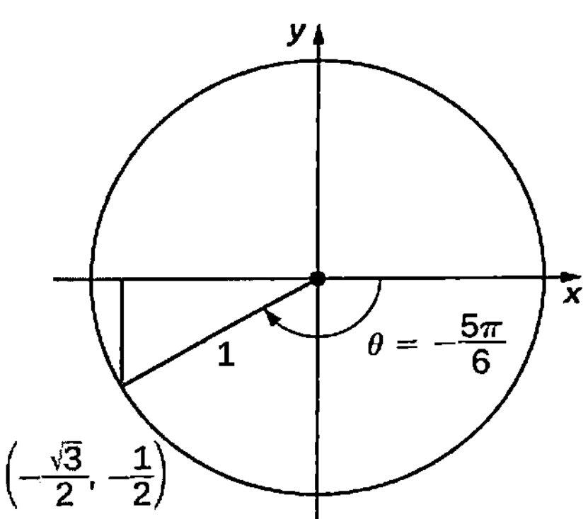

c. An angle $\theta = \frac{15\pi}{4} = 2\pi + \frac{7\pi}{4}$. Therefore, this angle corresponds to more than one revolution, as shown. Knowing the fact that an angle of $\frac{7\pi}{4}$ corresponds to the point $\left(\frac{\sqrt{2}}{2}, -\frac{\sqrt{2}}{2}\right)$, we can conclude that $\tan\left(\frac{15\pi}{4}\right) = \frac{y}{x} = -1$.

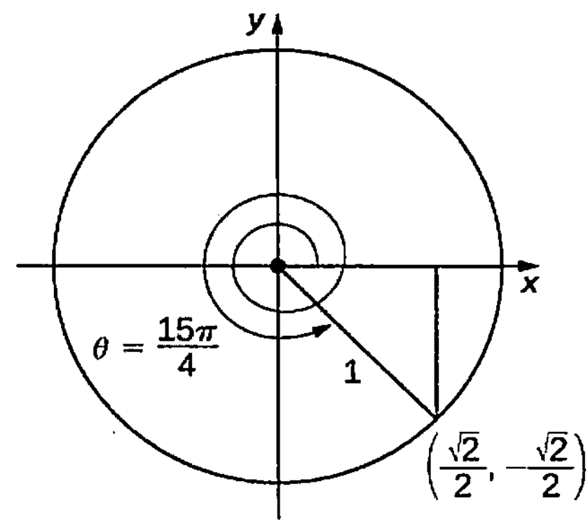

1.18 Evaluate $\cos(3\pi/4)$ and $\sin(-\pi/6)$.

As mentioned earlier, the ratios of the side lengths of a right triangle can be expressed in terms of the trigonometric functions evaluated at either of the acute angles of the triangle. Let θ be one of the acute angles. Let A be the length of the adjacent leg, O be the length of the opposite leg, and H be the length of the hypotenuse. By inscribing the triangle into a circle of radius H, as shown in **Figure 1.33**, we see that A, H, and O satisfy the following relationships with θ:

$$\sin\theta = \frac{O}{H} \qquad \csc\theta = \frac{H}{O}$$
$$\cos\theta = \frac{A}{H} \qquad \sec\theta = \frac{H}{A}$$
$$\tan\theta = \frac{O}{A} \qquad \cot\theta = \frac{A}{O}$$

Figure 1.33 By inscribing a right triangle in a circle, we can express the ratios of the side lengths in terms of the trigonometric functions evaluated at θ.

Example 1.24

Constructing a Wooden Ramp

A wooden ramp is to be built with one end on the ground and the other end at the top of a short staircase. If the top of the staircase is 4 ft from the ground and the angle between the ground and the ramp is to be $10°$, how long does the ramp need to be?

Solution

Let x denote the length of the ramp. In the following image, we see that x needs to satisfy the equation $\sin(10°) = 4/x$. Solving this equation for x, we see that $x = 4/\sin(10°) \approx 23.035$ ft.

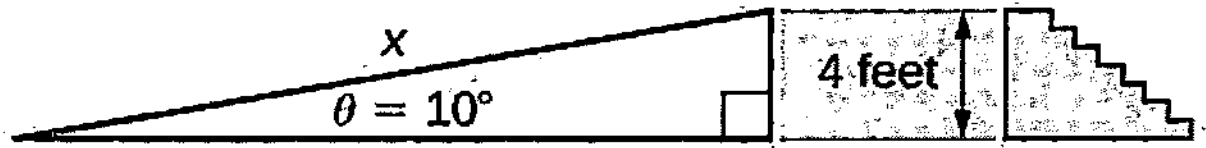

1.19 A house painter wants to lean a 20 -ft ladder against a house. If the angle between the base of the ladder and the ground is to be $60°$, how far from the house should she place the base of the ladder?

Trigonometric Identities

A **trigonometric identity** is an equation involving trigonometric functions that is true for all angles θ for which the functions are defined. We can use the identities to help us solve or simplify equations. The main trigonometric identities are listed next.

Rule: Trigonometric Identities

Reciprocal identities

$$\tan\theta = \frac{\sin\theta}{\cos\theta} \qquad \cot\theta = \frac{\cos\theta}{\sin\theta}$$

$$\csc\theta = \frac{1}{\sin\theta} \qquad \sec\theta = \frac{1}{\cos\theta}$$

Pythagorean identities

$$\sin^2\theta + \cos^2\theta = 1 \qquad 1 + \tan^2\theta = \sec^2\theta \qquad 1 + \cot^2\theta = \csc^2\theta$$

Addition and subtraction formulas

$$\sin(\alpha \pm \beta) = \sin\alpha\cos\beta \pm \cos\alpha\sin\beta$$

$$\cos(\alpha \pm \beta) = \cos\alpha\cos\beta \mp \sin\alpha\sin\beta$$

Double-angle formulas

$$\sin(2\theta) = 2\sin\theta\cos\theta$$

$$\cos(2\theta) = 2\cos^2\theta - 1 = 1 - 2\sin^2\theta = \cos^2\theta - \sin^2\theta$$

Example 1.25

Solving Trigonometric Equations

For each of the following equations, use a trigonometric identity to find all solutions.

a. $1 + \cos(2\theta) = \cos\theta$

b. $\sin(2\theta) = \tan\theta$

Solution

a. Using the double-angle formula for $\cos(2\theta)$, we see that θ is a solution of

$$1 + \cos(2\theta) = \cos\theta$$

if and only if

$$1 + 2\cos^2\theta - 1 = \cos\theta,$$

which is true if and only if

$$2\cos^2\theta - \cos\theta = 0.$$

To solve this equation, it is important to note that we need to factor the left-hand side and not divide both sides of the equation by $\cos\theta$. The problem with dividing by $\cos\theta$ is that it is possible that $\cos\theta$ is zero. In fact, if we did divide both sides of the equation by $\cos\theta$, we would miss some of the solutions of the original equation. Factoring the left-hand side of the equation, we see that θ is a solution of this equation if and only if

$$\cos\theta(2\cos\theta - 1) = 0.$$

Since $\cos\theta = 0$ when

$$\theta = \frac{\pi}{2}, \frac{\pi}{2} \pm \pi, \frac{\pi}{2} \pm 2\pi, \ldots,$$

and $\cos\theta = 1/2$ when

$$\theta = \frac{\pi}{3}, \frac{\pi}{3} \pm 2\pi, \ldots \text{ or } \theta = -\frac{\pi}{3}, -\frac{\pi}{3} \pm 2\pi, \ldots,$$

we conclude that the set of solutions to this equation is

$$\theta = \frac{\pi}{2} + n\pi, \theta = \frac{\pi}{3} + 2n\pi, \text{ and } \theta = -\frac{\pi}{3} + 2n\pi, n = 0, \pm 1, \pm 2, \ldots.$$

b. Using the double-angle formula for $\sin(2\theta)$ and the reciprocal identity for $\tan(\theta)$, the equation can be written as

$$2\sin\theta\cos\theta = \frac{\sin\theta}{\cos\theta}.$$

To solve this equation, we multiply both sides by $\cos\theta$ to eliminate the denominator, and say that if θ satisfies this equation, then θ satisfies the equation

$$2\sin\theta\cos^2\theta - \sin\theta = 0.$$

However, we need to be a little careful here. Even if θ satisfies this new equation, it may not satisfy the original equation because, to satisfy the original equation, we would need to be able to divide both sides of the equation by $\cos\theta$. However, if $\cos\theta = 0$, we cannot divide both sides of the equation by $\cos\theta$. Therefore, it is possible that we may arrive at extraneous solutions. So, at the end, it is important to check for extraneous solutions. Returning to the equation, it is important that we factor $\sin\theta$ out of both terms on the left-hand side instead of dividing both sides of the equation by $\sin\theta$. Factoring the left-hand side of the equation, we can rewrite this equation as

$$\sin\theta(2\cos^2\theta - 1) = 0.$$

Therefore, the solutions are given by the angles θ such that $\sin\theta = 0$ or $\cos^2\theta = 1/2$. The solutions of the first equation are $\theta = 0, \ \pm\pi, \ \pm 2\pi, \ldots$ The solutions of the second equation are $\theta = \pi/4, \ (\pi/4) \pm (\pi/2), \ (\pi/4) \pm \pi, \ldots$ After checking for extraneous solutions, the set of solutions to the equation is

$$\theta = n\pi \quad \text{and} \quad \theta = \frac{\pi}{4} + \frac{n\pi}{2}, \ n = 0, \ \pm 1, \ \pm 2, \ldots$$

1.20 Find all solutions to the equation $\cos(2\theta) = \sin\theta$.

Example 1.26

Proving a Trigonometric Identity

Prove the trigonometric identity $1 + \tan^2\theta = \sec^2\theta$.

Solution

We start with the identity

$$\sin^2\theta + \cos^2\theta = 1.$$

Dividing both sides of this equation by $\cos^2\theta$, we obtain

$$\frac{\sin^2\theta}{\cos^2\theta} + 1 = \frac{1}{\cos^2\theta}.$$

Since $\sin\theta/\cos\theta = \tan\theta$ and $1/\cos\theta = \sec\theta$, we conclude that

$$\tan^2\theta + 1 = \sec^2\theta.$$

1.21 Prove the trigonometric identity $1 + \cot^2\theta = \csc^2\theta$.

Graphs and Periods of the Trigonometric Functions

We have seen that as we travel around the unit circle, the values of the trigonometric functions repeat. We can see this pattern in the graphs of the functions. Let $P = (x, \ y)$ be a point on the unit circle and let θ be the corresponding angle . Since the angle θ and $\theta + 2\pi$ correspond to the same point P, the values of the trigonometric functions at θ and at $\theta + 2\pi$ are the same. Consequently, the trigonometric functions are **periodic functions.** The period of a function f is defined to be the smallest positive value p such that $f(x + p) = f(x)$ for all values x in the domain of f. The sine, cosine, secant, and cosecant functions have a period of 2π. Since the tangent and cotangent functions repeat on an interval of length π, their period is π (**Figure 1.34**).

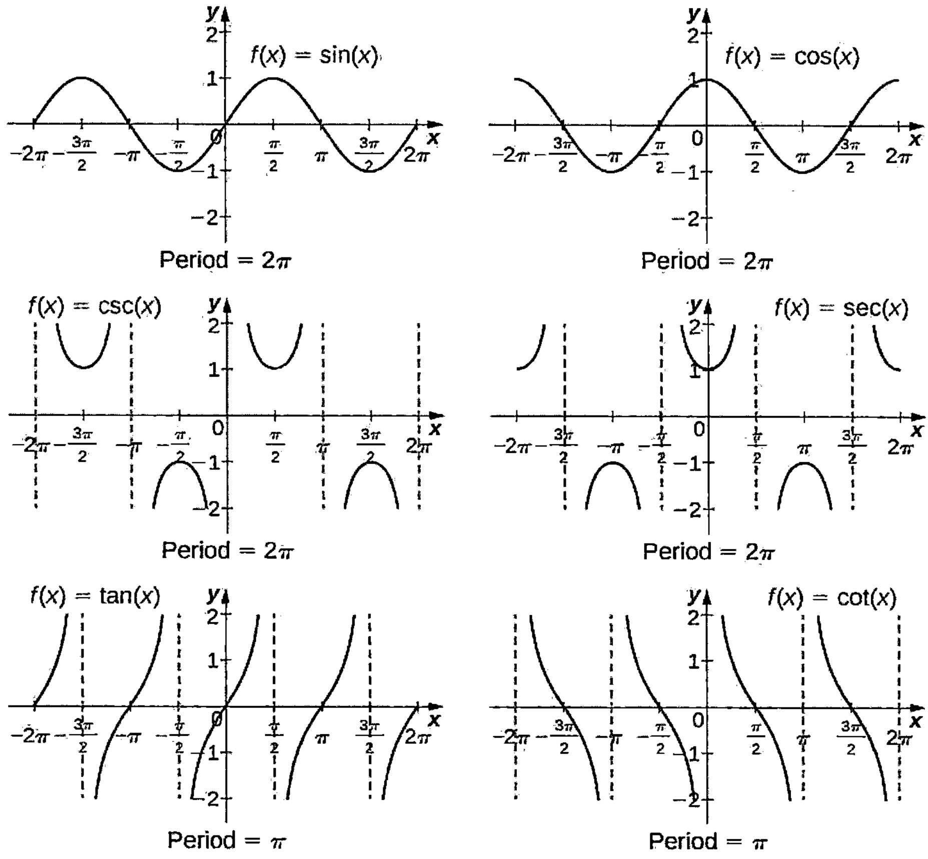

Figure 1.34 The six trigonometric functions are periodic.

Just as with algebraic functions, we can apply transformations to trigonometric functions. In particular, consider the following function:

$$f(x) = A\sin(B(x - \alpha)) + C. \tag{1.10}$$

In **Figure 1.35**, the constant α causes a horizontal or phase shift. The factor B changes the period. This transformed sine function will have a period $2\pi/|B|$. The factor A results in a vertical stretch by a factor of $|A|$. We say $|A|$ is the "amplitude of f." The constant C causes a vertical shift.

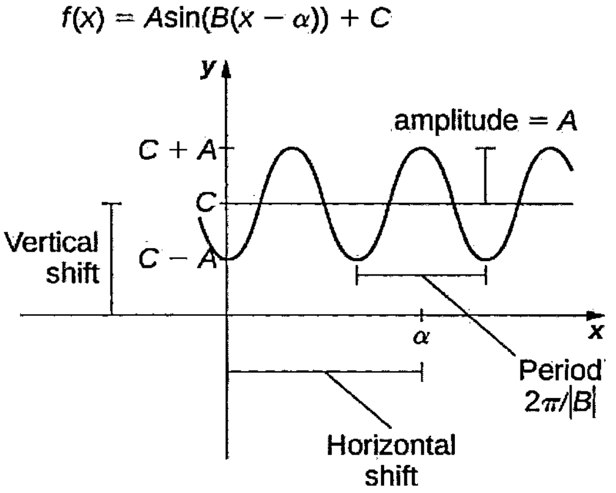

Figure 1.35 A graph of a general sine function.

Notice in **Figure 1.34** that the graph of $y = \cos x$ is the graph of $y = \sin x$ shifted to the left $\pi/2$ units. Therefore, we can write $\cos x = \sin(x + \pi/2)$. Similarly, we can view the graph of $y = \sin x$ as the graph of $y = \cos x$ shifted right $\pi/2$ units, and state that $\sin x = \cos(x - \pi/2)$.

A shifted sine curve arises naturally when graphing the number of hours of daylight in a given location as a function of the day of the year. For example, suppose a city reports that June 21 is the longest day of the year with 15.7 hours and December 21 is the shortest day of the year with 8.3 hours. It can be shown that the function

$$h(t) = 3.7\sin\left(\frac{2\pi}{365}(x - 80.5)\right) + 12$$

is a model for the number of hours of daylight h as a function of day of the year t (**Figure 1.36**).

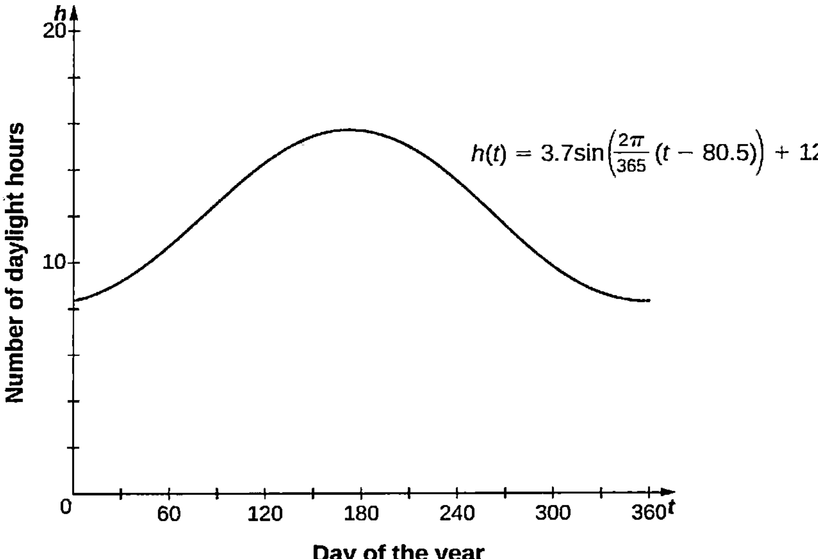

Figure 1.36 The hours of daylight as a function of day of the year can be modeled by a shifted sine curve.

Example 1.27

Sketching the Graph of a Transformed Sine Curve

Sketch a graph of $f(x) = 3\sin\left(2\left(x - \frac{\pi}{4}\right)\right) + 1$.

Solution

This graph is a phase shift of $y = \sin(x)$ to the right by $\pi/4$ units, followed by a horizontal compression by a factor of 2, a vertical stretch by a factor of 3, and then a vertical shift by 1 unit. The period of f is π.

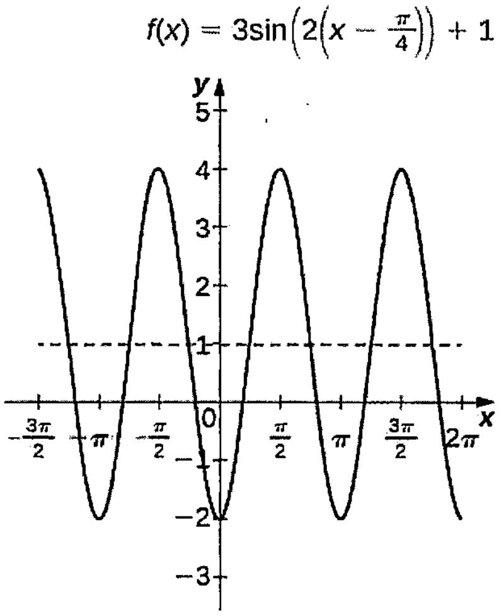

$f(x) = 3\sin\left(2\left(x - \frac{\pi}{4}\right)\right) + 1$

1.22 Describe the relationship between the graph of $f(x) = 3\sin(4x) - 5$ and the graph of $y = \sin(x)$.

1.3 EXERCISES

For the following exercises, convert each angle in degrees to radians. Write the answer as a multiple of π.

113. 240°

114. 15°

115. −60°

116. −225°

117. 330°

For the following exercises, convert each angle in radians to degrees.

118. $\frac{\pi}{2}$ rad

119. $\frac{7\pi}{6}$ rad

120. $\frac{11\pi}{2}$ rad

121. -3π rad

122. $\frac{5\pi}{12}$ rad

Evaluate the following functional values.

123. $\cos\left(\frac{4\pi}{3}\right)$

124. $\tan\left(\frac{19\pi}{4}\right)$

125. $\sin\left(-\frac{3\pi}{4}\right)$

126. $\sec\left(\frac{\pi}{6}\right)$

127. $\sin\left(\frac{\pi}{12}\right)$

128. $\cos\left(\frac{5\pi}{12}\right)$

For the following exercises, consider triangle *ABC*, a right triangle with a right angle at *C*. a. Find the missing side of the triangle. b. Find the six trigonometric function values for the angle at *A*. Where necessary, round to one decimal place.

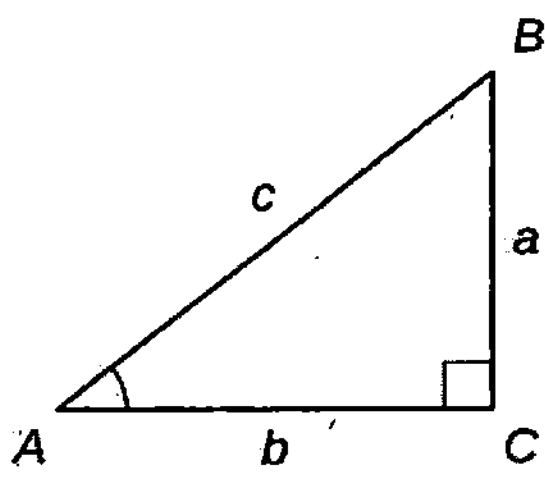

129. $a = 4, c = 7$

130. $a = 21, c = 29$

131. $a = 85.3, b = 125.5$

132. $b = 40, c = 41$

133. $a = 84, b = 13$

134. $b = 28, c = 35$

For the following exercises, P is a point on the unit circle. a. Find the (exact) missing coordinate value of each point and b. find the values of the six trigonometric functions for the angle θ with a terminal side that passes through point P. Rationalize denominators.

135. $P\left(\frac{7}{25}, y\right), y > 0$

136. $P\left(\frac{-15}{17}, y\right), y < 0$

137. $P\left(x, \frac{\sqrt{7}}{3}\right), x < 0$

138. $P\left(x, \frac{-\sqrt{15}}{4}\right), x > 0$

For the following exercises, simplify each expression by writing it in terms of sines and cosines, then simplify. The final answer does not have to be in terms of sine and cosine only.

139. $\tan^2 x + \sin x \csc x$

140. $\sec x \sin x \cot x$

141. $\frac{\tan^2 x}{\sec^2 x}$

142. $\sec x - \cos x$

143. $(1 + \tan\theta)^2 - 2\tan\theta$

144. $\sin x(\csc x - \sin x)$

145. $\frac{\cos t}{\sin t} + \frac{\sin t}{1 + \cos t}$

146. $\frac{1 + \tan^2 \alpha}{1 + \cot^2 \alpha}$

For the following exercises, verify that each equation is an identity.

147. $\frac{\tan\theta\cot\theta}{\csc\theta} = \sin\theta$

148. $\frac{\sec^2\theta}{\tan\theta} = \sec\theta\csc\theta$

149. $\frac{\sin t}{\csc t} + \frac{\cos t}{\sec t} = 1$

150. $\frac{\sin x}{\cos x + 1} + \frac{\cos x - 1}{\sin x} = 0$

151. $\cot\gamma + \tan\gamma = \sec\gamma\csc\gamma$

152. $\sin^2\beta + \tan^2\beta + \cos^2\beta = \sec^2\beta$

153. $\frac{1}{1 - \sin\alpha} + \frac{1}{1 + \sin\alpha} = 2\sec^2\alpha$

154. $\frac{\tan\theta - \cot\theta}{\sin\theta\cos\theta} = \sec^2\theta - \csc^2\theta$

For the following exercises, solve the trigonometric equations on the interval $0 \le \theta < 2\pi$.

155. $2\sin\theta - 1 = 0$

156. $1 + \cos\theta = \frac{1}{2}$

157. $2\tan^2\theta = 2$

158. $4\sin^2\theta - 2 = 0$

159. $\sqrt{3}\cot\theta + 1 = 0$

160. $3\sec\theta - 2\sqrt{3} = 0$

161. $2\cos\theta\sin\theta = \sin\theta$

162. $\csc^2\theta + 2\csc\theta + 1 = 0$

For the following exercises, each graph is of the form $y = A\sin Bx$ or $y = A\cos Bx$, where $B > 0$. Write the equation of the graph.

163.

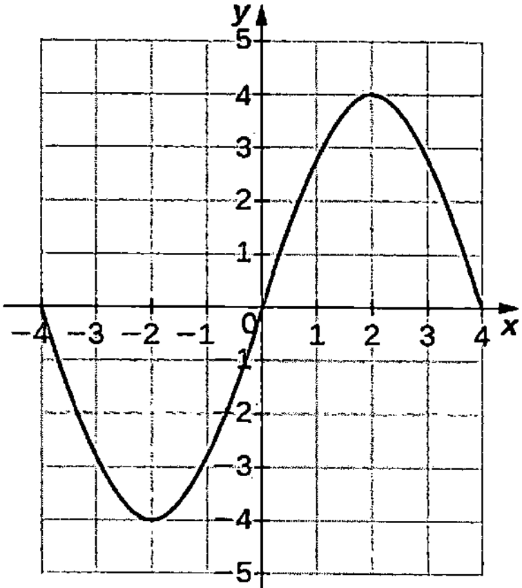

164.

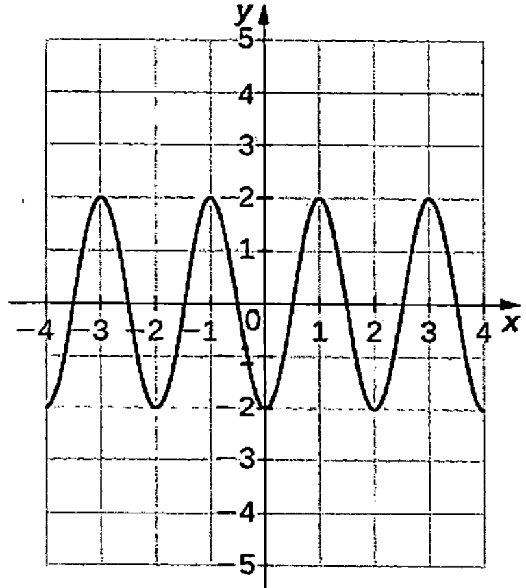

165.

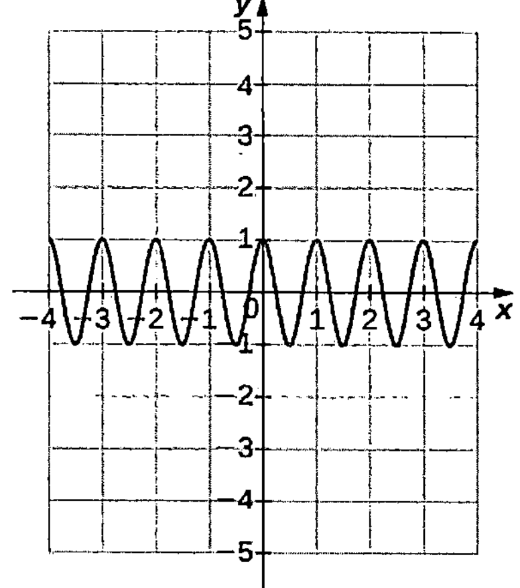

166.

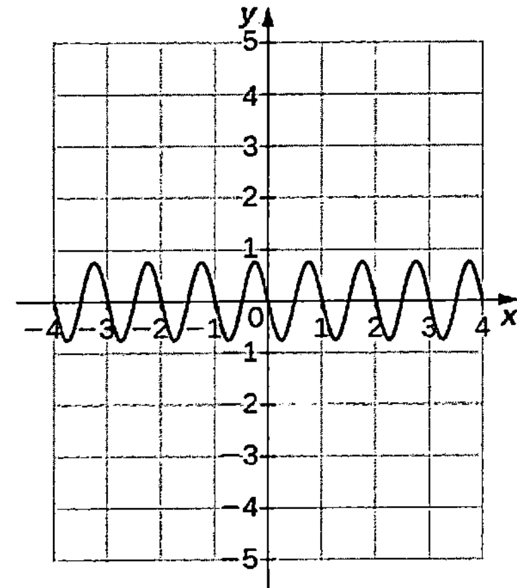

For the following exercises, find a. the amplitude, b. the period, and c. the phase shift with direction for each function.

167. $y = \sin\left(x - \frac{\pi}{4}\right)$

168. $y = 3\cos(2x + 3)$

169. $y = \frac{-1}{2}\sin\left(\frac{1}{4}x\right)$

170. $y = 2\cos\left(x - \frac{\pi}{3}\right)$

171. $y = -3\sin(\pi x + 2)$

172. $y = 4\cos\left(2x - \frac{\pi}{2}\right)$

173. **[T]** The diameter of a wheel rolling on the ground is 40 in. If the wheel rotates through an angle of $120°$, how many inches does it move? Approximate to the nearest whole inch.

174. **[T]** Find the length of the arc intercepted by central angle θ in a circle of radius r. Round to the nearest hundredth. a. $r = 12.8$ cm, $\theta = \frac{5\pi}{6}$ rad b. $r = 4.378$ cm, $\theta = \frac{7\pi}{6}$ rad c. $r = 0.964$ cm, $\theta = 50°$ d. $r = 8.55$ cm, $\theta = 325°$

175. **[T]** As a point P moves around a circle, the measure of the angle changes. The measure of how fast the angle is changing is called *angular speed*, ω, and is given by $\omega = \theta/t$, where θ is in radians and t is time. Find the angular speed for the given data. Round to the nearest thousandth. a. $\theta = \frac{7\pi}{4}\text{rad}, t = 10$ sec b. $\theta = \frac{3\pi}{5}\text{rad}, t = 8$ sec c. $\theta = \frac{2\pi}{9}\text{rad}, t = 1$ min d. $\theta = 23.76\text{rad}, t = 14$ min

176. **[T]** A total of 250,000 m^2 of land is needed to build a nuclear power plant. Suppose it is decided that the area on which the power plant is to be built should be circular.

a. Find the radius of the circular land area.
b. If the land area is to form a $45°$ sector of a circle instead of a whole circle, find the length of the curved side.

177. **[T]** The area of an isosceles triangle with equal sides of length x is $\frac{1}{2}x^2 \sin\theta$, where θ is the angle formed by the two sides. Find the area of an isosceles triangle with equal sides of length 8 in. and angle $\theta = 5\pi/12$ rad.

178. **[T]** A particle travels in a circular path at a constant angular speed ω. The angular speed is modeled by the function $\omega = 9|\cos(\pi t - \pi/12)|$. Determine the angular speed at $t = 9$ sec.

179. **[T]** An alternating current for outlets in a home has voltage given by the function $V(t) = 150\cos 368t$, where V is the voltage in volts at time t in seconds.

a. Find the period of the function and interpret its meaning.
b. Determine the number of periods that occur when 1 sec has passed.

180. **[T]** The number of hours of daylight in a northeast city is modeled by the function

$$N(t) = 12 + 3\sin\left[\frac{2\pi}{365}(t - 79)\right],$$

where t is the number of days after January 1.

a. Find the amplitude and period.
b. Determine the number of hours of daylight on the longest day of the year.
c. Determine the number of hours of daylight on the shortest day of the year.
d. Determine the number of hours of daylight 90 days after January 1.
e. Sketch the graph of the function for one period starting on January 1.

181. **[T]** Suppose that $T = 50 + 10\sin\left[\frac{\pi}{12}(t - 8)\right]$ is a mathematical model of the temperature (in degrees Fahrenheit) at *t* hours after midnight on a certain day of the week.

a. Determine the amplitude and period.
b. Find the temperature 7 hours after midnight.
c. At what time does $T = 60°$?
d. Sketch the graph of T over $0 \le t \le 24$.

182. **[T]** The function $H(t) = 8\sin\left(\frac{\pi}{6}t\right)$ models the height *H* (in feet) of the tide *t* hours after midnight. Assume that $t = 0$ is midnight.

a. Find the amplitude and period.
b. Graph the function over one period.
c. What is the height of the tide at 4:30 a.m.?

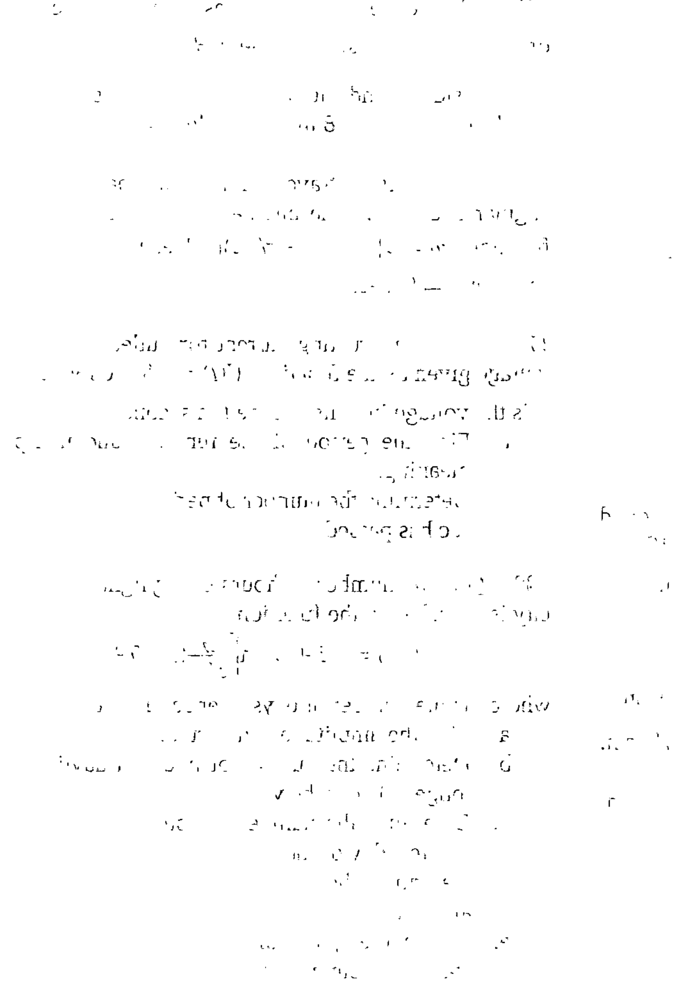

1.4 | Inverse Functions

Learning Objectives

1.4.1 Determine the conditions for when a function has an inverse.
1.4.2 Use the horizontal line test to recognize when a function is one-to-one.
1.4.3 Find the inverse of a given function.
1.4.4 Draw the graph of an inverse function.
1.4.5 Evaluate inverse trigonometric functions.

An inverse function reverses the operation done by a particular function. In other words, whatever a function does, the inverse function undoes it. In this section, we define an inverse function formally and state the necessary conditions for an inverse function to exist. We examine how to find an inverse function and study the relationship between the graph of a function and the graph of its inverse. Then we apply these ideas to define and discuss properties of the inverse trigonometric functions.

Existence of an Inverse Function

We begin with an example. Given a function f and an output $y = f(x)$, we are often interested in finding what value or values x were mapped to y by f. For example, consider the function $f(x) = x^3 + 4$. Since any output $y = x^3 + 4$, we can solve this equation for x to find that the input is $x = \sqrt[3]{y-4}$. This equation defines x as a function of y. Denoting this function as f^{-1}, and writing $x = f^{-1}(y) = \sqrt[3]{y-4}$, we see that for any x in the domain of f, $f^{-1}(f(x)) = f^{-1}\left(x^3 + 4\right) = x$. Thus, this new function, f^{-1}, "undid" what the original function f did. A function with this property is called the inverse function of the original function.

Definition

Given a function f with domain D and range R, its **inverse function** (if it exists) is the function f^{-1} with domain R and range D such that $f^{-1}(y) = x$ if $f(x) = y$. In other words, for a function f and its inverse f^{-1},

$$f^{-1}(f(x)) = x \text{ for all } x \text{ in } D, \text{ and } f\left(f^{-1}(y)\right) = y \text{ for all } y \text{ in } R. \tag{1.11}$$

Note that f^{-1} is read as "f inverse." Here, the -1 is not used as an exponent and $f^{-1}(x) \neq 1/f(x)$. **Figure 1.37** shows the relationship between the domain and range of f and the domain and range of f^{-1}.

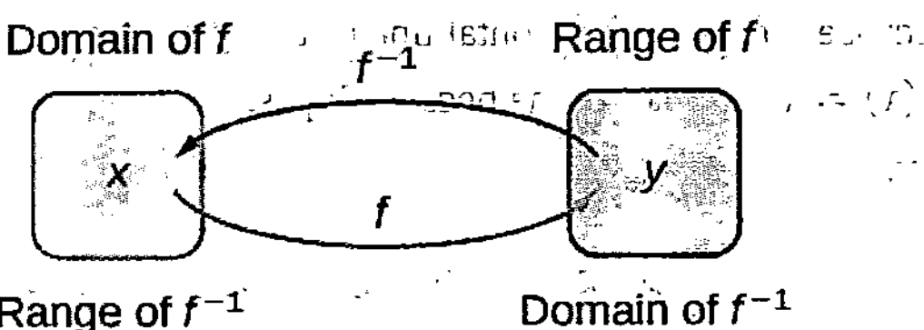

Figure 1.37 Given a function f and its inverse f^{-1}, $f^{-1}(y) = x$ if and only if $f(x) = y$. The range of f becomes the domain of f^{-1} and the domain of f becomes the range of f^{-1}.

Recall that a function has exactly one output for each input. Therefore, to define an inverse function, we need to map each input to exactly one output. For example, let's try to find the inverse function for $f(x) = x^2$. Solving the equation $y = x^2$ for x, we arrive at the equation $x = \pm\sqrt{y}$. This equation does not describe x as a function of y because there are two solutions to this equation for every $y > 0$. The problem with trying to find an inverse function for $f(x) = x^2$ is that two inputs are sent to the same output for each output $y > 0$. The function $f(x) = x^3 + 4$ discussed earlier did not have this problem. For that function, each input was sent to a different output. A function that sends each input to a *different* output is called a one-to-one function.

Definition

We say a f is a **one-to-one function** if $f(x_1) \neq f(x_2)$ when $x_1 \neq x_2$.

One way to determine whether a function is one-to-one is by looking at its graph. If a function is one-to-one, then no two inputs can be sent to the same output. Therefore, if we draw a horizontal line anywhere in the xy-plane, according to the **horizontal line test**, it cannot intersect the graph more than once. We note that the horizontal line test is different from the vertical line test. The vertical line test determines whether a graph is the graph of a function. The horizontal line test determines whether a function is one-to-one (**Figure 1.38**).

Rule: Horizontal Line Test

A function f is one-to-one if and only if every horizontal line intersects the graph of f no more than once.

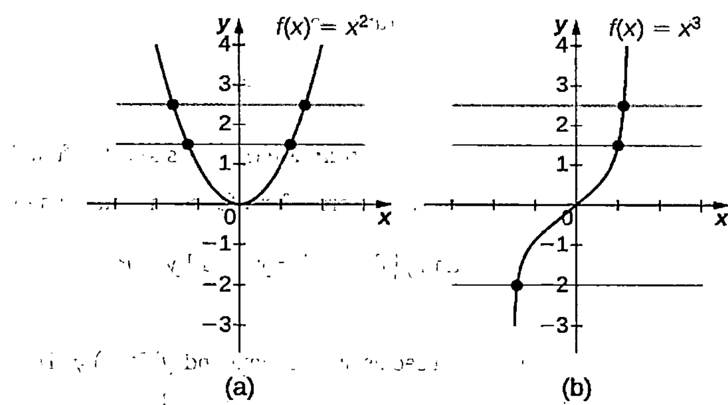

Figure 1.38 (a) The function $f(x) = x^2$ is not one-to-one because it fails the horizontal line test. (b) The function $f(x) = x^3$ is one-to-one because it passes the horizontal line test.

Example 1.28

Determining Whether a Function Is One-to-One

For each of the following functions, use the horizontal line test to determine whether it is one-to-one.

a.

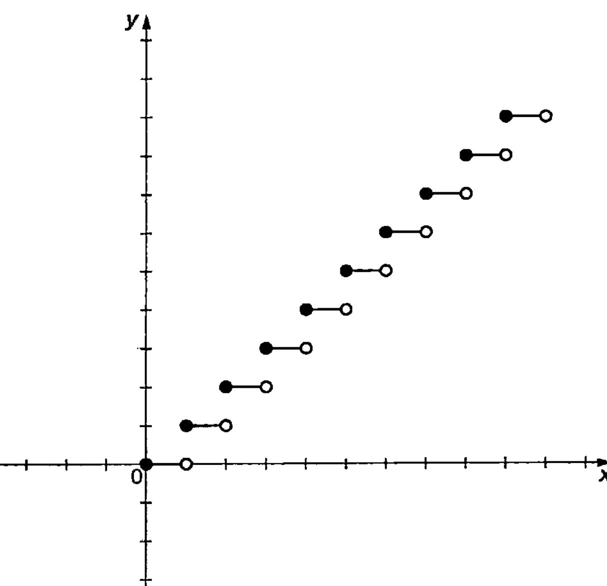

b.

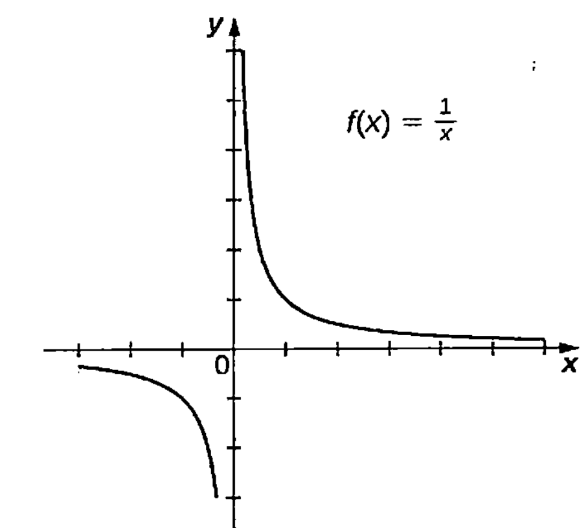

Solution

a. Since the horizontal line $y = n$ for any integer $n \geq 0$ intersects the graph more than once, this function is not one-to-one.

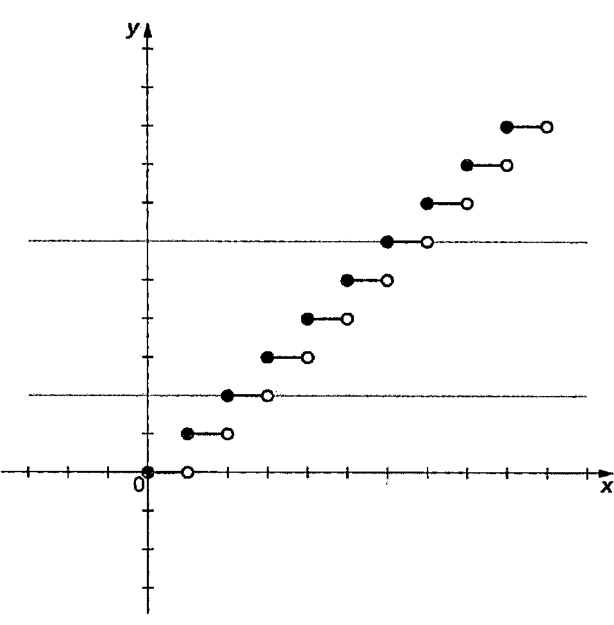

b. Since every horizontal line intersects the graph once (at most), this function is one-to-one.

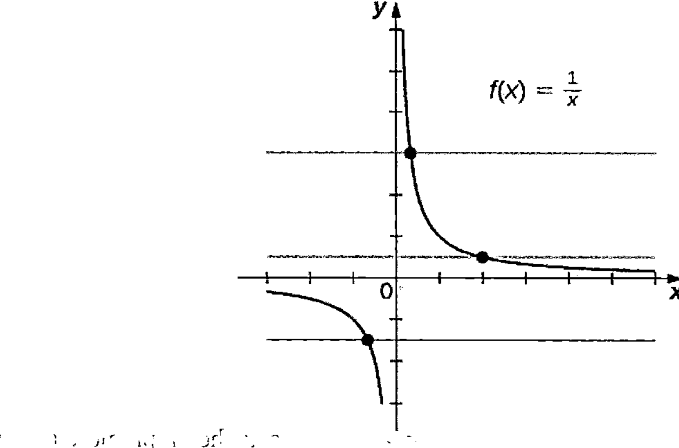

1.23 Is the function f graphed in the following image one-to-one?

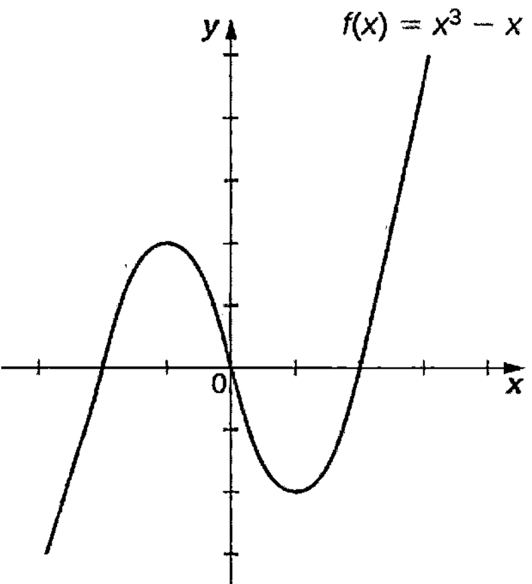

Finding a Function's Inverse

We can now consider one-to-one functions and show how to find their inverses. Recall that a function maps elements in the domain of f to elements in the range of f. The inverse function maps each element from the range of f back to its corresponding element from the domain of f. Therefore, to find the inverse function of a one-to-one function f, given any y in the range of f, we need to determine which x in the domain of f satisfies $f(x) = y$. Since f is one-to-one, there is exactly one such value x. We can find that value x by solving the equation $f(x) = y$ for x. Doing so, we are able to write x as a function of y where the domain of this function is the range of f and the range of this new function is the domain of f. Consequently, this function is the inverse of f, and we write $x = f^{-1}(y)$. Since we typically use the variable x to denote the independent variable and y to denote the dependent variable, we often interchange the roles of x and y, and write $y = f^{-1}(x)$. Representing the inverse function in this way is also helpful later when we graph a function f and its inverse f^{-1} on the same axes.

Problem-Solving Strategy: Finding an Inverse Function

1. Solve the equation $y = f(x)$ for x.
2. Interchange the variables x and y and write $y = f^{-1}(x)$.

Example 1.29

Finding an Inverse Function

Find the inverse for the function $f(x) = 3x - 4$. State the domain and range of the inverse function. Verify that $f^{-1}(f(x)) = x$.

Solution

Follow the steps outlined in the strategy.

Step 1. If $y = 3x - 4$, then $3x = y + 4$ and $x = \frac{1}{3}y + \frac{4}{3}$.

Step 2. Rewrite as $y = \frac{1}{3}x + \frac{4}{3}$ and let $y = f^{-1}(x)$.

Therefore, $f^{-1}(x) = \frac{1}{3}x + \frac{4}{3}$.

Since the domain of f is $(-\infty, \infty)$, the range of f^{-1} is $(-\infty, \infty)$. Since the range of f is $(-\infty, \infty)$, the domain of f^{-1} is $(-\infty, \infty)$.

You can verify that $f^{-1}(f(x)) = x$ by writing

$$f^{-1}(f(x)) = f^{-1}(3x - 4) = \frac{1}{3}(3x - 4) + \frac{4}{3} = x - \frac{4}{3} + \frac{4}{3} = x.$$

Note that for $f^{-1}(x)$ to be the inverse of $f(x)$, both $f^{-1}(f(x)) = x$ and $f(f^{-1}(x)) = x$ for all x in the domain of the inside function.

1.24 Find the inverse of the function $f(x) = 3x/(x - 2)$. State the domain and range of the inverse function.

Graphing Inverse Functions

Let's consider the relationship between the graph of a function f and the graph of its inverse. Consider the graph of f shown in **Figure 1.39** and a point (a, b) on the graph. Since $b = f(a)$, then $f^{-1}(b) = a$. Therefore, when we graph f^{-1}, the point (b, a) is on the graph. As a result, the graph of f^{-1} is a reflection of the graph of f about the line $y = x$.

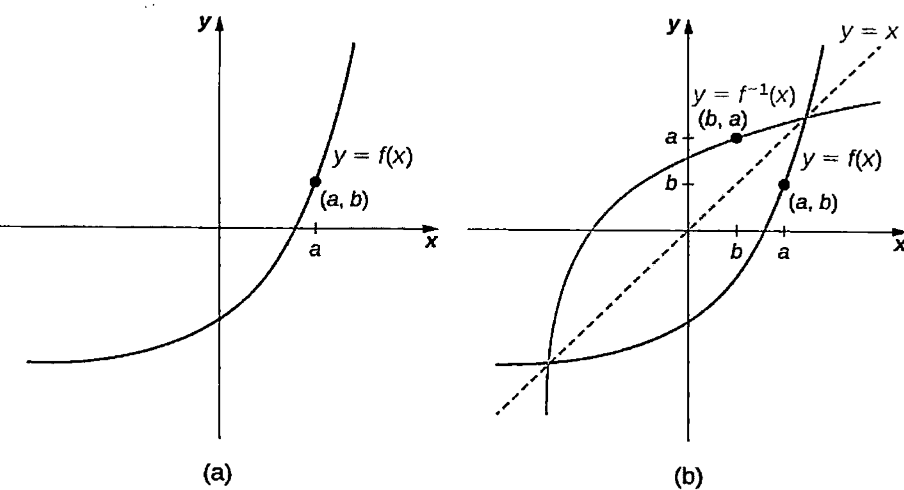

Figure 1.39 (a) The graph of this function f shows point (a, b) on the graph of f. (b) Since (a, b) is on the graph of f, the point (b, a) is on the graph of f^{-1}. The graph of f^{-1} is a reflection of the graph of f about the line $y = x$.

Example 1.30

Sketching Graphs of Inverse Functions

For the graph of f in the following image, sketch a graph of f^{-1} by sketching the line $y = x$ and using symmetry. Identify the domain and range of f^{-1}.

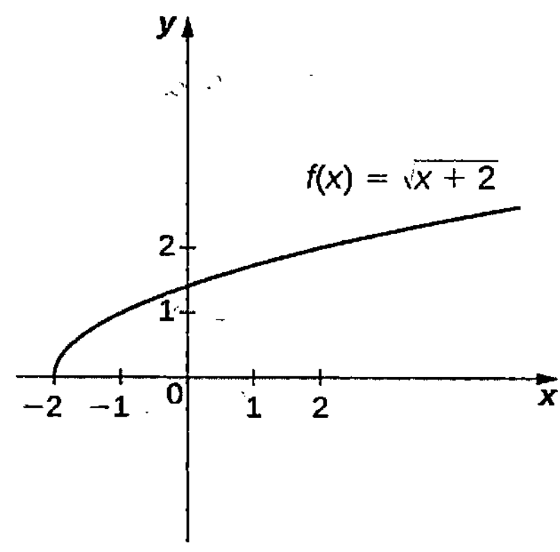

Solution

Reflect the graph about the line $y = x$. The domain of f^{-1} is $[0, \infty)$. The range of f^{-1} is $[-2, \infty)$. By using the preceding strategy for finding inverse functions, we can verify that the inverse function is $f^{-1}(x) = x^2 - 2$, as shown in the graph.

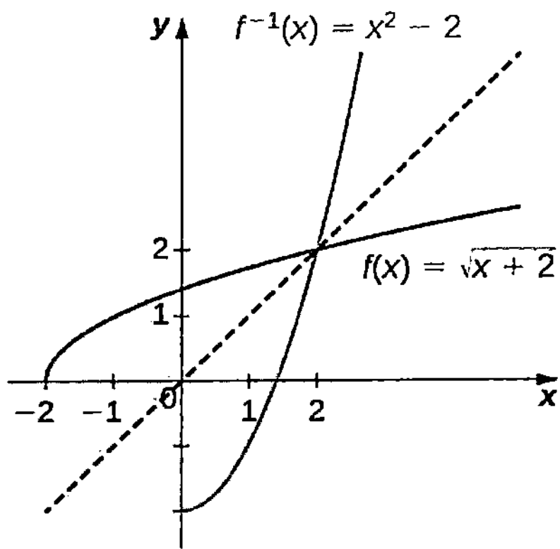

1.25 Sketch the graph of $f(x) = 2x + 3$ and the graph of its inverse using the symmetry property of inverse functions.

Restricting Domains

As we have seen, $f(x) = x^2$ does not have an inverse function because it is not one-to-one. However, we can choose a subset of the domain of f such that the function is one-to-one. This subset is called a **restricted domain**. By restricting the domain of $f,$ we can define a new function g such that the domain of g is the restricted domain of f and $g(x) = f(x)$ for all x in the domain of g. Then we can define an inverse function for g on that domain. For example, since $f(x) = x^2$ is one-to-one on the interval $[0, \infty),$ we can define a new function g such that the domain of g is $[0, \infty)$ and $g(x) = x^2$ for all x in its domain. Since g is a one-to-one function, it has an inverse function, given by the formula $g^{-1}(x) = \sqrt{x}$. On the other hand, the function $f(x) = x^2$ is also one-to-one on the domain $(-\infty, 0]$. Therefore, we could also define a new function h such that the domain of h is $(-\infty, 0]$ and $h(x) = x^2$ for all x in the domain of h. Then h is a one-to-one function and must also have an inverse. Its inverse is given by the formula $h^{-1}(x) = -\sqrt{x}$ (**Figure 1.40**).

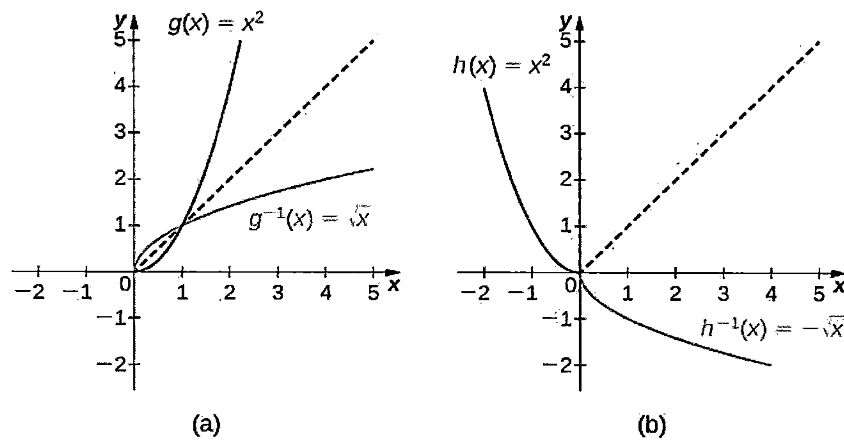

Figure 1.40 (a) For $g(x) = x^2$ restricted to $[0, \infty)$, $g^{-1}(x) = \sqrt{x}$. (b) For $h(x) = x^2$ restricted to $(-\infty, 0]$, $h^{-1}(x) = -\sqrt{x}$.

Example 1.31

Restricting the Domain

Consider the function $f(x) = (x + 1)^2$.

a. Sketch the graph of f and use the horizontal line test to show that f is not one-to-one.

b. Show that f is one-to-one on the restricted domain $[-1, \infty)$. Determine the domain and range for the inverse of f on this restricted domain and find a formula for f^{-1}.

Solution

a. The graph of f is the graph of $y = x^2$ shifted left 1 unit. Since there exists a horizontal line intersecting the graph more than once, f is not one-to-one.

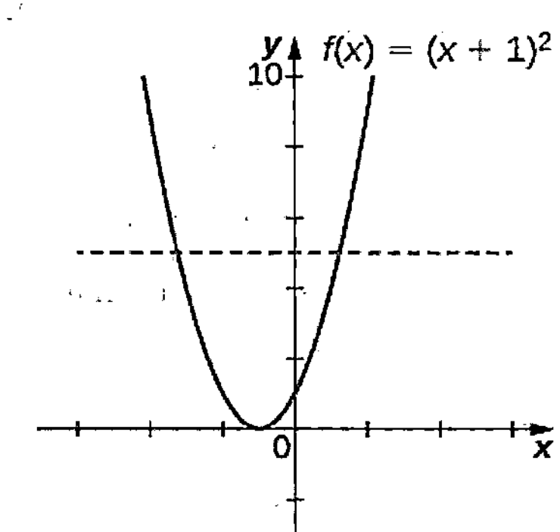

b. On the interval $[-1, \infty)$, f is one-to-one.

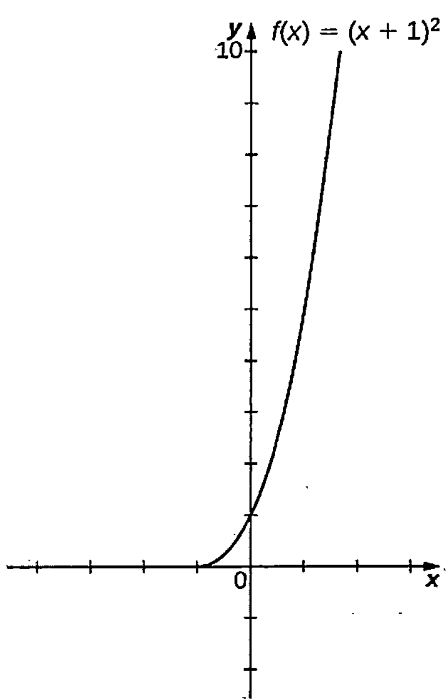

The domain and range of f^{-1} are given by the range and domain of f, respectively. Therefore, the domain of f^{-1} is $[0, \infty)$ and the range of f^{-1} is $[-1, \infty)$. To find a formula for f^{-1}, solve the equation $y = (x+1)^2$ for x. If $y = (x+1)^2$, then $x = -1 \pm \sqrt{y}$. Since we are restricting the domain to the interval where $x \geq -1$, we need $\pm\sqrt{y} \geq 0$. Therefore, $x = -1 + \sqrt{y}$. Interchanging x and y, we write $y = -1 + \sqrt{x}$ and conclude that $f^{-1}(x) = -1 + \sqrt{x}$.

1.26 Consider $f(x) = 1/x^2$ restricted to the domain $(-\infty, 0)$. Verify that f is one-to-one on this domain. Determine the domain and range of the inverse of f and find a formula for f^{-1}.

Inverse Trigonometric Functions

The six basic trigonometric functions are periodic, and therefore they are not one-to-one. However, if we restrict the domain of a trigonometric function to an interval where it is one-to-one, we can define its inverse. Consider the sine function (**Figure 1.34**). The sine function is one-to-one on an infinite number of intervals, but the standard convention is to restrict the domain to the interval $\left[-\frac{\pi}{2}, \frac{\pi}{2}\right]$. By doing so, we define the inverse sine function on the domain $[-1, 1]$ such that for any x in the interval $[-1, 1]$, the inverse sine function tells us which angle θ in the interval $\left[-\frac{\pi}{2}, \frac{\pi}{2}\right]$ satisfies $\sin\theta = x$. Similarly, we can restrict the domains of the other trigonometric functions to define **inverse trigonometric functions**, which are functions that tell us which angle in a certain interval has a specified trigonometric value.

Definition

The inverse sine function, denoted $\sin^{-1}$ or arcsin, and the inverse cosine function, denoted $\cos^{-1}$ or arccos, are defined on the domain $D = \{x | -1 \leq x \leq 1\}$ as follows:

$$\sin^{-1}(x) = y \text{ if and only if } \sin(y) = x \text{ and } -\frac{\pi}{2} \le y \le \frac{\pi}{2};$$ **(1.12)**
$$\cos^{-1}(x) = y \text{ if and only if } \cos(y) = x \text{ and } 0 \le y \le \pi.$$

The inverse tangent function, denoted $\tan^{-1}$ or arctan, and inverse cotangent function, denoted $\cot^{-1}$ or arccot, are defined on the domain $D = \{x| - \infty < x < \infty\}$ as follows:

$$\tan^{-1}(x) = y \text{ if and only if } \tan(y) = x \text{ and } -\frac{\pi}{2} < y < \frac{\pi}{2};$$ **(1.13)**
$$\cot^{-1}(x) = y \text{ if and only if } \cot(y) = x \text{ and } 0 < y < \pi.$$

The inverse cosecant function, denoted $\csc^{-1}$ or arccsc, and inverse secant function, denoted $\sec^{-1}$ or arcsec, are defined on the domain $D = \{x||x| \ge 1\}$ as follows:

$$\csc^{-1}(x) = y \text{ if and only if } \csc(y) = x \text{ and } -\frac{\pi}{2} \le y \le \frac{\pi}{2},\ y \ne 0;$$ **(1.14)**
$$\sec^{-1}(x) = y \text{ if and only if } \sec(y) = x \text{ and } 0 \le y \le \pi,\ y \ne \pi/2.$$

To graph the inverse trigonometric functions, we use the graphs of the trigonometric functions restricted to the domains defined earlier and reflect the graphs about the line $y = x$ (**Figure 1.41**).

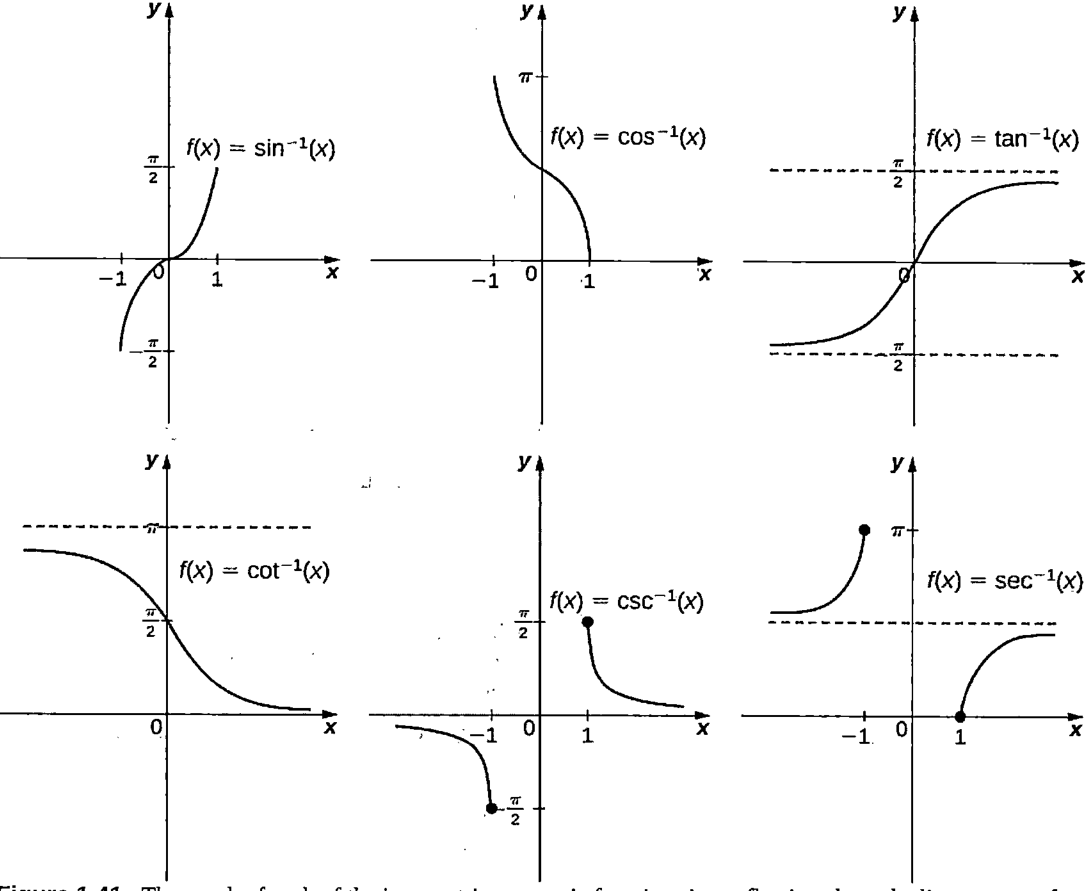

Figure 1.41 The graph of each of the inverse trigonometric functions is a reflection about the line $y = x$ of the corresponding restricted trigonometric function.

Go to the **following site (http://www.openstaxcollege.org/l/20_inversefun)** for more comparisons of functions and their inverses.

When evaluating an inverse trigonometric function, the output is an angle. For example, to evaluate $\cos^{-1}\left(\frac{1}{2}\right)$, we need to find an angle θ such that $\cos\theta = \frac{1}{2}$. Clearly, many angles have this property. However, given the definition of $\cos^{-1}$, we need the angle θ that not only solves this equation, but also lies in the interval $[0, \pi]$. We conclude that $\cos^{-1}\left(\frac{1}{2}\right) = \frac{\pi}{3}$.

We now consider a composition of a trigonometric function and its inverse. For example, consider the two expressions $\sin\left(\sin^{-1}\left(\frac{\sqrt{2}}{2}\right)\right)$ and $\sin^{-1}(\sin(\pi))$. For the first one, we simplify as follows:

$$\sin\left(\sin^{-1}\left(\frac{\sqrt{2}}{2}\right)\right) = \sin\left(\frac{\pi}{4}\right) = \frac{\sqrt{2}}{2}.$$

For the second one, we have

$$\sin^{-1}(\sin(\pi)) = \sin^{-1}(0) = 0.$$

The inverse function is supposed to "undo" the original function, so why isn't $\sin^{-1}(\sin(\pi)) = \pi$? Recalling our definition of inverse functions, a function f and its inverse f^{-1} satisfy the conditions $f\left(f^{-1}(y)\right) = y$ for all y in the domain of f^{-1} and $f^{-1}(f(x)) = x$ for all x in the domain of f, so what happened here? The issue is that the inverse sine function, $\sin^{-1}$, is the inverse of the *restricted* sine function defined on the domain $\left[-\frac{\pi}{2}, \frac{\pi}{2}\right]$. Therefore, for x in the interval $\left[-\frac{\pi}{2}, \frac{\pi}{2}\right]$, it is true that $\sin^{-1}(\sin x) = x$. However, for values of x outside this interval, the equation does not hold, even though $\sin^{-1}(\sin x)$ is defined for all real numbers x.

What about $\sin(\sin^{-1} y)$? Does that have a similar issue? The answer is *no*. Since the domain of $\sin^{-1}$ is the interval $[-1, 1]$, we conclude that $\sin(\sin^{-1} y) = y$ if $-1 \le y \le 1$ and the expression is not defined for other values of y. To summarize,

$$\sin(\sin^{-1} y) = y \text{ if } -1 \le y \le 1$$

and

$$\sin^{-1}(\sin x) = x \text{ if } -\frac{\pi}{2} \le x \le \frac{\pi}{2}.$$

Similarly, for the cosine function,

$$\cos(\cos^{-1} y) = y \text{ if } -1 \le y \le 1$$

and

$$\cos^{-1}(\cos x) = x \text{ if } 0 \le x \le \pi.$$

Similar properties hold for the other trigonometric functions and their inverses.

Example 1.32

Evaluating Expressions Involving Inverse Trigonometric Functions

Evaluate each of the following expressions.

a. $\sin^{-1}\left(-\frac{\sqrt{3}}{2}\right)$

b. $\tan\left(\tan^{-1}\left(-\frac{1}{\sqrt{3}}\right)\right)$

c. $\cos^{-1}\left(\cos\left(\frac{5\pi}{4}\right)\right)$

d. $\sin^{-1}\left(\cos\left(\frac{2\pi}{3}\right)\right)$

Solution

a. Evaluating $\sin^{-1}(-\sqrt{3}/2)$ is equivalent to finding the angle θ such that $\sin\theta = -\sqrt{3}/2$ and $-\pi/2 \leq \theta \leq \pi/2$. The angle $\theta = -\pi/3$ satisfies these two conditions. Therefore, $\sin^{-1}(-\sqrt{3}/2) = -\pi/3$.

b. First we use the fact that $\tan^{-1}(-1/\sqrt{3}) = -\pi/6$. Then $\tan(\pi/6) = -1/\sqrt{3}$. Therefore, $\tan\left(\tan^{-1}(-1/\sqrt{3})\right) = -1/\sqrt{3}$.

c. To evaluate $\cos^{-1}(\cos(5\pi/4))$, first use the fact that $\cos(5\pi/4) = -\sqrt{2}/2$. Then we need to find the angle θ such that $\cos(\theta) = -\sqrt{2}/2$ and $0 \leq \theta \leq \pi$. Since $3\pi/4$ satisfies both these conditions, we have $\cos\left(\cos^{-1}(5\pi/4)\right) = \cos\left(\cos^{-1}(-\sqrt{2}/2)\right) = 3\pi/4$.

d. Since $\cos(2\pi/3) = -1/2$, we need to evaluate $\sin^{-1}(-1/2)$. That is, we need to find the angle θ such that $\sin(\theta) = -1/2$ and $-\pi/2 \leq \theta \leq \pi/2$. Since $-\pi/6$ satisfies both these conditions, we can conclude that $\sin^{-1}(\cos(2\pi/3)) = \sin^{-1}(-1/2) = -\pi/6$.

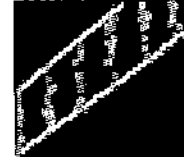

Student PROJECT

The Maximum Value of a Function

In many areas of science, engineering, and mathematics, it is useful to know the maximum value a function can obtain, even if we don't know its exact value at a given instant. For instance, if we have a function describing the strength of a roof beam, we would want to know the maximum weight the beam can support without breaking. If we have a function that describes the speed of a train, we would want to know its maximum speed before it jumps off the rails. Safe design often depends on knowing maximum values.

This project describes a simple example of a function with a maximum value that depends on two equation coefficients. We will see that maximum values can depend on several factors other than the independent variable x.

1. Consider the graph in **Figure 1.42** of the function $y = \sin x + \cos x$. Describe its overall shape. Is it periodic? How do you know?

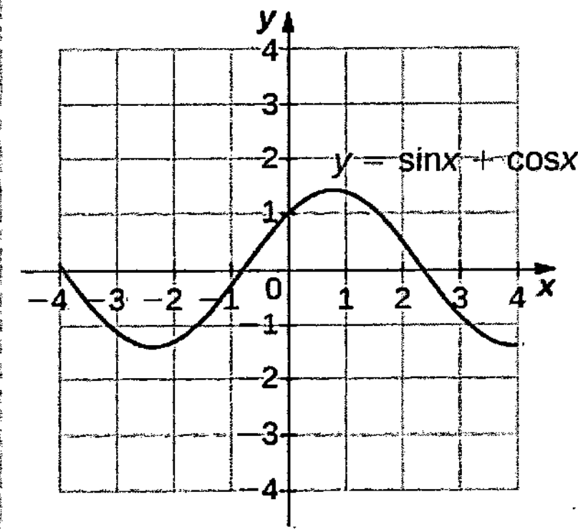

Figure 1.42 The graph of $y = \sin x + \cos x$.

Using a graphing calculator or other graphing device, estimate the x- and y-values of the maximum point for the graph (the first such point where $x > 0$). It may be helpful to express the x-value as a multiple of π.

2. Now consider other graphs of the form $y = A\sin x + B\cos x$ for various values of A and B. Sketch the graph when $A = 2$ and $B = 1$, and find the x- and y-values for the maximum point. (Remember to express the x-value as a multiple of π, if possible.) Has it moved?
3. Repeat for $A = 1$, $B = 2$. Is there any relationship to what you found in part (2)?
4. Complete the following table, adding a few choices of your own for A and B:

A	B	x	y		A	B	x	y
0	1				$\sqrt{3}$	1		
1	0				1	$\sqrt{3}$		
1	1				12	5		
1	2				5	12		
2	1							
2	2							
3	4							
4	3							

5. Try to figure out the formula for the y-values.
6. The formula for the x-values is a little harder. The most helpful points from the table are $(1, 1)$, $(1, \sqrt{3})$, $(\sqrt{3}, 1)$. (*Hint*: Consider inverse trigonometric functions.)
7. If you found formulas for parts (5) and (6), show that they work together. That is, substitute the x-value formula you found into $y = A\sin x + B\cos x$ and simplify it to arrive at the y-value formula you found.

1.4 EXERCISES

For the following exercises, use the horizontal line test to determine whether each of the given graphs is one-to-one.

183.

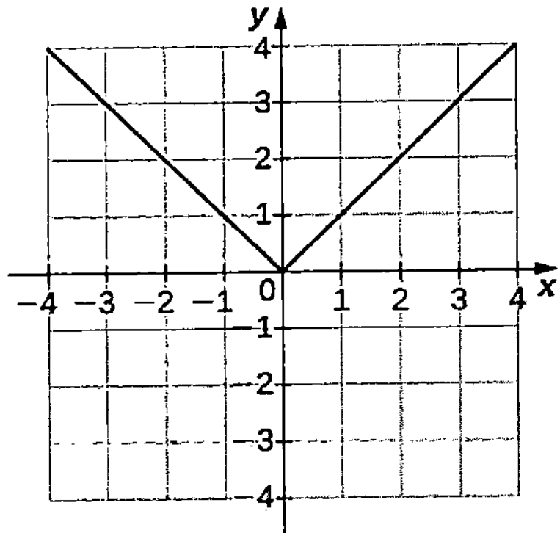

184.

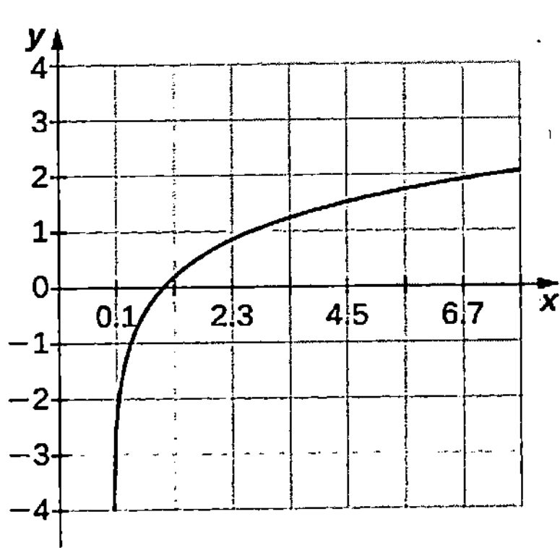

185.

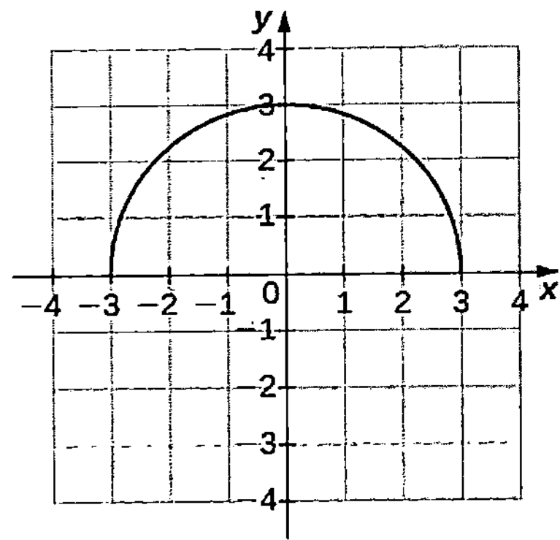

186.

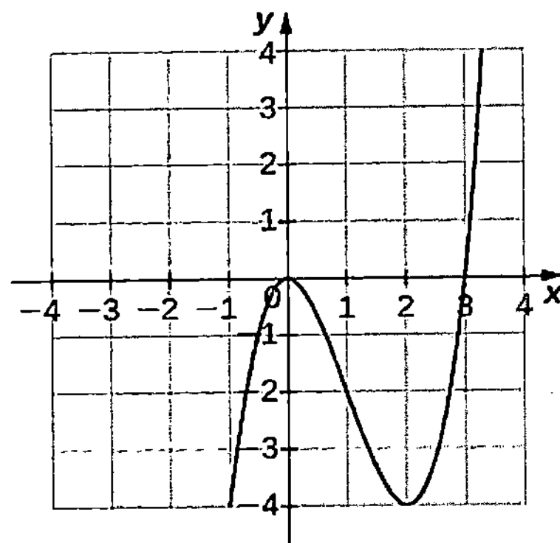

187.

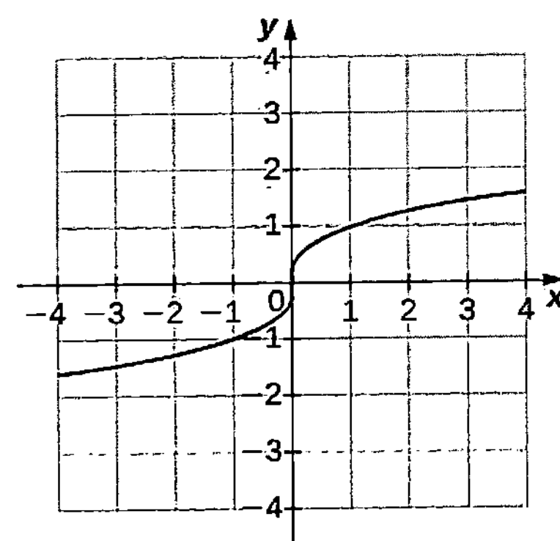

188.

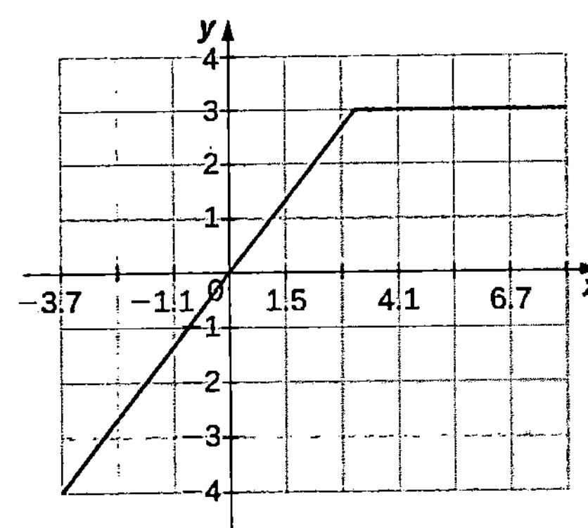

For the following exercises, a. find the inverse function, and b. find the domain and range of the inverse function.

189. $f(x) = x^2 - 4,\ x \geq 0$

190. $f(x) = \sqrt[3]{x - 4}$

191. $f(x) = x^3 + 1$

192. $f(x) = (x - 1)^2,\ x \leq 1$

193. $f(x) = \sqrt{x-1}$

194. $f(x) = \dfrac{1}{x+2}$

For the following exercises, use the graph of f to sketch the graph of its inverse function.

195.

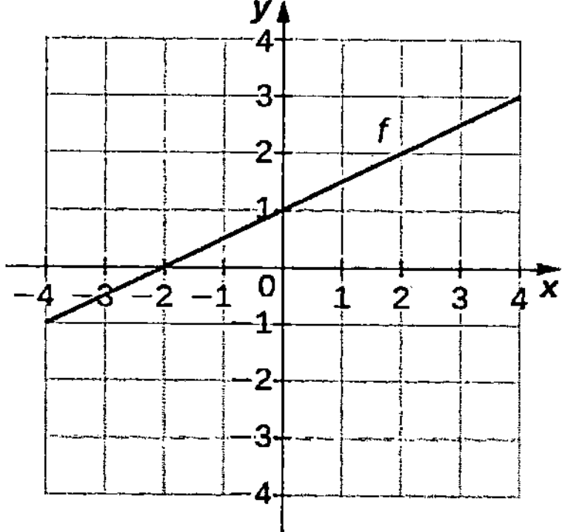

196.

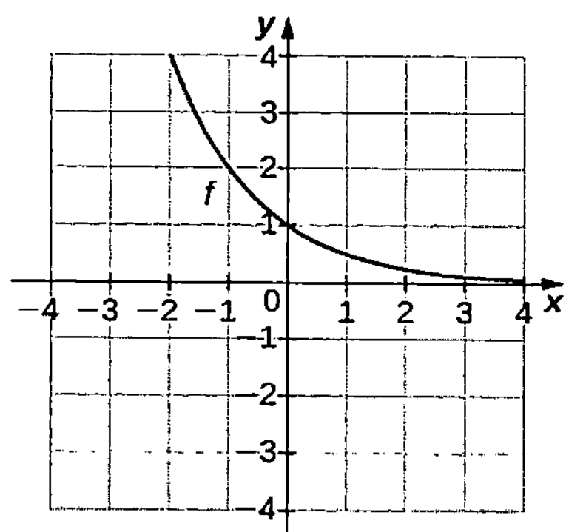

197.

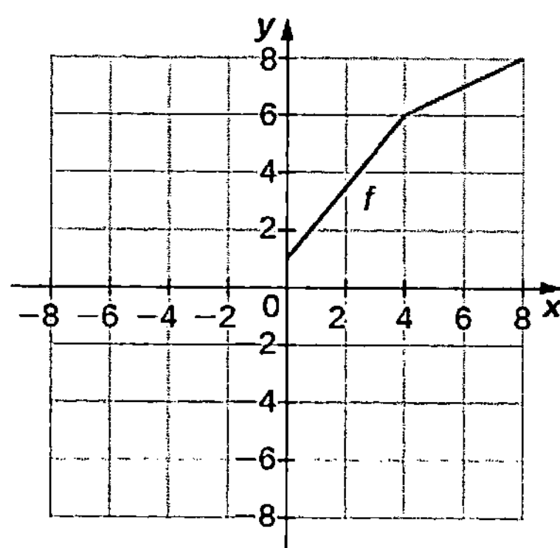

198.

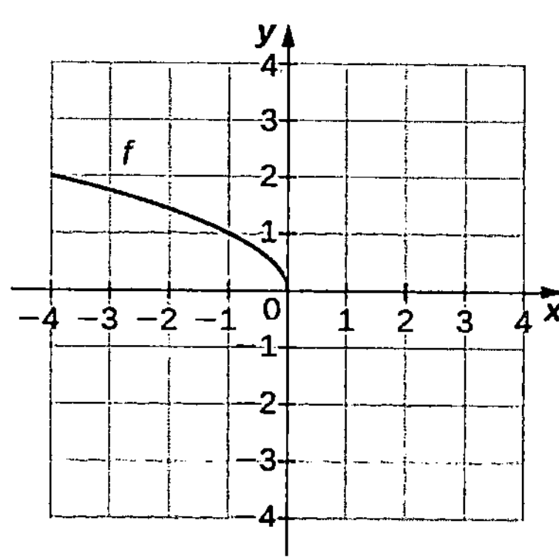

For the following exercises, use composition to determine which pairs of functions are inverses.

199. $f(x) = 8x,\ g(x) = \frac{x}{8}$

200. $f(x) = 8x + 3,\ g(x) = \dfrac{x-3}{8}$

201. $f(x) = 5x - 7,\ g(x) = \dfrac{x+5}{7}$

202. $f(x) = \frac{2}{3}x + 2,\ g(x) = \frac{3}{2}x + 3$

203. $f(x) = \dfrac{1}{x-1},\ x \neq 1,\ g(x) = \frac{1}{x} + 1,\ x \neq 0$

204. $f(x) = x^3 + 1,\ g(x) = (x-1)^{1/3}$

205.
$f(x) = x^2 + 2x + 1,\ x \geq -1, \quad g(x) = -1 + \sqrt{x},\ x \geq 0$

206.
$f(x) = \sqrt{4 - x^2},\ 0 \leq x \leq 2,\ g(x) = \sqrt{4 - x^2},\ 0 \leq x \leq 2$

For the following exercises, evaluate the functions. Give the exact value.

207. $\tan^{-1}\left(\frac{\sqrt{3}}{3}\right)$

208. $\cos^{-1}\left(-\frac{\sqrt{2}}{2}\right)$

209. $\cot^{-1}(1)$

210. $\sin^{-1}(-1)$

211. $\cos^{-1}\left(\frac{\sqrt{3}}{2}\right)$

212. $\cos\left(\tan^{-1}(\sqrt{3})\right)$

213. $\sin\left(\cos^{-1}\left(\frac{\sqrt{2}}{2}\right)\right)$

214. $\sin^{-1}\left(\sin\left(\frac{\pi}{3}\right)\right)$

215. $\tan^{-1}\left(\tan\left(-\frac{\pi}{6}\right)\right)$

216. The function $C = T(F) = (5/9)(F - 32)$ converts degrees Fahrenheit to degrees Celsius.

a. Find the inverse function $F = T^{-1}(C)$
b. What is the inverse function used for?

217. **[T]** The velocity V (in centimeters per second) of blood in an artery at a distance x cm from the center of the artery can be modeled by the function $V = f(x) = 500(0.04 - x^2)$ for $0 \le x \le 0.2$.

a. Find $x = f^{-1}(V)$.
b. Interpret what the inverse function is used for.
c. Find the distance from the center of an artery with a velocity of 15 cm/sec, 10 cm/sec, and 5 cm/sec.

218. A function that converts dress sizes in the United States to those in Europe is given by $D(x) = 2x + 24$.

a. Find the European dress sizes that correspond to sizes 6, 8, 10, and 12 in the United States.
b. Find the function that converts European dress sizes to U.S. dress sizes.
c. Use part b. to find the dress sizes in the United States that correspond to 46, 52, 62, and 70.

219. **[T]** The cost to remove a toxin from a lake is modeled by the function $C(p) = 75p/(85 - p)$, where C is the cost (in thousands of dollars) and p is the amount of toxin in a small lake (measured in parts per billion [ppb]). This model is valid only when the amount of toxin is less than 85 ppb.

a. Find the cost to remove 25 ppb, 40 ppb, and 50 ppb of the toxin from the lake.
b. Find the inverse function. c. Use part b. to determine how much of the toxin is removed for $50,000.

220. **[T]** A race car is accelerating at a velocity given by $v(t) = \frac{25}{4}t + 54$, where v is the velocity (in feet per second) at time t.

a. Find the velocity of the car at 10 sec.
b. Find the inverse function.
c. Use part b. to determine how long it takes for the car to reach a speed of 150 ft/sec.

221. **[T]** An airplane's Mach number M is the ratio of its speed to the speed of sound. When a plane is flying at a constant altitude, then its Mach angle is given by $\mu = 2\sin^{-1}\left(\frac{1}{M}\right)$. Find the Mach angle (to the nearest degree) for the following Mach numbers.

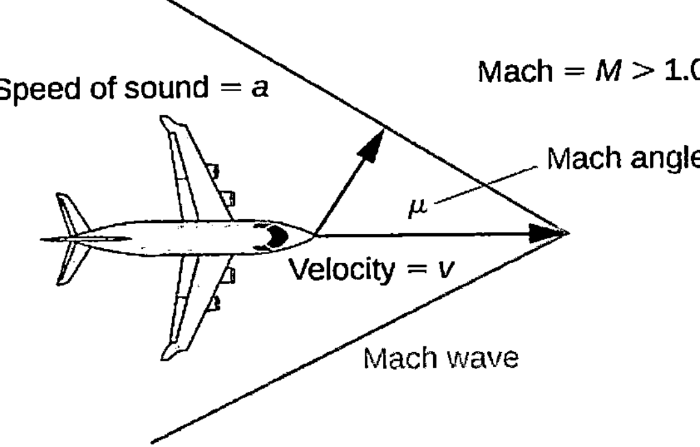

a. $\mu = 1.4$
b. $\mu = 2.8$
c. $\mu = 4.3$

222. **[T]** Using $\mu = 2\sin^{-1}\left(\frac{1}{M}\right)$, find the Mach number M for the following angles.

a. $\mu = \frac{\pi}{6}$
b. $\mu = \frac{2\pi}{7}$
c. $\mu = \frac{3\pi}{8}$

223. **[T]** The temperature (in degrees Celsius) of a city in the northern United States can be modeled by the function $T(x) = 5 + 18\sin\left[\frac{\pi}{6}(x - 4.6)\right]$, where x is time in months and $x = 1.00$ corresponds to January 1. Determine the month and day when the temperature is $21°C$.

224. **[T]** The depth (in feet) of water at a dock changes with the rise and fall of tides. It is modeled by the function $D(t) = 5\sin\left(\frac{\pi}{6}t - \frac{7\pi}{6}\right) + 8$, where t is the number of hours after midnight. Determine the first time after midnight when the depth is 11.75 ft.

225. **[T]** An object moving in simple harmonic motion is modeled by the function $s(t) = -6\cos\left(\frac{\pi t}{2}\right)$, where s is measured in inches and t is measured in seconds. Determine the first time when the distance moved is 4.5 in.

226. **[T]** A local art-gallery has a portrait 3 ft in height that is hung 2.5 ft above the eye level of an average person. The viewing angle θ can be modeled by the function $\theta = \tan^{-1}\frac{5.5}{x} - \tan^{-1}\frac{2.5}{x}$, where x is the distance (in feet) from the portrait. Find the viewing angle when a person is 4 ft from the portrait.

227. **[T]** Use a calculator to evaluate $\tan^{-1}(\tan(2.1))$ and $\cos^{-1}(\cos(2.1))$. Explain the results of each.

228. **[T]** Use a calculator to evaluate $\sin(\sin^{-1}(-2))$ and $\tan(\tan^{-1}(-2))$. Explain the results of each.

1.5 | Exponential and Logarithmic Functions

Learning Objectives

1.5.1 Identify the form of an exponential function.
1.5.2 Explain the difference between the graphs of x^b and b^x.
1.5.3 Recognize the significance of the number e.
1.5.4 Identify the form of a logarithmic function.
1.5.5 Explain the relationship between exponential and logarithmic functions.
1.5.6 Describe how to calculate a logarithm to a different base.
1.5.7 Identify the hyperbolic functions, their graphs, and basic identities.

In this section we examine exponential and logarithmic functions. We use the properties of these functions to solve equations involving exponential or logarithmic terms, and we study the meaning and importance of the number e. We also define hyperbolic and inverse hyperbolic functions, which involve combinations of exponential and logarithmic functions. (Note that we present alternative definitions of exponential and logarithmic functions in the chapter **Applications of Integrations**, and prove that the functions have the same properties with either definition.)

Exponential Functions

Exponential functions arise in many applications. One common example is population growth.

For example, if a population starts with P_0 individuals and then grows at an annual rate of $2\%,$ its population after 1 year is

$$P(1) = P_0 + 0.02P_0 = P_0(1 + 0.02) = P_0(1.02).$$

Its population after 2 years is

$$P(2) = P(1) + 0.02P(1) = P(1)(1.02) = P_0(1.02)^2.$$

In general, its population after t years is

$$P(t) = P_0(1.02)^t,$$

which is an exponential function. More generally, any function of the form $f(x) = b^x,$ where $b > 0, b \neq 1,$ is an exponential function with **base** b and **exponent** x. Exponential functions have constant bases and variable exponents. Note that a function of the form $f(x) = x^b$ for some constant b is not an exponential function but a power function.

To see the difference between an exponential function and a power function, we compare the functions $y = x^2$ and $y = 2^x$. In **Table 1.10**, we see that both 2^x and x^2 approach infinity as $x \to \infty$. Eventually, however, 2^x becomes larger than x^2 and grows more rapidly as $x \to \infty$. In the opposite direction, as $x \to -\infty, x^2 \to \infty,$ whereas $2^x \to 0$. The line $y = 0$ is a horizontal asymptote for $y = 2^x$.

x	−3	−2	−1	0	1	2	3	4	5	6
x^2	9	4	1	0	1	4	9	16	25	36
2^x	1/8	1/4	1/2	1	2	4	8	16	32	64

Table 1.10 Values of x^2 and 2^x

In **Figure 1.43**, we graph both $y = x^2$ and $y = 2^x$ to show how the graphs differ.

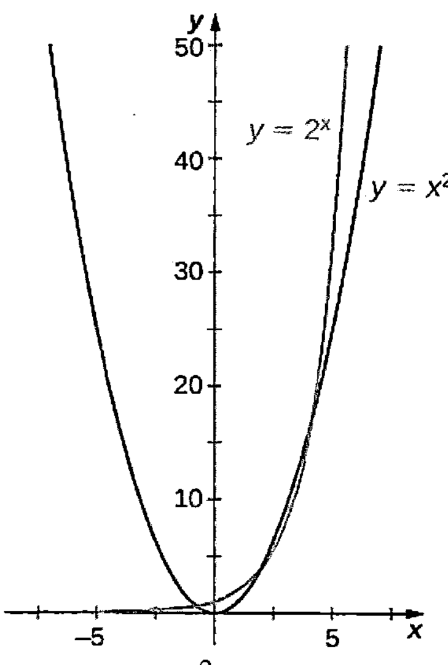

Figure 1.43 Both 2^x and x^2 approach infinity as $x \to \infty$, but 2^x grows more rapidly than x^2. As $x \to -\infty$, $x^2 \to \infty$, whereas $2^x \to 0$.

Evaluating Exponential Functions

Recall the properties of exponents: If x is a positive integer, then we define $b^x = b \cdot b \cdots b$ (with x factors of b). If x is a negative integer, then $x = -y$ for some positive integer y, and we define $b^x = b^{-y} = 1/b^y$. Also, b^0 is defined to be 1. If x is a rational number, then $x = p/q$, where p and q are integers and $b^x = b^{p/q} = \sqrt[q]{b^p}$. For example, $9^{3/2} = \sqrt{9^3} = 27$. However, how is b^x defined if x is an irrational number? For example, what do we mean by $2^{\sqrt{2}}$? This is too complex a question for us to answer fully right now; however, we can make an approximation. In **Table 1.11**, we list some rational numbers approaching $\sqrt{2}$, and the values of 2^x for each rational number x are presented as well. We claim that if we choose rational numbers x getting closer and closer to $\sqrt{2}$, the values of 2^x get closer and closer to some number L. We define that number L to be $2^{\sqrt{2}}$.

x	1.4	1.41	1.414	1.4142	1.41421	1.414213
2^x	2.639	2.65737	2.66475	2.665119	2.665138	2.665143

Table 1.11 Values of 2^x for a List of Rational Numbers Approximating $\sqrt{2}$

Example 1.33

Bacterial Growth

Suppose a particular population of bacteria is known to double in size every 4 hours. If a culture starts with 1000 bacteria, the number of bacteria after 4 hours is $n(4) = 1000 \cdot 2$. The number of bacteria after 8 hours is $n(8) = n(4) \cdot 2 = 1000 \cdot 2^2$. In general, the number of bacteria after $4m$ hours is $n(4m) = 1000 \cdot 2^m$. Letting

$t = 4m,$ we see that the number of bacteria after t hours is $n(t) = 1000 \cdot 2^{t/4}$. Find the number of bacteria after 6 hours, 10 hours, and 24 hours.

Solution

The number of bacteria after 6 hours is given by $n(6) = 1000 \cdot 2^{6/4} \approx 2828$ bacteria. The number of bacteria after 10 hours is given by $n(10) = 1000 \cdot 2^{10/4} \approx 5657$ bacteria. The number of bacteria after 24 hours is given by $n(24) = 1000 \cdot 2^6 = 64{,}000$ bacteria.

1.27 Given the exponential function $f(x) = 100 \cdot 3^{x/2}$, evaluate $f(4)$ and $f(10)$.

Go to **World Population Balance (http://www.openstaxcollege.org/l/20_exponengrow)** for another example of exponential population growth.

Graphing Exponential Functions

For any base $b > 0, b \neq 1,$ the exponential function $f(x) = b^x$ is defined for all real numbers x and $b^x > 0$. Therefore, the domain of $f(x) = b^x$ is $(-\infty, \infty)$ and the range is $(0, \infty)$. To graph b^x, we note that for $b > 1$, b^x is increasing on $(-\infty, \infty)$ and $b^x \to \infty$ as $x \to \infty$, whereas $b^x \to 0$ as $x \to -\infty$. On the other hand, if $0 < b < 1$, $f(x) = b^x$ is decreasing on $(-\infty, \infty)$ and $b^x \to 0$ as $x \to \infty$ whereas $b^x \to \infty$ as $x \to -\infty$ (**Figure 1.44**).

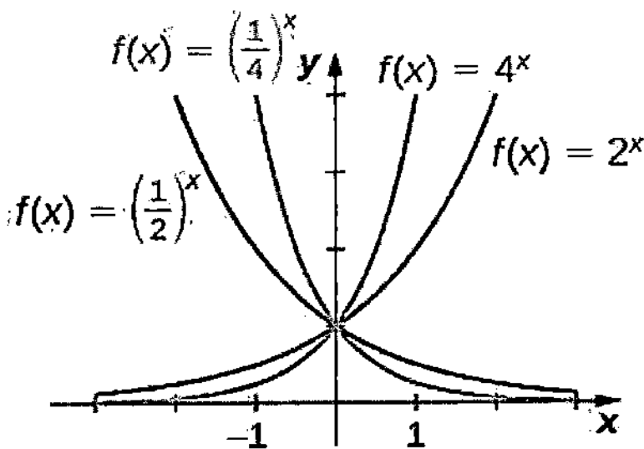

Figure 1.44 If $b > 1$, then b^x is increasing on $(-\infty, \infty)$. If $0 < b < 1$, then b^x is decreasing on $(-\infty, \infty)$.

Visit this **site (http://www.openstaxcollege.org/l/20_inverse)** for more exploration of the graphs of exponential functions.

Note that exponential functions satisfy the general laws of exponents. To remind you of these laws, we state them as rules.

Rule: Laws of Exponents

For any constants $a > 0$, $b > 0$, and for all x and y,

1. $b^x \cdot b^y = b^{x+y}$
2. $\dfrac{b^x}{b^y} = b^{x-y}$

3. $(b^x)^y = b^{xy}$
4. $(ab)^x = a^x b^x$
5. $\frac{a^x}{b^x} = \left(\frac{a}{b}\right)^x$

Example 1.34

Using the Laws of Exponents

Use the laws of exponents to simplify each of the following expressions.

a. $\frac{\left(2x^{2/3}\right)^3}{\left(4x^{-1/3}\right)^2}$

b. $\frac{\left(x^3 y^{-1}\right)^2}{\left(xy^2\right)^{-2}}$

Solution

a. We can simplify as follows:

$$\frac{\left(2x^{2/3}\right)^3}{\left(4x^{-1/3}\right)^2} = \frac{2^3\left(x^{2/3}\right)^3}{4^2\left(x^{-1/3}\right)^2} = \frac{8x^2}{16x^{-2/3}} = \frac{x^2 x^{2/3}}{2} = \frac{x^{8/3}}{2}.$$

b. We can simplify as follows:

$$\frac{\left(x^3 y^{-1}\right)^2}{\left(xy^2\right)^{-2}} = \frac{\left(x^3\right)^2\left(y^{-1}\right)^2}{x^{-2}\left(y^2\right)^{-2}} = \frac{x^6 y^{-2}}{x^{-2} y^{-4}} = x^6 x^2 y^{-2} y^4 = x^8 y^2.$$

1.28 Use the laws of exponents to simplify $\left(6x^{-3} y^2\right)/\left(12x^{-4} y^5\right)$.

The Number e

A special type of exponential function appears frequently in real-world applications. To describe it, consider the following example of exponential growth, which arises from compounding interest in a savings account. Suppose a person invests P dollars in a savings account with an annual interest rate $r,$ compounded annually. The amount of money after 1 year is

$$A(1) = P + rP = P(1 + r).$$

The amount of money after 2 years is

$$A(2) = A(1) + rA(1) = P(1 + r) + rP(1 + r) = P(1 + r)^2.$$

More generally, the amount after t years is

$$A(t) = P(1 + r)^t.$$

If the money is compounded 2 times per year, the amount of money after half a year is

$$A\left(\frac{1}{2}\right) = P + \left(\frac{r}{2}\right)P = P\left(1 + \left(\frac{r}{2}\right)\right).$$

The amount of money after 1 year is

$$A(1) = A\left(\frac{1}{2}\right) + \left(\frac{r}{2}\right)A\left(\frac{1}{2}\right) = P\left(1 + \frac{r}{2}\right) + \frac{r}{2}\left(P\left(1 + \frac{r}{2}\right)\right) = P\left(1 + \frac{r}{2}\right)^2.$$

After t years, the amount of money in the account is

$$A(t) = P\left(1 + \frac{r}{2}\right)^{2t}.$$

More generally, if the money is compounded n times per year, the amount of money in the account after t years is given by the function

$$A(t) = P\left(1 + \frac{r}{n}\right)^{nt}.$$

What happens as $n \to \infty$? To answer this question, we let $m = n/r$ and write

$$\left(1 + \frac{r}{n}\right)^{nt} = \left(1 + \frac{1}{m}\right)^{mrt},$$

and examine the behavior of $(1 + 1/m)^m$ as $m \to \infty$, using a table of values (**Table 1.12**).

m	10	100	1000	10,000	100,000	1,000,000
$\left(1 + \frac{1}{m}\right)^m$	2.5937	2.7048	2.71692	2.71815	2.718268	2.718280

Table 1.12 Values of $\left(1 + \frac{1}{m}\right)^m$ as $m \to \infty$

Looking at this table, it appears that $(1 + 1/m)^m$ is approaching a number between 2.7 and 2.8 as $m \to \infty$. In fact, $(1 + 1/m)^m$ does approach some number as $m \to \infty$. We call this **number** $\boldsymbol{e}$. To six decimal places of accuracy,

$$e \approx 2.718282.$$

The letter e was first used to represent this number by the Swiss mathematician Leonhard Euler during the 1720s. Although Euler did not discover the number, he showed many important connections between e and logarithmic functions. We still use the notation e today to honor Euler's work because it appears in many areas of mathematics and because we can use it in many practical applications.

Returning to our savings account example, we can conclude that if a person puts P dollars in an account at an annual interest rate r, compounded continuously, then $A(t) = Pe^{rt}$. This function may be familiar. Since functions involving base e arise often in applications, we call the function $f(x) = e^x$ the **natural exponential function**. Not only is this function interesting because of the definition of the number e, but also, as discussed next, its graph has an important property.

Since $e > 1$, we know e^x is increasing on $(-\infty, \infty)$. In **Figure 1.45**, we show a graph of $f(x) = e^x$ along with a *tangent line* to the graph of at $x = 0$. We give a precise definition of tangent line in the next chapter; but, informally, we say a tangent line to a graph of f at $x = a$ is a line that passes through the point $(a, f(a))$ and has the same "slope" as f at that point . The function $f(x) = e^x$ is the only exponential function b^x with tangent line at $x = 0$ that has a slope of 1. As we see later in the text, having this property makes the natural exponential function the most simple exponential function to use in many instances.

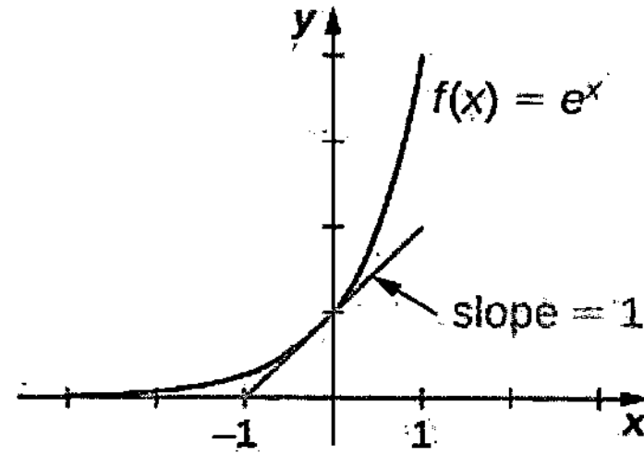

Figure 1.45 The graph of $f(x) = e^x$ has a tangent line with slope 1 at $x = 0$.

Example 1.35

Compounding Interest

Suppose $\$500$ is invested in an account at an annual interest rate of $r = 5.5\%$, compounded continuously.

a. Let t denote the number of years after the initial investment and $A(t)$ denote the amount of money in the account at time t. Find a formula for $A(t)$.

b. Find the amount of money in the account after 10 years and after 20 years.

Solution

a. If P dollars are invested in an account at an annual interest rate r, compounded continuously, then $A(t) = Pe^{rt}$. Here $P = \$500$ and $r = 0.055$. Therefore, $A(t) = 500e^{0.055t}$.

b. After 10 years, the amount of money in the account is

$$A(10) = 500e^{0.055 \cdot 10} = 500e^{0.55} \approx \$866.63.$$

After 20 years, the amount of money in the account is

$$A(20) = 500e^{0.055 \cdot 20} = 500e^{1.1} \approx \$1,502.08.$$

1.29 If $\$750$ is invested in an account at an annual interest rate of 4%, compounded continuously, find a formula for the amount of money in the account after t years. Find the amount of money after 30 years.

Logarithmic Functions

Using our understanding of exponential functions, we can discuss their inverses, which are the logarithmic functions. These come in handy when we need to consider any phenomenon that varies over a wide range of values, such as pH in chemistry or decibels in sound levels.

The exponential function $f(x) = b^x$ is one-to-one, with domain $(-\infty, \infty)$ and range $(0, \infty)$. Therefore, it has an inverse function, called the *logarithmic function with base* b. For any $b > 0, b \neq 1$, the logarithmic function with base b, denoted $\log_b$, has domain $(0, \infty)$ and range $(-\infty, \infty)$, and satisfies

$$\log_b(x) = y \text{ if and only if } b^y = x.$$

For example,

$$\log_2(8) = 3 \quad \text{since} \quad 2^3 = 8,$$
$$\log_{10}\left(\frac{1}{100}\right) = -2 \quad \text{since} \quad 10^{-2} = \frac{1}{10^2} = \frac{1}{100},$$
$$\log_b(1) = 0 \quad \text{since} \quad b^0 = 1 \text{ for any base } b > 0.$$

Furthermore, since $y = \log_b(x)$ and $y = b^x$ are inverse functions,

$$\log_b(b^x) = x \text{ and } b^{\log_b(x)} = x.$$

The most commonly used logarithmic function is the function $\log_e$. Since this function uses natural e as its base, it is called the **natural logarithm**. Here we use the notation $\ln(x)$ or $\ln x$ to mean $\log_e(x)$. For example,

$$\ln(e) = \log_e(e) = 1, \ \ln(e^3) = \log_e(e^3) = 3, \ \ln(1) = \log_e(1) = 0.$$

Since the functions $f(x) = e^x$ and $g(x) = \ln(x)$ are inverses of each other,

$$\ln(e^x) = x \text{ and } e^{\ln x} = x,$$

and their graphs are symmetric about the line $y = x$ (**Figure 1.46**).

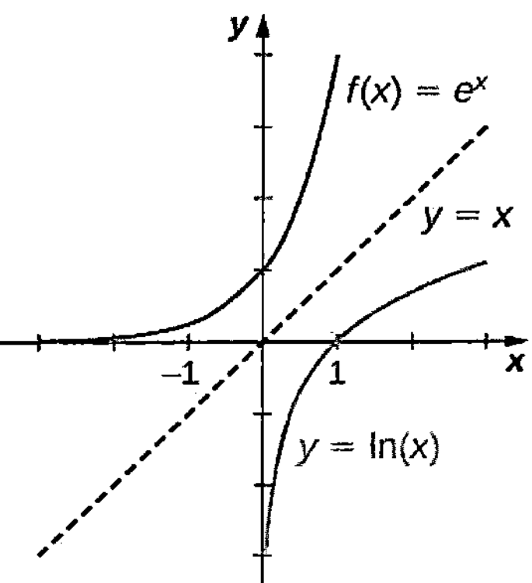

Figure 1.46 The functions $y = e^x$ and $y = \ln(x)$ are inverses of each other, so their graphs are symmetric about the line $y = x$.

At this **site (http://www.openstaxcollege.org/l/20_logscale)** you can see an example of a base-10 logarithmic scale.

In general, for any base $b > 0, b \neq 1,$ the function $g(x) = \log_b(x)$ is symmetric about the line $y = x$ with the function $f(x) = b^x$. Using this fact and the graphs of the exponential functions, we graph functions $\log_b$ for several values of $b > 1$ (**Figure 1.47**).

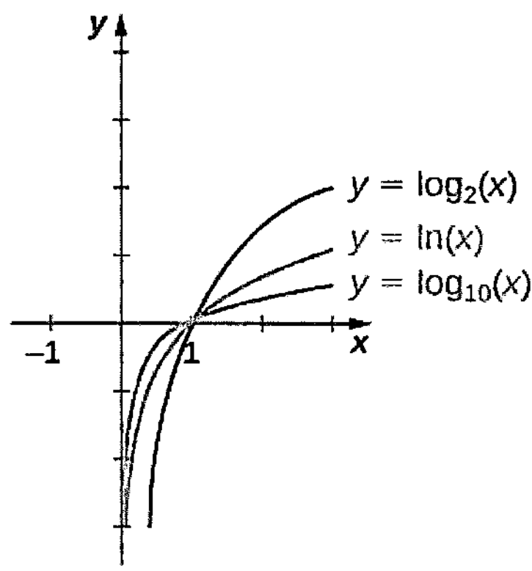

Figure 1.47 Graphs of $y = \log_b(x)$ are depicted for $b = 2, e, 10.$

Before solving some equations involving exponential and logarithmic functions, let's review the basic properties of logarithms.

Rule: Properties of Logarithms

If $a, b, c > 0, b \neq 1,$ and r is any real number, then

1. $\log_b(ac) = \log_b(a) + \log_b(c)$ (Product property)
2. $\log_b\left(\frac{a}{c}\right) = \log_b(a) - \log_b(c)$ (Quotient property)
3. $\log_b(a^r) = r\log_b(a)$ (Power property)

Example 1.36

Solving Equations Involving Exponential Functions

Solve each of the following equations for x.

a. $5^x = 2$

b. $e^x + 6e^{-x} = 5$

Solution

a. Applying the natural logarithm function to both sides of the equation, we have

$$\ln 5^x = \ln 2.$$

Using the power property of logarithms,

$$x\ln 5 = \ln 2.$$

Therefore, $x = \ln 2/\ln 5$.

b. Multiplying both sides of the equation by e^x, we arrive at the equation

$$e^{2x} + 6 = 5e^x.$$

Rewriting this equation as

$$e^{2x} - 5e^x + 6 = 0,$$

we can then rewrite it as a quadratic equation in e^x:

$$(e^x)^2 - 5(e^x) + 6 = 0.$$

Now we can solve the quadratic equation. Factoring this equation, we obtain

$$(e^x - 3)(e^x - 2) = 0.$$

Therefore, the solutions satisfy $e^x = 3$ and $e^x = 2.$ Taking the natural logarithm of both sides gives us the solutions $x = \ln 3, \ln 2.$

1.30 Solve $e^{2x}/(3 + e^{2x}) = 1/2.$

Example 1.37

Solving Equations Involving Logarithmic Functions

Solve each of the following equations for $x.$

a. $\ln\left(\frac{1}{x}\right) = 4$

b. $\log_{10}\sqrt{x} + \log_{10}x = 2$

c. $\ln(2x) - 3\ln\left(x^2\right) = 0$

Solution

a. By the definition of the natural logarithm function,

$$\ln\left(\frac{1}{x}\right) = 4 \text{ if and only if } e^4 = \frac{1}{x}.$$

Therefore, the solution is $x = 1/e^4.$

b. Using the product and power properties of logarithmic functions, rewrite the left-hand side of the equation as

$$\log_{10}\sqrt{x} + \log_{10}x = \log_{10}x\sqrt{x} = \log_{10}x^{3/2} = \frac{3}{2}\log_{10}x.$$

Therefore, the equation can be rewritten as

$$\frac{3}{2}\log_{10}x = 2 \text{ or } \log_{10}x = \frac{4}{3}.$$

The solution is $x = 10^{4/3} = 10\sqrt[3]{10}.$

c. Using the power property of logarithmic functions, we can rewrite the equation as $\ln(2x) - \ln\left(x^6\right) = 0.$ Using the quotient property, this becomes

$$\ln\left(\frac{2}{x^5}\right) = 0.$$

Therefore, $2/x^5 = 1,$ which implies $x = \sqrt[5]{2}.$ We should then check for any extraneous solutions.

 **1.31** Solve $\ln\left(x^3\right) - 4\ln(x) = 1.$

When evaluating a logarithmic function with a calculator, you may have noticed that the only options are $\log_{10}$ or log, called the *common logarithm*, or *ln*, which is the natural logarithm. However, exponential functions and logarithm functions can be expressed in terms of any desired base $b.$ If you need to use a calculator to evaluate an expression with a different base, you can apply the change-of-base formulas first. Using this change of base, we typically write a given exponential or logarithmic function in terms of the natural exponential and natural logarithmic functions.

Rule: Change-of-Base Formulas

Let $a > 0,\ b > 0,$ and $a \neq 1,\ b \neq 1.$

1. $a^x = b^{x\log_b a}$ for any real number $x.$

   If $b = e,$ this equation reduces to $a^x = e^{x\log_e a} = e^{x\ln a}.$

2. $\log_a x = \dfrac{\log_b x}{\log_b a}$ for any real number $x > 0.$

   If $b = e,$ this equation reduces to $\log_a x = \dfrac{\ln x}{\ln a}.$

Proof

For the first change-of-base formula, we begin by making use of the power property of logarithmic functions. We know that for any base $b > 0,\ b \neq 1,\ \log_b(a^x) = x\log_b a.$ Therefore,

$$b^{\log_b(a^x)} = b^{x\log_b a}.$$

In addition, we know that b^x and $\log_b(x)$ are inverse functions. Therefore,

$$b^{\log_b(a^x)} = a^x.$$

Combining these last two equalities, we conclude that $a^x = b^{x\log_b a}.$

To prove the second property, we show that

$$(\log_b a) \cdot (\log_a x) = \log_b x.$$

Let $u = \log_b a,\ v = \log_a x,$ and $w = \log_b x.$ We will show that $u \cdot v = w.$ By the definition of logarithmic functions, we know that $b^u = a,\ a^v = x,$ and $b^w = x.$ From the previous equations, we see that

$$b^{uv} = (b^u)^v = a^v = x = b^w.$$

Therefore, $b^{uv} = b^w.$ Since exponential functions are one-to-one, we can conclude that $u \cdot v = w.$

□

Example 1.38

Changing Bases

Use a calculating utility to evaluate $\log_3 7$ with the change-of-base formula presented earlier.

Solution

Use the second equation with $a = 3$ and $e = 3$:

$\log_3 7 = \frac{\ln 7}{\ln 3} \approx 1.77124.$

1.32 Use the change-of-base formula and a calculating utility to evaluate $\log_4 6.$

Example 1.39

Chapter Opener: The Richter Scale for Earthquakes

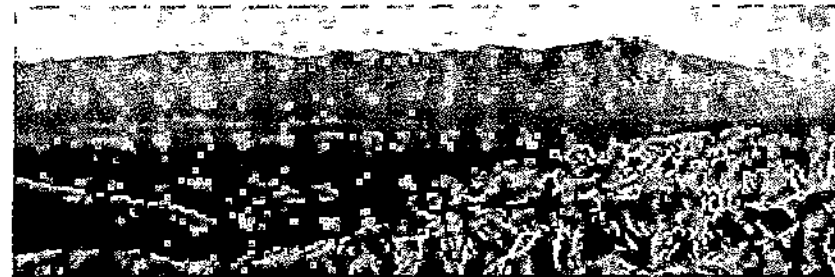

Figure 1.48 (credit: modification of work by Robb Hannawacker, NPS)

In 1935, Charles Richter developed a scale (now known as the *Richter scale*) to measure the magnitude of an earthquake. The scale is a base-10 logarithmic scale, and it can be described as follows: Consider one earthquake with magnitude R_1 on the Richter scale and a second earthquake with magnitude R_2 on the Richter scale. Suppose $R_1 > R_2,$ which means the earthquake of magnitude R_1 is stronger, but how much stronger is it than the other earthquake? A way of measuring the intensity of an earthquake is by using a seismograph to measure the amplitude of the earthquake waves. If A_1 is the amplitude measured for the first earthquake and A_2 is the amplitude measured for the second earthquake, then the amplitudes and magnitudes of the two earthquakes satisfy the following equation:

$$R_1 - R_2 = \log_{10}\left(\frac{A_1}{A_2}\right).$$

Consider an earthquake that measures 8 on the Richter scale and an earthquake that measures 7 on the Richter scale. Then,

$$8 - 7 = \log_{10}\left(\frac{A_1}{A_2}\right).$$

Therefore,

$$\log_{10}\left(\frac{A_1}{A_2}\right) = 1,$$

which implies $A_1/A_2 = 10$ or $A_1 = 10A_2$. Since A_1 is 10 times the size of A_2, we say that the first earthquake is 10 times as intense as the second earthquake. On the other hand, if one earthquake measures 8 on the Richter scale and another measures 6, then the relative intensity of the two earthquakes satisfies the equation

$$\log_{10}\left(\frac{A_1}{A_2}\right) = 8 - 6 = 2.$$

Therefore, $A_1 = 100A_2$. That is, the first earthquake is 100 times more intense than the second earthquake.

How can we use logarithmic functions to compare the relative severity of the magnitude 9 earthquake in Japan in 2011 with the magnitude 7.3 earthquake in Haiti in 2010?

Solution

To compare the Japan and Haiti earthquakes, we can use an equation presented earlier:

$$9 - 7.3 = \log_{10}\left(\frac{A_1}{A_2}\right).$$

Therefore, $A_1/A_2 = 10^{1.7}$, and we conclude that the earthquake in Japan was approximately 50 times more intense than the earthquake in Haiti.

1.33 Compare the relative severity of a magnitude 8.4 earthquake with a magnitude 7.4 earthquake.

Hyperbolic Functions

The hyperbolic functions are defined in terms of certain combinations of e^x and e^{-x}. These functions arise naturally in various engineering and physics applications, including the study of water waves and vibrations of elastic membranes. Another common use for a hyperbolic function is the representation of a hanging chain or cable, also known as a catenary (**Figure 1.49**). If we introduce a coordinate system so that the low point of the chain lies along the y-axis, we can describe the height of the chain in terms of a hyperbolic function. First, we define the **hyperbolic functions**.

Figure 1.49 The shape of a strand of silk in a spider's web can be described in terms of a hyperbolic function. The same shape applies to a chain or cable hanging from two supports with only its own weight. (credit: "Mtpaley", Wikimedia Commons)

Definition

Hyperbolic cosine

$$\cosh x = \frac{e^x + e^{-x}}{2}$$

Hyperbolic sine

$$\sinh x = \frac{e^x - e^{-x}}{2}$$

Hyperbolic tangent

$$\tanh x = \frac{\sinh x}{\cosh x} = \frac{e^x - e^{-x}}{e^x + e^{-x}}$$

Hyperbolic cosecant

$$\operatorname{csch} x = \frac{1}{\sinh x} = \frac{2}{e^x - e^{-x}}$$

Hyperbolic secant

$$\operatorname{sech} x = \frac{1}{\cosh x} = \frac{2}{e^x + e^{-x}}$$

Hyperbolic cotangent

$$\coth x = \frac{\cosh x}{\sinh x} = \frac{e^x + e^{-x}}{e^x - e^{-x}}$$

The name *cosh* rhymes with "gosh," whereas the name *sinh* is pronounced "cinch." *Tanh, sech, csch,* and *coth* are pronounced "tanch," "seech," "coseech," and "cotanch," respectively.

Using the definition of $\cosh(x)$ and principles of physics, it can be shown that the height of a hanging chain, such as the one in **Figure 1.49**, can be described by the function $h(x) = a\cosh(x/a) + c$ for certain constants a and c.

But why are these functions called *hyperbolic functions*? To answer this question, consider the quantity $\cosh^2 t - \sinh^2 t$. Using the definition of $\cosh$ and $\sinh,$ we see that

$$\cosh^2 t - \sinh^2 t = \frac{e^{2t} + 2 + e^{-2t}}{4} - \frac{e^{2t} - 2 + e^{-2t}}{4} = 1.$$

This identity is the analog of the trigonometric identity $\cos^2 t + \sin^2 t = 1$. Here, given a value t, the point $(x, y) = (\cosh t, \sinh t)$ lies on the unit hyperbola $x^2 - y^2 = 1$ (**Figure 1.50**).

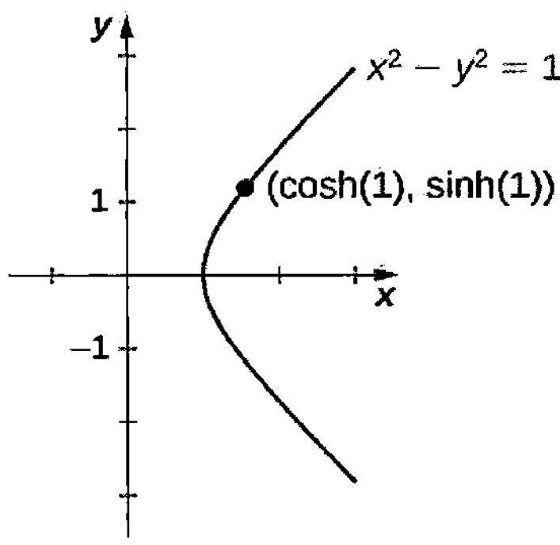

Figure 1.50 The unit hyperbola $\cosh^2 t - \sinh^2 t = 1$.

Graphs of Hyperbolic Functions

To graph $\cosh x$ and $\sinh x$, we make use of the fact that both functions approach $(1/2)e^x$ as $x \to \infty$, since $e^{-x} \to 0$ as $x \to \infty$. As $x \to -\infty$, $\cosh x$ approaches $1/2e^{-x}$, whereas $\sinh x$ approaches $-1/2e^{-x}$. Therefore, using the graphs of $1/2e^x$, $1/2e^{-x}$, and $-1/2e^{-x}$ as guides, we graph $\cosh x$ and $\sinh x$. To graph $\tanh x$, we use the fact that $\tanh(0) = 1$, $-1 < \tanh(x) < 1$ for all x, $\tanh x \to 1$ as $x \to \infty$, and $\tanh x \to -1$ as $x \to -\infty$. The graphs of the other three hyperbolic functions can be sketched using the graphs of $\cosh x$, $\sinh x$, and $\tanh x$ (**Figure 1.51**).

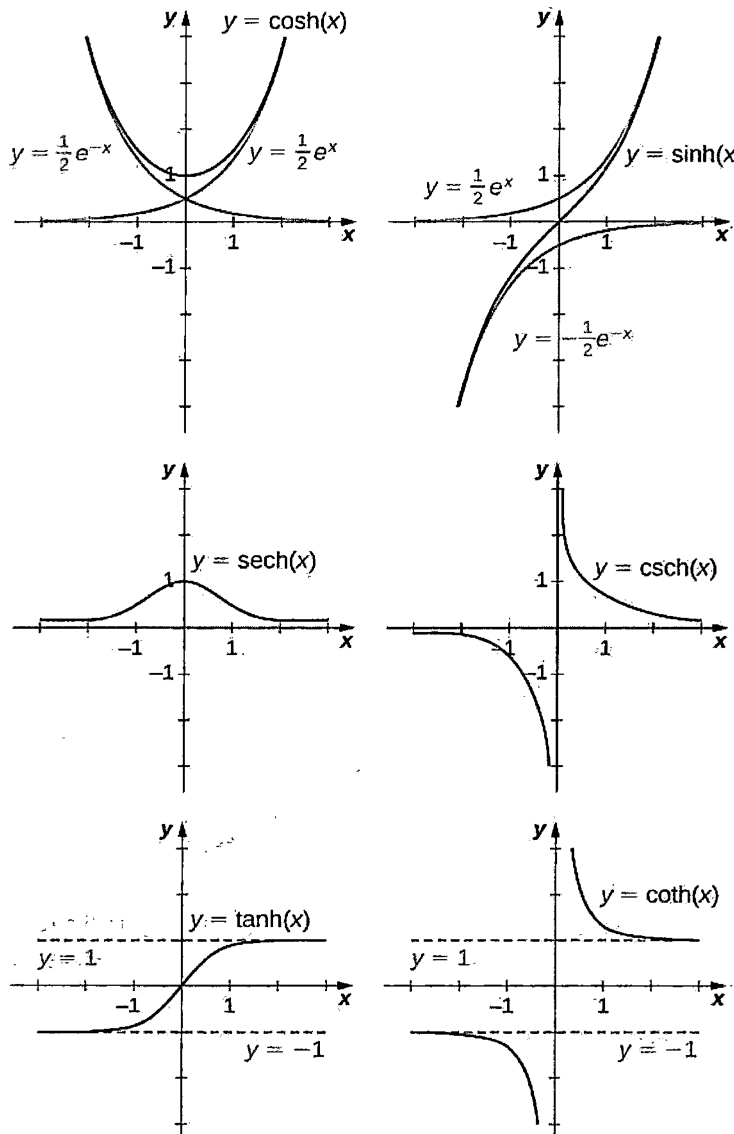

Figure 1.51 The hyperbolic functions involve combinations of e^x and e^{-x}.

Identities Involving Hyperbolic Functions

The identity $\cosh^2 t - \sinh^2 t$, shown in **Figure 1.50**, is one of several identities involving the hyperbolic functions, some of which are listed next. The first four properties follow easily from the definitions of hyperbolic sine and hyperbolic cosine. Except for some differences in signs, most of these properties are analogous to identities for trigonometric functions.

Rule: Identities Involving Hyperbolic Functions

1. $\cosh(-x) = \cosh x$
2. $\sinh(-x) = -\sinh x$
3. $\cosh x + \sinh x = e^x$
4. $\cosh x - \sinh x = e^{-x}$

5. $\cosh^2 x - \sinh^2 x = 1$
6. $1 - \tanh^2 x = \text{sech}^2 x$
7. $\coth^2 x - 1 = \text{csch}^2 x$
8. $\sinh(x \pm y) = \sinh x \cosh y \pm \cosh x \sinh y$
9. $\cosh(x \pm y) = \cosh x \cosh y \pm \sinh x \sinh y$

Example 1.40

Evaluating Hyperbolic Functions

a. Simplify $\sinh(5 \ln x)$.

b. If $\sinh x = 3/4$, find the values of the remaining five hyperbolic functions.

Solution

a. Using the definition of the sinh function, we write

$$\sinh(5 \ln x) = \frac{e^{5 \ln x} - e^{-5 \ln x}}{2} = \frac{e^{\ln(x^5)} - e^{\ln(x^{-5})}}{2} = \frac{x^5 - x^{-5}}{2}.$$

b. Using the identity $\cosh^2 x - \sinh^2 x = 1$, we see that

$$\cosh^2 x = 1 + \left(\frac{3}{4}\right)^2 = \frac{25}{16}.$$

Since $\cosh x \geq 1$ for all x, we must have $\cosh x = 5/4$. Then, using the definitions for the other hyperbolic functions, we conclude that $\tanh x = 3/5$, $\text{csch}\, x = 4/3$, $\text{sech}\, x = 4/5$, and $\coth x = 5/3$.

1.34 Simplify $\cosh(2 \ln x)$.

Inverse Hyperbolic Functions

From the graphs of the hyperbolic functions, we see that all of them are one-to-one except $\cosh x$ and $\text{sech}\, x$. If we restrict the domains of these two functions to the interval $[0, \infty)$, then all the hyperbolic functions are one-to-one, and we can define the **inverse hyperbolic functions**. Since the hyperbolic functions themselves involve exponential functions, the inverse hyperbolic functions involve logarithmic functions.

Definition

Inverse Hyperbolic Functions

$$\sinh^{-1} x = \text{arcsinh}\, x = \ln\left(x + \sqrt{x^2 + 1}\right) \qquad \cosh^{-1} x = \text{arccosh}\, x = \ln\left(x + \sqrt{x^2 - 1}\right)$$

$$\tanh^{-1} x = \text{arctanh}\, x = \frac{1}{2}\ln\left(\frac{1 + x}{1 - x}\right) \qquad \coth^{-1} x = \text{arccot}\, x = \frac{1}{2}\ln\left(\frac{x + 1}{x - 1}\right)$$

$$\text{sech}^{-1} x = \text{arcsech}\, x = \ln\left(\frac{1 + \sqrt{1 - x^2}}{x}\right) \qquad \text{csch}^{-1} x = \text{arccsch}\, x = \ln\left(\frac{1}{x} + \frac{\sqrt{1 + x^2}}{|x|}\right)$$

Let's look at how to derive the first equation. The others follow similarly. Suppose $y = \sinh^{-1} x$. Then, $x = \sinh y$ and, by the definition of the hyperbolic sine function, $x = \frac{e^y - e^{-y}}{2}$. Therefore,

$$e^y - 2x - e^{-y} = 0.$$

Multiplying this equation by e^y, we obtain

$$e^{2y} - 2xe^y - 1 = 0.$$

This can be solved like a quadratic equation, with the solution

$$e^y = \frac{2x \pm \sqrt{4x^2 + 4}}{2} = x \pm \sqrt{x^2 + 1}.$$

Since $e^y > 0$, the only solution is the one with the positive sign. Applying the natural logarithm to both sides of the equation, we conclude that

$$y = \ln\left(x + \sqrt{x^2 + 1}\right).$$

Example 1.41

Evaluating Inverse Hyperbolic Functions

Evaluate each of the following expressions.

$$\sinh^{-1}(2)$$
$$\tanh^{-1}(1/4)$$

Solution

$$\sinh^{-1}(2) = \ln\left(2 + \sqrt{2^2 + 1}\right) = \ln(2 + \sqrt{5}) \approx 1.4436$$

$$\tanh^{-1}(1/4) = \frac{1}{2}\ln\left(\frac{1 + 1/4}{1 - 1/4}\right) = \frac{1}{2}\ln\left(\frac{5/4}{3/4}\right) = \frac{1}{2}\ln\left(\frac{5}{3}\right) \approx 0.2554$$

1.35 Evaluate $\tanh^{-1}(1/2)$.

1.5 EXERCISES

For the following exercises, evaluate the given exponential functions as indicated, accurate to two significant digits after the decimal.

229. $f(x) = 5^x$ a. $x = 3$ b. $x = \frac{1}{2}$ c. $x = \sqrt{2}$

230. $f(x) = (0.3)^x$ a. $x = -1$ b. $x = 4$ c. $x = -1.5$

231. $f(x) = 10^x$ a. $x = -2$ b. $x = 4$ c. $x = \frac{5}{3}$

232. $f(x) = e^x$ a. $x = 2$ b. $x = -3.2$ c. $x = \pi$

For the following exercises, match the exponential equation to the correct graph.

a. $y = 4^{-x}$

b. $y = 3^{x-1}$

c. $y = 2^{x+1}$

d. $y = \left(\frac{1}{2}\right)^x + 2$

e. $y = -3^{-x}$

f. $y = 1 - 5^x$

233.

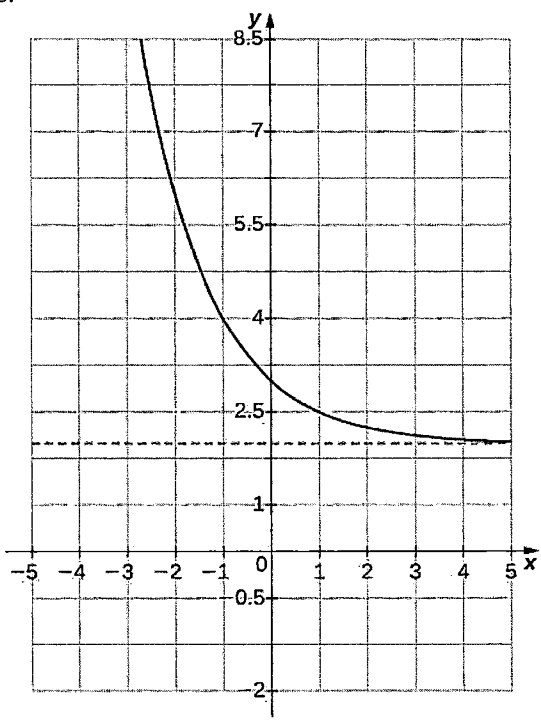

234.

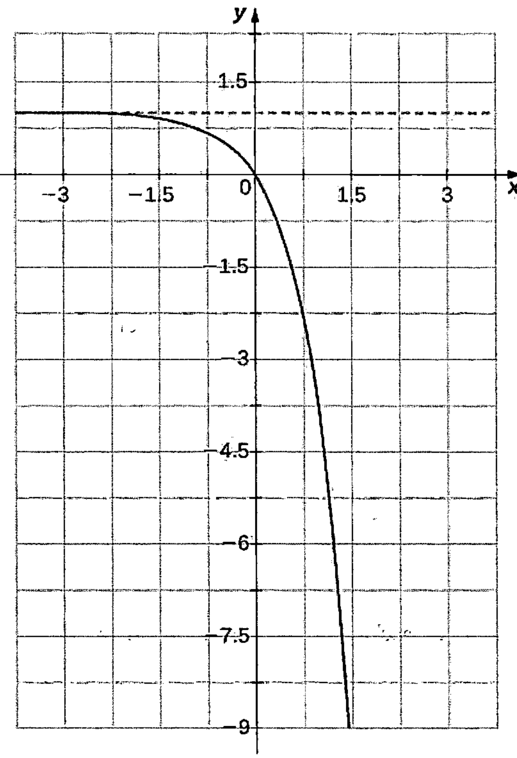

235.

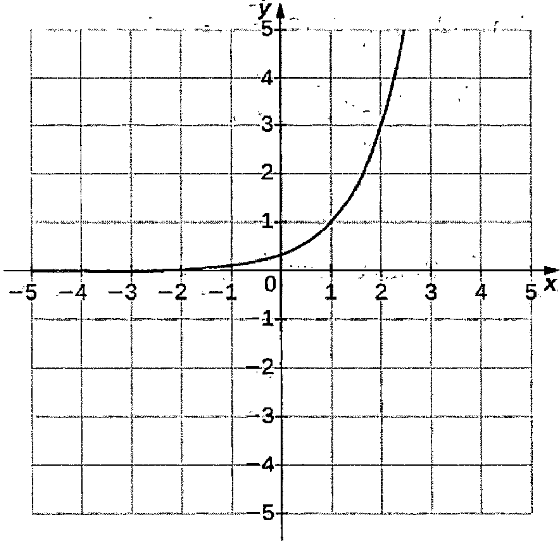

236.

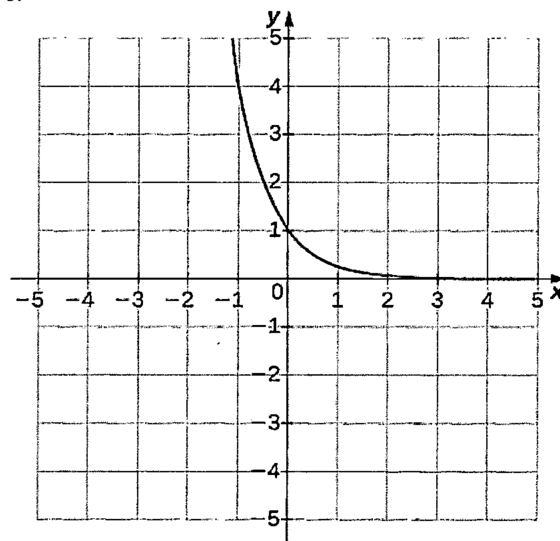

237.

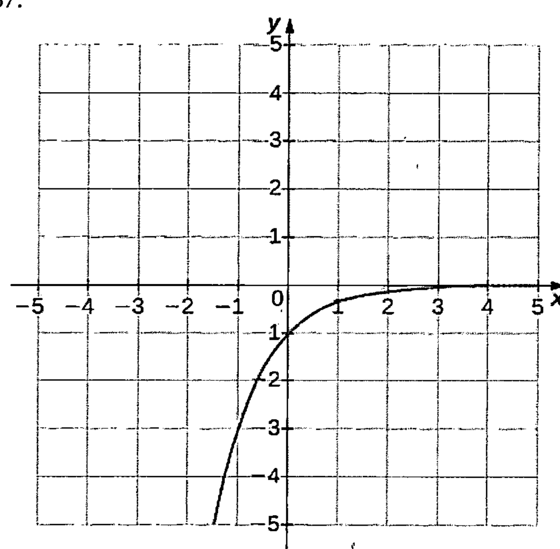

238.

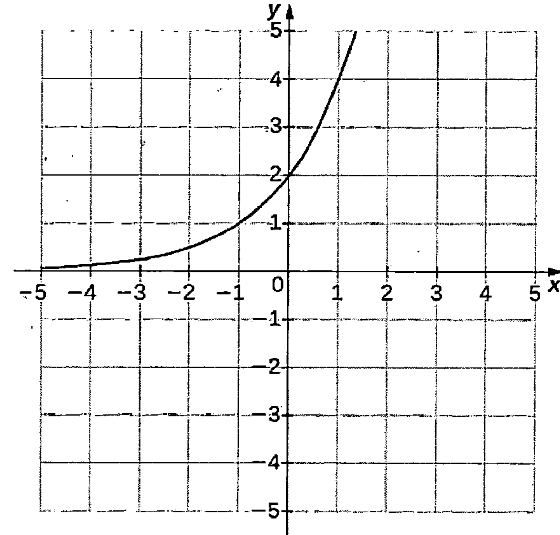

For the following exercises, sketch the graph of the exponential function. Determine the domain, range, and horizontal asymptote.

239. $f(x) = e^x + 2$

240. $f(x) = -2^x$

241. $f(x) = 3^{x+1}$

242. $f(x) = 4^x - 1$

243. $f(x) = 1 - 2^{-x}$

244. $f(x) = 5^{x+1} + 2$

245. $f(x) = e^{-x} - 1$

For the following exercises, write the equation in equivalent exponential form.

246. $\log_3 81 = 4$

247. $\log_8 2 = \frac{1}{3}$

248. $\log_5 1 = 0$

249. $\log_5 25 = 2$

250. $\log 0.1 = -1$

251. $\ln\left(\frac{1}{e^3}\right) = -3$

252. $\log_9 3 = 0.5$

253. $\ln 1 = 0$

For the following exercises, write the equation in equivalent logarithmic form.

254. $2^3 = 8$

255. $4^{-2} = \frac{1}{16}$

256. $10^2 = 100$

257. $9^0 = 1$

258. $\left(\frac{1}{3}\right)^3 = \frac{1}{27}$

259. $\sqrt[3]{64} = 4$

260. $e^x = y$

261. $9^y = 150$

262. $b^3 = 45$

263. $4^{-3/2} = 0.125$

For the following exercises, sketch the graph of the logarithmic function. Determine the domain, range, and vertical asymptote.

264. $f(x) = 3 + \ln x$

265. $f(x) = \ln(x - 1)$

266. $f(x) = \ln(-x)$

267. $f(x) = 1 - \ln x$

268. $f(x) = \log x - 1$

269. $f(x) = \ln(x + 1)$

For the following exercises, use properties of logarithms to write the expressions as a sum, difference, and/or product of logarithms.

270. $\log x^4 y$

271. $\log_3 \frac{9a^3}{b}$

272. $\ln a\sqrt[3]{b}$

273. $\log_5 \sqrt{125xy^3}$

274. $\log_4 \frac{\sqrt[3]{xy}}{64}$

275. $\ln\left(\frac{6}{\sqrt{e^3}}\right)$

For the following exercises, solve the exponential equation exactly.

276. $5^x = 125$

277. $e^{3x} - 15 = 0$

278. $8^x = 4$

279. $4^{x+1} - 32 = 0$

280. $3^{x/14} = \frac{1}{10}$

281. $10^x = 7.21$

282. $4 \cdot 2^{3x} - 20 = 0$

283. $7^{3x-2} = 11$

For the following exercises, solve the logarithmic equation exactly, if possible.

284. $\log_3 x = 0$

285. $\log_5 x = -2$

286. $\log_4 (x + 5) = 0$

287. $\log(2x - 7) = 0$

288. $\ln\sqrt{x + 3} = 2$

289. $\log_6 (x + 9) + \log_6 x = 2$

290. $\log_4 (x + 2) - \log_4 (x - 1) = 0$

291. $\ln x + \ln(x - 2) = \ln 4$

For the following exercises, use the change-of-base formula and either base 10 or base e to evaluate the given expressions. Answer in exact form and in approximate form, rounding to four decimal places.

292. $\log_5 47$

293. $\log_7 82$

294. $\log_6 103$

295. $\log_{0.5} 211$

296. $\log_2 \pi$

297. $\log_{0.2} 0.452$

298. Rewrite the following expressions in terms of exponentials and simplify. a. $2\cosh(\ln x)$ b. $\cosh 4x + \sinh 4x$ c. $\cosh 2x - \sinh 2x$ d. $\ln(\cosh x + \sinh x) + \ln(\cosh x - \sinh x)$

299. **[T]** The number of bacteria N in a culture after t days can be modeled by the function $N(t) = 1300 \cdot (2)^{t/4}$. Find the number of bacteria present after 15 days.

300. **[T]** The demand D (in millions of barrels) for oil in an oil-rich country is given by the function $D(p) = 150 \cdot (2.7)^{-0.25p}$, where p is the price (in dollars) of a barrel of oil. Find the amount of oil demanded (to the nearest million barrels) when the price is between \$15 and \$20.

301. **[T]** The amount A of a \$100,000 investment paying continuously and compounded for t years is given by $A(t) = 100{,}000 \cdot e^{0.055t}$. Find the amount A accumulated in 5 years.

302. **[T]** An investment is compounded monthly, quarterly, or yearly and is given by the function $A = P\left(1 + \frac{j}{n}\right)^{nt}$, where A is the value of the investment at time t, P is the initial principle that was invested, j is the annual interest rate, and n is the number of time the interest is compounded per year. Given a yearly interest rate of 3.5% and an initial principle of \$100,000, find the amount A accumulated in 5 years for interest that is compounded a. daily, b., monthly, c. quarterly, and d. yearly.

303. **[T]** The concentration of hydrogen ions in a substance is denoted by $[\mathrm{H}^+]$, measured in moles per liter. The pH of a substance is defined by the logarithmic function $\mathrm{pH} = -\log[\mathrm{H}^+]$. This function is used to measure the acidity of a substance. The pH of water is 7. A substance with a pH less than 7 is an acid, whereas one that has a pH of more than 7 is a base.

a. Find the pH of the following substances. Round answers to one digit.
b. Determine whether the substance is an acid or a base.

i. Eggs: $[\mathrm{H}^+] = 1.6 \times 10^{-8}$ mol/L
ii. Beer: $[\mathrm{H}^+] = 3.16 \times 10^{-3}$ mol/L
iii. Tomato Juice: $[\mathrm{H}^+] = 7.94 \times 10^{-5}$ mol/L

304. **[T]** Iodine-131 is a radioactive substance that decays according to the function $Q(t) = Q_0 \cdot e^{-0.08664t}$, where Q_0 is the initial quantity of a sample of the substance and t is in days. Determine how long it takes (to the nearest day) for 95% of a quantity to decay.

305. **[T]** According to the World Bank, at the end of 2013 ($t = 0$) the U.S. population was 316 million and was increasing according to the following model: $P(t) = 316e^{0.0074t}$, where P is measured in millions of people and t is measured in years after 2013.

a. Based on this model, what will be the population of the United States in 2020?
b. Determine when the U.S. population will be twice what it is in 2013.

306. **[T]** The amount A accumulated after 1000 dollars is invested for t years at an interest rate of 4% is modeled by the function $A(t) = 1000(1.04)^t$.

a. Find the amount accumulated after 5 years and 10 years.
b. Determine how long it takes for the original investment to triple.

307. **[T]** A bacterial colony grown in a lab is known to double in number in 12 hours. Suppose, initially, there are 1000 bacteria present.

a. Use the exponential function $Q = Q_0 e^{kt}$ to determine the value k, which is the growth rate of the bacteria. Round to four decimal places.
b. Determine approximately how long it takes for 200,000 bacteria to grow.

308. **[T]** The rabbit population on a game reserve doubles every 6 months. Suppose there were 120 rabbits initially.

a. Use the exponential function $P = P_0 a^t$ to determine the growth rate constant a. Round to four decimal places.
b. Use the function in part a. to determine approximately how long it takes for the rabbit population to reach 3500.

309. **[T]** The 1906 earthquake in San Francisco had a magnitude of 8.3 on the Richter scale. At the same time, in Japan, an earthquake with magnitude 4.9 caused only minor damage. Approximately how much more energy was released by the San Francisco earthquake than by the Japanese earthquake?

CHAPTER 1 REVIEW

KEY TERMS

absolute value function $f(x) = \begin{cases} -x, & x < 0 \\ x, & x \geq 0 \end{cases}$

algebraic function a function involving any combination of only the basic operations of addition, subtraction, multiplication, division, powers, and roots applied to an input variable x

base the number b in the exponential function $f(x) = b^x$ and the logarithmic function $f(x) = \log_b x$

composite function given two functions f and g, a new function, denoted $g \circ f$, such that $(g \circ f)(x) = g(f(x))$

cubic function a polynomial of degree 3; that is, a function of the form $f(x) = ax^3 + bx^2 + cx + d$, where $a \neq 0$

decreasing on the interval I a function decreasing on the interval I if, for all $x_1, x_2 \in I$, $f(x_1) \geq f(x_2)$ if $x_1 < x_2$

degree for a polynomial function, the value of the largest exponent of any term

dependent variable the output variable for a function

domain the set of inputs for a function

even function a function is even if $f(-x) = f(x)$ for all x in the domain of f

exponent the value x in the expression b^x

function a set of inputs, a set of outputs, and a rule for mapping each input to exactly one output

graph of a function the set of points (x, y) such that x is in the domain of f and $y = f(x)$

horizontal line test a function f is one-to-one if and only if every horizontal line intersects the graph of f, at most, once

hyperbolic functions the functions denoted $\sinh, \cosh, \tanh, \text{csch}, \text{sech},$ and $\coth,$ which involve certain combinations of e^x and e^{-x}

increasing on the interval I a function increasing on the interval I if for all $x_1, x_2 \in I$, $f(x_1) \leq f(x_2)$ if $x_1 < x_2$

independent variable the input variable for a function

inverse function for a function f, the inverse function f^{-1} satisfies $f^{-1}(y) = x$ if $f(x) = y$

inverse hyperbolic functions the inverses of the hyperbolic functions where $\cosh$ and sech are restricted to the domain $[0, \infty)$; each of these functions can be expressed in terms of a composition of the natural logarithm function and an algebraic function

inverse trigonometric functions the inverses of the trigonometric functions are defined on restricted domains where they are one-to-one functions

linear function a function that can be written in the form $f(x) = mx + b$

logarithmic function a function of the form $f(x) = \log_b(x)$ for some base $b > 0, b \neq 1$ such that $y = \log_b(x)$ if and only if $b^y = x$

mathematical model A method of simulating real-life situations with mathematical equations

natural exponential function the function $f(x) = e^x$

natural logarithm the function $\ln x = \log_e x$

number e as m gets larger, the quantity $(1 + (1/m))^m$ gets closer to some real number; we define that real number to be e; the value of e is approximately 2.718282

odd function a function is odd if $f(-x) = -f(x)$ for all x in the domain of f

one-to-one function a function f is one-to-one if $f(x_1) \neq f(x_2)$ if $x_1 \neq x_2$

periodic function a function is periodic if it has a repeating pattern as the values of x move from left to right

piecewise-defined function a function that is defined differently on different parts of its domain

point-slope equation equation of a linear function indicating its slope and a point on the graph of the function

polynomial function a function of the form $f(x) = a_n x^n + a_{n-1} x^{n-1} + \ldots + a_1 x + a_0$

power function a function of the form $f(x) = x^n$ for any positive integer $n \geq 1$

quadratic function a polynomial of degree 2; that is, a function of the form $f(x) = ax^2 + bx + c$ where $a \neq 0$

radians for a circular arc of length s on a circle of radius 1, the radian measure of the associated angle θ is s

range the set of outputs for a function

rational function a function of the form $f(x) = p(x)/q(x)$, where $p(x)$ and $q(x)$ are polynomials

restricted domain a subset of the domain of a function f

root function a function of the form $f(x) = x^{1/n}$ for any integer $n \geq 2$

slope the change in y for each unit change in x

slope-intercept form equation of a linear function indicating its slope and y-intercept

symmetry about the origin the graph of a function f is symmetric about the origin if $(-x, -y)$ is on the graph of f whenever (x, y) is on the graph

symmetry about the *y*-axis the graph of a function f is symmetric about the y-axis if $(-x, y)$ is on the graph of f whenever (x, y) is on the graph

table of values a table containing a list of inputs and their corresponding outputs

transcendental function a function that cannot be expressed by a combination of basic arithmetic operations

transformation of a function a shift, scaling, or reflection of a function

trigonometric functions functions of an angle defined as ratios of the lengths of the sides of a right triangle

trigonometric identity an equation involving trigonometric functions that is true for all angles θ for which the functions in the equation are defined

vertical line test given the graph of a function, every vertical line intersects the graph, at most, once

zeros of a function when a real number x is a zero of a function f, $f(x) = 0$

KEY EQUATIONS

- **Composition of two functions**
  $(g \circ f)(x) = g(f(x))$
- **Absolute value function**
  $f(x) = \begin{cases} -x, & x < 0 \\ x, & x \geq 0 \end{cases}$

- **Point-slope equation of a line**
  $y - y_1 = m(x - x_1)$
- **Slope-intercept form of a line**
  $y = mx + b$
- **Standard form of a line**
  $ax + by = c$
- **Polynomial function**
  $f(x) = a_n x^n + a_{n-1} x^{n-1} + \cdots + a_1 x + a_0$
- **Generalized sine function**
  $f(x) = A\sin(B(x - \alpha)) + C$
- **Inverse functions**
  $f^{-1}(f(x)) = x$ for all x in D, and $f\big(f^{-1}(y)\big) = y$ for all y in R.

KEY CONCEPTS

1.1 Review of Functions

- A function is a mapping from a set of inputs to a set of outputs with exactly one output for each input.
- If no domain is stated for a function $y = f(x)$, the domain is considered to be the set of all real numbers x for which the function is defined.
- When sketching the graph of a function f, each vertical line may intersect the graph, at most, once.
- A function may have any number of zeros, but it has, at most, one y-intercept.
- To define the composition $g \circ f$, the range of f must be contained in the domain of g.
- Even functions are symmetric about the y-axis whereas odd functions are symmetric about the origin.

1.2 Basic Classes of Functions

- The power function $f(x) = x^n$ is an even function if n is even and $n \neq 0$, and it is an odd function if n is odd.
- The root function $f(x) = x^{1/n}$ has the domain $[0, \infty)$ if n is even and the domain $(-\infty, \infty)$ if n is odd. If n is odd, then $f(x) = x^{1/n}$ is an odd function.
- The domain of the rational function $f(x) = p(x)/q(x)$, where $p(x)$ and $q(x)$ are polynomial functions, is the set of x such that $q(x) \neq 0$.
- Functions that involve the basic operations of addition, subtraction, multiplication, division, and powers are algebraic functions. All other functions are transcendental. Trigonometric, exponential, and logarithmic functions are examples of transcendental functions.
- A polynomial function f with degree $n \geq 1$ satisfies $f(x) \to \pm\infty$ as $x \to \pm\infty$. The sign of the output as $x \to \infty$ depends on the sign of the leading coefficient only and on whether n is even or odd.
- Vertical and horizontal shifts, vertical and horizontal scalings, and reflections about the x- and y-axes are examples of transformations of functions.

1.3 Trigonometric Functions

- Radian measure is defined such that the angle associated with the arc of length 1 on the unit circle has radian measure 1. An angle with a degree measure of $180°$ has a radian measure of π rad.

- For acute angles $\theta,$ the values of the trigonometric functions are defined as ratios of two sides of a right triangle in which one of the acute angles is $\theta.$
- For a general angle $\theta,$ let (x, y) be a point on a circle of radius r corresponding to this angle $\theta.$ The trigonometric functions can be written as ratios involving $x, y,$ and $r.$
- The trigonometric functions are periodic. The sine, cosine, secant, and cosecant functions have period $2\pi.$ The tangent and cotangent functions have period $\pi.$

1.4 Inverse Functions

- For a function to have an inverse, the function must be one-to-one. Given the graph of a function, we can determine whether the function is one-to-one by using the horizontal line test.
- If a function is not one-to-one, we can restrict the domain to a smaller domain where the function is one-to-one and then define the inverse of the function on the smaller domain.
- For a function f and its inverse $f^{-1}, f\left(f^{-1}(x)\right) = x$ for all x in the domain of f^{-1} and $f^{-1}(f(x)) = x$ for all x in the domain of $f.$
- Since the trigonometric functions are periodic, we need to restrict their domains to define the inverse trigonometric functions.
- The graph of a function f and its inverse f^{-1} are symmetric about the line $y = x.$

1.5 Exponential and Logarithmic Functions

- The exponential function $y = b^x$ is increasing if $b > 1$ and decreasing if $0 < b < 1.$ Its domain is $(-\infty, \infty)$ and its range is $(0, \infty).$
- The logarithmic function $y = \log_b(x)$ is the inverse of $y = b^x.$ Its domain is $(0, \infty)$ and its range is $(-\infty, \infty).$
- The natural exponential function is $y = e^x$ and the natural logarithmic function is $y = \ln x = \log_e x.$
- Given an exponential function or logarithmic function in base $a,$ we can make a change of base to convert this function to any base $b > 0, b \neq 1.$ We typically convert to base $e.$
- The hyperbolic functions involve combinations of the exponential functions e^x and $e^{-x}.$ As a result, the inverse hyperbolic functions involve the natural logarithm.

CHAPTER 1 REVIEW EXERCISES

True or False? Justify your answer with a proof or a counterexample.

310. A function is always one-to-one.

311. $f \circ g = g \circ f,$ assuming *f* and *g* are functions.

312. A relation that passes the horizontal and vertical line tests is a one-to-one function.

313. A relation passing the horizontal line test is a function.

For the following problems, state the domain and range of the given functions:

$f = x^2 + 2x - 3,$ $g = \ln(x - 5),$ $h = \frac{1}{x + 4}$

314. h

315. g

316. $h \circ f$

317. $g \circ f$

Find the degree, *y*-intercept, and zeros for the following polynomial functions.

318. $f(x) = 2x^2 + 9x - 5$

319. $f(x) = x^3 + 2x^2 - 2x$

Simplify the following trigonometric expressions.

320. $\frac{\tan^2 x}{\sec^2 x} + \cos^2 x$

321. $\cos(2x) = \sin^2 x$

Solve the following trigonometric equations on the interval $\theta = [-2\pi, 2\pi]$ exactly.

322. $6\cos^2 x - 3 = 0$

323. $\sec^2 x - 2\sec x + 1 = 0$

Solve the following logarithmic equations.

324. $5^x = 16$

325. $\log_2(x + 4) = 3$

Are the following functions one-to-one over their domain of existence? Does the function have an inverse? If so, find the inverse $f^{-1}(x)$ of the function. Justify your answer.

326. $f(x) = x^2 + 2x + 1$

327. $f(x) = \frac{1}{x}$

For the following problems, determine the largest domain on which the function is one-to-one and find the inverse on that domain.

328. $f(x) = \sqrt{9 - x}$

329. $f(x) = x^2 + 3x + 4$

330. A car is racing along a circular track with diameter of 1 mi. A trainer standing in the center of the circle marks his progress every 5 sec. After 5 sec, the trainer has to turn 55° to keep up with the car. How fast is the car traveling?

For the following problems, consider a restaurant owner who wants to sell T-shirts advertising his brand. He recalls that there is a fixed cost and variable cost, although he does not remember the values. He does know that the T-shirt printing company charges $440 for 20 shirts and $1000 for 100 shirts.

331. a. Find the equation $C = f(x)$ that describes the total cost as a function of number of shirts and b. determine how many shirts he must sell to break even if he sells the shirts for $10 each.

332. a. Find the inverse function $x = f^{-1}(C)$ and describe the meaning of this function. b. Determine how many shirts the owner can buy if he has $8000 to spend.

For the following problems, consider the population of Ocean City, New Jersey, which is cyclical by season.

333. The population can be modeled by $P(t) = 82.5 - 67.5\cos[(\pi/6)t]$, where t is time in months ($t = 0$ represents January 1) and P is population (in thousands). During a year, in what intervals is the population less than 20,000? During what intervals is the population more than 140,000?

334. In reality, the overall population is most likely increasing or decreasing throughout each year. Let's reformulate the model as $P(t) = 82.5 - 67.5\cos[(\pi/6)t] + t$, where t is time in months ($t = 0$ represents January 1) and P is population (in thousands). When is the first time the population reaches 200,000?

For the following problems, consider radioactive dating. A human skeleton is found in an archeological dig. Carbon dating is implemented to determine how old the skeleton is by using the equation $y = e^{rt}$, where y is the percentage of radiocarbon still present in the material, t is the number of years passed, and $r = -0.0001210$ is the decay rate of radiocarbon.

335. If the skeleton is expected to be 2000 years old, what percentage of radiocarbon should be present?

336. Find the inverse of the carbon-dating equation. What does it mean? If there is 25% radiocarbon, how old is the skeleton?

2 | LIMITS

Figure 2.1 The vision of human exploration by the National Aeronautics and Space Administration (NASA) to distant parts of the universe illustrates the idea of space travel at high speeds. But, is there a limit to how fast a spacecraft can go? (credit: NASA)

Chapter Outline

Introduction

Science fiction writers often imagine spaceships that can travel to far-off planets in distant galaxies. However, back in 1905, Albert Einstein showed that a limit exists to how fast any object can travel. The problem is that the faster an object moves, the more mass it attains (in the form of energy), according to the equation

$$m = \frac{m_0}{\sqrt{1 - \frac{v^2}{c^2}}},$$

where m_0 is the object's mass at rest, v is its speed, and c is the speed of light. What is this speed limit? (We explore this problem further in **Example 2.12.**)

The idea of a limit is central to all of calculus. We begin this chapter by examining why limits are so important. Then, we go on to describe how to find the limit of a function at a given point. Not all functions have limits at all points, and we discuss what this means and how we can tell if a function does or does not have a limit at a particular value. This chapter has been created in an informal, intuitive fashion, but this is not always enough if we need to prove a mathematical statement involving limits. The last section of this chapter presents the more precise definition of a limit and shows how to prove whether a function has a limit.

2.1 | A Preview of Calculus

Learning Objectives

2.1.1 Describe the tangent problem and how it led to the idea of a derivative.
2.1.2 Explain how the idea of a limit is involved in solving the tangent problem.
2.1.3 Recognize a tangent to a curve at a point as the limit of secant lines.
2.1.4 Identify instantaneous velocity as the limit of average velocity over a small time interval.
2.1.5 Describe the area problem and how it was solved by the integral.
2.1.6 Explain how the idea of a limit is involved in solving the area problem.
2.1.7 Recognize how the ideas of limit, derivative, and integral led to the studies of infinite series and multivariable calculus.

As we embark on our study of calculus, we shall see how its development arose from common solutions to practical problems in areas such as engineering physics—like the space travel problem posed in the chapter opener. Two key problems led to the initial formulation of calculus: (1) the tangent problem, or how to determine the slope of a line tangent to a curve at a point; and (2) the area problem, or how to determine the area under a curve.

The Tangent Problem and Differential Calculus

Rate of change is one of the most critical concepts in calculus. We begin our investigation of rates of change by looking at the graphs of the three lines $f(x) = -2x - 3$, $g(x) = \frac{1}{2}x + 1$, and $h(x) = 2$, shown in **Figure 2.2**.

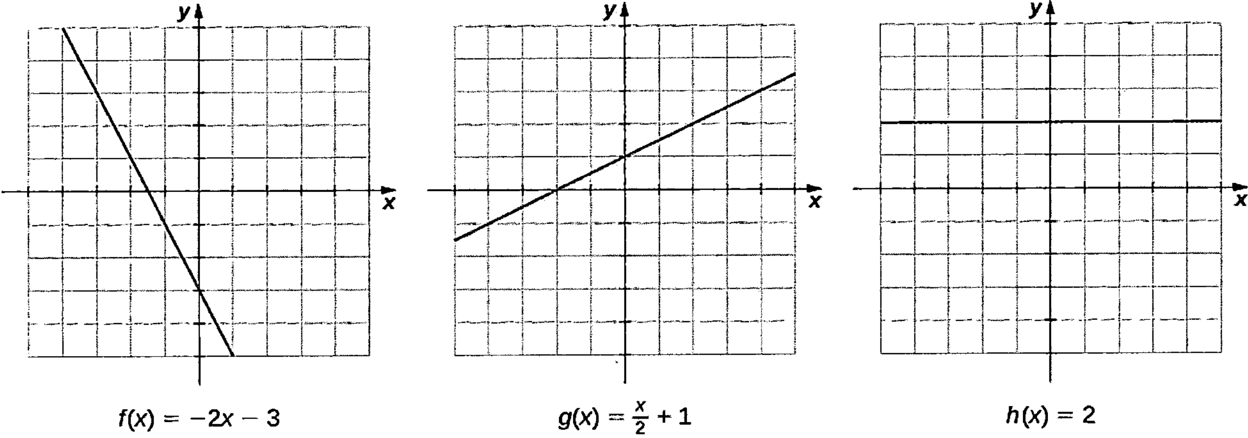

Figure 2.2 The rate of change of a linear function is constant in each of these three graphs, with the constant determined by the slope.

As we move from left to right along the graph of $f(x) = -2x - 3$, we see that the graph decreases at a constant rate. For every 1 unit we move to the right along the x-axis, the y-coordinate decreases by 2 units. This rate of change is determined by the slope (−2) of the line. Similarly, the slope of 1/2 in the function $g(x)$ tells us that for every change in x of 1 unit there is a corresponding change in y of 1/2 unit. The function $h(x) = 2$ has a slope of zero, indicating that the values of the function remain constant. We see that the slope of each linear function indicates the rate of change of the function.

Compare the graphs of these three functions with the graph of $k(x) = x^2$ (**Figure 2.3**). The graph of $k(x) = x^2$ starts from the left by decreasing rapidly, then begins to decrease more slowly and level off, and then finally begins to increase—slowly at first, followed by an increasing rate of increase as it moves toward the right. Unlike a linear function, no single number represents the rate of change for this function. We quite naturally ask: How do we measure the rate of change of a nonlinear function?

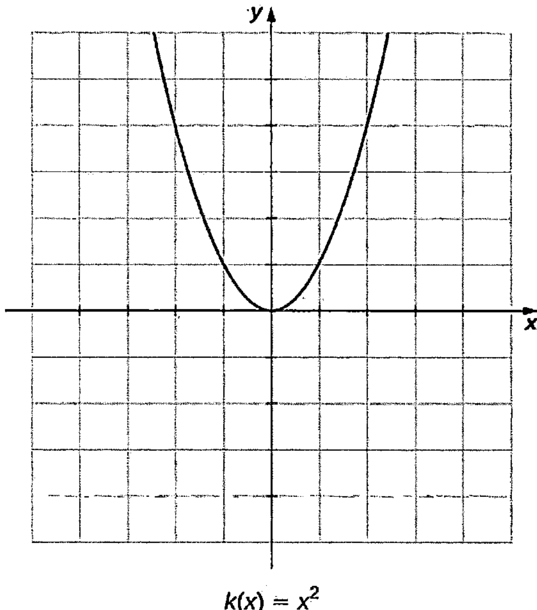

Figure 2.3 The function $k(x) = x^2$ does not have a constant rate of change.

We can approximate the rate of change of a function $f(x)$ at a point $(a, f(a))$ on its graph by taking another point $(x, f(x))$ on the graph of $f(x)$, drawing a line through the two points, and calculating the slope of the resulting line. Such a line is called a **secant** line. **Figure 2.4** shows a secant line to a function $f(x)$ at a point $(a, f(a))$.

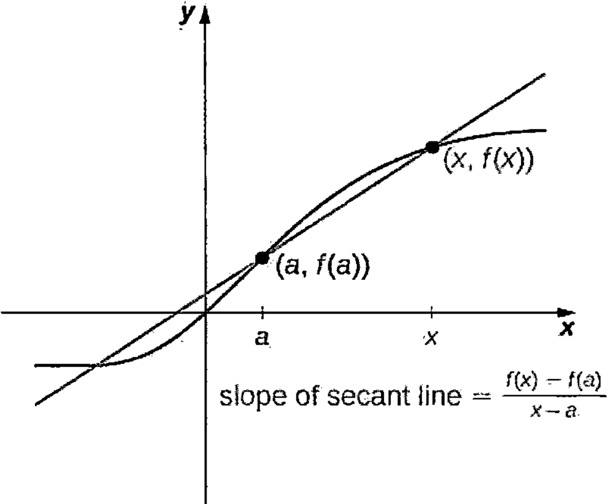

Figure 2.4 The slope of a secant line through a point $(a, f(a))$ estimates the rate of change of the function at the point $(a, f(a))$.

We formally define a secant line as follows:

Definition

The **secant** to the function $f(x)$ through the points $(a, f(a))$ and $(x, f(x))$ is the line passing through these points. Its slope is given by

$$m_{\text{sec}} = \frac{f(x) - f(a)}{x - a}. \quad (2.1)$$

The accuracy of approximating the rate of change of the function with a secant line depends on how close x is to a. As we see in **Figure 2.5**, if x is closer to a, the slope of the secant line is a better measure of the rate of change of $f(x)$ at a.

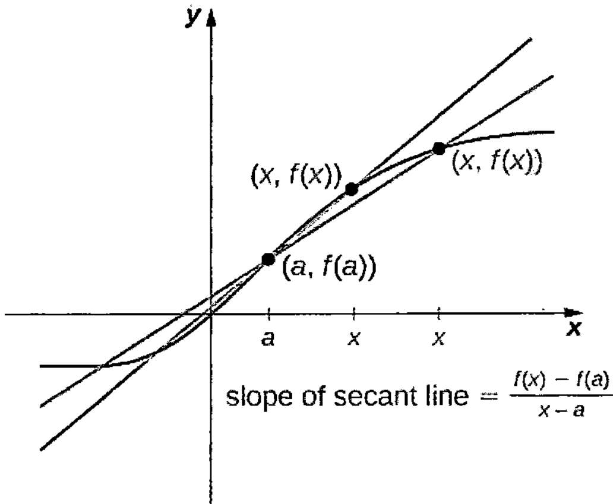

Figure 2.5 As x gets closer to a, the slope of the secant line becomes a better approximation to the rate of change of the function $f(x)$ at a.

The secant lines themselves approach a line that is called the **tangent** to the function $f(x)$ at a (**Figure 2.6**). The slope of the tangent line to the graph at a measures the rate of change of the function at a. This value also represents the derivative of the function $f(x)$ at a, or the rate of change of the function at a. This derivative is denoted by $f'(a)$. **Differential calculus** is the field of calculus concerned with the study of derivatives and their applications.

For an interactive demonstration of the slope of a secant line that you can manipulate yourself, visit this applet (*Note:* this site requires a Java browser plugin): **Math Insight (http://www.openstaxcollege.org/l/20_mathinsight)**.

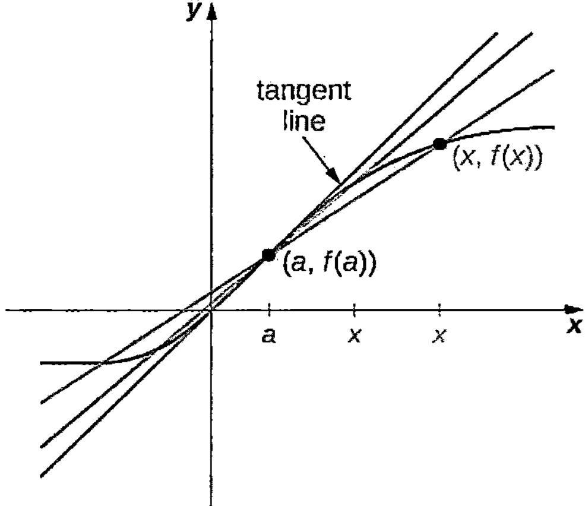

Figure 2.6 Solving the Tangent Problem: As x approaches a, the secant lines approach the tangent line.

Example 2.1 illustrates how to find slopes of secant lines. These slopes estimate the slope of the tangent line or, equivalently, the rate of change of the function at the point at which the slopes are calculated.

Example 2.1

Finding Slopes of Secant Lines

Estimate the slope of the tangent line (rate of change) to $f(x) = x^2$ at $x = 1$ by finding slopes of secant lines through $(1, 1)$ and each of the following points on the graph of $f(x) = x^2$.

a. $(2, 4)$

b. $\left(\frac{3}{2}, \frac{9}{4}\right)$

Solution

Use the formula for the slope of a secant line from the definition.

a. $m_{\text{sec}} = \frac{4-1}{2-1} = 3$

b. $m_{\text{sec}} = \frac{\frac{9}{4}-1}{\frac{3}{2}-1} = \frac{5}{2} = 2.5$

The point in part b. is closer to the point $(1, 1)$, so the slope of 2.5 is closer to the slope of the tangent line. A good estimate for the slope of the tangent would be in the range of 2 to 2.5 (**Figure 2.7**).

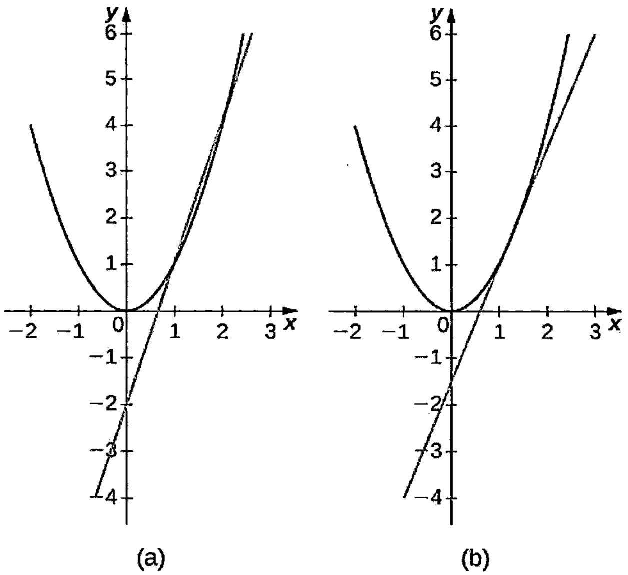

Figure 2.7 The secant lines to $f(x) = x^2$ at $(1, 1)$ through (a) $(2, 4)$ and (b) $\left(\frac{3}{2}, \frac{9}{4}\right)$ provide successively closer approximations to the tangent line to $f(x) = x^2$ at $(1, 1)$.

2.1 Estimate the slope of the tangent line (rate of change) to $f(x) = x^2$ at $x = 1$ by finding slopes of secant lines through $(1, 1)$ and the point $\left(\frac{5}{4}, \frac{25}{16}\right)$ on the graph of $f(x) = x^2$.

We continue our investigation by exploring a related question. Keeping in mind that velocity may be thought of as the rate of change of position, suppose that we have a function, $s(t)$, that gives the position of an object along a coordinate axis at any given time *t*. Can we use these same ideas to create a reasonable definition of the instantaneous velocity at a given time $t = a$? We start by approximating the instantaneous velocity with an average velocity. First, recall that the speed of an object traveling at a constant rate is the ratio of the distance traveled to the length of time it has traveled. We define the **average velocity** of an object over a time period to be the change in its position divided by the length of the time period.

Definition

Let $s(t)$ be the position of an object moving along a coordinate axis at time *t*. The **average velocity** of the object over a time interval $[a, t]$ where $a < t$ (or $[t, a]$ if $t < a$) is

$$v_{\text{ave}} = \frac{s(t) - s(a)}{t - a}. \tag{2.2}$$

As *t* is chosen closer to *a*, the average velocity becomes closer to the instantaneous velocity. Note that finding the average velocity of a position function over a time interval is essentially the same as finding the slope of a secant line to a function. Furthermore, to find the slope of a tangent line at a point *a*, we let the *x*-values approach *a* in the slope of the secant line. Similarly, to find the instantaneous velocity at time *a*, we let the *t*-values approach *a* in the average velocity. This process of letting *x* or *t* approach *a* in an expression is called taking a **limit**. Thus, we may define the **instantaneous velocity** as follows.

Definition

For a position function $s(t)$, the **instantaneous velocity** at a time $t = a$ is the value that the average velocities approach on intervals of the form $[a, t]$ and $[t, a]$ as the values of *t* become closer to *a*, provided such a value exists.

Example 2.2 illustrates this concept of limits and average velocity.

Example 2.2

Finding Average Velocity

A rock is dropped from a height of 64 ft. It is determined that its height (in feet) above ground *t* seconds later (for $0 \le t \le 2$) is given by $s(t) = -16t^2 + 64$. Find the average velocity of the rock over each of the given time intervals. Use this information to guess the instantaneous velocity of the rock at time $t = 0.5$.

a. $[0.49, 0.5]$

b. $[0.5, 0.51]$

Solution

Substitute the data into the formula for the definition of average velocity.

a. $v_{\text{ave}} = \dfrac{s(0.49) - s(0.5)}{0.49 - 0.5} = -15.84$

b. $v_{\text{ave}} = \dfrac{s(0.51) - s(0.5)}{0.51 - 0.5} = -16.016$

The instantaneous velocity is somewhere between −15.84 and −16.16 ft/sec. A good guess might be −16 ft/sec.

2.2 An object moves along a coordinate axis so that its position at time t is given by $s(t) = t^3$. Estimate its instantaneous velocity at time $t = 2$ by computing its average velocity over the time interval $[2, 2.001]$.

The Area Problem and Integral Calculus

We now turn our attention to a classic question from calculus. Many quantities in physics—for example, quantities of work—may be interpreted as the area under a curve. This leads us to ask the question: How can we find the area between the graph of a function and the x-axis over an interval (**Figure 2.8**)?

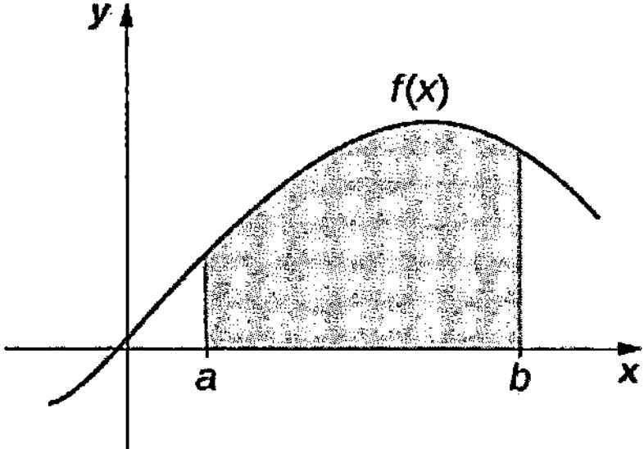

Figure 2.8 The Area Problem: How do we find the area of the shaded region?

As in the answer to our previous questions on velocity, we first try to approximate the solution. We approximate the area by dividing up the interval $[a, b]$ into smaller intervals in the shape of rectangles. The approximation of the area comes from adding up the areas of these rectangles (**Figure 2.9**).

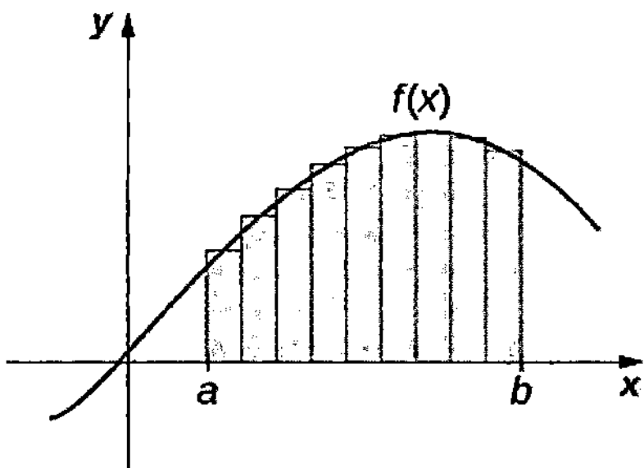

Figure 2.9 The area of the region under the curve is approximated by summing the areas of thin rectangles.

As the widths of the rectangles become smaller (approach zero), the sums of the areas of the rectangles approach the area between the graph of $f(x)$ and the x-axis over the interval $[a, b]$. Once again, we find ourselves taking a limit. Limits of this type serve as a basis for the definition of the definite integral. **Integral calculus** is the study of integrals and their applications.

Example 2.3

Estimation Using Rectangles

Estimate the area between the x-axis and the graph of $f(x) = x^2 + 1$ over the interval $[0, 3]$ by using the three rectangles shown in **Figure 2.10**.

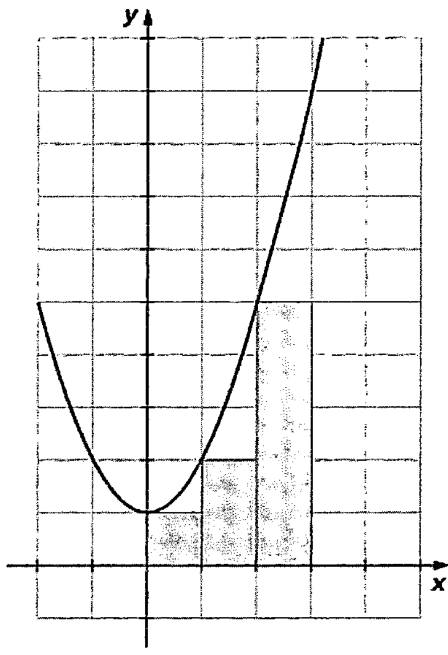

Figure 2.10 The area of the region under the curve of $f(x) = x^2 + 1$ can be estimated using rectangles.

Solution

The areas of the three rectangles are 1 unit^2, 2 unit^2, and 5 unit^2. Using these rectangles, our area estimate is 8 unit^2.

2.3 Estimate the area between the x-axis and the graph of $f(x) = x^2 + 1$ over the interval $[0, 3]$ by using the three rectangles shown here:

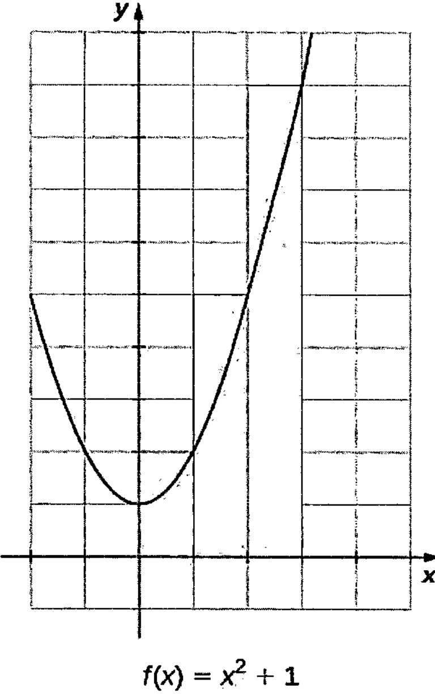

Other Aspects of Calculus

So far, we have studied functions of one variable only. Such functions can be represented visually using graphs in two dimensions; however, there is no good reason to restrict our investigation to two dimensions. Suppose, for example, that instead of determining the velocity of an object moving along a coordinate axis, we want to determine the velocity of a rock fired from a catapult at a given time, or of an airplane moving in three dimensions. We might want to graph real-value functions of two variables or determine volumes of solids of the type shown in **Figure 2.11**. These are only a few of the types of questions that can be asked and answered using **multivariable calculus**. Informally, multivariable calculus can be characterized as the study of the calculus of functions of two or more variables. However, before exploring these and other ideas, we must first lay a foundation for the study of calculus in one variable by exploring the concept of a limit.

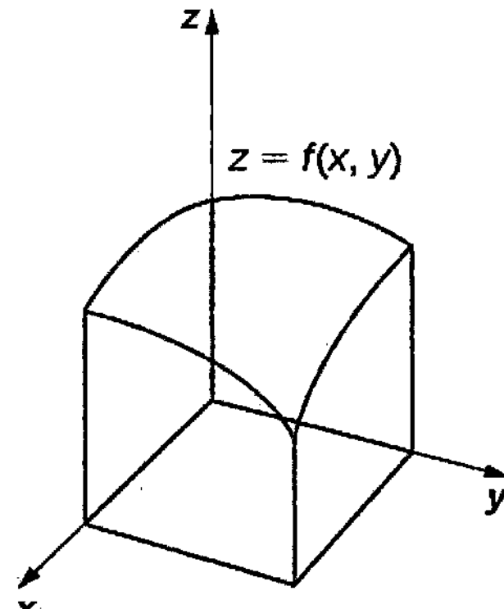

Figure 2.11 We can use multivariable calculus to find the volume between a surface defined by a function of two variables and a plane.

2.1 EXERCISES

For the following exercises, points $P(1, 2)$ and $Q(x, y)$ are on the graph of the function $f(x) = x^2 + 1$.

1. **[T]** Complete the following table with the appropriate values: y-coordinate of Q, the point $Q(x, y)$, and the slope of the secant line passing through points P and Q. Round your answer to eight significant digits.

x	y	$Q(x, y)$	m_{sec}
1.1	a.	e.	i.
1.01	b.	f.	j.
1.001	c.	g.	k.
1.0001	d.	h.	l.

2. Use the values in the right column of the table in the preceding exercise to guess the value of the slope of the line tangent to f at $x = 1$.

3. Use the value in the preceding exercise to find the equation of the tangent line at point P. Graph $f(x)$ and the tangent line.

For the following exercises, points $P(1, 1)$ and $Q(x, y)$ are on the graph of the function $f(x) = x^3$.

4. **[T]** Complete the following table with the appropriate values: y-coordinate of Q, the point $Q(x, y)$, and the slope of the secant line passing through points P and Q. Round your answer to eight significant digits.

x	y	$Q(x, y)$	m_{sec}
1.1	a.	e.	i.
1.01	b.	f.	j.
1.001	c.	g.	k.
1.0001	d.	h.	l.

5. Use the values in the right column of the table in the preceding exercise to guess the value of the slope of the tangent line to f at $x = 1$.

6. Use the value in the preceding exercise to find the equation of the tangent line at point P. Graph $f(x)$ and the tangent line.

For the following exercises, points $P(4, 2)$ and $Q(x, y)$ are on the graph of the function $f(x) = \sqrt{x}$.

7. **[T]** Complete the following table with the appropriate values: y-coordinate of Q, the point $Q(x, y)$, and the slope of the secant line passing through points P and Q. Round your answer to eight significant digits.

x	y	$Q(x, y)$	m_{sec}
4.1	a.	e.	i.
4.01	b.	f.	j.
4.001	c.	g.	k.
4.0001	d.	h.	l.

8. Use the values in the right column of the table in the preceding exercise to guess the value of the slope of the tangent line to f at $x = 4$.

9. Use the value in the preceding exercise to find the equation of the tangent line at point P.

For the following exercises, points $P(1.5, 0)$ and $Q(\phi, y)$ are on the graph of the function $f(\phi) = \cos(\pi\phi)$.

10. **[T]** Complete the following table with the appropriate values: y-coordinate of Q, the point $Q(x, y)$, and the slope of the secant line passing through points P and Q. Round your answer to eight significant digits.

x	y	$Q(\phi, y)$	m_{sec}
1.4	a.	e.	i.
1.49	b.	f.	j.
1.499	c.	g.	k.
1.4999	d.	h.	l.

11. Use the values in the right column of the table in the preceding exercise to guess the value of the slope of the tangent line to f at $x = 4$.

12. Use the value in the preceding exercise to find the equation of the tangent line at point P.

For the following exercises, points $P(-1, -1)$ and $Q(x, y)$ are on the graph of the function $f(x) = \frac{1}{x}$.

13. **[T]** Complete the following table with the appropriate values: y-coordinate of Q, the point $Q(x, y)$, and the slope of the secant line passing through points P and Q. Round your answer to eight significant digits.

x	y	$Q(x, y)$	m_{sec}
−1.05	a.	e.	i.
−1.01	b.	f.	j.
−1.005	c.	g.	k.
−1.001	d.	h.	l.

14. Use the values in the right column of the table in the preceding exercise to guess the value of the slope of the line tangent to f at $x = -1$.

15. Use the value in the preceding exercise to find the equation of the tangent line at point P.

For the following exercises, the position function of a ball dropped from the top of a 200-meter tall building is given by $s(t) = 200 - 4.9t^2$, where position s is measured in meters and time t is measured in seconds. Round your answer to eight significant digits.

16. **[T]** Compute the average velocity of the ball over the given time intervals.
   a. [4.99, 5]
   b. [5, 5.01]
   c. [4.999, 5]
   d. [5, 5.001]

17. Use the preceding exercise to guess the instantaneous velocity of the ball at $t = 5$ sec.

For the following exercises, consider a stone tossed into the air from ground level with an initial velocity of 15 m/sec. Its height in meters at time t seconds is $h(t) = 15t - 4.9t^2$.

18. **[T]** Compute the average velocity of the stone over the given time intervals.
   a. [1, 1.05]
   b. [1, 1.01]
   c. [1, 1.005]
   d. [1, 1.001]

19. Use the preceding exercise to guess the instantaneous velocity of the stone at $t = 1$ sec.

For the following exercises, consider a rocket shot into the air that then returns to Earth. The height of the rocket in meters is given by $h(t) = 600 + 78.4t - 4.9t^2$, where t is measured in seconds.

20. **[T]** Compute the average velocity of the rocket over the given time intervals.
   a. [9, 9.01]
   b. [8.99, 9]
   c. [9, 9.001]
   d. [8.999, 9]

21. Use the preceding exercise to guess the instantaneous velocity of the rocket at $t = 9$ sec.

For the following exercises, consider an athlete running a 40-m dash. The position of the athlete is given by $d(t) = \frac{t^3}{6} + 4t$, where d is the position in meters and t is the time elapsed, measured in seconds.

22. **[T]** Compute the average velocity of the runner over the given time intervals.
   a. [1.95, 2.05]
   b. [1.995, 2.005]
   c. [1.9995, 2.0005]
   d. [2, 2.00001]

23. Use the preceding exercise to guess the instantaneous velocity of the runner at $t = 2$ sec.

For the following exercises, consider the function $f(x) = |x|$.

24. Sketch the graph of f over the interval $[-1, 2]$ and shade the region above the x-axis.

25. Use the preceding exercise to find the exact value of the area between the x-axis and the graph of f over the interval $[-1, 2]$ using rectangles. For the rectangles, use the square units, and approximate both above and below the lines. Use geometry to find the exact answer.

For the following exercises, consider the function $f(x) = \sqrt{1 - x^2}$. (*Hint*: This is the upper half of a circle of radius 1 positioned at $(0, 0)$.)

26. Sketch the graph of f over the interval $[-1, 1]$.

27. Use the preceding exercise to find the exact area between the x-axis and the graph of f over the interval $[-1, 1]$ using rectangles. For the rectangles, use squares 0.4 by 0.4 units, and approximate both above and below the lines. Use geometry to find the exact answer.

For the following exercises, consider the function $f(x) = -x^2 + 1$.

28. Sketch the graph of f over the interval $[-1, 1]$.

29. Approximate the area of the region between the x-axis and the graph of f over the interval $[-1, 1]$.

2.2 | The Limit of a Function

Learning Objectives

2.2.1 Using correct notation, describe the limit of a function.
2.2.2 Use a table of values to estimate the limit of a function or to identify when the limit does not exist.
2.2.3 Use a graph to estimate the limit of a function or to identify when the limit does not exist.
2.2.4 Define one-sided limits and provide examples.
2.2.5 Explain the relationship between one-sided and two-sided limits.
2.2.6 Using correct notation, describe an infinite limit.
2.2.7 Define a vertical asymptote.

The concept of a limit or limiting process, essential to the understanding of calculus, has been around for thousands of years. In fact, early mathematicians used a limiting process to obtain better and better approximations of areas of circles. Yet, the formal definition of a limit—as we know and understand it today—did not appear until the late 19th century. We therefore begin our quest to understand limits, as our mathematical ancestors did, by using an intuitive approach. At the end of this chapter, armed with a conceptual understanding of limits, we examine the formal definition of a limit.

We begin our exploration of limits by taking a look at the graphs of the functions

$$f(x) = \frac{x^2 - 4}{x - 2},\ g(x) = \frac{|x - 2|}{x - 2},\ \text{and } h(x) = \frac{1}{(x - 2)^2},$$

which are shown in **Figure 2.12**. In particular, let's focus our attention on the behavior of each graph at and around $x = 2$.

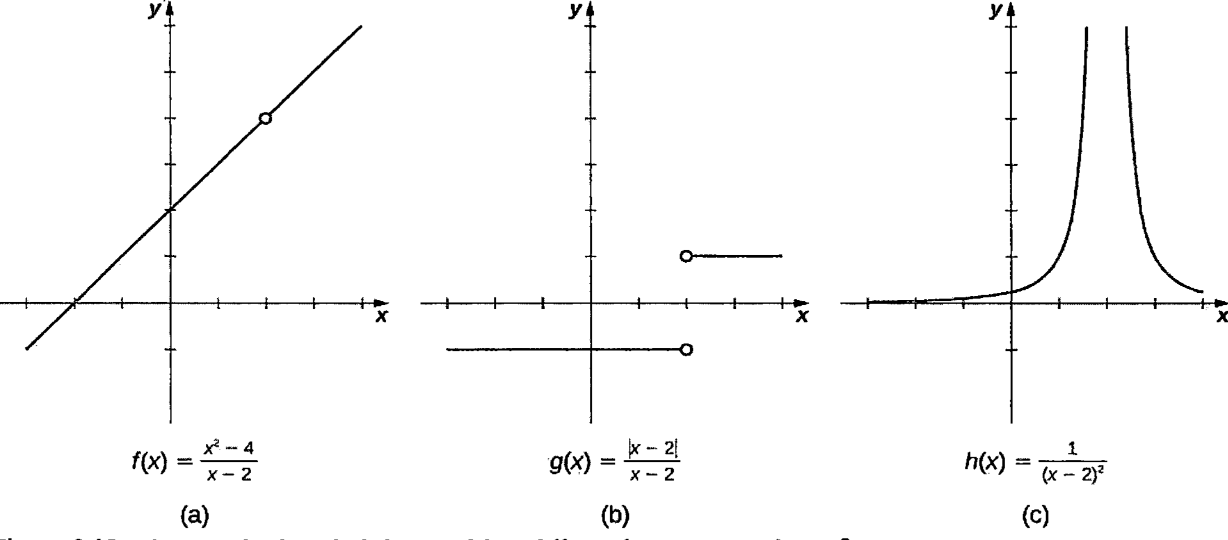

Figure 2.12 These graphs show the behavior of three different functions around $x = 2$.

Each of the three functions is undefined at $x = 2$, but if we make this statement and no other, we give a very incomplete picture of how each function behaves in the vicinity of $x = 2$. To express the behavior of each graph in the vicinity of 2 more completely, we need to introduce the concept of a limit.

Intuitive Definition of a Limit

Let's first take a closer look at how the function $f(x) = (x^2 - 4)/(x - 2)$ behaves around $x = 2$ in **Figure 2.12**. As the values of x approach 2 from either side of 2, the values of $y = f(x)$ approach 4. Mathematically, we say that the limit of $f(x)$ as x approaches 2 is 4. Symbolically, we express this limit as

$$\lim_{x \to 2} f(x) = 4.$$

From this very brief informal look at one limit, let's start to develop an **intuitive definition of the limit**. We can think of the limit of a function at a number a as being the one real number L that the functional values approach as the x-values approach a, provided such a real number L exists. Stated more carefully, we have the following definition:

Definition

Let $f(x)$ be a function defined at all values in an open interval containing a, with the possible exception of a itself, and let L be a real number. If *all* values of the function $f(x)$ approach the real number L as the values of $x(\neq a)$ approach the number a, then we say that the limit of $f(x)$ as x approaches a is L. (More succinct, as x gets closer to a, $f(x)$ gets closer and stays close to L.) Symbolically, we express this idea as

$$\lim_{x \to a} f(x) = L. \quad \textbf{(2.3)}$$

We can estimate limits by constructing tables of functional values and by looking at their graphs. This process is described in the following Problem-Solving Strategy.

Problem-Solving Strategy: Evaluating a Limit Using a Table of Functional Values

1. To evaluate $\lim_{x \to a} f(x)$, we begin by completing a table of functional values. We should choose two sets of x-values—one set of values approaching a and less than a, and another set of values approaching a and greater than a. **Table 2.1** demonstrates what your tables might look like.

x	$f(x)$		x	$f(x)$
$a-0.1$	$f(a-0.1)$		$a+0.1$	$f(a+0.1)$
$a-0.01$	$f(a-0.01)$		$a+0.01$	$f(a+0.01)$
$a-0.001$	$f(a-0.001)$		$a+0.001$	$f(a+0.001)$
$a-0.0001$	$f(a-0.0001)$		$a+0.0001$	$f(a+0.0001)$
Use additional values as necessary.			Use additional values as necessary.	

Table 2.1 Table of Functional Values for $\lim_{x \to a} f(x)$

2. Next, let's look at the values in each of the $f(x)$ columns and determine whether the values seem to be approaching a single value as we move down each column. In our columns, we look at the sequence $f(a-0.1)$, $f(a-0.01)$, $f(a-0.001)$., $f(a-0.0001)$, and so on, and $f(a+0.1)$, $f(a+0.01)$, $f(a+0.001)$, $f(a+0.0001)$, and so on. (*Note*: Although we have chosen the x-values $a \pm 0.1$, $a \pm 0.01$, $a \pm 0.001$, $a \pm 0.0001$, and so forth, and these values will probably work nearly every time, on very rare occasions we may need to modify our choices.)
3. If both columns approach a common y-value L, we state $\lim_{x \to a} f(x) = L$. We can use the following strategy to confirm the result obtained from the table or as an alternative method for estimating a limit.

4. Using a graphing calculator or computer software that allows us graph functions, we can plot the function $f(x)$, making sure the functional values of $f(x)$ for x-values near a are in our window. We can use the trace feature to move along the graph of the function and watch the y-value readout as the x-values approach a. If the y-values approach L as our x-values approach a from both directions, then $\lim_{x \to a} f(x) = L$. We may need to zoom in on our graph and repeat this process several times.

We apply this Problem-Solving Strategy to compute a limit in **Example 2.4**.

Example 2.4

Evaluating a Limit Using a Table of Functional Values 1

Evaluate $\lim_{x \to 0} \frac{\sin x}{x}$ using a table of functional values.

Solution

We have calculated the values of $f(x) = (\sin x)/x$ for the values of x listed in **Table 2.2**.

x	$\frac{\sin x}{x}$		x	$\frac{\sin x}{x}$
−0.1	0.998334166468		0.1	0.998334166468
−0.01	0.999983333417		0.01	0.999983333417
−0.001	0.999999833333		0.001	0.999999833333
−0.0001	0.999999998333		0.0001	0.999999998333

Table 2.2
Table of Functional Values for $\lim_{x \to 0} \frac{\sin x}{x}$

Note: The values in this table were obtained using a calculator and using all the places given in the calculator output.

As we read down each $\frac{(\sin x)}{x}$ column, we see that the values in each column appear to be approaching one. Thus, it is fairly reasonable to conclude that $\lim_{x \to 0} \frac{\sin x}{x} = 1$. A calculator-or computer-generated graph of $f(x) = \frac{(\sin x)}{x}$ would be similar to that shown in **Figure 2.13**, and it confirms our estimate.

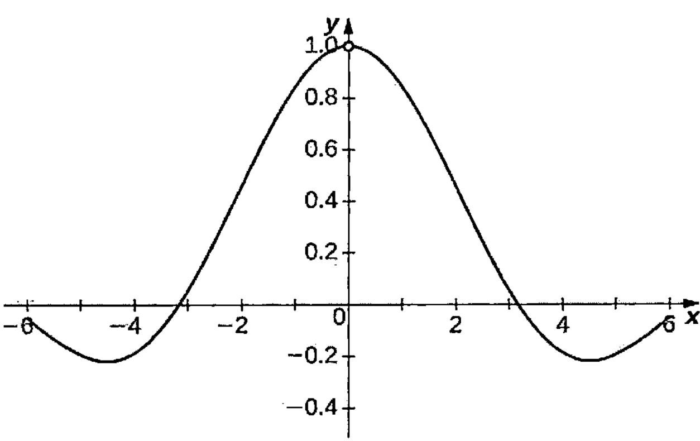

Figure 2.13 The graph of $f(x) = (\sin x)/x$ confirms the estimate from **Table 2.2**.

Example 2.5

Evaluating a Limit Using a Table of Functional Values 2

Evaluate $\lim_{x \to 4} \frac{\sqrt{x} - 2}{x - 4}$ using a table of functional values.

Solution

As before, we use a table—in this case, **Table 2.3**—to list the values of the function for the given values of x.

x	$\frac{\sqrt{x}-2}{x-4}$		x	$\frac{\sqrt{x}-2}{x-4}$
3.9	0.251582341869		4.1	0.248456731317
3.99	0.25015644562		4.01	0.24984394501
3.999	0.250015627		4.001	0.249984377
3.9999	0.250001563		4.0001	0.249998438
3.99999	0.25000016		4.00001	0.24999984

Table 2.3
Table of Functional Values for $\lim_{x \to 4} \frac{\sqrt{x} - 2}{x - 4}$

After inspecting this table, we see that the functional values less than 4 appear to be decreasing toward 0.25 whereas the functional values greater than 4 appear to be increasing toward 0.25. We conclude that

$\lim_{x \to 4} \frac{\sqrt{x} - 2}{x - 4} = 0.25$. We confirm this estimate using the graph of $f(x) = \frac{\sqrt{x} - 2}{x - 4}$ shown in **Figure 2.14**.

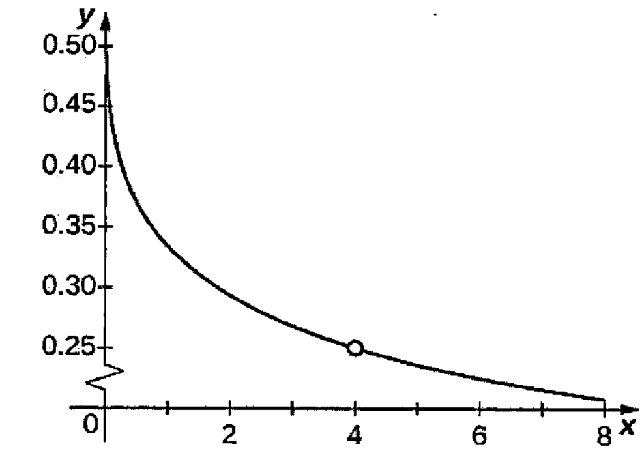

Figure 2.14 The graph of $f(x) = \frac{\sqrt{x} - 2}{x - 4}$ confirms the estimate from **Table 2.3**.

2.4 Estimate $\lim_{x \to 1} \frac{\frac{1}{x} - 1}{x - 1}$ using a table of functional values. Use a graph to confirm your estimate.

At this point, we see from **Example 2.4** and **Example 2.5** that it may be just as easy, if not easier, to estimate a limit of a function by inspecting its graph as it is to estimate the limit by using a table of functional values. In **Example 2.6**, we evaluate a limit exclusively by looking at a graph rather than by using a table of functional values.

Example 2.6

Evaluating a Limit Using a Graph

For $g(x)$ shown in **Figure 2.15**, evaluate $\lim_{x \to -1} g(x)$.

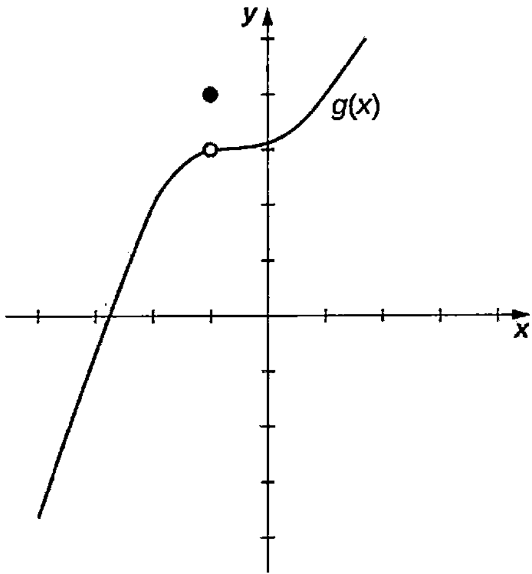

Figure 2.15 The graph of $g(x)$ includes one value not on a smooth curve.

Solution

Despite the fact that $g(-1) = 4$, as the x-values approach -1 from either side, the $g(x)$ values approach 3. Therefore, $\lim_{x \to -1} g(x) = 3$. Note that we can determine this limit without even knowing the algebraic expression of the function.

Based on **Example 2.6**, we make the following observation: It is possible for the limit of a function to exist at a point, and for the function to be defined at this point, but the limit of the function and the value of the function at the point may be different.

2.5 Use the graph of $h(x)$ in **Figure 2.16** to evaluate $\lim_{x \to 2} h(x)$, if possible.

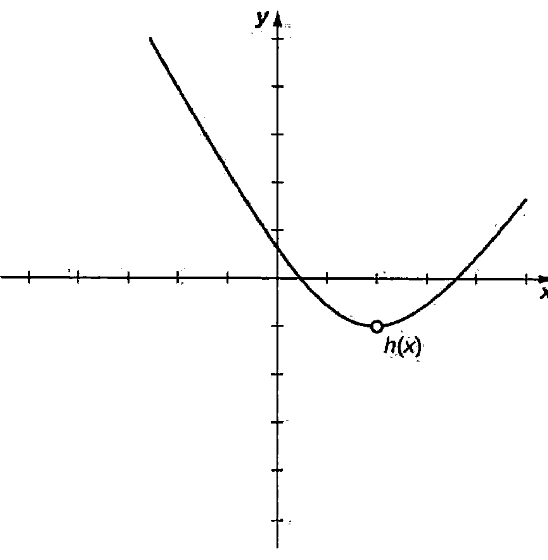

Figure 2.16

Looking at a table of functional values or looking at the graph of a function provides us with useful insight into the value of the limit of a function at a given point. However, these techniques rely too much on guesswork. We eventually need to develop alternative methods of evaluating limits. These new methods are more algebraic in nature and we explore them in the next section; however, at this point we introduce two special limits that are foundational to the techniques to come.

Theorem 2.1: Two Important Limits

Let a be a real number and c be a constant.

i. $\lim_{x \to a} x = a$ **(2.4)**

ii. $\lim_{x \to a} c = c$ **(2.5)**

We can make the following observations about these two limits.

i. For the first limit, observe that as x approaches a, so does $f(x)$, because $f(x) = x$. Consequently, $\lim_{x \to a} x = a$.

ii. For the second limit, consider **Table 2.4**.

x	$f(x) = c$		x	$f(x) = c$
$a - 0.1$	c		$a + 0.1$	c
$a - 0.01$	c		$a + 0.01$	c
$a - 0.001$	c		$a + 0.001$	c
$a - 0.0001$	c		$a + 0.0001$	c

Table 2.4 Table of Functional Values for $\lim_{x \to a} c = c$

Observe that for all values of x (regardless of whether they are approaching a), the values $f(x)$ remain constant at c. We have no choice but to conclude $\lim_{x \to a} c = c$.

The Existence of a Limit

As we consider the limit in the next example, keep in mind that for the limit of a function to exist at a point, the functional values must approach a single real-number value at that point. If the functional values do not approach a single value, then the limit does not exist.

Example 2.7

Evaluating a Limit That Fails to Exist

Evaluate $\lim_{x \to 0} \sin(1/x)$ using a table of values.

Solution

Table 2.5 lists values for the function $\sin(1/x)$ for the given values of x.

x	$\sin\left(\frac{1}{x}\right)$		x	$\sin\left(\frac{1}{x}\right)$
−0.1	0.544021110889		0.1	−0.544021110889
−0.01	0.50636564111		0.01	−0.50636564111
−0.001	−0.8268795405312		0.001	0.826879540532
−0.0001	0.305614388888		0.0001	−0.305614388888
−0.00001	−0.035748797987		0.00001	0.035748797987
−0.000001	0.349993504187		0.000001	−0.349993504187

Table 2.5
Table of Functional Values for $\lim_{x \to 0} \sin\left(\frac{1}{x}\right)$

After examining the table of functional values, we can see that the y-values do not seem to approach any one single value. It appears the limit does not exist. Before drawing this conclusion, let's take a more systematic approach. Take the following sequence of x-values approaching 0:

$$\frac{2}{\pi}, \frac{2}{3\pi}, \frac{2}{5\pi}, \frac{2}{7\pi}, \frac{2}{9\pi}, \frac{2}{11\pi}, \ldots.$$

The corresponding y-values are

$$1, -1, 1, -1, 1, -1, \ldots.$$

At this point we can indeed conclude that $\lim_{x \to 0} \sin(1/x)$ does not exist. (Mathematicians frequently abbreviate "does not exist" as DNE. Thus, we would write $\lim_{x \to 0} \sin(1/x)$ DNE.) The graph of $f(x) = \sin(1/x)$ is shown in **Figure 2.17** and it gives a clearer picture of the behavior of $\sin(1/x)$ as x approaches 0. You can see that $\sin(1/x)$ oscillates ever more wildly between −1 and 1 as x approaches 0.

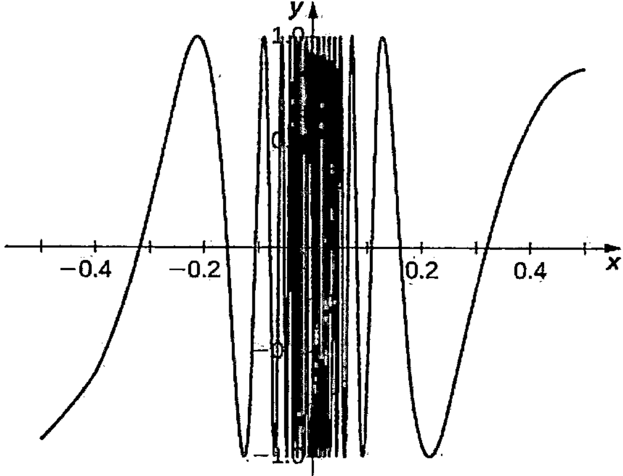

Figure 2.17 The graph of $f(x) = \sin(1/x)$ oscillates rapidly between −1 and 1 as x approaches 0.

2.6 Use a table of functional values to evaluate $\lim_{x \to 2} \frac{|x^2 - 4|}{x - 2}$, if possible.

One-Sided Limits

Sometimes indicating that the limit of a function fails to exist at a point does not provide us with enough information about the behavior of the function at that particular point. To see this, we now revisit the function $g(x) = |x - 2|/(x - 2)$ introduced at the beginning of the section (see **Figure 2.12**(b)). As we pick values of x close to 2, $g(x)$ does not approach a single value, so the limit as x approaches 2 does not exist—that is, $\lim_{x \to 2} g(x)$ DNE. However, this statement alone does not give us a complete picture of the behavior of the function around the x-value 2. To provide a more accurate description, we introduce the idea of a **one-sided limit**. For all values to the left of 2 (or *the negative side of* 2), $g(x) = -1$. Thus, as x approaches 2 from the left, $g(x)$ approaches −1. Mathematically, we say that the limit as x approaches 2 from the left is −1. Symbolically, we express this idea as

$$\lim_{x \to 2^-} g(x) = -1.$$

Similarly, as x approaches 2 from the right (or *from the positive side*), $g(x)$ approaches 1. Symbolically, we express this idea as

$$\lim_{x \to 2^+} g(x) = 1.$$

We can now present an informal definition of one-sided limits.

Definition

We define two types of **one-sided limits**.

Limit from the left: Let $f(x)$ be a function defined at all values in an open interval of the form z, and let L be a real number. If the values of the function $f(x)$ approach the real number L as the values of x (where $x < a$) approach the number a, then we say that L is the limit of $f(x)$ as x approaches a from the left. Symbolically, we express this idea as

$$\lim_{x \to a^-} f(x) = L. \quad (2.6)$$

Limit from the right: Let $f(x)$ be a function defined at all values in an open interval of the form (a, c), and let L be a real number. If the values of the function $f(x)$ approach the real number L as the values of x (where $x > a$) approach the number a, then we say that L is the limit of $f(x)$ as x approaches a from the right. Symbolically, we express this idea as

$$\lim_{x \to a^+} f(x) = L. \quad (2.7)$$

Example 2.8

Evaluating One-Sided Limits

For the function $f(x) = \begin{cases} x+1 & \text{if } x < 2 \\ x^2 - 4 & \text{if } x \geq 2 \end{cases}$, evaluate each of the following limits.

a. $\lim_{x \to 2^-} f(x)$

b. $\lim_{x \to 2^+} f(x)$

Solution

We can use tables of functional values again **Table 2.6**. Observe that for values of x less than 2, we use $f(x) = x + 1$ and for values of x greater than 2, we use $f(x) = x^2 - 4$.

x	$f(x) = x+1$		x	$f(x) = x^2 - 4$
1.9	2.9		2.1	0.41
1.99	2.99		2.01	0.0401
1.999	2.999		2.001	0.004001
1.9999	2.9999		2.0001	0.00040001
1.99999	2.99999		2.00001	0.0000400001

Table 2.6
Table of Functional Values for $f(x) = \begin{cases} x+1 \text{ if } x < 2 \\ x^2 - 4 \text{ if } x \geq 2 \end{cases}$

Based on this table, we can conclude that a. $\lim_{x \to 2^-} f(x) = 3$ and b. $\lim_{x \to 2^+} f(x) = 0$. Therefore, the (two-sided) limit of $f(x)$ does not exist at $x = 2$. **Figure 2.18** shows a graph of $f(x)$ and reinforces our conclusion about these limits.

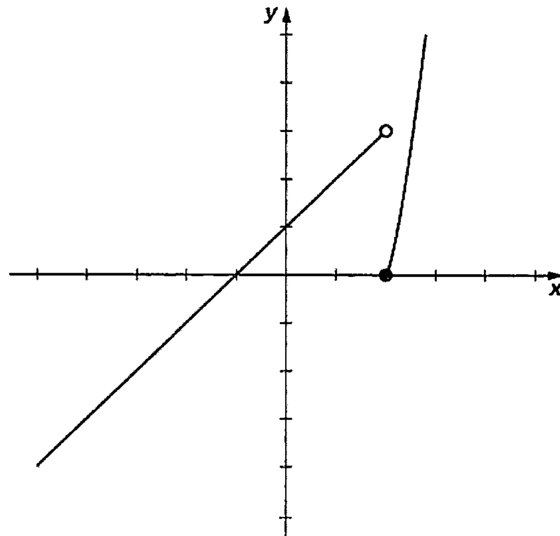

Figure 2.18 The graph of $f(x) = \begin{cases} x + 1 \text{ if } x < 2 \\ x^2 - 4 \text{ if } x \geq 2 \end{cases}$ has a break at $x = 2$.

2.7 Use a table of functional values to estimate the following limits, if possible.

a. $\lim_{x \to 2^-} \frac{|x^2 - 4|}{x - 2}$

b. $\lim_{x \to 2^+} \frac{|x^2 - 4|}{x - 2}$

Let us now consider the relationship between the limit of a function at a point and the limits from the right and left at that point. It seems clear that if the limit from the right and the limit from the left have a common value, then that common value is the limit of the function at that point. Similarly, if the limit from the left and the limit from the right take on different values, the limit of the function does not exist. These conclusions are summarized in **Relating One-Sided and Two-Sided Limits.**

Theorem 2.2: Relating One-Sided and Two-Sided Limits

Let $f(x)$ be a function defined at all values in an open interval containing a, with the possible exception of a itself, and let L be a real number. Then,

$$\lim_{x \to a} f(x) = L \text{ if and only if } \lim_{x \to a^-} f(x) = L \text{ and } \lim_{x \to a^+} f(x) = L.$$

Infinite Limits

Evaluating the limit of a function at a point or evaluating the limit of a function from the right and left at a point helps us to characterize the behavior of a function around a given value. As we shall see, we can also describe the behavior of functions that do not have finite limits.

We now turn our attention to $h(x) = 1/(x-2)^2$, the third and final function introduced at the beginning of this section (see **Figure 2.12**(c)). From its graph we see that as the values of x approach 2, the values of $h(x) = 1/(x-2)^2$ become larger and larger and, in fact, become infinite. Mathematically, we say that the limit of $h(x)$ as x approaches 2 is positive infinity. Symbolically, we express this idea as

$$\lim_{x \to 2} h(x) = +\infty.$$

More generally, we define **infinite limits** as follows:

Definition

We define three types of **infinite limits.**

Infinite limits from the left: Let $f(x)$ be a function defined at all values in an open interval of the form (b, a).

i. If the values of $f(x)$ increase without bound as the values of x (where $x < a$) approach the number a, then we say that the limit as x approaches a from the left is positive infinity and we write

$$\lim_{x \to a^-} f(x) = +\infty. \quad \textbf{(2.8)}$$

ii. If the values of $f(x)$ decrease without bound as the values of x (where $x < a$) approach the number a, then we say that the limit as x approaches a from the left is negative infinity and we write

$$\lim_{x \to a^-} f(x) = -\infty. \quad \textbf{(2.9)}$$

Infinite limits from the right: Let $f(x)$ be a function defined at all values in an open interval of the form (a, c).

i. If the values of $f(x)$ increase without bound as the values of x (where $x > a$) approach the number a, then we say that the limit as x approaches a from the left is positive infinity and we write

$$\lim_{x \to a^+} f(x) = +\infty. \quad \textbf{(2.10)}$$

ii. If the values of $f(x)$ decrease without bound as the values of x (where $x > a$) approach the number a, then we say that the limit as x approaches a from the left is negative infinity and we write

$$\lim_{x \to a^+} f(x) = -\infty. \quad \textbf{(2.11)}$$

Two-sided infinite limit: Let $f(x)$ be defined for all $x \neq a$ in an open interval containing a.

i. If the values of $f(x)$ increase without bound as the values of x (where $x \neq a$) approach the number a, then we say that the limit as x approaches a is positive infinity and we write

$$\lim_{x \to a} f(x) = +\infty. \quad \textbf{(2.12)}$$

ii. If the values of $f(x)$ decrease without bound as the values of x (where $x \neq a$) approach the number a, then we say that the limit as x approaches a is negative infinity and we write

$$\lim_{x \to a} f(x) = -\infty. \quad \textbf{(2.13)}$$

It is important to understand that when we write statements such as $\lim_{x \to a} f(x) = +\infty$ or $\lim_{x \to a} f(x) = -\infty$ we are describing the behavior of the function, as we have just defined it. We are not asserting that a limit exists. For the limit of a function $f(x)$ to exist at a, it must approach a real number L as x approaches a. That said, if, for example, $\lim_{x \to a} f(x) = +\infty$, we always write $\lim_{x \to a} f(x) = +\infty$ rather than $\lim_{x \to a} f(x)$ DNE.

Example 2.9

Recognizing an Infinite Limit

Evaluate each of the following limits, if possible. Use a table of functional values and graph $f(x) = 1/x$ to confirm your conclusion.

a. $\lim_{x \to 0^-} \frac{1}{x}$

b. $\lim_{x \to 0^+} \frac{1}{x}$

c. $\lim_{x \to 0} \frac{1}{x}$

Solution

Begin by constructing a table of functional values.

x	$\frac{1}{x}$		x	$\frac{1}{x}$
−0.1	−10		0.1	10
−0.01	−100		0.01	100
−0.001	−1000		0.001	1000
−0.0001	−10,000		0.0001	10,000
−0.00001	−100,000		0.00001	100,000
−0.000001	−1,000,000		0.000001	1,000,000

Table 2.7
Table of Functional Values for $f(x) = \frac{1}{x}$

a. The values of $1/x$ decrease without bound as x approaches 0 from the left. We conclude that

$$\lim_{x \to 0^-} \frac{1}{x} = -\infty.$$

b. The values of $1/x$ increase without bound as x approaches 0 from the right. We conclude that

$$\lim_{x \to 0^+} \frac{1}{x} = +\infty.$$

c. Since $\lim_{x \to 0^-} \frac{1}{x} = -\infty$ and $\lim_{x \to 0^+} \frac{1}{x} = +\infty$ have different values, we conclude that

$$\lim_{x \to 0} \frac{1}{x} \text{ DNE.}$$

The graph of $f(x) = 1/x$ in **Figure 2.19** confirms these conclusions.

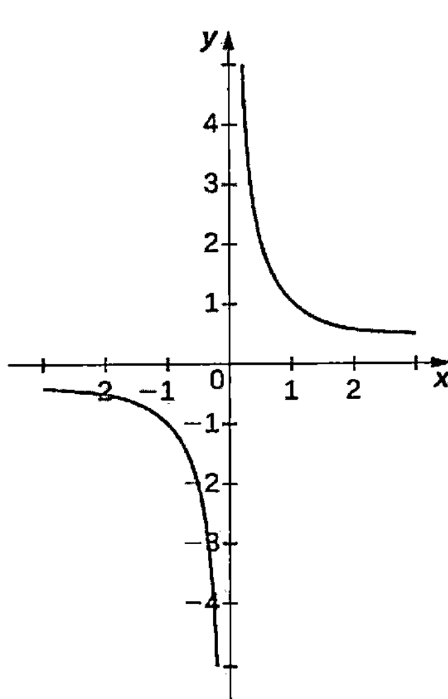

Figure 2.19 The graph of $f(x) = 1/x$ confirms that the limit as x approaches 0 does not exist.

2.8 Evaluate each of the following limits, if possible. Use a table of functional values and graph $f(x) = 1/x^2$ to confirm your conclusion.

a. $\lim\limits_{x \to 0^-} \frac{1}{x^2}$

b. $\lim\limits_{x \to 0^+} \frac{1}{x^2}$

c. $\lim\limits_{x \to 0} \frac{1}{x^2}$

It is useful to point out that functions of the form $f(x) = 1/(x-a)^n$, where n is a positive integer, have infinite limits as x approaches a from either the left or right (**Figure 2.20**). These limits are summarized in **Infinite Limits from Positive Integers**.

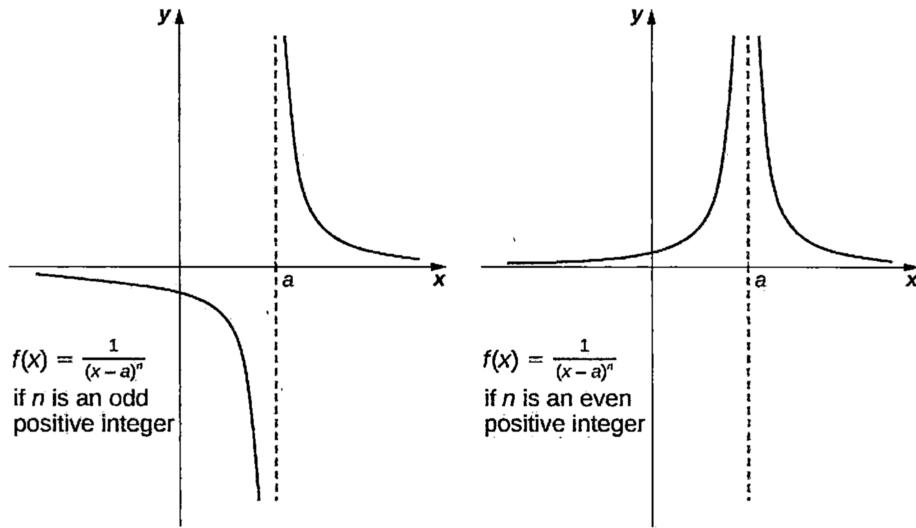

Figure 2.20 The function $f(x) = 1/(x - a)^n$ has infinite limits at a.

Theorem 2.3: Infinite Limits from Positive Integers

If n is a positive even integer, then

$$\lim_{x \to a} \frac{1}{(x-a)^n} = +\infty.$$

If n is a positive odd integer, then

$$\lim_{x \to a^+} \frac{1}{(x-a)^n} = +\infty$$

and

$$\lim_{x \to a^-} \frac{1}{(x-a)^n} = -\infty.$$

We should also point out that in the graphs of $f(x) = 1/(x - a)^n$, points on the graph having x-coordinates very near to a are very close to the vertical line $x = a$. That is, as x approaches a, the points on the graph of $f(x)$ are closer to the line $x = a$. The line $x = a$ is called a **vertical asymptote** of the graph. We formally define a vertical asymptote as follows:

Definition

Let $f(x)$ be a function. If any of the following conditions hold, then the line $x = a$ is a **vertical asymptote** of $f(x)$.

$$\lim_{x \to a^-} f(x) = +\infty \text{ or } -\infty$$
$$\lim_{x \to a^+} f(x) = +\infty \text{ or } -\infty$$
or
$$\lim_{x \to a} f(x) = +\infty \text{ or } -\infty$$

Example 2.10

Finding a Vertical Asymptote

Evaluate each of the following limits using **Infinite Limits from Positive Integers**. Identify any vertical asymptotes of the function $f(x) = 1/(x+3)^4$.

a. $\lim_{x \to -3^-} \frac{1}{(x+3)^4}$

b. $\lim_{x \to -3^+} \frac{1}{(x+3)^4}$

c. $\lim_{x \to -3} \frac{1}{(x+3)^4}$

Solution

We can use **Infinite Limits from Positive Integers** directly.

a. $\lim_{x \to -3^-} \frac{1}{(x+3)^4} = +\infty$

b. $\lim_{x \to -3^+} \frac{1}{(x+3)^4} = +\infty$

c. $\lim_{x \to -3} \frac{1}{(x+3)^4} = +\infty$

The function $f(x) = 1/(x+3)^4$ has a vertical asymptote of $x = -3$.

2.9 Evaluate each of the following limits. Identify any vertical asymptotes of the function $f(x) = \frac{1}{(x-2)^3}$.

a. $\lim_{x \to 2^-} \frac{1}{(x-2)^3}$

b. $\lim_{x \to 2^+} \frac{1}{(x-2)^3}$

c. $\lim_{x \to 2} \frac{1}{(x-2)^3}$

In the next example we put our knowledge of various types of limits to use to analyze the behavior of a function at several different points.

Example 2.11

Behavior of a Function at Different Points

Use the graph of $f(x)$ in **Figure 2.21** to determine each of the following values:

a. $\lim_{x \to -4^-} f(x)$; $\lim_{x \to -4^+} f(x)$; $\lim_{x \to -4} f(x)$; $f(-4)$

b. $\lim_{x \to -2^-} f(x)$; $\lim_{x \to -2^+} f(x)$; $\lim_{x \to -2} f(x)$; $f(-2)$

c. $\lim_{x \to 1^-} f(x)$; $\lim_{x \to 1^+} f(x)$; $\lim_{x \to 1} f(x)$; $f(1)$

d. $\lim_{x \to 3^-} f(x)$; $\lim_{x \to 3^+} f(x)$; $\lim_{x \to 3} f(x)$; $f(3)$

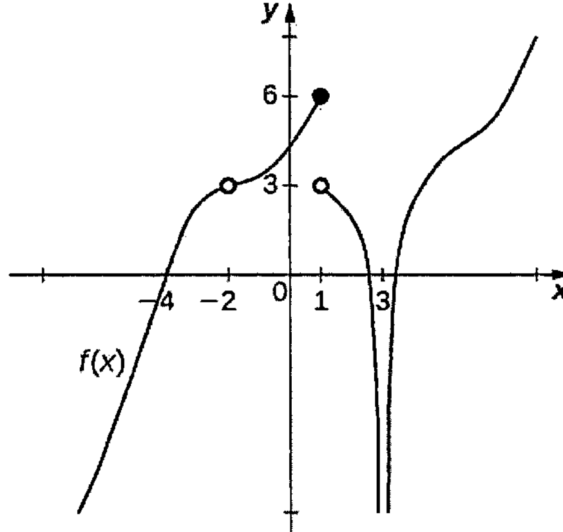

Figure 2.21 The graph shows $f(x)$.

Solution

Using **Infinite Limits from Positive Integers** and the graph for reference, we arrive at the following values:

a. $\lim_{x \to -4^-} f(x) = 0$; $\lim_{x \to -4^+} f(x) = 0$; $\lim_{x \to -4} f(x) = 0$; $f(-4) = 0$

b. $\lim_{x \to -2^-} f(x) = 3.$; $\lim_{x \to -2^+} f(x) = 3$; $\lim_{x \to -2} f(x) = 3$; $f(-2)$ is undefined

c. $\lim_{x \to 1^-} f(x) = 6$; $\lim_{x \to 1^+} f(x) = 3$; $\lim_{x \to 1} f(x)$ DNE; $f(1) = 6$

d. $\lim_{x \to 3^-} f(x) = -\infty$; $\lim_{x \to 3^+} f(x) = -\infty$; $\lim_{x \to 3} f(x) = -\infty$; $f(3)$ is undefined

2.10 Evaluate $\lim_{x \to 1} f(x)$ for $f(x)$ shown here:

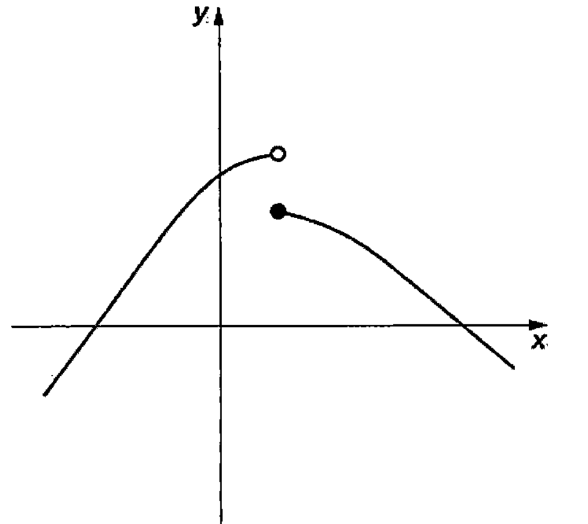

Example 2.12

Chapter Opener: Einstein's Equation

Figure 2.22 (credit: NASA)

In the chapter opener we mentioned briefly how Albert Einstein showed that a limit exists to how fast any object can travel. Given Einstein's equation for the mass of a moving object, what is the value of this bound?

Solution

Our starting point is Einstein's equation for the mass of a moving object,

$$m = \frac{m_0}{\sqrt{1 - \frac{v^2}{c^2}}},$$

where m_0 is the object's mass at rest, v is its speed, and c is the speed of light. To see how the mass changes at high speeds, we can graph the ratio of masses m/m_0 as a function of the ratio of speeds, v/c (**Figure 2.23**).

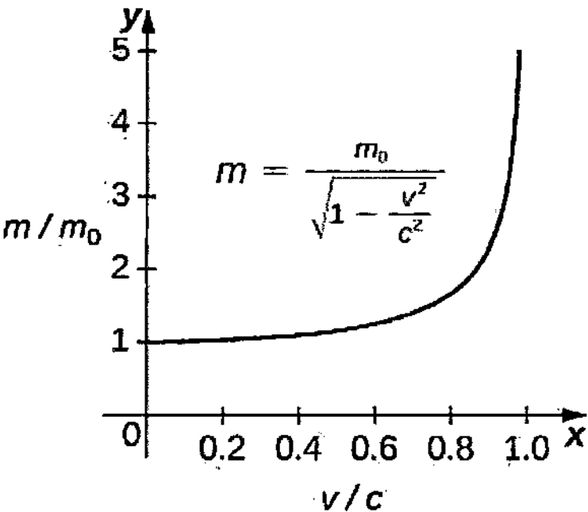

Figure 2.23 This graph shows the ratio of masses as a function of the ratio of speeds in Einstein's equation for the mass of a moving object.

We can see that as the ratio of speeds approaches 1—that is, as the speed of the object approaches the speed of light—the ratio of masses increases without bound. In other words, the function has a vertical asymptote at $v/c = 1$. We can try a few values of this ratio to test this idea.

$\frac{v}{c}$	$\sqrt{1 - \frac{v^2}{c^2}}$	$\frac{m}{m_0}$
0.99	0.1411	7.089
0.999	0.0447	22.37
0.9999	0.0141	70.71

Table 2.8
Ratio of Masses and Speeds for a Moving Object

Thus, according to **Table 2.8**, if an object with mass 100 kg is traveling at 0.9999c, its mass becomes 7071 kg. Since no object can have an infinite mass, we conclude that no object can travel at or more than the speed of light.

2.2 EXERCISES

For the following exercises, consider the function $f(x) = \frac{x^2 - 1}{|x - 1|}$.

30. **[T]** Complete the following table for the function. Round your solutions to four decimal places.

x	*f(x)*	*x*	*f(x)*
0.9	a.	1.1	e.
0.99	b.	1.01	f.
0.999	c.	1.001	g.
0.9999	d.	1.0001	h.

31. What do your results in the preceding exercise indicate about the two-sided limit $\lim_{x \to 1} f(x)$? Explain your response.

For the following exercises, consider the function $f(x) = (1 + x)^{1/x}$.

32. **[T]** Make a table showing the values of f for $x = -0.01, -0.001, -0.0001, -0.00001$ and for $x = 0.01, 0.001, 0.0001, 0.00001$. Round your solutions to five decimal places.

x	*f(x)*	*x*	*f(x)*
−0.01	a.	0.01	e.
−0.001	b.	0.001	f.
−0.0001	c.	0.0001	g.
−0.00001	d.	0.00001	h.

33. What does the table of values in the preceding exercise indicate about the function $f(x) = (1 + x)^{1/x}$?

34. To which mathematical constant does the limit in the preceding exercise appear to be getting closer?

In the following exercises, use the given values to set up a table to evaluate the limits. Round your solutions to eight decimal places.

35. **[T]** $\lim_{x \to 0} \frac{\sin 2x}{x}$; $\pm 0.1, \pm 0.01, \pm 0.001, \pm .0001$

x	$\frac{\sin 2x}{x}$	*x*	$\frac{\sin 2x}{x}$
−0.1	a.	0.1	e.
−0.01	b.	0.01	f.
−0.001	c.	0.001	g.
−0.0001	d.	0.0001	h.

36. **[T]** $\lim_{x \to 0} \frac{\sin 3x}{x}$ $\pm 0.1, \pm 0.01, \pm 0.001, \pm 0.0001$

X	$\frac{\sin 3x}{x}$	*x*	$\frac{\sin 3x}{x}$
−0.1	a.	0.1	e.
−0.01	b.	0.01	f.
−0.001	c.	0.001	g.
−0.0001	d.	0.0001	h.

37. Use the preceding two exercises to conjecture (guess) the value of the following limit: $\lim_{x \to 0} \frac{\sin ax}{x}$ for a, a positive real value.

[T] In the following exercises, set up a table of values to find the indicated limit. Round to eight digits.

38. $\lim_{x \to 2} \frac{x^2 - 4}{x^2 + x - 6}$

x	$\frac{x^2 - 4}{x^2 + x - 6}$	x	$\frac{x^2 - 4}{x^2 + x - 6}$
1.9	a.	2.1	e.
1.99	b.	2.01	f.
1.999	c.	2.001	g.
1.9999	d.	2.0001	h.

39. $\lim_{x \to 1} (1 - 2x)$

x	$1 - 2x$	x	$1 - 2x$
0.9	a.	1.1	e.
0.99	b.	1.01	f.
0.999	c.	1.001	g.
0.9999	d.	1.0001	h.

40. $\lim_{x \to 0} \frac{5}{1 - e^{1/x}}$

x	$\frac{5}{1 - e^{1/x}}$	x	$\frac{5}{1 - e^{1/x}}$
−0.1	a.	0.1	e.
−0.01	b.	0.01	f.
−0.001	c.	0.001	g.
−0.0001	d.	0.0001	h.

41. $\lim_{z \to 0} \frac{z - 1}{z^2 (z + 3)}$

z	$\frac{z - 1}{z^2 (z + 3)}$	z	$\frac{z - 1}{z^2 (z + 3)}$
−0.1	a.	0.1	e.
−0.01	b.	0.01	f.
−0.001	c.	0.001	g.
−0.0001	d.	0.0001	h.

42. $\lim_{t \to 0^+} \frac{\cos t}{t}$

t	$\frac{\cos t}{t}$
0.1	a.
0.01	b.
0.001	c.
0.0001	d.

43. $\lim_{x \to 2} \frac{1 - \frac{2}{x}}{x^2 - 4}$

x	$\frac{1 - \frac{2}{x}}{x^2 - 4}$	x	$\frac{1 - \frac{2}{x}}{x^2 - 4}$
1.9	a.	2.1	e.
1.99	b.	2.01	f.
1.999	c.	2.001	g.
1.9999	d.	2.0001	h.

[T] In the following exercises, set up a table of values and round to eight significant digits. Based on the table of values, make a guess about what the limit is. Then, use a calculator to graph the function and determine the limit. Was the conjecture correct? If not, why does the method of tables fail?

44. $\lim_{\theta \to 0} \sin\left(\frac{\pi}{\theta}\right)$

θ	$\sin\left(\frac{\pi}{\theta}\right)$	θ	$\sin\left(\frac{\pi}{\theta}\right)$
−0.1	a.	0.1	e.
−0.01	b.	0.01	f.
−0.001	c.	0.001	g.
−0.0001	d.	0.0001	h.

45. $\lim_{\alpha \to 0^+} \frac{1}{\alpha}\cos\left(\frac{\pi}{\alpha}\right)$

a	$\frac{1}{\alpha}\cos\left(\frac{\pi}{\alpha}\right)$
0.1	a.
0.01	b.
0.001	c.
0.0001	d.

In the following exercises, consider the graph of the function $y = f(x)$ shown here. Which of the statements about $y = f(x)$ are true and which are false? Explain why a statement is false.

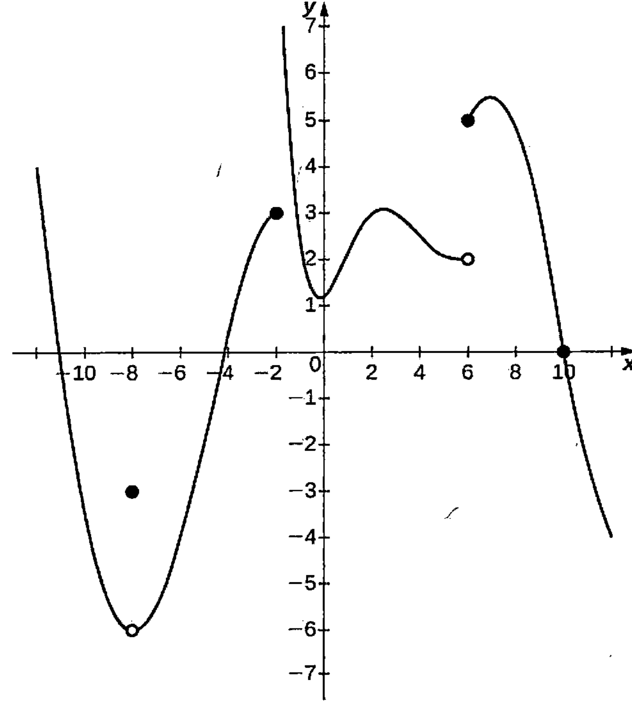

46. $\lim_{x \to 10} f(x) = 0$

47. $\lim_{x \to -2^+} f(x) = 3$

48. $\lim_{x \to -8} f(x) = f(-8)$

49. $\lim_{x \to 6} f(x) = 5$

In the following exercises, use the following graph of the function $y = f(x)$ to find the values, if possible. Estimate when necessary.

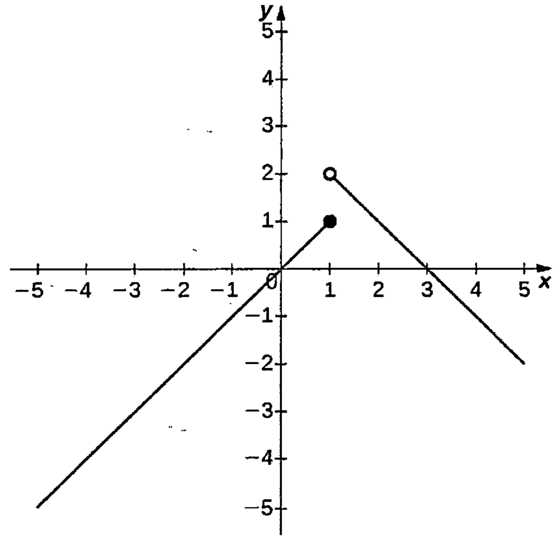

50. $\lim_{x \to 1^-} f(x)$

51. $\lim_{x \to 1^+} f(x)$

52. $\lim_{x \to 1} f(x)$

53. $\lim_{x \to 2} f(x)$

54. $f(1)$

In the following exercises, use the graph of the function $y = f(x)$ shown here to find the values, if possible. Estimate when necessary.

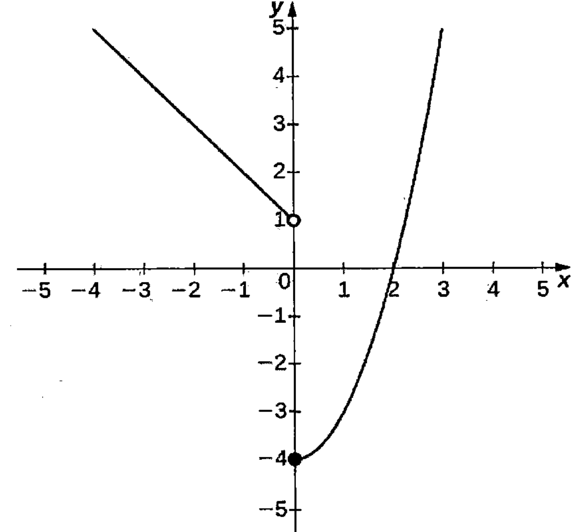

55. $\lim_{x \to 0^-} f(x)$

56. $\lim_{x \to 0^+} f(x)$

57. $\lim_{x \to 0} f(x)$

58. $\lim_{x \to 2} f(x)$

In the following exercises, use the graph of the function $y = f(x)$ shown here to find the values, if possible. Estimate when necessary.

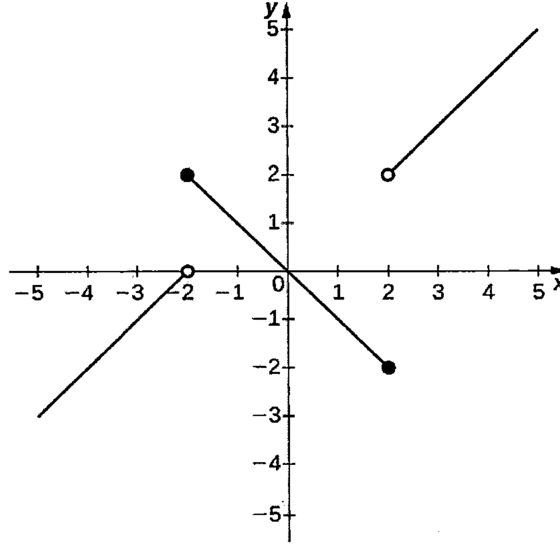

59. $\lim_{x \to -2^-} f(x)$

60. $\lim_{x \to -2^+} f(x)$

61. $\lim_{x \to -2} f(x)$

62. $\lim_{x \to 2^-} f(x)$

63. $\lim_{x \to 2^+} f(x)$

64. $\lim_{x \to 2} f(x)$

In the following exercises, use the graph of the function $y = g(x)$ shown here to find the values, if possible. Estimate when necessary.

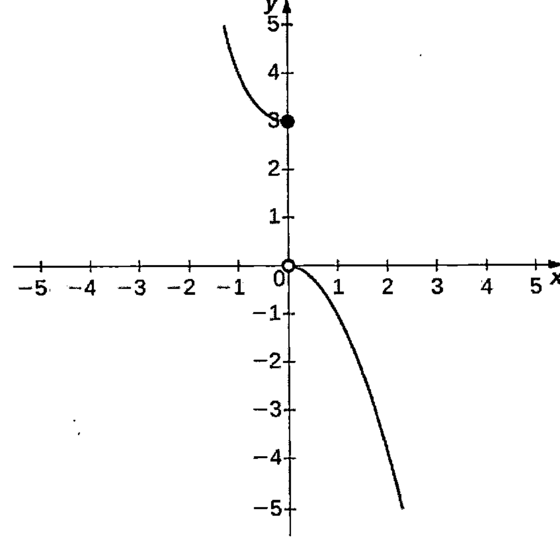

65. $\lim_{x \to 0^-} g(x)$

66. $\lim_{x \to 0^+} g(x)$

67. $\lim_{x \to 0} g(x)$

In the following exercises, use the graph of the function $y = h(x)$ shown here to find the values, if possible. Estimate when necessary.

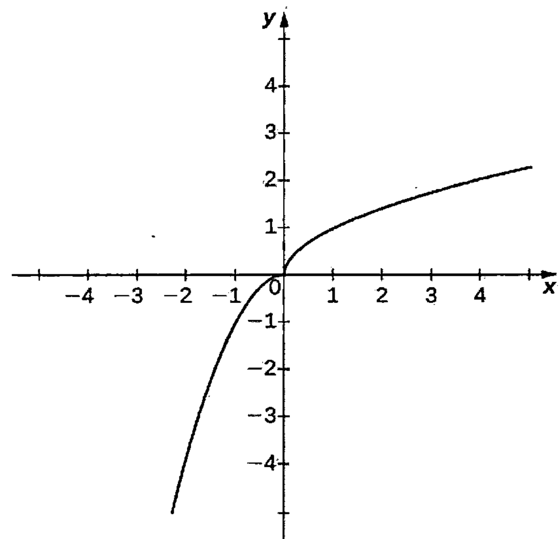

68. $\lim_{x \to 0^-} h(x)$

69. $\lim_{x \to 0^+} h(x)$

70. $\lim_{x \to 0} h(x)$

In the following exercises, use the graph of the function $y = f(x)$ shown here to find the values, if possible. Estimate when necessary.

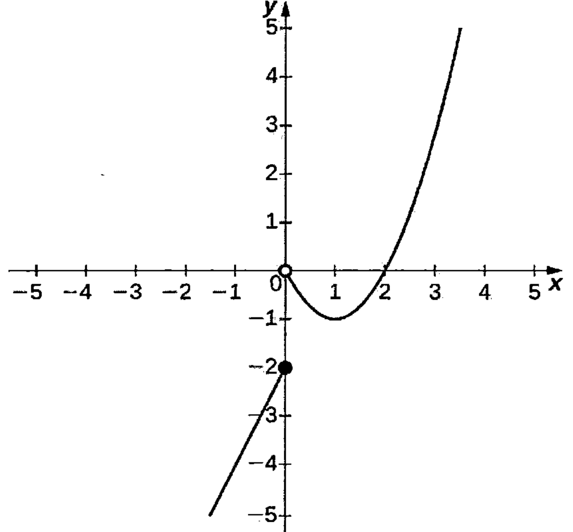

71. $\lim_{x \to 0^-} f(x)$

72. $\lim_{x \to 0^+} f(x)$

73. $\lim_{x \to 0} f(x)$

74. $\lim_{x \to 1} f(x)$

75. $\lim_{x \to 2} f(x)$

In the following exercises, sketch the graph of a function with the given properties.

76. $\lim_{x \to 2} f(x) = 1$, $\lim_{x \to 4^-} f(x) = 3$, $\lim_{x \to 4^+} f(x) = 6$, $x = 4$ is not defined.

77. $\lim_{x \to -\infty} f(x) = 0$, $\lim_{x \to -1^-} f(x) = -\infty$, $\lim_{x \to -1^+} f(x) = \infty$, $\lim_{x \to 0} f(x) = f(0)$, $f(0) = 1$, $\lim_{x \to \infty} f(x) = -\infty$

78. $\lim_{x \to -\infty} f(x) = 2$, $\lim_{x \to 3^-} f(x) = -\infty$, $\lim_{x \to 3^+} f(x) = \infty$, $\lim_{x \to \infty} f(x) = 2$, $f(0) = \frac{-1}{3}$

79. $\lim_{x \to -\infty} f(x) = 2$, $\lim_{x \to -2} f(x) = -\infty$, $\lim_{x \to \infty} f(x) = 2$, $f(0) = 0$

80. $\lim_{x \to -\infty} f(x) = 0$, $\lim_{x \to -1^-} f(x) = \infty$, $\lim_{x \to -1^+} f(x) = -\infty$, $f(0) = -1$, $\lim_{x \to 1^-} f(x) = -\infty$, $\lim_{x \to 1^+} f(x) = \infty$, $\lim_{x \to \infty} f(x) = 0$

81. Shock waves arise in many physical applications, ranging from supernovas to detonation waves. A graph of the density of a shock wave with respect to distance, x, is shown here. We are mainly interested in the location of the front of the shock, labeled x_{SF} in the diagram.

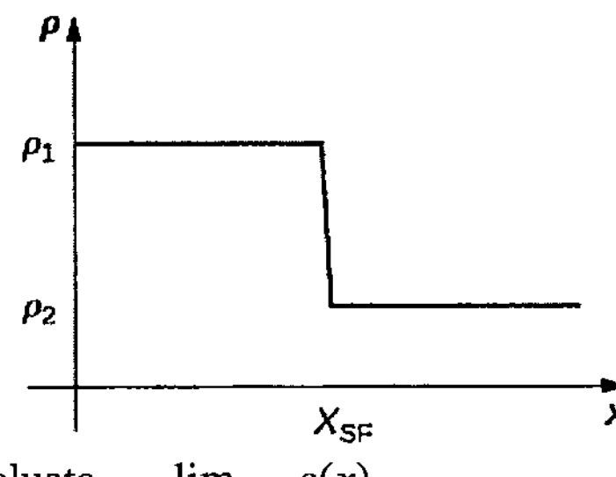

a. Evaluate $\lim_{x \to x_{SF}^+} \rho(x)$.

b. Evaluate $\lim_{x \to x_{SF}^-} \rho(x)$.

c. Evaluate $\lim_{x \to x_{SF}} \rho(x)$. Explain the physical meanings behind your answers.

82. A track coach uses a camera with a fast shutter to estimate the position of a runner with respect to time. A table of the values of position of the athlete versus time is given here, where x is the position in meters of the runner and t is time in seconds. What is $\lim_{t \to 2} x(t)$? What does it mean physically?

t (sec)	x (m)
1.75	4.5
1.95	6.1
1.99	6.42
2.01	6.58
2.05	6.9
2.25	8.5

2.3 | The Limit Laws

Learning Objectives

2.3.1 Recognize the basic limit laws.
2.3.2 Use the limit laws to evaluate the limit of a function.
2.3.3 Evaluate the limit of a function by factoring.
2.3.4 Use the limit laws to evaluate the limit of a polynomial or rational function.
2.3.5 Evaluate the limit of a function by factoring or by using conjugates.
2.3.6 Evaluate the limit of a function by using the squeeze theorem.

In the previous section, we evaluated limits by looking at graphs or by constructing a table of values. In this section, we establish laws for calculating limits and learn how to apply these laws. In the Student Project at the end of this section, you have the opportunity to apply these limit laws to derive the formula for the area of a circle by adapting a method devised by the Greek mathematician Archimedes. We begin by restating two useful limit results from the previous section. These two results, together with the limit laws, serve as a foundation for calculating many limits.

Evaluating Limits with the Limit Laws

The first two limit laws were stated in **Two Important Limits** and we repeat them here. These basic results, together with the other limit laws, allow us to evaluate limits of many algebraic functions.

Theorem 2.4: Basic Limit Results

For any real number a and any constant c,

i. $\lim\limits_{x \to a} x = a$ **(2.14)**

ii. $\lim\limits_{x \to a} c = c$ **(2.15)**

Example 2.13

Evaluating a Basic Limit

Evaluate each of the following limits using **Basic Limit Results**.

a. $\lim\limits_{x \to 2} x$

b. $\lim\limits_{x \to 2} 5$

Solution

a. The limit of x as x approaches a is a: $\lim\limits_{x \to 2} x = 2$.

b. The limit of a constant is that constant: $\lim\limits_{x \to 2} 5 = 5$.

We now take a look at the **limit laws**, the individual properties of limits. The proofs that these laws hold are omitted here.

Theorem 2.5: Limit Laws

Let $f(x)$ and $g(x)$ be defined for all $x \neq a$ over some open interval containing a. Assume that L and M are real numbers such that $\lim_{x \to a} f(x) = L$ and $\lim_{x \to a} g(x) = M$. Let c be a constant. Then, each of the following statements holds:

Sum law for limits: $\lim_{x \to a}(f(x) + g(x)) = \lim_{x \to a} f(x) + \lim_{x \to a} g(x) = L + M$

Difference law for limits: $\lim_{x \to a}(f(x) - g(x)) = \lim_{x \to a} f(x) - \lim_{x \to a} g(x) = L - M$

Constant multiple law for limits: $\lim_{x \to a} cf(x) = c \cdot \lim_{x \to a} f(x) = cL$

Product law for limits: $\lim_{x \to a}(f(x) \cdot g(x)) = \lim_{x \to a} f(x) \cdot \lim_{x \to a} g(x) = L \cdot M$

Quotient law for limits: $\lim_{x \to a} \frac{f(x)}{g(x)} = \frac{\lim_{x \to a} f(x)}{\lim_{x \to a} g(x)} = \frac{L}{M}$ for $M \neq 0$

Power law for limits: $\lim_{x \to a}(f(x))^n = \left(\lim_{x \to a} f(x)\right)^n = L^n$ for every positive integer n.

Root law for limits: $\lim_{x \to a} \sqrt[n]{f(x)} = \sqrt[n]{\lim_{x \to a} f(x)} = \sqrt[n]{L}$ for all L if n is odd and for $L \geq 0$ if n is even.

We now practice applying these limit laws to evaluate a limit.

Example 2.14

Evaluating a Limit Using Limit Laws

Use the limit laws to evaluate $\lim_{x \to -3}(4x + 2)$.

Solution

Let's apply the limit laws one step at a time to be sure we understand how they work. We need to keep in mind the requirement that, at each application of a limit law, the new limits must exist for the limit law to be applied.

$$\begin{aligned} \lim_{x \to -3}(4x + 2) &= \lim_{x \to -3} 4x + \lim_{x \to -3} 2 && \text{Apply the sum law.} \\ &= 4 \cdot \lim_{x \to -3} x + \lim_{x \to -3} 2 && \text{Apply the constant multiple law.} \\ &= 4 \cdot (-3) + 2 = -10. && \text{Apply the basic limit results and simplify.} \end{aligned}$$

Example 2.15

Using Limit Laws Repeatedly

Use the limit laws to evaluate $\lim_{x \to 2} \frac{2x^2 - 3x + 1}{x^3 + 4}$.

Solution

To find this limit, we need to apply the limit laws several times. Again, we need to keep in mind that as we rewrite the limit in terms of other limits, each new limit must exist for the limit law to be applied.

$$\begin{aligned}
\lim_{x \to 2} \frac{2x^2 - 3x + 1}{x^3 + 4} &= \frac{\lim_{x \to 2}\left(2x^2 - 3x + 1\right)}{\lim_{x \to 2}\left(x^3 + 4\right)} && \text{Apply the quotient law, making sure that. } (2)^3 + 4 \neq 0 \\
&= \frac{2 \cdot \lim_{x \to 2} x^2 - 3 \cdot \lim_{x \to 2} x + \lim_{x \to 2} 1}{\lim_{x \to 2} x^3 + \lim_{x \to 2} 4} && \text{Apply the sum law and constant multiple law.} \\
&= \frac{2 \cdot \left(\lim_{x \to 2} x\right)^2 - 3 \cdot \lim_{x \to 2} x + \lim_{x \to 2} 1}{\left(\lim_{x \to 2} x\right)^3 + \lim_{x \to 2} 4} && \text{Apply the power law.} \\
&= \frac{2(4) - 3(2) + 1}{(2)^3 + 4} = \frac{1}{4}. && \text{Apply the basic limit laws and simplify.}
\end{aligned}$$

2.11 Use the limit laws to evaluate $\lim_{x \to 6} (2x - 1)\sqrt{x + 4}$. In each step, indicate the limit law applied.

Limits of Polynomial and Rational Functions

By now you have probably noticed that, in each of the previous examples, it has been the case that $\lim_{x \to a} f(x) = f(a)$. This is not always true, but it does hold for all polynomials for any choice of a and for all rational functions at all values of a for which the rational function is defined.

Theorem 2.6: Limits of Polynomial and Rational Functions

Let $p(x)$ and $q(x)$ be polynomial functions. Let a be a real number. Then,

$$\lim_{x \to a} p(x) = p(a)$$

$$\lim_{x \to a} \frac{p(x)}{q(x)} = \frac{p(a)}{q(a)} \text{ when } q(a) \neq 0.$$

To see that this theorem holds, consider the polynomial $p(x) = c_n x^n + c_{n-1} x^{n-1} + \cdots + c_1 x + c_0$. By applying the sum, constant multiple, and power laws, we end up with

$$\begin{aligned}
\lim_{x \to a} p(x) &= \lim_{x \to a}\left(c_n x^n + c_{n-1} x^{n-1} + \cdots + c_1 x + c_0\right) \\
&= c_n\left(\lim_{x \to a} x\right)^n + c_{n-1}\left(\lim_{x \to a} x\right)^{n-1} + \cdots + c_1\left(\lim_{x \to a} x\right) + \lim_{x \to a} c_0 \\
&= c_n a^n + c_{n-1} a^{n-1} + \cdots + c_1 a + c_0 \\
&= p(a).
\end{aligned}$$

It now follows from the quotient law that if $p(x)$ and $q(x)$ are polynomials for which $q(a) \neq 0$, then

$$\lim_{x \to a} \frac{p(x)}{q(x)} = \frac{p(a)}{q(a)}.$$

Example 2.16 applies this result.

Example 2.16

Evaluating a Limit of a Rational Function

Evaluate the $\lim_{x \to 3} \frac{2x^2 - 3x + 1}{5x + 4}$.

Solution

Since 3 is in the domain of the rational function $f(x) = \frac{2x^2 - 3x + 1}{5x + 4}$, we can calculate the limit by substituting 3 for x into the function. Thus,

$$\lim_{x \to 3} \frac{2x^2 - 3x + 1}{5x + 4} = \frac{10}{19}.$$

2.12 Evaluate $\lim_{x \to -2} (3x^3 - 2x + 7)$.

Additional Limit Evaluation Techniques

As we have seen, we may evaluate easily the limits of polynomials and limits of some (but not all) rational functions by direct substitution. However, as we saw in the introductory section on limits, it is certainly possible for $\lim_{x \to a} f(x)$ to exist when $f(a)$ is undefined. The following observation allows us to evaluate many limits of this type:

If for all $x \neq a$, $f(x) = g(x)$ over some open interval containing a, then $\lim_{x \to a} f(x) = \lim_{x \to a} g(x)$.

To understand this idea better, consider the limit $\lim_{x \to 1} \frac{x^2 - 1}{x - 1}$.

The function

$$\begin{aligned} f(x) &= \frac{x^2 - 1}{x - 1} \\ &= \frac{(x - 1)(x + 1)}{x - 1} \end{aligned}$$

and the function $g(x) = x + 1$ are identical for all values of $x \neq 1$. The graphs of these two functions are shown in **Figure 2.24**.

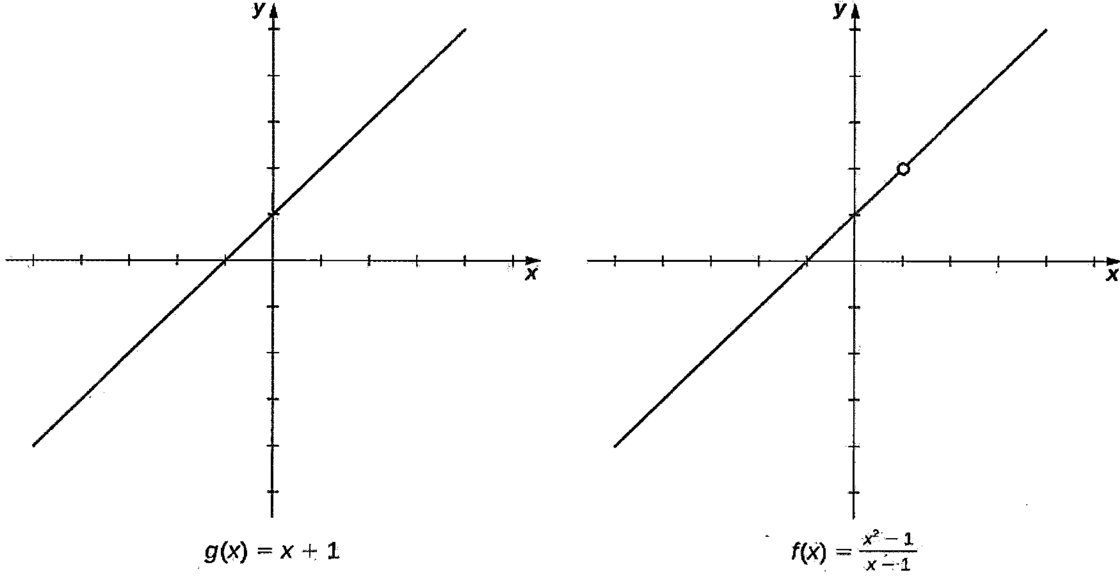

Figure 2.24 The graphs of $f(x)$ and $g(x)$ are identical for all $x \neq 1$. Their limits at 1 are equal.

We see that

$$\begin{aligned}\lim_{x \to 1} \frac{x^2-1}{x-1} &= \lim_{x \to 1} \frac{(x-1)(x+1)}{x-1} \\ &= \lim_{x \to 1} (x+1) \\ &= 2.\end{aligned}$$

The limit has the form $\lim_{x \to a} \frac{f(x)}{g(x)}$, where $\lim_{x \to a} f(x) = 0$ and $\lim_{x \to a} g(x) = 0$. (In this case, we say that $f(x)/g(x)$ has the indeterminate form $0/0$.) The following Problem-Solving Strategy provides a general outline for evaluating limits of this type.

Problem-Solving Strategy: Calculating a Limit When $f(x)/g(x)$ has the Indeterminate Form 0/0

1. First, we need to make sure that our function has the appropriate form and cannot be evaluated immediately using the limit laws.
2. We then need to find a function that is equal to $h(x) = f(x)/g(x)$ for all $x \neq a$ over some interval containing a. To do this, we may need to try one or more of the following steps:
   a. If $f(x)$ and $g(x)$ are polynomials, we should factor each function and cancel out any common factors.
   b. If the numerator or denominator contains a difference involving a square root, we should try multiplying the numerator and denominator by the conjugate of the expression involving the square root.
   c. If $f(x)/g(x)$ is a complex fraction, we begin by simplifying it.
3. Last, we apply the limit laws.

The next examples demonstrate the use of this Problem-Solving Strategy. **Example 2.17** illustrates the factor-and-cancel technique; **Example 2.18** shows multiplying by a conjugate. In **Example 2.19**, we look at simplifying a complex fraction.

Example 2.17

Evaluating a Limit by Factoring and Canceling

Evaluate $\lim_{x \to 3} \frac{x^2 - 3x}{2x^2 - 5x - 3}$.

Solution

Step 1. The function $f(x) = \frac{x^2 - 3x}{2x^2 - 5x - 3}$ is undefined for $x = 3$. In fact, if we substitute 3 into the function we get $0/0$, which is undefined. Factoring and canceling is a good strategy:

$$\lim_{x \to 3} \frac{x^2 - 3x}{2x^2 - 5x - 3} = \lim_{x \to 3} \frac{x(x-3)}{(x-3)(2x+1)}$$

Step 2. For all $x \neq 3$, $\frac{x^2 - 3x}{2x^2 - 5x - 3} = \frac{x}{2x+1}$. Therefore,

$$\lim_{x \to 3} \frac{x(x-3)}{(x-3)(2x+1)} = \lim_{x \to 3} \frac{x}{2x+1}.$$

Step 3. Evaluate using the limit laws:

$$\lim_{x \to 3} \frac{x}{2x+1} = \frac{3}{7}.$$

2.13 Evaluate $\lim_{x \to -3} \frac{x^2 + 4x + 3}{x^2 - 9}$.

Example 2.18

Evaluating a Limit by Multiplying by a Conjugate

Evaluate $\lim_{x \to -1} \frac{\sqrt{x+2} - 1}{x+1}$.

Solution

Step 1. $\frac{\sqrt{x+2} - 1}{x+1}$ has the form $0/0$ at -1. Let's begin by multiplying by $\sqrt{x+2} + 1$, the conjugate of $\sqrt{x+2} - 1$, on the numerator and denominator:

$$\lim_{x \to -1} \frac{\sqrt{x+2} - 1}{x+1} = \lim_{x \to -1} \frac{\sqrt{x+2} - 1}{x+1} \cdot \frac{\sqrt{x+2} + 1}{\sqrt{x+2} + 1}.$$

Step 2. We then multiply out the numerator. We don't multiply out the denominator because we are hoping that the $(x+1)$ in the denominator cancels out in the end:

$$= \lim_{x \to -1} \frac{x+1}{(x+1)(\sqrt{x+2} + 1)}.$$

Step 3. Then we cancel:

$$= \lim_{x \to -1} \frac{1}{\sqrt{x+2}+1}.$$

Step 4. Last, we apply the limit laws:

$$\lim_{x \to -1} \frac{1}{\sqrt{x+2}+1} = \frac{1}{2}.$$

2.14 Evaluate $\lim_{x \to 5} \frac{\sqrt{x-1}-2}{x-5}$.

Example 2.19

Evaluating a Limit by Simplifying a Complex Fraction

Evaluate $\lim_{x \to 1} \frac{\frac{1}{x+1} - \frac{1}{2}}{x-1}$.

Solution

Step 1. $\frac{\frac{1}{x+1} - \frac{1}{2}}{x-1}$ has the form $0/0$ at 1. We simplify the algebraic fraction by multiplying by $2(x+1)/2(x+1)$:

$$\lim_{x \to 1} \frac{\frac{1}{x+1} - \frac{1}{2}}{x-1} = \lim_{x \to 1} \frac{\frac{1}{x+1} - \frac{1}{2}}{x-1} \cdot \frac{2(x+1)}{2(x+1)}.$$

Step 2. Next, we multiply through the numerators. Do not multiply the denominators because we want to be able to cancel the factor $(x-1)$:

$$= \lim_{x \to 1} \frac{2-(x+1)}{2(x-1)(x+1)}.$$

Step 3. Then, we simplify the numerator:

$$= \lim_{x \to 1} \frac{-x+1}{2(x-1)(x+1)}.$$

Step 4. Now we factor out −1 from the numerator:

$$= \lim_{x \to 1} \frac{-(x-1)}{2(x-1)(x+1)}.$$

Step 5. Then, we cancel the common factors of $(x-1)$:

$$= \lim_{x \to 1} \frac{-1}{2(x+1)}.$$

Step 6. Last, we evaluate using the limit laws:

$$\lim_{x \to 1} \frac{-1}{2(x+1)} = -\frac{1}{4}.$$

2.15 Evaluate $\lim_{x \to -3} \frac{\frac{1}{x+2} + 1}{x+3}$.

Example 2.20 does not fall neatly into any of the patterns established in the previous examples. However, with a little creativity, we can still use these same techniques.

Example 2.20

Evaluating a Limit When the Limit Laws Do Not Apply

Evaluate $\lim_{x \to 0} \left(\frac{1}{x} + \frac{5}{x(x-5)} \right)$.

Solution

Both $1/x$ and $5/x(x-5)$ fail to have a limit at zero. Since neither of the two functions has a limit at zero, we cannot apply the sum law for limits; we must use a different strategy. In this case, we find the limit by performing addition and then applying one of our previous strategies. Observe that

$$\begin{aligned} \frac{1}{x} + \frac{5}{x(x-5)} &= \frac{x-5+5}{x(x-5)} \\ &= \frac{x}{x(x-5)}. \end{aligned}$$

Thus,

$$\begin{aligned} \lim_{x \to 0} \left(\frac{1}{x} + \frac{5}{x(x-5)} \right) &= \lim_{x \to 0} \frac{x}{x(x-5)} \\ &= \lim_{x \to 0} \frac{1}{x-5} \\ &= -\frac{1}{5}. \end{aligned}$$

2.16 Evaluate $\lim_{x \to 3} \left(\frac{1}{x-3} - \frac{4}{x^2 - 2x - 3} \right)$.

Let's now revisit one-sided limits. Simple modifications in the limit laws allow us to apply them to one-sided limits. For example, to apply the limit laws to a limit of the form $\lim_{x \to a^-} h(x)$, we require the function $h(x)$ to be defined over an open interval of the form (b, a); for a limit of the form $\lim_{x \to a^+} h(x)$, we require the function $h(x)$ to be defined over an open interval of the form (a, c). **Example 2.21** illustrates this point.

Example 2.21

Evaluating a One-Sided Limit Using the Limit Laws

Evaluate each of the following limits, if possible.

a. $\lim_{x \to 3^-} \sqrt{x-3}$

b. $\lim\limits_{x \to 3^+} \sqrt{x-3}$

Solution

Figure 2.25 illustrates the function $f(x) = \sqrt{x-3}$ and aids in our understanding of these limits.

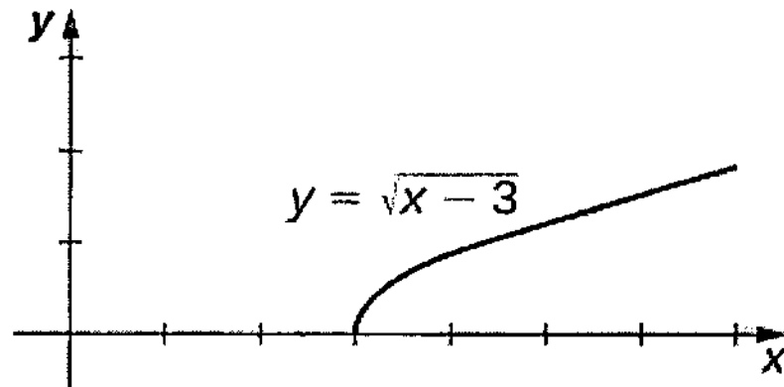

Figure 2.25 The graph shows the function $f(x) = \sqrt{x-3}$.

a. The function $f(x) = \sqrt{x-3}$ is defined over the interval $[3, +\infty)$. Since this function is not defined to the left of 3, we cannot apply the limit laws to compute $\lim\limits_{x \to 3^-} \sqrt{x-3}$. In fact, since $f(x) = \sqrt{x-3}$ is undefined to the left of 3, $\lim\limits_{x \to 3^-} \sqrt{x-3}$ does not exist.

b. Since $f(x) = \sqrt{x-3}$ is defined to the right of 3, the limit laws do apply to $\lim\limits_{x \to 3^+} \sqrt{x-3}$. By applying these limit laws we obtain $\lim\limits_{x \to 3^+} \sqrt{x-3} = 0$.

In **Example 2.22** we look at one-sided limits of a piecewise-defined function and use these limits to draw a conclusion about a two-sided limit of the same function.

Example 2.22

Evaluating a Two-Sided Limit Using the Limit Laws

For $f(x) = \begin{cases} 4x-3 & \text{if } x < 2 \\ (x-3)^2 & \text{if } x \geq 2 \end{cases}$, evaluate each of the following limits:

a. $\lim\limits_{x \to 2^-} f(x)$

b. $\lim\limits_{x \to 2^+} f(x)$

c. $\lim\limits_{x \to 2} f(x)$

Solution

Figure 2.26 illustrates the function $f(x)$ and aids in our understanding of these limits.

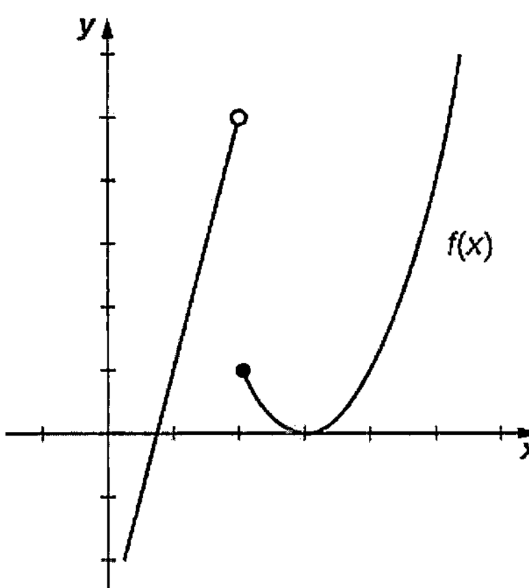

Figure 2.26 This graph shows a function $f(x)$.

a. Since $f(x) = 4x - 3$ for all x in $(-\infty, 2)$, replace $f(x)$ in the limit with $4x - 3$ and apply the limit laws:

$$\lim_{x \to 2^-} f(x) = \lim_{x \to 2^-} (4x - 3) = 5.$$

b. Since $f(x) = (x - 3)^2$ for all x in $(2, +\infty)$, replace $f(x)$ in the limit with $(x - 3)^2$ and apply the limit laws:

$$\lim_{x \to 2^+} f(x) = \lim_{x \to 2^-} (x - 3)^2 = 1.$$

c. Since $\lim_{x \to 2^-} f(x) = 5$ and $\lim_{x \to 2^+} f(x) = 1$, we conclude that $\lim_{x \to 2} f(x)$ does not exist.

 **2.17** Graph $f(x) = \begin{cases} -x - 2 \text{ if } x < -1 \\ 2 \text{ if } x = -1 \\ x^3 \text{ if } x > -1 \end{cases}$ and evaluate $\lim_{x \to -1^-} f(x)$.

We now turn our attention to evaluating a limit of the form $\lim_{x \to a} \frac{f(x)}{g(x)}$, where $\lim_{x \to a} f(x) = K$, where $K \neq 0$ and $\lim_{x \to a} g(x) = 0$. That is, $f(x)/g(x)$ has the form $K/0, K \neq 0$ at a.

Example 2.23

Evaluating a Limit of the Form $K/0, K \neq 0$ Using the Limit Laws

Evaluate $\lim_{x \to 2^-} \frac{x - 3}{x^2 - 2x}$.

Solution

Step 1. After substituting in $x = 2$, we see that this limit has the form $-1/0$. That is, as x approaches 2 from the left, the numerator approaches -1; and the denominator approaches 0. Consequently, the magnitude of $\frac{x-3}{x(x-2)}$ becomes infinite. To get a better idea of what the limit is, we need to factor the denominator:

$$\lim_{x \to 2^-} \frac{x-3}{x^2-2x} = \lim_{x \to 2^-} \frac{x-3}{x(x-2)}.$$

Step 2. Since $x-2$ is the only part of the denominator that is zero when 2 is substituted, we then separate $1/(x-2)$ from the rest of the function:

$$= \lim_{x \to 2^-} \frac{x-3}{x} \cdot \frac{1}{x-2}.$$

Step 3. $\lim_{x \to 2^-} \frac{x-3}{x} = -\frac{1}{2}$ and $\lim_{x \to 2^-} \frac{1}{x-2} = -\infty$. Therefore, the product of $(x-3)/x$ and $1/(x-2)$ has a limit of $+\infty$:

$$\lim_{x \to 2^-} \frac{x-3}{x^2-2x} = +\infty.$$

2.18 Evaluate $\lim_{x \to 1} \frac{x+2}{(x-1)^2}$.

The Squeeze Theorem

The techniques we have developed thus far work very well for algebraic functions, but we are still unable to evaluate limits of very basic trigonometric functions. The next theorem, called the **squeeze theorem**, proves very useful for establishing basic trigonometric limits. This theorem allows us to calculate limits by “squeezing” a function, with a limit at a point a that is unknown, between two functions having a common known limit at a. **Figure 2.27** illustrates this idea.

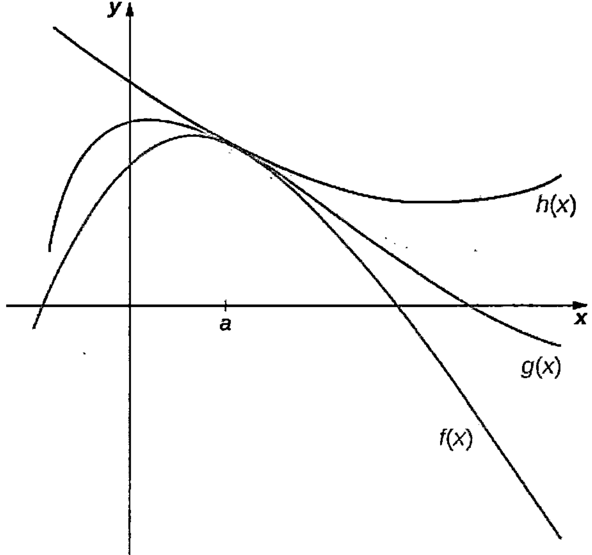

Figure 2.27 The Squeeze Theorem applies when $f(x) \le g(x) \le h(x)$ and $\lim_{x \to a} f(x) = \lim_{x \to a} h(x)$.

Theorem 2.7: The Squeeze Theorem

Let $f(x)$, $g(x)$, and $h(x)$ be defined for all $x \neq a$ over an open interval containing a. If

$$f(x) \leq g(x) \leq h(x)$$

for all $x \neq a$ in an open interval containing a and

$$\lim_{x \to a} f(x) = L = \lim_{x \to a} h(x)$$

where L is a real number, then $\lim_{x \to a} g(x) = L$.

Example 2.24

Applying the Squeeze Theorem

Apply the squeeze theorem to evaluate $\lim_{x \to 0} x \cos x$.

Solution

Because $-1 \leq \cos x \leq 1$ for all x, we have $-|x| \leq x \cos x \leq |x|$. Since $\lim_{x \to 0} (-|x|) = 0 = \lim_{x \to 0} |x|$, from the squeeze theorem, we obtain $\lim_{x \to 0} x \cos x = 0$. The graphs of $f(x) = -|x|$, $g(x) = x \cos x$, and $h(x) = |x|$ are shown in **Figure 2.28**.

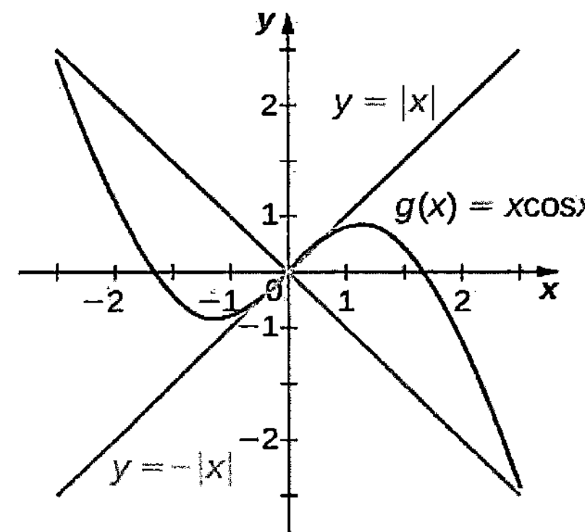

Figure 2.28 The graphs of $f(x)$, $g(x)$, and $h(x)$ are shown around the point $x = 0$.

2.19 Use the squeeze theorem to evaluate $\lim_{x \to 0} x^2 \sin \frac{1}{x}$.

We now use the squeeze theorem to tackle several very important limits. Although this discussion is somewhat lengthy, these limits prove invaluable for the development of the material in both the next section and the next chapter. The first of these limits is $\lim_{\theta \to 0} \sin \theta$. Consider the unit circle shown in **Figure 2.29**. In the figure, we see that $\sin \theta$ is the y-coordinate on the unit circle and it corresponds to the line segment shown in blue. The radian measure of angle θ is the length of the arc it subtends on the unit circle. Therefore, we see that for $0 < \theta < \frac{\pi}{2}$, $0 < \sin \theta < \theta$.

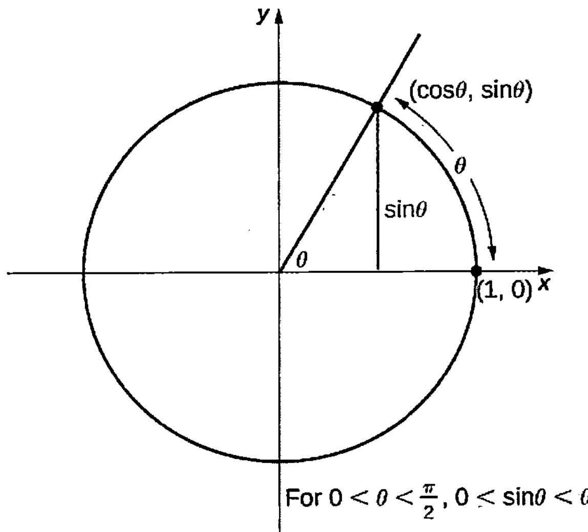

Figure 2.29 The sine function is shown as a line on the unit circle.

Because $\lim\limits_{\theta \to 0^+} 0 = 0$ and $\lim\limits_{\theta \to 0^+} \theta = 0,$ by using the squeeze theorem we conclude that

$$\lim_{\theta \to 0^+} \sin\theta = 0.$$

To see that $\lim\limits_{\theta \to 0^-} \sin\theta = 0$ as well, observe that for $-\frac{\pi}{2} < \theta < 0,\ 0 < -\theta < \frac{\pi}{2}$ and hence, $0 < \sin(-\theta) < -\theta.$ Consequently, $0 < -\sin\theta < -\theta.$ It follows that $0 > \sin\theta > \theta.$ An application of the squeeze theorem produces the desired limit. Thus, since $\lim\limits_{\theta \to 0^+} \sin\theta = 0$ and $\lim\limits_{\theta \to 0^-} \sin\theta = 0,$

$$\lim_{\theta \to 0} \sin\theta = 0. \tag{2.16}$$

Next, using the identity $\cos\theta = \sqrt{1 - \sin^2\theta}$ for $-\frac{\pi}{2} < \theta < \frac{\pi}{2},$ we see that

$$\lim_{\theta \to 0} \cos\theta = \lim_{\theta \to 0} \sqrt{1 - \sin^2\theta} = 1. \tag{2.17}$$

We now take a look at a limit that plays an important role in later chapters—namely, $\lim\limits_{\theta \to 0} \frac{\sin\theta}{\theta}.$ To evaluate this limit, we use the unit circle in **Figure 2.30**. Notice that this figure adds one additional triangle to **Figure 2.30**. We see that the length of the side opposite angle θ in this new triangle is $\tan\theta.$ Thus, we see that for $0 < \theta < \frac{\pi}{2},\ \sin\theta < \theta < \tan\theta.$

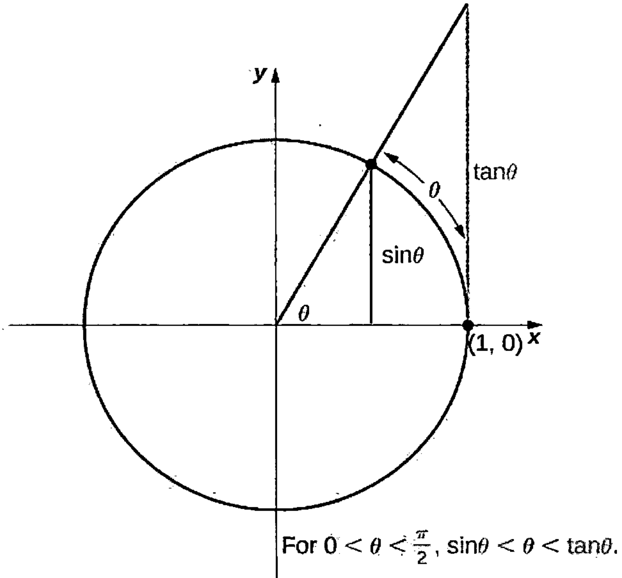

Figure 2.30 The sine and tangent functions are shown as lines on the unit circle.

By dividing by $\sin\theta$ in all parts of the inequality, we obtain

$$1 < \frac{\theta}{\sin\theta} < \frac{1}{\cos\theta}.$$

Equivalently, we have

$$1 > \frac{\sin\theta}{\theta} > \cos\theta.$$

Since $\lim_{\theta \to 0^+} 1 = 1 = \lim_{\theta \to 0^+} \cos\theta,$ we conclude that $\lim_{\theta \to 0^+} \frac{\sin\theta}{\theta} = 1.$ By applying a manipulation similar to that used in demonstrating that $\lim_{\theta \to 0^-} \sin\theta = 0,$ we can show that $\lim_{\theta \to 0^-} \frac{\sin\theta}{\theta} = 1.$ Thus,

$$\lim_{\theta \to 0} \frac{\sin\theta}{\theta} = 1. \quad \textbf{(2.18)}$$

In **Example 2.25** we use this limit to establish $\lim_{\theta \to 0} \frac{1 - \cos\theta}{\theta} = 0.$ This limit also proves useful in later chapters.

Example 2.25

Evaluating an Important Trigonometric Limit

Evaluate $\lim_{\theta \to 0} \frac{1 - \cos\theta}{\theta}.$

Solution

In the first step, we multiply by the conjugate so that we can use a trigonometric identity to convert the cosine in the numerator to a sine:

$$\begin{aligned}\lim_{\theta \to 0} \frac{1 - \cos\theta}{\theta} &= \lim_{\theta \to 0} \frac{1 - \cos\theta}{\theta} \cdot \frac{1 + \cos\theta}{1 + \cos\theta} \\ &= \lim_{\theta \to 0} \frac{1 - \cos^2\theta}{\theta(1 + \cos\theta)} \\ &= \lim_{\theta \to 0} \frac{\sin^2\theta}{\theta(1 + \cos\theta)} \\ &= \lim_{\theta \to 0} \frac{\sin\theta}{\theta} \cdot \frac{\sin\theta}{1 + \cos\theta} \\ &= 1 \cdot \frac{0}{2} = 0.\end{aligned}$$

Therefore,

$$\lim_{\theta \to 0} \frac{1 - \cos\theta}{\theta} = 0. \tag{2.19}$$

2.20 Evaluate $\lim\limits_{\theta \to 0} \frac{1 - \cos\theta}{\sin\theta}$.

Student PROJECT

Deriving the Formula for the Area of a Circle

Some of the geometric formulas we take for granted today were first derived by methods that anticipate some of the methods of calculus. The Greek mathematician Archimedes (ca. 287−212; BCE) was particularly inventive, using polygons inscribed within circles to approximate the area of the circle as the number of sides of the polygon increased. He never came up with the idea of a limit, but we can use this idea to see what his geometric constructions could have predicted about the limit.

We can estimate the area of a circle by computing the area of an inscribed regular polygon. Think of the regular polygon as being made up of n triangles. By taking the limit as the vertex angle of these triangles goes to zero, you can obtain the area of the circle. To see this, carry out the following steps:

1. Express the height h and the base b of the isosceles triangle in **Figure 2.31** in terms of θ and r.

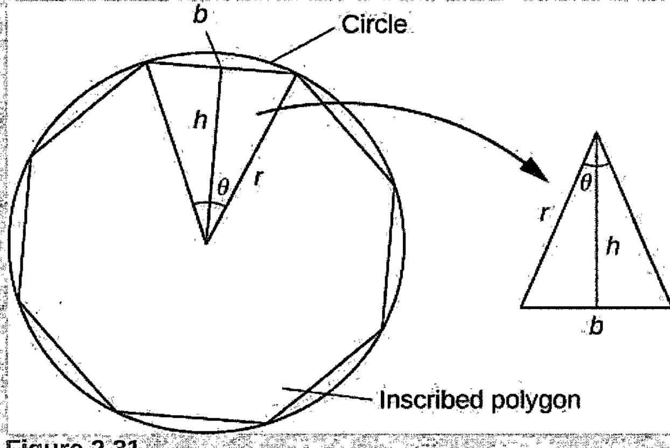

Figure 2.31

2. Using the expressions that you obtained in step 1, express the area of the isosceles triangle in terms of θ and r. (Substitute $(1/2)\sin\theta$ for $\sin(\theta/2)\cos(\theta/2)$ in your expression.)
3. If an n-sided regular polygon is inscribed in a circle of radius r, find a relationship between θ and n. Solve this for n. Keep in mind there are 2π radians in a circle. (Use radians, not degrees.)
4. Find an expression for the area of the n-sided polygon in terms of r and θ.
5. To find a formula for the area of the circle, find the limit of the expression in step 4 as θ goes to zero. (*Hint:* $\lim_{\theta \to 0} \frac{(\sin\theta)}{\theta} = 1$).

The technique of estimating areas of regions by using polygons is revisited in **Introduction to Integration**.

2.3 EXERCISES

In the following exercises, use the limit laws to evaluate each limit. Justify each step by indicating the appropriate limit law(s).

83. $\lim_{x \to 0}\left(4x^2 - 2x + 3\right)$

84. $\lim_{x \to 1}\frac{x^3 + 3x^2 + 5}{4 - 7x}$

85. $\lim_{x \to -2}\sqrt{x^2 - 6x + 3}$

86. $\lim_{x \to -1}(9x + 1)^2$

In the following exercises, use direct substitution to evaluate each limit.

87. $\lim_{x \to 7}x^2$

88. $\lim_{x \to -2}\left(4x^2 - 1\right)$

89. $\lim_{x \to 0}\frac{1}{1 + \sin x}$

90. $\lim_{x \to 2}e^{2x - x^2}$

91. $\lim_{x \to 1}\frac{2 - 7x}{x + 6}$

92. $\lim_{x \to 3}\ln e^{3x}$

In the following exercises, use direct substitution to show that each limit leads to the indeterminate form 0/0. Then, evaluate the limit.

93. $\lim_{x \to 4}\frac{x^2 - 16}{x - 4}$

94. $\lim_{x \to 2}\frac{x - 2}{x^2 - 2x}$

95. $\lim_{x \to 6}\frac{3x - 18}{2x - 12}$

96. $\lim_{h \to 0}\frac{(1 + h)^2 - 1}{h}$

97. $\lim_{t \to 9}\frac{t - 9}{\sqrt{t} - 3}$

98. $\lim_{h \to 0}\frac{\frac{1}{a + h} - \frac{1}{a}}{h}$, where a is a real-valued constant

99. $\lim_{\theta \to \pi}\frac{\sin\theta}{\tan\theta}$

100. $\lim_{x \to 1}\frac{x^3 - 1}{x^2 - 1}$

101. $\lim_{x \to 1/2}\frac{2x^2 + 3x - 2}{2x - 1}$

102. $\lim_{x \to -3}\frac{\sqrt{x + 4} - 1}{x + 3}$

In the following exercises, use direct substitution to obtain an undefined expression. Then, use the method of **Example 2.23** to simplify the function to help determine the limit.

103. $\lim_{x \to -2^-}\frac{2x^2 + 7x - 4}{x^2 + x - 2}$

104. $\lim_{x \to -2^+}\frac{2x^2 + 7x - 4}{x^2 + x - 2}$

105. $\lim_{x \to 1^-}\frac{2x^2 + 7x - 4}{x^2 + x - 2}$

106. $\lim_{x \to 1^+}\frac{2x^2 + 7x - 4}{x^2 + x - 2}$

In the following exercises, assume that $\lim_{x \to 6}f(x) = 4$, $\lim_{x \to 6}g(x) = 9$, and $\lim_{x \to 6}h(x) = 6$. Use these three facts and the limit laws to evaluate each limit.

107. $\lim_{x \to 6}2f(x)g(x)$

108. $\lim_{x \to 6}\frac{g(x) - 1}{f(x)}$

109. $\lim_{x \to 6}\left(f(x) + \frac{1}{3}g(x)\right)$

110. $\lim_{x \to 6}\frac{(h(x))^3}{2}$

111. $\lim_{x \to 6}\sqrt{g(x) - f(x)}$

112. $\lim_{x \to 6}x \cdot h(x)$

113. $\lim_{x \to 6} [(x + 1) \cdot f(x)]$

114. $\lim_{x \to 6} (f(x) \cdot g(x) - h(x))$

[T] In the following exercises, use a calculator to draw the graph of each piecewise-defined function and study the graph to evaluate the given limits.

115. $f(x) = \begin{cases} x^2, & x \le 3 \\ x + 4, & x > 3 \end{cases}$

a. $\lim_{x \to 3^-} f(x)$

b. $\lim_{x \to 3^+} f(x)$

116. $g(x) = \begin{cases} x^3 - 1, & x \le 0 \\ 1, & x > 0 \end{cases}$

a. $\lim_{x \to 0^-} g(x)$

b. $\lim_{x \to 0^+} g(x)$

117. $h(x) = \begin{cases} x^2 - 2x + 1, & x < 2 \\ 3 - x, & x \ge 2 \end{cases}$

a. $\lim_{x \to 2^-} h(x)$

b. $\lim_{x \to 2^+} h(x)$

In the following exercises, use the following graphs and the limit laws to evaluate each limit.

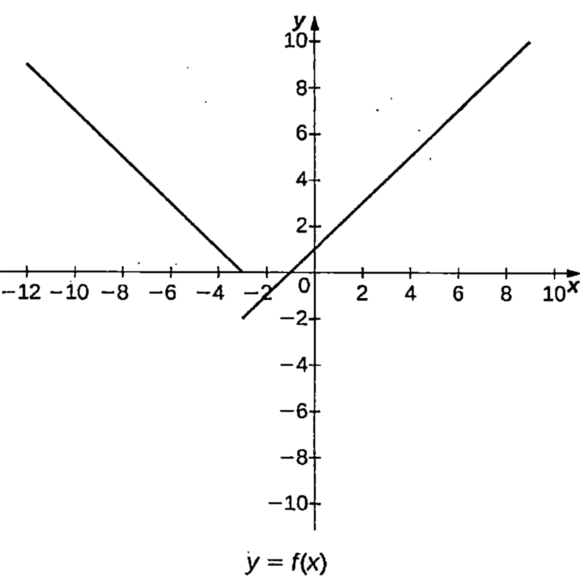

$y = f(x)$

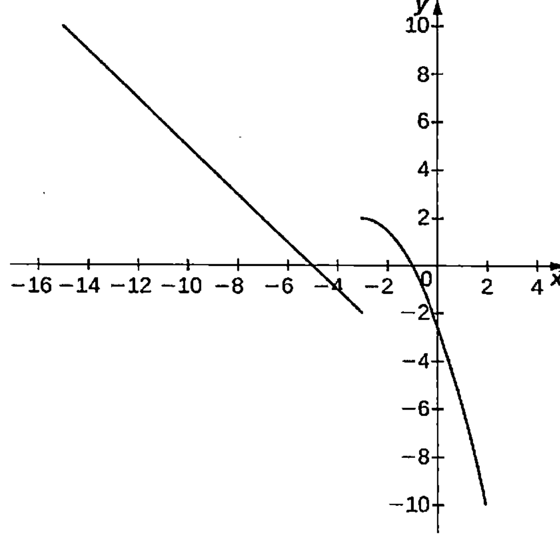

$y = g(x)$

118. $\lim_{x \to -3^+} (f(x) + g(x))$

119. $\lim_{x \to -3^-} (f(x) - 3g(x))$

120. $\lim_{x \to 0} \frac{f(x)g(x)}{3}$

121. $\lim_{x \to -5} \frac{2 + g(x)}{f(x)}$

122. $\lim_{x \to 1} (f(x))^2$

123. $\lim_{x \to 1} \sqrt{f(x) - g(x)}$

124. $\lim_{x \to -7} (x \cdot g(x))$

125. $\lim_{x \to -9} [x \cdot f(x) + 2 \cdot g(x)]$

For the following problems, evaluate the limit using the squeeze theorem. Use a calculator to graph the functions $f(x)$, $g(x)$, and $h(x)$ when possible.

126. **[T]** True or False? If $2x - 1 \leq g(x) \leq x^2 - 2x + 3$, then $\lim_{x \to 2} g(x) = 0$.

127. **[T]** $\lim_{\theta \to 0} \theta^2 \cos\left(\frac{1}{\theta}\right)$

128. $\lim_{x \to 0} f(x)$, where $f(x) = \begin{cases} 0, & x \text{ rational} \\ x^2, & x \text{ irrrational} \end{cases}$

129. **[T]** In physics, the magnitude of an electric field generated by a point charge at a distance r in vacuum is governed by Coulomb's law: $E(r) = \frac{q}{4\pi\varepsilon_0 r^2}$, where E represents the magnitude of the electric field, q is the charge of the particle, r is the distance between the particle and where the strength of the field is measured, and $\frac{1}{4\pi\varepsilon_0}$ is Coulomb's constant: $8.988 \times 10^9 \text{ N} \cdot \text{m}^2/\text{C}^2$.

a. Use a graphing calculator to graph $E(r)$ given that the charge of the particle is $q = 10^{-10}$.

b. Evaluate $\lim_{r \to 0^+} E(r)$. What is the physical meaning of this quantity? Is it physically relevant? Why are you evaluating from the right?

130. **[T]** The density of an object is given by its mass divided by its volume: $\rho = m/V$.

a. Use a calculator to plot the volume as a function of density $(V = m/\rho)$, assuming you are examining something of mass 8 kg ($m = 8$).

b. Evaluate $\lim_{\rho \to 0^+} V(\rho)$ and explain the physical meaning.

2.4 | Continuity

Learning Objectives

2.4.1 Explain the three conditions for continuity at a point.
2.4.2 Describe three kinds of discontinuities.
2.4.3 Define continuity on an interval.
2.4.4 State the theorem for limits of composite functions.
2.4.5 Provide an example of the intermediate value theorem.

Many functions have the property that their graphs can be traced with a pencil without lifting the pencil from the page. Such functions are called *continuous*. Other functions have points at which a break in the graph occurs, but satisfy this property over intervals contained in their domains. They are continuous on these intervals and are said to have a *discontinuity at a point* where a break occurs.

We begin our investigation of continuity by exploring what it means for a function to have *continuity at a point*. Intuitively, a function is continuous at a particular point if there is no break in its graph at that point.

Continuity at a Point

Before we look at a formal definition of what it means for a function to be continuous at a point, let's consider various functions that fail to meet our intuitive notion of what it means to be continuous at a point. We then create a list of conditions that prevent such failures.

Our first function of interest is shown in **Figure 2.32**. We see that the graph of $f(x)$ has a hole at a. In fact, $f(a)$ is undefined. At the very least, for $f(x)$ to be continuous at a, we need the following condition:

i. $f(a)$ is defined.

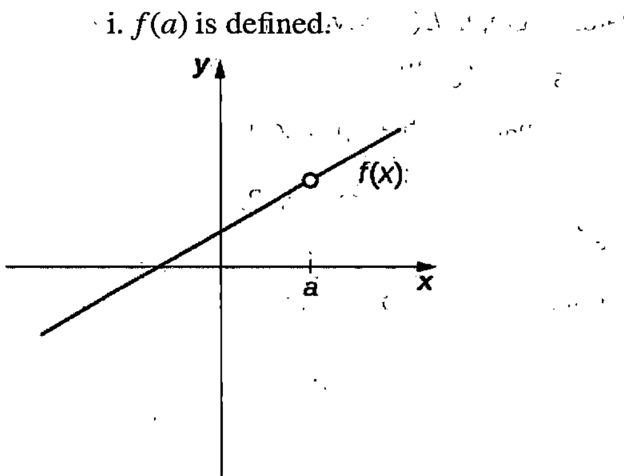

Figure 2.32 The function $f(x)$ is not continuous at a because $f(a)$ is undefined.

However, as we see in **Figure 2.33**, this condition alone is insufficient to guarantee continuity at the point a. Although $f(a)$ is defined, the function has a gap at a. In this example, the gap exists because $\lim_{x \to a} f(x)$ does not exist. We must add another condition for continuity at a—namely,

ii. $\lim_{x \to a} f(x)$ exists.

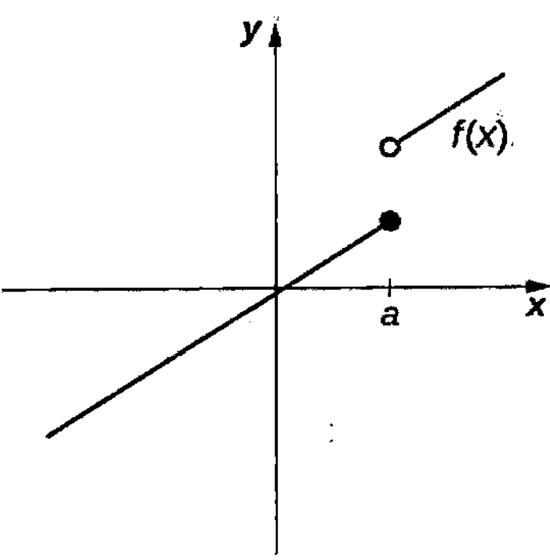

Figure 2.33 The function $f(x)$ is not continuous at a because $\lim_{x \to a} f(x)$ does not exist.

However, as we see in **Figure 2.34**, these two conditions by themselves do not guarantee continuity at a point. The function in this figure satisfies both of our first two conditions, but is still not continuous at a. We must add a third condition to our list:

iii. $\lim_{x \to a} f(x) = f(a)$.

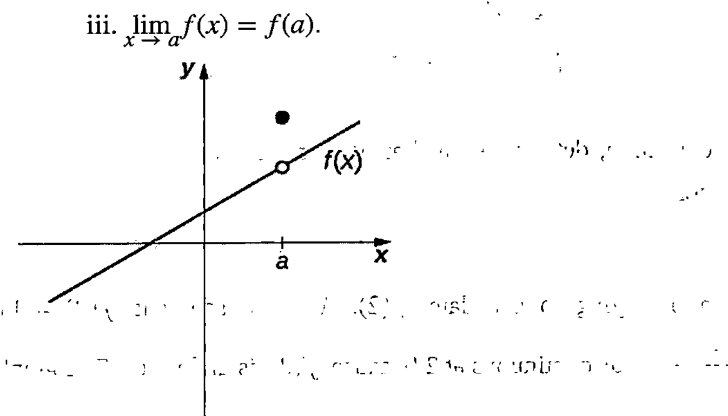

Figure 2.34 The function $f(x)$ is not continuous at a because $\lim_{x \to a} f(x) \neq f(a)$.

Now we put our list of conditions together and form a definition of continuity at a point.

Definition

A function $f(x)$ is **continuous at a point** a if and only if the following three conditions are satisfied:

i. $f(a)$ is defined

ii. $\lim_{x \to a} f(x)$ exists

iii. $\lim_{x \to a} f(x) = f(a)$

A function is **discontinuous at a point** a if it fails to be continuous at a.

The following procedure can be used to analyze the continuity of a function at a point using this definition.

Problem-Solving Strategy: Determining Continuity at a Point

1. Check to see if $f(a)$ is defined. If $f(a)$ is undefined, we need go no further. The function is not continuous at a. If $f(a)$ is defined, continue to step 2.
2. Compute $\lim_{x \to a} f(x)$. In some cases, we may need to do this by first computing $\lim_{x \to a^-} f(x)$ and $\lim_{x \to a^+} f(x)$. If $\lim_{x \to a} f(x)$ does not exist (that is, it is not a real number), then the function is not continuous at a and the problem is solved. If $\lim_{x \to a} f(x)$ exists, then continue to step 3.
3. Compare $f(a)$ and $\lim_{x \to a} f(x)$. If $\lim_{x \to a} f(x) \neq f(a)$, then the function is not continuous at a. If $\lim_{x \to a} f(x) = f(a)$, then the function is continuous at a.

The next three examples demonstrate how to apply this definition to determine whether a function is continuous at a given point. These examples illustrate situations in which each of the conditions for continuity in the definition succeed or fail.

Example 2.26

Determining Continuity at a Point, Condition 1

Using the definition, determine whether the function $f(x) = (x^2 - 4)/(x - 2)$ is continuous at $x = 2$. Justify the conclusion.

Solution

Let's begin by trying to calculate $f(2)$. We can see that $f(2) = 0/0$, which is undefined. Therefore, $f(x) = \frac{x^2 - 4}{x - 2}$ is discontinuous at 2 because $f(2)$ is undefined. The graph of $f(x)$ is shown in **Figure 2.35**.

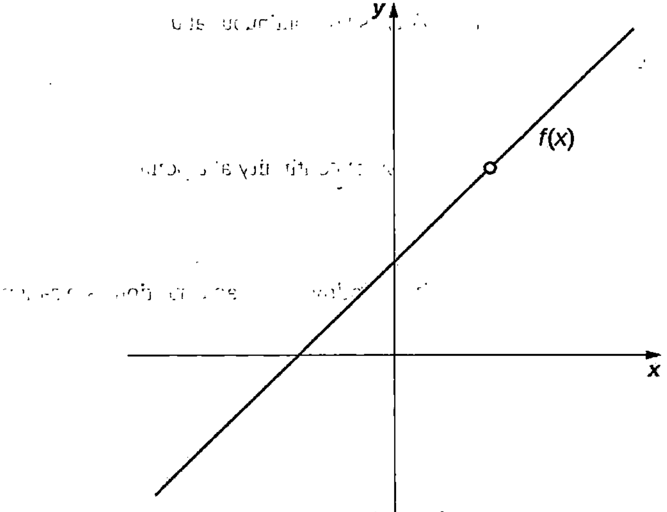

Figure 2.35 The function $f(x)$ is discontinuous at 2 because $f(2)$ is undefined.

Example 2.27

Determining Continuity at a Point, Condition 2

Using the definition, determine whether the function $f(x) = \begin{cases} -x^2 + 4 & \text{if } x \le 3 \\ 4x - 8 & \text{if } x > 3 \end{cases}$ is continuous at $x = 3$. Justify the conclusion.

Solution

Let's begin by trying to calculate $f(3)$.

$$f(3) = -(3^2) + 4 = -5.$$

Thus, $f(3)$ is defined. Next, we calculate $\lim_{x \to 3} f(x)$. To do this, we must compute $\lim_{x \to 3^-} f(x)$ and $\lim_{x \to 3^+} f(x)$:

$$\lim_{x \to 3^-} f(x) = -(3^2) + 4 = -5$$

and

$$\lim_{x \to 3^+} f(x) = 4(3) - 8 = 4.$$

Therefore, $\lim_{x \to 3} f(x)$ does not exist. Thus, $f(x)$ is not continuous at 3. The graph of $f(x)$ is shown in **Figure 2.36**.

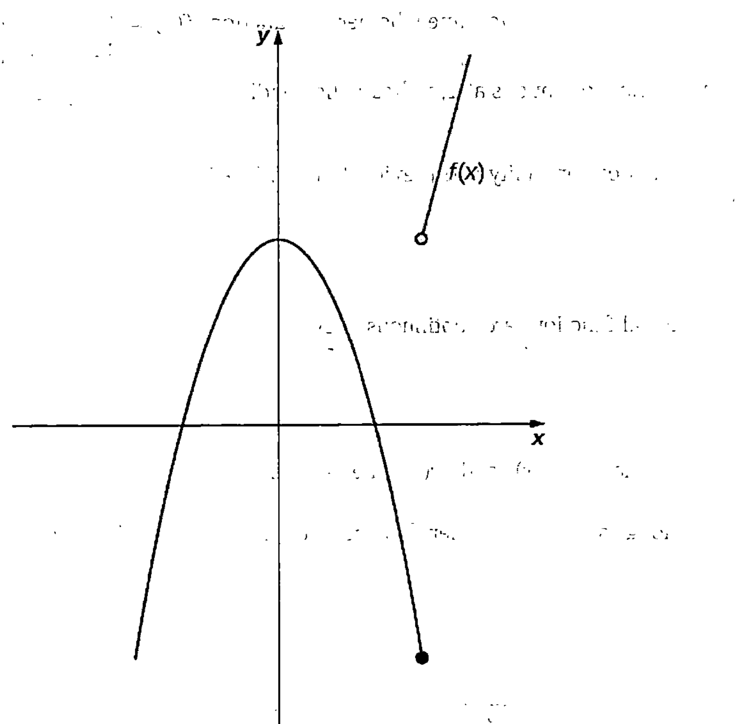

Figure 2.36 The function $f(x)$ is not continuous at 3 because $\lim_{x \to 3} f(x)$ does not exist.

Example 2.28

Determining Continuity at a Point, Condition 3

Using the definition, determine whether the function $f(x) = \begin{cases} \frac{\sin x}{x} & \text{if } x \neq 0 \\ 1 & \text{if } x = 0 \end{cases}$ is continuous at $x = 0$.

Solution

First, observe that

$$f(0) = 1.$$

Next,

$$\lim_{x \to 0} f(x) = \lim_{x \to 0} \frac{\sin x}{x} = 1.$$

Last, compare $f(0)$ and $\lim_{x \to 1} f(x)$. We see that

$$f(0) = 1 = \lim_{x \to 0} f(x).$$

Since all three of the conditions in the definition of continuity are satisfied, $f(x)$ is continuous at $x = 0$.

2.21 Using the definition, determine whether the function $f(x) = \begin{cases} 2x + 1 & \text{if } x < 1 \\ 2 & \text{if } x = 1 \\ -x + 4 & \text{if } x > 1 \end{cases}$ is continuous at $x = 1$.

If the function is not continuous at 1, indicate the condition for continuity at a point that fails to hold.

By applying the definition of continuity and previously established theorems concerning the evaluation of limits, we can state the following theorem.

Theorem 2.8: Continuity of Polynomials and Rational Functions

Polynomials and rational functions are continuous at every point in their domains.

Proof

Previously, we showed that if $p(x)$ and $q(x)$ are polynomials, $\lim_{x \to a} p(x) = p(a)$ for every polynomial $p(x)$ and $\lim_{x \to a} \frac{p(x)}{q(x)} = \frac{p(a)}{q(a)}$ as long as $q(a) \neq 0$. Therefore, polynomials and rational functions are continuous on their domains.

□

We now apply **Continuity of Polynomials and Rational Functions** to determine the points at which a given rational function is continuous.

Example 2.29

Continuity of a Rational Function

For what values of x is $f(x) = \frac{x+1}{x-5}$ continuous?

Solution

The rational function $f(x) = \frac{x+1}{x-5}$ is continuous for every value of x except $x = 5$.

2.22 For what values of x is $f(x) = 3x^4 - 4x^2$ continuous?

Types of Discontinuities

As we have seen in **Example 2.26** and **Example 2.27**, discontinuities take on several different appearances. We classify the types of discontinuities we have seen thus far as removable discontinuities, infinite discontinuities, or jump discontinuities. Intuitively, a **removable discontinuity** is a discontinuity for which there is a hole in the graph, a **jump discontinuity** is a noninfinite discontinuity for which the sections of the function do not meet up, and an **infinite discontinuity** is a discontinuity located at a vertical asymptote. **Figure 2.37** illustrates the differences in these types of discontinuities. Although these terms provide a handy way of describing three common types of discontinuities, keep in mind that not all discontinuities fit neatly into these categories.

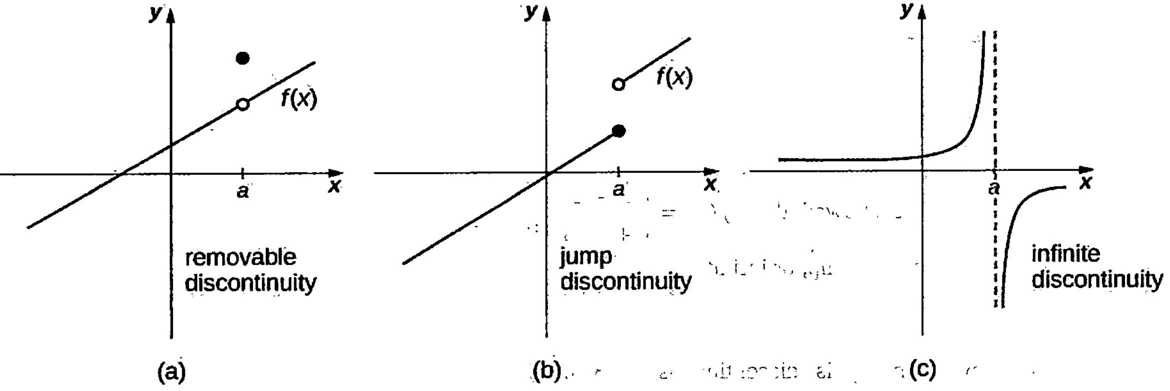

Figure 2.37 Discontinuities are classified as (a) removable, (b) jump, or (c) infinite.

These three discontinuities are formally defined as follows:

Definition

If $f(x)$ is discontinuous at a, then

1. f has a **removable discontinuity** at a if $\lim_{x \to a} f(x)$ exists. (Note: When we state that $\lim_{x \to a} f(x)$ exists, we mean that $\lim_{x \to a} f(x) = L$, where L is a real number.)
2. f has a **jump discontinuity** at a if $\lim_{x \to a^-} f(x)$ and $\lim_{x \to a^+} f(x)$ both exist, but $\lim_{x \to a^-} f(x) \neq \lim_{x \to a^+} f(x)$. (Note: When we state that $\lim_{x \to a^-} f(x)$ and $\lim_{x \to a^+} f(x)$ both exist, we mean that both are real-valued and that neither take on the values $\pm\infty$.)
3. f has an **infinite discontinuity** at a if $\lim_{x \to a^-} f(x) = \pm\infty$ or $\lim_{x \to a^+} f(x) = \pm\infty$.

Example 2.30

Classifying a Discontinuity

In **Example 2.26**, we showed that $f(x) = \frac{x^2 - 4}{x - 2}$ is discontinuous at $x = 2$. Classify this discontinuity as removable, jump, or infinite.

Solution

To classify the discontinuity at 2 we must evaluate $\lim_{x \to 2} f(x)$:

$$\begin{aligned} \lim_{x \to 2} f(x) &= \lim_{x \to 2} \frac{x^2 - 4}{x - 2} \\ &= \lim_{x \to 2} \frac{(x-2)(x+2)}{x - 2} \\ &= \lim_{x \to 2} (x + 2) \\ &= 4. \end{aligned}$$

Since f is discontinuous at 2 and $\lim_{x \to 2} f(x)$ exists, f has a removable discontinuity at $x = 2$.

Example 2.31

Classifying a Discontinuity

In **Example 2.27**, we showed that $f(x) = \begin{cases} -x^2 + 4 & \text{if } x \le 3 \\ 4x - 8 & \text{if } x > 3 \end{cases}$ is discontinuous at $x = 3$. Classify this discontinuity as removable, jump, or infinite.

Solution

Earlier, we showed that f is discontinuous at 3 because $\lim_{x \to 3} f(x)$ does not exist. However, since $\lim_{x \to 3^-} f(x) = -5$ and $\lim_{x \to 3^-} f(x) = 4$ both exist, we conclude that the function has a jump discontinuity at 3.

Example 2.32

Classifying a Discontinuity

Determine whether $f(x) = \frac{x + 2}{x + 1}$ is continuous at −1. If the function is discontinuous at −1, classify the discontinuity as removable, jump, or infinite.

Solution

The function value $f(-1)$ is undefined. Therefore, the function is not continuous at −1. To determine the type of discontinuity, we must determine the limit at −1. We see that $\lim_{x \to -1^-} \frac{x+2}{x+1} = -\infty$ and $\lim_{x \to -1^+} \frac{x+2}{x+1} = +\infty$. Therefore, the function has an infinite discontinuity at −1.

2.23 For $f(x) = \begin{cases} x^2 & \text{if } x \neq 1 \\ 3 & \text{if } x = 1 \end{cases}$, decide whether f is continuous at 1. If f is not continuous at 1, classify the discontinuity as removable, jump, or infinite.

Continuity over an Interval

Now that we have explored the concept of continuity at a point, we extend that idea to **continuity over an interval**. As we develop this idea for different types of intervals, it may be useful to keep in mind the intuitive idea that a function is continuous over an interval if we can use a pencil to trace the function between any two points in the interval without lifting the pencil from the paper. In preparation for defining continuity on an interval, we begin by looking at the definition of what it means for a function to be continuous from the right at a point and continuous from the left at a point.

Continuity from the Right and from the Left

A function $f(x)$ is said to be **continuous from the right** at a if $\lim_{x \to a^+} f(x) = f(a)$.

A function $f(x)$ is said to be **continuous from the left** at a if $\lim_{x \to a^-} f(x) = f(a)$.

A function is continuous over an open interval if it is continuous at every point in the interval. A function $f(x)$ is continuous over a closed interval of the form $[a, b]$ if it is continuous at every point in (a, b) and is continuous from the right at a and is continuous from the left at b. Analogously, a function $f(x)$ is continuous over an interval of the form $(a, b]$ if it is continuous over (a, b) and is continuous from the left at b. Continuity over other types of intervals are defined in a similar fashion.

Requiring that $\lim_{x \to a^+} f(x) = f(a)$ and $\lim_{x \to b^-} f(x) = f(b)$ ensures that we can trace the graph of the function from the point $(a, f(a))$ to the point $(b, f(b))$ without lifting the pencil. If, for example, $\lim_{x \to a^+} f(x) \neq f(a)$, we would need to lift our pencil to jump from $f(a)$ to the graph of the rest of the function over $(a, b]$.

Example 2.33

Continuity on an Interval

State the interval(s) over which the function $f(x) = \frac{x-1}{x^2+2x}$ is continuous.

Solution

Since $f(x) = \frac{x-1}{x^2+2x}$ is a rational function, it is continuous at every point in its domain. The domain of $f(x)$ is the set $(-\infty, -2) \cup (-2, 0) \cup (0, +\infty)$. Thus, $f(x)$ is continuous over each of the intervals

$(-\infty, -2), (-2, 0)$, and $(0, +\infty)$.

Example 2.34

Continuity over an Interval

State the interval(s) over which the function $f(x) = \sqrt{4 - x^2}$ is continuous.

Solution

From the limit laws, we know that $\lim_{x \to a} \sqrt{4 - x^2} = \sqrt{4 - a^2}$ for all values of a in $(-2, 2)$. We also know that $\lim_{x \to -2^+} \sqrt{4 - x^2} = 0$ exists and $\lim_{x \to 2^-} \sqrt{4 - x^2} = 0$ exists. Therefore, $f(x)$ is continuous over the interval $[-2, 2]$.

2.24 State the interval(s) over which the function $f(x) = \sqrt{x + 3}$ is continuous.

The **Composite Function Theorem** allows us to expand our ability to compute limits. In particular, this theorem ultimately allows us to demonstrate that trigonometric functions are continuous over their domains.

Theorem 2.9: Composite Function Theorem

If $f(x)$ is continuous at L and $\lim_{x \to a} g(x) = L$, then

$$\lim_{x \to a} f(g(x)) = f\left(\lim_{x \to a} g(x)\right) = f(L).$$

Before we move on to **Example 2.35**, recall that earlier, in the section on limit laws, we showed $\lim_{x \to 0} \cos x = 1 = \cos(0)$. Consequently, we know that $f(x) = \cos x$ is continuous at 0. In **Example 2.35** we see how to combine this result with the composite function theorem.

Example 2.35

Limit of a Composite Cosine Function

Evaluate $\lim_{x \to \pi/2} \cos\left(x - \frac{\pi}{2}\right)$.

Solution

The given function is a composite of $\cos x$ and $x - \frac{\pi}{2}$. Since $\lim_{x \to \pi/2} \left(x - \frac{\pi}{2}\right) = 0$ and $\cos x$ is continuous at 0, we may apply the composite function theorem. Thus,

$$\lim_{x \to \pi/2} \cos\left(x - \frac{\pi}{2}\right) = \cos\left(\lim_{x \to \pi/2}\left(x - \frac{\pi}{2}\right)\right) = \cos(0) = 1.$$

2.25 Evaluate $\lim_{x \to \pi} \sin(x - \pi)$.

The proof of the next theorem uses the composite function theorem as well as the continuity of $f(x) = \sin x$ and $g(x) = \cos x$ at the point 0 to show that trigonometric functions are continuous over their entire domains.

Theorem 2.10: Continuity of Trigonometric Functions

Trigonometric functions are continuous over their entire domains.

Proof

We begin by demonstrating that $\cos x$ is continuous at every real number. To do this, we must show that $\lim_{x \to a} \cos x = \cos a$ for all values of a.

$$\begin{aligned}
\lim_{x \to a} \cos x &= \lim_{x \to a} \cos((x - a) + a) && \text{rewrite } x = x - a + a \\
&= \lim_{x \to a} (\cos(x - a)\cos a - \sin(x - a)\sin a) && \text{apply the identity for the cosine of the sum of two angles} \\
&= \cos\left(\lim_{x \to a}(x - a)\right)\cos a - \sin\left(\lim_{x \to a}(x - a)\right)\sin a && \lim_{x \to a}(x - a) = 0, \text{ and } \sin x \text{ and } \cos x \text{ are continuous at 0} \\
&= \cos(0)\cos a - \sin(0)\sin a && \text{evaluate } \cos(0) \text{ and } \sin(0) \text{ and simplify} \\
&= 1 \cdot \cos a - 0 \cdot \sin a = \cos a.
\end{aligned}$$

The proof that $\sin x$ is continuous at every real number is analogous. Because the remaining trigonometric functions may be expressed in terms of $\sin x$ and $\cos x$, their continuity follows from the quotient limit law.

□

As you can see, the composite function theorem is invaluable in demonstrating the continuity of trigonometric functions. As we continue our study of calculus, we revisit this theorem many times.

The Intermediate Value Theorem

Functions that are continuous over intervals of the form $[a, b]$, where a and b are real numbers, exhibit many useful properties. Throughout our study of calculus, we will encounter many powerful theorems concerning such functions. The first of these theorems is the **Intermediate Value Theorem**.

Theorem 2.11: The Intermediate Value Theorem

Let f be continuous over a closed, bounded interval $[a, b]$. If z is any real number between $f(a)$ and $f(b)$, then there is a number c in $[a, b]$ satisfying $f(c) = z$ in **Figure 2.38**.

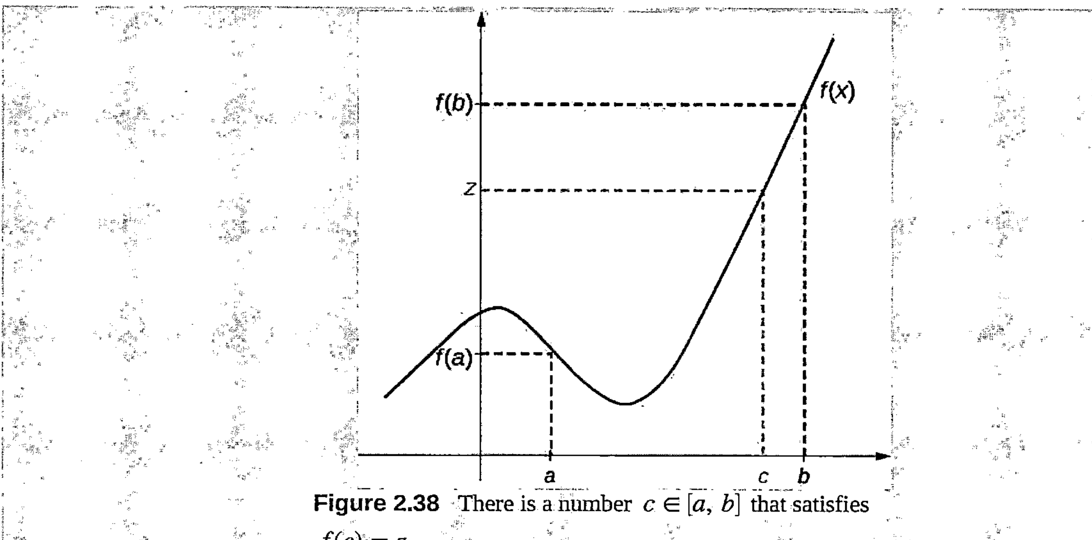

Figure 2.38 There is a number $c \in [a, b]$ that satisfies $f(c) = z$.

Example 2.36

Application of the Intermediate Value Theorem

Show that $f(x) = x - \cos x$ has at least one zero.

Solution

Since $f(x) = x - \cos x$ is continuous over $(-\infty, +\infty)$, it is continuous over any closed interval of the form $[a, b]$. If you can find an interval $[a, b]$ such that $f(a)$ and $f(b)$ have opposite signs, you can use the Intermediate Value Theorem to conclude there must be a real number c in (a, b) that satisfies $f(c) = 0$. Note that

$$f(0) = 0 - \cos(0) = -1 < 0$$

and

$$f\left(\frac{\pi}{2}\right) = \frac{\pi}{2} - \cos\frac{\pi}{2} = \frac{\pi}{2} > 0.$$

Using the Intermediate Value Theorem, we can see that there must be a real number c in $[0, \pi/2]$ that satisfies $f(c) = 0$. Therefore, $f(x) = x - \cos x$ has at least one zero.

Example 2.37

When Can You Apply the Intermediate Value Theorem?

If $f(x)$ is continuous over $[0, 2]$, $f(0) > 0$ and $f(2) > 0$, can we use the Intermediate Value Theorem to conclude that $f(x)$ has no zeros in the interval $[0, 2]$? Explain.

Solution

No. The Intermediate Value Theorem only allows us to conclude that we can find a value between $f(0)$ and $f(2)$; it doesn't allow us to conclude that we can't find other values. To see this more clearly, consider the function $f(x) = (x-1)^2$. It satisfies $f(0) = 1 > 0, f(2) = 1 > 0,$ and $f(1) = 0.$

Example 2.38

When Can You Apply the Intermediate Value Theorem?

For $f(x) = 1/x, f(-1) = -1 < 0$ and $f(1) = 1 > 0.$ Can we conclude that $f(x)$ has a zero in the interval $[-1, 1]$?

Solution

No. The function is not continuous over $[-1, 1]$. The Intermediate Value Theorem does not apply here.

2.26 Show that $f(x) = x^3 - x^2 - 3x + 1$ has a zero over the interval $[0, 1]$.

2.4 EXERCISES

For the following exercises, determine the point(s), if any, at which each function is discontinuous. Classify any discontinuity as jump, removable, infinite, or other.

131. $f(x) = \frac{1}{\sqrt{x}}$

132. $f(x) = \frac{2}{x^2 + 1}$

133. $f(x) = \frac{x}{x^2 - x}$

134. $g(t) = t^{-1} + 1$

135. $f(x) = \frac{5}{e^x - 2}$

136. $f(x) = \frac{|x-2|}{x-2}$

137. $H(x) = \tan 2x$

138. $f(t) = \frac{t+3}{t^2 + 5t + 6}$

For the following exercises, decide if the function continuous at the given point. If it is discontinuous, what type of discontinuity is it?

139. $\frac{2x^2 - 5x + 3}{x - 1}$ at $x = 1$

140. $h(\theta) = \frac{\sin\theta - \cos\theta}{\tan\theta}$ at $\theta = \pi$

141. $g(u) = \begin{cases} \frac{6u^2 + u - 2}{2u - 1} & \text{if } u \neq \frac{1}{2} \\ \frac{7}{2} & \text{if } u = \frac{1}{2} \end{cases}$, at $u = \frac{1}{2}$

142. $f(y) = \frac{\sin(\pi y)}{\tan(\pi y)}$, at $y = 1$

143. $f(x) = \begin{cases} x^2 - e^x & \text{if } x < 0 \\ x - 1 & \text{if } x \geq 0 \end{cases}$, at $x = 0$

144. $f(x) = \begin{cases} x\sin(x) \text{ if } x \leq \pi \\ x\tan(x) \text{ if } x > \pi \end{cases}$, at $x = \pi$

In the following exercises, find the value(s) of k that makes each function continuous over the given interval.

145. $f(x) = \begin{cases} 3x + 2, & x < k \\ 2x - 3, & k \leq x \leq 8 \end{cases}$

146. $f(\theta) = \begin{cases} \sin\theta, & 0 \leq \theta < \frac{\pi}{2} \\ \cos(\theta + k), & \frac{\pi}{2} \leq \theta \leq \pi \end{cases}$

147. $f(x) = \begin{cases} \frac{x^2 + 3x + 2}{x + 2}, & x \neq -2 \\ k, & x = -2 \end{cases}$

148. $f(x) = \begin{cases} e^{kx}, & 0 \leq x < 4 \\ x + 3, & 4 \leq x \leq 8 \end{cases}$

149. $f(x) = \begin{cases} \sqrt{kx}, & 0 \leq x \leq 3 \\ x + 1, & 3 < x \leq 10 \end{cases}$

In the following exercises, use the Intermediate Value Theorem (IVT).

150. Let $h(x) = \begin{cases} 3x^2 - 4, & x \leq 2 \\ 5 + 4x, & x > 2 \end{cases}$ Over the interval $[0, 4]$, there is no value of x such that $h(x) = 10$, although $h(0) < 10$ and $h(4) > 10$. Explain why this does not contradict the IVT.

151. A particle moving along a line has at each time t a position function $s(t)$, which is continuous. Assume $s(2) = 5$ and $s(5) = 2$. Another particle moves such that its position is given by $h(t) = s(t) - t$. Explain why there must be a value c for $2 < c < 5$ such that $h(c) = 0$.

152. **[T]** Use the statement "The cosine of t is equal to t cubed."

a. Write a mathematical equation of the statement.
b. Prove that the equation in part a. has at least one real solution.
c. Use a calculator to find an interval of length 0.01 that contains a solution.

153. Apply the IVT to determine whether $2^x = x^3$ has a solution in one of the intervals $[1.25, 1.375]$ or $[1.375, 1.5]$. Briefly explain your response for each interval.

154. Consider the graph of the function $y = f(x)$ shown in the following graph.

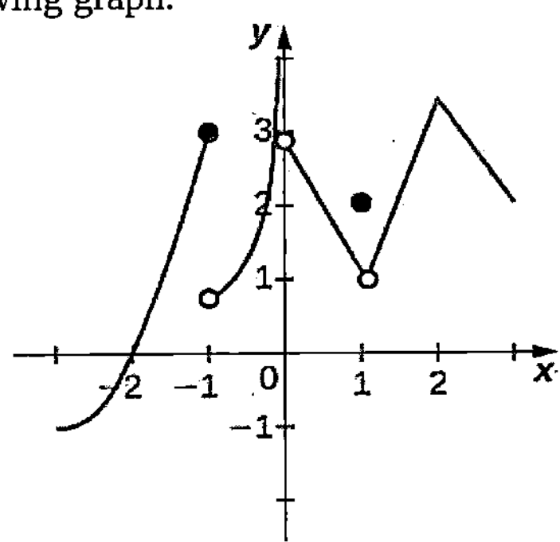

a. Find all values for which the function is discontinuous.
b. For each value in part a., state why the formal definition of continuity does not apply.
c. Classify each discontinuity as either jump, removable, or infinite.

155. Let $f(x) = \begin{cases} 3x, & x > 1 \\ x^3, & x < 1 \end{cases}$.

a. Sketch the graph of f.
b. Is it possible to find a value k such that $f(1) = k$, which makes $f(x)$ continuous for all real numbers? Briefly explain.

156. Let $f(x) = \dfrac{x^4 - 1}{x^2 - 1}$ for $x \neq -1, 1$.

a. Sketch the graph of f.
b. Is it possible to find values k_1 and k_2 such that $f(-1) = k$ and $f(1) = k_2$, and that makes $f(x)$ continuous for all real numbers? Briefly explain.

157. Sketch the graph of the function $y = f(x)$ with properties i. through vii.

i. The domain of f is $(-\infty, +\infty)$.
ii. f has an infinite discontinuity at $x = -6$.
iii. $f(-6) = 3$
iv. $\lim\limits_{x \to -3^-} f(x) = \lim\limits_{x \to -3^+} f(x) = 2$
v. $f(-3) = 3$
vi. f is left continuous but not right continuous at $x = 3$.
vii. $\lim\limits_{x \to -\infty} f(x) = -\infty$ and $\lim\limits_{x \to +\infty} f(x) = +\infty$

158. Sketch the graph of the function $y = f(x)$ with properties i. through iv.

i. The domain of f is $[0, 5]$.
ii. $\lim\limits_{x \to 1^+} f(x)$ and $\lim\limits_{x \to 1^-} f(x)$ exist and are equal.
iii. $f(x)$ is left continuous but not continuous at $x = 2$, and right continuous but not continuous at $x = 3$.
iv. $f(x)$ has a removable discontinuity at $x = 1$, a jump discontinuity at $x = 2$, and the following limits hold: $\lim\limits_{x \to 3^-} f(x) = -\infty$ and $\lim\limits_{x \to 3^+} f(x) = 2$.

In the following exercises, suppose $y = f(x)$ is defined for all x. For each description, sketch a graph with the indicated property.

159. Discontinuous at $x = 1$ with $\lim\limits_{x \to -1} f(x) = -1$ and $\lim\limits_{x \to 2} f(x) = 4$

160. Discontinuous at $x = 2$ but continuous elsewhere with $\lim\limits_{x \to 0} f(x) = \frac{1}{2}$

Determine whether each of the given statements is true. Justify your response with an explanation or counterexample.

161. $f(t) = \dfrac{2}{e^t - e^{-t}}$ is continuous everywhere.

162. If the left- and right-hand limits of $f(x)$ as $x \to a$ exist and are equal, then f cannot be discontinuous at $x = a$.

163. If a function is not continuous at a point, then it is not defined at that point.

164. According to the IVT, $\cos x - \sin x - x = 2$ has a solution over the interval $[-1, 1]$.

165. If $f(x)$ is continuous such that $f(a)$ and $f(b)$ have opposite signs, then $f(x) = 0$ has exactly one solution in $[a, b]$.

166. The function $f(x) = \dfrac{x^2 - 4x + 3}{x^2 - 1}$ is continuous over the interval $[0, 3]$.

167. If $f(x)$ is continuous everywhere and $f(a), f(b) > 0,$ then there is no root of $f(x)$ in the interval $[a, b]$.

[T] The following problems consider the scalar form of Coulomb's law, which describes the electrostatic force between two point charges, such as electrons. It is given by the equation $F(r) = k_e \frac{|q_1 q_2|}{r^2}$, where k_e is Coulomb's constant, q_i are the magnitudes of the charges of the two particles, and r is the distance between the two particles.

168. To simplify the calculation of a model with many interacting particles, after some threshold value $r = R,$ we approximate F as zero.

a. Explain the physical reasoning behind this assumption.
b. What is the force equation?
c. Evaluate the force F using both Coulomb's law and our approximation, assuming two protons with a charge magnitude of 1.6022×10^{-19} coulombs (C), and the Coulomb constant $k_e = 8.988 \times 10^9 \text{Nm}^2/\text{C}^2$ are 1 m apart. Also, assume $R < 1$ m. How much inaccuracy does our approximation generate? Is our approximation reasonable?
d. Is there any finite value of R for which this system remains continuous at R?

169. Instead of making the force 0 at R, instead we let the force be 10^{-20} for $r \geq R$. Assume two protons, which have a magnitude of charge 1.6022×10^{-19} C, and the Coulomb constant $k_e = 8.988 \times 10^9 \text{Nm}^2/\text{C}^2$. Is there a value R that can make this system continuous? If so, find it.

Recall the discussion on spacecraft from the chapter opener. The following problems consider a rocket launch from Earth's surface. The force of gravity on the rocket is given by $F(d) = -mk/d^2$, where m is the mass of the rocket, d is the distance of the rocket from the center of Earth, and k is a constant.

170. **[T]** Determine the value and units of k given that the mass of the rocket on Earth is 3 million kg. (*Hint*: The distance from the center of Earth to its surface is 6378 km.)

171. **[T]** After a certain distance D has passed, the gravitational effect of Earth becomes quite negligible, so we can approximate the force function by $F(d) = \begin{cases} -\frac{mk}{d^2} & \text{if } d < D \\ 10{,}000 & \text{if } d \geq D \end{cases}$. Find the necessary condition D such that the force function remains continuous.

172. As the rocket travels away from Earth's surface, there is a distance D where the rocket sheds some of its mass, since it no longer needs the excess fuel storage. We can write this function as $F(d) = \begin{cases} -\frac{m_1 k}{d^2} \text{ if } d < D \\ -\frac{m_2 k}{d^2} \text{ if } d \geq D \end{cases}$. Is there a D value such that this function is continuous, assuming $m_1 \neq m_2$?

Prove the following functions are continuous everywhere

173. $f(\theta) = \sin\theta$

174. $g(x) = |x|$

175. Where is $f(x) = \begin{cases} 0 \text{ if } x \text{ is irrational} \\ 1 \text{ if } x \text{ is rational} \end{cases}$ continuous?

2.5 | The Precise Definition of a Limit

Learning Objectives

2.5.1 Describe the epsilon-delta definition of a limit.
2.5.2 Apply the epsilon-delta definition to find the limit of a function.
2.5.3 Describe the epsilon-delta definitions of one-sided limits and infinite limits.
2.5.4 Use the epsilon-delta definition to prove the limit laws.

By now you have progressed from the very informal definition of a limit in the introduction of this chapter to the intuitive understanding of a limit. At this point, you should have a very strong intuitive sense of what the limit of a function means and how you can find it. In this section, we convert this intuitive idea of a limit into a formal definition using precise mathematical language. The formal definition of a limit is quite possibly one of the most challenging definitions you will encounter early in your study of calculus; however, it is well worth any effort you make to reconcile it with your intuitive notion of a limit. Understanding this definition is the key that opens the door to a better understanding of calculus.

Quantifying Closeness

Before stating the formal definition of a limit, we must introduce a few preliminary ideas. Recall that the distance between two points a and b on a number line is given by $|a-b|$.

- The statement $|f(x)-L|<\varepsilon$ may be interpreted as: *The distance between* $f(x)$ *and L is less than ε.*
- The statement $0<|x-a|<\delta$ may be interpreted as: $x \neq a$ *and the distance between x and a is less than δ.*

It is also important to look at the following equivalences for absolute value:

- The statement $|f(x)-L|<\varepsilon$ is equivalent to the statement $L-\varepsilon<f(x)<L+\varepsilon$.
- The statement $0<|x-a|<\delta$ is equivalent to the statement $a-\delta<x<a+\delta$ and $x \neq a$.

With these clarifications, we can state the formal **epsilon-delta definition of the limit**.

Definition

Let $f(x)$ be defined for all $x \neq a$ over an open interval containing a. Let L be a real number. Then

$$\lim_{x \to a} f(x) = L$$

if, for every $\varepsilon>0$, there exists a $\delta>0$, such that if $0<|x-a|<\delta$, then $|f(x)-L|<\varepsilon$.

This definition may seem rather complex from a mathematical point of view, but it becomes easier to understand if we break it down phrase by phrase. The statement itself involves something called a *universal quantifier* (for every $\varepsilon>0$), an *existential quantifier* (there exists a $\delta>0$), and, last, a *conditional statement* (if $0<|x-a|<\delta$, then $|f(x)-L|<\varepsilon$). Let's take a look at **Table 2.9**, which breaks down the definition and translates each part.

Definition	Translation
1. For every $\varepsilon > 0,$	1. For every positive distance ε from L,
2. there exists a $\delta > 0,$	2. There is a positive distance δ from a,
3. such that	3. such that
4. if $0 < \lvert x - a \rvert < \delta,$ then $\lvert f(x) - L \rvert < \varepsilon.$	4. if x is closer than δ to a and $x \neq a,$ then $f(x)$ is closer than ε to L.

Table 2.9 Translation of the Epsilon-Delta Definition of the Limit

We can get a better handle on this definition by looking at the definition geometrically. **Figure 2.39** shows possible values of δ for various choices of $\varepsilon > 0$ for a given function $f(x),$ a number $a,$ and a limit L at $a.$ Notice that as we choose smaller values of ε (the distance between the function and the limit), we can always find a δ small enough so that if we have chosen an x value within δ of a, then the value of $f(x)$ is within ε of the limit L.

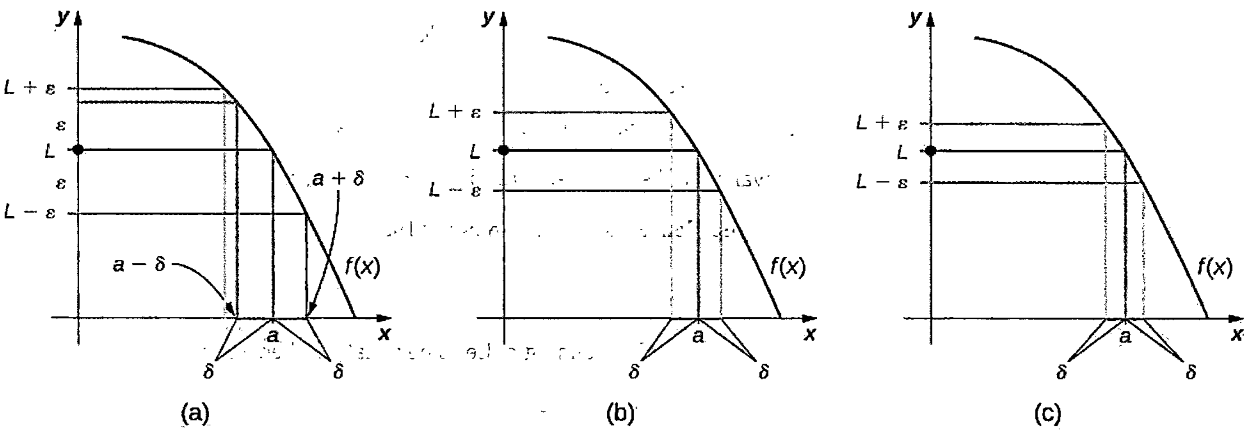

Figure 2.39 These graphs show possible values of δ, given successively smaller choices of ε.

Visit the following applet to experiment with finding values of δ for selected values of ε:

- **The epsilon-delta definition of limit (http://www.openstaxcollege.org/l/20_epsilondelt)**

Example 2.39 shows how you can use this definition to prove a statement about the limit of a specific function at a specified value.

Example 2.39

Proving a Statement about the Limit of a Specific Function

Prove that $\lim\limits_{x \to 1} (2x + 1) = 3.$

Solution

Let $\varepsilon > 0$.

The first part of the definition begins "For every $\varepsilon > 0$." This means we must prove that whatever follows is true no matter what positive value of ε is chosen. By stating "Let $\varepsilon > 0$," we signal our intent to do so.

Choose $\delta = \frac{\varepsilon}{2}$.

The definition continues with "there exists a $\delta > 0$." The phrase "there exists" in a mathematical statement is always a signal for a scavenger hunt. In other words, we must go and find δ. So, where exactly did $\delta = \varepsilon/2$ come from? There are two basic approaches to tracking down δ. One method is purely algebraic and the other is geometric.

We begin by tackling the problem from an algebraic point of view. Since ultimately we want $|(2x+1)-3| < \varepsilon$, we begin by manipulating this expression: $|(2x+1)-3| < \varepsilon$ is equivalent to $|2x-2| < \varepsilon$, which in turn is equivalent to $|2||x-1| < \varepsilon$. Last, this is equivalent to $|x-1| < \varepsilon/2$. Thus, it would seem that $\delta = \varepsilon/2$ is appropriate.

We may also find δ through geometric methods. **Figure 2.40** demonstrates how this is done.

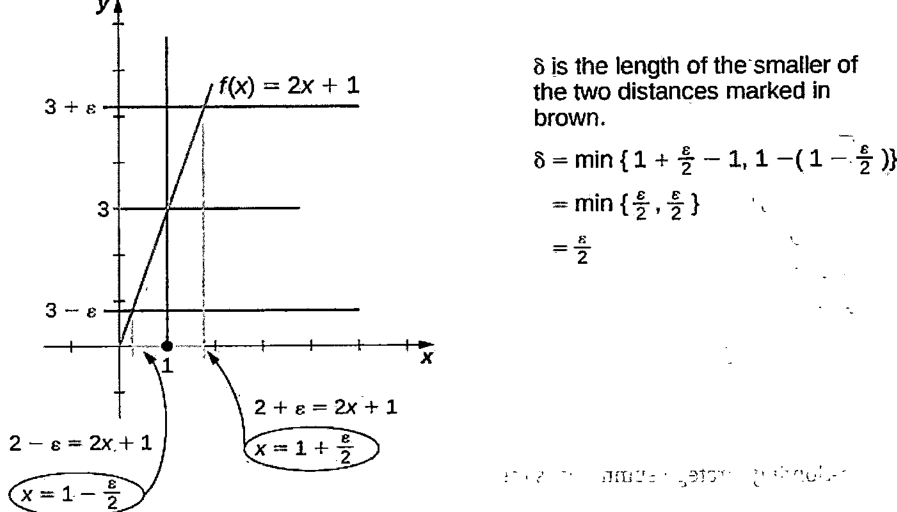

Figure 2.40 This graph shows how we find δ geometrically.

Assume $0 < |x-1| < \delta$. When δ has been chosen, our goal is to show that if $0 < |x-1| < \delta$, then $|(2x+1)-3| < \varepsilon$. To prove any statement of the form "If this, then that," we begin by assuming "this" and trying to get "that."

Thus,

$$\begin{aligned} |(2x+1)-3| &= |2x-2| && \text{property of absolute value} \\ &= |2(x-1)| \\ &= |2||x-1| && |2| = 2 \\ &= 2|x-1| \\ &< 2 \cdot \delta && \text{here's where we use the assumption that } 0 < |x-1| < \delta \\ &= 2 \cdot \frac{\varepsilon}{2} = \varepsilon && \text{here's where we use our choice of } \delta = \varepsilon/2 \end{aligned}$$

Analysis

In this part of the proof, we started with $|(2x+1)-3|$ and used our assumption $0 < |x-1| < \delta$ in a key part of the chain of inequalities to get $|(2x+1)-3|$ to be less than ε. We could just as easily have manipulated the assumed inequality $0 < |x-1| < \delta$ to arrive at $|(2x+1)-3| < \varepsilon$ as follows:

$$\begin{aligned} 0 < |x-1| < \delta &\Rightarrow |x-1| < \delta \\ &\Rightarrow -\delta < x-1 < \delta \\ &\Rightarrow -\frac{\varepsilon}{2} < x-1 < \frac{\varepsilon}{2} \\ &\Rightarrow -\varepsilon < 2x-2 < \varepsilon \\ &\Rightarrow -\varepsilon < 2x-2 < \varepsilon \\ &\Rightarrow |2x-2| < \varepsilon \\ &\Rightarrow |(2x+1)-3| < \varepsilon. \end{aligned}$$

Therefore, $\lim\limits_{x \to 1}(2x+1) = 3$. (Having completed the proof, we state what we have accomplished.)

After removing all the remarks, here is a final version of the proof:

Let $\varepsilon > 0$.

Choose $\delta = \varepsilon/2$.

Assume $0 < |x-1| < \delta$.

Thus,

$$\begin{aligned} |(2x+1)-3| &= |2x-2| \\ &= |2(x-1)| \\ &= |2||x-1| \\ &= 2|x-1| \\ &< 2 \cdot \delta \\ &= 2 \cdot \frac{\varepsilon}{2} \\ &= \varepsilon. \end{aligned}$$

Therefore, $\lim\limits_{x \to 1}(2x+1) = 3$.

The following Problem-Solving Strategy summarizes the type of proof we worked out in **Example 2.39**.

Problem-Solving Strategy: Proving That $\lim\limits_{x \to a} f(x) = L$ for a Specific Function $f(x)$

1. Let's begin the proof with the following statement: Let $\varepsilon > 0$.
2. Next, we need to obtain a value for δ. After we have obtained this value, we make the following statement, filling in the blank with our choice of δ: Choose $\delta =$ _______.
3. The next statement in the proof should be (at this point, we fill in our given value for a):
   Assume $0 < |x-a| < \delta$.
4. Next, based on this assumption, we need to show that $|f(x)-L| < \varepsilon$, where $f(x)$ and L are our function $f(x)$ and our limit L. At some point, we need to use $0 < |x-a| < \delta$.
5. We conclude our proof with the statement: Therefore, $\lim\limits_{x \to a} f(x) = L$.

Example 2.40

Proving a Statement about a Limit

Complete the proof that $\lim_{x \to -1} (4x + 1) = -3$ by filling in the blanks.

Let _____.

Choose $\delta =$ _______.

Assume $0 < |x -$ _______$| < \delta$.

Thus, $|$________ $-$ ________$| =$ ____ε.

Solution

We begin by filling in the blanks where the choices are specified by the definition. Thus, we have

Let $\varepsilon > 0$.

Choose $\delta =$ _______.

Assume $0 < |x - (-1)| < \delta$. (or equivalently, $0 < |x + 1| < \delta$.)

Thus, $|(4x + 1) - (-3)| = |4x + 4| = |4||x + 1| < 4\delta$_______$\varepsilon$.

Focusing on the final line of the proof, we see that we should choose $\delta = \frac{\varepsilon}{4}$.

We now complete the final write-up of the proof:

Let $\varepsilon > 0$.

Choose $\delta = \frac{\varepsilon}{4}$.

Assume $0 < |x - (-1)| < \delta$ (or equivalently, $0 < |x + 1| < \delta$.)

Thus, $|(4x + 1) - (-3)| = |4x + 4| = |4||x + 1| < 4\delta = 4(\varepsilon/4) = \varepsilon$.

2.27 Complete the proof that $\lim_{x \to 2} (3x - 2) = 4$ by filling in the blanks.

Let _______.

Choose $\delta =$ _______.

Assume $0 < |x -$ ____$| <$ ____.

Thus,

$|$_______ $-$ ____$| =$ ________________________________ε.

Therefore, $\lim_{x \to 2} (3x - 2) = 4$.

In **Example 2.39** and **Example 2.40**, the proofs were fairly straightforward, since the functions with which we were working were linear. In **Example 2.41**, we see how to modify the proof to accommodate a nonlinear function.

Example 2.41

Proving a Statement about the Limit of a Specific Function (Geometric Approach)

Prove that $\lim_{x \to 2} x^2 = 4$.

Solution

1. Let $\varepsilon > 0$. The first part of the definition begins "For every $\varepsilon > 0$," so we must prove that whatever follows is true no matter what positive value of ε is chosen. By stating "Let $\varepsilon > 0$," we signal our intent to do so.
2. Without loss of generality, assume $\varepsilon \leq 4$. Two questions present themselves: Why do we want $\varepsilon \leq 4$ and why is it okay to make this assumption? In answer to the first question: Later on, in the process of solving for δ, we will discover that δ involves the quantity $\sqrt{4-\varepsilon}$. Consequently, we need $\varepsilon \leq 4$. In answer to the second question: If we can find $\delta > 0$ that "works" for $\varepsilon \leq 4$, then it will "work" for any $\varepsilon > 4$ as well. Keep in mind that, although it is always okay to put an upper bound on ε, it is never okay to put a lower bound (other than zero) on ε.
3. Choose $\delta = \min\{2-\sqrt{4-\varepsilon}, \sqrt{4+\varepsilon}-2\}$. **Figure 2.41** shows how we made this choice of δ.

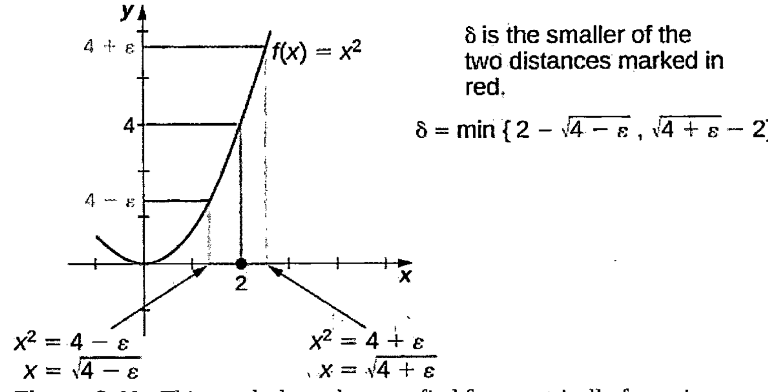

Figure 2.41 This graph shows how we find δ geometrically for a given ε for the proof in **Example 2.41**.

4. We must show: If $0 < |x-2| < \delta$, then $|x^2-4| < \varepsilon$, so we must begin by assuming

$$0 < |x-2| < \delta.$$

We don't really need $0 < |x-2|$ (in other words, $x \neq 2$) for this proof. Since $0 < |x-2| < \delta \Rightarrow |x-2| < \delta$, it is okay to drop $0 < |x-2|$.

$$|x-2| < \delta.$$

Hence,

$$-\delta < x-2 < \delta.$$

Recall that $\delta = \min\{2-\sqrt{4-\varepsilon}, \sqrt{4+\varepsilon}-2\}$. Thus, $\delta \geq 2-\sqrt{4-\varepsilon}$ and consequently $-(2-\sqrt{4-\varepsilon}) \leq -\delta$. We also use $\delta \leq \sqrt{4+\varepsilon}-2$ here. We might ask at this point: Why did we substitute $2-\sqrt{4-\varepsilon}$ for δ on the left-hand side of the inequality and $\sqrt{4+\varepsilon}-2$ on the right-hand side of the inequality? If we look at **Figure 2.41**, we see that $2-\sqrt{4-\varepsilon}$ corresponds to the distance on the left of 2 on the x-axis and $\sqrt{4+\varepsilon}-2$ corresponds to the distance on the right. Thus,

$$-\left(2-\sqrt{4-\varepsilon}\right) \leq -\delta < x-2 < \delta \leq \sqrt{4+\varepsilon}-2.$$

We simplify the expression on the left:

$$-2+\sqrt{4-\varepsilon} < x-2 < \sqrt{4+\varepsilon}-2.$$

Then, we add 2 to all parts of the inequality:

$$\sqrt{4-\varepsilon} < x < \sqrt{4+\varepsilon}.$$

We square all parts of the inequality. It is okay to do so, since all parts of the inequality are positive:

$$4-\varepsilon < x^2 < 4+\varepsilon.$$

We subtract 4 from all parts of the inequality:

$$-\varepsilon < x^2-4 < \varepsilon.$$

Last,

$$|x^2-4| < \varepsilon.$$

5. Therefore,

$$\lim_{x \to 2} x^2 = 4.$$

2.28 Find δ corresponding to $\varepsilon > 0$ for a proof that $\lim_{x \to 9} \sqrt{x} = 3$.

The geometric approach to proving that the limit of a function takes on a specific value works quite well for some functions. Also, the insight into the formal definition of the limit that this method provides is invaluable. However, we may also approach limit proofs from a purely algebraic point of view. In many cases, an algebraic approach may not only provide us with additional insight into the definition, it may prove to be simpler as well. Furthermore, an algebraic approach is the primary tool used in proofs of statements about limits. For **Example 2.42**, we take on a purely algebraic approach.

Example 2.42

Proving a Statement about the Limit of a Specific Function (Algebraic Approach)

Prove that $\lim_{x \to -1} \left(x^2-2x+3\right) = 6.$

Solution

Let's use our outline from the Problem-Solving Strategy:

1. Let $\varepsilon > 0$.
2. Choose $\delta = \min\{1, \varepsilon/5\}$. This choice of δ may appear odd at first glance, but it was obtained by

taking a look at our ultimate desired inequality: $\left|\left(x^2 - 2x + 3\right) - 6\right| < \varepsilon$. This inequality is equivalent to $|x + 1| \cdot |x - 3| < \varepsilon$. At this point, the temptation simply to choose $\delta = \frac{\varepsilon}{x - 3}$ is very strong. Unfortunately, our choice of δ must depend on ε only and no other variable. If we can replace $|x - 3|$ by a numerical value, our problem can be resolved. This is the place where assuming $\delta \le 1$ comes into play. The choice of $\delta \le 1$ here is arbitrary. We could have just as easily used any other positive number. In some proofs, greater care in this choice may be necessary. Now, since $\delta \le 1$ and $|x + 1| < \delta \le 1$, we are able to show that $|x - 3| < 5$. Consequently, $|x + 1| \cdot |x - 3| < |x + 1| \cdot 5$. At this point we realize that we also need $\delta \le \varepsilon/5$. Thus, we choose $\delta = \min\{1, \varepsilon/5\}$.

3. Assume $0 < |x + 1| < \delta$. Thus,

$$|x + 1| < 1 \text{ and } |x + 1| < \frac{\varepsilon}{5}.$$

Since $|x + 1| < 1$, we may conclude that $-1 < x + 1 < 1$. Thus, by subtracting 4 from all parts of the inequality, we obtain $-5 < x - 3 < -1$. Consequently, $|x - 3| < 5$. This gives us

$$\left|\left(x^2 - 2x + 3\right) - 6\right| = |x + 1| \cdot |x - 3| < \frac{\varepsilon}{5} \cdot 5 = \varepsilon.$$

Therefore,

$$\lim_{x \to -1}\left(x^2 - 2x + 3\right) = 6.$$

2.29 Complete the proof that $\lim_{x \to 1} x^2 = 1$.

Let $\varepsilon > 0$; choose $\delta = \min\{1, \varepsilon/3\}$; assume $0 < |x - 1| < \delta$.

Since $|x - 1| < 1$, we may conclude that $-1 < x - 1 < 1$. Thus, $1 < x + 1 < 3$. Hence, $|x + 1| < 3$.

You will find that, in general, the more complex a function, the more likely it is that the algebraic approach is the easiest to apply. The algebraic approach is also more useful in proving statements about limits.

Proving Limit Laws

We now demonstrate how to use the epsilon-delta definition of a limit to construct a rigorous proof of one of the limit laws. The **triangle inequality** is used at a key point of the proof, so we first review this key property of absolute value.

Definition

The **triangle inequality** states that if a and b are any real numbers, then $|a + b| \le |a| + |b|$.

Proof

We prove the following limit law: If $\lim_{x \to a} f(x) = L$ and $\lim_{x \to a} g(x) = M$, then $\lim_{x \to a}(f(x) + g(x)) = L + M$.

Let $\varepsilon > 0$.

Choose $\delta_1 > 0$ so that if $0 < |x - a| < \delta_1$, then $|f(x) - L| < \varepsilon/2$.

Choose $\delta_2 > 0$ so that if $0 < |x - a| < \delta_2$, then $|g(x) - M| < \varepsilon/2$.

Choose $\delta = \min\{\delta_1, \delta_2\}$.

Assume $0 < |x - a| < \delta$.

Thus,

$$0 < |x - a| < \delta_1 \text{ and } 0 < |x - a| < \delta_2.$$

Hence,

$$\begin{aligned} |(f(x) + g(x)) - (L + M)| &= |(f(x) - L) + (g(x) - M)| \\ &\leq |f(x) - L| + |g(x) - M| \\ &< \frac{\varepsilon}{2} + \frac{\varepsilon}{2} = \varepsilon. \end{aligned}$$

□

We now explore what it means for a limit not to exist. The limit $\lim_{x \to a} f(x)$ does not exist if there is no real number L for which $\lim_{x \to a} f(x) = L$. Thus, for all real numbers L, $\lim_{x \to a} f(x) \neq L$. To understand what this means, we look at each part of the definition of $\lim_{x \to a} f(x) = L$ together with its opposite. A translation of the definition is given in **Table 2.10**.

Definition	**Opposite**
1. For every $\varepsilon > 0$,	1. There exists $\varepsilon > 0$ so that
2. there exists a $\delta > 0$, so that	2. for every $\delta > 0$,
3. if $0 < |x - a| < \delta$, then $|f(x) - L| < \varepsilon$.	3. There is an *x* satisfying $0 < |x - a| < \delta$ so that $|f(x) - L| \geq \varepsilon$.

Table 2.10 Translation of the Definition of $\lim_{x \to a} f(x) = L$ and its Opposite

Finally, we may state what it means for a limit not to exist. The limit $\lim_{x \to a} f(x)$ does not exist if for every real number L, there exists a real number $\varepsilon > 0$ so that for all $\delta > 0$, there is an *x* satisfying $0 < |x - a| < \delta$, so that $|f(x) - L| \geq \varepsilon$. Let's apply this in **Example 2.43** to show that a limit does not exist.

Example 2.43

Showing That a Limit Does Not Exist

Show that $\lim_{x \to 0} \frac{|x|}{x}$ does not exist. The graph of $f(x) = |x|/x$ is shown here:

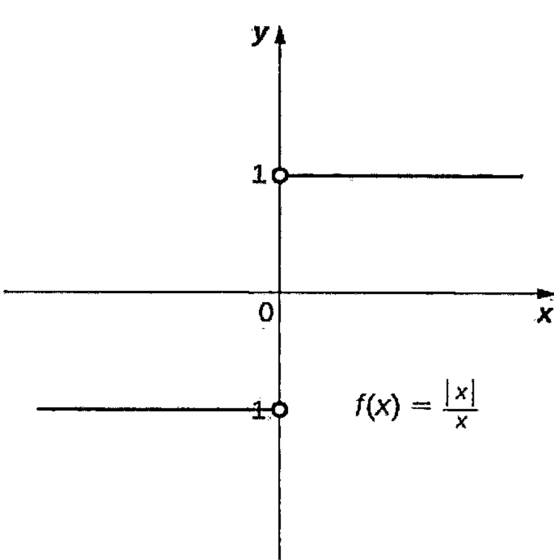

Solution

Suppose that L is a candidate for a limit. Choose $\varepsilon = 1/2$.

Let $\delta > 0$. Either $L \geq 0$ or $L < 0$. If $L \geq 0$, then let $x = -\delta/2$. Thus,

$$|x - 0| = \left|-\frac{\delta}{2} - 0\right| = \frac{\delta}{2} < \delta$$

and

$$\left|\frac{\left|-\frac{\delta}{2}\right|}{-\frac{\delta}{2}} - L\right| = |-1 - L| = L + 1 \geq 1 > \frac{1}{2} = \varepsilon.$$

On the other hand, if $L < 0$, then let $x = \delta/2$. Thus,

$$|x - 0| = \left|\frac{\delta}{2} - 0\right| = \frac{\delta}{2} < \delta$$

and

$$\left|\frac{\left|\frac{\delta}{2}\right|}{\frac{\delta}{2}} - L\right| = |1 - L| = |L| + 1 \geq 1 > \frac{1}{2} = \varepsilon.$$

Thus, for any value of L, $\lim\limits_{x \to 0} \frac{|x|}{x} \neq L$.

One-Sided and Infinite Limits

Just as we first gained an intuitive understanding of limits and then moved on to a more rigorous definition of a limit, we now revisit one-sided limits. To do this, we modify the epsilon-delta definition of a limit to give formal epsilon-delta definitions for limits from the right and left at a point. These definitions only require slight modifications from the definition of the limit. In the definition of the limit from the right, the inequality $0 < x - a < \delta$ replaces $0 < |x - a| < \delta$, which ensures that we only consider values of x that are greater than (to the right of) a. Similarly, in the definition of the limit from the left, the inequality $-\delta < x - a < 0$ replaces $0 < |x - a| < \delta$, which ensures that we only consider values of x that are less than (to the left of) a.

Definition

Limit from the Right: Let $f(x)$ be defined over an open interval of the form (a, b) where $a < b$. Then,

$$\lim_{x \to a^+} f(x) = L$$

if for every $\varepsilon > 0$, there exists a $\delta > 0$ such that if $0 < x - a < \delta$, then $|f(x) - L| < \varepsilon$.

Limit from the Left: Let $f(x)$ be defined over an open interval of the form (b, c) where $b < c$. Then,

$$\lim_{x \to a^-} f(x) = L$$

if for every $\varepsilon > 0$, there exists a $\delta > 0$ such that if $-\delta < x - a < 0$, then $|f(x) - L| < \varepsilon$.

Example 2.44

Proving a Statement about a Limit From the Right

Prove that $\lim_{x \to 4^+} \sqrt{x - 4} = 0$.

Solution

Let $\varepsilon > 0$.

Choose $\delta = \varepsilon^2$. Since we ultimately want $\left|\sqrt{x - 4} - 0\right| < \varepsilon$, we manipulate this inequality to get $\sqrt{x - 4} < \varepsilon$ or, equivalently, $0 < x - 4 < \varepsilon^2$, making $\delta = \varepsilon^2$ a clear choice. We may also determine δ geometrically, as shown in **Figure 2.42**.

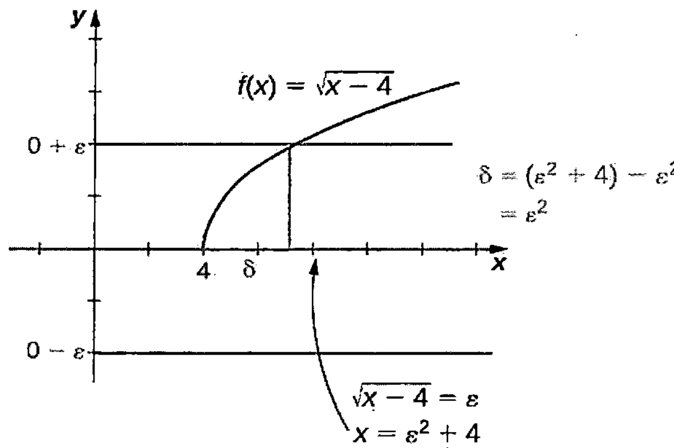

Figure 2.42 This graph shows how we find δ for the proof in **Example 2.44**.

Assume $0 < x - 4 < \delta$. Thus, $0 < x - 4 < \varepsilon^2$. Hence, $0 < \sqrt{x - 4} < \varepsilon$. Finally, $\left|\sqrt{x - 4} - 0\right| < \varepsilon$.

Therefore, $\lim_{x \to 4^+} \sqrt{x - 4} = 0$.

2.30 Find δ corresponding to ε for a proof that $\lim_{x \to 1^-} \sqrt{1 - x} = 0$.

We conclude the process of converting our intuitive ideas of various types of limits to rigorous formal definitions by pursuing a formal definition of infinite limits. To have $\lim_{x \to a} f(x) = +\infty,$ we want the values of the function $f(x)$ to get larger and larger as x approaches a. Instead of the requirement that $|f(x) - L| < \varepsilon$ for arbitrarily small ε when $0 < |x - a| < \delta$ for small enough $\delta,$ we want $f(x) > M$ for arbitrarily large positive M when $0 < |x - a| < \delta$ for small enough δ. **Figure 2.43** illustrates this idea by showing the value of δ for successively larger values of M.

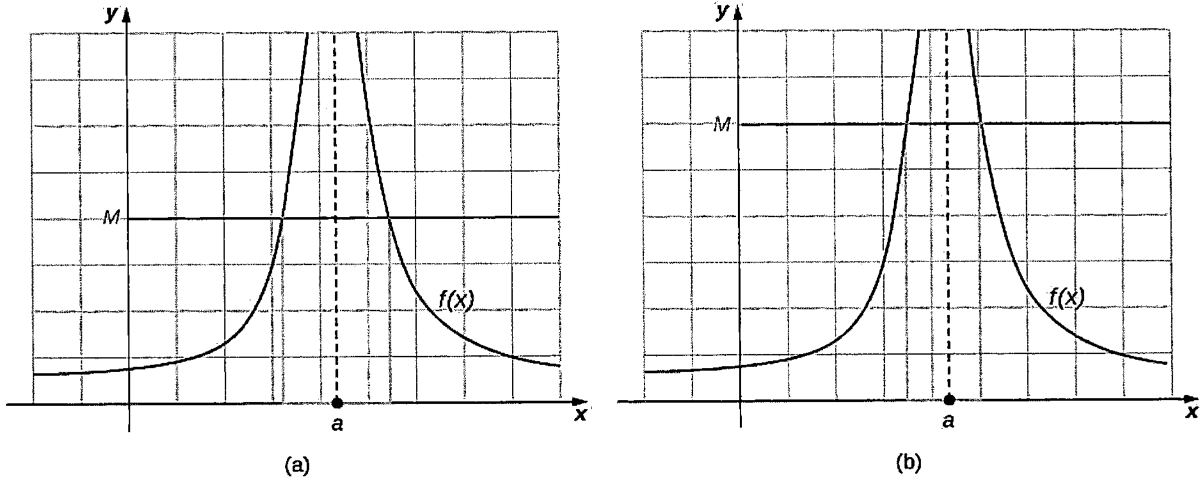
y
M
f(x)
a
x
(a)
y
M
f(x)
a
x
(b)
In each graph, δ is the smaller of the lengths of the two brown intervals.

Figure 2.43 These graphs plot values of δ for M to show that $\lim_{x \to a} f(x) = +\infty.$

Definition

Let $f(x)$ be defined for all $x \neq a$ in an open interval containing a. Then, we have an infinite limit

$$\lim_{x \to a} f(x) = +\infty$$

if for every $M > 0,$ there exists $\delta > 0$ such that if $0 < |x - a| < \delta,$ then $f(x) > M$.

Let $f(x)$ be defined for all $x \neq a$ in an open interval containing a. Then, we have a negative infinite limit

$$\lim_{x \to a} f(x) = -\infty$$

if for every $M > 0,$ there exists $\delta > 0$ such that if $0 < |x - a| < \delta,$ then $f(x) < -M$.

2.5 EXERCISES

In the following exercises, write the appropriate $\varepsilon - \delta$ definition for each of the given statements.

176. $\lim_{x \to a} f(x) = N$

177. $\lim_{t \to b} g(t) = M$

178. $\lim_{x \to c} h(x) = L$

179. $\lim_{x \to a} \varphi(x) = A$

The following graph of the function f satisfies $\lim_{x \to 2} f(x) = 2$. In the following exercises, determine a value of $\delta > 0$ that satisfies each statement.

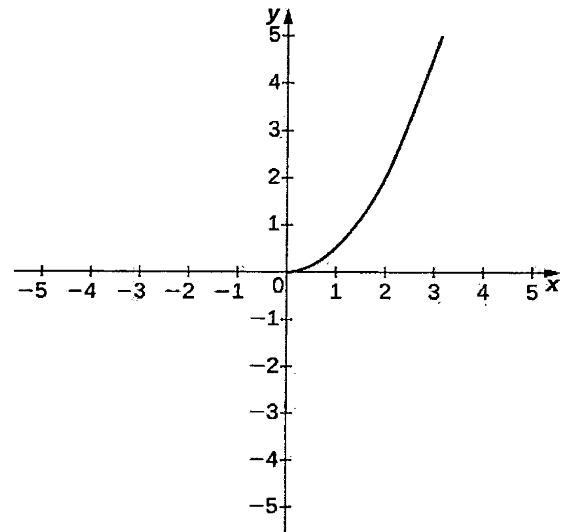

180. If $0 < |x - 2| < \delta$, then $|f(x) - 2| < 1$.

181. If $0 < |x - 2| < \delta$, then $|f(x) - 2| < 0.5$.

The following graph of the function f satisfies $\lim_{x \to 3} f(x) = -1$. In the following exercises, determine a value of $\delta > 0$ that satisfies each statement.

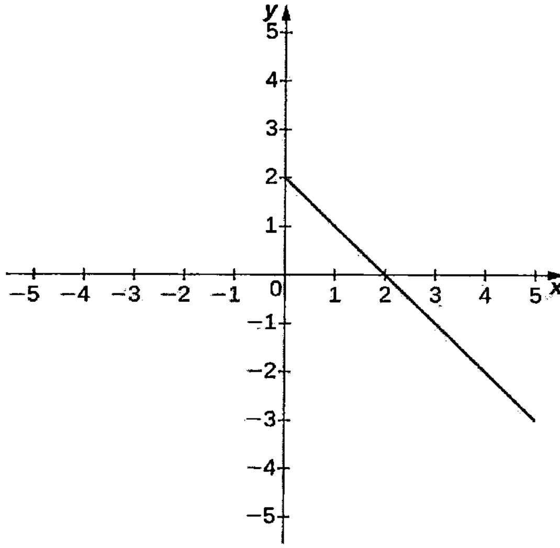

182. If $0 < |x - 3| < \delta$, then $|f(x) + 1| < 1$.

183. If $0 < |x - 3| < \delta$, then $|f(x) + 1| < 2$.

The following graph of the function f satisfies $\lim_{x \to 3} f(x) = 2$. In the following exercises, for each value of ε, find a value of $\delta > 0$ such that the precise definition of limit holds true.

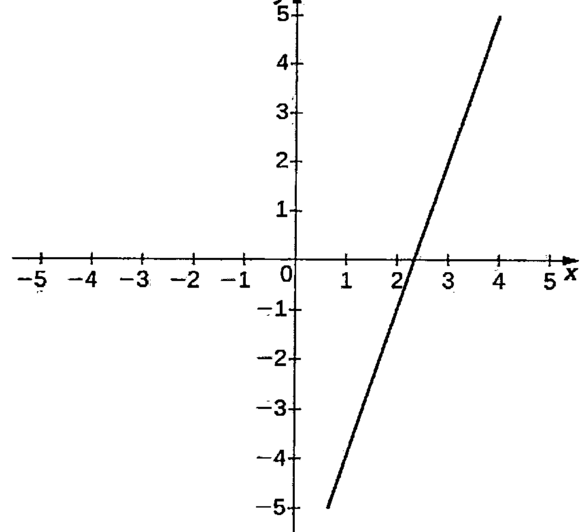

184. $\varepsilon = 1.5$

185. $\varepsilon = 3$

[T] In the following exercises, use a graphing calculator to find a number δ such that the statements hold true.

186. $\left|\sin(2x) - \frac{1}{2}\right| < 0.1$, whenever $\left|x - \frac{\pi}{12}\right| < \delta$

187. $\left|\sqrt{x-4}-2\right| < 0.1$, whenever $|x-8| < \delta$

In the following exercises, use the precise definition of limit to prove the given limits.

188. $\lim_{x \to 2} (5x + 8) = 18$

189. $\lim_{x \to 3} \frac{x^2 - 9}{x - 3} = 6$

190. $\lim_{x \to 2} \frac{2x^2 - 3x - 2}{x - 2} = 5$

191. $\lim_{x \to 0} x^4 = 0$

192. $\lim_{x \to 2} (x^2 + 2x) = 8$

In the following exercises, use the precise definition of limit to prove the given one-sided limits.

193. $\lim_{x \to 5^-} \sqrt{5 - x} = 0$

194.
$\lim_{x \to 0^+} f(x) = -2$, where $f(x) = \begin{cases} 8x - 3, & \text{if } x < 0 \\ 4x - 2, & \text{if } x \ge 0 \end{cases}$.

195. $\lim_{x \to 1^-} f(x) = 3$, where $f(x) = \begin{cases} 5x - 2, & \text{if } x < 1 \\ 7x - 1, & \text{if } x \ge 1 \end{cases}$.

In the following exercises, use the precise definition of limit to prove the given infinite limits.

196. $\lim_{x \to 0} \frac{1}{x^2} = \infty$

197. $\lim_{x \to -1} \frac{3}{(x + 1)^2} = \infty$

198. $\lim_{x \to 2} -\frac{1}{(x - 2)^2} = -\infty$

199. An engineer is using a machine to cut a flat square of Aerogel of area 144 cm^2. If there is a maximum error tolerance in the area of 8 cm^2, how accurately must the engineer cut on the side, assuming all sides have the same length? How do these numbers relate to δ, ε, a, and L?

200. Use the precise definition of limit to prove that the following limit does not exist: $\lim_{x \to 1} \frac{|x - 1|}{x - 1}$.

201. Using precise definitions of limits, prove that $\lim_{x \to 0} f(x)$ does not exist, given that $f(x)$ is the ceiling function. (*Hint*: Try any $\delta < 1$.)

202. Using precise definitions of limits, prove that $\lim_{x \to 0} f(x)$ does not exist: $f(x) = \begin{cases} 1 \text{ if } x \text{ is rational} \\ 0 \text{ if } x \text{ is irrational} \end{cases}$. (*Hint*: Think about how you can always choose a rational number $0 < r < d$, but $|f(r) - 0| = 1$.)

203. Using precise definitions of limits, determine $\lim_{x \to 0} f(x)$ for $f(x) = \begin{cases} x \text{ if } x \text{ is rational} \\ 0 \text{ if } x \text{ is irrational} \end{cases}$. (*Hint*: Break into two cases, *x* rational and *x* irrational.)

204. Using the function from the previous exercise, use the precise definition of limits to show that $\lim_{x \to a} f(x)$ does not exist for $a \ne 0$.

For the following exercises, suppose that $\lim_{x \to a} f(x) = L$ and $\lim_{x \to a} g(x) = M$ both exist. Use the precise definition of limits to prove the following limit laws:

205. $\lim_{x \to a} (f(x) - g(x)) = L - M$

206. $\lim_{x \to a} [cf(x)] = cL$ for any real constant c (*Hint*: Consider two cases: $c = 0$ and $c \ne 0$.)

207. $\lim_{x \to a} [f(x)g(x)] = LM$. (*Hint*: $|f(x)g(x) - LM| = |f(x)g(x) - f(x)M + f(x)M - LM| \le |f(x)||g(x) - M| + |M||f(x) - L|$.)

CHAPTER 2 REVIEW

KEY TERMS

average velocity the change in an object's position divided by the length of a time period; the average velocity of an object over a time interval $[t, a]$ (if $t < a$ or $[a, t]$ if $t > a$), with a position given by $s(t)$, that is $v_{\text{ave}} = \frac{s(t) - s(a)}{t - a}$

constant multiple law for limits the limit law $\lim\limits_{x \to a} cf(x) = c \cdot \lim\limits_{x \to a} f(x) = cL$

continuity at a point A function $f(x)$ is continuous at a point a if and only if the following three conditions are satisfied: (1) $f(a)$ is defined, (2) $\lim\limits_{x \to a} f(x)$ exists, and (3) $\lim\limits_{x \to a} f(x) = f(a)$

continuity from the left A function is continuous from the left at b if $\lim\limits_{x \to b^-} f(x) = f(b)$

continuity from the right A function is continuous from the right at a if $\lim\limits_{x \to a^+} f(x) = f(a)$

continuity over an interval a function that can be traced with a pencil without lifting the pencil; a function is continuous over an open interval if it is continuous at every point in the interval; a function $f(x)$ is continuous over a closed interval of the form $[a, b]$ if it is continuous at every point in (a, b), and it is continuous from the right at a and from the left at b

difference law for limits the limit law $\lim\limits_{x \to a}(f(x) - g(x)) = \lim\limits_{x \to a} f(x) - \lim\limits_{x \to a} g(x) = L - M$

differential calculus the field of calculus concerned with the study of derivatives and their applications

discontinuity at a point A function is discontinuous at a point or has a discontinuity at a point if it is not continuous at the point

epsilon-delta definition of the limit $\lim\limits_{x \to a} f(x) = L$ if for every $\varepsilon > 0$, there exists a $\delta > 0$ such that if $0 < |x - a| < \delta$, then $|f(x) - L| < \varepsilon$

infinite discontinuity An infinite discontinuity occurs at a point a if $\lim\limits_{x \to a^-} f(x) = \pm\infty$ or $\lim\limits_{x \to a^+} f(x) = \pm\infty$

infinite limit A function has an infinite limit at a point a if it either increases or decreases without bound as it approaches a

instantaneous velocity The instantaneous velocity of an object with a position function that is given by $s(t)$ is the value that the average velocities on intervals of the form $[t, a]$ and $[a, t]$ approach as the values of t move closer to a, provided such a value exists

integral calculus the study of integrals and their applications

Intermediate Value Theorem Let f be continuous over a closed bounded interval [a, b]; if z is any real number between $f(a)$ and $f(b)$, then there is a number c in $[a, b]$ satisfying $f(c) = z$

intuitive definition of the limit If all values of the function $f(x)$ approach the real number L as the values of $x(\neq a)$ approach a, $f(x)$ approaches L

jump discontinuity A jump discontinuity occurs at a point a if $\lim\limits_{x \to a^-} f(x)$ and $\lim\limits_{x \to a^+} f(x)$ both exist, but $\lim\limits_{x \to a^-} f(x) \neq \lim\limits_{x \to a^+} f(x)$

limit the process of letting x or t approach a in an expression; the limit of a function $f(x)$ as x approaches a is the value that $f(x)$ approaches as x approaches a

limit laws the individual properties of limits; for each of the individual laws, let $f(x)$ and $g(x)$ be defined for all $x \neq a$ over some open interval containing a; assume that L and M are real numbers so that $\lim_{x \to a} f(x) = L$ and $\lim_{x \to a} g(x) = M$; let c be a constant

multivariable calculus the study of the calculus of functions of two or more variables

one-sided limit A one-sided limit of a function is a limit taken from either the left or the right

power law for limits the limit law $\lim_{x \to a} (f(x))^n = \left(\lim_{x \to a} f(x)\right)^n = L^n$ for every positive integer n

product law for limits the limit law $\lim_{x \to a} (f(x) \cdot g(x)) = \lim_{x \to a} f(x) \cdot \lim_{x \to a} g(x) = L \cdot M$

quotient law for limits the limit law $\lim_{x \to a} \frac{f(x)}{g(x)} = \frac{\lim_{x \to a} f(x)}{\lim_{x \to a} g(x)} = \frac{L}{M}$ for $M \neq 0$

removable discontinuity A removable discontinuity occurs at a point a if $f(x)$ is discontinuous at a, but $\lim_{x \to a} f(x)$ exists

root law for limits the limit law $\lim_{x \to a} \sqrt[n]{f(x)} = \sqrt[n]{\lim_{x \to a} f(x)} = \sqrt[n]{L}$ for all L if n is odd and for $L \geq 0$ if n is even

secant A secant line to a function $f(x)$ at a is a line through the point $(a, f(a))$ and another point on the function; the slope of the secant line is given by $m_{\text{sec}} = \frac{f(x) - f(a)}{x - a}$

squeeze theorem states that if $f(x) \leq g(x) \leq h(x)$ for all $x \neq a$ over an open interval containing a and $\lim_{x \to a} f(x) = L = \lim_{x \to a} h(x)$ where L is a real number, then $\lim_{x \to a} g(x) = L$

sum law for limits The limit law $\lim_{x \to a} (f(x) + g(x)) = \lim_{x \to a} f(x) + \lim_{x \to a} g(x) = L + M$

tangent A tangent line to the graph of a function at a point $(a, f(a))$ is the line that secant lines through $(a, f(a))$ approach as they are taken through points on the function with x-values that approach a; the slope of the tangent line to a graph at a measures the rate of change of the function at a

triangle inequality If a and b are any real numbers, then $|a + b| \leq |a| + |b|$

vertical asymptote A function has a vertical asymptote at $x = a$ if the limit as x approaches a from the right or left is infinite

KEY EQUATIONS

- **Slope of a Secant Line**
  $m_{\text{sec}} = \frac{f(x) - f(a)}{x - a}$
- **Average Velocity over Interval** $[a, t]$
  $v_{\text{ave}} = \frac{s(t) - s(a)}{t - a}$
- **Intuitive Definition of the Limit**
  $\lim_{x \to a} f(x) = L$
- **Two Important Limits**
  $\lim_{x \to a} x = a \quad \lim_{x \to a} c = c$
- **One-Sided Limits**

$\lim_{x \to a^-} f(x) = L \quad \lim_{x \to a^+} f(x) = L$

- **Infinite Limits from the Left**
  $\lim_{x \to a^-} f(x) = +\infty \quad \lim_{x \to a^-} f(x) = -\infty$
- **Infinite Limits from the Right**
  $\lim_{x \to a^+} f(x) = +\infty \quad \lim_{x \to a^+} f(x) = -\infty$
- **Two-Sided Infinite Limits**
  $\lim_{x \to a} f(x) = +\infty : \lim_{x \to a^-} f(x) = +\infty$ and $\lim_{x \to a^+} f(x) = +\infty$

  $\lim_{x \to a} f(x) = -\infty : \lim_{x \to a^-} f(x) = -\infty$ and $\lim_{x \to a^+} f(x) = -\infty$
- **Basic Limit Results**
  $\lim_{x \to a} x = a \; \lim_{x \to a} c = c$
- **Important Limits**
  $\lim_{\theta \to 0} \sin\theta = 0$

  $\lim_{\theta \to 0} \cos\theta = 1$

  $\lim_{\theta \to 0} \frac{\sin\theta}{\theta} = 1$

  $\lim_{\theta \to 0} \frac{1 - \cos\theta}{\theta} = 0$

KEY CONCEPTS

2.1 A Preview of Calculus

- Differential calculus arose from trying to solve the problem of determining the slope of a line tangent to a curve at a point. The slope of the tangent line indicates the rate of change of the function, also called the *derivative*. Calculating a derivative requires finding a limit.
- Integral calculus arose from trying to solve the problem of finding the area of a region between the graph of a function and the x-axis. We can approximate the area by dividing it into thin rectangles and summing the areas of these rectangles. This summation leads to the value of a function called the *integral*. The integral is also calculated by finding a limit and, in fact, is related to the derivative of a function.
- Multivariable calculus enables us to solve problems in three-dimensional space, including determining motion in space and finding volumes of solids.

2.2 The Limit of a Function

- A table of values or graph may be used to estimate a limit.
- If the limit of a function at a point does not exist, it is still possible that the limits from the left and right at that point may exist.
- If the limits of a function from the left and right exist and are equal, then the limit of the function is that common value.
- We may use limits to describe infinite behavior of a function at a point.

2.3 The Limit Laws

- The limit laws allow us to evaluate limits of functions without having to go through step-by-step processes each time.
- For polynomials and rational functions, $\lim_{x \to a} f(x) = f(a)$.

- You can evaluate the limit of a function by factoring and canceling, by multiplying by a conjugate, or by simplifying a complex fraction.
- The squeeze theorem allows you to find the limit of a function if the function is always greater than one function and less than another function with limits that are known.

2.4 Continuity

- For a function to be continuous at a point, it must be defined at that point, its limit must exist at the point, and the value of the function at that point must equal the value of the limit at that point.
- Discontinuities may be classified as removable, jump, or infinite.
- A function is continuous over an open interval if it is continuous at every point in the interval. It is continuous over a closed interval if it is continuous at every point in its interior and is continuous at its endpoints.
- The composite function theorem states: If $f(x)$ is continuous at L and $\lim_{x \to a} g(x) = L,$ then $\lim_{x \to a} f(g(x)) = f\left(\lim_{x \to a} g(x)\right) = f(L).$
- The Intermediate Value Theorem guarantees that if a function is continuous over a closed interval, then the function takes on every value between the values at its endpoints.

2.5 The Precise Definition of a Limit

- The intuitive notion of a limit may be converted into a rigorous mathematical definition known as the *epsilon-delta definition of the limit.*
- The epsilon-delta definition may be used to prove statements about limits.
- The epsilon-delta definition of a limit may be modified to define one-sided limits.

CHAPTER 2 REVIEW EXERCISES

True or False. In the following exercises, justify your answer with a proof or a counterexample.

208. A function has to be continuous at $x = a$ if the $\lim_{x \to a} f(x)$ exists.

209. You can use the quotient rule to evaluate $\lim_{x \to 0} \frac{\sin x}{x}.$

210. If there is a vertical asymptote at $x = a$ for the function $f(x),$ then f is undefined at the point $x = a.$

211. If $\lim_{x \to a} f(x)$ does not exist, then f is undefined at the point $x = a.$

212. Using the graph, find each limit or explain why the limit does not exist.

a. $\lim_{x \to -1} f(x)$

b. $\lim_{x \to 1} f(x)$

c. $\lim_{x \to 0^+} f(x)$

d. $\lim_{x \to 2} f(x)$

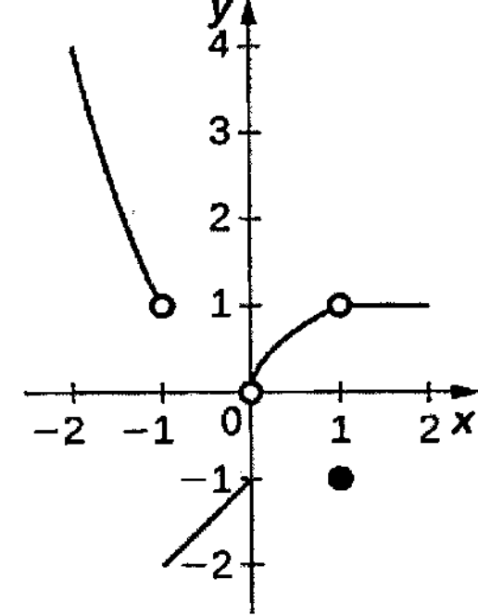

In the following exercises, evaluate the limit algebraically or explain why the limit does not exist.

213. $\lim_{x \to 2} \frac{2x^2 - 3x - 2}{x - 2}$

214. $\lim_{x \to 0} 3x^2 - 2x + 4$

215. $\lim_{x \to 3} \frac{x^3 - 2x^2 - 1}{3x - 2}$

216. $\lim_{x \to \pi/2} \frac{\cot x}{\cos x}$

217. $\lim_{x \to -5} \frac{x^2 + 25}{x + 5}$

218. $\lim_{x \to 2} \frac{3x^2 - 2x - 8}{x^2 - 4}$

219. $\lim_{x \to 1} \frac{x^2 - 1}{x^3 - 1}$

220. $\lim_{x \to 1} \frac{x^2 - 1}{\sqrt{x} - 1}$

221. $\lim_{x \to 4} \frac{4 - x}{\sqrt{x} - 2}$

222. $\lim_{x \to 4} \frac{1}{\sqrt{x} - 2}$

In the following exercises, use the squeeze theorem to prove the limit.

223. $\lim_{x \to 0} x^2 \cos(2\pi x) = 0$

224. $\lim_{x \to 0} x^3 \sin\left(\frac{\pi}{x}\right) = 0$

225. Determine the domain such that the function $f(x) = \sqrt{x - 2} + xe^x$ is continuous over its domain.

In the following exercises, determine the value of c such that the function remains continuous. Draw your resulting function to ensure it is continuous.

226. $f(x) = \begin{cases} x^2 + 1, & x > c \\ 2x, & x \le c \end{cases}$

227. $f(x) = \begin{cases} \sqrt{x + 1}, & x > -1 \\ x^2 + c, & x \le -1 \end{cases}$

In the following exercises, use the precise definition of limit to prove the limit.

228. $\lim_{x \to 1} (8x + 16) = 24$

229. $\lim_{x \to 0} x^3 = 0$

230. A ball is thrown into the air and the vertical position is given by $x(t) = -4.9t^2 + 25t + 5$. Use the Intermediate Value Theorem to show that the ball must land on the ground sometime between 5 sec and 6 sec after the throw.

231. A particle moving along a line has a displacement according to the function $x(t) = t^2 - 2t + 4$, where x is measured in meters and t is measured in seconds. Find the average velocity over the time period $t = [0, 2]$.

232. From the previous exercises, estimate the instantaneous velocity at $t = 2$ by checking the average velocity within $t = 0.01$ sec.

3 | DERIVATIVES

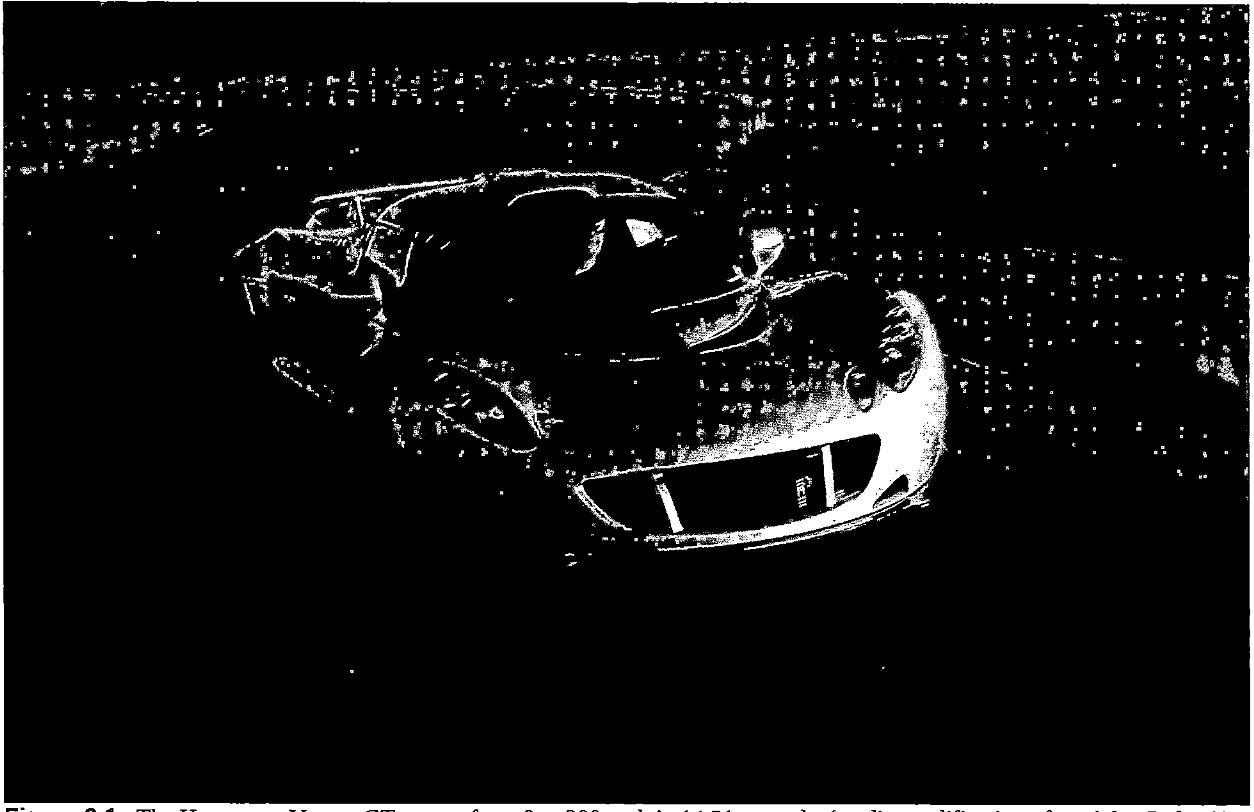

Figure 3.1 The Hennessey Venom GT can go from 0 to 200 mph in 14.51 seconds. (credit: modification of work by Codex41, Flickr)

Chapter Outline

Introduction

The Hennessey Venom GT is one of the fastest cars in the world. In 2014, it reached a record-setting speed of 270.49 mph. It can go from 0 to 200 mph in 14.51 seconds. The techniques in this chapter can be used to calculate the acceleration the Venom achieves in this feat (see **Example 3.8**.)

Calculating velocity and changes in velocity are important uses of calculus, but it is far more widespread than that. Calculus is important in all branches of mathematics, science, and engineering, and it is critical to analysis in business and health as well. In this chapter, we explore one of the main tools of calculus, the derivative, and show convenient ways to calculate derivatives. We apply these rules to a variety of functions in this chapter so that we can then explore applications of these techniques.

3.1 | Defining the Derivative

Learning Objectives

3.1.1 Recognize the meaning of the tangent to a curve at a point.
3.1.2 Calculate the slope of a tangent line.
3.1.3 Identify the derivative as the limit of a difference quotient.
3.1.4 Calculate the derivative of a given function at a point.
3.1.5 Describe the velocity as a rate of change.
3.1.6 Explain the difference between average velocity and instantaneous velocity.
3.1.7 Estimate the derivative from a table of values.

Now that we have both a conceptual understanding of a limit and the practical ability to compute limits, we have established the foundation for our study of calculus, the branch of mathematics in which we compute derivatives and integrals. Most mathematicians and historians agree that calculus was developed independently by the Englishman Isaac Newton (1643–1727) and the German Gottfried Leibniz (1646–1716), whose images appear in **Figure 3.2**. When we credit Newton and Leibniz with developing calculus, we are really referring to the fact that Newton and Leibniz were the first to understand the relationship between the derivative and the integral. Both mathematicians benefited from the work of predecessors, such as Barrow, Fermat, and Cavalieri. The initial relationship between the two mathematicians appears to have been amicable; however, in later years a bitter controversy erupted over whose work took precedence. Although it seems likely that Newton did, indeed, arrive at the ideas behind calculus first, we are indebted to Leibniz for the notation that we commonly use today.

Figure 3.2 Newton and Leibniz are credited with developing calculus independently.

Tangent Lines

We begin our study of calculus by revisiting the notion of secant lines and tangent lines. Recall that we used the slope of a secant line to a function at a point $(a, f(a))$ to estimate the rate of change, or the rate at which one variable changes in relation to another variable. We can obtain the slope of the secant by choosing a value of x near a and drawing a line through the points $(a, f(a))$ and $(x, f(x))$, as shown in **Figure 3.3**. The slope of this line is given by an equation in the form of a difference quotient:

$$m_{\text{sec}} = \frac{f(x) - f(a)}{x - a}.$$

We can also calculate the slope of a secant line to a function at a value a by using this equation and replacing x with $a + h$, where h is a value close to 0. We can then calculate the slope of the line through the points $(a, f(a))$ and $(a + h, f(a + h))$. In this case, we find the secant line has a slope given by the following difference quotient with increment h:

$$m_{\text{sec}} = \frac{f(a+h) - f(a)}{a + h - a} = \frac{f(a+h) - f(a)}{h}.$$

Definition

Let f be a function defined on an interval I containing a. If $x \neq a$ is in I, then

$$Q = \frac{f(x) - f(a)}{x - a} \tag{3.1}$$

is a **difference quotient**.

Also, if $h \neq 0$ is chosen so that $a + h$ is in I, then

$$Q = \frac{f(a+h) - f(a)}{h} \tag{3.2}$$

is a difference quotient with increment h.

View the development of the **derivative (http://www.openstaxcollege.org/l/20_calcapplets)** with this applet.

These two expressions for calculating the slope of a secant line are illustrated in **Figure 3.3**. We will see that each of these two methods for finding the slope of a secant line is of value. Depending on the setting, we can choose one or the other. The primary consideration in our choice usually depends on ease of calculation.

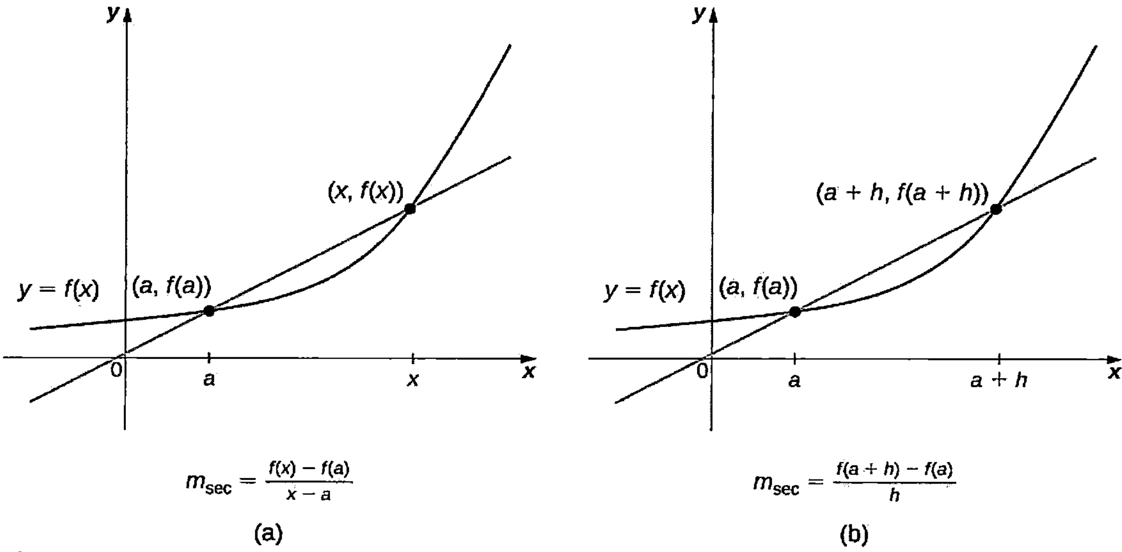

Figure 3.3 We can calculate the slope of a secant line in either of two ways.

In **Figure 3.4**(a) we see that, as the values of x approach a, the slopes of the secant lines provide better estimates of the rate of change of the function at a. Furthermore, the secant lines themselves approach the tangent line to the function at a, which represents the limit of the secant lines. Similarly, **Figure 3.4**(b) shows that as the values of h get closer to 0, the secant lines also approach the tangent line. The slope of the tangent line at a is the rate of change of the function at a, as shown in **Figure 3.4**(c).

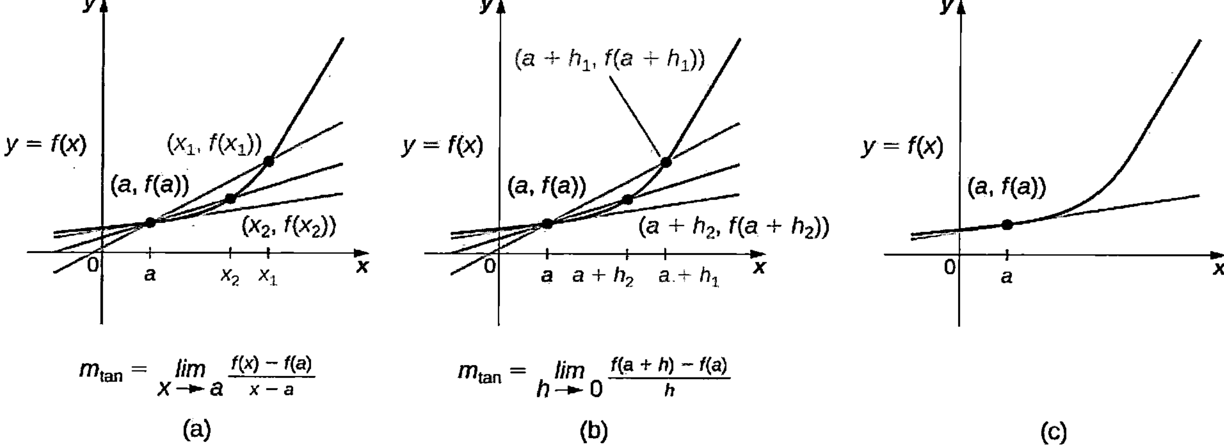

Figure 3.4 The secant lines approach the tangent line (shown in green) as the second point approaches the first.

You can use this **site (http://www.openstaxcollege.org/l/20_diffmicros)** to explore graphs to see if they have a tangent line at a point.

In **Figure 3.5** we show the graph of $f(x) = \sqrt{x}$ and its tangent line at $(1, 1)$ in a series of tighter intervals about $x = 1$. As the intervals become narrower, the graph of the function and its tangent line appear to coincide, making the values on the tangent line a good approximation to the values of the function for choices of x close to 1. In fact, the graph of $f(x)$ itself appears to be locally linear in the immediate vicinity of $x = 1$.

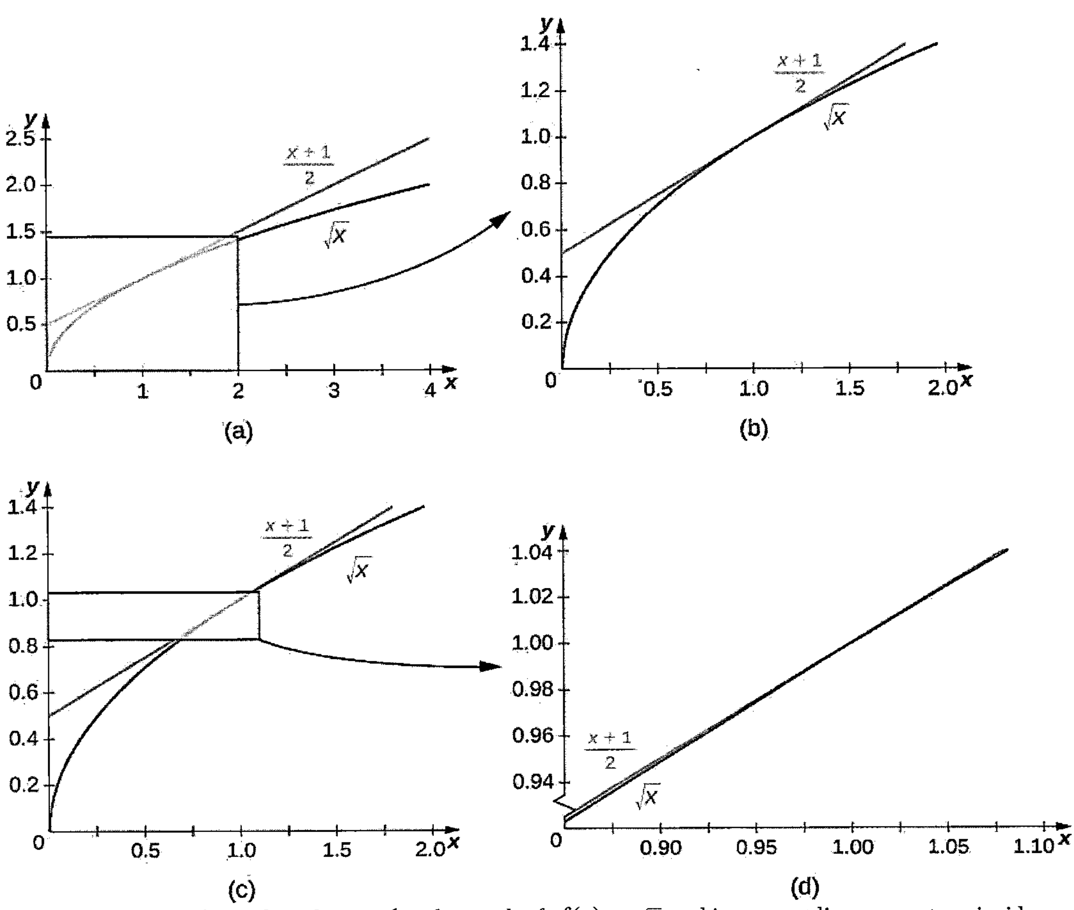

Figure 3.5 For values of x close to 1, the graph of $f(x) = \sqrt{x}$ and its tangent line appear to coincide.

Formally we may define the tangent line to the graph of a function as follows.

Definition

Let $f(x)$ be a function defined in an open interval containing a. The *tangent line* to $f(x)$ at a is the line passing through the point $(a, f(a))$ having slope

$$m_{\tan} = \lim_{x \to a} \frac{f(x) - f(a)}{x - a} \tag{3.3}$$

provided this limit exists.

Equivalently, we may define the tangent line to $f(x)$ at a to be the line passing through the point $(a, f(a))$ having slope

$$m_{\tan} = \lim_{h \to 0} \frac{f(a + h) - f(a)}{h} \tag{3.4}$$

provided this limit exists.

Just as we have used two different expressions to define the slope of a secant line, we use two different forms to define the slope of the tangent line. In this text we use both forms of the definition. As before, the choice of definition will depend on the setting. Now that we have formally defined a tangent line to a function at a point, we can use this definition to find equations of tangent lines.

Example 3.1

Finding a Tangent Line

Find the equation of the line tangent to the graph of $f(x) = x^2$ at $x = 3$.

Solution

First find the slope of the tangent line. In this example, use **Equation 3.3**.

$$\begin{aligned} m_{\tan} &= \lim_{x \to 3} \frac{f(x) - f(3)}{x - 3} && \text{Apply the definition.} \\ &= \lim_{x \to 3} \frac{x^2 - 9}{x - 3} && \text{Substitute } f(x) = x^2 \text{ and } f(3) = 9. \\ &= \lim_{x \to 3} \frac{(x-3)(x+3)}{x-3} = \lim_{x \to 3}(x+3) = 6 && \text{Factor the numerator to evaluate the limit.} \end{aligned}$$

Next, find a point on the tangent line. Since the line is tangent to the graph of $f(x)$ at $x = 3$, it passes through the point $(3, f(3))$. We have $f(3) = 9$, so the tangent line passes through the point $(3, 9)$.

Using the point-slope equation of the line with the slope $m = 6$ and the point $(3, 9)$, we obtain the line $y - 9 = 6(x - 3)$. Simplifying, we have $y = 6x - 9$. The graph of $f(x) = x^2$ and its tangent line at 3 are shown in **Figure 3.6**.

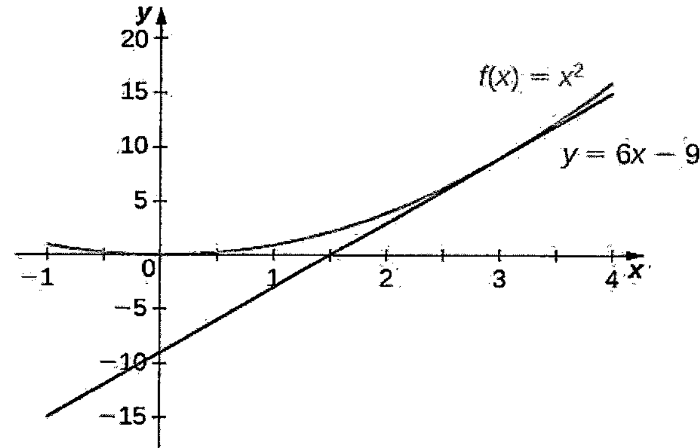

Figure 3.6 The tangent line to $f(x)$ at $x = 3$.

Example 3.2

The Slope of a Tangent Line Revisited

Use **Equation 3.4** to find the slope of the line tangent to the graph of $f(x) = x^2$ at $x = 3$.

Solution

The steps are very similar to **Example 3.1**. See **Equation 3.4** for the definition.

$$\begin{aligned} m_{\tan} &= \lim_{h \to 0} \frac{f(3+h) - f(3)}{h} && \text{Apply the definition.} \\ &= \lim_{h \to 0} \frac{(3+h)^2 - 9}{h} && \text{Substitute } f(3+h) = (3+h)^2 \text{ and } f(3) = 9. \\ &= \lim_{h \to 0} \frac{9 + 6h + h^2 - 9}{h} && \text{Expand and simplify to evaluate the limit.} \\ &= \lim_{h \to 0} \frac{h(6+h)}{h} = \lim_{h \to 0} (6+h) = 6 \end{aligned}$$

We obtained the same value for the slope of the tangent line by using the other definition, demonstrating that the formulas can be interchanged.

Example 3.3

Finding the Equation of a Tangent Line

Find the equation of the line tangent to the graph of $f(x) = 1/x$ at $x = 2$.

Solution

We can use **Equation 3.3**, but as we have seen, the results are the same if we use **Equation 3.4**.

$$\begin{aligned} m_{\tan} &= \lim_{x \to 2} \frac{f(x) - f(2)}{x - 2} && \text{Apply the definition.} \\ &= \lim_{x \to 2} \frac{\frac{1}{x} - \frac{1}{2}}{x - 2} && \text{Substitute } f(x) = \tfrac{1}{x} \text{ and } f(2) = \tfrac{1}{2}. \\ &= \lim_{x \to 2} \frac{\frac{1}{x} - \frac{1}{2}}{x - 2} \cdot \frac{2x}{2x} && \text{Multiply numerator and denominator by } 2x \text{ to simplify fractions.} \\ &= \lim_{x \to 2} \frac{(2 - x)}{(x - 2)(2x)} && \text{Simplify.} \\ &= \lim_{x \to 2} \frac{-1}{2x} && \text{Simplify using } \tfrac{2 - x}{x - 2} = -1, \text{ for } x \neq 2. \\ &= -\frac{1}{4} && \text{Evaluate the limit.} \end{aligned}$$

We now know that the slope of the tangent line is $-\frac{1}{4}$. To find the equation of the tangent line, we also need a point on the line. We know that $f(2) = \frac{1}{2}$. Since the tangent line passes through the point $(2, \frac{1}{2})$ we can use the point-slope equation of a line to find the equation of the tangent line. Thus the tangent line has the equation $y = -\frac{1}{4}x + 1$. The graphs of $f(x) = \frac{1}{x}$ and $y = -\frac{1}{4}x + 1$ are shown in **Figure 3.7**.

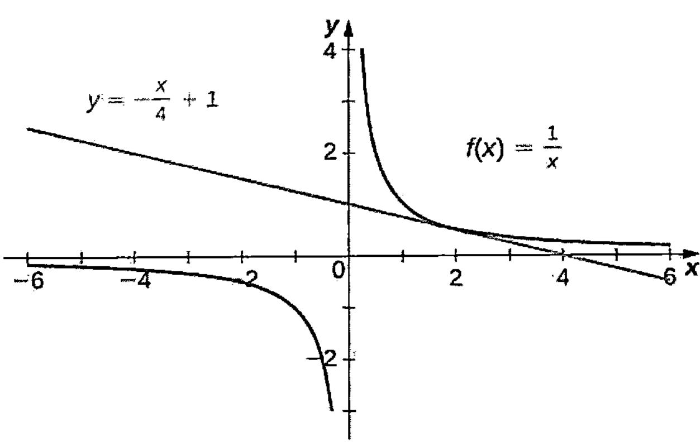

Figure 3.7 The line is tangent to $f(x)$ at $x = 2$.

3.1 Find the slope of the line tangent to the graph of $f(x) = \sqrt{x}$ at $x = 4$.

The Derivative of a Function at a Point

The type of limit we compute in order to find the slope of the line tangent to a function at a point occurs in many applications across many disciplines. These applications include velocity and acceleration in physics, marginal profit functions in business, and growth rates in biology. This limit occurs so frequently that we give this value a special name: the **derivative.** The process of finding a derivative is called **differentiation.**

Definition

Let $f(x)$ be a function defined in an open interval containing a. The derivative of the function $f(x)$ at a, denoted by $f'(a)$, is defined by

$$f'(a) = \lim_{x \to a} \frac{f(x) - f(a)}{x - a} \tag{3.5}$$

provided this limit exists.

Alternatively, we may also define the derivative of $f(x)$ at a as

$$f'(a) = \lim_{h \to 0} \frac{f(a + h) - f(a)}{h}. \tag{3.6}$$

Example 3.4

Estimating a Derivative

For $f(x) = x^2$, use a table to estimate $f'(3)$ using **Equation 3.5.**

Solution

Create a table using values of x just below 3 and just above 3.

x	$\frac{x^2-9}{x-3}$
2.9	5.9
2.99	5.99
2.999	5.999
3.001	6.001
3.01	6.01
3.1	6.1

After examining the table, we see that a good estimate is $f'(3) = 6$.

3.2 For $f(x) = x^2$, use a table to estimate $f'(3)$ using **Equation 3.6**.

Example 3.5

Finding a Derivative

For $f(x) = 3x^2 - 4x + 1$, find $f'(2)$ by using **Equation 3.5.**

Solution

Substitute the given function and value directly into the equation.

$$\begin{aligned} f'(x) &= \lim_{x \to 2} \frac{f(x) - f(2)}{x - 2} && \text{Apply the definition.} \\ &= \lim_{x \to 2} \frac{\left(3x^2 - 4x + 1\right) - 5}{x - 2} && \text{Substitute } f(x) = 3x^2 - 4x + 1 \text{ and } f(2) = 5. \\ &= \lim_{x \to 2} \frac{(x-2)(3x+2)}{x-2} && \text{Simplify and factor the numerator.} \\ &= \lim_{x \to 2} (3x + 2) && \text{Cancel the common factor.} \\ &= 8 && \text{Evaluate the limit.} \end{aligned}$$

Example 3.6

Revisiting the Derivative

For $f(x) = 3x^2 - 4x + 1,$ find $f'(2)$ by using **Equation 3.6**.

Solution

Using this equation, we can substitute two values of the function into the equation, and we should get the same value as in **Example 3.5**.

$$\begin{aligned} f'(2) &= \lim_{h \to 0} \frac{f(2+h) - f(2)}{h} && \text{Apply the definition.} \\ &= \lim_{h \to 0} \frac{(3(2+h)^2 - 4(2+h) + 1) - 5}{h} && \text{Substitute } f(2) = 5 \text{ and } f(2+h) = 3(2+h)^2 - 4(2+h) + 1. \\ &= \lim_{h \to 0} \frac{3h^2 + 8h}{h} && \text{Simplify the numerator.} \\ &= \lim_{h \to 0} \frac{h(3h+8)}{h} && \text{Factor the numerator.} \\ &= \lim_{h \to 0} (3h+8) && \text{Cancel the common factor.} \\ &= 8 && \text{Evaluate the limit.} \end{aligned}$$

The results are the same whether we use **Equation 3.5** or **Equation 3.6**.

3.3 For $f(x) = x^2 + 3x + 2,$ find $f'(1)$.

Velocities and Rates of Change

Now that we can evaluate a derivative, we can use it in velocity applications. Recall that if $s(t)$ is the position of an object moving along a coordinate axis, the average velocity of the object over a time interval $[a, t]$ if $t > a$ or $[t, a]$ if $t < a$ is given by the difference quotient

$$v_{\text{ave}} = \frac{s(t) - s(a)}{t - a}. \quad \textbf{(3.7)}$$

As the values of t approach $a,$ the values of v_{ave} approach the value we call the instantaneous velocity at $a.$ That is, instantaneous velocity at $a,$ denoted $v(a),$ is given by

$$v(a) = s'(a) = \lim_{t \to a} \frac{s(t) - s(a)}{t - a}. \quad \textbf{(3.8)}$$

To better understand the relationship between average velocity and instantaneous velocity, see **Figure 3.8**. In this figure, the slope of the tangent line (shown in red) is the instantaneous velocity of the object at time $t = a$ whose position at time t is given by the function $s(t)$. The slope of the secant line (shown in green) is the average velocity of the object over the time interval $[a, t]$.

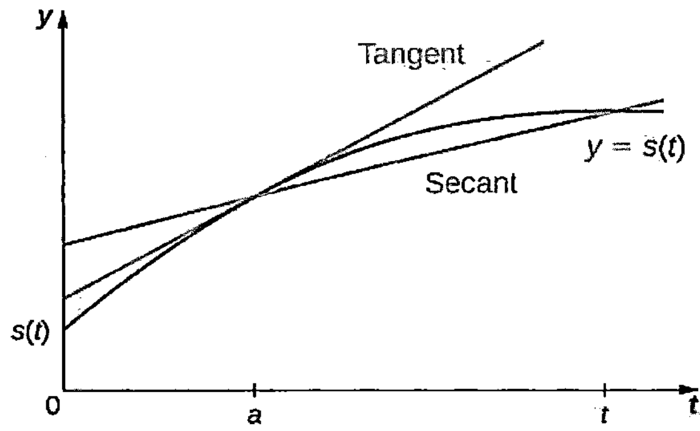

Figure 3.8 The slope of the secant line is the average velocity over the interval $[a,\ t]$. The slope of the tangent line is the instantaneous velocity.

We can use **Equation 3.5** to calculate the instantaneous velocity, or we can estimate the velocity of a moving object by using a table of values. We can then confirm the estimate by using **Equation 3.7**.

Example 3.7

Estimating Velocity

A lead weight on a spring is oscillating up and down. Its position at time t with respect to a fixed horizontal line is given by $s(t) = \sin t$ (**Figure 3.9**). Use a table of values to estimate $v(0)$. Check the estimate by using **Equation 3.5**.

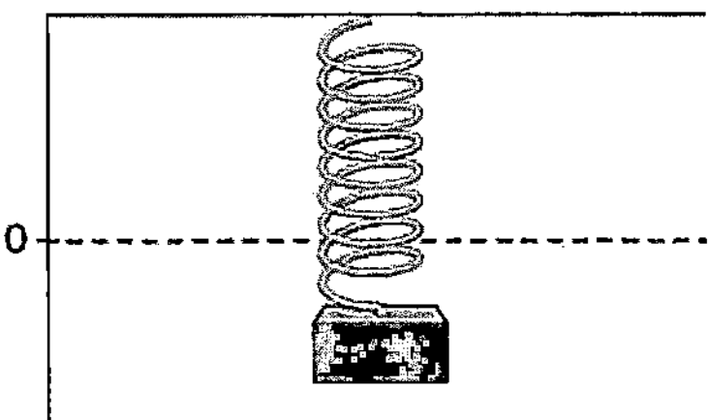

Figure 3.9 A lead weight suspended from a spring in vertical oscillatory motion.

Solution

We can estimate the instantaneous velocity at $t = 0$ by computing a table of average velocities using values of t approaching $0,$ as shown in **Table 3.2**.

t	$\frac{\sin t - \sin 0}{t - 0} = \frac{\sin t}{t}$
−0.1	0.998334166
−0.01	0.9999833333
−0.001	0.999999833
0.001	0.999999833
0.01	0.9999833333
0.1	0.998334166

Table 3.2
Average velocities using values of t approaching 0

From the table we see that the average velocity over the time interval $[-0.1, 0]$ is $0.998334166,$ the average velocity over the time interval $[-0.01, 0]$ is $0.9999833333,$ and so forth. Using this table of values, it appears that a good estimate is $v(0) = 1.$

By using **Equation 3.5**, we can see that

$$v(0) = s'(0) = \lim_{t \to 0} \frac{\sin t - \sin 0}{t - 0} = \lim_{t \to 0} \frac{\sin t}{t} = 1.$$

Thus, in fact, $v(0) = 1.$

3.4 A rock is dropped from a height of 64 feet. Its height above ground at time t seconds later is given by $s(t) = -16t^2 + 64, 0 \le t \le 2.$ Find its instantaneous velocity 1 second after it is dropped, using **Equation 3.5.**

As we have seen throughout this section, the slope of a tangent line to a function and instantaneous velocity are related concepts. Each is calculated by computing a derivative and each measures the instantaneous rate of change of a function, or the rate of change of a function at any point along the function.

Definition

The **instantaneous rate of change** of a function $f(x)$ at a value a is its derivative $f'(a).$

Example 3.8

Chapter Opener: Estimating Rate of Change of Velocity

Figure 3.10 (credit: modification of work by Codex41, Flickr)

Reaching a top speed of 270.49 mph, the Hennessey Venom GT is one of the fastest cars in the world. In tests it went from 0 to 60 mph in 3.05 seconds, from 0 to 100 mph in 5.88 seconds, from 0 to 200 mph in 14.51 seconds, and from 0 to 229.9 mph in 19.96 seconds. Use this data to draw a conclusion about the rate of change of velocity (that is, its acceleration) as it approaches 229.9 mph. Does the rate at which the car is accelerating appear to be increasing, decreasing, or constant?

Solution

First observe that 60 mph = 88 ft/s, 100 mph $\approx$ 146.67 ft/s, 200 mph $\approx$ 293.33 ft/s, and 229.9 mph $\approx$ 337.19 ft/s. We can summarize the information in a table.

t	$v(t)$
0	0
3.05	88
5.88	147.67
14.51	293.33
19.96	337.19

Table 3.3 $v(t)$ at different values of t

Now compute the average acceleration of the car in feet per second on intervals of the form $[t, 19.96]$ as t approaches 19.96, as shown in the following table.

t	$\frac{v(t) - v(19.96)}{t - 19.96} = \frac{v(t) - 337.19}{t - 19.96}$
0.0	16.89
3.05	14.74
5.88	13.46
14.51	8.05

Table 3.4
Average acceleration

The rate at which the car is accelerating is decreasing as its velocity approaches 229.9 mph (337.19 ft/s).

Example 3.9

Rate of Change of Temperature

A homeowner sets the thermostat so that the temperature in the house begins to drop from 70°F at 9 p.m., reaches a low of 60° during the night, and rises back to 70° by 7 a.m. the next morning. Suppose that the temperature in the house is given by $T(t) = 0.4t^2 - 4t + 70$ for $0 \le t \le 10$, where t is the number of hours past 9 p.m. Find the instantaneous rate of change of the temperature at midnight.

Solution

Since midnight is 3 hours past 9 p.m., we want to compute $T'(3)$. Refer to **Equation 3.5**.

$$\begin{aligned} T'(3) &= \lim_{t \to 3} \frac{T(t) - T(3)}{t - 3} && \text{Apply the definition.} \\ &= \lim_{t \to 3} \frac{0.4t^2 - 4t + 70 - 61.6}{t - 3} && \text{Substitute } T(t) = 0.4t^2 - 4t + 70 \text{ and } T(3) = 61.6. \\ &= \lim_{t \to 3} \frac{0.4t^2 - 4t + 8.4}{t - 3} && \text{Simplify.} \\ &= \lim_{t \to 3} \frac{0.4(t-3)(t-7)}{t - 3} && = \lim_{t \to 3} \frac{0.4(t-3)(t-7)}{t - 3} \\ &= \lim_{t \to 3} 0.4(t - 7) && \text{Cancel.} \\ &= -1.6 && \text{Evaluate the limit.} \end{aligned}$$

The instantaneous rate of change of the temperature at midnight is -1.6°F per hour.

Example 3.10

Rate of Change of Profit

A toy company can sell x electronic gaming systems at a price of $p = -0.01x + 400$ dollars per gaming system. The cost of manufacturing x systems is given by $C(x) = 100x + 10{,}000$ dollars. Find the rate of change of profit when 10,000 games are produced. Should the toy company increase or decrease production?

Solution

The profit $P(x)$ earned by producing x gaming systems is $R(x) - C(x)$, where $R(x)$ is the revenue obtained from the sale of x games. Since the company can sell x games at $p = -0.01x + 400$ per game,

$$R(x) = xp = x(-0.01x + 400) = -0.01x^2 + 400x.$$

Consequently,

$$P(x) = -0.01x^2 + 300x - 10{,}000.$$

Therefore, evaluating the rate of change of profit gives

$$\begin{aligned} P'(10000) &= \lim_{x \to 10000} \frac{P(x) - P(10000)}{x - 10000} \\ &= \lim_{x \to 10000} \frac{-0.01x^2 + 300x - 10000 - 1990000}{x - 10000} \\ &= \lim_{x \to 10000} \frac{-0.01x^2 + 300x - 2000000}{x - 10000} \\ &= 100. \end{aligned}$$

Since the rate of change of profit $P'(10{,}000) > 0$ and $P(10{,}000) > 0$, the company should increase production.

3.5 A coffee shop determines that the daily profit on scones obtained by charging s dollars per scone is $P(s) = -20s^2 + 150s - 10$. The coffee shop currently charges \$3.25 per scone. Find $P'(3.25)$, the rate of change of profit when the price is \$3.25 and decide whether or not the coffee shop should consider raising or lowering its prices on scones.

3.1 EXERCISES

For the following exercises, use **Equation 3.3** to find the slope of the secant line between the values x_1 and x_2 for each function $y = f(x)$.

1. $f(x) = 4x + 7;\ x_1 = 2,\ x_2 = 5$

2. $f(x) = 8x - 3;\ x_1 = -1,\ x_2 = 3$

3. $f(x) = x^2 + 2x + 1;\ x_1 = 3,\ x_2 = 3.5$

4. $f(x) = -x^2 + x + 2;\ x_1 = 0.5,\ x_2 = 1.5$

5. $f(x) = \frac{4}{3x - 1};\ x_1 = 1,\ x_2 = 3$

6. $f(x) = \frac{x - 7}{2x + 1};\ x_1 = -2,\ x_2 = 0$

7. $f(x) = \sqrt{x};\ x_1 = 1,\ x_2 = 16$

8. $f(x) = \sqrt{x - 9};\ x_1 = 10,\ x_2 = 13$

9. $f(x) = x^{1/3} + 1;\ x_1 = 0,\ x_2 = 8$

10. $f(x) = 6x^{2/3} + 2x^{1/3};\ x_1 = 1,\ x_2 = 27$

For the following functions,

a. use **Equation 3.4** to find the slope of the tangent line $m_{\tan} = f'(a)$, and

b. find the equation of the tangent line to f at $x = a$.

11. $f(x) = 3 - 4x,\ a = 2$

12. $f(x) = \frac{x}{5} + 6,\ a = -1$

13. $f(x) = x^2 + x,\ a = 1$

14. $f(x) = 1 - x - x^2,\ a = 0$

15. $f(x) = \frac{7}{x},\ a = 3$

16. $f(x) = \sqrt{x + 8},\ a = 1$

17. $f(x) = 2 - 3x^2,\ a = -2$

18. $f(x) = \frac{-3}{x - 1},\ a = 4$

19. $f(x) = \frac{2}{x + 3},\ a = -4$

20. $f(x) = \frac{3}{x^2},\ a = 3$

For the following functions $y = f(x)$, find $f'(a)$ using **Equation 3.3**.

21. $f(x) = 5x + 4,\ a = -1$

22. $f(x) = -7x + 1,\ a = 3$

23. $f(x) = x^2 + 9x,\ a = 2$

24. $f(x) = 3x^2 - x + 2,\ a = 1$

25. $f(x) = \sqrt{x},\ a = 4$

26. $f(x) = \sqrt{x - 2},\ a = 6$

27. $f(x) = \frac{1}{x},\ a = 2$

28. $f(x) = \frac{1}{x - 3},\ a = -1$

29. $f(x) = \frac{1}{x^3},\ a = 1$

30. $f(x) = \frac{1}{\sqrt{x}},\ a = 4$

For the following exercises, given the function $y = f(x)$,

a. find the slope of the secant line PQ for each point $Q(x,\ f(x))$ with x value given in the table.

b. Use the answers from a. to estimate the value of the slope of the tangent line at P.

c. Use the answer from b. to find the equation of the tangent line to f at point P.

31. **[T]** $f(x) = x^2 + 3x + 4,\ P(1, 8)$ (Round to 6 decimal places.)

x	Slope m_{PQ}	x	Slope m_{PQ}
1.1	(i)	0.9	(vii)
1.01	(ii)	0.99	(viii)
1.001	(iii)	0.999	(ix)
1.0001	(iv)	0.9999	(x)
1.00001	(v)	0.99999	(xi)
1.000001	(vi)	0.999999	(xii)

32. **[T]** $f(x) = \frac{x+1}{x^2 - 1},\ P(0, -1)$

x	Slope m_{PQ}	x	Slope m_{PQ}
0.1	(i)	−0.1	(vii)
0.01	(ii)	−0.01	(viii)
0.001	(iii)	−0.001	(ix)
0.0001	(iv)	−0.0001	(x)
0.00001	(v)	−0.00001	(xi)
0.000001	(vi)	−0.000001	(xii)

33. **[T]** $f(x) = 10e^{0.5x},\ P(0, 10)$ (Round to 4 decimal places.)

x	Slope m_{PQ}
−0.1	(i)
−0.01	(ii)
−0.001	(iii)
−0.0001	(iv)
−0.00001	(v)
−0.000001	(vi)

34. **[T]** $f(x) = \tan(x),\ P(\pi, 0)$

x	Slope m_{PQ}
3.1	(i)
3.14	(ii)
3.141	(iii)
3.1415	(iv)
3.14159	(v)
3.141592	(vi)

[T] For the following position functions $y = s(t)$, an object is moving along a straight line, where t is in seconds and s is in meters. Find

a. the simplified expression for the average velocity from $t = 2$ to $t = 2 + h$;

b. the average velocity between $t = 2$ and $t = 2 + h$, where (i) $h = 0.1$, (ii) $h = 0.01$, (iii) $h = 0.001$, and (iv) $h = 0.0001$; and

c. use the answer from a. to estimate the instantaneous

velocity at $t = 2$ second.

35. $s(t) = \frac{1}{3}t + 5$

36. $s(t) = t^2 - 2t$

37. $s(t) = 2t^3 + 3$

38. $s(t) = \frac{16}{t^2} - \frac{4}{t}$

39. Use the following graph to evaluate a. $f'(1)$ and b. $f'(6)$.

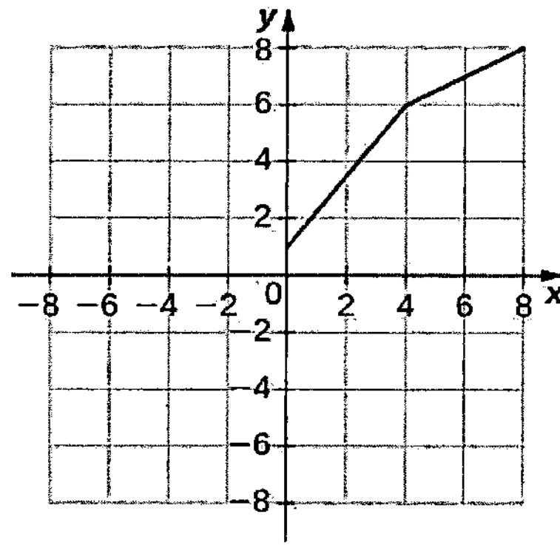

40. Use the following graph to evaluate a. $f'(-3)$ and b. $f'(1.5)$.

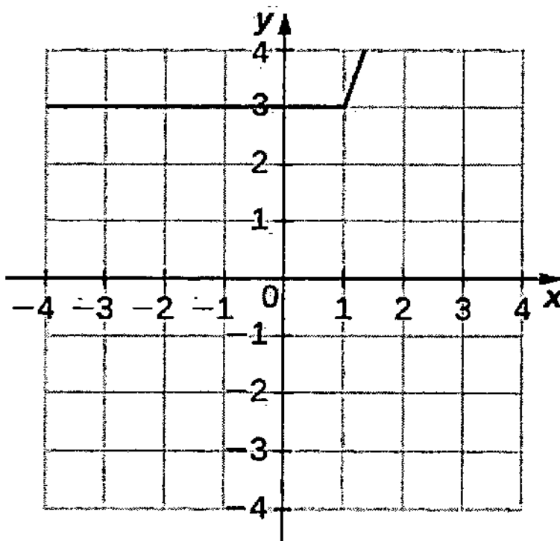

For the following exercises, use the limit definition of derivative to show that the derivative does not exist at $x = a$ for each of the given functions.

41. $f(x) = x^{1/3}, x = 0$

42. $f(x) = x^{2/3}, x = 0$

43. $f(x) = \begin{cases} 1, & x < 1 \\ x, & x \geq 1 \end{cases}, x = 1$

44. $f(x) = \frac{|x|}{x}, x = 0$

45. **[T]** The position in feet of a race car along a straight track after t seconds is modeled by the function $s(t) = 8t^2 - \frac{1}{16}t^3$.

a. Find the average velocity of the vehicle over the following time intervals to four decimal places:
   i. [4, 4.1]
   ii. [4, 4.01]
   iii. [4, 4.001]
   iv. [4, 4.0001]

b. Use a. to draw a conclusion about the instantaneous velocity of the vehicle at $t = 4$ seconds.

46. **[T]** The distance in feet that a ball rolls down an incline is modeled by the function $s(t) = 14t^2$, where t is seconds after the ball begins rolling.

a. Find the average velocity of the ball over the following time intervals:
   i. [5, 5.1]
   ii. [5, 5.01]
   iii. [5, 5.001]
   iv. [5, 5.0001]

b. Use the answers from a. to draw a conclusion about the instantaneous velocity of the ball at $t = 5$ seconds.

47. Two vehicles start out traveling side by side along a straight road. Their position functions, shown in the following graph, are given by $s = f(t)$ and $s = g(t)$, where s is measured in feet and t is measured in seconds.

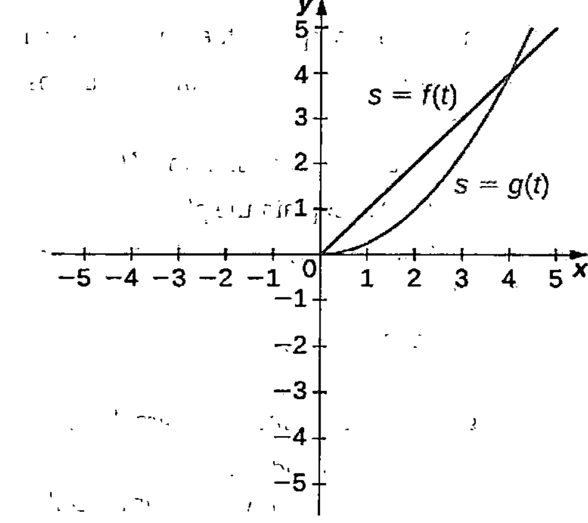

a. Which vehicle has traveled farther at $t = 2$ seconds?

b. What is the approximate velocity of each vehicle at $t = 3$ seconds?

c. Which vehicle is traveling faster at $t = 4$ seconds?

d. What is true about the positions of the vehicles at $t = 4$ seconds?

48. **[T]** The total cost $C(x)$, in hundreds of dollars, to produce x jars of mayonnaise is given by $C(x) = 0.000003x^3 + 4x + 300$.

a. Calculate the average cost per jar over the following intervals:
   i. [100, 100.1]
   ii. [100, 100.01]
   iii. [100, 100.001]
   iv. [100, 100.0001]
b. Use the answers from a. to estimate the average cost to produce 100 jars of mayonnaise.

49. **[T]** For the function $f(x) = x^3 - 2x^2 - 11x + 12$, do the following.

a. Use a graphing calculator to graph f in an appropriate viewing window.
b. Use the ZOOM feature on the calculator to approximate the two values of $x = a$ for which $m_{\tan} = f'(a) = 0$.

50. **[T]** For the function $f(x) = \frac{x}{1 + x^2}$, do the following.

a. Use a graphing calculator to graph f in an appropriate viewing window.
b. Use the ZOOM feature on the calculator to approximate the values of $x = a$ for which $m_{\tan} = f'(a) = 0$.

51. Suppose that $N(x)$ computes the number of gallons of gas used by a vehicle traveling x miles. Suppose the vehicle gets 30 mpg.

a. Find a mathematical expression for $N(x)$.
b. What is $N(100)$? Explain the physical meaning.
c. What is $N'(100)$? Explain the physical meaning.

52. **[T]** For the function $f(x) = x^4 - 5x^2 + 4$, do the following.

a. Use a graphing calculator to graph f in an appropriate viewing window.
b. Use the nDeriv function, which numerically finds the derivative, on a graphing calculator to estimate $f'(-2)$, $f'(-0.5)$, $f'(1.7)$, and $f'(2.718)$.

53. **[T]** For the function $f(x) = \frac{x^2}{x^2 + 1}$, do the following.

a. Use a graphing calculator to graph f in an appropriate viewing window.
b. Use the nDeriv function on a graphing calculator to find $f'(-4)$, $f'(-2)$, $f'(2)$, and $f'(4)$.

3.2 | The Derivative as a Function

Learning Objectives

3.2.1 Define the derivative function of a given function.
3.2.2 Graph a derivative function from the graph of a given function.
3.2.3 State the connection between derivatives and continuity.
3.2.4 Describe three conditions for when a function does not have a derivative.
3.2.5 Explain the meaning of a higher-order derivative.

As we have seen, the derivative of a function at a given point gives us the rate of change or slope of the tangent line to the function at that point. If we differentiate a position function at a given time, we obtain the velocity at that time. It seems reasonable to conclude that knowing the derivative of the function at every point would produce valuable information about the behavior of the function. However, the process of finding the derivative at even a handful of values using the techniques of the preceding section would quickly become quite tedious. In this section we define the derivative function and learn a process for finding it.

Derivative Functions

The derivative function gives the derivative of a function at each point in the domain of the original function for which the derivative is defined. We can formally define a derivative function as follows.

Definition

Let f be a function. The **derivative function**, denoted by f', is the function whose domain consists of those values of x such that the following limit exists:

$$f'(x) = \lim_{h \to 0} \frac{f(x+h) - f(x)}{h}. \quad (3.9)$$

A function $f(x)$ is said to be **differentiable at** a if $f'(a)$ exists. More generally, a function is said to be **differentiable on** S if it is differentiable at every point in an open set S, and a **differentiable function** is one in which $f'(x)$ exists on its domain.

In the next few examples we use **Equation 3.9** to find the derivative of a function.

Example 3.11

Finding the Derivative of a Square-Root Function

Find the derivative of $f(x) = \sqrt{x}$.

Solution

Start directly with the definition of the derivative function. Use **Equation 3.1**.

$$
\begin{aligned}
f'(x) &= \lim_{h \to 0} \frac{\sqrt{x+h} - \sqrt{x}}{h} && \text{Substitute } f(x+h) = \sqrt{x+h} \text{ and } f(x) = \sqrt{x} \text{ into } f'(x) = \lim_{h \to 0} \frac{f(x+h) - f(x)}{h}. \\
&= \lim_{h \to 0} \frac{\sqrt{x+h} - \sqrt{x}}{h} \cdot \frac{\sqrt{x+h} + \sqrt{x}}{\sqrt{x+h} + \sqrt{x}} && \text{Multiply numerator and denominator by } \sqrt{x+h} + \sqrt{x} \text{ without distributing in the denominator.} \\
&= \lim_{h \to 0} \frac{h}{h(\sqrt{x+h} + \sqrt{x})} && \text{Multiply the numerators and simplify.} \\
&= \lim_{h \to 0} \frac{1}{(\sqrt{x+h} + \sqrt{x})} && \text{Cancel the } h. \\
&= \frac{1}{2\sqrt{x}} && \text{Evaluate the limit.}
\end{aligned}
$$

Example 3.12

Finding the Derivative of a Quadratic Function

Find the derivative of the function $f(x) = x^2 - 2x$.

Solution

Follow the same procedure here, but without having to multiply by the conjugate.

$$
\begin{aligned}
f'(x) &= \lim_{h \to 0} \frac{((x+h)^2 - 2(x+h)) - (x^2 - 2x)}{h} && \text{Substitute } f(x+h) = (x+h)^2 - 2(x+h) \text{ and } f(x) = x^2 - 2x \text{ into } f'(x) = \lim_{h \to 0} \frac{f(x+h) - f(x)}{h}. \\
&= \lim_{h \to 0} \frac{x^2 + 2xh + h^2 - 2x - 2h - x^2 + 2x}{h} && \text{Expand } (x+h)^2 - 2(x+h). \\
&= \lim_{h \to 0} \frac{2xh - 2h + h^2}{h} && \text{Simplify.} \\
&= \lim_{h \to 0} \frac{h(2x - 2 + h)}{h} && \text{Factor out } h \text{ from the numerator.} \\
&= \lim_{h \to 0} (2x - 2 + h) && \text{Cancel the common factor of } h. \\
&= 2x - 2 && \text{Evaluate the limit.}
\end{aligned}
$$

 **3.6** Find the derivative of $f(x) = x^2$.

We use a variety of different notations to express the derivative of a function. In **Example 3.12** we showed that if $f(x) = x^2 - 2x$, then $f'(x) = 2x - 2$. If we had expressed this function in the form $y = x^2 - 2x$, we could have expressed the derivative as $y' = 2x - 2$ or $\frac{dy}{dx} = 2x - 2$. We could have conveyed the same information by writing $\frac{d}{dx}\left(x^2 - 2x\right) = 2x - 2$. Thus, for the function $y = f(x)$, each of the following notations represents the derivative of $f(x)$:

$$f'(x),\ \frac{dy}{dx},\ y',\ \frac{d}{dx}(f(x)).$$

In place of $f'(a)$ we may also use $\left.\frac{dy}{dx}\right|_{x=a}$ Use of the $\frac{dy}{dx}$ notation (called Leibniz notation) is quite common in engineering and physics. To understand this notation better, recall that the derivative of a function at a point is the limit of the slopes of secant lines as the secant lines approach the tangent line. The slopes of these secant lines are often expressed in the form $\frac{\Delta y}{\Delta x}$ where Δy is the difference in the y values corresponding to the difference in the x values, which are expressed as Δx (**Figure 3.11**). Thus the derivative, which can be thought of as the instantaneous rate of change of y with respect to x, is expressed as

$$\frac{dy}{dx} = \lim_{\Delta x \to 0} \frac{\Delta y}{\Delta x}.$$

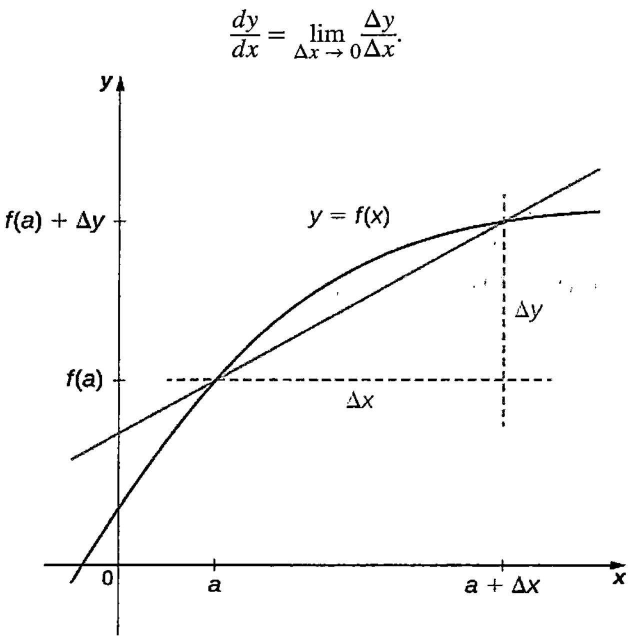

Figure 3.11 The derivative is expressed as $\frac{dy}{dx} = \lim_{\Delta x \to 0} \frac{\Delta y}{\Delta x}$.

Graphing a Derivative

We have already discussed how to graph a function, so given the equation of a function or the equation of a derivative function, we could graph it. Given both, we would expect to see a correspondence between the graphs of these two functions, since $f'(x)$ gives the rate of change of a function $f(x)$ (or slope of the tangent line to $f(x)$).

In **Example 3.11** we found that for $f(x) = \sqrt{x}$, $f'(x) = 1/2\sqrt{x}$. If we graph these functions on the same axes, as in **Figure 3.12**, we can use the graphs to understand the relationship between these two functions. First, we notice that $f(x)$ is increasing over its entire domain, which means that the slopes of its tangent lines at all points are positive. Consequently, we expect $f'(x) > 0$ for all values of x in its domain. Furthermore, as x increases, the slopes of the tangent lines to $f(x)$ are decreasing and we expect to see a corresponding decrease in $f'(x)$. We also observe that $f(0)$ is undefined and that $\lim_{x \to 0^+} f'(x) = +\infty$, corresponding to a vertical tangent to $f(x)$ at 0.

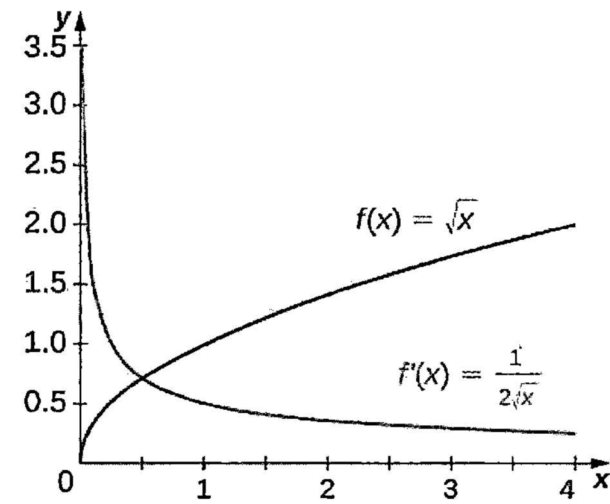

Figure 3.12 The derivative $f'(x)$ is positive everywhere because the function $f(x)$ is increasing.

In **Example 3.12** we found that for $f(x) = x^2 - 2x$, $f'(x) = 2x - 2$. The graphs of these functions are shown in **Figure 3.13**. Observe that $f(x)$ is decreasing for $x < 1$. For these same values of x, $f'(x) < 0$. For values of $x > 1$, $f(x)$ is increasing and $f'(x) > 0$. Also, $f(x)$ has a horizontal tangent at $x = 1$ and $f'(1) = 0$.

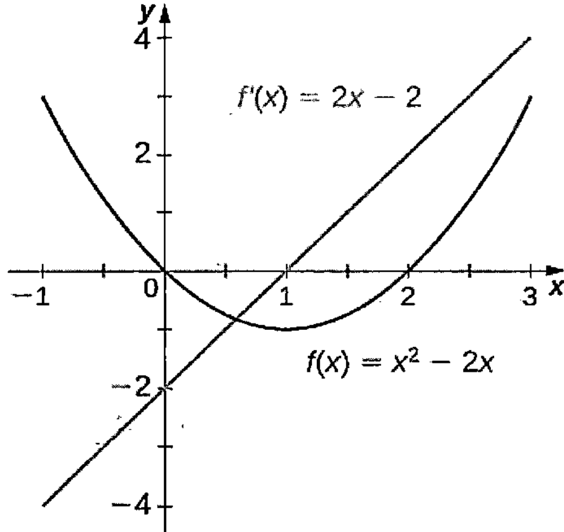

Figure 3.13 The derivative $f'(x) < 0$ where the function $f(x)$ is decreasing and $f'(x) > 0$ where $f(x)$ is increasing. The derivative is zero where the function has a horizontal tangent.

Example 3.13

Sketching a Derivative Using a Function

Use the following graph of $f(x)$ to sketch a graph of $f'(x)$.

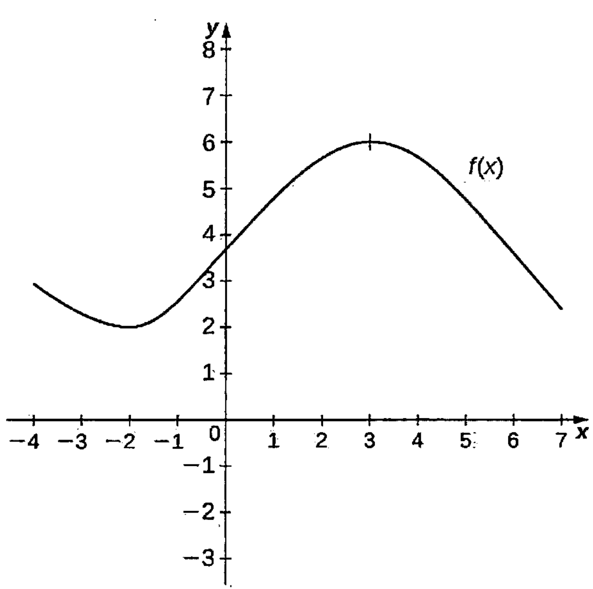

Solution

The solution is shown in the following graph. Observe that $f(x)$ is increasing and $f'(x) > 0$ on $(-2, 3)$. Also, $f(x)$ is decreasing and $f'(x) < 0$ on $(-\infty, -2)$ and on $(3, +\infty)$. Also note that $f(x)$ has horizontal tangents at -2 and $3,$ and $f'(-2) = 0$ and $f'(3) = 0.$

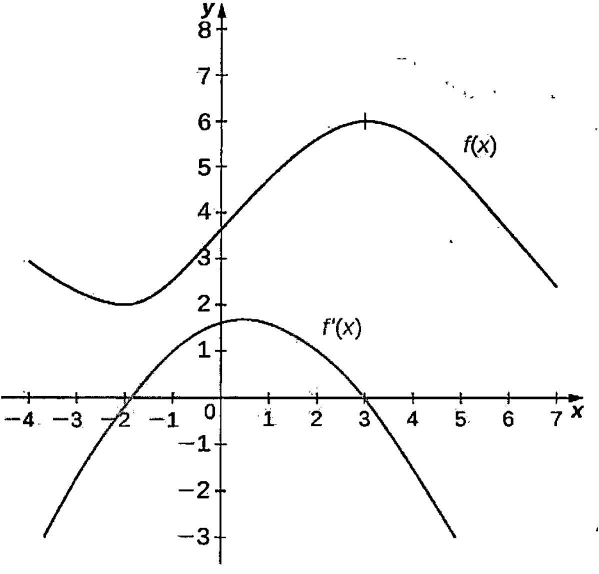

3.7 Sketch the graph of $f(x) = x^2 - 4.$ On what interval is the graph of $f'(x)$ above the x-axis?

Derivatives and Continuity

Now that we can graph a derivative, let's examine the behavior of the graphs. First, we consider the relationship between differentiability and continuity. We will see that if a function is differentiable at a point, it must be continuous there;

however, a function that is continuous at a point need not be differentiable at that point. In fact, a function may be continuous at a point and fail to be differentiable at the point for one of several reasons.

Theorem 3.1: Differentiability Implies Continuity

Let $f(x)$ be a function and a be in its domain. If $f(x)$ is differentiable at a, then f is continuous at a.

Proof

If $f(x)$ is differentiable at a, then $f'(a)$ exists and

$$f'(a) = \lim_{x \to a} \frac{f(x) - f(a)}{x - a}.$$

We want to show that $f(x)$ is continuous at a by showing that $\lim_{x \to a} f(x) = f(a)$. Thus,

$$\begin{aligned}
\lim_{x \to a} f(x) &= \lim_{x \to a} (f(x) - f(a) + f(a)) \\
&= \lim_{x \to a} \left(\frac{f(x) - f(a)}{x - a} \cdot (x - a) + f(a) \right) && \text{Multiply and divide } f(x) - f(a) \text{ by } x - a. \\
&= \left(\lim_{x \to a} \frac{f(x) - f(a)}{x - a} \right) \cdot \left(\lim_{x \to a} (x - a) \right) + \lim_{x \to a} f(a) \\
&= f'(a) \cdot 0 + f(a) \\
&= f(a).
\end{aligned}$$

Therefore, since $f(a)$ is defined and $\lim_{x \to a} f(x) = f(a)$, we conclude that f is continuous at a.

□

We have just proven that differentiability implies continuity, but now we consider whether continuity implies differentiability. To determine an answer to this question, we examine the function $f(x) = |x|$. This function is continuous everywhere; however, $f'(0)$ is undefined. This observation leads us to believe that continuity does not imply differentiability. Let's explore further. For $f(x) = |x|$,

$$f'(0) = \lim_{x \to 0} \frac{f(x) - f(0)}{x - 0} = \lim_{x \to 0} \frac{|x| - |0|}{x - 0} = \lim_{x \to 0} \frac{|x|}{x}.$$

This limit does not exist because

$$\lim_{x \to 0^-} \frac{|x|}{x} = -1 \text{ and } \lim_{x \to 0^+} \frac{|x|}{x} = 1.$$

See **Figure 3.14**.

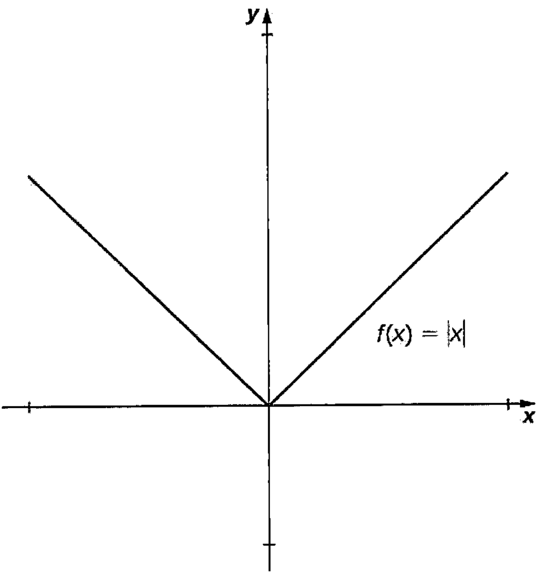

Figure 3.14 The function $f(x) = |x|$ is continuous at 0 but is not differentiable at 0.

Let's consider some additional situations in which a continuous function fails to be differentiable. Consider the function $f(x) = \sqrt[3]{x}$:

$$f'(0) = \lim_{x \to 0} \frac{\sqrt[3]{x} - 0}{x - 0} = \lim_{x \to 0} \frac{1}{\sqrt[3]{x^2}} = +\infty.$$

Thus $f'(0)$ does not exist. A quick look at the graph of $f(x) = \sqrt[3]{x}$ clarifies the situation. The function has a vertical tangent line at 0 (**Figure 3.15**).

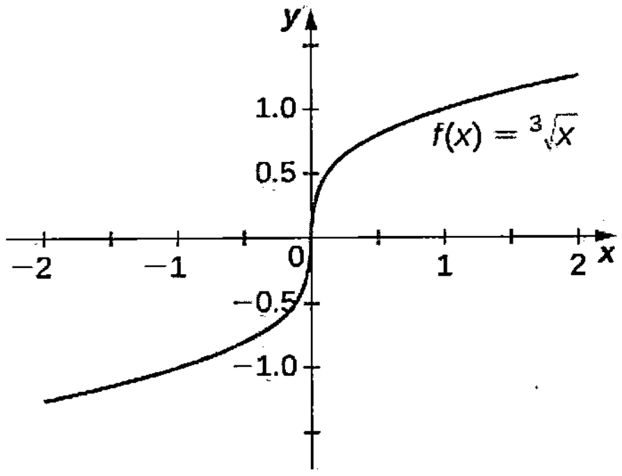

Figure 3.15 The function $f(x) = \sqrt[3]{x}$ has a vertical tangent at $x = 0$. It is continuous at 0 but is not differentiable at 0.

The function $f(x) = \begin{cases} x\sin\left(\frac{1}{x}\right) \text{ if } x \neq 0 \\ 0 \text{ if } x = 0 \end{cases}$ also has a derivative that exhibits interesting behavior at 0. We see that

$$f'(0) = \lim_{x \to 0} \frac{x\sin(1/x) - 0}{x - 0} = \lim_{x \to 0} \sin\left(\frac{1}{x}\right).$$

This limit does not exist, essentially because the slopes of the secant lines continuously change direction as they approach zero (**Figure 3.16**).

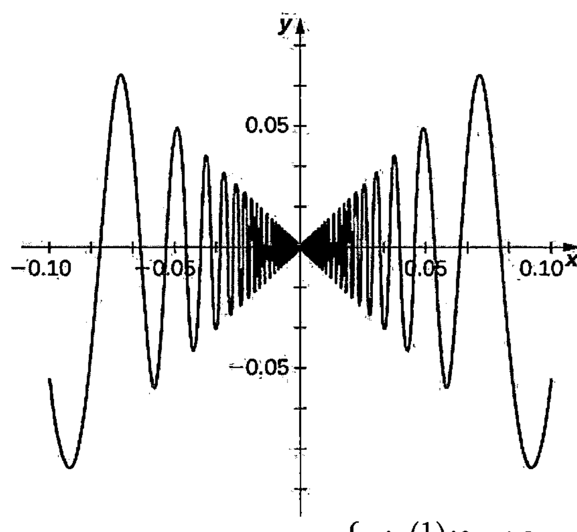

Figure 3.16 The function $f(x) = \begin{cases} x\sin\left(\frac{1}{x}\right) \text{ if } x \neq 0 \\ 0 \text{ if } x = 0 \end{cases}$ is not differentiable at 0.

In summary:

1. We observe that if a function is not continuous, it cannot be differentiable, since every differentiable function must be continuous. However, if a function is continuous, it may still fail to be differentiable.
2. We saw that $f(x) = |x|$ failed to be differentiable at 0 because the limit of the slopes of the tangent lines on the left and right were not the same. Visually, this resulted in a sharp corner on the graph of the function at $0.$ From this we conclude that in order to be differentiable at a point, a function must be "smooth" at that point.
3. As we saw in the example of $f(x) = \sqrt[3]{x},$ a function fails to be differentiable at a point where there is a vertical tangent line.
4. As we saw with $f(x) = \begin{cases} x\sin\left(\frac{1}{x}\right) \text{ if } x \neq 0 \\ 0 \text{ if } x = 0 \end{cases}$ a function may fail to be differentiable at a point in more complicated ways as well.

Example 3.14

A Piecewise Function that is Continuous and Differentiable

A toy company wants to design a track for a toy car that starts out along a parabolic curve and then converts to a straight line (**Figure 3.17**). The function that describes the track is to have the form $f(x) = \begin{cases} \frac{1}{10}x^2 + bx + c \text{ if } x < -10 \\ -\frac{1}{4}x + \frac{5}{2} \text{ if } x \geq -10 \end{cases}$ where x and $f(x)$ are in inches. For the car to move smoothly along the track, the function $f(x)$ must be both continuous and differentiable at $-10.$ Find values of b and c that make $f(x)$ both continuous and differentiable.

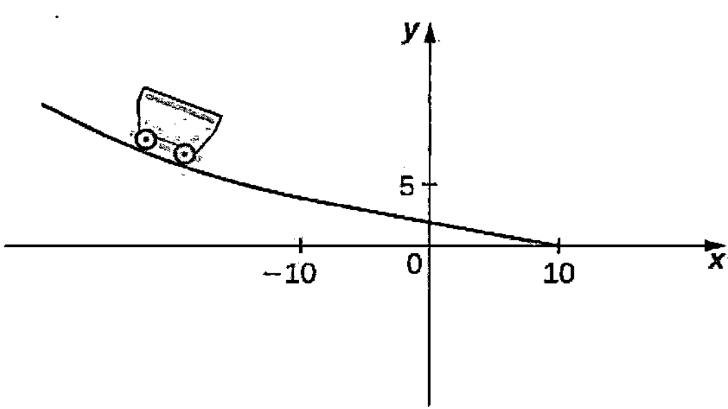

Figure 3.17 For the car to move smoothly along the track, the function must be both continuous and differentiable.

Solution

For the function to be continuous at $x = -10$, $\lim\limits_{x \to 10^-} f(x) = f(-10)$. Thus, since

$$\lim_{x \to -10^-} f(x) = \frac{1}{10}(-10)^2 - 10b + c = 10 - 10b + c$$

and $f(-10) = 5$, we must have $10 - 10b + c = 5$. Equivalently, we have $c = 10b - 5$.

For the function to be differentiable at -10,

$$f'(10) = \lim_{x \to -10} \frac{f(x) - f(-10)}{x + 10}$$

must exist. Since $f(x)$ is defined using different rules on the right and the left, we must evaluate this limit from the right and the left and then set them equal to each other:

$$\begin{aligned}
\lim_{x \to -10^-} \frac{f(x) - f(-10)}{x + 10} &= \lim_{x \to -10^-} \frac{\frac{1}{10}x^2 + bx + c - 5}{x + 10} \\
&= \lim_{x \to -10^-} \frac{\frac{1}{10}x^2 + bx + (10b - 5) - 5}{x + 10} && \text{Substitute } c = 10b - 5. \\
&= \lim_{x \to -10^-} \frac{x^2 - 100 + 10bx + 100b}{10(x + 10)} \\
&= \lim_{x \to -10^-} \frac{(x + 10)(x - 10 + 10b)}{10(x + 10)} && \text{Factor by grouping.} \\
&= b - 2.
\end{aligned}$$

We also have

$$\begin{aligned}
\lim_{x \to -10^+} \frac{f(x) - f(-10)}{x + 10} &= \lim_{x \to -10^+} \frac{-\frac{1}{4}x + \frac{5}{2} - 5}{x + 10} \\
&= \lim_{x \to -10^+} \frac{-(x + 10)}{4(x + 10)} \\
&= -\frac{1}{4}.
\end{aligned}$$

This gives us $b - 2 = -\frac{1}{4}$. Thus $b = \frac{7}{4}$ and $c = 10\left(\frac{7}{4}\right) - 5 = \frac{25}{2}$.

3.8 Find values of a and b that make $f(x) = \begin{cases} ax + b \text{ if } x < 3 \\ x^2 \text{ if } x \geq 3 \end{cases}$ both continuous and differentiable at 3.

Higher-Order Derivatives

The derivative of a function is itself a function, so we can find the derivative of a derivative. For example, the derivative of a position function is the rate of change of position, or velocity. The derivative of velocity is the rate of change of velocity, which is acceleration. The new function obtained by differentiating the derivative is called the second derivative. Furthermore, we can continue to take derivatives to obtain the third derivative, fourth derivative, and so on. Collectively, these are referred to as **higher-order derivatives**. The notation for the higher-order derivatives of $y = f(x)$ can be expressed in any of the following forms:

$$f''(x),\ f'''(x),\ f^{(4)}(x),\ldots,\ f^{(n)}(x)$$
$$y''(x),\ y'''(x),\ y^{(4)}(x),\ldots,\ y^{(n)}(x)$$
$$\frac{d^2y}{dx^2},\ \frac{d^3y}{dy^3},\ \frac{d^4y}{dy^4},\ldots,\ \frac{d^ny}{dy^n}.$$

It is interesting to note that the notation for $\frac{d^2y}{dx^2}$ may be viewed as an attempt to express $\frac{d}{dx}\left(\frac{dy}{dx}\right)$ more compactly. Analogously, $\frac{d}{dx}\left(\frac{d}{dx}\left(\frac{dy}{dx}\right)\right) = \frac{d}{dx}\left(\frac{d^2y}{dx^2}\right) = \frac{d^3y}{dx^3}$.

Example 3.15

Finding a Second Derivative

For $f(x) = 2x^2 - 3x + 1$, find $f''(x)$.

Solution

First find $f'(x)$.

$$f'(x) = \lim_{h \to 0} \frac{\left(2(x+h)^2 - 3(x+h) + 1\right) - (2x^2 - 3x + 1)}{h}$$

Substitute $f(x) = 2x^2 - 3x + 1$ and $f(x+h) = 2(x+h)^2 - 3(x+h) + 1$ into $f'(x) = \lim_{h \to 0} \frac{f(x+h) - f(x)}{h}$.

$$= \lim_{h \to 0} \frac{4xh + h^2 - 3h}{h}$$

Simplify the numerator.

$$= \lim_{h \to 0} (4x + h - 3)$$

Factor out the h in the numerator and cancel with the h in the denominator.

$$= 4x - 3$$

Take the limit.

Next, find $f''(x)$ by taking the derivative of $f'(x) = 4x - 3$.

$$f''(x) = \lim_{h \to 0} \frac{f'(x+h) - f'(x)}{h}$$

Use $f'(x) = \lim_{h \to 0} \frac{f(x+h) - f(x)}{h}$ with $f'(x)$ in place of $f(x)$.

$$= \lim_{h \to 0} \frac{(4(x+h) - 3) - (4x - 3)}{h}$$

Substitute $f'(x+h) = 4(x+h) - 3$ and $f'(x) = 4x - 3$.

$$= \lim_{h \to 0} 4$$

Simplify.

$$= 4$$

Take the limit.

3.9 Find $f''(x)$ for $f(x) = x^2$.

Example 3.16

Finding Acceleration

The position of a particle along a coordinate axis at time t (in seconds) is given by $s(t) = 3t^2 - 4t + 1$ (in meters). Find the function that describes its acceleration at time t.

Solution

Since $v(t) = s'(t)$ and $a(t) = v'(t) = s''(t)$, we begin by finding the derivative of $s(t)$:

$$\begin{aligned} s'(t) &= \lim_{h \to 0} \frac{s(t+h) - s(t)}{h} \\ &= \lim_{h \to 0} \frac{3(t+h)^2 - 4(t+h) + 1 - \left(3t^2 - 4t + 1\right)}{h} \\ &= 6t - 4. \end{aligned}$$

Next,

$$\begin{aligned} s''(t) &= \lim_{h \to 0} \frac{s'(t+h) - s'(t)}{h} \\ &= \lim_{h \to 0} \frac{6(t+h) - 4 - (6t - 4)}{h} \\ &= 6. \end{aligned}$$

Thus, $a = 6 \text{ m/s}^2$.

3.10 For $s(t) = t^3$, find $a(t)$.

3.2 EXERCISES

For the following exercises, use the definition of a derivative to find $f'(x)$.

54. $f(x) = 6$

55. $f(x) = 2 - 3x$

56. $f(x) = \frac{2x}{7} + 1$

57. $f(x) = 4x^2$

58. $f(x) = 5x - x^2$

59. $f(x) = \sqrt{2x}$

60. $f(x) = \sqrt{x - 6}$

61. $f(x) = \frac{9}{x}$

62. $f(x) = x + \frac{1}{x}$

63. $f(x) = \frac{1}{\sqrt{x}}$

For the following exercises, use the graph of $y = f(x)$ to sketch the graph of its derivative $f'(x)$.

64.

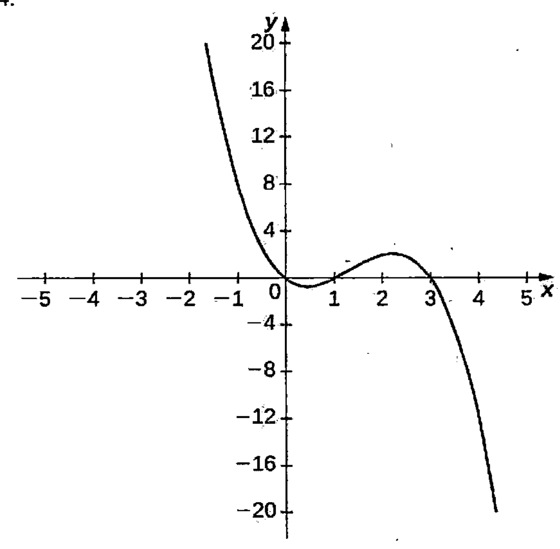

65.

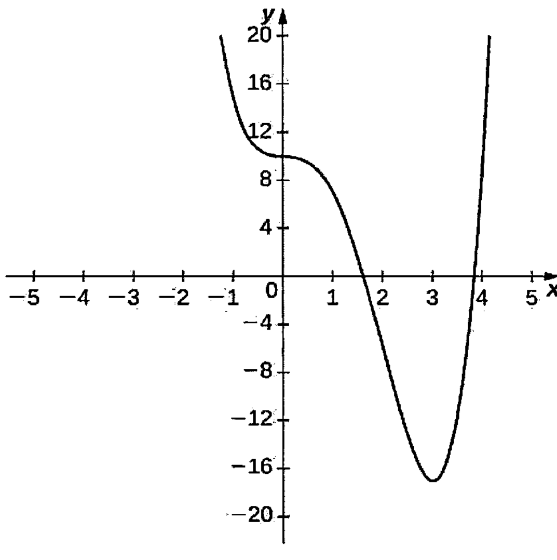

66.

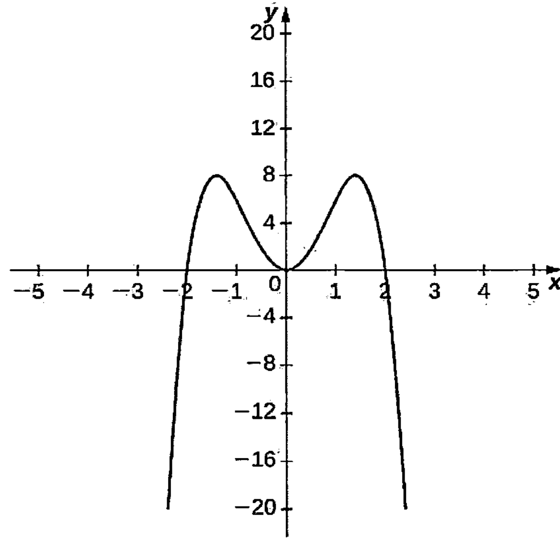

67.

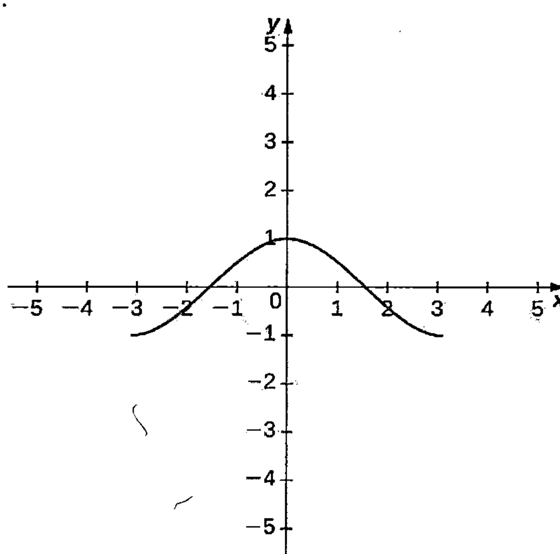

For the following exercises, the given limit represents the derivative of a function $y = f(x)$ at $x = a$. Find $f(x)$ and a.

68. $\lim_{h \to 0} \frac{(1+h)^{2/3} - 1}{h}$

69. $\lim_{h \to 0} \frac{\left[3(2+h)^2 + 2\right] - 14}{h}$

70. $\lim_{h \to 0} \frac{\cos(\pi + h) + 1}{h}$

71. $\lim_{h \to 0} \frac{(2+h)^4 - 16}{h}$

72. $\lim_{h \to 0} \frac{[2(3+h)^2 - (3+h)] - 15}{h}$

73. $\lim_{h \to 0} \frac{e^h - 1}{h}$

For the following functions,

a. sketch the graph and
b. use the definition of a derivative to show that the function is not differentiable at $x = 1$.

74. $f(x) = \begin{cases} 2\sqrt{x}, & 0 \le x \le 1 \\ 3x - 1, & x > 1 \end{cases}$

75. $f(x) = \begin{cases} 3, & x < 1 \\ 3x, & x \ge 1 \end{cases}$

76. $f(x) = \begin{cases} -x^2 + 2, & x \le 1 \\ x, & x > 1 \end{cases}$

77. $f(x) = \begin{cases} 2x, & x \le 1 \\ \frac{2}{x}, & x > 1 \end{cases}$

For the following graphs,

a. determine for which values of $x = a$ the $\lim_{x \to a} f(x)$ exists but f is not continuous at $x = a$, and
b. determine for which values of $x = a$ the function is continuous but not differentiable at $x = a$.

78.

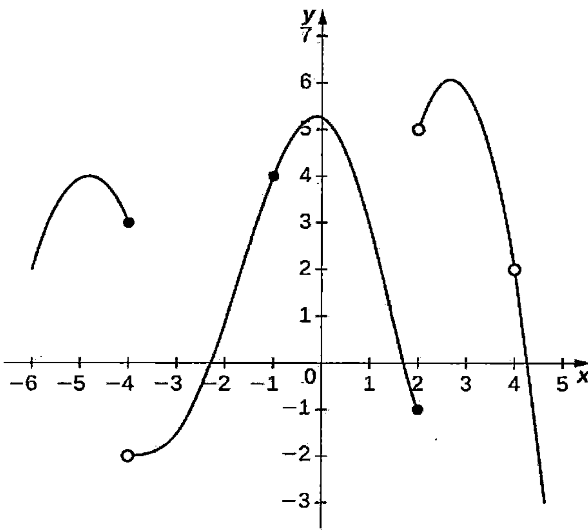

79.

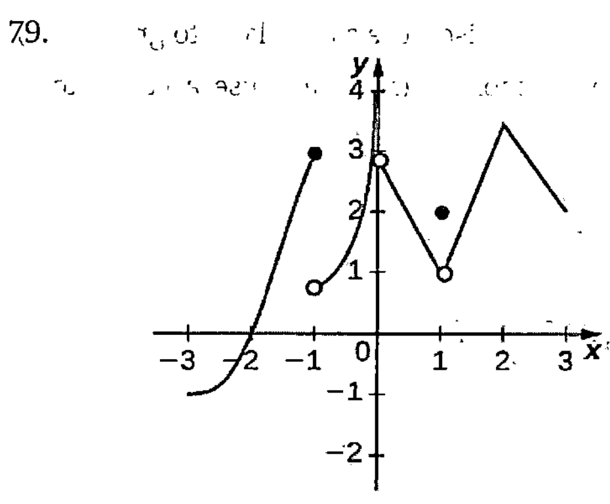

80. Use the graph to evaluate a. $f'(-0.5)$, b. $f'(0)$, c. $f'(1)$, d. $f'(2)$, and e. $f'(3)$, if it exists.

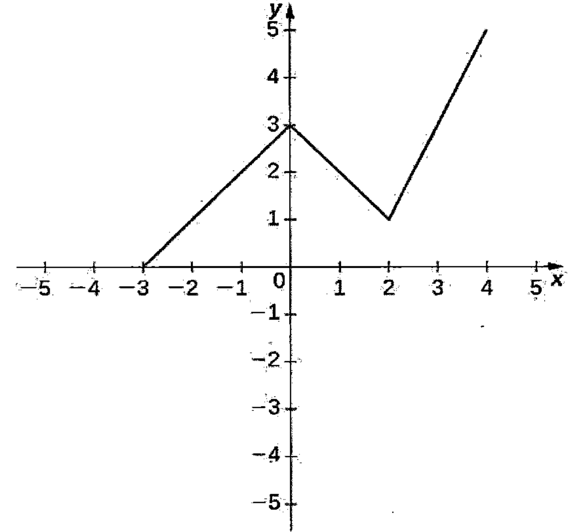

For the following functions, use $f''(x) = \lim_{h \to 0} \frac{f'(x+h) - f'(x)}{h}$ to find $f''(x)$.

81. $f(x) = 2 - 3x$

82. $f(x) = 4x^2$

83. $f(x) = x + \frac{1}{x}$

For the following exercises, use a calculator to graph $f(x)$. Determine the function $f'(x)$, then use a calculator to graph $f'(x)$.

84. **[T]** $f(x) = -\frac{5}{x}$

85. **[T]** $f(x) = 3x^2 + 2x + 4.$

86. **[T]** $f(x) = \sqrt{x} + 3x$

87. **[T]** $f(x) = \frac{1}{\sqrt{2x}}$

88. **[T]** $f(x) = 1 + x + \frac{1}{x}$

89. **[T]** $f(x) = x^3 + 1$

For the following exercises, describe what the two expressions represent in terms of each of the given situations. Be sure to include units.

a. $\frac{f(x+h) - f(x)}{h}$

b. $f'(x) = \lim_{h \to 0} \frac{f(x+h) - f(x)}{h}$

90. $P(x)$ denotes the population of a city at time x in years.

91. $C(x)$ denotes the total amount of money (in thousands of dollars) spent on concessions by x customers at an amusement park.

92. $R(x)$ denotes the total cost (in thousands of dollars) of manufacturing x clock radios.

93. $g(x)$ denotes the grade (in percentage points) received on a test, given x hours of studying.

94. $B(x)$ denotes the cost (in dollars) of a sociology textbook at university bookstores in the United States in x years since 1990.

95. $p(x)$ denotes atmospheric pressure at an altitude of x feet.

96. Sketch the graph of a function $y = f(x)$ with all of the following properties:

a. $f'(x) > 0$ for $-2 \le x < 1$
b. $f'(2) = 0$
c. $f'(x) > 0$ for $x > 2$
d. $f(2) = 2$ and $f(0) = 1$
e. $\lim_{x \to -\infty} f(x) = 0$ and $\lim_{x \to \infty} f(x) = \infty$
f. $f'(1)$ does not exist.

97. Suppose temperature T in degrees Fahrenheit at a height x in feet above the ground is given by $y = T(x)$.

a. Give a physical interpretation, with units, of $T'(x)$.
b. If we know that $T'(1000) = -0.1$, explain the physical meaning.

98. Suppose the total profit of a company is $y = P(x)$ thousand dollars when x units of an item are sold.

a. What does $\frac{P(b) - P(a)}{b - a}$ for $0 < a < b$ measure, and what are the units?
b. What does $P'(x)$ measure, and what are the units?
c. Suppose that $P'(30) = 5$, what is the approximate change in profit if the number of items sold increases from 30 to 31?

99. The graph in the following figure models the number of people $N(t)$ who have come down with the flu t weeks after its initial outbreak in a town with a population of 50,000 citizens.

a. Describe what $N'(t)$ represents and how it behaves as t increases.
b. What does the derivative tell us about how this town is affected by the flu outbreak?

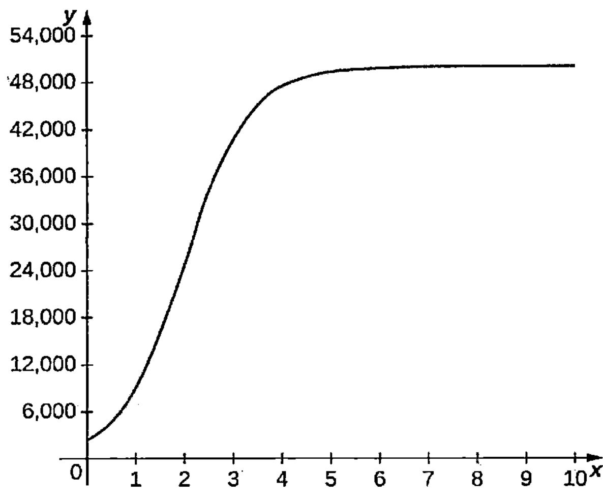

For the following exercises, use the following table, which shows the height h of the Saturn V rocket for the Apollo 11 mission t seconds after launch.

Time (seconds)	Height (meters)
0	0
1	2
2	4
3	13
4	25
5	32

100. What is the physical meaning of $h'(t)$? What are the units?

101. **[T]** Construct a table of values for $h'(t)$ and graph both $h(t)$ and $h'(t)$ on the same graph. (*Hint:* for interior points, estimate both the left limit and right limit and average them.)

102. **[T]** The best linear fit to the data is given by $H(t) = 7.229t - 4.905$, where H is the height of the rocket (in meters) and t is the time elapsed since takeoff. From this equation, determine $H'(t)$. Graph $H(t)$ with the given data and, on a separate coordinate plane, graph $H'(t)$.

103. **[T]** The best quadratic fit to the data is given by $G(t) = 1.429t^2 + 0.0857t - 0.1429$, where G is the height of the rocket (in meters) and t is the time elapsed since takeoff. From this equation, determine $G'(t)$. Graph $G(t)$ with the given data and, on a separate coordinate plane, graph $G'(t)$.

104. **[T]** The best cubic fit to the data is given by $F(t) = 0.2037t^3 + 2.956t^2 - 2.705t + 0.4683$, where F is the height of the rocket (in m) and t is the time elapsed since take off. From this equation, determine $F'(t)$. Graph $F(t)$ with the given data and, on a separate coordinate plane, graph $F'(t)$. Does the linear, quadratic, or cubic function fit the data best?

105. Using the best linear, quadratic, and cubic fits to the data, determine what $H''(t)$, $G''(t)$ and $F''(t)$ are. What are the physical meanings of $H''(t)$, $G''(t)$ and $F''(t)$, and what are their units?

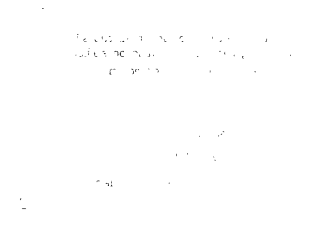

3.3 | Differentiation Rules

Learning Objectives

3.3.1 State the constant, constant multiple, and power rules.
3.3.2 Apply the sum and difference rules to combine derivatives.
3.3.3 Use the product rule for finding the derivative of a product of functions.
3.3.4 Use the quotient rule for finding the derivative of a quotient of functions.
3.3.5 Extend the power rule to functions with negative exponents.
3.3.6 Combine the differentiation rules to find the derivative of a polynomial or rational function.

Finding derivatives of functions by using the definition of the derivative can be a lengthy and, for certain functions, a rather challenging process. For example, previously we found that $\frac{d}{dx}(\sqrt{x}) = \frac{1}{2\sqrt{x}}$ by using a process that involved multiplying an expression by a conjugate prior to evaluating a limit. The process that we could use to evaluate $\frac{d}{dx}(\sqrt[3]{x})$ using the definition, while similar, is more complicated. In this section, we develop rules for finding derivatives that allow us to bypass this process. We begin with the basics.

The Basic Rules

The functions $f(x) = c$ and $g(x) = x^n$ where n is a positive integer are the building blocks from which all polynomials and rational functions are constructed. To find derivatives of polynomials and rational functions efficiently without resorting to the limit definition of the derivative, we must first develop formulas for differentiating these basic functions.

The Constant Rule

We first apply the limit definition of the derivative to find the derivative of the constant function, $f(x) = c$. For this function, both $f(x) = c$ and $f(x+h) = c$, so we obtain the following result:

$$\begin{aligned} f'(x) &= \lim_{h \to 0} \frac{f(x+h) - f(x)}{h} \\ &= \lim_{h \to 0} \frac{c-c}{h} \\ &= \lim_{h \to 0} \frac{0}{h} \\ &= \lim_{h \to 0} 0 = 0. \end{aligned}$$

The rule for differentiating constant functions is called the **constant rule**. It states that the derivative of a constant function is zero; that is, since a constant function is a horizontal line, the slope, or the rate of change, of a constant function is 0. We restate this rule in the following theorem.

Theorem 3.2: The Constant Rule

Let c be a constant.

If $f(x) = c$, then $f'(c) = 0$.

Alternatively, we may express this rule as

$$\frac{d}{dx}(c) = 0.$$

Example 3.17

Applying the Constant Rule

Find the derivative of $f(x) = 8$.

Solution

This is just a one-step application of the rule:

$$f'(8) = 0.$$

3.11 Find the derivative of $g(x) = -3$.

The Power Rule

We have shown that

$$\frac{d}{dx}\left(x^2\right) = 2x \text{ and } \frac{d}{dx}\left(x^{1/2}\right) = \frac{1}{2}x^{-1/2}.$$

At this point, you might see a pattern beginning to develop for derivatives of the form $\frac{d}{dx}(x^n)$. We continue our examination of derivative formulas by differentiating power functions of the form $f(x) = x^n$ where n is a positive integer. We develop formulas for derivatives of this type of function in stages, beginning with positive integer powers. Before stating and proving the general rule for derivatives of functions of this form, we take a look at a specific case, $\frac{d}{dx}(x^3)$. As we go through this derivation, pay special attention to the portion of the expression in boldface, as the technique used in this case is essentially the same as the technique used to prove the general case.

Example 3.18

Differentiating x^3

Find $\frac{d}{dx}\left(x^3\right)$.

Solution

$$\frac{d}{dx}(x^3) = \lim_{h \to 0} \frac{(x+h)^3 - x^3}{h}$$

$$= \lim_{h \to 0} \frac{x^3 + 3x^2h + 3xh^2 + h^3 - x^3}{h}$$

Notice that the first term in the expansion of $(x+h)^3$ is x^3 and the second term is $3x^2h$. All other terms contain powers of h that are two or greater.

$$= \lim_{h \to 0} \frac{3x^2h + 3xh^2 + h^3}{h}$$

In this step the x^3 terms have been cancelled, leaving only terms containing h.

$$= \lim_{h \to 0} \frac{h(3x^2 + 3xh + h^2)}{h}$$

Factor out the common factor of h.

$$= \lim_{h \to 0} (3x^2 + 3xh + h^2)$$

After cancelling the common factor of h, the only term not containing h is $3x^2$.

$$= 3x^2$$

Let h go to 0.

3.12 Find $\frac{d}{dx}(x^4)$.

As we shall see, the procedure for finding the derivative of the general form $f(x) = x^n$ is very similar. Although it is often unwise to draw general conclusions from specific examples, we note that when we differentiate $f(x) = x^3$, the power on x becomes the coefficient of x^2 in the derivative and the power on x in the derivative decreases by 1. The following theorem states that the **power rule** holds for all positive integer powers of x. We will eventually extend this result to negative integer powers. Later, we will see that this rule may also be extended first to rational powers of x and then to arbitrary powers of x. Be aware, however, that this rule does not apply to functions in which a constant is raised to a variable power, such as $f(x) = 3^x$.

Theorem 3.3: The Power Rule

Let n be a positive integer. If $f(x) = x^n$, then

$$f'(x) = nx^{n-1}.$$

Alternatively, we may express this rule as

$$\frac{d}{dx}x^n = nx^{n-1}.$$

Proof

For $f(x) = x^n$ where n is a positive integer, we have

$$f'(x) = \lim_{h \to 0} \frac{(x+h)^n - x^n}{h}.$$

$$\text{Since } (x+h)^n = x^n + nx^{n-1}h + \binom{n}{2}x^{n-2}h^2 + \binom{n}{3}x^{n-3}h^3 + \ldots + nxh^{n-1} + h^n,$$

we see that

$$(x+h)^n - x^n = nx^{n-1}h + \binom{n}{2}x^{n-2}h^2 + \binom{n}{3}x^{n-3}h^3 + \ldots + nxh^{n-1} + h^n.$$

Next, divide both sides by h:

$$\frac{(x+h)^n - x^n}{h} = \frac{nx^{n-1}h + \binom{n}{2}x^{n-2}h^2 + \binom{n}{3}x^{n-3}h^3 + \ldots + nxh^{n-1} + h^n}{h}.$$

Thus,

$$\frac{(x+h)^n - x^n}{h} = nx^{n-1} + \binom{n}{2}x^{n-2}h + \binom{n}{3}x^{n-3}h^2 + \ldots + nxh^{n-2} + h^{n-1}.$$

Finally,

$$\begin{aligned} f'(x) &= \lim_{h \to 0}\left(nx^{n-1} + \binom{n}{2}x^{n-2}h + \binom{n}{3}x^{n-3}h^2 + \ldots + nxh^{n-1} + h^n\right) \\ &= nx^{n-1}. \end{aligned}$$

□

Example 3.19

Applying the Power Rule

Find the derivative of the function $f(x) = x^{10}$ by applying the power rule.

Solution

Using the power rule with $n = 10$, we obtain

$$f'(x) = 10x^{10-1} = 10x^9.$$

3.13 Find the derivative of $f(x) = x^7$.

The Sum, Difference, and Constant Multiple Rules

We find our next differentiation rules by looking at derivatives of sums, differences, and constant multiples of functions. Just as when we work with functions, there are rules that make it easier to find derivatives of functions that we add, subtract, or multiply by a constant. These rules are summarized in the following theorem.

Theorem 3.4: Sum, Difference, and Constant Multiple Rules

Let $f(x)$ and $g(x)$ be differentiable functions and k be a constant. Then each of the following equations holds.

Sum Rule. The derivative of the sum of a function f and a function g is the same as the sum of the derivative of f and the derivative of g.

$$\frac{d}{dx}(f(x) + g(x)) = \frac{d}{dx}(f(x)) + \frac{d}{dx}(g(x));$$

that is,

$$\text{for } j(x) = f(x) + g(x),\ j'(x) = f'(x) + g'(x).$$

Difference Rule. The derivative of the difference of a function f and a function g is the same as the difference of the derivative of f and the derivative of g:

$$\frac{d}{dx}(f(x) - g(x)) = \frac{d}{dx}(f(x)) - \frac{d}{dx}(g(x));$$

that is,

$$\text{for } j(x) = f(x) - g(x),\ j'(x) = f'(x) - g'(x).$$

Constant Multiple Rule. The derivative of a constant k multiplied by a function f is the same as the constant multiplied by the derivative:

$$\frac{d}{dx}(kf(x)) = k\frac{d}{dx}(f(x));$$

that is,

$$\text{for } j(x) = kf(x),\ j'(x) = kf'(x).$$

Proof

We provide only the proof of the sum rule here. The rest follow in a similar manner.

For differentiable functions $f(x)$ and $g(x)$, we set $j(x) = f(x) + g(x)$. Using the limit definition of the derivative we have

$$j'(x) = \lim_{h \to 0} \frac{j(x+h) - j(x)}{h}.$$

By substituting $j(x+h) = f(x+h) + g(x+h)$ and $j(x) = f(x) + g(x)$, we obtain

$$j'(x) = \lim_{h \to 0} \frac{(f(x+h) + g(x+h)) - (f(x) + g(x))}{h}.$$

Rearranging and regrouping the terms, we have

$$j'(x) = \lim_{h \to 0}\left(\frac{f(x+h) - f(x)}{h} + \frac{g(x+h) - g(x)}{h}\right).$$

We now apply the sum law for limits and the definition of the derivative to obtain

$$j'(x) = \lim_{h \to 0}\left(\frac{f(x+h) - f(x)}{h}\right) + \lim_{h \to 0}\left(\frac{g(x+h) - g(x)}{h}\right) = f'(x) + g'(x).$$

□

Example 3.20

Applying the Constant Multiple Rule

Find the derivative of $g(x) = 3x^2$ and compare it to the derivative of $f(x) = x^2$.

Solution

We use the power rule directly:

$$g'(x) = \frac{d}{dx}(3x^2) = 3\frac{d}{dx}(x^2) = 3(2x) = 6x.$$

Since $f(x) = x^2$ has derivative $f'(x) = 2x$, we see that the derivative of $g(x)$ is 3 times the derivative of

$f(x)$. This relationship is illustrated in **Figure 3.18**.

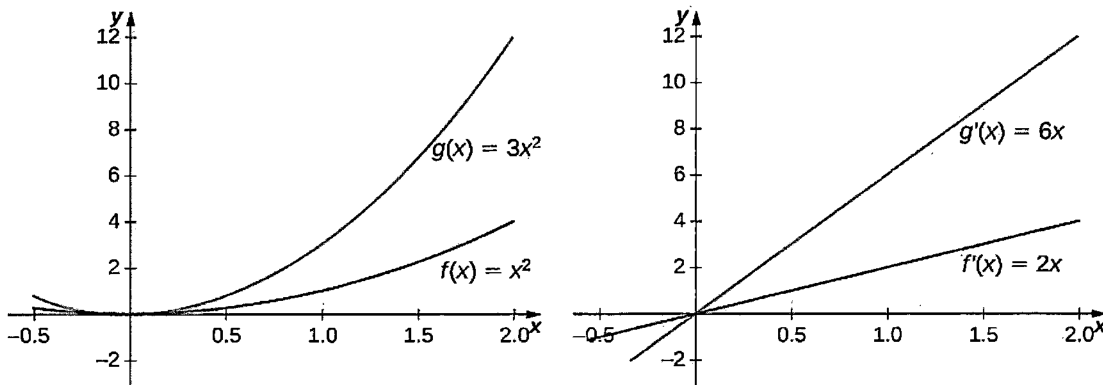

Figure 3.18 The derivative of $g(x)$ is 3 times the derivative of $f(x)$.

Example 3.21

Applying Basic Derivative Rules

Find the derivative of $f(x) = 2x^5 + 7$.

Solution

We begin by applying the rule for differentiating the sum of two functions, followed by the rules for differentiating constant multiples of functions and the rule for differentiating powers. To better understand the sequence in which the differentiation rules are applied, we use Leibniz notation throughout the solution:

$$\begin{aligned} f'(x) &= \frac{d}{dx}\left(2x^5 + 7\right) & \\ &= \frac{d}{dx}\left(2x^5\right) + \frac{d}{dx}(7) & \text{Apply the sum rule.} \\ &= 2\frac{d}{dx}\left(x^5\right) + \frac{d}{dx}(7) & \text{Apply the constant multiple rule.} \\ &= 2\left(5x^4\right) + 0 & \text{Apply the power rule and the constant rule.} \\ &= 10x^4. & \text{Simplify.} \end{aligned}$$

3.14 Find the derivative of $f(x) = 2x^3 - 6x^2 + 3$.

Example 3.22

Finding the Equation of a Tangent Line

Find the equation of the line tangent to the graph of $f(x) = x^2 - 4x + 6$ at $x = 1$.

Solution

To find the equation of the tangent line, we need a point and a slope. To find the point, compute

$$f(1) = 1^2 - 4(1) + 6 = 3.$$

This gives us the point $(1, 3)$. Since the slope of the tangent line at 1 is $f'(1)$, we must first find $f'(x)$. Using the definition of a derivative, we have

$$f'(x) = 2x - 4$$

so the slope of the tangent line is $f'(1) = -2$. Using the point-slope formula, we see that the equation of the tangent line is

$$y - 3 = -2(x - 1).$$

Putting the equation of the line in slope-intercept form, we obtain

$$y = -2x + 5.$$

3.15 Find the equation of the line tangent to the graph of $f(x) = 3x^2 - 11$ at $x = 2$. Use the point-slope form.

The Product Rule

Now that we have examined the basic rules, we can begin looking at some of the more advanced rules. The first one examines the derivative of the product of two functions. Although it might be tempting to assume that the derivative of the product is the product of the derivatives, similar to the sum and difference rules, the **product rule** does not follow this pattern. To see why we cannot use this pattern, consider the function $f(x) = x^2$, whose derivative is $f'(x) = 2x$ and not $\frac{d}{dx}(x) \cdot \frac{d}{dx}(x) = 1 \cdot 1 = 1$.

Theorem 3.5: Product Rule

Let $f(x)$ and $g(x)$ be differentiable functions. Then

$$\frac{d}{dx}(f(x)g(x)) = \frac{d}{dx}(f(x)) \cdot g(x) + \frac{d}{dx}(g(x)) \cdot f(x).$$

That is,

$$\text{if } j(x) = f(x)g(x), \text{ then } j'(x) = f'(x)g(x) + g'(x)f(x).$$

This means that the derivative of a product of two functions is the derivative of the first function times the second function plus the derivative of the second function times the first function.

Proof

We begin by assuming that $f(x)$ and $g(x)$ are differentiable functions. At a key point in this proof we need to use the fact that, since $g(x)$ is differentiable, it is also continuous. In particular, we use the fact that since $g(x)$ is continuous, $\lim_{h \to 0} g(x + h) = g(x)$.

By applying the limit definition of the derivative to $j(x) = f(x)g(x)$, we obtain

$$j'(x) = \lim_{h \to 0} \frac{f(x+h)g(x+h) - f(x)g(x)}{h}.$$

By adding and subtracting $f(x)g(x+h)$ in the numerator, we have

$$j'(x) = \lim_{h \to 0} \frac{f(x+h)g(x+h) - f(x)g(x+h) + f(x)g(x+h) - f(x)g(x)}{h}.$$

After breaking apart this quotient and applying the sum law for limits, the derivative becomes

$$j'(x) = \lim_{h \to 0}\left(\frac{f(x+h)g(x+h) - f(x)g(x+h)}{h}\right) + \lim_{h \to 0}\left(\frac{f(x)g(x+h) - f(x)g(x)}{h}\right).$$

Rearranging, we obtain

$$j'(x) = \lim_{h \to 0}\left(\frac{f(x+h) - f(x)}{h} \cdot g(x+h)\right) + \lim_{h \to 0}\left(\frac{g(x+h) - g(x)}{h} \cdot f(x)\right).$$

By using the continuity of $g(x)$, the definition of the derivatives of $f(x)$ and $g(x)$, and applying the limit laws, we arrive at the product rule,

$$j'(x) = f'(x)g(x) + g'(x)f(x).$$

□

Example 3.23

Applying the Product Rule to Functions at a Point

For $j(x) = f(x)g(x)$, use the product rule to find $j'(2)$ if $f(2) = 3$, $f'(2) = -4$, $g(2) = 1$, and $g'(2) = 6$.

Solution

Since $j(x) = f(x)g(x)$, $j'(x) = f'(x)g(x) + g'(x)f(x)$, and hence

$$j'(2) = f'(2)g(2) + g'(2)f(2) = (-4)(1) + (6)(3) = 14.$$

Example 3.24

Applying the Product Rule to Binomials

For $j(x) = (x^2 + 2)(3x^3 - 5x)$, find $j'(x)$ by applying the product rule. Check the result by first finding the product and then differentiating.

Solution

If we set $f(x) = x^2 + 2$ and $g(x) = 3x^3 - 5x$, then $f'(x) = 2x$ and $g'(x) = 9x^2 - 5$. Thus,

$$j'(x) = f'(x)g(x) + g'(x)f(x) = (2x)(3x^3 - 5x) + (9x^2 - 5)(x^2 + 2).$$

Simplifying, we have

$$j'(x) = 15x^4 + 3x^2 - 10.$$

To check, we see that $j(x) = 3x^5 + x^3 - 10x$ and, consequently, $j'(x) = 15x^4 + 3x^2 - 10$.

3.16 Use the product rule to obtain the derivative of $j(x) = 2x^5\left(4x^2 + x\right)$.

The Quotient Rule

Having developed and practiced the product rule, we now consider differentiating quotients of functions. As we see in the following theorem, the derivative of the quotient is not the quotient of the derivatives; rather, it is the derivative of the function in the numerator times the function in the denominator minus the derivative of the function in the denominator times the function in the numerator, all divided by the square of the function in the denominator. In order to better grasp why we cannot simply take the quotient of the derivatives, keep in mind that

$$\frac{d}{dx}\left(x^2\right) = 2x, \text{ not } \frac{\frac{d}{dx}\left(x^3\right)}{\frac{d}{dx}(x)} = \frac{3x^2}{1} = 3x^2.$$

Theorem 3.6: The Quotient Rule

Let $f(x)$ and $g(x)$ be differentiable functions. Then

$$\frac{d}{dx}\left(\frac{f(x)}{g(x)}\right) = \frac{\frac{d}{dx}(f(x)) \cdot g(x) - \frac{d}{dx}(g(x)) \cdot f(x)}{(g(x))^2}.$$

That is,

$$\text{if } j(x) = \frac{f(x)}{g(x)}, \text{ then } j'(x) = \frac{f'(x)g(x) - g'(x)f(x)}{(g(x))^2}.$$

The proof of the **quotient rule** is very similar to the proof of the product rule, so it is omitted here. Instead, we apply this new rule for finding derivatives in the next example.

Example 3.25

Applying the Quotient Rule

Use the quotient rule to find the derivative of $k(x) = \frac{5x^2}{4x + 3}$.

Solution

Let $f(x) = 5x^2$ and $g(x) = 4x + 3$. Thus, $f'(x) = 10x$ and $g'(x) = 4$. Substituting into the quotient rule, we have

$$k'(x) = \frac{f'(x)g(x) - g'(x)f(x)}{(g(x))^2} = \frac{10x(4x + 3) - 4(5x^2)}{(4x + 3)^2}.$$

Simplifying, we obtain

$$k'(x) = \frac{20x^2 + 30x}{(4x+3)^2}.$$

3.17 Find the derivative of $h(x) = \frac{3x+1}{4x-3}$.

It is now possible to use the quotient rule to extend the power rule to find derivatives of functions of the form x^k where k is a negative integer.

Theorem 3.7: Extended Power Rule

If k is a negative integer, then

$$\frac{d}{dx}\left(x^k\right) = kx^{k-1}.$$

Proof

If k is a negative integer, we may set $n = -k$, so that n is a positive integer with $k = -n$. Since for each positive integer n, $x^{-n} = \frac{1}{x^n}$, we may now apply the quotient rule by setting $f(x) = 1$ and $g(x) = x^n$. In this case, $f'(x) = 0$ and $g'(x) = nx^{n-1}$. Thus,

$$\frac{d}{d}(x^{-n}) = \frac{0(x^n) - 1\left(nx^{n-1}\right)}{(x^n)^2}.$$

Simplifying, we see that

$$\frac{d}{d}(x^{-n}) = \frac{-nx^{n-1}}{x^{2n}} = -nx^{(n-1)-2n} = -nx^{-n-1}.$$

Finally, observe that since $k = -n$, by substituting we have

$$\frac{d}{dx}\left(x^k\right) = kx^{k-1}.$$

□

Example 3.26

Using the Extended Power Rule

Find $\frac{d}{dx}\left(x^{-4}\right)$.

Solution

By applying the extended power rule with $k = -4$, we obtain

$$\frac{d}{dx}\left(x^{-4}\right) = -4x^{-4-1} = -4x^{-5}.$$

Example 3.27

Using the Extended Power Rule and the Constant Multiple Rule

Use the extended power rule and the constant multiple rule to find $f(x) = \frac{6}{x^2}$.

Solution

It may seem tempting to use the quotient rule to find this derivative, and it would certainly not be incorrect to do so. However, it is far easier to differentiate this function by first rewriting it as $f(x) = 6x^{-2}$.

$$\begin{aligned} f'(x) &= \frac{d}{dx}\left(\frac{6}{x^2}\right) = \frac{d}{dx}\left(6x^{-2}\right) && \text{Rewrite } \frac{6}{x^2} \text{ as } 6x^{-2}. \\ &= 6\frac{d}{dx}(x^{-2}) && \text{Apply the constant multiple rule.} \\ &= 6(-2x^{-3}) && \text{Use the extended power rule to differentiate } x^{-2}. \\ &= -12x^{-3} && \text{Simplify.} \end{aligned}$$

3.18 Find the derivative of $g(x) = \frac{1}{x^7}$ using the extended power rule.

Combining Differentiation Rules

As we have seen throughout the examples in this section, it seldom happens that we are called on to apply just one differentiation rule to find the derivative of a given function. At this point, by combining the differentiation rules, we may find the derivatives of any polynomial or rational function. Later on we will encounter more complex combinations of differentiation rules. A good rule of thumb to use when applying several rules is to apply the rules in reverse of the order in which we would evaluate the function.

Example 3.28

Combining Differentiation Rules

For $k(x) = 3h(x) + x^2 g(x)$, find $k'(x)$.

Solution

Finding this derivative requires the sum rule, the constant multiple rule, and the product rule.

$$\begin{aligned} k'(x) &= \frac{d}{dx}\left(3h(x) + x^2 g(x)\right) = \frac{d}{dx}(3h(x)) + \frac{d}{dx}\left(x^2 g(x)\right) \\ &= 3\frac{d}{dx}(h(x)) + \left(\frac{d}{dx}(x^2)g(x) + \frac{d}{dx}(g(x))x^2\right) \\ &= 3h'(x) + 2xg(x) + g'(x)x^2 \end{aligned}$$

Apply the sum rule.

Apply the constant multiple rule to differentiate $3h(x)$ and the product rule to differentiate $x^2 g(x)$.

Example 3.29

Extending the Product Rule

For $k(x) = f(x)g(x)h(x)$, express $k'(x)$ in terms of $f(x)$, $g(x)$, $h(x)$, and their derivatives.

Solution

We can think of the function $k(x)$ as the product of the function $f(x)g(x)$ and the function $h(x)$. That is, $k(x) = (f(x)g(x)) \cdot h(x)$. Thus,

$$\begin{aligned} k'(x) &= \frac{d}{dx}(f(x)g(x)) \cdot h(x) + \frac{d}{dx}(h(x)) \cdot (f(x)g(x)) \\ &= (f'(x)g(x) + g'(x)f(x))h(x) + h'(x)f(x)g(x) \\ &= f'(x)g(x)h(x) + f(x)g'(x)h(x) + f(x)g(x)h'(x). \end{aligned}$$

Apply the product rule to the product of $f(x)g(x)$ and $h(x)$.

Apply the product rule to $f(x)g(x)$.

Simplify.

Example 3.30

Combining the Quotient Rule and the Product Rule

For $h(x) = \dfrac{2x^3 k(x)}{3x+2}$, find $h'(x)$.

Solution

This procedure is typical for finding the derivative of a rational function.

$$\begin{aligned} h'(x) &= \frac{\frac{d}{dx}\left(2x^3 k(x)\right) \cdot (3x+2) - \frac{d}{dx}(3x+2) \cdot \left(2x^3 k(x)\right)}{(3x+2)^2} \\ &= \frac{\left(6x^2 k(x) + k'(x) \cdot 2x^3\right)(3x+2) - 3\left(2x^3 k(x)\right)}{(3x+2)^2} \\ &= \frac{-6x^3 k(x) + 18x^3 k(x) + 12x^2 k(x) + 6x^4 k'(x) + 4x^3 k'(x)}{(3x+2)^2} \end{aligned}$$

Apply the quotient rule.

Apply the product rule to find $\frac{d}{dx}\left(2x^3 k(x)\right)$. Use $\frac{d}{dx}(3x+2) = 3$.

Simplify.

3.19 Find $\frac{d}{dx}(3f(x) - 2g(x))$.

Example 3.31

Determining Where a Function Has a Horizontal Tangent

Determine the values of x for which $f(x) = x^3 - 7x^2 + 8x + 1$ has a horizontal tangent line.

Solution

To find the values of x for which $f(x)$ has a horizontal tangent line, we must solve $f'(x) = 0$. Since

$$f'(x) = 3x^2 - 14x + 8 = (3x - 2)(x - 4),$$

we must solve $(3x - 2)(x - 4) = 0$. Thus we see that the function has horizontal tangent lines at $x = \frac{2}{3}$ and $x = 4$ as shown in the following graph.

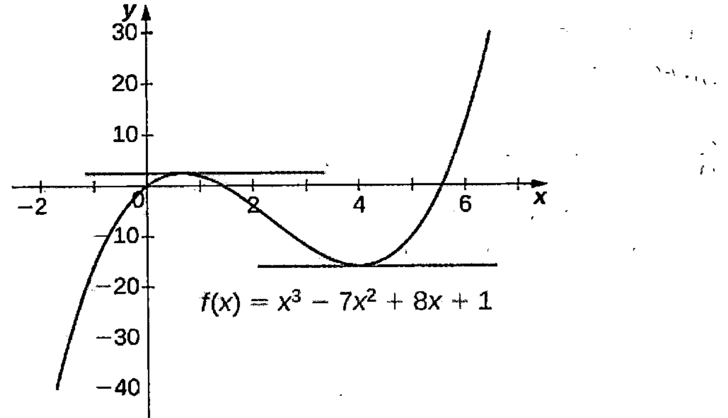

Figure 3.19 This function has horizontal tangent lines at $x = 2/3$ and $x = 4$.

Example 3.32

Finding a Velocity

The position of an object on a coordinate axis at time t is given by $s(t) = \frac{t}{t^2 + 1}$. What is the initial velocity of the object?

Solution

Since the initial velocity is $v(0) = s'(0)$, begin by finding $s'(t)$ by applying the quotient rule:

$$s'(t) = \frac{1(t^2 + 1) - 2t(t)}{(t^2 + 1)^2} = \frac{1 - t^2}{(t^2 + 1)^2}.$$

After evaluating, we see that $v(0) = 1$.

3.20 Find the values of x for which the line tangent to the graph of $f(x) = 4x^2 - 3x + 2$ has a tangent line parallel to the line $y = 2x + 3$.

Student PROJECT

Formula One Grandstands

Formula One car races can be very exciting to watch and attract a lot of spectators. Formula One track designers have to ensure sufficient grandstand space is available around the track to accommodate these viewers. However, car racing can be dangerous, and safety considerations are paramount. The grandstands must be placed where spectators will not be in danger should a driver lose control of a car (**Figure 3.20**).

Figure 3.20 The grandstand next to a straightaway of the Circuit de Barcelona-Catalunya race track, located where the spectators are not in danger.

Safety is especially a concern on turns. If a driver does not slow down enough before entering the turn, the car may slide off the racetrack. Normally, this just results in a wider turn, which slows the driver down. But if the driver loses control completely, the car may fly off the track entirely, on a path tangent to the curve of the racetrack.

Suppose you are designing a new Formula One track. One section of the track can be modeled by the function $f(x) = x^3 + 3x^2 + x$ (**Figure 3.21**). The current plan calls for grandstands to be built along the first straightaway and around a portion of the first curve. The plans call for the front corner of the grandstand to be located at the point $(-1.9, 2.8)$. We want to determine whether this location puts the spectators in danger if a driver loses control of the car.

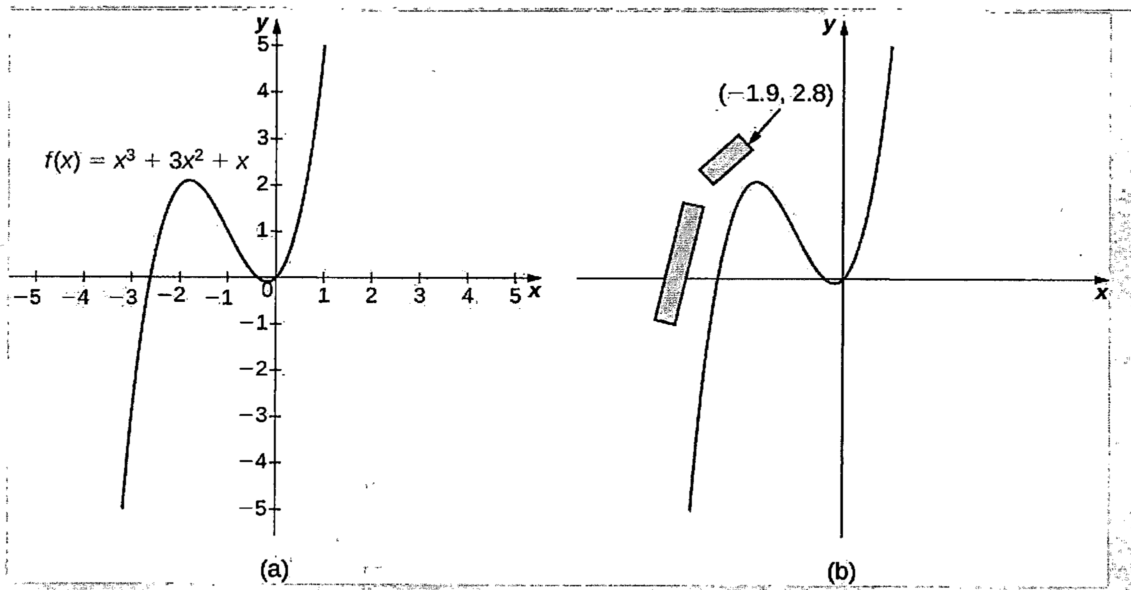

Figure 3.21 (a) One section of the racetrack can be modeled by the function $f(x) = x^3 + 3x^2 + x$. (b) The front corner of the grandstand is located at $(-1.9, 2.8)$.

1. Physicists have determined that drivers are most likely to lose control of their cars as they are coming into a turn, at the point where the slope of the tangent line is 1. Find the (x, y) coordinates of this point near the turn.
2. Find the equation of the tangent line to the curve at this point.
3. To determine whether the spectators are in danger in this scenario, find the *x*-coordinate of the point where the tangent line crosses the line $y = 2.8$. Is this point safely to the right of the grandstand? Or are the spectators in danger?
4. What if a driver loses control earlier than the physicists project? Suppose a driver loses control at the point $(-2.5, 0.625)$. What is the slope of the tangent line at this point?
5. If a driver loses control as described in part 4, are the spectators safe?
6. Should you proceed with the current design for the grandstand, or should the grandstands be moved?

3.3 EXERCISES

For the following exercises, find $f'(x)$ for each function.

106. $f(x) = x^7 + 10$

107. $f(x) = 5x^3 - x + 1$

108. $f(x) = 4x^2 - 7x$

109. $f(x) = 8x^4 + 9x^2 - 1$

110. $f(x) = x^4 + \frac{2}{x}$

111. $f(x) = 3x\left(18x^4 + \frac{13}{x+1}\right)$

112. $f(x) = (x+2)\left(2x^2 - 3\right)$

113. $f(x) = x^2\left(\frac{2}{x^2} + \frac{5}{x^3}\right)$

114. $f(x) = \frac{x^3 + 2x^2 - 4}{3}$

115. $f(x) = \frac{4x^3 - 2x + 1}{x^2}$

116. $f(x) = \frac{x^2 + 4}{x^2 - 4}$

117. $f(x) = \frac{x + 9}{x^2 - 7x + 1}$

For the following exercises, find the equation of the tangent line $T(x)$ to the graph of the given function at the indicated point. Use a graphing calculator to graph the function and the tangent line.

118. **[T]** $y = 3x^2 + 4x + 1$ at $(0, 1)$

119. **[T]** $y = 2\sqrt{x} + 1$ at $(4, 5)$

120. **[T]** $y = \frac{2x}{x-1}$ at $(-1, 1)$

121. **[T]** $y = \frac{2}{x} - \frac{3}{x^2}$ at $(1, -1)$

For the following exercises, assume that $f(x)$ and $g(x)$ are both differentiable functions for all x. Find the derivative of each of the functions $h(x)$.

122. $h(x) = 4f(x) + \frac{g(x)}{7}$

123. $h(x) = x^3 f(x)$

124. $h(x) = \frac{f(x)g(x)}{2}$

125. $h(x) = \frac{3f(x)}{g(x) + 2}$

For the following exercises, assume that $f(x)$ and $g(x)$ are both differentiable functions with values as given in the following table. Use the following table to calculate the following derivatives.

x	1	2	3	4
$f(x)$	3	5	−2	0
$g(x)$	2	3	−4	6
$f'(x)$	−1	7	8	−3
$g'(x)$	4	1	2	9

126. Find $h'(1)$ if $h(x) = xf(x) + 4g(x)$.

127. Find $h'(2)$ if $h(x) = \frac{f(x)}{g(x)}$.

128. Find $h'(3)$ if $h(x) = 2x + f(x)g(x)$.

129. Find $h'(4)$ if $h(x) = \frac{1}{x} + \frac{g(x)}{f(x)}$.

For the following exercises, use the following figure to find the indicated derivatives, if they exist.

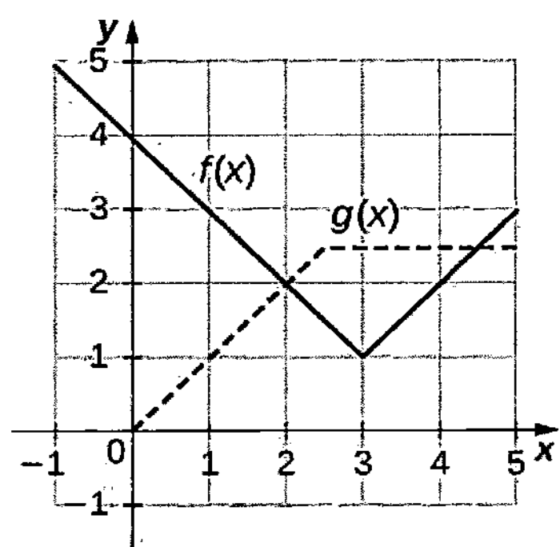

130. Let $h(x) = f(x) + g(x)$. Find

a. $h'(1)$,

b. $h'(3)$, and

c. $h'(4)$.

131. Let $h(x) = f(x)g(x)$. Find

a. $h'(1)$,

b. $h'(3)$, and

c. $h'(4)$.

132. Let $h(x) = \frac{f(x)}{g(x)}$. Find

a. $h'(1)$,

b. $h'(3)$, and

c. $h'(4)$.

For the following exercises,

a. evaluate $f'(a)$, and

b. graph the function $f(x)$ and the tangent line at $x = a$.

133. **[T]** $f(x) = 2x^3 + 3x - x^2,\ a = 2$

134. **[T]** $f(x) = \frac{1}{x} - x^2,\ a = 1$

135. **[T]** $f(x) = x^2 - x^{12} + 3x + 2,\ a = 0$

136. **[T]** $f(x) = \frac{1}{x} - x^{2/3},\ a = -1$

137. Find the equation of the tangent line to the graph of $f(x) = 2x^3 + 4x^2 - 5x - 3$ at $x = -1$.

138. Find the equation of the tangent line to the graph of $f(x) = x^2 + \frac{4}{x} - 10$ at $x = 8$.

139. Find the equation of the tangent line to the graph of $f(x) = (3x - x^2)(3 - x - x^2)$ at $x = 1$.

140. Find the point on the graph of $f(x) = x^3$ such that the tangent line at that point has an x intercept of 6.

141. Find the equation of the line passing through the point $P(3,\ 3)$ and tangent to the graph of $f(x) = \frac{6}{x-1}$.

142. Determine all points on the graph of $f(x) = x^3 + x^2 - x - 1$ for which the slope of the tangent line is

a. horizontal

b. -1.

143. Find a quadratic polynomial such that $f(1) = 5,\ f'(1) = 3$ and $f''(1) = -6$.

144. A car driving along a freeway with traffic has traveled $s(t) = t^3 - 6t^2 + 9t$ meters in t seconds.

a. Determine the time in seconds when the velocity of the car is 0.

b. Determine the acceleration of the car when the velocity is 0.

145. **[T]** A herring swimming along a straight line has traveled $s(t) = \frac{t^2}{t^2 + 2}$ feet in t seconds. Determine the velocity of the herring when it has traveled 3 seconds.

146. The population in millions of arctic flounder in the Atlantic Ocean is modeled by the function $P(t) = \frac{8t + 3}{0.2t^2 + 1}$, where t is measured in years.

a. Determine the initial flounder population.

b. Determine $P'(10)$ and briefly interpret the result.

147. **[T]** The concentration of antibiotic in the bloodstream t hours after being injected is given by the function $C(t) = \frac{2t^2 + t}{t^3 + 50}$, where C is measured in milligrams per liter of blood.

a. Find the rate of change of $C(t)$.

b. Determine the rate of change for $t = 8,\ 12,\ 24,$ and 36.

c. Briefly describe what seems to be occurring as the number of hours increases.

148. A book publisher has a cost function given by $C(x) = \frac{x^3 + 2x + 3}{x^2}$, where x is the number of copies of a book in thousands and C is the cost, per book, measured in dollars. Evaluate $C'(2)$ and explain its meaning.

149. **[T]** According to Newton's law of universal gravitation, the force F between two bodies of constant mass m_1 and m_2 is given by the formula $F = \frac{Gm_1 m_2}{d^2}$, where G is the gravitational constant and d is the distance between the bodies.

a. Suppose that $G, m_1,$ and m_2 are constants. Find the rate of change of force F with respect to distance d.

b. Find the rate of change of force F with gravitational constant $G = 6.67 \times 10^{-11}$ Nm^2/kg^2, on two bodies 10 meters apart, each with a mass of 1000 kilograms.

3.4 | Derivatives as Rates of Change

Learning Objectives

3.4.1 Determine a new value of a quantity from the old value and the amount of change.
3.4.2 Calculate the average rate of change and explain how it differs from the instantaneous rate of change.
3.4.3 Apply rates of change to displacement, velocity, and acceleration of an object moving along a straight line.
3.4.4 Predict the future population from the present value and the population growth rate.
3.4.5 Use derivatives to calculate marginal cost and revenue in a business situation.

In this section we look at some applications of the derivative by focusing on the interpretation of the derivative as the rate of change of a function. These applications include **acceleration** and velocity in physics, **population growth rates** in biology, and marginal functions in economics.

Amount of Change Formula

One application for derivatives is to estimate an unknown value of a function at a point by using a known value of a function at some given point together with its rate of change at the given point. If $f(x)$ is a function defined on an interval $[a, a+h]$, then the **amount of change** of $f(x)$ over the interval is the change in the y values of the function over that interval and is given by

$$f(a+h) - f(a).$$

The **average rate of change** of the function f over that same interval is the ratio of the amount of change over that interval to the corresponding change in the x values. It is given by

$$\frac{f(a+h) - f(a)}{h}.$$

As we already know, the instantaneous rate of change of $f(x)$ at a is its derivative

$$f'(a) = \lim_{h \to 0} \frac{f(a+h) - f(a)}{h}.$$

For small enough values of h, $f'(a) \approx \frac{f(a+h) - f(a)}{h}$. We can then solve for $f(a+h)$ to get the amount of change formula:

$$f(a+h) \approx f(a) + f'(a)h. \tag{3.10}$$

We can use this formula if we know only $f(a)$ and $f'(a)$ and wish to estimate the value of $f(a+h)$. For example, we may use the current population of a city and the rate at which it is growing to estimate its population in the near future. As we can see in **Figure 3.22**, we are approximating $f(a+h)$ by the y coordinate at $a+h$ on the line tangent to $f(x)$ at $x = a$. Observe that the accuracy of this estimate depends on the value of h as well as the value of $f'(a)$.

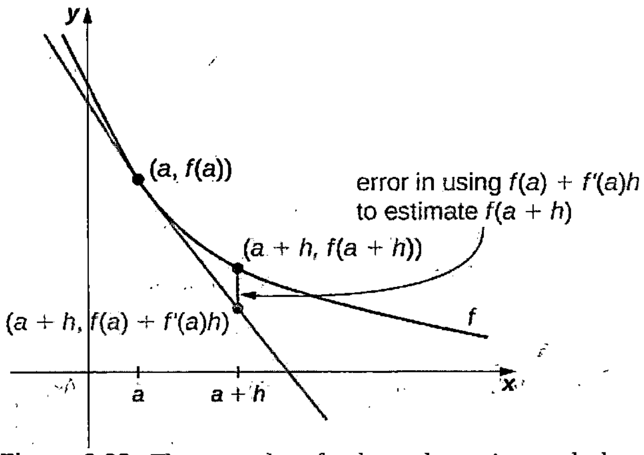

Figure 3.22 The new value of a changed quantity equals the original value plus the rate of change times the interval of change: $f(a+h) \approx f(a) + f'(a)$h.

 Here is an interesting **demonstration (http://www.openstaxcollege.org/l/20_chainrule)** of rate of change.

Example 3.33

Estimating the Value of a Function

If $f(3) = 2$ and $f'(3) = 5$, estimate $f(3.2)$.

Solution

Begin by finding h. We have $h = 3.2 - 3 = 0.2$. Thus,

$$f(3.2) = f(3 + 0.2) \approx f(3) + (0.2)f'(3) = 2 + 0.2(5) = 3.$$

 **3.21** Given $f(10) = -5$ and $f'(10) = 6$, estimate $f(10.1)$.

Motion along a Line

Another use for the derivative is to analyze motion along a line. We have described velocity as the rate of change of position. If we take the derivative of the velocity, we can find the acceleration, or the rate of change of velocity. It is also important to introduce the idea of **speed**, which is the magnitude of velocity. Thus, we can state the following mathematical definitions.

Definition

Let $s(t)$ be a function giving the position of an object at time t.

The velocity of the object at time t is given by $v(t) = s'(t)$.

The speed of the object at time t is given by $|v(t)|$.

The acceleration of the object at t is given by $a(t) = v'(t) = s''(t)$.

Example 3.34

Comparing Instantaneous Velocity and Average Velocity

A ball is dropped from a height of 64 feet. Its height above ground (in feet) t seconds later is given by $s(t) = -16t^2 + 64.$

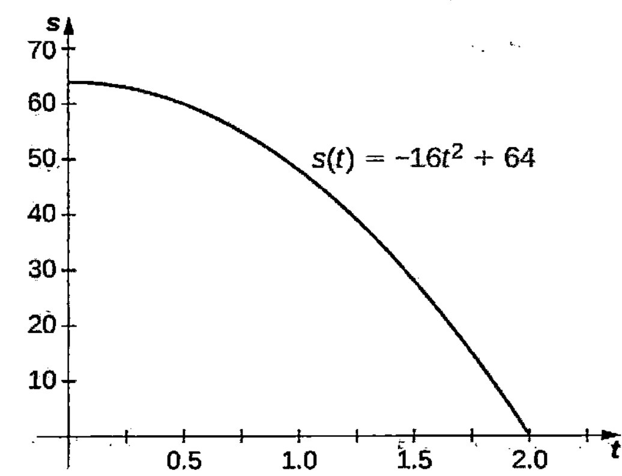

a. What is the instantaneous velocity of the ball when it hits the ground?
b. What is the average velocity during its fall?

Solution

The first thing to do is determine how long it takes the ball to reach the ground. To do this, set $s(t) = 0.$ Solving $-16t^2 + 64 = 0,$ we get $t = 2,$ so it take 2 seconds for the ball to reach the ground.

a. The instantaneous velocity of the ball as it strikes the ground is $v(2).$ Since $v(t) = s'(t) = -32t,$ we obtain $v(t) = -64$ ft/s.

b. The average velocity of the ball during its fall is

$$v_{ave} = \frac{s(2) - s(0)}{2 - 0} = \frac{0 - 64}{2} = -32 \text{ ft/s.}$$

Example 3.35

Interpreting the Relationship between $v(t)$ and $a(t)$

A particle moves along a coordinate axis in the positive direction to the right. Its position at time t is given by $s(t) = t^3 - 4t + 2.$ Find $v(1)$ and $a(1)$ and use these values to answer the following questions.

a. Is the particle moving from left to right or from right to left at time $t = 1$?
b. Is the particle speeding up or slowing down at time $t = 1$?

Solution

Begin by finding $v(t)$ and $a(t).$

and $a(t) = v'(t) = s''(t) = 6t.$

Evaluating these functions at $t = 1,$ we obtain $v(1) = -1$ and $a(1) = 6.$

a. Because $v(1) < 0,$ the particle is moving from right to left.

b. Because $v(1) < 0$ and $a(1) > 0,$ velocity and acceleration are acting in opposite directions. In other words, the particle is being accelerated in the direction opposite the direction in which it is traveling, causing $|v(t)|$ to decrease. The particle is slowing down.

Example 3.36

Position and Velocity

The position of a particle moving along a coordinate axis is given by $s(t) = t^3 - 9t^2 + 24t + 4,\ t \geq 0.$

a. Find $v(t)$.

b. At what time(s) is the particle at rest?

c. On what time intervals is the particle moving from left to right? From right to left?

d. Use the information obtained to sketch the path of the particle along a coordinate axis.

Solution

a. The velocity is the derivative of the position function:

$$v(t) = s'(t) = 3t^2 - 18t + 24.$$

b. The particle is at rest when $v(t) = 0,$ so set $3t^2 - 18t + 24 = 0.$ Factoring the left-hand side of the equation produces $3(t - 2)(t - 4) = 0.$ Solving, we find that the particle is at rest at $t = 2$ and $t = 4.$

c. The particle is moving from left to right when $v(t) > 0$ and from right to left when $v(t) < 0.$ **Figure 3.23** gives the analysis of the sign of $v(t)$ for $t \geq 0,$ but it does not represent the axis along which the particle is moving.

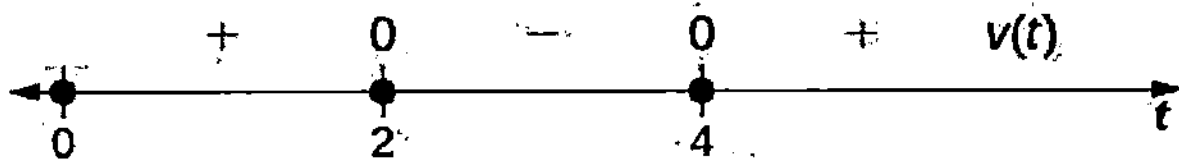

Figure 3.23 The sign of v(t) determines the direction of the particle.

Since $3t^2 - 18t + 24 > 0$ on $[0, 2) \cup (2, +\infty),$ the particle is moving from left to right on these intervals.

Since $3t^2 - 18t + 24 < 0$ on $(2, 4),$ the particle is moving from right to left on this interval.

d. Before we can sketch the graph of the particle, we need to know its position at the time it starts moving $(t = 0)$ and at the times that it changes direction $(t = 2, 4).$ We have $s(0) = 4,\ s(2) = 24,$ and $s(4) = 20.$ This means that the particle begins on the coordinate axis at 4 and changes direction at 0 and

20 on the coordinate axis. The path of the particle is shown on a coordinate axis in **Figure 3.24**.

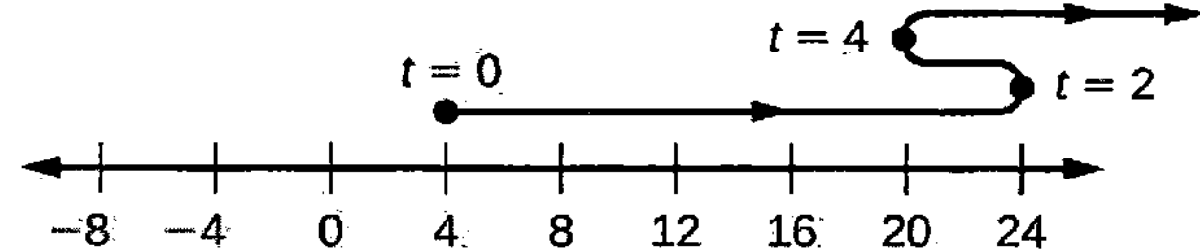

Figure 3.24 The path of the particle can be determined by analyzing v(t).

3.22 A particle moves along a coordinate axis. Its position at time t is given by $s(t) = t^2 - 5t + 1$. Is the particle moving from right to left or from left to right at time $t = 3$?

Population Change

In addition to analyzing velocity, speed, acceleration, and position, we can use derivatives to analyze various types of populations, including those as diverse as bacteria colonies and cities. We can use a current population, together with a growth rate, to estimate the size of a population in the future. The population growth rate is the rate of change of a population and consequently can be represented by the derivative of the size of the population.

Definition

If $P(t)$ is the number of entities present in a population, then the population growth rate of $P(t)$ is defined to be $P'(t)$.

Example 3.37

Estimating a Population

The population of a city is tripling every 5 years. If its current population is 10,000, what will be its approximate population 2 years from now?

Solution

Let $P(t)$ be the population (in thousands) t years from now. Thus, we know that $P(0) = 10$ and based on the information, we anticipate $P(5) = 30$. Now estimate $P'(0)$, the current growth rate, using

$$P'(0) \approx \frac{P(5) - P(0)}{5 - 0} = \frac{30 - 10}{5} = 4.$$

By applying **Equation 3.10** to $P(t)$, we can estimate the population 2 years from now by writing

$$P(2) \approx P(0) + (2)P'(0) \approx 10 + 2(4) = 18;$$

thus, in 2 years the population will be 18,000.

3.23 The current population of a mosquito colony is known to be 3,000; that is, $P(0) = 3{,}000$. If $P'(0) = 100$, estimate the size of the population in 3 days, where t is measured in days.

Changes in Cost and Revenue

In addition to analyzing motion along a line and population growth, derivatives are useful in analyzing changes in cost, revenue, and profit. The concept of a marginal function is common in the fields of business and economics and implies the use of derivatives. The marginal cost is the derivative of the cost function. The marginal revenue is the derivative of the revenue function. The marginal profit is the derivative of the profit function, which is based on the cost function and the revenue function.

Definition

If $C(x)$ is the cost of producing x items, then the **marginal cost** $MC(x)$ is $MC(x) = C'(x)$.

If $R(x)$ is the revenue obtained from selling x items, then the marginal revenue $MR(x)$ is $MR(x) = R'(x)$.

If $P(x) = R(x) - C(x)$ is the profit obtained from selling x items, then the **marginal profit** $MP(x)$ is defined to be $MP(x) = P'(x) = MR(x) - MC(x) = R'(x) - C'(x)$.

We can roughly approximate

$$MC(x) = C'(x) = \lim_{h \to 0} \frac{C(x+h) - C(x)}{h}$$

by choosing an appropriate value for h. Since x represents objects, a reasonable and small value for h is 1. Thus, by substituting $h = 1$, we get the approximation $MC(x) = C'(x) \approx C(x+1) - C(x)$. Consequently, $C'(x)$ for a given value of x can be thought of as the change in cost associated with producing one additional item. In a similar way, $MR(x) = R'(x)$ approximates the revenue obtained by selling one additional item, and $MP(x) = P'(x)$ approximates the profit obtained by producing and selling one additional item.

Example 3.38

Applying Marginal Revenue

Assume that the number of barbeque dinners that can be sold, x, can be related to the price charged, p, by the equation $p(x) = 9 - 0.03x,\ 0 \le x \le 300$.

In this case, the revenue in dollars obtained by selling x barbeque dinners is given by

$$R(x) = xp(x) = x(9 - 0.03x) = -0.03x^2 + 9x \text{ for } 0 \le x \le 300.$$

Use the marginal revenue function to estimate the revenue obtained from selling the 101st barbeque dinner. Compare this to the actual revenue obtained from the sale of this dinner.

Solution

First, find the marginal revenue function: $MR(x) = R'(x) = -0.06x + 9$.

Next, use $R'(100)$ to approximate $R(101) - R(100)$, the revenue obtained from the sale of the 101st dinner. Since $R'(100) = 3$, the revenue obtained from the sale of the 101st dinner is approximately \$3.

The actual revenue obtained from the sale of the 101st dinner is

$$R(101) - R(100) = 602.97 - 600 = 2.97, \text{ or } \$2.97.$$

The marginal revenue is a fairly good estimate in this case and has the advantage of being easy to compute.

3.24 Suppose that the profit obtained from the sale of x fish-fry dinners is given by $P(x) = -0.03x^2 + 8x - 50$. Use the marginal profit function to estimate the profit from the sale of the 101st fish-fry dinner.

3.4 EXERCISES

For the following exercises, the given functions represent the position of a particle traveling along a horizontal line.

a. Find the velocity and acceleration functions.

b. Determine the time intervals when the object is slowing down or speeding up.

150. $s(t) = 2t^3 - 3t^2 - 12t + 8$

151. $s(t) = 2t^3 - 15t^2 + 36t - 10$

152. $s(t) = \frac{t}{1+t^2}$

153. A rocket is fired vertically upward from the ground. The distance s in feet that the rocket travels from the ground after t seconds is given by $s(t) = -16t^2 + 560t$.

a. Find the velocity of the rocket 3 seconds after being fired.

b. Find the acceleration of the rocket 3 seconds after being fired.

154. A ball is thrown downward with a speed of 8 ft/s from the top of a 64-foot-tall building. After t seconds, its height above the ground is given by $s(t) = -16t^2 - 8t + 64$.

a. Determine how long it takes for the ball to hit the ground.

b. Determine the velocity of the ball when it hits the ground.

155. The position function $s(t) = t^2 - 3t - 4$ represents the position of the back of a car backing out of a driveway and then driving in a straight line, where s is in feet and t is in seconds. In this case, $s(t) = 0$ represents the time at which the back of the car is at the garage door, so $s(0) = -4$ is the starting position of the car, 4 feet inside the garage.

a. Determine the velocity of the car when $s(t) = 0$.

b. Determine the velocity of the car when $s(t) = 14$.

156. The position of a hummingbird flying along a straight line in t seconds is given by $s(t) = 3t^3 - 7t$ meters.

a. Determine the velocity of the bird at $t = 1$ sec.

b. Determine the acceleration of the bird at $t = 1$ sec.

c. Determine the acceleration of the bird when the velocity equals 0.

157. A potato is launched vertically upward with an initial velocity of 100 ft/s from a potato gun at the top of an 85-foot-tall building. The distance in feet that the potato travels from the ground after t seconds is given by $s(t) = -16t^2 + 100t + 85$.

a. Find the velocity of the potato after 0.5 s and 5.75 s.

b. Find the speed of the potato at 0.5 s and 5.75 s.

c. Determine when the potato reaches its maximum height.

d. Find the acceleration of the potato at 0.5 s and 1.5 s.

e. Determine how long the potato is in the air.

f. Determine the velocity of the potato upon hitting the ground.

158. The position function $s(t) = t^3 - 8t$ gives the position in miles of a freight train where east is the positive direction and t is measured in hours.

a. Determine the direction the train is traveling when $s(t) = 0$.

b. Determine the direction the train is traveling when $a(t) = 0$.

c. Determine the time intervals when the train is slowing down or speeding up.

159. The following graph shows the position $y = s(t)$ of an object moving along a straight line.

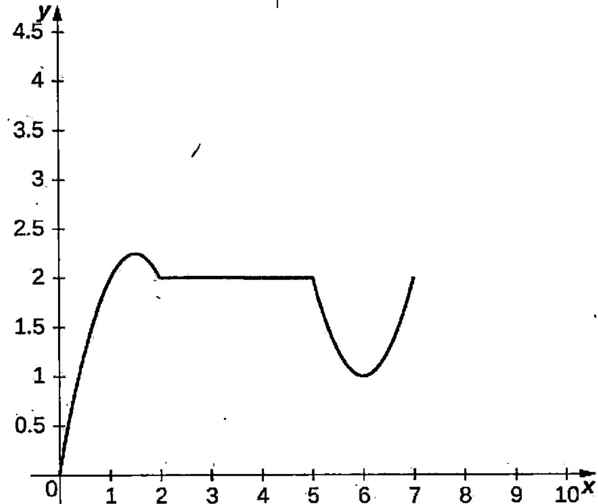

a. Use the graph of the position function to determine the time intervals when the velocity is positive, negative, or zero.

b. Sketch the graph of the velocity function.

c. Use the graph of the velocity function to determine the time intervals when the acceleration is positive, negative, or zero.

d. Determine the time intervals when the object is speeding up or slowing down.

160. The cost function, in dollars, of a company that manufactures food processors is given by $C(x) = 200 + \frac{7}{x} + \frac{x^2}{7}$, where x is the number of food processors manufactured.

a. Find the marginal cost function.
b. Find the marginal cost of manufacturing 12 food processors.
c. Find the actual cost of manufacturing the thirteenth food processor.

161. The price p (in dollars) and the demand x for a certain digital clock radio is given by the price–demand function $p = 10 - 0.001x$.

a. Find the revenue function $R(x)$.
b. Find the marginal revenue function.
c. Find the marginal revenue at $x = 2000$ and 5000.

162. **[T]** A profit is earned when revenue exceeds cost. Suppose the profit function for a skateboard manufacturer is given by $P(x) = 30x - 0.3x^2 - 250$, where x is the number of skateboards sold.

a. Find the exact profit from the sale of the thirtieth skateboard.
b. Find the marginal profit function and use it to estimate the profit from the sale of the thirtieth skateboard.

163. **[T]** In general, the profit function is the difference between the revenue and cost functions: $P(x) = R(x) - C(x)$. Suppose the price-demand and cost functions for the production of cordless drills is given respectively by $p = 143 - 0.03x$ and $C(x) = 75{,}000 + 65x$, where x is the number of cordless drills that are sold at a price of p dollars per drill and $C(x)$ is the cost of producing x cordless drills.

a. Find the marginal cost function.
b. Find the revenue and marginal revenue functions.
c. Find $R'(1000)$ and $R'(4000)$. Interpret the results.
d. Find the profit and marginal profit functions.
e. Find $P'(1000)$ and $P'(4000)$. Interpret the results.

164. A small town in Ohio commissioned an actuarial firm to conduct a study that modeled the rate of change of the town's population. The study found that the town's population (measured in thousands of people) can be modeled by the function $P(t) = -\frac{1}{3}t^3 + 64t + 3000$, where t is measured in years.

a. Find the rate of change function $P'(t)$ of the population function.
b. Find $P'(1)$, $P'(2)$, $P'(3)$, and $P'(4)$. Interpret what the results mean for the town.
c. Find $P''(1)$, $P''(2)$, $P''(3)$, and $P''(4)$. Interpret what the results mean for the town's population.

165. **[T]** A culture of bacteria grows in number according to the function $N(t) = 3000\left(1 + \frac{4t}{t^2 + 100}\right)$, where t is measured in hours.

a. Find the rate of change of the number of bacteria.
b. Find $N'(0)$, $N'(10)$, $N'(20)$, and $N'(30)$.
c. Interpret the results in (b).
d. Find $N''(0)$, $N''(10)$, $N''(20)$, and $N''(30)$. Interpret what the answers imply about the bacteria population growth.

166. The centripetal force of an object of mass m is given by $F(r) = \frac{mv^2}{r}$, where v is the speed of rotation and r is the distance from the center of rotation.

a. Find the rate of change of centripetal force with respect to the distance from the center of rotation.
b. Find the rate of change of centripetal force of an object with mass 1000 kilograms, velocity of 13.89 m/s, and a distance from the center of rotation of 200 meters.

The following questions concern the population (in millions) of London by decade in the 19th century, which is listed in the following table.

Years since 1800	Population (millions)
1	0.8795
11	1.040
21	1.264
31	1.516
41	1.661
51	2.000
61	2.634
71	3.272
81	3.911
91	4.422

Table 3.5 Population of London **Source: http://en.wikipedia.org/wiki/Demographics_of_London.**

167. **[T]**
  a. Using a calculator or a computer program, find the best-fit linear function to measure the population.
  b. Find the derivative of the equation in a. and explain its physical meaning.
  c. Find the second derivative of the equation and explain its physical meaning.

168. **[T]**
  a. Using a calculator or a computer program, find the best-fit quadratic curve through the data.
  b. Find the derivative of the equation and explain its physical meaning.
  c. Find the second derivative of the equation and explain its physical meaning.

For the following exercises, consider an astronaut on a large planet in another galaxy. To learn more about the composition of this planet, the astronaut drops an electronic sensor into a deep trench. The sensor transmits its vertical position every second in relation to the astronaut's position. The summary of the falling sensor data is displayed in the following table.

Time after dropping (s)	Position (m)
0	0
1	−1
2	−2
3	−5
4	−7
5	−14

169. **[T]**
  a. Using a calculator or computer program, find the best-fit quadratic curve to the data.
  b. Find the derivative of the position function and explain its physical meaning.
  c. Find the second derivative of the position function and explain its physical meaning.

170. **[T]**
  a. Using a calculator or computer program, find the best-fit cubic curve to the data.
  b. Find the derivative of the position function and explain its physical meaning.
  c. Find the second derivative of the position function and explain its physical meaning.
  d. Using the result from c. explain why a cubic function is not a good choice for this problem.

The following problems deal with the Holling type I, II, and III equations. These equations describe the ecological event of growth of a predator population given the amount of prey available for consumption.

171. **[T]** The Holling type I equation is described by $f(x) = ax,$ where x is the amount of prey available and $a > 0$ is the rate at which the predator meets the prey for consumption.
  a. Graph the Holling type I equation, given $a = 0.5.$
  b. Determine the first derivative of the Holling type I equation and explain physically what the derivative implies.
  c. Determine the second derivative of the Holling type I equation and explain physically what the derivative implies.
  d. Using the interpretations from b. and c. explain why the Holling type I equation may not be realistic.

172. **[T]** The Holling type II equation is described by $f(x) = \frac{ax}{n + x}$, where x is the amount of prey available and $a > 0$ is the maximum consumption rate of the predator.

a. Graph the Holling type II equation given $a = 0.5$ and $n = 5$. What are the differences between the Holling type I and II equations?
b. Take the first derivative of the Holling type II equation and interpret the physical meaning of the derivative.
c. Show that $f(n) = \frac{1}{2}a$ and interpret the meaning of the parameter n.
d. Find and interpret the meaning of the second derivative. What makes the Holling type II function more realistic than the Holling type I function?

173. **[T]** The Holling type III equation is described by $f(x) = \frac{ax^2}{n^2 + x^2}$, where x is the amount of prey available and $a > 0$ is the maximum consumption rate of the predator.

a. Graph the Holling type III equation given $a = 0.5$ and $n = 5$. What are the differences between the Holling type II and III equations?
b. Take the first derivative of the Holling type III equation and interpret the physical meaning of the derivative.
c. Find and interpret the meaning of the second derivative (it may help to graph the second derivative).
d. What additional ecological phenomena does the Holling type III function describe compared with the Holling type II function?

174. **[T]** The populations of the snowshoe hare (in thousands) and the lynx (in hundreds) collected over 7 years from 1937 to 1943 are shown in the following table. The snowshoe hare is the primary prey of the lynx.

Population of snowshoe hare (thousands)	**Population of lynx (hundreds)**
20	10
55	15
65	55
95	60

Table 3.6 Snowshoe Hare and Lynx Populations **Source: http://www.biotopics.co.uk/newgcse/predatorprey.html.**

a. Graph the data points and determine which Holling-type function fits the data best.
b. Using the meanings of the parameters a and n, determine values for those parameters by examining a graph of the data. Recall that n measures what prey value results in the half-maximum of the predator value.
c. Plot the resulting Holling-type I, II, and III functions on top of the data. Was the result from part a. correct?

3.5 | Derivatives of Trigonometric Functions

Learning Objectives

3.5.1 Find the derivatives of the sine and cosine function.
3.5.2 Find the derivatives of the standard trigonometric functions.
3.5.3 Calculate the higher-order derivatives of the sine and cosine.

One of the most important types of motion in physics is simple harmonic motion, which is associated with such systems as an object with mass oscillating on a spring. Simple harmonic motion can be described by using either sine or cosine functions. In this section we expand our knowledge of derivative formulas to include derivatives of these and other trigonometric functions. We begin with the derivatives of the sine and cosine functions and then use them to obtain formulas for the derivatives of the remaining four trigonometric functions. Being able to calculate the derivatives of the sine and cosine functions will enable us to find the velocity and acceleration of simple harmonic motion.

Derivatives of the Sine and Cosine Functions

We begin our exploration of the derivative for the sine function by using the formula to make a reasonable guess at its derivative. Recall that for a function $f(x)$,

$$f'(x) = \lim_{h \to 0} \frac{f(x+h) - f(x)}{h}.$$

Consequently, for values of h very close to 0, $f'(x) \approx \frac{f(x+h) - f(x)}{h}$. We see that by using $h = 0.01$,

$$\frac{d}{dx}(\sin x) \approx \frac{\sin(x + 0.01) - \sin x}{0.01}$$

By setting $D(x) = \frac{\sin(x + 0.01) - \sin x}{0.01}$ and using a graphing utility, we can get a graph of an approximation to the derivative of $\sin x$ (**Figure 3.25**).

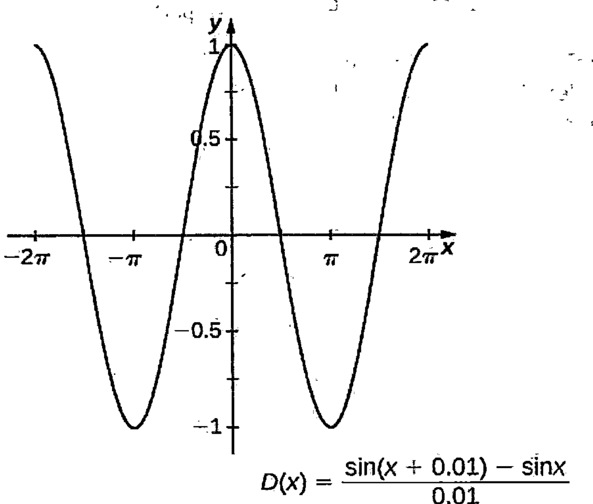

Figure 3.25 The graph of the function $D(x)$ looks a lot like a cosine curve.

Upon inspection, the graph of $D(x)$ appears to be very close to the graph of the cosine function. Indeed, we will show that

$$\frac{d}{dx}(\sin x) = \cos x.$$

If we were to follow the same steps to approximate the derivative of the cosine function, we would find that

$$\frac{d}{dx}(\cos x) = -\sin x.$$

Theorem 3.8: The Derivatives of sin x and cos x

The derivative of the sine function is the cosine and the derivative of the cosine function is the negative sine.

$$\frac{d}{dx}(\sin x) = \cos x \tag{3.11}$$

$$\frac{d}{dx}(\cos x) = -\sin x \tag{3.12}$$

Proof

Because the proofs for $\frac{d}{dx}(\sin x) = \cos x$ and $\frac{d}{dx}(\cos x) = -\sin x$ use similar techniques, we provide only the proof for $\frac{d}{dx}(\sin x) = \cos x$. Before beginning, recall two important trigonometric limits we learned in **Introduction to Limits**:

$$\lim_{h \to 0} \frac{\sin h}{h} = 1 \text{ and } \lim_{h \to 0} \frac{\cos h - 1}{h} = 0.$$

The graphs of $y = \frac{(\sin h)}{h}$ and $y = \frac{(\cos h - 1)}{h}$ are shown in **Figure 3.26**.

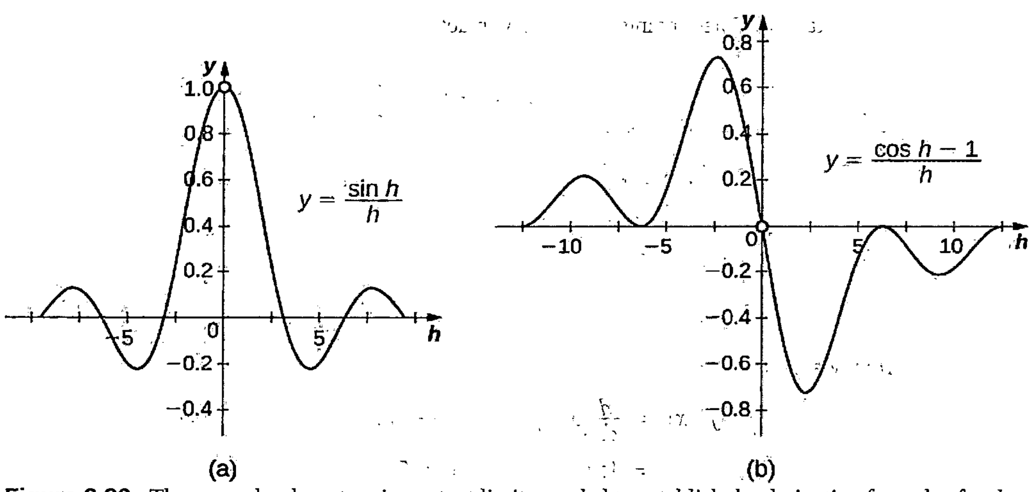

Figure 3.26 These graphs show two important limits needed to establish the derivative formulas for the sine and cosine functions.

We also recall the following trigonometric identity for the sine of the sum of two angles:

$$\sin(x + h) = \sin x \cos h + \cos x \sin h.$$

Now that we have gathered all the necessary equations and identities, we proceed with the proof.

$$\begin{aligned}
\frac{d}{dx}\sin x &= \lim_{h \to 0} \frac{\sin(x+h) - \sin x}{h} && \text{Apply the definition of the derivative.} \\
&= \lim_{h \to 0} \frac{\sin x \cos h + \cos x \sin h - \sin x}{h} && \text{Use trig identity for the sine of the sum of two angles.} \\
&= \lim_{h \to 0}\left(\frac{\sin x \cos h - \sin x}{h} + \frac{\cos x \sin h}{h}\right) && \text{Regroup.} \\
&= \lim_{h \to 0}\left(\sin x\left(\frac{\cos h - 1}{h}\right) + \cos x\left(\frac{\sin h}{h}\right)\right) && \text{Factor out } \sin x \text{ and } \cos x. \\
&= \sin x(0) + \cos x(1) && \text{Apply trig limit formulas.} \\
&= \cos x && \text{Simplify.}
\end{aligned}$$

□

Figure 3.27 shows the relationship between the graph of $f(x) = \sin x$ and its derivative $f'(x) = \cos x$. Notice that at the points where $f(x) = \sin x$ has a horizontal tangent, its derivative $f'(x) = \cos x$ takes on the value zero. We also see that where $f(x) = \sin x$ is increasing, $f'(x) = \cos x > 0$ and where $f(x) = \sin x$ is decreasing, $f'(x) = \cos x < 0$.

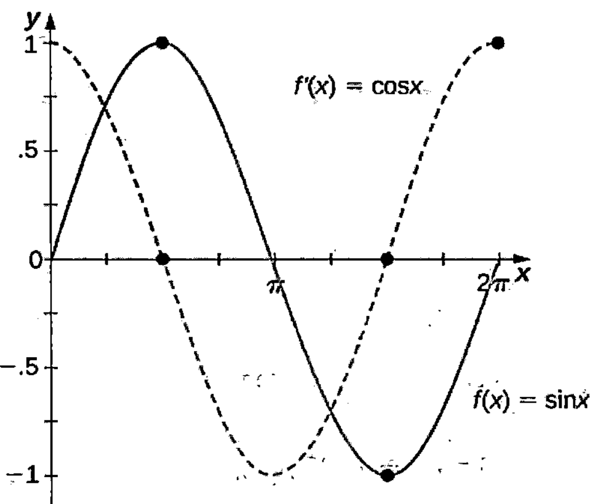

Figure 3.27 Where $f(x)$ has a maximum or a minimum, $f'(x) = 0$ that is, $f'(x) = 0$ where $f(x)$ has a horizontal tangent. These points are noted with dots on the graphs.

Example 3.39

Differentiating a Function Containing sin *x*

Find the derivative of $f(x) = 5x^3 \sin x$.

Solution

Using the product rule, we have

$$\begin{aligned} f'(x) &= \frac{d}{dx}\left(5x^3\right) \cdot \sin x + \frac{d}{dx}(\sin x) \cdot 5x^3 \\ &= 15x^2 \cdot \sin x + \cos x \cdot 5x^3. \end{aligned}$$

After simplifying, we obtain

$$f'(x) = 15x^2 \sin x + 5x^3 \cos x.$$

3.25 Find the derivative of $f(x) = \sin x \cos x$.

Example 3.40

Finding the Derivative of a Function Containing cos *x*

Find the derivative of $g(x) = \frac{\cos x}{4x^2}$.

Solution

By applying the quotient rule, we have

$$g'(x) = \frac{(-\sin x)4x^2 - 8x(\cos x)}{\left(4x^2\right)^2}.$$

Simplifying, we obtain

$$\begin{aligned} g'(x) &= \frac{-4x^2 \sin x - 8x \cos x}{16x^4} \\ &= \frac{-x \sin x - 2\cos x}{4x^3}. \end{aligned}$$

3.26 Find the derivative of $f(x) = \frac{x}{\cos x}$.

Example 3.41

An Application to Velocity

A particle moves along a coordinate axis in such a way that its position at time t is given by $s(t) = 2\sin t - t$ for $0 \le t \le 2\pi$. At what times is the particle at rest?

Solution

To determine when the particle is at rest, set $s'(t) = v(t) = 0$. Begin by finding $s'(t)$. We obtain

$$s'(t) = 2\cos t - 1,$$

so we must solve

$$2\cos t - 1 = 0 \text{ for } 0 \le t \le 2\pi.$$

The solutions to this equation are $t = \frac{\pi}{3}$ and $t = \frac{5\pi}{3}$. Thus the particle is at rest at times $t = \frac{\pi}{3}$ and $t = \frac{5\pi}{3}$.

3.27 A particle moves along a coordinate axis. Its position at time t is given by $s(t) = \sqrt{3}t + 2\cos t$ for $0 \le t \le 2\pi$. At what times is the particle at rest?

Derivatives of Other Trigonometric Functions

Since the remaining four trigonometric functions may be expressed as quotients involving sine, cosine, or both, we can use the quotient rule to find formulas for their derivatives.

Example 3.42

The Derivative of the Tangent Function

Find the derivative of $f(x) = \tan x$.

Solution

Start by expressing $\tan x$ as the quotient of $\sin x$ and $\cos x$:

$$f(x) = \tan x = \frac{\sin x}{\cos x}.$$

Now apply the quotient rule to obtain

$$f'(x) = \frac{\cos x \cos x - (-\sin x)\sin x}{(\cos x)^2}.$$

Simplifying, we obtain

$$f'(x) = \frac{\cos^2 x + \sin^2 x}{\cos^2 x}.$$

Recognizing that $\cos^2 x + \sin^2 x = 1,$ by the Pythagorean theorem, we now have

$$f'(x) = \frac{1}{\cos^2 x}.$$

Finally, use the identity $\sec x = \frac{1}{\cos x}$ to obtain

$$f'(x) = \sec^2 x.$$

3.28 Find the derivative of $f(x) = \cot x$.

The derivatives of the remaining trigonometric functions may be obtained by using similar techniques. We provide these formulas in the following theorem.

Theorem 3.9: Derivatives of $\tan x$, $\cot x$, $\sec x$, and $\csc x$

The derivatives of the remaining trigonometric functions are as follows:

$$\frac{d}{dx}(\tan x) = \sec^2 x \quad (3.13)$$

$$\frac{d}{dx}(\cot x) = -\csc^2 x \quad (3.14)$$

$$\frac{d}{dx}(\sec x) = \sec x \tan x \quad (3.15)$$

$$\frac{d}{dx}(\csc x) = -\csc x \cot x. \quad (3.16)$$

Example 3.43

Finding the Equation of a Tangent Line

Find the equation of a line tangent to the graph of $f(x) = \cot x$ at $x = \frac{\pi}{4}$.

Solution

To find the equation of the tangent line, we need a point and a slope at that point. To find the point, compute

$$f\left(\frac{\pi}{4}\right) = \cot\frac{\pi}{4} = 1.$$

Thus the tangent line passes through the point $\left(\frac{\pi}{4}, 1\right)$. Next, find the slope by finding the derivative of $f(x) = \cot x$ and evaluating it at $\frac{\pi}{4}$:

$$f'(x) = -\csc^2 x \text{ and } f'\left(\frac{\pi}{4}\right) = -\csc^2\left(\frac{\pi}{4}\right) = -2.$$

Using the point-slope equation of the line, we obtain

$$y - 1 = -2\left(x - \frac{\pi}{4}\right)$$

or equivalently,

$$y = -2x + 1 + \frac{\pi}{2}.$$

Example 3.44

Finding the Derivative of Trigonometric Functions

Find the derivative of $f(x) = \csc x + x\tan x.$

Solution

To find this derivative, we must use both the sum rule and the product rule. Using the sum rule, we find

$$f'(x) = \frac{d}{dx}(\csc x) + \frac{d}{dx}(x\tan x).$$

In the first term, $\frac{d}{dx}(\csc x) = -\csc x\cot x,$ and by applying the product rule to the second term we obtain

$$\frac{d}{dx}(x\tan x) = (1)(\tan x) + (\sec^2 x)(x).$$

Therefore, we have

$$f'(x) = -\csc x\cot x + \tan x + x\sec^2 x.$$

3.29 Find the derivative of $f(x) = 2\tan x - 3\cot x.$

3.30 Find the slope of the line tangent to the graph of $f(x) = \tan x$ at $x = \frac{\pi}{6}$.

Higher-Order Derivatives

The higher-order derivatives of $\sin x$ and $\cos x$ follow a repeating pattern. By following the pattern, we can find any higher-order derivative of $\sin x$ and $\cos x$.

Example 3.45

Finding Higher-Order Derivatives of $y = \sin x$

Find the first four derivatives of $y = \sin x$.

Solution

Each step in the chain is straightforward:

$$\begin{aligned} y &= \sin x \\ \frac{dy}{dx} &= \cos x \\ \frac{d^2 y}{dx^2} &= -\sin x \\ \frac{d^3 y}{dx^3} &= -\cos x \\ \frac{d^4 y}{dx^4} &= \sin x. \end{aligned}$$

Analysis

Once we recognize the pattern of derivatives, we can find any higher-order derivative by determining the step in the pattern to which it corresponds. For example, every fourth derivative of sin x equals sin x, so

$$\frac{d^4}{dx^4}(\sin x) = \frac{d^8}{dx^8}(\sin x) = \frac{d^{12}}{dx^{12}}(\sin x) = \ldots = \frac{d^{4n}}{dx^{4n}}(\sin x) = \sin x$$
$$\frac{d^5}{dx^5}(\sin x) = \frac{d^9}{dx^9}(\sin x) = \frac{d^{13}}{dx^{13}}(\sin x) = \ldots = \frac{d^{4n+1}}{dx^{4n+1}}(\sin x) = \cos x.$$

3.31 For $y = \cos x$, find $\frac{d^4 y}{dx^4}$.

Example 3.46

Using the Pattern for Higher-Order Derivatives of $y = \sin x$

Find $\frac{d^{74}}{dx^{74}}(\sin x)$.

Solution

We can see right away that for the 74th derivative of $\sin x$, $74 = 4(18) + 2$, so

$$\frac{d^{74}}{dx^{74}}(\sin x) = \frac{d^{72+2}}{dx^{72+2}}(\sin x) = \frac{d^2}{dx^2}(\sin x) = -\sin x.$$

3.32 For $y = \sin x$, find $\frac{d^{59}}{dx^{59}}(\sin x)$.

Example 3.47

An Application to Acceleration

A particle moves along a coordinate axis in such a way that its position at time t is given by $s(t) = 2 - \sin t$. Find $v(\pi/4)$ and $a(\pi/4)$. Compare these values and decide whether the particle is speeding up or slowing down.

Solution

First find $v(t) = s'(t)$:

$$v(t) = s'(t) = -\cos t.$$

Thus,

$$v\left(\frac{\pi}{4}\right) = -\frac{1}{\sqrt{2}}.$$

Next, find $a(t) = v'(t)$. Thus, $a(t) = v'(t) = \sin t$ and we have

$$a\left(\frac{\pi}{4}\right) = \frac{1}{\sqrt{2}}.$$

Since $v\left(\frac{\pi}{4}\right) = -\frac{1}{\sqrt{2}} < 0$ and $a\left(\frac{\pi}{4}\right) = \frac{1}{\sqrt{2}} > 0$, we see that velocity and acceleration are acting in opposite directions; that is, the object is being accelerated in the direction opposite to the direction in which it is travelling. Consequently, the particle is slowing down.

3.33 A block attached to a spring is moving vertically. Its position at time t is given by $s(t) = 2\sin t$. Find $v\left(\frac{5\pi}{6}\right)$ and $a\left(\frac{5\pi}{6}\right)$. Compare these values and decide whether the block is speeding up or slowing down.

3.5 EXERCISES

For the following exercises, find $\frac{dy}{dx}$ for the given functions.

175. $y = x^2 - \sec x + 1$

176. $y = 3\csc x + \frac{5}{x}$

177. $y = x^2 \cot x$

178. $y = x - x^3 \sin x$

179. $y = \frac{\sec x}{x}$

180. $y = \sin x \tan x$

181. $y = (x + \cos x)(1 - \sin x)$

182. $y = \frac{\tan x}{1 - \sec x}$

183. $y = \frac{1 - \cot x}{1 + \cot x}$

184. $y = \cos x(1 + \csc x)$

For the following exercises, find the equation of the tangent line to each of the given functions at the indicated values of x. Then use a calculator to graph both the function and the tangent line to ensure the equation for the tangent line is correct.

185. **[T]** $f(x) = -\sin x,\ x = 0$

186. **[T]** $f(x) = \csc x,\ x = \frac{\pi}{2}$

187. **[T]** $f(x) = 1 + \cos x,\ x = \frac{3\pi}{2}$

188. **[T]** $f(x) = \sec x,\ x = \frac{\pi}{4}$

189. **[T]** $f(x) = x^2 - \tan x\, x = 0$

190. **[T]** $f(x) = 5\cot x\, x = \frac{\pi}{4}$

For the following exercises, find $\frac{d^2y}{dx^2}$ for the given functions.

191. $y = x\sin x - \cos x$

192. $y = \sin x \cos x$

193. $y = x - \frac{1}{2}\sin x$

194. $y = \frac{1}{x} + \tan x$

195. $y = 2\csc x$

196. $y = \sec^2 x$

197. Find all x values on the graph of $f(x) = -3\sin x \cos x$ where the tangent line is horizontal.

198. Find all x values on the graph of $f(x) = x - 2\cos x$ for $0 < x < 2\pi$ where the tangent line has slope 2.

199. Let $f(x) = \cot x$. Determine the points on the graph of f for $0 < x < 2\pi$ where the tangent line(s) is (are) parallel to the line $y = -2x$.

200. **[T]** A mass on a spring bounces up and down in simple harmonic motion, modeled by the function $s(t) = -6\cos t$ where s is measured in inches and t is measured in seconds. Find the rate at which the spring is oscillating at $t = 5$ s.

201. Let the position of a swinging pendulum in simple harmonic motion be given by $s(t) = a\cos t + b\sin t$. Find the constants a and b such that when the velocity is 3 cm/s, $s = 0$ and $t = 0$.

202. After a diver jumps off a diving board, the edge of the board oscillates with position given by $s(t) = -5\cos t$ cm at t seconds after the jump.

a. Sketch one period of the position function for $t \geq 0$.
b. Find the velocity function.
c. Sketch one period of the velocity function for $t \geq 0$.
d. Determine the times when the velocity is 0 over one period.
e. Find the acceleration function.
f. Sketch one period of the acceleration function for $t \geq 0$.

203. The number of hamburgers sold at a fast-food restaurant in Pasadena, California, is given by $y = 10 + 5\sin x$ where y is the number of hamburgers sold and x represents the number of hours after the restaurant opened at 11 a.m. until 11 p.m., when the store closes. Find y' and determine the intervals where the number of burgers being sold is increasing.

204. **[T]** The amount of rainfall per month in Phoenix, Arizona, can be approximated by $y(t) = 0.5 + 0.3\cos t$, where t is months since January. Find y' and use a calculator to determine the intervals where the amount of rain falling is decreasing.

For the following exercises, use the quotient rule to derive the given equations.

205. $\frac{d}{dx}(\cot x) = -\csc^2 x$

206. $\frac{d}{dx}(\sec x) = \sec x \tan x$

207. $\frac{d}{dx}(\csc x) = -\csc x \cot x$

208. Use the definition of derivative and the identity $\cos(x + h) = \cos x \cos h - \sin x \sin h$ to prove that $\frac{d(\cos x)}{dx} = -\sin x$.

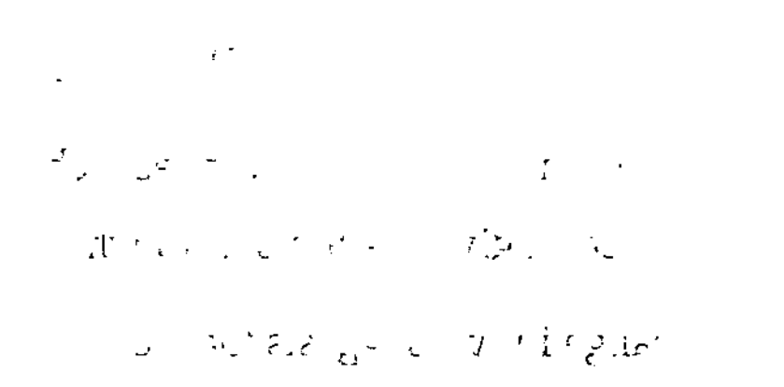

For the following exercises, find the requested higher-order derivative for the given functions.

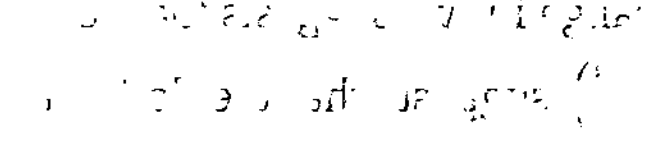

209. $\frac{d^3 y}{dx^3}$ of $y = 3\cos x$

210. $\frac{d^2 y}{dx^2}$ of $y = 3\sin x + x^2 \cos x$

211. $\frac{d^4 y}{dx^4}$ of $y = 5\cos x$

212. $\frac{d^2 y}{dx^2}$ of $y = \sec x + \cot x$

213. $\frac{d^3 y}{dx^3}$ of $y = x^{10} - \sec x$

3.6 | The Chain Rule

Learning Objectives

3.6.1 State the chain rule for the composition of two functions.

3.6.2 Apply the chain rule together with the power rule.

3.6.3 Apply the chain rule and the product/quotient rules correctly in combination when both are necessary.

3.6.4 Recognize the chain rule for a composition of three or more functions.

3.6.5 Describe the proof of the chain rule.

We have seen the techniques for differentiating basic functions $(x^n, \sin x, \cos x, \text{etc.})$ as well as sums, differences, products, quotients, and constant multiples of these functions. However, these techniques do not allow us to differentiate compositions of functions, such as $h(x) = \sin\left(x^3\right)$ or $k(x) = \sqrt{3x^2 + 1}$. In this section, we study the rule for finding the derivative of the composition of two or more functions.

Deriving the Chain Rule

When we have a function that is a composition of two or more functions, we could use all of the techniques we have already learned to differentiate it. However, using all of those techniques to break down a function into simpler parts that we are able to differentiate can get cumbersome. Instead, we use the **chain rule**, which states that the derivative of a composite function is the derivative of the outer function evaluated at the inner function times the derivative of the inner function.

To put this rule into context, let's take a look at an example: $h(x) = \sin\left(x^3\right)$. We can think of the derivative of this function with respect to x as the rate of change of $\sin\left(x^3\right)$ relative to the change in x. Consequently, we want to know how $\sin\left(x^3\right)$ changes as x changes. We can think of this event as a chain reaction: As x changes, x^3 changes, which leads to a change in $\sin\left(x^3\right)$. This chain reaction gives us hints as to what is involved in computing the derivative of $\sin\left(x^3\right)$. First of all, a change in x forcing a change in x^3 suggests that somehow the derivative of x^3 is involved. In addition, the change in x^3 forcing a change in $\sin\left(x^3\right)$ suggests that the derivative of $\sin(u)$ with respect to u, where $u = x^3$, is also part of the final derivative.

We can take a more formal look at the derivative of $h(x) = \sin\left(x^3\right)$ by setting up the limit that would give us the derivative at a specific value a in the domain of $h(x) = \sin\left(x^3\right)$.

$$h'(a) = \lim_{x \to a} \frac{\sin\left(x^3\right) - \sin\left(a^3\right)}{x - a}.$$

This expression does not seem particularly helpful; however, we can modify it by multiplying and dividing by the expression $x^3 - a^3$ to obtain

$$h'(a) = \lim_{x \to a} \frac{\sin\left(x^3\right) - \sin\left(a^3\right)}{x^3 - a^3} \cdot \frac{x^3 - a^3}{x - a}.$$

From the definition of the derivative, we can see that the second factor is the derivative of x^3 at $x = a$. That is,

$$\lim_{x \to a} \frac{x^3 - a^3}{x - a} = \frac{d}{dx}\left(x^3\right) = 3a^2.$$

However, it might be a little more challenging to recognize that the first term is also a derivative. We can see this by letting $u = x^3$ and observing that as $x \to a$, $u \to a^3$:

$$\lim_{x \to a} \frac{\sin(x^3) - \sin(a^3)}{x^3 - a^3} = \lim_{u \to a^3} \frac{\sin u - \sin(a^3)}{u - a^3}$$

$$= \frac{d}{du}(\sin u)_{u = a^3}$$

$$= \cos(a^3).$$

Thus, $h'(a) = \cos(a^3) \cdot 3a^2$.

In other words, if $h(x) = \sin(x^3)$, then $h'(x) = \cos(x^3) \cdot 3x^2$. Thus, if we think of $h(x) = \sin(x^3)$ as the composition $(f \circ g)(x) = f(g(x))$ where $f(x) = \sin x$ and $g(x) = x^3$, then the derivative of $h(x) = \sin(x^3)$ is the product of the derivative of $g(x) = x^3$ and the derivative of the function $f(x) = \sin x$ evaluated at the function $g(x) = x^3$. At this point, we anticipate that for $h(x) = \sin(g(x))$, it is quite likely that $h'(x) = \cos(g(x))g'(x)$. As we determined above, this is the case for $h(x) = \sin(x^3)$.

Now that we have derived a special case of the chain rule, we state the general case and then apply it in a general form to other composite functions. An informal proof is provided at the end of the section.

Rule: The Chain Rule

Let f and g be functions. For all x in the domain of g for which g is differentiable at x and f is differentiable at $g(x)$, the derivative of the composite function

$$h(x) = (f \circ g)(x) = f(g(x))$$

is given by

$$h'(x) = f'(g(x))g'(x). \quad \textbf{(3.17)}$$

Alternatively, if y is a function of u, and u is a function of x, then

$$\frac{dy}{dx} = \frac{dy}{du} \cdot \frac{du}{dx}.$$

Watch an **animation (http://www.openstaxcollege.org/l/20_chainrule2)** of the chain rule.

Problem-Solving Strategy: Applying the Chain Rule

1. To differentiate $h(x) = f(g(x))$, begin by identifying $f(x)$ and $g(x)$.
2. Find $f'(x)$ and evaluate it at $g(x)$ to obtain $f'(g(x))$.
3. Find $g'(x)$.
4. Write $h'(x) = f'(g(x)) \cdot g'(x)$.

Note: When applying the chain rule to the composition of two or more functions, keep in mind that we work our way from the outside function in. It is also useful to remember that the derivative of the composition of two functions can be thought of as having two parts; the derivative of the composition of three functions has three parts; and so on. Also, remember that we never evaluate a derivative at a derivative.

The Chain and Power Rules Combined

We can now apply the chain rule to composite functions, but note that we often need to use it with other rules. For example, to find derivatives of functions of the form $h(x) = (g(x))^n$, we need to use the chain rule combined with the power rule. To do so, we can think of $h(x) = (g(x))^n$ as $f(g(x))$ where $f(x) = x^n$. Then $f'(x) = nx^{n-1}$. Thus, $f'(g(x)) = n(g(x))^{n-1}$. This leads us to the derivative of a power function using the chain rule,

$$h'(x) = n(g(x))^{n-1} g'(x)$$

Rule: Power Rule for Composition of Functions

For all values of x for which the derivative is defined, if

$$h(x) = (g(x))^n.$$

Then

$$h'(x) = n(g(x))^{n-1} g'(x). \quad (3.18)$$

Example 3.48

Using the Chain and Power Rules

Find the derivative of $h(x) = \frac{1}{(3x^2 + 1)^2}$.

Solution

First, rewrite $h(x) = \frac{1}{(3x^2 + 1)^2} = (3x^2 + 1)^{-2}$.

Applying the power rule with $g(x) = 3x^2 + 1$, we have

$$h'(x) = -2(3x^2 + 1)^{-3}(6x).$$

Rewriting back to the original form gives us

$$h'(x) = \frac{-12x}{(3x^2 + 1)^3}.$$

 **3.34** Find the derivative of $h(x) = (2x^3 + 2x - 1)^4$.

Example 3.49

Using the Chain and Power Rules with a Trigonometric Function

Find the derivative of $h(x) = \sin^3 x$.

Solution

First recall that $\sin^3 x = (\sin x)^3$, so we can rewrite $h(x) = \sin^3 x$ as $h(x) = (\sin x)^3$.

Applying the power rule with $g(x) = \sin x$, we obtain

$$h'(x) = 3(\sin x)^2 \cos x = 3\sin^2 x \cos x.$$

Example 3.50

Finding the Equation of a Tangent Line

Find the equation of a line tangent to the graph of $h(x) = \frac{1}{(3x-5)^2}$ at $x = 2$.

Solution

Because we are finding an equation of a line, we need a point. The x-coordinate of the point is 2. To find the y-coordinate, substitute 2 into $h(x)$. Since $h(2) = \frac{1}{(3(2)-5)^2} = 1$, the point is $(2, 1)$.

For the slope, we need $h'(2)$. To find $h'(x)$, first we rewrite $h(x) = (3x-5)^{-2}$ and apply the power rule to obtain

$$h'(x) = -2(3x-5)^{-3}(3) = -6(3x-5)^{-3}.$$

By substituting, we have $h'(2) = -6(3(2)-5)^{-3} = -6$. Therefore, the line has equation $y - 1 = -6(x-2)$. Rewriting, the equation of the line is $y = -6x + 13$.

3.35 Find the equation of the line tangent to the graph of $f(x) = \left(x^2 - 2\right)^3$ at $x = -2$.

Combining the Chain Rule with Other Rules

Now that we can combine the chain rule and the power rule, we examine how to combine the chain rule with the other rules we have learned. In particular, we can use it with the formulas for the derivatives of trigonometric functions or with the product rule.

Example 3.51

Using the Chain Rule on a General Cosine Function

Find the derivative of $h(x) = \cos(g(x))$.

Solution

Think of $h(x) = \cos(g(x))$ as $f(g(x))$ where $f(x) = \cos x$. Since $f'(x) = -\sin x$. we have $f'(g(x)) = -\sin(g(x))$. Then we do the following calculation.

$$\begin{aligned} h'(x) &= f'(g(x))g'(x) && \text{Apply the chain rule.} \\ &= -\sin(g(x))g'(x) && \text{Substitute } f'(g(x)) = -\sin(g(x)). \end{aligned}$$

Thus, the derivative of $h(x) = \cos(g(x))$ is given by $h'(x) = -\sin(g(x))g'(x)$.

In the following example we apply the rule that we have just derived.

Example 3.52

Using the Chain Rule on a Cosine Function

Find the derivative of $h(x) = \cos\left(5x^2\right)$.

Solution

Let $g(x) = 5x^2$. Then $g'(x) = 10x$. Using the result from the previous example,

$$\begin{aligned} h'(x) &= -\sin\left(5x^2\right) \cdot 10x \\ &= -10x\sin\left(5x^2\right). \end{aligned}$$

Example 3.53

Using the Chain Rule on Another Trigonometric Function

Find the derivative of $h(x) = \sec\left(4x^5 + 2x\right)$.

Solution

Apply the chain rule to $h(x) = \sec(g(x))$ to obtain

$$h'(x) = \sec(g(x)\tan(g(x))g'(x).$$

In this problem, $g(x) = 4x^5 + 2x$, so we have $g'(x) = 20x^4 + 2$. Therefore, we obtain

$$\begin{aligned} h'(x) &= \sec\left(4x^5 + 2x\right)\tan\left(4x^5 + 2x\right)\left(20x^4 + 2\right) \\ &= (20x^4 + 2)\sec\left(4x^5 + 2x\right)\tan\left(4x^5 + 2x\right). \end{aligned}$$

3.36 Find the derivative of $h(x) = \sin(7x + 2)$.

At this point we provide a list of derivative formulas that may be obtained by applying the chain rule in conjunction with the formulas for derivatives of trigonometric functions. Their derivations are similar to those used in **Example 3.51** and **Example 3.53**. For convenience, formulas are also given in Leibniz's notation, which some students find easier to remember. (We discuss the chain rule using Leibniz's notation at the end of this section.) It is not absolutely necessary to memorize these as separate formulas as they are all applications of the chain rule to previously learned formulas.

Theorem 3.10: Using the Chain Rule with Trigonometric Functions

For all values of x for which the derivative is defined,

$$\begin{aligned}
\frac{d}{dx}(\sin(g(x)) &= \cos(g(x))g'(x) & \frac{d}{dx}\sin u &= \cos u\frac{du}{dx}\\
\frac{d}{dx}(\cos(g(x)) &= -\sin(g(x))g'(x) & \frac{d}{dx}\cos u &= -\sin u\frac{du}{dx}\\
\frac{d}{dx}(\tan(g(x)) &= \sec^2(g(x))g'(x) & \frac{d}{dx}\tan u &= \sec^2 u\frac{du}{dx}\\
\frac{d}{dx}(\cot(g(x)) &= -\csc^2(g(x))g'(x) & \frac{d}{dx}\cot u &= -\csc^2 u\frac{du}{dx}\\
\frac{d}{dx}(\sec(g(x)) &= \sec(g(x)\tan(g(x))g'(x) & \frac{d}{dx}\sec u &= \sec u\tan u\frac{du}{dx}\\
\frac{d}{dx}(\csc(g(x)) &= -\csc(g(x))\cot(g(x))g'(x) & \frac{d}{dx}\csc u &= -\csc u\cot u\frac{du}{dx}.
\end{aligned}$$

Example 3.54

Combining the Chain Rule with the Product Rule

Find the derivative of $h(x) = (2x+1)^5(3x-2)^7$.

Solution

First apply the product rule, then apply the chain rule to each term of the product.

$$\begin{aligned}
h'(x) &= \frac{d}{dx}\left((2x+1)^5\right)\cdot(3x-2)^7 + \frac{d}{dx}\left((3x-2)^7\right)\cdot(2x+1)^5 && \text{Apply the product rule.}\\
&= 5(2x+1)^4\cdot 2\cdot(3x-2)^7 + 7(3x-2)^6\cdot 3\cdot(2x+1)^5 && \text{Apply the chain rule.}\\
&= 10(2x+1)^4(3x-2)^7 + 21(3x-2)^6(2x+1)^5 && \text{Simplify.}\\
&= (2x+1)^4(3x-2)^6(10(3x-7)+21(2x+1)) && \text{Factor out } (2x+1)^4(3x-2)^6.\\
&= (2x+1)^4(3x-2)^6(72x-49) && \text{Simplify.}
\end{aligned}$$

3.37 Find the derivative of $h(x) = \dfrac{x}{(2x+3)^3}$.

Composites of Three or More Functions

We can now combine the chain rule with other rules for differentiating functions, but when we are differentiating the composition of three or more functions, we need to apply the chain rule more than once. If we look at this situation in general terms, we can generate a formula, but we do not need to remember it, as we can simply apply the chain rule multiple times.

In general terms, first we let

$$k(x) = h(f(g(x))).$$

Then, applying the chain rule once we obtain

$$k'(x) = \frac{d}{dx}(h(f(g(x))) = h'(f(g(x))) \cdot \frac{d}{dx}f((g(x))).$$

Applying the chain rule again, we obtain

$$k'(x) = h'(f(g(x))f'(g(x))g'(x)).$$

Rule: Chain Rule for a Composition of Three Functions

For all values of x for which the function is differentiable, if

$$k(x) = h(f(g(x))),$$

then

$$k'(x) = h'(f(g(x)))f'(g(x))g'(x).$$

In other words, we are applying the chain rule twice.

Notice that the derivative of the composition of three functions has three parts. (Similarly, the derivative of the composition of four functions has four parts, and so on.) Also, *remember, we can always work from the outside in, taking one derivative at a time.*

Example 3.55

Differentiating a Composite of Three Functions

Find the derivative of $k(x) = \cos^4(7x^2 + 1)$.

Solution

First, rewrite $k(x)$ as

$$k(x) = \left(\cos(7x^2 + 1)\right)^4.$$

Then apply the chain rule several times.

$$\begin{aligned} k'(x) &= 4\left(\cos(7x^2+1)\right)^3 \left(\frac{d}{dx}(\cos(7x^2+1))\right) && \text{Apply the chain rule.} \\ &= 4\left(\cos(7x^2+1)\right)^3 \left(-\sin(7x^2+1)\right)\left(\frac{d}{dx}(7x^2+1)\right) && \text{Apply the chain rule.} \\ &= 4\left(\cos(7x^2+1)\right)^3 \left(-\sin(7x^2+1)\right)(14x) && \text{Apply the chain rule.} \\ &= -56x\sin(7x^2+1)\cos^3(7x^2+1) && \text{Simplify.} \end{aligned}$$

3.38 Find the derivative of $h(x) = \sin^6(x^3)$.

Example 3.56

Using the Chain Rule in a Velocity Problem

A particle moves along a coordinate axis. Its position at time t is given by $s(t) = \sin(2t) + \cos(3t)$. What is the velocity of the particle at time $t = \frac{\pi}{6}$?

Solution

To find $v(t)$, the velocity of the particle at time t, we must differentiate $s(t)$. Thus,

$$v(t) = s'(t) = 2\cos(2t) - 3\sin(3t).$$

Substituting $t = \frac{\pi}{6}$ into $v(t)$, we obtain $v\left(\frac{\pi}{6}\right) = -2.$

3.39 A particle moves along a coordinate axis. Its position at time t is given by $s(t) = \sin(4t)$. Find its acceleration at time t.

Proof

At this point, we present a very informal proof of the chain rule. For simplicity's sake we ignore certain issues: For example, we assume that $g(x) \neq g(a)$ for $x \neq a$ in some open interval containing a. We begin by applying the limit definition of the derivative to the function $h(x)$ to obtain $h'(a)$:

$$h'(a) = \lim_{x \to a} \frac{f(g(x)) - f(g(a))}{x - a}.$$

Rewriting, we obtain

$$h'(a) = \lim_{x \to a} \frac{f(g(x)) - f(g(a))}{g(x) - g(a)} \cdot \frac{g(x) - g(a)}{x - a}.$$

Although it is clear that

$$\lim_{x \to a} \frac{g(x) - g(a)}{x - a} = g'(a),$$

it is not obvious that

$$\lim_{x \to a} \frac{f(g(x)) - f(g(a))}{g(x) - g(a)} = f'(g(a)).$$

To see that this is true, first recall that since g is differentiable at a, g is also continuous at a. Thus,

$$\lim_{x \to a} g(x) = g(a).$$

Next, make the substitution $y = g(x)$ and $b = g(a)$ and use change of variables in the limit to obtain

$$\lim_{x \to a} \frac{f(g(x)) - f(g(a))}{g(x) - g(a)} = \lim_{y \to b} \frac{f(y) - f(b)}{y - b} = f'(b) = f'(g(a)).$$

Finally,

$$h'(a) = \lim_{x \to a} \frac{f(g(x)) - f(g(a))}{g(x) - g(a)} \cdot \frac{g(x) - g(a)}{x - a} = f'(g(a))g'(a).$$

□

Example 3.57

Using the Chain Rule with Functional Values

Let $h(x) = f(g(x))$. If $g(1) = 4,\ g'(1) = 3,$ and $f'(4) = 7,$ find $h'(1)$.

Solution

Use the chain rule, then substitute.

$$\begin{aligned} h'(1) &= f'(g(1))g'(1) && \text{Apply the chain rule.} \\ &= f'(4) \cdot 3 && \text{Substitute } g(1) = 4 \text{ and } g'(1) = 3. \\ &= 7 \cdot 3 && \text{Substitute } f'(4) = 7. \\ &= 21 && \text{Simplify.} \end{aligned}$$

3.40 Given $h(x) = f(g(x))$. If $g(2) = -3,\ g'(2) = 4,$ and $f'(-3) = 7,$ find $h'(2)$.

The Chain Rule Using Leibniz's Notation

As with other derivatives that we have seen, we can express the chain rule using Leibniz's notation. This notation for the chain rule is used heavily in physics applications.

For $h(x) = f(g(x)),$ let $u = g(x)$ and $y = h(x) = g(u)$. Thus,

$$h'(x) = \frac{dy}{dx},\ f'(g(x)) = f'(u) = \frac{dy}{du} \text{ and } g'(x) = \frac{du}{dx}.$$

Consequently,

$$\frac{dy}{dx} = h'(x) = f'(g(x))g'(x) = \frac{dy}{du} \cdot \frac{du}{dx}.$$

Rule: Chain Rule Using Leibniz's Notation

If y is a function of u, and u is a function of x, then

$$\frac{dy}{dx} = \frac{dy}{du} \cdot \frac{du}{dx}.$$

Example 3.58

Taking a Derivative Using Leibniz's Notation, Example 1

Find the derivative of $y = \left(\frac{x}{3x+2}\right)^5$.

Solution

First, let $u = \frac{x}{3x+2}$. Thus, $y = u^5$. Next, find $\frac{du}{dx}$ and $\frac{dy}{du}$. Using the quotient rule,

$$\frac{du}{dx} = \frac{2}{(3x+2)^2}$$

and

$$\frac{dy}{du} = 5u^4.$$

Finally, we put it all together.

$$\begin{aligned}
\frac{dy}{dx} &= \frac{dy}{du} \cdot \frac{du}{dx} && \text{Apply the chain rule.} \\
&= 5u^4 \cdot \frac{2}{(3x+2)^2} && \text{Substitute } \frac{dy}{du} = 5u^4 \text{ and } \frac{du}{dx} = \frac{2}{(3x+2)^2}. \\
&= 5\left(\frac{x}{3x+2}\right)^4 \cdot \frac{2}{(3x+2)^2} && \text{Substitute } u = \frac{x}{3x+2}. \\
&= \frac{10x^4}{(3x+2)^6} && \text{Simplify.}
\end{aligned}$$

It is important to remember that, when using the Leibniz form of the chain rule, the final answer must be expressed entirely in terms of the original variable given in the problem.

Example 3.59

Taking a Derivative Using Leibniz's Notation, Example 2

Find the derivative of $y = \tan\left(4x^2 - 3x + 1\right)$.

Solution

First, let $u = 4x^2 - 3x + 1$. Then $y = \tan u$. Next, find $\frac{du}{dx}$ and $\frac{dy}{du}$:

$$\frac{du}{dx} = 8x - 3 \text{ and } \frac{dy}{du} = \sec^2 u.$$

Finally, we put it all together.

$$\begin{aligned}
\frac{dy}{dx} &= \frac{dy}{du} \cdot \frac{du}{dx} && \text{Apply the chain rule.} \\
&= \sec^2 u \cdot (8x-3) && \text{Use } \frac{du}{dx} = 8x-3 \text{ and } \frac{dy}{du} = \sec^2 u. \\
&= \sec^2(4x^2 - 3x + 1) \cdot (8x - 3) && \text{Substitute } u = 4x^2 - 3x + 1.
\end{aligned}$$

3.41 Use Leibniz's notation to find the derivative of $y = \cos\left(x^3\right)$. Make sure that the final answer is expressed entirely in terms of the variable x.

3.6 EXERCISES

For the following exercises, given $y = f(u)$ and $u = g(x)$, find $\frac{dy}{dx}$ by using Leibniz's notation for the chain rule: $\frac{dy}{dx} = \frac{dy}{du}\frac{du}{dx}$.

214. $y = 3u - 6,\ u = 2x^2$

215. $y = 6u^3,\ u = 7x - 4$

216. $y = \sin u,\ u = 5x - 1$

217. $y = \cos u,\ u = \frac{-x}{8}$

218. $y = \tan u,\ u = 9x + 2$

219. $y = \sqrt{4u + 3},\ u = x^2 - 6x$

For each of the following exercises,

a. decompose each function in the form $y = f(u)$ and $u = g(x)$, and

b. find $\frac{dy}{dx}$ as a function of x.

220. $y = (3x - 2)^6$

221. $y = \left(3x^2 + 1\right)^3$

222. $y = \sin^5(x)$

223. $y = \left(\frac{x}{7} + \frac{7}{x}\right)^7$

224. $y = \tan(\sec x)$

225. $y = \csc(\pi x + 1)$

226. $y = \cot^2 x$

227. $y = -6\sin^{-3} x$

For the following exercises, find $\frac{dy}{dx}$ for each function.

228. $y = \left(3x^2 + 3x - 1\right)^4$

229. $y = (5 - 2x)^{-2}$

230. $y = \cos^3(\pi x)$

231. $y = \left(2x^3 - x^2 + 6x + 1\right)^3$

232. $y = \frac{1}{\sin^2(x)}$

233. $y = (\tan x + \sin x)^{-3}$

234. $y = x^2\cos^4 x$

235. $y = \sin(\cos 7x)$

236. $y = \sqrt{6 + \sec \pi x^2}$

237. $y = \cot^3(4x + 1)$

238. Let $y = [f(x)]^3$ and suppose that $f'(1) = 4$ and $\frac{dy}{dx} = 10$ for $x = 1$. Find $f(1)$.

239. Let $y = \left(f(x) + 5x^2\right)^4$ and suppose that $f(-1) = -4$ and $\frac{dy}{dx} = 3$ when $x = -1$. Find $f'(-1)$

240. Let $y = (f(u) + 3x)^2$ and $u = x^3 - 2x$. If $f(4) = 6$ and $\frac{dy}{dx} = 18$ when $x = 2$, find $f'(4)$.

241. **[T]** Find the equation of the tangent line to $y = -\sin\left(\frac{x}{2}\right)$ at the origin. Use a calculator to graph the function and the tangent line together.

242. **[T]** Find the equation of the tangent line to $y = \left(3x + \frac{1}{x}\right)^2$ at the point $(1, 16)$. Use a calculator to graph the function and the tangent line together.

243. Find the x-coordinates at which the tangent line to $y = \left(x - \frac{6}{x}\right)^8$ is horizontal.

244. **[T]** Find an equation of the line that is normal to $g(\theta) = \sin^2(\pi\theta)$ at the point $\left(\frac{1}{4}, \frac{1}{2}\right)$. Use a calculator to graph the function and the normal line together.

For the following exercises, use the information in the following table to find $h'(a)$ at the given value for a.

x	$f(x)$	$f'(x)$	$g(x)$	$g'(x)$
0	2	5	0	2
1	1	−2	3	0
2	4	4	1	−1
3	3	−3	2	3

245. $h(x) = f(g(x)); a = 0$

246. $h(x) = g(f(x)); a = 0$

247. $h(x) = \left(x^4 + g(x)\right)^{-2}; a = 1$

248. $h(x) = \left(\frac{f(x)}{g(x)}\right)^2; a = 3$

249. $h(x) = f(x + f(x)); a = 1$

250. $h(x) = (1 + g(x))^3; a = 2$

251. $h(x) = g\left(2 + f\left(x^2\right)\right); a = 1$

252. $h(x) = f(g(\sin x)); a = 0$

253. **[T]** The position function of a freight train is given by $s(t) = 100(t + 1)^{-2}$, with s in meters and t in seconds. At time $t = 6$ s, find the train's

a. velocity and
b. acceleration.
c. Using a. and b. is the train speeding up or slowing down?

254. **[T]** A mass hanging from a vertical spring is in simple harmonic motion as given by the following position function, where t is measured in seconds and s is in inches: $s(t) = -3\cos\left(\pi t + \frac{\pi}{4}\right)$.

a. Determine the position of the spring at $t = 1.5$ s.
b. Find the velocity of the spring at $t = 1.5$ s.

255. **[T]** The total cost to produce x boxes of Thin Mint Girl Scout cookies is C dollars, where $C = 0.0001x^3 - 0.02x^2 + 3x + 300.$ In t weeks production is estimated to be $x = 1600 + 100t$ boxes.

a. Find the marginal cost $C'(x)$.
b. Use Leibniz's notation for the chain rule, $\frac{dC}{dt} = \frac{dC}{dx} \cdot \frac{dx}{dt}$, to find the rate with respect to time t that the cost is changing.
c. Use b. to determine how fast costs are increasing when $t = 2$ weeks. Include units with the answer.

256. **[T]** The formula for the area of a circle is $A = \pi r^2$, where r is the radius of the circle. Suppose a circle is expanding, meaning that both the area A and the radius r (in inches) are expanding.

a. Suppose $r = 2 - \frac{100}{(t + 7)^2}$ where t is time in seconds. Use the chain rule $\frac{dA}{dt} = \frac{dA}{dr} \cdot \frac{dr}{dt}$ to find the rate at which the area is expanding.
b. Use a. to find the rate at which the area is expanding at $t = 4$ s.

257. **[T]** The formula for the volume of a sphere is $S = \frac{4}{3}\pi r^3$, where r (in feet) is the radius of the sphere. Suppose a spherical snowball is melting in the sun.

a. Suppose $r = \frac{1}{(t + 1)^2} - \frac{1}{12}$ where t is time in minutes. Use the chain rule $\frac{dS}{dt} = \frac{dS}{dr} \cdot \frac{dr}{dt}$ to find the rate at which the snowball is melting.
b. Use a. to find the rate at which the volume is changing at $t = 1$ min.

258. **[T]** The daily temperature in degrees Fahrenheit of Phoenix in the summer can be modeled by the function $T(x) = 94 - 10\cos\left[\frac{\pi}{12}(x - 2)\right]$, where x is hours after midnight. Find the rate at which the temperature is changing at 4 p.m.

259. **[T]** The depth (in feet) of water at a dock changes with the rise and fall of tides. The depth is modeled by the function $D(t) = 5\sin\left(\frac{\pi}{6}t - \frac{7\pi}{6}\right) + 8$, where t is the number of hours after midnight. Find the rate at which the depth is changing at 6 a.m.

3.7 | Derivatives of Inverse Functions

Learning Objectives

3.7.1 Calculate the derivative of an inverse function.
3.7.2 Recognize the derivatives of the standard inverse trigonometric functions.

In this section we explore the relationship between the derivative of a function and the derivative of its inverse. For functions whose derivatives we already know, we can use this relationship to find derivatives of inverses without having to use the limit definition of the derivative. In particular, we will apply the formula for derivatives of inverse functions to trigonometric functions. This formula may also be used to extend the power rule to rational exponents.

The Derivative of an Inverse Function

We begin by considering a function and its inverse. If $f(x)$ is both invertible and differentiable, it seems reasonable that the inverse of $f(x)$ is also differentiable. **Figure 3.28** shows the relationship between a function $f(x)$ and its inverse $f^{-1}(x)$. Look at the point $\left(a,\ f^{-1}(a)\right)$ on the graph of $f^{-1}(x)$ having a tangent line with a slope of $\left(f^{-1}\right)'(a) = \frac{p}{q}$. This point corresponds to a point $\left(f^{-1}(a),\ a\right)$ on the graph of $f(x)$ having a tangent line with a slope of $f'\left(f^{-1}(a)\right) = \frac{q}{p}$. Thus, if $f^{-1}(x)$ is differentiable at a, then it must be the case that

$$\left(f^{-1}\right)'(a) = \frac{1}{f'\left(f^{-1}(a)\right)}.$$

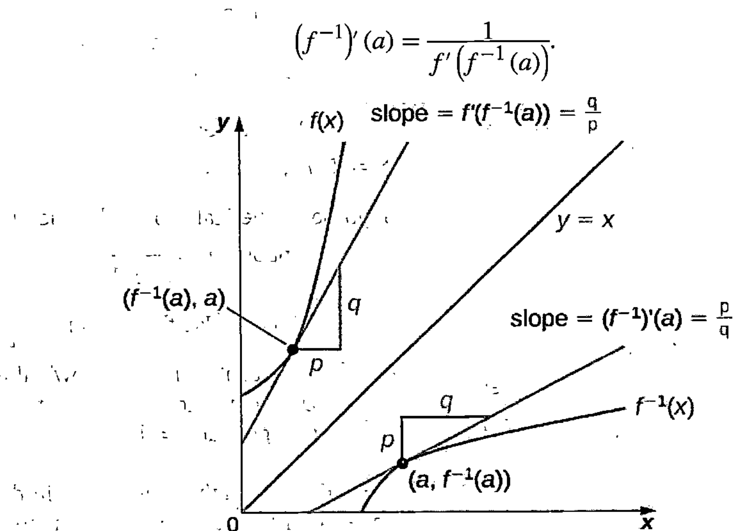

Figure 3.28 The tangent lines of a function and its inverse are related; so, too, are the derivatives of these functions.

We may also derive the formula for the derivative of the inverse by first recalling that $x = f\left(f^{-1}(x)\right)$. Then by differentiating both sides of this equation (using the chain rule on the right), we obtain

$$1 = f'\left(f^{-1}(x)\right)\left(f^{-1}\right)'(x)\Big).$$

Solving for $(f^{-1})'(x)$, we obtain

$$\left(f^{-1}\right)'(x) = \frac{1}{f'\left(f^{-1}(x)\right)}. \quad \textbf{(3.19)}$$

We summarize this result in the following theorem.

Theorem 3.11: Inverse Function Theorem

Let $f(x)$ be a function that is both invertible and differentiable. Let $y = f^{-1}(x)$ be the inverse of $f(x)$. For all x satisfying $f'\left(f^{-1}(x)\right) \neq 0$,

$$\frac{dy}{dx} = \frac{d}{dx}\left(f^{-1}(x)\right) = \left(f^{-1}\right)'(x) = \frac{1}{f'\left(f^{-1}(x)\right)}.$$

Alternatively, if $y = g(x)$ is the inverse of $f(x)$, then

$$g(x) = \frac{1}{f'(g(x))}.$$

Example 3.60

Applying the Inverse Function Theorem

Use the inverse function theorem to find the derivative of $g(x) = \frac{x+2}{x}$. Compare the resulting derivative to that obtained by differentiating the function directly.

Solution

The inverse of $g(x) = \frac{x+2}{x}$ is $f(x) = \frac{2}{x-1}$. Since $g'(x) = \frac{1}{f'(g(x))}$, begin by finding $f'(x)$. Thus,

$$f'(x) = \frac{-2}{(x-1)^2} \text{ and } f'(g(x)) = \frac{-2}{(g(x)-1)^2} = \frac{-2}{\left(\frac{x+2}{x} - 1\right)^2} = -\frac{x^2}{2}.$$

Finally,

$$g'(x) = \frac{1}{f'(g(x))} = -\frac{2}{x^2}.$$

We can verify that this is the correct derivative by applying the quotient rule to $g(x)$ to obtain

$$g'(x) = -\frac{2}{x^2}.$$

3.42 Use the inverse function theorem to find the derivative of $g(x) = \frac{1}{x+2}$. Compare the result obtained by differentiating $g(x)$ directly.

Example 3.61

Applying the Inverse Function Theorem

Use the inverse function theorem to find the derivative of $g(x) = \sqrt[3]{x}$.

Solution

The function $g(x) = \sqrt[3]{x}$ is the inverse of the function $f(x) = x^3$. Since $g'(x) = \frac{1}{f'(g(x))}$, begin by finding $f'(x)$. Thus,

$$f'(x) = 3x^3 \text{ and } f'(g(x)) = 3\left(\sqrt[3]{x}\right)^2 = 3x^{2/3}.$$

Finally,

$$g'(x) = \frac{1}{3x^{2/3}} = \frac{1}{3}x^{-2/3}.$$

3.43 Find the derivative of $g(x) = \sqrt[5]{x}$ by applying the inverse function theorem.

From the previous example, we see that we can use the inverse function theorem to extend the power rule to exponents of the form $\frac{1}{n}$, where n is a positive integer. This extension will ultimately allow us to differentiate x^q, where q is any rational number.

Theorem 3.12: Extending the Power Rule to Rational Exponents

The power rule may be extended to rational exponents. That is, if n is a positive integer, then

$$\frac{d}{dx}\left(x^{1/n}\right) = \frac{1}{n}x^{(1/n)-1}. \quad (3.20)$$

Also, if n is a positive integer and m is an arbitrary integer, then

$$\frac{d}{dx}\left(x^{m/n}\right) = \frac{m}{n}x^{(m/n)-1}. \quad (3.21)$$

Proof

The function $g(x) = x^{1/n}$ is the inverse of the function $f(x) = x^n$. Since $g'(x) = \frac{1}{f'(g(x))}$, begin by finding $f'(x)$.

Thus,

$$f'(x) = nx^{n-1} \text{ and } f'(g(x)) = n\left(x^{1/n}\right)^{n-1} = nx^{(n-1)/n}.$$

Finally,

$$g'(x) = \frac{1}{nx^{(n-1)/n}} = \frac{1}{n}x^{(1-n)/n} = \frac{1}{n}x^{(1/n)-1}.$$

To differentiate $x^{m/n}$ we must rewrite it as $\left(x^{1/n}\right)^m$ and apply the chain rule. Thus,

$$\frac{d}{dx}\left(x^{m/n}\right) = \frac{d}{dx}\left(\left(x^{1/n}\right)^m\right) = m\left(x^{1/n}\right)^{m-1} \cdot \frac{1}{n}x^{(1/n)-1} = \frac{m}{n}x^{(m/n)-1}.$$

□

Example 3.62

Applying the Power Rule to a Rational Power

Find the equation of the line tangent to the graph of $y = x^{2/3}$ at $x = 8$.

Solution

First find $\frac{dy}{dx}$ and evaluate it at $x = 8$. Since

$$\frac{dy}{dx} = \frac{2}{3}x^{-1/3} \text{ and } \frac{dy}{dx}\bigg|_{x=8} = \frac{1}{3}$$

the slope of the tangent line to the graph at $x = 8$ is $\frac{1}{3}$.

Substituting $x = 8$ into the original function, we obtain $y = 4$. Thus, the tangent line passes through the point $(8, 4)$. Substituting into the point-slope formula for a line, we obtain the tangent line

$$y = \frac{1}{3}x + \frac{4}{3}.$$

3.44 Find the derivative of $s(t) = \sqrt{2t + 1}$.

Derivatives of Inverse Trigonometric Functions

We now turn our attention to finding derivatives of inverse trigonometric functions. These derivatives will prove invaluable in the study of integration later in this text. The derivatives of inverse trigonometric functions are quite surprising in that their derivatives are actually algebraic functions. Previously, derivatives of algebraic functions have proven to be algebraic functions and derivatives of trigonometric functions have been shown to be trigonometric functions. Here, for the first time, we see that the derivative of a function need not be of the same type as the original function.

Example 3.63

Derivative of the Inverse Sine Function

Use the inverse function theorem to find the derivative of $g(x) = \sin^{-1} x$.

Solution

Since for x in the interval $\left[-\frac{\pi}{2}, \frac{\pi}{2}\right]$, $f(x) = \sin x$ is the inverse of $g(x) = \sin^{-1} x$, begin by finding $f'(x)$. Since

$$f'(x) = \cos x \text{ and } f'(g(x)) = \cos\left(\sin^{-1} x\right) = \sqrt{1 - x^2},$$

we see that

$$g'(x) = \frac{d}{dx}\left(\sin^{-1} x\right) = \frac{1}{f'(g(x))} = \frac{1}{\sqrt{1 - x^2}}.$$

Analysis

To see that $\cos\left(\sin^{-1} x\right) = \sqrt{1 - x^2}$, consider the following argument. Set $\sin^{-1} x = \theta$. In this case, $\sin\theta = x$ where $-\frac{\pi}{2} \le \theta \le \frac{\pi}{2}$. We begin by considering the case where $0 < \theta < \frac{\pi}{2}$. Since θ is an acute angle, we may construct a right triangle having acute angle θ, a hypotenuse of length 1 and the side opposite angle θ having length x. From the Pythagorean theorem, the side adjacent to angle θ has length $\sqrt{1 - x^2}$. This triangle is shown in **Figure 3.29**. Using the triangle, we see that $\cos\left(\sin^{-1} x\right) = \cos\theta = \sqrt{1 - x^2}$.

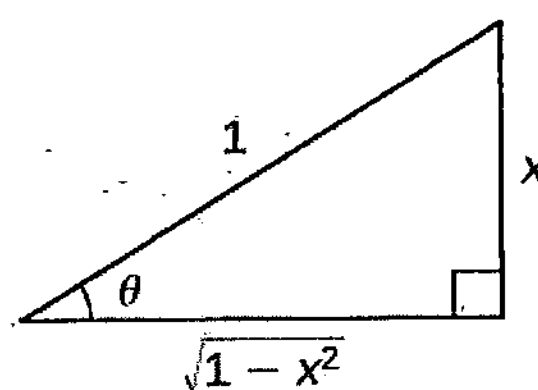

Figure 3.29 Using a right triangle having acute angle θ, a hypotenuse of length 1, and the side opposite angle θ having length x, we can see that $\cos\left(\sin^{-1} x\right) = \cos\theta = \sqrt{1 - x^2}$.

In the case where $-\frac{\pi}{2} < \theta < 0$, we make the observation that $0 < -\theta < \frac{\pi}{2}$ and hence

$$\cos\left(\sin^{-1} x\right) = \cos\theta = \cos(-\theta) = \sqrt{1 - x^2}.$$

Now if $\theta = \frac{\pi}{2}$ or $\theta = -\frac{\pi}{2}$, $x = 1$ or $x = -1$, and since in either case $\cos\theta = 0$ and $\sqrt{1 - x^2} = 0$, we have

$$\cos\left(\sin^{-1} x\right) = \cos\theta = \sqrt{1 - x^2}.$$

Consequently, in all cases, $\cos\left(\sin^{-1} x\right) = \sqrt{1 - x^2}$.

Example 3.64

Applying the Chain Rule to the Inverse Sine Function

Apply the chain rule to the formula derived in **Example 3.61** to find the derivative of $h(x) = \sin^{-1}(g(x))$ and use this result to find the derivative of $h(x) = \sin^{-1}\left(2x^3\right)$.

Solution

Applying the chain rule to $h(x) = \sin^{-1}(g(x))$, we have

$$h'(x) = \frac{1}{\sqrt{1 - (g(x))^2}} g'(x).$$

Now let $g(x) = 2x^3$, so $g'(x) = 6x^2$. Substituting into the previous result, we obtain

$$\begin{aligned} h'(x) &= \frac{1}{\sqrt{1-4x^6}} \cdot 6x^2 \\ &= \frac{6x^2}{\sqrt{1-4x^6}}. \end{aligned}$$

3.45 Use the inverse function theorem to find the derivative of $g(x) = \tan^{-1} x$.

The derivatives of the remaining inverse trigonometric functions may also be found by using the inverse function theorem. These formulas are provided in the following theorem.

Theorem 3.13: Derivatives of Inverse Trigonometric Functions

$$\frac{d}{dx}\sin^{-1} x = \frac{1}{\sqrt{1-(x)^2}} \quad (3.22)$$

$$\frac{d}{dx}\cos^{-1} x = \frac{-1}{\sqrt{1-(x)^2}} \quad (3.23)$$

$$\frac{d}{dx}\tan^{-1} x = \frac{1}{1+(x)^2} \quad (3.24)$$

$$\frac{d}{dx}\cot^{-1} x = \frac{-1}{1+(x)^2} \quad (3.25)$$

$$\frac{d}{dx}\sec^{-1} x = \frac{1}{|x|\sqrt{(x)^2-1}} \quad (3.26)$$

$$\frac{d}{dx}\csc^{-1} x = \frac{-1}{|x|\sqrt{(x)^2-1}} \quad (3.27)$$

Example 3.65

Applying Differentiation Formulas to an Inverse Tangent Function

Find the derivative of $f(x) = \tan^{-1}\left(x^2\right)$.

Solution

Let $g(x) = x^2$, so $g'(x) = 2x$. Substituting into **Equation 3.24**, we obtain

$$f'(x) = \frac{1}{1+\left(x^2\right)^2} \cdot (2x).$$

Simplifying, we have

$$f'(x) = \frac{2x}{1+x^4}.$$

Example 3.66

Applying Differentiation Formulas to an Inverse Sine Function

Find the derivative of $h(x) = x^2 \sin^{-1} x$.

Solution

By applying the product rule, we have

$$h'(x) = 2x\sin^{-1} x + \frac{1}{\sqrt{1-x^2}} \cdot x^2.$$

3.46 Find the derivative of $h(x) = \cos^{-1}(3x - 1)$.

Example 3.67

Applying the Inverse Tangent Function

The position of a particle at time t is given by $s(t) = \tan^{-1}\left(\frac{1}{t}\right)$ for $t \geq \frac{1}{2}$. Find the velocity of the particle at time $t = 1$.

Solution

Begin by differentiating $s(t)$ in order to find $v(t)$. Thus,

$$v(t) = s'(t) = \frac{1}{1 + \left(\frac{1}{t}\right)^2} \cdot \frac{-1}{t^2}.$$

Simplifying, we have

$$v(t) = -\frac{1}{t^2 + 1}.$$

Thus, $v(1) = -\frac{1}{2}$.

3.47 Find the equation of the line tangent to the graph of $f(x) = \sin^{-1} x$ at $x = 0$.

3.7 EXERCISES

For the following exercises, use the graph of $y = f(x)$ to

a. sketch the graph of $y = f^{-1}(x)$, and

b. use part a. to estimate $\left(f^{-1}\right)'(1)$.

260.

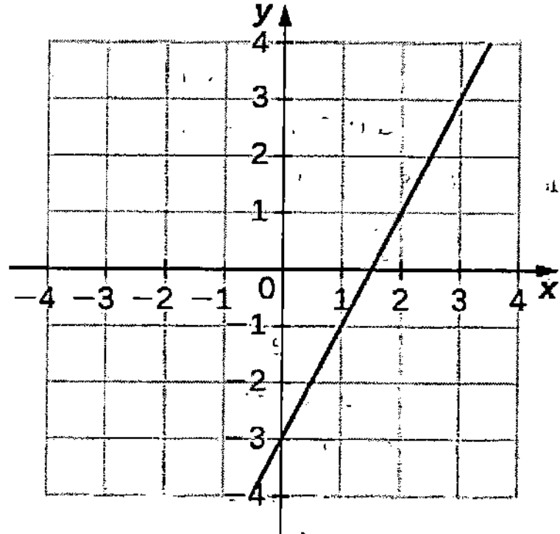

261.

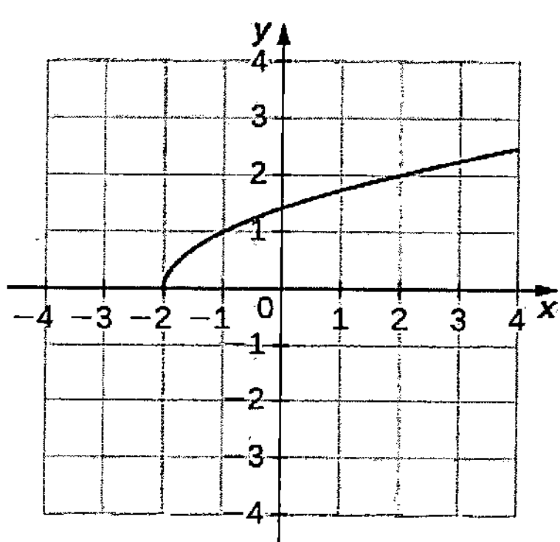

262.

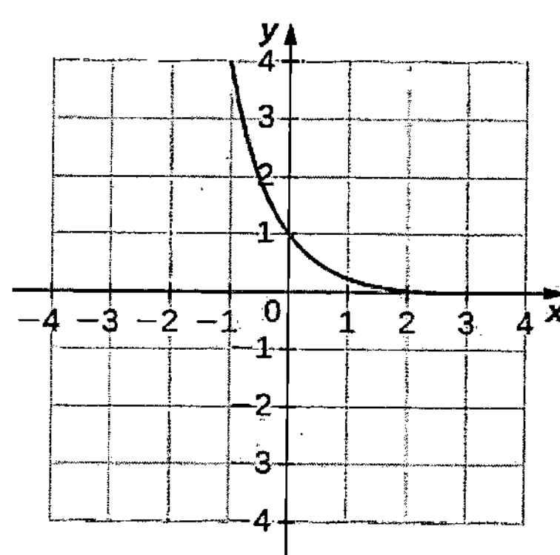

263.

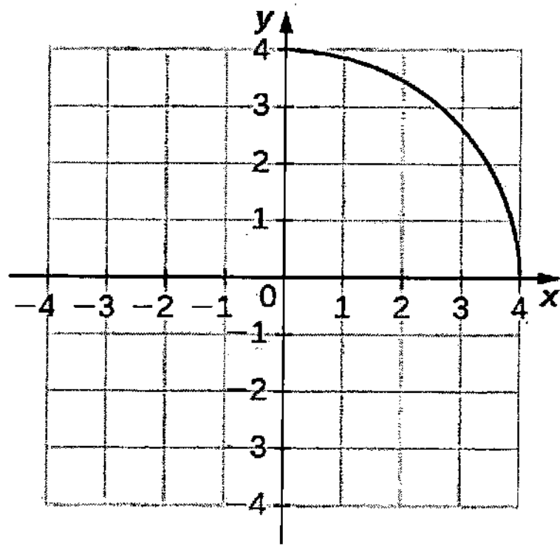

For the following exercises, use the functions $y = f(x)$ to find

a. $\frac{df}{dx}$ at $x = a$ and

b. $x = f^{-1}(y)$.

c. Then use part b. to find $\frac{df^{-1}}{dy}$ at $y = f(a)$.

264. $f(x) = 6x - 1,\ x = -2$

265. $f(x) = 2x^3 - 3,\ x = 1$

266. $f(x) = 9 - x^2,\ 0 \le x \le 3,\ x = 2$

267. $f(x) = \sin x,\ x = 0$

For each of the following functions, find $\left(f^{-1}\right)'(a)$.

268. $f(x) = x^2 + 3x + 2,\ x \ge -1,\ a = 2$

269. $f(x) = x^3 + 2x + 3,\ a = 0$

270. $f(x) = x + \sqrt{x},\ a = 2$

271. $f(x) = x - \frac{2}{x},\ x < 0,\ a = 1$

272. $f(x) = x + \sin x,\ a = 0$

273. $f(x) = \tan x + 3x^2,\ a = 0$

For each of the given functions $y = f(x)$,

a. find the slope of the tangent line to its inverse function f^{-1} at the indicated point P, and

b. find the equation of the tangent line to the graph of f^{-1} at the indicated point.

274. $f(x) = \frac{4}{1+x^2}$, $P(2, 1)$

275. $f(x) = \sqrt{x-4}$, $P(2, 8)$

276. $f(x) = \left(x^3+1\right)^4$, $P(16, 1)$

277. $f(x) = -x^3 - x + 2$, $P(-8, 2)$

278. $f(x) = x^5 + 3x^3 - 4x - 8$, $P(-8, 1)$

For the following exercises, find $\frac{dy}{dx}$ for the given function.

279. $y = \sin^{-1}\left(x^2\right)$

280. $y = \cos^{-1}(\sqrt{x})$

281. $y = \sec^{-1}\left(\frac{1}{x}\right)$

282. $y = \sqrt{\csc^{-1} x}$

283. $y = \left(1 + \tan^{-1} x\right)^3$

284. $y = \cos^{-1}(2x) \cdot \sin^{-1}(2x)$

285. $y = \frac{1}{\tan^{-1}(x)}$

286. $y = \sec^{-1}(-x)$

287. $y = \cot^{-1}\sqrt{4-x^2}$

288. $y = x \cdot \csc^{-1} x$

For the following exercises, use the given values to find $\left(f^{-1}\right)'(a)$.

289. $f(\pi) = 0$, $f'(\pi) = -1$, $a = 0$

290. $f(6) = 2$, $f'(6) = \frac{1}{3}$, $a = 2$

291. $f\left(\frac{1}{3}\right) = -8$, $f'\left(\frac{1}{3}\right) = 2$, $a = -8$

292. $f(\sqrt{3}) = \frac{1}{2}$, $f'(\sqrt{3}) = \frac{2}{3}$, $a = \frac{1}{2}$

293. $f(1) = -3$, $f'(1) = 10$, $a = -3$

294. $f(1) = 0$, $f'(1) = -2$, $a = 0$

295. **[T]** The position of a moving hockey puck after t seconds is $s(t) = \tan^{-1} t$ where s is in meters.

a. Find the velocity of the hockey puck at any time t.
b. Find the acceleration of the puck at any time t.
c. Evaluate a. and b. for $t = 2, 4,$ and 6 seconds.
d. What conclusion can be drawn from the results in c.?

296. **[T]** A building that is 225 feet tall casts a shadow of various lengths x as the day goes by. An angle of elevation θ is formed by lines from the top and bottom of the building to the tip of the shadow, as seen in the following figure. Find the rate of change of the angle of elevation $\frac{d\theta}{dx}$ when $x = 272$ feet.

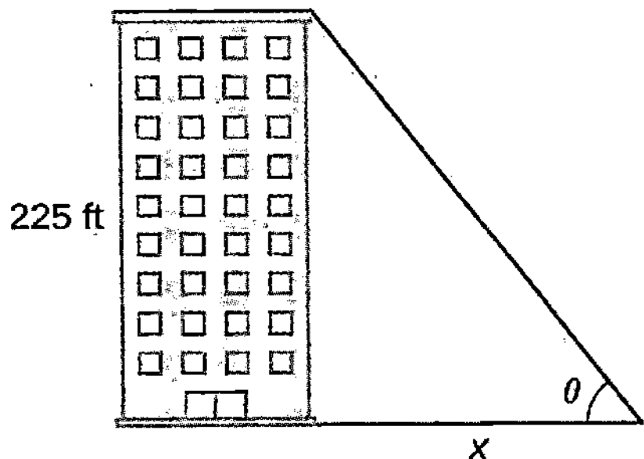

297. **[T]** A pole stands 75 feet tall. An angle θ is formed when wires of various lengths of x feet are attached from the ground to the top of the pole, as shown in the following figure. Find the rate of change of the angle $\frac{d\theta}{dx}$ when a wire of length 90 feet is attached.

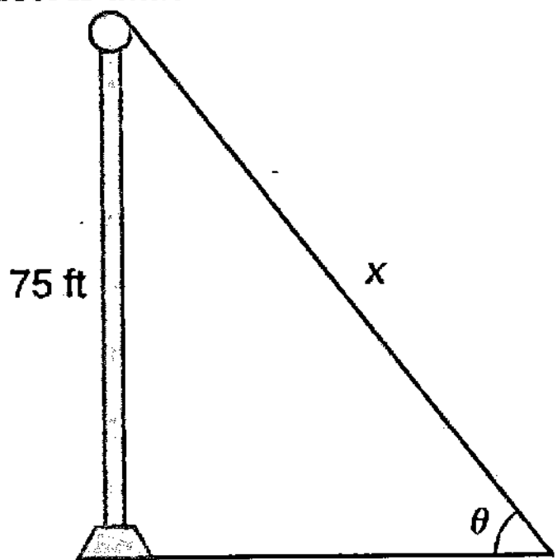

298. **[T]** A television camera at ground level is 2000 feet away from the launching pad of a space rocket that is set to take off vertically, as seen in the following figure. The angle of elevation of the camera can be found by $\theta = \tan^{-1}\left(\frac{x}{2000}\right)$, where x is the height of the rocket. Find the rate of change of the angle of elevation after launch when the camera and the rocket are 5000 feet apart.

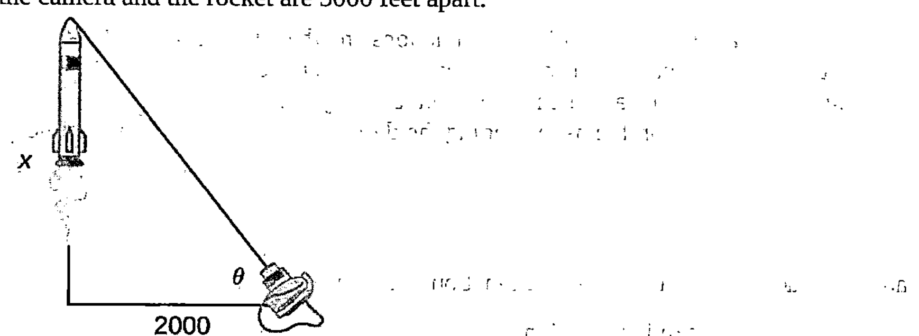

299. **[T]** A local movie theater with a 30-foot-high screen that is 10 feet above a person's eye level when seated has a viewing angle θ (in radians) given by $\theta = \cot^{-1}\frac{x}{40} - \cot^{-1}\frac{x}{10}$, where x is the distance in feet away from the movie screen that the person is sitting, as shown in the following figure.

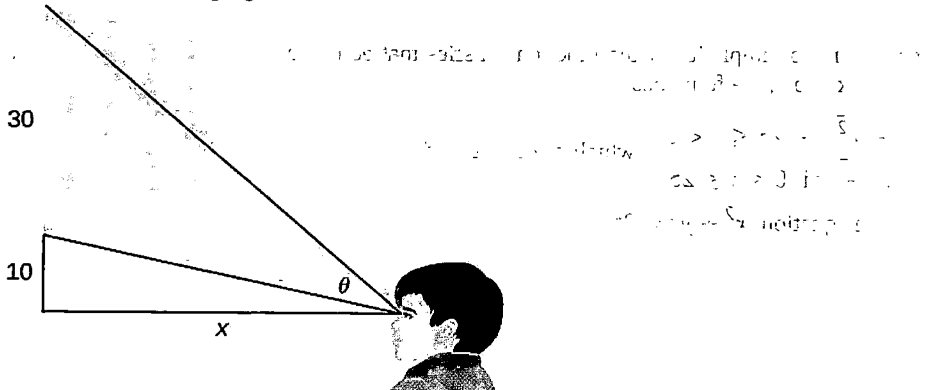

a. Find $\frac{d\theta}{dx}$.

b. Evaluate $\frac{d\theta}{dx}$ for $x = 5, 10, 15,$ and 20.

c. Interpret the results in b..

d. Evaluate $\frac{d\theta}{dx}$ for $x = 25, 30, 35,$ and 40

e. Interpret the results in d. At what distance x should the person stand to maximize his or her viewing angle?

3.8 | Implicit Differentiation

Learning Objectives

3.8.1 Find the derivative of a complicated function by using implicit differentiation.
3.8.2 Use implicit differentiation to determine the equation of a tangent line.

We have already studied how to find equations of tangent lines to functions and the rate of change of a function at a specific point. In all these cases we had the explicit equation for the function and differentiated these functions explicitly. Suppose instead that we want to determine the equation of a tangent line to an arbitrary curve or the rate of change of an arbitrary curve at a point. In this section, we solve these problems by finding the derivatives of functions that define y implicitly in terms of x.

Implicit Differentiation

In most discussions of math, if the dependent variable y is a function of the independent variable x, we express y in terms of x. If this is the case, we say that y is an explicit function of x. For example, when we write the equation $y = x^2 + 1$, we are defining y explicitly in terms of x. On the other hand, if the relationship between the function y and the variable x is expressed by an equation where y is not expressed entirely in terms of x, we say that the equation defines y implicitly in terms of x. For example, the equation $y - x^2 = 1$ defines the function $y = x^2 + 1$ implicitly.

Implicit differentiation allows us to find slopes of tangents to curves that are clearly not functions (they fail the vertical line test). We are using the idea that portions of y are functions that satisfy the given equation, but that y is not actually a function of x.

In general, an equation defines a function implicitly if the function satisfies that equation. An equation may define many different functions implicitly. For example, the functions

$y = \sqrt{25 - x^2}$ and $y = \begin{cases} \sqrt{25 - x^2} \text{ if } -25 \le x < 0 \\ -\sqrt{25 - x^2} \text{ if } 0 \le x \le 25 \end{cases}$, which are illustrated in **Figure 3.30**, are just three of the many functions defined implicitly by the equation $x^2 + y^2 = 25$.

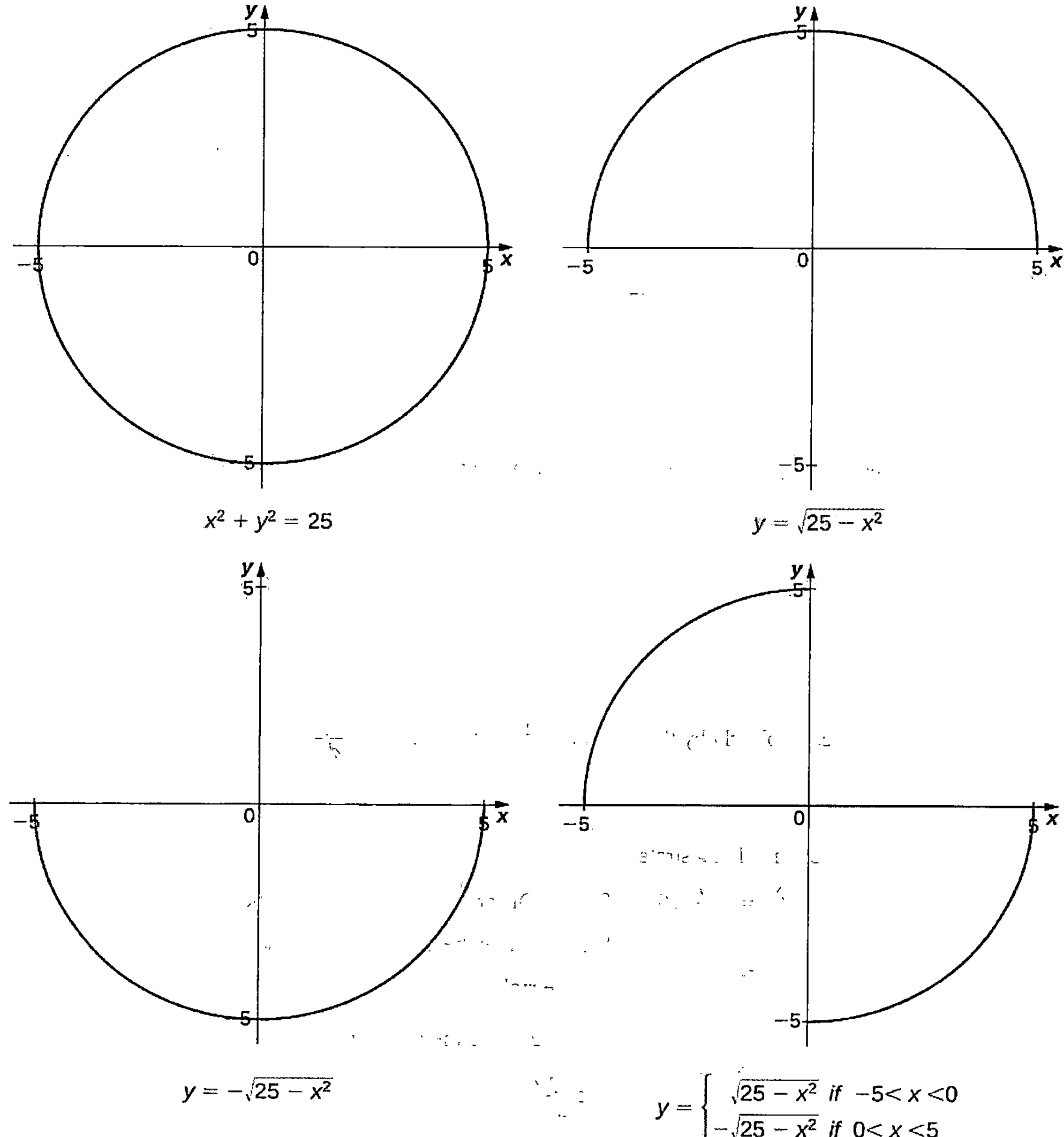

Figure 3.30 The equation $x^2 + y^2 = 25$ defines many functions implicitly.

If we want to find the slope of the line tangent to the graph of $x^2 + y^2 = 25$ at the point $(3, 4)$, we could evaluate the derivative of the function $y = \sqrt{25 - x^2}$ at $x = 3$. On the other hand, if we want the slope of the tangent line at the point $(3, -4)$, we could use the derivative of $y = -\sqrt{25 - x^2}$. However, it is not always easy to solve for a function defined implicitly by an equation. Fortunately, the technique of **implicit differentiation** allows us to find the derivative of an implicitly defined function without ever solving for the function explicitly. The process of finding $\frac{dy}{dx}$ using implicit differentiation is described in the following problem-solving strategy.

Problem-Solving Strategy: Implicit Differentiation

To perform implicit differentiation on an equation that defines a function y implicitly in terms of a variable x, use the following steps:

1. Take the derivative of both sides of the equation. Keep in mind that y is a function of x. Consequently, whereas $\frac{d}{dx}(\sin x) = \cos x$, $\frac{d}{dx}(\sin y) = \cos y \frac{dy}{dx}$ because we must use the chain rule to differentiate $\sin y$ with respect to x.
2. Rewrite the equation so that all terms containing $\frac{dy}{dx}$ are on the left and all terms that do not contain $\frac{dy}{dx}$ are on the right.
3. Factor out $\frac{dy}{dx}$ on the left.
4. Solve for $\frac{dy}{dx}$ by dividing both sides of the equation by an appropriate algebraic expression.

Example 3.68

Using Implicit Differentiation

Assuming that y is defined implicitly by the equation $x^2 + y^2 = 25$, find $\frac{dy}{dx}$.

Solution

Follow the steps in the problem-solving strategy.

$$\frac{d}{dx}\left(x^2 + y^2\right) = \frac{d}{dx}(25)$$ Step 1. Differentiate both sides of the equation.

Step 1.1. Use the sum rule on the left.

$$\frac{d}{dx}\left(x^2\right) + \frac{d}{dx}\left(y^2\right) = 0$$ On the right $\frac{d}{dx}(25) = 0$.

Step 1.2. Take the derivatives, so $\frac{d}{dx}\left(x^2\right) = 2x$

$$2x + 2y\frac{dy}{dx} = 0$$ and $\frac{d}{dx}\left(y^2\right) = 2y\frac{dy}{dx}$.

$$2y\frac{dy}{dx} = -2x$$ Step 2. Keep the terms with $\frac{dy}{dx}$ on the left. Move the remaining terms to the right.

$$\frac{dy}{dx} = -\frac{x}{y}$$ Step 4. Divide both sides of the equation by $2y$. (Step 3 does not apply in this case.)

Analysis

Note that the resulting expression for $\frac{dy}{dx}$ is in terms of both the independent variable x and the dependent variable y. Although in some cases it may be possible to express $\frac{dy}{dx}$ in terms of x only, it is generally not possible to do so.

Example 3.69

Using Implicit Differentiation and the Product Rule

Assuming that y is defined implicitly by the equation $x^3 \sin y + y = 4x + 3$, find $\frac{dy}{dx}$.

Solution

$$\frac{d}{dx}\left(x^3 \sin y + y\right) = \frac{d}{dx}(4x + 3)$$

Step 1: Differentiate both sides of the equation.

$$\frac{d}{dx}\left(x^3 \sin y\right) + \frac{d}{dx}(y) = 4$$

Step 1.1: Apply the sum rule on the left. On the right, $\frac{d}{dx}(4x + 3) = 4$.

$$\left(\frac{d}{dx}\left(x^3\right) \cdot \sin y + \frac{d}{dx}(\sin y) \cdot x^3\right) + \frac{dy}{dx} = 4$$

Step 1.2: Use the product rule to find $\frac{d}{dx}\left(x^3 \sin y\right)$. Observe that $\frac{d}{dx}(y) = \frac{dy}{dx}$.

$$3x^2 \sin y + \left(\cos y \frac{dy}{dx}\right) \cdot x^3 + \frac{dy}{dx} = 4$$

Step 1.3: We know $\frac{d}{dx}\left(x^3\right) = 3x^2$. Use the chain rule to obtain $\frac{d}{dx}(\sin y) = \cos y \frac{dy}{dx}$.

$$x^3 \cos y \frac{dy}{dx} + \frac{dy}{dx} = 4 - 3x^2 \sin y$$

Step 2: Keep all terms containing $\frac{dy}{dx}$ on the left. Move all other terms to the right.

$$\frac{dy}{dx}\left(x^3 \cos y + 1\right) = 4 - 3x^2 \sin y$$

Step 3: Factor out $\frac{dy}{dx}$ on the left.

$$\frac{dy}{dx} = \frac{4 - 3x^2 \sin y}{x^3 \cos y + 1}$$

Step 4: Solve for $\frac{dy}{dx}$ by dividing both sides of the equation by $x^3 \cos y + 1$.

Example 3.70

Using Implicit Differentiation to Find a Second Derivative

Find $\frac{d^2 y}{dx^2}$ if $x^2 + y^2 = 25$.

Solution

In **Example 3.68**, we showed that $\frac{dy}{dx} = -\frac{x}{y}$. We can take the derivative of both sides of this equation to find $\frac{d^2 y}{dx^2}$.

$$\begin{aligned}\frac{d^2y}{dx^2} &= \frac{d}{dy}\left(-\frac{x}{y}\right) && \text{Differentiate both sides of } \frac{dy}{dx} = -\frac{x}{y}.\\ &= -\frac{\left(1 \cdot y - x\frac{dy}{dx}\right)}{y^2} && \text{Use the quotient rule to find } \frac{d}{dy}\left(-\frac{x}{y}\right).\\ &= \frac{-y + x\frac{dy}{dx}}{y^2} && \text{Simplify.}\\ &= \frac{-y + x\left(-\frac{x}{y}\right)}{y^2} && \text{Substitute } \frac{dy}{dx} = -\frac{x}{y}.\\ &= \frac{-y^2 - x^2}{y^3} && \text{Simplify.}\end{aligned}$$

At this point we have found an expression for $\frac{d^2y}{dx^2}$. If we choose, we can simplify the expression further by recalling that $x^2 + y^2 = 25$ and making this substitution in the numerator to obtain $\frac{d^2y}{dx^2} = -\frac{25}{y^3}$.

3.48 Find $\frac{dy}{dx}$ for y defined implicitly by the equation $4x^5 + \tan y = y^2 + 5x$.

Finding Tangent Lines Implicitly

Now that we have seen the technique of implicit differentiation, we can apply it to the problem of finding equations of tangent lines to curves described by equations.

Example 3.71

Finding a Tangent Line to a Circle

Find the equation of the line tangent to the curve $x^2 + y^2 = 25$ at the point $(3, -4)$.

Solution

Although we could find this equation without using implicit differentiation, using that method makes it much easier. In **Example 3.68**, we found $\frac{dy}{dx} = -\frac{x}{y}$.

The slope of the tangent line is found by substituting $(3, -4)$ into this expression. Consequently, the slope of the tangent line is $\left.\frac{dy}{dx}\right|_{(3,\,-4)} = -\frac{3}{-4} = \frac{3}{4}$.

Using the point $(3, -4)$ and the slope $\frac{3}{4}$ in the point-slope equation of the line, we obtain the equation $y = \frac{3}{4}x - \frac{25}{4}$ (**Figure 3.31**).

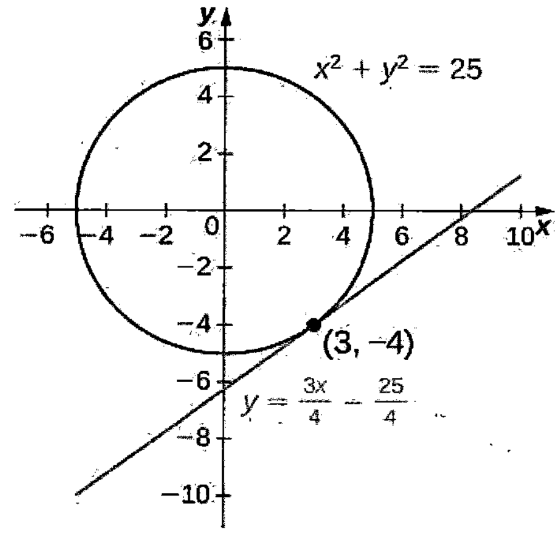

Figure 3.31 The line $y = \frac{3}{4}x - \frac{25}{4}$ is tangent to $x^2 + y^2 = 25$ at the point (3, −4).

Example 3.72

Finding the Equation of the Tangent Line to a Curve

Find the equation of the line tangent to the graph of $y^3 + x^3 - 3xy = 0$ at the point $\left(\frac{3}{2}, \frac{3}{2}\right)$ (**Figure 3.32**). This curve is known as the folium (or leaf) of Descartes.

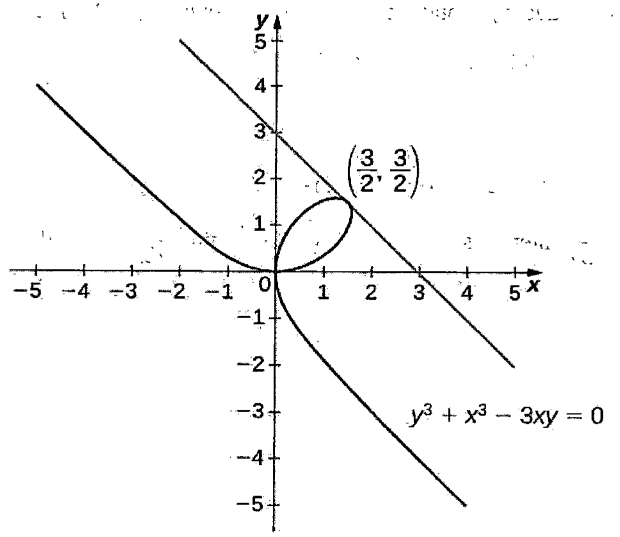

Figure 3.32 Finding the tangent line to the folium of Descartes at $\left(\frac{3}{2}, \frac{3}{2}\right)$.

Solution

Begin by finding $\frac{dy}{dx}$.

$$\begin{aligned} \frac{d}{dx}\left(y^3 + x^3 - 3xy\right) &= \frac{d}{dx}(0) \\ 3y^2\frac{dy}{dx} + 3x^2 - \left(3y + \frac{dy}{dx}3x\right) &= 0 \\ \frac{dy}{dx} &= \frac{3y - 3x^2}{3y^2 - 3x}. \end{aligned}$$

Next, substitute $\left(\frac{3}{2}, \frac{3}{2}\right)$ into $\frac{dy}{dx} = \frac{3y - 3x^2}{3y^2 - 3x}$ to find the slope of the tangent line:

$$\left.\frac{dy}{dx}\right|_{\left(\frac{3}{2}, \frac{3}{2}\right)} = -1.$$

Finally, substitute into the point-slope equation of the line to obtain

$$y = -x + 3.$$

Example 3.73

Applying Implicit Differentiation

In a simple video game, a rocket travels in an elliptical orbit whose path is described by the equation $4x^2 + 25y^2 = 100$. The rocket can fire missiles along lines tangent to its path. The object of the game is to destroy an incoming asteroid traveling along the positive x-axis toward $(0, 0)$. If the rocket fires a missile when it is located at $\left(3, \frac{8}{3}\right)$, where will it intersect the x-axis?

Solution

To solve this problem, we must determine where the line tangent to the graph of

$4x^2 + 25y^2 = 100$ at $\left(3, \frac{8}{3}\right)$ intersects the x-axis. Begin by finding $\frac{dy}{dx}$ implicitly.

Differentiating, we have

$$8x + 50y\frac{dy}{dx} = 0.$$

Solving for $\frac{dy}{dx}$, we have

$$\frac{dy}{dx} = -\frac{4x}{25y}.$$

The slope of the tangent line is $\left.\frac{dy}{dx}\right|_{\left(3, \frac{8}{3}\right)} = -\frac{9}{50}$. The equation of the tangent line is $y = -\frac{9}{50}x + \frac{183}{200}$. To determine where the line intersects the x-axis, solve $0 = -\frac{9}{50}x + \frac{183}{200}$. The solution is $x = \frac{61}{3}$. The missile intersects the x-axis at the point $\left(\frac{61}{3}, 0\right)$.

3.49 Find the equation of the line tangent to the hyperbola $x^2 - y^2 = 16$ at the point $(5, 3)$.

3.8 EXERCISES

For the following exercises, use implicit differentiation to find $\frac{dy}{dx}$.

300. $x^2 - y^2 = 4$

301. $6x^2 + 3y^2 = 12$

302. $x^2 y = y - 7$

303. $3x^3 + 9xy^2 = 5x^3$

304. $xy - \cos(xy) = 1$

305. $y\sqrt{x+4} = xy + 8$

306. $-xy - 2 = \frac{x}{7}$

307. $y\sin(xy) = y^2 + 2$

308. $(xy)^2 + 3x = y^2$

309. $x^3 y + xy^3 = -8$

For the following exercises, find the equation of the tangent line to the graph of the given equation at the indicated point. Use a calculator or computer software to graph the function and the tangent line.

310. **[T]** $x^4 y - xy^3 = -2, (-1, -1)$

311. **[T]** $x^2 y^2 + 5xy = 14, (2, 1)$

312. **[T]** $\tan(xy) = y, \left(\frac{\pi}{4}, 1\right)$

313. **[T]** $xy^2 + \sin(\pi y) - 2x^2 = 10, (2, -3)$

314. **[T]** $\frac{x}{y} + 5x - 7 = -\frac{3}{4}y, (1, 2)$

315. **[T]** $xy + \sin(x) = 1, \left(\frac{\pi}{2}, 0\right)$

316. **[T]** The graph of a folium of Descartes with equation $2x^3 + 2y^3 - 9xy = 0$ is given in the following graph.

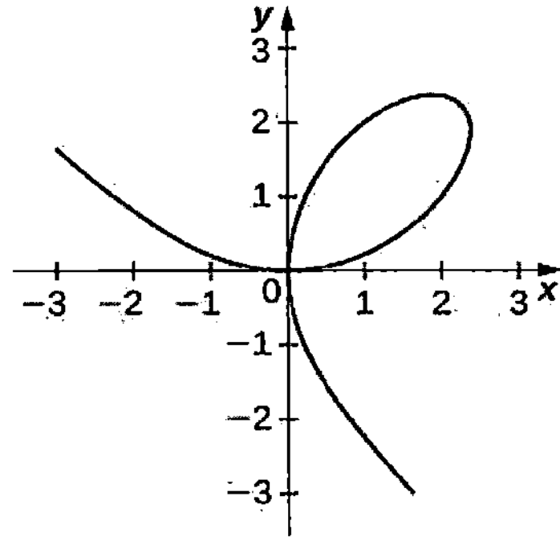

a. Find the equation of the tangent line at the point $(2, 1)$. Graph the tangent line along with the folium.
b. Find the equation of the normal line to the tangent line in a. at the point $(2, 1)$.

317. For the equation $x^2 + 2xy - 3y^2 = 0,$

a. Find the equation of the normal to the tangent line at the point $(1, 1)$.
b. At what other point does the normal line in a. intersect the graph of the equation?

318. Find all points on the graph of $y^3 - 27y = x^2 - 90$ at which the tangent line is vertical.

319. For the equation $x^2 + xy + y^2 = 7,$

a. Find the x-intercept(s).
b. Find the slope of the tangent line(s) at the x-intercept(s).
c. What does the value(s) in b. indicate about the tangent line(s)?

320. Find the equation of the tangent line to the graph of the equation $\sin^{-1} x + \sin^{-1} y = \frac{\pi}{6}$ at the point $\left(0, \frac{1}{2}\right)$.

321. Find the equation of the tangent line to the graph of the equation $\tan^{-1}(x + y) = x^2 + \frac{\pi}{4}$ at the point $(0, 1)$.

322. Find y' and y'' for $x^2 + 6xy - 2y^2 = 3$.

323. **[T]** The number of cell phones produced when x dollars is spent on labor and y dollars is spent on capital invested by a manufacturer can be modeled by the equation $60x^{3/4}y^{1/4} = 3240$.

a. Find $\frac{dy}{dx}$ and evaluate at the point $(81, 16)$.

b. Interpret the result of a.

324. **[T]** The number of cars produced when x dollars is spent on labor and y dollars is spent on capital invested by a manufacturer can be modeled by the equation $30x^{1/3}y^{2/3} = 360$. (Both x and y are measured in thousands of dollars.)

a. Find $\frac{dy}{dx}$ and evaluate at the point $(27, 8)$.

b. Interpret the result of a.

325. The volume of a right circular cone of radius x and height y is given by $V = \frac{1}{3}\pi x^2 y$. Suppose that the volume of the cone is $85\pi\,\text{cm}^3$. Find $\frac{dy}{dx}$ when $x = 4$ and $y = 16$.

For the following exercises, consider a closed rectangular box with a square base with side x and height y.

326. Find an equation for the surface area of the rectangular box, $S(x, y)$.

327. If the surface area of the rectangular box is 78 square feet, find $\frac{dy}{dx}$ when $x = 3$ feet and $y = 5$ feet.

For the following exercises, use implicit differentiation to determine y'. Does the answer agree with the formulas we have previously determined?

328. $x = \sin y$

329. $x = \cos y$

330. $x = \tan y$

3.9 | Derivatives of Exponential and Logarithmic Functions

Learning Objectives

3.9.1 Find the derivative of exponential functions.
3.9.2 Find the derivative of logarithmic functions.
3.9.3 Use logarithmic differentiation to determine the derivative of a function.

So far, we have learned how to differentiate a variety of functions, including trigonometric, inverse, and implicit functions. In this section, we explore derivatives of exponential and logarithmic functions. As we discussed in **Introduction to Functions and Graphs**, exponential functions play an important role in modeling population growth and the decay of radioactive materials. Logarithmic functions can help rescale large quantities and are particularly helpful for rewriting complicated expressions.

Derivative of the Exponential Function

Just as when we found the derivatives of other functions, we can find the derivatives of exponential and logarithmic functions using formulas. As we develop these formulas, we need to make certain basic assumptions. The proofs that these assumptions hold are beyond the scope of this course.

First of all, we begin with the assumption that the function $B(x) = b^x,\ b > 0,$ is defined for every real number and is continuous. In previous courses, the values of exponential functions for all rational numbers were defined—beginning with the definition of $b^n,$ where n is a positive integer—as the product of b multiplied by itself n times. Later, we defined $b^0 = 1,\ b^{-n} = \frac{1}{b^n},$ for a positive integer $n,$ and $b^{s/t} = (\sqrt[t]{b})^s$ for positive integers s and $t.$ These definitions leave open the question of the value of b^r where r is an arbitrary real number. By assuming the *continuity* of $B(x) = b^x,\ b > 0,$ we may interpret b^r as $\lim\limits_{x \to r} b^x$ where the values of x as we take the limit are rational. For example, we may view 4^π as the number satisfying

$$4^3 < 4^\pi < 4^4,\ 4^{3.1} < 4^\pi < 4^{3.2},\ 4^{3.14} < 4^\pi < 4^{3.15},$$
$$4^{3.141} < 4^\pi < 4^{3.142},\ 4^{3.1415} < 4^\pi < 4^{3.1416},\ldots.$$

As we see in the following table, $4^\pi \approx 77.88.$

x	4^x	x	4^x
4^3	64	$4^{3.141593}$	77.8802710486
$4^{3.1}$	73.5166947198	$4^{3.1416}$	77.8810268071
$4^{3.14}$	77.7084726013	$4^{3.142}$	77.9242251944
$4^{3.141}$	77.8162741237	$4^{3.15}$	78.7932424541
$4^{3.1415}$	77.8702309526	$4^{3.2}$	84.4485062895
$4^{3.14159}$	77.8799471543	4^4	256

Table 3.7 Approximating a Value of 4^{π}

We also assume that for $B(x) = b^x, b > 0,$ the value $B'(0)$ of the derivative exists. In this section, we show that by making this one additional assumption, it is possible to prove that the function $B(x)$ is differentiable everywhere.

We make one final assumption: that there is a unique value of $b > 0$ for which $B'(0) = 1.$ We define e to be this unique value, as we did in **Introduction to Functions and Graphs. Figure 3.33** provides graphs of the functions $y = 2^x, y = 3^x, y = 2.7^x,$ and $y = 2.8^x.$ A visual estimate of the slopes of the tangent lines to these functions at 0 provides evidence that the value of e lies somewhere between 2.7 and 2.8. The function $E(x) = e^x$ is called the **natural exponential function**. Its inverse, $L(x) = \log_e x = \ln x$ is called the **natural logarithmic function**.

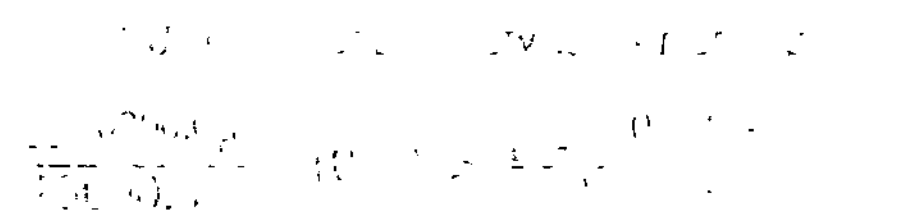

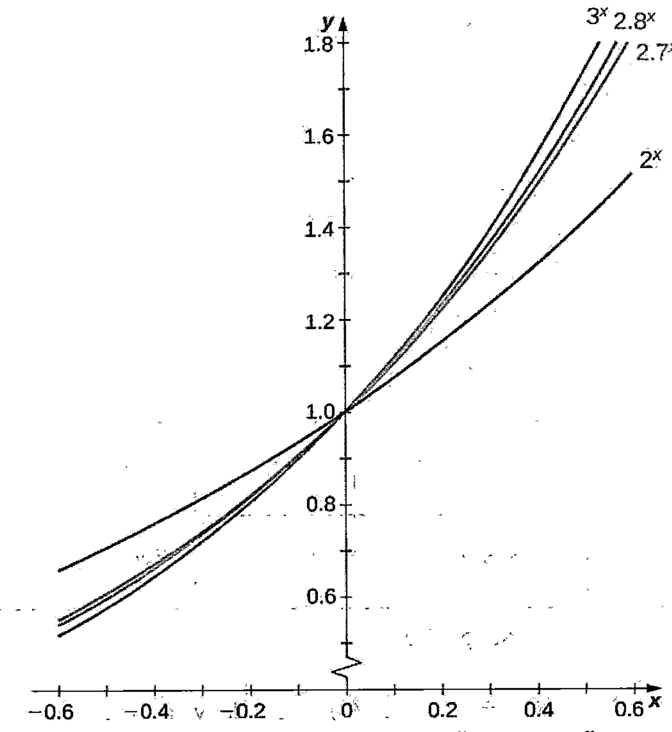

Figure 3.33 The graph of $E(x) = e^x$ is between $y = 2^x$ and $y = 3^x$.

For a better estimate of e, we may construct a table of estimates of $B'(0)$ for functions of the form $B(x) = b^x$. Before doing this, recall that

$$B'(0) = \lim_{x \to 0} \frac{b^x - b^0}{x - 0} = \lim_{x \to 0} \frac{b^x - 1}{x} \approx \frac{b^x - 1}{x}$$

for values of x very close to zero. For our estimates, we choose $x = 0.00001$ and $x = -0.00001$ to obtain the estimate

$$\frac{b^{-0.00001} - 1}{-0.00001} < B'(0) < \frac{b^{0.00001} - 1}{0.00001}.$$

See the following table.

b	$\frac{b^{-0.00001}-1}{-0.00001} < B'(0) < \frac{b^{0.00001}-1}{0.00001}$	b	$\frac{b^{-0.00001}-1}{-0.00001} < B'(0) < \frac{b^{0.00001}-1}{0.00001}$
2	$0.693145 < B'(0) < 0.69315$	2.7183	$1.000002 < B'(0) < 1.000012$
2.7	$0.993247 < B'(0) < 0.993257$	2.719	$1.000259 < B'(0) < 1.000269$
2.71	$0.996944 < B'(0) < 0.996954$	2.72	$1.000627 < B'(0) < 1.000637$
2.718	$0.999891 < B'(0) < 0.999901$	2.8	$1.029614 < B'(0) < 1.029625$
2.7182	$0.999965 < B'(0) < 0.999975$	3	$1.098606 < B'(0) < 1.098618$

Table 3.8 Estimating a Value of e

The evidence from the table suggests that $2.7182 < e < 2.7183$.

The graph of $E(x) = e^x$ together with the line $y = x + 1$ are shown in **Figure 3.34**. This line is tangent to the graph of $E(x) = e^x$ at $x = 0$.

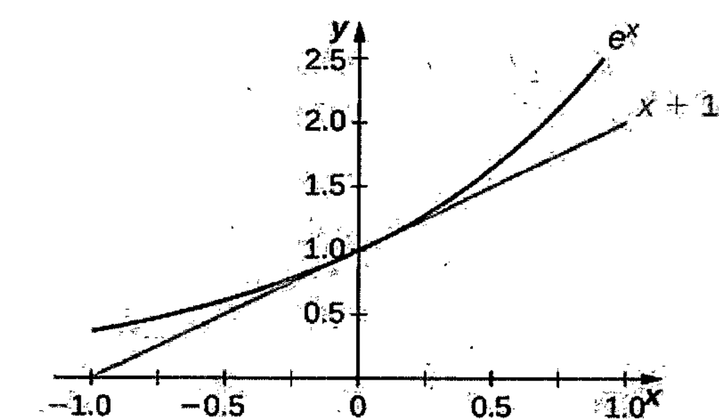

Figure 3.34 The tangent line to $E(x) = e^x$ at $x = 0$ has slope 1.

Now that we have laid out our basic assumptions, we begin our investigation by exploring the derivative of $B(x) = b^x, b > 0$. Recall that we have assumed that $B'(0)$ exists. By applying the limit definition to the derivative we conclude that

$$B'(0) = \lim_{h \to 0} \frac{b^{0+h} - b^0}{h} = \lim_{h \to 0} \frac{b^h - 1}{h}. \tag{3.28}$$

Turning to $B'(x)$, we obtain the following.

$$\begin{aligned} B'(x) &= \lim_{h \to 0} \frac{b^{x+h} - b^x}{h} && \text{Apply the limit definition of the derivative.} \\ &= \lim_{h \to 0} \frac{b^x b^h - b^x}{h} && \text{Note that } b^{x+h} = b^x b^h. \\ &= \lim_{h \to 0} \frac{b^x (b^h - 1)}{h} && \text{Factor out } b^x. \\ &= b^x \lim_{h \to 0} \frac{b^h - 1}{h} && \text{Apply a property of limits.} \\ &= b^x B'(0) && \text{Use } B'(0) = \lim_{h \to 0} \frac{b^{0+h} - b^0}{h} = \lim_{h \to 0} \frac{b^h - 1}{h}. \end{aligned}$$

We see that on the basis of the assumption that $B(x) = b^x$ is differentiable at 0, $B(x)$ is not only differentiable everywhere, but its derivative is

$$B'(x) = b^x B'(0). \tag{3.29}$$

For $E(x) = e^x$, $E'(0) = 1$. Thus, we have $E'(x) = e^x$. (The value of $B'(0)$ for an arbitrary function of the form $B(x) = b^x$, $b > 0$, will be derived later.)

Theorem 3.14: Derivative of the Natural Exponential Function

Let $E(x) = e^x$ be the natural exponential function. Then

$$E'(x) = e^x.$$

In general,

$$\frac{d}{dx}\left(e^{g(x)}\right) = e^{g(x)} g'(x).$$

Example 3.74

Derivative of an Exponential Function

Find the derivative of $f(x) = e^{\tan(2x)}$.

Solution

Using the derivative formula and the chain rule,

$$\begin{aligned} f'(x) &= e^{\tan(2x)} \frac{d}{dx}(\tan(2x)) \\ &= e^{\tan(2x)} \sec^2(2x) \cdot 2. \end{aligned}$$

Example 3.75

Combining Differentiation Rules

Find the derivative of $y = \frac{e^{x^2}}{x}$.

Solution

Use the derivative of the natural exponential function, the quotient rule, and the chain rule.

$$\begin{aligned} y' &= \frac{\left(e^{x^2} \cdot 2\right)x \cdot x - 1 \cdot e^{x^2}}{x^2} && \text{Apply the quotient rule.} \\ &= \frac{e^{x^2}\left(2x^2 - 1\right)}{x^2} && \text{Simplify.} \end{aligned}$$

3.50 Find the derivative of $h(x) = xe^{2x}$.

Example 3.76

Applying the Natural Exponential Function

A colony of mosquitoes has an initial population of 1000. After t days, the population is given by $A(t) = 1000e^{0.3t}$. Show that the ratio of the rate of change of the population, $A'(t)$, to the population, $A(t)$ is constant.

Solution

First find $A'(t)$. By using the chain rule, we have $A'(t) = 300e^{0.3t}$. Thus, the ratio of the rate of change of the population to the population is given by

$$A'(t) = \frac{300e^{0.3t}}{1000e^{0.3t}} = 0.3.$$

The ratio of the rate of change of the population to the population is the constant 0.3.

3.51 If $A(t) = 1000e^{0.3t}$ describes the mosquito population after t days, as in the preceding example, what is the rate of change of $A(t)$ after 4 days?

Derivative of the Logarithmic Function

Now that we have the derivative of the natural exponential function, we can use implicit differentiation to find the derivative of its inverse, the natural logarithmic function.

Theorem 3.15: The Derivative of the Natural Logarithmic Function

If $x > 0$ and $y = \ln x$, then

$$\frac{dy}{dx} = \frac{1}{x}. \tag{3.30}$$

More generally, let $g(x)$ be a differentiable function. For all values of x for which $g'(x) > 0$, the derivative of

$h(x) = \ln(g(x))$ is given by

$$h'(x) = \frac{1}{g(x)} g'(x). \quad (3.31)$$

Proof

If $x > 0$ and $y = \ln x$, then $e^y = x$. Differentiating both sides of this equation results in the equation

$$e^y \frac{dy}{dx} = 1.$$

Solving for $\frac{dy}{dx}$ yields

$$\frac{dy}{dx} = \frac{1}{e^y}.$$

Finally, we substitute $x = e^y$ to obtain

$$\frac{dy}{dx} = \frac{1}{x}.$$

We may also derive this result by applying the inverse function theorem, as follows. Since $y = g(x) = \ln x$ is the inverse of $f(x) = e^x$, by applying the inverse function theorem we have

$$\frac{dy}{dx} = \frac{1}{f'(g(x))} = \frac{1}{e^{\ln x}} = \frac{1}{x}.$$

Using this result and applying the chain rule to $h(x) = \ln(g(x))$ yields

$$h'(x) = \frac{1}{g(x)} g'(x).$$

□

The graph of $y = \ln x$ and its derivative $\frac{dy}{dx} = \frac{1}{x}$ are shown in **Figure 3.35**.

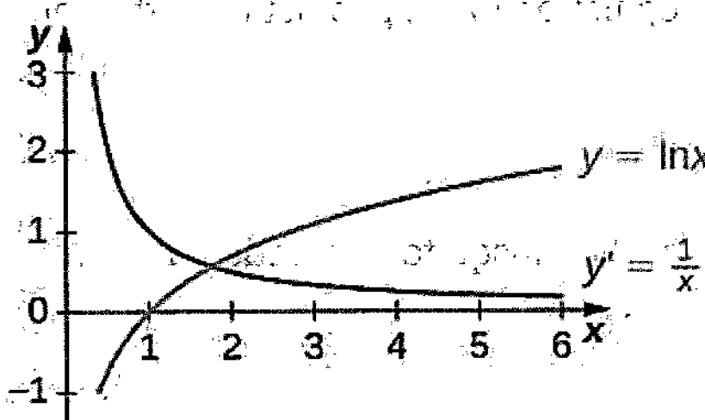

Figure 3.35 The function $y = \ln x$ is increasing on $(0, +\infty)$. Its derivative $y' = \frac{1}{x}$ is greater than zero on $(0, +\infty)$.

Example 3.77

Taking a Derivative of a Natural Logarithm

Find the derivative of $f(x) = \ln\left(x^3 + 3x - 4\right)$.

Solution

Use **Equation 3.31** directly.

$$\begin{aligned} f'(x) &= \frac{1}{x^3 + 3x - 4} \cdot \left(3x^2 + 3\right) && \text{Use } g(x) = x^3 + 3x - 4 \text{ in } h'(x) = \frac{1}{g(x)} g'(x). \\ &= \frac{3x^2 + 3}{x^3 + 3x - 4} && \text{Rewrite.} \end{aligned}$$

Example 3.78

Using Properties of Logarithms in a Derivative

Find the derivative of $f(x) = \ln\left(\frac{x^2 \sin x}{2x + 1}\right)$.

Solution

At first glance, taking this derivative appears rather complicated. However, by using the properties of logarithms prior to finding the derivative, we can make the problem much simpler.

$$\begin{aligned} f(x) &= \ln\left(\frac{x^2 \sin x}{2x + 1}\right) = 2\ln x + \ln(\sin x) - \ln(2x + 1) && \text{Apply properties of logarithms.} \\ f'(x) &= \frac{2}{x} + \cot x - \frac{2}{2x + 1} && \text{Apply sum rule and } h'(x) = \frac{1}{g(x)} g'(x). \end{aligned}$$

3.52 Differentiate: $f(x) = \ln(3x + 2)^5$.

Now that we can differentiate the natural logarithmic function, we can use this result to find the derivatives of $y = log_b x$ and $y = b^x$ for $b > 0,\ b \neq 1$.

Theorem 3.16: Derivatives of General Exponential and Logarithmic Functions

Let $b > 0,\ b \neq 1,$ and let $g(x)$ be a differentiable function.

i. If, $y = \log_b x,$ then

$$\frac{dy}{dx} = \frac{1}{x \ln b}. \tag{3.32}$$

More generally, if $h(x) = \log_b (g(x)),$ then for all values of x for which $g(x) > 0,$

$$h'(x) = \frac{g'(x)}{g(x) \ln b}. \tag{3.33}$$

ii. If $y = b^x,$ then

$$\frac{dy}{dx} = b^x \ln b. \quad (3.34)$$

More generally, if $h(x) = b^{g(x)}$, then

$$h'(x) = b^{g(x)} g'(x) \ln b. \quad (3.35)$$

Proof

If $y = \log_b x$, then $b^y = x$. It follows that $\ln(b^y) = \ln x$. Thus $y \ln b = \ln x$. Solving for y, we have $y = \frac{\ln x}{\ln b}$. Differentiating and keeping in mind that $\ln b$ is a constant, we see that

$$\frac{dy}{dx} = \frac{1}{x \ln b}.$$

The derivative in **Equation 3.33** now follows from the chain rule.

If $y = b^x$, then $\ln y = x \ln b$. Using implicit differentiation, again keeping in mind that $\ln b$ is constant, it follows that $\frac{1}{y}\frac{dy}{dx} = \ln b$. Solving for $\frac{dy}{dx}$ and substituting $y = b^x$, we see that

$$\frac{dy}{dx} = y \ln b = b^x \ln b.$$

The more general derivative (**Equation 3.35**) follows from the chain rule.

□

Example 3.79

Applying Derivative Formulas

Find the derivative of $h(x) = \frac{3^x}{3^x + 2}$.

Solution

Use the quotient rule and **Derivatives of General Exponential and Logarithmic Functions**.

$$\begin{aligned} h'(x) &= \frac{3^x \ln 3(3^x + 2) - 3^x \ln 3(3^x)}{(3^x + 2)^2} && \text{Apply the quotient rule.} \\ &= \frac{2 \cdot 3^x \ln 3}{(3^x + 2)^2} && \text{Simplify.} \end{aligned}$$

Example 3.80

Finding the Slope of a Tangent Line

Find the slope of the line tangent to the graph of $y = \log_2(3x + 1)$ at $x = 1$.

Solution

To find the slope, we must evaluate $\frac{dy}{dx}$ at $x = 1$. Using **Equation 3.33**, we see that

$$\frac{dy}{dx} = \frac{3}{\ln 2(3x+1)}.$$

By evaluating the derivative at $x = 1$, we see that the tangent line has slope

$$\left.\frac{dy}{dx}\right|_{x=1} = \frac{3}{4\ln 2} = \frac{3}{\ln 16}.$$

 **3.53** Find the slope for the line tangent to $y = 3^x$ at $x = 2$.

Logarithmic Differentiation

At this point, we can take derivatives of functions of the form $y = (g(x))^n$ for certain values of n, as well as functions of the form $y = b^{g(x)}$, where $b > 0$ and $b \neq 1$. Unfortunately, we still do not know the derivatives of functions such as $y = x^x$ or $y = x^{\pi}$. These functions require a technique called **logarithmic differentiation**, which allows us to differentiate any function of the form $h(x) = g(x)^{f(x)}$. It can also be used to convert a very complex differentiation problem into a simpler one, such as finding the derivative of $y = \frac{x\sqrt{2x+1}}{e^x \sin^3 x}$. We outline this technique in the following problem-solving strategy.

Problem-Solving Strategy: Using Logarithmic Differentiation

1. To differentiate $y = h(x)$ using logarithmic differentiation, take the natural logarithm of both sides of the equation to obtain $\ln y = \ln(h(x))$.
2. Use properties of logarithms to expand $\ln(h(x))$ as much as possible.
3. Differentiate both sides of the equation. On the left we will have $\frac{1}{y}\frac{dy}{dx}$.
4. Multiply both sides of the equation by y to solve for $\frac{dy}{dx}$.
5. Replace y by $h(x)$.

Example 3.81

Using Logarithmic Differentiation

Find the derivative of $y = \left(2x^4 + 1\right)^{\tan x}$.

Solution

Use logarithmic differentiation to find this derivative.

$$\ln y = \ln\left(2x^4+1\right)^{\tan x}$$ Step 1. Take the natural logarithm of both sides.

$$\ln y = \tan x \ln\left(2x^4+1\right)$$ Step 2. Expand using properties of logarithms.

$$\frac{1}{y}\frac{dy}{dx} = \sec^2 x \ln\left(2x^4+1\right) + \frac{8x^3}{2x^4+1}\cdot\tan x$$ Step 3. Differentiate both sides. Use the product rule on the right.

$$\frac{dy}{dx} = y\cdot\left(\sec^2 x \ln\left(2x^4+1\right) + \frac{8x^3}{2x^4+1}\cdot\tan x\right)$$ Step 4. Multiply by y on both sides.

$$\frac{dy}{dx} = \left(2x^4+1\right)^{\tan x}\left(\sec^2 x \ln\left(2x^4+1\right) + \frac{8x^3}{2x^4+1}\cdot\tan x\right)$$ Step 5. Substitute $y=\left(2x^4+1\right)^{\tan x}$.

Example 3.82

Using Logarithmic Differentiation

Find the derivative of $y=\dfrac{x\sqrt{2x+1}}{e^x \sin^3 x}$.

Solution

This problem really makes use of the properties of logarithms and the differentiation rules given in this chapter.

$$\ln y = \ln\frac{x\sqrt{2x+1}}{e^x\sin^3 x}$$ Step 1. Take the natural logarithm of both sides.

$$\ln y = \ln x + \frac{1}{2}\ln(2x+1) - x\ln e - 3\ln\sin x$$ Step 2. Expand using properties of logarithms.

$$\frac{1}{y}\frac{dy}{dx} = \frac{1}{x} + \frac{1}{2x+1} - 1 - 3\frac{\cos x}{\sin x}$$ Step 3. Differentiate both sides.

$$\frac{dy}{dx} = y\left(\frac{1}{x} + \frac{1}{2x+1} - 1 - 3\cot x\right)$$ Step 4. Multiply by y on both sides.

$$\frac{dy}{dx} = \frac{x\sqrt{2x+1}}{e^x\sin^3 x}\left(\frac{1}{x} + \frac{1}{2x+1} - 1 - 3\cot x\right)$$ Step 5. Substitute $y=\dfrac{x\sqrt{2x+1}}{e^x\sin^3 x}$.

Example 3.83

Extending the Power Rule

Find the derivative of $y=x^r$ where r is an arbitrary real number.

Solution

The process is the same as in **Example 3.82**, though with fewer complications.

$$\begin{aligned}
\ln y &= \ln x^r && \text{Step 1. Take the natural logarithm of both sides.}\\
\ln y &= r\ln x && \text{Step 2. Expand using properties of logarithms.}\\
\frac{1}{y}\frac{dy}{dx} &= r\frac{1}{x} && \text{Step 3. Differentiate both sides.}\\
\frac{dy}{dx} &= y\frac{r}{x} && \text{Step 4. Multiply by } y \text{ on both sides.}\\
\frac{dy}{dx} &= x^r\frac{r}{x} && \text{Step 5. Substitute } y = x^r.\\
\frac{dy}{dx} &= rx^{r-1} && \text{Simplify.}
\end{aligned}$$

3.54 Use logarithmic differentiation to find the derivative of $y = x^x$.

3.55 Find the derivative of $y = (\tan x)^{\pi}$.

3.9 EXERCISES

For the following exercises, find $f'(x)$ for each function.

331. $f(x) = x^2 e^x$

332. $f(x) = \frac{e^{-x}}{x}$

333. $f(x) = e^{x^3 \ln x}$

334. $f(x) = \sqrt{e^{2x} + 2x}$

335. $f(x) = \frac{e^x - e^{-x}}{e^x + e^{-x}}$

336. $f(x) = \frac{10^x}{\ln 10}$

337. $f(x) = 2^{4x} + 4x^2$

338. $f(x) = 3^{\sin 3x}$

339. $f(x) = x^{\pi} \cdot \pi^x$

340. $f(x) = \ln\left(4x^3 + x\right)$

341. $f(x) = \ln\sqrt{5x - 7}$

342. $f(x) = x^2 \ln 9x$

343. $f(x) = \log(\sec x)$

344. $f(x) = \log_7\left(6x^4 + 3\right)^5$

345. $f(x) = 2^x \cdot \log_3 7^{x^2 - 4}$

For the following exercises, use logarithmic differentiation to find $\frac{dy}{dx}$.

346. $y = x^{\sqrt{x}}$

347. $y = (\sin 2x)^{4x}$

348. $y = (\ln x)^{\ln x}$

349. $y = x^{\log_2 x}$

350. $y = \left(x^2 - 1\right)^{\ln x}$

351. $y = x^{\cot x}$

352. $y = \frac{x + 11}{\sqrt[3]{x^2 - 4}}$

353. $y = x^{-1/2}\left(x^2 + 3\right)^{2/3}(3x - 4)^4$

354. **[T]** Find an equation of the tangent line to the graph of $f(x) = 4xe^{\left(x^2 - 1\right)}$ at the point where $x = -1$. Graph both the function and the tangent line.

355. **[T]** Find the equation of the line that is normal to the graph of $f(x) = x \cdot 5^x$ at the point where $x = 1$. Graph both the function and the normal line.

356. **[T]** Find the equation of the tangent line to the graph of $x^3 - x\ln y + y^3 = 2x + 5$ at the point where $x = 2$. (*Hint*: Use implicit differentiation to find $\frac{dy}{dx}$.) Graph both the curve and the tangent line.

357. Consider the function $y = x^{1/x}$ for $x > 0$.

a. Determine the points on the graph where the tangent line is horizontal.
b. Determine the points on the graph where $y' > 0$ and those where $y' < 0$.

358. The formula $I(t) = \frac{\sin t}{e^t}$ is the formula for a decaying alternating current.

a. Complete the following table with the appropriate values.

t	$\frac{\sin t}{e^t}$
0	(i)
$\frac{\pi}{2}$	(ii)
π	(iii)
$\frac{3\pi}{2}$	(iv)
2π	(v)
2π	(vi)
3π	(vii)
$\frac{7\pi}{2}$	(viii)
4π	(ix)

b. Using only the values in the table, determine where the tangent line to the graph of $I(t)$ is horizontal.

359. **[T]** The population of Toledo, Ohio, in 2000 was approximately 500,000. Assume the population is increasing at a rate of 5% per year.

a. Write the exponential function that relates the total population as a function of t.
b. Use a. to determine the rate at which the population is increasing in t years.
c. Use b. to determine the rate at which the population is increasing in 10 years.

360. **[T]** An isotope of the element erbium has a half-life of approximately 12 hours. Initially there are 9 grams of the isotope present.

a. Write the exponential function that relates the amount of substance remaining as a function of t, measured in hours.
b. Use a. to determine the rate at which the substance is decaying in t hours.
c. Use b. to determine the rate of decay at $t = 4$ hours.

361. **[T]** The number of cases of influenza in New York City from the beginning of 1960 to the beginning of 1961 is modeled by the function $N(t) = 5.3e^{0.093t^2 - 0.87t}$, $(0 \le t \le 4)$, where $N(t)$ gives the number of cases (in thousands) and t is measured in years, with $t = 0$ corresponding to the beginning of 1960.

a. Show work that evaluates $N(0)$ and $N(4)$. Briefly describe what these values indicate about the disease in New York City.
b. Show work that evaluates $N'(0)$ and $N'(3)$. Briefly describe what these values indicate about the disease in the United States.

362. **[T]** The *relative rate of change* of a differentiable function $y = f(x)$ is given by $\frac{100 \cdot f'(x)}{f(x)}\%$. One model for population growth is a Gompertz growth function, given by $P(x) = ae^{-b \cdot e^{-cx}}$ where a, b, and c are constants.

a. Find the relative rate of change formula for the generic Gompertz function.
b. Use a. to find the relative rate of change of a population in $x = 20$ months when $a = 204$, $b = 0.0198$, and $c = 0.15$.
c. Briefly interpret what the result of b. means.

For the following exercises, use the population of New York City from 1790 to 1860, given in the following table.

Years since 1790	Population
0	33,131
10	60,515
20	96,373
30	123,706
40	202,300
50	312,710
60	515,547
70	813,669

Table 3.9 New York City Population Over Time **Source: http://en.wikipedia.org/wiki/Largest_cities_in_the_United_States_by_population_by_decade.**

363. **[T]** Using a computer program or a calculator, fit a growth curve to the data of the form $p = ab^t$.

364. **[T]** Using the exponential best fit for the data, write a table containing the derivatives evaluated at each year.

365. **[T]** Using the exponential best fit for the data, write a table containing the second derivatives evaluated at each year.

366. **[T]** Using the tables of first and second derivatives and the best fit, answer the following questions:
   a. Will the model be accurate in predicting the future population of New York City? Why or why not?
   b. Estimate the population in 2010. Was the prediction correct from a.?

CHAPTER 3 REVIEW

KEY TERMS

acceleration is the rate of change of the velocity, that is, the derivative of velocity

amount of change the amount of a function $f(x)$ over an interval $[x, x+h]$ is $f(x+h) - f(x)$

average rate of change is a function $f(x)$ over an interval $[x, x+h]$ is $\frac{f(x+h) - f(a)}{b - a}$

chain rule the chain rule defines the derivative of a composite function as the derivative of the outer function evaluated at the inner function times the derivative of the inner function

constant multiple rule the derivative of a constant *c* multiplied by a function *f* is the same as the constant multiplied by the derivative: $\frac{d}{dx}(cf(x)) = cf'(x)$

constant rule the derivative of a constant function is zero: $\frac{d}{dx}(c) = 0,$ where *c* is a constant

derivative the slope of the tangent line to a function at a point, calculated by taking the limit of the difference quotient, is the derivative

derivative function gives the derivative of a function at each point in the domain of the original function for which the derivative is defined

difference quotient of a function $f(x)$ at a is given by

$$\frac{f(a+h) - f(a)}{h} \text{ or } \frac{f(x) - f(a)}{x - a}$$

difference rule the derivative of the difference of a function *f* and a function *g* is the same as the difference of the derivative of *f* and the derivative of *g*: $\frac{d}{dx}(f(x) - g(x)) = f'(x) - g'(x)$

differentiable at *a* a function for which $f'(a)$ exists is differentiable at a

differentiable function a function for which $f'(x)$ exists is a differentiable function

differentiable on *S* a function for which $f'(x)$ exists for each x in the open set S is differentiable on S

differentiation the process of taking a derivative

higher-order derivative a derivative of a derivative, from the second derivative to the *n*th derivative, is called a higher-order derivative

implicit differentiation is a technique for computing $\frac{dy}{dx}$ for a function defined by an equation, accomplished by differentiating both sides of the equation (remembering to treat the variable y as a function) and solving for $\frac{dy}{dx}$

instantaneous rate of change the rate of change of a function at any point along the function $a,$ also called $f'(a),$ or the derivative of the function at a

logarithmic differentiation is a technique that allows us to differentiate a function by first taking the natural logarithm of both sides of an equation, applying properties of logarithms to simplify the equation, and differentiating implicitly

marginal cost is the derivative of the cost function, or the approximate cost of producing one more item

marginal profit is the derivative of the profit function, or the approximate profit obtained by producing and selling one more item

marginal revenue is the derivative of the revenue function, or the approximate revenue obtained by selling one more item

population growth rate is the derivative of the population with respect to time

power rule the derivative of a power function is a function in which the power on x becomes the coefficient of the term and the power on x in the derivative decreases by 1: If n is an integer, then $\frac{d}{dx}x^n = nx^{n-1}$

product rule the derivative of a product of two functions is the derivative of the first function times the second function plus the derivative of the second function times the first function: $\frac{d}{dx}(f(x)g(x)) = f'(x)g(x) + g'(x)f(x)$

quotient rule the derivative of the quotient of two functions is the derivative of the first function times the second function minus the derivative of the second function times the first function, all divided by the square of the second function: $\frac{d}{dx}\left(\frac{f(x)}{g(x)}\right) = \frac{f'(x)g(x) - g'(x)f(x)}{(g(x))^2}$

speed is the absolute value of velocity, that is, $|v(t)|$ is the speed of an object at time t whose velocity is given by $v(t)$

sum rule the derivative of the sum of a function f and a function g is the same as the sum of the derivative of f and the derivative of g: $\frac{d}{dx}(f(x) + g(x)) = f'(x) + g'(x)$

KEY EQUATIONS

- **Difference quotient**
  $Q = \frac{f(x) - f(a)}{x - a}$
- **Difference quotient with increment h**
  $Q = \frac{f(a+h) - f(a)}{a+h-a} = \frac{f(a+h) - f(a)}{h}$
- **Slope of tangent line**
  $m_{\tan} = \lim\limits_{x \to a} \frac{f(x) - f(a)}{x - a}$
  $m_{\tan} = \lim\limits_{h \to 0} \frac{f(a+h) - f(a)}{h}$
- **Derivative of $f(x)$ at a**
  $f'(a) = \lim\limits_{x \to a} \frac{f(x) - f(a)}{x - a}$
  $f'(a) = \lim\limits_{h \to 0} \frac{f(a+h) - f(a)}{h}$
- **Average velocity**
  $v_{\text{ave}} = \frac{s(t) - s(a)}{t - a}$
- **Instantaneous velocity**
  $v(a) = s'(a) = \lim\limits_{t \to a} \frac{s(t) - s(a)}{t - a}$
- **The derivative function**
  $f'(x) = \lim\limits_{h \to 0} \frac{f(x+h) - f(x)}{h}$
- **Derivative of sine function**
  $\frac{d}{dx}(\sin x) = \cos x$
- **Derivative of cosine function**
  $\frac{d}{dx}(\cos x) = -\sin x$
- **Derivative of tangent function**

$\frac{d}{dx}(\tan x) = \sec^2 x$

- **Derivative of cotangent function**
  $\frac{d}{dx}(\cot x) = -\csc^2 x$
- **Derivative of secant function**
  $\frac{d}{dx}(\sec x) = \sec x \tan x$
- **Derivative of cosecant function**
  $\frac{d}{dx}(\csc x) = -\csc x \cot x$
- **The chain rule**
  $h'(x) = f'(g(x))g'(x)$
- **The power rule for functions**
  $h'(x) = n(g(x))^{n-1} g'(x)$
- **Inverse function theorem**
  $\left(f^{-1}\right)'(x) = \frac{1}{f'\left(f^{-1}(x)\right)}$ whenever $f'\left(f^{-1}(x)\right) \neq 0$ and $f(x)$ is differentiable.
- **Power rule with rational exponents**
  $\frac{d}{dx}\left(x^{m/n}\right) = \frac{m}{n} x^{(m/n)-1}.$
- **Derivative of inverse sine function**
  $\frac{d}{dx}\sin^{-1} x = \frac{1}{\sqrt{1-(x)^2}}$
- **Derivative of inverse cosine function**
  $\frac{d}{dx}\cos^{-1} x = \frac{-1}{\sqrt{1-(x)^2}}$
- **Derivative of inverse tangent function**
  $\frac{d}{dx}\tan^{-1} x = \frac{1}{1+(x)^2}$
- **Derivative of inverse cotangent function**
  $\frac{d}{dx}\cot^{-1} x = \frac{-1}{1+(x)^2}$
- **Derivative of inverse secant function**
  $\frac{d}{dx}\sec^{-1} x = \frac{1}{|x|\sqrt{(x)^2-1}}$
- **Derivative of inverse cosecant function**
  $\frac{d}{dx}\csc^{-1} x = \frac{-1}{|x|\sqrt{(x)^2-1}}$
- **Derivative of the natural exponential function**
  $\frac{d}{dx}\left(e^{g(x)}\right) = e^{g(x)} g'(x)$
- **Derivative of the natural logarithmic function**
  $\frac{d}{dx}(\ln g(x)) = \frac{1}{g(x)} g'(x)$
- **Derivative of the general exponential function**

$$\frac{d}{dx}\left(b^{g(x)}\right) = b^{g(x)} g'(x) \ln b$$

- **Derivative of the general logarithmic function**

$$\frac{d}{dx}(\log_b g(x)) = \frac{g'(x)}{g(x) \ln b}$$

KEY CONCEPTS

3.1 Defining the Derivative

- The slope of the tangent line to a curve measures the instantaneous rate of change of a curve. We can calculate it by finding the limit of the difference quotient or the difference quotient with increment h.
- The derivative of a function $f(x)$ at a value a is found using either of the definitions for the slope of the tangent line.
- Velocity is the rate of change of position. As such, the velocity $v(t)$ at time t is the derivative of the position $s(t)$ at time t. Average velocity is given by

$$v_{\text{ave}} = \frac{s(t) - s(a)}{t - a}.$$

  Instantaneous velocity is given by

$$v(a) = s'(a) = \lim_{t \to a} \frac{s(t) - s(a)}{t - a}.$$

- We may estimate a derivative by using a table of values.

3.2 The Derivative as a Function

- The derivative of a function $f(x)$ is the function whose value at x is $f'(x)$.
- The graph of a derivative of a function $f(x)$ is related to the graph of $f(x)$. Where $f(x)$ has a tangent line with positive slope, $f'(x) > 0$. Where $f(x)$ has a tangent line with negative slope, $f'(x) < 0$. Where $f(x)$ has a horizontal tangent line, $f'(x) = 0$.
- If a function is differentiable at a point, then it is continuous at that point. A function is not differentiable at a point if it is not continuous at the point, if it has a vertical tangent line at the point, or if the graph has a sharp corner or cusp.
- Higher-order derivatives are derivatives of derivatives, from the second derivative to the nth derivative.

3.3 Differentiation Rules

- The derivative of a constant function is zero.
- The derivative of a power function is a function in which the power on x becomes the coefficient of the term and the power on x in the derivative decreases by 1.
- The derivative of a constant c multiplied by a function f is the same as the constant multiplied by the derivative.
- The derivative of the sum of a function f and a function g is the same as the sum of the derivative of f and the derivative of g.
- The derivative of the difference of a function f and a function g is the same as the difference of the derivative of f and the derivative of g.
- The derivative of a product of two functions is the derivative of the first function times the second function plus the derivative of the second function times the first function.
- The derivative of the quotient of two functions is the derivative of the first function times the second function minus

the derivative of the second function times the first function, all divided by the square of the second function.

- We used the limit definition of the derivative to develop formulas that allow us to find derivatives without resorting to the definition of the derivative. These formulas can be used singly or in combination with each other.

3.4 Derivatives as Rates of Change

- Using $f(a+h) \approx f(a) + f'(a)h,$ it is possible to estimate $f(a+h)$ given $f'(a)$ and $f(a)$.
- The rate of change of position is velocity, and the rate of change of velocity is acceleration. Speed is the absolute value, or magnitude, of velocity.
- The population growth rate and the present population can be used to predict the size of a future population.
- Marginal cost, marginal revenue, and marginal profit functions can be used to predict, respectively, the cost of producing one more item, the revenue obtained by selling one more item, and the profit obtained by producing and selling one more item.

3.5 Derivatives of Trigonometric Functions

- We can find the derivatives of sin x and cos x by using the definition of derivative and the limit formulas found earlier. The results are

$$\frac{d}{dx}\sin x = \cos x \frac{d}{dx}\cos x = -\sin x.$$

- With these two formulas, we can determine the derivatives of all six basic trigonometric functions.

3.6 The Chain Rule

- The chain rule allows us to differentiate compositions of two or more functions. It states that for $h(x) = f(g(x)),$

$$h'(x) = f'(g(x))g'(x).$$

In Leibniz's notation this rule takes the form

$$\frac{dy}{dx} = \frac{dy}{du} \cdot \frac{du}{dx}.$$

- We can use the chain rule with other rules that we have learned, and we can derive formulas for some of them.
- The chain rule combines with the power rule to form a new rule:

$$\text{If } h(x) = (g(x))^n, \text{ then } h'(x) = n(g(x))^{n-1} g'(x).$$

- When applied to the composition of three functions, the chain rule can be expressed as follows: If $h(x) = f(g(k(x))),$ then $h'(x) = f'(g(k(x))g'(k(x))k'(x).$

3.7 Derivatives of Inverse Functions

- The inverse function theorem allows us to compute derivatives of inverse functions without using the limit definition of the derivative.
- We can use the inverse function theorem to develop differentiation formulas for the inverse trigonometric functions.

3.8 Implicit Differentiation

- We use implicit differentiation to find derivatives of implicitly defined functions (functions defined by equations).
- By using implicit differentiation, we can find the equation of a tangent line to the graph of a curve.

3.9 Derivatives of Exponential and Logarithmic Functions

- On the basis of the assumption that the exponential function $y = b^x, b > 0$ is continuous everywhere and differentiable at 0, this function is differentiable everywhere and there is a formula for its derivative.

- We can use a formula to find the derivative of $y = \ln x$, and the relationship $\log_b x = \frac{\ln x}{\ln b}$ allows us to extend our differentiation formulas to include logarithms with arbitrary bases.
- Logarithmic differentiation allows us to differentiate functions of the form $y = g(x)^{f(x)}$ or very complex functions by taking the natural logarithm of both sides and exploiting the properties of logarithms before differentiating.

CHAPTER 3 REVIEW EXERCISES

True or False? Justify the answer with a proof or a counterexample.

367. Every function has a derivative.

368. A continuous function has a continuous derivative.

369. A continuous function has a derivative.

370. If a function is differentiable, it is continuous.

Use the limit definition of the derivative to exactly evaluate the derivative.

371. $f(x) = \sqrt{x+4}$

372. $f(x) = \frac{3}{x}$

Find the derivatives of the following functions.

373. $f(x) = 3x^3 - \frac{4}{x^2}$

374. $f(x) = \left(4 - x^2\right)^3$

375. $f(x) = e^{\sin x}$

376. $f(x) = \ln(x+2)$

377. $f(x) = x^2 \cos x + x \tan(x)$

378. $f(x) = \sqrt{3x^2 + 2}$

379. $f(x) = \frac{x}{4}\sin^{-1}(x)$

380. $x^2 y = (y+2) + xy\sin(x)$

Find the following derivatives of various orders.

381. First derivative of $y = x\ln(x)\cos x$

382. Third derivative of $y = (3x+2)^2$

383. Second derivative of $y = 4^x + x^2 \sin(x)$

Find the equation of the tangent line to the following equations at the specified point.

384. $y = \cos^{-1}(x) + x$ at $x = 0$

385. $y = x + e^x - \frac{1}{x}$ at $x = 1$

Draw the derivative for the following graphs.

386.

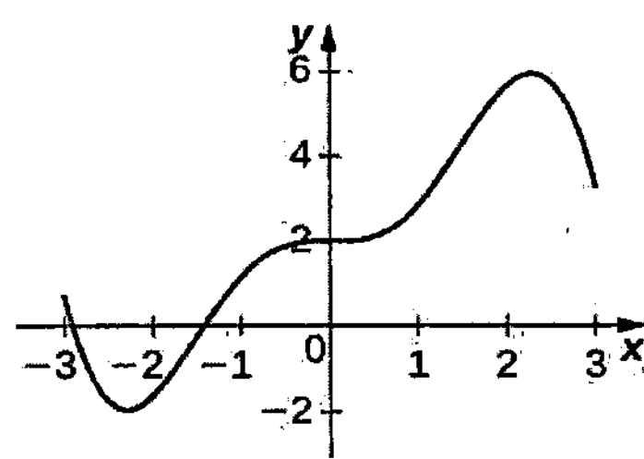

387.

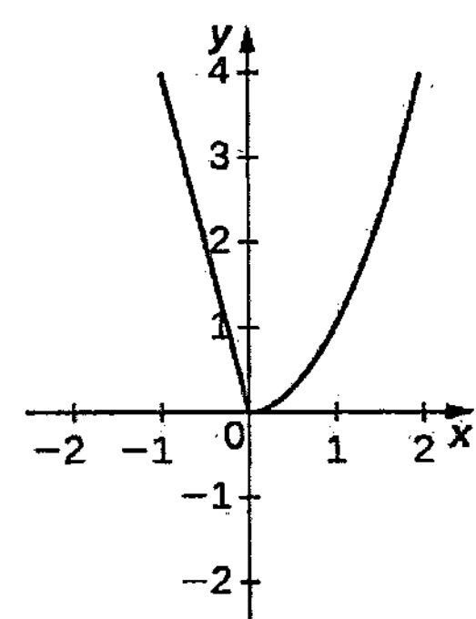

The following questions concern the water level in Ocean City, New Jersey, in January, which can be approximated by $w(t) = 1.9 + 2.9\cos\left(\frac{\pi}{6}t\right)$, where t is measured in hours after midnight, and the height is measured in feet.

388. Find and graph the derivative. What is the physical meaning?

389. Find $w'(3)$. What is the physical meaning of this value?

The following questions consider the wind speeds of Hurricane Katrina, which affected New Orleans, Louisiana, in August 2005. The data are displayed in a table.

Hours after Midnight, August 26	Wind Speed (mph)
1	45
5	75
11	100
29	115
49	145
58	175
73	155
81	125
85	95
107	35

Table 3.10 Wind Speeds of Hurricane Katrina **Source: http://news.nationalgeographic.com/news/2005/09/0914_050914_katrina_timeline.html.**

390. Using the table, estimate the derivative of the wind speed at hour 39. What is the physical meaning?

391. Estimate the derivative of the wind speed at hour 83. What is the physical meaning?

4 | APPLICATIONS OF DERIVATIVES

Figure 4.1 As a rocket is being launched, at what rate should the angle of a video camera change to continue viewing the rocket? (credit: modification of work by Steve Jurvetson, Wikimedia Commons)

Chapter Outline

Introduction

A rocket is being launched from the ground and cameras are recording the event. A video camera is located on the ground a certain distance from the launch pad. At what rate should the angle of inclination (the angle the camera makes with the ground) change to allow the camera to record the flight of the rocket as it heads upward? (See **Example 4.3**.)

A rocket launch involves two related quantities that change over time. Being able to solve this type of problem is just one application of derivatives introduced in this chapter. We also look at how derivatives are used to find maximum and minimum values of functions. As a result, we will be able to solve applied optimization problems, such as maximizing revenue and minimizing surface area. In addition, we examine how derivatives are used to evaluate complicated limits, to approximate roots of functions, and to provide accurate graphs of functions.

4.1 | Related Rates

Learning Objectives

4.1.1 Express changing quantities in terms of derivatives.

4.1.2 Find relationships among the derivatives in a given problem.

4.1.3 Use the chain rule to find the rate of change of one quantity that depends on the rate of change of other quantities.

We have seen that for quantities that are changing over time, the rates at which these quantities change are given by derivatives. If two related quantities are changing over time, the rates at which the quantities change are related. For example, if a balloon is being filled with air, both the radius of the balloon and the volume of the balloon are increasing. In this section, we consider several problems in which two or more related quantities are changing and we study how to determine the relationship between the rates of change of these quantities.

Setting up Related-Rates Problems

In many real-world applications, related quantities are changing with respect to time. For example, if we consider the balloon example again, we can say that the rate of change in the volume, V, is related to the rate of change in the radius, r. In this case, we say that $\frac{dV}{dt}$ and $\frac{dr}{dt}$ are **related rates** because V is related to r. Here we study several examples of related quantities that are changing with respect to time and we look at how to calculate one rate of change given another rate of change.

Example 4.1

Inflating a Balloon

A spherical balloon is being filled with air at the constant rate of $2\text{ cm}^3/\text{sec}$ (**Figure 4.2**). How fast is the radius increasing when the radius is 3 cm?

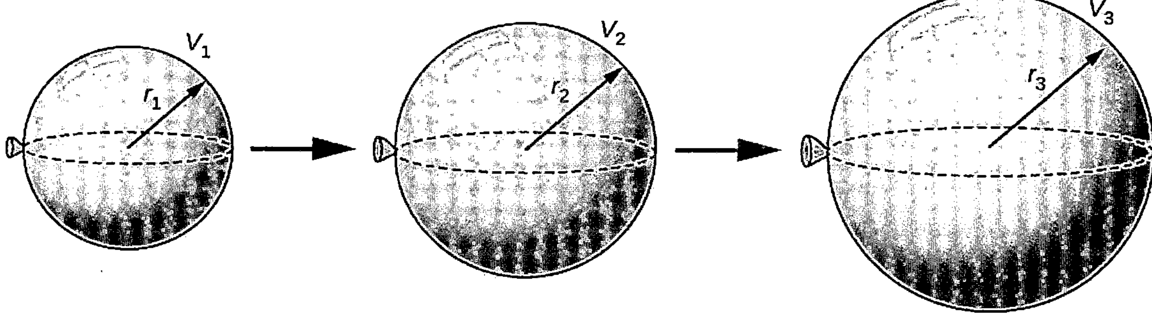

Figure 4.2 As the balloon is being filled with air, both the radius and the volume are increasing with respect to time.

Solution

The volume of a sphere of radius r centimeters is

$$V = \frac{4}{3}\pi r^3 \text{ cm}^3.$$

Since the balloon is being filled with air, both the volume and the radius are functions of time. Therefore, t seconds after beginning to fill the balloon with air, the volume of air in the balloon is

$$V(t) = \frac{4}{3}\pi[r(t)]^3 \text{ cm}^3.$$

Differentiating both sides of this equation with respect to time and applying the chain rule, we see that the rate of change in the volume is related to the rate of change in the radius by the equation

$$V'(t) = 4\pi[r(t)]^2 r'(t).$$

The balloon is being filled with air at the constant rate of 2 cm³/sec, so $V'(t) = 2 \text{ cm}^3/\text{sec}$. Therefore,

$$2\text{cm}^3/\text{sec} = \left(4\pi[r(t)]^2 \text{ cm}^2\right) \cdot (r'(t)\text{cm/s}),$$

which implies

$$r'(t) = \frac{1}{2\pi[r(t)]^2} \text{cm/sec}.$$

When the radius $r = 3$ cm,

$$r'(t) = \frac{1}{18\pi} \text{cm/sec}.$$

4.1 What is the instantaneous rate of change of the radius when $r = 6$ cm?

Before looking at other examples, let's outline the problem-solving strategy we will be using to solve related-rates problems.

Problem-Solving Strategy: Solving a Related-Rates Problem

1. Assign symbols to all variables involved in the problem. Draw a figure if applicable.
2. State, in terms of the variables, the information that is given and the rate to be determined.
3. Find an equation relating the variables introduced in step 1.
4. Using the chain rule, differentiate both sides of the equation found in step 3 with respect to the independent variable. This new equation will relate the derivatives.
5. Substitute all known values into the equation from step 4, then solve for the unknown rate of change.

Note that when solving a related-rates problem, it is crucial not to substitute known values too soon. For example, if the value for a changing quantity is substituted into an equation before both sides of the equation are differentiated, then that quantity will behave as a constant and its derivative will not appear in the new equation found in step 4. We examine this potential error in the following example.

Examples of the Process

Let's now implement the strategy just described to solve several related-rates problems. The first example involves a plane flying overhead. The relationship we are studying is between the speed of the plane and the rate at which the distance between the plane and a person on the ground is changing.

Example 4.2

An Airplane Flying at a Constant Elevation

An airplane is flying overhead at a constant elevation of 4000 ft. A man is viewing the plane from a position 3000 ft from the base of a radio tower. The airplane is flying horizontally away from the man. If the plane is flying at the rate of 600 ft/sec, at what rate is the distance between the man and the plane increasing when the plane passes over the radio tower?

Solution

Step 1. Draw a picture, introducing variables to represent the different quantities involved.

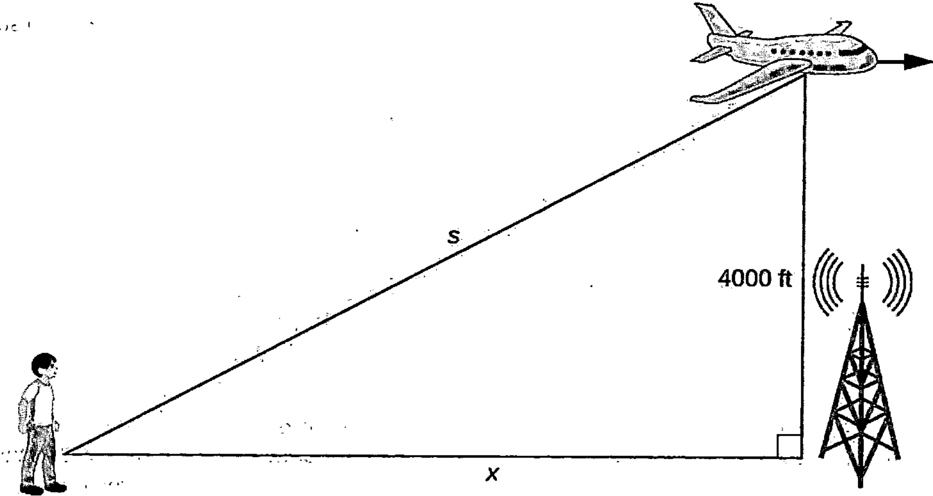

Figure 4.3 An airplane is flying at a constant height of 4000 ft. The distance between the person and the airplane and the person and the place on the ground directly below the airplane are changing. We denote those quantities with the variables s and $x,$ respectively.

As shown, x denotes the distance between the man and the position on the ground directly below the airplane. The variable s denotes the distance between the man and the plane. Note that both x and s are functions of time. We do not introduce a variable for the height of the plane because it remains at a constant elevation of 4000 ft. Since an object's height above the ground is measured as the shortest distance between the object and the ground, the line segment of length 4000 ft is perpendicular to the line segment of length x feet, creating a right triangle.

Step 2. Since x denotes the horizontal distance between the man and the point on the ground below the plane, dx/dt represents the speed of the plane. We are told the speed of the plane is 600 ft/sec. Therefore, $\frac{dx}{dt} = 600$ ft/sec. Since we are asked to find the rate of change in the distance between the man and the plane when the plane is directly above the radio tower, we need to find ds/dt when $x = 3000$ ft.

Step 3. From the figure, we can use the Pythagorean theorem to write an equation relating x and s:

$$[x(t)]^2 + 4000^2 = [s(t)]^2.$$

Step 4. Differentiating this equation with respect to time and using the fact that the derivative of a constant is zero, we arrive at the equation

$$x\frac{dx}{dt} = s\frac{ds}{dt}.$$

Step 5. Find the rate at which the distance between the man and the plane is increasing when the plane is directly over the radio tower. That is, find $\frac{ds}{dt}$ when $x = 3000$ ft. Since the speed of the plane is 600 ft/sec, we know that $\frac{dx}{dt} = 600$ ft/sec. We are not given an explicit value for s; however, since we are trying to find $\frac{ds}{dt}$ when $x = 3000$ ft, we can use the Pythagorean theorem to determine the distance s when $x = 3000$ and the height is 4000 ft. Solving the equation

$$3000^2 + 4000^2 = s^2$$

for s, we have $s = 5000$ ft at the time of interest. Using these values, we conclude that ds/dt is a solution of the equation

$$(3000)(600) = (5000) \cdot \frac{ds}{dt}.$$

Therefore,

$$\frac{ds}{dt} = \frac{3000 \cdot 600}{5000} = 360 \text{ ft/sec}.$$

Note: When solving related-rates problems, it is important not to substitute values for the variables too soon. For example, in step 3, we related the variable quantities $x(t)$ and $s(t)$ by the equation

$$[x(t)]^2 + 4000^2 = [s(t)]^2.$$

Since the plane remains at a constant height, it is not necessary to introduce a variable for the height, and we are allowed to use the constant 4000 to denote that quantity. However, the other two quantities are changing. If we mistakenly substituted $x(t) = 3000$ into the equation before differentiating, our equation would have been

$$3000^2 + 4000^2 = [s(t)]^2.$$

After differentiating, our equation would become

$$0 = s(t)\frac{ds}{dt}.$$

As a result, we would incorrectly conclude that $\frac{ds}{dt} = 0.$

4.2 What is the speed of the plane if the distance between the person and the plane is increasing at the rate of 300 ft/sec?

We now return to the problem involving the rocket launch from the beginning of the chapter.

Example 4.3

Chapter Opener: A Rocket Launch

Figure 4.4 (credit: modification of work by Steve Jurvetson, Wikimedia Commons)

A rocket is launched so that it rises vertically. A camera is positioned 5000 ft from the launch pad. When the rocket is 1000 ft above the launch pad, its velocity is $600\text{ ft/sec}.$ Find the necessary rate of change of the camera's angle as a function of time so that it stays focused on the rocket.

Solution

Step 1. Draw a picture introducing the variables.

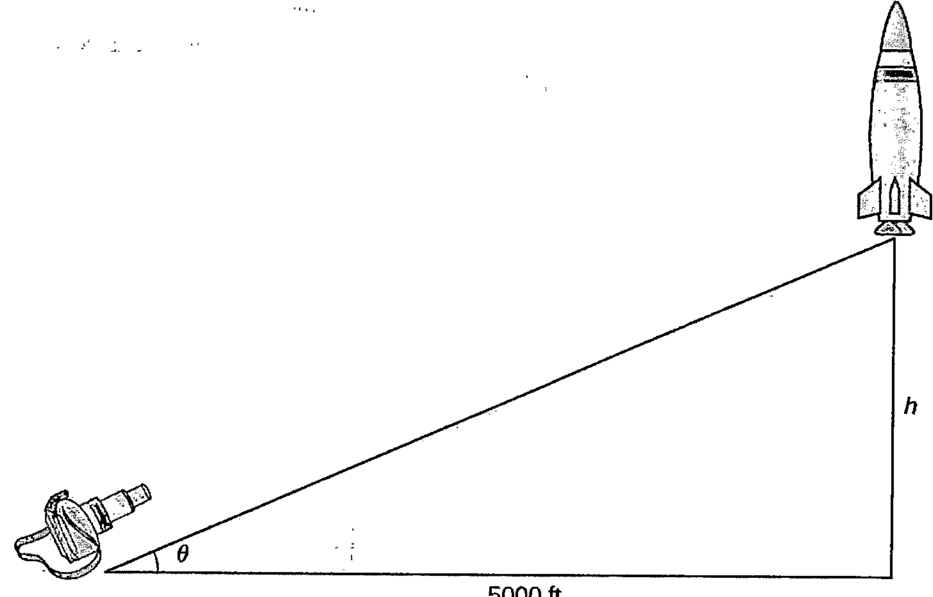

Figure 4.5 A camera is positioned 5000 ft from the launch pad of the rocket. The height of the rocket and the angle of the camera are changing with respect to time. We denote those quantities with the variables h and $\theta,$ respectively.

Let h denote the height of the rocket above the launch pad and θ be the angle between the camera lens and the ground.

Step 2. We are trying to find the rate of change in the angle of the camera with respect to time when the rocket is 1000 ft off the ground. That is, we need to find $\frac{d\theta}{dt}$ when $h = 1000$ ft. At that time, we know the velocity of the rocket is $\frac{dh}{dt} = 600$ ft/sec.

Step 3. Now we need to find an equation relating the two quantities that are changing with respect to time: h and θ. How can we create such an equation? Using the fact that we have drawn a right triangle, it is natural to think about trigonometric functions. Recall that $\tan\theta$ is the ratio of the length of the opposite side of the triangle to the length of the adjacent side. Thus, we have

$$\tan\theta = \frac{h}{5000}.$$

This gives us the equation

$$h = 5000\tan\theta.$$

Step 4. Differentiating this equation with respect to time t, we obtain

$$\frac{dh}{dt} = 5000\sec^2\theta\frac{d\theta}{dt}.$$

Step 5. We want to find $\frac{d\theta}{dt}$ when $h = 1000$ ft. At this time, we know that $\frac{dh}{dt} = 600$ ft/sec. We need to determine $\sec^2\theta$. Recall that $\sec\theta$ is the ratio of the length of the hypotenuse to the length of the adjacent side. We know the length of the adjacent side is 5000 ft. To determine the length of the hypotenuse, we use the Pythagorean theorem, where the length of one leg is 5000 ft, the length of the other leg is $h = 1000$ ft, and the length of the hypotenuse is c feet as shown in the following figure.

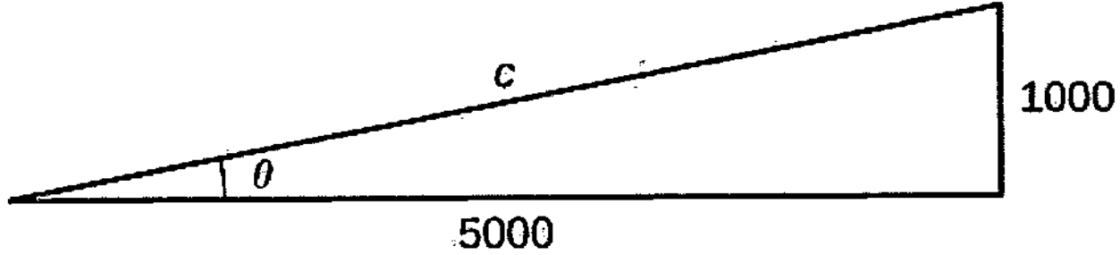

We see that

$$1000^2 + 5000^2 = c^2$$

and we conclude that the hypotenuse is

$$c = 1000\sqrt{26}\text{ ft}.$$

Therefore, when $h = 1000$, we have

$$\sec^2\theta = \left(\frac{1000\sqrt{26}}{5000}\right)^2 = \frac{26}{25}.$$

Recall from step 4 that the equation relating $\frac{d\theta}{dt}$ to our known values is

$$\frac{dh}{dt} = 5000\sec^2\theta\frac{d\theta}{dt}.$$

When $h = 1000$ ft, we know that $\frac{dh}{dt} = 600$ ft/sec and $\sec^2\theta = \frac{26}{25}$. Substituting these values into the previous equation, we arrive at the equation

$$600 = 5000\left(\frac{26}{25}\right)\frac{d\theta}{dt}.$$

Therefore, $\frac{d\theta}{dt} = \frac{3}{26}$ rad/sec.

4.3 What rate of change is necessary for the elevation angle of the camera if the camera is placed on the ground at a distance of 4000 ft from the launch pad and the velocity of the rocket is 500 ft/sec when the rocket is 2000 ft off the ground?

In the next example, we consider water draining from a cone-shaped funnel. We compare the rate at which the level of water in the cone is decreasing with the rate at which the volume of water is decreasing.

Example 4.4

Water Draining from a Funnel

Water is draining from the bottom of a cone-shaped funnel at the rate of $0.03\ \text{ft}^3/\text{sec}$. The height of the funnel is 2 ft and the radius at the top of the funnel is 1 ft. At what rate is the height of the water in the funnel changing when the height of the water is $\frac{1}{2}$ ft?

Solution

Step 1: Draw a picture introducing the variables.

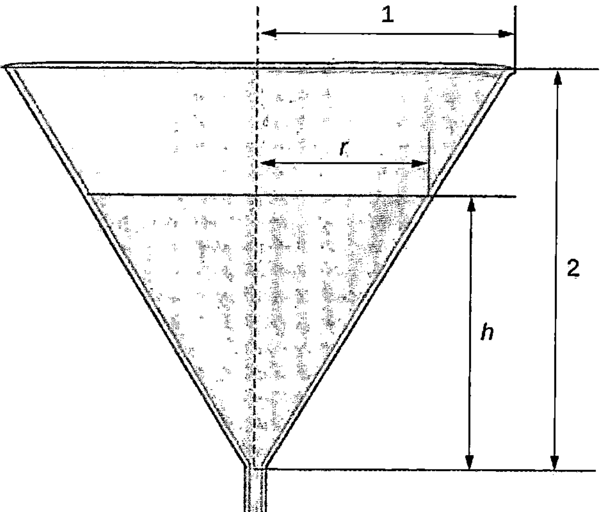

Figure 4.6 Water is draining from a funnel of height 2 ft and radius 1 ft. The height of the water and the radius of water are changing over time. We denote these quantities with the variables h and $r,$ respectively.

Let h denote the height of the water in the funnel, r denote the radius of the water at its surface, and V denote the volume of the water.

Step 2: We need to determine $\frac{dh}{dt}$ when $h = \frac{1}{2}$ ft. We know that $\frac{dV}{dt} = -0.03$ ft/sec.

Step 3: The volume of water in the cone is

$$V = \frac{1}{3}\pi r^2 h.$$

From the figure, we see that we have similar triangles. Therefore, the ratio of the sides in the two triangles is the same. Therefore, $\frac{r}{h} = \frac{1}{2}$ or $r = \frac{h}{2}$. Using this fact, the equation for volume can be simplified to

$$V = \frac{1}{3}\pi\left(\frac{h}{2}\right)^2 h = \frac{\pi}{12}h^3.$$

Step 4: Applying the chain rule while differentiating both sides of this equation with respect to time t, we obtain

$$\frac{dV}{dt} = \frac{\pi}{4}h^2\frac{dh}{dt}.$$

Step 5: We want to find $\frac{dh}{dt}$ when $h = \frac{1}{2}$ ft. Since water is leaving at the rate of $0.03\ \text{ft}^3/\text{sec}$, we know that $\frac{dV}{dt} = -0.03\ \text{ft}^3/\text{sec}$. Therefore,

$$-0.03 = \frac{\pi}{4}\left(\frac{1}{2}\right)^2\frac{dh}{dt},$$

which implies

$$-0.03 = \frac{\pi}{16}\frac{dh}{dt}.$$

It follows that

$$\frac{dh}{dt} = -\frac{0.48}{\pi} = -0.153\ \text{ft/sec}.$$

4.4 At what rate is the height of the water changing when the height of the water is $\frac{1}{4}$ ft?

4.1 EXERCISES

For the following exercises, find the quantities for the given equation.

1. Find $\frac{dy}{dt}$ at $x = 1$ and $y = x^2 + 3$ if $\frac{dx}{dt} = 4$.

2. Find $\frac{dx}{dt}$ at $x = -2$ and $y = 2x^2 + 1$ if $\frac{dy}{dt} = -1$.

3. Find $\frac{dz}{dt}$ at $(x, y) = (1, 3)$ and $z^2 = x^2 + y^2$ if $\frac{dx}{dt} = 4$ and $\frac{dy}{dt} = 3$.

For the following exercises, sketch the situation if necessary and used related rates to solve for the quantities.

4. **[T]** If two electrical resistors are connected in parallel, the total resistance (measured in ohms, denoted by the Greek capital letter omega, Ω) is given by the equation $\frac{1}{R} = \frac{1}{R_1} + \frac{1}{R_2}$. If R_1 is increasing at a rate of $0.5\ \Omega/\text{min}$ and R_2 decreases at a rate of $1.1\Omega/\text{min}$, at what rate does the total resistance change when $R_1 = 20\Omega$ and $R_2 = 50\Omega/\text{min}$?

5. A 10-ft ladder is leaning against a wall. If the top of the ladder slides down the wall at a rate of 2 ft/sec, how fast is the bottom moving along the ground when the bottom of the ladder is 5 ft from the wall?

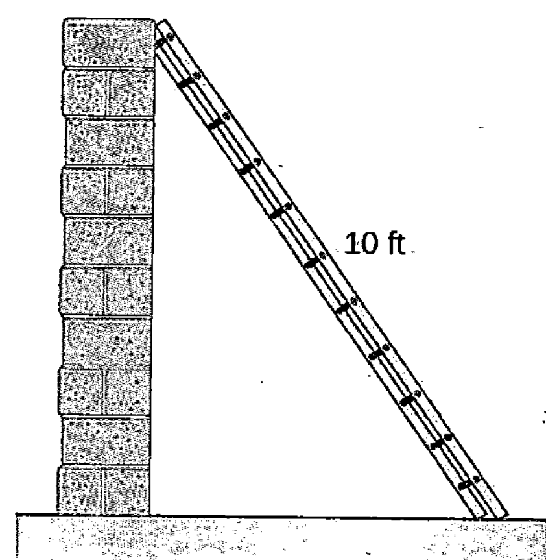

6. A 25-ft ladder is leaning against a wall. If we push the ladder toward the wall at a rate of 1 ft/sec, and the bottom of the ladder is initially 20 ft away from the wall, how fast does the ladder move up the wall 5 sec after we start pushing?

7. Two airplanes are flying in the air at the same height: airplane A is flying east at 250 mi/h and airplane B is flying north at 300 mi/h. If they are both heading to the same airport, located 30 miles east of airplane A and 40 miles north of airplane B, at what rate is the distance between the airplanes changing?

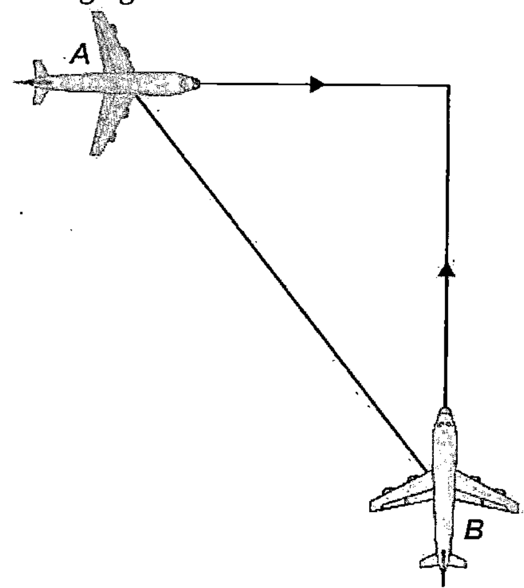

8. You and a friend are riding your bikes to a restaurant that you think is east; your friend thinks the restaurant is north. You both leave from the same point, with you riding at 16 mph east and your friend riding 12 mph north. After you traveled 4 mi, at what rate is the distance between you changing?

9. Two buses are driving along parallel freeways that are 5 mi apart, one heading east and the other heading west. Assuming that each bus drives a constant 55 mph, find the rate at which the distance between the buses is changing when they are 13 mi apart, heading toward each other.

10. A 6-ft-tall person walks away from a 10-ft lamppost at a constant rate of 3 ft/sec. What is the rate that the tip of the shadow moves away from the pole when the person is 10 ft away from the pole?

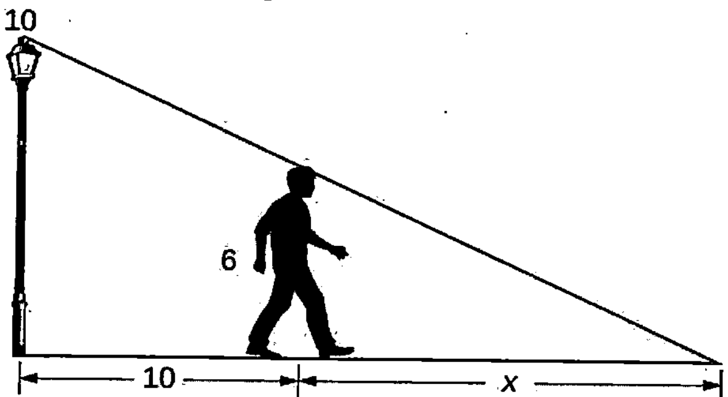

11. Using the previous problem, what is the rate at which the tip of the shadow moves away from the person when the person is 10 ft from the pole?

12. A 5-ft-tall person walks toward a wall at a rate of 2 ft/sec. A spotlight is located on the ground 40 ft from the wall. How fast does the height of the person's shadow on the wall change when the person is 10 ft from the wall?

13. Using the previous problem, what is the rate at which the shadow changes when the person is 10 ft from the wall, if the person is walking away from the wall at a rate of 2 ft/sec?

14. A helicopter starting on the ground is rising directly into the air at a rate of 25 ft/sec. You are running on the ground starting directly under the helicopter at a rate of 10 ft/sec. Find the rate of change of the distance between the helicopter and yourself after 5 sec.

15. Using the previous problem, what is the rate at which the distance between you and the helicopter is changing when the helicopter has risen to a height of 60 ft in the air, assuming that, initially, it was 30 ft above you?

For the following exercises, draw and label diagrams to help solve the related-rates problems.

16. The side of a cube increases at a rate of $\frac{1}{2}$ m/sec. Find the rate at which the volume of the cube increases when the side of the cube is 4 m.

17. The volume of a cube decreases at a rate of 10 m/sec. Find the rate at which the side of the cube changes when the side of the cube is 2 m.

18. The radius of a circle increases at a rate of 2 m/sec. Find the rate at which the area of the circle increases when the radius is 5 m.

19. The radius of a sphere decreases at a rate of 3 m/sec. Find the rate at which the surface area decreases when the radius is 10 m.

20. The radius of a sphere increases at a rate of 1 m/sec. Find the rate at which the volume increases when the radius is 20 m.

21. The radius of a sphere is increasing at a rate of 9 cm/sec. Find the radius of the sphere when the volume and the radius of the sphere are increasing at the same numerical rate.

22. The base of a triangle is shrinking at a rate of 1 cm/min and the height of the triangle is increasing at a rate of 5 cm/min. Find the rate at which the area of the triangle changes when the height is 22 cm and the base is 10 cm.

23. A triangle has two constant sides of length 3 ft and 5 ft. The angle between these two sides is increasing at a rate of 0.1 rad/sec. Find the rate at which the area of the triangle is changing when the angle between the two sides is $\pi/6$.

24. A triangle has a height that is increasing at a rate of 2 cm/sec and its area is increasing at a rate of 4 cm^2/sec. Find the rate at which the base of the triangle is changing when the height of the triangle is 4 cm and the area is 20 cm^2.

For the following exercises, consider a right cone that is leaking water. The dimensions of the conical tank are a height of 16 ft and a radius of 5 ft.

25. How fast does the depth of the water change when the water is 10 ft high if the cone leaks water at a rate of 10 ft^3/min?

26. Find the rate at which the surface area of the water changes when the water is 10 ft high if the cone leaks water at a rate of 10 ft^3/min.

27. If the water level is decreasing at a rate of 3 in./min when the depth of the water is 8 ft, determine the rate at which water is leaking out of the cone.

28. A vertical cylinder is leaking water at a rate of 1 ft^3/sec. If the cylinder has a height of 10 ft and a radius of 1 ft, at what rate is the height of the water changing when the height is 6 ft?

29. A cylinder is leaking water but you are unable to determine at what rate. The cylinder has a height of 2 m and a radius of 2 m. Find the rate at which the water is leaking out of the cylinder if the rate at which the height is decreasing is 10 cm/min when the height is 1 m.

30. A trough has ends shaped like isosceles triangles, with width 3 m and height 4 m, and the trough is 10 m long. Water is being pumped into the trough at a rate of 5 m^3/min. At what rate does the height of the water change when the water is 1 m deep?

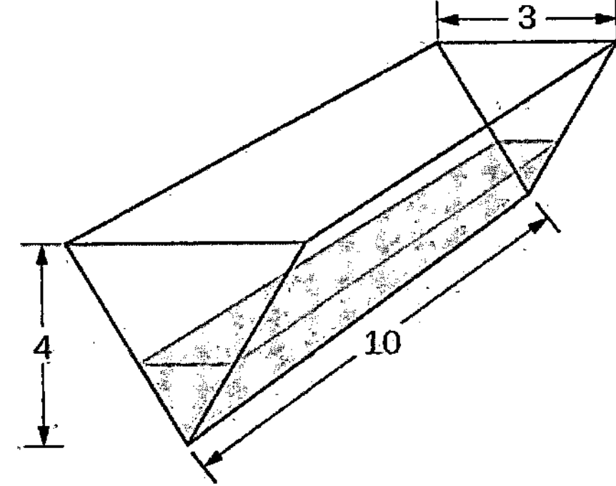

31. A tank is shaped like an upside-down square pyramid, with base of 4 m by 4 m and a height of 12 m (see the following figure). How fast does the height increase when the water is 2 m deep if water is being pumped in at a rate of $\frac{2}{3}$ m/sec?

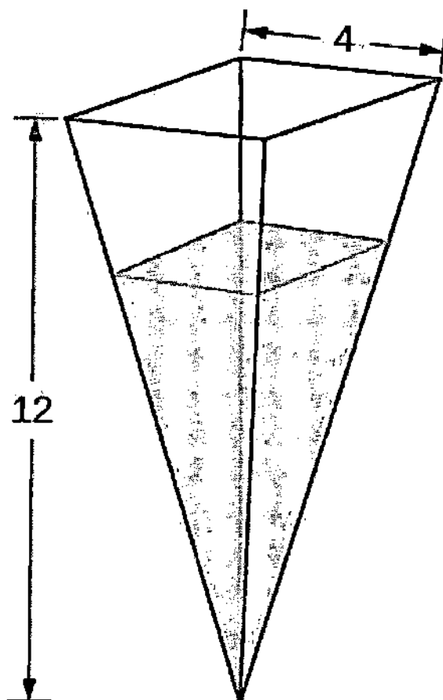

For the following problems, consider a pool shaped like the bottom half of a sphere, that is being filled at a rate of 25 ft^3/min. The radius of the pool is 10 ft.

32. Find the rate at which the depth of the water is changing when the water has a depth of 5 ft.

33. Find the rate at which the depth of the water is changing when the water has a depth of 1 ft.

34. If the height is increasing at a rate of 1 in./sec when the depth of the water is 2 ft, find the rate at which water is being pumped in.

35. Gravel is being unloaded from a truck and falls into a pile shaped like a cone at a rate of 10 ft^3/min. The radius of the cone base is three times the height of the cone. Find the rate at which the height of the gravel changes when the pile has a height of 5 ft.

36. Using a similar setup from the preceding problem, find the rate at which the gravel is being unloaded if the pile is 5 ft high and the height is increasing at a rate of 4 in./min.

For the following exercises, draw the situations and solve the related-rate problems.

37. You are stationary on the ground and are watching a bird fly horizontally at a rate of 10 m/sec. The bird is located 40 m above your head. How fast does the angle of elevation change when the horizontal distance between you and the bird is 9 m?

38. You stand 40 ft from a bottle rocket on the ground and watch as it takes off vertically into the air at a rate of 20 ft/sec. Find the rate at which the angle of elevation changes when the rocket is 30 ft in the air.

39. A lighthouse, L, is on an island 4 mi away from the closest point, P, on the beach (see the following image). If the lighthouse light rotates clockwise at a constant rate of 10 revolutions/min, how fast does the beam of light move across the beach 2 mi away from the closest point on the beach?

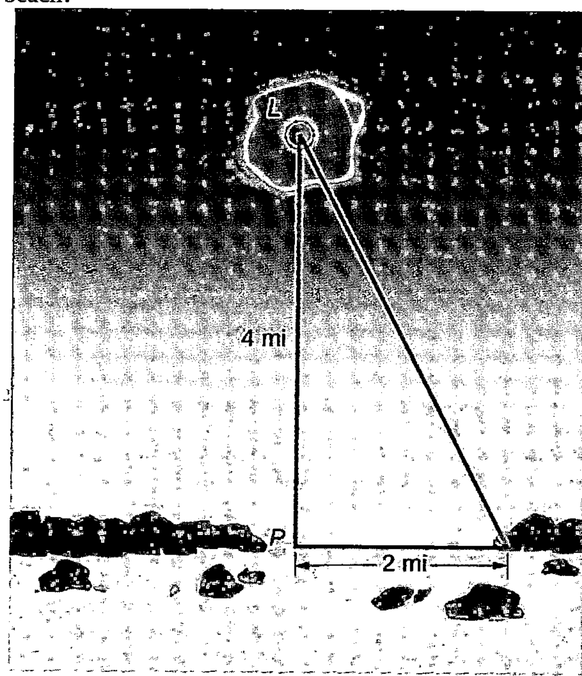

40. Using the same setup as the previous problem, determine at what rate the beam of light moves across the beach 1 mi away from the closest point on the beach.

41. You are walking to a bus stop at a right-angle corner. You move north at a rate of 2 m/sec and are 20 m south of the intersection. The bus travels west at a rate of 10 m/sec away from the intersection – you have missed the bus! What is the rate at which the angle between you and the bus is changing when you are 20 m south of the intersection and the bus is 10 m west of the intersection?

For the following exercises, refer to the figure of baseball diamond, which has sides of 90 ft.

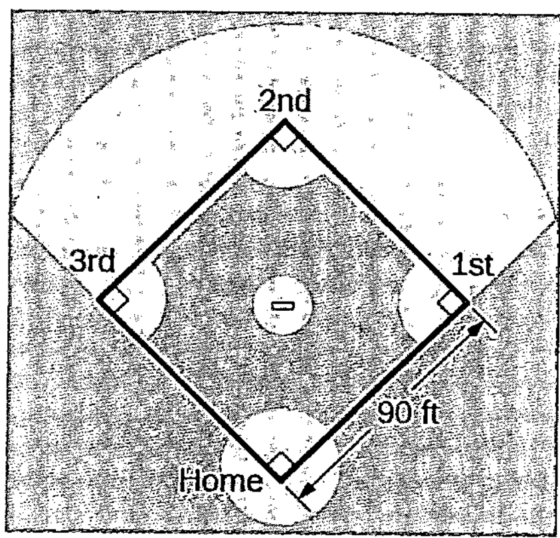

42. **[T]** A batter hits a ball toward third base at 75 ft/sec and runs toward first base at a rate of 24 ft/sec. At what rate does the distance between the ball and the batter change when 2 sec have passed?

43. **[T]** A batter hits a ball toward second base at 80 ft/sec and runs toward first base at a rate of 30 ft/sec. At what rate does the distance between the ball and the batter change when the runner has covered one-third of the distance to first base? (*Hint*: Recall the law of cosines.)

44. **[T]** A batter hits the ball and runs toward first base at a speed of 22 ft/sec. At what rate does the distance between the runner and second base change when the runner has run 30 ft?

45. **[T]** Runners start at first and second base. When the baseball is hit, the runner at first base runs at a speed of 18 ft/sec toward second base and the runner at second base runs at a speed of 20 ft/sec toward third base. How fast is the distance between runners changing 1 sec after the ball is hit?

4.2 | Linear Approximations and Differentials

Learning Objectives

4.2.1 Describe the linear approximation to a function at a point.
4.2.2 Write the linearization of a given function.
4.2.3 Draw a graph that illustrates the use of differentials to approximate the change in a quantity.
4.2.4 Calculate the relative error and percentage error in using a differential approximation.

We have just seen how derivatives allow us to compare related quantities that are changing over time. In this section, we examine another application of derivatives: the ability to approximate functions locally by linear functions. Linear functions are the easiest functions with which to work, so they provide a useful tool for approximating function values. In addition, the ideas presented in this section are generalized later in the text when we study how to approximate functions by higher-degree polynomials **Introduction to Power Series and Functions (http://cnx.org/content/m53760/latest/)** .

Linear Approximation of a Function at a Point

Consider a function f that is differentiable at a point $x = a.$ Recall that the tangent line to the graph of f at a is given by the equation

$$y = f(a) + f'(a)(x - a).$$

For example, consider the function $f(x) = \frac{1}{x}$ at $a = 2.$ Since f is differentiable at $x = 2$ and $f'(x) = -\frac{1}{x^2},$ we see that $f'(2) = -\frac{1}{4}.$ Therefore, the tangent line to the graph of f at $a = 2$ is given by the equation

$$y = \frac{1}{2} - \frac{1}{4}(x - 2).$$

Figure 4.7(a) shows a graph of $f(x) = \frac{1}{x}$ along with the tangent line to f at $x = 2.$ Note that for x near 2, the graph of the tangent line is close to the graph of $f.$ As a result, we can use the equation of the tangent line to approximate $f(x)$ for x near 2. For example, if $x = 2.1,$ the y value of the corresponding point on the tangent line is

$$y = \frac{1}{2} - \frac{1}{4}(2.1 - 2) = 0.475.$$

The actual value of $f(2.1)$ is given by

$$f(2.1) = \frac{1}{2.1} \approx 0.47619.$$

Therefore, the tangent line gives us a fairly good approximation of $f(2.1)$ (**Figure 4.7**(b)). However, note that for values of x far from 2, the equation of the tangent line does not give us a good approximation. For example, if $x = 10,$ the y -value of the corresponding point on the tangent line is

$$y = \frac{1}{2} - \frac{1}{4}(10 - 2) = \frac{1}{2} - 2 = -1.5,$$

whereas the value of the function at $x = 10$ is $f(10) = 0.1.$

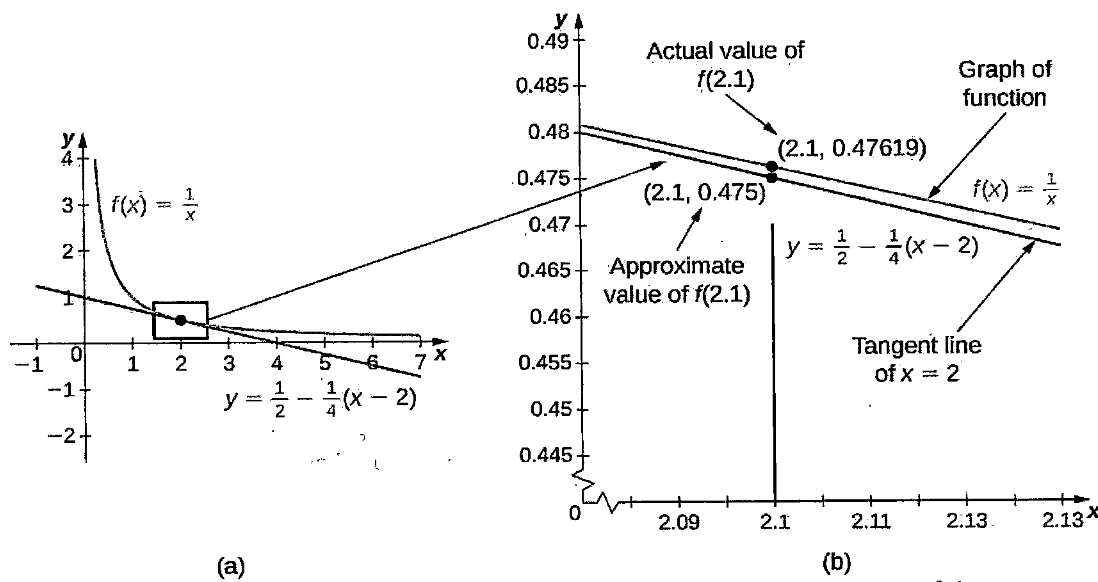

Figure 4.7 (a) The tangent line to $f(x) = 1/x$ at $x = 2$ provides a good approximation to f for x near 2. (b) At $x = 2.1,$ the value of y on the tangent line to $f(x) = 1/x$ is 0.475. The actual value of $f(2.1)$ is $1/2.1,$ which is approximately 0.47619.

In general, for a differentiable function $f,$ the equation of the tangent line to f at $x = a$ can be used to approximate $f(x)$ for x near a. Therefore, we can write

$$f(x) \approx f(a) + f'(a)(x - a) \text{ for } x \text{ near } a.$$

We call the linear function

$$L(x) = f(a) + f'(a)(x - a) \tag{4.1}$$

the **linear approximation**, or **tangent line approximation**, of f at $x = a$. This function L is also known as the **linearization** of f at $x = a$.

To show how useful the linear approximation can be, we look at how to find the linear approximation for $f(x) = \sqrt{x}$ at $x = 9$.

Example 4.5

Linear Approximation of $\sqrt{x}$

Find the linear approximation of $f(x) = \sqrt{x}$ at $x = 9$ and use the approximation to estimate $\sqrt{9.1}$.

Solution

Since we are looking for the linear approximation at $x = 9,$ using **Equation 4.1** we know the linear approximation is given by

$$L(x) = f(9) + f'(9)(x - 9).$$

We need to find $f(9)$ and $f'(9)$.

$$f(x) = \sqrt{x} \Rightarrow f(9) = \sqrt{9} = 3$$
$$f'(x) = \frac{1}{2\sqrt{x}} \Rightarrow f'(9) = \frac{1}{2\sqrt{9}} = \frac{1}{6}$$

Therefore, the linear approximation is given by **Figure 4.8**.

$$L(x) = 3 + \frac{1}{6}(x - 9)$$

Using the linear approximation, we can estimate $\sqrt{9.1}$ by writing

$$\sqrt{9.1} = f(9.1) \approx L(9.1) = 3 + \frac{1}{6}(9.1 - 9) \approx 3.0167.$$

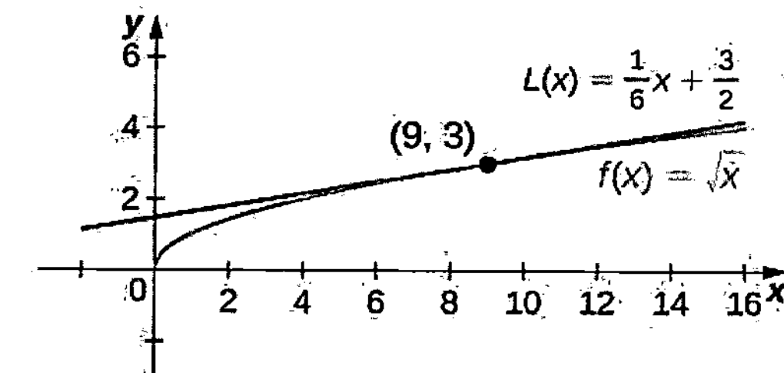

Figure 4.8 The local linear approximation to $f(x) = \sqrt{x}$ at $x = 9$ provides an approximation to f for x near 9.

Analysis

Using a calculator, the value of $\sqrt{9.1}$ to four decimal places is 3.0166. The value given by the linear approximation, 3.0167, is very close to the value obtained with a calculator, so it appears that using this linear approximation is a good way to estimate $\sqrt{x}$, at least for x near 9. At the same time, it may seem odd to use a linear approximation when we can just push a few buttons on a calculator to evaluate $\sqrt{9.1}$. However, how does the calculator evaluate $\sqrt{9.1}$? The calculator uses an approximation! In fact, calculators and computers use approximations all the time to evaluate mathematical expressions; they just use higher-degree approximations.

4.5 Find the local linear approximation to $f(x) = \sqrt[3]{x}$ at $x = 8$. Use it to approximate $\sqrt[3]{8.1}$ to five decimal places.

Example 4.6

Linear Approximation of $\sin x$

Find the linear approximation of $f(x) = \sin x$ at $x = \frac{\pi}{3}$ and use it to approximate $\sin(62°)$.

Solution

First we note that since $\frac{\pi}{3}$ rad is equivalent to $60°$, using the linear approximation at $x = \pi/3$ seems reasonable. The linear approximation is given by

$$L(x) = f\left(\frac{\pi}{3}\right) + f'\left(\frac{\pi}{3}\right)\left(x - \frac{\pi}{3}\right).$$

We see that

$$f(x) = \sin x \;\Rightarrow\; f\left(\frac{\pi}{3}\right) = \sin\left(\frac{\pi}{3}\right) = \frac{\sqrt{3}}{2}$$
$$f'(x) = \cos x \;\Rightarrow\; f'\left(\frac{\pi}{3}\right) = \cos\left(\frac{\pi}{3}\right) = \frac{1}{2}$$

Therefore, the linear approximation of f at $x = \pi/3$ is given by **Figure 4.9**.

$$L(x) = \frac{\sqrt{3}}{2} + \frac{1}{2}\left(x - \frac{\pi}{3}\right)$$

To estimate $\sin(62°)$ using $L,$ we must first convert $62°$ to radians. We have $62° = \frac{62\pi}{180}$ radians, so the estimate for $\sin(62°)$ is given by

$$\sin(62°) = f\left(\frac{62\pi}{180}\right) \approx L\left(\frac{62\pi}{180}\right) = \frac{\sqrt{3}}{2} + \frac{1}{2}\left(\frac{62\pi}{180} - \frac{\pi}{3}\right) = \frac{\sqrt{3}}{2} + \frac{1}{2}\left(\frac{2\pi}{180}\right) = \frac{\sqrt{3}}{2} + \frac{\pi}{180} \approx 0.88348.$$

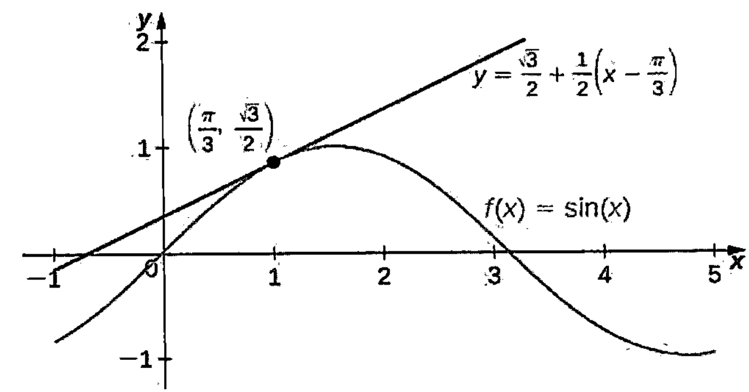

Figure 4.9 The linear approximation to $f(x) = \sin x$ at $x = \pi/3$ provides an approximation to $\sin x$ for x near $\pi/3$.

4.6 Find the linear approximation for $f(x) = \cos x$ at $x = \frac{\pi}{2}$.

Linear approximations may be used in estimating roots and powers. In the next example, we find the linear approximation for $f(x) = (1 + x)^n$ at $x = 0,$ which can be used to estimate roots and powers for real numbers near 1. The same idea can be extended to a function of the form $f(x) = (m + x)^n$ to estimate roots and powers near a different number m.

Example 4.7

Approximating Roots and Powers

Find the linear approximation of $f(x) = (1 + x)^n$ at $x = 0.$ Use this approximation to estimate $(1.01)^3$.

Solution

The linear approximation at $x = 0$ is given by

$$L(x) = f(0) + f'(0)(x - 0).$$

Because

$$f(x) = (1 + x)^n \Rightarrow f(0) = 1$$
$$f'(x) = n(1 + x)^{n-1} \Rightarrow f'(0) = n,$$

the linear approximation is given by **Figure 4.10**(a).

$$L(x) = 1 + n(x - 0) = 1 + nx$$

We can approximate $(1.01)^3$ by evaluating $L(0.01)$ when $n = 3$. We conclude that

$$(1.01)^3 = f(1.01) \approx L(1.01) = 1 + 3(0.01) = 1.03.$$

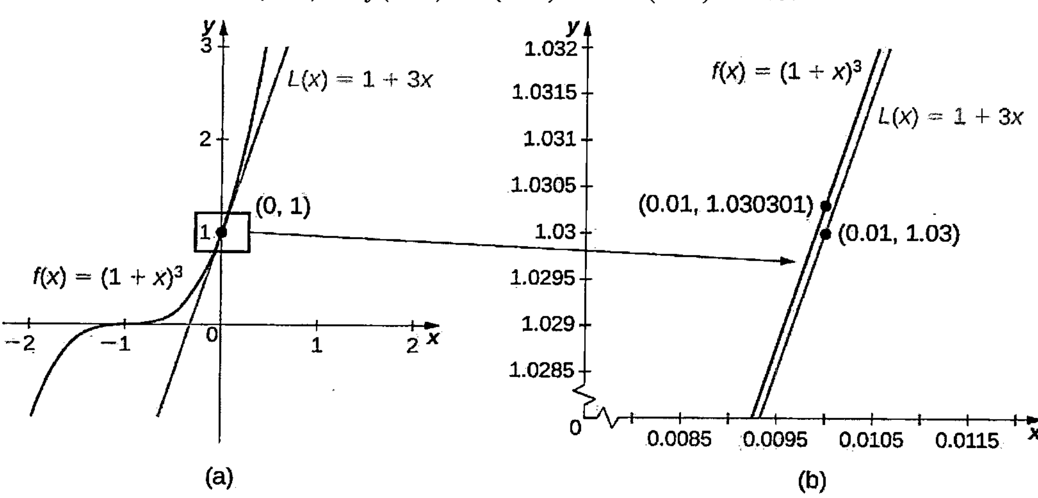

Figure 4.10 (a) The linear approximation of $f(x)$ at $x = 0$ is $L(x)$. (b) The actual value of 1.01^3 is 1.030301. The linear approximation of $f(x)$ at $x = 0$ estimates 1.01^3 to be 1.03.

4.7 Find the linear approximation of $f(x) = (1 + x)^4$ at $x = 0$ without using the result from the preceding example.

Differentials

We have seen that linear approximations can be used to estimate function values. They can also be used to estimate the amount a function value changes as a result of a small change in the input. To discuss this more formally, we define a related concept: **differentials**. Differentials provide us with a way of estimating the amount a function changes as a result of a small change in input values.

When we first looked at derivatives, we used the Leibniz notation dy/dx to represent the derivative of y with respect to x. Although we used the expressions *dy* and *dx* in this notation, they did not have meaning on their own. Here we see a meaning to the expressions *dy* and *dx*. Suppose $y = f(x)$ is a differentiable function. Let *dx* be an independent variable that can be assigned any nonzero real number, and define the dependent variable dy by

$$dy = f'(x)dx. \qquad \textbf{(4.2)}$$

It is important to notice that dy is a function of both x and dx. The expressions *dy* and *dx* are called *differentials*. We can divide both sides of **Equation 4.2** by $dx,$ which yields

$$\frac{dy}{dx} = f'(x). \tag{4.3}$$

This is the familiar expression we have used to denote a derivative. **Equation 4.2** is known as the **differential form** of **Equation 4.3**.

Example 4.8

Computing differentials

For each of the following functions, find dy and evaluate when $x = 3$ and $dx = 0.1$.

a. $y = x^2 + 2x$

b. $y = \cos x$

Solution

The key step is calculating the derivative. When we have that, we can obtain dy directly.

a. Since $f(x) = x^2 + 2x,$ we know $f'(x) = 2x + 2,$ and therefore

$$dy = (2x + 2)dx.$$

When $x = 3$ and $dx = 0.1,$

$$dy = (2 \cdot 3 + 2)(0.1) = 0.8.$$

b. Since $f(x) = \cos x,$ $f'(x) = -\sin(x).$ This gives us

$$dy = -\sin x dx.$$

When $x = 3$ and $dx = 0.1,$

$$dy = -\sin(3)(0.1) = -0.1 \sin(3).$$

4.8 For $y = e^{x^2},$ find $dy.$

We now connect differentials to linear approximations. Differentials can be used to estimate the change in the value of a function resulting from a small change in input values. Consider a function f that is differentiable at point $a.$ Suppose the input x changes by a small amount. We are interested in how much the output y changes. If x changes from a to $a + dx,$ then the change in x is dx (also denoted $\Delta x),$ and the change in y is given by

$$\Delta y = f(a + dx) - f(a).$$

Instead of calculating the exact change in $y,$ however, it is often easier to approximate the change in y by using a linear approximation. For x near $a,$ $f(x)$ can be approximated by the linear approximation

$$L(x) = f(a) + f'(a)(x - a).$$

Therefore, if dx is small,

$$f(a + dx) \approx L(a + dx) = f(a) + f'(a)(a + dx - a).$$

That is,

$$f(a+dx)-f(a)\approx L(a+dx)-f(a)=f'(a)dx.$$

In other words, the actual change in the function f if x increases from a to $a+dx$ is approximately the difference between $L(a+dx)$ and $f(a)$, where $L(x)$ is the linear approximation of f at a. By definition of $L(x)$, this difference is equal to $f'(a)dx$. In summary,

$$\Delta y=f(a+dx)-f(a)\approx L(a+dx)-f(a)=f'(a)dx=dy.$$

Therefore, we can use the differential $dy=f'(a)dx$ to approximate the change in y if x increases from $x=a$ to $x=a+dx$. We can see this in the following graph.

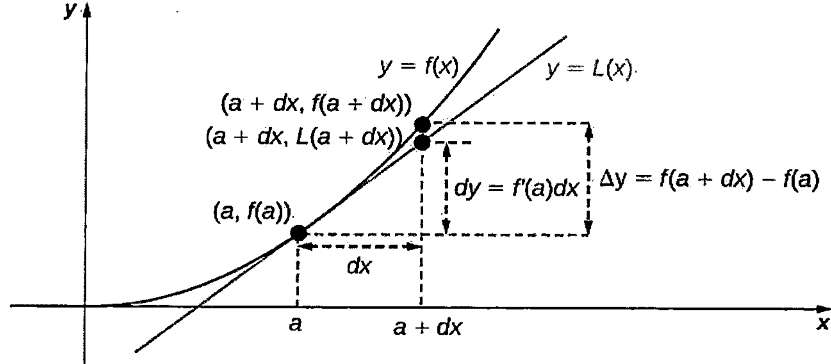

Figure 4.11 The differential $dy=f'(a)dx$ is used to approximate the actual change in y if x increases from a to $a+dx$.

We now take a look at how to use differentials to approximate the change in the value of the function that results from a small change in the value of the input. Note the calculation with differentials is much simpler than calculating actual values of functions and the result is very close to what we would obtain with the more exact calculation.

Example 4.9

Approximating Change with Differentials

Let $y=x^2+2x$. Compute Δy and dy at $x=3$ if $dx=0.1$.

Solution

The actual change in y if x changes from $x=3$ to $x=3.1$ is given by

$$\Delta y=f(3.1)-f(3)=[(3.1)^2+2(3.1)]-[3^2+2(3)]=0.81.$$

The approximate change in y is given by $dy=f'(3)dx$. Since $f'(x)=2x+2$, we have

$$dy=f'(3)dx=(2(3)+2)(0.1)=0.8.$$

4.9 For $y=x^2+2x$, find Δy and dy at $x=3$ if $dx=0.2$.

Calculating the Amount of Error

Any type of measurement is prone to a certain amount of error. In many applications, certain quantities are calculated based on measurements. For example, the area of a circle is calculated by measuring the radius of the circle. An error in the measurement of the radius leads to an error in the computed value of the area. Here we examine this type of error and study how differentials can be used to estimate the error.

Consider a function f with an input that is a measured quantity. Suppose the exact value of the measured quantity is a, but the measured value is $a + dx$. We say the measurement error is dx (or Δx). As a result, an error occurs in the calculated quantity $f(x)$. This type of error is known as a **propagated error** and is given by

$$\Delta y = f(a + dx) - f(a).$$

Since all measurements are prone to some degree of error, we do not know the exact value of a measured quantity, so we cannot calculate the propagated error exactly. However, given an estimate of the accuracy of a measurement, we can use differentials to approximate the propagated error Δy. Specifically, if f is a differentiable function at a, the propagated error is

$$\Delta y \approx dy = f'(a)dx.$$

Unfortunately, we do not know the exact value a. However, we can use the measured value $a + dx$, and estimate

$$\Delta y \approx dy \approx f'(a + dx)dx.$$

In the next example, we look at how differentials can be used to estimate the error in calculating the volume of a box if we assume the measurement of the side length is made with a certain amount of accuracy.

Example 4.10

Volume of a Cube

Suppose the side length of a cube is measured to be 5 cm with an accuracy of 0.1 cm.

a. Use differentials to estimate the error in the computed volume of the cube.
b. Compute the volume of the cube if the side length is (i) 4.9 cm and (ii) 5.1 cm to compare the estimated error with the actual potential error.

Solution

a. The measurement of the side length is accurate to within ± 0.1 cm. Therefore,

$$-0.1 \leq dx \leq 0.1.$$

The volume of a cube is given by $V = x^3$, which leads to

$$dV = 3x^2 dx.$$

Using the measured side length of 5 cm, we can estimate that

$$-3(5)^2(0.1) \leq dV \leq 3(5)^2(0.1).$$

Therefore,

$$-7.5 \leq dV \leq 7.5.$$

b. If the side length is actually 4.9 cm, then the volume of the cube is

$$V(4.9) = (4.9)^3 = 117.649 \text{ cm}^3.$$

If the side length is actually 5.1 cm, then the volume of the cube is

$$V(5.1) = (5.1)^3 = 132.651 \text{ cm}^3.$$

Therefore, the actual volume of the cube is between 117.649 and 132.651. Since the side length is measured to be 5 cm, the computed volume is $V(5) = 5^3 = 125.$ Therefore, the error in the computed volume is

$$117.649 - 125 \leq \Delta V \leq 132.651 - 125.$$

That is,

$$-7.351 \leq \Delta V \leq 7.651.$$

We see the estimated error dV is relatively close to the actual potential error in the computed volume.

4.10 Estimate the error in the computed volume of a cube if the side length is measured to be 6 cm with an accuracy of 0.2 cm.

The measurement error dx $(=\Delta x)$ and the propagated error Δy are absolute errors. We are typically interested in the size of an error relative to the size of the quantity being measured or calculated. Given an absolute error Δq for a particular quantity, we define the **relative error** as $\frac{\Delta q}{q},$ where q is the actual value of the quantity. The **percentage error** is the relative error expressed as a percentage. For example, if we measure the height of a ladder to be 63 in. when the actual height is 62 in., the absolute error is 1 in. but the relative error is $\frac{1}{62} = 0.016,$ or $1.6\%.$ By comparison, if we measure the width of a piece of cardboard to be 8.25 in. when the actual width is 8 in., our absolute error is $\frac{1}{4}$ in., whereas the relative error is $\frac{0.25}{8} = \frac{1}{32},$ or $3.1\%.$ Therefore, the percentage error in the measurement of the cardboard is larger, even though 0.25 in. is less than 1 in.

Example 4.11

Relative and Percentage Error

An astronaut using a camera measures the radius of Earth as 4000 mi with an error of ± 80 mi. Let's use differentials to estimate the relative and percentage error of using this radius measurement to calculate the volume of Earth, assuming the planet is a perfect sphere.

Solution

If the measurement of the radius is accurate to within $\pm 80,$ we have

$$-80 \leq dr \leq 80.$$

Since the volume of a sphere is given by $V = \left(\frac{4}{3}\right)\pi r^3,$ we have

$$dV = 4\pi r^2\,dr.$$

Using the measured radius of 4000 mi, we can estimate

$$-4\pi(4000)^2(80) \le dV \le 4\pi(4000)^2(80).$$

To estimate the relative error, consider $\frac{dV}{V}$. Since we do not know the exact value of the volume V, use the measured radius $r = 4000$ mi to estimate V. We obtain $V \approx \left(\frac{4}{3}\right)\pi(4000)^3$. Therefore the relative error satisfies

$$\frac{-4\pi(4000)^2(80)}{4\pi(4000)^3/3} \le \frac{dV}{V} \le \frac{4\pi(4000)^2(80)}{4\pi(4000)^3/3},$$

which simplifies to

$$-0.06 \le \frac{dV}{V} \le 0.06.$$

The relative error is 0.06 and the percentage error is 6%.

4.11 Determine the percentage error if the radius of Earth is measured to be 3950 mi with an error of ± 100 mi.

4.2 EXERCISES

46. What is the linear approximation for any generic linear function $y = mx + b$?

47. Determine the necessary conditions such that the linear approximation function is constant. Use a graph to prove your result.

48. Explain why the linear approximation becomes less accurate as you increase the distance between x and a. Use a graph to prove your argument.

49. When is the linear approximation exact?

For the following exercises, find the linear approximation $L(x)$ to $y = f(x)$ near $x = a$ for the function.

50. **[T]** $f(x) = x + x^4, a = 0$

51. **[T]** $f(x) = \frac{1}{x}, a = 2$

52. **[T]** $f(x) = \tan x, a = \frac{\pi}{4}$

53. **[T]** $f(x) = \sin x, a = \frac{\pi}{2}$

54. **[T]** $f(x) = x\sin x, a = 2\pi$

55. **[T]** $f(x) = \sin^2 x, a = 0$

For the following exercises, compute the values given within 0.01 by deciding on the appropriate $f(x)$ and a, and evaluating $L(x) = f(a) + f'(a)(x - a)$. Check your answer using a calculator.

56. **[T]** $(2.001)^6$

57. **[T]** $\sin(0.02)$

58. **[T]** $\cos(0.03)$

59. **[T]** $(15.99)^{1/4}$

60. **[T]** $\frac{1}{0.98}$

61. **[T]** $\sin(3.14)$

For the following exercises, determine the appropriate $f(x)$ and a, and evaluate $L(x) = f(a) + f'(a)(x - a)$. Calculate the numerical error in the linear approximations that follow.

62. $(1.01)^3$

63. $\cos(0.01)$

64. $(\sin(0.01))^2$

65. $(1.01)^{-3}$

66. $\left(1 + \frac{1}{10}\right)^{10}$

67. $\sqrt{8.99}$

For the following exercises, find the differential of the function.

68. $y = 3x^4 + x^2 - 2x + 1$

69. $y = x\cos x$

70. $y = \sqrt{1 + x}$

71. $y = \frac{x^2 + 2}{x - 1}$

For the following exercises, find the differential and evaluate for the given x and dx.

72. $y = 3x^2 - x + 6, \quad x = 2, \quad dx = 0.1$

73. $y = \frac{1}{x + 1}, \quad x = 1, \quad dx = 0.25$

74. $y = \tan x, \quad x = 0, \quad dx = \frac{\pi}{10}$

75. $y = \frac{3x^2 + 2}{\sqrt{x + 1}}, \quad x = 0, \quad dx = 0.1$

76. $y = \frac{\sin(2x)}{x}, \quad x = \pi, \quad dx = 0.25$

77. $y = x^3 + 2x + \frac{1}{x}, \quad x = 1, \quad dx = 0.05$

For the following exercises, find the change in volume dV or in surface area dA.

78. dV if the sides of a cube change from 10 to 10.1.

79. dA if the sides of a cube change from x to $x + dx$.

80. dA if the radius of a sphere changes from r by dr.

81. dV if the radius of a sphere changes from r by dr.

82. dV if a circular cylinder with $r = 2$ changes height from 3 cm to 3.05 cm.

83. dV if a circular cylinder of height 3 changes from $r = 2$ to $r = 1.9$ cm.

For the following exercises, use differentials to estimate the maximum and relative error when computing the surface area or volume.

84. A spherical golf ball is measured to have a radius of 5 mm, with a possible measurement error of 0.1 mm. What is the possible change in volume?

85. A pool has a rectangular base of 10 ft by 20 ft and a depth of 6 ft. What is the change in volume if you only fill it up to 5.5 ft?

86. An ice cream cone has height 4 in. and radius 1 in. If the cone is 0.1 in. thick, what is the difference between the volume of the cone, including the shell, and the volume of the ice cream you can fit inside the shell?

For the following exercises, confirm the approximations by using the linear approximation at $x = 0$.

87. $\sqrt{1 - x} \approx 1 - \frac{1}{2}x$

88. $\frac{1}{\sqrt{1 - x^2}} \approx 1$

89. $\sqrt{c^2 + x^2} \approx c$

4.3 | Maxima and Minima

Learning Objectives

- **4.3.1** Define absolute extrema.
- **4.3.2** Define local extrema.
- **4.3.3** Explain how to find the critical points of a function over a closed interval.
- **4.3.4** Describe how to use critical points to locate absolute extrema over a closed interval.

Given a particular function, we are often interested in determining the largest and smallest values of the function. This information is important in creating accurate graphs. Finding the maximum and minimum values of a function also has practical significance because we can use this method to solve optimization problems, such as maximizing profit, minimizing the amount of material used in manufacturing an aluminum can, or finding the maximum height a rocket can reach. In this section, we look at how to use derivatives to find the largest and smallest values for a function.

Absolute Extrema

Consider the function $f(x) = x^2 + 1$ over the interval $(-\infty, \infty)$. As $x \to \pm\infty$, $f(x) \to \infty$. Therefore, the function does not have a largest value. However, since $x^2 + 1 \geq 1$ for all real numbers x and $x^2 + 1 = 1$ when $x = 0$, the function has a smallest value, 1, when $x = 0$. We say that 1 is the absolute minimum of $f(x) = x^2 + 1$ and it occurs at $x = 0$. We say that $f(x) = x^2 + 1$ does not have an absolute maximum (see the following figure).

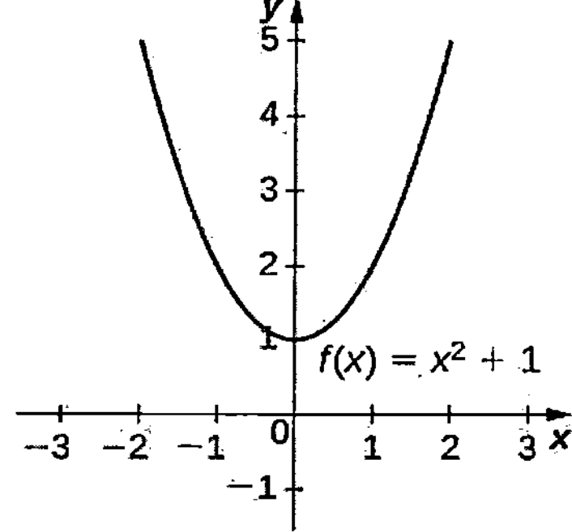

Figure 4.12 The given function has an absolute minimum of 1 at $x = 0$. The function does not have an absolute maximum.

Definition

Let f be a function defined over an interval I and let $c \in I$. We say f has an **absolute maximum** on I at c if $f(c) \geq f(x)$ for all $x \in I$. We say f has an **absolute minimum** on I at c if $f(c) \leq f(x)$ for all $x \in I$. If f has an absolute maximum on I at c or an absolute minimum on I at c, we say f has an **absolute extremum** on I at c.

Before proceeding, let's note two important issues regarding this definition. First, the term *absolute* here does not refer to absolute value. An absolute extremum may be positive, negative, or zero. Second, if a function f has an absolute extremum over an interval I at c, the absolute extremum is $f(c)$. The real number c is a point in the domain at which the absolute extremum occurs. For example, consider the function $f(x) = 1/(x^2 + 1)$ over the interval $(-\infty, \infty)$. Since

$$f(0) = 1 \geq \frac{1}{x^2 + 1} = f(x)$$

for all real numbers x, we say f has an absolute maximum over $(-\infty, \infty)$ at $x = 0$. The absolute maximum is

$f(0) = 1.$ It occurs at $x = 0,$ as shown in **Figure 4.13**(b).

A function may have both an absolute maximum and an absolute minimum, just one extremum, or neither. **Figure 4.13** shows several functions and some of the different possibilities regarding absolute extrema. However, the following theorem, called the **Extreme Value Theorem**, guarantees that a continuous function f over a closed, bounded interval $[a, b]$ has both an absolute maximum and an absolute minimum.

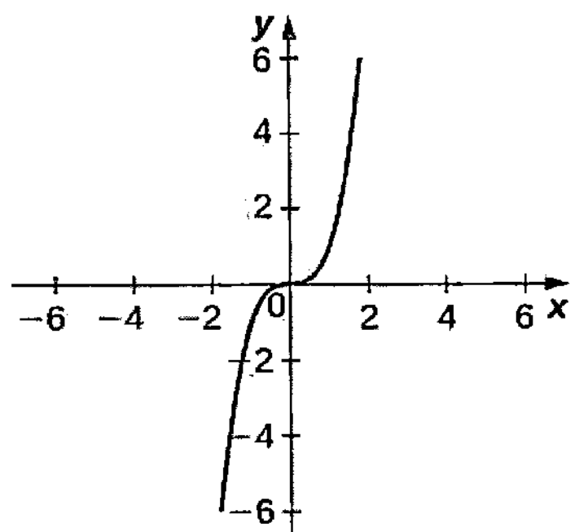

$f(x) = x^3$ on $(-\infty, \infty)$
No absolute maximum
No absolute minimum

(a)

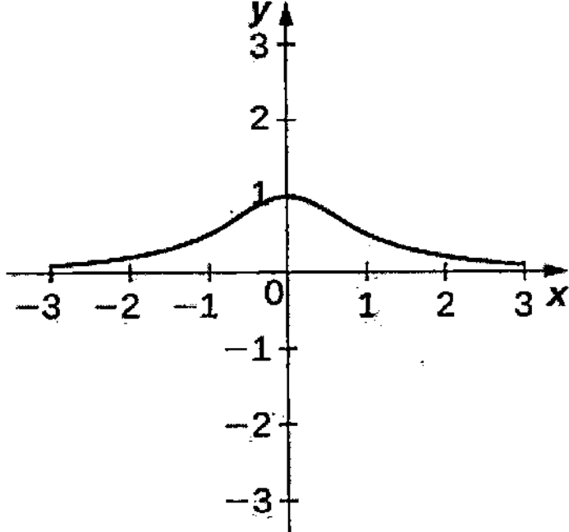

$f(x) = \frac{-1}{x^2+1}$ on $(-\infty, \infty)$
Absolute maximum of 1 at $x = 0$
No absolute minimum

(b)

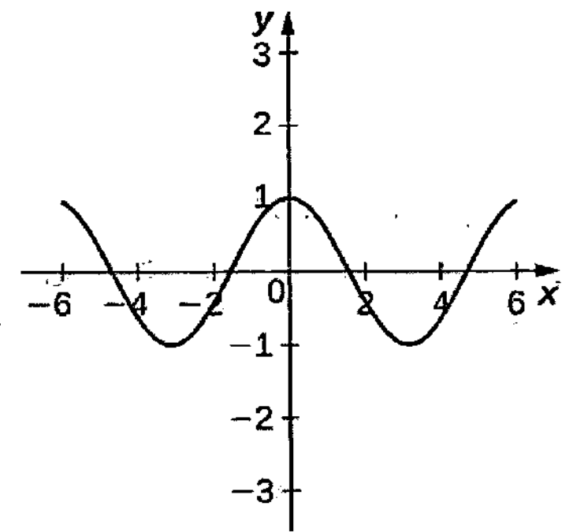

$f(x) = \cos(x)$ on $(-\infty, \infty)$
Absolute maximum of 1 at $x = 0, \pm 2\pi, \pm 4\pi \ldots$
Absolute minimum of -1 at $x = \pm\pi, \pm 3\pi \ldots$

(c)

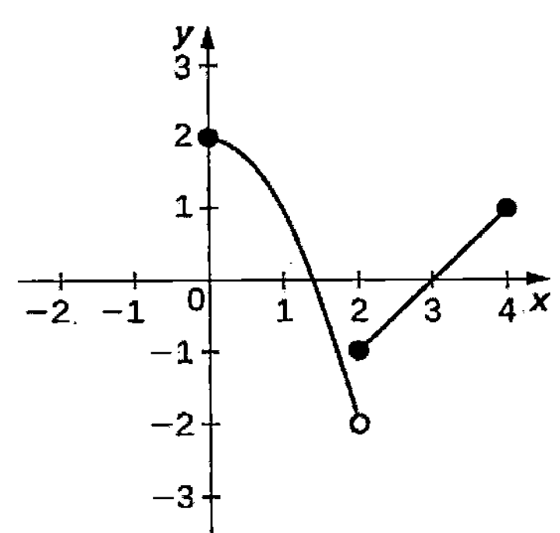

$f(x) = \begin{cases} 2 - x^2 & 0 \le x < 2 \\ x - 3 & 2 \le x \le 4 \end{cases}$
Absolute maximum of 2 at $x = 0$
No absolute minimum

(d)

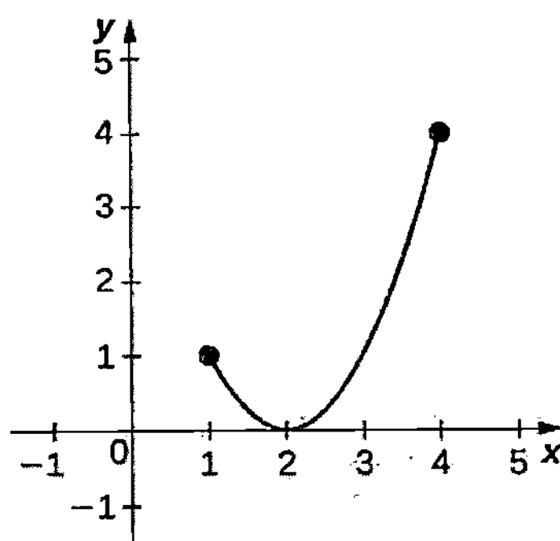

$f(x) = (x - 2)^2$ on $[1, 4]$
Absolute maximum of 4 at $x = 4$
Absolute minimum of 0 at $x = 2$

(e)

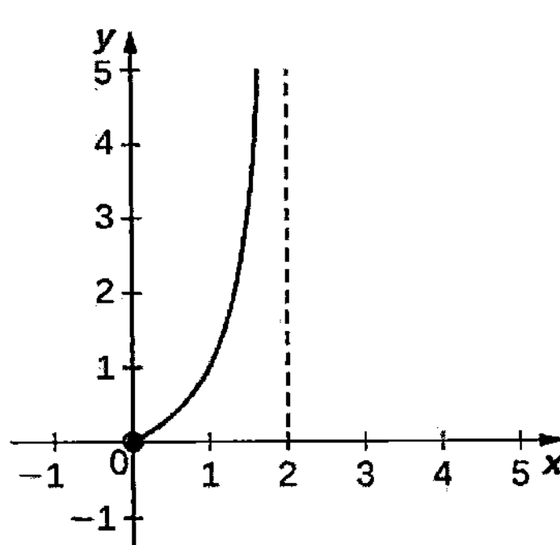

$f(x) = \frac{x}{2-x}$ on $[0, 2)$
No absolute maximum
Absolute minimum of 0 at $x = 0$

(f)

Figure 4.13 Graphs (a), (b), and (c) show several possibilities for absolute extrema for functions with a domain of $(-\infty, \infty)$. Graphs (d), (e), and (f) show several possibilities for absolute extrema for functions with a domain that is a bounded interval.

Theorem 4.1: Extreme Value Theorem

If f is a continuous function over the closed, bounded interval $[a, b]$, then there is a point in $[a, b]$ at which f has an absolute maximum over $[a, b]$ and there is a point in $[a, b]$ at which f has an absolute minimum over $[a, b]$.

The proof of the extreme value theorem is beyond the scope of this text. Typically, it is proved in a course on real analysis. There are a couple of key points to note about the statement of this theorem. For the extreme value theorem to apply, the function must be continuous over a closed, bounded interval. If the interval I is open or the function has even one point of discontinuity, the function may not have an absolute maximum or absolute minimum over I. For example, consider the functions shown in **Figure 4.13**(d), (e), and (f). All three of these functions are defined over bounded intervals. However, the function in graph (e) is the only one that has both an absolute maximum and an absolute minimum over its domain. The extreme value theorem cannot be applied to the functions in graphs (d) and (f) because neither of these functions is continuous over a closed, bounded interval. Although the function in graph (d) is defined over the closed interval $[0, 4]$, the function is discontinuous at $x = 2$. The function has an absolute maximum over $[0, 4]$ but does not have an absolute minimum. The function in graph (f) is continuous over the half-open interval $[0, 2)$, but is not defined at $x = 2$, and therefore is not continuous over a closed, bounded interval. The function has an absolute minimum over $[0, 2)$, but does not have an absolute maximum over $[0, 2)$. These two graphs illustrate why a function over a bounded interval may fail to have an absolute maximum and/or absolute minimum.

Before looking at how to find absolute extrema, let's examine the related concept of local extrema. This idea is useful in determining where absolute extrema occur.

Local Extrema and Critical Points

Consider the function f shown in **Figure 4.14**. The graph can be described as two mountains with a valley in the middle. The absolute maximum value of the function occurs at the higher peak, at $x = 2$. However, $x = 0$ is also a point of interest. Although $f(0)$ is not the largest value of f, the value $f(0)$ is larger than $f(x)$ for all x near 0. We say f has a local maximum at $x = 0$. Similarly, the function f does not have an absolute minimum, but it does have a local minimum at $x = 1$ because $f(1)$ is less than $f(x)$ for x near 1.

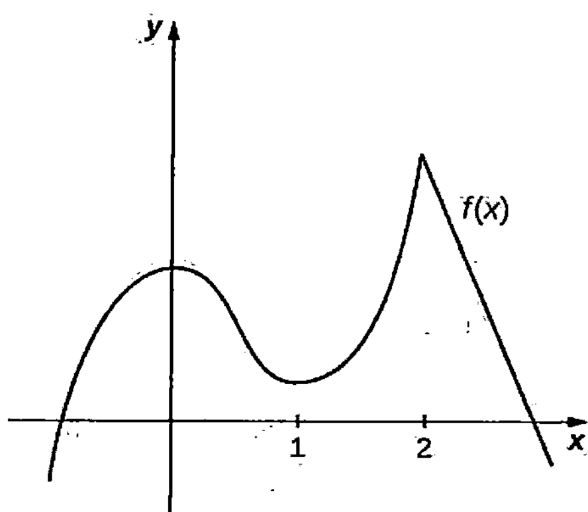

Figure 4.14 This function f has two local maxima and one local minimum. The local maximum at $x = 2$ is also the absolute maximum.

Definition

A function f has a **local maximum** at c if there exists an open interval I containing c such that I is contained in the domain of f and $f(c) \geq f(x)$ for all $x \in I$. A function f has a **local minimum** at c if there exists an open interval I containing c such that I is contained in the domain of f and $f(c) \leq f(x)$ for all $x \in I$. A function f has a **local extremum** at c if f has a local maximum at c or f has a local minimum at c.

Note that if f has an absolute extremum at c and f is defined over an interval containing c, then $f(c)$ is also considered a local extremum. If an absolute extremum for a function f occurs at an endpoint, we do not consider that to be a local extremum, but instead refer to that as an endpoint extremum.

Given the graph of a function f, it is sometimes easy to see where a local maximum or local minimum occurs. However, it is not always easy to see, since the interesting features on the graph of a function may not be visible because they occur at a very small scale. Also, we may not have a graph of the function. In these cases, how can we use a formula for a function to determine where these extrema occur?

To answer this question, let's look at **Figure 4.14** again. The local extrema occur at $x = 0,$ $x = 1,$ and $x = 2.$ Notice that at $x = 0$ and $x = 1,$ the derivative $f'(x) = 0.$ At $x = 2,$ the derivative $f'(x)$ does not exist, since the function f has a corner there. In fact, if f has a local extremum at a point $x = c,$ the derivative $f'(c)$ must satisfy one of the following conditions: either $f'(c) = 0$ or $f'(c)$ is undefined. Such a value c is known as a critical point and it is important in finding extreme values for functions.

Definition

Let c be an interior point in the domain of $f.$ We say that c is a **critical point** of f if $f'(c) = 0$ or $f'(c)$ is undefined.

As mentioned earlier, if f has a local extremum at a point $x = c,$ then c must be a critical point of $f.$ This fact is known as **Fermat's theorem**.

Theorem 4.2: Fermat's Theorem

If f has a local extremum at c and f is differentiable at $c,$ then $f'(c) = 0.$

Proof

Suppose f has a local extremum at c and f is differentiable at $c.$ We need to show that $f'(c) = 0.$ To do this, we will show that $f'(c) \geq 0$ and $f'(c) \leq 0,$ and therefore $f'(c) = 0.$ Since f has a local extremum at $c,$ f has a local maximum or local minimum at $c.$ Suppose f has a local maximum at $c.$ The case in which f has a local minimum at c can be handled similarly. There then exists an open interval I such that $f(c) \geq f(x)$ for all $x \in I.$ Since f is differentiable at $c,$ from the definition of the derivative, we know that

$$f'(c) = \lim_{x \to c} \frac{f(x) - f(c)}{x - c}.$$

Since this limit exists, both one-sided limits also exist and equal $f'(c).$ Therefore,

$$f'(c) = \lim_{x \to c^+} \frac{f(x) - f(c)}{x - c}, \tag{4.4}$$

and

$$f'(c) = \lim_{x \to c^-} \frac{f(x) - f(c)}{x - c}. \tag{4.5}$$

Since $f(c)$ is a local maximum, we see that $f(x) - f(c) \leq 0$ for x near $c.$ Therefore, for x near $c,$ but $x > c,$ we have $\frac{f(x) - f(c)}{x - c} \leq 0.$ From **Equation 4.4** we conclude that $f'(c) \leq 0.$ Similarly, it can be shown that $f'(c) \geq 0.$ Therefore, $f'(c) = 0.$

□

From Fermat's theorem, we conclude that if f has a local extremum at $c,$ then either $f'(c) = 0$ or $f'(c)$ is undefined. In other words, local extrema can only occur at critical points.

Note this theorem does not claim that a function f must have a local extremum at a critical point. Rather, it states that critical points are candidates for local extrema. For example, consider the function $f(x) = x^3$. We have $f'(x) = 3x^2 = 0$ when $x = 0$. Therefore, $x = 0$ is a critical point. However, $f(x) = x^3$ is increasing over $(-\infty, \infty)$, and thus f does not have a local extremum at $x = 0$. In **Figure 4.15**, we see several different possibilities for critical points. In some of these cases, the functions have local extrema at critical points, whereas in other cases the functions do not. Note that these graphs do not show all possibilities for the behavior of a function at a critical point.

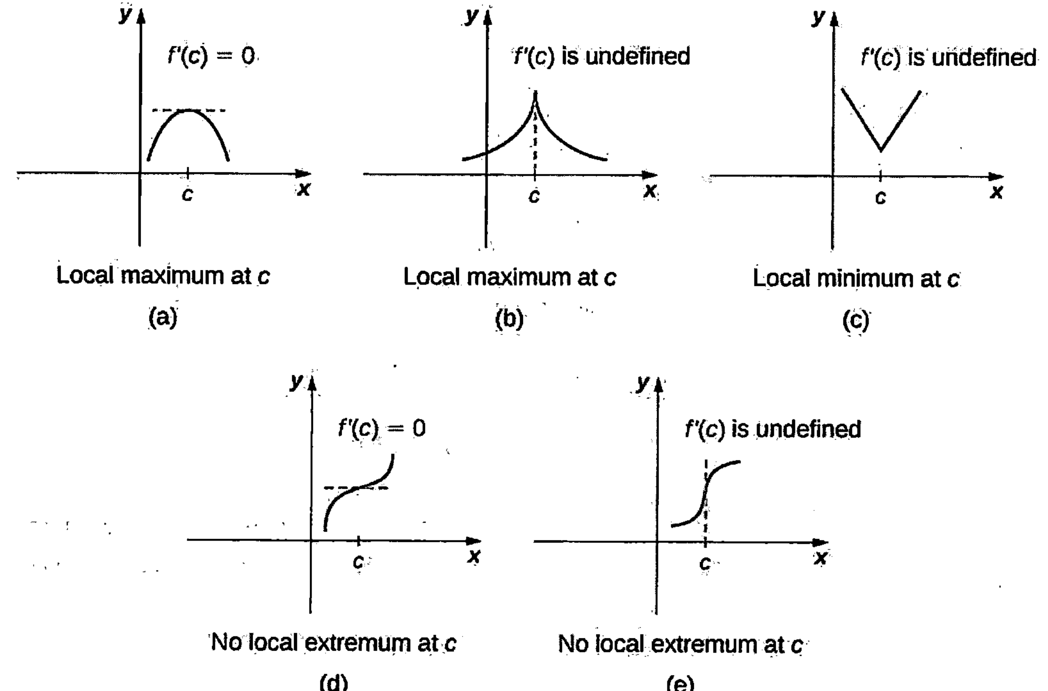

Figure 4.15 (a–e) A function f has a critical point at c if $f'(c) = 0$ or $f'(c)$ is undefined. A function may or may not have a local extremum at a critical point.

Later in this chapter we look at analytical methods for determining whether a function actually has a local extremum at a critical point. For now, let's turn our attention to finding critical points. We will use graphical observations to determine whether a critical point is associated with a local extremum.

Example 4.12

Locating Critical Points

For each of the following functions, find all critical points. Use a graphing utility to determine whether the function has a local extremum at each of the critical points.

a. $f(x) = \frac{1}{3}x^3 - \frac{5}{2}x^2 + 4x$

b. $f(x) = \left(x^2 - 1\right)^3$

c. $f(x) = \frac{4x}{1 + x^2}$

Solution

a. The derivative $f'(x) = x^2 - 5x + 4$ is defined for all real numbers x. Therefore, we only need to find the values for x where $f'(x) = 0$. Since $f'(x) = x^2 - 5x + 4 = (x - 4)(x - 1)$, the critical points are $x = 1$ and $x = 4$. From the graph of f in **Figure 4.16**, we see that f has a local maximum at $x = 1$ and a local minimum at $x = 4$.

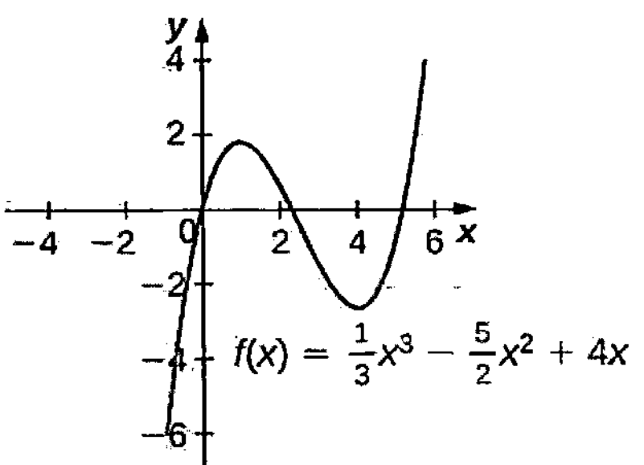

Figure 4.16 This function has a local maximum and a local minimum.

b. Using the chain rule, we see the derivative is

$$f'(x) = 3\left(x^2 - 1\right)^2 (2x) = 6x\left(x^2 - 1\right)^2.$$

Therefore, f has critical points when $x = 0$ and when $x^2 - 1 = 0$. We conclude that the critical points are $x = 0, \pm 1$. From the graph of f in **Figure 4.17**, we see that f has a local (and absolute) minimum at $x = 0$, but does not have a local extremum at $x = 1$ or $x = -1$.

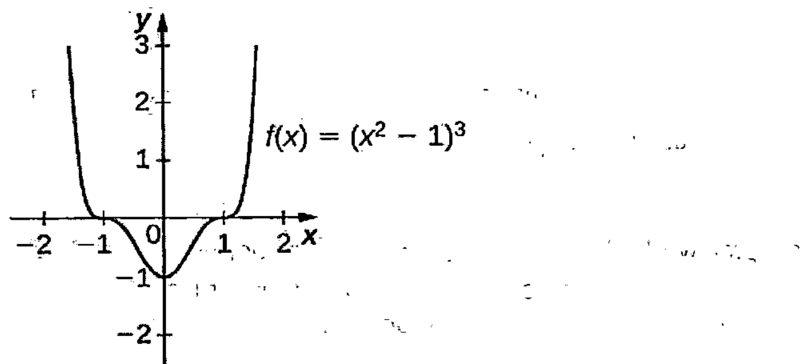

Figure 4.17 This function has three critical points: $x = 0$, $x = 1$, and $x = -1$. The function has a local (and absolute) minimum at $x = 0$, but does not have extrema at the other two critical points.

c. By the chain rule, we see that the derivative is

$$f'(x) = \frac{\left(1 + x^2 4\right) - 4x(2x)}{\left(1 + x^2\right)^2} = \frac{4 - 4x^2}{\left(1 + x^2\right)^2}.$$

The derivative is defined everywhere. Therefore, we only need to find values for x where $f'(x) = 0$. Solving $f'(x) = 0$, we see that $4 - 4x^2 = 0$, which implies $x = \pm 1$. Therefore, the critical points are $x = \pm 1$. From the graph of f in **Figure 4.18**, we see that f has an absolute maximum at $x = 1$

and an absolute minimum at $x = -1$. Hence, f has a local maximum at $x = 1$ and a local minimum at $x = -1$. (Note that if f has an absolute extremum over an interval I at a point c that is not an endpoint of I, then f has a local extremum at c.)

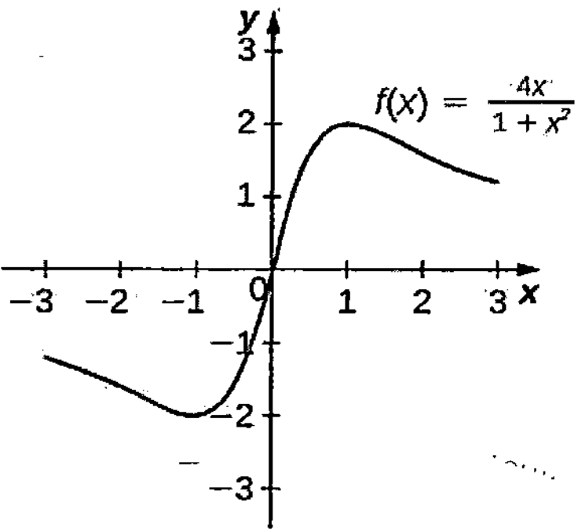

Figure 4.18 This function has an absolute maximum and an absolute minimum.

4.12 Find all critical points for $f(x) = x^3 - \frac{1}{2}x^2 - 2x + 1$.

Locating Absolute Extrema

The extreme value theorem states that a continuous function over a closed, bounded interval has an absolute maximum and an absolute minimum. As shown in **Figure 4.13**, one or both of these absolute extrema could occur at an endpoint. If an absolute extremum does not occur at an endpoint, however, it must occur at an interior point, in which case the absolute extremum is a local extremum. Therefore, by **Fermat's Theorem**, the point c at which the local extremum occurs must be a critical point. We summarize this result in the following theorem.

Theorem 4.3: Location of Absolute Extrema

Let f be a continuous function over a closed, bounded interval I. The absolute maximum of f over I and the absolute minimum of f over I must occur at endpoints of I or at critical points of f in I.

With this idea in mind, let's examine a procedure for locating absolute extrema.

Problem-Solving Strategy: Locating Absolute Extrema over a Closed Interval

Consider a continuous function f defined over the closed interval $[a, b]$.

1. Evaluate f at the endpoints $x = a$ and $x = b$.
2. Find all critical points of f that lie over the interval (a, b) and evaluate f at those critical points.
3. Compare all values found in (1) and (2). From **Location of Absolute Extrema**, the absolute extrema must occur at endpoints or critical points. Therefore, the largest of these values is the absolute maximum of f. The smallest of these values is the absolute minimum of f.

Now let's look at how to use this strategy to find the absolute maximum and absolute minimum values for continuous functions.

Example 4.13

Locating Absolute Extrema

For each of the following functions, find the absolute maximum and absolute minimum over the specified interval and state where those values occur.

a. $f(x) = -x^2 + 3x - 2$ over $[1, 3]$.

b. $f(x) = x^2 - 3x^{2/3}$ over $[0, 2]$.

Solution

a. Step 1. Evaluate f at the endpoints $x = 1$ and $x = 3$.

$$f(1) = 0 \text{ and } f(3) = -2$$

Step 2. Since $f'(x) = -2x + 3$, f' is defined for all real numbers x. Therefore, there are no critical points where the derivative is undefined. It remains to check where $f'(x) = 0$. Since $f'(x) = -2x + 3 = 0$ at $x = \frac{3}{2}$ and $\frac{3}{2}$ is in the interval $[1, 3]$, $f\left(\frac{3}{2}\right)$ is a candidate for an absolute extremum of f over $[1, 3]$. We evaluate $f\left(\frac{3}{2}\right)$ and find

$$f\left(\frac{3}{2}\right) = \frac{1}{4}.$$

Step 3. We set up the following table to compare the values found in steps 1 and 2.

x	$f(x)$	Conclusion
0	0	
$\frac{3}{2}$	$\frac{1}{4}$	Absolute maximum
3	-2	Absolute minimum

From the table, we find that the absolute maximum of f over the interval [1, 3] is $\frac{1}{4}$, and it occurs at $x = \frac{3}{2}$. The absolute minimum of f over the interval [1, 3] is -2, and it occurs at $x = 3$ as shown in the following graph.

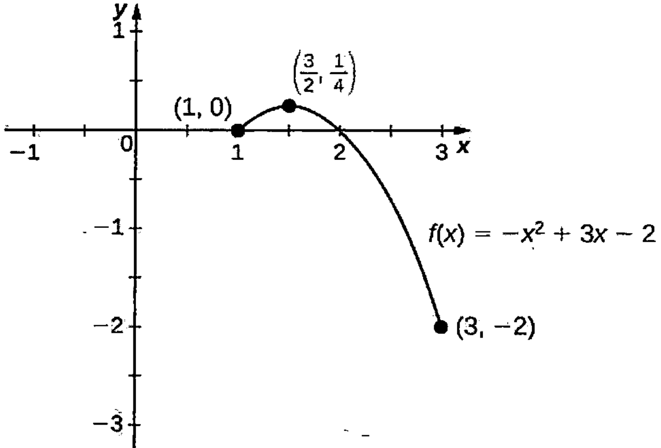

Figure 4.19 This function has both an absolute maximum and an absolute minimum.

b. Step 1. Evaluate f at the endpoints $x = 0$ and $x = 2$.

$$f(0) = 0 \text{ and } f(2) = 4 - 3\sqrt[3]{4} \approx -0.762$$

Step 2. The derivative of f is given by

$$f'(x) = 2x - \frac{2}{x^{1/3}} = \frac{2x^{4/3} - 2}{x^{1/3}}$$

for $x \neq 0$. The derivative is zero when $2x^{4/3} - 2 = 0$, which implies $x = \pm 1$. The derivative is undefined at $x = 0$. Therefore, the critical points of f are $x = 0, 1, -1$. The point $x = 0$ is an endpoint, so we already evaluated $f(0)$ in step 1. The point $x = -1$ is not in the interval of interest, so we need only evaluate $f(1)$. We find that

$$f(1) = -2.$$

Step 3. We compare the values found in steps 1 and 2, in the following table.

x	$f(x)$	**Conclusion**
0	0	Absolute maximum
1	−2	Absolute minimum
2	−0.762	

We conclude that the absolute maximum of f over the interval [0, 2] is zero, and it occurs at $x = 0$. The absolute minimum is −2, and it occurs at $x = 1$ as shown in the following graph.

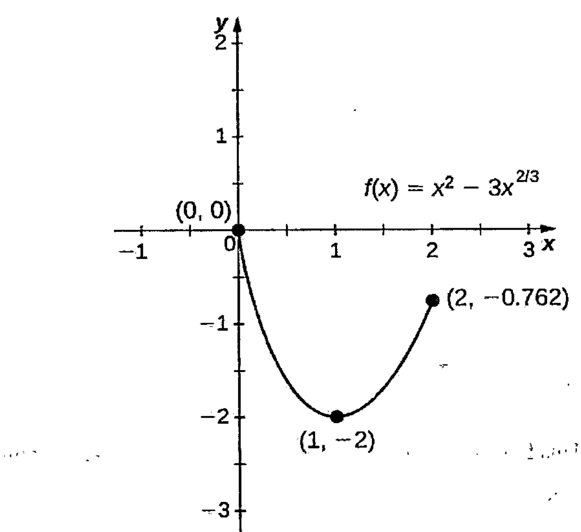

Figure 4.20 This function has an absolute maximum at an endpoint of the interval.

4.13 Find the absolute maximum and absolute minimum of $f(x) = x^2 - 4x + 3$ over the interval $[1, 4]$.

At this point, we know how to locate absolute extrema for continuous functions over closed intervals. We have also defined local extrema and determined that if a function f has a local extremum at a point $c,$ then c must be a critical point of $f.$ However, c being a critical point is not a sufficient condition for f to have a local extremum at $c.$ Later in this chapter, we show how to determine whether a function actually has a local extremum at a critical point. First, however, we need to introduce the Mean Value Theorem, which will help as we analyze the behavior of the graph of a function.

4.3 EXERCISES

90. In precalculus, you learned a formula for the position of the maximum or minimum of a quadratic equation $y = ax^2 + bx + c$, which was $m = -\frac{b}{(2a)}$. Prove this formula using calculus.

91. If you are finding an absolute minimum over an interval $[a, b]$, why do you need to check the endpoints? Draw a graph that supports your hypothesis.

92. If you are examining a function over an interval (a, b), for a and b finite, is it possible not to have an absolute maximum or absolute minimum?

93. When you are checking for critical points, explain why you also need to determine points where $f(x)$ is undefined. Draw a graph to support your explanation.

94. Can you have a finite absolute maximum for $y = ax^2 + bx + c$ over $(-\infty, \infty)$? Explain why or why not using graphical arguments.

95. Can you have a finite absolute maximum for $y = ax^3 + bx^2 + cx + d$ over $(-\infty, \infty)$ assuming a is non-zero? Explain why or why not using graphical arguments.

96. Let m be the number of local minima and M be the number of local maxima. Can you create a function where $M > m + 2$? Draw a graph to support your explanation.

97. Is it possible to have more than one absolute maximum? Use a graphical argument to prove your hypothesis.

98. Is it possible to have no absolute minimum or maximum for a function? If so, construct such a function. If not, explain why this is not possible.

99. **[T]** Graph the function $y = e^{ax}$. For which values of a, on any infinite domain, will you have an absolute minimum and absolute maximum?

For the following exercises, determine where the local and absolute maxima and minima occur on the graph given. Assume domains are closed intervals unless otherwise specified.

100.

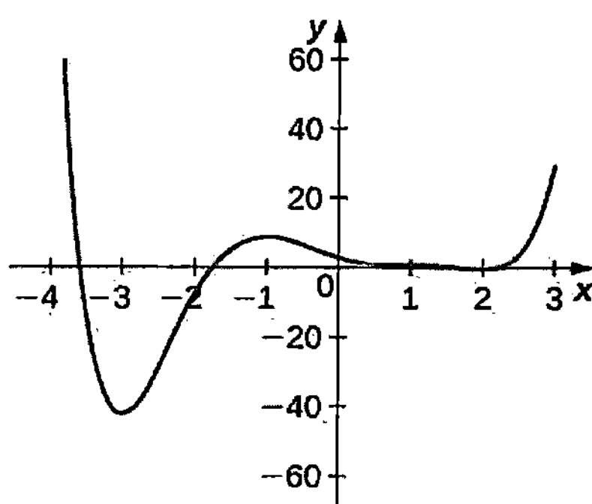

101.

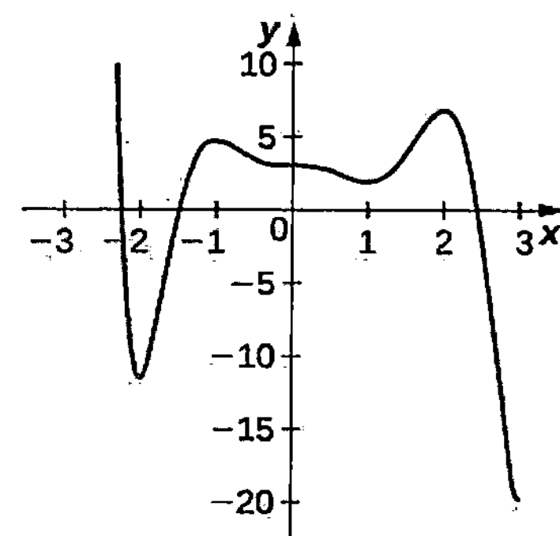

102.

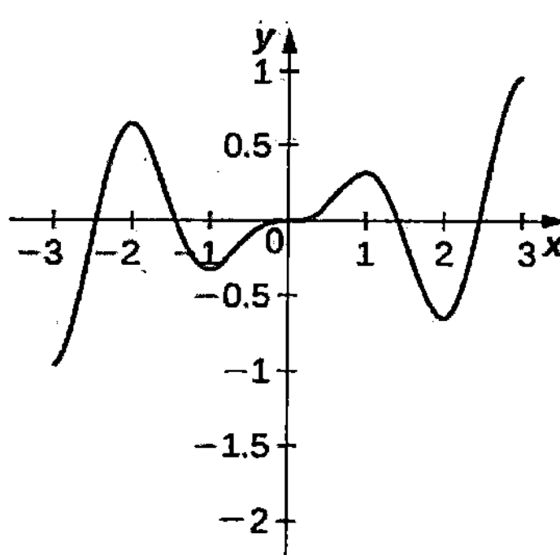

103.

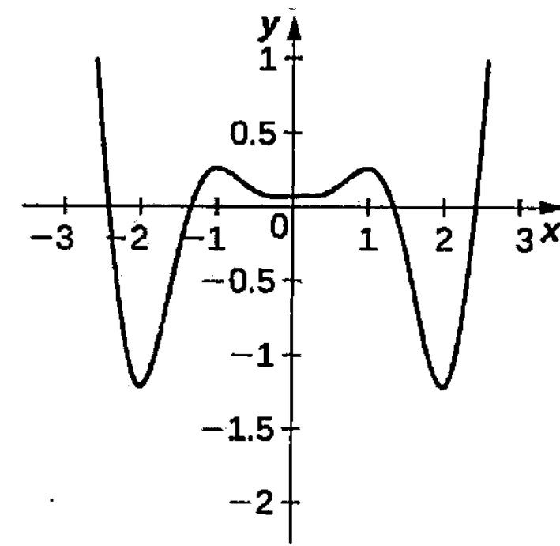

For the following problems, draw graphs of $f(x)$, which is continuous, over the interval $[-4, 4]$ with the following properties:

104. Absolute maximum at $x = 2$ and absolute minima at $x = \pm 3$

105. Absolute minimum at $x = 1$ and absolute maximum at $x = 2$

106. Absolute maximum at $x = 4$, absolute minimum at $x = -1$, local maximum at $x = -2$, and a critical point that is not a maximum or minimum at $x = 2$

107. Absolute maxima at $x = 2$ and $x = -3$, local minimum at $x = 1$, and absolute minimum at $x = 4$

For the following exercises, find the critical points in the domains of the following functions.

108. $y = 4x^3 - 3x$

109. $y = 4\sqrt{x} - x^2$

110. $y = \frac{1}{x-1}$

111. $y = \ln(x-2)$

112. $y = \tan(x)$

113. $y = \sqrt{4 - x^2}$

114. $y = x^{3/2} - 3x^{5/2}$

115. $y = \frac{x^2 - 1}{x^2 + 2x - 3}$

116. $y = \sin^2(x)$

117. $y = x + \frac{1}{x}$

For the following exercises, find the local and/or absolute maxima for the functions over the specified domain.

118. $f(x) = x^2 + 3$ over $[-1, 4]$

119. $y = x^2 + \frac{2}{x}$ over $[1, 4]$

120. $y = \left(x - x^2\right)^2$ over $[-1, 1]$

121. $y = \frac{1}{\left(x - x^2\right)}$ over $[0, 1]$

122. $y = \sqrt{9 - x}$ over $[1, 9]$

123. $y = x + \sin(x)$ over $[0, 2\pi]$

124. $y = \frac{x}{1+x}$ over $[0, 100]$

125. $y = |x+1| + |x-1|$ over $[-3, 2]$

126. $y = \sqrt{x} - \sqrt{x^3}$ over $[0, 4]$

127. $y = \sin x + \cos x$ over $[0, 2\pi]$

128. $y = 4\sin\theta - 3\cos\theta$ over $[0, 2\pi]$

For the following exercises, find the local and absolute minima and maxima for the functions over $(-\infty, \infty)$.

129. $y = x^2 + 4x + 5$

130. $y = x^3 - 12x$

131. $y = 3x^4 + 8x^3 - 18x^2$

132. $y = x^3(1-x)^6$

133. $y = \frac{x^2 + x + 6}{x - 1}$

134. $y = \frac{x^2 - 1}{x - 1}$

For the following functions, use a calculator to graph the function and to estimate the absolute and local maxima and minima. Then, solve for them explicitly.

135. **[T]** $y = 3x\sqrt{1 - x^2}$

136. **[T]** $y = x + \sin(x)$

137. **[T]** $y = 12x^5 + 45x^4 + 20x^3 - 90x^2 - 120x + 3$

138. **[T]** $y = \frac{x^3 + 6x^2 - x - 30}{x - 2}$

139. **[T]** $y = \frac{\sqrt{4 - x^2}}{\sqrt{4 + x^2}}$

140. A company that produces cell phones has a cost function of $C = x^2 - 1200x + 36{,}400$, where C is cost in dollars and x is number of cell phones produced (in thousands). How many units of cell phone (in thousands) minimizes this cost function?

141. A ball is thrown into the air and its position is given by $h(t) = -4.9t^2 + 60t + 5$ m. Find the height at which the ball stops ascending. How long after it is thrown does this happen?

For the following exercises, consider the production of gold during the California gold rush (1848–1888). The production of gold can be modeled by $G(t) = \frac{(25t)}{(t^2 + 16)}$, where t is the number of years since the rush began $(0 \leq t \leq 40)$ and G is ounces of gold produced (in millions). A summary of the data is shown in the following figure.

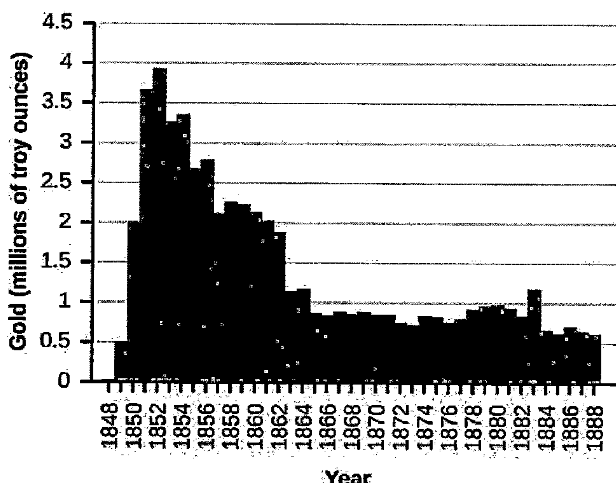

142. Find when the maximum (local and global) gold production occurred, and the amount of gold produced during that maximum.

143. Find when the minimum (local and global) gold production occurred. What was the amount of gold produced during this minimum?

Find the critical points, maxima, and minima for the following piecewise functions.

144. $y = \begin{cases} x^2 - 4x & 0 \leq x \leq 1 \\ x^2 - 4 & 1 < x \leq 2 \end{cases}$

145. $y = \begin{cases} x^2 + 1 & x \leq 1 \\ x^2 - 4x + 5 & x > 1 \end{cases}$

For the following exercises, find the critical points of the following generic functions. Are they maxima, minima, or neither? State the necessary conditions.

146. $y = ax^2 + bx + c$, given that $a > 0$

147. $y = (x - 1)^a$, given that $a > 1$

4.4 | The Mean Value Theorem

Learning Objectives

4.4.1 Explain the meaning of Rolle's theorem.
4.4.2 Describe the significance of the Mean Value Theorem.
4.4.3 State three important consequences of the Mean Value Theorem.

The **Mean Value Theorem** is one of the most important theorems in calculus. We look at some of its implications at the end of this section. First, let's start with a special case of the Mean Value Theorem, called Rolle's theorem.

Rolle's Theorem

Informally, **Rolle's theorem** states that if the outputs of a differentiable function f are equal at the endpoints of an interval, then there must be an interior point c where $f'(c) = 0.$ Figure 4.21 illustrates this theorem.

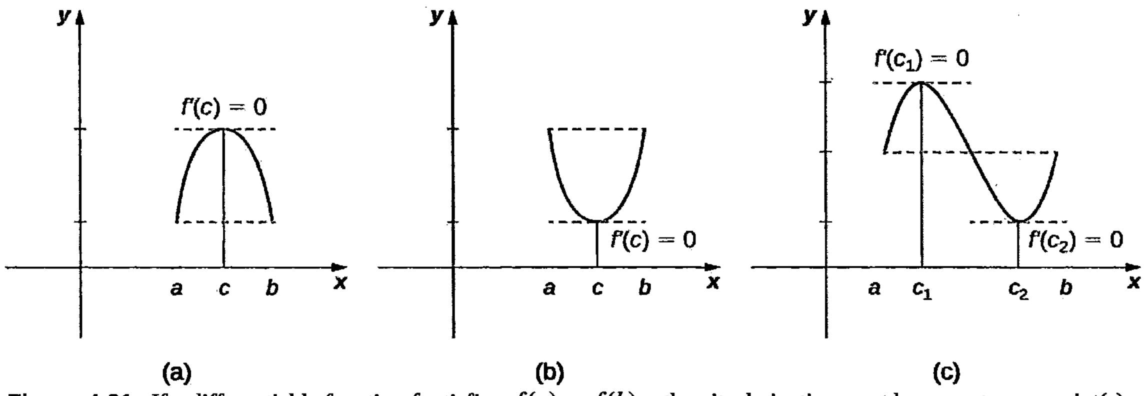

Figure 4.21 If a differentiable function f satisfies $f(a) = f(b),$ then its derivative must be zero at some point(s) between a and b.

Theorem 4.4: Rolle's Theorem

Let f be a continuous function over the closed interval $[a, b]$ and differentiable over the open interval (a, b) such that $f(a) = f(b).$ There then exists at least one $c \in (a, b)$ such that $f'(c) = 0.$

Proof

Let $k = f(a) = f(b).$ We consider three cases:

1. $f(x) = k$ for all $x \in (a, b).$
2. There exists $x \in (a, b)$ such that $f(x) > k.$
3. There exists $x \in (a, b)$ such that $f(x) < k.$

Case 1: If $f(x) = 0$ for all $x \in (a, b),$ then $f'(x) = 0$ for all $x \in (a, b).$

Case 2: Since f is a continuous function over the closed, bounded interval $[a, b],$ by the extreme value theorem, it has an absolute maximum. Also, since there is a point $x \in (a, b)$ such that $f(x) > k,$ the absolute maximum is greater than $k.$ Therefore, the absolute maximum does not occur at either endpoint. As a result, the absolute maximum must occur at an interior point $c \in (a, b).$ Because f has a maximum at an interior point $c,$ and f is differentiable at $c,$ by Fermat's theorem, $f'(c) = 0.$

Case 3: The case when there exists a point $x \in (a, b)$ such that $f(x) < k$ is analogous to case 2, with maximum replaced by minimum.

□

An important point about Rolle's theorem is that the differentiability of the function f is critical. If f is not differentiable, even at a single point, the result may not hold. For example, the function $f(x) = |x| - 1$ is continuous over $[-1, 1]$ and $f(-1) = 0 = f(1)$, but $f'(c) \neq 0$ for any $c \in (-1, 1)$ as shown in the following figure.

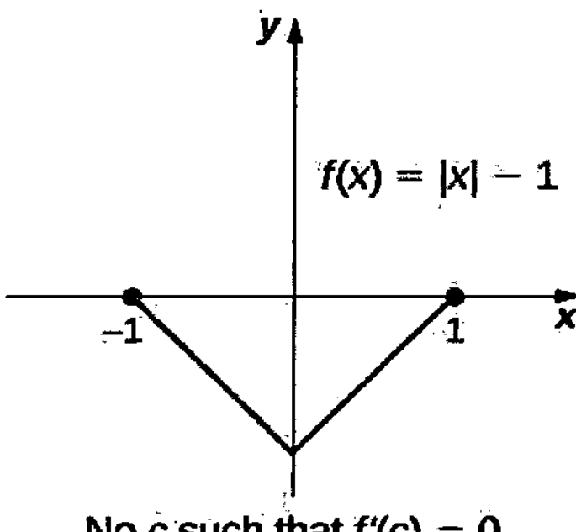

Figure 4.22 Since $f(x) = |x| - 1$ is not differentiable at $x = 0$, the conditions of Rolle's theorem are not satisfied. In fact, the conclusion does not hold here; there is no $c \in (-1, 1)$ such that $f'(c) = 0$.

Let's now consider functions that satisfy the conditions of Rolle's theorem and calculate explicitly the points c where $f'(c) = 0$.

Example 4.14

Using Rolle's Theorem

For each of the following functions, verify that the function satisfies the criteria stated in Rolle's theorem and find all values c in the given interval where $f'(c) = 0$.

a. $f(x) = x^2 + 2x$ over $[-2, 0]$

b. $f(x) = x^3 - 4x$ over $[-2, 2]$

Solution

a. Since f is a polynomial, it is continuous and differentiable everywhere. In addition, $f(-2) = 0 = f(0)$. Therefore, f satisfies the criteria of Rolle's theorem. We conclude that there exists at least one value $c \in (-2, 0)$ such that $f'(c) = 0$. Since $f'(x) = 2x + 2 = 2(x + 1)$, we see that $f'(c) = 2(c + 1) = 0$ implies $c = -1$ as shown in the following graph.

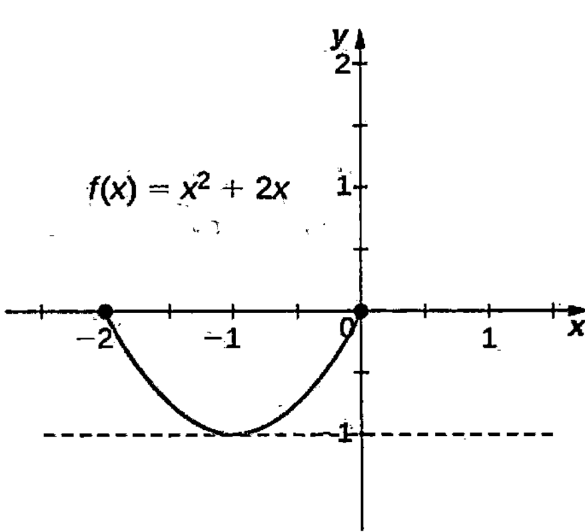

Figure 4.23 This function is continuous and differentiable over $[-2, 0]$, $f'(c) = 0$ when $c = -1$.

b. As in part a. f is a polynomial and therefore is continuous and differentiable everywhere. Also, $f(-2) = 0 = f(2)$. That said, f satisfies the criteria of Rolle's theorem. Differentiating, we find that $f'(x) = 3x^2 - 4$. Therefore, $f'(c) = 0$ when $x = \pm\frac{2}{\sqrt{3}}$. Both points are in the interval $[-2, 2]$, and, therefore, both points satisfy the conclusion of Rolle's theorem as shown in the following graph.

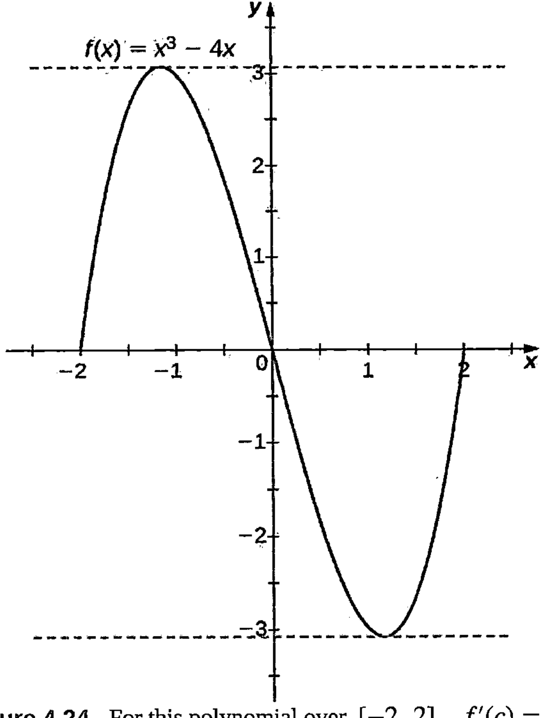

Figure 4.24 For this polynomial over $[-2, 2]$, $f'(c) = 0$ at $x = \pm 2/\sqrt{3}$.

4.14 Verify that the function $f(x) = 2x^2 - 8x + 6$ defined over the interval $[1, 3]$ satisfies the conditions of Rolle's theorem. Find all points c guaranteed by Rolle's theorem.

The Mean Value Theorem and Its Meaning

Rolle's theorem is a special case of the Mean Value Theorem. In Rolle's theorem, we consider differentiable functions f defined on a closed interval $[a, b]$ with $f(a) = f(b)$. The Mean Value Theorem generalizes Rolle's theorem by considering functions that do not necessarily have equal value at the endpoints. Consequently, we can view the Mean Value Theorem as a slanted version of Rolle's theorem (**Figure 4.25**). The Mean Value Theorem states that if f is continuous over the closed interval $[a, b]$ and differentiable over the open interval $(a, b),$ then there exists a point $c \in (a, b)$ such that the tangent line to the graph of f at c is parallel to the secant line connecting $(a, f(a))$ and $(b, f(b))$.

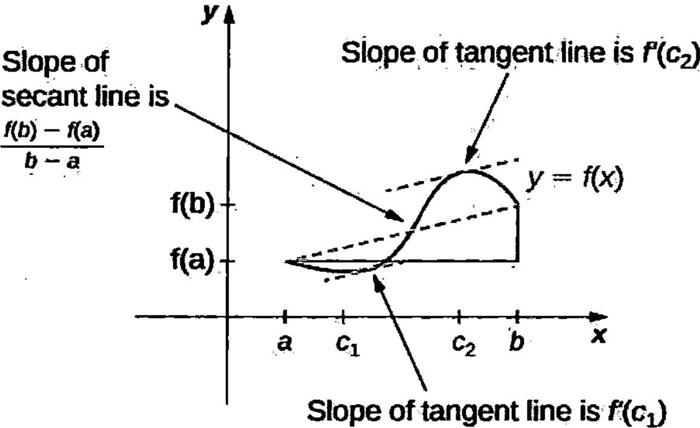

Figure 4.25 The Mean Value Theorem says that for a function that meets its conditions, at some point the tangent line has the same slope as the secant line between the ends. For this function, there are two values c_1 and c_2 such that the tangent line to f at c_1 and c_2 has the same slope as the secant line.

Theorem 4.5: Mean Value Theorem

Let f be continuous over the closed interval $[a, b]$ and differentiable over the open interval (a, b). Then, there exists at least one point $c \in (a, b)$ such that

$$f'(c) = \frac{f(b) - f(a)}{b - a}.$$

Proof

The proof follows from Rolle's theorem by introducing an appropriate function that satisfies the criteria of Rolle's theorem. Consider the line connecting $(a, f(a))$ and $(b, f(b))$. Since the slope of that line is

$$\frac{f(b) - f(a)}{b - a}$$

and the line passes through the point $(a, f(a)),$ the equation of that line can be written as

$$y = \frac{f(b) - f(a)}{b - a}(x - a) + f(a).$$

Let $g(x)$ denote the vertical difference between the point $(x, f(x))$ and the point (x, y) on that line. Therefore,

$$g(x) = f(x) - \left[\frac{f(b) - f(a)}{b - a}(x - a) + f(a)\right].$$

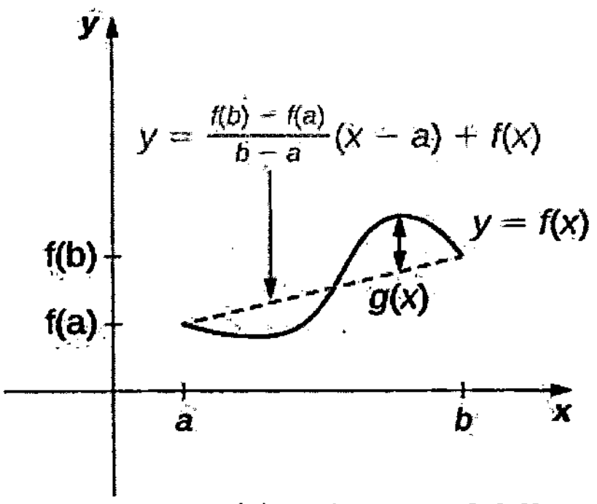

Figure 4.26 The value $g(x)$ is the vertical difference between the point $(x, f(x))$ and the point (x, y) on the secant line connecting $(a, f(a))$ and $(b, f(b))$.

Since the graph of f intersects the secant line when $x = a$ and $x = b$, we see that $g(a) = 0 = g(b)$. Since f is a differentiable function over (a, b), g is also a differentiable function over (a, b). Furthermore, since f is continuous over $[a, b]$, g is also continuous over $[a, b]$. Therefore, g satisfies the criteria of Rolle's theorem. Consequently, there exists a point $c \in (a, b)$ such that $g'(c) = 0$. Since

$$g'(x) = f'(x) - \frac{f(b) - f(a)}{b - a},$$

we see that

$$g'(c) = f'(c) - \frac{f(b) - f(a)}{b - a}.$$

Since $g'(c) = 0$, we conclude that

$$f'(c) = \frac{f(b) - f(a)}{b - a}.$$

□

In the next example, we show how the Mean Value Theorem can be applied to the function $f(x) = \sqrt{x}$ over the interval $[0, 9]$. The method is the same for other functions, although sometimes with more interesting consequences.

Example 4.15

Verifying that the Mean Value Theorem Applies

For $f(x) = \sqrt{x}$ over the interval $[0, 9]$, show that f satisfies the hypothesis of the Mean Value Theorem, and therefore there exists at least one value $c \in (0, 9)$ such that $f'(c)$ is equal to the slope of the line connecting $(0, f(0))$ and $(9, f(9))$. Find these values c guaranteed by the Mean Value Theorem.

Solution

We know that $f(x) = \sqrt{x}$ is continuous over $[0, 9]$ and differentiable over $(0, 9)$. Therefore, f satisfies the hypotheses of the Mean Value Theorem, and there must exist at least one value $c \in (0, 9)$ such that $f'(c)$ is equal to the slope of the line connecting $(0, f(0))$ and $(9, f(9))$ (**Figure 4.27**). To determine which value(s) of c are guaranteed, first calculate the derivative of f. The derivative $f'(x) = \frac{1}{(2\sqrt{x})}$. The slope of the line connecting $(0, f(0))$ and $(9, f(9))$ is given by

$$\frac{f(9) - f(0)}{9 - 0} = \frac{\sqrt{9} - \sqrt{0}}{9 - 0} = \frac{3}{9} = \frac{1}{3}.$$

We want to find c such that $f'(c) = \frac{1}{3}$. That is, we want to find c such that

$$\frac{1}{2\sqrt{c}} = \frac{1}{3}.$$

Solving this equation for c, we obtain $c = \frac{9}{4}$. At this point, the slope of the tangent line equals the slope of the line joining the endpoints.

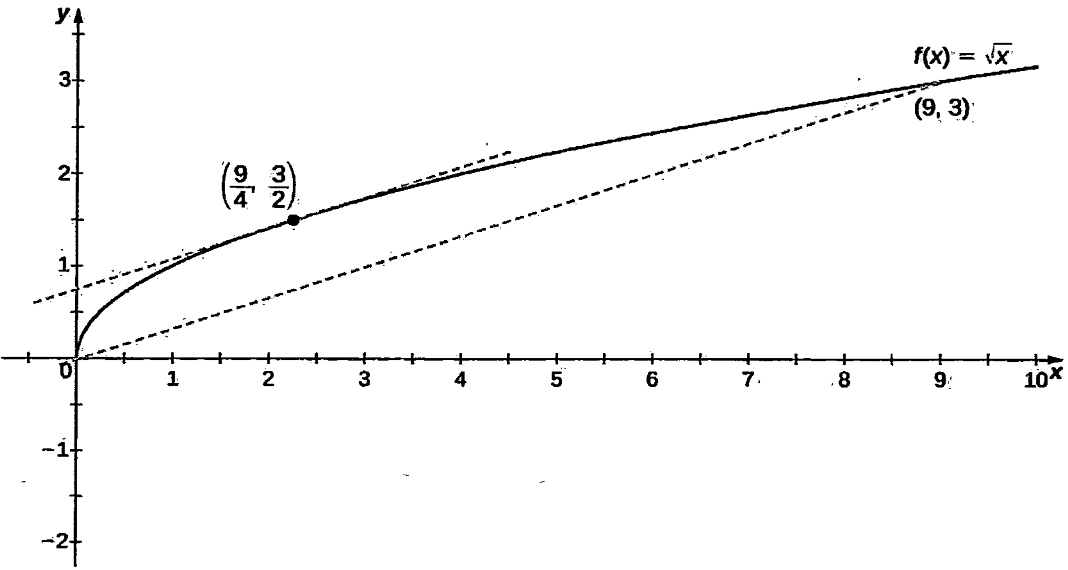

Figure 4.27 The slope of the tangent line at $c = 9/4$ is the same as the slope of the line segment connecting $(0, 0)$ and $(9, 3)$.

One application that helps illustrate the Mean Value Theorem involves velocity. For example, suppose we drive a car for 1 h down a straight road with an average velocity of 45 mph. Let $s(t)$ and $v(t)$ denote the position and velocity of the car, respectively, for $0 \le t \le 1$ h. Assuming that the position function $s(t)$ is differentiable, we can apply the Mean Value Theorem to conclude that, at some time $c \in (0, 1)$, the speed of the car was exactly

$$v(c) = s'(c) = \frac{s(1) - s(0)}{1 - 0} = 45 \text{ mph}.$$

Example 4.16

Mean Value Theorem and Velocity

If a rock is dropped from a height of 100 ft, its position t seconds after it is dropped until it hits the ground is given by the function $s(t) = -16t^2 + 100$.

a. Determine how long it takes before the rock hits the ground.

b. Find the average velocity v_{avg} of the rock for when the rock is released and the rock hits the ground.

c. Find the time t guaranteed by the Mean Value Theorem when the instantaneous velocity of the rock is v_{avg}.

Solution

a. When the rock hits the ground, its position is $s(t) = 0$. Solving the equation $-16t^2 + 100 = 0$ for t, we find that $t = \pm\frac{5}{2}$ sec. Since we are only considering $t \geq 0$, the ball will hit the ground $\frac{5}{2}$ sec after it is dropped.

b. The average velocity is given by

$$v_{avg} = \frac{s(5/2) - s(0)}{5/2 - 0} = \frac{1 - 100}{5/2} = -40 \text{ ft/sec.}$$

c. The instantaneous velocity is given by the derivative of the position function. Therefore, we need to find a time t such that $v(t) = s'(t) = v_{avg} = -40$ ft/sec. Since $s(t)$ is continuous over the interval $[0, 5/2]$ and differentiable over the interval $(0, 5/2)$, by the Mean Value Theorem, there is guaranteed to be a point $c \in (0, 5/2)$ such that

$$s'(c) = \frac{s(5/2) - s(0)}{5/2 - 0} = -40.$$

Taking the derivative of the position function $s(t)$, we find that $s'(t) = -32t$. Therefore, the equation reduces to $s'(c) = -32c = -40$. Solving this equation for c, we have $c = \frac{5}{4}$. Therefore, $\frac{5}{4}$ sec after the rock is dropped, the instantaneous velocity equals the average velocity of the rock during its free fall: -40 ft/sec.

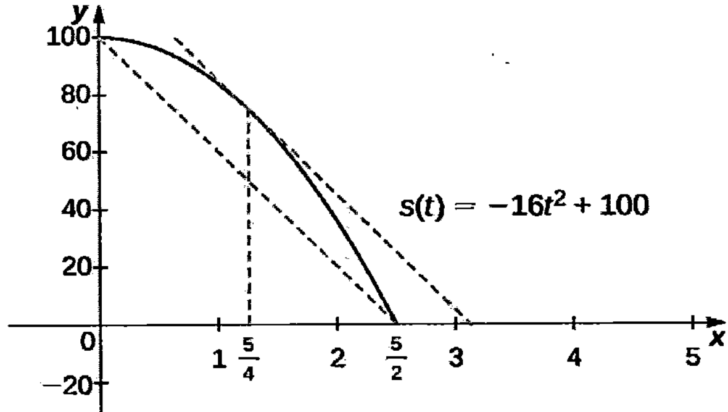

Figure 4.28 At time $t = 5/4$ sec, the velocity of the rock is equal to its average velocity from the time it is dropped until it hits the ground.

4.15 Suppose a ball is dropped from a height of 200 ft. Its position at time t is $s(t) = -16t^2 + 200$. Find the time t when the instantaneous velocity of the ball equals its average velocity.

Corollaries of the Mean Value Theorem

Let's now look at three corollaries of the Mean Value Theorem. These results have important consequences, which we use in upcoming sections.

At this point, we know the derivative of any constant function is zero. The Mean Value Theorem allows us to conclude that the converse is also true. In particular, if $f'(x) = 0$ for all x in some interval $I,$ then $f(x)$ is constant over that interval. This result may seem intuitively obvious, but it has important implications that are not obvious, and we discuss them shortly.

Theorem 4.6: Corollary 1: Functions with a Derivative of Zero

Let f be differentiable over an interval $I.$ If $f'(x) = 0$ for all $x \in I,$ then $f(x) =$ constant for all $x \in I.$

Proof

Since f is differentiable over $I,$ f must be continuous over $I.$ Suppose $f(x)$ is not constant for all x in $I.$ Then there exist $a, b \in I,$ where $a \neq b$ and $f(a) \neq f(b).$ Choose the notation so that $a < b.$ Therefore,

$$\frac{f(b) - f(a)}{b - a} \neq 0.$$

Since f is a differentiable function, by the Mean Value Theorem, there exists $c \in (a, b)$ such that

$$f'(c) = \frac{f(b) - f(a)}{b - a}.$$

Therefore, there exists $c \in I$ such that $f'(c) \neq 0,$ which contradicts the assumption that $f'(x) = 0$ for all $x \in I.$

□

From **Corollary 1: Functions with a Derivative of Zero**, it follows that if two functions have the same derivative, they differ by, at most, a constant.

Theorem 4.7: Corollary 2: Constant Difference Theorem

If f and g are differentiable over an interval I and $f'(x) = g'(x)$ for all $x \in I,$ then $f(x) = g(x) + C$ for some constant $C.$

Proof

Let $h(x) = f(x) - g(x).$ Then, $h'(x) = f'(x) - g'(x) = 0$ for all $x \in I.$ By Corollary 1, there is a constant C such that $h(x) = C$ for all $x \in I.$ Therefore, $f(x) = g(x) + C$ for all $x \in I.$

□

The third corollary of the Mean Value Theorem discusses when a function is increasing and when it is decreasing. Recall that a function f is increasing over I if $f(x_1) < f(x_2)$ whenever $x_1 < x_2,$ whereas f is decreasing over I if $f(x)_1 > f(x_2)$ whenever $x_1 < x_2.$ Using the Mean Value Theorem, we can show that if the derivative of a function is positive, then the function is increasing; if the derivative is negative, then the function is decreasing (**Figure 4.29**). We make use of this fact in the next section, where we show how to use the derivative of a function to locate local maximum and minimum values of the function, and how to determine the shape of the graph.

This fact is important because it means that for a given function $f,$ if there exists a function F such that $F'(x) = f(x);$ then, the only other functions that have a derivative equal to f are $F(x) + C$ for some constant $C.$ We discuss this result in more detail later in the chapter.

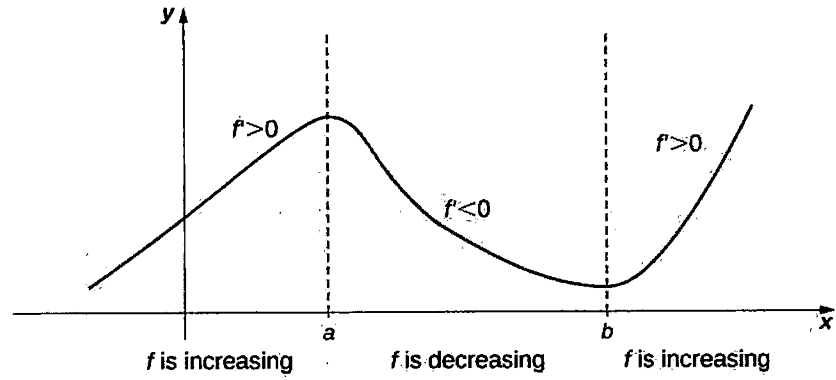

Figure 4.29 If a function has a positive derivative over some interval $I,$ then the function increases over that interval $I;$ if the derivative is negative over some interval $I,$ then the function decreases over that interval $I.$

Theorem 4.8: Corollary 3: Increasing and Decreasing Functions

Let f be continuous over the closed interval $[a, b]$ and differentiable over the open interval $(a, b).$

i. If $f'(x) > 0$ for all $x \in (a, b),$ then f is an increasing function over $[a, b].$

ii. If $f'(x) < 0$ for all $x \in (a, b),$ then f is a decreasing function over $[a, b].$

Proof

We will prove i.; the proof of ii. is similar. Suppose f is not an increasing function on $I.$ Then there exist a and b in I such that $a < b,$ but $f(a) \geq f(b).$ Since f is a differentiable function over $I,$ by the Mean Value Theorem there exists $c \in (a, b)$ such that

$$f'(c) = \frac{f(b) - f(a)}{b - a}.$$

Since $f(a) \geq f(b),$ we know that $f(b) - f(a) \leq 0.$ Also, $a < b$ tells us that $b - a > 0.$ We conclude that

$$f'(c) = \frac{f(b) - f(a)}{b - a} \leq 0.$$

However, $f'(x) > 0$ for all $x \in I.$ This is a contradiction, and therefore f must be an increasing function over $I.$

□

4.4 EXERCISES

148. Why do you need continuity to apply the Mean Value Theorem? Construct a counterexample.

149. Why do you need differentiability to apply the Mean Value Theorem? Find a counterexample.

150. When are Rolle's theorem and the Mean Value Theorem equivalent?

151. If you have a function with a discontinuity, is it still possible to have $f'(c)(b-a) = f(b) - f(a)$? Draw such an example or prove why not.

For the following exercises, determine over what intervals (if any) the Mean Value Theorem applies. Justify your answer.

152. $y = \sin(\pi x)$

153. $y = \frac{1}{x^3}$

154. $y = \sqrt{4 - x^2}$

155. $y = \sqrt{x^2 - 4}$

156. $y = \ln(3x - 5)$

For the following exercises, graph the functions on a calculator and draw the secant line that connects the endpoints. Estimate the number of points c such that $f'(c)(b-a) = f(b) - f(a)$.

157. **[T]** $y = 3x^3 + 2x + 1$ over $[-1, 1]$

158. **[T]** $y = \tan\left(\frac{\pi}{4}x\right)$ over $\left[-\frac{3}{2}, \frac{3}{2}\right]$

159. **[T]** $y = x^2\cos(\pi x)$ over $[-2, 2]$

160. **[T]** $y = x^6 - \frac{3}{4}x^5 - \frac{9}{8}x^4 + \frac{15}{16}x^3 + \frac{3}{32}x^2 + \frac{3}{16}x + \frac{1}{32}$ over $[-1, 1]$

For the following exercises, use the Mean Value Theorem and find all points $0 < c < 2$ such that $f(2) - f(0) = f'(c)(2-0)$.

161. $f(x) = x^3$

162. $f(x) = \sin(\pi x)$

163. $f(x) = \cos(2\pi x)$

164. $f(x) = 1 + x + x^2$

165. $f(x) = (x-1)^{10}$

166. $f(x) = (x-1)^9$

For the following exercises, show there is no c such that $f(1) - f(-1) = f'(c)(2)$. Explain why the Mean Value Theorem does not apply over the interval $[-1, 1]$.

167. $f(x) = \left|x - \frac{1}{2}\right|$

168. $f(x) = \frac{1}{x^2}$

169. $f(x) = \sqrt{|x|}$

170. $f(x) = \lfloor x \rfloor$ (*Hint*: This is called the *floor function* and it is defined so that $f(x)$ is the largest integer less than or equal to x.)

For the following exercises, determine whether the Mean Value Theorem applies for the functions over the given interval $[a, b]$. Justify your answer.

171. $y = e^x$ over $[0, 1]$

172. $y = \ln(2x + 3)$ over $\left[-\frac{3}{2}, 0\right]$

173. $f(x) = \tan(2\pi x)$ over $[0, 2]$

174. $y = \sqrt{9 - x^2}$ over $[-3, 3]$

175. $y = \frac{1}{|x+1|}$ over $[0, 3]$

176. $y = x^3 + 2x + 1$ over $[0, 6]$

177. $y = \frac{x^2 + 3x + 2}{x}$ over $[-1, 1]$

178. $y = \frac{x}{\sin(\pi x) + 1}$ over $[0, 1]$

179. $y = \ln(x + 1)$ over $[0, e - 1]$

180. $y = x\sin(\pi x)$ over $[0, 2]$

181. $y = 5 + |x|$ over $[-1, 1]$

For the following exercises, consider the roots of the equation.

182. Show that the equation $y = x^3 + 3x^2 + 16$ has exactly one real root. What is it?

183. Find the conditions for exactly one root (double root) for the equation $y = x^2 + bx + c$

184. Find the conditions for $y = e^x - b$ to have one root. Is it possible to have more than one root?

For the following exercises, use a calculator to graph the function over the interval $[a, b]$ and graph the secant line from a to b. Use the calculator to estimate all values of c as guaranteed by the Mean Value Theorem. Then, find the exact value of c, if possible, or write the final equation and use a calculator to estimate to four digits.

185. **[T]** $y = \tan(\pi x)$ over $\left[-\frac{1}{4}, \frac{1}{4}\right]$

186. **[T]** $y = \frac{1}{\sqrt{x+1}}$ over $[0, 3]$

187. **[T]** $y = \left|x^2 + 2x - 4\right|$ over $[-4, 0]$

188. **[T]** $y = x + \frac{1}{x}$ over $\left[\frac{1}{2}, 4\right]$

189. **[T]** $y = \sqrt{x+1} + \frac{1}{x^2}$ over $[3, 8]$

190. At 10:17 a.m., you pass a police car at 55 mph that is stopped on the freeway. You pass a second police car at 55 mph at 10:53 a.m., which is located 39 mi from the first police car. If the speed limit is 60 mph, can the police cite you for speeding?

191. Two cars drive from one spotlight to the next, leaving at the same time and arriving at the same time. Is there ever a time when they are going the same speed? Prove or disprove.

192. Show that $y = \sec^2 x$ and $y = \tan^2 x$ have the same derivative. What can you say about $y = \sec^2 x - \tan^2 x$?

193. Show that $y = \csc^2 x$ and $y = \cot^2 x$ have the same derivative. What can you say about $y = \csc^2 x - \cot^2 x$?

4.5 | Derivatives and the Shape of a Graph

Learning Objectives

4.5.1 Explain how the sign of the first derivative affects the shape of a function's graph.
4.5.2 State the first derivative test for critical points.
4.5.3 Use concavity and inflection points to explain how the sign of the second derivative affects the shape of a function's graph.
4.5.4 Explain the concavity test for a function over an open interval.
4.5.5 Explain the relationship between a function and its first and second derivatives.
4.5.6 State the second derivative test for local extrema.

Earlier in this chapter we stated that if a function f has a local extremum at a point c, then c must be a critical point of f. However, a function is not guaranteed to have a local extremum at a critical point. For example, $f(x) = x^3$ has a critical point at $x = 0$ since $f'(x) = 3x^2$ is zero at $x = 0$, but f does not have a local extremum at $x = 0$. Using the results from the previous section, we are now able to determine whether a critical point of a function actually corresponds to a local extreme value. In this section, we also see how the second derivative provides information about the shape of a graph by describing whether the graph of a function curves upward or curves downward.

The First Derivative Test

Corollary 3 of the Mean Value Theorem showed that if the derivative of a function is positive over an interval I then the function is increasing over I. On the other hand, if the derivative of the function is negative over an interval I, then the function is decreasing over I as shown in the following figure.

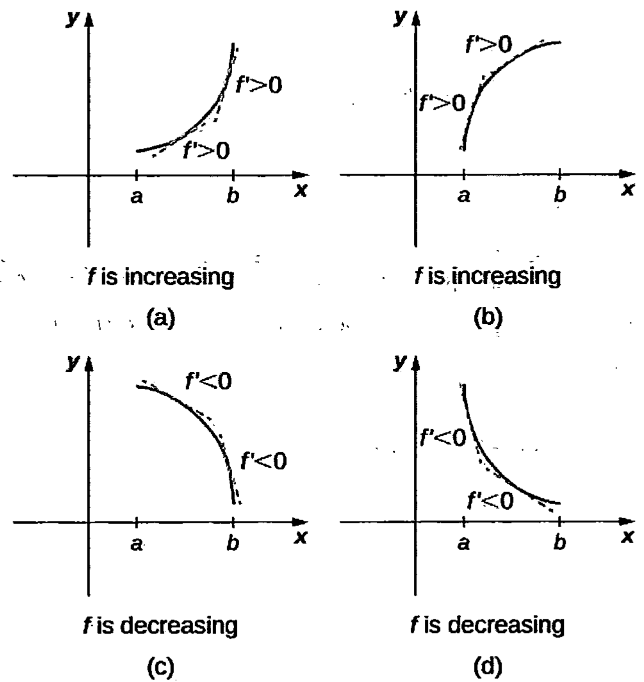

Figure 4.30 Both functions are increasing over the interval (a, b). At each point x, the derivative $f'(x) > 0$. Both functions are decreasing over the interval (a, b). At each point x, the derivative $f'(x) < 0$.

A continuous function f has a local maximum at point c if and only if f switches from increasing to decreasing at point c. Similarly, f has a local minimum at c if and only if f switches from decreasing to increasing at c. If f is a continuous function over an interval I containing c and differentiable over I, except possibly at c, the only way f can switch from increasing to decreasing (or vice versa) at point c is if f' changes sign as x increases through c. If f is differentiable at c, the only way that f'. can change sign as x increases through c is if $f'(c) = 0$. Therefore, for a function f that is continuous over an interval I containing c and differentiable over I, except possibly at c, the only way f can switch from increasing to decreasing (or vice versa) is if $f'(c) = 0$ or $f'(c)$ is undefined. Consequently, to locate local extrema for a function f, we look for points c in the domain of f such that $f'(c) = 0$ or $f'(c)$ is undefined. Recall that such points are called critical points of f.

Note that f need not have a local extrema at a critical point. The critical points are candidates for local extrema only. In **Figure 4.31**, we show that if a continuous function f has a local extremum, it must occur at a critical point, but a function may not have a local extremum at a critical point. We show that if f has a local extremum at a critical point, then the sign of f' switches as x increases through that point.

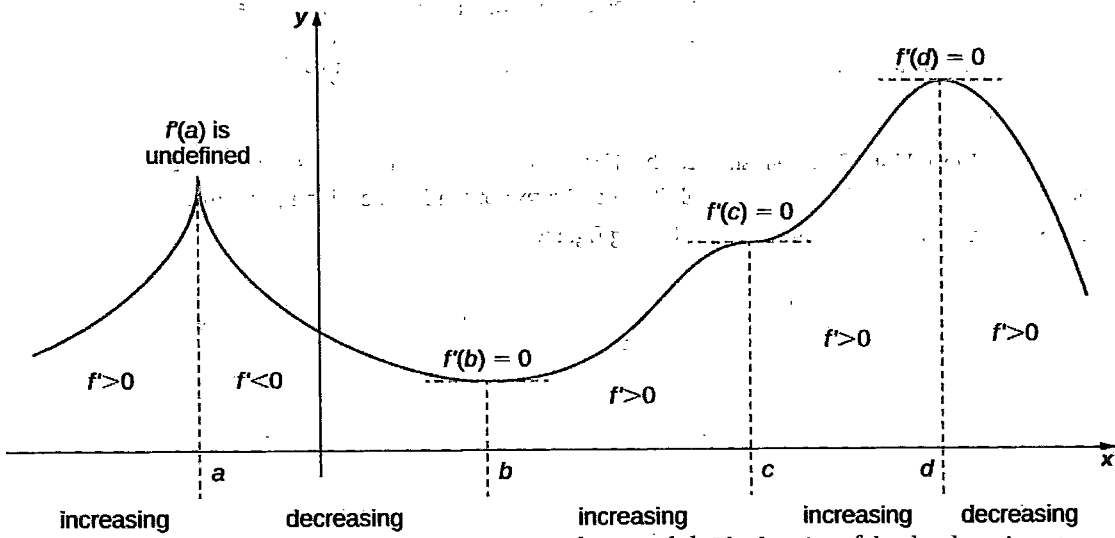

Figure 4.31 The function f has four critical points: a, b, c, and d. The function f has local maxima at a and d, and a local minimum at b. The function f does not have a local extremum at c. The sign of f' changes at all local extrema.

Using **Figure 4.31**, we summarize the main results regarding local extrema.

- If a continuous function f has a local extremum, it must occur at a critical point c.
- The function has a local extremum at the critical point c if and only if the derivative f' switches sign as x increases through c.
- Therefore, to test whether a function has a local extremum at a critical point c, we must determine the sign of $f'(x)$ to the left and right of c.

This result is known as the **first derivative test**.

Theorem 4.9: First Derivative Test

Suppose that f is a continuous function over an interval I containing a critical point c. If f is differentiable over I, except possibly at point c, then $f(c)$ satisfies one of the following descriptions:

i. If f' changes sign from positive when $x < c$ to negative when $x > c$, then $f(c)$ is a local maximum of f.

ii. If f' changes sign from negative when $x < c$ to positive when $x > c$, then $f(c)$ is a local minimum of f.

iii. If f' has the same sign for $x < c$ and $x > c$, then $f(c)$ is neither a local maximum nor a local minimum of f.

We can summarize the first derivative test as a strategy for locating local extrema.

Problem-Solving Strategy: Using the First Derivative Test

Consider a function f that is continuous over an interval I.

1. Find all critical points of f and divide the interval I into smaller intervals using the critical points as endpoints.
2. Analyze the sign of f' in each of the subintervals. If f' is continuous over a given subinterval (which is typically the case), then the sign of f' in that subinterval does not change and, therefore, can be determined by choosing an arbitrary test point x in that subinterval and by evaluating the sign of f' at that test point. Use the sign analysis to determine whether f is increasing or decreasing over that interval.
3. Use **First Derivative Test** and the results of step 2 to determine whether f has a local maximum, a local minimum, or neither at each of the critical points.

Now let's look at how to use this strategy to locate all local extrema for particular functions.

Example 4.17

Using the First Derivative Test to Find Local Extrema

Use the first derivative test to find the location of all local extrema for $f(x) = x^3 - 3x^2 - 9x - 1$. Use a graphing utility to confirm your results.

Solution

Step 1. The derivative is $f'(x) = 3x^2 - 6x - 9$. To find the critical points, we need to find where $f'(x) = 0$. Factoring the polynomial, we conclude that the critical points must satisfy

$$3(x^2 - 2x - 3) = 3(x - 3)(x + 1) = 0.$$

Therefore, the critical points are $x = 3, -1$. Now divide the interval $(-\infty, \infty)$ into the smaller intervals $(-\infty, -1)$, $(-1, 3)$ and $(3, \infty)$.

Step 2. Since f' is a continuous function, to determine the sign of $f'(x)$ over each subinterval, it suffices to choose a point over each of the intervals $(-\infty, -1)$, $(-1, 3)$ and $(3, \infty)$ and determine the sign of f' at each of these points. For example, let's choose $x = -2$, $x = 0$, and $x = 4$ as test points.

Interval	Test Point	Sign of $f'(x) = 3(x-3)(x+1)$ at Test Point	Conclusion
$(-\infty, -1)$	$x = -2$	$(+)(-)(-) = +$	f is increasing.
$(-1, 3)$	$x = 0$	$(+)(-)(+) = -$	f is decreasing.
$(3, \infty)$	$x = 4$	$(+)(+)(+) = +$	f is increasing.

Step 3. Since f' switches sign from positive to negative as x increases through 1, f has a local maximum at $x = -1$. Since f' switches sign from negative to positive as x increases through 3, f has a local minimum at $x = 3$. These analytical results agree with the following graph.

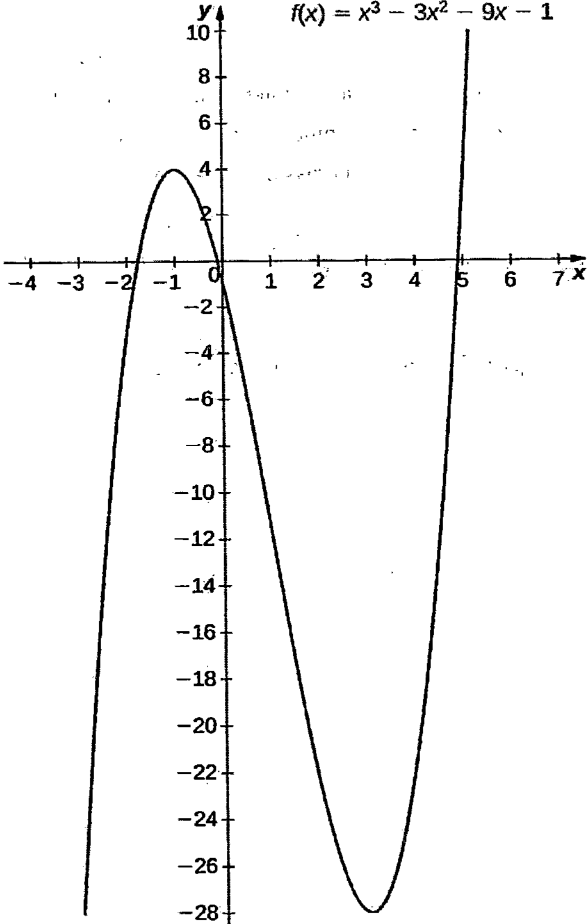

Figure 4.32 The function f has a maximum at $x = -1$ and a minimum at $x = 3$

 **4.16** Use the first derivative test to locate all local extrema for $f(x) = -x^3 + \frac{3}{2}x^2 + 18x.$

Example 4.18

Using the First Derivative Test

Use the first derivative test to find the location of all local extrema for $f(x) = 5x^{1/3} - x^{5/3}$. Use a graphing utility to confirm your results.

Solution

Step 1. The derivative is

$$f'(x) = \frac{5}{3}x^{-2/3} - \frac{5}{3}x^{2/3} = \frac{5}{3x^{2/3}} - \frac{5x^{2/3}}{3} = \frac{5 - 5x^{4/3}}{3x^{2/3}} = \frac{5\left(1 - x^{4/3}\right)}{3x^{2/3}}.$$

The derivative $f'(x) = 0$ when $1 - x^{4/3} = 0$. Therefore, $f'(x) = 0$ at $x = \pm 1$. The derivative $f'(x)$ is undefined at $x = 0$. Therefore, we have three critical points: $x = 0$, $x = 1$, and $x = -1$. Consequently, divide the interval $(-\infty, \infty)$ into the smaller intervals $(-\infty, -1)$, $(-1, 0)$, $(0, 1)$, and $(1, \infty)$.

Step 2: Since f' is continuous over each subinterval, it suffices to choose a test point x in each of the intervals from step 1 and determine the sign of f' at each of these points. The points $x = -2$, $x = -\frac{1}{2}$, $x = \frac{1}{2}$, and $x = 2$ are test points for these intervals.

Interval	Test Point	Sign of $f'(x) = \frac{5\left(1 - x^{4/3}\right)}{3x^{2/3}}$ at Test Point	Conclusion
$(-\infty, -1)$	$x = -2$	$\frac{(+)(-)}{+} = -$	f is decreasing.
$(-1, 0)$	$x = -\frac{1}{2}$	$\frac{(+)(+)}{+} = +$	f is increasing.
$(0, 1)$	$x = \frac{1}{2}$	$\frac{(+)(+)}{+} = +$	f is increasing.
$(1, \infty)$	$x = 2$	$\frac{(+)(-)}{+} = -$	f is decreasing.

Step 3: Since f is decreasing over the interval $(-\infty, -1)$ and increasing over the interval $(-1, 0)$, f has a local minimum at $x = -1$. Since f is increasing over the interval $(-1, 0)$ and the interval $(0, 1)$, f does not have a local extremum at $x = 0$. Since f is increasing over the interval $(0, 1)$ and decreasing over the interval $(1, \infty)$, f has a local maximum at $x = 1$. The analytical results agree with the following graph.

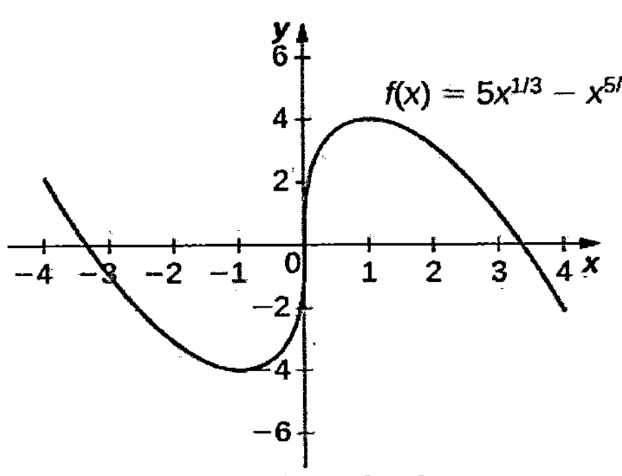

Figure 4.33 The function f has a local minimum at $x = -1$ and a local maximum at $x = 1$.

4.17 Use the first derivative test to find all local extrema for $f(x) = \sqrt[3]{x-1}.$

Concavity and Points of Inflection

We now know how to determine where a function is increasing or decreasing. However, there is another issue to consider regarding the shape of the graph of a function. If the graph curves, does it curve upward or curve downward? This notion is called the **concavity** of the function.

Figure 4.34(a) shows a function f with a graph that curves upward. As x increases, the slope of the tangent line increases. Thus, since the derivative increases as x increases, f' is an increasing function. We say this function f is concave up. **Figure 4.34**(b) shows a function f that curves downward. As x increases, the slope of the tangent line decreases. Since the derivative decreases as x increases, f' is a decreasing function. We say this function f is concave down.

Definition

Let f be a function that is differentiable over an open interval $I.$ If f' is increasing over $I,$ we say f is **concave up** over $I.$ If f' is decreasing over $I,$ we say f is **concave down** over $I.$

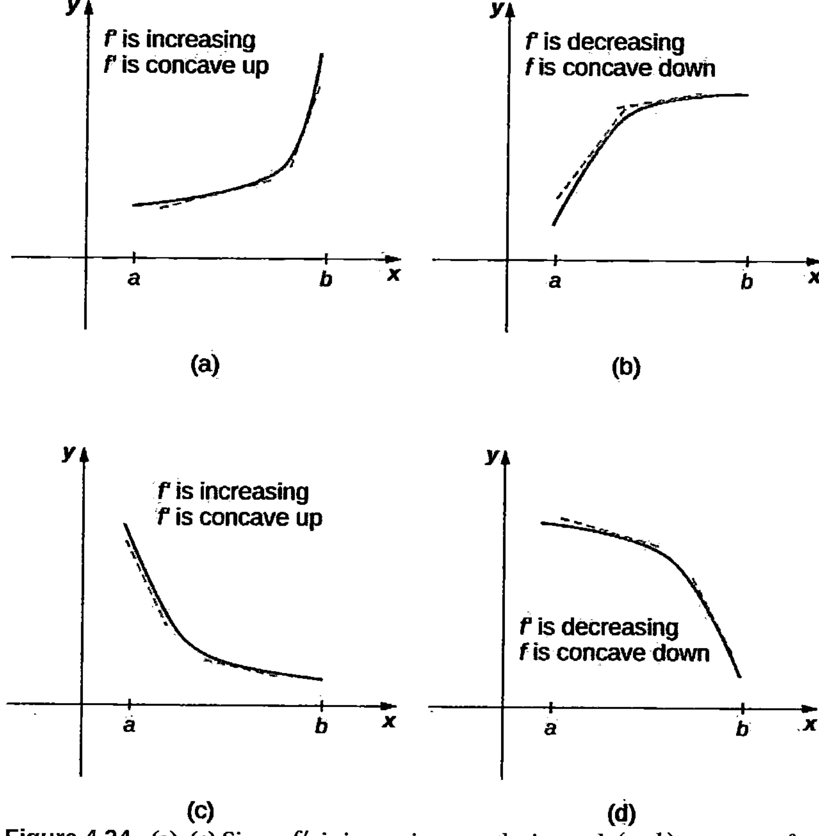

Figure 4.34 (a), (c) Since f' is increasing over the interval (a, b), we say f is concave up over (a, b). (b), (d) Since f' is decreasing over the interval (a, b), we say f is concave down over (a, b).

In general, without having the graph of a function f, how can we determine its concavity? By definition, a function f is concave up if f' is increasing. From Corollary 3, we know that if f' is a differentiable function, then f' is increasing if its derivative $f''(x) > 0$. Therefore, a function f that is twice differentiable is concave up when $f''(x) > 0$. Similarly, a function f is concave down if f' is decreasing. We know that a differentiable function f' is decreasing if its derivative $f''(x) < 0$. Therefore, a twice-differentiable function f is concave down when $f''(x) < 0$. Applying this logic is known as the **concavity test**.

Theorem 4.10: Test for Concavity

Let f be a function that is twice differentiable over an interval I.

i. If $f''(x) > 0$ for all $x \in I$, then f is concave up over I.

ii. If $f''(x) < 0$ for all $x \in I$, then f is concave down over I.

We conclude that we can determine the concavity of a function f by looking at the second derivative of f. In addition, we observe that a function f can switch concavity (**Figure 4.35**). However, a continuous function can switch concavity only at a point x if $f''(x) = 0$ or $f''(x)$ is undefined. Consequently, to determine the intervals where a function f is concave up and concave down, we look for those values of x where $f''(x) = 0$ or $f''(x)$ is undefined. When we have determined these points, we divide the domain of f into smaller intervals and determine the sign of f'' over each of these smaller intervals. If f'' changes sign as we pass through a point x, then f changes concavity. It is important to remember that a function f may not change concavity at a point x even if $f''(x) = 0$ or $f''(x)$ is undefined. If, however, f does change concavity at a point a and f is continuous at a, we say the point $(a, f(a))$ is an inflection point of f.

Definition

If f is continuous at a and f changes concavity at a, the point $(a, f(a))$ is an **inflection point** of f.

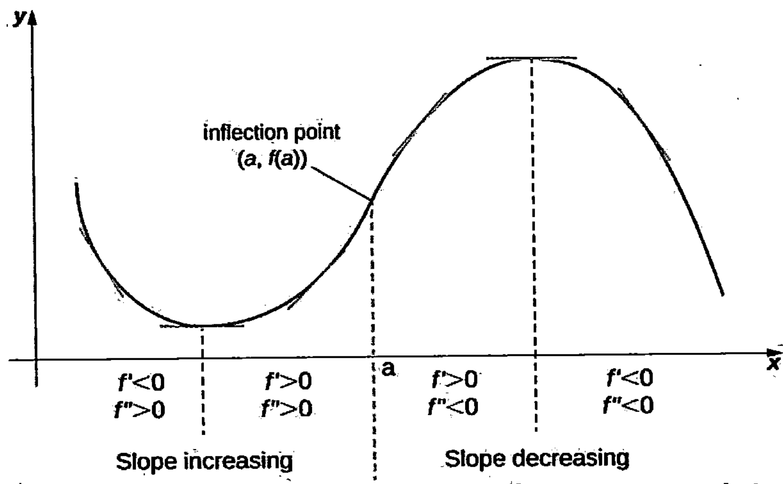

Figure 4.35 Since $f''(x) > 0$ for $x < a$, the function f is concave up over the interval $(-\infty, a)$. Since $f''(x) < 0$ for $x > a$, the function f is concave down over the interval (a, ∞). The point $(a, f(a))$ is an inflection point of f.

Example 4.19

Testing for Concavity

For the function $f(x) = x^3 - 6x^2 + 9x + 30$, determine all intervals where f is concave up and all intervals where f is concave down. List all inflection points for f. Use a graphing utility to confirm your results.

Solution

To determine concavity, we need to find the second derivative $f''(x)$. The first derivative is $f'(x) = 3x^2 - 12x + 9$, so the second derivative is $f''(x) = 6x - 12$. If the function changes concavity, it occurs either when $f''(x) = 0$ or $f''(x)$ is undefined. Since f'' is defined for all real numbers x, we need only find where $f''(x) = 0$. Solving the equation $6x - 12 = 0$, we see that $x = 2$ is the only place where f could change concavity. We now test points over the intervals $(-\infty, 2)$ and $(2, \infty)$ to determine the concavity of f. The points $x = 0$ and $x = 3$ are test points for these intervals.

Interval	Test Point	Sign of $f''(x) = 6x - 12$ at Test Point	Conclusion
$(-\infty, 2)$	$x = 0$	$-$	f is concave down
$(2, \infty)$	$x = 3$	$+$	f is concave up.

We conclude that f is concave down over the interval $(-\infty, 2)$ and concave up over the interval $(2, \infty)$. Since f changes concavity at $x = 2$, the point $(2, f(2)) = (2, 32)$ is an inflection point. **Figure 4.36** confirms the analytical results.

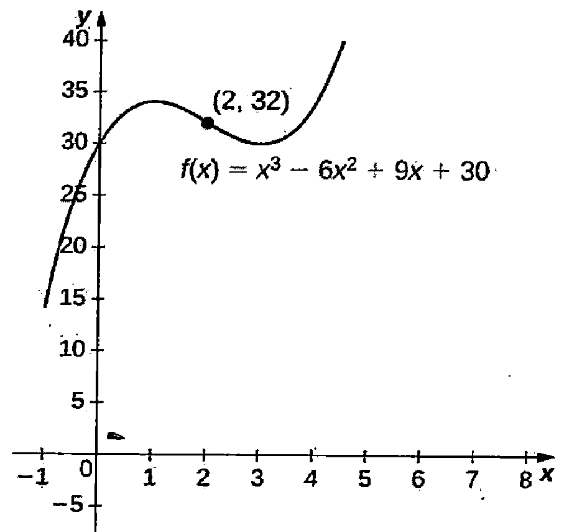

Figure 4.36 The given function has a point of inflection at $(2, 32)$ where the graph changes concavity.

4.18 For $f(x) = -x^3 + \frac{3}{2}x^2 + 18x$, find all intervals where f is concave up and all intervals where f is concave down.

We now summarize, in **Table 4.6**, the information that the first and second derivatives of a function f provide about the graph of f, and illustrate this information in **Figure 4.37**.

Sign of f'	Sign of f''	Is f increasing or decreasing?	Concavity
Positive	Positive	Increasing	Concave up
Positive	Negative	Increasing	Concave down
Negative	Positive	Decreasing	Concave up
Negative	Negative	Decreasing	Concave down

Table 4.6 What Derivatives Tell Us about Graphs

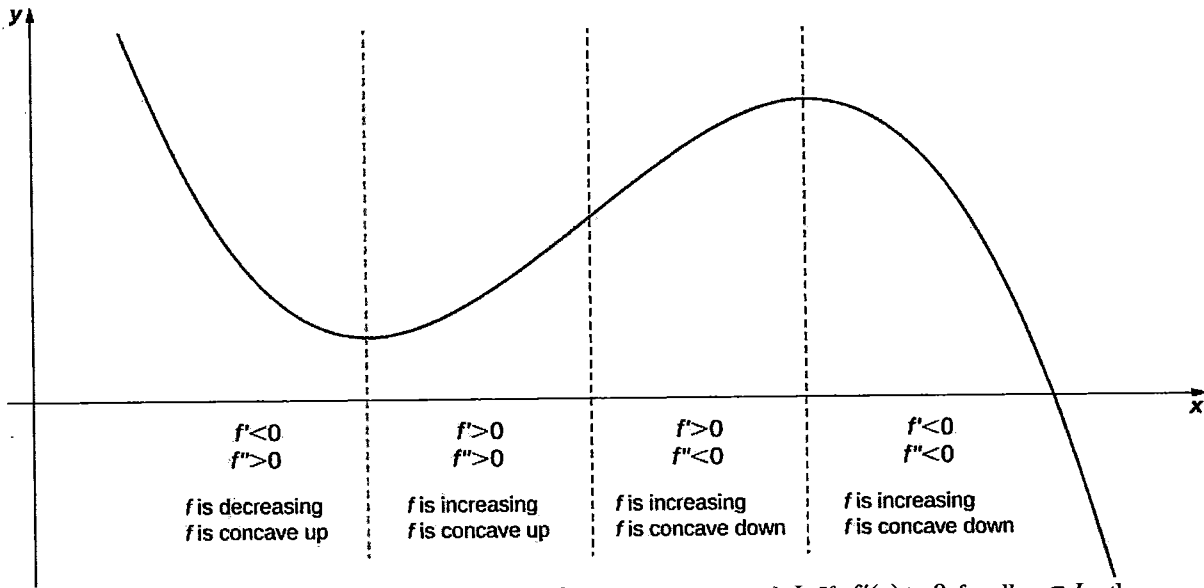

Figure 4.37 Consider a twice-differentiable function f over an open interval I. If $f'(x) > 0$ for all $x \in I$, the function is increasing over I. If $f'(x) < 0$ for all $x \in I$, the function is decreasing over I. If $f''(x) > 0$ for all $x \in I$, the function is concave up. If $f''(x) < 0$ for all $x \in I$, the function is concave down on I.

The Second Derivative Test

The first derivative test provides an analytical tool for finding local extrema, but the second derivative can also be used to locate extreme values. Using the second derivative can sometimes be a simpler method than using the first derivative.

We know that if a continuous function has a local extrema, it must occur at a critical point. However, a function need not have a local extrema at a critical point. Here we examine how the **second derivative test** can be used to determine whether a function has a local extremum at a critical point. Let f be a twice-differentiable function such that $f'(a) = 0$ and f'' is continuous over an open interval I containing a. Suppose $f''(a) < 0$. Since f'' is continuous over I, $f''(x) < 0$ for all $x \in I$ (**Figure 4.38**). Then, by Corollary 3, f' is a decreasing function over I. Since $f'(a) = 0$, we conclude that for all $x \in I$, $f'(x) > 0$ if $x < a$ and $f'(x) < 0$ if $x > a$. Therefore, by the first derivative test, f has a local maximum at $x = a$. On the other hand, suppose there exists a point b such that $f'(b) = 0$ but $f''(b) > 0$. Since f'' is continuous over an open interval I containing b, then $f''(x) > 0$ for all $x \in I$ (**Figure 4.38**). Then, by Corollary 3, f' is an increasing function over I. Since $f'(b) = 0$, we conclude that for all $x \in I$, $f'(x) < 0$ if $x < b$ and $f'(x) > 0$ if $x > b$. Therefore, by the first derivative test, f has a local minimum at $x = b$.

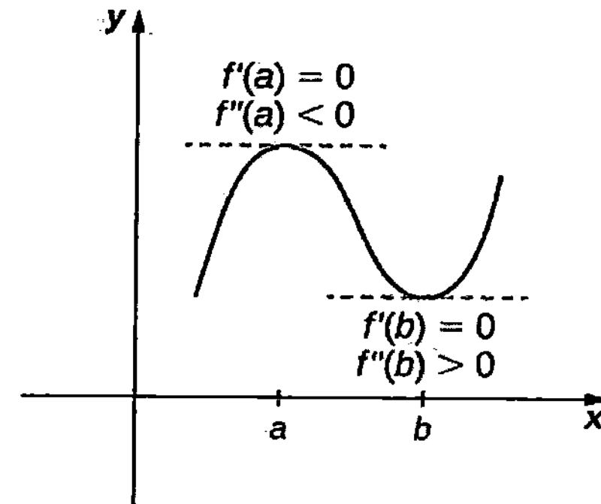

Figure 4.38 Consider a twice-differentiable function f such that f'' is continuous. Since $f'(a) = 0$ and $f''(a) < 0$, there is an interval I containing a such that for all x in I, f is increasing if $x < a$ and f is decreasing if $x > a$. As a result, f has a local maximum at $x = a$. Since $f'(b) = 0$ and $f''(b) > 0$, there is an interval I containing b such that for all x in I, f is decreasing if $x < b$ and f is increasing if $x > b$. As a result, f has a local minimum at $x = b$.

Theorem 4.11: Second Derivative Test

Suppose $f'(c) = 0$, f'' is continuous over an interval containing c.

i. If $f''(c) > 0$, then f has a local minimum at c.
ii. If $f''(c) < 0$, then f has a local maximum at c.
iii. If $f''(c) = 0$, then the test is inconclusive.

Note that for case iii. when $f''(c) = 0$, then f may have a local maximum, local minimum, or neither at c. For example, the functions $f(x) = x^3$, $f(x) = x^4$, and $f(x) = -x^4$ all have critical points at $x = 0$. In each case, the second derivative is zero at $x = 0$. However, the function $f(x) = x^4$ has a local minimum at $x = 0$ whereas the function $f(x) = -x^4$ has a local maximum at x, and the function $f(x) = x^3$ does not have a local extremum at $x = 0$.

Let's now look at how to use the second derivative test to determine whether f has a local maximum or local minimum at a critical point c where $f'(c) = 0$.

Example 4.20

Using the Second Derivative Test

Use the second derivative to find the location of all local extrema for $f(x) = x^5 - 5x^3$.

Solution

To apply the second derivative test, we first need to find critical points c where $f'(c) = 0$. The derivative is

$f'(x) = 5x^4 - 15x^2$. Therefore, $f'(x) = 5x^4 - 15x^2 = 5x^2(x^2 - 3) = 0$ when $x = 0, \pm\sqrt{3}$.

To determine whether f has a local extrema at any of these points, we need to evaluate the sign of f'' at these points. The second derivative is

$$f''(x) = 20x^3 - 30x = 10x(2x^2 - 3).$$

In the following table, we evaluate the second derivative at each of the critical points and use the second derivative test to determine whether f has a local maximum or local minimum at any of these points.

x	$f''(x)$	**Conclusion**
$-\sqrt{3}$	$-30\sqrt{3}$	Local maximum
0	0	Second derivative test is inconclusive
$\sqrt{3}$	$30\sqrt{3}$	Local minimum

By the second derivative test, we conclude that f has a local maximum at $x = -\sqrt{3}$ and f has a local minimum at $x = \sqrt{3}$. The second derivative test is inconclusive at $x = 0$. To determine whether f has a local extrema at $x = 0$, we apply the first derivative test. To evaluate the sign of $f'(x) = 5x^2(x^2 - 3)$ for $x \in (-\sqrt{3}, 0)$ and $x \in (0, \sqrt{3})$, let $x = -1$ and $x = 1$ be the two test points. Since $f'(-1) < 0$ and $f'(1) < 0$, we conclude that f is decreasing on both intervals and, therefore, f does not have a local extrema at $x = 0$ as shown in the following graph.

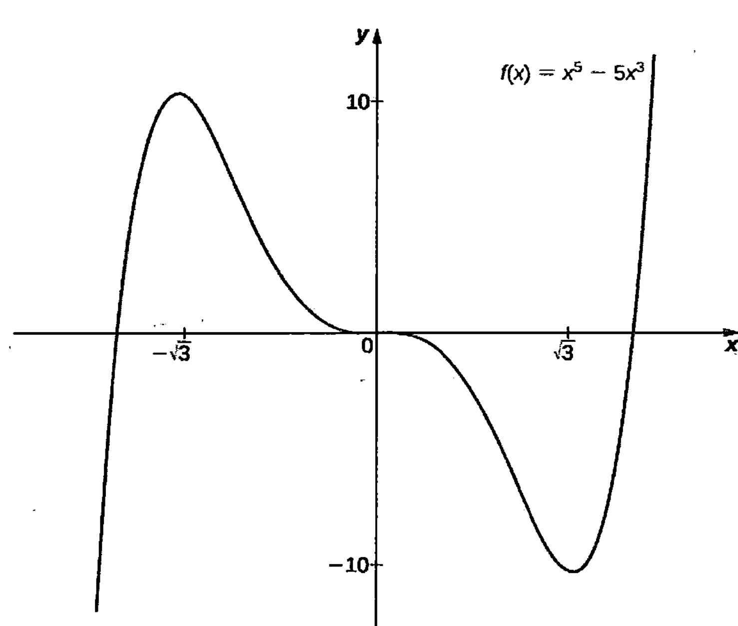

Figure 4.39 The function f has a local maximum at $x = -\sqrt{3}$ and a local minimum at $x = \sqrt{3}$

4.19 Consider the function $f(x) = x^3 - \left(\frac{3}{2}\right)x^2 - 18x$. The points $c = 3, -2$ satisfy $f'(c) = 0$. Use the second derivative test to determine whether f has a local maximum or local minimum at those points.

We have now developed the tools we need to determine where a function is increasing and decreasing, as well as acquired an understanding of the basic shape of the graph. In the next section we discuss what happens to a function as $x \to \pm\infty$. At that point, we have enough tools to provide accurate graphs of a large variety of functions.

4.5 EXERCISES

194. If c is a critical point of $f(x)$, when is there no local maximum or minimum at c? Explain.

195. For the function $y = x^3$, is $x = 0$ both an inflection point and a local maximum/minimum?

196. For the function $y = x^3$, is $x = 0$ an inflection point?

197. Is it possible for a point c to be both an inflection point and a local extrema of a twice differentiable function?

198. Why do you need continuity for the first derivative test? Come up with an example.

199. Explain whether a concave-down function has to cross $y = 0$ for some value of x.

200. Explain whether a polynomial of degree 2 can have an inflection point.

For the following exercises, analyze the graphs of f', then list all intervals where f is increasing or decreasing.

201.

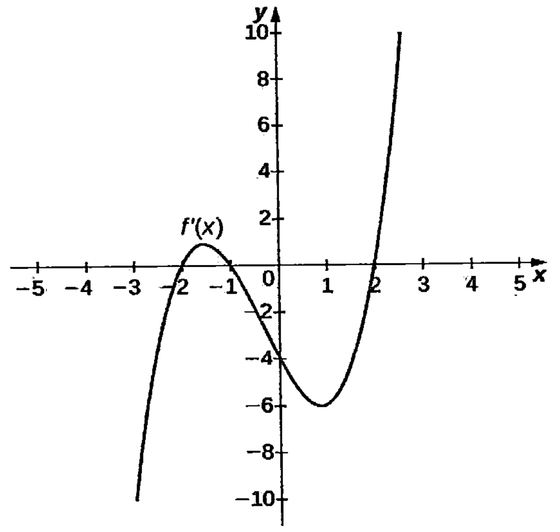

202.

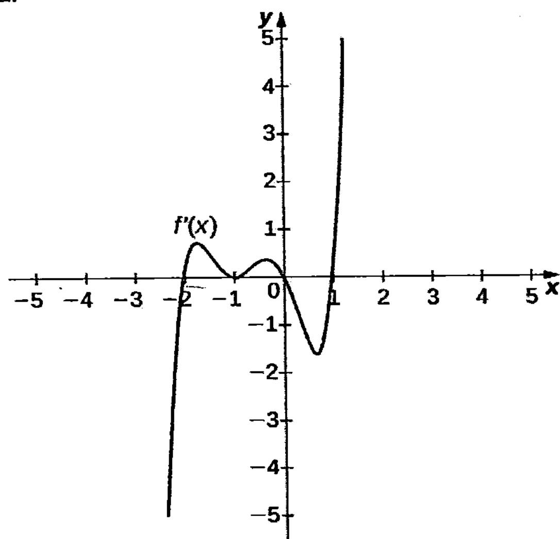

203.

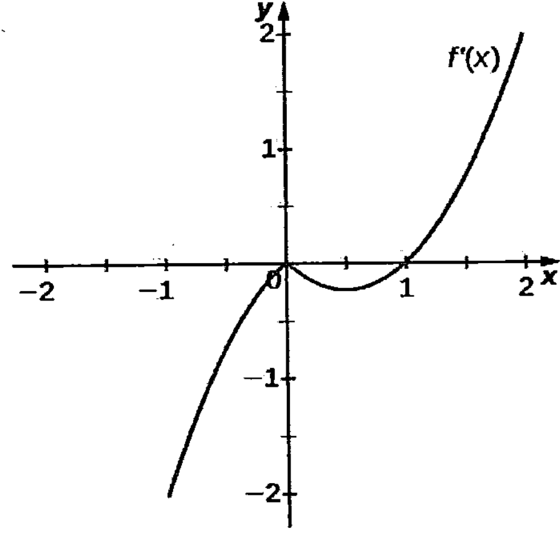

204.

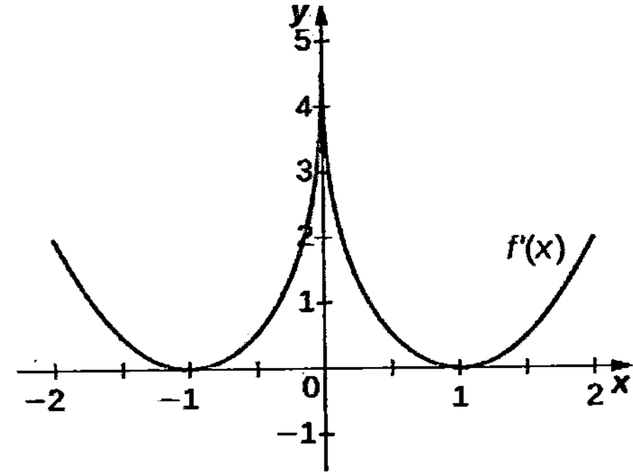

205.

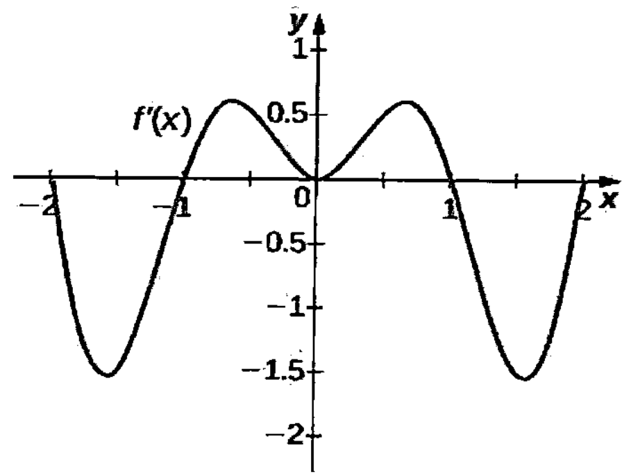

For the following exercises, analyze the graphs of f', then list all intervals where

a. f is increasing and decreasing and

b. the minima and maxima are located.

206.

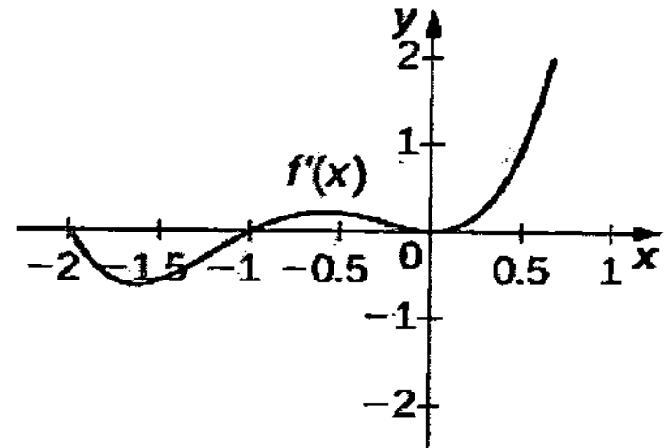

207.

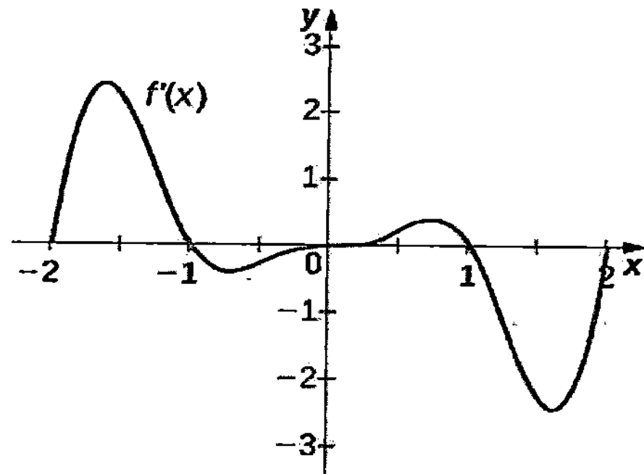

208.

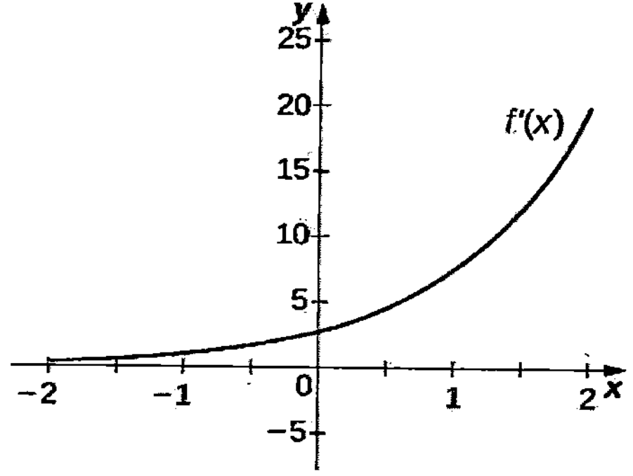

209.

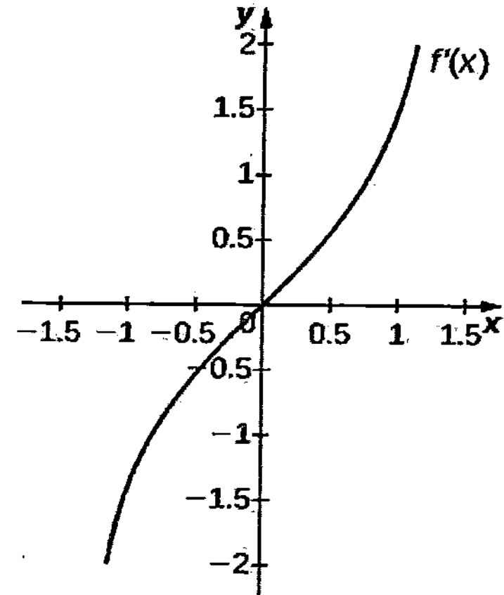

210.

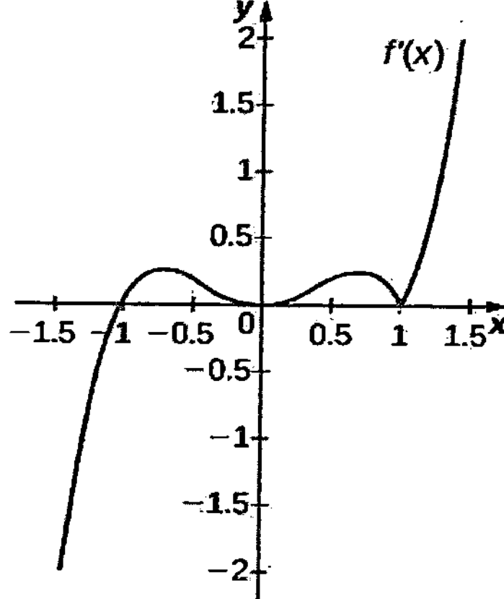

For the following exercises, analyze the graphs of f', then list all inflection points and intervals f that are concave up and concave down.

211.

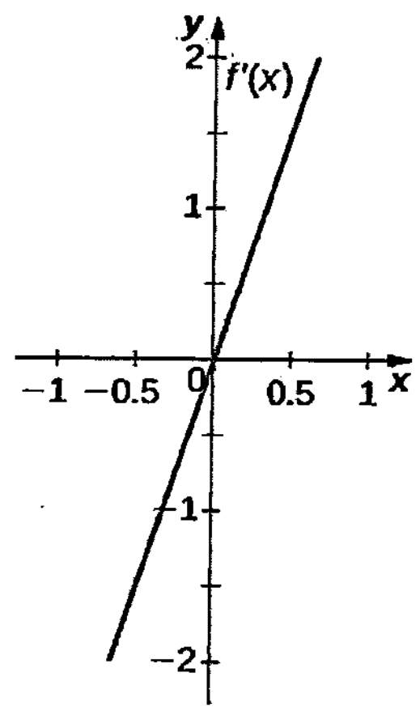

212.

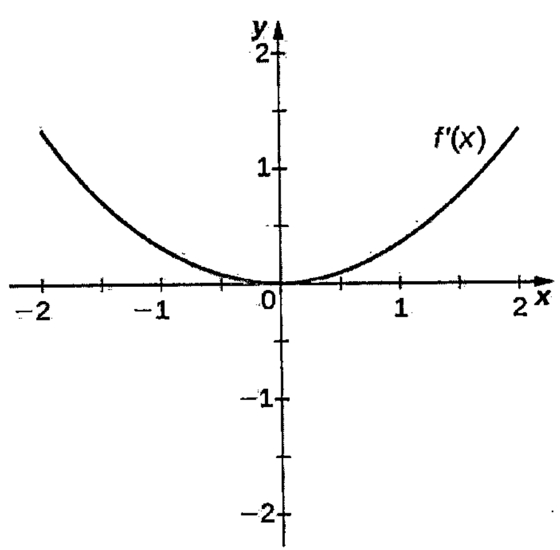

213.

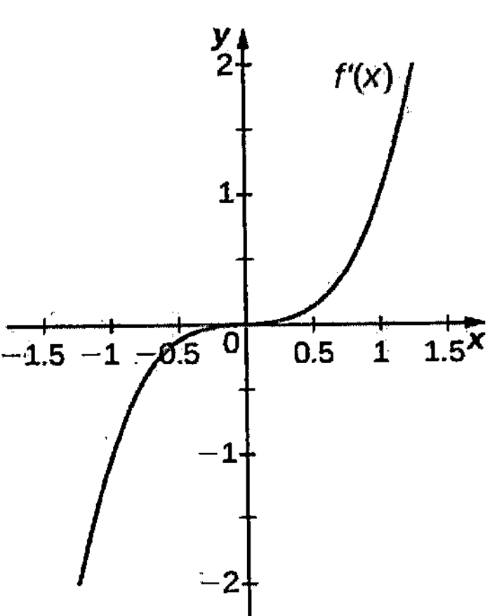

214.

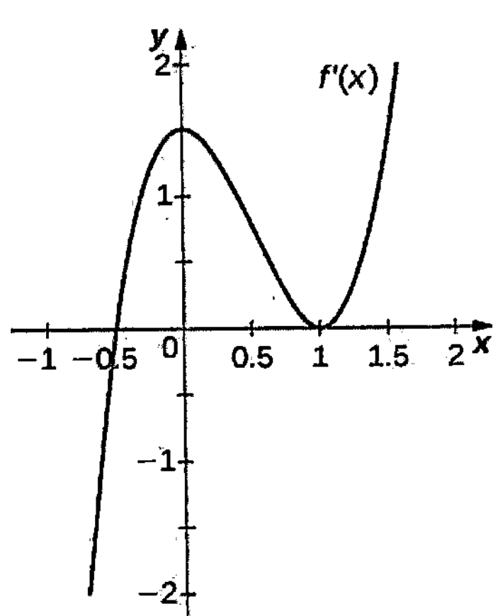

215.

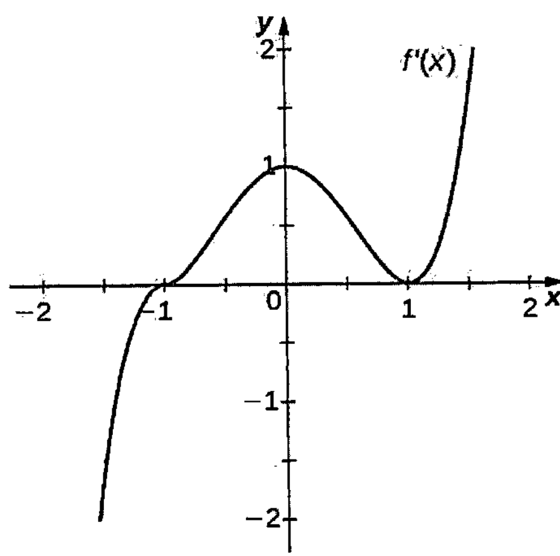

For the following exercises, draw a graph that satisfies the given specifications for the domain $x = [-3, 3]$. The function does not have to be continuous or differentiable.

216. $f(x) > 0,\ f'(x) > 0$ over $x > 1,\ -3 < x < 0,\ f'(x) = 0$ over $0 < x < 1$

217. $f'(x) > 0$ over $x > 2,\ -3 < x < -1,\ f'(x) < 0$ over $-1 < x < 2,\ f''(x) < 0$ for all x

218. $f''(x) < 0$ over $-1 < x < 1,\ f''(x) > 0,\ -3 < x < -1,\ 1 < x < 3,$ local maximum at $x = 0,$ local minima at $x = \pm 2$

219. There is a local maximum at $x = 2,$ local minimum at $x = 1,$ and the graph is neither concave up nor concave down.

220. There are local maxima at $x = \pm 1,$ the function is concave up for all $x,$ and the function remains positive for all $x.$

For the following exercises, determine

a. intervals where f is increasing or decreasing and

b. local minima and maxima of f.

221. $f(x) = \sin x + \sin^3 x$ over $-\pi < x < \pi$

222. $f(x) = x^2 + \cos x$

For the following exercises, determine a. intervals where f is concave up or concave down, and b. the inflection points of f.

223. $f(x) = x^3 - 4x^2 + x + 2$

For the following exercises, determine

a. intervals where f is increasing or decreasing,

b. local minima and maxima of f,

c. intervals where f is concave up and concave down, and

d. the inflection points of f.

224. $f(x) = x^2 - 6x$

225. $f(x) = x^3 - 6x^2$

226. $f(x) = x^4 - 6x^3$

227. $f(x) = x^{11} - 6x^{10}$

228. $f(x) = x + x^2 - x^3$

229. $f(x) = x^2 + x + 1$

230. $f(x) = x^3 + x^4$

For the following exercises, determine

a. intervals where f is increasing or decreasing,

b. local minima and maxima of f,

c. intervals where f is concave up and concave down, and

d. the inflection points of f. Sketch the curve, then use a calculator to compare your answer. If you cannot determine the exact answer analytically, use a calculator.

231. **[T]** $f(x) = \sin(\pi x) - \cos(\pi x)$ over $x = [-1, 1]$

232. **[T]** $f(x) = x + \sin(2x)$ over $x = \left[-\frac{\pi}{2}, \frac{\pi}{2}\right]$

233. **[T]** $f(x) = \sin x + \tan x$ over $\left(-\frac{\pi}{2}, \frac{\pi}{2}\right)$

234. **[T]** $f(x) = (x-2)^2(x-4)^2$

235. **[T]** $f(x) = \frac{1}{1-x}, x \neq 1$

236. **[T]** $f(x) = \frac{\sin x}{x}$ over $x = [-2\pi, 2\pi]$ $[2\pi, 0) \cup (0, 2\pi]$

237. $f(x) = \sin(x)e^x$ over $x = [-\pi, \pi]$

238. $f(x) = \ln x\sqrt{x}, x > 0$

239. $f(x) = \frac{1}{4}\sqrt{x} + \frac{1}{x}, x > 0$

240. $f(x) = \frac{e^x}{x}, x \neq 0$

For the following exercises, interpret the sentences in terms of $f, f',$ and f''.

241. The population is growing more slowly. Here f is the population.

242. A bike accelerates faster, but a car goes faster. Here $f =$ Bike's position minus Car's position.

243. The airplane lands smoothly. Here f is the plane's altitude.

244. Stock prices are at their peak. Here f is the stock price.

245. The economy is picking up speed. Here f is a measure of the economy, such as GDP.

For the following exercises, consider a third-degree polynomial $f(x)$, which has the properties $f'(1) = 0, f'(3) = 0$. Determine whether the following statements are *true or false*. Justify your answer.

246. $f(x) = 0$ for some $1 \leq x \leq 3$

247. $f''(x) = 0$ for some $1 \leq x \leq 3$

248. There is no absolute maximum at $x = 3$

249. If $f(x)$ has three roots, then it has 1 inflection point.

250. If $f(x)$ has one inflection point, then it has three real roots.

4.6 | Limits at Infinity and Asymptotes

Learning Objectives

4.6.1 Calculate the limit of a function as x increases or decreases without bound.
4.6.2 Recognize a horizontal asymptote on the graph of a function.
4.6.3 Estimate the end behavior of a function as x increases or decreases without bound.
4.6.4 Recognize an oblique asymptote on the graph of a function.
4.6.5 Analyze a function and its derivatives to draw its graph.

We have shown how to use the first and second derivatives of a function to describe the shape of a graph. To graph a function f defined on an unbounded domain, we also need to know the behavior of f as $x \to \pm\infty$. In this section, we define limits at infinity and show how these limits affect the graph of a function. At the end of this section, we outline a strategy for graphing an arbitrary function f.

Limits at Infinity

We begin by examining what it means for a function to have a finite limit at infinity. Then we study the idea of a function with an infinite limit at infinity. Back in **Introduction to Functions and Graphs**, we looked at vertical asymptotes; in this section we deal with horizontal and oblique asymptotes.

Limits at Infinity and Horizontal Asymptotes

Recall that $\lim_{x \to a} f(x) = L$ means $f(x)$ becomes arbitrarily close to L as long as x is sufficiently close to a. We can extend this idea to limits at infinity. For example, consider the function $f(x) = 2 + \frac{1}{x}$. As can be seen graphically in **Figure 4.40** and numerically in **Table 4.8**, as the values of x get larger, the values of $f(x)$ approach 2. We say the limit as x approaches ∞ of $f(x)$ is 2 and write $\lim_{x \to \infty} f(x) = 2$. Similarly, for $x < 0$, as the values $|x|$ get larger, the values of $f(x)$ approaches 2. We say the limit as x approaches $-\infty$ of $f(x)$ is 2 and write $\lim_{x \to a} f(x) = 2$.

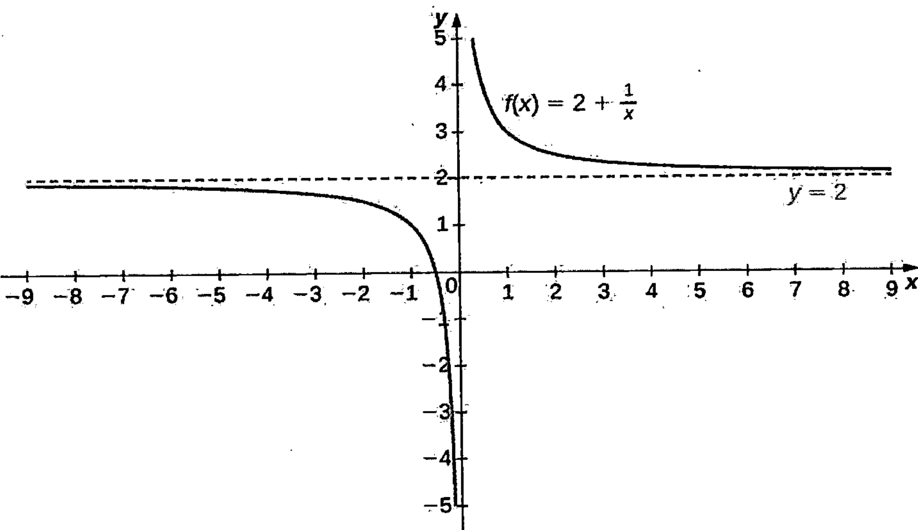

Figure 4.40 The function approaches the asymptote $y = 2$ as x approaches $\pm\infty$.

x	10	100	1,000	10,000
$2+\frac{1}{x}$	2.1	2.01	2.001	2.0001
x	−10	−100	−1000	−10,000
$2+\frac{1}{x}$	1.9	1.99	1.999	1.9999

Table 4.8 Values of a function f as $x \to \pm\infty$

More generally, for any function f, we say the limit as $x \to \infty$ of $f(x)$ is L if $f(x)$ becomes arbitrarily close to L as long as x is sufficiently large. In that case, we write $\lim_{x\to\infty} f(x) = L$. Similarly, we say the limit as $x \to -\infty$ of $f(x)$ is L if $f(x)$ becomes arbitrarily close to L as long as $x < 0$ and $|x|$ is sufficiently large. In that case, we write $\lim_{x\to-\infty} f(x) = L$. We now look at the definition of a function having a limit at infinity.

Definition

(Informal) If the values of $f(x)$ become arbitrarily close to L as x becomes sufficiently large, we say the function f has a **limit at infinity** and write

$$\lim_{x\to\infty} f(x) = L.$$

If the values of $f(x)$ becomes arbitrarily close to L for $x < 0$ as $|x|$ becomes sufficiently large, we say that the function f has a limit at negative infinity and write

$$\lim_{x\to-\infty} f(x) = L.$$

If the values $f(x)$ are getting arbitrarily close to some finite value L as $x \to \infty$ or $x \to -\infty$, the graph of f approaches the line $y = L$. In that case, the line $y = L$ is a horizontal asymptote of f (**Figure 4.41**). For example, for the function $f(x) = \frac{1}{x}$, since $\lim_{x\to\infty} f(x) = 0$, the line $y = 0$ is a horizontal asymptote of $f(x) = \frac{1}{x}$.

Definition

If $\lim_{x\to\infty} f(x) = L$ or $\lim_{x\to-\infty} f(x) = L$, we say the line $y = L$ is a **horizontal asymptote** of f.

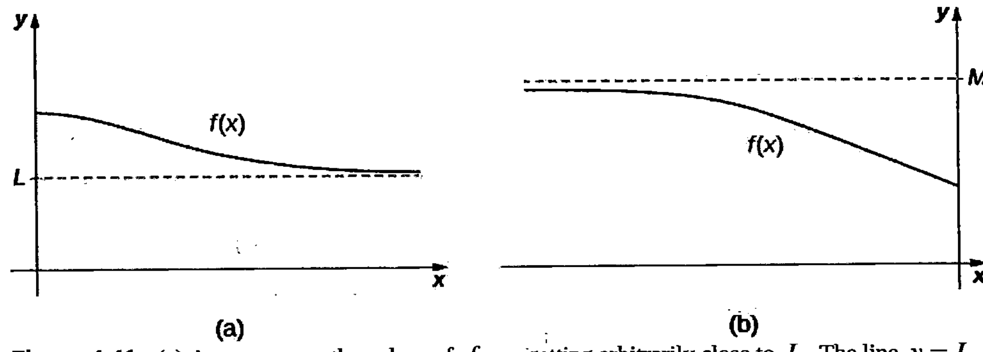

Figure 4.41 (a) As $x \to \infty$, the values of f are getting arbitrarily close to L. The line $y = L$ is a horizontal asymptote of f. (b) As $x \to -\infty$, the values of f are getting arbitrarily close to M. The line $y = M$ is a horizontal asymptote of f.

A function cannot cross a vertical asymptote because the graph must approach infinity (or $-\infty$) from at least one direction as x approaches the vertical asymptote. However, a function may cross a horizontal asymptote. In fact, a function may cross a horizontal asymptote an unlimited number of times. For example, the function $f(x) = \frac{(\cos x)}{x} + 1$ shown in **Figure 4.42** intersects the horizontal asymptote $y = 1$ an infinite number of times as it oscillates around the asymptote with ever-decreasing amplitude.

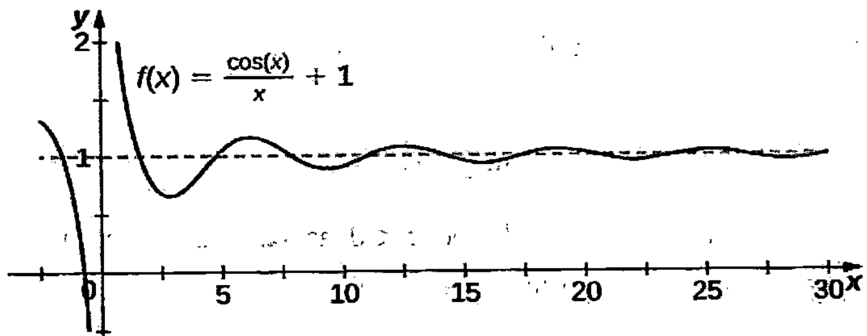

Figure 4.42 The graph of $f(x) = (\cos x)/x + 1$ crosses its horizontal asymptote $y = 1$ an infinite number of times.

The algebraic limit laws and squeeze theorem we introduced in **Introduction to Limits** also apply to limits at infinity. We illustrate how to use these laws to compute several limits at infinity.

Example 4.21

Computing Limits at Infinity

For each of the following functions f, evaluate $\lim\limits_{x \to \infty} f(x)$ and $\lim\limits_{x \to -\infty} f(x)$. Determine the horizontal asymptote(s) for f.

a. $f(x) = 5 - \frac{2}{x^2}$

b. $f(x) = \frac{\sin x}{x}$

c. $f(x) = \tan^{-1}(x)$

Solution

a. Using the algebraic limit laws, we have $\lim_{x \to \infty}\left(5 - \frac{2}{x^2}\right) = \lim_{x \to \infty} 5 - 2\left(\lim_{x \to \infty}\frac{1}{x}\right).\left(\lim_{x \to \infty}\frac{1}{x}\right) = 5 - 2 \cdot 0 = 5.$

Similarly, $\lim_{x \to -\infty} f(x) = 5$. Therefore, $f(x) = 5 - \frac{2}{x^2}$ has a horizontal asymptote of $y = 5$ and f approaches this horizontal asymptote as $x \to \pm\infty$ as shown in the following graph.

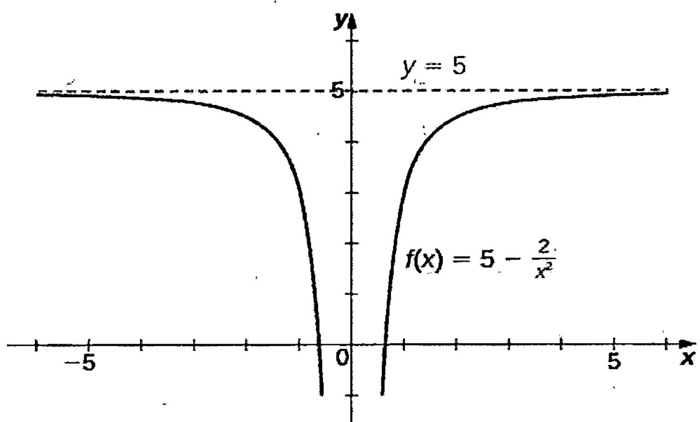

Figure 4.43 This function approaches a horizontal asymptote as $x \to \pm\infty$.

b. Since $-1 \le \sin x \le 1$ for all x, we have

$$\frac{-1}{x} \le \frac{\sin x}{x} \le \frac{1}{x}$$

for all $x \ne 0$. Also, since

$$\lim_{x \to \infty}\frac{-1}{x} = 0 = \lim_{x \to \infty}\frac{1}{x},$$

we can apply the squeeze theorem to conclude that

$$\lim_{x \to \infty}\frac{\sin x}{x} = 0.$$

Similarly,

$$\lim_{x \to -\infty}\frac{\sin x}{x} = 0.$$

Thus, $f(x) = \frac{\sin x}{x}$ has a horizontal asymptote of $y = 0$ and $f(x)$ approaches this horizontal asymptote as $x \to \pm\infty$ as shown in the following graph.

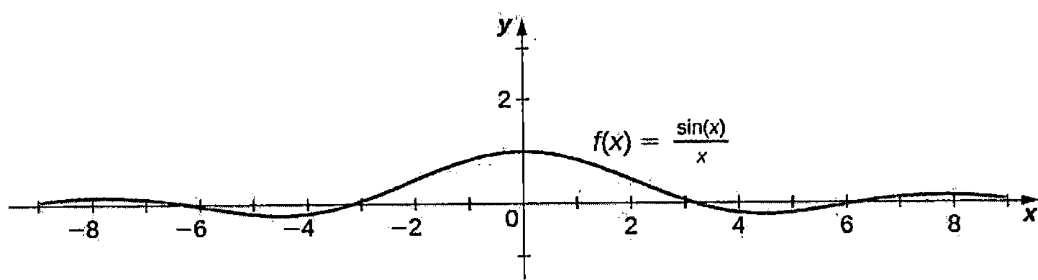

Figure 4.44 This function crosses its horizontal asymptote multiple times.

c. To evaluate $\lim\limits_{x \to \infty} \tan^{-1}(x)$ and $\lim\limits_{x \to -\infty} \tan^{-1}(x)$, we first consider the graph of $y = \tan(x)$ over the interval $(-\pi/2, \pi/2)$ as shown in the following graph.

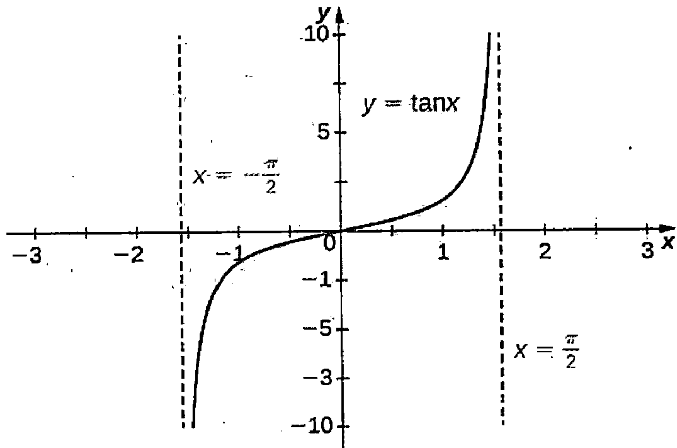

Figure 4.45 The graph of $\tan x$ has vertical asymptotes at $x = \pm\frac{\pi}{2}$

Since

$$\lim_{x \to (\pi/2)^-} \tan x = \infty,$$

it follows that

$$\lim_{x \to \infty} \tan^{-1}(x) = \frac{\pi}{2}.$$

Similarly, since

$$\lim_{x \to (\pi/2)^+} \tan x = -\infty,$$

it follows that

$$\lim_{x \to -\infty} \tan^{-1}(x) = -\frac{\pi}{2}.$$

As a result, $y = \frac{\pi}{2}$ and $y = -\frac{\pi}{2}$ are horizontal asymptotes of $f(x) = \tan^{-1}(x)$ as shown in the following graph.

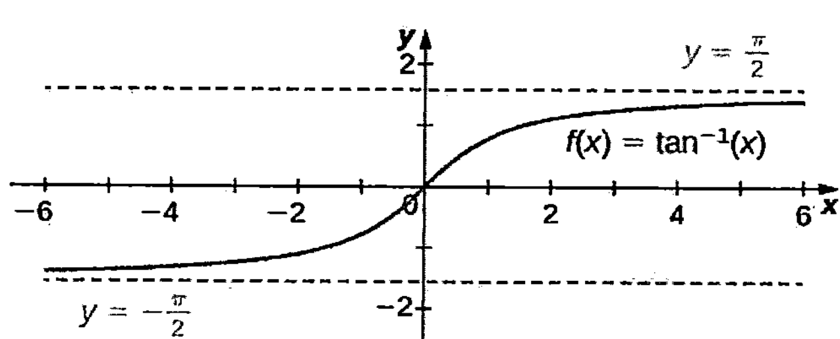

Figure 4.46 This function has two horizontal asymptotes.

4.20 Evaluate $\lim_{x \to -\infty}\left(3 + \frac{4}{x}\right)$ and $\lim_{x \to \infty}\left(3 + \frac{4}{x}\right)$. Determine the horizontal asymptotes of $f(x) = 3 + \frac{4}{x}$, if any.

Infinite Limits at Infinity

Sometimes the values of a function f become arbitrarily large as $x \to \infty$ (or as $x \to -\infty$). In this case, we write $\lim_{x \to \infty} f(x) = \infty$ (or $\lim_{x \to -\infty} f(x) = \infty$). On the other hand, if the values of f are negative but become arbitrarily large in magnitude as $x \to \infty$ (or as $x \to -\infty$), we write $\lim_{x \to \infty} f(x) = -\infty$ (or $\lim_{x \to -\infty} f(x) = -\infty$).

For example, consider the function $f(x) = x^3$. As seen in **Table 4.9** and **Figure 4.47**, as $x \to \infty$ the values $f(x)$ become arbitrarily large. Therefore, $\lim_{x \to \infty} x^3 = \infty$. On the other hand, as $x \to -\infty$, the values of $f(x) = x^3$ are negative but become arbitrarily large in magnitude. Consequently, $\lim_{x \to -\infty} x^3 = -\infty$.

x	10	20	50	100	1000
x^3	1000	8000	125,000	1,000,000	1,000,000,000
x	−10	−20	−50	−100	−1000
x^3	−1000	−8000	−125,000	−1,000,000	−1,000,000,000

Table 4.9 Values of a power function as $x \to \pm\infty$

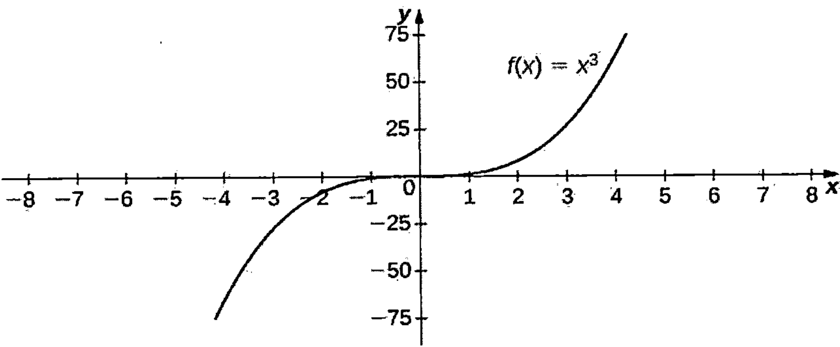

Figure 4.47 For this function, the functional values approach infinity as $x \to \pm\infty$.

Definition

(Informal) We say a function f has an infinite limit at infinity and write

$$\lim_{x \to \infty} f(x) = \infty.$$

if $f(x)$ becomes arbitrarily large for x sufficiently large. We say a function has a negative infinite limit at infinity and write

$$\lim_{x \to \infty} f(x) = -\infty.$$

if $f(x) < 0$ and $|f(x)|$ becomes arbitrarily large for x sufficiently large. Similarly, we can define infinite limits as $x \to -\infty$.

Formal Definitions

Earlier, we used the terms *arbitrarily close*, *arbitrarily large*, and *sufficiently large* to define limits at infinity informally. Although these terms provide accurate descriptions of limits at infinity, they are not precise mathematically. Here are more formal definitions of limits at infinity. We then look at how to use these definitions to prove results involving limits at infinity.

Definition

(Formal) We say a function f has a **limit at infinity**, if there exists a real number L such that for all $\varepsilon > 0$, there exists $N > 0$ such that

$$|f(x) - L| < \varepsilon$$

for all $x > N$. In that case, we write

$$\lim_{x \to \infty} f(x) = L$$

(see **Figure 4.48**).

We say a function f has a limit at negative infinity if there exists a real number L such that for all $\varepsilon > 0$, there exists $N < 0$ such that

$$|f(x) - L| < \varepsilon$$

for all $x < N$. In that case, we write

$$\lim_{x \to -\infty} f(x) = L.$$

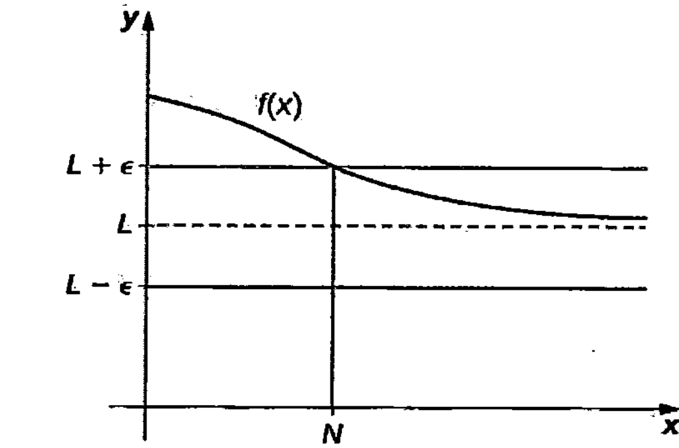

Figure 4.48 For a function with a limit at infinity, for all $x > N,\ |f(x) - L| < \varepsilon.$

Earlier in this section, we used graphical evidence in **Figure 4.40** and numerical evidence in **Table 4.8** to conclude that $\lim_{x \to \infty}\left(\frac{2+1}{x}\right) = 2.$ Here we use the formal definition of limit at infinity to prove this result rigorously.

Example 4.22 A Finite Limit at Infinity Example

Use the formal definition of limit at infinity to prove that $\lim_{x \to \infty}\left(2 + \frac{1}{x}\right) = 2.$

Solution

Let $\varepsilon > 0.$ Let $N = \frac{1}{\varepsilon}.$ Therefore, for all $x > N,$ we have

$$\left|2 + \frac{1}{x} - 2\right| = \left|\frac{1}{x}\right| = \frac{1}{x} < \frac{1}{N} = \varepsilon.$$

4.21 Use the formal definition of limit at infinity to prove that $\lim_{x \to \infty}\left(3 - \frac{1}{x^2}\right) = 3.$

We now turn our attention to a more precise definition for an infinite limit at infinity.

Definition

(Formal) We say a function f has an **infinite limit at infinity** and write

$$\lim_{x \to \infty} f(x) = \infty$$

if for all $M > 0,$ there exists an $N > 0$ such that

$$f(x) > M$$

for all $x > N$ (see **Figure 4.49**).

We say a function has a negative infinite limit at infinity and write

$$\lim_{x \to \infty} f(x) = -\infty$$

if for all $M < 0,$ there exists an $N > 0$ such that

$$f(x) < M$$

for all $x > N$.

Similarly we can define limits as $x \to -\infty$.

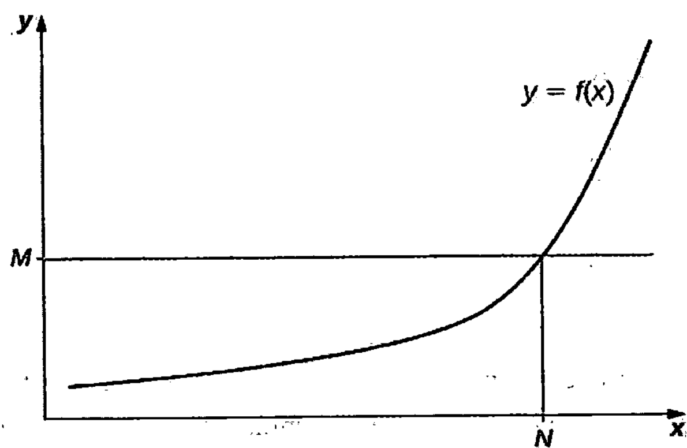

Figure 4.49 For a function with an infinite limit at infinity, for all $x > N, \ \ f(x) > M$.

Earlier, we used graphical evidence (**Figure 4.47**) and numerical evidence (**Table 4.9**) to conclude that $\lim_{x \to \infty} x^3 = \infty$. Here we use the formal definition of infinite limit at infinity to prove that result.

Example 4.23 An Infinite Limit at Infinity

Use the formal definition of infinite limit at infinity to prove that $\lim_{x \to \infty} x^3 = \infty$.

Solution

Let $M > 0$. Let $N = \sqrt[3]{M}$. Then, for all $x > N$, we have

$$x^3 > N^3 = \left(\sqrt[3]{M}\right)^3 = M.$$

Therefore, $\lim_{x \to \infty} x^3 = \infty$.

 **4.22** Use the formal definition of infinite limit at infinity to prove that $\lim_{x \to \infty} 3x^2 = \infty$.

End Behavior

The behavior of a function as $x \to \pm\infty$ is called the function's **end behavior**. At each of the function's ends, the function could exhibit one of the following types of behavior:

1. The function $f(x)$ approaches a horizontal asymptote $y = L$.
2. The function $f(x) \to \infty$ or $f(x) \to -\infty$.
3. The function does not approach a finite limit, nor does it approach ∞ or $-\infty$. In this case, the function may have some oscillatory behavior.

Let's consider several classes of functions here and look at the different types of end behaviors for these functions.

End Behavior for Polynomial Functions

Consider the power function $f(x) = x^n$ where n is a positive integer. From **Figure 4.50** and **Figure 4.51**, we see that

$$\lim_{x \to \infty} x^n = \infty; n = 1, 2, 3,\ldots$$

and

$$\lim_{x \to -\infty} x^n = \begin{cases} \infty; n = 2, 4, 6,\ldots \\ -\infty; n = 1, 3, 5,\ldots \end{cases}.$$

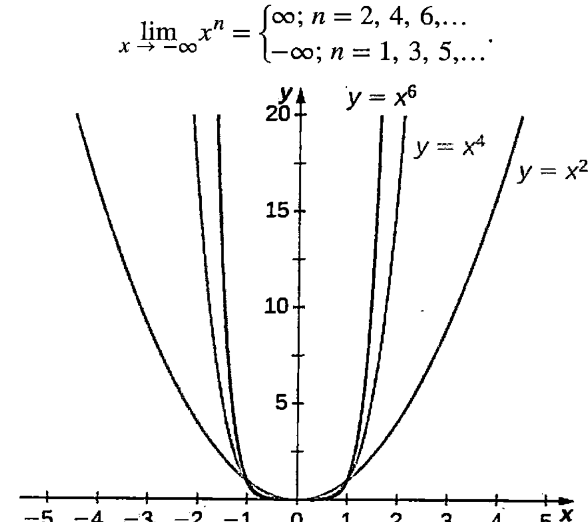

Figure 4.50 For power functions with an even power of n, $\lim_{x \to \infty} x^n = \infty = \lim_{x \to -\infty} x^n$.

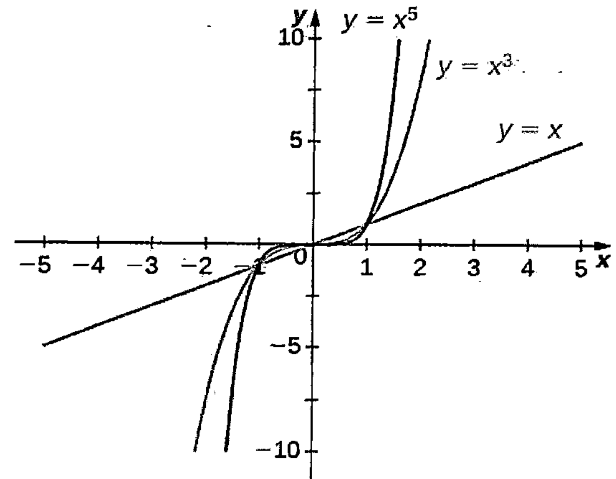

Figure 4.51 For power functions with an odd power of n, $\lim_{x \to \infty} x^n = \infty$ and $\lim_{x \to -\infty} x^n = -\infty$.

Using these facts, it is not difficult to evaluate $\lim_{x \to \infty} cx^n$ and $\lim_{x \to -\infty} cx^n$, where c is any constant and n is a positive integer. If $c > 0$, the graph of $y = cx^n$ is a vertical stretch or compression of $y = x^n$, and therefore

$$\lim_{x \to \infty} cx^n = \lim_{x \to \infty} x^n \text{ and } \lim_{x \to -\infty} cx^n = \lim_{x \to -\infty} x^n \text{ if } c > 0.$$

If $c < 0$, the graph of $y = cx^n$ is a vertical stretch or compression combined with a reflection about the x-axis, and therefore

$$\lim_{x \to \infty} cx^n = -\lim_{x \to \infty} x^n \text{ and } \lim_{x \to -\infty} cx^n = -\lim_{x \to -\infty} x^n \text{ if } c < 0.$$

If $c = 0, y = cx^n = 0,$ in which case $\lim_{x \to \infty} cx^n = 0 = \lim_{x \to -\infty} cx^n.$

Example 4.24

Limits at Infinity for Power Functions

For each function $f,$ evaluate $\lim_{x \to \infty} f(x)$ and $\lim_{x \to -\infty} f(x).$

a. $f(x) = -5x^3$

b. $f(x) = 2x^4$

Solution

a. Since the coefficient of x^3 is $-5,$ the graph of $f(x) = -5x^3$ involves a vertical stretch and reflection of the graph of $y = x^3$ about the x-axis. Therefore, $\lim_{x \to \infty}\left(-5x^3\right) = -\infty$ and $\lim_{x \to -\infty}\left(-5x^3\right) = \infty.$

b. Since the coefficient of x^4 is $2,$ the graph of $f(x) = 2x^4$ is a vertical stretch of the graph of $y = x^4.$ Therefore, $\lim_{x \to \infty} 2x^4 = \infty$ and $\lim_{x \to -\infty} 2x^4 = \infty.$

4.23 Let $f(x) = -3x^4.$ Find $\lim_{x \to \infty} f(x).$

We now look at how the limits at infinity for power functions can be used to determine $\lim_{x \to \pm\infty} f(x)$ for any polynomial function $f.$ Consider a polynomial function

$$f(x) = a_n x^n + a_{n-1} x^{n-1} + \ldots + a_1 x + a_0$$

of degree $n \geq 1$ so that $a_n \neq 0.$ Factoring, we see that

$$f(x) = a_n x^n \left(1 + \frac{a_{n-1}}{a_n}\frac{1}{x} + \ldots + \frac{a_1}{a_n}\frac{1}{x^{n-1}} + \frac{a_0}{a_n}\frac{1}{x^n}\right).$$

As $x \to \pm\infty,$ all the terms inside the parentheses approach zero except the first term. We conclude that

$$\lim_{x \to \pm\infty} f(x) = \lim_{x \to \pm\infty} a_n x^n.$$

For example, the function $f(x) = 5x^3 - 3x^2 + 4$ behaves like $g(x) = 5x^3$ as $x \to \pm\infty$ as shown in **Figure 4.52** and **Table 4.10**.

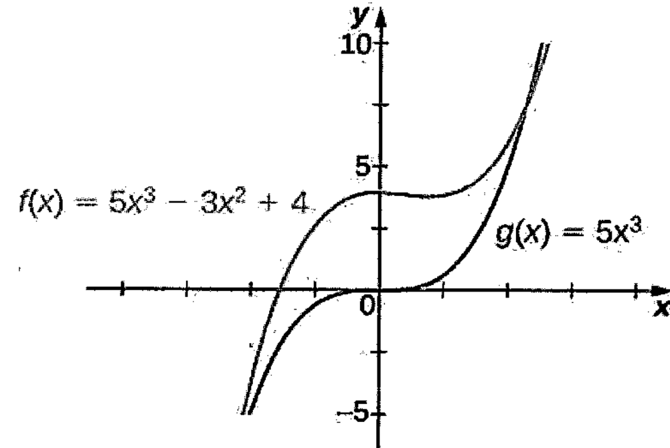

Figure 4.52 The end behavior of a polynomial is determined by the behavior of the term with the largest exponent.

x	10	100	1000
$f(x) = 5x^3 - 3x^2 + 4$	4704	4,970,004	4,997,000,004
$g(x) = 5x^3$	5000	5,000,000	5,000,000,000
x	−10	−100	−1000
$f(x) = 5x^3 - 3x^2 + 4$	−5296	−5,029,996	−5,002,999,996
$g(x) = 5x^3$	−5000	−5,000,000	−5,000,000,000

Table 4.10 A polynomial's end behavior is determined by the term with the largest exponent.

End Behavior for Algebraic Functions

The end behavior for rational functions and functions involving radicals is a little more complicated than for polynomials. In **Example 4.25**, we show that the limits at infinity of a rational function $f(x) = \frac{p(x)}{q(x)}$ depend on the relationship between the degree of the numerator and the degree of the denominator. To evaluate the limits at infinity for a rational function, we divide the numerator and denominator by the highest power of x appearing in the denominator. This determines which term in the overall expression dominates the behavior of the function at large values of x.

Example 4.25

Determining End Behavior for Rational Functions

For each of the following functions, determine the limits as $x \to \infty$ and $x \to -\infty$. Then, use this information to describe the end behavior of the function.

a. $f(x) = \frac{3x - 1}{2x + 5}$ (*Note:* The degree of the numerator and the denominator are the same.)

b. $f(x) = \dfrac{3x^2 + 2x}{4x^3 - 5x + 7}$ (*Note:* The degree of numerator is less than the degree of the denominator.)

c. $f(x) = \dfrac{3x^2 + 4x}{x + 2}$ (*Note:* The degree of numerator is greater than the degree of the denominator.)

Solution

a. The highest power of x in the denominator is x. Therefore, dividing the numerator and denominator by x and applying the algebraic limit laws, we see that

$$\begin{aligned}\lim_{x \to \pm\infty} \frac{3x - 1}{2x + 5} &= \lim_{x \to \pm\infty} \frac{3 - 1/x}{2 + 5/x} \\ &= \frac{\lim_{x \to \pm\infty} (3 - 1/x)}{\lim_{x \to \pm\infty} (2 + 5/x)} \\ &= \frac{\lim_{x \to \pm\infty} 3 - \lim_{x \to \pm\infty} 1/x}{\lim_{x \to \pm\infty} 2 + \lim_{x \to \pm\infty} 5/x} \\ &= \frac{3 - 0}{2 + 0} = \frac{3}{2}.\end{aligned}$$

Since $\lim_{x \to \pm\infty} f(x) = \frac{3}{2}$, we know that $y = \frac{3}{2}$ is a horizontal asymptote for this function as shown in the following graph.

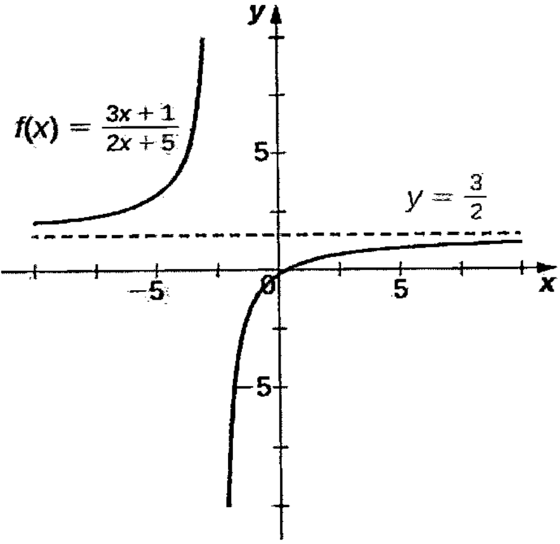

Figure 4.53 The graph of this rational function approaches a horizontal asymptote as $x \to \pm\infty$.

b. Since the largest power of x appearing in the denominator is x^3, divide the numerator and denominator by x^3. After doing so and applying algebraic limit laws, we obtain

$$\lim_{x \to \pm\infty} \frac{3x^2 + 2x}{4x^3 - 5x + 7} = \lim_{x \to \pm\infty} \frac{3/x + 2/x^2}{4 - 5/x^2 + 7/x^3} = \frac{3(0) + 2(0)}{4 - 5(0) + 7(0)} = 0.$$

Therefore f has a horizontal asymptote of $y = 0$ as shown in the following graph.

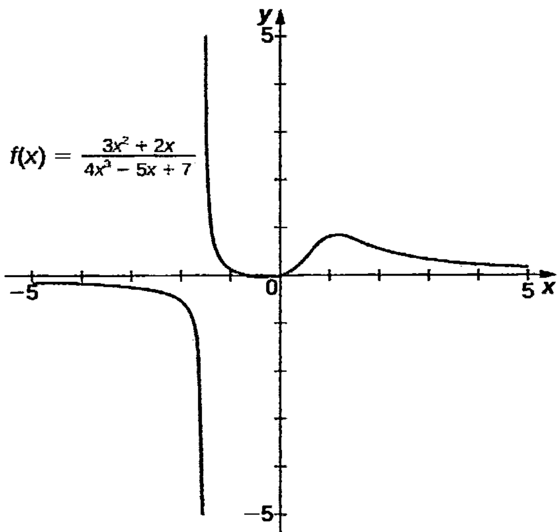

Figure 4.54 The graph of this rational function approaches the horizontal asymptote $y = 0$ as $x \to \pm\infty$.

c. Dividing the numerator and denominator by x, we have

$$\lim_{x \to \pm\infty} \frac{3x^2 + 4x}{x + 2} = \lim_{x \to \pm\infty} \frac{3x + 4}{1 + 2/x}.$$

As $x \to \pm\infty$, the denominator approaches 1. As $x \to \infty$, the numerator approaches $+\infty$. As $x \to -\infty$, the numerator approaches $-\infty$. Therefore $\lim_{x \to \infty} f(x) = \infty$, whereas $\lim_{x \to -\infty} f(x) = -\infty$ as shown in the following figure.

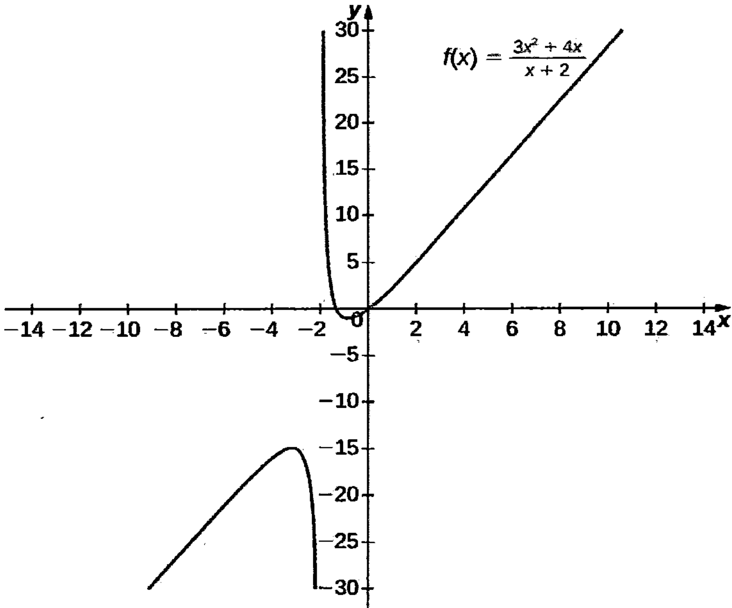

Figure 4.55 As $x \to \infty$, the values $f(x) \to \infty$. As $x \to -\infty$, the values $f(x) \to -\infty$.

 **4.24** Evaluate $\lim_{x \to \pm\infty} \frac{3x^2 + 2x - 1}{5x^2 - 4x + 7}$ and use these limits to determine the end behavior of $f(x) = \frac{3x^2 + 2x - 1}{5x^2 - 4x + 7}$.

Before proceeding, consider the graph of $f(x) = \frac{(3x^2 + 4x)}{(x + 2)}$ shown in **Figure 4.56**. As $x \to \infty$ and $x \to -\infty$, the graph of f appears almost linear. Although f is certainly not a linear function, we now investigate why the graph of f seems to be approaching a linear function. First, using long division of polynomials, we can write

$$f(x) = \frac{3x^2 + 4x}{x + 2} = 3x - 2 + \frac{4}{x + 2}.$$

Since $\frac{4}{(x + 2)} \to 0$ as $x \to \pm\infty$, we conclude that

$$\lim_{x \to \pm\infty} (f(x) - (3x - 2)) = \lim_{x \to \pm\infty} \frac{4}{x + 2} = 0.$$

Therefore, the graph of f approaches the line $y = 3x - 2$ as $x \to \pm\infty$. This line is known as an **oblique asymptote** for f **(Figure 4.56)**.

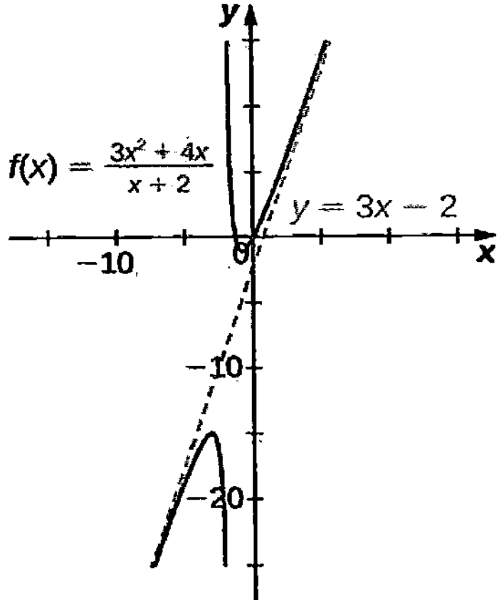

Figure 4.56 The graph of the rational function $f(x) = (3x^2 + 4x)/(x + 2)$ approaches the oblique asymptote $y = 3x - 2$ as $x \to \pm\infty$.

We can summarize the results of **Example 4.25** to make the following conclusion regarding end behavior for rational functions. Consider a rational function

$$f(x) = \frac{p(x)}{q(x)} = \frac{a_n x^n + a_{n-1} x^{n-1} + \ldots + a_1 x + a_0}{b_m x^m + b_{m-1} x^{m-1} + \ldots + b_1 x + b_0},$$

where $a_n \neq 0$ and $b_m \neq 0$.

1. If the degree of the numerator is the same as the degree of the denominator $(n = m)$, then f has a horizontal asymptote of $y = a_n / b_m$ as $x \to \pm\infty$.
2. If the degree of the numerator is less than the degree of the denominator $(n < m)$, then f has a horizontal asymptote of $y = 0$ as $x \to \pm\infty$.
3. If the degree of the numerator is greater than the degree of the denominator $(n > m)$, then f does not have a

horizontal asymptote. The limits at infinity are either positive or negative infinity, depending on the signs of the leading terms. In addition, using long division, the function can be rewritten as

$$f(x) = \frac{p(x)}{q(x)} = g(x) + \frac{r(x)}{q(x)},$$

where the degree of $r(x)$ is less than the degree of $q(x)$. As a result, $\lim_{x \to \pm\infty} r(x)/q(x) = 0$. Therefore, the values of $[f(x) - g(x)]$ approach zero as $x \to \pm\infty$. If the degree of $p(x)$ is exactly one more than the degree of $q(x)$ $(n = m + 1)$, the function $g(x)$ is a linear function. In this case, we call $g(x)$ an oblique asymptote.

Now let's consider the end behavior for functions involving a radical.

Example 4.26

Determining End Behavior for a Function Involving a Radical

Find the limits as $x \to \infty$ and $x \to -\infty$ for $f(x) = \frac{3x - 2}{\sqrt{4x^2 + 5}}$ and describe the end behavior of f.

Solution

Let's use the same strategy as we did for rational functions: divide the numerator and denominator by a power of x. To determine the appropriate power of x, consider the expression $\sqrt{4x^2 + 5}$ in the denominator. Since

$$\sqrt{4x^2 + 5} \approx \sqrt{4x^2} = 2|x|$$

for large values of x in effect x appears just to the first power in the denominator. Therefore, we divide the numerator and denominator by $|x|$. Then, using the fact that $|x| = x$ for $x > 0$, $|x| = -x$ for $x < 0$, and $|x| = \sqrt{x^2}$ for all x, we calculate the limits as follows:

$$\begin{aligned}
\lim_{x \to \infty} \frac{3x - 2}{\sqrt{4x^2 + 5}} &= \lim_{x \to \infty} \frac{(1/|x|)(3x - 2)}{(1/|x|)\sqrt{4x^2 + 5}} \\
&= \lim_{x \to \infty} \frac{(1/x)(3x - 2)}{\sqrt{(1/x^2)(4x^2 + 5)}} \\
&= \lim_{x \to \infty} \frac{3 - 2/x}{\sqrt{4 + 5/x^2}} = \frac{3}{\sqrt{4}} = \frac{3}{2} \\
\lim_{x \to -\infty} \frac{3x - 2}{\sqrt{4x^2 + 5}} &= \lim_{x \to -\infty} \frac{(1/|x|)(3x - 2)}{(1/|x|)\sqrt{4x^2 + 5}} \\
&= \lim_{x \to -\infty} \frac{(-1/x)(3x - 2)}{\sqrt{(1/x^2)(4x^2 + 5)}} \\
&= \lim_{x \to -\infty} \frac{-3 + 2/x}{\sqrt{4 + 5/x^2}} = \frac{-3}{\sqrt{4}} = \frac{-3}{2}.
\end{aligned}$$

Therefore, $f(x)$ approaches the horizontal asymptote $y = \frac{3}{2}$ as $x \to \infty$ and the horizontal asymptote $y = -\frac{3}{2}$ as $x \to -\infty$ as shown in the following graph.

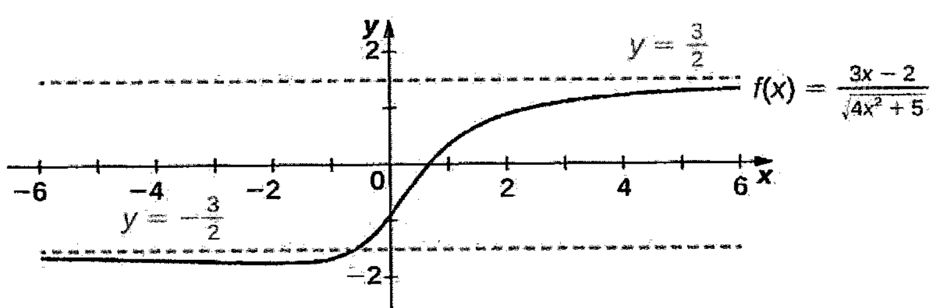

Figure 4.57 This function has two horizontal asymptotes and it crosses one of the asymptotes.

4.25 Evaluate $\lim_{x \to \infty} \frac{\sqrt{3x^2+4}}{x+6}$.

Determining End Behavior for Transcendental Functions

The six basic trigonometric functions are periodic and do not approach a finite limit as $x \to \pm\infty$. For example, $\sin x$ oscillates between $1 \text{ and } -1$ (**Figure 4.58**). The tangent function x has an infinite number of vertical asymptotes as $x \to \pm\infty$; therefore, it does not approach a finite limit nor does it approach $\pm\infty$ as $x \to \pm\infty$ as shown in **Figure 4.59**.

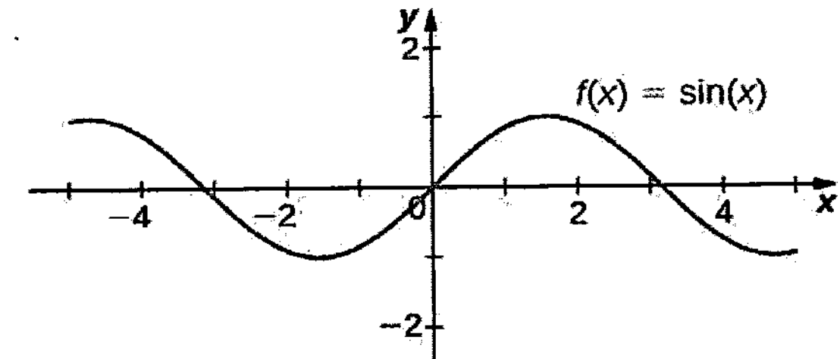

Figure 4.58 The function $f(x) = \sin x$ oscillates between $1 \text{ and } -1$ as $x \to \pm\infty$

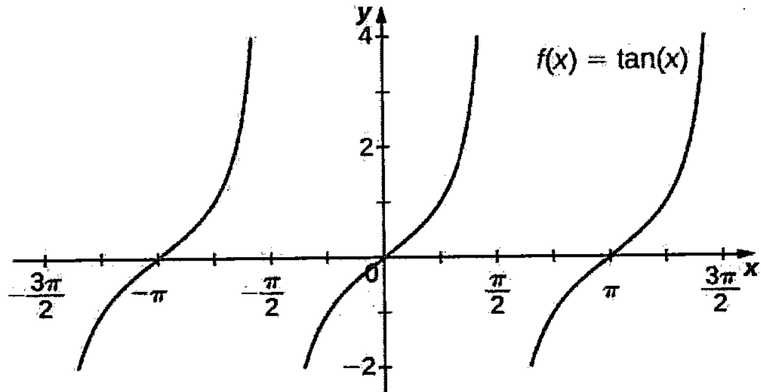

Figure 4.59 The function $f(x) = \tan x$ does not approach a limit and does not approach $\pm\infty$ as $x \to \pm\infty$

Recall that for any base $b > 0, b \neq 1,$ the function $y = b^x$ is an exponential function with domain $(-\infty, \infty)$ and range $(0, \infty)$. If $b > 1, y = b^x$ is increasing over $(-\infty, \infty)$. If $0 < b < 1,$ $y = b^x$ is decreasing over $(-\infty, \infty)$. For the natural exponential function $f(x) = e^x,$ $e \approx 2.718 > 1$. Therefore, $f(x) = e^x$ is increasing on $(-\infty, \infty)$ and the range is $(0, \infty)$. The exponential function $f(x) = e^x$ approaches ∞ as $x \to \infty$ and approaches 0 as $x \to -\infty$ as shown in **Table 4.11** and **Figure 4.60**.

x	−5	−2	0	2	5
e^x	0.00674	0.135	1	7.389	148.413

Table 4.11 End behavior of the natural exponential function

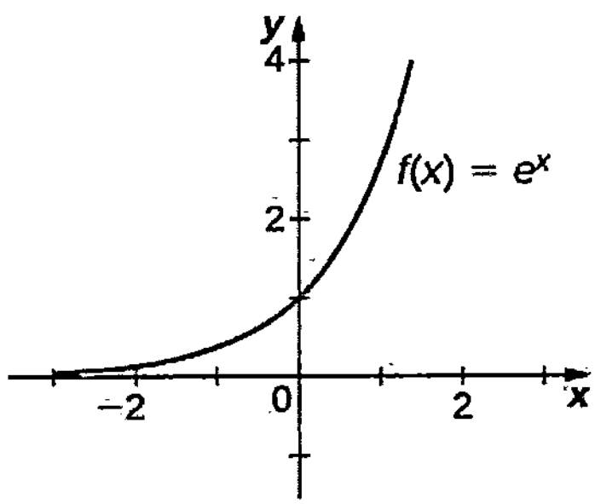

Figure 4.60 The exponential function approaches zero as $x \to -\infty$ and approaches ∞ as $x \to \infty$.

Recall that the natural logarithm function $f(x) = \ln(x)$ is the inverse of the natural exponential function $y = e^x$. Therefore, the domain of $f(x) = \ln(x)$ is $(0, \infty)$ and the range is $(-\infty, \infty)$. The graph of $f(x) = \ln(x)$ is the reflection of the graph of $y = e^x$ about the line $y = x$. Therefore, $\ln(x) \to -\infty$ as $x \to 0^+$ and $\ln(x) \to \infty$ as $x \to \infty$ as shown in **Figure 4.61** and **Table 4.12**.

x	0.01	0.1	1	10	100
$\ln(x)$	−4.605	−2.303	0	2.303	4.605

Table 4.12 End behavior of the natural logarithm function

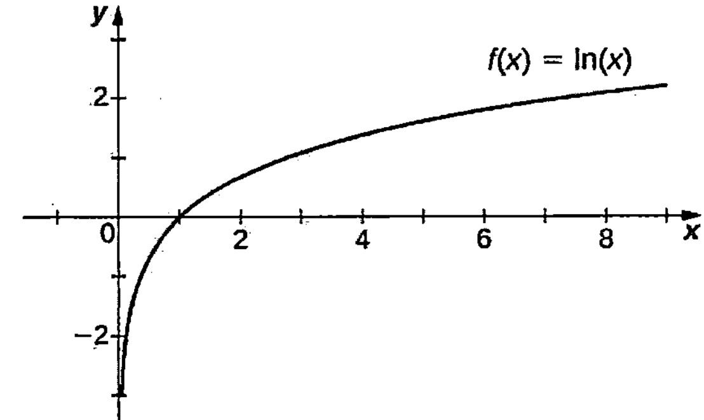

Figure 4.61 The natural logarithm function approaches ∞ as $x \to \infty$.

Example 4.27

Determining End Behavior for a Transcendental Function

Find the limits as $x \to \infty$ and $x \to -\infty$ for $f(x) = \frac{(2+3e^x)}{(7-5e^x)}$ and describe the end behavior of f.

Solution

To find the limit as $x \to \infty$, divide the numerator and denominator by e^x:

$$\begin{aligned}\lim_{x\to\infty} f(x) &= \lim_{x\to\infty}\frac{2+3e^x}{7-5e^x}\\ &= \lim_{x\to\infty}\frac{(2/e^x)+3}{(7/e^x)-5}.\end{aligned}$$

As shown in **Figure 4.60**, $e^x \to \infty$ as $x \to \infty$. Therefore,

$$\lim_{x\to\infty}\frac{2}{e^x} = 0 = \lim_{x\to\infty}\frac{7}{e^x}.$$

We conclude that $\lim_{x\to\infty} f(x) = -\frac{3}{5}$, and the graph of f approaches the horizontal asymptote $y = -\frac{3}{5}$ as $x \to \infty$. To find the limit as $x \to -\infty$, use the fact that $e^x \to 0$ as $x \to -\infty$ to conclude that $\lim_{x\to\infty} f(x) = \frac{2}{7}$, and therefore the graph of approaches the horizontal asymptote $y = \frac{2}{7}$ as $x \to -\infty$.

4.26 Find the limits as $x \to \infty$ and $x \to -\infty$ for $f(x) = \frac{(3e^x-4)}{(5e^x+2)}$.

Guidelines for Drawing the Graph of a Function

We now have enough analytical tools to draw graphs of a wide variety of algebraic and transcendental functions. Before showing how to graph specific functions, let's look at a general strategy to use when graphing any function.

Problem-Solving Strategy: Drawing the Graph of a Function

Given a function f, use the following steps to sketch a graph of f:

1. Determine the domain of the function.
2. Locate the x- and y-intercepts.
3. Evaluate $\lim_{x\to\infty} f(x)$ and $\lim_{x\to-\infty} f(x)$ to determine the end behavior. If either of these limits is a finite number L, then $y = L$ is a horizontal asymptote. If either of these limits is ∞ or $-\infty$, determine whether f has an oblique asymptote. If f is a rational function such that $f(x) = \frac{p(x)}{q(x)}$, where the degree of the numerator is greater than the degree of the denominator, then f can be written as

$$f(x) = \frac{p(x)}{q(x)} = g(x) + \frac{r(x)}{q(x)},$$

where the degree of $r(x)$ is less than the degree of $q(x)$. The values of $f(x)$ approach the values of $g(x)$ as

$x \to \pm\infty$. If $g(x)$ is a linear function, it is known as an *oblique asymptote*.

4. Determine whether f has any vertical asymptotes.
5. Calculate f'. Find all critical points and determine the intervals where f is increasing and where f is decreasing. Determine whether f has any local extrema.
6. Calculate f''. Determine the intervals where f is concave up and where f is concave down. Use this information to determine whether f has any inflection points. The second derivative can also be used as an alternate means to determine or verify that f has a local extremum at a critical point.

Now let's use this strategy to graph several different functions. We start by graphing a polynomial function.

Example 4.28

Sketching a Graph of a Polynomial

Sketch a graph of $f(x) = (x-1)^2(x+2)$.

Solution

Step 1. Since f is a polynomial, the domain is the set of all real numbers.

Step 2. When $x = 0$, $f(x) = 2$. Therefore, the y-intercept is $(0, 2)$. To find the x-intercepts, we need to solve the equation $(x-1)^2(x+2) = 0$, gives us the x-intercepts $(1, 0)$ and $(-2, 0)$

Step 3. We need to evaluate the end behavior of f. As $x \to \infty$, $(x-1)^2 \to \infty$ and $(x+2) \to \infty$. Therefore, $\lim_{x\to\infty} f(x) = \infty$. As $x \to -\infty$, $(x-1)^2 \to \infty$ and $(x+2) \to -\infty$. Therefore, $\lim_{x\to-\infty} f(x) = -\infty$. To get even more information about the end behavior of f, we can multiply the factors of f. When doing so, we see that

$$f(x) = (x-1)^2(x+2) = x^3 - 3x + 2.$$

Since the leading term of f is x^3, we conclude that f behaves like $y = x^3$ as $x \to \pm\infty$.

Step 4. Since f is a polynomial function, it does not have any vertical asymptotes.

Step 5. The first derivative of f is

$$f'(x) = 3x^2 - 3.$$

Therefore, f has two critical points: $x = 1, -1$. Divide the interval $(-\infty, \infty)$ into the three smaller intervals: $(-\infty, -1)$, $(-1, 1)$, and $(1, \infty)$. Then, choose test points $x = -2$, $x = 0$, and $x = 2$ from these intervals and evaluate the sign of $f'(x)$ at each of these test points, as shown in the following table.

Interval	Test Point	Sign of Derivative $f'(x) = 3x^2 - 3 = 3(x-1)(x+1)$	Conclusion
$(-\infty, -1)$	$x = -2$	$(+)(-)(-) = +$	f is increasing.
$(-1, 1)$	$x = 0$	$(+)(-)(+) = -$	f is decreasing.
$(1, \infty)$	$x = 2$	$(+)(+)(+) = +$	f is increasing.

From the table, we see that f has a local maximum at $x = -1$ and a local minimum at $x = 1$. Evaluating $f(x)$ at those two points, we find that the local maximum value is $f(-1) = 4$ and the local minimum value is $f(1) = 0$.

Step 6. The second derivative of f is

$$f''(x) = 6x.$$

The second derivative is zero at $x = 0$. Therefore, to determine the concavity of f, divide the interval $(-\infty, \infty)$ into the smaller intervals $(-\infty, 0)$ and $(0, \infty)$, and choose test points $x = -1$ and $x = 1$ to determine the concavity of f on each of these smaller intervals as shown in the following table.

Interval	Test Point	Sign of $f''(x) = 6x$	Conclusion
$(-\infty, 0)$	$x = -1$	$-$	f is concave down.
$(0, \infty)$	$x = 1$	$+$	f is concave up.

We note that the information in the preceding table confirms the fact, found in step 5, that f has a local maximum at $x = -1$ and a local minimum at $x = 1$. In addition, the information found in step 5—namely, f has a local maximum at $x = -1$ and a local minimum at $x = 1$, and $f'(x) = 0$ at those points—combined with the fact that f'' changes sign only at $x = 0$ confirms the results found in step 6 on the concavity of f.

Combining this information, we arrive at the graph of $f(x) = (x-1)^2(x+2)$ shown in the following graph.

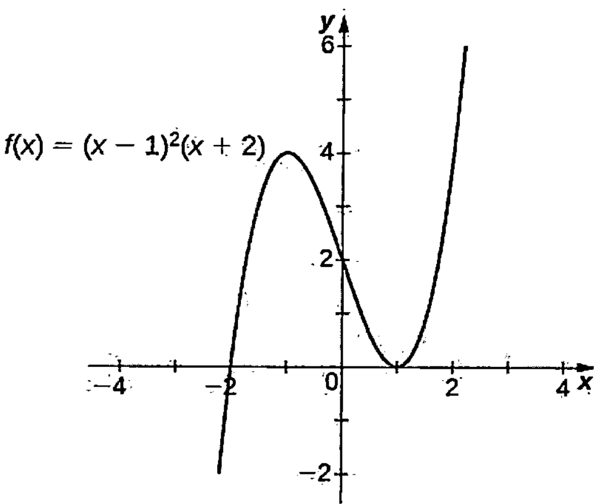

4.27 Sketch a graph of $f(x) = (x-1)^3(x+2)$.

Example 4.29

Sketching a Rational Function

Sketch the graph of $f(x) = \frac{x^2}{(1-x^2)}$.

Solution

Step 1. The function f is defined as long as the denominator is not zero. Therefore, the domain is the set of all real numbers x except $x = \pm 1$.

Step 2. Find the intercepts. If $x = 0$, then $f(x) = 0$, so 0 is an intercept. If $y = 0$, then $\frac{x^2}{(1-x^2)} = 0$, which implies $x = 0$. Therefore, $(0, 0)$ is the only intercept.

Step 3. Evaluate the limits at infinity. Since f is a rational function, divide the numerator and denominator by the highest power in the denominator: x^2. We obtain

$$\lim_{x \to \pm\infty} \frac{x^2}{1-x^2} = \lim_{x \to \pm\infty} \frac{1}{\frac{1}{x^2} - 1} = -1.$$

Therefore, f has a horizontal asymptote of $y = -1$ as $x \to \infty$ and $x \to -\infty$.

Step 4. To determine whether f has any vertical asymptotes, first check to see whether the denominator has any zeroes. We find the denominator is zero when $x = \pm 1$. To determine whether the lines $x = 1$ or $x = -1$ are vertical asymptotes of f, evaluate $\lim_{x \to 1} f(x)$ and $\lim_{x \to -1} f(x)$. By looking at each one-sided limit as $x \to 1$, we see that

$$\lim_{x \to 1^+} \frac{x^2}{1 - x^2} = -\infty \text{ and } \lim_{x \to 1^-} \frac{x^2}{1 - x^2} = \infty.$$

In addition, by looking at each one-sided limit as $x \to -1,$ we find that

$$\lim_{x \to -1^+} \frac{x^2}{1 - x^2} = \infty \text{ and } \lim_{x \to -1^-} \frac{x^2}{1 - x^2} = -\infty.$$

Step 5. Calculate the first derivative:

$$f'(x) = \frac{(1 - x^2)(2x) - x^2(-2x)}{(1 - x^2)^2} = \frac{2x}{(1 - x^2)^2}.$$

Critical points occur at points x where $f'(x) = 0$ or $f'(x)$ is undefined. We see that $f'(x) = 0$ when $x = 0$. The derivative f' is not undefined at any point in the domain of f. However, $x = \pm 1$ are not in the domain of f. Therefore, to determine where f is increasing and where f is decreasing, divide the interval $(-\infty, \infty)$ into four smaller intervals: $(-\infty, -1),$ $(-1, 0),$ $(0, 1),$ and $(1, \infty),$ and choose a test point in each interval to determine the sign of $f'(x)$ in each of these intervals. The values $x = -2,$ $x = -\frac{1}{2},$ $x = \frac{1}{2},$ and $x = 2$ are good choices for test points as shown in the following table.

Interval	**Test Point**	**Sign of** $f'(x) = \frac{2x}{(1 - x^2)^2}$	**Conclusion**
$(-\infty, -1)$	$x = -2$	$-/+ = -$	f is decreasing.
$(-1, 0)$	$x = -1/2$	$-/+ = -$	f is decreasing.
$(0, 1)$	$x = 1/2$	$+/+ = +$	f is increasing.
$(1, \infty)$	$x = 2$	$+/+ = +$	f is increasing.

From this analysis, we conclude that f has a local minimum at $x = 0$ but no local maximum.

Step 6. Calculate the second derivative:

$$\begin{aligned} f''(x) &= \frac{\left(1-x^2\right)^2(2) - 2x\left(2\left(1-x^2\right)(-2x)\right)}{\left(1-x^2\right)^4} \\ &= \frac{\left(1-x^2\right)\left[2\left(1-x^2\right)+8x^2\right]}{\left(1-x^2\right)^4} \\ &= \frac{2\left(1-x^2\right)+8x^2}{\left(1-x^2\right)^3} \\ &= \frac{6x^2+2}{\left(1-x^2\right)^3}. \end{aligned}$$

To determine the intervals where f is concave up and where f is concave down, we first need to find all points x where $f''(x)=0$ or $f''(x)$ is undefined. Since the numerator $6x^2+2 \neq 0$ for any $x,$ $f''(x)$ is never zero. Furthermore, f'' is not undefined for any x in the domain of $f.$ However, as discussed earlier, $x=\pm 1$ are not in the domain of $f.$ Therefore, to determine the concavity of $f,$ we divide the interval $(-\infty, \infty)$ into the three smaller intervals $(-\infty, -1),$ $(-1, -1),$ and $(1, \infty),$ and choose a test point in each of these intervals to evaluate the sign of $f''(x).$ in each of these intervals. The values $x=-2,$ $x=0,$ and $x=2$ are possible test points as shown in the following table.

Interval	**Test Point**	**Sign of $f''(x) = \frac{6x^2+2}{\left(1-x^2\right)^3}$**	**Conclusion**
$(-\infty, -1)$	$x=-2$	$+/- = -$	f is concave down.
$(-1, -1)$	$x=0$	$+/+ = +$	f is concave up.
$(1, \infty)$.	$x=2$	$+/- = -$	f is concave down.

Combining all this information, we arrive at the graph of f shown below. Note that, although f changes concavity at $x=-1$ and $x=1,$ there are no inflection points at either of these places because f is not continuous at $x=-1$ or $x=1.$

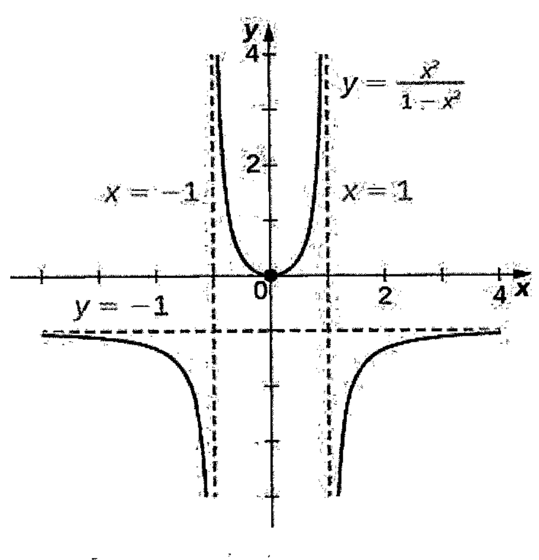

4.28 Sketch a graph of $f(x) = \frac{(3x+5)}{(8+4x)}$.

Example 4.30

Sketching a Rational Function with an Oblique Asymptote

Sketch the graph of $f(x) = \frac{x^2}{(x-1)}$

Solution

Step 1. The domain of f is the set of all real numbers x except $x = 1$.

Step 2. Find the intercepts. We can see that when $x = 0$, $f(x) = 0$, so $(0, 0)$ is the only intercept.

Step 3. Evaluate the limits at infinity. Since the degree of the numerator is one more than the degree of the denominator, f must have an oblique asymptote. To find the oblique asymptote, use long division of polynomials to write

$$f(x) = \frac{x^2}{x-1} = x + 1 + \frac{1}{x-1}.$$

Since $1/(x-1) \to 0$ as $x \to \pm\infty$, $f(x)$ approaches the line $y = x + 1$ as $x \to \pm\infty$. The line $y = x + 1$ is an oblique asymptote for f.

Step 4. To check for vertical asymptotes, look at where the denominator is zero. Here the denominator is zero at $x = 1$. Looking at both one-sided limits as $x \to 1$, we find

$$\lim_{x \to 1^+} \frac{x^2}{x-1} = \infty \text{ and } \lim_{x \to 1^-} \frac{x^2}{x-1} = -\infty.$$

Therefore, $x = 1$ is a vertical asymptote, and we have determined the behavior of f as x approaches 1 from the right and the left.

Step 5. Calculate the first derivative:

$$f'(x) = \frac{(x-1)(2x) - x^2(1)}{(x-1)^2} = \frac{x^2 - 2x}{(x-1)^2}.$$

We have $f'(x) = 0$ when $x^2 - 2x = x(x-2) = 0$. Therefore, $x = 0$ and $x = 2$ are critical points. Since f is undefined at $x = 1$, we need to divide the interval $(-\infty, \infty)$ into the smaller intervals $(-\infty, 0)$, $(0, 1)$, $(1, 2)$, and $(2, \infty)$, and choose a test point from each interval to evaluate the sign of $f'(x)$ in each of these smaller intervals. For example, let $x = -1$, $x = \frac{1}{2}$, $x = \frac{3}{2}$, and $x = 3$ be the test points as shown in the following table.

Interval	**Test Point**	**Sign of $f'(x) = \frac{x^2 - 2x}{(x-1)^2} = \frac{x(x-2)}{(x-1)^2}$**	**Conclusion**
$(-\infty, 0)$	$x = -1$	$(-)(-)/+ = +$	f is increasing.
$(0, 1)$	$x = 1/2$	$(+)(-)/+ = -$	f is decreasing.
$(1, 2)$	$x = 3/2$	$(+)(-)/+ = -$	f is decreasing.
$(2, \infty)$	$x = 3$	$(+)(+)/+ = +$	f is increasing.

From this table, we see that f has a local maximum at $x = 0$ and a local minimum at $x = 2$. The value of f at the local maximum is $f(0) = 0$ and the value of f at the local minimum is $f(2) = 4$. Therefore, $(0, 0)$ and $(2, 4)$ are important points on the graph.

Step 6. Calculate the second derivative:

$$\begin{aligned} f''(x) &= \frac{(x-1)^2(2x-2) - \left(x^2 - 2x\right)(2(x-1))}{(x-1)^4} \\ &= \frac{(x-1)\left[(x-1)(2x-2) - 2\left(x^2 - 2x\right)\right]}{(x-1)^4} \\ &= \frac{(x-1)(2x-2) - 2\left(x^2 - 2x\right)}{(x-1)^3} \\ &= \frac{2x^2 - 4x + 2 - \left(2x^2 - 4x\right)}{(x-1)^3} \\ &= \frac{2}{(x-1)^3}. \end{aligned}$$

We see that $f''(x)$ is never zero or undefined for x in the domain of f. Since f is undefined at $x = 1$, to check concavity we just divide the interval $(-\infty, \infty)$ into the two smaller intervals $(-\infty, 1)$ and $(1, \infty)$, and choose a test point from each interval to evaluate the sign of $f''(x)$ in each of these intervals. The values $x = 0$

and $x = 2$ are possible test points as shown in the following table.

Interval	Test Point	Sign of $f''(x) = \frac{2}{(x-1)^3}$	Conclusion
$(-\infty, 1)$	$x = 0$	$+/- = -$	f is concave down.
$(1, \infty)$	$x = 2$	$+/+ = +$	f is concave up.

From the information gathered, we arrive at the following graph for f.

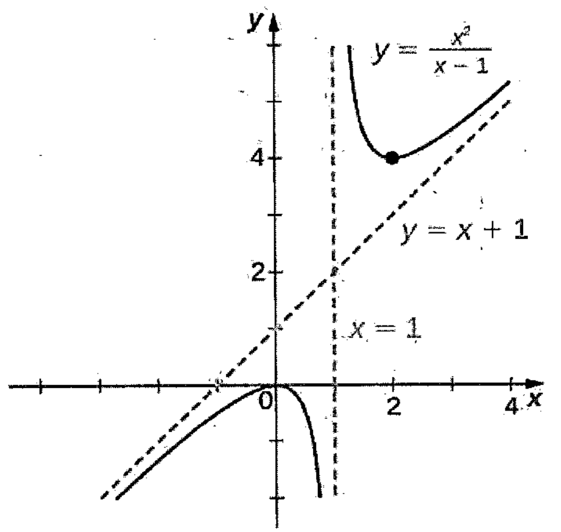

4.29 Find the oblique asymptote for $f(x) = \frac{(3x^3 - 2x + 1)}{(2x^2 - 4)}$.

Example 4.31

Sketching the Graph of a Function with a Cusp

Sketch a graph of $f(x) = (x-1)^{2/3}$.

Solution

Step 1. Since the cube-root function is defined for all real numbers x and $(x-1)^{2/3} = \left(\sqrt[3]{x-1}\right)^2$, the domain of f is all real numbers.

Step 2: To find the y-intercept, evaluate $f(0)$. Since $f(0) = 1$, the y-intercept is $(0, 1)$. To find the x-intercept, solve $(x-1)^{2/3} = 0$. The solution of this equation is $x = 1$, so the x-intercept is $(1, 0)$.

Step 3: Since $\lim_{x \to \pm\infty} (x-1)^{2/3} = \infty$, the function continues to grow without bound as $x \to \infty$ and $x \to -\infty$.

Step 4: The function has no vertical asymptotes.

Step 5: To determine where f is increasing or decreasing, calculate f'. We find

$$f'(x) = \frac{2}{3}(x-1)^{-1/3} = \frac{2}{3(x-1)^{1/3}}.$$

This function is not zero anywhere, but it is undefined when $x = 1$. Therefore, the only critical point is $x = 1$. Divide the interval $(-\infty, \infty)$ into the smaller intervals $(-\infty, 1)$ and $(1, \infty)$, and choose test points in each of these intervals to determine the sign of $f'(x)$ in each of these smaller intervals. Let $x = 0$ and $x = 2$ be the test points as shown in the following table.

Interval	**Test Point**	**Sign of $f'(x) = \frac{2}{3(x-1)^{1/3}}$**	**Conclusion**
$(-\infty, 1)$	$x = 0$	$+/- = -$	f is decreasing.
$(1, \infty)$	$x = 2$	$+/+ = +$	f is increasing.

We conclude that f has a local minimum at $x = 1$. Evaluating f at $x = 1$, we find that the value of f at the local minimum is zero. Note that $f'(1)$ is undefined, so to determine the behavior of the function at this critical point, we need to examine $\lim_{x \to 1} f'(x)$. Looking at the one-sided limits, we have

$$\lim_{x \to 1^+} \frac{2}{3(x-1)^{1/3}} = \infty \text{ and } \lim_{x \to 1^-} \frac{2}{3(x-1)^{1/3}} = -\infty.$$

Therefore, f has a cusp at $x = 1$.

Step 6: To determine concavity, we calculate the second derivative of f:

$$f''(x) = -\frac{2}{9}(x-1)^{-4/3} = \frac{-2}{9(x-1)^{4/3}}.$$

We find that $f''(x)$ is defined for all x, but is undefined when $x = 1$. Therefore, divide the interval $(-\infty, \infty)$ into the smaller intervals $(-\infty, 1)$ and $(1, \infty)$, and choose test points to evaluate the sign of $f''(x)$ in each of these intervals. As we did earlier, let $x = 0$ and $x = 2$ be test points as shown in the following table.

Interval	**Test Point**	**Sign of $f''(x) = \frac{-2}{9(x-1)^{4/3}}$**	**Conclusion**
$(-\infty, 1)$	$x = 0$	$-/+ = -$	f is concave down.
$(1, \infty)$	$x = 2$	$-/+ = -$	f is concave down.

From this table, we conclude that f is concave down everywhere. Combining all of this information, we arrive at the following graph for f.

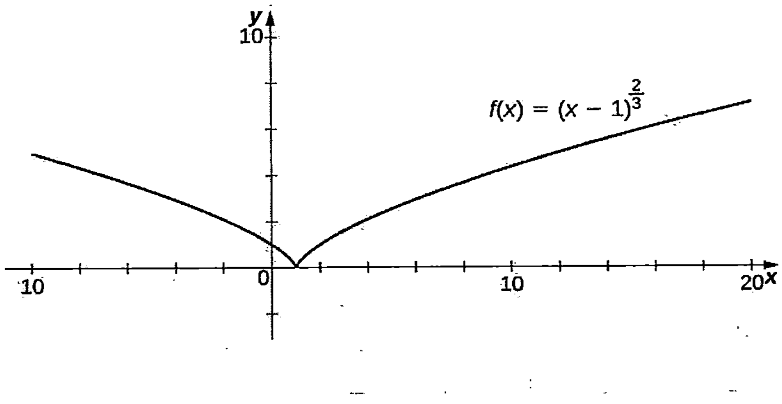

4.30 Consider the function $f(x) = 5 - x^{2/3}$. Determine the point on the graph where a cusp is located. Determine the end behavior of f.

4.6 EXERCISES

For the following exercises, examine the graphs. Identify where the vertical asymptotes are located.

251.

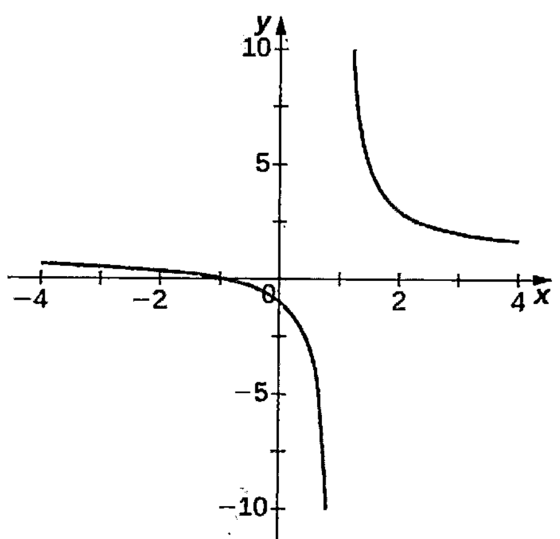

252.

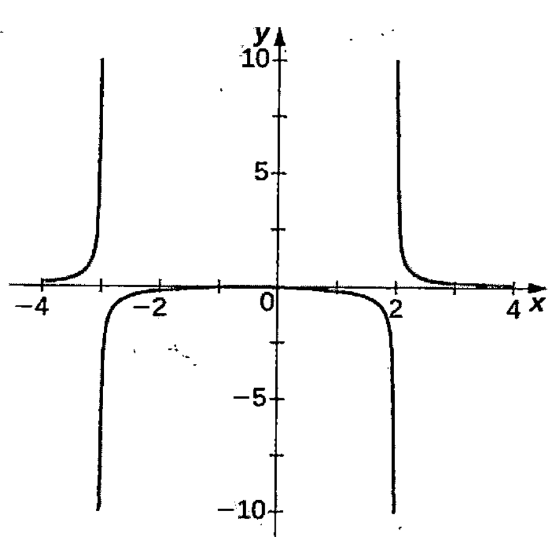

253.

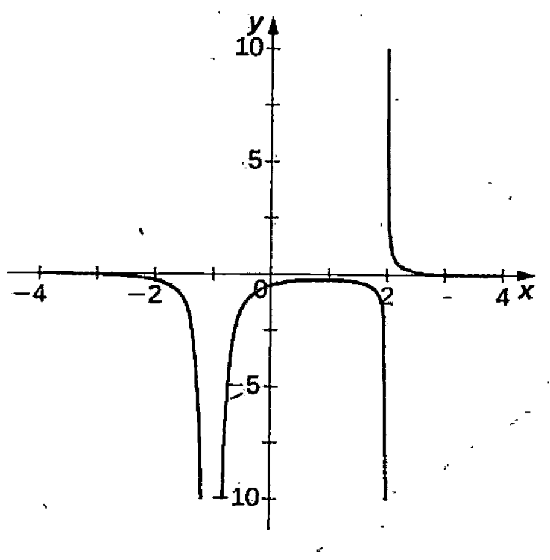

254.

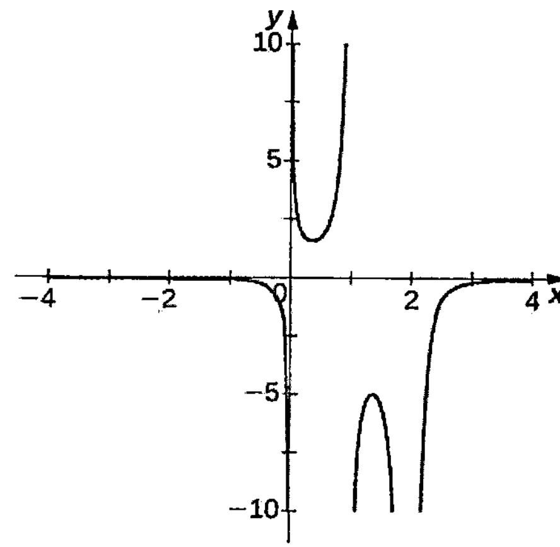

255.

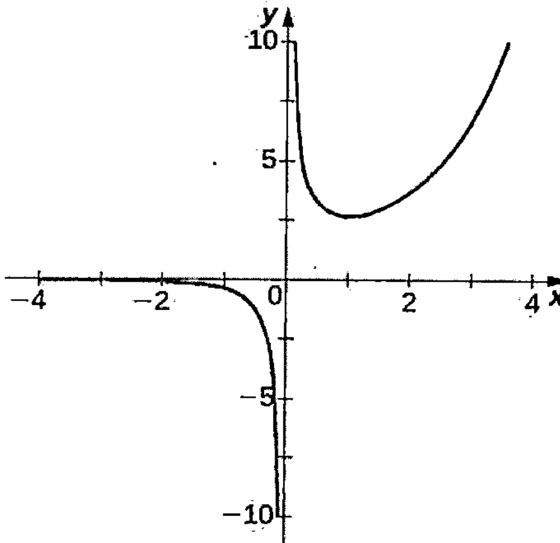

For the following functions $f(x)$, determine whether there is an asymptote at $x = a$. Justify your answer without graphing on a calculator.

256. $f(x) = \frac{x+1}{x^2 + 5x + 4}$, $a = -1$

257. $f(x) = \frac{x}{x-2}$, $a = 2$

258. $f(x) = (x+2)^{3/2}$, $a = -2$

259. $f(x) = (x-1)^{-1/3}$, $a = 1$

260. $f(x) = 1 + x^{-2/5}$, $a = 1$

For the following exercises, evaluate the limit.

261. $\lim_{x \to \infty} \frac{1}{3x+6}$

262. $\lim_{x \to \infty} \frac{2x - 5}{4x}$

263. $\lim_{x \to \infty} \frac{x^2 - 2x + 5}{x + 2}$

264. $\lim_{x \to -\infty} \frac{3x^3 - 2x}{x^2 + 2x + 8}$

265. $\lim_{x \to -\infty} \frac{x^4 - 4x^3 + 1}{2 - 2x^2 - 7x^4}$

266. $\lim_{x \to \infty} \frac{3x}{\sqrt{x^2 + 1}}$

267. $\lim_{x \to -\infty} \frac{\sqrt{4x^2 - 1}}{x + 2}$

268. $\lim_{x \to \infty} \frac{4x}{\sqrt{x^2 - 1}}$

269. $\lim_{x \to -\infty} \frac{4x}{\sqrt{x^2 - 1}}$

270. $\lim_{x \to \infty} \frac{2\sqrt{x}}{x - \sqrt{x} + 1}$

For the following exercises, find the horizontal and vertical asymptotes.

271. $f(x) = x - \frac{9}{x}$

272. $f(x) = \frac{1}{1 - x^2}$

273. $f(x) = \frac{x^3}{4 - x^2}$

274. $f(x) = \frac{x^2 + 3}{x^2 + 1}$

275. $f(x) = \sin(x)\sin(2x)$

276. $f(x) = \cos x + \cos(3x) + \cos(5x)$

277. $f(x) = \frac{x\sin(x)}{x^2 - 1}$

278. $f(x) = \frac{x}{\sin(x)}$

279. $f(x) = \frac{1}{x^3 + x^2}$

280. $f(x) = \frac{1}{x - 1} - 2x$

281. $f(x) = \frac{x^3 + 1}{x^3 - 1}$

282. $f(x) = \frac{\sin x + \cos x}{\sin x - \cos x}$

283. $f(x) = x - \sin x$

284. $f(x) = \frac{1}{x} - \sqrt{x}$

For the following exercises, construct a function $f(x)$ that has the given asymptotes.

285. $x = 1$ and $y = 2$

286. $x = 1$ and $y = 0$

287. $y = 4, \quad x = -1$

288. $x = 0$

For the following exercises, graph the function on a graphing calculator on the window $x = [-5, 5]$ and estimate the horizontal asymptote or limit. Then, calculate the actual horizontal asymptote or limit.

289. **[T]** $f(x) = \frac{1}{x + 10}$

290. **[T]** $f(x) = \frac{x + 1}{x^2 + 7x + 6}$

291. **[T]** $\lim_{x \to -\infty} x^2 + 10x + 25$

292. **[T]** $\lim_{x \to -\infty} \frac{x + 2}{x^2 + 7x + 6}$

293. **[T]** $\lim_{x \to \infty} \frac{3x + 2}{x + 5}$

For the following exercises, draw a graph of the functions without using a calculator. Be sure to notice all important features of the graph: local maxima and minima, inflection points, and asymptotic behavior.

294. $y = 3x^2 + 2x + 4$

295. $y = x^3 - 3x^2 + 4$

296. $y = \frac{2x + 1}{x^2 + 6x + 5}$

297. $y = \frac{x^3 + 4x^2 + 3x}{3x + 9}$

298. $y = \frac{x^2 + x - 2}{x^2 - 3x - 4}$

299. $y = \sqrt{x^2 - 5x + 4}$

300. $y = 2x\sqrt{16 - x^2}$

301. $y = \frac{\cos x}{x}$, on $x = [-2\pi, 2\pi]$

302. $y = e^x - x^3$

303. $y = x\tan x$, $x = [-\pi, \pi]$

304. $y = x\ln(x)$, $x > 0$

305. $y = x^2\sin(x)$, $x = [-2\pi, 2\pi]$

306. For $f(x) = \frac{P(x)}{Q(x)}$ to have an asymptote at $y = 2$ then the polynomials $P(x)$ and $Q(x)$ must have what relation?

307. For $f(x) = \frac{P(x)}{Q(x)}$ to have an asymptote at $x = 0$, then the polynomials $P(x)$ and $Q(x)$. must have what relation?

308. If $f'(x)$ has asymptotes at $y = 3$ and $x = 1$, then $f(x)$ has what asymptotes?

309. Both $f(x) = \frac{1}{(x-1)}$ and $g(x) = \frac{1}{(x-1)^2}$ have asymptotes at $x = 1$ and $y = 0$. What is the most obvious difference between these two functions?

310. True or false: Every ratio of polynomials has vertical asymptotes.

4.7 | Applied Optimization Problems

Learning Objectives

4.7.1 Set up and solve optimization problems in several applied fields.

One common application of calculus is calculating the minimum or maximum value of a function. For example, companies often want to minimize production costs or maximize revenue. In manufacturing, it is often desirable to minimize the amount of material used to package a product with a certain volume. In this section, we show how to set up these types of minimization and maximization problems and solve them by using the tools developed in this chapter.

Solving Optimization Problems over a Closed, Bounded Interval

The basic idea of the **optimization problems** that follow is the same. We have a particular quantity that we are interested in maximizing or minimizing. However, we also have some auxiliary condition that needs to be satisfied. For example, in **Example 4.32**, we are interested in maximizing the area of a rectangular garden. Certainly, if we keep making the side lengths of the garden larger, the area will continue to become larger. However, what if we have some restriction on how much fencing we can use for the perimeter? In this case, we cannot make the garden as large as we like. Let's look at how we can maximize the area of a rectangle subject to some constraint on the perimeter.

Example 4.32

Maximizing the Area of a Garden

A rectangular garden is to be constructed using a rock wall as one side of the garden and wire fencing for the other three sides (**Figure 4.62**). Given 100 ft of wire fencing, determine the dimensions that would create a garden of maximum area. What is the maximum area?

Figure 4.62 We want to determine the measurements x and y that will create a garden with a maximum area using 100 ft of fencing.

Solution

Let x denote the length of the side of the garden perpendicular to the rock wall and y denote the length of the side parallel to the rock wall. Then the area of the garden is

$$A = x \cdot y.$$

We want to find the maximum possible area subject to the constraint that the total fencing is 100 ft. From **Figure 4.62**, the total amount of fencing used will be $2x + y$. Therefore, the constraint equation is

$$2x + y = 100.$$

Solving this equation for y, we have $y = 100 - 2x$. Thus, we can write the area as

$$A(x) = x \cdot (100 - 2x) = 100x - 2x^2.$$

Before trying to maximize the area function $A(x) = 100x - 2x^2$, we need to determine the domain under consideration. To construct a rectangular garden, we certainly need the lengths of both sides to be positive. Therefore, we need $x > 0$ and $y > 0$. Since $y = 100 - 2x$, if $y > 0$, then $x < 50$. Therefore, we are trying to determine the maximum value of $A(x)$ for x over the open interval $(0, 50)$. We do not know that a function necessarily has a maximum value over an open interval. However, we do know that a continuous function has an absolute maximum (and absolute minimum) over a closed interval. Therefore, let's consider the function $A(x) = 100x - 2x^2$ over the closed interval $[0, 50]$. If the maximum value occurs at an interior point, then we have found the value x in the open interval $(0, 50)$ that maximizes the area of the garden. Therefore, we consider the following problem:

Maximize $A(x) = 100x - 2x^2$ over the interval $[0, 50]$.

As mentioned earlier, since A is a continuous function on a closed, bounded interval, by the extreme value theorem, it has a maximum and a minimum. These extreme values occur either at endpoints or critical points. At the endpoints, $A(x) = 0$. Since the area is positive for all x in the open interval $(0, 50)$, the maximum must occur at a critical point. Differentiating the function $A(x)$, we obtain

$$A'(x) = 100 - 4x.$$

Therefore, the only critical point is $x = 25$ (**Figure 4.63**). We conclude that the maximum area must occur when $x = 25$. Then we have $y = 100 - 2x = 100 - 2(25) = 50$. To maximize the area of the garden, let $x = 25$ ft and $y = 50$ ft. The area of this garden is $1250\ \text{ft}^2$.

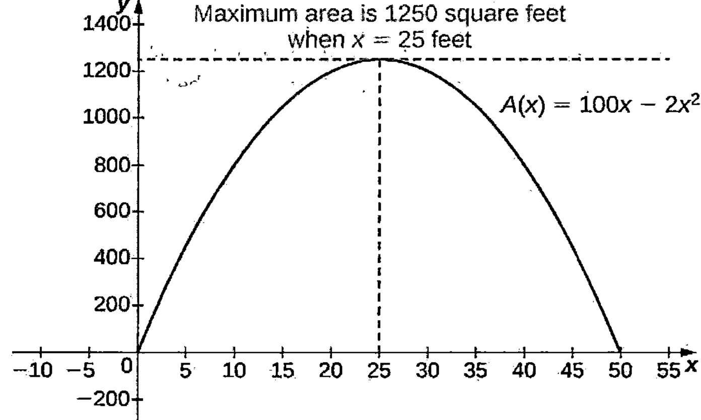

Figure 4.63 To maximize the area of the garden, we need to find the maximum value of the function $A(x) = 100x - 2x^2$.

4.31 Determine the maximum area if we want to make the same rectangular garden as in **Figure 4.63**, but we have 200 ft of fencing.

Now let's look at a general strategy for solving optimization problems similar to **Example 4.32**.

Problem-Solving Strategy: Solving Optimization Problems

1. Introduce all variables. If applicable, draw a figure and label all variables.
2. Determine which quantity is to be maximized or minimized, and for what range of values of the other variables (if this can be determined at this time).
3. Write a formula for the quantity to be maximized or minimized in terms of the variables. This formula may involve more than one variable.
4. Write any equations relating the independent variables in the formula from step 3. Use these equations to write the quantity to be maximized or minimized as a function of one variable.
5. Identify the domain of consideration for the function in step 4 based on the physical problem to be solved.
6. Locate the maximum or minimum value of the function from step 4. This step typically involves looking for critical points and evaluating a function at endpoints.

Now let's apply this strategy to maximize the volume of an open-top box given a constraint on the amount of material to be used.

Example 4.33

Maximizing the Volume of a Box

An open-top box is to be made from a 24 in. by 36 in. piece of cardboard by removing a square from each corner of the box and folding up the flaps on each side. What size square should be cut out of each corner to get a box with the maximum volume?

Solution

Step 1: Let x be the side length of the square to be removed from each corner (**Figure 4.64**). Then, the remaining four flaps can be folded up to form an open-top box. Let V be the volume of the resulting box.

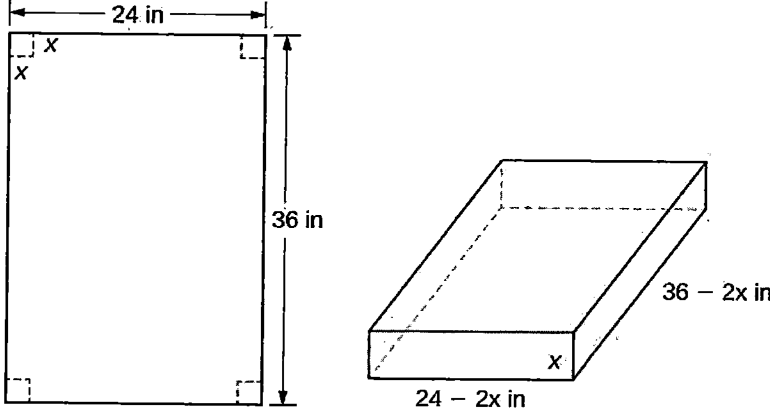

Figure 4.64 A square with side length x inches is removed from each corner of the piece of cardboard. The remaining flaps are folded to form an open-top box.

Step 2: We are trying to maximize the volume of a box. Therefore, the problem is to maximize V.

Step 3: As mentioned in step 2, are trying to maximize the volume of a box. The volume of a box is $V = L \cdot W \cdot H,$ where $L,$ $W,$ and H are the length, width, and height, respectively.

Step 4: From **Figure 4.64**, we see that the height of the box is x inches, the length is $36 - 2x$ inches, and the width is $24 - 2x$ inches. Therefore, the volume of the box is

$$V(x) = (36 - 2x)(24 - 2x)x = 4x^3 - 120x^2 + 864x.$$

Step 5: To determine the domain of consideration, let's examine **Figure 4.64**. Certainly, we need $x > 0.$ Furthermore, the side length of the square cannot be greater than or equal to half the length of the shorter side, 24 in.; otherwise, one of the flaps would be completely cut off. Therefore, we are trying to determine whether there is a maximum volume of the box for x over the open interval $(0, 12).$ Since V is a continuous function over the closed interval $[0, 12],$ we know V will have an absolute maximum over the closed interval. Therefore, we consider V over the closed interval $[0, 12]$ and check whether the absolute maximum occurs at an interior point.

Step 6: Since $V(x)$ is a continuous function over the closed, bounded interval $[0, 12],$ V must have an absolute maximum (and an absolute minimum). Since $V(x) = 0$ at the endpoints and $V(x) > 0$ for $0 < x < 12,$ the maximum must occur at a critical point. The derivative is

$$V'(x) = 12x^2 - 240x + 864.$$

To find the critical points, we need to solve the equation

$$12x^2 - 240x + 864 = 0.$$

Dividing both sides of this equation by $12,$ the problem simplifies to solving the equation

$$x^2 - 20x + 72 = 0.$$

Using the quadratic formula, we find that the critical points are

$$x = \frac{20 \pm \sqrt{(-20)^2 - 4(1)(72)}}{2} = \frac{20 \pm \sqrt{112}}{2} = \frac{20 \pm 4\sqrt{7}}{2} = 10 \pm 2\sqrt{7}.$$

Since $10 + 2\sqrt{7}$ is not in the domain of consideration, the only critical point we need to consider is $10 - 2\sqrt{7}$. Therefore, the volume is maximized if we let $x = 10 - 2\sqrt{7}$ in. The maximum volume is $V(10 - 2\sqrt{7}) = 640 + 448\sqrt{7} \approx 1825 \text{ in.}^3$ as shown in the following graph.

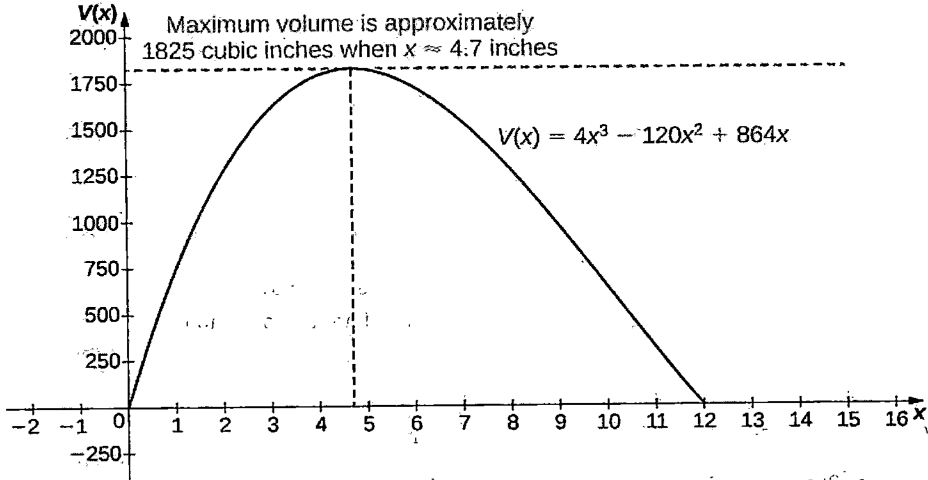

Figure 4.65 Maximizing the volume of the box leads to finding the maximum value of a cubic polynomial.

Watch a **video (http://www.openstaxcollege.org/l/20_boxvolume)** about optimizing the volume of a box.

4.32 Suppose the dimensions of the cardboard in **Example 4.33** are 20 in. by 30 in. Let x be the side length of each square and write the volume of the open-top box as a function of x. Determine the domain of consideration for x.

Example 4.34

Minimizing Travel Time

An island is 2 mi due north of its closest point along a straight shoreline. A visitor is staying at a cabin on the shore that is 6 mi west of that point. The visitor is planning to go from the cabin to the island. Suppose the visitor runs at a rate of 8 mph and swims at a rate of 3 mph. How far should the visitor run before swimming to minimize the time it takes to reach the island?

Solution

Step 1: Let x be the distance running and let y be the distance swimming (**Figure 4.66**). Let T be the time it takes to get from the cabin to the island.

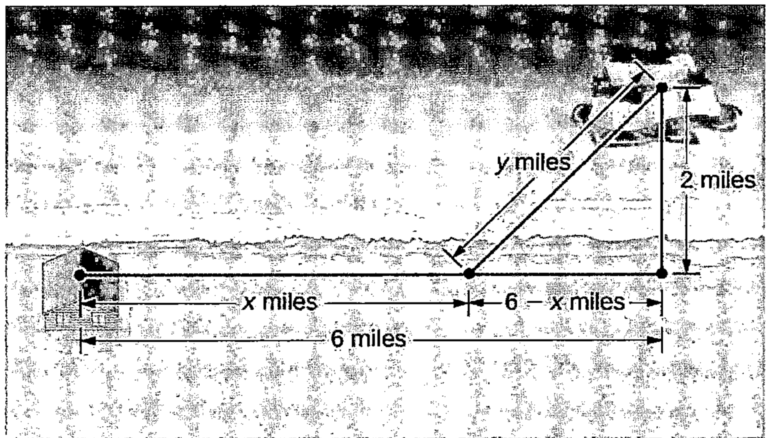

Figure 4.66 How can we choose x and y to minimize the travel time from the cabin to the island?

Step 2: The problem is to minimize T.

Step 3: To find the time spent traveling from the cabin to the island, add the time spent running and the time spent swimming. Since Distance $=$ Rate $\times$ Time $(D = R \times T)$, the time spent running is

$$T_{\text{running}} = \frac{D_{\text{running}}}{R_{\text{running}}} = \frac{x}{8},$$

and the time spent swimming is

$$T_{\text{swimming}} = \frac{D_{\text{swimming}}}{R_{\text{swimming}}} = \frac{y}{3}.$$

Therefore, the total time spent traveling is

$$T = \frac{x}{8} + \frac{y}{3}.$$

Step 4: From **Figure 4.66**, the line segment of y miles forms the hypotenuse of a right triangle with legs of length 2 mi and $6 - x\text{ mi}$. Therefore, by the Pythagorean theorem, $2^2 + (6 - x)^2 = y^2$, and we obtain $y = \sqrt{(6 - x)^2 + 4}$. Thus, the total time spent traveling is given by the function

$$T(x) = \frac{x}{8} + \frac{\sqrt{(6 - x)^2 + 4}}{3}.$$

Step 5: From **Figure 4.66**, we see that $0 \le x \le 6$. Therefore, $[0, 6]$ is the domain of consideration.

Step 6: Since $T(x)$ is a continuous function over a closed, bounded interval, it has a maximum and a minimum. Let's begin by looking for any critical points of T over the interval $[0, 6]$. The derivative is

$$T'(x) = \frac{1}{8} - \frac{1}{2}\frac{\left[(6 - x)^2 + 4\right]^{-1/2}}{3} \cdot 2(6 - x) = \frac{1}{8} - \frac{(6 - x)}{3\sqrt{(6 - x)^2 + 4}}.$$

If $T'(x) = 0$, then

$$\frac{1}{8} = \frac{6-x}{3\sqrt{(6-x)^2+4}}.$$

Therefore,

$$3\sqrt{(6-x)^2+4} = 8(6-x). \tag{4.6}$$

Squaring both sides of this equation, we see that if x satisfies this equation, then x must satisfy

$$9\left[(6-x)^2+4\right] = 64(6-x)^2,$$

which implies

$$55(6-x)^2 = 36.$$

We conclude that if x is a critical point, then x satisfies

$$(x-6)^2 = \frac{36}{55}.$$

Therefore, the possibilities for critical points are

$$x = 6 \pm \frac{6}{\sqrt{55}}.$$

Since $x = 6 + 6/\sqrt{55}$ is not in the domain, it is not a possibility for a critical point. On the other hand, $x = 6 - 6/\sqrt{55}$ is in the domain. Since we squared both sides of **Equation 4.6** to arrive at the possible critical points, it remains to verify that $x = 6 - 6/\sqrt{55}$ satisfies **Equation 4.6**. Since $x = 6 - 6/\sqrt{55}$ does satisfy that equation, we conclude that $x = 6 - 6/\sqrt{55}$ is a critical point, and it is the only one. To justify that the time is minimized for this value of x, we just need to check the values of $T(x)$ at the endpoints $x = 0$ and $x = 6$, and compare them with the value of $T(x)$ at the critical point $x = 6 - 6/\sqrt{55}$. We find that $T(0) \approx 2.108$ h and $T(6) \approx 1.417$ h, whereas $T\left(6 - 6/\sqrt{55}\right) \approx 1.368$ h. Therefore, we conclude that T has a local minimum at $x \approx 5.19$ mi.

4.33 Suppose the island is 1 mi from shore, and the distance from the cabin to the point on the shore closest to the island is 15 mi. Suppose a visitor swims at the rate of 2.5 mph and runs at a rate of 6 mph. Let x denote the distance the visitor will run before swimming, and find a function for the time it takes the visitor to get from the cabin to the island.

In business, companies are interested in maximizing revenue. In the following example, we consider a scenario in which a company has collected data on how many cars it is able to lease, depending on the price it charges its customers to rent a car. Let's use these data to determine the price the company should charge to maximize the amount of money it brings in.

Example 4.35

Maximizing Revenue

Owners of a car rental company have determined that if they charge customers p dollars per day to rent a car, where $50 \leq p \leq 200$, the number of cars n they rent per day can be modeled by the linear function

$n(p) = 1000 - 5p.$ If they charge $50 per day or less, they will rent all their cars. If they charge $200 per day or more, they will not rent any cars. Assuming the owners plan to charge customers between $50 per day and $200 per day to rent a car, how much should they charge to maximize their revenue?

Solution

Step 1: Let p be the price charged per car per day and let n be the number of cars rented per day. Let R be the revenue per day.

Step 2: The problem is to maximize $R.$

Step 3: The revenue (per day) is equal to the number of cars rented per day times the price charged per car per day—that is, $R = n \times p.$

Step 4: Since the number of cars rented per day is modeled by the linear function $n(p) = 1000 - 5p,$ the revenue R can be represented by the function

$$R(p) = n \times p = (1000 - 5p)p = -5p^2 + 1000p.$$

Step 5: Since the owners plan to charge between $50 per car per day and $200 per car per day, the problem is to find the maximum revenue $R(p)$ for p in the closed interval $[50, 200]$.

Step 6: Since R is a continuous function over the closed, bounded interval $[50, 200]$, it has an absolute maximum (and an absolute minimum) in that interval. To find the maximum value, look for critical points. The derivative is $R'(p) = -10p + 1000.$ Therefore, the critical point is $p = 100$ When $p = 100,$ $R(100) = \$50{,}000.$ When $p = 50,$ $R(p) = \$37{,}500.$ When $p = 200,$ $R(p) = \$0.$ Therefore, the absolute maximum occurs at $p = \$100.$ The car rental company should charge $100 per day per car to maximize revenue as shown in the following figure.

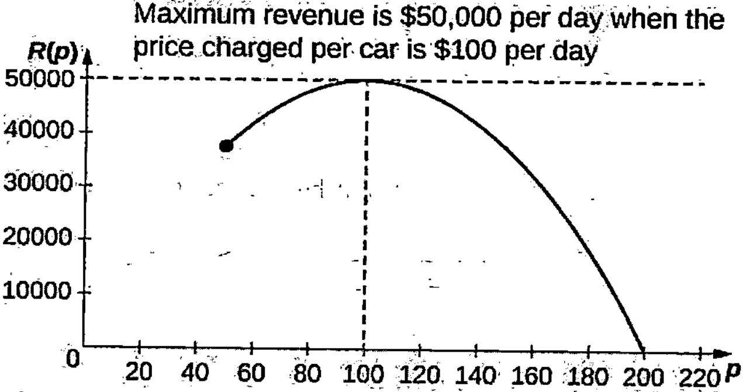

Figure 4.67 To maximize revenue, a car rental company has to balance the price of a rental against the number of cars people will rent at that price.

4.34 A car rental company charges its customers p dollars per day, where $60 \le p \le 150.$ It has found that the number of cars rented per day can be modeled by the linear function $n(p) = 750 - 5p.$ How much should the company charge each customer to maximize revenue?

Example 4.36

Maximizing the Area of an Inscribed Rectangle

A rectangle is to be inscribed in the ellipse

$$\frac{x^2}{4} + y^2 = 1.$$

What should the dimensions of the rectangle be to maximize its area? What is the maximum area?

Solution

Step 1: For a rectangle to be inscribed in the ellipse, the sides of the rectangle must be parallel to the axes. Let L be the length of the rectangle and W be its width. Let A be the area of the rectangle.

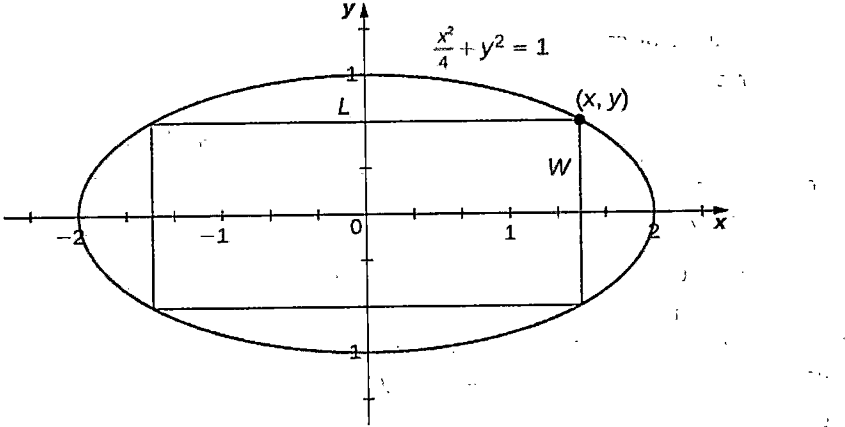

Figure 4.68 We want to maximize the area of a rectangle inscribed in an ellipse.

Step 2: The problem is to maximize A.

Step 3: The area of the rectangle is $A = LW$.

Step 4: Let (x, y) be the corner of the rectangle that lies in the first quadrant, as shown in **Figure 4.68**. We can write length $L = 2x$ and width $W = 2y$. Since $\frac{x^2}{4 + y^2 = 1}$ and $y > 0$, we have $y = \sqrt{\frac{1 - x^2}{4}}$. Therefore, the area is

$$A = LW = (2x)(2y) = 4x\sqrt{\frac{1 - x^2}{4}} = 2x\sqrt{4 - x^2}.$$

Step 5: From **Figure 4.68**, we see that to inscribe a rectangle in the ellipse, the x-coordinate of the corner in the first quadrant must satisfy $0 < x < 2$. Therefore, the problem reduces to looking for the maximum value of $A(x)$ over the open interval $(0, 2)$. Since $A(x)$ will have an absolute maximum (and absolute minimum) over the closed interval $[0, 2]$, we consider $A(x) = 2x\sqrt{4 - x^2}$ over the interval $[0, 2]$. If the absolute maximum occurs at an interior point, then we have found an absolute maximum in the open interval.

Step 6: As mentioned earlier, $A(x)$ is a continuous function over the closed, bounded interval $[0, 2]$. Therefore, it has an absolute maximum (and absolute minimum). At the endpoints $x = 0$ and $x = 2$, $A(x) = 0$. For $0 < x < 2$, $A(x) > 0$. Therefore, the maximum must occur at a critical point. Taking the derivative of $A(x)$, we obtain

$$\begin{aligned} A'(x) &= 2\sqrt{4-x^2} + 2x \cdot \frac{1}{2\sqrt{4-x^2}}(-2x) \\ &= 2\sqrt{4-x^2} - \frac{2x^2}{\sqrt{4-x^2}} \\ &= \frac{8-4x^2}{\sqrt{4-x^2}}. \end{aligned}$$

To find critical points, we need to find where $A'(x) = 0$. We can see that if x is a solution of

$$\frac{8-4x^2}{\sqrt{4-x^2}} = 0, \quad (4.7)$$

then x must satisfy

$$8 - 4x^2 = 0.$$

Therefore, $x^2 = 2$. Thus, $x = \pm\sqrt{2}$ are the possible solutions of **Equation 4.7**. Since we are considering x over the interval $[0, 2]$, $x = \sqrt{2}$ is a possibility for a critical point, but $x = -\sqrt{2}$ is not. Therefore, we check whether $\sqrt{2}$ is a solution of **Equation 4.7**. Since $x = \sqrt{2}$ is a solution of **Equation 4.7**, we conclude that $\sqrt{2}$ is the only critical point of $A(x)$ in the interval $[0, 2]$. Therefore, $A(x)$ must have an absolute maximum at the critical point $x = \sqrt{2}$. To determine the dimensions of the rectangle, we need to find the length L and the width W. If $x = \sqrt{2}$ then

$$y = \sqrt{1 - \frac{(\sqrt{2})^2}{4}} = \sqrt{1 - \frac{1}{2}} = \frac{1}{\sqrt{2}}.$$

Therefore, the dimensions of the rectangle are $L = 2x = 2\sqrt{2}$ and $W = 2y = \frac{2}{\sqrt{2}} = \sqrt{2}$. The area of this rectangle is $A = LW = (2\sqrt{2})(\sqrt{2}) = 4$.

4.35 Modify the area function A if the rectangle is to be inscribed in the unit circle $x^2 + y^2 = 1$. What is the domain of consideration?

Solving Optimization Problems when the Interval Is Not Closed or Is Unbounded

In the previous examples, we considered functions on closed, bounded domains. Consequently, by the extreme value theorem, we were guaranteed that the functions had absolute extrema. Let's now consider functions for which the domain is neither closed nor bounded.

Many functions still have at least one absolute extrema, even if the domain is not closed or the domain is unbounded. For example, the function $f(x) = x^2 + 4$ over $(-\infty, \infty)$ has an absolute minimum of 4 at $x = 0$. Therefore, we can still consider functions over unbounded domains or open intervals and determine whether they have any absolute extrema. In the next example, we try to minimize a function over an unbounded domain. We will see that, although the domain of consideration is $(0, \infty)$, the function has an absolute minimum.

In the following example, we look at constructing a box of least surface area with a prescribed volume. It is not difficult to show that for a closed-top box, by symmetry, among all boxes with a specified volume, a cube will have the smallest surface area. Consequently, we consider the modified problem of determining which open-topped box with a specified volume has the smallest surface area.

Example 4.37

Minimizing Surface Area

A rectangular box with a square base, an open top, and a volume of 216 in.^{3} is to be constructed. What should the dimensions of the box be to minimize the surface area of the box? What is the minimum surface area?

Solution

Step 1: Draw a rectangular box and introduce the variable x to represent the length of each side of the square base; let y represent the height of the box. Let S denote the surface area of the open-top box.

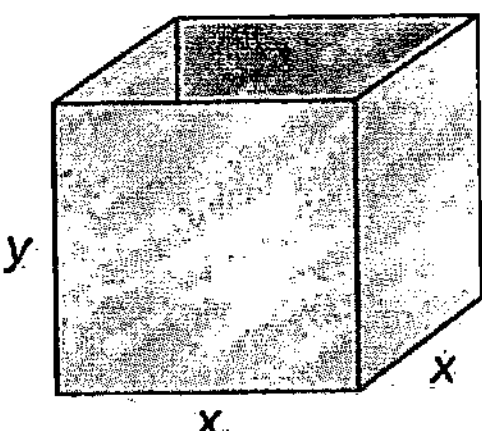

Figure 4.69 We want to minimize the surface area of a square-based box with a given volume.

Step 2: We need to minimize the surface area. Therefore, we need to minimize S.

Step 3: Since the box has an open top, we need only determine the area of the four vertical sides and the base. The area of each of the four vertical sides is $x \cdot y$. The area of the base is x^2. Therefore, the surface area of the box is

$$S = 4xy + x^2.$$

Step 4: Since the volume of this box is $x^2 y$ and the volume is given as 216 in.^3, the constraint equation is

$$x^2 y = 216.$$

Solving the constraint equation for y, we have $y = \frac{216}{x^2}$. Therefore, we can write the surface area as a function of x only:

$$S(x) = 4x\left(\frac{216}{x^2}\right) + x^2.$$

Therefore, $S(x) = \frac{864}{x} + x^2$.

Step 5: Since we are requiring that $x^2 y = 216$, we cannot have $x = 0$. Therefore, we need $x > 0$. On the other hand, x is allowed to have any positive value. Note that as x becomes large, the height of the box y becomes correspondingly small so that $x^2 y = 216$. Similarly, as x becomes small, the height of the box becomes correspondingly large. We conclude that the domain is the open, unbounded interval $(0, \infty)$. Note that, unlike the previous examples, we cannot reduce our problem to looking for an absolute maximum or absolute minimum over a closed, bounded interval. However, in the next step, we discover why this function must have an absolute minimum over the interval $(0, \infty)$.

Step 6: Note that as $x \to 0^+$, $S(x) \to \infty$. Also, as $x \to \infty$, $S(x) \to \infty$. Since S is a continuous function that approaches infinity at the ends, it must have an absolute minimum at some $x \in (0, \infty)$. This minimum must occur at a critical point of S. The derivative is

$$S'(x) = -\frac{864}{x^2} + 2x.$$

Therefore, $S'(x) = 0$ when $2x = \frac{864}{x^2}$. Solving this equation for x, we obtain $x^3 = 432$, so $x = \sqrt[3]{432} = 6\sqrt[3]{2}$. Since this is the only critical point of S, the absolute minimum must occur at $x = 6\sqrt[3]{2}$ (see **Figure 4.70**). When $x = 6\sqrt[3]{2}$, $y = \frac{216}{\left(6\sqrt[3]{2}\right)^2} = 3\sqrt[3]{2}$ in. Therefore, the dimensions of the box should be $x = 6\sqrt[3]{2}$ in. and $y = 3\sqrt[3]{2}$ in. With these dimensions, the surface area is

$$S\left(6\sqrt[3]{2}\right) = \frac{864}{6\sqrt[3]{2}} + \left(6\sqrt[3]{2}\right)^2 = 108\sqrt[3]{4}\text{ in.}^2$$

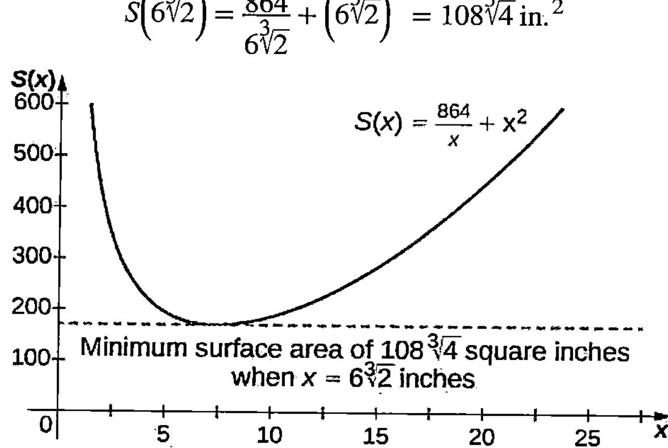

Figure 4.70 We can use a graph to determine the dimensions of a box of given the volume and the minimum surface area.

4.36 Consider the same open-top box, which is to have volume 216 in.^3. Suppose the cost of the material for the base is $20\,¢/\text{in.}^2$ and the cost of the material for the sides is $30\,¢/\text{in.}^2$ and we are trying to minimize the cost of this box. Write the cost as a function of the side lengths of the base. (Let x be the side length of the base and y be the height of the box.)

4.7 EXERCISES

For the following exercises, answer by proof, counterexample, or explanation.

311. When you find the maximum for an optimization problem, why do you need to check the sign of the derivative around the critical points?

312. Why do you need to check the endpoints for optimization problems?

313. *True or False*. For every continuous nonlinear function, you can find the value x that maximizes the function.

314. *True or False*. For every continuous nonconstant function on a closed, finite domain, there exists at least one x that minimizes or maximizes the function.

For the following exercises, set up and evaluate each optimization problem.

315. To carry a suitcase on an airplane, the length $+\text{width}+$ height of the box must be less than or equal to 62 in. Assuming the height is fixed, show that the maximum volume is $V = h\left(31 - \left(\frac{1}{2}\right)h\right)^2$. What height allows you to have the largest volume?

316. You are constructing a cardboard box with the dimensions 2 m by 4 m. You then cut equal-size squares from each corner so you may fold the edges. What are the dimensions of the box with the largest volume?

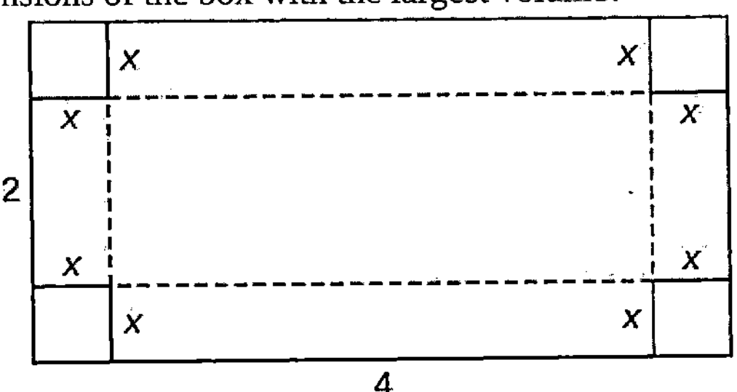

317. Find the positive integer that minimizes the sum of the number and its reciprocal.

318. Find two positive integers such that their sum is 10, and minimize and maximize the sum of their squares.

For the following exercises, consider the construction of a pen to enclose an area.

319. You have 400 ft of fencing to construct a rectangular pen for cattle. What are the dimensions of the pen that maximize the area?

320. You have 800 ft of fencing to make a pen for hogs. If you have a river on one side of your property, what is the dimension of the rectangular pen that maximizes the area?

321. You need to construct a fence around an area of 1600 ft. What are the dimensions of the rectangular pen to minimize the amount of material needed?

322. Two poles are connected by a wire that is also connected to the ground. The first pole is 20 ft tall and the second pole is 10 ft tall. There is a distance of 30 ft between the two poles. Where should the wire be anchored to the ground to minimize the amount of wire needed?

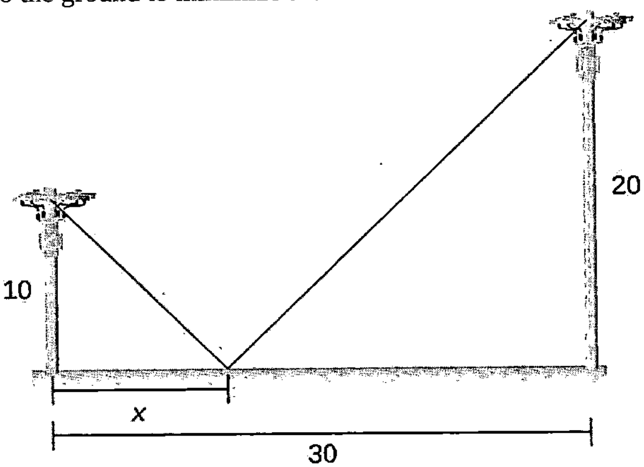

323. **[T]** You are moving into a new apartment and notice there is a corner where the hallway narrows from 8 ft to 6 ft. What is the length of the longest item that can be carried horizontally around the corner?

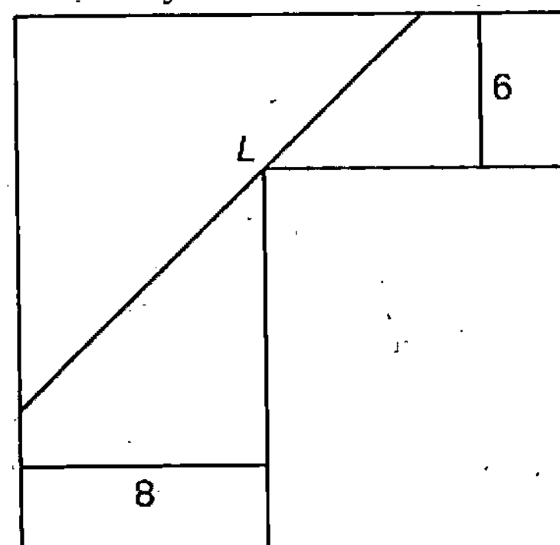

324. A patient's pulse measures 70 bpm, 80 bpm, then 120 bpm. To determine an accurate measurement of pulse, the doctor wants to know what value minimizes the expression $(x-70)^2 + (x-80)^2 + (x-120)^2$? What value minimizes it?

325. In the previous problem, assume the patient was nervous during the third measurement, so we only weight that value half as much as the others. What is the value that minimizes $(x-70)^2+(x-80)^2+\frac{1}{2}(x-120)^2$?

326. You can run at a speed of 6 mph and swim at a speed of 3 mph and are located on the shore, 4 miles east of an island that is 1 mile north of the shoreline. How far should you run west to minimize the time needed to reach the island?

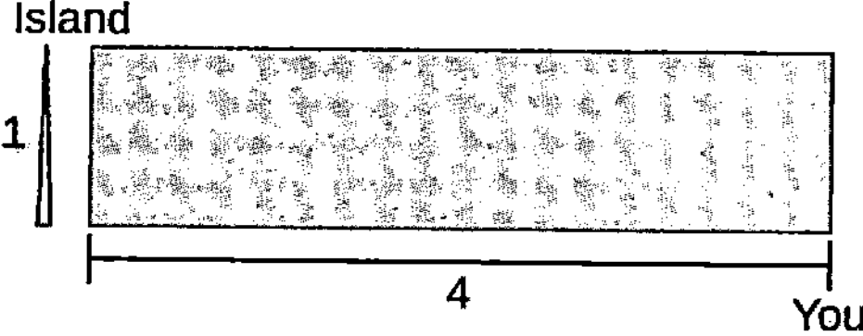

For the following problems, consider a lifeguard at a circular pool with diameter 40 m. He must reach someone who is drowning on the exact opposite side of the pool, at position C. The lifeguard swims with a speed v and runs around the pool at speed $w=3v$.

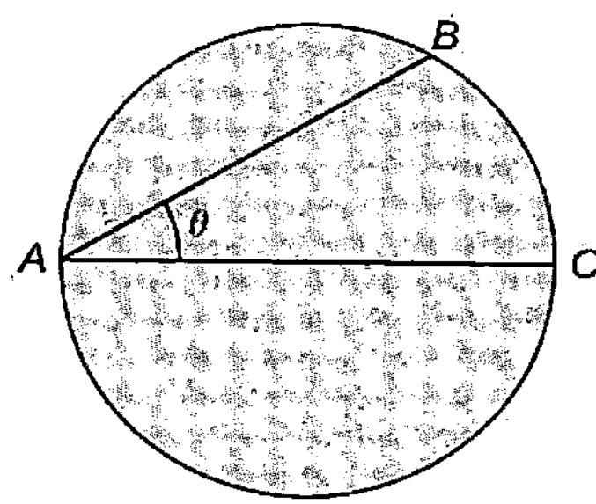

327. Find a function that measures the total amount of time it takes to reach the drowning person as a function of the swim angle, θ.

328. Find at what angle θ the lifeguard should swim to reach the drowning person in the least amount of time.

329. A truck uses gas as $g(v)=av+\frac{b}{v}$, where v represents the speed of the truck and g represents the gallons of fuel per mile. At what speed is fuel consumption minimized?

For the following exercises, consider a limousine that gets $m(v)=\frac{(120-2v)}{5}$ mi/gal at speed v, the chauffeur costs \$15/h, and gas is \$3.5/gal.

330. Find the cost per mile at speed v.

331. Find the cheapest driving speed.

For the following exercises, consider a pizzeria that sell pizzas for a revenue of $R(x)=ax$ and costs $C(x)=b+cx+dx^2$, where x represents the number of pizzas.

332. Find the profit function for the number of pizzas. How many pizzas gives the largest profit per pizza?

333. Assume that $R(x)=10x$ and $C(x)=2x+x^2$. How many pizzas sold maximizes the profit?

334. Assume that $R(x)=15x$, and $C(x)=60+3x+\frac{1}{2}x^2$. How many pizzas sold maximizes the profit?

For the following exercises, consider a wire 4 ft long cut into two pieces. One piece forms a circle with radius r and the other forms a square of side x.

335. Choose x to maximize the sum of their areas.

336. Choose x to minimize the sum of their areas.

For the following exercises, consider two nonnegative numbers x and y such that $x+y=10$. Maximize and minimize the quantities.

337. xy

338. x^2y^2

339. $y-\frac{1}{x}$

340. x^2-y

For the following exercises, draw the given optimization problem and solve.

341. Find the volume of the largest right circular cylinder that fits in a sphere of radius 1.

342. Find the volume of the largest right cone that fits in a sphere of radius 1.

343. Find the area of the largest rectangle that fits into the triangle with sides $x=0$, $y=0$ and $\frac{x}{4}+\frac{y}{6}=1$.

344. Find the largest volume of a cylinder that fits into a cone that has base radius R and height h.

345. Find the dimensions of the closed cylinder volume $V=16\pi$ that has the least amount of surface area.

346. Find the dimensions of a right cone with surface area $S=4\pi$ that has the largest volume.

For the following exercises, consider the points on the given graphs. Use a calculator to graph the functions.

347. **[T]** Where is the line $y = 5 - 2x$ closest to the origin?

348. **[T]** Where is the line $y = 5 - 2x$ closest to point $(1, 1)$?

349. **[T]** Where is the parabola $y = x^2$ closest to point $(2, 0)$?

350. **[T]** Where is the parabola $y = x^2$ closest to point $(0, 3)$?

For the following exercises, set up, but do not evaluate, each optimization problem.

351. A window is composed of a semicircle placed on top of a rectangle. If you have 20 ft of window-framing materials for the outer frame, what is the maximum size of the window you can create? Use r to represent the radius of the semicircle.

352. You have a garden row of 20 watermelon plants that produce an average of 30 watermelons apiece. For any additional watermelon plants planted, the output per watermelon plant drops by one watermelon. How many extra watermelon plants should you plant?

353. You are constructing a box for your cat to sleep in. The plush material for the square bottom of the box costs $\$5/\text{ft}^2$ and the material for the sides costs $\$2/\text{ft}^2$. You need a box with volume $4\ \text{ft}^2$. Find the dimensions of the box that minimize cost. Use x to represent the length of the side of the box.

354. You are building five identical pens adjacent to each other with a total area of $1000\ \text{m}^2$, as shown in the following figure. What dimensions should you use to minimize the amount of fencing?

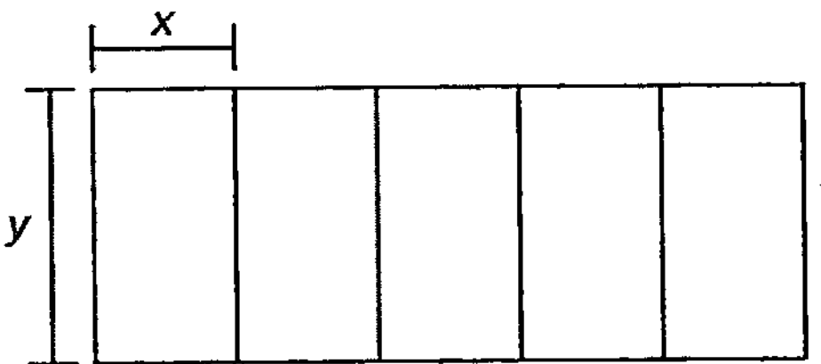

355. You are the manager of an apartment complex with 50 units. When you set rent at \$800/month, all apartments are rented. As you increase rent by \$25/month, one fewer apartment is rented. Maintenance costs run \$50/month for each occupied unit. What is the rent that maximizes the total amount of profit?

4.8 | L'Hôpital's Rule

Learning Objectives

4.8.1 Recognize when to apply L'Hôpital's rule.
4.8.2 Identify indeterminate forms produced by quotients, products, subtractions, and powers, and apply L'Hôpital's rule in each case.
4.8.3 Describe the relative growth rates of functions.

In this section, we examine a powerful tool for evaluating limits. This tool, known as **L'Hôpital's rule**, uses derivatives to calculate limits. With this rule, we will be able to evaluate many limits we have not yet been able to determine. Instead of relying on numerical evidence to conjecture that a limit exists, we will be able to show definitively that a limit exists and to determine its exact value.

Applying L'Hôpital's Rule

L'Hôpital's rule can be used to evaluate limits involving the quotient of two functions. Consider

$$\lim_{x \to a} \frac{f(x)}{g(x)}.$$

If $\lim_{x \to a} f(x) = L_1$ and $\lim_{x \to a} g(x) = L_2 \neq 0$, then

$$\lim_{x \to a} \frac{f(x)}{g(x)} = \frac{L_1}{L_2}.$$

However, what happens if $\lim_{x \to a} f(x) = 0$ and $\lim_{x \to a} g(x) = 0$? We call this one of the **indeterminate forms**, of type $\frac{0}{0}$. This is considered an indeterminate form because we cannot determine the exact behavior of $\frac{f(x)}{g(x)}$ as $x \to a$ without further analysis. We have seen examples of this earlier in the text. For example, consider

$$\lim_{x \to 2} \frac{x^2 - 4}{x - 2} \text{ and } \lim_{x \to 0} \frac{\sin x}{x}.$$

For the first of these examples, we can evaluate the limit by factoring the numerator and writing

$$\lim_{x \to 2} \frac{x^2 - 4}{x - 2} = \lim_{x \to 2} \frac{(x + 2)(x - 2)}{x - 2} = \lim_{x \to 2} (x + 2) = 2 + 2 = 4.$$

For $\lim_{x \to 0} \frac{\sin x}{x}$ we were able to show, using a geometric argument, that

$$\lim_{x \to 0} \frac{\sin x}{x} = 1.$$

Here we use a different technique for evaluating limits such as these. Not only does this technique provide an easier way to evaluate these limits, but also, and more important, it provides us with a way to evaluate many other limits that we could not calculate previously.

The idea behind L'Hôpital's rule can be explained using local linear approximations. Consider two differentiable functions f and g such that $\lim_{x \to a} f(x) = 0 = \lim_{x \to a} g(x)$ and such that $g'(a) \neq 0$ For x near a, we can write

$$f(x) \approx f(a) + f'(a)(x - a)$$

and

$$g(x) \approx g(a) + g'(a)(x - a).$$

Therefore,

$$\frac{f(x)}{g(x)} \approx \frac{f(a) + f'(a)(x - a)}{g(a) + g'(a)(x - a)}.$$

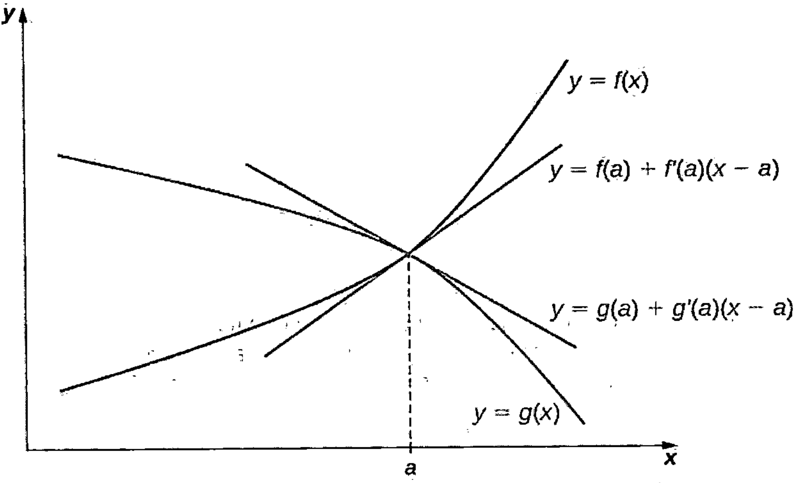

Figure 4.71 If $\lim_{x \to a} f(x) = \lim_{x \to a} g(x)$, then the ratio $f(x)/g(x)$ is approximately equal to the ratio of their linear approximations near a.

Since f is differentiable at a, then f is continuous at a, and therefore $f(a) = \lim_{x \to a} f(x) = 0$. Similarly, $g(a) = \lim_{x \to a} g(x) = 0$. If we also assume that f' and g' are continuous at $x = a$, then $f'(a) = \lim_{x \to a} f'(x)$ and $g'(a) = \lim_{x \to a} g'(x)$. Using these ideas, we conclude that

$$\lim_{x \to a} \frac{f(x)}{g(x)} = \lim_{x \to a} \frac{f'(x)(x-a)}{g'(x)(x-a)} = \lim_{x \to a} \frac{f'(x)}{g'(x)}.$$

Note that the assumption that f' and g' are continuous at a and $g'(a) \neq 0$ can be loosened. We state L'Hôpital's rule formally for the indeterminate form $\frac{0}{0}$. Also note that the notation $\frac{0}{0}$ does not mean we are actually dividing zero by zero. Rather, we are using the notation $\frac{0}{0}$ to represent a quotient of limits, each of which is zero.

Theorem 4.12: L'Hôpital's Rule (0/0 Case)

Suppose f and g are differentiable functions over an open interval containing a, except possibly at a. If $\lim_{x \to a} f(x) = 0$ and $\lim_{x \to a} g(x) = 0$, then

$$\lim_{x \to a} \frac{f(x)}{g(x)} = \lim_{x \to a} \frac{f'(x)}{g'(x)},$$

assuming the limit on the right exists or is ∞ or $-\infty$. This result also holds if we are considering one-sided limits, or if $a = \infty$ and $-\infty$.

Proof

We provide a proof of this theorem in the special case when f, g, f', and g' are all continuous over an open interval containing a. In that case, since $\lim_{x \to a} f(x) = 0 = \lim_{x \to a} g(x)$ and f and g are continuous at a, it follows that $f(a) = 0 = g(a)$. Therefore,

$$\begin{aligned}
\lim_{x \to a} \frac{f(x)}{g(x)} &= \lim_{x \to a} \frac{f(x) - f(a)}{g(x) - g(a)} && \text{since } f(a) = 0 = g(a) \\
&= \lim_{x \to a} \frac{\frac{f(x) - f(a)}{x - a}}{\frac{g(x) - g(a)}{x - a}} && \text{algebra} \\
&= \frac{\lim_{x \to a} \frac{f(x) - f(a)}{x - a}}{\lim_{x \to a} \frac{g(x) - g(a)}{x - a}} && \text{limit of a quotient} \\
&= \frac{f'(a)}{g'(a)} && \text{definition of the derivative} \\
&= \frac{\lim_{x \to a} f'(x)}{\lim_{x \to a} g'(x)} && \text{continuity of } f' \text{ and } g' \\
&= \lim_{x \to a} \frac{f'(x)}{g'(x)}. && \text{limit of a quotient}
\end{aligned}$$

Note that L'Hôpital's rule states we can calculate the limit of a quotient $\frac{f}{g}$ by considering the limit of the quotient of the derivatives $\frac{f'}{g'}$. It is important to realize that we are not calculating the derivative of the quotient $\frac{f}{g}$.

□

Example 4.38

Applying L'Hôpital's Rule (0/0 Case)

Evaluate each of the following limits by applying L'Hôpital's rule.

a. $\lim_{x \to 0} \frac{1 - \cos x}{x}$

b. $\lim_{x \to 1} \frac{\sin(\pi x)}{\ln x}$

c. $\lim_{x \to \infty} \frac{e^{1/x} - 1}{1/x}$

d. $\lim_{x \to 0} \frac{\sin x - x}{x^2}$

Solution

a. Since the numerator $1 - \cos x \to 0$ and the denominator $x \to 0,$ we can apply L'Hôpital's rule to evaluate this limit. We have

$$\begin{aligned}
\lim_{x \to 0} \frac{1 - \cos x}{x} &= \lim_{x \to 0} \frac{\frac{d}{dx}(1 - \cos x)}{\frac{d}{dx}(x)} \\
&= \lim_{x \to 0} \frac{\sin x}{1} \\
&= \frac{\lim_{x \to 0} (\sin x)}{\lim_{x \to 0} (1)} \\
&= \frac{0}{1} = 0.
\end{aligned}$$

b. As $x \to 1,$ the numerator $\sin(\pi x) \to 0$ and the denominator $\ln(x) \to 0.$ Therefore, we can apply L'Hôpital's rule. We obtain

$$\begin{aligned}\lim_{x \to 1} \frac{\sin(\pi x)}{\ln x} &= \lim_{x \to 1} \frac{\pi \cos(\pi x)}{1/x} \\ &= \lim_{x \to 1} (\pi x)\cos(\pi x) \\ &= (\pi \cdot 1)(-1) = -\pi.\end{aligned}$$

c. As $x \to \infty,$ the numerator $e^{1/x} - 1 \to 0$ and the denominator $\left(\frac{1}{x}\right) \to 0.$ Therefore, we can apply L'Hôpital's rule. We obtain

$$\lim_{x \to \infty} \frac{e^{1/x} - 1}{\frac{1}{x}} = \lim_{x \to \infty} \frac{e^{1/x}\left(\frac{-1}{x^2}\right)}{\left(\frac{-1}{x^2}\right)} = \lim_{x \to \infty} e^{1/x} = e^0 = 1.$$

d. As $x \to 0,$ both the numerator and denominator approach zero. Therefore, we can apply L'Hôpital's rule. We obtain

$$\lim_{x \to 0} \frac{\sin x - x}{x^2} = \lim_{x \to 0} \frac{\cos x - 1}{2x}.$$

Since the numerator and denominator of this new quotient both approach zero as $x \to 0,$ we apply L'Hôpital's rule again. In doing so, we see that

$$\lim_{x \to 0} \frac{\cos x - 1}{2x} = \lim_{x \to 0} \frac{-\sin x}{2} = 0.$$

Therefore, we conclude that

$$\lim_{x \to 0} \frac{\sin x - x}{x^2} = 0.$$

4.37 Evaluate $\lim_{x \to 0} \frac{x}{\tan x}.$

We can also use L'Hôpital's rule to evaluate limits of quotients $\frac{f(x)}{g(x)}$ in which $f(x) \to \pm\infty$ and $g(x) \to \pm\infty.$ Limits of this form are classified as *indeterminate forms of type* $\infty/\infty.$ Again, note that we are not actually dividing ∞ by $\infty.$ Since ∞ is not a real number, that is impossible; rather, $\infty/\infty.$ is used to represent a quotient of limits, each of which is ∞ or $-\infty.$

Theorem 4.13: L'Hôpital's Rule (∞/∞ Case)

Suppose f and g are differentiable functions over an open interval containing $a,$ except possibly at $a.$ Suppose $\lim_{x \to a} f(x) = \infty$ (or $-\infty$) and $\lim_{x \to a} g(x) = \infty$ (or $-\infty$). Then,

$$\lim_{x \to a} \frac{f(x)}{g(x)} = \lim_{x \to a} \frac{f'(x)}{g'(x)},$$

assuming the limit on the right exists or is ∞ or $-\infty.$ This result also holds if the limit is infinite, if $a = \infty$ or

$-\infty$, or the limit is one-sided.

Example 4.39

Applying L'Hôpital's Rule (∞/∞ Case)

Evaluate each of the following limits by applying L'Hôpital's rule.

a. $\lim_{x \to \infty} \frac{3x+5}{2x+1}$

b. $\lim_{x \to 0^+} \frac{\ln x}{\cot x}$

Solution

a. Since $3x+5$ and $2x+1$ are first-degree polynomials with positive leading coefficients, $\lim_{x \to \infty}(3x+5) = \infty$ and $\lim_{x \to \infty}(2x+1) = \infty$. Therefore, we apply L'Hôpital's rule and obtain

$$\lim_{x \to \infty} \frac{3x+5}{2x+1} = \lim_{x \to \infty} \frac{3}{2} = \frac{3}{2}.$$

Note that this limit can also be calculated without invoking L'Hôpital's rule. Earlier in the chapter we showed how to evaluate such a limit by dividing the numerator and denominator by the highest power of x in the denominator. In doing so, we saw that

$$\lim_{x \to \infty} \frac{3x+5}{2x+1} = \lim_{x \to \infty} \frac{3+5/x}{2x+1/x} = \frac{3}{2}.$$

L'Hôpital's rule provides us with an alternative means of evaluating this type of limit.

b. Here, $\lim_{x \to 0^+} \ln x = -\infty$ and $\lim_{x \to 0^+} \cot x = \infty$. Therefore, we can apply L'Hôpital's rule and obtain

$$\lim_{x \to 0^+} \frac{\ln x}{\cot x} = \lim_{x \to 0^+} \frac{1/x}{-\csc^2 x} = \lim_{x \to 0^+} \frac{1}{-x\csc^2 x}.$$

Now as $x \to 0^+$, $\csc^2 x \to \infty$. Therefore, the first term in the denominator is approaching zero and the second term is getting really large. In such a case, anything can happen with the product. Therefore, we cannot make any conclusion yet. To evaluate the limit, we use the definition of $\csc x$ to write

$$\lim_{x \to 0^+} \frac{1}{-x\csc^2 x} = \lim_{x \to 0^+} \frac{\sin^2 x}{-x}.$$

Now $\lim_{x \to 0^+} \sin^2 x = 0$ and $\lim_{x \to 0^+} x = 0$, so we apply L'Hôpital's rule again. We find

$$\lim_{x \to 0^+} \frac{\sin^2 x}{-x} = \lim_{x \to 0^+} \frac{2\sin x \cos x}{-1} = \frac{0}{-1} = 0.$$

We conclude that

$$\lim_{x \to 0^+} \frac{\ln x}{\cot x} = 0.$$

4.38 Evaluate $\lim_{x \to \infty} \frac{\ln x}{5x}$.

As mentioned, L'Hôpital's rule is an extremely useful tool for evaluating limits. It is important to remember, however, that to apply L'Hôpital's rule to a quotient $\frac{f(x)}{g(x)}$, it is essential that the limit of $\frac{f(x)}{g(x)}$ be of the form $\frac{0}{0}$ or ∞/∞. Consider the following example.

Example 4.40

When L'Hôpital's Rule Does Not Apply

Consider $\lim_{x \to 1} \frac{x^2+5}{3x+4}$. Show that the limit cannot be evaluated by applying L'Hôpital's rule.

Solution

Because the limits of the numerator and denominator are not both zero and are not both infinite, we cannot apply L'Hôpital's rule. If we try to do so, we get

$$\frac{d}{dx}\left(x^2+5\right) = 2x$$

and

$$\frac{d}{dx}(3x+4) = 3.$$

At which point we would conclude erroneously that

$$\lim_{x \to 1} \frac{x^2+5}{3x+4} = \lim_{x \to 1} \frac{2x}{3} = \frac{2}{3}.$$

However, since $\lim_{x \to 1}\left(x^2+5\right) = 6$ and $\lim_{x \to 1}(3x+4) = 7$, we actually have

$$\lim_{x \to 1} \frac{x^2+5}{3x+4} = \frac{6}{7}.$$

We can conclude that

$$\lim_{x \to 1} \frac{x^2+5}{3x+4} \neq \lim_{x \to 1} \frac{\frac{d}{dx}\left(x^2+5\right)}{\frac{d}{dx}(3x+4)}.$$

4.39 Explain why we cannot apply L'Hôpital's rule to evaluate $\lim_{x \to 0^+} \frac{\cos x}{x}$. Evaluate $\lim_{x \to 0^+} \frac{\cos x}{x}$ by other means.

Other Indeterminate Forms

L'Hôpital's rule is very useful for evaluating limits involving the indeterminate forms $\frac{0}{0}$ and ∞/∞. However, we can also use L'Hôpital's rule to help evaluate limits involving other indeterminate forms that arise when evaluating limits. The expressions $0 \cdot \infty$, $\infty - \infty$, 1^∞, ∞^0, and 0^0 are all considered indeterminate forms. These expressions are not real numbers. Rather, they represent forms that arise when trying to evaluate certain limits. Next we realize why these are indeterminate forms and then understand how to use L'Hôpital's rule in these cases. The key idea is that we must rewrite the indeterminate forms in such a way that we arrive at the indeterminate form $\frac{0}{0}$ or ∞/∞.

Indeterminate Form of Type $0 \cdot \infty$

Suppose we want to evaluate $\lim_{x \to a}(f(x) \cdot g(x))$, where $f(x) \to 0$ and $g(x) \to \infty$ (or $-\infty$) as $x \to a$. Since one term in the product is approaching zero but the other term is becoming arbitrarily large (in magnitude), anything can happen to the product. We use the notation $0 \cdot \infty$ to denote the form that arises in this situation. The expression $0 \cdot \infty$ is considered indeterminate because we cannot determine without further analysis the exact behavior of the product $f(x)g(x)$ as $x \to a$. For example, let n be a positive integer and consider

$$f(x) = \frac{1}{(x^n + 1)} \text{ and } g(x) = 3x^2.$$

As $x \to \infty$, $f(x) \to 0$ and $g(x) \to \infty$. However, the limit as $x \to \infty$ of $f(x)g(x) = \frac{3x^2}{(x^n + 1)}$ varies, depending on n. If $n = 2$, then $\lim_{x \to \infty} f(x)g(x) = 3$. If $n = 1$, then $\lim_{x \to \infty} f(x)g(x) = \infty$. If $n = 3$, then $\lim_{x \to \infty} f(x)g(x) = 0$. Here we consider another limit involving the indeterminate form $0 \cdot \infty$ and show how to rewrite the function as a quotient to use L'Hôpital's rule.

Example 4.41

Indeterminate Form of Type $0 \cdot \infty$

Evaluate $\lim_{x \to 0^+} x \ln x$.

Solution

First, rewrite the function $x \ln x$ as a quotient to apply L'Hôpital's rule. If we write

$$x \ln x = \frac{\ln x}{1/x},$$

we see that $\ln x \to -\infty$ as $x \to 0^+$ and $\frac{1}{x} \to \infty$ as $x \to 0^+$. Therefore, we can apply L'Hôpital's rule and obtain

$$\lim_{x \to 0^+} \frac{\ln x}{1/x} = \lim_{x \to 0^+} \frac{\frac{d}{dx}(\ln x)}{\frac{d}{dx}(1/x)} = \lim_{x \to 0^+} \frac{1/x}{-1/x^2} = \lim_{x \to 0^+} (-x) = 0.$$

We conclude that

$$\lim_{x \to 0^+} x \ln x = 0.$$

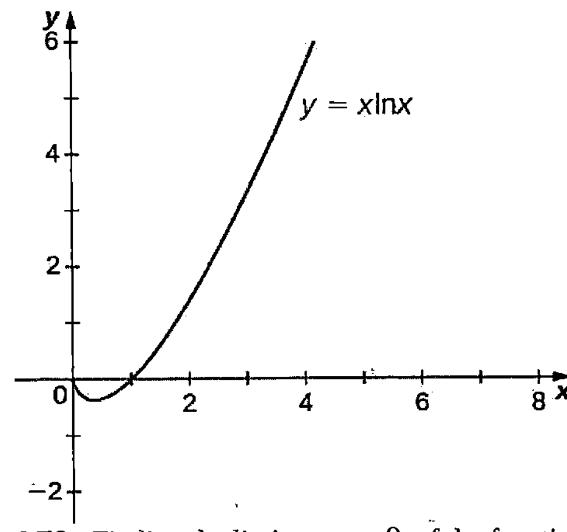

Figure 4.72 Finding the limit at $x = 0$ of the function $f(x) = x\ln x$.

4.40 Evaluate $\lim_{x \to 0} x\cot x$.

Indeterminate Form of Type $\infty - \infty$

Another type of indeterminate form is $\infty - \infty$. Consider the following example. Let n be a positive integer and let $f(x) = 3x^n$ and $g(x) = 3x^2 + 5$. As $x \to \infty$, $f(x) \to \infty$ and $g(x) \to \infty$. We are interested in $\lim_{x \to \infty}(f(x) - g(x))$. Depending on whether $f(x)$ grows faster, $g(x)$ grows faster, or they grow at the same rate, as we see next, anything can happen in this limit. Since $f(x) \to \infty$ and $g(x) \to \infty$, we write $\infty - \infty$ to denote the form of this limit. As with our other indeterminate forms, $\infty - \infty$ has no meaning on its own and we must do more analysis to determine the value of the limit. For example, suppose the exponent n in the function $f(x) = 3x^n$ is $n = 3$, then

$$\lim_{x \to \infty}(f(x) - g(x)) = \lim_{x \to \infty}\left(3x^3 - 3x^2 - 5\right) = \infty.$$

On the other hand, if $n = 2$, then

$$\lim_{x \to \infty}(f(x) - g(x)) = \lim_{x \to \infty}\left(3x^2 - 3x^2 - 5\right) = -5.$$

However, if $n = 1$, then

$$\lim_{x \to \infty}(f(x) - g(x)) = \lim_{x \to \infty}\left(3x - 3x^2 - 5\right) = -\infty.$$

Therefore, the limit cannot be determined by considering only $\infty - \infty$. Next we see how to rewrite an expression involving the indeterminate form $\infty - \infty$ as a fraction to apply L'Hôpital's rule.

Example 4.42

Indeterminate Form of Type $\infty - \infty$

Evaluate $\lim_{x \to 0^+} \left(\frac{1}{x^2} - \frac{1}{\tan x}\right)$.

Solution

By combining the fractions, we can write the function as a quotient. Since the least common denominator is $x^2 \tan x$, we have

$$\frac{1}{x^2} - \frac{1}{\tan x} = \frac{(\tan x) - x^2}{x^2 \tan x}.$$

As $x \to 0^+$, the numerator $\tan x - x^2 \to 0$ and the denominator $x^2 \tan x \to 0$. Therefore, we can apply L'Hôpital's rule. Taking the derivatives of the numerator and the denominator, we have

$$\lim_{x \to 0^+} \frac{(\tan x) - x^2}{x^2 \tan x} = \lim_{x \to 0^+} \frac{\left(\sec^2 x\right) - 2x}{x^2 \sec^2 x + 2x \tan x}.$$

As $x \to 0^+$, $\left(\sec^2 x\right) - 2x \to 1$ and $x^2 \sec^2 x + 2x \tan x \to 0$. Since the denominator is positive as x approaches zero from the right, we conclude that

$$\lim_{x \to 0^+} \frac{\left(\sec^2 x\right) - 2x}{x^2 \sec^2 x + 2x \tan x} = \infty.$$

Therefore,

$$\lim_{x \to 0^+} \left(\frac{1}{x^2} - \frac{1}{\tan x}\right) = \infty.$$

 **4.41** Evaluate $\lim_{x \to 0^+} \left(\frac{1}{x} - \frac{1}{\sin x}\right)$.

Another type of indeterminate form that arises when evaluating limits involves exponents. The expressions 0^0, ∞^0, and 1^∞ are all indeterminate forms. On their own, these expressions are meaningless because we cannot actually evaluate these expressions as we would evaluate an expression involving real numbers. Rather, these expressions represent forms that arise when finding limits. Now we examine how L'Hôpital's rule can be used to evaluate limits involving these indeterminate forms.

Since L'Hôpital's rule applies to quotients, we use the natural logarithm function and its properties to reduce a problem evaluating a limit involving exponents to a related problem involving a limit of a quotient. For example, suppose we want to evaluate $\lim_{x \to a} f(x)^{g(x)}$ and we arrive at the indeterminate form ∞^0. (The indeterminate forms 0^0 and 1^∞ can be handled similarly.) We proceed as follows. Let

$$y = f(x)^{g(x)}.$$

Then,

$$\ln y = \ln\left(f(x)^{g(x)}\right) = g(x)\ln(f(x)).$$

Therefore,

$$\lim_{x \to a}[\ln(y)] = \lim_{x \to a}[g(x)\ln(f(x))].$$

Since $\lim_{x \to a} f(x) = \infty$, we know that $\lim_{x \to a} \ln(f(x)) = \infty$. Therefore, $\lim_{x \to a} g(x)\ln(f(x))$ is of the indeterminate form

$0 \cdot \infty$, and we can use the techniques discussed earlier to rewrite the expression $g(x)\ln(f(x))$ in a form so that we can apply L'Hôpital's rule. Suppose $\lim_{x \to a} g(x)\ln(f(x)) = L$, where L may be ∞ or $-\infty$. Then

$$\lim_{x \to a} [\ln(y)] = L.$$

Since the natural logarithm function is continuous, we conclude that

$$\ln\left(\lim_{x \to a} y\right) = L,$$

which gives us

$$\lim_{x \to a} y = \lim_{x \to a} f(x)^{g(x)} = e^L.$$

Example 4.43

Indeterminate Form of Type ∞^0

Evaluate $\lim_{x \to \infty} x^{1/x}$.

Solution

Let $y = x^{1/x}$. Then,

$$\ln\left(x^{1/x}\right) = \frac{1}{x}\ln x = \frac{\ln x}{x}.$$

We need to evaluate $\lim_{x \to \infty} \frac{\ln x}{x}$. Applying L'Hôpital's rule, we obtain

$$\lim_{x \to \infty} \ln y = \lim_{x \to \infty} \frac{\ln x}{x} = \lim_{x \to \infty} \frac{1/x}{1} = 0.$$

Therefore, $\lim_{x \to \infty} \ln y = 0$. Since the natural logarithm function is continuous, we conclude that

$$\ln\left(\lim_{x \to \infty} y\right) = 0,$$

which leads to

$$\lim_{x \to \infty} y = \lim_{x \to \infty} \frac{\ln x}{x} = e^0 = 1.$$

Hence,

$$\lim_{x \to \infty} x^{1/x} = 1.$$

4.42 Evaluate $\lim_{x \to \infty} x^{1/\ln(x)}$.

Example 4.44

Indeterminate Form of Type 0^0

Evaluate $\lim_{x \to 0^+} x^{\sin x}$.

Solution

Let

$$y = x^{\sin x}.$$

Therefore,

$$\ln y = \ln\left(x^{\sin x}\right) = \sin x \ln x.$$

We now evaluate $\lim_{x \to 0^+} \sin x \ln x$. Since $\lim_{x \to 0^+} \sin x = 0$ and $\lim_{x \to 0^+} \ln x = -\infty$, we have the indeterminate form $0 \cdot \infty$. To apply L'Hôpital's rule, we need to rewrite $\sin x \ln x$ as a fraction. We could write

$$\sin x \ln x = \frac{\sin x}{1/\ln x}$$

or

$$\sin x \ln x = \frac{\ln x}{1/\sin x} = \frac{\ln x}{\csc x}.$$

Let's consider the first option. In this case, applying L'Hôpital's rule, we would obtain

$$\lim_{x \to 0^+} \sin x \ln x = \lim_{x \to 0^+} \frac{\sin x}{1/\ln x} = \lim_{x \to 0^+} \frac{\cos x}{-1/\left(x(\ln x)^2\right)} = \lim_{x \to 0^+} \left(-x(\ln x)^2 \cos x\right).$$

Unfortunately, we not only have another expression involving the indeterminate form $0 \cdot \infty$, but the new limit is even more complicated to evaluate than the one with which we started. Instead, we try the second option. By writing

$$\sin x \ln x = \frac{\ln x}{1/\sin x} = \frac{\ln x}{\csc x},$$

and applying L'Hôpital's rule, we obtain

$$\lim_{x \to 0^+} \sin x \ln x = \lim_{x \to 0^+} \frac{\ln x}{\csc x} = \lim_{x \to 0^+} \frac{1/x}{-\csc x \cot x} = \lim_{x \to 0^+} \frac{-1}{x \csc x \cot x}.$$

Using the fact that $\csc x = \frac{1}{\sin x}$ and $\cot x = \frac{\cos x}{\sin x}$, we can rewrite the expression on the right-hand side as

$$\lim_{x \to 0^+} \frac{-\sin^2 x}{x \cos x} = \lim_{x \to 0^+} \left[\frac{\sin x}{x} \cdot (-\tan x)\right] = \left(\lim_{x \to 0^+} \frac{\sin x}{x}\right) \cdot \left(\lim_{x \to 0^+} (-\tan x)\right) = 1 \cdot 0 = 0.$$

We conclude that $\lim_{x \to 0^+} \ln y = 0$. Therefore, $\ln\left(\lim_{x \to 0^+} y\right) = 0$ and we have

$$\lim_{x \to 0^+} y = \lim_{x \to 0^+} x^{\sin x} = e^0 = 1.$$

Hence,

$$\lim_{x \to 0^+} x^{\sin x} = 1.$$

4.43 Evaluate $\lim_{x \to 0^+} x^x$.

Growth Rates of Functions

Suppose the functions f and g both approach infinity as $x \to \infty$. Although the values of both functions become arbitrarily large as the values of x become sufficiently large, sometimes one function is growing more quickly than the other. For example, $f(x) = x^2$ and $g(x) = x^3$ both approach infinity as $x \to \infty$. However, as shown in the following table, the values of x^3 are growing much faster than the values of x^2.

x	10	100	1000	10,000
$f(x) = x^2$	100	10,000	1,000,000	100,000,000
$g(x) = x^3$	1000	1,000,000	1,000,000,000	1,000,000,000,000

Table 4.21 Comparing the Growth Rates of x^2 and x^3

In fact,

$$\lim_{x \to \infty} \frac{x^3}{x^2} = \lim_{x \to \infty} x = \infty. \text{ or, equivalently, } \lim_{x \to \infty} \frac{x^2}{x^3} = \lim_{x \to \infty} \frac{1}{x} = 0.$$

As a result, we say x^3 is growing more rapidly than x^2 as $x \to \infty$. On the other hand, for $f(x) = x^2$ and $g(x) = 3x^2 + 4x + 1$, although the values of $g(x)$ are always greater than the values of $f(x)$ for $x > 0$, each value of $g(x)$ is roughly three times the corresponding value of $f(x)$ as $x \to \infty$, as shown in the following table. In fact,

$$\lim_{x \to \infty} \frac{x^2}{3x^2 + 4x + 1} = \frac{1}{3}.$$

x	10	100	1000	10,000
$f(x) = x^2$	100	10,000	1,000,000	100,000,000
$g(x) = 3x^2 + 4x + 1$	341	30,401	3,004,001	300,040,001

Table 4.22 Comparing the Growth Rates of x^2 and $3x^2 + 4x + 1$

In this case, we say that x^2 and $3x^2 + 4x + 1$ are growing at the same rate as $x \to \infty$.

More generally, suppose f and g are two functions that approach infinity as $x \to \infty$. We say g grows more rapidly than f as $x \to \infty$ if

$$\lim_{x \to \infty} \frac{g(x)}{f(x)} = \infty; \text{ or, equivalently, } \lim_{x \to \infty} \frac{f(x)}{g(x)} = 0.$$

On the other hand, if there exists a constant $M \neq 0$ such that

$$\lim_{x \to \infty} \frac{f(x)}{g(x)} = M,$$

we say f and g grow at the same rate as $x \to \infty$.

Next we see how to use L'Hôpital's rule to compare the growth rates of power, exponential, and logarithmic functions.

Example 4.45

Comparing the Growth Rates of $\ln(x)$, x^2, and e^x

For each of the following pairs of functions, use L'Hôpital's rule to evaluate $\lim_{x \to \infty}\left(\frac{f(x)}{g(x)}\right)$.

a. $f(x) = x^2$ and $g(x) = e^x$

b. $f(x) = \ln(x)$ and $g(x) = x^2$

Solution

a. Since $\lim_{x \to \infty} x^2 = \infty$ and $\lim_{x \to \infty} e^x = \infty$, we can use L'Hôpital's rule to evaluate $\lim_{x \to \infty}\left[\frac{x^2}{e^x}\right]$. We obtain

$$\lim_{x \to \infty} \frac{x^2}{e^x} = \lim_{x \to \infty} \frac{2x}{e^x}.$$

Since $\lim_{x \to \infty} 2x = \infty$ and $\lim_{x \to \infty} e^x = \infty$, we can apply L'Hôpital's rule again. Since

$$\lim_{x \to \infty} \frac{2x}{e^x} = \lim_{x \to \infty} \frac{2}{e^x} = 0,$$

we conclude that

$$\lim_{x \to \infty} \frac{x^2}{e^x} = 0.$$

Therefore, e^x grows more rapidly than x^2 as $x \to \infty$ (See **Figure 4.73** and **Table 4.23**).

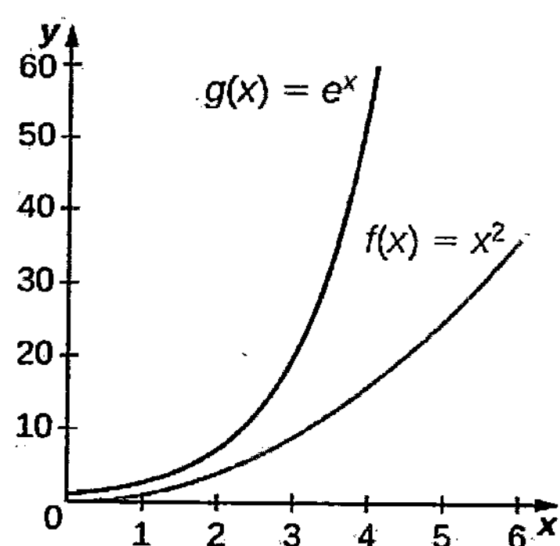

Figure 4.73 An exponential function grows at a faster rate than a power function.

x	5	10	15	20
x^2	25	100	225	400
e^x	148	22,026	3,269,017	485,165,195

Table 4.23
Growth rates of a power function and an exponential function.

b. Since $\lim_{x \to \infty} \ln x = \infty$ and $\lim_{x \to \infty} x^2 = \infty$, we can use L'Hôpital's rule to evaluate $\lim_{x \to \infty} \frac{\ln x}{x^2}$. We obtain

$$\lim_{x \to \infty} \frac{\ln x}{x^2} = \lim_{x \to \infty} \frac{1/x}{2x} = \lim_{x \to \infty} \frac{1}{2x^2} = 0.$$

Thus, x^2 grows more rapidly than $\ln x$ as $x \to \infty$ (see **Figure 4.74** and **Table 4.24**).

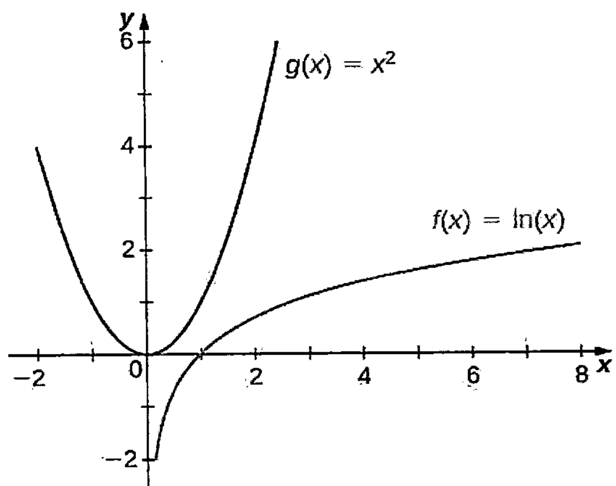

Figure 4.74 A power function grows at a faster rate than a logarithmic function.

x	10	100	1000	10,000
$\ln(x)$	2.303	4.605	6.908	9.210
x^2	100	10,000	1,000,000	100,000,000

Table 4.24
Growth rates of a power function and a logarithmic function

4.44 Compare the growth rates of x^{100} and 2^x.

Using the same ideas as in **Example 4.45**a. it is not difficult to show that e^x grows more rapidly than x^p for any $p > 0$. In **Figure 4.75** and **Table 4.25**, we compare e^x with x^3 and x^4 as $x \to \infty$.

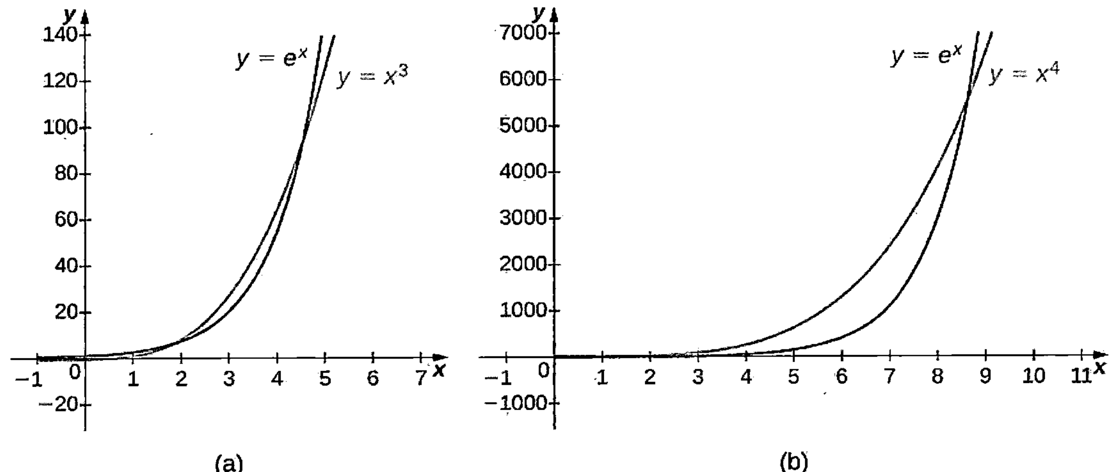

Figure 4.75 The exponential function e^x grows faster than x^p for any $p > 0$. (a) A comparison of e^x with x^3. (b) A comparison of e^x with x^4.

x	5	10	15	20
x^3	125	1000	3375	8000
x^4	625	10,000	50,625	160,000
e^x	148	22,026	3,269,017	485,165,195

Table 4.25 An exponential function grows at a faster rate than any power function

Similarly, it is not difficult to show that x^p grows more rapidly than $\ln x$ for any $p > 0$. In **Figure 4.76** and **Table 4.26**, we compare $\ln x$ with $\sqrt[3]{x}$ and $\sqrt{x}$.

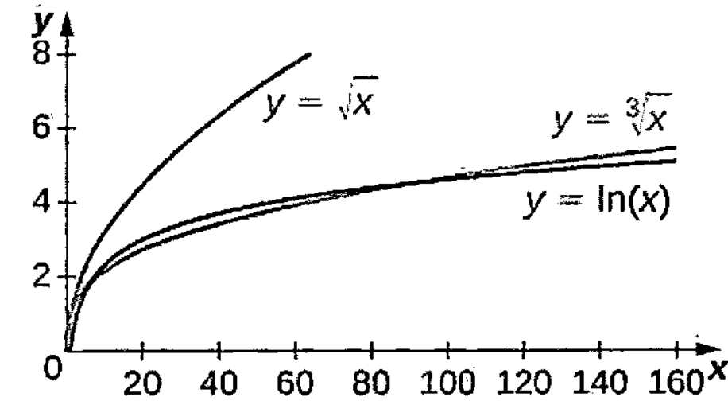

Figure 4.76 The function $y = \ln(x)$ grows more slowly than x^p for any $p > 0$ as $x \to \infty$.

x	10	100	1000	10,000
$\ln(x)$	2.303	4.605	6.908	9.210
$\sqrt[3]{x}$	2.154	4.642	10	21.544
$\sqrt{x}$	3.162	10	31.623	100

Table 4.26 A logarithmic function grows at a slower rate than any root function

4.8 EXERCISES

For the following exercises, evaluate the limit.

356. Evaluate the limit $\lim_{x \to \infty} \frac{e^x}{x}$.

357. Evaluate the limit $\lim_{x \to \infty} \frac{e^x}{x^k}$.

358. Evaluate the limit $\lim_{x \to \infty} \frac{\ln x}{x^k}$.

359. Evaluate the limit $\lim_{x \to a} \frac{x - a}{x^2 - a^2}$, $a \neq 0$.

360. Evaluate the limit $\lim_{x \to a} \frac{x - a}{x^3 - a^3}$, $a \neq 0$.

361. Evaluate the limit $\lim_{x \to a} \frac{x - a}{x^n - a^n}$, $a \neq 0$.

For the following exercises, determine whether you can apply L'Hôpital's rule directly. Explain why or why not. Then, indicate if there is some way you can alter the limit so you can apply L'Hôpital's rule.

362. $\lim_{x \to 0^+} x^2 \ln x$

363. $\lim_{x \to \infty} x^{1/x}$

364. $\lim_{x \to 0} x^{2/x}$

365. $\lim_{x \to 0} \frac{x^2}{1/x}$

366. $\lim_{x \to \infty} \frac{e^x}{x}$

For the following exercises, evaluate the limits with either L'Hôpital's rule or previously learned methods.

367. $\lim_{x \to 3} \frac{x^2 - 9}{x - 3}$

368. $\lim_{x \to 3} \frac{x^2 - 9}{x + 3}$

369. $\lim_{x \to 0} \frac{(1 + x)^{-2} - 1}{x}$

370. $\lim_{x \to \pi/2} \frac{\cos x}{\frac{\pi}{2} - x}$

371. $\lim_{x \to \pi} \frac{x - \pi}{\sin x}$

372. $\lim_{x \to 1} \frac{x - 1}{\sin x}$

373. $\lim_{x \to 0} \frac{(1 + x)^n - 1}{x}$

374. $\lim_{x \to 0} \frac{(1 + x)^n - 1 - nx}{x^2}$

375. $\lim_{x \to 0} \frac{\sin x - \tan x}{x^3}$

376. $\lim_{x \to 0} \frac{\sqrt{1 + x} - \sqrt{1 - x}}{x}$

377. $\lim_{x \to 0} \frac{e^x - x - 1}{x^2}$

378. $\lim_{x \to 0} \frac{\tan x}{\sqrt{x}}$

379. $\lim_{x \to 1} \frac{x - 1}{\ln x}$

380. $\lim_{x \to 0} (x + 1)^{1/x}$

381. $\lim_{x \to 1} \frac{\sqrt{x} - \sqrt[3]{x}}{x - 1}$

382. $\lim_{x \to 0^+} x^{2x}$

383. $\lim_{x \to \infty} x \sin\left(\frac{1}{x}\right)$

384. $\lim_{x \to 0} \frac{\sin x - x}{x^2}$

385. $\lim_{x \to 0^+} x \ln\left(x^4\right)$

386. $\lim_{x \to \infty} (x - e^x)$

387. $\lim_{x \to \infty} x^2 e^{-x}$

388. $\lim_{x \to 0} \frac{3^x - 2^x}{x}$

389. $\lim_{x \to 0} \frac{1 + 1/x}{1 - 1/x}$

390. $\lim_{x \to \pi/4} (1 - \tan x) \cot x$

391. $\lim_{x \to \infty} xe^{1/x}$

392. $\lim_{x \to 0} x^{1/\cos x}$

393. $\lim_{x \to 0} x^{1/x}$

394. $\lim_{x \to 0} \left(1 - \frac{1}{x}\right)^x$

395. $\lim_{x \to \infty} \left(1 - \frac{1}{x}\right)^x$

For the following exercises, use a calculator to graph the function and estimate the value of the limit, then use L'Hôpital's rule to find the limit directly.

396. **[T]** $\lim_{x \to 0} \frac{e^x - 1}{x}$

397. **[T]** $\lim_{x \to 0} x\sin\left(\frac{1}{x}\right)$

398. **[T]** $\lim_{x \to 1} \frac{x - 1}{1 - \cos(\pi x)}$

399. **[T]** $\lim_{x \to 1} \frac{e^{(x-1)} - 1}{x - 1}$

400. **[T]** $\lim_{x \to 1} \frac{(x - 1)^2}{\ln x}$

401. **[T]** $\lim_{x \to \pi} \frac{1 + \cos x}{\sin x}$

402. **[T]** $\lim_{x \to 0} \left(\csc x - \frac{1}{x}\right)$

403. **[T]** $\lim_{x \to 0^+} \tan(x^x)$

404. **[T]** $\lim_{x \to 0^+} \frac{\ln x}{\sin x}$

405. **[T]** $\lim_{x \to 0} \frac{e^x - e^{-x}}{x}$

4.9 | Newton's Method

Learning Objectives

- **4.9.1** Describe the steps of Newton's method.
- **4.9.2** Explain what an iterative process means.
- **4.9.3** Recognize when Newton's method does not work.
- **4.9.4** Apply iterative processes to various situations.

In many areas of pure and applied mathematics, we are interested in finding solutions to an equation of the form $f(x) = 0$. For most functions, however, it is difficult—if not impossible—to calculate their zeroes explicitly. In this section, we take a look at a technique that provides a very efficient way of approximating the zeroes of functions. This technique makes use of tangent line approximations and is behind the method used often by calculators and computers to find zeroes.

Describing Newton's Method

Consider the task of finding the solutions of $f(x) = 0$. If f is the first-degree polynomial $f(x) = ax + b$, then the solution of $f(x) = 0$ is given by the formula $x = -\frac{b}{a}$. If f is the second-degree polynomial $f(x) = ax^2 + bx + c$, the solutions of $f(x) = 0$ can be found by using the quadratic formula. However, for polynomials of degree 3 or more, finding roots of f becomes more complicated. Although formulas exist for third- and fourth-degree polynomials, they are quite complicated. Also, if f is a polynomial of degree 5 or greater, it is known that no such formulas exist. For example, consider the function

$$f(x) = x^5 + 8x^4 + 4x^3 - 2x - 7.$$

No formula exists that allows us to find the solutions of $f(x) = 0$. Similar difficulties exist for nonpolynomial functions. For example, consider the task of finding solutions of $\tan(x) - x = 0$. No simple formula exists for the solutions of this equation. In cases such as these, we can use Newton's method to approximate the roots.

Newton's method makes use of the following idea to approximate the solutions of $f(x) = 0$. By sketching a graph of f, we can estimate a root of $f(x) = 0$. Let's call this estimate x_0. We then draw the tangent line to f at x_0. If $f'(x_0) \neq 0$, this tangent line intersects the x-axis at some point $(x_1, 0)$. Now let x_1 be the next approximation to the actual root. Typically, x_1 is closer than x_0 to an actual root. Next we draw the tangent line to f at x_1. If $f'(x_1) \neq 0$, this tangent line also intersects the x-axis, producing another approximation, x_2. We continue in this way, deriving a list of approximations: $x_0, x_1, x_2, \ldots$. Typically, the numbers $x_0, x_1, x_2, \ldots$ quickly approach an actual root x^*, as shown in the following figure.

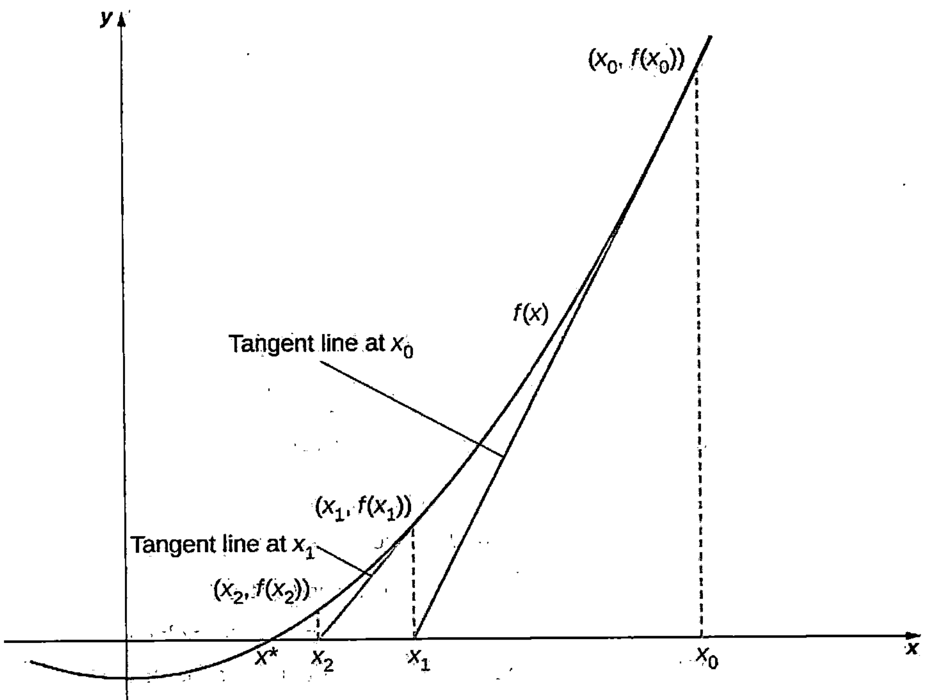

Figure 4.77 The approximations $x_0, x_1, x_2, \ldots$ approach the actual root x^*. The approximations are derived by looking at tangent lines to the graph of f.

Now let's look at how to calculate the approximations $x_0, x_1, x_2, \ldots$. If x_0 is our first approximation, the approximation x_1 is defined by letting $(x_1, 0)$ be the x-intercept of the tangent line to f at x_0. The equation of this tangent line is given by

$$y = f(x_0) + f'(x_0)(x - x_0).$$

Therefore, x_1 must satisfy

$$f(x_0) + f'(x_0)(x_1 - x_0) = 0.$$

Solving this equation for x_1, we conclude that

$$x_1 = x_0 - \frac{f(x_0)}{f'(x_0)}.$$

Similarly, the point $(x_2, 0)$ is the x-intercept of the tangent line to f at x_1. Therefore, x_2 satisfies the equation

$$x_2 = x_1 - \frac{f(x_1)}{f'(x_1)}.$$

In general, for $n > 0$, x_n satisfies

$$x_n = x_{n-1} - \frac{f(x_{n-1})}{f'(x_{n-1})}. \qquad \textbf{(4.8)}$$

Next we see how to make use of this technique to approximate the root of the polynomial $f(x) = x^3 - 3x + 1$.

Example 4.46

Finding a Root of a Polynomial

Use Newton's method to approximate a root of $f(x) = x^3 - 3x + 1$ in the interval $[1, 2]$. Let $x_0 = 2$ and find $x_1, x_2, x_3, x_4,$ and x_5.

Solution

From **Figure 4.78**, we see that f has one root over the interval $(1, 2)$. Therefore $x_0 = 2$ seems like a reasonable first approximation. To find the next approximation, we use **Equation 4.8**. Since $f(x) = x^3 - 3x + 1,$ the derivative is $f'(x) = 3x^2 - 3$. Using **Equation 4.8** with $n = 1$ (and a calculator that displays 10 digits), we obtain

$$x_1 = x_0 - \frac{f(x_0)}{f'(x_0)} = 2 - \frac{f(2)}{f'(2)} = 2 - \frac{3}{9} \approx 1.666666667.$$

To find the next approximation, $x_2,$ we use **Equation 4.8** with $n = 2$ and the value of x_1 stored on the calculator. We find that

$$x_2 = x_1 = \frac{f(x_1)}{f'(x_1)} \approx 1.548611111.$$

Continuing in this way, we obtain the following results:

$$\begin{aligned} x_1 &\approx 1.666666667 \\ x_2 &\approx 1.548611111 \\ x_3 &\approx 1.532390162 \\ x_4 &\approx 1.532088989 \\ x_5 &\approx 1.532088886 \\ x_6 &\approx 1.532088886. \end{aligned}$$

We note that we obtained the same value for x_5 and x_6. Therefore, any subsequent application of Newton's method will most likely give the same value for x_n.

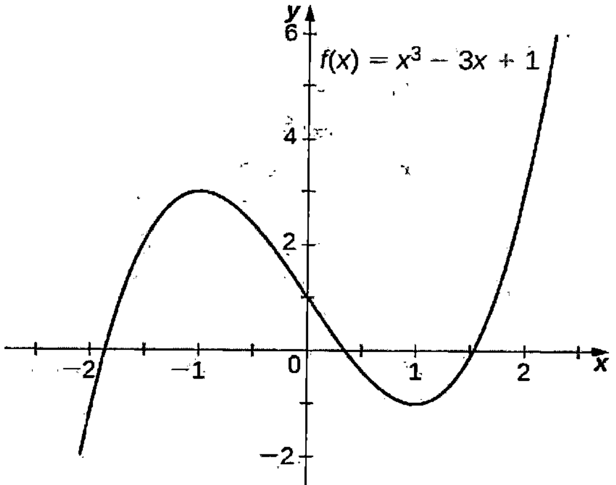

Figure 4.78 The function $f(x) = x^3 - 3x + 1$ has one root over the interval $[1, 2]$.

4.45 Letting $x_0 = 0,$ let's use Newton's method to approximate the root of $f(x) = x^3 - 3x + 1$ over the interval $[0, 1]$ by calculating x_1 and $x_2.$

Newton's method can also be used to approximate square roots. Here we show how to approximate $\sqrt{2}.$ This method can be modified to approximate the square root of any positive number.

Example 4.47

Finding a Square Root

Use Newton's method to approximate $\sqrt{2}$ (**Figure 4.79**). Let $f(x) = x^2 - 2,$ let $x_0 = 2,$ and calculate $x_1, x_2, x_3, x_4, x_5.$ (We note that since $f(x) = x^2 - 2$ has a zero at $\sqrt{2},$ the initial value $x_0 = 2$ is a reasonable choice to approximate $\sqrt{2}.$)

Solution

For $f(x) = x^2 - 2,\ f'(x) = 2x.$ From **Equation 4.8**, we know that

$$\begin{aligned} x_n &= x_{n-1} - \frac{f(x_{n-1})}{f'(x_{n-1})} \\ &= x_{n-1} - \frac{x^2{}_{n-1} - 2}{2x_{n-1}} \\ &= \frac{1}{2}x_{n-1} + \frac{1}{x_{n-1}} \\ &= \frac{1}{2}\left(x_{n-1} + \frac{2}{x_{n-1}}\right). \end{aligned}$$

Therefore,

$$\begin{aligned} x_1 &= \frac{1}{2}\left(x_0 + \frac{2}{x_0}\right) = \frac{1}{2}\left(2 + \frac{2}{2}\right) = 1.5 \\ x_2 &= \frac{1}{2}\left(x_1 + \frac{2}{x_1}\right) = \frac{1}{2}\left(1.5 + \frac{2}{1.5}\right) \approx 1.416666667. \end{aligned}$$

Continuing in this way, we find that

$$\begin{aligned} x_1 &= 1.5 \\ x_2 &\approx 1.416666667 \\ x_3 &\approx 1.414215686 \\ x_4 &\approx 1.414213562 \\ x_5 &\approx 1.414213562. \end{aligned}$$

Since we obtained the same value for x_4 and $x_5,$ it is unlikely that the value x_n will change on any subsequent application of Newton's method. We conclude that $\sqrt{2} \approx 1.414213562.$

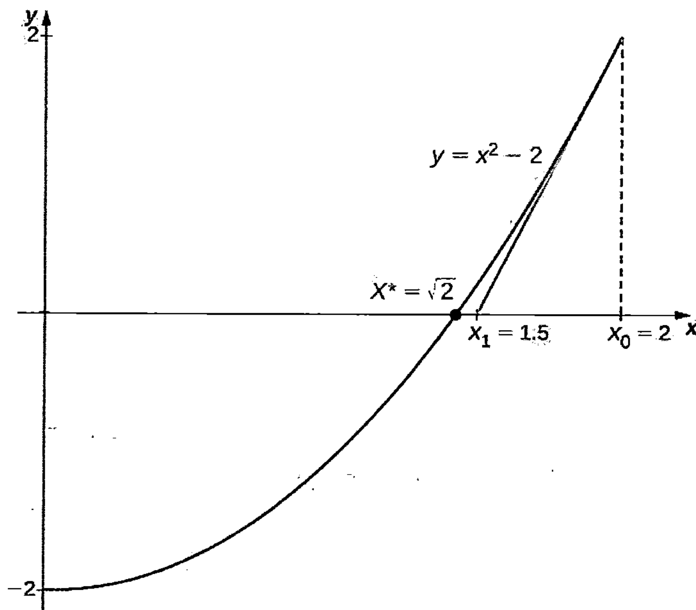

Figure 4.79 We can use Newton's method to find $\sqrt{2}$.

4.46 Use Newton's method to approximate $\sqrt{3}$ by letting $f(x) = x^2 - 3$ and $x_0 = 3$. Find x_1 and x_2.

When using Newton's method, each approximation after the initial guess is defined in terms of the previous approximation by using the same formula. In particular, by defining the function $F(x) = x - \left[\frac{f(x)}{f'(x)}\right]$, we can rewrite **Equation 4.8** as $x_n = F(x_{n-1})$. This type of process, where each x_n is defined in terms of x_{n-1} by repeating the same function, is an example of an **iterative process**. Shortly, we examine other iterative processes. First, let's look at the reasons why Newton's method could fail to find a root.

Failures of Newton's Method

Typically, Newton's method is used to find roots fairly quickly. However, things can go wrong. Some reasons why Newton's method might fail include the following:

1. At one of the approximations x_n, the derivative f' is zero at x_n, but $f(x_n) \neq 0$. As a result, the tangent line of f at x_n does not intersect the x-axis. Therefore, we cannot continue the iterative process.
2. The approximations $x_0, x_1, x_2, \ldots$ may approach a different root. If the function f has more than one root, it is possible that our approximations do not approach the one for which we are looking, but approach a different root (see **Figure 4.80**). This event most often occurs when we do not choose the approximation x_0 close enough to the desired root.
3. The approximations may fail to approach a root entirely. In **Example 4.48**, we provide an example of a function and an initial guess x_0 such that the successive approximations never approach a root because the successive approximations continue to alternate back and forth between two values.

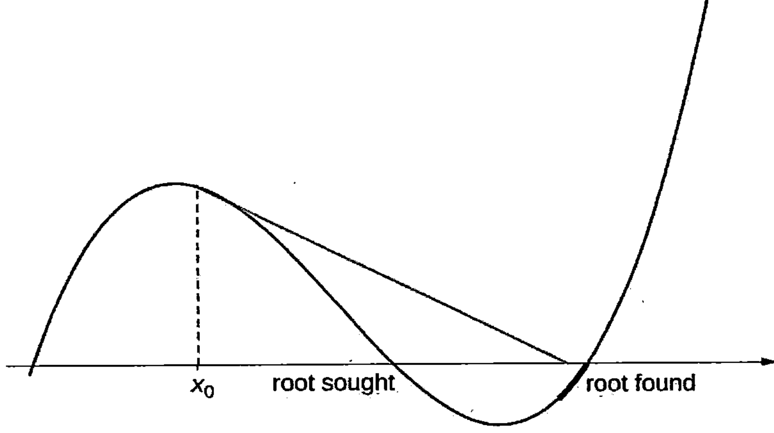

Figure 4.80 If the initial guess x_0 is too far from the root sought, it may lead to approximations that approach a different root.

Example 4.48

When Newton's Method Fails

Consider the function $f(x) = x^3 - 2x + 2$. Let $x_0 = 0$. Show that the sequence $x_1, x_2, \ldots$ fails to approach a root of f.

Solution

For $f(x) = x^3 - 2x + 2$, the derivative is $f'(x) = 3x^2 - 2$. Therefore,

$$x_1 = x_0 - \frac{f(x_0)}{f'(x_0)} = 0 - \frac{f(0)}{f'(0)} = -\frac{2}{-2} = 1.$$

In the next step,

$$x_2 = x_1 - \frac{f(x_1)}{f'(x_1)} = 1 - \frac{f(1)}{f'(1)} = 1 - \frac{1}{1} = 0.$$

Consequently, the numbers $x_0, x_1, x_2, \ldots$ continue to bounce back and forth between 0 and 1 and never get closer to the root of f which is over the interval $[-2, -1]$ (see **Figure 4.81**). Fortunately, if we choose an initial approximation x_0 closer to the actual root, we can avoid this situation.

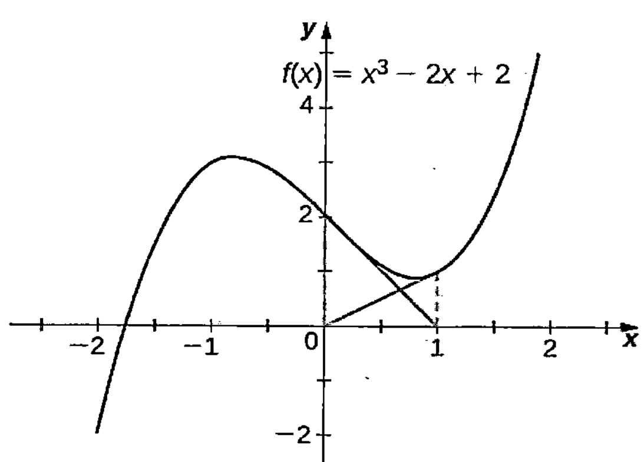

Figure 4.81 The approximations continue to alternate between 0 and 1 and never approach the root of f.

4.47 For $f(x) = x^3 - 2x + 2,$ let $x_0 = -1.5,$ and find x_1 and x_2.

From **Example 4.48**, we see that Newton's method does not always work. However, when it does work, the sequence of approximations approaches the root very quickly. Discussions of how quickly the sequence of approximations approach a root found using Newton's method are included in texts on numerical analysis.

Other Iterative Processes

As mentioned earlier, Newton's method is a type of iterative process. We now look at an example of a different type of iterative process.

Consider a function F and an initial number x_0. Define the subsequent numbers x_n by the formula $x_n = F(x_{n-1})$. This process is an iterative process that creates a list of numbers $x_0, x_1, x_2, \ldots, x_n, \ldots$. This list of numbers may approach a finite number x^* as n gets larger, or it may not. In **Example 4.49**, we see an example of a function F and an initial guess x_0 such that the resulting list of numbers approaches a finite value.

Example 4.49

Finding a Limit for an Iterative Process

Let $F(x) = \frac{1}{2}x + 4$ and let $x_0 = 0.$ For all $n \geq 1,$ let $x_n = F(x_{n-1})$. Find the values x_1, x_2, x_3, x_4, x_5. Make a conjecture about what happens to this list of numbers $x_1, x_2, x_3 \ldots, x_n, \ldots$ as $n \to \infty$. If the list of numbers $x_1, x_2, x_3, \ldots$ approaches a finite number x^*, then x^* satisfies $x^* = F(x^*)$, and x^* is called a fixed point of F.

Solution

If $x_0 = 0,$ then

$$\begin{aligned}
x_1 &= \frac{1}{2}(0) + 4 = 4 \\
x_2 &= \frac{1}{2}(4) + 4 = 6 \\
x_3 &= \frac{1}{2}(6) + 4 = 7 \\
x_4 &= \frac{1}{2}(7) + 4 = 7.5 \\
x_5 &= \frac{1}{2}(7.5) + 4 = 7.75 \\
x_6 &= \frac{1}{2}(7.75) + 4 = 7.875 \\
x_7 &= \frac{1}{2}(7.875) + 4 = 7.9375 \\
x_8 &= \frac{1}{2}(7.9375) + 4 = 7.96875 \\
x_9 &= \frac{1}{2}(7.96875) + 4 = 7.984375.
\end{aligned}$$

From this list, we conjecture that the values x_n approach 8.

Figure 4.82 provides a graphical argument that the values approach 8 as $n \to \infty$. Starting at the point (x_0, x_0), we draw a vertical line to the point $(x_0, F(x_0))$. The next number in our list is $x_1 = F(x_0)$. We use x_1 to calculate x_2. Therefore, we draw a horizontal line connecting (x_0, x_1) to the point (x_1, x_1) on the line $y = x$, and then draw a vertical line connecting (x_1, x_1) to the point $(x_1, F(x_1))$. The output $F(x_1)$ becomes x_2. Continuing in this way, we could create an infinite number of line segments. These line segments are trapped between the lines $F(x) = \frac{x}{2} + 4$ and $y = x$. The line segments get closer to the intersection point of these two lines, which occurs when $x = F(x)$. Solving the equation $x = \frac{x}{2} + 4$, we conclude they intersect at $x = 8$. Therefore, our graphical evidence agrees with our numerical evidence that the list of numbers $x_0, x_1, x_2, \ldots$ approaches $x^* = 8$ as $n \to \infty$.

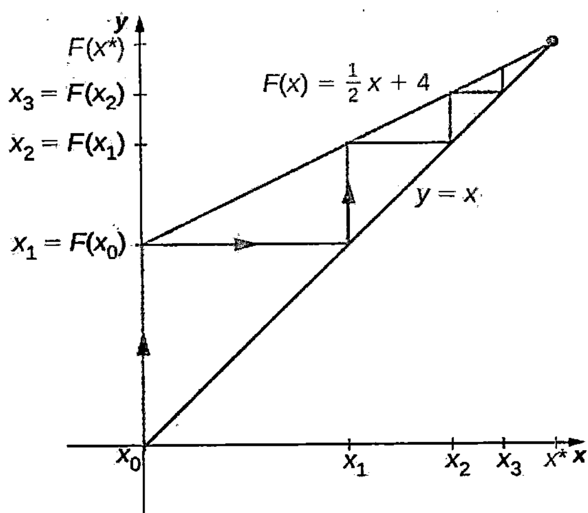

Figure 4.82 This iterative process approaches the value $x^* = 8$.

4.48 Consider the function $F(x)=\frac{1}{3}x+6$. Let $x_0=0$ and let $x_n=F(x_{n-1})$ for $n\geq 2$. Find x_1, x_2, x_3, x_4, x_5. Make a conjecture about what happens to the list of numbers $x_1, x_2, x_3, \ldots x_n, \ldots$ as $n\to\infty$.

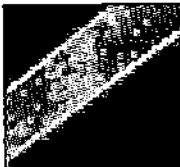

Student PROJECT

Iterative Processes and Chaos

Iterative processes can yield some very interesting behavior. In this section, we have seen several examples of iterative processes that converge to a fixed point. We also saw in **Example 4.48** that the iterative process bounced back and forth between two values. We call this kind of behavior a 2-*cycle*. Iterative processes can converge to cycles with various periodicities, such as $2-$cycles, $4-$cycles (where the iterative process repeats a sequence of four values), 8-cycles, and so on.

Some iterative processes yield what mathematicians call *chaos*. In this case, the iterative process jumps from value to value in a seemingly random fashion and never converges or settles into a cycle. Although a complete exploration of chaos is beyond the scope of this text, in this project we look at one of the key properties of a chaotic iterative process: sensitive dependence on initial conditions. This property refers to the concept that small changes in initial conditions can generate drastically different behavior in the iterative process.

Probably the best-known example of chaos is the Mandelbrot set (see **Figure 4.83**), named after Benoit Mandelbrot (1924–2010), who investigated its properties and helped popularize the field of chaos theory. The Mandelbrot set is usually generated by computer and shows fascinating details on enlargement, including self-replication of the set. Several colorized versions of the set have been shown in museums and can be found online and in popular books on the subject.

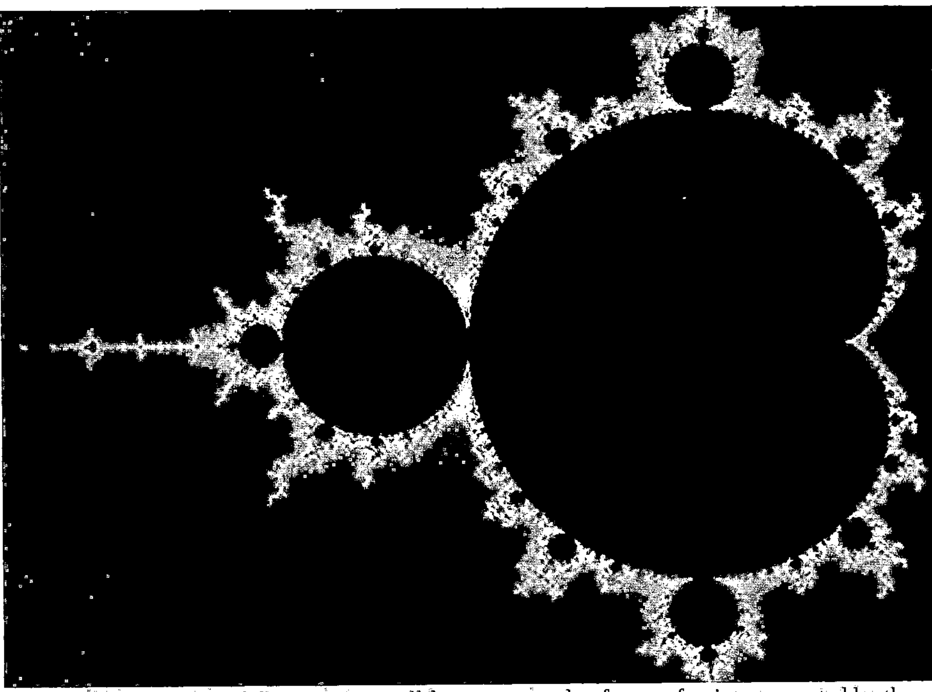

Figure 4.83 The Mandelbrot set is a well-known example of a set of points generated by the iterative chaotic behavior of a relatively simple function.

In this project we use the logistic map

$$f(x) = rx(1-x), \text{ where } x \in [0, 1] \text{ and } r > 0$$

as the function in our iterative process. The logistic map is a deceptively simple function; but, depending on the value of r, the resulting iterative process displays some very interesting behavior. It can lead to fixed points, cycles, and even chaos.

To visualize the long-term behavior of the iterative process associated with the logistic map, we will use a tool called a *cobweb diagram*. As we did with the iterative process we examined earlier in this section, we first draw a vertical line from the point $(x_0, 0)$ to the point $(x_0, f(x_0)) = (x_0, x_1)$. We then draw a horizontal line from that point to the point (x_1, x_1), then draw a vertical line to $(x_1, f(x_1)) = (x_1, x_2)$, and continue the process until the long-term behavior of the system becomes apparent. **Figure 4.84** shows the long-term behavior of the logistic map when $r = 3.55$ and $x_0 = 0.2$. (The first 100 iterations are not plotted.) The long-term behavior of this iterative process is an 8 -cycle.

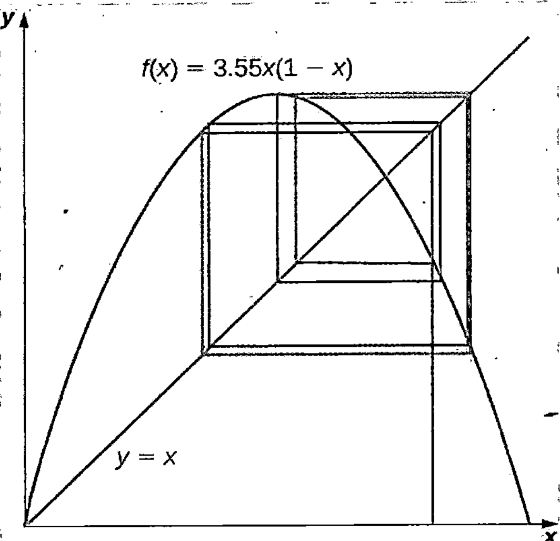

Figure 4.84 A cobweb diagram for $f(x) = 3.55x(1 - x)$ is presented here. The sequence of values results in an 8 -cycle.

1. Let $r = 0.5$ and choose $x_0 = 0.2$. Either by hand or by using a computer, calculate the first 10 values in the sequence. Does the sequence appear to converge? If so, to what value? Does it result in a cycle? If so, what kind of cycle (for example, $2 - \text{cycle}, 4 - \text{cycle}.$)?
2. What happens when $r = 2$?
3. For $r = 3.2$ and $r = 3.5$, calculate the first 100 sequence values. Generate a cobweb diagram for each iterative process. (Several free applets are available online that generate cobweb diagrams for the logistic map.) What is the long-term behavior in each of these cases?
4. Now let $r = 4$. Calculate the first 100 sequence values and generate a cobweb diagram. What is the long-term behavior in this case?
5. Repeat the process for $r = 4$, but let $x_0 = 0.201$. How does this behavior compare with the behavior for $x_0 = 0.2$?

4.9 EXERCISES

For the following exercises, write Newton's formula as $x_{n+1} = F(x_n)$ for solving $f(x) = 0$.

406. $f(x) = x^2 + 1$

407. $f(x) = x^3 + 2x + 1$

408. $f(x) = \sin x$

409. $f(x) = e^x$

410. $f(x) = x^3 + 3xe^x$

For the following exercises, solve $f(x) = 0$ using the iteration $x_{n+1} = x_n - cf(x_n)$, which differs slightly from Newton's method. Find a c that works and a c that fails to converge, with the exception of $c = 0$.

411. $f(x) = x^2 - 4$, with $x_0 = 0$

412. $f(x) = x^2 - 4x + 3$, with $x_0 = 2$

413. What is the value of "c" for Newton's method?

For the following exercises, start at

a. $x_0 = 0.6$ and

b. $x_0 = 2$.

Compute x_1 and x_2 using the specified iterative method.

414. $x_{n+1} = {x_n}^2 - \frac{1}{2}$

415. $x_{n+1} = 2x_n(1 - x_n)$

416. $x_{n+1} = \sqrt{x_n}$

417. $x_{n+1} = \frac{1}{\sqrt{x_n}}$

418. $x_{n+1} = 3x_n(1 - x_n)$

419. $x_{n+1} = {x_n}^2 + x_n - 2$

420. $x_{n+1} = \frac{1}{2}x_n - 1$

421. $x_{n+1} = |x_n|$

For the following exercises, solve to four decimal places using Newton's method and a computer or calculator. Choose any initial guess x_0 that is not the exact root.

422. $x^2 - 10 = 0$

423. $x^4 - 100 = 0$

424. $x^2 - x = 0$

425. $x^3 - x = 0$

426. $x + 5\cos(x) = 0$

427. $x + \tan(x) = 0$, choose $x_0 \in \left(-\frac{\pi}{2}, \frac{\pi}{2}\right)$

428. $\frac{1}{1-x} = 2$

429. $1 + x + x^2 + x^3 + x^4 = 2$

430. $x^3 + (x+1)^3 = 10^3$

431. $x = \sin^2(x)$

For the following exercises, use Newton's method to find the fixed points of the function where $f(x) = x$; round to three decimals.

432. $\sin x$

433. $\tan(x)$ on $x = \left(\frac{\pi}{2}, \frac{3\pi}{2}\right)$

434. $e^x - 2$

435. $\ln(x) + 2$

Newton's method can be used to find maxima and minima of functions in addition to the roots. In this case apply Newton's method to the derivative function $f'(x)$ to find its roots, instead of the original function. For the following exercises, consider the formulation of the method.

436. To find candidates for maxima and minima, we need to find the critical points $f'(x) = 0$. Show that to solve for the critical points of a function $f(x)$, Newton's method is given by $x_{n+1} = x_n - \frac{f'(x_n)}{f''(x_n)}$.

437. What additional restrictions are necessary on the function f?

For the following exercises, use Newton's method to find the location of the local minima and/or maxima of the following functions; round to three decimals.

438. Minimum of $f(x) = x^2 + 2x + 4$

439. Minimum of $f(x) = 3x^3 + 2x^2 - 16$

440. Minimum of $f(x) = x^2 e^x$

441. Maximum of $f(x) = x + \frac{1}{x}$

442. Maximum of $f(x) = x^3 + 10x^2 + 15x - 2$

443. Maximum of $f(x) = \frac{\sqrt{x} - \sqrt[3]{x}}{x}$

444. Minimum of $f(x) = x^2 \sin x$, closest non-zero minimum to $x = 0$

445. Minimum of $f(x) = x^4 + x^3 + 3x^2 + 12x + 6$

For the following exercises, use the specified method to solve the equation. If it does not work, explain why it does not work.

446. Newton's method, $x^2 + 2 = 0$

447. Newton's method, $0 = e^x$

448. Newton's method, $0 = 1 + x^2$ starting at $x_0 = 0$

449. Solving $x_{n+1} = -x_n{}^3$ starting at $x_0 = -1$

For the following exercises, use the secant method, an alternative iterative method to Newton's method. The formula is given by

$$x_n = x_{n-1} - f(x_{n-1})\frac{x_{n-1} - x_{n-2}}{f(x_{n-1}) - f(x_{n-2})}.$$

450. Find a root to $0 = x^2 - x - 3$ accurate to three decimal places.

451. Find a root to $0 = \sin x + 3x$ accurate to four decimal places.

452. Find a root to $0 = e^x - 2$ accurate to four decimal places.

453. Find a root to $\ln(x + 2) = \frac{1}{2}$ accurate to four decimal places.

454. Why would you use the secant method over Newton's method? What are the necessary restrictions on f?

For the following exercises, use both Newton's method and the secant method to calculate a root for the following equations. Use a calculator or computer to calculate how many iterations of each are needed to reach within three decimal places of the exact answer. For the secant method, use the first guess from Newton's method.

455. $f(x) = x^2 + 2x + 1,\ x_0 = 1$

456. $f(x) = x^2,\ x_0 = 1$

457. $f(x) = \sin x,\ x_0 = 1$

458. $f(x) = e^x - 1,\ x_0 = 2$

459. $f(x) = x^3 + 2x + 4,\ x_0 = 0$

In the following exercises, consider Kepler's equation regarding planetary orbits, $M = E - \varepsilon \sin(E)$, where M is the mean anomaly, E is eccentric anomaly, and ε measures eccentricity.

460. Use Newton's method to solve for the eccentric anomaly E when the mean anomaly $M = \frac{\pi}{3}$ and the eccentricity of the orbit $\varepsilon = 0.25$; round to three decimals.

461. Use Newton's method to solve for the eccentric anomaly E when the mean anomaly $M = \frac{3\pi}{2}$ and the eccentricity of the orbit $\varepsilon = 0.8$; round to three decimals.

The following two exercises consider a bank investment. The initial investment is $10,000. After 25 years, the investment has tripled to $30,000.

462. Use Newton's method to determine the interest rate if the interest was compounded annually.

463. Use Newton's method to determine the interest rate if the interest was compounded continuously.

464. The cost for printing a book can be given by the equation $C(x) = 1000 + 12x + \left(\frac{1}{2}\right)x^{2/3}$. Use Newton's method to find the break-even point if the printer sells each book for $20.

4.10 | Antiderivatives

Learning Objectives

4.10.1 Find the general antiderivative of a given function.
4.10.2 Explain the terms and notation used for an indefinite integral.
4.10.3 State the power rule for integrals.
4.10.4 Use antidifferentiation to solve simple initial-value problems.

At this point, we have seen how to calculate derivatives of many functions and have been introduced to a variety of their applications. We now ask a question that turns this process around: Given a function f, how do we find a function with the derivative f and why would we be interested in such a function?

We answer the first part of this question by defining antiderivatives. The antiderivative of a function f is a function with a derivative f. Why are we interested in antiderivatives? The need for antiderivatives arises in many situations, and we look at various examples throughout the remainder of the text. Here we examine one specific example that involves rectilinear motion. In our examination in **Derivatives** of rectilinear motion, we showed that given a position function $s(t)$ of an object, then its velocity function $v(t)$ is the derivative of $s(t)$—that is, $v(t) = s'(t)$. Furthermore, the acceleration $a(t)$ is the derivative of the velocity $v(t)$—that is, $a(t) = v'(t) = s''(t)$. Now suppose we are given an acceleration function a, but not the velocity function v or the position function s. Since $a(t) = v'(t)$, determining the velocity function requires us to find an antiderivative of the acceleration function. Then, since $v(t) = s'(t)$, determining the position function requires us to find an antiderivative of the velocity function. Rectilinear motion is just one case in which the need for antiderivatives arises. We will see many more examples throughout the remainder of the text. For now, let's look at the terminology and notation for antiderivatives, and determine the antiderivatives for several types of functions. We examine various techniques for finding antiderivatives of more complicated functions later in the text (**Introduction to Techniques of Integration (http://cnx.org/content/m53654/latest/)**).

The Reverse of Differentiation

At this point, we know how to find derivatives of various functions. We now ask the opposite question. Given a function f, how can we find a function with derivative f? If we can find a function F derivative f, we call F an antiderivative of f.

Definition

A function F is an **antiderivative** of the function f if

$$F'(x) = f(x)$$

for all x in the domain of f.

Consider the function $f(x) = 2x$. Knowing the power rule of differentiation, we conclude that $F(x) = x^2$ is an antiderivative of f since $F'(x) = 2x$. Are there any other antiderivatives of f? Yes; since the derivative of any constant C is zero, $x^2 + C$ is also an antiderivative of $2x$. Therefore, $x^2 + 5$ and $x^2 - \sqrt{2}$ are also antiderivatives. Are there any others that are not of the form $x^2 + C$ for some constant C? The answer is no. From Corollary 2 of the Mean Value Theorem, we know that if F and G are differentiable functions such that $F'(x) = G'(x)$, then $F(x) - G(x) = C$ for some constant C. This fact leads to the following important theorem.

Theorem 4.14: General Form of an Antiderivative

Let F be an antiderivative of f over an interval I. Then,

i. for each constant C, the function $F(x)+C$ is also an antiderivative of f over I;

ii. if G is an antiderivative of f over I, there is a constant C for which $G(x)=F(x)+C$ over I.

In other words, the most general form of the antiderivative of f over I is $F(x)+C$.

We use this fact and our knowledge of derivatives to find all the antiderivatives for several functions.

Example 4.50

Finding Antiderivatives

For each of the following functions, find all antiderivatives.

a. $f(x)=3x^2$

b. $f(x)=\frac{1}{x}$

c. $f(x)=\cos x$

d. $f(x)=e^x$

Solution

a. Because

$$\frac{d}{dx}\left(x^3\right)=3x^2$$

then $F(x)=x^3$ is an antiderivative of $3x^2$. Therefore, every antiderivative of $3x^2$ is of the form x^3+C for some constant C, and every function of the form x^3+C is an antiderivative of $3x^2$.

b. Let $f(x)=\ln|x|$. For $x>0$, $f(x)=\ln(x)$ and

$$\frac{d}{dx}(\ln x)=\frac{1}{x}.$$

For $x<0$, $f(x)=\ln(-x)$ and

$$\frac{d}{dx}(\ln(-x))=-\frac{1}{-x}=\frac{1}{x}.$$

Therefore,

$$\frac{d}{dx}(\ln|x|)=\frac{1}{x}.$$

Thus, $F(x)=\ln|x|$ is an antiderivative of $\frac{1}{x}$. Therefore, every antiderivative of $\frac{1}{x}$ is of the form $\ln|x|+C$ for some constant C and every function of the form $\ln|x|+C$ is an antiderivative of $\frac{1}{x}$.

c. We have

$$\frac{d}{dx}(\sin x) = \cos x,$$

so $F(x) = \sin x$ is an antiderivative of $\cos x$. Therefore, every antiderivative of $\cos x$ is of the form $\sin x + C$ for some constant C and every function of the form $\sin x + C$ is an antiderivative of $\cos x$.

d. Since

$$\frac{d}{dx}(e^x) = e^x,$$

then $F(x) = e^x$ is an antiderivative of e^x. Therefore, every antiderivative of e^x is of the form $e^x + C$ for some constant C and every function of the form $e^x + C$ is an antiderivative of e^x.

 **4.49** Find all antiderivatives of $f(x) = \sin x$.

Indefinite Integrals

We now look at the formal notation used to represent antiderivatives and examine some of their properties. These properties allow us to find antiderivatives of more complicated functions. Given a function f, we use the notation $f'(x)$ or $\frac{df}{dx}$ to denote the derivative of f. Here we introduce notation for antiderivatives. If F is an antiderivative of f, we say that $F(x) + C$ is the most general antiderivative of f and write

$$\int f(x)dx = F(x) + C.$$

The symbol $\int$ is called an *integral sign,* and $\int f(x)dx$ is called the indefinite integral of f.

Definition

Given a function f, the **indefinite integral** of f, denoted

$$\int f(x)dx,$$

is the most general antiderivative of f. If F is an antiderivative of f, then

$$\int f(x)dx = F(x) + C.$$

The expression $f(x)$ is called the *integrand* and the variable x is the *variable of integration.*

Given the terminology introduced in this definition, the act of finding the antiderivatives of a function f is usually referred to as *integrating* f.

For a function f and an antiderivative F, the functions $F(x) + C$, where C is any real number, is often referred to as *the family of antiderivatives of* f. For example, since x^2 is an antiderivative of $2x$ and any antiderivative of $2x$ is of the form $x^2 + C$, we write

$$\int 2x\,dx = x^2 + C.$$

The collection of all functions of the form $x^2 + C$, where C is any real number, is known as the *family of antiderivatives of* $2x$. **Figure 4.85** shows a graph of this family of antiderivatives.

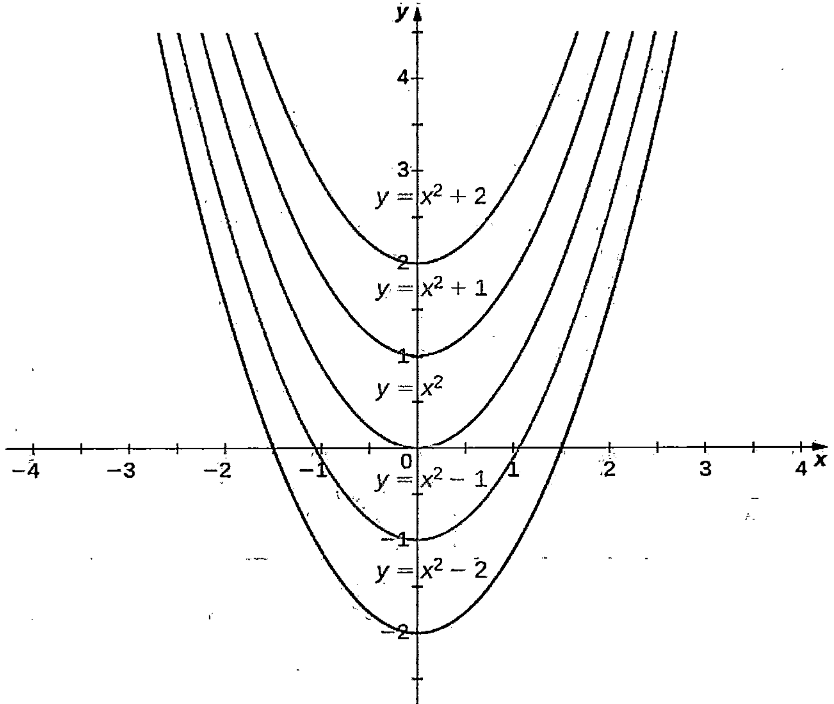

Figure 4.85 The family of antiderivatives of $2x$ consists of all functions of the form $x^2 + C$, where C is any real number.

For some functions, evaluating indefinite integrals follows directly from properties of derivatives. For example, for $n \neq -1$,

$$\int x^n\,dx = \frac{x^{n+1}}{n+1} + C,$$

which comes directly from

$$\frac{d}{dx}\left(\frac{x^{n+1}}{n+1}\right) = (n+1)\frac{x^n}{n+1} = x^n.$$

This fact is known as *the power rule for integrals.*

Theorem 4.15: Power Rule for Integrals

For $n \neq -1$,

$$\int x^n\,dx = \frac{x^{n+1}}{n+1} + C.$$

Evaluating indefinite integrals for some other functions is also a straightforward calculation. The following table lists the indefinite integrals for several common functions. A more complete list appears in **Appendix B.**

Differentiation Formula	Indefinite Integral
$\frac{d}{dx}(k) = 0$	$\int k dx = \int kx^0 dx = kx + C$
$\frac{d}{dx}(x^n) = nx^{n-1}$	$\int x^n dn = \frac{x^{n+1}}{n+1} + C$ for $n \neq -1$
$\frac{d}{dx}(\ln\|x\|) = \frac{1}{x}$	$\int \frac{1}{x} dx = \ln\|x\| + C$
$\frac{d}{dx}(e^x) = e^x$	$\int e^x dx = e^x + C$
$\frac{d}{dx}(\sin x) = \cos x$	$\int \cos x dx = \sin x + C$
$\frac{d}{dx}(\cos x) = -\sin x$	$\int \sin x dx = -\cos x + C$
$\frac{d}{dx}(\tan x) = \sec^2 x$	$\int \sec^2 x dx = \tan x + C$
$\frac{d}{dx}(\csc x) = -\csc x \cot x$	$\int \csc x \cot x dx = -\csc x + C$
$\frac{d}{dx}(\sec x) = \sec x \tan x$	$\int \sec x \tan x dx = \sec x + C$
$\frac{d}{dx}(\cot x) = -\csc^2 x$	$\int \csc^2 x dx = -\cot x + C$
$\frac{d}{dx}\left(\sin^{-1} x\right) = \frac{1}{\sqrt{1-x^2}}$	$\int \frac{1}{\sqrt{1-x^2}} = \sin^{-1} x + C$
$\frac{d}{dx}\left(\tan^{-1} x\right) = \frac{1}{1+x^2}$	$\int \frac{1}{1+x^2} dx = \tan^{-1} x + C$
$\frac{d}{dx}\left(\sec^{-1}\|x\|\right) = \frac{1}{x\sqrt{x^2-1}}$	$\int \frac{1}{x\sqrt{x^2-1}} dx = \sec^{-1}\|x\| + C$

Table 4.27 Integration Formulas

From the definition of indefinite integral of f, we know

$$\int f(x)dx = F(x) + C$$

if and only if F is an antiderivative of f. Therefore, when claiming that

$$\int f(x)dx = F(x) + C$$

it is important to check whether this statement is correct by verifying that $F'(x) = f(x)$.

Example 4.51

Verifying an Indefinite Integral

Each of the following statements is of the form $\int f(x)dx = F(x) + C$. Verify that each statement is correct by showing that $F'(x) = f(x)$.

a. $\int (x + e^x)dx = \frac{x^2}{2} + e^x + C$

b. $\int xe^x dx = xe^x - e^x + C$

Solution

a. Since

$$\frac{d}{dx}\left(\frac{x^2}{2} + e^x + C\right) = x + e^x,$$

the statement

$$\int (x + e^x)dx = \frac{x^2}{2} + e^x + C$$

is correct.

Note that we are verifying an indefinite integral for a sum. Furthermore, $\frac{x^2}{2}$ and e^x are antiderivatives of x and e^x, respectively, and the sum of the antiderivatives is an antiderivative of the sum. We discuss this fact again later in this section.

b. Using the product rule, we see that

$$\frac{d}{dx}(xe^x - e^x + C) = e^x + xe^x - e^x = xe^x.$$

Therefore, the statement

$$\int xe^x dx = xe^x - e^x + C$$

is correct.

Note that we are verifying an indefinite integral for a product. The antiderivative $xe^x - e^x$ is not a product of the antiderivatives. Furthermore, the product of antiderivatives, $x^2e^x/2$ is not an antiderivative of xe^x since

$$\frac{d}{dx}\left(\frac{x^2e^x}{2}\right) = xe^x + \frac{x^2e^x}{2} \neq xe^x.$$

In general, the product of antiderivatives is not an antiderivative of a product.

4.50 Verify that $\int x \cos x dx = x \sin x + \cos x + C$.

In **Table 4.27**, we listed the indefinite integrals for many elementary functions. Let's now turn our attention to evaluating indefinite integrals for more complicated functions. For example, consider finding an antiderivative of a sum $f+g$. In **Example 4.51**a. we showed that an antiderivative of the sum $x+e^x$ is given by the sum $\left(\frac{x^2}{2}\right)+e^x$—that is, an antiderivative of a sum is given by a sum of antiderivatives. This result was not specific to this example. In general, if F and G are antiderivatives of any functions f and g, respectively, then

$$\frac{d}{dx}(F(x)+G(x)) = F'(x)+G'(x) = f(x)+g(x).$$

Therefore, $F(x)+G(x)$ is an antiderivative of $f(x)+g(x)$ and we have

$$\int (f(x)+g(x))dx = F(x)+G(x)+C.$$

Similarly,

$$\int (f(x)-g(x))dx = F(x)-G(x)+C.$$

In addition, consider the task of finding an antiderivative of $kf(x)$, where k is any real number. Since

$$\frac{d}{dx}(kf(x)) = k\frac{d}{dx}F(x) = kF'(x)$$

for any real number k, we conclude that

$$\int kf(x)dx = kF(x)+C.$$

These properties are summarized next.

Theorem 4.16: Properties of Indefinite Integrals

Let F and G be antiderivatives of f and g, respectively, and let k be any real number.

Sums and Differences

$$\int (f(x) \pm g(x))dx = F(x) \pm G(x)+C$$

Constant Multiples

$$\int kf(x)dx = kF(x)+C$$

From this theorem, we can evaluate any integral involving a sum, difference, or constant multiple of functions with antiderivatives that are known. Evaluating integrals involving products, quotients, or compositions is more complicated (see **Example 4.51**b. for an example involving an antiderivative of a product.) We look at and address integrals involving these more complicated functions in **Introduction to Integration**. In the next example, we examine how to use this theorem to calculate the indefinite integrals of several functions.

Example 4.52

Evaluating Indefinite Integrals

Evaluate each of the following indefinite integrals:

a. $\int \left(5x^3 - 7x^2 + 3x + 4\right) dx$

b. $\int \frac{x^2 + 4\sqrt[3]{x}}{x} dx$

c. $\int \frac{4}{1 + x^2} dx$

d. $\int \tan x \cos x \, dx$

Solution

a. Using **Properties of Indefinite Integrals**, we can integrate each of the four terms in the integrand separately. We obtain

$$\int \left(5x^3 - 7x^2 + 3x + 4\right) dx = \int 5x^3 \, dx - \int 7x^2 \, dx + \int 3x \, dx + \int 4 \, dx.$$

From the second part of **Properties of Indefinite Integrals**, each coefficient can be written in front of the integral sign, which gives

$$\int 5x^3 \, dx - \int 7x^2 \, dx + \int 3x \, dx + \int 4 \, dx = 5\int x^3 \, dx - 7\int x^2 \, dx + 3\int x \, dx + 4\int 1 \, dx.$$

Using the power rule for integrals, we conclude that

$$\int \left(5x^3 - 7x^2 + 3x + 4\right) dx = \frac{5}{4}x^4 - \frac{7}{3}x^3 + \frac{3}{2}x^2 + 4x + C.$$

b. Rewrite the integrand as

$$\frac{x^2 + 4\sqrt[3]{x}}{x} = \frac{x^2}{x} + \frac{4\sqrt[3]{x}}{x} = 0.$$

Then, to evaluate the integral, integrate each of these terms separately. Using the power rule, we have

$$\begin{aligned} \int \left(x + \frac{4}{x^{2/3}}\right) dx &= \int x \, dx + 4\int x^{-2/3} \, dx \\ &= \frac{1}{2}x^2 + 4\frac{1}{\left(\frac{-2}{3}\right) + 1} x^{(-2/3) + 1} + C \\ &= \frac{1}{2}x^2 + 12x^{1/3} + C. \end{aligned}$$

c. Using **Properties of Indefinite Integrals**, write the integral as

$$4\int \frac{1}{1 + x^2} dx.$$

Then, use the fact that $\tan^{-1}(x)$ is an antiderivative of $\frac{1}{\left(1 + x^2\right)}$ to conclude that

$$\int \frac{4}{1 + x^2} dx = 4\tan^{-1}(x) + C.$$

d. Rewrite the integrand as

$$\tan x \cos x = \frac{\sin x}{\cos x} \cos x = \sin x.$$

Therefore,

$$\int \tan x \cos x = \int \sin x = -\cos x + C.$$

 **4.51** Evaluate $\int \left(4x^3 - 5x^2 + x - 7\right)dx.$

Initial-Value Problems

We look at techniques for integrating a large variety of functions involving products, quotients, and compositions later in the text. Here we turn to one common use for antiderivatives that arises often in many applications: solving differential equations.

A *differential equation* is an equation that relates an unknown function and one or more of its derivatives. The equation

$$\frac{dy}{dx} = f(x) \tag{4.9}$$

is a simple example of a differential equation. Solving this equation means finding a function y with a derivative $f.$ Therefore, the solutions of **Equation 4.9** are the antiderivatives of $f.$ If F is one antiderivative of $f,$ every function of the form $y = F(x) + C$ is a solution of that differential equation. For example, the solutions of

$$\frac{dy}{dx} = 6x^2$$

are given by

$$y = \int 6x^2\,dx = 2x^3 + C.$$

Sometimes we are interested in determining whether a particular solution curve passes through a certain point (x_0, y_0) —that is, $y(x_0) = y_0.$ The problem of finding a function y that satisfies a differential equation

$$\frac{dy}{dx} = f(x) \tag{4.10}$$

with the additional condition

$$y(x_0) = y_0 \tag{4.11}$$

is an example of an **initial-value problem**. The condition $y(x_0) = y_0$ is known as an *initial condition*. For example, looking for a function y that satisfies the differential equation

$$\frac{dy}{dx} = 6x^2$$

and the initial condition

$$y(1) = 5$$

is an example of an initial-value problem. Since the solutions of the differential equation are $y = 2x^3 + C,$ to find a function y that also satisfies the initial condition, we need to find C such that $y(1) = 2(1)^3 + C = 5.$ From this equation, we see that $C = 3,$ and we conclude that $y = 2x^3 + 3$ is the solution of this initial-value problem as shown in the following graph.

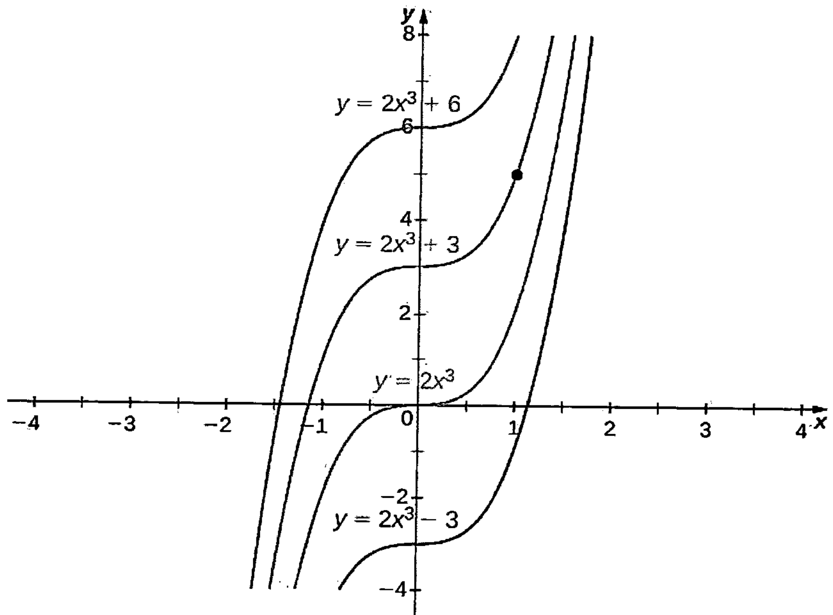

Figure 4.86 Some of the solution curves of the differential equation $\frac{dy}{dx} = 6x^2$ are displayed. The function $y = 2x^3 + 3$ satisfies the differential equation and the initial condition $y(1) = 5$.

Example 4.53

Solving an Initial-Value Problem

Solve the initial-value problem

$$\frac{dy}{dx} = \sin x,\ y(0) = 5.$$

Solution

First we need to solve the differential equation. If $\frac{dy}{dx} = \sin x,$ then

$$y = \int \sin(x)dx = -\cos x + C.$$

Next we need to look for a solution y that satisfies the initial condition. The initial condition $y(0) = 5$ means we need a constant C such that $-\cos x + C = 5.$ Therefore,

$$C = 5 + \cos(0) = 6.$$

The solution of the initial-value problem is $y = -\cos x + 6.$

 **4.52** Solve the initial value problem $\frac{dy}{dx} = 3x^{-2},\ y(1) = 2.$

Initial-value problems arise in many applications. Next we consider a problem in which a driver applies the brakes in a car.

We are interested in how long it takes for the car to stop. Recall that the velocity function $v(t)$ is the derivative of a position function $s(t)$, and the acceleration $a(t)$ is the derivative of the velocity function. In earlier examples in the text, we could calculate the velocity from the position and then compute the acceleration from the velocity. In the next example we work the other way around. Given an acceleration function, we calculate the velocity function. We then use the velocity function to determine the position function.

Example 4.54

Decelerating Car

A car is traveling at the rate of 88 ft/sec (60 mph) when the brakes are applied. The car begins decelerating at a constant rate of 15 ft/sec^2.

a. How many seconds elapse before the car stops?
b. How far does the car travel during that time?

Solution

a. First we introduce variables for this problem. Let t be the time (in seconds) after the brakes are first applied. Let $a(t)$ be the acceleration of the car (in feet per seconds squared) at time t. Let $v(t)$ be the velocity of the car (in feet per second) at time t. Let $s(t)$ be the car's position (in feet) beyond the point where the brakes are applied at time t.
The car is traveling at a rate of 88 ft/sec. Therefore, the initial velocity is $v(0) = 88$ ft/sec. Since the car is decelerating, the acceleration is

$$a(t) = -15 \text{ ft/s}^2.$$

The acceleration is the derivative of the velocity,

$$v'(t) = -15.$$

Therefore, we have an initial-value problem to solve:

$$v'(t) = -15, \; v(0) = 88.$$

Integrating, we find that

$$v(t) = -15t + C.$$

Since $v(0) = 88$, $C = 88$. Thus, the velocity function is

$$v(t) = -15t + 88.$$

To find how long it takes for the car to stop, we need to find the time t such that the velocity is zero. Solving $-15t + 88 = 0$, we obtain $t = \frac{88}{15}$ sec.

b. To find how far the car travels during this time, we need to find the position of the car after $\frac{88}{15}$ sec. We know the velocity $v(t)$ is the derivative of the position $s(t)$. Consider the initial position to be $s(0) = 0$. Therefore, we need to solve the initial-value problem

$$s'(t) = -15t + 88, \; s(0) = 0.$$

Integrating, we have

$$s(t) = -\frac{15}{2}t^2 + 88t + C.$$

Since $s(0) = 0,$ the constant is $C = 0.$ Therefore, the position function is

$$s(t) = -\frac{15}{2}t^2 + 88t.$$

After $t = \frac{88}{15}$ sec, the position is $s\left(\frac{88}{15}\right) \approx 258.133$ ft.

4.53 Suppose the car is traveling at the rate of 44 ft/sec. How long does it take for the car to stop? How far will the car travel?

4.10 EXERCISES

For the following exercises, show that $F(x)$ are antiderivatives of $f(x)$.

465. $F(x) = 5x^3 + 2x^2 + 3x + 1,\ f(x) = 15x^2 + 4x + 3$

466. $F(x) = x^2 + 4x + 1,\ f(x) = 2x + 4$

467. $F(x) = x^2 e^x,\ f(x) = e^x\left(x^2 + 2x\right)$

468. $F(x) = \cos x,\ f(x) = -\sin x$

469. $F(x) = e^x,\ f(x) = e^x$

For the following exercises, find the antiderivative of the function.

470. $f(x) = \frac{1}{x^2} + x$

471. $f(x) = e^x - 3x^2 + \sin x$

472. $f(x) = e^x + 3x - x^2$

473. $f(x) = x - 1 + 4\sin(2x)$

For the following exercises, find the antiderivative $F(x)$ of each function $f(x)$.

474. $f(x) = 5x^4 + 4x^5$

475. $f(x) = x + 12x^2$

476. $f(x) = \frac{1}{\sqrt{x}}$

477. $f(x) = (\sqrt{x})^3$

478. $f(x) = x^{1/3} + (2x)^{1/3}$

479. $f(x) = \frac{x^{1/3}}{x^{2/3}}$

480. $f(x) = 2\sin(x) + \sin(2x)$

481. $f(x) = \sec^2(x) + 1$

482. $f(x) = \sin x \cos x$

483. $f(x) = \sin^2(x)\cos(x)$

484. $f(x) = 0$

485. $f(x) = \frac{1}{2}\csc^2(x) + \frac{1}{x^2}$

486. $f(x) = \csc x \cot x + 3x$

487. $f(x) = 4\csc x \cot x - \sec x \tan x$

488. $f(x) = 8\sec x(\sec x - 4\tan x)$

489. $f(x) = \frac{1}{2}e^{-4x} + \sin x$

For the following exercises, evaluate the integral.

490. $\int (-1)dx$

491. $\int \sin x\, dx$

492. $\int (4x + \sqrt{x})dx$

493. $\int \frac{3x^2 + 2}{x^2} dx$

494. $\int (\sec x \tan x + 4x)dx$

495. $\int \left(4\sqrt{x} + \sqrt[4]{x}\right)dx$

496. $\int \left(x^{-1/3} - x^{2/3}\right)dx$

497. $\int \frac{14x^3 + 2x + 1}{x^3} dx$

498. $\int (e^x + e^{-x})dx$

For the following exercises, solve the initial value problem.

499. $f'(x) = x^{-3},\ f(1) = 1$

500. $f'(x) = \sqrt{x} + x^2,\ f(0) = 2$

501. $f'(x) = \cos x + \sec^2(x),\ f\left(\frac{\pi}{4}\right) = 2 + \frac{\sqrt{2}}{2}$

502. $f'(x) = x^3 - 8x^2 + 16x + 1,\ f(0) = 0$

503. $f'(x) = \frac{2}{x^2} - \frac{x^2}{2},\ f(1) = 0$

For the following exercises, find two possible functions f given the second- or third-order derivatives.

504. $f''(x) = x^2 + 2$

505. $f''(x) = e^{-x}$

506. $f''(x) = 1 + x$

507. $f'''(x) = \cos x$

508. $f'''(x) = 8e^{-2x} - \sin x$

509. A car is being driven at a rate of 40 mph when the brakes are applied. The car decelerates at a constant rate of 10 ft/sec^2. How long before the car stops?

510. In the preceding problem, calculate how far the car travels in the time it takes to stop.

511. You are merging onto the freeway, accelerating at a constant rate of 12 ft/sec^2. How long does it take you to reach merging speed at 60 mph?

512. Based on the previous problem, how far does the car travel to reach merging speed?

513. A car company wants to ensure its newest model can stop in 8 sec when traveling at 75 mph. If we assume constant deceleration, find the value of deceleration that accomplishes this.

514. A car company wants to ensure its newest model can stop in less than 450 ft when traveling at 60 mph. If we assume constant deceleration, find the value of deceleration that accomplishes this.

For the following exercises, find the antiderivative of the function, assuming $F(0) = 0$.

515. **[T]** $f(x) = x^2 + 2$

516. **[T]** $f(x) = 4x - \sqrt{x}$

517. **[T]** $f(x) = \sin x + 2x$

518. **[T]** $f(x) = e^x$

519. **[T]** $f(x) = \frac{1}{(x+1)^2}$

520. **[T]** $f(x) = e^{-2x} + 3x^2$

For the following exercises, determine whether the statement is true or false. Either prove it is true or find a counterexample if it is false.

521. If $f(x)$ is the antiderivative of $v(x)$, then $2f(x)$ is the antiderivative of $2v(x)$.

522. If $f(x)$ is the antiderivative of $v(x)$, then $f(2x)$ is the antiderivative of $v(2x)$.

523. If $f(x)$ is the antiderivative of $v(x)$, then $f(x) + 1$ is the antiderivative of $v(x) + 1$.

524. If $f(x)$ is the antiderivative of $v(x)$, then $(f(x))^2$ is the antiderivative of $(v(x))^2$.

CHAPTER 4 REVIEW

KEY TERMS

absolute extremum if f has an absolute maximum or absolute minimum at $c,$ we say f has an absolute extremum at c

absolute maximum if $f(c) \geq f(x)$ for all x in the domain of $f,$ we say f has an absolute maximum at c

absolute minimum if $f(c) \leq f(x)$ for all x in the domain of $f,$ we say f has an absolute minimum at c

antiderivative a function F such that $F'(x) = f(x)$ for all x in the domain of f is an antiderivative of f

concave down if f is differentiable over an interval I and f' is decreasing over $I,$ then f is concave down over I

concave up if f is differentiable over an interval I and f' is increasing over $I,$ then f is concave up over I

concavity the upward or downward curve of the graph of a function

concavity test suppose f is twice differentiable over an interval I; if $f'' > 0$ over $I,$ then f is concave up over I; if $f'' < 0$ over $I,$ then f is concave down over I

critical point if $f'(c) = 0$ or $f'(c)$ is undefined, we say that c is a critical point of f

differential the differential dx is an independent variable that can be assigned any nonzero real number; the differential dy is defined to be $dy = f'(x)dx$

differential form given a differentiable function $y = f'(x),$ the equation $dy = f'(x)dx$ is the differential form of the derivative of y with respect to x

end behavior the behavior of a function as $x \to \infty$ and $x \to -\infty$

extreme value theorem if f is a continuous function over a finite, closed interval, then f has an absolute maximum and an absolute minimum

Fermat's theorem if f has a local extremum at $c,$ then c is a critical point of f

first derivative test let f be a continuous function over an interval I containing a critical point c such that f is differentiable over I except possibly at c; if f' changes sign from positive to negative as x increases through $c,$ then f has a local maximum at c; if f' changes sign from negative to positive as x increases through $c,$ then f has a local minimum at c; if f' does not change sign as x increases through $c,$ then f does not have a local extremum at c

horizontal asymptote if $\lim_{x \to \infty} f(x) = L$ or $\lim_{x \to -\infty} f(x) = L,$ then $y = L$ is a horizontal asymptote of f

indefinite integral the most general antiderivative of $f(x)$ is the indefinite integral of f; we use the notation $\int f(x)dx$ to denote the indefinite integral of f

indeterminate forms when evaluating a limit, the forms $\frac{0}{0},$ $\infty/\infty,$ $0 \cdot \infty,$ $\infty - \infty,$ $0^0,$ $\infty^0,$ and 1^∞ are considered indeterminate because further analysis is required to determine whether the limit exists and, if so, what its value is

infinite limit at infinity a function that becomes arbitrarily large as x becomes large

inflection point if f is continuous at c and f changes concavity at $c,$ the point $(c, f(c))$ is an inflection point of f

initial value problem a problem that requires finding a function y that satisfies the differential equation $\frac{dy}{dx} = f(x)$ together with the initial condition $y(x_0) = y_0$

iterative process process in which a list of numbers $x_0, x_1, x_2, x_3 \ldots$ is generated by starting with a number x_0 and defining $x_n = F(x_{n-1})$ for $n \geq 1$

limit at infinity the limiting value, if it exists, of a function as $x \to \infty$ or $x \to -\infty$

linear approximation the linear function $L(x) = f(a) + f'(a)(x - a)$ is the linear approximation of f at $x = a$

local extremum if f has a local maximum or local minimum at c, we say f has a local extremum at c

local maximum if there exists an interval I such that $f(c) \geq f(x)$ for all $x \in I$, we say f has a local maximum at c

local minimum if there exists an interval I such that $f(c) \leq f(x)$ for all $x \in I$, we say f has a local minimum at c

L'Hôpital's rule if f and g are differentiable functions over an interval a, except possibly at a, and $\lim_{x \to a} f(x) = 0 = \lim_{x \to a} g(x)$ or $\lim_{x \to a} f(x)$ and $\lim_{x \to a} g(x)$ are infinite, then $\lim_{x \to a} \frac{f(x)}{g(x)} = \lim_{x \to a} \frac{f'(x)}{g'(x)}$, assuming the limit on the right exists or is ∞ or $-\infty$

mean value theorem if f is continuous over $[a, b]$ and differentiable over (a, b), then there exists $c \in (a, b)$ such that

$$f'(c) = \frac{f(b) - f(a)}{b - a}$$

Newton's method method for approximating roots of $f(x) = 0$; using an initial guess x_0; each subsequent approximation is defined by the equation $x_n = x_{n-1} - \frac{f(x_{n-1})}{f'(x_{n-1})}$

oblique asymptote the line $y = mx + b$ if $f(x)$ approaches it as $x \to \infty$ or $x \to -\infty$

optimization problems problems that are solved by finding the maximum or minimum value of a function

percentage error the relative error expressed as a percentage

propagated error the error that results in a calculated quantity $f(x)$ resulting from a measurement error dx

related rates are rates of change associated with two or more related quantities that are changing over time

relative error given an absolute error Δq for a particular quantity, $\frac{\Delta q}{q}$ is the relative error.

rolle's theorem if f is continuous over $[a, b]$ and differentiable over (a, b), and if $f(a) = f(b)$, then there exists $c \in (a, b)$ such that $f'(c) = 0$

second derivative test suppose $f'(c) = 0$ and f'' is continuous over an interval containing c; if $f''(c) > 0$, then f has a local minimum at c; if $f''(c) < 0$, then f has a local maximum at c; if $f''(c) = 0$, then the test is inconclusive

tangent line approximation (linearization) since the linear approximation of f at $x = a$ is defined using the equation of the tangent line, the linear approximation of f at $x = a$ is also known as the tangent line approximation to f at $x = a$

KEY EQUATIONS

- **Linear approximation**

$L(x) = f(a) + f'(a)(x - a)$

- **A differential**
  $dy = f'(x)dx.$

KEY CONCEPTS

4.1 Related Rates

- To solve a related rates problem, first draw a picture that illustrates the relationship between the two or more related quantities that are changing with respect to time.
- In terms of the quantities, state the information given and the rate to be found.
- Find an equation relating the quantities.
- Use differentiation, applying the chain rule as necessary, to find an equation that relates the rates.
- Be sure not to substitute a variable quantity for one of the variables until after finding an equation relating the rates.

4.2 Linear Approximations and Differentials

- A differentiable function $y = f(x)$ can be approximated at a by the linear function
$$L(x) = f(a) + f'(a)(x - a).$$
- For a function $y = f(x)$, if x changes from a to $a + dx$, then
$$dy = f'(x)dx$$
is an approximation for the change in y. The actual change in y is
$$\Delta y = f(a + dx) - f(a).$$
- A measurement error dx can lead to an error in a calculated quantity $f(x)$. The error in the calculated quantity is known as the *propagated error*. The propagated error can be estimated by
$$dy \approx f'(x)dx.$$
- To estimate the relative error of a particular quantity q, we estimate $\frac{\Delta q}{q}$.

4.3 Maxima and Minima

- A function may have both an absolute maximum and an absolute minimum, have just one absolute extremum, or have no absolute maximum or absolute minimum.
- If a function has a local extremum, the point at which it occurs must be a critical point. However, a function need not have a local extremum at a critical point.
- A continuous function over a closed, bounded interval has an absolute maximum and an absolute minimum. Each extremum occurs at a critical point or an endpoint.

4.4 The Mean Value Theorem

- If f is continuous over $[a, b]$ and differentiable over (a, b) and $f(a) = 0 = f(b)$, then there exists a point $c \in (a, b)$ such that $f'(c) = 0$. This is Rolle's theorem.
- If f is continuous over $[a, b]$ and differentiable over (a, b), then there exists a point $c \in (a, b)$ such that
$$f'(c) = \frac{f(b) - f(a)}{b - a}.$$

This is the Mean Value Theorem.

- If $f'(x) = 0$ over an interval I, then f is constant over I.
- If two differentiable functions f and g satisfy $f'(x) = g'(x)$ over I, then $f(x) = g(x) + C$ for some constant C.
- If $f'(x) > 0$ over an interval I, then f is increasing over I. If $f'(x) < 0$ over I, then f is decreasing over I.

4.5 Derivatives and the Shape of a Graph

- If c is a critical point of f and $f'(x) > 0$ for $x < c$ and $f'(x) < 0$ for $x > c$, then f has a local maximum at c.
- If c is a critical point of f and $f'(x) < 0$ for $x < c$ and $f'(x) > 0$ for $x > c$, then f has a local minimum at c.
- If $f''(x) > 0$ over an interval I, then f is concave up over I.
- If $f''(x) < 0$ over an interval I, then f is concave down over I.
- If $f'(c) = 0$ and $f''(c) > 0$, then f has a local minimum at c.
- If $f'(c) = 0$ and $f''(c) < 0$, then f has a local maximum at c.
- If $f'(c) = 0$ and $f''(c) = 0$, then evaluate $f'(x)$ at a test point x to the left of c and a test point x to the right of c, to determine whether f has a local extremum at c.

4.6 Limits at Infinity and Asymptotes

- The limit of $f(x)$ is L as $x \to \infty$ (or as $x \to -\infty$) if the values $f(x)$ become arbitrarily close to L as x becomes sufficiently large.
- The limit of $f(x)$ is ∞ as $x \to \infty$ if $f(x)$ becomes arbitrarily large as x becomes sufficiently large. The limit of $f(x)$ is $-\infty$ as $x \to \infty$ if $f(x) < 0$ and $|f(x)|$ becomes arbitrarily large as x becomes sufficiently large. We can define the limit of $f(x)$ as x approaches $-\infty$ similarly.
- For a polynomial function $p(x) = a_n x^n + a_{n-1} x^{n-1} + \ldots + a_1 x + a_0$, where $a_n \neq 0$, the end behavior is determined by the leading term $a_n x^n$. If $n \neq 0$, $p(x)$ approaches ∞ or $-\infty$ at each end.
- For a rational function $f(x) = \frac{p(x)}{q(x)}$, the end behavior is determined by the relationship between the degree of p and the degree of q. If the degree of p is less than the degree of q, the line $y = 0$ is a horizontal asymptote for f. If the degree of p is equal to the degree of q, then the line $y = \frac{a_n}{b_n}$ is a horizontal asymptote, where a_n and b_n are the leading coefficients of p and q, respectively. If the degree of p is greater than the degree of q, then f approaches ∞ or $-\infty$ at each end.

4.7 Applied Optimization Problems

- To solve an optimization problem, begin by drawing a picture and introducing variables.
- Find an equation relating the variables.
- Find a function of one variable to describe the quantity that is to be minimized or maximized.

- Look for critical points to locate local extrema.

4.8 L'Hôpital's Rule

- L'Hôpital's rule can be used to evaluate the limit of a quotient when the indeterminate form $\frac{0}{0}$ or ∞/∞ arises.
- L'Hôpital's rule can also be applied to other indeterminate forms if they can be rewritten in terms of a limit involving a quotient that has the indeterminate form $\frac{0}{0}$ or ∞/∞.
- The exponential function e^x grows faster than any power function x^p, $p > 0$.
- The logarithmic function $\ln x$ grows more slowly than any power function x^p, $p > 0$.

4.9 Newton's Method

- Newton's method approximates roots of $f(x) = 0$ by starting with an initial approximation x_0, then uses tangent lines to the graph of f to create a sequence of approximations $x_1, x_2, x_3, \ldots$.
- Typically, Newton's method is an efficient method for finding a particular root. In certain cases, Newton's method fails to work because the list of numbers $x_0, x_1, x_2, \ldots$ does not approach a finite value or it approaches a value other than the root sought.
- Any process in which a list of numbers $x_0, x_1, x_2, \ldots$ is generated by defining an initial number x_0 and defining the subsequent numbers by the equation $x_n = F(x_{n-1})$ for some function F is an iterative process. Newton's method is an example of an iterative process, where the function $F(x) = x - \left[\frac{f(x)}{f'(x)}\right]$ for a given function f.

4.10 Antiderivatives

- If F is an antiderivative of f, then every antiderivative of f is of the form $F(x) + C$ for some constant C.
- Solving the initial-value problem

$$\frac{dy}{dx} = f(x), \ y(x_0) = y_0$$

requires us first to find the set of antiderivatives of f and then to look for the particular antiderivative that also satisfies the initial condition.

CHAPTER 4 REVIEW EXERCISES

True or False? Justify your answer with a proof or a counterexample. Assume that $f(x)$ is continuous and differentiable unless stated otherwise.

525. If $f(-1) = -6$ and $f(1) = 2$, then there exists at least one point $x \in [-1, 1]$ such that $f'(x) = 4$.

526. If $f'(c) = 0$, there is a maximum or minimum at $x = c$.

527. There is a function such that $f(x) < 0$, $f'(x) > 0$, and $f''(x) < 0$. (A graphical "proof" is acceptable for this answer.)

528. There is a function such that there is both an inflection point and a critical point for some value $x = a$.

529. Given the graph of f', determine where f is increasing or decreasing.

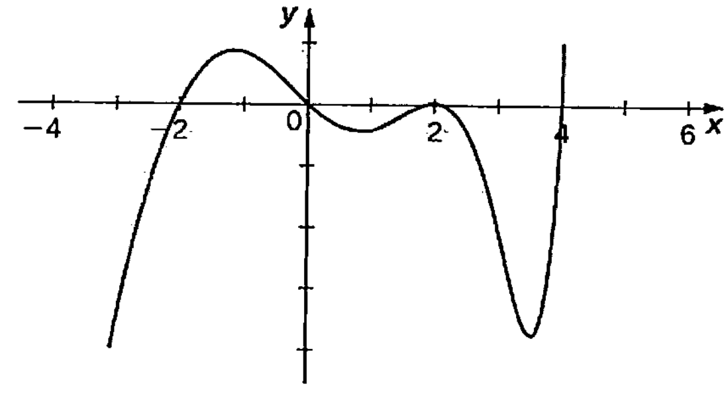

530. The graph of f is given below. Draw f'.

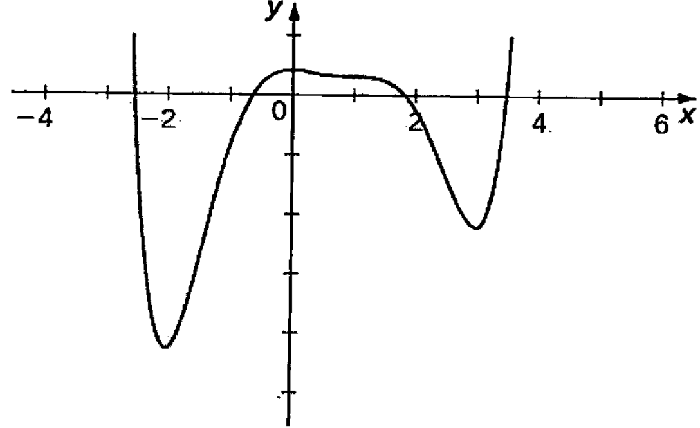

531. Find the linear approximation $L(x)$ to $y = x^2 + \tan(\pi x)$ near $x = \frac{1}{4}$.

532. Find the differential of $y = x^2 - 5x - 6$ and evaluate for $x = 2$ with $dx = 0.1$.

Find the critical points and the local and absolute extrema of the following functions on the given interval.

533. $f(x) = x + \sin^2(x)$ over $[0, \pi]$

534. $f(x) = 3x^4 - 4x^3 - 12x^2 + 6$ over $[-3, 3]$

Determine over which intervals the following functions are increasing, decreasing, concave up, and concave down.

535. $x(t) = 3t^4 - 8t^3 - 18t^2$

536. $y = x + \sin(\pi x)$

537. $g(x) = x - \sqrt{x}$

538. $f(\theta) = \sin(3\theta)$

Evaluate the following limits.

539. $\lim_{x \to \infty} \frac{3x\sqrt{x^2 + 1}}{\sqrt{x^4 - 1}}$

540. $\lim_{x \to \infty} \cos\left(\frac{1}{x}\right)$

541. $\lim_{x \to 1} \frac{x - 1}{\sin(\pi x)}$

542. $\lim_{x \to \infty} (3x)^{1/x}$

Use Newton's method to find the first two iterations, given the starting point.

543. $y = x^3 + 1,\ x_0 = 0.5$

544. $\frac{1}{x + 1} = \frac{1}{2},\ x_0 = 0$

Find the antiderivatives $F(x)$ of the following functions.

545. $g(x) = \sqrt{x} - \frac{1}{x^2}$

546. $f(x) = 2x + 6\cos x,\ F(\pi) = \pi^2 + 2$

Graph the following functions by hand. Make sure to label the inflection points, critical points, zeros, and asymptotes.

547. $y = \frac{1}{x(x + 1)^2}$

548. $y = x - \sqrt{4 - x^2}$

549. A car is being compacted into a rectangular solid. The volume is decreasing at a rate of 2 m^3/sec. The length and width of the compactor are square, but the height is not the same length as the length and width. If the length and width walls move toward each other at a rate of 0.25 m/sec, find the rate at which the height is changing when the length and width are 2 m and the height is 1.5 m.

550. A rocket is launched into space; its kinetic energy is given by $K(t) = \left(\frac{1}{2}\right)m(t)v(t)^2$, where K is the kinetic energy in joules, m is the mass of the rocket in kilograms, and v is the velocity of the rocket in meters/second. Assume the velocity is increasing at a rate of 15 m/sec^2 and the mass is decreasing at a rate of 10 kg/sec because the fuel is being burned. At what rate is the rocket's kinetic energy changing when the mass is 2000 kg and the velocity is 5000 m/sec? Give your answer in mega-Joules (MJ), which is equivalent to 10^6 J.

551. The famous Regiomontanus' problem for angle maximization was proposed during the 15 th century. A painting hangs on a wall with the bottom of the painting a distance a feet above eye level, and the top b feet above eye level. What distance x (in feet) from the wall should the viewer stand to maximize the angle subtended by the painting, θ?

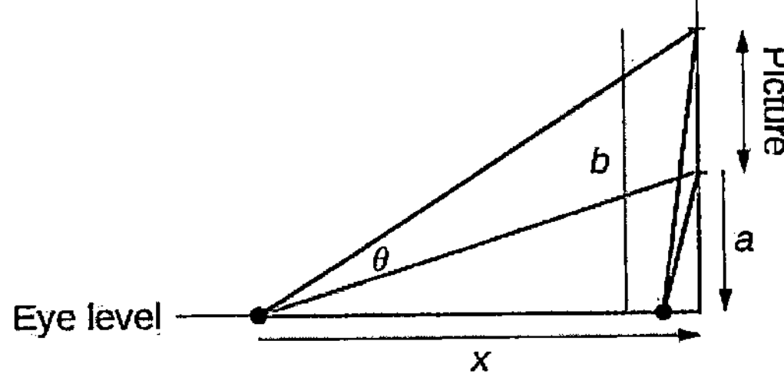

552. An airline sells tickets from Tokyo to Detroit for $\$1200$. There are 500 seats available and a typical flight books 350 seats. For every $\$10$ decrease in price, the airline observes an additional five seats sold. What should the fare be to maximize profit? How many passengers would be onboard?

5 | INTEGRATION

Figure 5.1 Iceboating is a popular winter sport in parts of the northern United States and Europe. (credit: modification of work by Carter Brown, Flickr)

Chapter Outline

Introduction

Iceboats are a common sight on the lakes of Wisconsin and Minnesota on winter weekends. Iceboats are similar to sailboats, but they are fitted with runners, or "skates," and are designed to run over the ice, rather than on water. Iceboats can move very quickly, and many ice boating enthusiasts are drawn to the sport because of the speed. Top iceboat racers can attain speeds up to five times the wind speed. If we know how fast an iceboat is moving, we can use integration to determine how far it travels. We revisit this question later in the chapter (see **Example 5.27**).

Determining distance from velocity is just one of many applications of integration. In fact, integrals are used in a wide variety of mechanical and physical applications. In this chapter, we first introduce the theory behind integration and use integrals to calculate areas. From there, we develop the Fundamental Theorem of Calculus, which relates differentiation and integration. We then study some basic integration techniques and briefly examine some applications.

5.1 | Approximating Areas

Learning Objectives

5.1.1 Use sigma (summation) notation to calculate sums and powers of integers.
5.1.2 Use the sum of rectangular areas to approximate the area under a curve.
5.1.3 Use Riemann sums to approximate area.

Archimedes was fascinated with calculating the areas of various shapes—in other words, the amount of space enclosed by the shape. He used a process that has come to be known as the *method of exhaustion*, which used smaller and smaller shapes, the areas of which could be calculated exactly, to fill an irregular region and thereby obtain closer and closer approximations to the total area. In this process, an area bounded by curves is filled with rectangles, triangles, and shapes with exact area formulas. These areas are then summed to approximate the area of the curved region.

In this section, we develop techniques to approximate the area between a curve, defined by a function $f(x)$, and the x-axis on a closed interval $[a, b]$. Like Archimedes, we first approximate the area under the curve using shapes of known area (namely, rectangles). By using smaller and smaller rectangles, we get closer and closer approximations to the area. Taking a limit allows us to calculate the exact area under the curve.

Let's start by introducing some notation to make the calculations easier. We then consider the case when $f(x)$ is continuous and nonnegative. Later in the chapter, we relax some of these restrictions and develop techniques that apply in more general cases.

Sigma (Summation) Notation

As mentioned, we will use shapes of known area to approximate the area of an irregular region bounded by curves. This process often requires adding up long strings of numbers. To make it easier to write down these lengthy sums, we look at some new notation here, called **sigma notation** (also known as **summation notation**). The Greek capital letter Σ, sigma, is used to express long sums of values in a compact form. For example, if we want to add all the integers from 1 to 20 without sigma notation, we have to write

$$1 + 2 + 3 + 4 + 5 + 6 + 7 + 8 + 9 + 10 + 11 + 12 + 13 + 14 + 15 + 16 + 17 + 18 + 19 + 20.$$

We could probably skip writing a couple of terms and write

$$1 + 2 + 3 + 4 + \cdots + 19 + 20,$$

which is better, but still cumbersome. With sigma notation, we write this sum as

$$\sum_{i=1}^{20} i,$$

which is much more compact.

Typically, sigma notation is presented in the form

$$\sum_{i=1}^{n} a_i$$

where a_i describes the terms to be added, and the i is called the *index*. Each term is evaluated, then we sum all the values, beginning with the value when $i = 1$ and ending with the value when $i = n$. For example, an expression like $\sum_{i=2}^{7} s_i$ is interpreted as $s_2 + s_3 + s_4 + s_5 + s_6 + s_7$. Note that the index is used only to keep track of the terms to be added; it does not factor into the calculation of the sum itself. The index is therefore called a *dummy variable*. We can use any letter we like for the index. Typically, mathematicians use *i*, *j*, *k*, *m*, and *n* for indices.

Let's try a couple of examples of using sigma notation.

Example 5.1

Using Sigma Notation

a. Write in sigma notation and evaluate the sum of terms 3^i for $i = 1, 2, 3, 4, 5$.

b. Write the sum in sigma notation:

$$1 + \frac{1}{4} + \frac{1}{9} + \frac{1}{16} + \frac{1}{25}.$$

Solution

a. Write

$$\begin{aligned}\sum_{i=1}^{5} 3^i &= 3 + 3^2 + 3^3 + 3^4 + 3^5 \\ &= 363.\end{aligned}$$

b. The denominator of each term is a perfect square. Using sigma notation, this sum can be written as $\sum_{i=1}^{5} \frac{1}{i^2}$.

5.1 Write in sigma notation and evaluate the sum of terms 2^i for $i = 3, 4, 5, 6$.

The properties associated with the summation process are given in the following rule.

Rule: Properties of Sigma Notation

Let $a_1, a_2, \ldots, a_n$ and $b_1, b_2, \ldots, b_n$ represent two sequences of terms and let c be a constant. The following properties hold for all positive integers n and for integers m, with $1 \le m \le n$.

1.
$$\sum_{i=1}^{n} c = nc \tag{5.1}$$

2.
$$\sum_{i=1}^{n} ca_i = c\sum_{i=1}^{n} a_i \tag{5.2}$$

3.
$$\sum_{i=1}^{n} (a_i + b_i) = \sum_{i=1}^{n} a_i + \sum_{i=1}^{n} b_i \tag{5.3}$$

4.
$$\sum_{i=1}^{n} (a_i - b_i) = \sum_{i=1}^{n} a_i - \sum_{i=1}^{n} b_i \tag{5.4}$$

5.

$$\sum_{i=1}^{n} a_i = \sum_{i=1}^{m} a_i + \sum_{i=m+1}^{n} a_i \tag{5.5}$$

Proof

We prove properties 2. and 3. here, and leave proof of the other properties to the Exercises.

2. We have

$$\begin{aligned}\sum_{i=1}^{n} ca_i &= ca_1 + ca_2 + ca_3 + \cdots + ca_n \\ &= c(a_1 + a_2 + a_3 + \cdots + a_n) \\ &= c\sum_{i=1}^{n} a_i.\end{aligned}$$

3. We have

$$\begin{aligned}\sum_{i=1}^{n} (a_i + b_i) &= (a_1 + b_1) + (a_2 + b_2) + (a_3 + b_3) + \cdots + (a_n + b_n) \\ &= (a_1 + a_2 + a_3 + \cdots + a_n) + (b_1 + b_2 + b_3 + \cdots + b_n) \\ &= \sum_{i=1}^{n} a_i + \sum_{i=1}^{n} b_i.\end{aligned}$$

□

A few more formulas for frequently found functions simplify the summation process further. These are shown in the next rule, for **sums and powers of integers**, and we use them in the next set of examples.

Rule: Sums and Powers of Integers

1. The sum of n integers is given by

$$\sum_{i=1}^{n} i = 1 + 2 + \cdots + n = \frac{n(n+1)}{2}.$$

2. The sum of consecutive integers squared is given by

$$\sum_{i=1}^{n} i^2 = 1^2 + 2^2 + \cdots + n^2 = \frac{n(n+1)(2n+1)}{6}.$$

3. The sum of consecutive integers cubed is given by

$$\sum_{i=1}^{n} i^3 = 1^3 + 2^3 + \cdots + n^3 = \frac{n^2(n+1)^2}{4}.$$

Example 5.2

Evaluation Using Sigma Notation

Write using sigma notation and evaluate:

a. The sum of the terms $(i-3)^2$ for $i = 1, 2, \ldots, 200$.

b. The sum of the terms $\left(i^3 - i^2\right)$ for $i = 1, 2, 3, 4, 5, 6.$

Solution

a. Multiplying out $(i-3)^2,$ we can break the expression into three terms.

$$\begin{aligned}
\sum_{i=1}^{200} (i-3)^2 &= \sum_{i=1}^{200} \left(i^2 - 6i + 9\right) \\
&= \sum_{i=1}^{200} i^2 - \sum_{i=1}^{200} 6i + \sum_{i=1}^{200} 9 \\
&= \sum_{i=1}^{200} i^2 - 6\sum_{i=1}^{200} i + \sum_{i=1}^{200} 9 \\
&= \frac{200(200+1)(400+1)}{6} - 6\left[\frac{200(200+1)}{2}\right] + 9(200) \\
&= 2{,}686{,}700 - 120{,}600 + 1800 \\
&= 2{,}567{,}900
\end{aligned}$$

b. Use sigma notation property iv. and the rules for the sum of squared terms and the sum of cubed terms.

$$\begin{aligned}
\sum_{i=1}^{6} \left(i^3 - i^2\right) &= \sum_{i=1}^{6} i^3 - \sum_{i=1}^{6} i^2 \\
&= \frac{6^2(6+1)^2}{4} - \frac{6(6+1)(2(6)+1)}{6} \\
&= \frac{1764}{4} - \frac{546}{6} \\
&= 350
\end{aligned}$$

5.2 Find the sum of the values of $4 + 3i$ for $i = 1, 2, \ldots, 100.$

Example 5.3

Finding the Sum of the Function Values

Find the sum of the values of $f(x) = x^3$ over the integers $1, 2, 3, \ldots, 10.$

Solution

Using the formula, we have

$$\begin{aligned}
\sum_{i=0}^{10} i^3 &= \frac{(10)^2(10+1)^2}{4} \\
&= \frac{100(121)}{4} \\
&= 3025.
\end{aligned}$$

5.3 Evaluate the sum indicated by the notation $\sum_{k=1}^{20}(2k+1)$.

Approximating Area

Now that we have the necessary notation, we return to the problem at hand: approximating the area under a curve. Let $f(x)$ be a continuous, nonnegative function defined on the closed interval $[a, b]$. We want to approximate the area A bounded by $f(x)$ above, the x-axis below, the line $x = a$ on the left, and the line $x = b$ on the right (**Figure 5.2**).

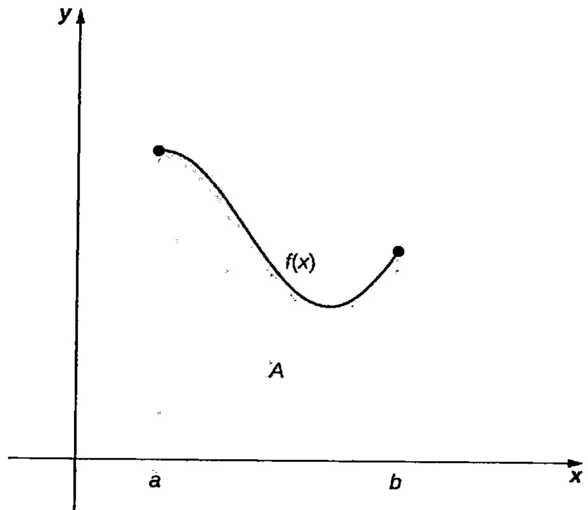

Figure 5.2 An area (shaded region) bounded by the curve $f(x)$ at top, the x-axis at bottom, the line $x = a$ to the left, and the line $x = b$ at right.

How do we approximate the area under this curve? The approach is a geometric one. By dividing a region into many small shapes that have known area formulas, we can sum these areas and obtain a reasonable estimate of the true area. We begin by dividing the interval $[a, b]$ into n subintervals of equal width, $\frac{b-a}{n}$. We do this by selecting equally spaced points $x_0, x_1, x_2,\ldots, x_n$ with $x_0 = a, x_n = b,$ and

$$x_i - x_{i-1} = \frac{b-a}{n}$$

for $i = 1, 2, 3,\ldots, n$.

We denote the width of each subinterval with the notation Δx, so $\Delta x = \frac{b-a}{n}$ and

$$x_i = x_0 + i\Delta x$$

for $i = 1, 2, 3,\ldots, n$. This notion of dividing an interval $[a, b]$ into subintervals by selecting points from within the interval is used quite often in approximating the area under a curve, so let's define some relevant terminology.

Definition

A set of points $P = \{x_i\}$ for $i = 0, 1, 2,\ldots, n$ with $a = x_0 < x_1 < x_2 < \cdots < x_n = b,$ which divides the interval $[a, b]$ into subintervals of the form $[x_0, x_1], [x_1, x_2],\ldots, [x_{n-1}, x_n]$ is called a **partition** of $[a, b]$. If the subintervals all have the same width, the set of points forms a **regular partition** of the interval $[a, b]$.

We can use this regular partition as the basis of a method for estimating the area under the curve. We next examine two methods: the left-endpoint approximation and the right-endpoint approximation.

Rule: Left-Endpoint Approximation

On each subinterval $[x_{i-1}, x_i]$ (for $i = 1, 2, 3, \ldots, n$), construct a rectangle with width Δx and height equal to $f(x_{i-1})$, which is the function value at the left endpoint of the subinterval. Then the area of this rectangle is $f(x_{i-1})\Delta x$. Adding the areas of all these rectangles, we get an approximate value for A (**Figure 5.3**). We use the notation L_n to denote that this is a **left-endpoint approximation** of A using n subintervals.

$$A \approx L_n = f(x_0)\Delta x + f(x_1)\Delta x + \cdots + f(x_{n-1})\Delta x \tag{5.6}$$

$$= \sum_{i=1}^{n} f(x_{i-1})\Delta x$$

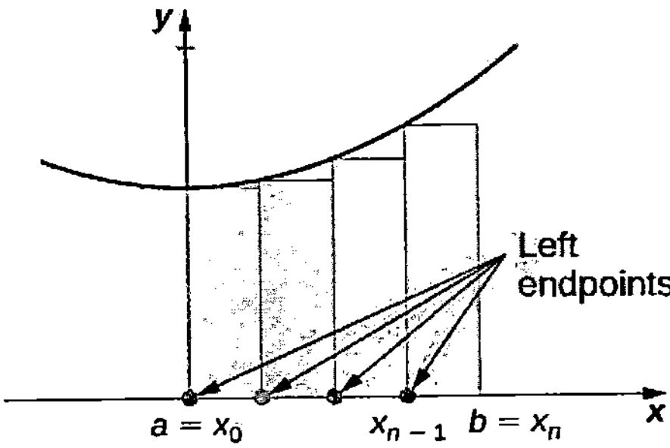

Figure 5.3 In the left-endpoint approximation of area under a curve, the height of each rectangle is determined by the function value at the left of each subinterval.

The second method for approximating area under a curve is the right-endpoint approximation. It is almost the same as the left-endpoint approximation, but now the heights of the rectangles are determined by the function values at the right of each subinterval.

Rule: Right-Endpoint Approximation

Construct a rectangle on each subinterval $[x_{i-1}, x_i]$, only this time the height of the rectangle is determined by the function value $f(x_i)$ at the right endpoint of the subinterval. Then, the area of each rectangle is $f(x_i)\Delta x$ and the approximation for A is given by

$$A \approx R_n = f(x_1)\Delta x + f(x_2)\Delta x + \cdots + f(x_n)\Delta x \tag{5.7}$$

$$= \sum_{i=1}^{n} f(x_i)\Delta x.$$

The notation R_n indicates this is a **right-endpoint approximation** for A (**Figure 5.4**).

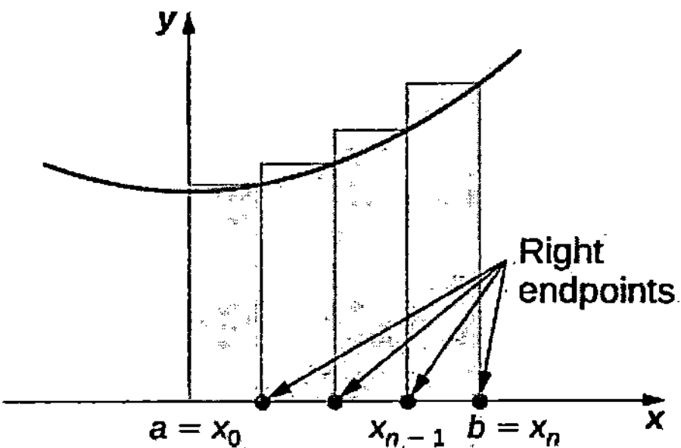

Figure 5.4 In the right-endpoint approximation of area under a curve, the height of each rectangle is determined by the function value at the right of each subinterval. Note that the right-endpoint approximation differs from the left-endpoint approximation in **Figure 5.3**.

The graphs in **Figure 5.5** represent the curve $f(x) = \frac{x^2}{2}$. In graph (a) we divide the region represented by the interval $[0, 3]$ into six subintervals, each of width 0.5. Thus, $\Delta x = 0.5$. We then form six rectangles by drawing vertical lines perpendicular to x_{i-1}, the left endpoint of each subinterval. We determine the height of each rectangle by calculating $f(x_{i-1})$ for $i = 1, 2, 3, 4, 5, 6$. The intervals are $[0, 0.5], [0.5, 1], [1, 1.5], [1.5, 2], [2, 2.5], [2.5, 3]$. We find the area of each rectangle by multiplying the height by the width. Then, the sum of the rectangular areas approximates the area between $f(x)$ and the x-axis. When the left endpoints are used to calculate height, we have a left-endpoint approximation. Thus,

$$\begin{aligned} A \approx L_6 &= \sum_{i=1}^{6} f(x_{i-1})\Delta x = f(x_0)\Delta x + f(x_1)\Delta x + f(x_2)\Delta x + f(x_3)\Delta x + f(x_4)\Delta x + f(x_5)\Delta x \\ &= f(0)0.5 + f(0.5)0.5 + f(1)0.5 + f(1.5)0.5 + f(2)0.5 + f(2.5)0.5 \\ &= (0)0.5 + (0.125)0.5 + (0.5)0.5 + (1.125)0.5 + (2)0.5 + (3.125)0.5 \\ &= 0 + 0.0625 + 0.25 + 0.5625 + 1 + 1.5625 \\ &= 3.4375. \end{aligned}$$

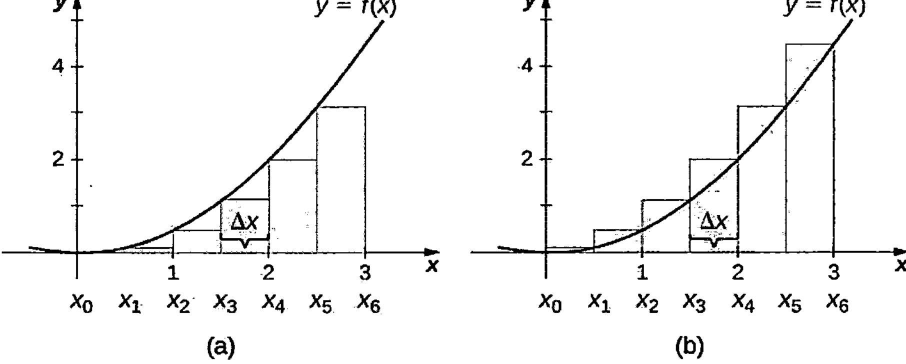

Figure 5.5 Methods of approximating the area under a curve by using (a) the left endpoints and (b) the right endpoints.

In **Figure 5.5**(b), we draw vertical lines perpendicular to x_i such that x_i is the right endpoint of each subinterval, and calculate $f(x_i)$ for $i = 1, 2, 3, 4, 5, 6$. We multiply each $f(x_i)$ by Δx to find the rectangular areas, and then add them. This is a right-endpoint approximation of the area under $f(x)$. Thus,

$$
\begin{aligned}
A \approx R_6 &= \sum_{i=1}^{6} f(x_i)\Delta x = f(x_1)\Delta x + f(x_2)\Delta x + f(x_3)\Delta x + f(x_4)\Delta x + f(x_5)\Delta x + f(x_6)\Delta x \\
&= f(0.5)0.5 + f(1)0.5 + f(1.5)0.5 + f(2)0.5 + f(2.5)0.5 + f(3)0.5 \\
&= (0.125)0.5 + (0.5)0.5 + (1.125)0.5 + (2)0.5 + (3.125)0.5 + (4.5)0.5 \\
&= 0.0625 + 0.25 + 0.5625 + 1 + 1.5625 + 2.25 \\
&= 5.6875.
\end{aligned}
$$

Example 5.4

Approximating the Area Under a Curve

Use both left-endpoint and right-endpoint approximations to approximate the area under the curve of $f(x) = x^2$ on the interval $[0, 2]$; use $n = 4$.

Solution

First, divide the interval $[0, 2]$ into n equal subintervals. Using $n = 4$, $\Delta x = \frac{(2-0)}{4} = 0.5$. This is the width of each rectangle. The intervals $[0, 0.5]$, $[0.5, 1]$, $[1, 1.5]$, $[1.5, 2]$ are shown in **Figure 5.6**. Using a left-endpoint approximation, the heights are $f(0) = 0$, $f(0.5) = 0.25$, $f(1) = 1$, $f(1.5) = 2.25$. Then,

$$
\begin{aligned}
L_4 &= f(x_0)\Delta x + f(x_1)\Delta x + f(x_2)\Delta x + f(x_3)\Delta x \\
&= 0(0.5) + 0.25(0.5) + 1(0.5) + 2.25(0.5) \\
&= 1.75.
\end{aligned}
$$

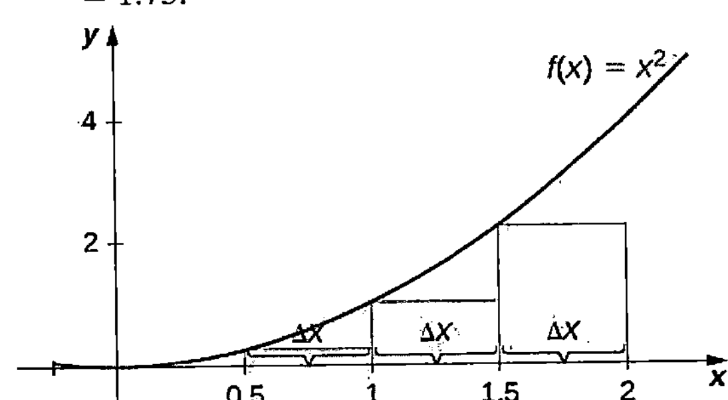

Figure 5.6 The graph shows the left-endpoint approximation of the area under $f(x) = x^2$ from 0 to 2.

The right-endpoint approximation is shown in **Figure 5.7**. The intervals are the same, $\Delta x = 0.5$, but now use the right endpoint to calculate the height of the rectangles. We have

$$
\begin{aligned}
R_4 &= f(x_1)\Delta x + f(x_2)\Delta x + f(x_3)\Delta x + f(x_4)\Delta x \\
&= 0.25(0.5) + 1(0.5) + 2.25(0.5) + 4(0.5) \\
&= 3.75.
\end{aligned}
$$

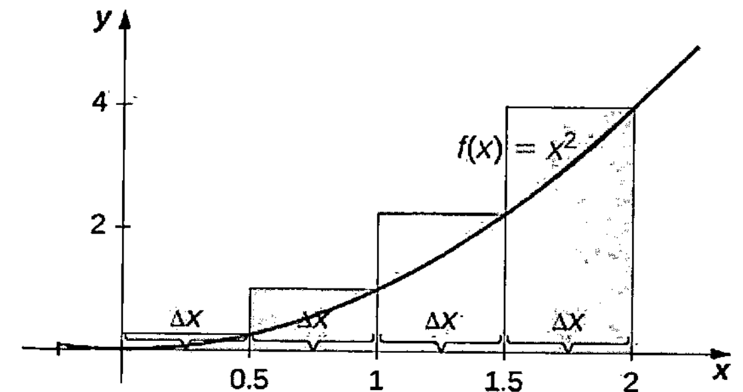

Figure 5.7 The graph shows the right-endpoint approximation of the area under $f(x) = x^2$ from 0 to 2.

The left-endpoint approximation is 1.75; the right-endpoint approximation is 3.75.

5.4 Sketch left-endpoint and right-endpoint approximations for $f(x) = \frac{1}{x}$ on $[1, 2]$; use $n = 4$. Approximate the area using both methods.

Looking at **Figure 5.5** and the graphs in **Example 5.4**, we can see that when we use a small number of intervals, neither the left-endpoint approximation nor the right-endpoint approximation is a particularly accurate estimate of the area under the curve. However, it seems logical that if we increase the number of points in our partition, our estimate of A will improve. We will have more rectangles, but each rectangle will be thinner, so we will be able to fit the rectangles to the curve more precisely.

We can demonstrate the improved approximation obtained through smaller intervals with an example. Let's explore the idea of increasing n, first in a left-endpoint approximation with four rectangles, then eight rectangles, and finally 32 rectangles. Then, let's do the same thing in a right-endpoint approximation, using the same sets of intervals, of the same curved region. **Figure 5.8** shows the area of the region under the curve $f(x) = (x-1)^3 + 4$ on the interval $[0, 2]$ using a left-endpoint approximation where $n = 4$. The width of each rectangle is

$$\Delta x = \frac{2-0}{4} = \frac{1}{2}.$$

The area is approximated by the summed areas of the rectangles, or

$$\begin{aligned} L_4 &= f(0)(0.5) + f(0.5)(0.5) + f(1)(0.5) + f(1.5)0.5 \\ &= 7.5. \end{aligned}$$

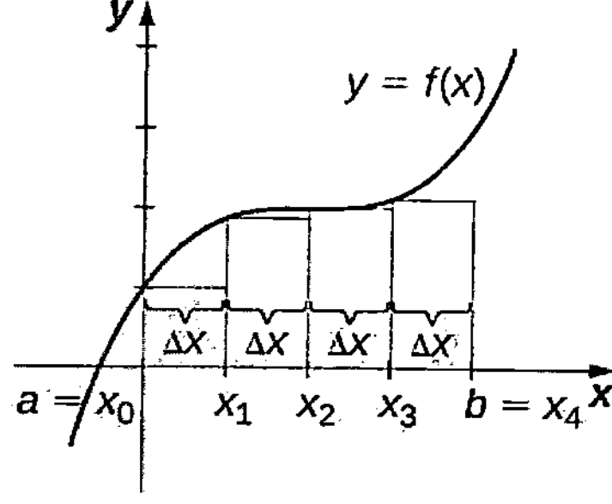

Figure 5.8 With a left-endpoint approximation and dividing the region from a to b into four equal intervals, the area under the curve is approximately equal to the sum of the areas of the rectangles.

Figure 5.9 shows the same curve divided into eight subintervals. Comparing the graph with four rectangles in **Figure 5.8** with this graph with eight rectangles, we can see there appears to be less white space under the curve when $n = 8$. This white space is area under the curve we are unable to include using our approximation. The area of the rectangles is

$$\begin{aligned} L_8 &= f(0)(0.25) + f(0.25)(0.25) + f(0.5)(0.25) + f(0.75)(0.25) \\ &\quad + f(1)(0.25) + f(1.25)(0.25) + f(1.5)(0.25) + f(1.75)(0.25) \\ &= 7.75. \end{aligned}$$

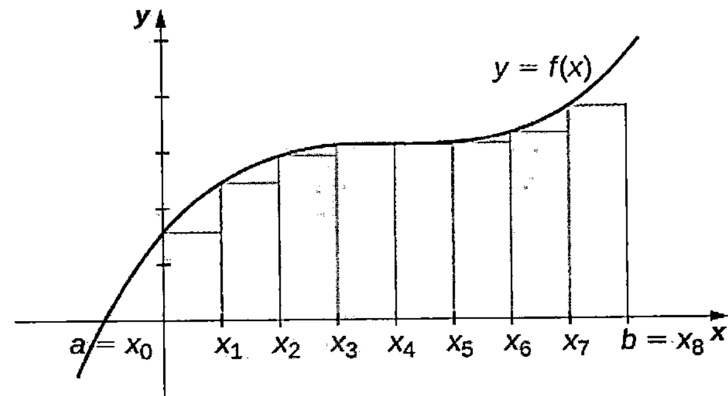

Figure 5.9 The region under the curve is divided into $n = 8$ rectangular areas of equal width for a left-endpoint approximation.

The graph in **Figure 5.10** shows the same function with 32 rectangles inscribed under the curve. There appears to be little white space left. The area occupied by the rectangles is

$$\begin{aligned} L_{32} &= f(0)(0.0625) + f(0.0625)(0.0625) + f(0.125)(0.0625) + \cdots + f(1.9375)(0.0625) \\ &= 7.9375. \end{aligned}$$

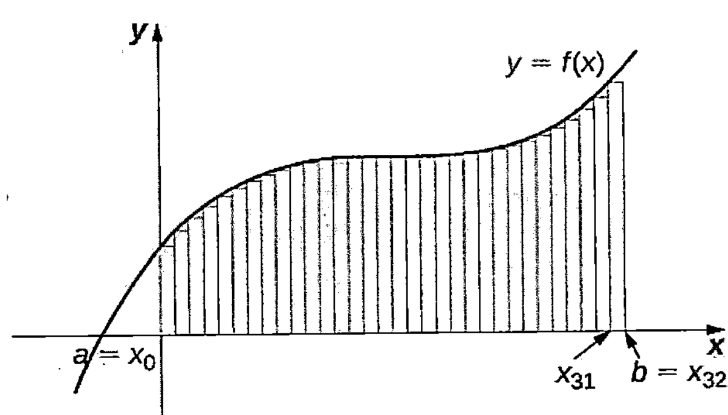

Figure 5.10 Here, 32 rectangles are inscribed under the curve for a left-endpoint approximation.

We can carry out a similar process for the right-endpoint approximation method. A right-endpoint approximation of the same curve, using four rectangles (**Figure 5.11**), yields an area

$$\begin{aligned} R_4 &= f(0.5)(0.5) + f(1)(0.5) + f(1.5)(0.5) + f(2)(0.5) \\ &= 8.5. \end{aligned}$$

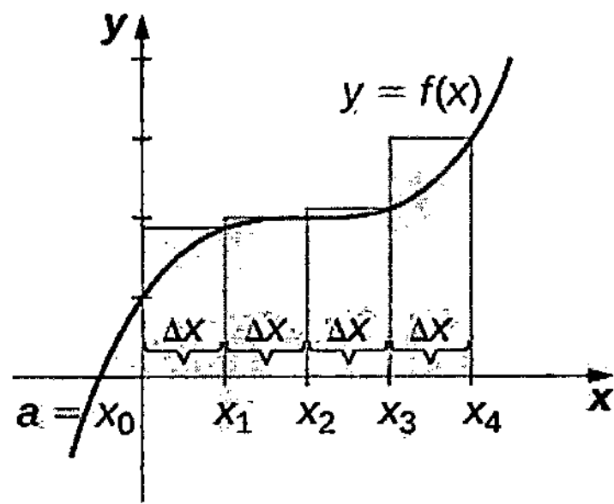

Figure 5.11 Now we divide the area under the curve into four equal subintervals for a right-endpoint approximation.

Dividing the region over the interval $[0, 2]$ into eight rectangles results in $\Delta x = \frac{2-0}{8} = 0.25$. The graph is shown in **Figure 5.12**. The area is

$$\begin{aligned} R_8 &= f(0.25)(0.25) + f(0.5)(0.25) + f(0.75)(0.25) + f(1)(0.25) \\ &\quad + f(1.25)(0.25) + f(1.5)(0.25) + f(1.75)(0.25) + f(2)(0.25) \\ &= 8.25. \end{aligned}$$

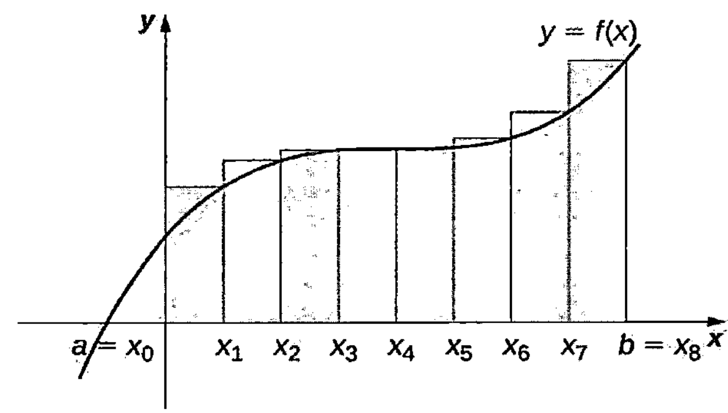

Figure 5.12 Here we use right-endpoint approximation for a region divided into eight equal subintervals.

Last, the right-endpoint approximation with $n = 32$ is close to the actual area (**Figure 5.13**). The area is approximately

$$\begin{aligned} R_{32} &= f(0.0625)(0.0625) + f(0.125)(0.0625) + f(0.1875)(0.0625) + \cdots + f(2)(0.0625) \\ &= 8.0625. \end{aligned}$$

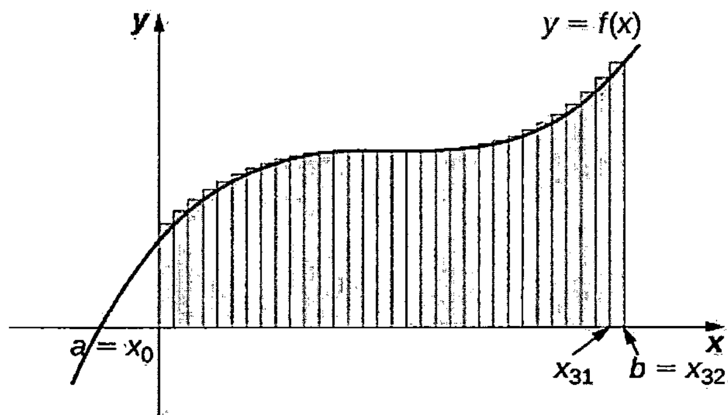

Figure 5.13 The region is divided into 32 equal subintervals for a right-endpoint approximation.

Based on these figures and calculations, it appears we are on the right track; the rectangles appear to approximate the area under the curve better as n gets larger. Furthermore, as n increases, both the left-endpoint and right-endpoint approximations appear to approach an area of 8 square units. **Table 5.1** shows a numerical comparison of the left- and right-endpoint methods. The idea that the approximations of the area under the curve get better and better as n gets larger and larger is very important, and we now explore this idea in more detail.

Values of n	Approximate Area L_n	Approximate Area R_n
$n = 4$	7.5	8.5
$n = 8$	7.75	8.25
$n = 32$	7.94	8.06

Table 5.1 Converging Values of Left- and Right-Endpoint Approximations as n Increases

Forming Riemann Sums

So far we have been using rectangles to approximate the area under a curve. The heights of these rectangles have been determined by evaluating the function at either the right or left endpoints of the subinterval $[x_{i-1}, x_i]$. In reality, there is no reason to restrict evaluation of the function to one of these two points only. We could evaluate the function at any point c_i in the subinterval $[x_{i-1}, x_i]$, and use $f(x_i^*)$ as the height of our rectangle. This gives us an estimate for the area of the form

$$A \approx \sum_{i=1}^{n} f(x_i^*)\Delta x.$$

A sum of this form is called a Riemann sum, named for the 19th-century mathematician Bernhard Riemann, who developed the idea.

Definition

Let $f(x)$ be defined on a closed interval $[a, b]$ and let P be a regular partition of $[a, b]$. Let Δx be the width of each subinterval $[x_{i-1}, x_i]$ and for each i, let x_i^* be any point in $[x_{i-1}, x_i]$. A **Riemann sum** is defined for $f(x)$ as

$$\sum_{i=1}^{n} f(x_i^*)\Delta x.$$

Recall that with the left- and right-endpoint approximations, the estimates seem to get better and better as n get larger and larger. The same thing happens with Riemann sums. Riemann sums give better approximations for larger values of n. We are now ready to define the area under a curve in terms of Riemann sums.

Definition

Let $f(x)$ be a continuous, nonnegative function on an interval $[a, b]$, and let $\sum_{i=1}^{n} f(x_i^*)\Delta x$ be a Riemann sum for $f(x)$. Then, the **area under the curve** $y = f(x)$ on $[a, b]$ is given by

$$A = \lim_{n\to\infty} \sum_{i=1}^{n} f(x_i^*)\Delta x.$$

 See a **graphical demonstration (http://www.openstaxcollege.org/l/20_riemannsums)** of the construction of a Riemann sum.

Some subtleties here are worth discussing. First, note that taking the limit of a sum is a little different from taking the limit of a function $f(x)$ as x goes to infinity. Limits of sums are discussed in detail in the chapter on **Sequences and Series (http://cnx.org/content/m53756/latest/)** ; however, for now we can assume that the computational techniques we used to compute limits of functions can also be used to calculate limits of sums.

Second, we must consider what to do if the expression converges to different limits for different choices of $\{x_i^*\}$. Fortunately, this does not happen. Although the proof is beyond the scope of this text, it can be shown that if $f(x)$ is continuous on the closed interval $[a, b]$, then $\lim_{n \to \infty} \sum_{i=1}^{n} f(x_i^*)\Delta x$ exists and is unique (in other words, it does not depend on the choice of $\{x_i^*\}$).

We look at some examples shortly. But, before we do, let's take a moment and talk about some specific choices for $\{x_i^*\}$. Although any choice for $\{x_i^*\}$ gives us an estimate of the area under the curve, we don't necessarily know whether that estimate is too high (overestimate) or too low (underestimate). If it is important to know whether our estimate is high or low, we can select our value for $\{x_i^*\}$ to guarantee one result or the other.

If we want an overestimate, for example, we can choose $\{x_i^*\}$ such that for $i = 1, 2, 3,\ldots, n,$ $f(x_i^*) \geq f(x)$ for all $x \in [x_{i-1}, x_i]$. In other words, we choose $\{x_i^*\}$ so that for $i = 1, 2, 3,\ldots, n,$ $f(x_i^*)$ is the maximum function value on the interval $[x_{i-1}, x_i]$. If we select $\{x_i^*\}$ in this way, then the Riemann sum $\sum_{i=1}^{n} f(x_i^*)\Delta x$ is called an **upper sum**. Similarly, if we want an underestimate, we can choose $\{x_i^*\}$ so that for $i = 1, 2, 3,\ldots, n,$ $f(x_i^*)$ is the minimum function value on the interval $[x_{i-1}, x_i]$. In this case, the associated Riemann sum is called a **lower sum**. Note that if $f(x)$ is either increasing or decreasing throughout the interval $[a, b]$, then the maximum and minimum values of the function occur at the endpoints of the subintervals, so the upper and lower sums are just the same as the left- and right-endpoint approximations.

Example 5.5

Finding Lower and Upper Sums

Find a lower sum for $f(x) = 10 - x^2$ on $[1, 2]$; let $n = 4$ subintervals.

Solution

With $n = 4$ over the interval $[1, 2]$, $\Delta x = \frac{1}{4}$. We can list the intervals as $[1, 1.25], [1.25, 1.5], [1.5, 1.75], [1.75, 2]$. Because the function is decreasing over the interval $[1, 2]$, **Figure 5.14** shows that a lower sum is obtained by using the right endpoints.

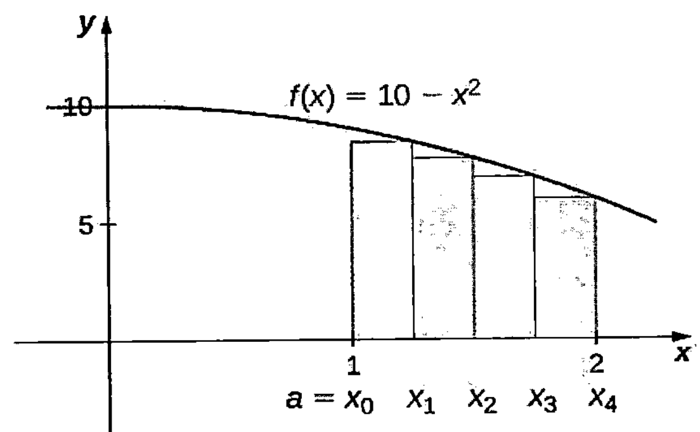

Figure 5.14 The graph of $f(x) = 10 - x^2$ is set up for a right-endpoint approximation of the area bounded by the curve and the x-axis on $[1, 2]$, and it shows a lower sum.

The Riemann sum is

$$\begin{aligned}\sum_{k=1}^{4}\left(10 - x^2\right)(0.25) &= 0.25\left[10 - (1.25)^2 + 10 - (1.5)^2 + 10 - (1.75)^2 + 10 - (2)^2\right] \\ &= 0.25[8.4375 + 7.75 + 6.9375 + 6] \\ &= 7.28.\end{aligned}$$

The area of 7.28 is a lower sum and an underestimate.

5.5 a. Find an upper sum for $f(x) = 10 - x^2$ on $[1, 2]$; let $n = 4$.

b. Sketch the approximation.

Example 5.6

Finding Lower and Upper Sums for $f(x) = \sin x$

Find a lower sum for $f(x) = \sin x$ over the interval $[a, b] = \left[0, \frac{\pi}{2}\right]$; let $n = 6$.

Solution

Let's first look at the graph in **Figure 5.15** to get a better idea of the area of interest.

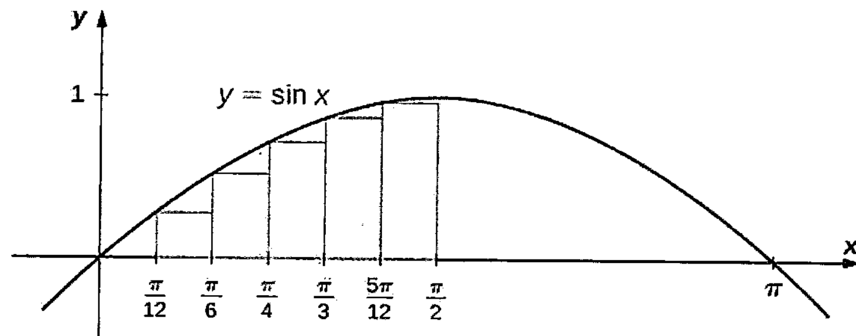

Figure 5.15 The graph of $y = \sin x$ is divided into six regions: $\Delta x = \frac{\pi/2}{6} = \frac{\pi}{12}$.

The intervals are $\left[0, \frac{\pi}{12}\right], \left[\frac{\pi}{12}, \frac{\pi}{6}\right], \left[\frac{\pi}{6}, \frac{\pi}{4}\right], \left[\frac{\pi}{4}, \frac{\pi}{3}\right], \left[\frac{\pi}{3}, \frac{5\pi}{12}\right]$, and $\left[\frac{5\pi}{12}, \frac{\pi}{2}\right]$. Note that $f(x) = \sin x$ is increasing on the interval $\left[0, \frac{\pi}{2}\right]$, so a left-endpoint approximation gives us the lower sum. A left-endpoint approximation is the Riemann sum $\sum_{i=0}^{5} \sin x_i \left(\frac{\pi}{12}\right)$. We have

$$\begin{aligned} A &\approx \sin(0)\left(\frac{\pi}{12}\right) + \sin\left(\frac{\pi}{12}\right)\left(\frac{\pi}{12}\right) + \sin\left(\frac{\pi}{6}\right)\left(\frac{\pi}{12}\right) + \sin\left(\frac{\pi}{4}\right)\left(\frac{\pi}{12}\right) + \sin\left(\frac{\pi}{3}\right)\left(\frac{\pi}{12}\right) + \sin\left(\frac{5\pi}{12}\right)\left(\frac{\pi}{12}\right) \\ &= 0.863. \end{aligned}$$

 **5.6** Using the function $f(x) = \sin x$ over the interval $\left[0, \frac{\pi}{2}\right]$, find an upper sum; let $n = 6$.

5.1 EXERCISES

1. State whether the given sums are equal or unequal.

   a. $\sum_{i=1}^{10} i$ and $\sum_{k=1}^{10} k$

   b. $\sum_{i=1}^{10} i$ and $\sum_{i=6}^{15} (i-5)$

   c. $\sum_{i=1}^{10} i(i-1)$ and $\sum_{j=0}^{9} (j+1)j$

   d. $\sum_{i=1}^{10} i(i-1)$ and $\sum_{k=1}^{10} \left(k^2-k\right)$

In the following exercises, use the rules for sums of powers of integers to compute the sums.

2. $\sum_{i=5}^{10} i$

3. $\sum_{i=5}^{10} i^2$

Suppose that $\sum_{i=1}^{100} a_i = 15$ and $\sum_{i=1}^{100} b_i = -12$. In the following exercises, compute the sums.

4. $\sum_{i=1}^{100} (a_i + b_i)$

5. $\sum_{i=1}^{100} (a_i - b_i)$

6. $\sum_{i=1}^{100} (3a_i - 4b_i)$

7. $\sum_{i=1}^{100} (5a_i + 4b_i)$

In the following exercises, use summation properties and formulas to rewrite and evaluate the sums.

8. $\sum_{k=1}^{20} 100\left(k^2 - 5k + 1\right)$

9. $\sum_{j=1}^{50} \left(j^2 - 2j\right)$

10. $\sum_{j=11}^{20} \left(j^2 - 10j\right)$

11. $\sum_{k=1}^{25} \left[(2k)^2 - 100k\right]$

Let L_n denote the left-endpoint sum using n subintervals and let R_n denote the corresponding right-endpoint sum. In the following exercises, compute the indicated left and right sums for the given functions on the indicated interval.

12. L_4 for $f(x) = \frac{1}{x-1}$ on $[2, 3]$

13. R_4 for $g(x) = \cos(\pi x)$ on $[0, 1]$

14. L_6 for $f(x) = \frac{1}{x(x-1)}$ on $[2, 5]$

15. R_6 for $f(x) = \frac{1}{x(x-1)}$ on $[2, 5]$

16. R_4 for $\frac{1}{x^2+1}$ on $[-2, 2]$

17. L_4 for $\frac{1}{x^2+1}$ on $[-2, 2]$

18. R_4 for $x^2 - 2x + 1$ on $[0, 2]$

19. L_8 for $x^2 - 2x + 1$ on $[0, 2]$

20. Compute the left and right Riemann sums—L_4 and R_4, respectively—for $f(x) = (2 - |x|)$ on $[-2, 2]$. Compute their average value and compare it with the area under the graph of f.

21. Compute the left and right Riemann sums—L_6 and R_6, respectively—for $f(x) = (3 - |3 - x|)$ on $[0, 6]$. Compute their average value and compare it with the area under the graph of f.

22. Compute the left and right Riemann sums—L_4 and R_4, respectively—for $f(x) = \sqrt{4 - x^2}$ on $[-2, 2]$ and compare their values.

23. Compute the left and right Riemann sums—L_6 and R_6, respectively—for $f(x) = \sqrt{9 - (x-3)^2}$ on $[0, 6]$ and compare their values.

Express the following endpoint sums in sigma notation but do not evaluate them.

24. L_{30} for $f(x) = x^2$ on $[1, 2]$

25. L_{10} for $f(x) = \sqrt{4 - x^2}$ on $[-2, 2]$

26. R_{20} for $f(x) = \sin x$ on $[0, \pi]$

27. R_{100} for $\ln x$ on $[1, e]$

In the following exercises, graph the function then use a calculator or a computer program to evaluate the following left and right endpoint sums. Is the area under the curve between the left and right endpoint sums?

28. **[T]** L_{100} and R_{100} for $y = x^2 - 3x + 1$ on the interval $[-1, 1]$

29. **[T]** L_{100} and R_{100} for $y = x^2$ on the interval $[0, 1]$

30. **[T]** L_{50} and R_{50} for $y = \frac{x+1}{x^2-1}$ on the interval $[2, 4]$

31. **[T]** L_{100} and R_{100} for $y = x^3$ on the interval $[-1, 1]$

32. **[T]** L_{50} and R_{50} for $y = \tan(x)$ on the interval $\left[0, \frac{\pi}{4}\right]$

33. **[T]** L_{100} and R_{100} for $y = e^{2x}$ on the interval $[-1, 1]$

34. Let t_j denote the time that it took Tejay van Garteren to ride the jth stage of the Tour de France in 2014. If there were a total of 21 stages, interpret $\sum_{j=1}^{21} t_j$.

35. Let r_j denote the total rainfall in Portland on the jth day of the year in 2009. Interpret $\sum_{j=1}^{31} r_j$.

36. Let d_j denote the hours of daylight and δ_j denote the increase in the hours of daylight from day $j - 1$ to day j in Fargo, North Dakota, on the jth day of the year. Interpret $d_1 + \sum_{j=2}^{365} \delta_j$.

37. To help get in shape, Joe gets a new pair of running shoes. If Joe runs 1 mi each day in week 1 and adds $\frac{1}{10}$ mi to his daily routine each week, what is the total mileage on Joe's shoes after 25 weeks?

38. The following table gives approximate values of the average annual atmospheric rate of increase in carbon dioxide (CO_2) each decade since 1960, in parts per million (ppm). Estimate the total increase in atmospheric CO_2 between 1964 and 2013.

Decade	Ppm/y
1964–1973	1.07
1974–1983	1.34
1984–1993	1.40
1994–2003	1.87
2004–2013	2.07

Table 5.2 Average Annual Atmospheric CO_2 Increase, 1964–2013 ***Source*:** **http://www.esrl.noaa.gov/gmd/ccgg/trends/.**

39. The following table gives the approximate increase in sea level in inches over 20 years starting in the given year. Estimate the net change in mean sea level from 1870 to 2010.

Starting Year	20-Year Change
1870	0.3
1890	1.5
1910	0.2
1930	2.8
1950	0.7
1970	1.1
1990	1.5

Table 5.3 Approximate 20-Year Sea Level Increases, 1870–1990 ***Source*:** **http://link.springer.com/article/10.1007%2Fs10712-011-9119-1**

40. The following table gives the approximate increase in dollars in the average price of a gallon of gas per decade since 1950. If the average price of a gallon of gas in 2010 was $2.60, what was the average price of a gallon of gas in 1950?

Starting Year	10-Year Change
1950	0.03
1960	0.05
1970	0.86
1980	−0.03
1990	0.29
2000	1.12

Table 5.4 Approximate 10-Year Gas Price Increases, 1950–2000 ***Source*:** **http://epb.lbl.gov/homepages/Rick_Diamond/docs/lbnl55011-trends.pdf.**

41. The following table gives the percent growth of the U.S. population beginning in July of the year indicated. If the U.S. population was 281,421,906 in July 2000, estimate the U.S. population in July 2010.

Year	% Change/Year
2000	1.12
2001	0.99
2002	0.93
2003	0.86
2004	0.93
2005	0.93
2006	0.97
2007	0.96
2008	0.95
2009	0.88

Table 5.5 Annual Percentage Growth of U.S. Population, 2000–2009 ***Source*:** **http://www.census.gov/popest/data.**

(*Hint:* To obtain the population in July 2001, multiply the population in July 2000 by 1.0112 to get 284,573,831.)

In the following exercises, estimate the areas under the curves by computing the left Riemann sums, L_8.

42.

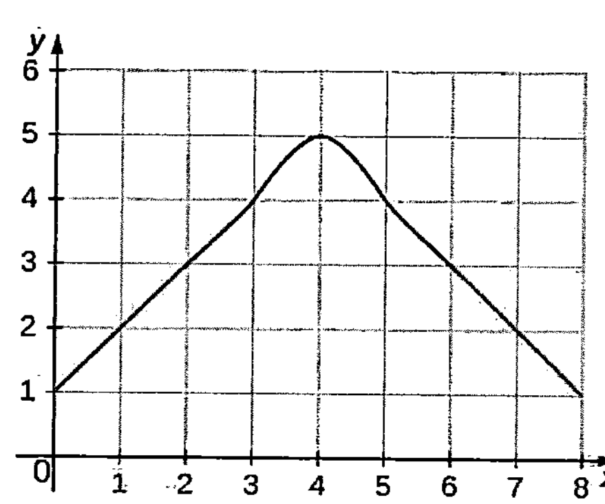

43.

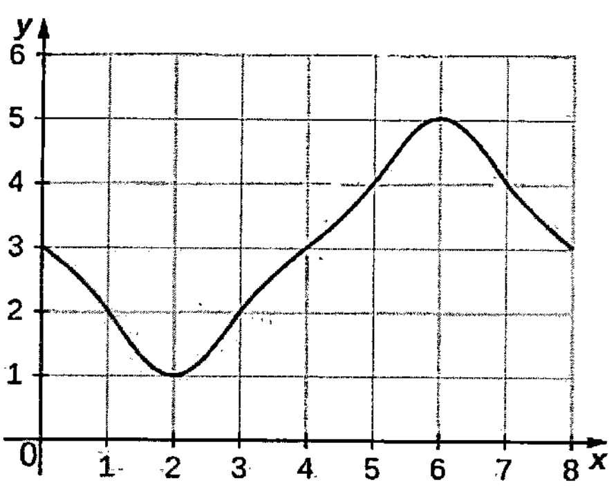

44.

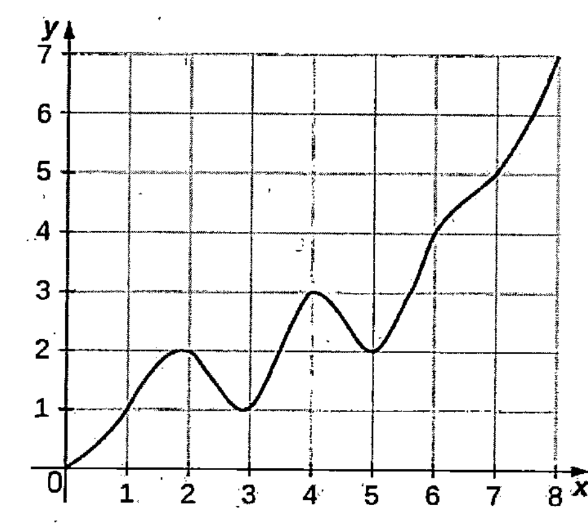

45.

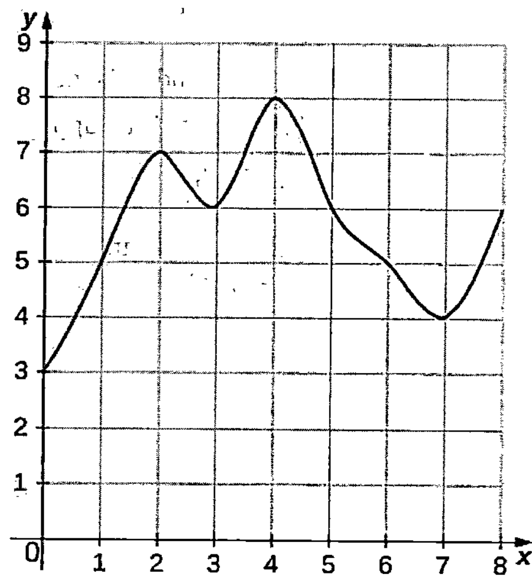

46. **[T]** Use a computer algebra system to compute the Riemann sum, L_N, for $N = 10, 30, 50$ for $f(x) = \sqrt{1 - x^2}$ on $[-1, 1]$.

47. **[T]** Use a computer algebra system to compute the Riemann sum, L_N, for $N = 10, 30, 50$ for $f(x) = \frac{1}{\sqrt{1 + x^2}}$ on $[-1, 1]$.

48. **[T]** Use a computer algebra system to compute the Riemann sum, L_N, for $N = 10, 30, 50$ for $f(x) = \sin^2 x$ on $[0, 2\pi]$. Compare these estimates with π.

In the following exercises, use a calculator or a computer program to evaluate the endpoint sums R_N and L_N for $N = 1,10,100$. How do these estimates compare with the exact answers, which you can find via geometry?

49. **[T]** $y = \cos(\pi x)$ on the interval $[0, 1]$

50. **[T]** $y = 3x + 2$ on the interval $[3, 5]$

In the following exercises, use a calculator or a computer program to evaluate the endpoint sums R_N and L_N for $N = 1,10,100$.

51. **[T]** $y = x^4 - 5x^2 + 4$ on the interval $[-2, 2]$, which has an exact area of $\frac{32}{15}$

52. **[T]** $y = \ln x$ on the interval $[1, 2]$, which has an exact area of $2\ln(2) - 1$

53. Explain why, if $f(a) \geq 0$ and f is increasing on $[a, b]$, that the left endpoint estimate is a lower bound for the area below the graph of f on $[a, b]$.

54. Explain why, if $f(b) \geq 0$ and f is decreasing on $[a, b]$, that the left endpoint estimate is an upper bound for the area below the graph of f on $[a, b]$.

55. Show that, in general, $R_N - L_N = (b - a) \times \frac{f(b) - f(a)}{N}$.

56. Explain why, if f is increasing on $[a, b]$, the error between either L_N or R_N and the area A below the graph of f is at most $(b - a)\frac{f(b) - f(a)}{N}$.

57. For each of the three graphs:

a. Obtain a lower bound $L(A)$ for the area enclosed by the curve by adding the areas of the squares *enclosed completely* by the curve.

b. Obtain an upper bound $U(A)$ for the area by adding to $L(A)$ the areas $B(A)$ of the squares *enclosed partially* by the curve.

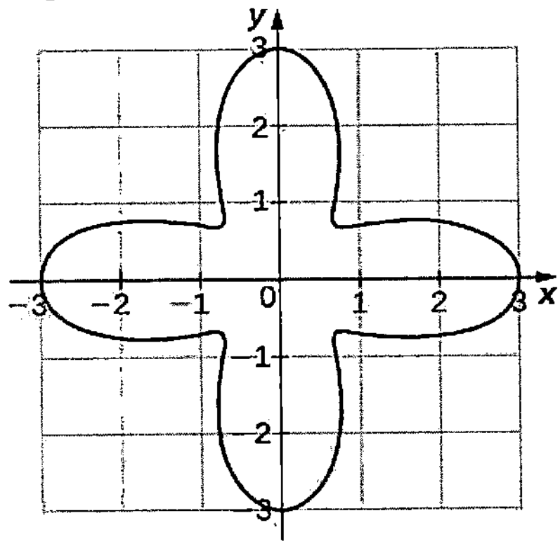

Graph 1

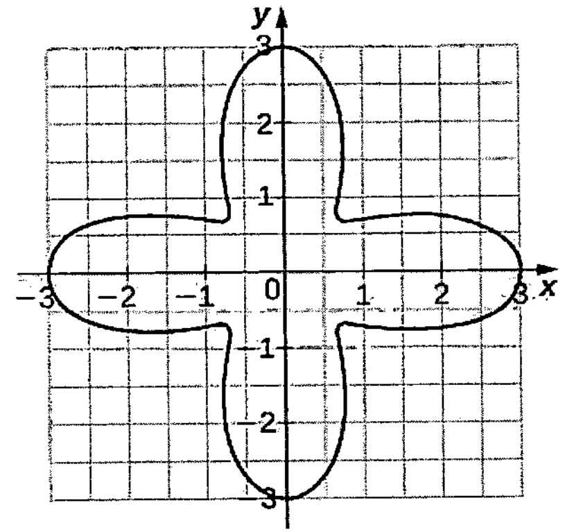

Graph 2

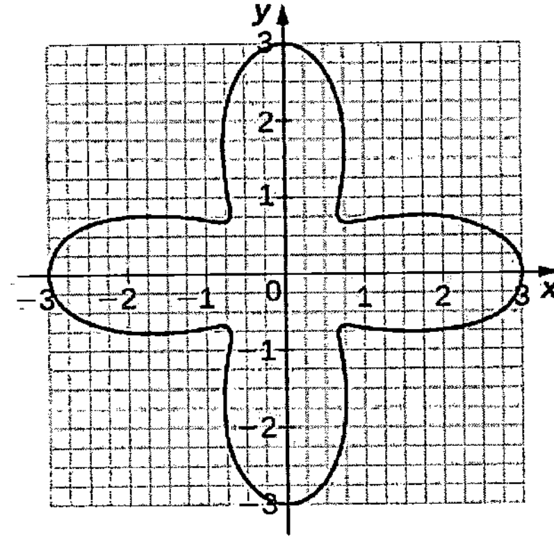

Graph 3

58. In the previous exercise, explain why $L(A)$ gets no smaller while $U(A)$ gets no larger as the squares are subdivided into four boxes of equal area.

59. A unit circle is made up of n wedges equivalent to the inner wedge in the figure. The base of the inner triangle is 1 unit and its height is $\sin\left(\frac{\pi}{n}\right)$. The base of the outer triangle is $B = \cos\left(\frac{\pi}{n}\right) + \sin\left(\frac{\pi}{n}\right)\tan\left(\frac{\pi}{n}\right)$ and the height is $H = B\sin\left(\frac{2\pi}{n}\right)$. Use this information to argue that the area of a unit circle is equal to π.

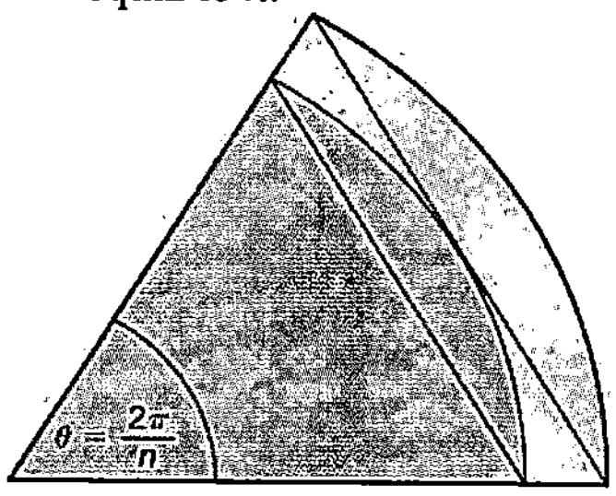

5.2 | The Definite Integral

Learning Objectives

5.2.1 State the definition of the definite integral.
5.2.2 Explain the terms integrand, limits of integration, and variable of integration.
5.2.3 Explain when a function is integrable.
5.2.4 Describe the relationship between the definite integral and net area.
5.2.5 Use geometry and the properties of definite integrals to evaluate them.
5.2.6 Calculate the average value of a function.

In the preceding section we defined the area under a curve in terms of Riemann sums:

$$A = \lim_{n \to \infty} \sum_{i=1}^{n} f(x_i^*)\Delta x.$$

However, this definition came with restrictions. We required $f(x)$ to be continuous and nonnegative. Unfortunately, real-world problems don't always meet these restrictions. In this section, we look at how to apply the concept of the area under the curve to a broader set of functions through the use of the definite integral.

Definition and Notation

The definite integral generalizes the concept of the area under a curve. We lift the requirements that $f(x)$ be continuous and nonnegative, and define the definite integral as follows.

Definition

If $f(x)$ is a function defined on an interval $[a, b]$, the **definite integral** of *f* from *a* to *b* is given by

$$\int_a^b f(x)dx = \lim_{n \to \infty} \sum_{i=1}^{n} f(x_i^*)\Delta x, \qquad (5.8)$$

provided the limit exists. If this limit exists, the function $f(x)$ is said to be integrable on $[a, b]$, or is an **integrable function**.

The integral symbol in the previous definition should look familiar. We have seen similar notation in the chapter on **Applications of Derivatives**, where we used the indefinite integral symbol (without the *a* and *b* above and below) to represent an antiderivative. Although the notation for indefinite integrals may look similar to the notation for a definite integral, they are not the same. A definite integral is a number. An indefinite integral is a family of functions. Later in this chapter we examine how these concepts are related. However, close attention should always be paid to notation so we know whether we're working with a definite integral or an indefinite integral.

Integral notation goes back to the late seventeenth century and is one of the contributions of Gottfried Wilhelm Leibniz, who is often considered to be the codiscoverer of calculus, along with Isaac Newton. The integration symbol ∫ is an elongated S, suggesting sigma or summation. On a definite integral, above and below the summation symbol are the boundaries of the interval, $[a, b]$. The numbers *a* and *b* are *x*-values and are called the **limits of integration**; specifically, *a* is the lower limit and *b* is the upper limit. To clarify, we are using the word *limit* in two different ways in the context of the definite integral. First, we talk about the limit of a sum as $n \to \infty$. Second, the boundaries of the region are called the *limits of integration*.

We call the function $f(x)$ the **integrand**, and the *dx* indicates that $f(x)$ is a function with respect to *x*, called the **variable of integration**. Note that, like the index in a sum, the variable of integration is a dummy variable, and has no impact on the computation of the integral. We could use any variable we like as the variable of integration:

$$\int_a^b f(x)dx = \int_a^b f(t)dt = \int_a^b f(u)du$$

Previously, we discussed the fact that if $f(x)$ is continuous on $[a, b]$, then the limit $\lim_{n \to \infty} \sum_{i=1}^{n} f(x_i^*)\Delta x$ exists and is unique. This leads to the following theorem, which we state without proof.

Theorem 5.1: Continuous Functions Are Integrable

If $f(x)$ is continuous on $[a, b]$, then f is integrable on $[a, b]$.

Functions that are not continuous on $[a, b]$ may still be integrable, depending on the nature of the discontinuities. For example, functions with a finite number of jump discontinuities on a closed interval are integrable.

It is also worth noting here that we have retained the use of a regular partition in the Riemann sums. This restriction is not strictly necessary. Any partition can be used to form a Riemann sum. However, if a nonregular partition is used to define the definite integral, it is not sufficient to take the limit as the number of subintervals goes to infinity. Instead, we must take the limit as the width of the largest subinterval goes to zero. This introduces a little more complex notation in our limits and makes the calculations more difficult without really gaining much additional insight, so we stick with regular partitions for the Riemann sums.

Example 5.7

Evaluating an Integral Using the Definition

Use the definition of the definite integral to evaluate $\int_0^2 x^2\, dx$. Use a right-endpoint approximation to generate the Riemann sum.

Solution

We first want to set up a Riemann sum. Based on the limits of integration, we have $a = 0$ and $b = 2$. For $i = 0, 1, 2,\ldots, n$, let $P = \{x_i\}$ be a regular partition of $[0, 2]$. Then

$$\Delta x = \frac{b-a}{n} = \frac{2}{n}.$$

Since we are using a right-endpoint approximation to generate Riemann sums, for each i, we need to calculate the function value at the right endpoint of the interval $[x_{i-1}, x_i]$. The right endpoint of the interval is x_i, and since P is a regular partition,

$$x_i = x_0 + i\Delta x = 0 + i\left[\frac{2}{n}\right] = \frac{2i}{n}.$$

Thus, the function value at the right endpoint of the interval is

$$f(x_i) = x_i^2 = \left(\frac{2i}{n}\right)^2 = \frac{4i^2}{n^2}.$$

Then the Riemann sum takes the form

$$\sum_{i=1}^{n} f(x_i)\Delta x = \sum_{i=1}^{n} \left(\frac{4i^2}{n^2}\right)\frac{2}{n} = \sum_{i=1}^{n} \frac{8i^2}{n^3} = \frac{8}{n^3}\sum_{i=1}^{n} i^2.$$

Using the summation formula for $\sum_{i=1}^{n} i^2$, we have

$$\begin{aligned}\sum_{i=1}^{n} f(x_i)\Delta x &= \frac{8}{n^3}\sum_{i=1}^{n} i^2 \\ &= \frac{8}{n^3}\left[\frac{n(n+1)(2n+1)}{6}\right] \\ &= \frac{8}{n^3}\left[\frac{2n^3+3n^2+n}{6}\right] \\ &= \frac{16n^3+24n^2+n}{6n^3} \\ &= \frac{8}{3}+\frac{4}{n}+\frac{1}{6n^2}.\end{aligned}$$

Now, to calculate the definite integral, we need to take the limit as $n \to \infty$. We get

$$\begin{aligned}\int_0^2 x^2\,dx &= \lim_{n\to\infty}\sum_{i=1}^{n} f(x_i)\Delta x \\ &= \lim_{n\to\infty}\left(\frac{8}{3}+\frac{4}{n}+\frac{1}{6n^2}\right) \\ &= \lim_{n\to\infty}\left(\frac{8}{3}\right)+\lim_{n\to\infty}\left(\frac{4}{n}\right)+\lim_{n\to\infty}\left(\frac{1}{6n^2}\right) \\ &= \frac{8}{3}+0+0=\frac{8}{3}.\end{aligned}$$

5.7 Use the definition of the definite integral to evaluate $\int_0^3 (2x-1)dx$. Use a right-endpoint approximation to generate the Riemann sum.

Evaluating Definite Integrals

Evaluating definite integrals this way can be quite tedious because of the complexity of the calculations. Later in this chapter we develop techniques for evaluating definite integrals *without* taking limits of Riemann sums. However, for now, we can rely on the fact that definite integrals represent the area under the curve, and we can evaluate definite integrals by using geometric formulas to calculate that area. We do this to confirm that definite integrals do, indeed, represent areas, so we can then discuss what to do in the case of a curve of a function dropping below the x-axis.

Example 5.8

Using Geometric Formulas to Calculate Definite Integrals

Use the formula for the area of a circle to evaluate $\int_3^6 \sqrt{9-(x-3)^2}\,dx$.

Solution

The function describes a semicircle with radius 3. To find

$$\int_3^6 \sqrt{9-(x-3)^2}dx,$$

we want to find the area under the curve over the interval $[3, 6]$. The formula for the area of a circle is $A = \pi r^2$. The area of a semicircle is just one-half the area of a circle, or $A = \left(\frac{1}{2}\right)\pi r^2$. The shaded area in **Figure 5.16** covers one-half of the semicircle, or $A = \left(\frac{1}{4}\right)\pi r^2$. Thus,

$$\begin{aligned}\int_3^6 \sqrt{9-(x-3)^2} &= \frac{1}{4}\pi(3)^2 \\ &= \frac{9}{4}\pi \\ &\approx 7.069.\end{aligned}$$

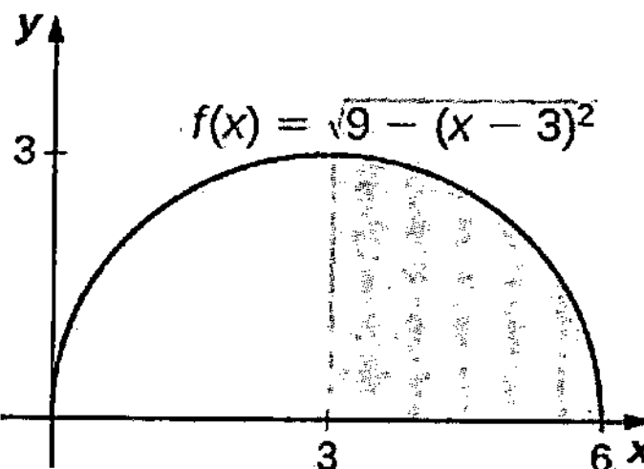

Figure 5.16 The value of the integral of the function $f(x)$ over the interval $[3, 6]$ is the area of the shaded region.

5.8 Use the formula for the area of a trapezoid to evaluate $\int_2^4 (2x+3)dx$.

Area and the Definite Integral

When we defined the definite integral, we lifted the requirement that $f(x)$ be nonnegative. But how do we interpret "the area under the curve" when $f(x)$ is negative?

Net Signed Area

Let us return to the Riemann sum. Consider, for example, the function $f(x) = 2 - 2x^2$ (shown in **Figure 5.17**) on the interval $[0, 2]$. Use $n = 8$ and choose $\{x_i^*\}$ as the left endpoint of each interval. Construct a rectangle on each subinterval of height $f(x_i^*)$ and width Δx. When $f(x_i^*)$ is positive, the product $f(x_i^*)\Delta x$ represents the area of the rectangle, as before. When $f(x_i^*)$ is negative, however, the product $f(x_i^*)\Delta x$ represents the *negative* of the area of the rectangle. The Riemann sum then becomes

$$\sum_{i=1}^{8} f(x_i^*)\Delta x = (\text{Area of rectangles above the } x\text{-axis}) - (\text{Area of rectangles below the } x\text{-axis})$$

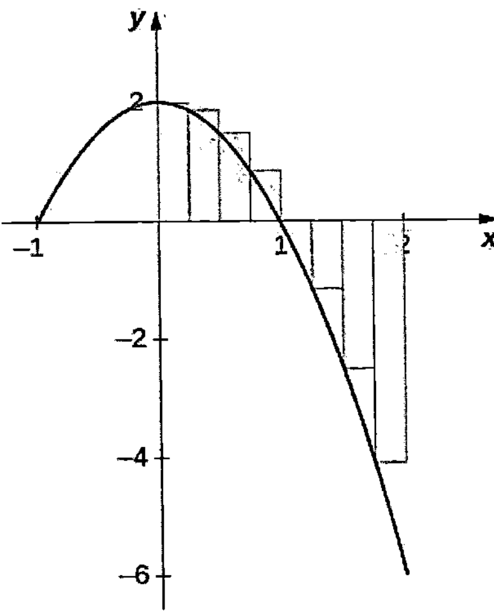

Figure 5.17 For a function that is partly negative, the Riemann sum is the area of the rectangles above the x-axis less the area of the rectangles below the x-axis.

Taking the limit as $n \to \infty$, the Riemann sum approaches the area between the curve above the x-axis and the x-axis, less the area between the curve below the x-axis and the x-axis, as shown in **Figure 5.18**. Then,

$$\begin{aligned} \int_0^2 f(x)dx &= \lim_{n \to \infty} \sum_{i=1}^{n} f(c_i)\Delta x \\ &= A_1 - A_2. \end{aligned}$$

The quantity $A_1 - A_2$ is called the **net signed area**.

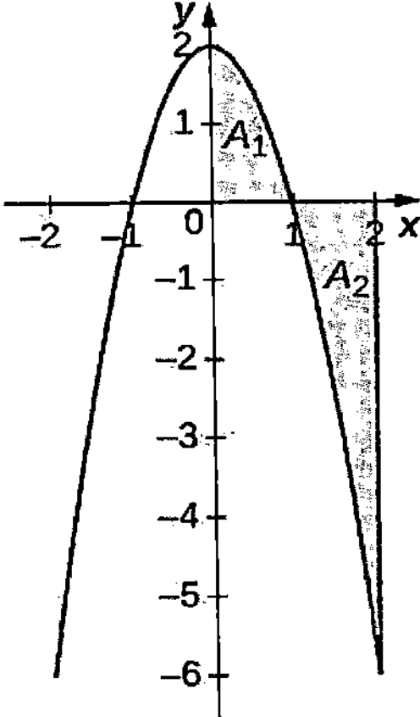

Figure 5.18 In the limit, the definite integral equals area A_1 less area A_2, or the net signed area.

Notice that net signed area can be positive, negative, or zero. If the area above the x-axis is larger, the net signed area is positive. If the area below the x-axis is larger, the net signed area is negative. If the areas above and below the x-axis are equal, the net signed area is zero.

Example 5.9

Finding the Net Signed Area

Find the net signed area between the curve of the function $f(x) = 2x$ and the x-axis over the interval $[-3, 3]$.

Solution

The function produces a straight line that forms two triangles: one from $x = -3$ to $x = 0$ and the other from $x = 0$ to $x = 3$ (**Figure 5.19**). Using the geometric formula for the area of a triangle, $A = \frac{1}{2}bh$, the area of triangle A_1, above the axis, is

$$A_1 = \frac{1}{2}3(6) = 9,$$

where 3 is the base and $2(3) = 6$ is the height. The area of triangle A_2, below the axis, is

$$A_2 = \frac{1}{2}(3)(6) = 9,$$

where 3 is the base and 6 is the height. Thus, the net area is

$$\int_{-3}^{3} 2x dx = A_1 - A_2 = 9 - 9 = 0.$$

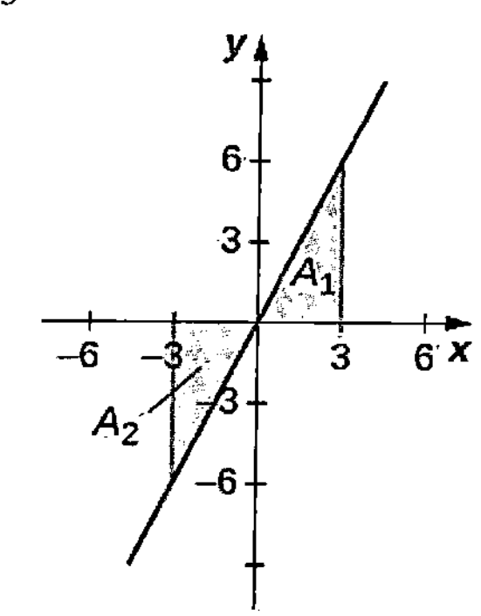

Figure 5.19 The area above the curve and below the x-axis equals the area below the curve and above the x-axis.

Analysis

If A_1 is the area above the x-axis and A_2 is the area below the x-axis, then the net area is $A_1 - A_2$. Since the areas of the two triangles are equal, the net area is zero.

 **5.9** Find the net signed area of $f(x) = x - 2$ over the interval $[0, 6]$, illustrated in the following image.

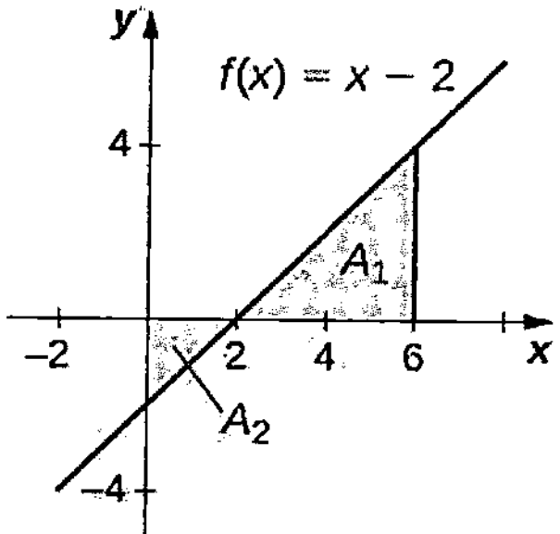

Total Area

One application of the definite integral is finding displacement when given a velocity function. If $v(t)$ represents the velocity of an object as a function of time, then the area under the curve tells us how far the object is from its original position. This is a very important application of the definite integral, and we examine it in more detail later in the chapter. For now, we're just going to look at some basics to get a feel for how this works by studying constant velocities.

When velocity is a constant, the area under the curve is just velocity times time. This idea is already very familiar. If a car travels away from its starting position in a straight line at a speed of 75 mph for 2 hours, then it is 150 mi away from its original position (**Figure 5.20**). Using integral notation, we have

$$\int_0^2 75dt = 150.$$

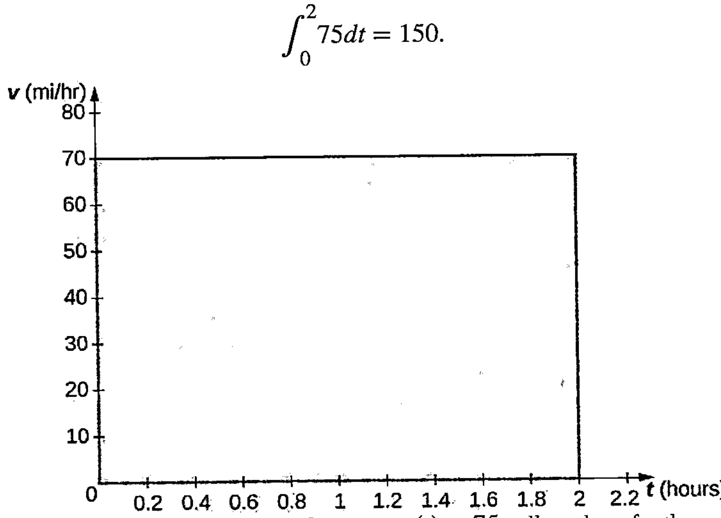

Figure 5.20 The area under the curve $v(t) = 75$ tells us how far the car is from its starting point at a given time.

In the context of displacement, net signed area allows us to take direction into account. If a car travels straight north at a speed of 60 mph for 2 hours, it is 120 mi north of its starting position. If the car then turns around and travels south at a speed of 40 mph for 3 hours, it will be back at it starting position (**Figure 5.21**). Again, using integral notation, we have

$$\begin{aligned} \int_0^2 60dt + \int_2^5 -40dt &= 120 - 120 \\ &= 0. \end{aligned}$$

In this case the displacement is zero.

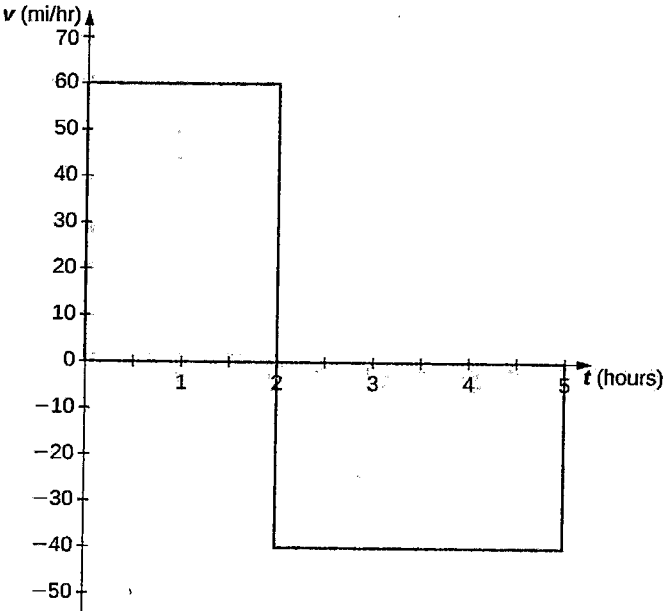

Figure 5.21 The area above the axis and the area below the axis are equal, so the net signed area is zero.

Suppose we want to know how far the car travels overall, regardless of direction. In this case, we want to know the area between the curve and the x-axis, regardless of whether that area is above or below the axis. This is called the **total area.**

Graphically, it is easiest to think of calculating total area by adding the areas above the axis and the areas below the axis (rather than subtracting the areas below the axis, as we did with net signed area). To accomplish this mathematically, we use the absolute value function. Thus, the total distance traveled by the car is

$$\begin{aligned}\int_0^2 |60|dt + \int_2^5 |-40|dt &= \int_0^2 60dt + \int_2^5 40dt \\ &= 120 + 120 \\ &= 240.\end{aligned}$$

Bringing these ideas together formally, we state the following definitions.

Definition

Let $f(x)$ be an integrable function defined on an interval $[a, b]$. Let A_1 represent the area between $f(x)$ and the x-axis that lies *above* the axis and let A_2 represent the area between $f(x)$ and the x-axis that lies *below* the axis. Then, the **net signed area** between $f(x)$ and the x-axis is given by

$$\int_a^b f(x)dx = A_1 - A_2.$$

The **total area** between $f(x)$ and the x-axis is given by

$$\int_a^b |f(x)|dx = A_1 + A_2.$$

Example 5.10

Finding the Total Area

Find the total area between $f(x) = x - 2$ and the x-axis over the interval $[0, 6]$.

Solution

Calculate the x-intercept as $(2, 0)$ (set $y = 0$, solve for x). To find the total area, take the area below the x-axis over the subinterval $[0, 2]$ and add it to the area above the x-axis on the subinterval $[2, 6]$ (**Figure 5.22**).

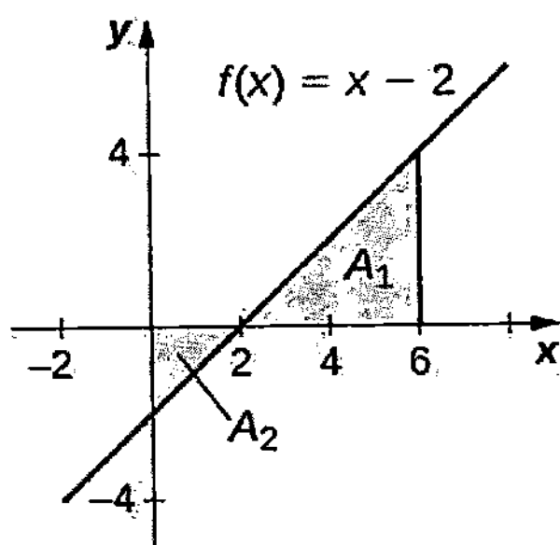

Figure 5.22 The total area between the line and the x-axis over $[0, 6]$ is A_2 plus A_1.

We have

$$\int_0^6 |(x-2)|dx = A_2 + A_1.$$

Then, using the formula for the area of a triangle, we obtain

$$A_2 = \frac{1}{2}bh = \frac{1}{2}\cdot 2\cdot 2 = 2$$
$$A_1 = \frac{1}{2}bh = \frac{1}{2}\cdot 4\cdot 4 = 8.$$

The total area, then, is

$$A_1 + A_2 = 8 + 2 = 10.$$

 **5.10** Find the total area between the function $f(x) = 2x$ and the x-axis over the interval $[-3, 3]$.

Properties of the Definite Integral

The properties of indefinite integrals apply to definite integrals as well. Definite integrals also have properties that relate to the limits of integration. These properties, along with the rules of integration that we examine later in this chapter, help us manipulate expressions to evaluate definite integrals.

Rule: Properties of the Definite Integral

1.
$$\int_a^a f(x)dx = 0 \tag{5.9}$$

If the limits of integration are the same, the integral is just a line and contains no area.

2.

$$\int_b^a f(x)dx = -\int_a^b f(x)dx \tag{5.10}$$

If the limits are reversed, then place a negative sign in front of the integral.

3.

$$\int_a^b [f(x) + g(x)]dx = \int_a^b f(x)dx + \int_a^b g(x)dx \tag{5.11}$$

The integral of a sum is the sum of the integrals.

4.

$$\int_a^b [f(x) - g(x)]dx = \int_a^b f(x)dx - \int_a^b g(x)dx \tag{5.12}$$

The integral of a difference is the difference of the integrals.

5.

$$\int_a^b cf(x)dx = c\int_a^b f(x) \tag{5.13}$$

for constant c. The integral of the product of a constant and a function is equal to the constant multiplied by the integral of the function.

6.

$$\int_a^b f(x)dx = \int_a^c f(x)dx + \int_c^b f(x)dx \tag{5.14}$$

Although this formula normally applies when c is between a and b, the formula holds for all values of a, b, and c, provided $f(x)$ is integrable on the largest interval.

Example 5.11

Using the Properties of the Definite Integral

Use the properties of the definite integral to express the definite integral of $f(x) = -3x^3 + 2x + 2$ over the interval $[-2, 1]$ as the sum of three definite integrals.

Solution

Using integral notation, we have $\int_{-2}^{1} \left(-3x^3 + 2x + 2\right)dx$. We apply properties 3. and 5. to get

$$\begin{aligned}\int_{-2}^{1}\left(-3x^3+2x+2\right)dx &= \int_{-2}^{1}-3x^3\,dx+\int_{-2}^{1}2x\,dx+\int_{-2}^{1}2\,dx \\ &= -3\int_{-2}^{1}x^3\,dx+2\int_{-2}^{1}x\,dx+\int_{-2}^{1}2\,dx.\end{aligned}$$

5.11 Use the properties of the definite integral to express the definite integral of $f(x)=6x^3-4x^2+2x-3$ over the interval $[1, 3]$ as the sum of four definite integrals.

Example 5.12

Using the Properties of the Definite Integral

If it is known that $\int_0^8 f(x)dx = 10$ and $\int_0^5 f(x)dx = 5,$ find the value of $\int_5^8 f(x)dx.$

Solution

By property 6.,

$$\int_a^b f(x)dx = \int_a^c f(x)dx + \int_c^b f(x)dx.$$

Thus,

$$\begin{aligned}\int_0^8 f(x)dx &= \int_0^5 f(x)dx + \int_5^8 f(x)dx \\ 10 &= 5 + \int_5^8 f(x)dx \\ 5 &= \int_5^8 f(x)dx.\end{aligned}$$

5.12 If it is known that $\int_1^5 f(x)dx = -3$ and $\int_2^5 f(x)dx = 4,$ find the value of $\int_1^2 f(x)dx.$

Comparison Properties of Integrals

A picture can sometimes tell us more about a function than the results of computations. Comparing functions by their graphs as well as by their algebraic expressions can often give new insight into the process of integration. Intuitively, we might say that if a function $f(x)$ is above another function $g(x),$ then the area between $f(x)$ and the x-axis is greater than the area between $g(x)$ and the x-axis. This is true depending on the interval over which the comparison is made. The properties of definite integrals are valid whether $a < b, a = b,$ or $a > b.$ The following properties, however, concern only the case $a \le b,$ and are used when we want to compare the sizes of integrals.

Theorem 5.2: Comparison Theorem

i. If $f(x) \geq 0$ for $a \leq x \leq b$, then

$$\int_a^b f(x)dx \geq 0.$$

ii. If $f(x) \geq g(x)$ for $a \leq x \leq b$, then

$$\int_a^b f(x)dx \geq \int_a^b g(x)dx.$$

iii. If m and M are constants such that $m \leq f(x) \leq M$ for $a \leq x \leq b$, then

$$\begin{aligned} m(b-a) &\leq \int_a^b f(x)dx \\ &\leq M(b-a). \end{aligned}$$

Example 5.13

Comparing Two Functions over a Given Interval

Compare $f(x) = \sqrt{1+x^2}$ and $g(x) = \sqrt{1+x}$ over the interval $[0, 1]$.

Solution

Graphing these functions is necessary to understand how they compare over the interval $[0, 1]$. Initially, when graphed on a graphing calculator, $f(x)$ appears to be above $g(x)$ everywhere. However, on the interval $[0, 1]$, the graphs appear to be on top of each other. We need to zoom in to see that, on the interval $[0, 1]$, $g(x)$ is above $f(x)$. The two functions intersect at $x = 0$ and $x = 1$ (**Figure 5.23**).

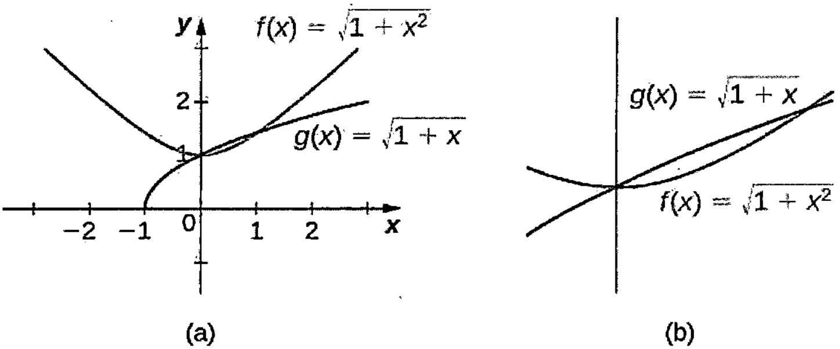

Figure 5.23 (a) The function $f(x)$ appears above the function $g(x)$ except over the interval $[0, 1]$ (b) Viewing the same graph with a greater zoom shows this more clearly.

We can see from the graph that over the interval $[0, 1]$, $g(x) \geq f(x)$. Comparing the integrals over the specified interval $[0, 1]$, we also see that $\int_0^1 g(x)dx \geq \int_0^1 f(x)dx$ (**Figure 5.24**). The thin, red-shaded area shows just how much difference there is between these two integrals over the interval $[0, 1]$.

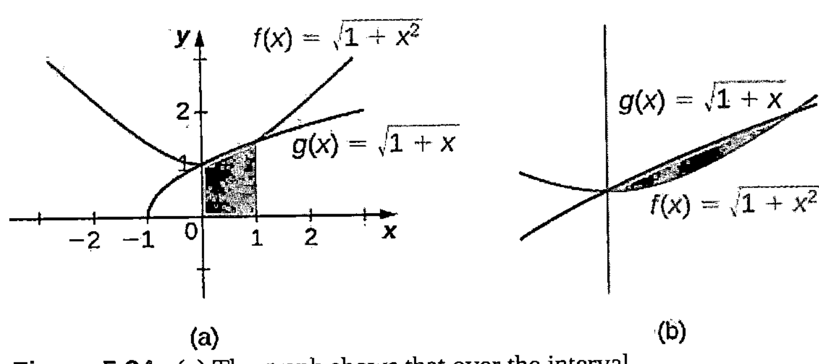

Figure 5.24 (a) The graph shows that over the interval $[0,\ 1],\ g(x) \geq f(x),$ where equality holds only at the endpoints of the interval. (b) Viewing the same graph with a greater zoom shows this more clearly.

Average Value of a Function

We often need to find the average of a set of numbers, such as an average test grade. Suppose you received the following test scores in your algebra class: 89, 90, 56, 78, 100, and 69. Your semester grade is your average of test scores and you want to know what grade to expect. We can find the average by adding all the scores and dividing by the number of scores. In this case, there are six test scores. Thus,

$$\frac{89 + 90 + 56 + 78 + 100 + 69}{6} = \frac{482}{6} \approx 80.33.$$

Therefore, your average test grade is approximately 80.33, which translates to a B− at most schools.

Suppose, however, that we have a function $v(t)$ that gives us the speed of an object at any time t, and we want to find the object's average speed. The function $v(t)$ takes on an infinite number of values, so we can't use the process just described. Fortunately, we can use a definite integral to find the average value of a function such as this.

Let $f(x)$ be continuous over the interval $[a,\ b]$ and let $[a,\ b]$ be divided into n subintervals of width $\Delta x = (b - a)/n.$ Choose a representative x_i^* in each subinterval and calculate $f(x_i^*)$ for $i = 1,\ 2, \ldots,\ n.$ In other words, consider each $f(x_i^*)$ as a sampling of the function over each subinterval. The average value of the function may then be approximated as

$$\frac{f(x_1^*) + f(x_2^*) + \cdots + f(x_n^*)}{n},$$

which is basically the same expression used to calculate the average of discrete values.

But we know $\Delta x = \frac{b - a}{n},$ so $n = \frac{b - a}{\Delta x},$ and we get

$$\frac{f(x_1^*) + f(x_2^*) + \cdots + f(x_n^*)}{n} = \frac{f(x_1^*) + f(x_2^*) + \cdots + f(x_n^*)}{\frac{(b - a)}{\Delta x}}.$$

Following through with the algebra, the numerator is a sum that is represented as $\sum_{i=1}^{n} f(x_i^*),$ and we are dividing by a fraction. To divide by a fraction, invert the denominator and multiply. Thus, an approximate value for the average value of the function is given by

$$\frac{\sum_{i=1}^{n} f(x_i^*)}{\frac{(b-a)}{\Delta x}} = \left(\frac{\Delta x}{b-a}\right)\sum_{i=1}^{n} f(x_i^*)$$
$$= \left(\frac{1}{b-a}\right)\sum_{i=1}^{n} f(x_i^*)\Delta x.$$

This is a Riemann sum. Then, to get the *exact* average value, take the limit as n goes to infinity. Thus, the average value of a function is given by

$$\frac{1}{b-a}\lim_{n\to\infty}\sum_{i=1}^{n} f(x_i)\Delta x = \frac{1}{b-a}\int_a^b f(x)dx.$$

Definition

Let $f(x)$ be continuous over the interval $[a, b]$. Then, the **average value of the function** $f(x)$ (or f_{ave}) on $[a, b]$ is given by

$$f_{\text{ave}} = \frac{1}{b-a}\int_a^b f(x)dx.$$

Example 5.14

Finding the Average Value of a Linear Function

Find the average value of $f(x) = x + 1$ over the interval $[0, 5]$.

Solution

First, graph the function on the stated interval, as shown in **Figure 5.25**.

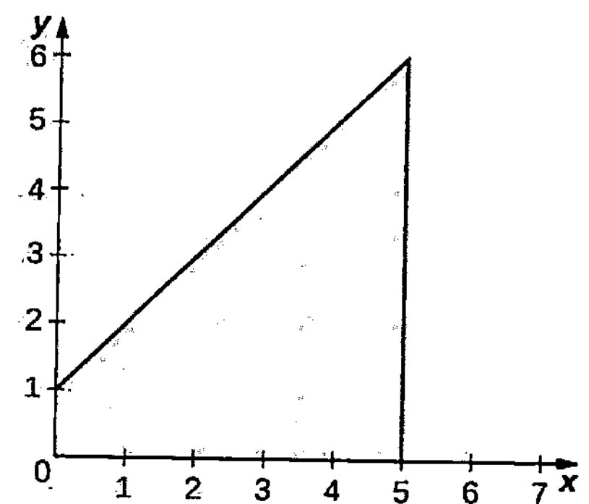

Figure 5.25 The graph shows the area under the function $f(x) = x + 1$ over $[0, 5]$.

The region is a trapezoid lying on its side, so we can use the area formula for a trapezoid $A = \frac{1}{2}h(a + b)$, where h represents height, and a and b represent the two parallel sides. Then,

$$\begin{aligned}\int_0^5 x + 1dx &= \frac{1}{2}h(a + b)\\ &= \frac{1}{2} \cdot 5 \cdot (1 + 6)\\ &= \frac{35}{2}.\end{aligned}$$

Thus the average value of the function is

$$\frac{1}{5 - 0}\int_0^5 x + 1dx = \frac{1}{5} \cdot \frac{35}{2} = \frac{7}{2}.$$

5.13 Find the average value of $f(x) = 6 - 2x$ over the interval $[0, 3]$.

5.2 EXERCISES

In the following exercises, express the limits as integrals.

60. $\lim_{n \to \infty} \sum_{i=1}^{n} (x_i^*)\Delta x$ over $[1, 3]$

61. $\lim_{n \to \infty} \sum_{i=1}^{n} \left(5(x_i^*)^2 - 3(x_i^*)^3\right)\Delta x$ over $[0, 2]$

62. $\lim_{n \to \infty} \sum_{i=1}^{n} \sin^2(2\pi x_i^*)\Delta x$ over $[0, 1]$

63. $\lim_{n \to \infty} \sum_{i=1}^{n} \cos^2(2\pi x_i^*)\Delta x$ over $[0, 1]$

In the following exercises, given L_n or R_n as indicated, express their limits as $n \to \infty$ as definite integrals, identifying the correct intervals.

64. $L_n = \frac{1}{n} \sum_{i=1}^{n} \frac{i-1}{n}$

65. $R_n = \frac{1}{n} \sum_{i=1}^{n} \frac{i}{n}$

66. $L_n = \frac{2}{n} \sum_{i=1}^{n} \left(1 + 2\frac{i-1}{n}\right)$

67. $R_n = \frac{3}{n} \sum_{i=1}^{n} \left(3 + 3\frac{i}{n}\right)$

68. $L_n = \frac{2\pi}{n} \sum_{i=1}^{n} 2\pi\frac{i-1}{n}\cos\left(2\pi\frac{i-1}{n}\right)$

69. $R_n = \frac{1}{n} \sum_{i=1}^{n} \left(1 + \frac{i}{n}\right)\log\left(\left(1 + \frac{i}{n}\right)^2\right)$

In the following exercises, evaluate the integrals of the functions graphed using the formulas for areas of triangles and circles, and subtracting the areas below the *x*-axis.

70.

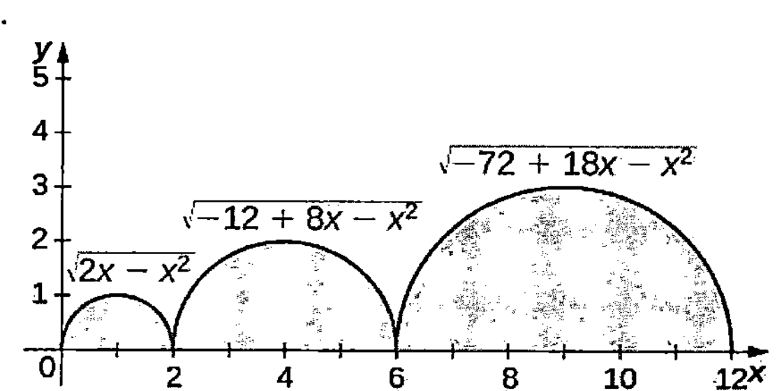

71.

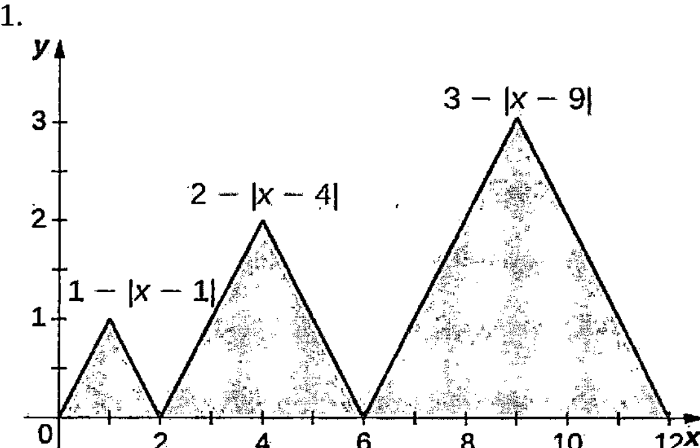

72.

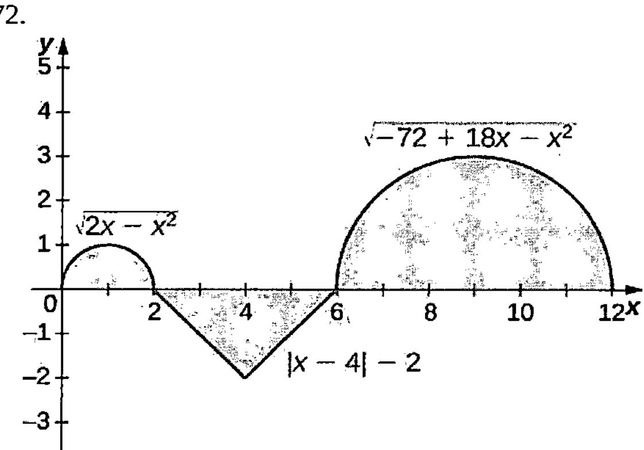

73.

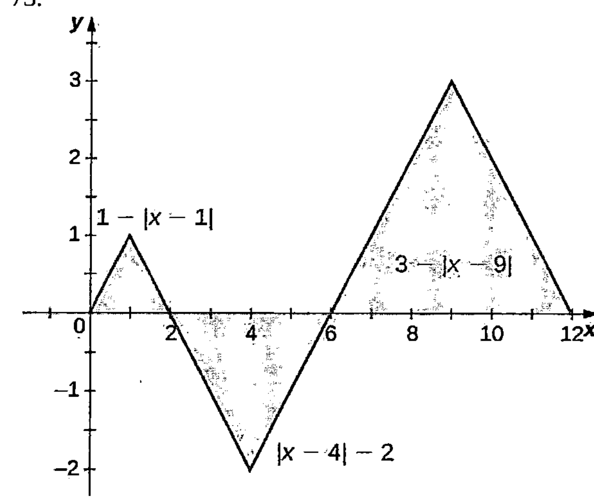

74.

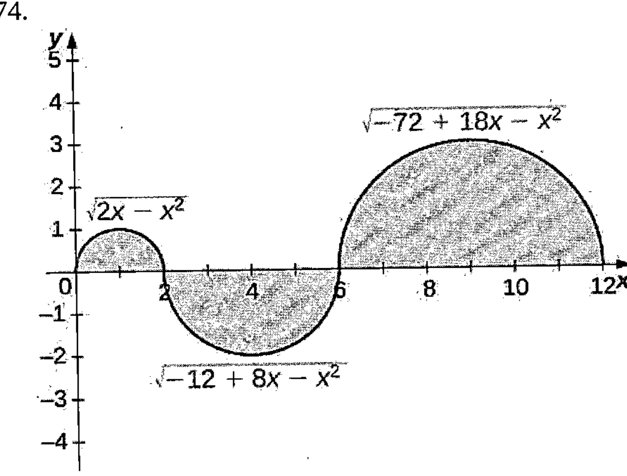

75.

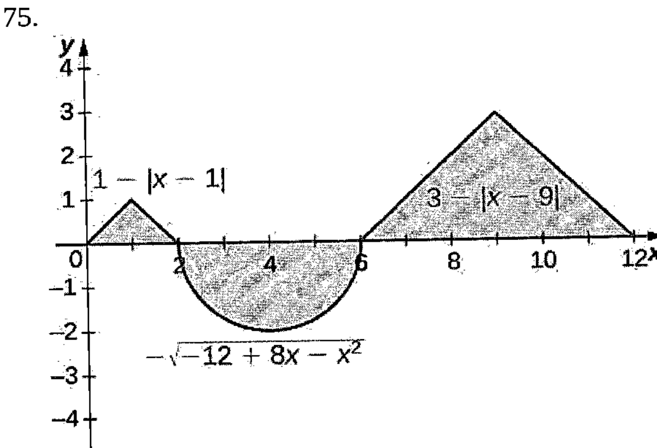

In the following exercises, evaluate the integral using area formulas.

76. $\int_0^3 (3 - x)dx$

77. $\int_2^3 (3 - x)dx$

78. $\int_{-3}^3 (3 - |x|)dx$

79. $\int_0^6 (3 - |x - 3|)dx$

80. $\int_{-2}^2 \sqrt{4 - x^2}dx$

81. $\int_1^5 \sqrt{4 - (x - 3)^2}dx$

82. $\int_0^{12} \sqrt{36 - (x - 6)^2}dx$

83. $\int_{-2}^3 (3 - |x|)dx$

In the following exercises, use averages of values at the left (L) and right (R) endpoints to compute the integrals of the piecewise linear functions with graphs that pass through the given list of points over the indicated intervals.

84. $\{(0, 0), (2, 1), (4, 3), (5, 0), (6, 0), (8, 3)\}$ over $[0, 8]$

85. $\{(0, 2), (1, 0), (3, 5), (5, 5), (6, 2), (8, 0)\}$ over $[0, 8]$

86. $\{(-4, -4), (-2, 0), (0, -2), (3, 3), (4, 3)\}$ over $[-4, 4]$

87. $\{(-4, 0), (-2, 2), (0, 0), (1, 2), (3, 2), (4, 0)\}$ over $[-4, 4]$

Suppose that $\int_0^4 f(x)dx = 5$ and $\int_0^2 f(x)dx = -3$, and $\int_0^4 g(x)dx = -1$ and $\int_0^2 g(x)dx = 2$. In the following exercises, compute the integrals.

88. $\int_0^4 (f(x) + g(x))dx$

89. $\int_2^4 (f(x) + g(x))dx$

90. $\int_0^2 (f(x) - g(x))dx$

91. $\int_2^4 (f(x) - g(x))dx$

92. $\int_0^2 (3f(x) - 4g(x))dx$

93. $\int_2^4 (4f(x) - 3g(x))dx$

In the following exercises, use the identity $\int_{-A}^A f(x)dx = \int_{-A}^0 f(x)dx + \int_0^A f(x)dx$ to compute the integrals.

94. $\int_{-\pi}^{\pi} \frac{\sin t}{1 + t^2}dt$ (*Hint*: $\sin(-t) = -\sin(t)$)

95. $\int_{-\sqrt{\pi}}^{\sqrt{\pi}} \frac{t}{1+\cos t} dt$

96. $\int_1^3 (2-x)dx$ (*Hint:* Look at the graph of *f*.)

97. $\int_2^4 (x-3)^3 dx$ (*Hint:* Look at the graph of *f*.)

In the following exercises, given that $\int_0^1 x dx = \frac{1}{2}$, $\int_0^1 x^2 dx = \frac{1}{3}$, and $\int_0^1 x^3 dx = \frac{1}{4}$, compute the integrals.

98. $\int_0^1 \left(1+x+x^2+x^3\right)dx$

99. $\int_0^1 \left(1-x+x^2-x^3\right)dx$

100. $\int_0^1 (1-x)^2 dx$

101. $\int_0^1 (1-2x)^3 dx$

102. $\int_0^1 \left(6x-\frac{4}{3}x^2\right)dx$

103. $\int_0^1 \left(7-5x^3\right)dx$

In the following exercises, use the **comparison theorem**.

104. Show that $\int_0^3 \left(x^2-6x+9\right)dx \geq 0$.

105. Show that $\int_{-2}^3 (x-3)(x+2)dx \leq 0$.

106. Show that $\int_0^1 \sqrt{1+x^3}dx \leq \int_0^1 \sqrt{1+x^2}dx$.

107. Show that $\int_1^2 \sqrt{1+x}dx \leq \int_1^2 \sqrt{1+x^2}dx$.

108. Show that $\int_0^{\pi/2} \sin t dt \geq \frac{\pi}{4}$. (*Hint*: $\sin t \geq \frac{2t}{\pi}$ over $\left[0, \frac{\pi}{2}\right]$)

109. Show that $\int_{-\pi/4}^{\pi/4} \cos t dt \geq \pi\sqrt{2}/4$.

In the following exercises, find the average value f_{ave} of f between a and b, and find a point c, where $f(c) = f_{\text{ave}}$.

110. $f(x) = x^2$, $a = -1$, $b = 1$

111. $f(x) = x^5$, $a = -1$, $b = 1$

112. $f(x) = \sqrt{4-x^2}$, $a = 0$, $b = 2$

113. $f(x) = (3-|x|)$, $a = -3$, $b = 3$

114. $f(x) = \sin x$, $a = 0$, $b = 2\pi$

115. $f(x) = \cos x$, $a = 0$, $b = 2\pi$

In the following exercises, approximate the average value using Riemann sums L_{100} and R_{100}. How does your answer compare with the exact given answer?

116. **[T]** $y = \ln(x)$ over the interval $[1, 4]$; the exact solution is $\frac{\ln(256)}{3} - 1$.

117. **[T]** $y = e^{x/2}$ over the interval $[0, 1]$; the exact solution is $2(\sqrt{e}-1)$.

118. **[T]** $y = \tan x$ over the interval $\left[0, \frac{\pi}{4}\right]$; the exact solution is $\frac{2\ln(2)}{\pi}$.

119. **[T]** $y = \frac{x+1}{\sqrt{4-x^2}}$ over the interval $[-1, 1]$; the exact solution is $\frac{\pi}{6}$.

In the following exercises, compute the average value using the left Riemann sums L_N for $N = 1, 10, 100$. How does the accuracy compare with the given exact value?

120. **[T]** $y = x^2 - 4$ over the interval $[0, 2]$; the exact solution is $-\frac{8}{3}$.

121. **[T]** $y = xe^{x^2}$ over the interval $[0, 2]$; the exact solution is $\frac{1}{4}\left(e^4 - 1\right)$.

122. **[T]** $y = \left(\frac{1}{2}\right)^x$ over the interval $[0, 4]$; the exact solution is $\frac{15}{64\ln(2)}$.

123. **[T]** $y = x\sin\left(x^2\right)$ over the interval $[-\pi, 0]$; the exact solution is $\frac{\cos\left(\pi^2\right) - 1}{2\pi}$.

124. Suppose that $A = \int_0^{2\pi} \sin^2 t dt$ and $B = \int_0^{2\pi} \cos^2 t dt$. Show that $A + B = 2\pi$ and $A = B$.

125. Suppose that $A = \int_{-\pi/4}^{\pi/4} \sec^2 t dt = \pi$ and $B = \int_{-\pi/4}^{\pi/4} \tan^2 t dt$. Show that $A - B = \frac{\pi}{2}$.

126. Show that the average value of $\sin^2 t$ over $[0, 2\pi]$ is equal to 1/2 Without further calculation, determine whether the average value of $\sin^2 t$ over $[0, \pi]$ is also equal to 1/2.

127. Show that the average value of $\cos^2 t$ over $[0, 2\pi]$ is equal to 1/2. Without further calculation, determine whether the average value of $\cos^2(t)$ over $[0, \pi]$ is also equal to 1/2.

128. Explain why the graphs of a quadratic function (parabola) $p(x)$ and a linear function $\ell(x)$ can intersect in at most two points. Suppose that $p(a) = \ell(a)$ and $p(b) = \ell(b)$, and that $\int_a^b p(t)dt > \int_a^b \ell(t)dt$. Explain why $\int_c^d p(t) > \int_c^d \ell(t)dt$ whenever $a \le c < d \le b$.

129. Suppose that parabola $p(x) = ax^2 + bx + c$ opens downward $(a < 0)$ and has a vertex of $y = \frac{-b}{2a} > 0$. For which interval $[A, B]$ is $\int_A^B \left(ax^2 + bx + c\right)dx$ as large as possible?

130. Suppose $[a, b]$ can be subdivided into subintervals $a = a_0 < a_1 < a_2 < \cdots < a_N = b$ such that either $f \ge 0$ over $[a_{i-1}, a_i]$ or $f \le 0$ over $[a_{i-1}, a_i]$. Set $A_i = \int_{a_{i-1}}^{a_i} f(t)dt$.

a. Explain why $\int_a^b f(t)dt = A_1 + A_2 + \cdots + A_N$.

b. Then, explain why $\left|\int_a^b f(t)dt\right| \le \int_a^b |f(t)|dt$.

131. Suppose f and g are continuous functions such that $\int_c^d f(t)dt \le \int_c^d g(t)dt$ for every subinterval $[c, d]$ of $[a, b]$. Explain why $f(x) \le g(x)$ for all values of x.

132. Suppose the average value of f over $[a, b]$ is 1 and the average value of f over $[b, c]$ is 1 where $a < c < b$. Show that the average value of f over $[a, c]$ is also 1.

133. Suppose that $[a, b]$ can be partitioned. taking $a = a_0 < a_1 < \cdots < a_N = b$ such that the average value of f over each subinterval $[a_{i-1}, a_i] = 1$ is equal to 1 for each $i = 1, \ldots, N$. Explain why the average value of f over $[a, b]$ is also equal to 1.

134. Suppose that for each i such that $1 \le i \le N$ one has $\int_{i-1}^{i} f(t)dt = i$. Show that $\int_0^N f(t)dt = \frac{N(N+1)}{2}$.

135. Suppose that for each i such that $1 \le i \le N$ one has $\int_{i-1}^{i} f(t)dt = i^2$. Show that $\int_0^N f(t)dt = \frac{N(N+1)(2N+1)}{6}$.

136. **[T]** Compute the left and right Riemann sums L_{10} and R_{10} and their average $\frac{L_{10} + R_{10}}{2}$ for $f(t) = t^2$ over $[0, 1]$. Given that $\int_0^1 t^2 dt = 0.\overline{33}$, to how many decimal places is $\frac{L_{10} + R_{10}}{2}$ accurate?

137. **[T]** Compute the left and right Riemann sums, L_{10} and R_{10}, and their average $\frac{L_{10} + R_{10}}{2}$ for $f(t) = \left(4 - t^2\right)$ over [1, 2]. Given that $\int_1^2 \left(4 - t^2\right)dt = 1.\overline{66}$, to how many decimal places is $\frac{L_{10} + R_{10}}{2}$ accurate?

138. If $\int_1^5 \sqrt{1 + t^4}dt = 41.7133...$, what is $\int_1^5 \sqrt{1 + u^4}du$?

139. Estimate $\int_0^1 tdt$ using the left and right endpoint sums, each with a single rectangle. How does the average of these left and right endpoint sums compare with the actual value $\int_0^1 tdt$?

140. Estimate $\int_0^1 tdt$ by comparison with the area of a single rectangle with height equal to the value of t at the midpoint $t = \frac{1}{2}$. How does this midpoint estimate compare with the actual value $\int_0^1 tdt$?

141. From the graph of $\sin(2\pi x)$ shown:

a. Explain why $\int_0^1 \sin(2\pi t)dt = 0$.

b. Explain why, in general, $\int_a^{a+1} \sin(2\pi t)dt = 0$ for any value of a.

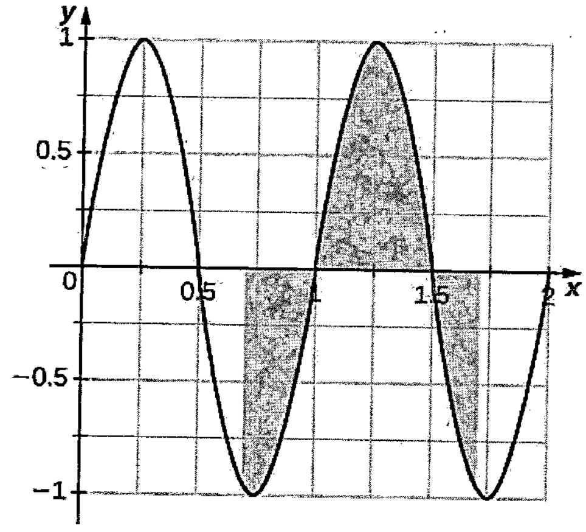

142. If f is 1-periodic $(f(t + 1) = f(t))$, odd, and integrable over [0, 1], is it always true that $\int_0^1 f(t)dt = 0$?

143. If f is 1-periodic and $\int_0^1 f(t)dt = A$, is it necessarily true that $\int_a^{1+a} f(t)dt = A$ for all A?

5.3 | The Fundamental Theorem of Calculus

Learning Objectives

- **5.3.1** Describe the meaning of the Mean Value Theorem for Integrals.
- **5.3.2** State the meaning of the Fundamental Theorem of Calculus, Part 1.
- **5.3.3** Use the Fundamental Theorem of Calculus, Part 1, to evaluate derivatives of integrals.
- **5.3.4** State the meaning of the Fundamental Theorem of Calculus, Part 2.
- **5.3.5** Use the Fundamental Theorem of Calculus, Part 2, to evaluate definite integrals.
- **5.3.6** Explain the relationship between differentiation and integration.

In the previous two sections, we looked at the definite integral and its relationship to the area under the curve of a function. Unfortunately, so far, the only tools we have available to calculate the value of a definite integral are geometric area formulas and limits of Riemann sums, and both approaches are extremely cumbersome. In this section we look at some more powerful and useful techniques for evaluating definite integrals.

These new techniques rely on the relationship between differentiation and integration. This relationship was discovered and explored by both Sir Isaac Newton and Gottfried Wilhelm Leibniz (among others) during the late 1600s and early 1700s, and it is codified in what we now call the **Fundamental Theorem of Calculus**, which has two parts that we examine in this section. Its very name indicates how central this theorem is to the entire development of calculus.

Isaac Newton's contributions to mathematics and physics changed the way we look at the world. The relationships he discovered, codified as Newton's laws and the law of universal gravitation, are still taught as foundational material in physics today, and his calculus has spawned entire fields of mathematics. To learn more, read a **brief biography (http://www.openstaxcollege.org/l/20_newtonbio)** of Newton with multimedia clips.

Before we get to this crucial theorem, however, let's examine another important theorem, the Mean Value Theorem for Integrals, which is needed to prove the Fundamental Theorem of Calculus.

The Mean Value Theorem for Integrals

The **Mean Value Theorem for Integrals** states that a continuous function on a closed interval takes on its average value at the same point in that interval. The theorem guarantees that if $f(x)$ is continuous, a point c exists in an interval $[a, b]$ such that the value of the function at c is equal to the average value of $f(x)$ over $[a, b]$. We state this theorem mathematically with the help of the formula for the average value of a function that we presented at the end of the preceding section.

Theorem 5.3: The Mean Value Theorem for Integrals

If $f(x)$ is continuous over an interval $[a, b]$, then there is at least one point $c \in [a, b]$ such that

$$f(c) = \frac{1}{b-a}\int_a^b f(x)dx. \tag{5.15}$$

This formula can also be stated as

$$\int_a^b f(x)dx = f(c)(b-a).$$

Proof

Since $f(x)$ is continuous on $[a, b]$, by the extreme value theorem (see **Maxima and Minima**), it assumes minimum and maximum values—m and M, respectively—on $[a, b]$. Then, for all x in $[a, b]$, we have $m \le f(x) \le M$. Therefore, by the comparison theorem (see **The Definite Integral**), we have

$$m(b-a) \le \int_a^b f(x)dx \le M(b-a).$$

Dividing by $b-a$ gives us

$$m \leq \frac{1}{b-a}\int_a^b f(x)dx \leq M.$$

Since $\frac{1}{b-a}\int_a^b f(x)dx$ is a number between m and M, and since $f(x)$ is continuous and assumes the values m and M over $[a, b]$, by the Intermediate Value Theorem (see **Continuity**), there is a number c over $[a, b]$ such that

$$f(c) = \frac{1}{b-a}\int_a^b f(x)dx,$$

and the proof is complete.

□

Example 5.15

Finding the Average Value of a Function

Find the average value of the function $f(x) = 8 - 2x$ over the interval $[0, 4]$ and find c such that $f(c)$ equals the average value of the function over $[0, 4]$.

Solution

The formula states the mean value of $f(x)$ is given by

$$\frac{1}{4-0}\int_0^4 (8-2x)dx.$$

We can see in **Figure 5.26** that the function represents a straight line and forms a right triangle bounded by the x- and y-axes. The area of the triangle is $A = \frac{1}{2}(\text{base})(\text{height})$. We have

$$A = \frac{1}{2}(4)(8) = 16.$$

The average value is found by multiplying the area by $1/(4-0)$. Thus, the average value of the function is

$$\frac{1}{4}(16) = 4.$$

Set the average value equal to $f(c)$ and solve for c.

$$\begin{aligned} 8 - 2c &= 4 \\ c &= 2 \end{aligned}$$

At $c = 2$, $f(2) = 4$.

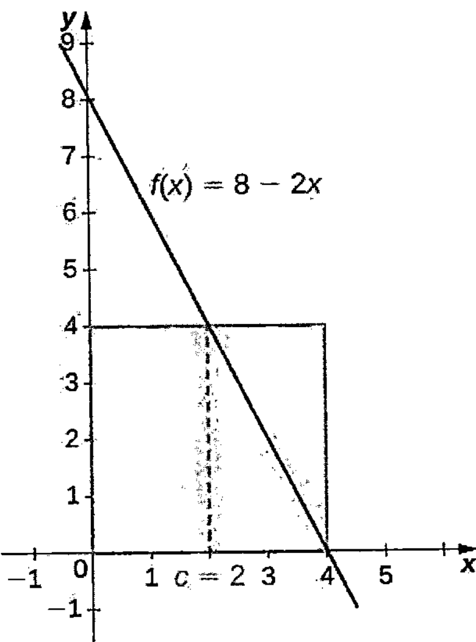

Figure 5.26 By the Mean Value Theorem, the continuous function $f(x)$ takes on its average value at c at least once over a closed interval.

5.14 Find the average value of the function $f(x) = \frac{x}{2}$ over the interval $[0, 6]$ and find c such that $f(c)$ equals the average value of the function over $[0, 6]$.

Example 5.16

Finding the Point Where a Function Takes on Its Average Value

Given $\int_0^3 x^2\,dx = 9,$ find c such that $f(c)$ equals the average value of $f(x) = x^2$ over $[0, 3]$.

Solution

We are looking for the value of c such that

$$f(c) = \frac{1}{3-0}\int_0^3 x^2\,dx = \frac{1}{3}(9) = 3.$$

Replacing $f(c)$ with c^2, we have

$$\begin{aligned} c^2 &= 3 \\ c &= \pm\sqrt{3}. \end{aligned}$$

Since $-\sqrt{3}$ is outside the interval, take only the positive value. Thus, $c = \sqrt{3}$ (**Figure 5.27**).

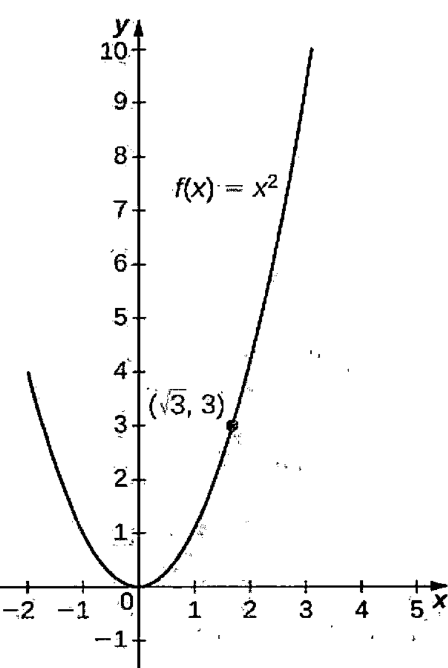

Figure 5.27 Over the interval $[0, 3],$ the function $f(x) = x^2$ takes on its average value at $c = \sqrt{3}.$

5.15 Given $\int_0^3 \left(2x^2 - 1\right)dx = 15,$ find c such that $f(c)$ equals the average value of $f(x) = 2x^2 - 1$ over $[0, 3].$

Fundamental Theorem of Calculus Part 1: Integrals and Antiderivatives

As mentioned earlier, the Fundamental Theorem of Calculus is an extremely powerful theorem that establishes the relationship between differentiation and integration, and gives us a way to evaluate definite integrals without using Riemann sums or calculating areas. The theorem is comprised of two parts, the first of which, the **Fundamental Theorem of Calculus, Part 1**, is stated here. Part 1 establishes the relationship between differentiation and integration.

Theorem 5.4: Fundamental Theorem of Calculus, Part 1

If $f(x)$ is continuous over an interval $[a, b],$ and the function $F(x)$ is defined by

$$F(x) = \int_a^x f(t)dt, \tag{5.16}$$

then $F'(x) = f(x)$ over $[a, b].$

Before we delve into the proof, a couple of subtleties are worth mentioning here. First, a comment on the notation. Note that we have defined a function, $F(x),$ as the definite integral of another function, $f(t),$ from the point a to the point x. At first glance, this is confusing, because we have said several times that a definite integral is a number, and here it looks like it's a function. The key here is to notice that for any particular value of x, the definite integral is a number. So the function $F(x)$ returns a number (the value of the definite integral) for each value of x.

Second, it is worth commenting on some of the key implications of this theorem. There is a reason it is called the *Fundamental* Theorem of Calculus. Not only does it establish a relationship between integration and differentiation, but also it guarantees that any integrable function has an antiderivative. Specifically, it guarantees that any continuous function has an antiderivative.

Proof

Applying the definition of the derivative, we have

$$\begin{aligned} F'(x) &= \lim_{h \to 0} \frac{F(x+h) - F(x)}{h} \\ &= \lim_{h \to 0} \frac{1}{h}\left[\int_a^{x+h} f(t)dt - \int_a^x f(t)dt\right] \\ &= \lim_{h \to 0} \frac{1}{h}\left[\int_a^{x+h} f(t)dt + \int_x^a f(t)dt\right] \\ &= \lim_{h \to 0} \frac{1}{h}\int_x^{x+h} f(t)dt. \end{aligned}$$

Looking carefully at this last expression, we see $\frac{1}{h}\int_x^{x+h} f(t)dt$ is just the average value of the function $f(x)$ over the interval $[x, x+h]$. Therefore, by **The Mean Value Theorem for Integrals**, there is some number c in $[x, x+h]$ such that

$$\frac{1}{h}\int_x^{x+h} f(x)dx = f(c).$$

In addition, since c is between x and $x + h$, c approaches x as h approaches zero. Also, since $f(x)$ is continuous, we have $\lim_{h \to 0} f(c) = \lim_{c \to x} f(c) = f(x)$. Putting all these pieces together, we have

$$\begin{aligned} F'(x) &= \lim_{h \to 0} \frac{1}{h}\int_x^{x+h} f(x)dx \\ &= \lim_{h \to 0} f(c) \\ &= f(x), \end{aligned}$$

and the proof is complete.

□

Example 5.17

Finding a Derivative with the Fundamental Theorem of Calculus

Use the **Fundamental Theorem of Calculus, Part 1** to find the derivative of

$$g(x) = \int_1^x \frac{1}{t^3 + 1}dt.$$

Solution

According to the Fundamental Theorem of Calculus, the derivative is given by

$$g'(x) = \frac{1}{x^3 + 1}.$$

5.16 Use the Fundamental Theorem of Calculus, Part 1 to find the derivative of $g(r) = \int_0^r \sqrt{x^2 + 4}dx.$

Example 5.18

Using the Fundamental Theorem and the Chain Rule to Calculate Derivatives

Let $F(x) = \int_1^{\sqrt{x}} \sin t dt.$ Find $F'(x).$

Solution

Letting $u(x) = \sqrt{x},$ we have $F(x) = \int_1^{u(x)} \sin t dt.$ Thus, by the Fundamental Theorem of Calculus and the chain rule,

$$\begin{aligned} F'(x) &= \sin(u(x))\frac{du}{dx} \\ &= \sin(u(x)) \cdot \left(\frac{1}{2}x^{-1/2}\right) \\ &= \frac{\sin\sqrt{x}}{2\sqrt{x}}. \end{aligned}$$

5.17 Let $F(x) = \int_1^{x^3} \cos t dt.$ Find $F'(x).$

Example 5.19

Using the Fundamental Theorem of Calculus with Two Variable Limits of Integration

Let $F(x) = \int_x^{2x} t^3 dt.$ Find $F'(x).$

Solution

We have $F(x) = \int_x^{2x} t^3 dt.$ Both limits of integration are variable, so we need to split this into two integrals. We get

$$\begin{aligned} F(x) &= \int_x^{2x} t^3 dt \\ &= \int_x^0 t^3 dt + \int_0^{2x} t^3 dt \\ &= -\int_0^x t^3 dt + \int_0^{2x} t^3 dt. \end{aligned}$$

Differentiating the first term, we obtain

$$\frac{d}{dx}\left[-\int_0^x t^3\,dt\right] = -x^3.$$

Differentiating the second term, we first let $u(x) = 2x$. Then,

$$\begin{aligned}\frac{d}{dx}\left[\int_0^{2x} t^3\,dt\right] &= \frac{d}{dx}\left[\int_0^{u(x)} t^3\,dt\right]\\ &= (u(x))^3\frac{du}{dx}\\ &= (2x)^3\cdot 2\\ &= 16x^3.\end{aligned}$$

Thus,

$$\begin{aligned}F'(x) &= \frac{d}{dx}\left[-\int_0^x t^3\,dt\right] + \frac{d}{dx}\left[\int_0^{2x} t^3\,dt\right]\\ &= -x^3 + 16x^3\\ &= 15x^3.\end{aligned}$$

5.18 Let $F(x) = \int_x^{x^2} \cos t\,dt$. Find $F'(x)$.

Fundamental Theorem of Calculus, Part 2: The Evaluation Theorem

The Fundamental Theorem of Calculus, Part 2, is perhaps the most important theorem in calculus. After tireless efforts by mathematicians for approximately 500 years, new techniques emerged that provided scientists with the necessary tools to explain many phenomena. Using calculus, astronomers could finally determine distances in space and map planetary orbits. Everyday financial problems such as calculating marginal costs or predicting total profit could now be handled with simplicity and accuracy. Engineers could calculate the bending strength of materials or the three-dimensional motion of objects. Our view of the world was forever changed with calculus.

After finding approximate areas by adding the areas of n rectangles, the application of this theorem is straightforward by comparison. It almost seems too simple that the area of an entire curved region can be calculated by just evaluating an antiderivative at the first and last endpoints of an interval.

Theorem 5.5: The Fundamental Theorem of Calculus, Part 2

If f is continuous over the interval $[a, b]$ and $F(x)$ is any antiderivative of $f(x)$, then

$$\int_a^b f(x)dx = F(b) - F(a). \tag{5.17}$$

We often see the notation $F(x)|_a^b$ to denote the expression $F(b) - F(a)$. We use this vertical bar and associated limits a and b to indicate that we should evaluate the function $F(x)$ at the upper limit (in this case, b), and subtract the value of the function $F(x)$ evaluated at the lower limit (in this case, a).

The **Fundamental Theorem of Calculus, Part 2** (also known as the **evaluation theorem**) states that if we can find an antiderivative for the integrand, then we can evaluate the definite integral by evaluating the antiderivative at the endpoints of the interval and subtracting.

Proof

Let $P = \{x_i\}, i = 0, 1,\ldots, n$ be a regular partition of $[a, b]$. Then, we can write

$$\begin{aligned} F(b) - F(a) &= F(x_n) - F(x_0) \\ &= [F(x_n) - F(x_{n-1})] + [F(x_{n-1}) - F(x_{n-2})] + \ldots + [F(x_1) - F(x_0)] \\ &= \sum_{i=1}^{n} [F(x_i) - F(x_{i-1})]. \end{aligned}$$

Now, we know F is an antiderivative of f over $[a, b]$, so by the Mean Value Theorem (see **The Mean Value Theorem**) for $i = 0, 1,\ldots, n$ we can find c_i in $[x_{i-1}, x_i]$ such that

$$F(x_i) - F(x_{i-1}) = F'(c_i)(x_i - x_{i-1}) = f(c_i)\Delta x.$$

Then, substituting into the previous equation, we have

$$F(b) - F(a) = \sum_{i=1}^{n} f(c_i)\Delta x.$$

Taking the limit of both sides as $n \to \infty$, we obtain

$$\begin{aligned} F(b) - F(a) &= \lim_{n \to \infty} \sum_{i=1}^{n} f(c_i)\Delta x \\ &= \int_a^b f(x)dx. \end{aligned}$$

□

Example 5.20

Evaluating an Integral with the Fundamental Theorem of Calculus

Use **The Fundamental Theorem of Calculus, Part 2** to evaluate

$$\int_{-2}^{2} (t^2 - 4)dt.$$

Solution

Recall the power rule for **Antiderivatives**:

$$\text{If } y = x^n, \int x^n\, dx = \frac{x^{n+1}}{n+1} + C.$$

Use this rule to find the antiderivative of the function and then apply the theorem. We have

$$\begin{aligned}\int_{-2}^{2}\left(t^2-4\right)dt &= \frac{t^3}{3}-4t\Big|_{-2}^{2}\\ &= \left[\frac{(2)^3}{3}-4(2)\right]-\left[\frac{(-2)^3}{3}-4(-2)\right]\\ &= \left(\frac{8}{3}-8\right)-\left(-\frac{8}{3}+8\right)\\ &= \frac{8}{3}-8+\frac{8}{3}-8\\ &= \frac{16}{3}-16\\ &= -\frac{32}{3}.\end{aligned}$$

Analysis

Notice that we did not include the "+ C" term when we wrote the antiderivative. The reason is that, according to the Fundamental Theorem of Calculus, Part 2, *any* antiderivative works. So, for convenience, we chose the antiderivative with $C = 0$. If we had chosen another antiderivative, the constant term would have canceled out. This always happens when evaluating a definite integral.

The region of the area we just calculated is depicted in **Figure 5.28**. Note that the region between the curve and the x-axis is all below the x-axis. Area is always positive, but a definite integral can still produce a negative number (a net signed area). For example, if this were a profit function, a negative number indicates the company is operating at a loss over the given interval.

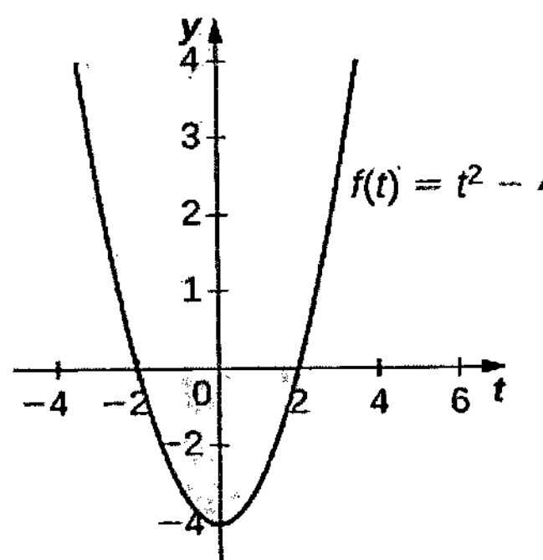

Figure 5.28 The evaluation of a definite integral can produce a negative value, even though area is always positive.

Example 5.21

Evaluating a Definite Integral Using the Fundamental Theorem of Calculus, Part 2

Evaluate the following integral using the Fundamental Theorem of Calculus, Part 2:

$$\int_{1}^{9}\frac{x-1}{\sqrt{x}}dx.$$

Solution

First, eliminate the radical by rewriting the integral using rational exponents. Then, separate the numerator terms by writing each one over the denominator:

$$\int_1^9 \frac{x-1}{x^{1/2}}dx = \int_1^9 \left(\frac{x}{x^{1/2}} - \frac{1}{x^{1/2}}\right)dx.$$

Use the properties of exponents to simplify:

$$\int_1^9 \left(\frac{x}{x^{1/2}} - \frac{1}{x^{1/2}}\right)dx = \int_1^9 \left(x^{1/2} - x^{-1/2}\right)dx.$$

Now, integrate using the power rule:

$$\begin{aligned}\int_1^9 \left(x^{1/2} - x^{-1/2}\right)dx &= \left(\frac{x^{3/2}}{\frac{3}{2}} - \frac{x^{1/2}}{\frac{1}{2}}\right)\Bigg|_1^9 \\ &= \left[\frac{(9)^{3/2}}{\frac{3}{2}} - \frac{(9)^{1/2}}{\frac{1}{2}}\right] - \left[\frac{(1)^{3/2}}{\frac{3}{2}} - \frac{(1)^{1/2}}{\frac{1}{2}}\right] \\ &= \left[\frac{2}{3}(27) - 2(3)\right] - \left[\frac{2}{3}(1) - 2(1)\right] \\ &= 18 - 6 - \frac{2}{3} + 2 \\ &= \frac{40}{3}.\end{aligned}$$

See **Figure 5.29**.

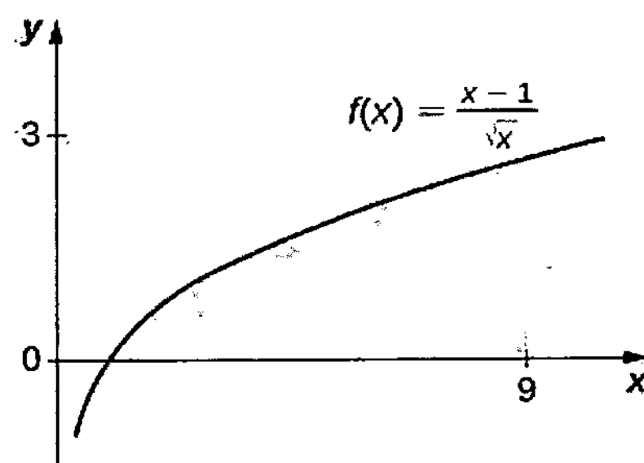

Figure 5.29 The area under the curve from $x = 1$ to $x = 9$ can be calculated by evaluating a definite integral.

5.19 Use **The Fundamental Theorem of Calculus, Part 2** to evaluate $\int_1^2 x^{-4}\,dx.$

Example 5.22

A Roller-Skating Race

James and Kathy are racing on roller skates. They race along a long, straight track, and whoever has gone the farthest after 5 sec wins a prize. If James can skate at a velocity of $f(t) = 5 + 2t$ ft/sec and Kathy can skate at a velocity of $g(t) = 10 + \cos\left(\frac{\pi}{2}t\right)$ ft/sec, who is going to win the race?

Solution

We need to integrate both functions over the interval $[0, 5]$ and see which value is bigger. For James, we want to calculate

$$\int_0^5 (5 + 2t)dt.$$

Using the power rule, we have

$$\begin{aligned}\int_0^5 (5 + 2t)dt &= \left(5t + t^2\right)\Big|_0^5 \\ &= (25 + 25) = 50.\end{aligned}$$

Thus, James has skated 50 ft after 5 sec. Turning now to Kathy, we want to calculate

$$\int_0^5 10 + \cos\left(\frac{\pi}{2}t\right)dt.$$

We know $\sin t$ is an antiderivative of $\cos t,$ so it is reasonable to expect that an antiderivative of $\cos\left(\frac{\pi}{2}t\right)$ would involve $\sin\left(\frac{\pi}{2}t\right)$. However, when we differentiate $\sin\left(\frac{\pi}{2}t\right),$ we get $\frac{\pi}{2}\cos\left(\frac{\pi}{2}t\right)$ as a result of the chain rule, so we have to account for this additional coefficient when we integrate. We obtain

$$\begin{aligned}\int_0^5 10 + \cos\left(\frac{\pi}{2}t\right)dt &= \left(10t + \frac{2}{\pi}\sin\left(\frac{\pi}{2}t\right)\right)\Big|_0^5 \\ &= \left(50 + \frac{2}{\pi}\right) - \left(0 - \frac{2}{\pi}\sin 0\right) \\ &\approx 50.6.\end{aligned}$$

Kathy has skated approximately 50.6 ft after 5 sec. Kathy wins, but not by much!

5.20 Suppose James and Kathy have a rematch, but this time the official stops the contest after only 3 sec. Does this change the outcome?

Student PROJECT

A Parachutist in Free Fall

Figure 5.30 Skydivers can adjust the velocity of their dive by changing the position of their body during the free fall. (credit: Jeremy T. Lock)

Julie is an avid skydiver. She has more than 300 jumps under her belt and has mastered the art of making adjustments to her body position in the air to control how fast she falls. If she arches her back and points her belly toward the ground, she reaches a terminal velocity of approximately 120 mph (176 ft/sec). If, instead, she orients her body with her head straight down, she falls faster, reaching a terminal velocity of 150 mph (220 ft/sec).

Since Julie will be moving (falling) in a downward direction, we assume the downward direction is positive to simplify our calculations. Julie executes her jumps from an altitude of 12,500 ft. After she exits the aircraft, she immediately starts falling at a velocity given by $v(t) = 32t.$ She continues to accelerate according to this velocity function until she reaches terminal velocity. After she reaches terminal velocity, her speed remains constant until she pulls her ripcord and slows down to land.

On her first jump of the day, Julie orients herself in the slower "belly down" position (terminal velocity is 176 ft/sec). Using this information, answer the following questions.

1. How long after she exits the aircraft does Julie reach terminal velocity?
2. Based on your answer to question 1, set up an expression involving one or more integrals that represents the distance Julie falls after 30 sec.
3. If Julie pulls her ripcord at an altitude of 3000 ft, how long does she spend in a free fall?
4. Julie pulls her ripcord at 3000 ft. It takes 5 sec for her parachute to open completely and for her to slow down, during which time she falls another 400 ft. After her canopy is fully open, her speed is reduced to 16 ft/sec. Find the total time Julie spends in the air, from the time she leaves the airplane until the time her feet touch the ground.

On Julie's second jump of the day, she decides she wants to fall a little faster and orients herself in the "head down" position. Her terminal velocity in this position is 220 ft/sec. Answer these questions based on this velocity:

5. How long does it take Julie to reach terminal velocity in this case?

6. Before pulling her ripcord, Julie reorients her body in the "belly down" position so she is not moving quite as fast when her parachute opens. If she begins this maneuver at an altitude of 4000 ft, how long does she spend in a free fall before beginning the reorientation?

Some jumpers wear " wingsuits" (see **Figure 5.31**). These suits have fabric panels between the arms and legs and allow the wearer to glide around in a free fall, much like a flying squirrel. (Indeed, the suits are sometimes called "flying squirrel suits.") When wearing these suits, terminal velocity can be reduced to about 30 mph (44 ft/sec), allowing the wearers a much longer time in the air. Wingsuit flyers still use parachutes to land; although the vertical velocities are within the margin of safety, horizontal velocities can exceed 70 mph, much too fast to land safely.

Figure 5.31 The fabric panels on the arms and legs of a wingsuit work to reduce the vertical velocity of a skydiver's fall. (credit: Richard Schneider)

Answer the following question based on the velocity in a wingsuit.

7. If Julie dons a wingsuit before her third jump of the day, and she pulls her ripcord at an altitude of 3000 ft, how long does she get to spend gliding around in the air?

5.3 EXERCISES

144. Consider two athletes running at variable speeds $v_1(t)$ and $v_2(t)$. The runners start and finish a race at exactly the same time. Explain why the two runners must be going the same speed at some point.

145. Two mountain climbers start their climb at base camp, taking two different routes, one steeper than the other, and arrive at the peak at exactly the same time. Is it necessarily true that, at some point, both climbers increased in altitude at the same rate?

146. To get on a certain toll road a driver has to take a card that lists the mile entrance point. The card also has a timestamp. When going to pay the toll at the exit, the driver is surprised to receive a speeding ticket along with the toll. Explain how this can happen.

147. Set $F(x) = \int_1^x (1-t)dt$. Find $F'(2)$ and the average value of F' over $[1, 2]$.

In the following exercises, use the Fundamental Theorem of Calculus, Part 1, to find each derivative.

148. $\frac{d}{dx}\int_1^x e^{-t^2}dt$

149. $\frac{d}{dx}\int_1^x e^{\cos t}dt$

150. $\frac{d}{dx}\int_3^x \sqrt{9-y^2}dy$

151. $\frac{d}{dx}\int_4^x \frac{ds}{\sqrt{16-s^2}}$

152. $\frac{d}{dx}\int_x^{2x} tdt$

153. $\frac{d}{dx}\int_0^{\sqrt{x}} tdt$

154. $\frac{d}{dx}\int_0^{\sin x} \sqrt{1-t^2}dt$

155. $\frac{d}{dx}\int_{\cos x}^1 \sqrt{1-t^2}dt$

156. $\frac{d}{dx}\int_1^{\sqrt{x}} \frac{t^2}{1+t^4}dt$

157. $\frac{d}{dx}\int_1^{x^2} \frac{\sqrt{t}}{1+t}dt$

158. $\frac{d}{dx}\int_0^{\ln x} e^t dt$

159. $\frac{d}{dx}\int_1^{e^2} \ln u^2 du$

160. The graph of $y = \int_0^x f(t)dt$, where f is a piecewise constant function, is shown here.

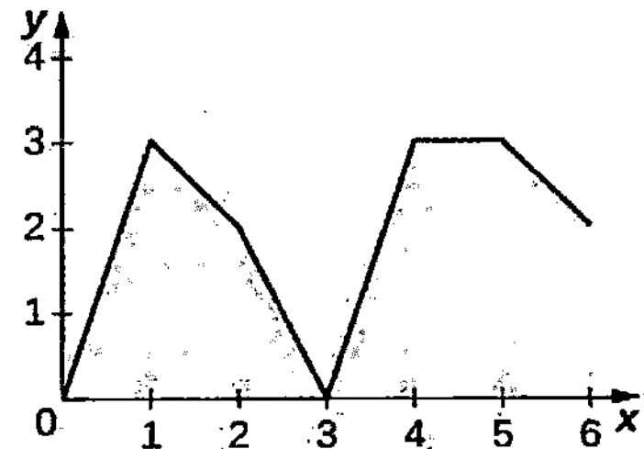

a. Over which intervals is f positive? Over which intervals is it negative? Over which intervals, if any, is it equal to zero?
b. What are the maximum and minimum values of f?
c. What is the average value of f?

161. The graph of $y = \int_0^x f(t)dt$, where f is a piecewise constant function, is shown here.

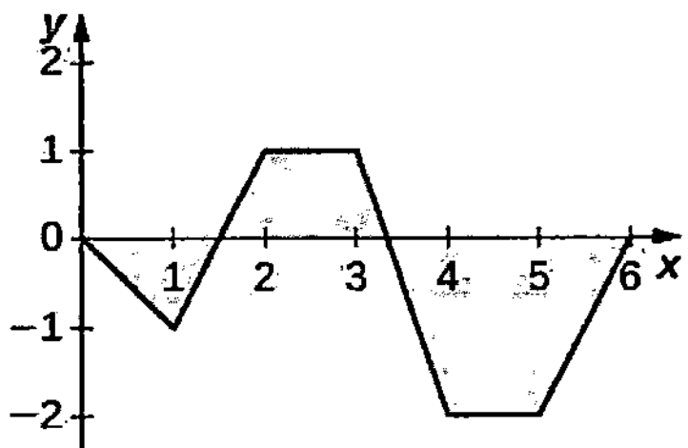

a. Over which intervals is f positive? Over which intervals is it negative? Over which intervals, if any, is it equal to zero?
b. What are the maximum and minimum values of f?
c. What is the average value of f?

162. The graph of $y = \int_0^x \ell(t)dt$, where ℓ is a piecewise linear function, is shown here.

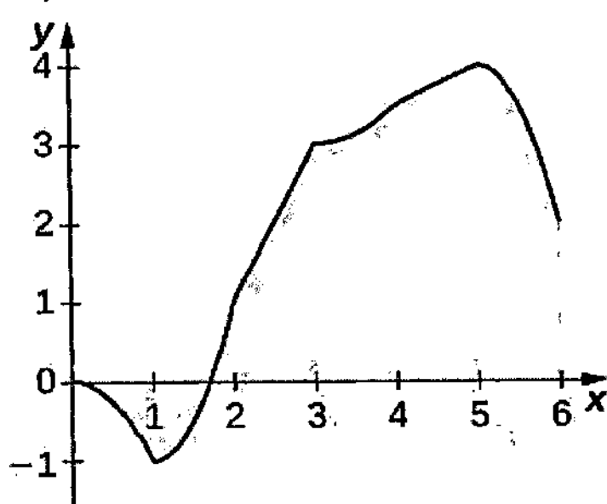

a. Over which intervals is ℓ positive? Over which intervals is it negative? Over which, if any, is it zero?
b. Over which intervals is ℓ increasing? Over which is it decreasing? Over which, if any, is it constant?
c. What is the average value of ℓ?

163. The graph of $y = \int_0^x \ell(t)dt$, where ℓ is a piecewise linear function, is shown here.

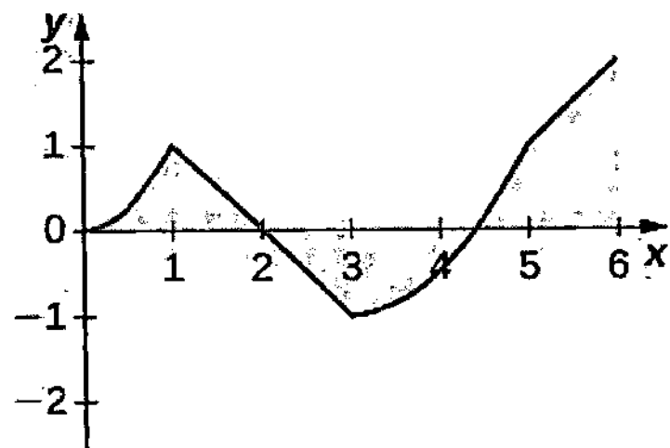

a. Over which intervals is ℓ positive? Over which intervals is it negative? Over which, if any, is it zero?
b. Over which intervals is ℓ increasing? Over which is it decreasing? Over which intervals, if any, is it constant?
c. What is the average value of ℓ?

In the following exercises, use a calculator to estimate the area under the curve by computing T_{10}, the average of the left- and right-endpoint Riemann sums using $N = 10$ rectangles. Then, using the Fundamental Theorem of Calculus, Part 2, determine the exact area.

164. **[T]** $y = x^2$ over $[0, 4]$

165. **[T]** $y = x^3 + 6x^2 + x - 5$ over $[-4, 2]$

166. **[T]** $y = \sqrt{x^3}$ over $[0, 6]$

167. **[T]** $y = \sqrt{x} + x^2$ over $[1, 9]$

168. **[T]** $\int (\cos x - \sin x)dx$ over $[0, \pi]$

169. **[T]** $\int \frac{4}{x^2}dx$ over $[1, 4]$

In the following exercises, evaluate each definite integral using the Fundamental Theorem of Calculus, Part 2.

170. $\int_{-1}^{2} \left(x^2 - 3x\right)dx$

171. $\int_{-2}^{3} \left(x^2 + 3x - 5\right)dx$

172. $\int_{-2}^{3} (t + 2)(t - 3)dt$

173. $\int_{2}^{3} \left(t^2 - 9\right)\left(4 - t^2\right)dt$

174. $\int_{1}^{2} x^9\, dx$

175. $\int_{0}^{1} x^{99}\, dx$

176. $\int_{4}^{8} \left(4t^{5/2} - 3t^{3/2}\right)dt$

177. $\int_{1/4}^{4} \left(x^2 - \frac{1}{x^2}\right)dx$

178. $\int_{1}^{2} \frac{2}{x^3}dx$

179. $\int_{1}^{4} \frac{1}{2\sqrt{x}}dx$

180. $\int_{1}^{4} \frac{2 - \sqrt{t}}{t^2}dt$

181. $\int_{1}^{16} \frac{dt}{t^{1/4}}$

182. $\int_{0}^{2\pi} \cos\theta d\theta$

183. $\int_{0}^{\pi/2} \sin\theta d\theta$

184. $\int_0^{\pi/4} \sec^2 \theta d\theta$

185. $\int_0^{\pi/4} \sec\theta \tan\theta$

186. $\int_{\pi/3}^{\pi/4} \csc\theta \cot\theta d\theta$

187. $\int_{\pi/4}^{\pi/2} \csc^2 \theta d\theta$

188. $\int_1^2 \left(\frac{1}{t^2} - \frac{1}{t^3}\right) dt$

189. $\int_{-2}^{-1} \left(\frac{1}{t^2} - \frac{1}{t^3}\right) dt$

In the following exercises, use the evaluation theorem to express the integral as a function $F(x)$.

190. $\int_a^x t^2 dt$

191. $\int_1^x e^t dt$

192. $\int_0^x \cos t dt$

193. $\int_{-x}^x \sin t dt$

In the following exercises, identify the roots of the integrand to remove absolute values, then evaluate using the Fundamental Theorem of Calculus, Part 2.

194. $\int_{-2}^3 |x| dx$

195. $\int_{-2}^4 \left|t^2 - 2t - 3\right| dt$

196. $\int_0^{\pi} |\cos t| dt$

197. $\int_{-\pi/2}^{\pi/2} |\sin t| dt$

198. Suppose that the number of hours of daylight on a given day in Seattle is modeled by the function $-3.75\cos\left(\frac{\pi t}{6}\right) + 12.25,$ with t given in months and $t = 0$ corresponding to the winter solstice.

a. What is the average number of daylight hours in a year?
b. At which times t_1 and $t_2,$ where $0 \le t_1 < t_2 < 12,$ do the number of daylight hours equal the average number?
c. Write an integral that expresses the total number of daylight hours in Seattle between t_1 and $t_2.$
d. Compute the mean hours of daylight in Seattle between t_1 and $t_2,$ where $0 \le t_1 < t_2 < 12,$ and then between t_2 and $t_1,$ and show that the average of the two is equal to the average day length.

199. Suppose the rate of gasoline consumption in the United States can be modeled by a sinusoidal function of the form $\left(11.21 - \cos\left(\frac{\pi t}{6}\right)\right) \times 10^9$ gal/mo.

a. What is the average monthly consumption, and for which values of t is the rate at time t equal to the average rate?
b. What is the number of gallons of gasoline consumed in the United States in a year?
c. Write an integral that expresses the average monthly U.S. gas consumption during the part of the year between the beginning of April $(t = 3)$ and the end of September $(t = 9)$.

200. Explain why, if f is continuous over $[a, b],$ there is at least one point $c \in [a, b]$ such that $f(c) = \frac{1}{b-a}\int_a^b f(t)dt.$

201. Explain why, if f is continuous over $[a, b]$ and is not equal to a constant, there is at least one point $M \in [a, b]$ such that $f(M) = \frac{1}{b-a}\int_a^b f(t)dt$ and at least one point $m \in [a, b]$ such that $f(m) < \frac{1}{b-a}\int_a^b f(t)dt.$

202. Kepler's first law states that the planets move in elliptical orbits with the Sun at one focus. The closest point of a planetary orbit to the Sun is called the *perihelion* (for Earth, it currently occurs around January 3) and the farthest point is called the *aphelion* (for Earth, it currently occurs around July 4). Kepler's second law states that planets sweep out equal areas of their elliptical orbits in equal times. Thus, the two arcs indicated in the following figure are swept out in equal times. At what time of year is Earth moving fastest in its orbit? When is it moving slowest?

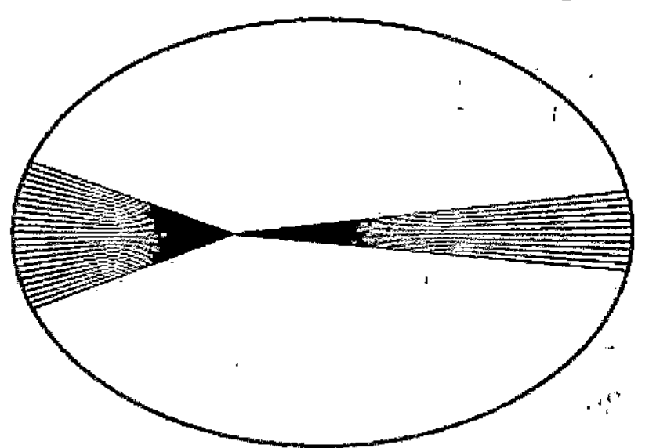

203. A point on an ellipse with major axis length $2a$ and minor axis length $2b$ has the coordinates $(a\cos\theta, b\sin\theta), 0 \le \theta \le 2\pi.$

a. Show that the distance from this point to the focus at $(-c, 0)$ is $d(\theta) = a + c\cos\theta,$ where $c = \sqrt{a^2 - b^2}.$

b. Use these coordinates to show that the average distance $\bar{d}$ from a point on the ellipse to the focus at $(-c, 0),$ with respect to angle θ, is a.

204. As implied earlier, according to Kepler's laws, Earth's orbit is an ellipse with the Sun at one focus. The perihelion for Earth's orbit around the Sun is 147,098,290 km and the aphelion is 152,098,232 km.

a. By placing the major axis along the x-axis, find the average distance from Earth to the Sun.

b. The classic definition of an astronomical unit (AU) is the distance from Earth to the Sun, and its value was computed as the average of the perihelion and aphelion distances. Is this definition justified?

205. The force of gravitational attraction between the Sun and a planet is $F(\theta) = \frac{GmM}{r^2(\theta)},$ where m is the mass of the planet, M is the mass of the Sun, G is a universal constant, and $r(\theta)$ is the distance between the Sun and the planet when the planet is at an angle θ with the major axis of its orbit. Assuming that M, m, and the ellipse parameters a and b (half-lengths of the major and minor axes) are given, set up—but do not evaluate—an integral that expresses in terms of G, m, M, a, b the average gravitational force between the Sun and the planet.

206. The displacement from rest of a mass attached to a spring satisfies the simple harmonic motion equation $x(t) = A\cos(\omega t - \phi),$ where ϕ is a phase constant, ω is the angular frequency, and A is the amplitude. Find the average velocity, the average speed (magnitude of velocity), the average displacement, and the average distance from rest (magnitude of displacement) of the mass.

5.4 | Integration Formulas and the Net Change Theorem

Learning Objectives

5.4.1 Apply the basic integration formulas.
5.4.2 Explain the significance of the net change theorem.
5.4.3 Use the net change theorem to solve applied problems.
5.4.4 Apply the integrals of odd and even functions.

In this section, we use some basic integration formulas studied previously to solve some key applied problems. It is important to note that these formulas are presented in terms of *indefinite* integrals. Although definite and indefinite integrals are closely related, there are some key differences to keep in mind. A definite integral is either a number (when the limits of integration are constants) or a single function (when one or both of the limits of integration are variables). An indefinite integral represents a family of functions, all of which differ by a constant. As you become more familiar with integration, you will get a feel for when to use definite integrals and when to use indefinite integrals. You will naturally select the correct approach for a given problem without thinking too much about it. However, until these concepts are cemented in your mind, think carefully about whether you need a definite integral or an indefinite integral and make sure you are using the proper notation based on your choice.

Basic Integration Formulas

Recall the integration formulas given in the **table in Antiderivatives** and the rule on properties of definite integrals. Let's look at a few examples of how to apply these rules.

Example 5.23

Integrating a Function Using the Power Rule

Use the power rule to integrate the function $\int_1^4 \sqrt{t}(1+t)dt.$

Solution

The first step is to rewrite the function and simplify it so we can apply the power rule:

$$\begin{aligned} \int_1^4 \sqrt{t}(1+t)dt &= \int_1^4 t^{1/2}(1+t)dt \\ &= \int_1^4 \left(t^{1/2}+t^{3/2}\right)dt. \end{aligned}$$

Now apply the power rule:

$$\begin{aligned} \int_1^4 \left(t^{1/2}+t^{3/2}\right)dt &= \left(\frac{2}{3}t^{3/2}+\frac{2}{5}t^{5/2}\right)\Big|_1^4 \\ &= \left[\frac{2}{3}(4)^{3/2}+\frac{2}{5}(4)^{5/2}\right]-\left[\frac{2}{3}(1)^{3/2}+\frac{2}{5}(1)^{5/2}\right] \\ &= \frac{256}{15}. \end{aligned}$$

5.21 Find the definite integral of $f(x)=x^2-3x$ over the interval $[1, 3]$.

The Net Change Theorem

The **net change theorem** considers the integral of a *rate of change*. It says that when a quantity changes, the new value equals the initial value plus the integral of the rate of change of that quantity. The formula can be expressed in two ways. The second is more familiar; it is simply the definite integral.

Theorem 5.6: Net Change Theorem

The new value of a changing quantity equals the initial value plus the integral of the rate of change:

$$F(b) = F(a) + \int_a^b F'(x)dx \tag{5.18}$$

or

$$\int_a^b F'(x)dx = F(b) - F(a).$$

Subtracting $F(a)$ from both sides of the first equation yields the second equation. Since they are equivalent formulas, which one we use depends on the application.

The significance of the net change theorem lies in the results. Net change can be applied to area, distance, and volume, to name only a few applications. Net change accounts for negative quantities automatically without having to write more than one integral. To illustrate, let's apply the net change theorem to a velocity function in which the result is displacement.

We looked at a simple example of this in **The Definite Integral**. Suppose a car is moving due north (the positive direction) at 40 mph between 2 p.m. and 4 p.m., then the car moves south at 30 mph between 4 p.m. and 5 p.m. We can graph this motion as shown in **Figure 5.32**.

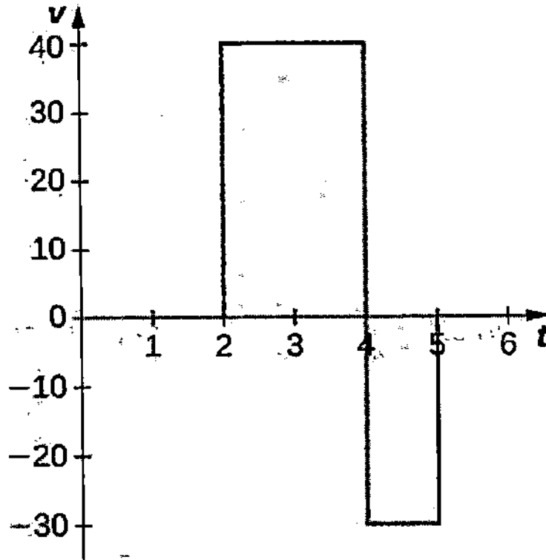

Figure 5.32 The graph shows speed versus time for the given motion of a car.

Just as we did before, we can use definite integrals to calculate the net displacement as well as the total distance traveled. The net displacement is given by

$$\begin{aligned}\int_2^5 v(t)dt &= \int_2^4 40dt + \int_4^5 -30dt \\ &= 80 - 30 \\ &= 50.\end{aligned}$$

Thus, at 5 p.m. the car is 50 mi north of its starting position. The total distance traveled is given by

$$\begin{aligned}\int_2^5 |v(t)|dt &= \int_2^4 40dt + \int_4^5 30dt \\ &= 80 + 30 \\ &= 110.\end{aligned}$$

Therefore, between 2 p.m. and 5 p.m., the car traveled a total of 110 mi.

To summarize, net displacement may include both positive and negative values. In other words, the velocity function accounts for both forward distance and backward distance. To find net displacement, integrate the velocity function over the interval. Total distance traveled, on the other hand, is always positive. To find the total distance traveled by an object, regardless of direction, we need to integrate the absolute value of the velocity function.

Example 5.24

Finding Net Displacement

Given a velocity function $v(t) = 3t - 5$ (in meters per second) for a particle in motion from time $t = 0$ to time $t = 3$, find the net displacement of the particle.

Solution

Applying the net change theorem, we have

$$\begin{aligned}\int_0^3 (3t - 5)dt &= \frac{3t^2}{2} - 5t\Big|_0^3 \\ &= \left[\frac{3(3)^2}{2} - 5(3)\right] - 0 \\ &= \frac{27}{2} - 15 \\ &= \frac{27}{2} - \frac{30}{2} \\ &= -\frac{3}{2}.\end{aligned}$$

The net displacement is $-\frac{3}{2}$ m (**Figure 5.33**).

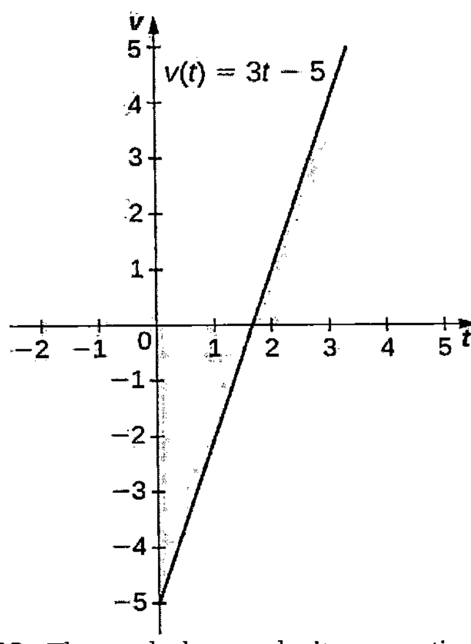

Figure 5.33 The graph shows velocity versus time for a particle moving with a linear velocity function.

Example 5.25

Finding the Total Distance Traveled

Use **Example 5.24** to find the total distance traveled by a particle according to the velocity function $v(t) = 3t - 5$ m/sec over a time interval $[0, 3]$.

Solution

The total distance traveled includes both the positive and the negative values. Therefore, we must integrate the absolute value of the velocity function to find the total distance traveled.

To continue with the example, use two integrals to find the total distance. First, find the t-intercept of the function, since that is where the division of the interval occurs. Set the equation equal to zero and solve for t. Thus,

$$\begin{aligned} 3t - 5 &= 0 \\ 3t &= 5 \\ t &= \frac{5}{3}. \end{aligned}$$

The two subintervals are $\left[0, \frac{5}{3}\right]$ and $\left[\frac{5}{3}, 3\right]$. To find the total distance traveled, integrate the absolute value of the function. Since the function is negative over the interval $\left[0, \frac{5}{3}\right]$, we have $|v(t)| = -v(t)$ over that interval. Over $\left[\frac{5}{3}, 3\right]$, the function is positive, so $|v(t)| = v(t)$. Thus, we have

$$\begin{aligned}\int_0^3 |v(t)|dt &= \int_0^{5/3} -v(t)dt + \int_{5/3}^3 v(t)dt \\ &= \int_0^{5/3} 5 - 3tdt + \int_{5/3}^3 3t - 5dt \\ &= \left(5t - \frac{3t^2}{2}\right)\Big|_0^{5/3} + \left(\frac{3t^2}{2} - 5t\right)\Big|_{5/3}^3 \\ &= \left[5\left(\frac{5}{3}\right) - \frac{3(5/3)^2}{2}\right] - 0 + \left[\frac{27}{2} - 15\right] - \left[\frac{3(5/3)^2}{2} - \frac{25}{3}\right] \\ &= \frac{25}{3} - \frac{25}{6} + \frac{27}{2} - 15 - \frac{25}{6} + \frac{25}{3} \\ &= \frac{41}{6}.\end{aligned}$$

So, the total distance traveled is $\frac{14}{6}$ m.

5.22 Find the net displacement and total distance traveled in meters given the velocity function $f(t) = \frac{1}{2}e^t - 2$ over the interval $[0, 2]$.

Applying the Net Change Theorem

The net change theorem can be applied to the flow and consumption of fluids, as shown in **Example 5.26**.

Example 5.26

How Many Gallons of Gasoline Are Consumed?

If the motor on a motorboat is started at $t = 0$ and the boat consumes gasoline at the rate of $5 - t^3$ gal/hr, how much gasoline is used in the first 2 hours?

Solution

Express the problem as a definite integral, integrate, and evaluate using the Fundamental Theorem of Calculus. The limits of integration are the endpoints of the interval $[0, 2]$. We have

$$\begin{aligned}\int_0^2 (5 - t^3)dt &= \left(5t - \frac{t^4}{4}\right)\Big|_0^2 \\ &= \left[5(2) - \frac{(2)^4}{4}\right] - 0 \\ &= 10 - \frac{16}{4} \\ &= 6.\end{aligned}$$

Thus, the motorboat uses 6 gal of gas in 2 hours.

Example 5.27

Chapter Opener: Iceboats

Figure 5.34 (credit: modification of work by Carter Brown, Flickr)

As we saw at the beginning of the chapter, top iceboat racers (**Figure 5.1**) can attain speeds of up to five times the wind speed. Andrew is an intermediate iceboater, though, so he attains speeds equal to only twice the wind speed. Suppose Andrew takes his iceboat out one morning when a light 5-mph breeze has been blowing all morning. As Andrew gets his iceboat set up, though, the wind begins to pick up. During his first half hour of iceboating, the wind speed increases according to the function $v(t) = 20t + 5.$ For the second half hour of Andrew's outing, the wind remains steady at 15 mph. In other words, the wind speed is given by

$$v(t) = \begin{cases} 20t + 5 & \text{for } 0 \le t \le \frac{1}{2} \\ 15 & \text{for } \frac{1}{2} \le t \le 1. \end{cases}$$

Recalling that Andrew's iceboat travels at twice the wind speed, and assuming he moves in a straight line away from his starting point, how far is Andrew from his starting point after 1 hour?

Solution

To figure out how far Andrew has traveled, we need to integrate his velocity, which is twice the wind speed. Then

$$\text{Distance } = \int_0^1 2v(t)dt.$$

Substituting the expressions we were given for $v(t),$ we get

$$\begin{aligned}\int_0^1 2v(t)dt &= \int_0^{1/2} 2v(t)dt + \int_{1/2}^1 2v(t)dt \\ &= \int_0^{1/2} 2(20t+5)dt + \int_{1/3}^1 2(15)dt \\ &= \int_0^{1/2} (40t+10)dt + \int_{1/2}^1 30dt \\ &= \left[20t^2+10t\right]\Big|_0^{1/2} + [30t]\Big|_{1/2}^1 \\ &= \left(\frac{20}{4}+5\right) - 0 + (30-15) \\ &= 25.\end{aligned}$$

Andrew is 25 mi from his starting point after 1 hour.

5.23 Suppose that, instead of remaining steady during the second half hour of Andrew's outing, the wind starts to die down according to the function $v(t) = -10t + 15$. In other words, the wind speed is given by

$$v(t) = \begin{cases} 20t+5 & \text{for } 0 \le t \le \frac{1}{2} \\ -10t+15 & \text{for } \frac{1}{2} \le t \le 1. \end{cases}$$

Under these conditions, how far from his starting point is Andrew after 1 hour?

Integrating Even and Odd Functions

We saw in **Functions and Graphs** that an even function is a function in which $f(-x) = f(x)$ for all x in the domain—that is, the graph of the curve is unchanged when x is replaced with $-x$. The graphs of even functions are symmetric about the y-axis. An odd function is one in which $f(-x) = -f(x)$ for all x in the domain, and the graph of the function is symmetric about the origin.

Integrals of even functions, when the limits of integration are from $-a$ to a, involve two equal areas, because they are symmetric about the y-axis. Integrals of odd functions, when the limits of integration are similarly $[-a, a]$, evaluate to zero because the areas above and below the x-axis are equal.

Rule: Integrals of Even and Odd Functions

For continuous even functions such that $f(-x) = f(x)$,

$$\int_{-a}^{a} f(x)dx = 2\int_0^a f(x)dx.$$

For continuous odd functions such that $f(-x) = -f(x)$,

$$\int_{-a}^{a} f(x)dx = 0.$$

Example 5.28

Integrating an Even Function

Integrate the even function $\int_{-2}^{2}\left(3x^8 - 2\right)dx$ and verify that the integration formula for even functions holds.

Solution

The symmetry appears in the graphs in **Figure 5.35**. Graph (a) shows the region below the curve and above the x-axis. We have to zoom in to this graph by a huge amount to see the region. Graph (b) shows the region above the curve and below the x-axis. The signed area of this region is negative. Both views illustrate the symmetry about the y-axis of an even function. We have

$$\begin{aligned}\int_{-2}^{2}\left(3x^8 - 2\right)dx &= \left(\frac{x^9}{3} - 2x\right)\Big|_{-2}^{2} \\ &= \left[\frac{(2)^9}{3} - 2(2)\right] - \left[\frac{(-2)^9}{3} - 2(-2)\right] \\ &= \left(\frac{512}{3} - 4\right) - \left(-\frac{512}{3} + 4\right) \\ &= \frac{1000}{3}.\end{aligned}$$

To verify the integration formula for even functions, we can calculate the integral from 0 to 2 and double it, then check to make sure we get the same answer.

$$\begin{aligned}\int_{0}^{2}\left(3x^8 - 2\right)dx &= \left(\frac{x^9}{3} - 2x\right)\Big|_{0}^{2} \\ &= \frac{512}{3} - 4 \\ &= \frac{500}{3}\end{aligned}$$

Since $2 \cdot \frac{500}{3} = \frac{1000}{3}$, we have verified the formula for even functions in this particular example.

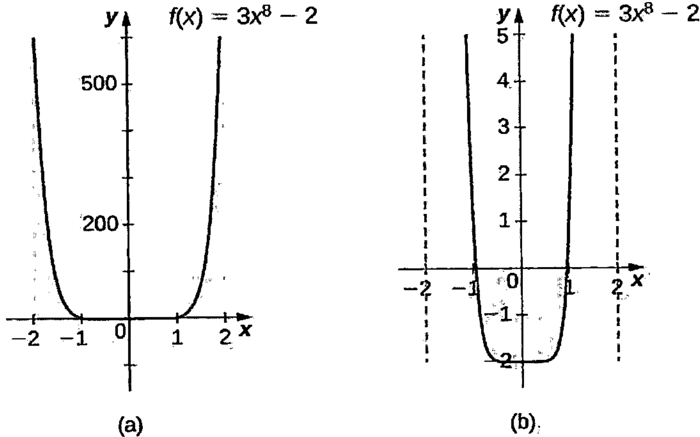

Figure 5.35 Graph (a) shows the positive area between the curve and the x-axis, whereas graph (b) shows the negative area between the curve and the x-axis. Both views show the symmetry about the y-axis.

Example 5.29

Integrating an Odd Function

Evaluate the definite integral of the odd function $-5\sin x$ over the interval $[-\pi, \pi]$.

Solution

The graph is shown in **Figure 5.36**. We can see the symmetry about the origin by the positive area above the x-axis over $[-\pi, 0]$, and the negative area below the x-axis over $[0, \pi]$. We have

$$\begin{aligned}\int_{-\pi}^{\pi} -5\sin x dx &= -5(-\cos x)|_{-\pi}^{\pi} \\ &= 5\cos x|_{-\pi}^{\pi} \\ &= [5\cos \pi] - [5\cos(-\pi)] \\ &= -5 - (-5) \\ &= 0.\end{aligned}$$

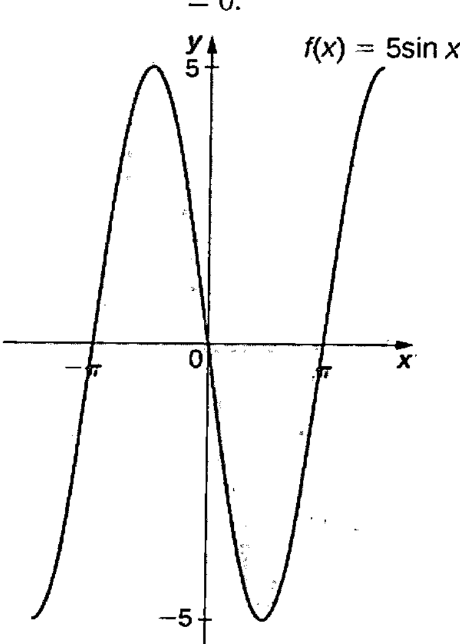

Figure 5.36 The graph shows areas between a curve and the x-axis for an odd function.

5.24 Integrate the function $\int_{-2}^{2} x^4 dx.$

5.4 EXERCISES

Use basic integration formulas to compute the following antiderivatives.

207. $\int\left(\sqrt{x}-\frac{1}{\sqrt{x}}\right)dx$

208. $\int\left(e^{2x}-\frac{1}{2}e^{x/2}\right)dx$

209. $\int\frac{dx}{2x}$

210. $\int\frac{x-1}{x^2}dx$

211. $\int_0^{\pi}(\sin x-\cos x)dx$

212. $\int_0^{\pi/2}(x-\sin x)dx$

213. Write an integral that expresses the increase in the perimeter $P(s)$ of a square when its side length s increases from 2 units to 4 units and evaluate the integral.

214. Write an integral that quantifies the change in the area $A(s)=s^2$ of a square when the side length doubles from S units to $2S$ units and evaluate the integral.

215. A regular N-gon (an N-sided polygon with sides that have equal length s, such as a pentagon or hexagon) has perimeter Ns. Write an integral that expresses the increase in perimeter of a regular N-gon when the length of each side increases from 1 unit to 2 units and evaluate the integral.

216. The area of a regular pentagon with side length $a>0$ is pa^2 with $p=\frac{1}{4}\sqrt{5+\sqrt{5+2\sqrt{5}}}$. The Pentagon in Washington, DC, has inner sides of length 360 ft and outer sides of length 920 ft. Write an integral to express the area of the roof of the Pentagon according to these dimensions and evaluate this area.

217. A dodecahedron is a Platonic solid with a surface that consists of 12 pentagons, each of equal area. By how much does the surface area of a dodecahedron increase as the side length of each pentagon doubles from 1 unit to 2 units?

218. An icosahedron is a Platonic solid with a surface that consists of 20 equilateral triangles. By how much does the surface area of an icosahedron increase as the side length of each triangle doubles from a unit to $2a$ units?

219. Write an integral that quantifies the change in the area of the surface of a cube when its side length doubles from s unit to $2s$ units and evaluate the integral.

220. Write an integral that quantifies the increase in the volume of a cube when the side length doubles from s unit to $2s$ units and evaluate the integral.

221. Write an integral that quantifies the increase in the surface area of a sphere as its radius doubles from R unit to $2R$ units and evaluate the integral.

222. Write an integral that quantifies the increase in the volume of a sphere as its radius doubles from R unit to $2R$ units and evaluate the integral.

223. Suppose that a particle moves along a straight line with velocity $v(t)=4-2t$, where $0\le t\le 2$ (in meters per second). Find the displacement at time t and the total distance traveled up to $t=2$.

224. Suppose that a particle moves along a straight line with velocity defined by $v(t)=t^2-3t-18$, where $0\le t\le 6$ (in meters per second). Find the displacement at time t and the total distance traveled up to $t=6$.

225. Suppose that a particle moves along a straight line with velocity defined by $v(t)=|2t-6|$, where $0\le t\le 6$ (in meters per second). Find the displacement at time t and the total distance traveled up to $t=6$.

226. Suppose that a particle moves along a straight line with acceleration defined by $a(t)=t-3$, where $0\le t\le 6$ (in meters per second). Find the velocity and displacement at time t and the total distance traveled up to $t=6$ if $v(0)=3$ and $d(0)=0$.

227. A ball is thrown upward from a height of 1.5 m at an initial speed of 40 m/sec. Acceleration resulting from gravity is -9.8 m/sec^2. Neglecting air resistance, solve for the velocity $v(t)$ and the height $h(t)$ of the ball t seconds after it is thrown and before it returns to the ground.

228. A ball is thrown upward from a height of 3 m at an initial speed of 60 m/sec. Acceleration resulting from gravity is -9.8 m/sec^2. Neglecting air resistance, solve for the velocity $v(t)$ and the height $h(t)$ of the ball t seconds after it is thrown and before it returns to the ground.

229. The area $A(t)$ of a circular shape is growing at a constant rate. If the area increases from 4π units to 9π units between times $t=2$ and $t=3$, find the net change in the radius during that time.

230. A spherical balloon is being inflated at a constant rate. If the volume of the balloon changes from 36π in.^{3} to 288π in.^{3} between time $t = 30$ and $t = 60$ seconds, find the net change in the radius of the balloon during that time.

231. Water flows into a conical tank with cross-sectional area πx^2 at height x and volume $\frac{\pi x^3}{3}$ up to height x. If water flows into the tank at a rate of 1 m^3/min, find the height of water in the tank after 5 min. Find the change in height between 5 min and 10 min.

232. A horizontal cylindrical tank has cross-sectional area $A(x) = 4(6x - x^2)m^2$ at height x meters above the bottom when $x \leq 3$.

a. The volume V between heights a and b is $\int_a^b A(x)dx$. Find the volume at heights between 2 m and 3 m.
b. Suppose that oil is being pumped into the tank at a rate of 50 L/min. Using the chain rule, $\frac{dx}{dt} = \frac{dx}{dV}\frac{dV}{dt}$, at how many meters per minute is the height of oil in the tank changing, expressed in terms of x, when the height is at x meters?
c. How long does it take to fill the tank to 3 m starting from a fill level of 2 m?

233. The following table lists the electrical power in gigawatts—the rate at which energy is consumed—used in a certain city for different hours of the day, in a typical 24-hour period, with hour 1 corresponding to midnight to 1 a.m.

Hour	**Power**	**Hour**	**Power**
1	28	13	48
2	25	14	49
3	24	15	49
4	23	16	50
5	24	17	50
6	27	18	50
7	29	19	46
8	32	20	43
9	34	21	42
10	39	22	40
11	42	23	37
12	46	24	34

Find the total amount of power in gigawatt-hours (gW-h) consumed by the city in a typical 24-hour period.

234. The average residential electrical power use (in hundreds of watts) per hour is given in the following table.

Hour	Power	Hour	Power
1	8	13	12
2	6	14	13
3	5	15	14
4	4	16	15
5	5	17	17
6	6	18	19
7	7	19	18
8	8	20	17
9	9	21	16
10	10	22	16
11	10	23	13
12	11	24	11

a. Compute the average total energy used in a day in kilowatt-hours (kWh).
b. If a ton of coal generates 1842 kWh, how long does it take for an average residence to burn a ton of coal?
c. Explain why the data might fit a plot of the form $p(t) = 11.5 - 7.5\sin\left(\frac{\pi t}{12}\right)$.

235. The data in the following table are used to estimate the average power output produced by Peter Sagan for each of the last 18 sec of Stage 1 of the 2012 Tour de France.

Second	Watts	Second	Watts
1	600	10	1200
2	500	11	1170
3	575	12	1125
4	1050	13	1100
5	925	14	1075
6	950	15	1000
7	1050	16	950
8	950	17	900
9	1100	18	780

Table 5.6 Average Power Output ***Source*****: sportsexercisengineering.com**

Estimate the net energy used in kilojoules (kJ), noting that 1W = 1 J/s, and the average power output by Sagan during this time interval.

236. The data in the following table are used to estimate the average power output produced by Peter Sagan for each 15-min interval of Stage 1 of the 2012 Tour de France.

Minutes	Watts	Minutes	Watts
15	200	165	170
30	180	180	220
45	190	195	140
60	230	210	225
75	240	225	170
90	210	240	210
105	210	255	200
120	220	270	220
135	210	285	250
150	150	300	400

Table 5.7 Average Power Output ***Source***: **sportsexercisengineering.com**

Estimate the net energy used in kilojoules, noting that 1W = 1 J/s.

237. The distribution of incomes as of 2012 in the United States in \$5000 increments is given in the following table. The kth row denotes the percentage of households with incomes between $\$5000xk$ and $5000xk + 4999$. The row $k = 40$ contains all households with income between \$200,000 and \$250,000 and $k = 41$ accounts for all households with income exceeding \$250,000.

0	3.5	21	1.5
1	4.1	22	1.4
2	5.9	23	1.3
3	5.7	24	1.3
4	5.9	25	1.1
5	5.4	26	1.0
6	5.5	27	0.75
7	5.1	28	0.8
8	4.8	29	1.0
9	4.1	30	0.6
10	4.3	31	0.6
11	3.5	32	0.5
12	3.7	33	0.5
13	3.2	34	0.4
14	3.0	35	0.3
15	2.8	36	0.3
16	2.5	37	0.3
17	2.2	38	0.2
18	2.2	39	1.8
19	1.8	40	2.3
20	2.1	41	

Table 5.8 Income Distributions ***Source*:** **http://www.census.gov/prod/2013pubs/p60-245.pdf**

Table 5.8 Income Distributions ***Source*:** **http://www.census.gov/prod/2013pubs/p60-245.pdf**

a. Estimate the percentage of U.S. households in 2012 with incomes less than $55,000.
b. What percentage of households had incomes exceeding $85,000?
c. Plot the data and try to fit its shape to that of a graph of the form $a(x+c)e^{-b(x+e)}$ for suitable a, b, c.

238. Newton's law of gravity states that the gravitational force exerted by an object of mass M and one of mass m with centers that are separated by a distance r is $F = G\frac{mM}{r^2}$, with G an empirical constant $G = 6.67x10^{-11}\ m^3/(kg \cdot s^2)$. The work done by a variable force over an interval $[a, b]$ is defined as $W = \int_a^b F(x)dx$. If Earth has mass 5.97219×10^{24} and radius 6371 km, compute the amount of work to elevate a polar weather satellite of mass 1400 kg to its orbiting altitude of 850 km above Earth.

239. For a given motor vehicle, the maximum achievable deceleration from braking is approximately 7 m/sec^2 on dry concrete. On wet asphalt, it is approximately 2.5 m/sec^2. Given that 1 mph corresponds to 0.447 m/sec, find the total distance that a car travels in meters on dry concrete after the brakes are applied until it comes to a complete stop if the initial velocity is 67 mph (30 m/sec) or if the initial braking velocity is 56 mph (25 m/sec). Find the corresponding distances if the surface is slippery wet asphalt.

240. John is a 25-year old man who weighs 160 lb. He burns $500 - 50t$ calories/hr while riding his bike for t hours. If an oatmeal cookie has 55 cal and John eats $4t$ cookies during the tth hour, how many net calories has he lost after 3 hours riding his bike?

241. Sandra is a 25-year old woman who weighs 120 lb. She burns $300 - 50t$ cal/hr while walking on her treadmill. Her caloric intake from drinking Gatorade is $100t$ calories during the tth hour. What is her net decrease in calories after walking for 3 hours?

242. A motor vehicle has a maximum efficiency of 33 mpg at a cruising speed of 40 mph. The efficiency drops at a rate of 0.1 mpg/mph between 40 mph and 50 mph, and at a rate of 0.4 mpg/mph between 50 mph and 80 mph. What is the efficiency in miles per gallon if the car is cruising at 50 mph? What is the efficiency in miles per gallon if the car is cruising at 80 mph? If gasoline costs $3.50/gal, what is the cost of fuel to drive 50 mi at 40 mph, at 50 mph, and at 80 mph?

243. Although some engines are more efficient at given a horsepower than others, on average, fuel efficiency decreases with horsepower at a rate of 1/25 mpg/horsepower. If a typical 50-horsepower engine has an average fuel efficiency of 32 mpg, what is the average fuel efficiency of an engine with the following horsepower: 150, 300, 450?

244. **[T]** The following table lists the 2013 schedule of federal income tax versus taxable income.

Taxable Income Range	The Tax Is ...	... Of the Amount Over
$0–$8925	10%	$0
$8925–$36,250	$892.50 + 15%	$8925
$36,250–$87,850	$4,991.25 + 25%	$36,250
$87,850–$183,250	$17,891.25 + 28%	$87,850
$183,250–$398,350	$44,603.25 + 33%	$183,250
$398,350–$400,000	$115,586.25 + 35%	$398,350
> $400,000	$116,163.75 + 39.6%	$400,000

Table 5.9 Federal Income Tax Versus Taxable Income ***Source*: http://www.irs.gov/pub/irs-prior/i1040tt--2013.pdf.**

Suppose that Steve just received a $10,000 raise. How much of this raise is left after federal taxes if Steve's salary before receiving the raise was $40,000? If it was $90,000? If it was $385,000?

245. **[T]** The following table provides hypothetical data regarding the level of service for a certain highway.

Highway Speed Range (mph)	Vehicles per Hour per Lane	Density Range (vehicles/mi)
> 60	< 600	< 10
60–57	600–1000	10–20
57–54	1000–1500	20–30
54–46	1500–1900	30–45
46–30	1900–2100	45–70
<30	Unstable	70–200

Table 5.10

a. Plot vehicles per hour per lane on the x-axis and highway speed on the y-axis.
b. Compute the average decrease in speed (in miles per hour) per unit increase in congestion (vehicles per hour per lane) as the latter increases from 600 to 1000, from 1000 to 1500, and from 1500 to 2100. Does the decrease in miles per hour depend linearly on the increase in vehicles per hour per lane?
c. Plot minutes per mile (60 times the reciprocal of miles per hour) as a function of vehicles per hour per lane. Is this function linear?

For the next two exercises use the data in the following table, which displays bald eagle populations from 1963 to 2000 in the continental United States.

Year	Population of Breeding Pairs of Bald Eagles
1963	487
1974	791
1981	1188
1986	1875
1992	3749
1996	5094
2000	6471

Table 5.11 Population of Breeding Bald Eagle Pairs ***Source*: http://www.fws.gov/Midwest/eagle/population/chtofprs.html.**

246. **[T]** The graph below plots the quadratic $p(t) = 6.48t^2 - 80.3\,1t + 585.69$ against the data in preceding table, normalized so that $t = 0$ corresponds to 1963. Estimate the average number of bald eagles per year present for the 37 years by computing the average value of p over $[0, 37]$.

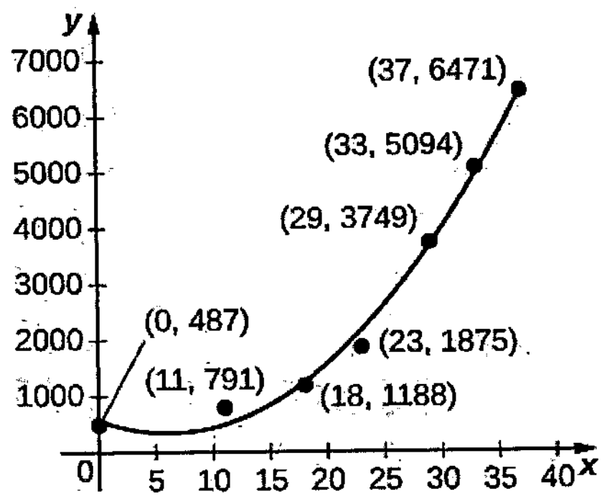

247. **[T]** The graph below plots the cubic $p(t) = 0.07t^3 + 2.42t^2 - 25.63t + 521.23$ against the data in the preceding table, normalized so that $t = 0$ corresponds to 1963. Estimate the average number of bald eagles per year present for the 37 years by computing the average value of p over $[0, 37]$.

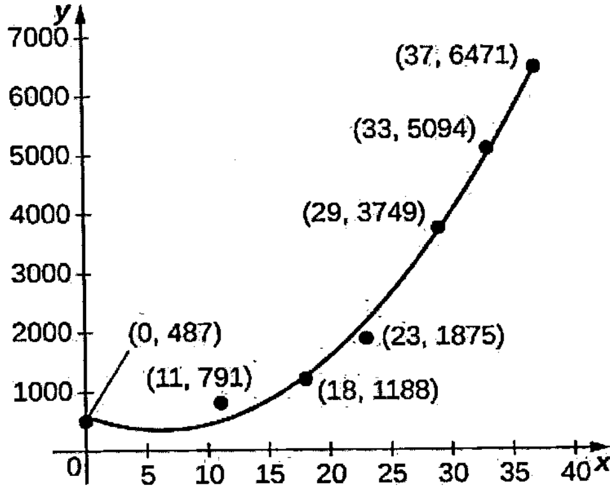

248. **[T]** Suppose you go on a road trip and record your speed at every half hour, as compiled in the following table. The best quadratic fit to the data is $q(t) = 5x^2 - 11x + 49$, shown in the accompanying graph. Integrate q to estimate the total distance driven over the 3 hours.

Time (hr)	Speed (mph)
0 (start)	50
1	40
2	50
3	60

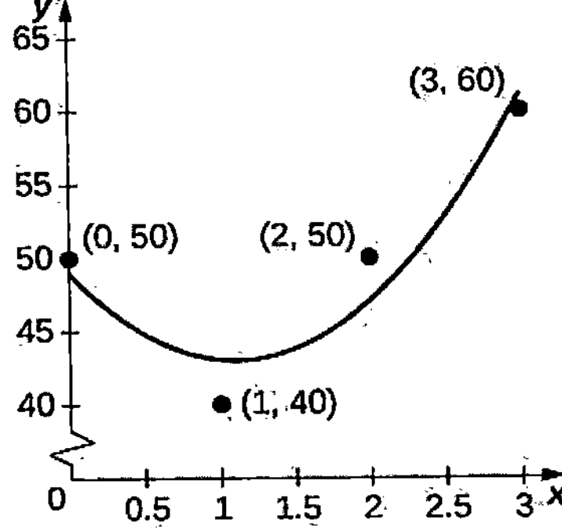

As a car accelerates, it does not accelerate at a constant rate; rather, the acceleration is variable. For the following exercises, use the following table, which contains the acceleration measured at every second as a driver merges onto a freeway.

Time (sec)	Acceleration (mph/sec)
1	11.2
2	10.6
3	8.1
4	5.4
5	0

249. **[T]** The accompanying graph plots the best quadratic fit, $a(t) = -0.70t^2 + 1.44t + 10.44,$ to the data from the preceding table. Compute the average value of $a(t)$ to estimate the average acceleration between $t = 0$ and $t = 5.$

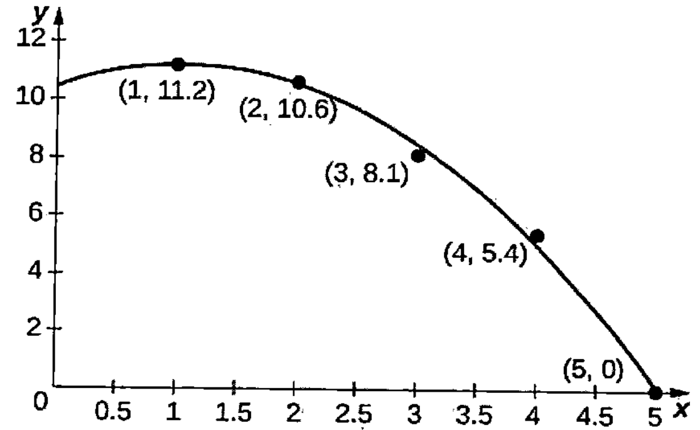

250. **[T]** Using your acceleration equation from the previous exercise, find the corresponding velocity equation. Assuming the final velocity is 0 mph, find the velocity at time $t = 0.$

251. **[T]** Using your velocity equation from the previous exercise, find the corresponding distance equation, assuming your initial distance is 0 mi. How far did you travel while you accelerated your car? (*Hint:* You will need to convert time units.)

252. **[T]** The number of hamburgers sold at a restaurant throughout the day is given in the following table, with the accompanying graph plotting the best cubic fit to the data, $b(t) = 0.12t^3 - 2.13t^3 + 12.13t + 3.91,$ with $t = 0$ corresponding to 9 a.m. and $t = 12$ corresponding to 9 p.m. Compute the average value of $b(t)$ to estimate the average number of hamburgers sold per hour.

Hours Past Midnight	No. of Burgers Sold
9	3
12	28
15	20
18	30
21	45

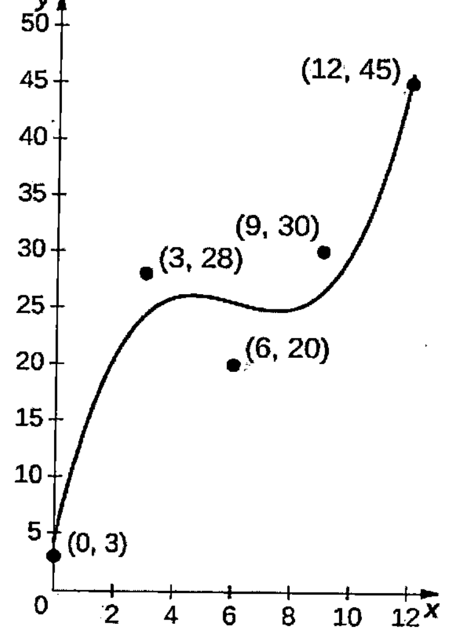

253. **[T]** An athlete runs by a motion detector, which records her speed, as displayed in the following table. The best linear fit to this data, $\ell(t) = -0.068t + 5.14$, is shown in the accompanying graph. Use the average value of $\ell(t)$ between $t = 0$ and $t = 40$ to estimate the runner's average speed.

Minutes	Speed (m/sec)
0	5
10	4.8
20	3.6
30	3.0
40	2.5

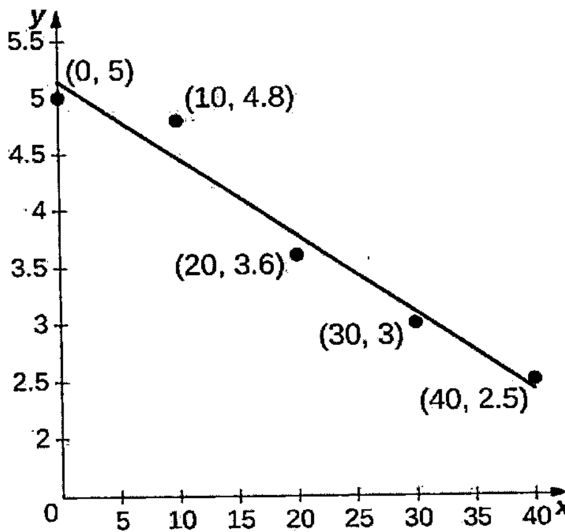

5.5 | Substitution

Learning Objectives

5.5.1 Use substitution to evaluate indefinite integrals.
5.5.2 Use substitution to evaluate definite integrals.

The Fundamental Theorem of Calculus gave us a method to evaluate integrals without using Riemann sums. The drawback of this method, though, is that we must be able to find an antiderivative, and this is not always easy. In this section we examine a technique, called **integration by substitution**, to help us find antiderivatives. Specifically, this method helps us find antiderivatives when the integrand is the result of a chain-rule derivative.

At first, the approach to the substitution procedure may not appear very obvious. However, it is primarily a visual task—that is, the integrand shows you what to do; it is a matter of recognizing the form of the function. So, what are we supposed to see? We are looking for an integrand of the form $f[g(x)]g'(x)dx.$ For example, in the integral $\int \left(x^2 - 3\right)^3 2x dx,$ we have $f(x) = x^3, g(x) = x^2 - 3,$ and $g'(x) = 2x.$ Then,

$$f[g(x)]g'(x) = \left(x^2 - 3\right)^3 (2x),$$

and we see that our integrand is in the correct form.

The method is called *substitution* because we substitute part of the integrand with the variable *u* and part of the integrand with *du*. It is also referred to as **change of variables** because we are changing variables to obtain an expression that is easier to work with for applying the integration rules.

Theorem 5.7: Substitution with Indefinite Integrals

Let $u = g(x),$, where $g'(x)$ is continuous over an interval, let $f(x)$ be continuous over the corresponding range of *g*, and let $F(x)$ be an antiderivative of $f(x).$ Then,

$$\begin{aligned} \int f[g(x)]g'(x)dx &= \int f(u)du \\ &= F(u) + C \\ &= F(g(x)) + C. \end{aligned} \quad (5.19)$$

Proof

Let *f*, *g*, *u*, and *F* be as specified in the theorem. Then

$$\begin{aligned} \frac{d}{dx}F(g(x)) &= F'(g(x))g'(x) \\ &= f[g(x)]g'(x). \end{aligned}$$

Integrating both sides with respect to *x*, we see that

$$\int f[g(x)]g'(x)dx = F(g(x)) + C.$$

If we now substitute $u = g(x),$ and $du = g'(x)dx,$ we get

$$\begin{aligned} \int f[g(x)]g'(x)dx &= \int f(u)du \\ &= F(u) + C \\ &= F(g(x)) + C. \end{aligned}$$

□

Returning to the problem we looked at originally, we let $u = x^2 - 3$ and then $du = 2xdx$. Rewrite the integral in terms of u:

$$\int \underbrace{\left(x^2 - 3\right)}_{u}^{3} \underbrace{(2xdx)}_{du} = \int u^3\,du.$$

Using the power rule for integrals, we have

$$\int u^3\,du = \frac{u^4}{4} + C.$$

Substitute the original expression for x back into the solution:

$$\frac{u^4}{4} + C = \frac{\left(x^2 - 3\right)^4}{4} + C.$$

We can generalize the procedure in the following Problem-Solving Strategy.

Problem-Solving Strategy: Integration by Substitution

1. Look carefully at the integrand and select an expression $g(x)$ within the integrand to set equal to u. Let's select $g(x)$. such that $g'(x)$ is also part of the integrand.
2. Substitute $u = g(x)$ and $du = g'(x)dx$. into the integral.
3. We should now be able to evaluate the integral with respect to u. If the integral can't be evaluated we need to go back and select a different expression to use as u.
4. Evaluate the integral in terms of u.
5. Write the result in terms of x and the expression $g(x)$.

Example 5.30

Using Substitution to Find an Antiderivative

Use substitution to find the antiderivative of $\int 6x\left(3x^2 + 4\right)^4 dx.$

Solution

The first step is to choose an expression for u. We choose $u = 3x^2 + 4.$ because then $du = 6xdx.$, and we already have du in the integrand. Write the integral in terms of u:

$$\int 6x\left(3x^2 + 4\right)^4 dx = \int u^4\,du.$$

Remember that du is the derivative of the expression chosen for u, regardless of what is inside the integrand. Now we can evaluate the integral with respect to u:

$$\begin{aligned}\int u^4\,du &= \frac{u^5}{5} + C \\ &= \frac{\left(3x^2+4\right)^5}{5} + C.\end{aligned}$$

Analysis

We can check our answer by taking the derivative of the result of integration. We should obtain the integrand. Picking a value for C of 1, we let $y = \frac{1}{5}\left(3x^2+4\right)^5 + 1$. We have

$$y = \frac{1}{5}\left(3x^2+4\right)^5 + 1,$$

so

$$\begin{aligned}y' &= \left(\frac{1}{5}\right)5\left(3x^2+4\right)^4 6x \\ &= 6x\left(3x^2+4\right)^4.\end{aligned}$$

This is exactly the expression we started with inside the integrand.

5.25 Use substitution to find the antiderivative of $\int 3x^2\left(x^3-3\right)^2 dx.$

Sometimes we need to adjust the constants in our integral if they don't match up exactly with the expressions we are substituting.

Example 5.31

Using Substitution with Alteration

Use substitution to find the antiderivative of $\int z\sqrt{z^2-5}\,dz.$

Solution

Rewrite the integral as $\int z\left(z^2-5\right)^{1/2} dz.$ Let $u = z^2 - 5$ and $du = 2z\,dz.$ Now we have a problem because $du = 2z\,dz$ and the original expression has only $z\,dz.$ We have to alter our expression for du or the integral in u will be twice as large as it should be. If we multiply both sides of the du equation by $\frac{1}{2}$. we can solve this problem. Thus,

$$\begin{aligned}u &= z^2 - 5 \\ du &= 2z\,dz \\ \frac{1}{2}du &= \frac{1}{2}(2z)dz = z\,dz.\end{aligned}$$

Write the integral in terms of u, but pull the $\frac{1}{2}$ outside the integration symbol:

$$\int z\left(z^2-5\right)^{1/2}dz = \frac{1}{2}\int u^{1/2}\,du.$$

Integrate the expression in u:

$$\begin{aligned}\frac{1}{2}\int u^{1/2}\,du &= \left(\frac{1}{2}\right)\frac{u^{3/2}}{\frac{3}{2}}+C\\ &= \left(\frac{1}{2}\right)\left(\frac{2}{3}\right)u^{3/2}+C\\ &= \frac{1}{3}u^{3/2}+C\\ &= \frac{1}{3}\left(z^2-5\right)^{3/2}+C.\end{aligned}$$

5.26 Use substitution to find the antiderivative of $\int x^2\left(x^3+5\right)^9 dx.$

Example 5.32

Using Substitution with Integrals of Trigonometric Functions

Use substitution to evaluate the integral $\int \frac{\sin t}{\cos^3 t}dt.$

Solution

We know the derivative of $\cos t$ is $-\sin t,$ so we set $u=\cos t.$ Then $du=-\sin t\,dt.$ Substituting into the integral, we have

$$\int \frac{\sin t}{\cos^3 t}dt = -\int \frac{du}{u^3}.$$

Evaluating the integral, we get

$$\begin{aligned}-\int \frac{du}{u^3} &= -\int u^{-3}\,du\\ &= -\left(-\frac{1}{2}\right)u^{-2}+C.\end{aligned}$$

Putting the answer back in terms of t, we get

$$\begin{aligned}\int \frac{\sin t}{\cos^3 t}dt &= \frac{1}{2u^2}+C\\ &= \frac{1}{2\cos^2 t}+C.\end{aligned}$$

5.27 Use substitution to evaluate the integral $\int \frac{\cos t}{\sin^2 t}dt.$

Sometimes we need to manipulate an integral in ways that are more complicated than just multiplying or dividing by a constant. We need to eliminate all the expressions within the integrand that are in terms of the original variable. When we are done, u should be the only variable in the integrand. In some cases, this means solving for the original variable in terms of u. This technique should become clear in the next example.

Example 5.33

Finding an Antiderivative Using *u*-Substitution

Use substitution to find the antiderivative of $\int \frac{x}{\sqrt{x-1}}dx.$

Solution

If we let $u = x - 1,$ then $du = dx.$ But this does not account for the x in the numerator of the integrand. We need to express x in terms of u. If $u = x - 1,$ then $x = u + 1.$ Now we can rewrite the integral in terms of u:

$$\begin{aligned}\int \frac{x}{\sqrt{x-1}}dx &= \int \frac{u+1}{\sqrt{u}}du \\ &= \int \sqrt{u} + \frac{1}{\sqrt{u}}du \\ &= \int \left(u^{1/2} + u^{-1/2}\right)du.\end{aligned}$$

Then we integrate in the usual way, replace u with the original expression, and factor and simplify the result. Thus,

$$\begin{aligned}\int \left(u^{1/2} + u^{-1/2}\right)du &= \frac{2}{3}u^{3/2} + 2u^{1/2} + C \\ &= \frac{2}{3}(x-1)^{3/2} + 2(x-1)^{1/2} + C \\ &= (x-1)^{1/2}\left[\frac{2}{3}(x-1) + 2\right] + C \\ &= (x-1)^{1/2}\left(\frac{2}{3}x - \frac{2}{3} + \frac{6}{3}\right) \\ &= (x-1)^{1/2}\left(\frac{2}{3}x + \frac{4}{3}\right) \\ &= \frac{2}{3}(x-1)^{1/2}(x+2) + C.\end{aligned}$$

5.28 Use substitution to evaluate the indefinite integral $\int \cos^3 t \sin t\, dt.$

Substitution for Definite Integrals

Substitution can be used with definite integrals, too. However, using substitution to evaluate a definite integral requires a change to the limits of integration. If we change variables in the integrand, the limits of integration change as well.

Theorem 5.8: Substitution with Definite Integrals

Let $u = g(x)$ and let g' be continuous over an interval $[a, b]$, and let f be continuous over the range of $u = g(x)$. Then,

$$\int_a^b f(g(x))g'(x)dx = \int_{g(a)}^{g(b)} f(u)du.$$

Although we will not formally prove this theorem, we justify it with some calculations here. From the substitution rule for indefinite integrals, if $F(x)$ is an antiderivative of $f(x)$, we have

$$\int f(g(x))g'(x)dx = F(g(x)) + C.$$

Then

$$\begin{aligned} \int_a^b f[g(x)]g'(x)dx &= F(g(x))\Big|_{x=a}^{x=b} \\ &= F(g(b)) - F(g(a)) \\ &= F(u)\Big|_{u=g(a)}^{u=g(b)} \\ &= \int_{g(a)}^{g(b)} f(u)du, \end{aligned} \tag{5.20}$$

and we have the desired result.

Example 5.34

Using Substitution to Evaluate a Definite Integral

Use substitution to evaluate $\int_0^1 x^2\left(1 + 2x^3\right)^5 dx.$

Solution

Let $u = 1 + 2x^3$, so $du = 6x^2 dx$. Since the original function includes one factor of x^2 and $du = 6x^2 dx$, multiply both sides of the du equation by $1/6$. Then,

$$\begin{aligned} du &= 6x^2 dx \\ \frac{1}{6}du &= x^2 dx. \end{aligned}$$

To adjust the limits of integration, note that when $x = 0, u = 1 + 2(0) = 1$, and when $x = 1, u = 1 + 2(1) = 3$. Then

$$\int_0^1 x^2\left(1 + 2x^3\right)^5 dx = \frac{1}{6}\int_1^3 u^5 du.$$

Evaluating this expression, we get

$$\frac{1}{6}\int_1^3 u^5\,du = \left(\frac{1}{6}\right)\left(\frac{u^6}{6}\right)\Big|_1^3 = \frac{1}{36}\left[(3)^6 - (1)^6\right] = \frac{182}{9}.$$

5.29 Use substitution to evaluate the definite integral $\int_{-1}^{0} y\left(2y^2 - 3\right)^5 dy.$

Example 5.35

Using Substitution with an Exponential Function

Use substitution to evaluate $\int_0^1 xe^{4x^2+3}\,dx.$

Solution

Let $u = 4x^3 + 3.$ Then, $du = 8xdx.$ To adjust the limits of integration, we note that when $x = 0,\ u = 3,$ and when $x = 1,\ u = 7.$ So our substitution gives

$$\int_0^1 xe^{4x^2+3}\,dx = \frac{1}{8}\int_3^7 e^u\,du = \frac{1}{8}e^u\Big|_3^7 = \frac{e^7 - e^3}{8} \approx 134.568.$$

5.30 Use substitution to evaluate $\int_0^1 x^2\cos\left(\frac{\pi}{2}x^3\right)dx.$

Substitution may be only one of the techniques needed to evaluate a definite integral. All of the properties and rules of integration apply independently, and trigonometric functions may need to be rewritten using a trigonometric identity before we can apply substitution. Also, we have the option of replacing the original expression for u after we find the antiderivative, which means that we do not have to change the limits of integration. These two approaches are shown in **Example 5.36**.

Example 5.36

Using Substitution to Evaluate a Trigonometric Integral

Use substitution to evaluate $\int_0^{\pi/2} \cos^2 \theta \, d\theta$.

Solution

Let us first use a trigonometric identity to rewrite the integral. The trig identity $\cos^2 \theta = \frac{1 + \cos 2\theta}{2}$ allows us to rewrite the integral as

$$\int_0^{\pi/2} \cos^2 \theta d\theta = \int_0^{\pi/2} \frac{1 + \cos 2\theta}{2} d\theta.$$

Then,

$$\begin{aligned} \int_0^{\pi/2} \left(\frac{1 + \cos 2\theta}{2}\right) d\theta &= \int_0^{\pi/2} \left(\frac{1}{2} + \frac{1}{2} \cos 2\theta\right) d\theta \\ &= \frac{1}{2} \int_0^{\pi/2} d\theta + \int_0^{\pi/2} \cos 2\theta d\theta. \end{aligned}$$

We can evaluate the first integral as it is, but we need to make a substitution to evaluate the second integral. Let $u = 2\theta$. Then, $du = 2d\theta$, or $\frac{1}{2} du = d\theta$. Also, when $\theta = 0$, $u = 0$, and when $\theta = \pi/2$, $u = \pi$. Expressing the second integral in terms of u, we have

$$\begin{aligned} \frac{1}{2} \int_0^{\pi/2} d\theta + \frac{1}{2} \int_0^{\pi/2} \cos 2\theta d\theta &= \frac{1}{2} \int_0^{\pi/2} d\theta + \frac{1}{2}\left(\frac{1}{2}\right) \int_0^{\pi} \cos u du \\ &= \frac{\theta}{2}\Big|_{\theta = 0}^{\theta = \pi/2} + \frac{1}{4} \sin u \Big|_{u = 0}^{u = \theta} \\ &= \left(\frac{\pi}{4} - 0\right) + (0 - 0) = \frac{\pi}{4}. \end{aligned}$$

5.5 EXERCISES

254. Why is *u*-substitution referred to as *change of variable*?

255. 2. If $f = g \circ h$, when reversing the chain rule, $\frac{d}{dx}(g \circ h)(x) = g'(h(x))h'(x)$, should you take $u = g(x)$ or $u = h(x)$?

In the following exercises, verify each identity using differentiation. Then, using the indicated *u*-substitution, identify *f* such that the integral takes the form $\int f(u)du$.

256. $\int x\sqrt{x+1}dx = \frac{2}{15}(x+1)^{3/2}(3x-2) + C;\ u = x+1$

257. $\int \frac{x^2}{\sqrt{x-1}}dx(x > 1) = \frac{2}{15}\sqrt{x-1}\left(3x^2+4x+8\right) + C;\ u = x-1$

258. $\int x\sqrt{4x^2+9}dx = \frac{1}{12}\left(4x^2+9\right)^{3/2} + C;\ u = 4x^2+9$

259. $\int \frac{x}{\sqrt{4x^2+9}}dx = \frac{1}{4}\sqrt{4x^2+9} + C;\ u = 4x^2+9$

260. $\int \frac{x}{(4x^2+9)^2}dx = -\frac{1}{8(4x^2+9)};\ u = 4x^2+9$

In the following exercises, find the antiderivative using the indicated substitution.

261. $\int (x+1)^4 dx;\ u = x+1$

262. $\int (x-1)^5 dx;\ u = x-1$

263. $\int (2x-3)^{-7} dx;\ u = 2x-3$

264. $\int (3x-2)^{-11} dx;\ u = 3x-2$

265. $\int \frac{x}{\sqrt{x^2+1}}dx;\ u = x^2+1$

266. $\int \frac{x}{\sqrt{1-x^2}}dx;\ u = 1-x^2$

267. $\int (x-1)\left(x^2-2x\right)^3 dx;\ u = x^2-2x$

268. $\int \left(x^2-2x\right)\left(x^3-3x^2\right)^2 dx;\ u = x^3 = 3x^2$

269. $\int \cos^3\theta d\theta;\ u = \sin\theta$ $(Hint\colon \cos^2\theta = 1-\sin^2\theta)$

270. $\int \sin^3\theta d\theta;\ u = \cos\theta$ $(Hint\colon \sin^2\theta = 1-\cos^2\theta)$

In the following exercises, use a suitable change of variables to determine the indefinite integral.

271. $\int x(1-x)^{99} dx$

272. $\int t\left(1-t^2\right)^{10} dt$

273. $\int (11x-7)^{-3} dx$

274. $\int (7x-11)^4 dx$

275. $\int \cos^3\theta\sin\theta d\theta$

276. $\int \sin^7\theta\cos\theta d\theta$

277. $\int \cos^2(\pi t)\sin(\pi t)dt$

278. $\int \sin^2 x\cos^3 x dx$ $(Hint\colon \sin^2 x + \cos^2 x = 1)$

279. $\int t\sin\left(t^2\right)\cos\left(t^2\right)dt$

280. $\int t^2\cos^2\left(t^3\right)\sin\left(t^3\right)dt$

281. $\int \frac{x^2}{\left(x^3-3\right)^2}dx$

282. $\int \frac{x^3}{\sqrt{1-x^2}}dx$

283. $\displaystyle\int \frac{y^5}{\left(1-y^3\right)^{3/2}}dy$

284. $\int \cos\theta(1-\cos\theta)^{99}\sin\theta d\theta$

285. $\int \left(1-\cos^3\theta\right)^{10}\cos^2\theta\sin\theta d\theta$

286. $\int (\cos\theta - 1)\left(\cos^2\theta - 2\cos\theta\right)^3 \sin\theta d\theta$

287. $\int \left(\sin^2\theta - 2\sin\theta\right)\left(\sin^3\theta - 3\sin^2\theta\right)^3 \cos\theta d\theta$

In the following exercises, use a calculator to estimate the area under the curve using left Riemann sums with 50 terms, then use substitution to solve for the exact answer.

288. **[T]** $y = 3(1-x)^2$ over $[0, 2]$

289. **[T]** $y = x\left(1-x^2\right)^3$ over $[-1, 2]$

290. **[T]** $y = \sin x(1-\cos x)^2$ over $[0, \pi]$

291. **[T]** $y = \dfrac{x}{\left(x^2+1\right)^2}$ over $[-1, 1]$

In the following exercises, use a change of variables to evaluate the definite integral.

292. $\int_0^1 x\sqrt{1-x^2}dx$

293. $\displaystyle\int_0^1 \frac{x}{\sqrt{1+x^2}}dx$

294. $\displaystyle\int_0^2 \frac{t}{\sqrt{5+t^2}}dt$

295. $\displaystyle\int_0^1 \frac{t^2}{\sqrt{1+t^3}}dt$

296. $\int_0^{\pi/4} \sec^2\theta\tan\theta d\theta$

297. $\displaystyle\int_0^{\pi/4} \frac{\sin\theta}{\cos^4\theta}d\theta$

In the following exercises, evaluate the indefinite integral $\int f(x)dx$ with constant $C=0$ using u-substitution. Then, graph the function and the antiderivative over the indicated interval. If possible, estimate a value of C that would need to be added to the antiderivative to make it equal to the definite integral $F(x) = \int_a^x f(t)dt,$ with a the left endpoint of the given interval.

298. **[T]** $\int (2x+1)e^{x^2+x-6}dx$ over $[-3, 2]$

299. **[T]** $\int \frac{\cos(\ln(2x))}{x}dx$ on $[0, 2]$

300. **[T]** $\displaystyle\int \frac{3x^2+2x+1}{\sqrt{x^3+x^2+x+4}}dx$ over $[-1, 2]$

301. **[T]** $\displaystyle\int \frac{\sin x}{\cos^3 x}dx$ over $\left[-\frac{\pi}{3}, \frac{\pi}{3}\right]$

302. **[T]** $\int (x+2)e^{-x^2-4x+3}dx$ over $[-5, 1]$

303. **[T]** $\int 3x^2\sqrt{2x^3+1}dx$ over $[0, 1]$

304. If $h(a) = h(b)$ in $\int_a^b g'(h(x))h(x)dx,$ what can you say about the value of the integral?

305. Is the substitution $u = 1-x^2$ in the definite integral $\displaystyle\int_0^2 \frac{x}{1-x^2}dx$ okay? If not, why not?

In the following exercises, use a change of variables to show that each definite integral is equal to zero.

306. $\int_0^{\pi} \cos^2(2\theta)\sin(2\theta)d\theta$

307. $\int_0^{\sqrt{\pi}} t\cos\left(t^2\right)\sin\left(t^2\right)dt$

308. $\int_0^1 (1-2t)dt$

309. $\displaystyle\int_0^1 \frac{1-2t}{\left(1+\left(t-\frac{1}{2}\right)^2\right)}dt$

310. $\displaystyle\int_0^{\pi} \sin\left(\left(t-\frac{\pi}{2}\right)^3\right)\cos\left(t-\frac{\pi}{2}\right)dt$

311. $\displaystyle\int_0^2 (1-t)\cos(\pi t)dt$

312. $\displaystyle\int_{\pi/4}^{3\pi/4} \sin^2 t\cos t dt$

313. Show that the average value of $f(x)$ over an interval $[a, b]$ is the same as the average value of $f(cx)$ over the interval $\left[\frac{a}{c}, \frac{b}{c}\right]$ for $c > 0$.

314. Find the area under the graph of $f(t) = \frac{t}{\left(1+t^2\right)^a}$ between $t = 0$ and $t = x$ where $a > 0$ and $a \neq 1$ is fixed, and evaluate the limit as $x \to \infty$.

315. Find the area under the graph of $g(t) = \frac{t}{\left(1-t^2\right)^a}$ between $t = 0$ and $t = x$, where $0 < x < 1$ and $a > 0$ is fixed. Evaluate the limit as $x \to 1$.

316. The area of a semicircle of radius 1 can be expressed as $\int_{-1}^{1} \sqrt{1-x^2}dx$. Use the substitution $x = \cos t$ to express the area of a semicircle as the integral of a trigonometric function. You do not need to compute the integral.

317. The area of the top half of an ellipse with a major axis that is the x-axis from $x = -1$ to a and with a minor axis that is the y-axis from $y = -b$ to b can be written as $\displaystyle\int_{-a}^{a} b\sqrt{1-\frac{x^2}{a^2}}dx$. Use the substitution $x = a\cos t$ to express this area in terms of an integral of a trigonometric function. You do not need to compute the integral.

318. **[T]** The following graph is of a function of the form $f(t) = a\sin(nt) + b\sin(mt)$. Estimate the coefficients a and b, and the frequency parameters n and m. Use these estimates to approximate $\int_0^{\pi} f(t)dt$.

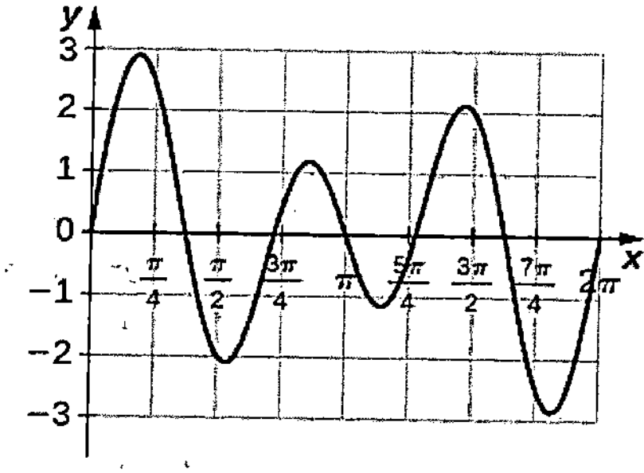

319. **[T]** The following graph is of a function of the form $f(x) = a\cos(nt) + b\cos(mt)$. Estimate the coefficients a and b and the frequency parameters n and m. Use these estimates to approximate $\int_0^{\pi} f(t)dt$.

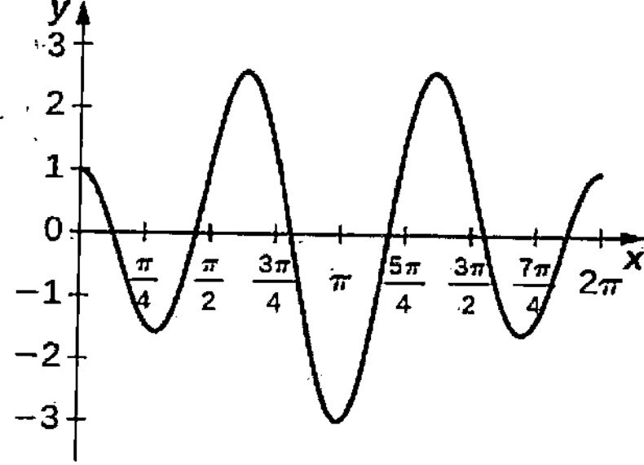

5.6 | Integrals Involving Exponential and Logarithmic Functions

Learning Objectives

5.6.1 Integrate functions involving exponential functions.
5.6.2 Integrate functions involving logarithmic functions.

Exponential and logarithmic functions are used to model population growth, cell growth, and financial growth, as well as depreciation, radioactive decay, and resource consumption, to name only a few applications. In this section, we explore integration involving exponential and logarithmic functions.

Integrals of Exponential Functions

The exponential function is perhaps the most efficient function in terms of the operations of calculus. The exponential function, $y = e^x$, is its own derivative and its own integral.

Rule: Integrals of Exponential Functions

Exponential functions can be integrated using the following formulas.

$$\begin{aligned} \int e^x dx &= e^x + C \\ \int a^x dx &= \frac{a^x}{\ln a} + C \end{aligned} \tag{5.21}$$

Example 5.37

Finding an Antiderivative of an Exponential Function

Find the antiderivative of the exponential function e^{-x}.

Solution

Use substitution, setting $u = -x$, and then $du = -1dx$. Multiply the du equation by -1, so you now have $-du = dx$. Then,

$$\begin{aligned} \int e^{-x}dx &= -\int e^u du \\ &= -e^u + C \\ &= -e^{-x} + C. \end{aligned}$$

5.31 Find the antiderivative of the function using substitution: $x^2 e^{-2x^3}$.

A common mistake when dealing with exponential expressions is treating the exponent on e the same way we treat exponents in polynomial expressions. We cannot use the power rule for the exponent on e. This can be especially confusing when we have both exponentials and polynomials in the same expression, as in the previous checkpoint. In these cases, we should always double-check to make sure we're using the right rules for the functions we're integrating.

Example 5.38

Square Root of an Exponential Function

Find the antiderivative of the exponential function $e^x\sqrt{1+e^x}$.

Solution

First rewrite the problem using a rational exponent:

$$\int e^x\sqrt{1+e^x}dx = \int e^x(1+e^x)^{1/2}dx.$$

Using substitution, choose $u = 1 + e^x.u = 1 + e^x$. Then, $du = e^x dx$. We have (**Figure 5.37**)

$$\int e^x(1+e^x)^{1/2}dx = \int u^{1/2}du.$$

Then

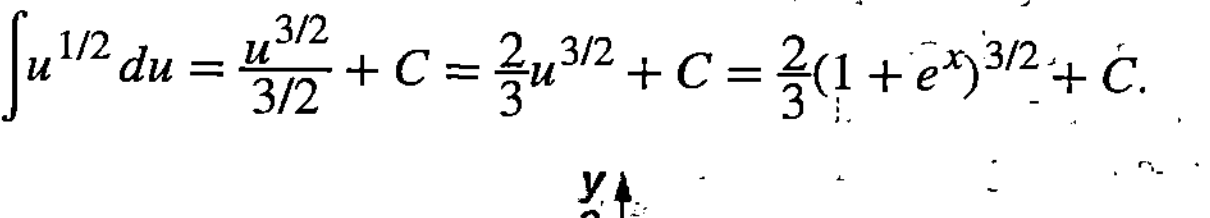

$$\int u^{1/2}du = \frac{u^{3/2}}{3/2} + C = \frac{2}{3}u^{3/2} + C = \frac{2}{3}(1+e^x)^{3/2} + C.$$

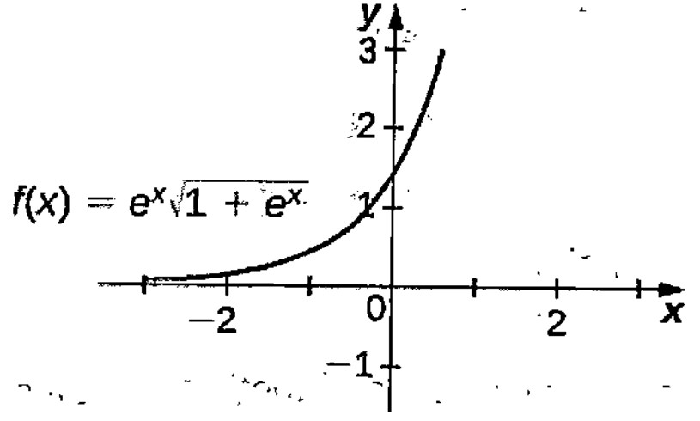

Figure 5.37 The graph shows an exponential function times the square root of an exponential function.

5.32 Find the antiderivative of $e^x(3e^x - 2)^2$.

Example 5.39

Using Substitution with an Exponential Function

Use substitution to evaluate the indefinite integral $\int 3x^2 e^{2x^3}dx$.

Solution

Here we choose to let u equal the expression in the exponent on e. Let $u = 2x^3$ and $du = 6x^2 dx$.. Again, du is off by a constant multiplier; the original function contains a factor of $3x^2$, not $6x^2$. Multiply both sides of the equation by $\frac{1}{2}$ so that the integrand in u equals the integrand in x. Thus,

$$\int 3x^2 e^{2x^3}dx = \frac{1}{2}\int e^u du.$$

Integrate the expression in u and then substitute the original expression in x back into the u integral:

$$\frac{1}{2}\int e^u du = \frac{1}{2}e^u + C = \frac{1}{2}e^{2x^3} + C.$$

5.33 Evaluate the indefinite integral $\int 2x^3 e^{x^4} dx$.

As mentioned at the beginning of this section, exponential functions are used in many real-life applications. The number e is often associated with compounded or accelerating growth, as we have seen in earlier sections about the derivative. Although the derivative represents a rate of change or a growth rate, the integral represents the total change or the total growth. Let's look at an example in which integration of an exponential function solves a common business application.

A price–demand function tells us the relationship between the quantity of a product demanded and the price of the product. In general, price decreases as quantity demanded increases. The marginal price–demand function is the derivative of the price–demand function and it tells us how fast the price changes at a given level of production. These functions are used in business to determine the price–elasticity of demand, and to help companies determine whether changing production levels would be profitable.

Example 5.40

Finding a Price–Demand Equation

Find the price–demand equation for a particular brand of toothpaste at a supermarket chain when the demand is 50 tubes per week at $2.35 per tube, given that the marginal price—demand function, $p'(x)$, for x number of tubes per week, is given as

$$p'(x) = -0.015e^{-0.01x}.$$

If the supermarket chain sells 100 tubes per week, what price should it set?

Solution

To find the price–demand equation, integrate the marginal price–demand function. First find the antiderivative, then look at the particulars. Thus,

$$\begin{aligned} p(x) &= \int -0.015e^{-0.01x} dx \\ &= -0.015\int e^{-0.01x} dx. \end{aligned}$$

Using substitution, let $u = -0.01x$ and $du = -0.01dx$. Then, divide both sides of the du equation by -0.01. This gives

$$\begin{aligned} \frac{-0.015}{-0.01}\int e^u du &= 1.5\int e^u du \\ &= 1.5e^u + C \\ &= 1.5e^{-0.01x} + C. \end{aligned}$$

The next step is to solve for C. We know that when the price is $2.35 per tube, the demand is 50 tubes per week. This means

$$\begin{aligned} p(50) &= 1.5e^{-0.01(50)} + C \\ &= 2.35. \end{aligned}$$

Now, just solve for C:

$$\begin{aligned} C &= 2.35 - 1.5e^{-0.5} \\ &= 2.35 - 0.91 \\ &= 1.44. \end{aligned}$$

Thus,

$$p(x) = 1.5e^{-0.01x} + 1.44.$$

If the supermarket sells 100 tubes of toothpaste per week, the price would be

$$p(100) = 1.5e^{-0.01(100)} + 1.44 = 1.5e^{-1} + 1.44 \approx 1.99.$$

The supermarket should charge $1.99 per tube if it is selling 100 tubes per week.

Example 5.41

Evaluating a Definite Integral Involving an Exponential Function

Evaluate the definite integral $\int_1^2 e^{1-x}\,dx.$

Solution

Again, substitution is the method to use. Let $u = 1 - x,$ so $du = -1dx$ or $-du = dx.$ Then $\int e^{1-x}\,dx = -\int e^u\,du.$ Next, change the limits of integration. Using the equation $u = 1 - x,$ we have

$$\begin{aligned} u &= 1 - (1) = 0 \\ u &= 1 - (2) = -1. \end{aligned}$$

The integral then becomes

$$\begin{aligned} \int_1^2 e^{1-x}\,dx &= -\int_0^{-1} e^u\,du \\ &= \int_{-1}^0 e^u\,du \\ &= e^u\big|_{-1}^0 \\ &= e^0 - \left(e^{-1}\right) \\ &= -e^{-1} + 1. \end{aligned}$$

See **Figure 5.38**.

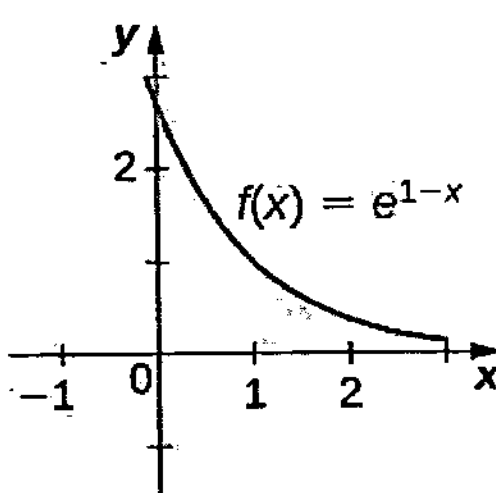

Figure 5.38 The indicated area can be calculated by evaluating a definite integral using substitution.

5.34 Evaluate $\int_0^2 e^{2x}\,dx.$

Example 5.42

Growth of Bacteria in a Culture

Suppose the rate of growth of bacteria in a Petri dish is given by $q(t) = 3^t,$ where t is given in hours and $q(t)$ is given in thousands of bacteria per hour. If a culture starts with 10,000 bacteria, find a function $Q(t)$ that gives the number of bacteria in the Petri dish at any time t. How many bacteria are in the dish after 2 hours?

Solution

We have

$$Q(t) = \int 3^t\,dt = \frac{3^t}{\ln 3} + C.$$

Then, at $t = 0$ we have $Q(0) = 10 = \frac{1}{\ln 3} + C,$ so $C \approx 9.090$ and we get

$$Q(t) = \frac{3^t}{\ln 3} + 9.090.$$

At time $t = 2,$ we have

$$\begin{aligned} Q(2) &= \frac{3^2}{\ln 3} + 9.090 \\ &= 17.282. \end{aligned}$$

After 2 hours, there are 17,282 bacteria in the dish.

5.35 From **Example 5.42**, suppose the bacteria grow at a rate of $q(t) = 2^t$. Assume the culture still starts with 10,000 bacteria. Find $Q(t)$. How many bacteria are in the dish after 3 hours?

Example 5.43

Fruit Fly Population Growth

Suppose a population of fruit flies increases at a rate of $g(t) = 2e^{0.02t}$, in flies per day. If the initial population of fruit flies is 100 flies, how many flies are in the population after 10 days?

Solution

Let $G(t)$ represent the number of flies in the population at time t. Applying the net change theorem, we have

$$\begin{aligned} G(10) &= G(0) + \int_0^{10} 2e^{0.02t}\,dt \\ &= 100 + \left[\frac{2}{0.02}e^{0.02t}\right]_0^{10} \\ &= 100 + \left[100e^{0.02t}\right]_0^{10} \\ &= 100 + 100e^{0.2} - 100 \\ &\approx 122. \end{aligned}$$

There are 122 flies in the population after 10 days.

5.36 Suppose the rate of growth of the fly population is given by $g(t) = e^{0.01t}$, and the initial fly population is 100 flies. How many flies are in the population after 15 days?

Example 5.44

Evaluating a Definite Integral Using Substitution

Evaluate the definite integral using substitution: $\displaystyle\int_1^2 \frac{e^{1/x}}{x^2}dx.$

Solution

This problem requires some rewriting to simplify applying the properties. First, rewrite the exponent on e as a power of x, then bring the x^2 in the denominator up to the numerator using a negative exponent. We have

$$\int_1^2 \frac{e^{1/x}}{x^2}dx = \int_1^2 e^{x^{-1}} x^{-2}\,dx.$$

Let $u = x^{-1}$, the exponent on e. Then

$$\begin{aligned} du &= -x^{-2}\,dx \\ -du &= x^{-2}\,dx. \end{aligned}$$

Bringing the negative sign outside the integral sign, the problem now reads

$$-\int e^u \, du.$$

Next, change the limits of integration:

$$u = (1)^{-1} = 1$$
$$u = (2)^{-1} = \frac{1}{2}.$$

Notice that now the limits begin with the larger number, meaning we must multiply by −1 and interchange the limits. Thus,

$$\begin{aligned} -\int_1^{1/2} e^u \, du &= \int_{1/2}^1 e^u \, du \\ &= e^u \Big|_{1/2}^1 \\ &= e - e^{1/2} \\ &= e - \sqrt{e}. \end{aligned}$$

 **5.37** Evaluate the definite integral using substitution: $\int_1^2 \frac{1}{x^3} e^{4x^{-2}} dx.$

Integrals Involving Logarithmic Functions

Integrating functions of the form $f(x) = x^{-1}$ result in the absolute value of the natural log function, as shown in the following rule. Integral formulas for other logarithmic functions, such as $f(x) = \ln x$ and $f(x) = \log_a x$, are also included in the rule.

Rule: Integration Formulas Involving Logarithmic Functions

The following formulas can be used to evaluate integrals involving logarithmic functions.

$$\begin{aligned} \int x^{-1} dx &= \ln|x| + C \\ \int \ln x \, dx &= x\ln x - x + C = x(\ln x - 1) + C \\ \int \log_a x \, dx &= \frac{x}{\ln a}(\ln x - 1) + C \end{aligned} \tag{5.22}$$

Example 5.45

Finding an Antiderivative Involving $\ln x$

Find the antiderivative of the function $\frac{3}{x - 10}$.

Solution

First factor the 3 outside the integral symbol. Then use the u^{-1} rule. Thus,

$$\begin{aligned}\int \frac{3}{x-10}dx &= 3\int \frac{1}{x-10}dx \\ &= 3\int \frac{du}{u} \\ &= 3\ln|u| + C \\ &= 3\ln|x-10| + C, \ x \neq 10.\end{aligned}$$

See **Figure 5.39**.

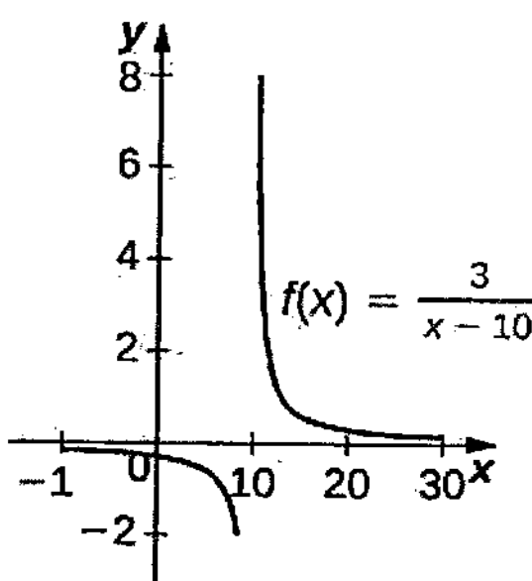

Figure 5.39 The domain of this function is $x \neq 10$.

5.38 Find the antiderivative of $\frac{1}{x+2}$.

Example 5.46

Finding an Antiderivative of a Rational Function

Find the antiderivative of $\frac{2x^3+3x}{x^4+3x^2}$.

Solution

This can be rewritten as $\int\left(2x^3+3x\right)\left(x^4+3x^2\right)^{-1}dx$. Use substitution. Let $u = x^4+3x^2$, then $du = 4x^3+6x$. Alter du by factoring out the 2. Thus,

$$\begin{aligned}du &= \left(4x^3+6x\right)dx \\ &= 2\left(2x^3+3x\right)dx \\ \frac{1}{2}du &= \left(2x^3+3x\right)dx.\end{aligned}$$

Rewrite the integrand in u:

$$\int (2x^3 + 3x)(x^4 + 3x^2)^{-1} dx = \frac{1}{2} \int u^{-1} du.$$

Then we have

$$\begin{aligned} \frac{1}{2} \int u^{-1} du &= \frac{1}{2} \ln |u| + C \\ &= \frac{1}{2} \ln |x^4 + 3x^2| + C. \end{aligned}$$

Example 5.47

Finding an Antiderivative of a Logarithmic Function

Find the antiderivative of the log function $\log_2 x$.

Solution

Follow the format in the formula listed in the rule on integration formulas involving logarithmic functions. Based on this format, we have

$$\int \log_2 x dx = \frac{x}{\ln 2} (\ln x - 1) + C.$$

5.39 Find the antiderivative of $\log_3 x$.

Example 5.48 is a definite integral of a trigonometric function. With trigonometric functions, we often have to apply a trigonometric property or an identity before we can move forward. Finding the right form of the integrand is usually the key to a smooth integration.

Example 5.48

Evaluating a Definite Integral

Find the definite integral of $\int_0^{\pi/2} \frac{\sin x}{1 + \cos x} dx$.

Solution

We need substitution to evaluate this problem. Let $u = 1 + \cos x$, , so $du = -\sin x \, dx$. Rewrite the integral in terms of u, changing the limits of integration as well. Thus,

$$\begin{aligned} u &= 1 + \cos(0) = 2 \\ u &= 1 + \cos\left(\frac{\pi}{2}\right) = 1. \end{aligned}$$

Then

$$\begin{aligned}\int_0^{\pi/2} \frac{\sin x}{1+\cos x} &= -\int_2^1 u^{-1}\,du \\ &= \int_1^2 u^{-1}\,du \\ &= \ln|u|\big|_1^2 \\ &= [\ln 2 - \ln 1] \\ &= \ln 2.\end{aligned}$$

5.6 EXERCISES

In the following exercises, compute each indefinite integral.

320. $\int e^{2x}dx$

321. $\int e^{-3x}dx$

322. $\int 2^x dx$

323. $\int 3^{-x}dx$

324. $\int \frac{1}{2x}dx$

325. $\int \frac{2}{x}dx$

326. $\int \frac{1}{x^2}dx$

327. $\int \frac{1}{\sqrt{x}}dx$

In the following exercises, find each indefinite integral by using appropriate substitutions.

328. $\int \frac{\ln x}{x}dx$

329. $\int \frac{dx}{x(\ln x)^2}$

330. $\int \frac{dx}{x\ln x}\ (x > 1)$

331. $\int \frac{dx}{x\ln x\ln(\ln x)}$

332. $\int \tan\theta\, d\theta$

333. $\int \frac{\cos x - x\sin x}{x\cos x}dx$

334. $\int \frac{\ln(\sin x)}{\tan x}dx$

335. $\int \ln(\cos x)\tan x dx$

336. $\int xe^{-x^2}dx$

337. $\int x^2 e^{-x^3}dx$

338. $\int e^{\sin x}\cos x dx$

339. $\int e^{\tan x}\sec^2 x dx$

340. $\int e^{\ln x}\frac{dx}{x}$

341. $\int \frac{e^{\ln(1-t)}}{1-t}dt$

In the following exercises, verify by differentiation that $\int \ln x\, dx = x(\ln x - 1) + C,$ then use appropriate changes of variables to compute the integral.

342. $\int \ln x dx$ (*Hint*: $\int \ln x dx = \frac{1}{2}\int x\ln\left(x^2\right)dx$)

343. $\int x^2 \ln^2 x\, dx$

344. $\int \frac{\ln x}{x^2}dx$ (*Hint*: Set $u = \frac{1}{x}$.)

345. $\int \frac{\ln x}{\sqrt{x}}dx$ (*Hint*: Set $u = \sqrt{x}$.)

346. Write an integral to express the area under the graph of $y = \frac{1}{t}$ from $t = 1$ to e^x and evaluate the integral.

347. Write an integral to express the area under the graph of $y = e^t$ between $t = 0$ and $t = \ln x,$ and evaluate the integral.

In the following exercises, use appropriate substitutions to express the trigonometric integrals in terms of compositions with logarithms.

348. $\int \tan(2x)dx$

349. $\int \frac{\sin(3x) - \cos(3x)}{\sin(3x) + \cos(3x)}dx$

350. $\int \frac{x\sin\left(x^2\right)}{\cos\left(x^2\right)}dx$

351. $\int x\csc\left(x^2\right)dx$

352. $\int \ln(\cos x)\tan x\, dx$

353. $\int \ln(\csc x)\cot x dx$

354. $\int \frac{e^x - e^{-x}}{e^x + e^{-x}} dx$

In the following exercises, evaluate the definite integral.

355. $\int_1^2 \frac{1 + 2x + x^2}{3x + 3x^2 + x^3} dx$

356. $\int_0^{\pi/4} \tan x\, dx$

357. $\int_0^{\pi/3} \frac{\sin x - \cos x}{\sin x + \cos x} dx$

358. $\int_{\pi/6}^{\pi/2} \csc x dx$

359. $\int_{\pi/4}^{\pi/3} \cot x dx$

In the following exercises, integrate using the indicated substitution.

360. $\int \frac{x}{x - 100} dx;\ u = x - 100$

361. $\int \frac{y - 1}{y + 1} dy;\ u = y + 1$

362. $\int \frac{1 - x^2}{3x - x^3} dx;\ u = 3x - x^3$

363. $\int \frac{\sin x + \cos x}{\sin x - \cos x} dx;\ u = \sin x - \cos x$

364. $\int e^{2x}\sqrt{1 - e^{2x}} dx;\ u = e^{2x}$

365. $\int \ln(x)\frac{\sqrt{1 - (\ln x)^2}}{x} dx;\ u = \ln x$

In the following exercises, does the right-endpoint approximation overestimate or underestimate the exact area? Calculate the right endpoint estimate R_{50} and solve for the exact area.

366. **[T]** $y = e^x$ over $[0, 1]$

367. **[T]** $y = e^{-x}$ over $[0, 1]$

368. **[T]** $y = \ln(x)$ over $[1, 2]$

369. **[T]** $y = \frac{x + 1}{x^2 + 2x + 6}$ over $[0, 1]$

370. **[T]** $y = 2^x$ over $[-1, 0]$

371. **[T]** $y = -2^{-x}$ over $[0, 1]$

In the following exercises, $f(x) \geq 0$ for $a \leq x \leq b$. Find the area under the graph of $f(x)$ between the given values a and b by integrating.

372. $f(x) = \frac{\log_{10}(x)}{x};\ a = 10, b = 100$

373. $f(x) = \frac{\log_2(x)}{x};\ a = 32, b = 64$

374. $f(x) = 2^{-x};\ a = 1, b = 2$

375. $f(x) = 2^{-x};\ a = 3, b = 4$

376. Find the area under the graph of the function $f(x) = xe^{-x^2}$ between $x = 0$ and $x = 5$.

377. Compute the integral of $f(x) = xe^{-x^2}$ and find the smallest value of N such that the area under the graph $f(x) = xe^{-x^2}$ between $x = N$ and $x = N + 10$ is, at most, 0.01.

378. Find the limit, as N tends to infinity, of the area under the graph of $f(x) = xe^{-x^2}$ between $x = 0$ and $x = 5$.

379. Show that $\int_a^b \frac{dt}{t} = \int_{1/b}^{1/a} \frac{dt}{t}$ when $0 < a \leq b$.

380. Suppose that $f(x) > 0$ for all x and that f and g are differentiable. Use the identity $f^g = e^{g \ln f}$ and the chain rule to find the derivative of f^g.

381. Use the previous exercise to find the antiderivative of $h(x) = x^x(1 + \ln x)$ and evaluate $\int_2^3 x^x(1 + \ln x)dx.$

382. Show that if $c > 0,$ then the integral of $1/x$ from ac to bc $(0 < a < b)$ is the same as the integral of $1/x$ from a to b.

The following exercises are intended to derive the fundamental properties of the natural log starting from the *definition* $\ln(x) = \int_1^x \frac{dt}{t}$, using properties of the definite integral and making no further assumptions.

383. Use the identity $\ln(x) = \int_1^x \frac{dt}{t}$ to derive the identity $\ln\left(\frac{1}{x}\right) = -\ln x$.

384. Use a change of variable in the integral $\int_1^{xy} \frac{1}{t}dt$ to show that $\ln xy = \ln x + \ln y$ for $x, y > 0$.

385. Use the identity $\ln x = \int_1^x \frac{dt}{x}$ to show that $\ln(x)$ is an increasing function of x on $[0, \infty)$, and use the previous exercises to show that the range of $\ln(x)$ is $(-\infty, \infty)$. Without any further assumptions, conclude that $\ln(x)$ has an inverse function defined on $(-\infty, \infty)$.

386. Pretend, for the moment, that we do not know that e^x is the inverse function of $\ln(x)$, but keep in mind that $\ln(x)$ has an inverse function defined on $(-\infty, \infty)$. Call it E. Use the identity $\ln xy = \ln x + \ln y$ to deduce that $E(a + b) = E(a)E(b)$ for any real numbers a, b.

387. Pretend, for the moment, that we do not know that e^x is the inverse function of $\ln x$, but keep in mind that $\ln x$ has an inverse function defined on $(-\infty, \infty)$. Call it E. Show that $E'(t) = E(t)$.

388. The sine integral, defined as $S(x) = \int_0^x \frac{\sin t}{t}dt$ is an important quantity in engineering. Although it does not have a simple closed formula, it is possible to estimate its behavior for large x. Show that for $k \geq 1$, $|S(2\pi k) - S(2\pi(k + 1))| \leq \frac{1}{k(2k + 1)\pi}$.

(*Hint*: $\sin(t + \pi) = -\sin t$)

389. **[T]** The normal distribution in probability is given by $p(x) = \frac{1}{\sigma\sqrt{2\pi}}e^{-(x - \mu)^2/2\sigma^2}$, where σ is the standard deviation and μ is the average. The *standard normal distribution* in probability, p_s, corresponds to $\mu = 0$ and $\sigma = 1$. Compute the left endpoint estimates R_{10} and R_{100} of $\int_{-1}^{1} \frac{1}{\sqrt{2\pi}}e^{-x^{2/2}}dx$.

390. **[T]** Compute the right endpoint estimates R_{50} and R_{100} of $\int_{-3}^{5} \frac{1}{2\sqrt{2\pi}}e^{-(x - 1)^2/8}$.

5.7 | Integrals Resulting in Inverse Trigonometric Functions

Learning Objectives

5.7.1 Integrate functions resulting in inverse trigonometric functions

In this section we focus on integrals that result in inverse trigonometric functions. We have worked with these functions before. Recall from **Functions and Graphs** that trigonometric functions are not one-to-one unless the domains are restricted. When working with inverses of trigonometric functions, we always need to be careful to take these restrictions into account. Also in **Derivatives**, we developed formulas for derivatives of inverse trigonometric functions. The formulas developed there give rise directly to integration formulas involving inverse trigonometric functions.

Integrals that Result in Inverse Sine Functions

Let us begin this last section of the chapter with the three formulas. Along with these formulas, we use substitution to evaluate the integrals. We prove the formula for the inverse sine integral.

Rule: Integration Formulas Resulting in Inverse Trigonometric Functions

The following integration formulas yield inverse trigonometric functions:

1.
$$\int \frac{du}{\sqrt{a^2 - u^2}} = \sin^{-1}\frac{u}{a} + C \tag{5.23}$$

2.
$$\int \frac{du}{a^2 + u^2} = \frac{1}{a}\tan^{-1}\frac{u}{a} + C \tag{5.24}$$

3.
$$\int \frac{du}{u\sqrt{u^2 - a^2}} = \frac{1}{a}\sec^{-1}\frac{u}{a} + C \tag{5.25}$$

Proof

Let $y = \sin^{-1}\frac{x}{a}$. Then $a\sin y = x$. Now let's use implicit differentiation. We obtain

$$\begin{aligned} \frac{d}{dx}(a\sin y) &= \frac{d}{dx}(x) \\ a\cos y\frac{dy}{dx} &= 1 \\ \frac{dy}{dx} &= \frac{1}{a\cos y}. \end{aligned}$$

For $-\frac{\pi}{2} \le y \le \frac{\pi}{2}$, $\cos y \ge 0$. Thus, applying the Pythagorean identity $\sin^2 y + \cos^2 y = 1$, we have $\cos y = \sqrt{1 = \sin^2 y}$. This gives

$$\begin{aligned}\frac{1}{a\cos y} &= \frac{1}{a\sqrt{1-\sin^2 y}} \\ &= \frac{1}{\sqrt{a^2 - a^2\sin^2 y}} \\ &= \frac{1}{\sqrt{a^2 - x^2}}.\end{aligned}$$

Then for $-a \le x \le a,$ we have

$$\int \frac{1}{\sqrt{a^2 - u^2}} du = \sin^{-1}\left(\frac{u}{a}\right) + C.$$

□

Example 5.49

Evaluating a Definite Integral Using Inverse Trigonometric Functions

Evaluate the definite integral $\displaystyle\int_0^1 \frac{dx}{\sqrt{1-x^2}}.$

Solution

We can go directly to the formula for the antiderivative in the rule on integration formulas resulting in inverse trigonometric functions, and then evaluate the definite integral. We have

$$\begin{aligned}\int_0^1 \frac{dx}{\sqrt{1-x^2}} &= \sin^{-1} x\Big|_0^1 \\ &= \sin^{-1} 1 - \sin^{-1} 0 \\ &= \frac{\pi}{2} - 0 \\ &= \frac{\pi}{2}.\end{aligned}$$

5.40 Find the antiderivative of $\displaystyle\int \frac{dx}{\sqrt{1-16x^2}}.$

Example 5.50

Finding an Antiderivative Involving an Inverse Trigonometric Function

Evaluate the integral $\displaystyle\int \frac{dx}{\sqrt{4-9x^2}}.$

Solution

Substitute $u = 3x$. Then $du = 3dx$ and we have

$$\int \frac{dx}{\sqrt{4 - 9x^2}} = \frac{1}{3} \int \frac{du}{\sqrt{4 - u^2}}.$$

Applying the formula with $a = 2$, we obtain

$$\begin{aligned}\int \frac{dx}{\sqrt{4 - 9x^2}} &= \frac{1}{3} \int \frac{du}{\sqrt{4 - u^2}} \\ &= \frac{1}{3} \sin^{-1}\left(\frac{u}{2}\right) + C \\ &= \frac{1}{3} \sin^{-1}\left(\frac{3x}{2}\right) + C.\end{aligned}$$

5.41 Find the indefinite integral using an inverse trigonometric function and substitution for $\int \frac{dx}{\sqrt{9 - x^2}}$.

Example 5.51

Evaluating a Definite Integral

Evaluate the definite integral $\int_0^{\sqrt{3}/2} \frac{du}{\sqrt{1 - u^2}}$.

Solution

The format of the problem matches the inverse sine formula. Thus,

$$\begin{aligned}\int_0^{\sqrt{3}/2} \frac{du}{\sqrt{1 - u^2}} &= \sin^{-1} u \Big|_0^{\sqrt{3}/2} \\ &= \left[\sin^{-1}\left(\frac{\sqrt{3}}{2}\right)\right] - \left[\sin^{-1}(0)\right] \\ &= \frac{\pi}{3}.\end{aligned}$$

Integrals Resulting in Other Inverse Trigonometric Functions

There are six inverse trigonometric functions. However, only three integration formulas are noted in the rule on integration formulas resulting in inverse trigonometric functions because the remaining three are negative versions of the ones we use. The only difference is whether the integrand is positive or negative. Rather than memorizing three more formulas, if the integrand is negative, simply factor out -1 and evaluate the integral using one of the formulas already provided. To close this section, we examine one more formula: the integral resulting in the inverse tangent function.

Example 5.52

Finding an Antiderivative Involving the Inverse Tangent Function

Find an antiderivative of $\int \frac{1}{1+4x^2}dx.$

Solution

Comparing this problem with the formulas stated in the rule on integration formulas resulting in inverse trigonometric functions, the integrand looks similar to the formula for $\tan^{-1} u + C.$ So we use substitution, letting $u = 2x,$ then $du = 2dx$ and $1/2du = dx.$ Then, we have

$$\frac{1}{2}\int \frac{1}{1+u^2}du = \frac{1}{2}\tan^{-1} u + C = \frac{1}{2}\tan^{-1}(2x) + C.$$

5.42 Use substitution to find the antiderivative of $\int \frac{dx}{25+4x^2}.$

Example 5.53

Applying the Integration Formulas

Find the antiderivative of $\int \frac{1}{9+x^2}dx.$

Solution

Apply the formula with $a = 3.$ Then,

$$\int \frac{dx}{9+x^2} = \frac{1}{3}\tan^{-1}\left(\frac{x}{3}\right) + C.$$

5.43 Find the antiderivative of $\int \frac{dx}{16+x^2}.$

Example 5.54

Evaluating a Definite Integral

Evaluate the definite integral $\int_{\sqrt{3}/3}^{\sqrt{3}} \frac{dx}{1+x^2}.$

Solution

Use the formula for the inverse tangent. We have

$$\begin{aligned}\int_{\sqrt{3}/3}^{\sqrt{3}} \frac{dx}{1+x^2} &= \tan^{-1} x \Big|_{\sqrt{3}/3}^{\sqrt{3}} \\ &= \left[\tan^{-1}(\sqrt{3})\right] - \left[\tan^{-1}\left(\frac{\sqrt{3}}{3}\right)\right] \\ &= \frac{\pi}{6}.\end{aligned}$$

5.44 Evaluate the definite integral $\int_0^2 \frac{dx}{4+x^2}$.

5.7 EXERCISES

In the following exercises, evaluate each integral in terms of an inverse trigonometric function.

391. $\displaystyle\int_0^{\sqrt{3}/2} \frac{dx}{\sqrt{1-x^2}}$

392. $\displaystyle\int_{-1/2}^{1/2} \frac{dx}{\sqrt{1-x^2}}$

393. $\displaystyle\int_{\sqrt{3}}^{1} \frac{dx}{\sqrt{1+x^2}}$

394. $\displaystyle\int_{1/\sqrt{3}}^{\sqrt{3}} \frac{dx}{1+x^2}$

395. $\displaystyle\int_1^{\sqrt{2}} \frac{dx}{|x|\sqrt{x^2-1}}$

396. $\displaystyle\int_1^{2/\sqrt{3}} \frac{dx}{|x|\sqrt{x^2-1}}$

In the following exercises, find each indefinite integral, using appropriate substitutions.

397. $\displaystyle\int \frac{dx}{\sqrt{9-x^2}}$

398. $\displaystyle\int \frac{dx}{\sqrt{1-16x^2}}$

399. $\displaystyle\int \frac{dx}{9+x^2}$

400. $\displaystyle\int \frac{dx}{25+16x^2}$

401. $\displaystyle\int \frac{dx}{|x|\sqrt{x^2-9}}$

402. $\displaystyle\int \frac{dx}{|x|\sqrt{4x^2-16}}$

403. Explain the relationship $-\cos^{-1} t + C = \displaystyle\int \frac{dt}{\sqrt{1-t^2}} = \sin^{-1} t + C.$ Is it true, in general, that $\cos^{-1} t = -\sin^{-1} t$?

404. Explain the relationship $\sec^{-1} t + C = \displaystyle\int \frac{dt}{|t|\sqrt{t^2-1}} = -\csc^{-1} t + C.$ Is it true, in general, that $\sec^{-1} t = -\csc^{-1} t$?

405. Explain what is wrong with the following integral: $\displaystyle\int_1^2 \frac{dt}{\sqrt{1-t^2}}.$

406. Explain what is wrong with the following integral: $\displaystyle\int_{-1}^1 \frac{dt}{|t|\sqrt{t^2-1}}.$

In the following exercises, solve for the antiderivative $\int f$ of f with $C = 0,$ then use a calculator to graph f and the antiderivative over the given interval $[a, b].$ Identify a value of C such that adding C to the antiderivative recovers the definite integral $F(x) = \int_a^x f(t)dt.$

407. **[T]** $\displaystyle\int \frac{1}{\sqrt{9-x^2}}dx$ over $[-3, 3]$

408. **[T]** $\displaystyle\int \frac{9}{9+x^2}dx$ over $[-6, 6]$

409. **[T]** $\displaystyle\int \frac{\cos x}{4+\sin^2 x}dx$ over $[-6, 6]$

410. **[T]** $\displaystyle\int \frac{e^x}{1+e^{2x}}dx$ over $[-6, 6]$

In the following exercises, compute the antiderivative using appropriate substitutions.

411. $\displaystyle\int \frac{\sin^{-1} t dt}{\sqrt{1-t^2}}$

412. $\displaystyle\int \frac{dt}{\sin^{-1} t\sqrt{1-t^2}}$

413. $\int \frac{\tan^{-1}(2t)}{1+4t^2} dt$

414. $\int \frac{t\tan^{-1}(t^2)}{1+t^4} dt$

415. $\int \frac{\sec^{-1}\left(\frac{t}{2}\right)}{|t|\sqrt{t^2-4}} dt$

416. $\int \frac{t\sec^{-1}(t^2)}{t^2\sqrt{t^4-1}} dt$

In the following exercises, use a calculator to graph the antiderivative $\int f$ with $C = 0$ over the given interval $[a, b]$. Approximate a value of C, if possible, such that adding C to the antiderivative gives the same value as the definite integral $F(x) = \int_a^x f(t)dt$.

417. **[T]** $\int \frac{1}{x\sqrt{x^2-4}} dx$ over $[2, 6]$

418. **[T]** $\int \frac{1}{(2x+2)\sqrt{x}} dx$ over $[0, 6]$

419. **[T]** $\int \frac{(\sin x + x\cos x)}{1 + x^2 \sin^2 x} dx$ over $[-6, 6]$

420. **[T]** $\int \frac{2e^{-2x}}{\sqrt{1-e^{-4x}}} dx$ over $[0, 2]$

421. **[T]** $\int \frac{1}{x + x\ln^2 x}$ over $[0, 2]$

422. **[T]** $\int \frac{\sin^{-1} x}{\sqrt{1-x^2}}$ over $[-1, 1]$

In the following exercises, compute each integral using appropriate substitutions.

423. $\int \frac{e^x}{\sqrt{1-e^{2t}}} dt$

424. $\int \frac{e^t}{1+e^{2t}} dt$

425. $\int \frac{dt}{t\sqrt{1-\ln^2 t}}$

426. $\int \frac{dt}{t\left(1+\ln^2 t\right)}$

427. $\int \frac{\cos^{-1}(2t)}{\sqrt{1-4t^2}} dt$

428. $\int \frac{e^t \cos^{-1}(e^t)}{\sqrt{1-e^{2t}}} dt$

In the following exercises, compute each definite integral.

429. $\int_0^{1/2} \frac{\tan\left(\sin^{-1} t\right)}{\sqrt{1-t^2}} dt$

430. $\int_{1/4}^{1/2} \frac{\tan\left(\cos^{-1} t\right)}{\sqrt{1-t^2}} dt$

431. $\int_0^{1/2} \frac{\sin\left(\tan^{-1} t\right)}{1+t^2} dt$

432. $\int_0^{1/2} \frac{\cos\left(\tan^{-1} t\right)}{1+t^2} dt$

433. For $A > 0$, compute $I(A) = \int_{-A}^{A} \frac{dt}{1+t^2}$ and evaluate $\lim_{a \to \infty} I(A)$, the area under the graph of $\frac{1}{1+t^2}$ on $[-\infty, \infty]$.

434. For $1 < B < \infty$, compute $I(B) = \int_1^B \frac{dt}{t\sqrt{t^2-1}}$ and evaluate $\lim_{B \to \infty} I(B)$, the area under the graph of $\frac{1}{t\sqrt{t^2-1}}$ over $[1, \infty)$.

435. Use the substitution $u = \sqrt{2}\cot x$ and the identity $1 + \cot^2 x = \csc^2 x$ to evaluate $\int \frac{dx}{1+\cos^2 x}$. (*Hint:* Multiply the top and bottom of the integrand by $\csc^2 x$.)

436. **[T]** Approximate the points at which the graphs of $f(x) = 2x^2 - 1$ and $g(x) = \left(1 + 4x^2\right)^{-3/2}$ intersect, and approximate the area between their graphs accurate to three decimal places.

437. 47. **[T]** Approximate the points at which the graphs of $f(x) = x^2 - 1$ and $f(x) = x^2 - 1$ intersect, and approximate the area between their graphs accurate to three decimal places.

438. Use the following graph to prove that $\int_0^x \sqrt{1 - t^2}dt = \frac{1}{2}x\sqrt{1 - x^2} + \frac{1}{2}\sin^{-1} x.$

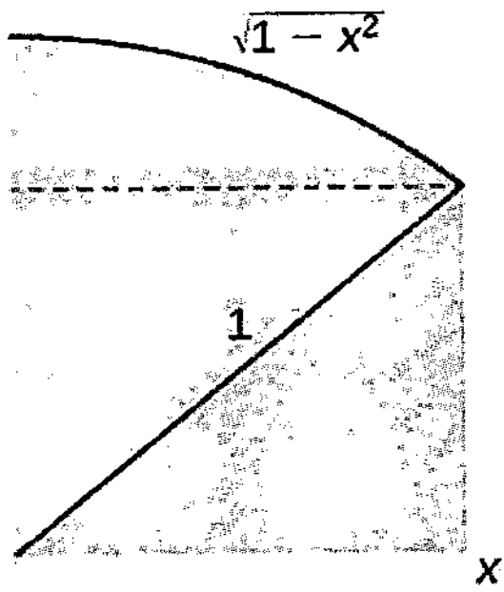

CHAPTER 5 REVIEW

KEY TERMS

average value of a function (or f_{ave}) the average value of a function on an interval can be found by calculating the definite integral of the function and dividing that value by the length of the interval

change of variables the substitution of a variable, such as u, for an expression in the integrand

definite integral a primary operation of calculus; the area between the curve and the x-axis over a given interval is a definite integral

fundamental theorem of calculus the theorem, central to the entire development of calculus, that establishes the relationship between differentiation and integration

fundamental theorem of calculus, part 1 uses a definite integral to define an antiderivative of a function

fundamental theorem of calculus, part 2 (also, **evaluation theorem**) we can evaluate a definite integral by evaluating the antiderivative of the integrand at the endpoints of the interval and subtracting

integrable function a function is integrable if the limit defining the integral exists; in other words, if the limit of the Riemann sums as n goes to infinity exists

integrand the function to the right of the integration symbol; the integrand includes the function being integrated

integration by substitution a technique for integration that allows integration of functions that are the result of a chain-rule derivative

left-endpoint approximation an approximation of the area under a curve computed by using the left endpoint of each subinterval to calculate the height of the vertical sides of each rectangle

limits of integration these values appear near the top and bottom of the integral sign and define the interval over which the function should be integrated

lower sum a sum obtained by using the minimum value of $f(x)$ on each subinterval

mean value theorem for integrals guarantees that a point c exists such that $f(c)$ is equal to the average value of the function

net change theorem if we know the rate of change of a quantity, the net change theorem says the future quantity is equal to the initial quantity plus the integral of the rate of change of the quantity

net signed area the area between a function and the x-axis such that the area below the x-axis is subtracted from the area above the x-axis; the result is the same as the definite integral of the function

partition a set of points that divides an interval into subintervals

regular partition a partition in which the subintervals all have the same width

riemann sum an estimate of the area under the curve of the form $A \approx \sum_{i=1}^{n} f(x_i^*)\Delta x$

right-endpoint approximation the right-endpoint approximation is an approximation of the area of the rectangles under a curve using the right endpoint of each subinterval to construct the vertical sides of each rectangle

sigma notation (also, **summation notation**) the Greek letter sigma (Σ) indicates addition of the values; the values of the index above and below the sigma indicate where to begin the summation and where to end it

total area total area between a function and the x-axis is calculated by adding the area above the x-axis and the area below the x-axis; the result is the same as the definite integral of the absolute value of the function

upper sum a sum obtained by using the maximum value of $f(x)$ on each subinterval

variable of integration indicates which variable you are integrating with respect to; if it is x, then the function in the integrand is followed by dx

KEY EQUATIONS

- **Properties of Sigma Notation**

$$\sum_{i=1}^{n} c = nc$$

$$\sum_{i=1}^{n} ca_i = c\sum_{i=1}^{n} a_i$$

$$\sum_{i=1}^{n} (a_i + b_i) = \sum_{i=1}^{n} a_i + \sum_{i=1}^{n} b_i$$

$$\sum_{i=1}^{n} (a_i - b_i) = \sum_{i=1}^{n} a_i - \sum_{i=1}^{n} b_i$$

$$\sum_{i=1}^{n} a_i = \sum_{i=1}^{m} a_i + \sum_{i=m+1}^{n} a_i$$

- **Sums and Powers of Integers**

$$\sum_{i=1}^{n} i = 1 + 2 + \cdots + n = \frac{n(n+1)}{2}$$

$$\sum_{i=1}^{n} i^2 = 1^2 + 2^2 + \cdots + n^2 = \frac{n(n+1)(2n+1)}{6}$$

$$\sum_{i=0}^{n} i^3 = 1^3 + 2^3 + \cdots + n^3 = \frac{n^2(n+1)^2}{4}$$

- **Left-Endpoint Approximation**

$$A \approx L_n = f(x_0)\Delta x + f(x_1)\Delta x + \cdots + f(x_{n-1})\Delta x = \sum_{i=1}^{n} f(x_{i-1})\Delta x$$

- **Right-Endpoint Approximation**

$$A \approx R_n = f(x_1)\Delta x + f(x_2)\Delta x + \cdots + f(x_n)\Delta x = \sum_{i=1}^{n} f(x_i)\Delta x$$

- **Definite Integral**

$$\int_a^b f(x)dx = \lim_{n \to \infty} \sum_{i=1}^{n} f(x_i^*)\Delta x$$

- **Properties of the Definite Integral**

$$\int_a^a f(x)dx = 0$$

$$\int_b^a f(x)dx = -\int_a^b f(x)dx$$

$$\int_a^b [f(x) + g(x)]dx = \int_a^b f(x)dx + \int_a^b g(x)dx$$

$$\int_a^b [f(x) - g(x)]dx = \int_a^b f(x)dx - \int_a^b g(x)dx$$

$$\int_a^b cf(x)dx = c\int_a^b f(x) \text{ for constant } c$$

$$\int_a^b f(x)dx = \int_a^c f(x)dx + \int_c^b f(x)dx$$

- **Mean Value Theorem for Integrals**

If $f(x)$ is continuous over an interval $[a, b]$, then there is at least one point $c \in [a, b]$ such that $f(c) = \frac{1}{b-a}\int_a^b f(x)dx.$

- **Fundamental Theorem of Calculus Part 1**
  If $f(x)$ is continuous over an interval $[a, b]$, and the function $F(x)$ is defined by $F(x) = \int_a^x f(t)dt,$ then $F'(x) = f(x).$
- **Fundamental Theorem of Calculus Part 2**
  If f is continuous over the interval $[a, b]$ and $F(x)$ is any antiderivative of $f(x)$, then $\int_a^b f(x)dx = F(b) - F(a).$
- **Net Change Theorem**
  $F(b) = F(a) + \int_a^b F'(x)dx$ or $\int_a^b F'(x)dx = F(b) - F(a)$
- **Substitution with Indefinite Integrals**
  $\int f[g(x)]g'(x)dx = \int f(u)du = F(u) + C = F(g(x)) + C$
- **Substitution with Definite Integrals**
  $\int_a^b f(g(x))g'(x)dx = \int_{g(a)}^{g(b)} f(u)du$
- **Integrals of Exponential Functions**
  $\int e^x\,dx = e^x + C$
  $\int a^x\,dx = \frac{a^x}{\ln a} + C$
- **Integration Formulas Involving Logarithmic Functions**
  $\int x^{-1}\,dx = \ln|x| + C$
  $\int \ln x\,dx = x\ln x - x + C = x(\ln x - 1) + C$
  $\int \log_a x\,dx = \frac{x}{\ln a}(\ln x - 1) + C$
- **Integrals That Produce Inverse Trigonometric Functions**
  $\int \frac{du}{\sqrt{a^2 - u^2}} = \sin^{-1}\left(\frac{u}{a}\right) + C$
  $\int \frac{du}{a^2 + u^2} = \frac{1}{a}\tan^{-1}\left(\frac{u}{a}\right) + C$
  $\int \frac{du}{u\sqrt{u^2 - a^2}} = \frac{1}{a}\sec^{-1}\left(\frac{u}{a}\right) + C$

KEY CONCEPTS

5.1 Approximating Areas

- The use of sigma (summation) notation of the form $\sum_{i=1}^{n} a_i$ is useful for expressing long sums of values in compact form.

- For a continuous function defined over an interval $[a, b]$, the process of dividing the interval into n equal parts, extending a rectangle to the graph of the function, calculating the areas of the series of rectangles, and then summing the areas yields an approximation of the area of that region.
- The width of each rectangle is $\Delta x = \frac{b-a}{n}$.
- Riemann sums are expressions of the form $\sum_{i=1}^{n} f(x_i^*)\Delta x$, and can be used to estimate the area under the curve $y = f(x)$. Left- and right-endpoint approximations are special kinds of Riemann sums where the values of $\{x_i^*\}$ are chosen to be the left or right endpoints of the subintervals, respectively.
- Riemann sums allow for much flexibility in choosing the set of points $\{x_i^*\}$ at which the function is evaluated, often with an eye to obtaining a lower sum or an upper sum.

5.2 The Definite Integral

- The definite integral can be used to calculate net signed area, which is the area above the x-axis less the area below the x-axis. Net signed area can be positive, negative, or zero.
- The component parts of the definite integral are the integrand, the variable of integration, and the limits of integration.
- Continuous functions on a closed interval are integrable. Functions that are not continuous may still be integrable, depending on the nature of the discontinuities.
- The properties of definite integrals can be used to evaluate integrals.
- The area under the curve of many functions can be calculated using geometric formulas.
- The average value of a function can be calculated using definite integrals.

5.3 The Fundamental Theorem of Calculus

- The Mean Value Theorem for Integrals states that for a continuous function over a closed interval, there is a value c such that $f(c)$ equals the average value of the function. See **The Mean Value Theorem for Integrals.**
- The Fundamental Theorem of Calculus, Part 1 shows the relationship between the derivative and the integral. See **Fundamental Theorem of Calculus, Part 1.**
- The Fundamental Theorem of Calculus, Part 2 is a formula for evaluating a definite integral in terms of an antiderivative of its integrand. The total area under a curve can be found using this formula. See **The Fundamental Theorem of Calculus, Part 2.**

5.4 Integration Formulas and the Net Change Theorem

- The net change theorem states that when a quantity changes, the final value equals the initial value plus the integral of the rate of change. Net change can be a positive number, a negative number, or zero.
- The area under an even function over a symmetric interval can be calculated by doubling the area over the positive x-axis. For an odd function, the integral over a symmetric interval equals zero, because half the area is negative.

5.5 Substitution

- Substitution is a technique that simplifies the integration of functions that are the result of a chain-rule derivative. The term 'substitution' refers to changing variables or substituting the variable u and du for appropriate expressions in the integrand.
- When using substitution for a definite integral, we also have to change the limits of integration.

5.6 Integrals Involving Exponential and Logarithmic Functions

- Exponential and logarithmic functions arise in many real-world applications, especially those involving growth and decay.
- Substitution is often used to evaluate integrals involving exponential functions or logarithms.

5.7 Integrals Resulting in Inverse Trigonometric Functions

- Formulas for derivatives of inverse trigonometric functions developed in **Derivatives of Exponential and Logarithmic Functions** lead directly to integration formulas involving inverse trigonometric functions.
- Use the formulas listed in the rule on integration formulas resulting in inverse trigonometric functions to match up the correct format and make alterations as necessary to solve the problem.
- Substitution is often required to put the integrand in the correct form.

CHAPTER 5 REVIEW EXERCISES

True or False. Justify your answer with a proof or a counterexample. Assume all functions f and g are continuous over their domains.

439. If $f(x) > 0, f'(x) > 0$ for all x, then the right-hand rule underestimates the integral $\int_a^b f(x)$. Use a graph to justify your answer.

440. $\int_a^b f(x)^2 dx = \int_a^b f(x)dx \int_a^b f(x)dx$

441. If $f(x) \le g(x)$ for all $x \in [a, b]$, then $\int_a^b f(x) \le \int_a^b g(x)$.

442. All continuous functions have an antiderivative.

Evaluate the Riemann sums L_4 and R_4 for the following functions over the specified interval. Compare your answer with the exact answer, when possible, or use a calculator to determine the answer.

443. $y = 3x^2 - 2x + 1$ over $[-1, 1]$

444. $y = \ln(x^2 + 1)$ over $[0, e]$

445. $y = x^2 \sin x$ over $[0, \pi]$

446. $y = \sqrt{x} + \frac{1}{x}$ over $[1, 4]$

Evaluate the following integrals.

447. $\int_{-1}^{1} (x^3 - 2x^2 + 4x)dx$

448. $\int_0^4 \frac{3t}{\sqrt{1 + 6t^2}}dt$

449. $\int_{\pi/3}^{\pi/2} 2\sec(2\theta)\tan(2\theta)d\theta$

450. $\int_0^{\pi/4} e^{\cos^2 x}\sin x \cos dx$

Find the antiderivative.

451. $\int \frac{dx}{(x + 4)^3}$

452. $\int x\ln(x^2)dx$

453. $\int \frac{4x^2}{\sqrt{1 - x^6}}dx$

454. $\int \frac{e^{2x}}{1 + e^{4x}}dx$

Find the derivative.

455. $\frac{d}{dt}\int_0^t \frac{\sin x}{\sqrt{1 + x^2}}dx$

456. $\frac{d}{dx}\int_1^{x^3} \sqrt{4 - t^2}dt$

457. $\frac{d}{dx}\int_1^{\ln(x)} (4t + e^t)dt$

458. $\frac{d}{dx}\int_0^{\cos x} e^{t^2} dt$

The following problems consider the historic average cost per gigabyte of RAM on a computer.

Year	5-Year Change ($)
1980	0
1985	−5,468,750
1990	−755,495
1995	−73,005
2000	−29,768
2005	−918
2010	−177

459. If the average cost per gigabyte of RAM in 2010 is $12, find the average cost per gigabyte of RAM in 1980.

460. The average cost per gigabyte of RAM can be approximated by the function $C(t) = 8,500,000(0.65)^t$, where t is measured in years since 1980, and C is cost in US$. Find the average cost per gigabyte of RAM for 1980 to 2010.

461. Find the average cost of 1GB RAM for 2005 to 2010.

462. The velocity of a bullet from a rifle can be approximated by $v(t) = 6400t^2 - 6505t + 2686$, where t is seconds after the shot and v is the velocity measured in feet per second. This equation only models the velocity for the first half-second after the shot: $0 \le t \le 0.5$. What is the total distance the bullet travels in 0.5 sec?

463. What is the average velocity of the bullet for the first half-second?

6 | APPLICATIONS OF INTEGRATION

Figure 6.1 Hoover Dam is one of the United States' iconic landmarks, and provides irrigation and hydroelectric power for millions of people in the southwest United States. (credit: modification of work by Lynn Betts, Wikimedia)

Chapter Outline

Introduction

The Hoover Dam is an engineering marvel. When Lake Mead, the reservoir behind the dam, is full, the dam withstands a great deal of force. However, water levels in the lake vary considerably as a result of droughts and varying water demands. Later in this chapter, we use definite integrals to calculate the force exerted on the dam when the reservoir is full and we examine how changing water levels affect that force (see **Example 6.28**).

Hydrostatic force is only one of the many applications of definite integrals we explore in this chapter. From geometric applications such as surface area and volume, to physical applications such as mass and work, to growth and decay models, definite integrals are a powerful tool to help us understand and model the world around us.

6.1 | Areas between Curves

Learning Objectives

6.1.1 Determine the area of a region between two curves by integrating with respect to the independent variable.

6.1.2 Find the area of a compound region.

6.1.3 Determine the area of a region between two curves by integrating with respect to the dependent variable.

In **Introduction to Integration**, we developed the concept of the definite integral to calculate the area below a curve on a given interval. In this section, we expand that idea to calculate the area of more complex regions. We start by finding the area between two curves that are functions of x, beginning with the simple case in which one function value is always greater than the other. We then look at cases when the graphs of the functions cross. Last, we consider how to calculate the area between two curves that are functions of y.

Area of a Region between Two Curves

Let $f(x)$ and $g(x)$ be continuous functions over an interval $[a, b]$ such that $f(x) \geq g(x)$ on $[a, b]$. We want to find the area between the graphs of the functions, as shown in the following figure.

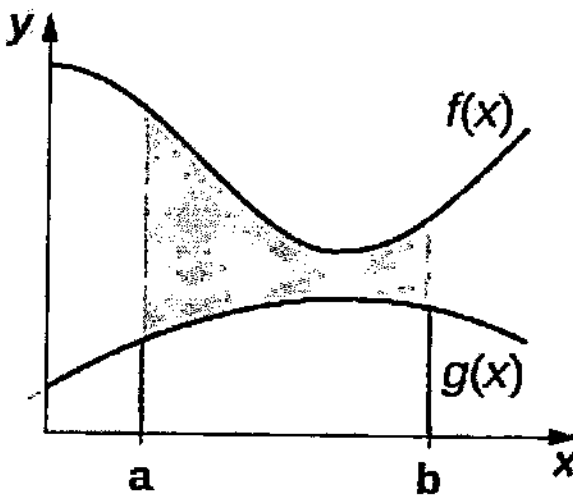

Figure 6.2 The area between the graphs of two functions, $f(x)$ and $g(x)$, on the interval $[a, b]$.

As we did before, we are going to partition the interval on the x-axis and approximate the area between the graphs of the functions with rectangles. So, for $i = 0, 1, 2, \ldots, n$, let $P = \{x_i\}$ be a regular partition of $[a, b]$. Then, for $i = 1, 2, \ldots, n$, choose a point $x_i^* \in [x_{i-1}, x_i]$, and on each interval $[x_{i-1}, x_i]$ construct a rectangle that extends vertically from $g(x_i^*)$ to $f(x_i^*)$. **Figure 6.3**(a) shows the rectangles when x_i^* is selected to be the left endpoint of the interval and $n = 10$. **Figure 6.3**(b) shows a representative rectangle in detail.

Use this **calculator (http://www.openstaxcollege.org/l/20_CurveCalc)** to learn more about the areas between two curves.

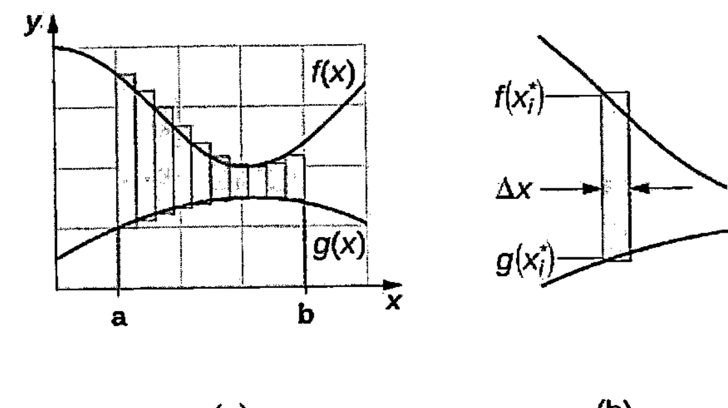

Figure 6.3 (a)We can approximate the area between the graphs of two functions, $f(x)$ and $g(x)$, with rectangles. (b) The area of a typical rectangle goes from one curve to the other.

The height of each individual rectangle is $f(x_i^*) - g(x_i^*)$ and the width of each rectangle is Δx. Adding the areas of all the rectangles, we see that the area between the curves is approximated by

$$A \approx \sum_{i=1}^{n} [f(x_i^*) - g(x_i^*)]\Delta x.$$

This is a Riemann sum, so we take the limit as $n \to \infty$ and we get

$$A = \lim_{n \to \infty} \sum_{i=1}^{n} [f(x_i^*) - g(x_i^*)]\Delta x = \int_a^b [f(x) - g(x)]dx.$$

These findings are summarized in the following theorem.

Theorem 6.1: Finding the Area between Two Curves

Let $f(x)$ and $g(x)$ be continuous functions such that $f(x) \geq g(x)$ over an interval $[a, b]$. Let R denote the region bounded above by the graph of $f(x)$, below by the graph of $g(x)$, and on the left and right by the lines $x = a$ and $x = b$, respectively. Then, the area of R is given by

$$A = \int_a^b [f(x) - g(x)]dx. \quad (6.1)$$

We apply this theorem in the following example.

Example 6.1

Finding the Area of a Region between Two Curves 1

If R is the region bounded above by the graph of the function $f(x) = x + 4$ and below by the graph of the function $g(x) = 3 - \frac{x}{2}$ over the interval $[1, 4]$, find the area of region R.

Solution

The region is depicted in the following figure.

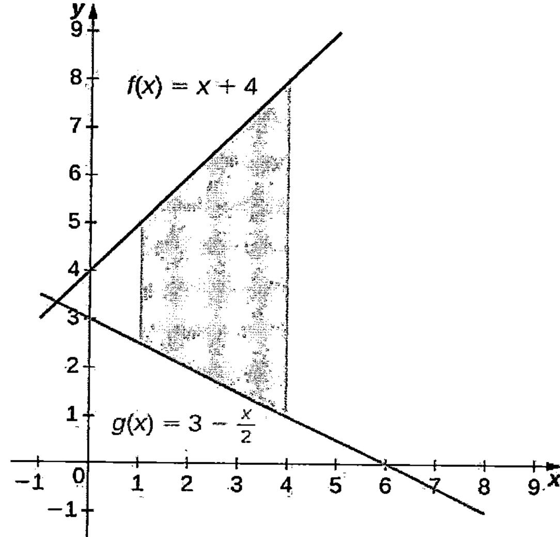

Figure 6.4 A region between two curves is shown where one curve is always greater than the other.

We have

$$\begin{aligned} A &= \int_a^b [f(x) - g(x)]dx \\ &= \int_1^4 \left[(x+4) - \left(3 - \frac{x}{2}\right)\right]dx = \int_1^4 \left[\frac{3x}{2} + 1\right]dx \\ &= \left[\frac{3x^2}{4} + x\right]\Big|_1^4 = \left(16 - \frac{7}{4}\right) = \frac{57}{4}. \end{aligned}$$

The area of the region is $\frac{57}{4}$ units^2.

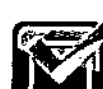

6.1 If R is the region bounded by the graphs of the functions $f(x) = \frac{x}{2} + 5$ and $g(x) = x + \frac{1}{2}$ over the interval $[1, 5]$, find the area of region R.

In **Example 6.1**, we defined the interval of interest as part of the problem statement. Quite often, though, we want to define our interval of interest based on where the graphs of the two functions intersect. This is illustrated in the following example.

Example 6.2

Finding the Area of a Region between Two Curves 2

If R is the region bounded above by the graph of the function $f(x) = 9 - (x/2)^2$ and below by the graph of the function $g(x) = 6 - x$, find the area of region R.

Solution

The region is depicted in the following figure.

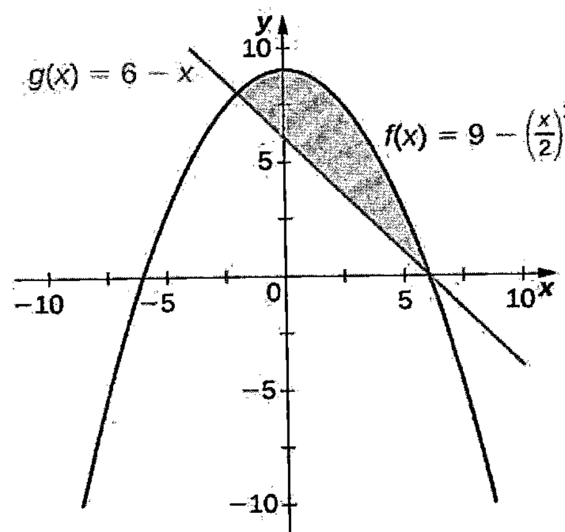

Figure 6.5 This graph shows the region below the graph of $f(x)$ and above the graph of $g(x)$.

We first need to compute where the graphs of the functions intersect. Setting $f(x) = g(x)$, we get

$$\begin{aligned}
f(x) &= g(x) \\
9 - \left(\frac{x}{2}\right)^2 &= 6 - x \\
9 - \frac{x^2}{4} &= 6 - x \\
36 - x^2 &= 24 - 4x \\
x^2 - 4x - 12 &= 0 \\
(x-6)(x+2) &= 0.
\end{aligned}$$

The graphs of the functions intersect when $x = 6$ or $x = -2$, so we want to integrate from -2 to 6. Since $f(x) \geq g(x)$ for $-2 \leq x \leq 6$, we obtain

$$\begin{aligned}
A &= \int_a^b [f(x) - g(x)]dx \\
&= \int_{-2}^{6} \left[9 - \left(\frac{x}{2}\right)^2 - (6 - x)\right]dx = \int_{-2}^{6} \left[3 - \frac{x^2}{4} + x\right]dx \\
&= \left[3x - \frac{x^3}{12} + \frac{x^2}{2}\right]\Bigg|_{-2}^{6} = \frac{64}{3}.
\end{aligned}$$

The area of the region is $64/3$ units^2.

6.2 If R is the region bounded above by the graph of the function $f(x) = x$ and below by the graph of the function $g(x) = x^4$, find the area of region R.

Areas of Compound Regions

So far, we have required $f(x) \geq g(x)$ over the entire interval of interest, but what if we want to look at regions bounded by the graphs of functions that cross one another? In that case, we modify the process we just developed by using the absolute value function.

Theorem 6.2: Finding the Area of a Region between Curves That Cross

Let $f(x)$ and $g(x)$ be continuous functions over an interval $[a, b]$. Let R denote the region between the graphs of $f(x)$ and $g(x)$, and be bounded on the left and right by the lines $x = a$ and $x = b$, respectively. Then, the area of R is given by

$$A = \int_a^b |f(x) - g(x)|dx.$$

In practice, applying this theorem requires us to break up the interval $[a, b]$ and evaluate several integrals, depending on which of the function values is greater over a given part of the interval. We study this process in the following example.

Example 6.3

Finding the Area of a Region Bounded by Functions That Cross

If R is the region between the graphs of the functions $f(x) = \sin x$ and $g(x) = \cos x$ over the interval $[0, \pi]$, find the area of region R.

Solution

The region is depicted in the following figure.

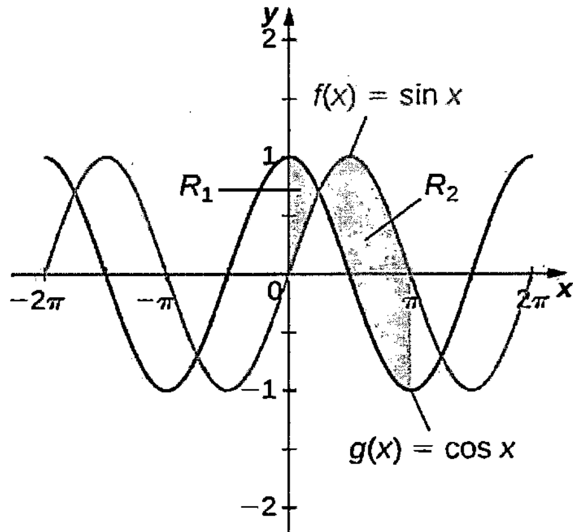

Figure 6.6 The region between two curves can be broken into two sub-regions.

The graphs of the functions intersect at $x = \pi/4$. For $x \in [0, \pi/4]$, $\cos x \geq \sin x$, so

$$|f(x) - g(x)| = |\sin x - \cos x| = \cos x - \sin x.$$

On the other hand, for $x \in [\pi/4, \pi]$, $\sin x \geq \cos x$, so

$$|f(x) - g(x)| = |\sin x - \cos x| = \sin x - \cos x.$$

Then

$$\begin{aligned} A &= \int_a^b |f(x) - g(x)| dx \\ &= \int_0^\pi |\sin x - \cos x| dx = \int_0^{\pi/4} (\cos x - \sin x) dx + \int_{\pi/4}^\pi (\sin x - \cos x) dx \\ &= [\sin x + \cos x] \Big|_0^{\pi/4} + [-\cos x - \sin x] \Big|_{\pi/4}^\pi \\ &= (\sqrt{2} - 1) + (1 + \sqrt{2}) = 2\sqrt{2}. \end{aligned}$$

The area of the region is $2\sqrt{2}$ units^2.

6.3 If R is the region between the graphs of the functions $f(x) = \sin x$ and $g(x) = \cos x$ over the interval $[\pi/2, 2\pi]$, find the area of region R.

Example 6.4

Finding the Area of a Complex Region

Consider the region depicted in **Figure 6.7**. Find the area of R.

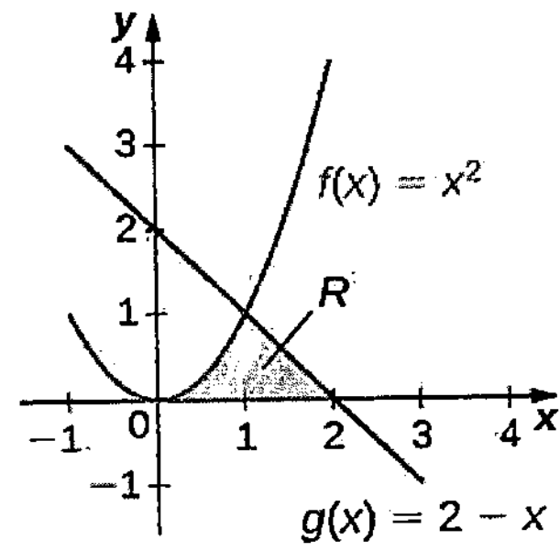

Figure 6.7 Two integrals are required to calculate the area of this region.

Solution

As with **Example 6.3**, we need to divide the interval into two pieces. The graphs of the functions intersect at $x = 1$ (set $f(x) = g(x)$ and solve for x), so we evaluate two separate integrals: one over the interval $[0, 1]$ and one over the interval $[1, 2]$.

Over the interval $[0, 1]$, the region is bounded above by $f(x) = x^2$ and below by the x-axis, so we have

$$A_1 = \int_0^1 x^2 dx = \frac{x^3}{3} \Big|_0^1 = \frac{1}{3}.$$

Over the interval $[1, 2]$, the region is bounded above by $g(x) = 2 - x$ and below by the x-axis, so we have

$$A_2 = \int_1^2 (2 - x)dx = \left[2x - \frac{x^2}{2}\right]\bigg|_1^2 = \frac{1}{2}.$$

Adding these areas together, we obtain

$$A = A_1 + A_2 = \frac{1}{3} + \frac{1}{2} = \frac{5}{6}.$$

The area of the region is $5/6$ units^2.

6.4 Consider the region depicted in the following figure. Find the area of R.

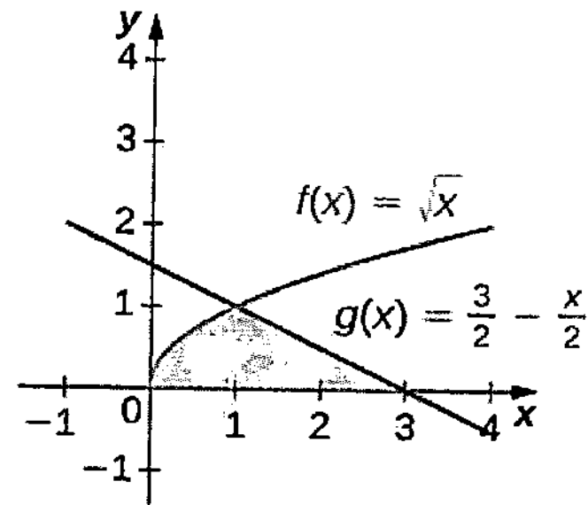

Regions Defined with Respect to y

In **Example 6.4**, we had to evaluate two separate integrals to calculate the area of the region. However, there is another approach that requires only one integral. What if we treat the curves as functions of y, instead of as functions of x?

Review **Figure 6.7**. Note that the left graph, shown in red, is represented by the function $y = f(x) = x^2$. We could just as easily solve this for x and represent the curve by the function $x = v(y) = \sqrt{y}$. (Note that $x = -\sqrt{y}$ is also a valid representation of the function $y = f(x) = x^2$ as a function of y. However, based on the graph, it is clear we are interested in the positive square root.) Similarly, the right graph is represented by the function $y = g(x) = 2 - x$, but could just as easily be represented by the function $x = u(y) = 2 - y$. When the graphs are represented as functions of y, we see the region is bounded on the left by the graph of one function and on the right by the graph of the other function. Therefore, if we integrate with respect to y, we need to evaluate one integral only. Let's develop a formula for this type of integration.

Let $u(y)$ and $v(y)$ be continuous functions over an interval $[c, d]$ such that $u(y) \geq v(y)$ for all $y \in [c, d]$. We want to find the area between the graphs of the functions, as shown in the following figure.

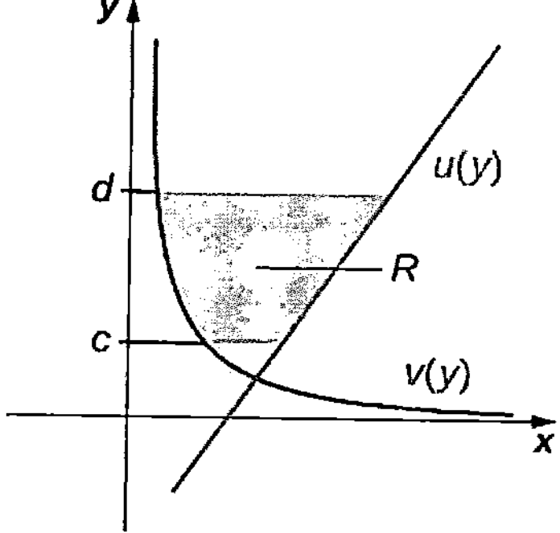

Figure 6.8 We can find the area between the graphs of two functions, $u(y)$ and $v(y)$.

This time, we are going to partition the interval on the y-axis and use horizontal rectangles to approximate the area between the functions. So, for $i = 0, 1, 2,\ldots, n,$ let $Q = \{y_i\}$ be a regular partition of $[c, d]$. Then, for $i = 1, 2,\ldots, n,$ choose a point $y_i^* \in [y_{i-1}, y_i],$ then over each interval $[y_{i-1}, y_i]$ construct a rectangle that extends horizontally from $v(y_i^*)$ to $u(y_i^*)$. **Figure 6.9**(a) shows the rectangles when y_i^* is selected to be the lower endpoint of the interval and $n = 10$. **Figure 6.9**(b) shows a representative rectangle in detail.

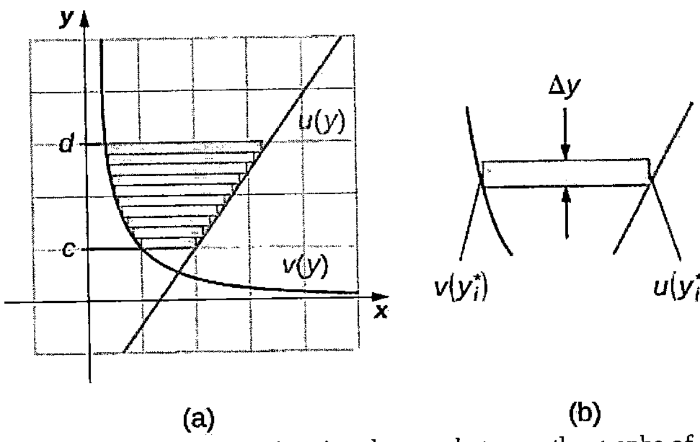

Figure 6.9 (a) Approximating the area between the graphs of two functions, $u(y)$ and $v(y)$, with rectangles. (b) The area of a typical rectangle.

The height of each individual rectangle is Δy and the width of each rectangle is $u(y_i^*) - v(y_i^*)$. Therefore, the area between the curves is approximately

$$A \approx \sum_{i=1}^{n} [u(y_i^*) - v(y_i^*)]\Delta y.$$

This is a Riemann sum, so we take the limit as $n \to \infty,$ obtaining

$$A = \lim_{n \to \infty} \sum_{i=1}^{n} [u(y_i^*) - v(y_i^*)]\Delta y = \int_c^d [u(y) - v(y)]dy.$$

These findings are summarized in the following theorem.

Theorem 6.3: Finding the Area between Two Curves, Integrating along the y-axis

Let $u(y)$ and $v(y)$ be continuous functions such that $u(y) \geq v(y)$ for all $y \in [c, d]$. Let R denote the region bounded on the right by the graph of $u(y),$ on the left by the graph of $v(y),$ and above and below by the lines $y = d$ and $y = c,$ respectively. Then, the area of R is given by

$$A = \int_c^d [u(y) - v(y)]dy. \tag{6.2}$$

Example 6.5

Integrating with Respect to y

Let's revisit **Example 6.4**, only this time let's integrate with respect to y. Let R be the region depicted in **Figure 6.10**. Find the area of R by integrating with respect to y.

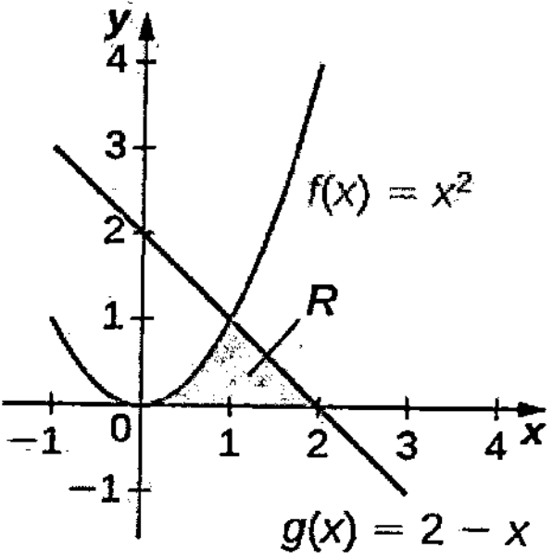

Figure 6.10 The area of region R can be calculated using one integral only when the curves are treated as functions of y.

Solution

We must first express the graphs as functions of y. As we saw at the beginning of this section, the curve on the left can be represented by the function $x = v(y) = \sqrt{y}$, and the curve on the right can be represented by the function $x = u(y) = 2 - y$.

Now we have to determine the limits of integration. The region is bounded below by the x-axis, so the lower limit of integration is $y = 0$. The upper limit of integration is determined by the point where the two graphs intersect, which is the point $(1, 1)$, so the upper limit of integration is $y = 1$. Thus, we have $[c, d] = [0, 1]$.

Calculating the area of the region, we get

$$\begin{aligned} A &= \int_c^d [u(y) - v(y)]dy \\ &= \int_0^1 [(2 - y) - \sqrt{y}]dy = \left[2y - \frac{y^2}{2} - \frac{2}{3}y^{3/2}\right]\Big|_0^1 \\ &= \frac{5}{6}. \end{aligned}$$

The area of the region is $5/6$ units^2.

6.5 Let's revisit the checkpoint associated with **Example 6.4**, only this time, let's integrate with respect to y. Let be the region depicted in the following figure. Find the area of R by integrating with respect to y.

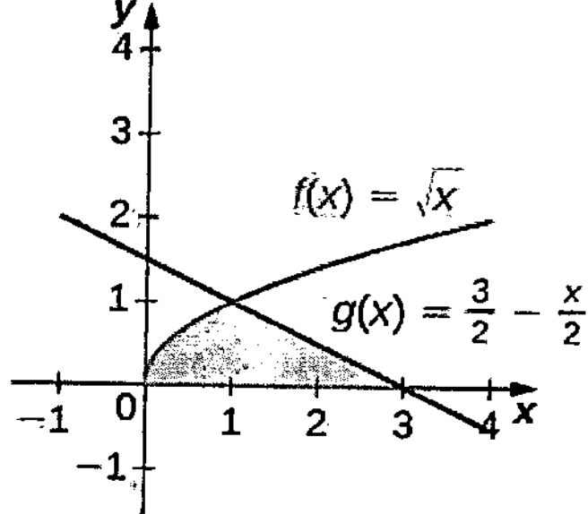

6.1 EXERCISES

For the following exercises, determine the area of the region between the two curves in the given figure by integrating over the x-axis.

1. $y = x^2 - 3$ and $y = 1$

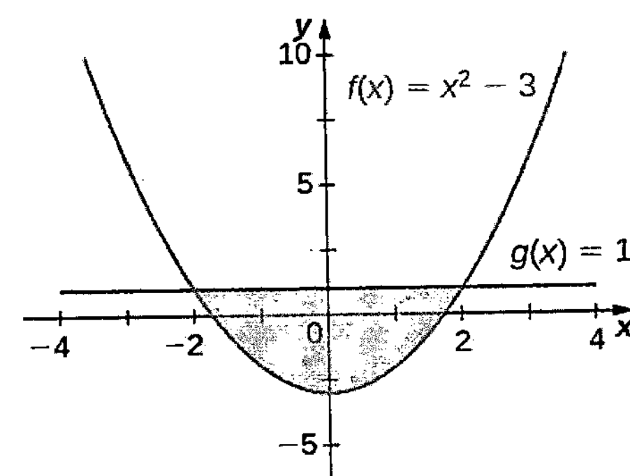

2. $y = x^2$ and $y = 3x + 4$

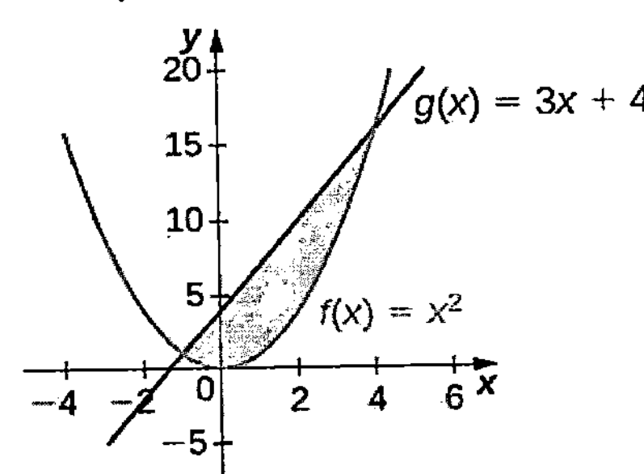

For the following exercises, split the region between the two curves into two smaller regions, then determine the area by integrating over the x-axis. Note that you will have two integrals to solve.

3. $y = x^3$ and $y = x^2 + x$

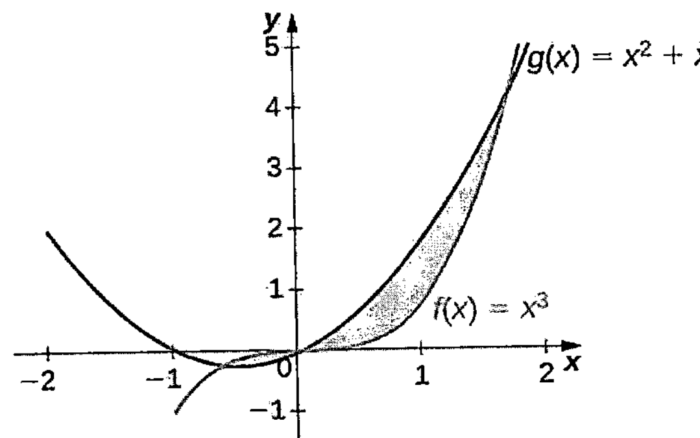

4. $y = \cos\theta$ and $y = 0.5$, for $0 \le \theta \le \pi$

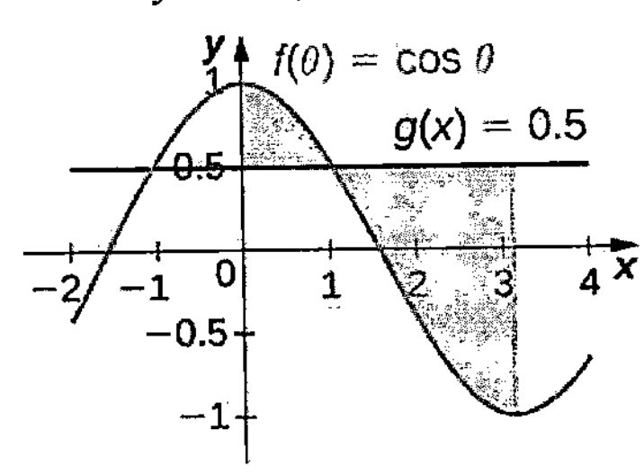

For the following exercises, determine the area of the region between the two curves by integrating over the y-axis.

5. $x = y^2$ and $x = 9$

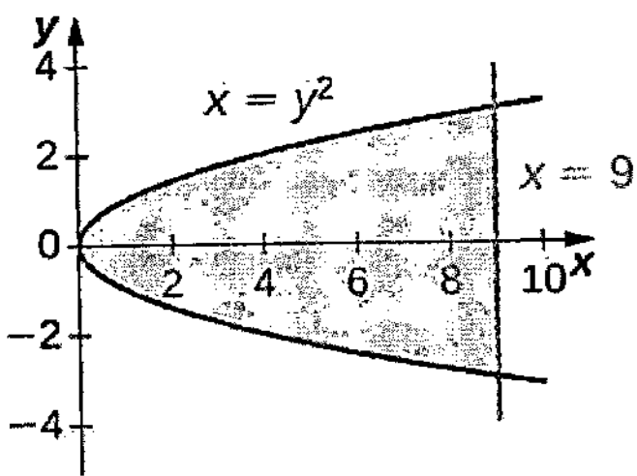

6. $y = x$ and $x = y^2$

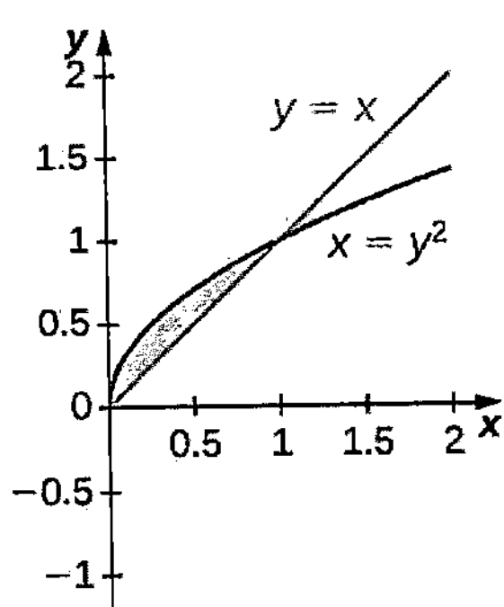

For the following exercises, graph the equations and shade the area of the region between the curves. Determine its area by integrating over the x-axis.

7. $y = x^2$ and $y = -x^2 + 18x$

8. $y = \frac{1}{x}$, $y = \frac{1}{x^2}$, and $x = 3$

9. $y = \cos x$ and $y = \cos^2 x$ on $x = [-\pi, \pi]$

10. $y = e^x$, $y = e^{2x-1}$, and $x = 0$

11. $y = e^x$, $y = e^{-x}$, $x = -1$ and $x = 1$

12. $y = e,\ y = e^x,$ and $y = e^{-x}$

13. $y = |x|$ and $y = x^2$

For the following exercises, graph the equations and shade the area of the region between the curves. If necessary, break the region into sub-regions to determine its entire area.

14. $y = \sin(\pi x),\ y = 2x,$ and $x > 0$

15. $y = 12 - x,\ y = \sqrt{x},$ and $y = 1$

16. $y = \sin x$ and $y = \cos x$ over $x = [-\pi, \pi]$

17. $y = x^3$ and $y = x^2 - 2x$ over $x = [-1, 1]$

18. $y = x^2 + 9$ and $y = 10 + 2x$ over $x = [-1, 3]$

19. $y = x^3 + 3x$ and $y = 4x$

For the following exercises, graph the equations and shade the area of the region between the curves. Determine its area by integrating over the y-axis.

20. $x = y^3$ and $x = 3y - 2$

21. $x = 2y$ and $x = y^3 - y$

22. $x = -3 + y^2$ and $x = y - y^2$

23. $y^2 = x$ and $x = y + 2$

24. $x = |y|$ and $2x = -y^2 + 2$

25. $x = \sin y,\ x = \cos(2y),\ y = \pi/2,$ and $y = -\pi/2$

For the following exercises, graph the equations and shade the area of the region between the curves. Determine its area by integrating over the x-axis or y-axis, whichever seems more convenient.

26. $x = y^4$ and $x = y^5$

27. $y = xe^x,\ y = e^x,\ x = 0,$ and $x = 1$

28. $y = x^6$ and $y = x^4$

29. $x = y^3 + 2y^2 + 1$ and $x = -y^2 + 1$

30. $y = |x|$ and $y = x^2 - 1$

31. $y = 4 - 3x$ and $y = \frac{1}{x}$

32. $y = \sin x,\ x = -\pi/6,\ x = \pi/6,$ and $y = \cos^3 x$

33. $y = x^2 - 3x + 2$ and $y = x^3 - 2x^2 - x + 2$

34. $y = 2\cos^3(3x),\ y = -1,\ x = \frac{\pi}{4},$ and $x = -\frac{\pi}{4}$

35. $y + y^3 = x$ and $2y = x$

36. $y = \sqrt{1 - x^2}$ and $y = x^2 - 1$

37. $y = \cos^{-1} x,\ y = \sin^{-1} x,\ x = -1,$ and $x = 1$

For the following exercises, find the exact area of the region bounded by the given equations if possible. If you are unable to determine the intersection points analytically, use a calculator to approximate the intersection points with three decimal places and determine the approximate area of the region.

38. **[T]** $x = e^y$ and $y = x - 2$

39. **[T]** $y = x^2$ and $y = \sqrt{1 - x^2}$

40. **[T]** $y = 3x^2 + 8x + 9$ and $3y = x + 24$

41. **[T]** $x = \sqrt{4 - y^2}$ and $y^2 = 1 + x^2$

42. **[T]** $x^2 = y^3$ and $x = 3y$

43. **[T]** $y = \sin^3 x + 2,\ y = \tan x,\ x = -1.5,$ and $x = 1.5$

44. **[T]** $y = \sqrt{1 - x^2}$ and $y^2 = x^2$

45. **[T]** $y = \sqrt{1 - x^2}$ and $y = x^2 + 2x + 1$

46. **[T]** $x = 4 - y^2$ and $x = 1 + 3y + y^2$

47. **[T]** $y = \cos x,\ y = e^x,\ x = -\pi,$ and $x = 0$

48. The largest triangle with a base on the x-axis that fits inside the upper half of the unit circle $y^2 + x^2 = 1$ is given by $y = 1 + x$ and $y = 1 - x$. See the following figure. What is the area inside the semicircle but outside the triangle?

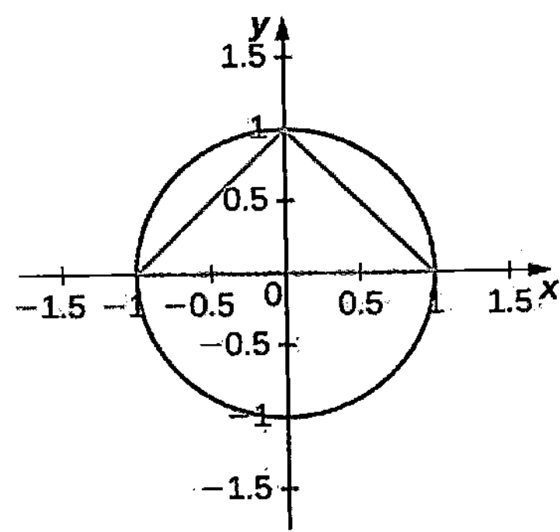

49. A factory selling cell phones has a marginal cost function $C(x) = 0.01x^2 - 3x + 229$, where x represents the number of cell phones, and a marginal revenue function given by $R(x) = 429 - 2x$. Find the area between the graphs of these curves and $x = 0$. What does this area represent?

50. An amusement park has a marginal cost function $C(x) = 1000e^{-x} + 5$, where x represents the number of tickets sold, and a marginal revenue function given by $R(x) = 60 - 0.1x$. Find the total profit generated when selling 550 tickets. Use a calculator to determine intersection points, if necessary, to two decimal places.

51. The tortoise versus the hare: The speed of the hare is given by the sinusoidal function $H(t) = 1 - \cos((\pi t)/2)$ whereas the speed of the tortoise is $T(t) = (1/2)\tan^{-1}(t/4)$, where t is time measured in hours and the speed is measured in miles per hour. Find the area between the curves from time $t = 0$ to the first time after one hour when the tortoise and hare are traveling at the same speed. What does it represent? Use a calculator to determine the intersection points, if necessary, accurate to three decimal places.

52. The tortoise versus the hare: The speed of the hare is given by the sinusoidal function $H(t) = (1/2) - (1/2)\cos(2\pi t)$ whereas the speed of the tortoise is $T(t) = \sqrt{t}$, where t is time measured in hours and speed is measured in kilometers per hour. If the race is over in 1 hour, who won the race and by how much? Use a calculator to determine the intersection points, if necessary, accurate to three decimal places.

For the following exercises, find the area between the curves by integrating with respect to x and then with respect to y. Is one method easier than the other? Do you obtain the same answer?

53. $y = x^2 + 2x + 1$ and $y = -x^2 - 3x + 4$

54. $y = x^4$ and $x = y^5$

55. $x = y^2 - 2$ and $x = 2y$

For the following exercises, solve using calculus, then check your answer with geometry.

56. Determine the equations for the sides of the square that touches the unit circle on all four sides, as seen in the following figure. Find the area between the perimeter of this square and the unit circle. Is there another way to solve this without using calculus?

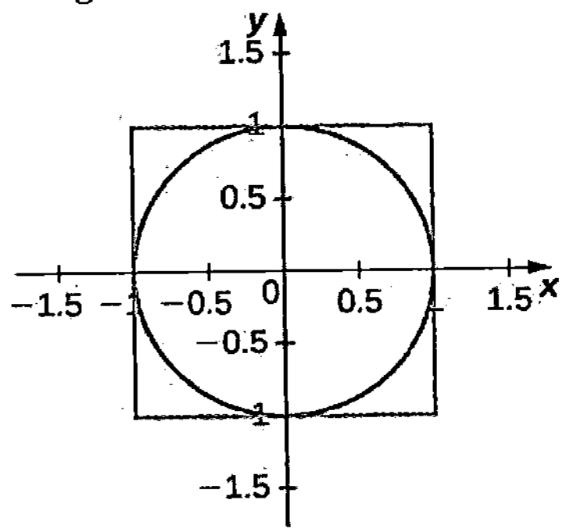

57. Find the area between the perimeter of the unit circle and the triangle created from $y = 2x + 1$, $y = 1 - 2x$ and $y = -\frac{3}{5}$, as seen in the following figure. Is there a way to solve this without using calculus?

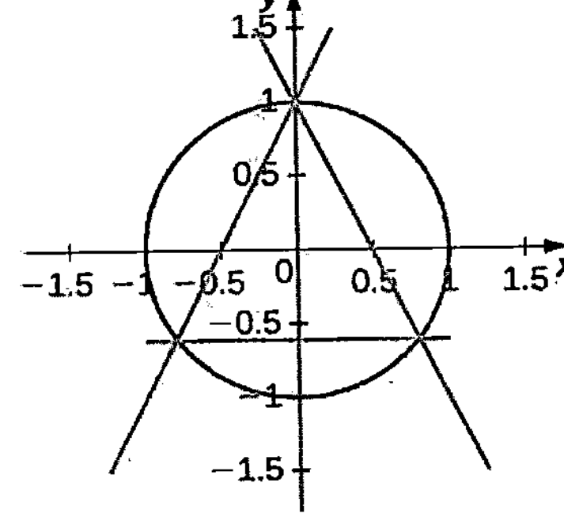

6.2 | Determining Volumes by Slicing

Learning Objectives

6.2.1 Determine the volume of a solid by integrating a cross-section (the slicing method).
6.2.2 Find the volume of a solid of revolution using the disk method.
6.2.3 Find the volume of a solid of revolution with a cavity using the washer method.

In the preceding section, we used definite integrals to find the area between two curves. In this section, we use definite integrals to find volumes of three-dimensional solids. We consider three approaches—slicing, disks, and washers—for finding these volumes, depending on the characteristics of the solid.

Volume and the Slicing Method

Just as area is the numerical measure of a two-dimensional region, volume is the numerical measure of a three-dimensional solid. Most of us have computed volumes of solids by using basic geometric formulas. The volume of a rectangular solid, for example, can be computed by multiplying length, width, and height: $V = lwh.$ The formulas for the volume of a sphere $\left(V = \frac{4}{3}\pi r^3\right),$ a cone $\left(V = \frac{1}{3}\pi r^2 h\right),$ and a pyramid $\left(V = \frac{1}{3}Ah\right)$ have also been introduced. Although some of these formulas were derived using geometry alone, all these formulas can be obtained by using integration.

We can also calculate the volume of a cylinder. Although most of us think of a cylinder as having a circular base, such as a soup can or a metal rod, in mathematics the word *cylinder* has a more general meaning. To discuss cylinders in this more general context, we first need to define some vocabulary.

We define the **cross-section** of a solid to be the intersection of a plane with the solid. A *cylinder* is defined as any solid that can be generated by translating a plane region along a line perpendicular to the region, called the *axis* of the cylinder. Thus, all cross-sections perpendicular to the axis of a cylinder are identical. The solid shown in **Figure 6.11** is an example of a cylinder with a noncircular base. To calculate the volume of a cylinder, then, we simply multiply the area of the cross-section by the height of the cylinder: $V = A \cdot h.$ In the case of a right circular cylinder (soup can), this becomes $V = \pi r^2 h.$

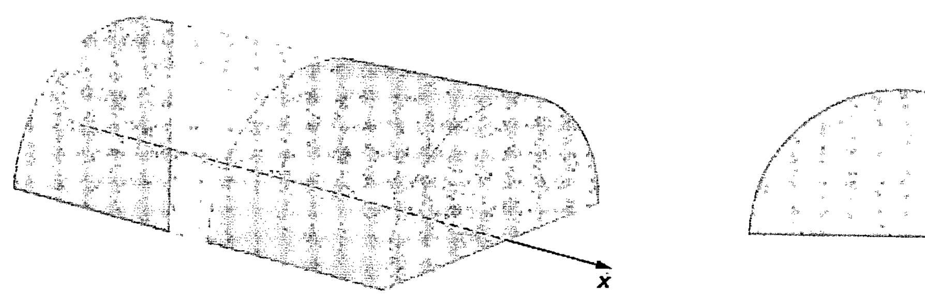

Figure 6.11 Each cross-section of a particular cylinder is identical to the others.

If a solid does not have a constant cross-section (and it is not one of the other basic solids), we may not have a formula for its volume. In this case, we can use a definite integral to calculate the volume of the solid. We do this by slicing the solid into pieces, estimating the volume of each slice, and then adding those estimated volumes together. The slices should all be parallel to one another, and when we put all the slices together, we should get the whole solid. Consider, for example, the solid S shown in **Figure 6.12**, extending along the x-axis.

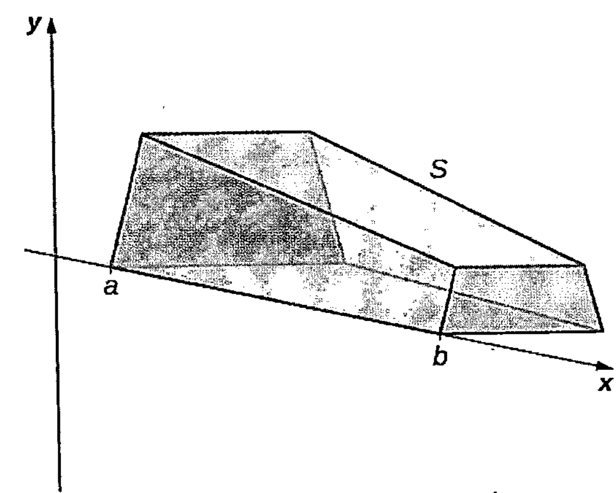

Figure 6.12 A solid with a varying cross-section.

We want to divide S into slices perpendicular to the x-axis. As we see later in the chapter, there may be times when we want to slice the solid in some other direction—say, with slices perpendicular to the y-axis. The decision of which way to slice the solid is very important. If we make the wrong choice, the computations can get quite messy. Later in the chapter, we examine some of these situations in detail and look at how to decide which way to slice the solid. For the purposes of this section, however, we use slices perpendicular to the x-axis.

Because the cross-sectional area is not constant, we let $A(x)$ represent the area of the cross-section at point x. Now let $P = \{x_0, x_1 \ldots, X_n\}$ be a regular partition of $[a, b]$, and for $i = 1, 2,\ldots n,$ let S_i represent the slice of S stretching from x_{i-1} to x_i. The following figure shows the sliced solid with $n = 3$.

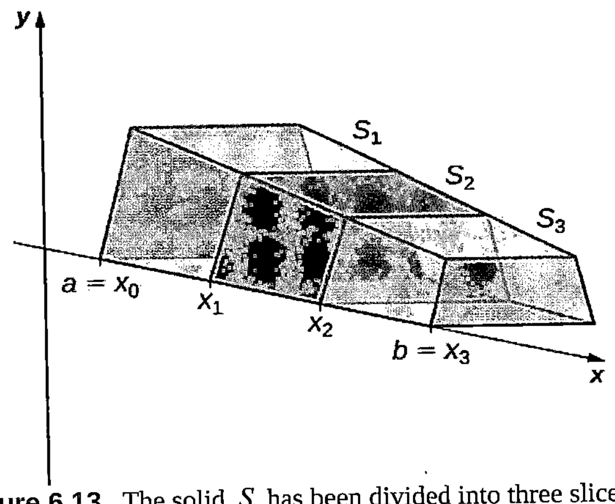

Figure 6.13 The solid S has been divided into three slices perpendicular to the x-axis.

Finally, for $i = 1, 2,\ldots n,$ let x_i^* be an arbitrary point in $[x_{i-1}, x_i]$. Then the volume of slice S_i can be estimated by $V(S_i) \approx A(x_i^*)\Delta x$. Adding these approximations together, we see the volume of the entire solid S can be approximated by

$$V(S) \approx \sum_{i=1}^{n} A(x_i^*)\Delta x.$$

By now, we can recognize this as a Riemann sum, and our next step is to take the limit as $n \to \infty$. Then we have

$$V(S) = \lim_{n \to \infty} \sum_{i=1}^{n} A(x_i^*)\Delta x = \int_a^b A(x)dx.$$

The technique we have just described is called the **slicing method**. To apply it, we use the following strategy.

Problem-Solving Strategy: Finding Volumes by the Slicing Method

1. Examine the solid and determine the shape of a cross-section of the solid. It is often helpful to draw a picture if one is not provided.
2. Determine a formula for the area of the cross-section.
3. Integrate the area formula over the appropriate interval to get the volume.

Recall that in this section, we assume the slices are perpendicular to the x-axis. Therefore, the area formula is in terms of x and the limits of integration lie on the x-axis. However, the problem-solving strategy shown here is valid regardless of how we choose to slice the solid.

Example 6.6

Deriving the Formula for the Volume of a Pyramid

We know from geometry that the formula for the volume of a pyramid is $V = \frac{1}{3}Ah.$ If the pyramid has a square base, this becomes $V = \frac{1}{3}a^2 h,$ where a denotes the length of one side of the base. We are going to use the slicing method to derive this formula.

Solution

We want to apply the slicing method to a pyramid with a square base. To set up the integral, consider the pyramid shown in **Figure 6.14**, oriented along the x-axis.

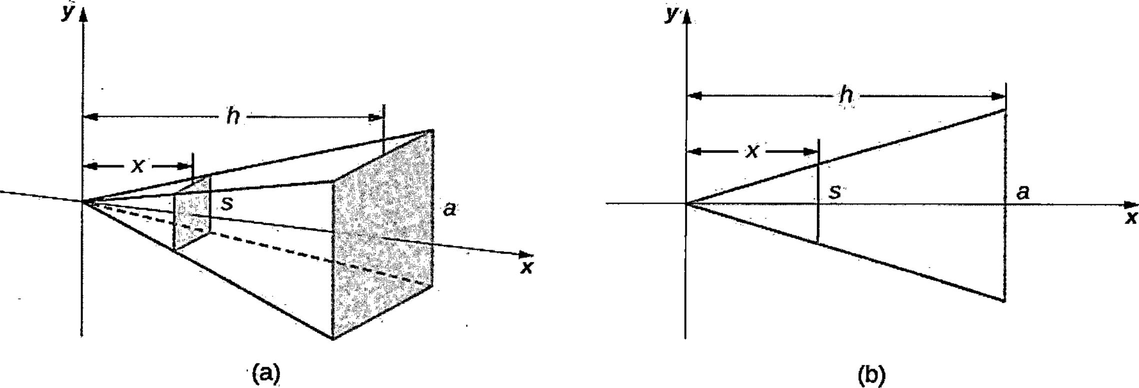

Figure 6.14 (a) A pyramid with a square base is oriented along the x-axis. (b) A two-dimensional view of the pyramid is seen from the side.

We first want to determine the shape of a cross-section of the pyramid. We are know the base is a square, so the cross-sections are squares as well (step 1). Now we want to determine a formula for the area of one of these cross-sectional squares. Looking at **Figure 6.14**(b), and using a proportion, since these are similar triangles, we have

$$\frac{s}{a} = \frac{x}{h} \text{ or } s = \frac{ax}{h}.$$

Therefore, the area of one of the cross-sectional squares is

$$A(x) = s^2 = \left(\frac{ax}{h}\right)^2 \text{ (step 2)}.$$

Then we find the volume of the pyramid by integrating from 0 to h (step 3):

$$\begin{aligned} V &= \int_0^h A(x)dx \\ &= \int_0^h \left(\frac{ax}{h}\right)^2 dx = \frac{a^2}{h^2}\int_0^h x^2 dx \\ &= \left[\frac{a^2}{h^2}\left(\frac{1}{3}x^3\right)\right]\Bigg|_0^h = \frac{1}{3}a^2 h. \end{aligned}$$

This is the formula we were looking for.

6.6 Use the slicing method to derive the formula $V = \frac{1}{3}\pi r^2 h$ for the volume of a circular cone.

Solids of Revolution

If a region in a plane is revolved around a line in that plane, the resulting solid is called a **solid of revolution**, as shown in the following figure.

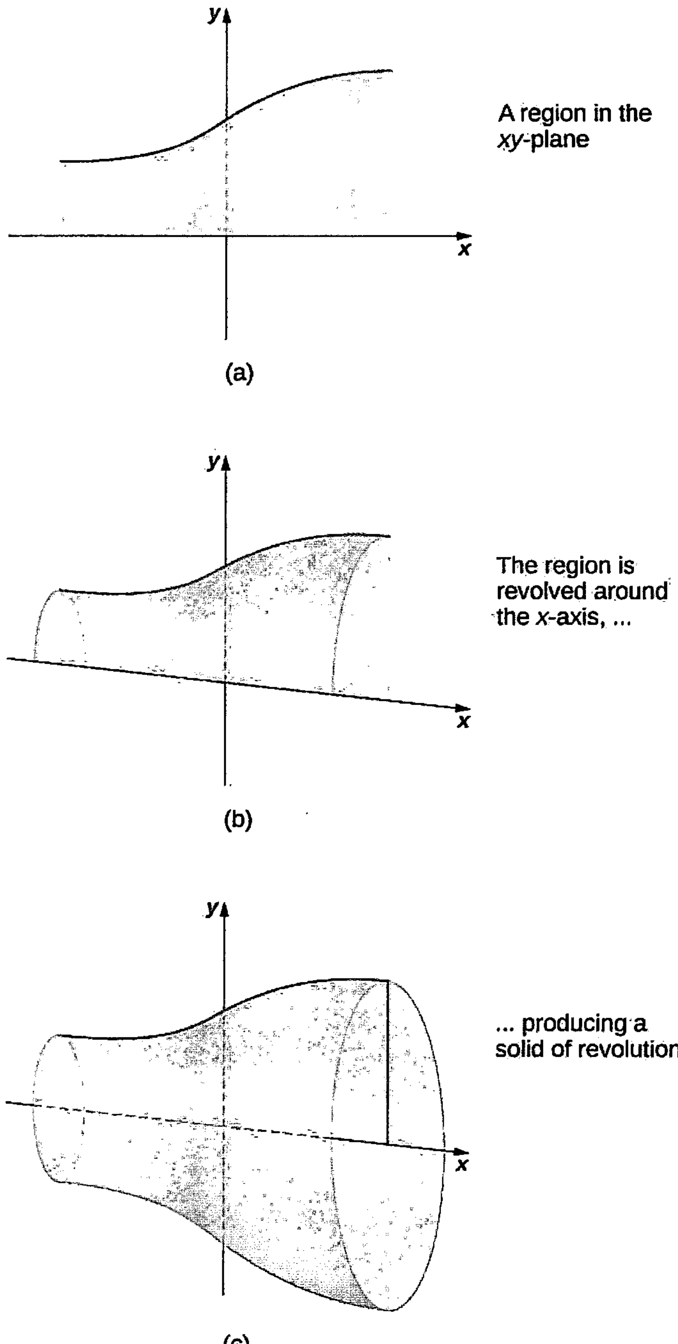

Figure 6.15 (a) This is the region that is revolved around the x-axis. (b) As the region begins to revolve around the axis, it sweeps out a solid of revolution. (c) This is the solid that results when the revolution is complete.

Solids of revolution are common in mechanical applications, such as machine parts produced by a lathe. We spend the rest of this section looking at solids of this type. The next example uses the slicing method to calculate the volume of a solid of revolution.

Use an online **integral calculator (http://www.openstaxcollege.org/l/20_IntCalc2)** to learn more.

Example 6.7

Using the Slicing Method to find the Volume of a Solid of Revolution

Use the slicing method to find the volume of the solid of revolution bounded by the graphs of $f(x) = x^2 - 4x + 5,\ x = 1,$ and $x = 4,$ and rotated about the x-axis.

Solution

Using the problem-solving strategy, we first sketch the graph of the quadratic function over the interval $[1, 4]$ as shown in the following figure.

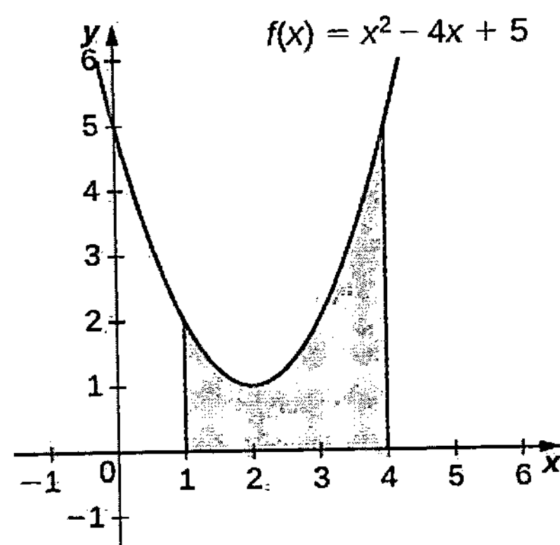

Figure 6.16 A region used to produce a solid of revolution.

Next, revolve the region around the x-axis, as shown in the following figure.

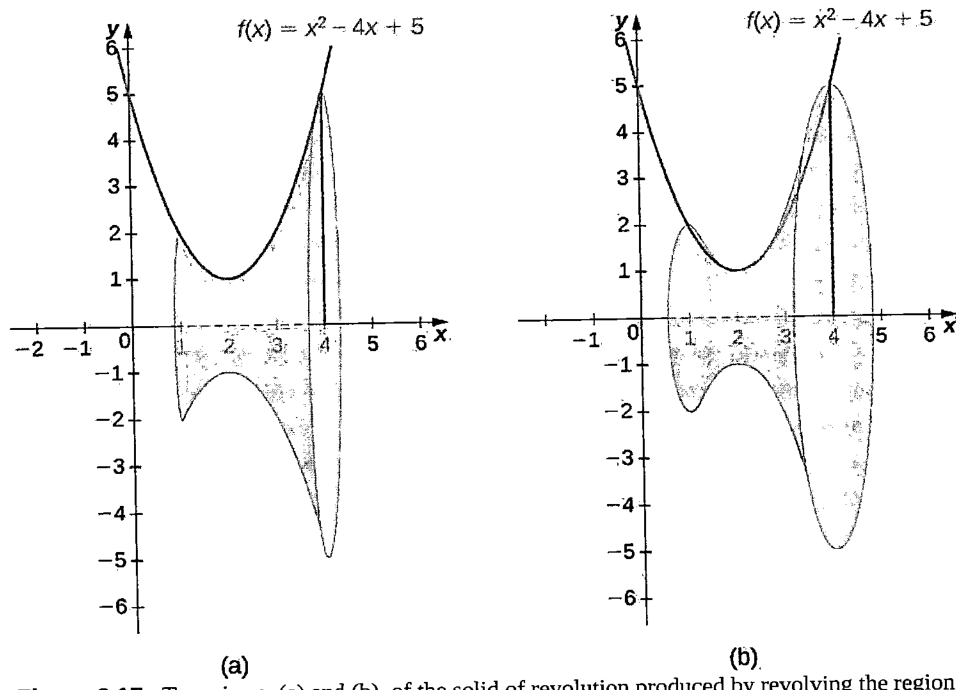

Figure 6.17 Two views, (a) and (b), of the solid of revolution produced by revolving the region in **Figure 6.16** about the x-axis.

Since the solid was formed by revolving the region around the x-axis, the cross-sections are circles (step 1). The area of the cross-section, then, is the area of a circle, and the radius of the circle is given by $f(x)$. Use the formula for the area of the circle:

$$A(x) = \pi r^2 = \pi[f(x)]^2 = \pi\left(x^2 - 4x + 5\right)^2 \text{ (step 2).}$$

The volume, then, is (step 3)

$$\begin{aligned} V &= \int_a^h A(x)dx \\ &= \int_1^4 \pi\left(x^2 - 4x + 5\right)^2 dx = \pi\int_1^4 \left(x^4 - 8x^3 + 26x^2 - 40x + 25\right)dx \\ &= \pi\left(\frac{x^5}{5} - 2x^4 + \frac{26x^3}{3} - 20x^2 + 25x\right)\Bigg|_1^4 = \frac{78}{5}\pi. \end{aligned}$$

The volume is $78\pi/5$.

6.7 Use the method of slicing to find the volume of the solid of revolution formed by revolving the region between the graph of the function $f(x) = 1/x$ and the x-axis over the interval $[1, 2]$ around the x-axis. See the following figure.

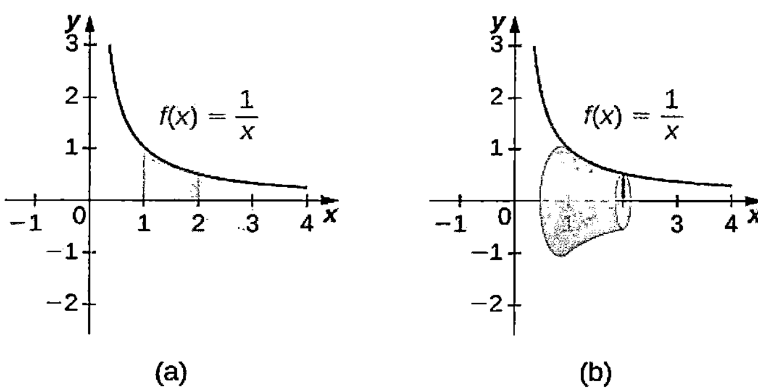

The Disk Method

When we use the slicing method with solids of revolution, it is often called the **disk method** because, for solids of revolution, the slices used to over approximate the volume of the solid are disks. To see this, consider the solid of revolution generated by revolving the region between the graph of the function $f(x) = (x - 1)^2 + 1$ and the x-axis over the interval $[-1, 3]$ around the x-axis. The graph of the function and a representative disk are shown in **Figure 6.18**(a) and (b). The region of revolution and the resulting solid are shown in **Figure 6.18**(c) and (d).

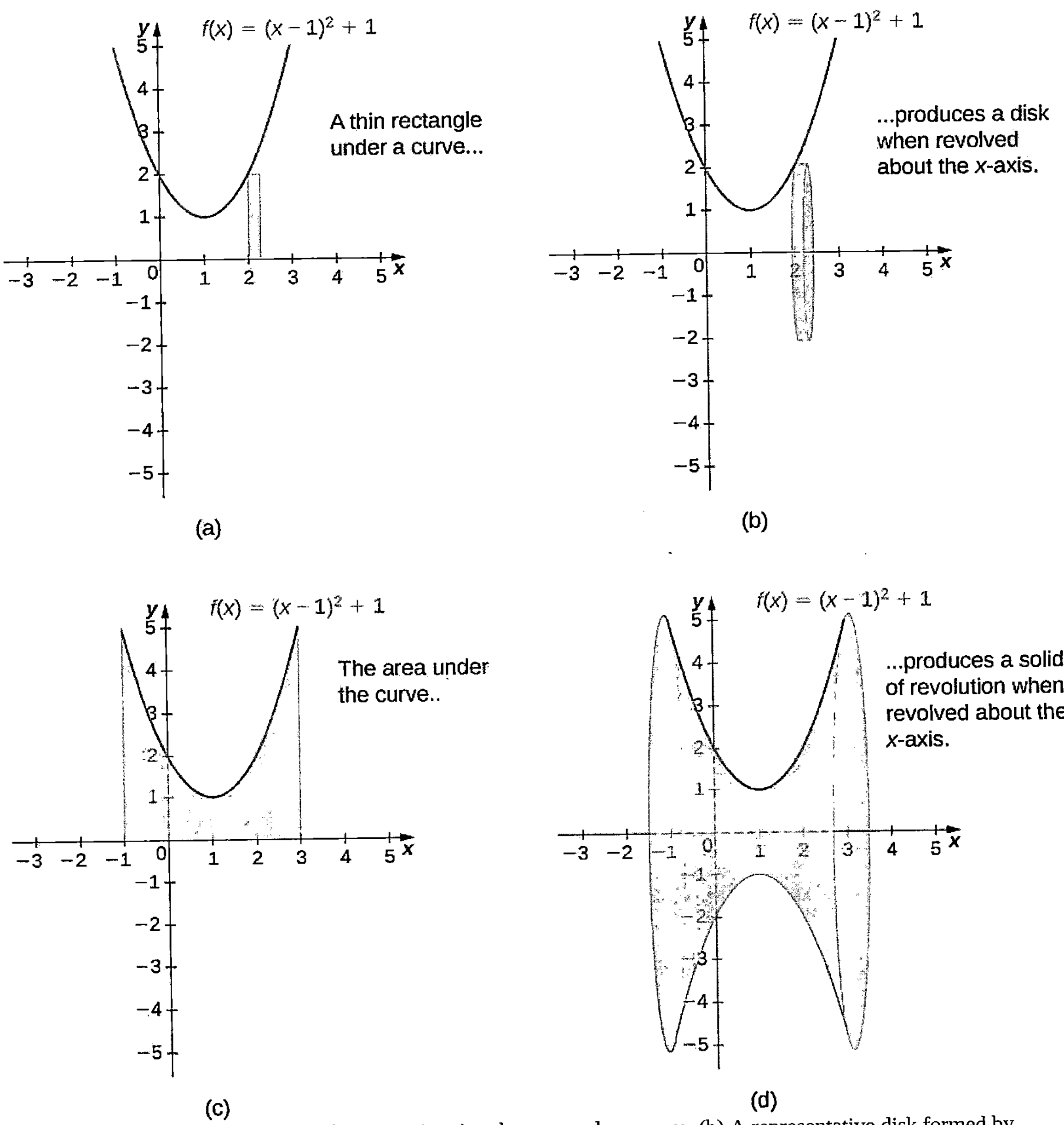

Figure 6.18 (a) A thin rectangle for approximating the area under a curve. (b) A representative disk formed by revolving the rectangle about the x-axis. (c) The region under the curve is revolved about the x-axis, resulting in (d) the solid of revolution.

We already used the formal Riemann sum development of the volume formula when we developed the slicing method. We know that

$$V = \int_a^b A(x)dx.$$

The only difference with the disk method is that we know the formula for the cross-sectional area ahead of time; it is the area of a circle. This gives the following rule.

Rule: The Disk Method

Let $f(x)$ be continuous and nonnegative. Define R as the region bounded above by the graph of $f(x)$, below by the

x-axis, on the left by the line $x = a,$ and on the right by the line $x = b.$ Then, the volume of the solid of revolution formed by revolving R around the x-axis is given by

$$V = \int_a^b \pi[f(x)]^2\, dx. \quad (6.3)$$

The volume of the solid we have been studying (**Figure 6.18**) is given by

$$\begin{aligned} V &= \int_a^b \pi[f(x)]^2\, dx \\ &= \int_{-1}^{3} \pi\left[(x-1)^2 + 1\right]^2 dx = \pi\int_{-1}^{3}\left[(x-1)^4 + 2(x-1)^2 + 1\right]^2 dx \\ &= \pi\left[\frac{1}{5}(x-1)^5 + \frac{2}{3}(x-1)^3 + x\right]\Big|_{-1}^{3} = \pi\left[\left(\frac{32}{5} + \frac{16}{3} + 3\right) - \left(-\frac{32}{5} - \frac{16}{3} - 1\right)\right] = \frac{412\pi}{15}\text{ units}^3. \end{aligned}$$

Let's look at some examples.

Example 6.8

Using the Disk Method to Find the Volume of a Solid of Revolution 1

Use the disk method to find the volume of the solid of revolution generated by rotating the region between the graph of $f(x) = \sqrt{x}$ and the x-axis over the interval $[1, 4]$ around the x-axis.

Solution

The graphs of the function and the solid of revolution are shown in the following figure.

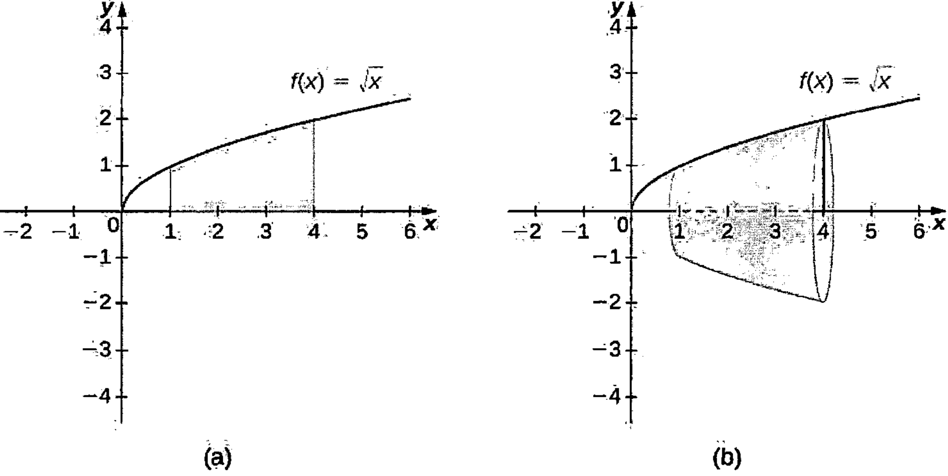

Figure 6.19 (a) The function $f(x) = \sqrt{x}$ over the interval $[1, 4]$. (b) The solid of revolution obtained by revolving the region under the graph of $f(x)$ about the x-axis.

We have

$$\begin{aligned} V &= \int_a^b \pi[f(x)]^2 dx \\ &= \int_1^4 \pi[\sqrt{x}]^2 dx = \pi \int_1^4 x\, dx \\ &= \frac{\pi}{2}x^2\Big|_1^4 = \frac{15\pi}{2}. \end{aligned}$$

The volume is $(15\pi)/2$ units^3.

6.8 Use the disk method to find the volume of the solid of revolution generated by rotating the region between the graph of $f(x) = \sqrt{4-x}$ and the x-axis over the interval $[0, 4]$ around the x-axis.

So far, our examples have all concerned regions revolved around the x-axis, but we can generate a solid of revolution by revolving a plane region around any horizontal or vertical line. In the next example, we look at a solid of revolution that has been generated by revolving a region around the y-axis. The mechanics of the disk method are nearly the same as when the x-axis is the axis of revolution, but we express the function in terms of y and we integrate with respect to y as well. This is summarized in the following rule.

Rule: The Disk Method for Solids of Revolution around the y-axis

Let $g(y)$ be continuous and nonnegative. Define Q as the region bounded on the right by the graph of $g(y)$, on the left by the y-axis, below by the line $y = c$, and above by the line $y = d$. Then, the volume of the solid of revolution formed by revolving Q around the y-axis is given by

$$V = \int_c^d \pi[g(y)]^2 dy. \tag{6.4}$$

The next example shows how this rule works in practice.

Example 6.9

Using the Disk Method to Find the Volume of a Solid of Revolution 2

Let R be the region bounded by the graph of $g(y) = \sqrt{4-y}$ and the y-axis over the y-axis interval $[0, 4]$. Use the disk method to find the volume of the solid of revolution generated by rotating R around the y-axis.

Solution

Figure 6.20 shows the function and a representative disk that can be used to estimate the volume. Notice that since we are revolving the function around the y-axis, the disks are horizontal, rather than vertical.

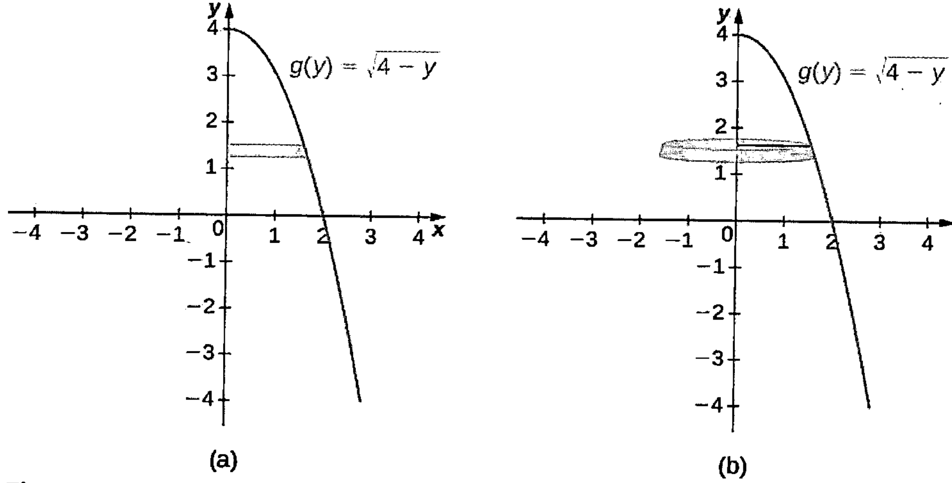

Figure 6.20 (a) Shown is a thin rectangle between the curve of the function $g(y) = \sqrt{4 - y}$ and the y-axis. (b) The rectangle forms a representative disk after revolution around the y-axis.

The region to be revolved and the full solid of revolution are depicted in the following figure.

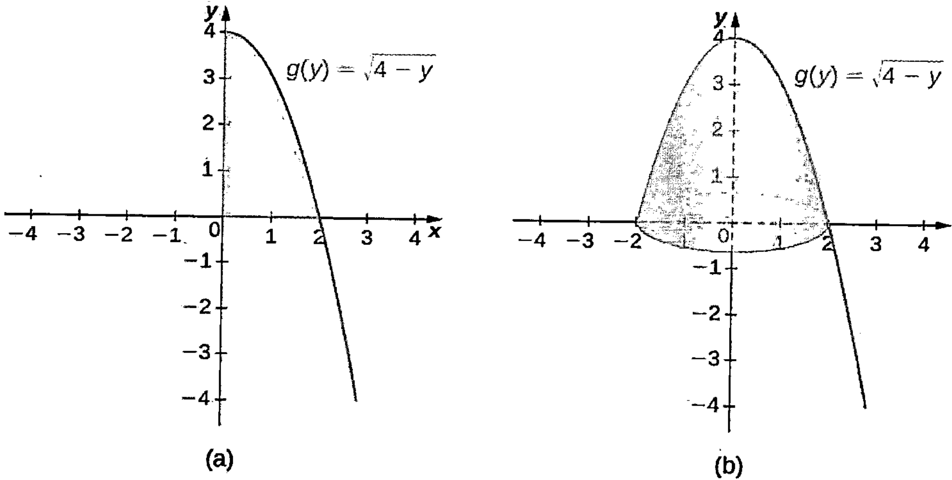

Figure 6.21 (a) The region to the left of the function $g(y) = \sqrt{4 - y}$ over the y-axis interval $[0, 4]$. (b) The solid of revolution formed by revolving the region about the y-axis.

To find the volume, we integrate with respect to y. We obtain

$$\begin{aligned} V &= \int_c^d \pi[g(y)]^2\,dy \\ &= \int_0^4 \pi\left[\sqrt{4 - y}\right]^2 dy = \pi\int_0^4 (4 - y)dy \\ &= \pi\left[4y - \frac{y^2}{2}\right]\Bigg|_0^4 = 8\pi. \end{aligned}$$

The volume is 8π units^3.

6.9 Use the disk method to find the volume of the solid of revolution generated by rotating the region between the graph of $g(y) = y$ and the y-axis over the interval $[1, 4]$ around the y-axis.

The Washer Method

Some solids of revolution have cavities in the middle; they are not solid all the way to the axis of revolution. Sometimes, this is just a result of the way the region of revolution is shaped with respect to the axis of revolution. In other cases, cavities arise when the region of revolution is defined as the region between the graphs of two functions. A third way this can happen is when an axis of revolution other than the x-axis or y-axis is selected.

When the solid of revolution has a cavity in the middle, the slices used to approximate the volume are not disks, but washers (disks with holes in the center). For example, consider the region bounded above by the graph of the function $f(x) = \sqrt{x}$ and below by the graph of the function $g(x) = 1$ over the interval $[1, 4]$. When this region is revolved around the x-axis, the result is a solid with a cavity in the middle, and the slices are washers. The graph of the function and a representative washer are shown in **Figure 6.22**(a) and (b). The region of revolution and the resulting solid are shown in **Figure 6.22**(c) and (d).

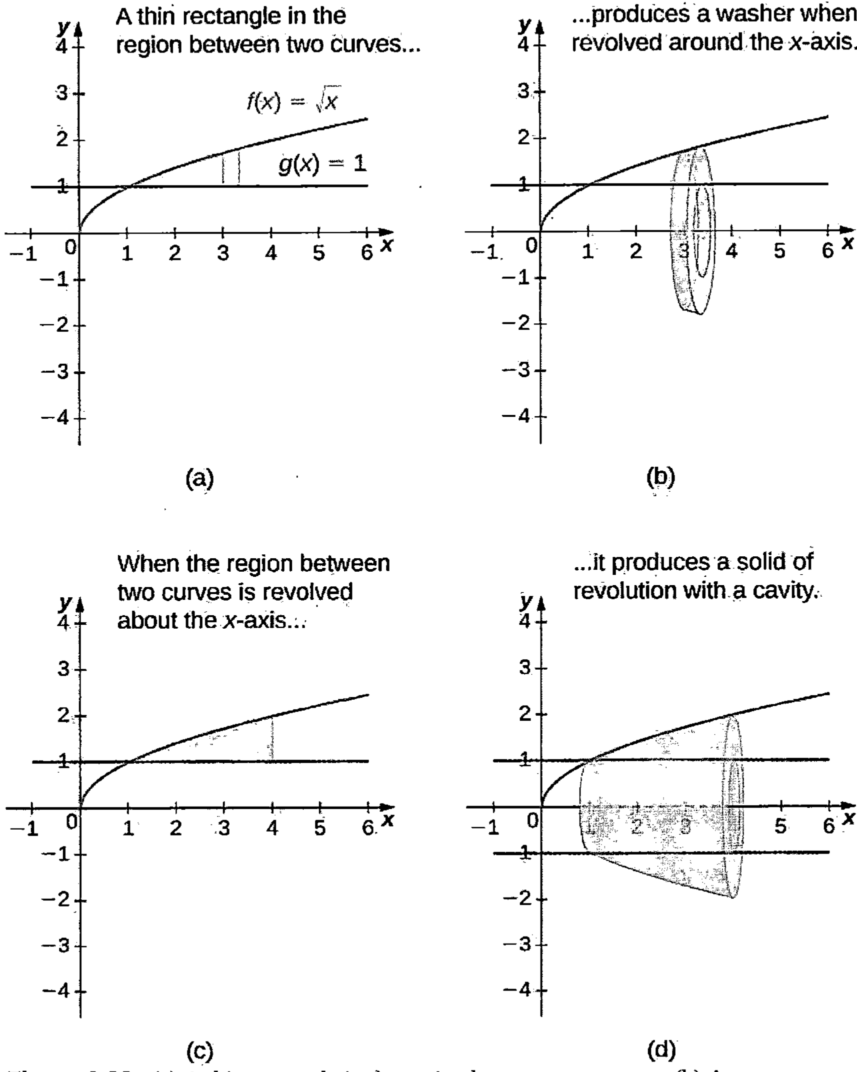

Figure 6.22 (a) A thin rectangle in the region between two curves. (b) A representative disk formed by revolving the rectangle about the x-axis. (c) The region between the curves over the given interval. (d) The resulting solid of revolution.

The cross-sectional area, then, is the area of the outer circle less the area of the inner circle. In this case,

$$A(x) = \pi(\sqrt{x})^2 - \pi(1)^2 = \pi(x - 1).$$

Then the volume of the solid is

$$\begin{aligned} V &= \int_a^b A(x)dx \\ &= \int_1^4 \pi(x-1)dx = \pi\left[\frac{x^2}{2} - x\right]\Big|_1^4 = \frac{9}{2}\pi \text{ units}^3. \end{aligned}$$

Generalizing this process gives the **washer method**.

Rule: The Washer Method

Suppose $f(x)$ and $g(x)$ are continuous, nonnegative functions such that $f(x) \geq g(x)$ over $[a, b]$. Let R denote the region bounded above by the graph of $f(x)$, below by the graph of $g(x)$, on the left by the line $x = a$, and on the right by the line $x = b$. Then, the volume of the solid of revolution formed by revolving R around the x-axis is given by

$$V = \int_a^b \pi\left[(f(x))^2 - (g(x))^2\right]dx. \tag{6.5}$$

Example 6.10

Using the Washer Method

Find the volume of a solid of revolution formed by revolving the region bounded above by the graph of $f(x) = x$ and below by the graph of $g(x) = 1/x$ over the interval $[1, 4]$ around the x-axis.

Solution

The graphs of the functions and the solid of revolution are shown in the following figure.

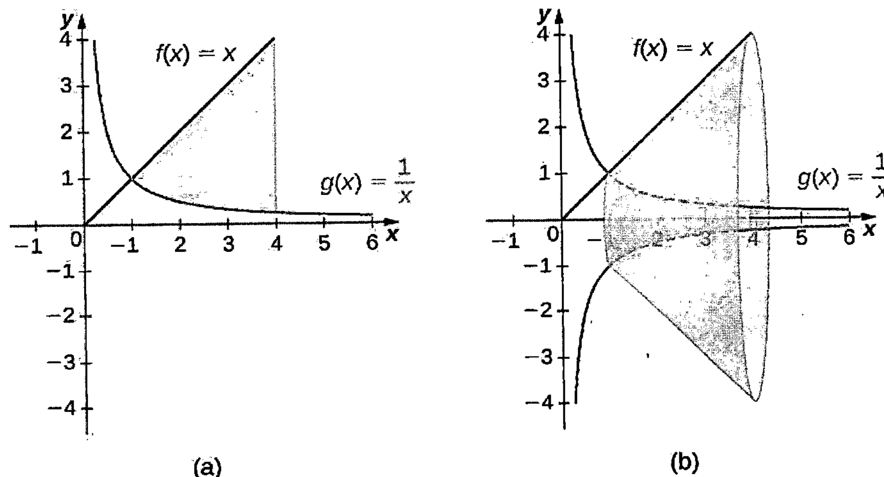

Figure 6.23 (a) The region between the graphs of the functions $f(x) = x$ and $g(x) = 1/x$ over the interval $[1, 4]$. (b) Revolving the region about the x-axis generates a solid of revolution with a cavity in the middle.

We have

$$\begin{aligned} V &= \int_a^b \pi\left[(f(x))^2 - (g(x))^2\right]dx \\ &= \pi\int_1^4 \left[x^2 - \left(\frac{1}{x}\right)^2\right]dx = \pi\left[\frac{x^3}{3} + \frac{1}{x}\right]\Big|_1^4 = \frac{81\pi}{4}\text{ units}^3. \end{aligned}$$

6.10 Find the volume of a solid of revolution formed by revolving the region bounded by the graphs of $f(x) = \sqrt{x}$ and $g(x) = 1/x$ over the interval $[1, 3]$ around the x-axis.

As with the disk method, we can also apply the washer method to solids of revolution that result from revolving a region around the y-axis. In this case, the following rule applies.

Rule: The Washer Method for Solids of Revolution around the y-axis

Suppose $u(y)$ and $v(y)$ are continuous, nonnegative functions such that $v(y) \le u(y)$ for $y \in [c, d]$. Let Q denote the region bounded on the right by the graph of $u(y)$, on the left by the graph of $v(y)$, below by the line $y = c$, and above by the line $y = d$. Then, the volume of the solid of revolution formed by revolving Q around the y-axis is given by

$$V = \int_c^d \pi\left[(u(y))^2 - (v(y))^2\right]dy.$$

Rather than looking at an example of the washer method with the y-axis as the axis of revolution, we now consider an example in which the axis of revolution is a line other than one of the two coordinate axes. The same general method applies, but you may have to visualize just how to describe the cross-sectional area of the volume.

Example 6.11

The Washer Method with a Different Axis of Revolution

Find the volume of a solid of revolution formed by revolving the region bounded above by $f(x) = 4 - x$ and below by the x-axis over the interval $[0, 4]$ around the line $y = -2$.

Solution

The graph of the region and the solid of revolution are shown in the following figure.

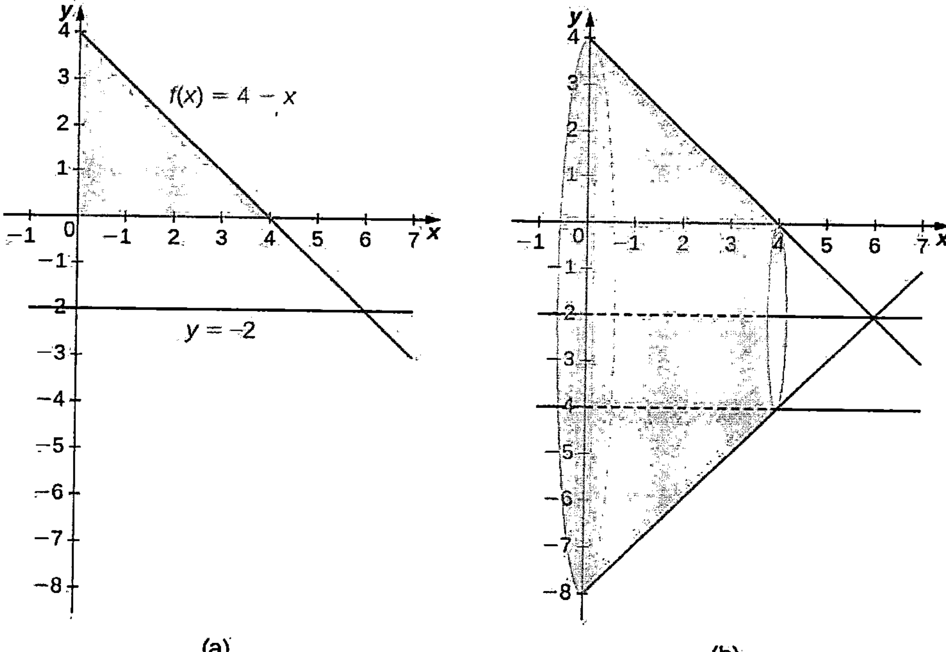

Figure 6.24 (a) The region between the graph of the function $f(x) = 4 - x$ and the x-axis over the interval $[0, 4]$. (b) Revolving the region about the line $y = -2$ generates a solid of revolution with a cylindrical hole through its middle.

We can't apply the volume formula to this problem directly because the axis of revolution is not one of the coordinate axes. However, we still know that the area of the cross-section is the area of the outer circle less the area of the inner circle. Looking at the graph of the function, we see the radius of the outer circle is given by $f(x)+2,$ which simplifies to

$$f(x)+2=(4-x)+2=6-x.$$

The radius of the inner circle is $g(x)=2.$ Therefore, we have

$$\begin{aligned} V &= \int_0^4 \pi\left[(6-x)^2-(2)^2\right]dx \\ &= \pi\int_0^4 \left(x^2-12x+32\right)dx = \pi\left[\frac{x^3}{3}-6x^2+32x\right]\Big|_0^4 = \frac{160\pi}{3}\text{ units}^3. \end{aligned}$$

6.11 Find the volume of a solid of revolution formed by revolving the region bounded above by the graph of $f(x)=x+2$ and below by the x-axis over the interval $[0,\ 3]$ around the line $y=-1.$

6.2 EXERCISES

58. Derive the formula for the volume of a sphere using the slicing method.

59. Use the slicing method to derive the formula for the volume of a cone.

60. Use the slicing method to derive the formula for the volume of a tetrahedron with side length a.

61. Use the disk method to derive the formula for the volume of a trapezoidal cylinder.

62. Explain when you would use the disk method versus the washer method. When are they interchangeable?

For the following exercises, draw a typical slice and find the volume using the slicing method for the given volume.

63. A pyramid with height 6 units and square base of side 2 units, as pictured here.

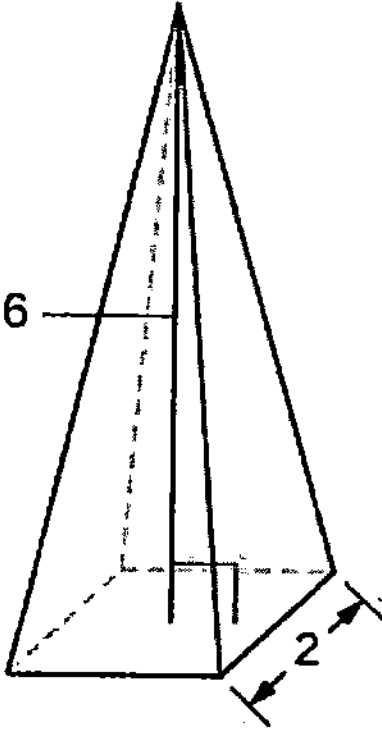

64. A pyramid with height 4 units and a rectangular base with length 2 units and width 3 units, as pictured here.

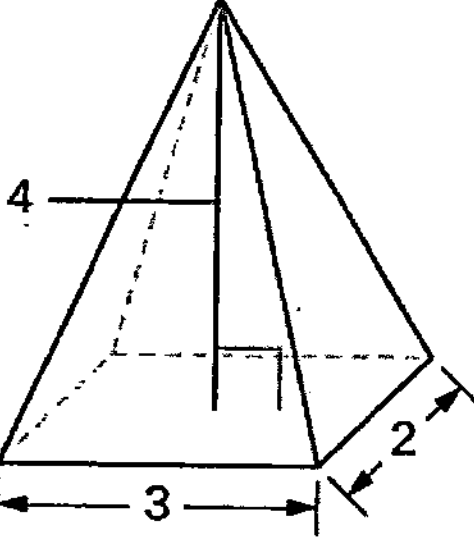

65. A tetrahedron with a base side of 4 units, as seen here.

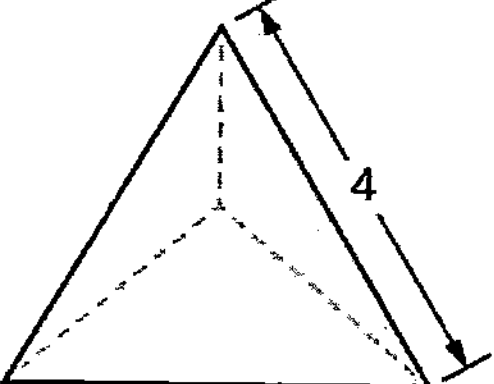

66. A pyramid with height 5 units, and an isosceles triangular base with lengths of 6 units and 8 units, as seen here.

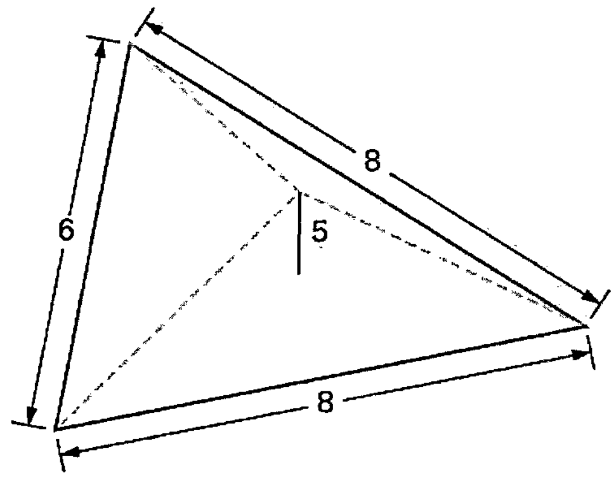

67. A cone of radius r and height h has a smaller cone of radius $r/2$ and height $h/2$ removed from the top, as seen here. The resulting solid is called a *frustum*.

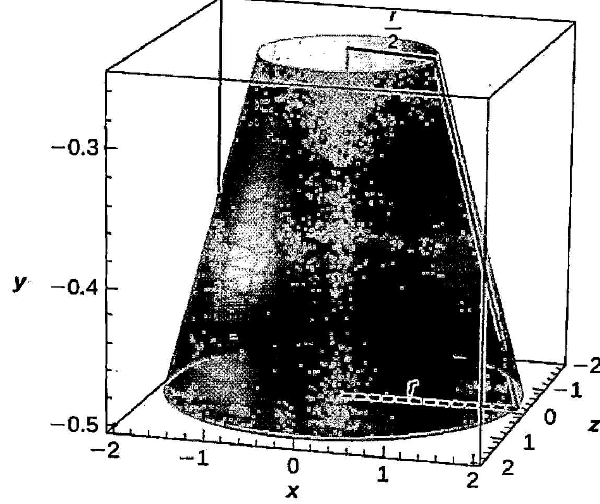

For the following exercises, draw an outline of the solid and find the volume using the slicing method.

68. The base is a circle of radius a. The slices perpendicular to the base are squares.

69. The base is a triangle with vertices $(0, 0)$, $(1, 0)$, and $(0, 1)$. Slices perpendicular to the xy-plane are semicircles.

70. The base is the region under the parabola $y = 1 - x^2$ in the first quadrant. Slices perpendicular to the xy-plane are squares.

71. The base is the region under the parabola $y = 1 - x^2$ and above the x-axis. Slices perpendicular to the y-axis are squares.

72. The base is the region enclosed by $y = x^2$ and $y = 9$. Slices perpendicular to the x-axis are right isosceles triangles.

73. The base is the area between $y = x$ and $y = x^2$. Slices perpendicular to the x-axis are semicircles.

For the following exercises, draw the region bounded by the curves. Then, use the disk method to find the volume when the region is rotated around the x-axis.

74. $x + y = 8,\ x = 0,$ and $y = 0$

75. $y = 2x^2,\ x = 0,\ x = 4,$ and $y = 0$

76. $y = e^x + 1,\ x = 0,\ x = 1,$ and $y = 0$

77. $y = x^4,\ x = 0,$ and $y = 1$

78. $y = \sqrt{x},\ x = 0,\ x = 4,$ and $y = 0$

79. $y = \sin x,\ y = \cos x,$ and $x = 0$

80. $y = \frac{1}{x},\ x = 2,$ and $y = 3$

81. $x^2 - y^2 = 9$ and $x + y = 9,\ y = 0$ and $x = 0$

For the following exercises, draw the region bounded by the curves. Then, find the volume when the region is rotated around the y-axis.

82. $y = 4 - \frac{1}{2}x,\ x = 0,$ and $y = 0$

83. $y = 2x^3,\ x = 0,\ x = 1,$ and $y = 0$

84. $y = 3x^2,\ x = 0,$ and $y = 3$

85. $y = \sqrt{4 - x^2},\ y = 0,$ and $x = 0$

86. $y = \frac{1}{\sqrt{x+1}},\ x = 0,$ and $x = 3$

87. $x = \sec(y)$ and $y = \frac{\pi}{4},\ y = 0$ and $x = 0$

88. $y = \frac{1}{x+1},\ x = 0,$ and $x = 2$

89. $y = 4 - x,\ y = x,$ and $x = 0$

For the following exercises, draw the region bounded by the curves. Then, find the volume when the region is rotated around the x-axis.

90. $y = x + 2,\ y = x + 6,\ x = 0,$ and $x = 5$

91. $y = x^2$ and $y = x + 2$

92. $x^2 = y^3$ and $x^3 = y^2$

93. $y = 4 - x^2$ and $y = 2 - x$

94. **[T]** $y = \cos x,\ y = e^{-x},\ x = 0,$ and $x = 1.2927$

95. $y = \sqrt{x}$ and $y = x^2$

96. $y = \sin x,\ y = 5\sin x,\ x = 0$ and $x = \pi$

97. $y = \sqrt{1 + x^2}$ and $y = \sqrt{4 - x^2}$

For the following exercises, draw the region bounded by the curves. Then, use the washer method to find the volume when the region is revolved around the y-axis.

98. $y = \sqrt{x},\ x = 4,$ and $y = 0$

99. $y = x + 2,\ y = 2x - 1,$ and $x = 0$

100. $y = \sqrt[3]{x}$ and $y = x^3$

101. $x = e^{2y},\ x = y^2,\ y = 0,$ and $y = \ln(2)$

102. $x = \sqrt{9 - y^2},\ x = e^{-y},\ y = 0,$ and $y = 3$

103. Yogurt containers can be shaped like frustums. Rotate the line $y = \frac{1}{m}x$ around the y-axis to find the volume between $y = a$ and $y = b$.

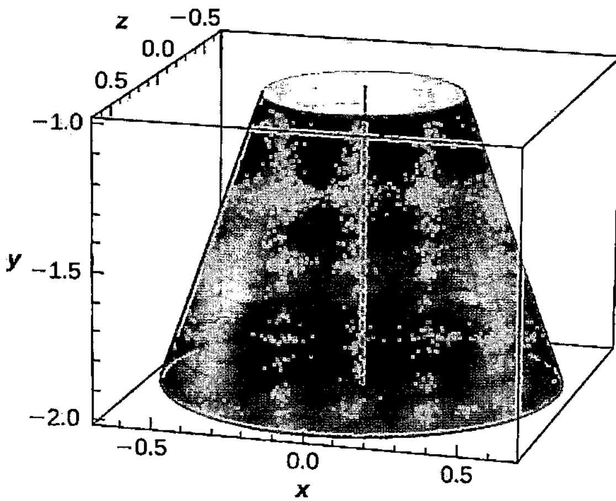

104. Rotate the ellipse $(x^2/a^2) + (y^2/b^2) = 1$ around the x-axis to approximate the volume of a football, as seen here.

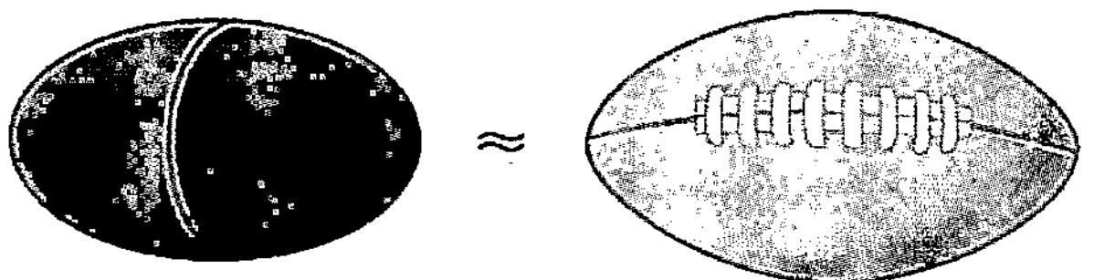

105. Rotate the ellipse $(x^2/a^2) + (y^2/b^2) = 1$ around the y-axis to approximate the volume of a football.

106. A better approximation of the volume of a football is given by the solid that comes from rotating $y = \sin x$ around the x-axis from $x = 0$ to $x = \pi$. What is the volume of this football approximation, as seen here?

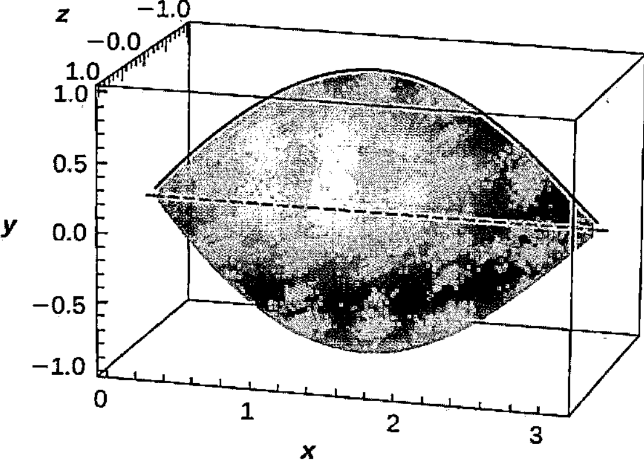

107. What is the volume of the Bundt cake that comes from rotating $y = \sin x$ around the y-axis from $x = 0$ to $x = \pi$?

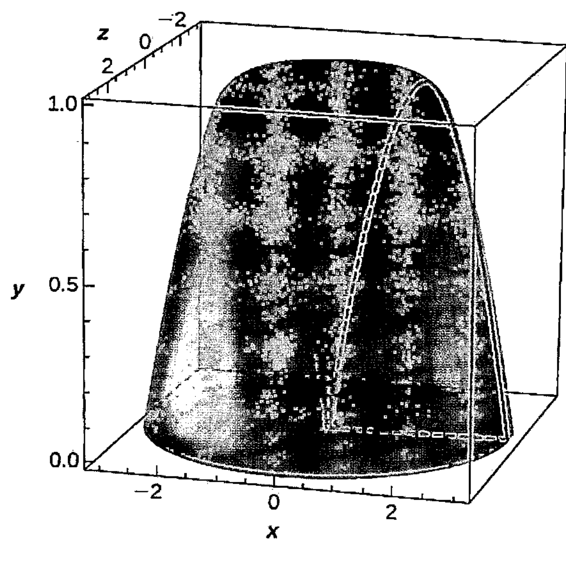

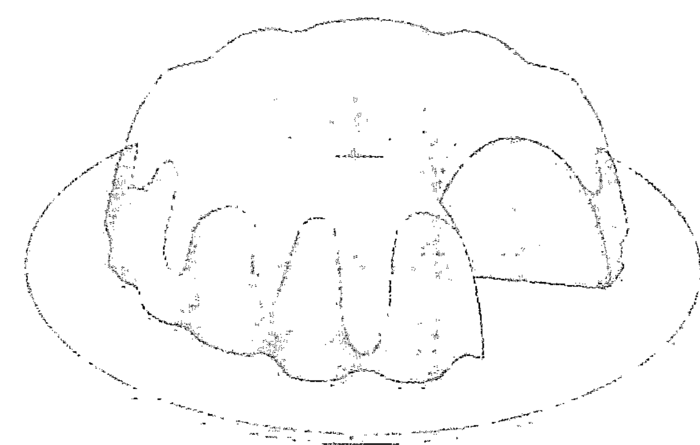

For the following exercises, find the volume of the solid described.

108. The base is the region between $y = x$ and $y = x^2$. Slices perpendicular to the x-axis are semicircles.

109. The base is the region enclosed by the generic ellipse $\left(x^2/a^2\right) + \left(y^2/b^2\right) = 1$. Slices perpendicular to the x-axis are semicircles.

110. Bore a hole of radius a down the axis of a right cone and through the base of radius b, as seen here.

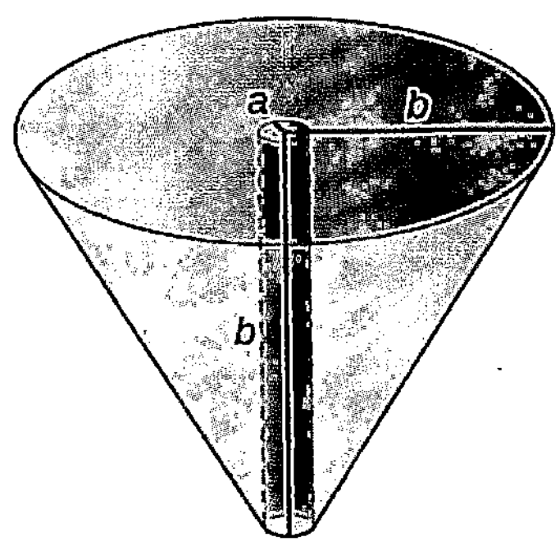

111. Find the volume common to two spheres of radius r with centers that are $2h$ apart, as shown here.

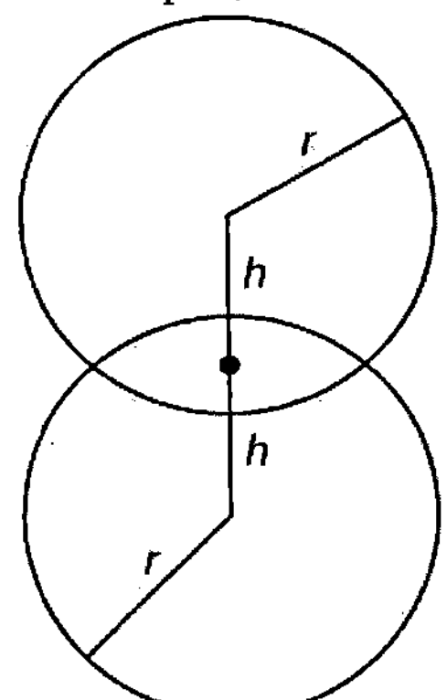

112. Find the volume of a spherical cap of height h and radius r where $h < r$, as seen here.

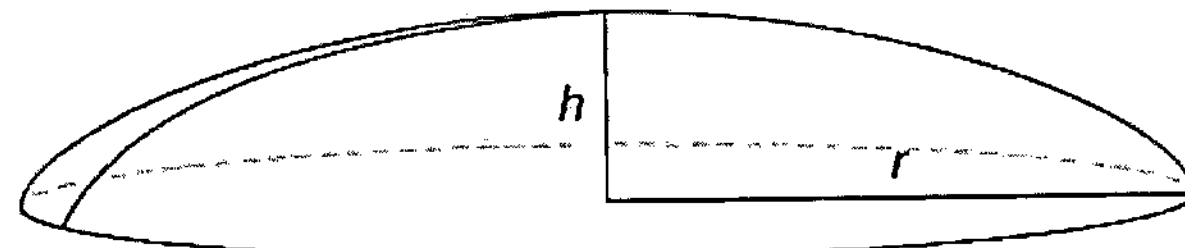

113. Find the volume of a sphere of radius R with a cap of height h removed from the top, as seen here.

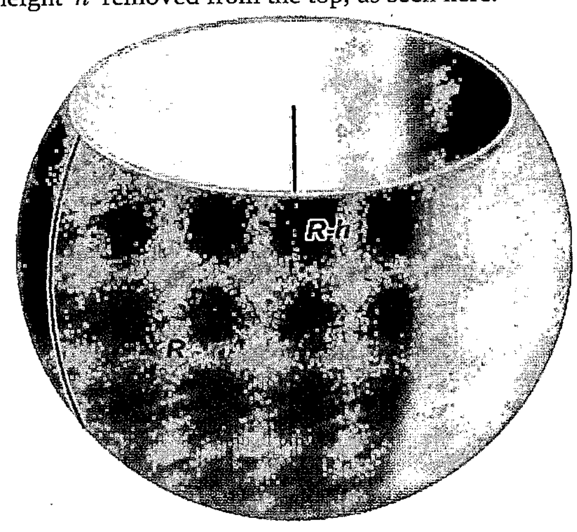

6.3 | Volumes of Revolution: Cylindrical Shells

Learning Objectives

6.3.1 Calculate the volume of a solid of revolution by using the method of cylindrical shells.
6.3.2 Compare the different methods for calculating a volume of revolution.

In this section, we examine the method of cylindrical shells, the final method for finding the volume of a solid of revolution. We can use this method on the same kinds of solids as the disk method or the washer method; however, with the disk and washer methods, we integrate along the coordinate axis parallel to the axis of revolution. With the method of cylindrical shells, we integrate along the coordinate axis *perpendicular* to the axis of revolution. The ability to choose which variable of integration we want to use can be a significant advantage with more complicated functions. Also, the specific geometry of the solid sometimes makes the method of using cylindrical shells more appealing than using the washer method. In the last part of this section, we review all the methods for finding volume that we have studied and lay out some guidelines to help you determine which method to use in a given situation.

The Method of Cylindrical Shells

Again, we are working with a solid of revolution. As before, we define a region R, bounded above by the graph of a function $y = f(x)$, below by the x-axis, and on the left and right by the lines $x = a$ and $x = b$, respectively, as shown in **Figure 6.25**(a). We then revolve this region around the y-axis, as shown in **Figure 6.25**(b). Note that this is different from what we have done before. Previously, regions defined in terms of functions of x were revolved around the x-axis or a line parallel to it.

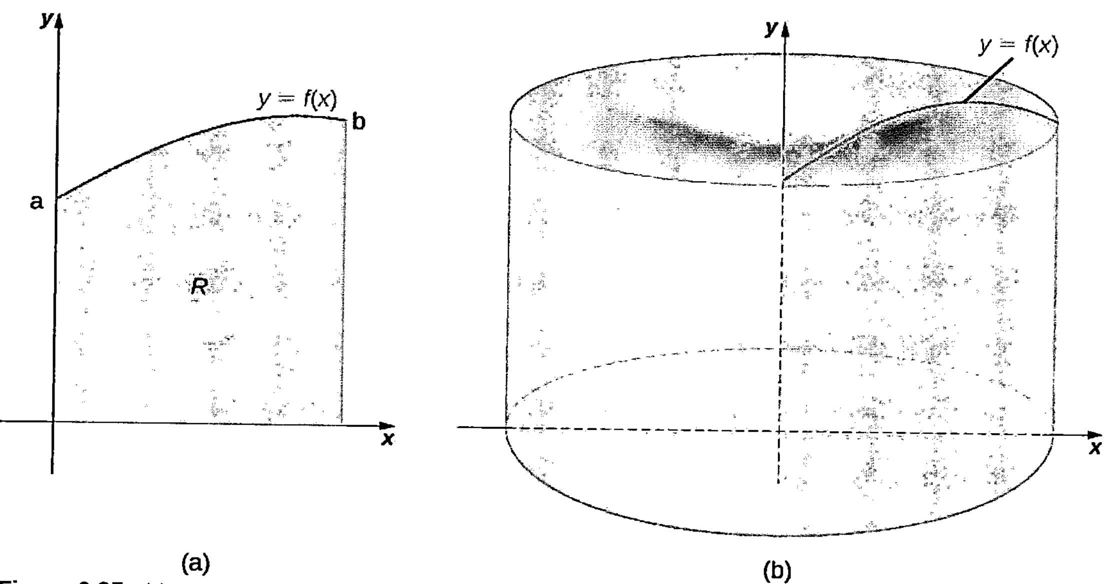

Figure 6.25 (a) A region bounded by the graph of a function of x. (b) The solid of revolution formed when the region is revolved around the y-axis.

As we have done many times before, partition the interval $[a, b]$ using a regular partition, $P = \{x_0, x_1, \ldots, x_n\}$ and, for $i = 1, 2, \ldots, n$, choose a point $x_i^* \in [x_{i-1}, x_i]$. Then, construct a rectangle over the interval $[x_{i-1}, x_i]$ of height $f(x_i^*)$ and width Δx. A representative rectangle is shown in **Figure 6.26**(a). When that rectangle is revolved around the y-axis, instead of a disk or a washer, we get a cylindrical shell, as shown in the following figure.

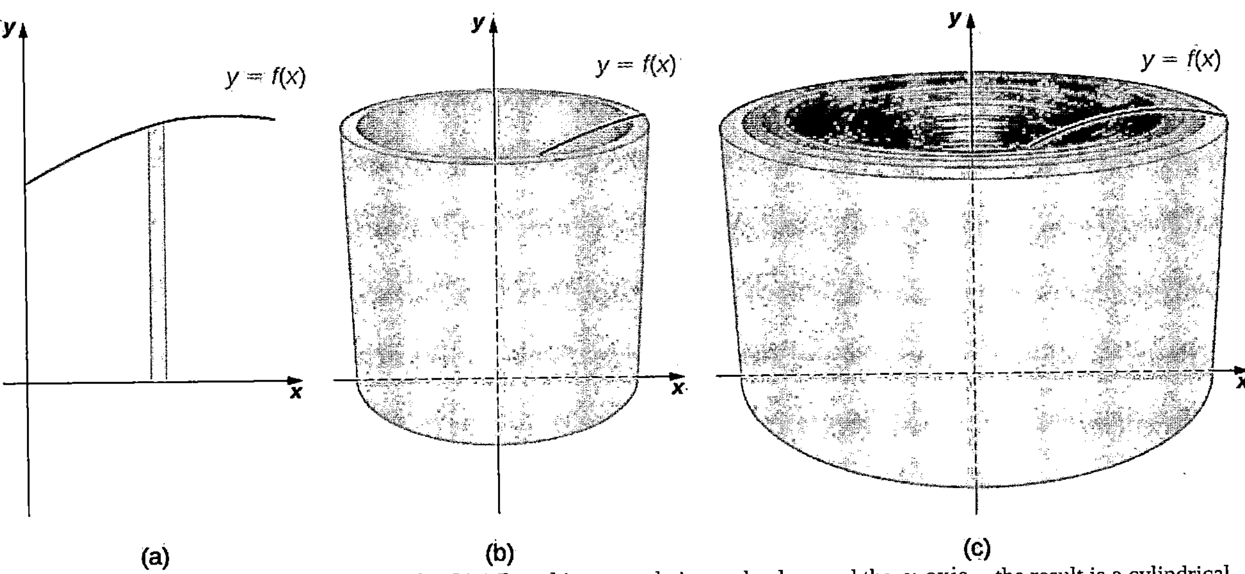

Figure 6.26 (a) A representative rectangle. (b) When this rectangle is revolved around the y-axis, the result is a cylindrical shell. (c) When we put all the shells together, we get an approximation of the original solid.

To calculate the volume of this shell, consider **Figure 6.27**.

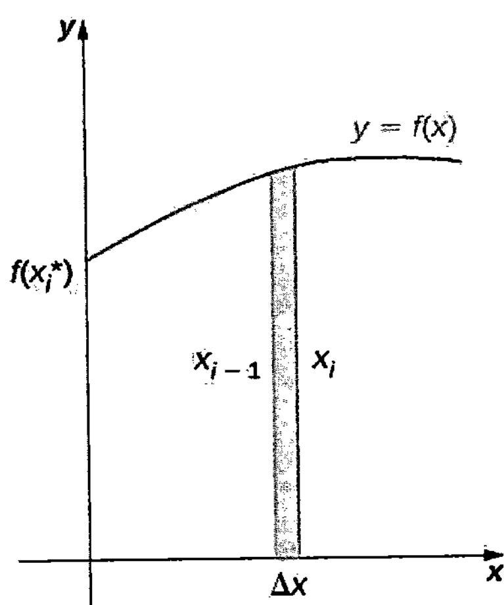

Figure 6.27 Calculating the volume of the shell.

The shell is a cylinder, so its volume is the cross-sectional area multiplied by the height of the cylinder. The cross-sections are annuli (ring-shaped regions—essentially, circles with a hole in the center), with outer radius x_i and inner radius x_{i-1}. Thus, the cross-sectional area is $\pi x_i^2 - \pi x_{i-1}^2$. The height of the cylinder is $f(x_i^*)$. Then the volume of the shell is

$$\begin{aligned} V_{\text{shell}} &= f(x_i^*)(\pi x_i^2 - \pi x_{i-1}^2) \\ &= \pi f(x_i^*)\left(x_i^2 - x_{i-1}^2\right) \\ &= \pi f(x_i^*)(x_i + x_{i-1})(x_i - x_{i-1}) \\ &= 2\pi f(x_i^*)\left(\frac{x_i + x_{i-1}}{2}\right)(x_i - x_{i-1}). \end{aligned}$$

Note that $x_i - x_{i-1} = \Delta x,$ so we have

$$V_{shell} = 2\pi f(x_i^*)\left(\frac{x_i + x_{i-1}}{2}\right)\Delta x.$$

Furthermore, $\frac{x_i + x_{i-1}}{2}$ is both the midpoint of the interval $[x_{i-1}, x_i]$ and the average radius of the shell, and we can approximate this by x_i^*. We then have

$$V_{shell} \approx 2\pi f(x_i^*)x_i^* \Delta x.$$

Another way to think of this is to think of making a vertical cut in the shell and then opening it up to form a flat plate (**Figure 6.28**).

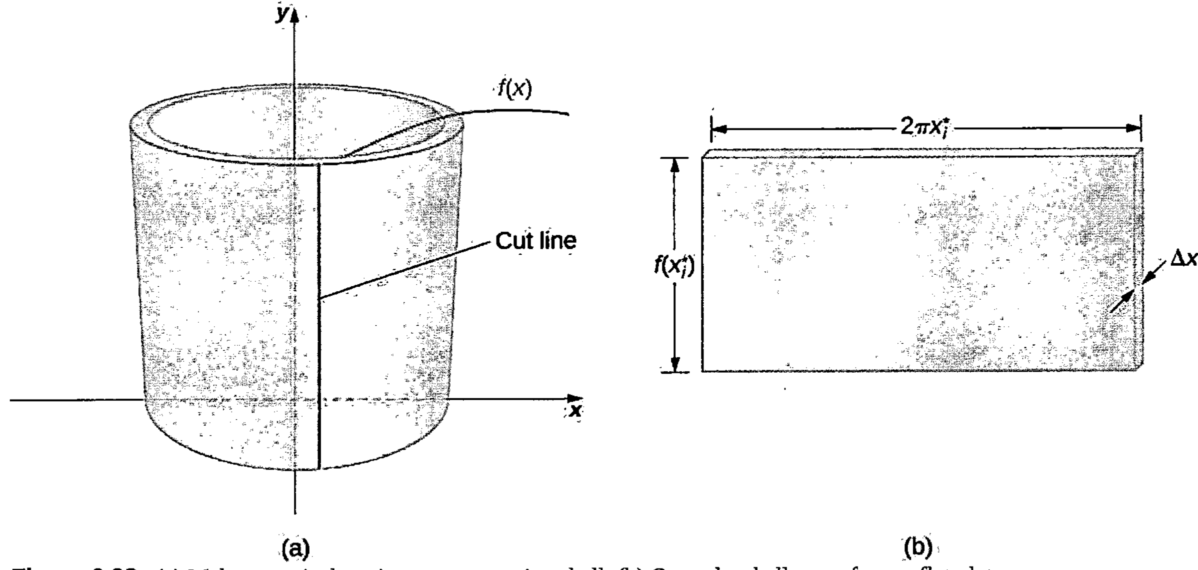

Figure 6.28 (a) Make a vertical cut in a representative shell. (b) Open the shell up to form a flat plate.

In reality, the outer radius of the shell is greater than the inner radius, and hence the back edge of the plate would be slightly longer than the front edge of the plate. However, we can approximate the flattened shell by a flat plate of height $f(x_i^*)$, width $2\pi x_i^*$, and thickness Δx (**Figure 6.28**). The volume of the shell, then, is approximately the volume of the flat plate. Multiplying the height, width, and depth of the plate, we get

$$V_{shell} \approx f(x_i^*)(2\pi x_i^*)\Delta x,$$

which is the same formula we had before.

To calculate the volume of the entire solid, we then add the volumes of all the shells and obtain

$$V \approx \sum_{i=1}^{n} (2\pi x_i^* f(x_i^*)\Delta x).$$

Here we have another Riemann sum, this time for the function $2\pi x f(x)$. Taking the limit as $n \to \infty$ gives us

$$V = \lim_{n \to \infty} \sum_{i=1}^{n} (2\pi x_i^* f(x_i^*)\Delta x) = \int_a^b (2\pi x f(x))dx.$$

This leads to the following rule for the **method of cylindrical shells.**

Rule: The Method of Cylindrical Shells

Let $f(x)$ be continuous and nonnegative. Define R as the region bounded above by the graph of $f(x)$, below by the x-axis, on the left by the line $x = a$, and on the right by the line $x = b$. Then the volume of the solid of revolution formed by revolving R around the y-axis is given by

$$V = \int_a^b (2\pi x f(x))dx. \quad (6.6)$$

Now let's consider an example.

Example 6.12

The Method of Cylindrical Shells 1

Define R as the region bounded above by the graph of $f(x) = 1/x$ and below by the x-axis over the interval $[1, 3]$. Find the volume of the solid of revolution formed by revolving R around the y-axis.

Solution

First we must graph the region R and the associated solid of revolution, as shown in the following figure.

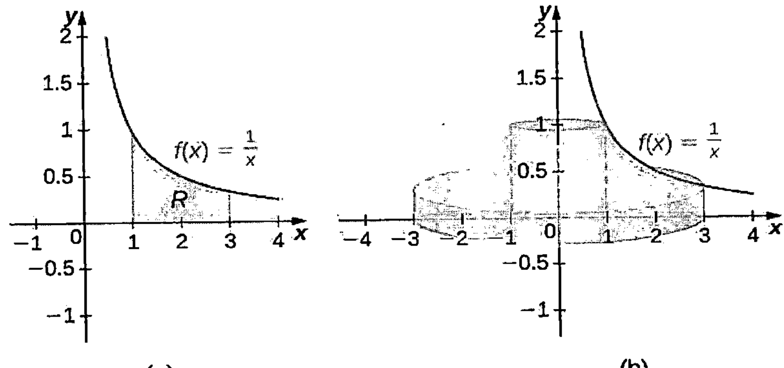

Figure 6.29 (a) The region R under the graph of $f(x) = 1/x$ over the interval $[1, 3]$. (b) The solid of revolution generated by revolving R about the y-axis.

Then the volume of the solid is given by

$$\begin{aligned} V &= \int_a^b (2\pi x f(x))dx \\ &= \int_1^3 \left(2\pi x\left(\frac{1}{x}\right)\right)dx \\ &= \int_1^3 2\pi\, dx = 2\pi x\big|_1^3 = 4\pi \text{ units}^3. \end{aligned}$$

6.12 Define R as the region bounded above by the graph of $f(x) = x^2$ and below by the x-axis over the interval $[1, 2]$. Find the volume of the solid of revolution formed by revolving R around the y-axis.

Example 6.13

The Method of Cylindrical Shells 2

Define R as the region bounded above by the graph of $f(x) = 2x - x^2$ and below by the x-axis over the interval $[0, 2]$. Find the volume of the solid of revolution formed by revolving R around the y-axis.

Solution

First graph the region R and the associated solid of revolution, as shown in the following figure.

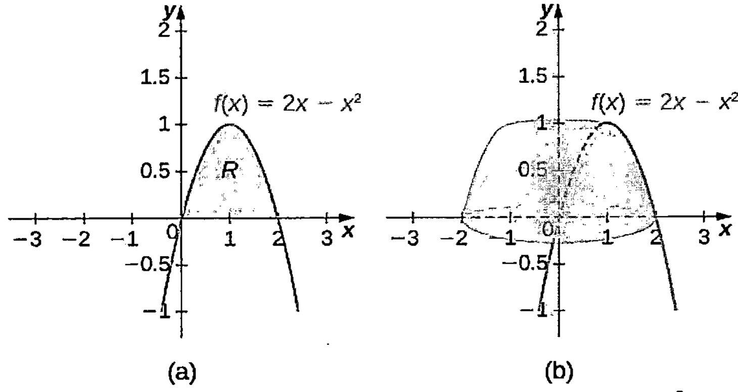

Figure 6.30 (a) The region R under the graph of $f(x) = 2x - x^2$ over the interval $[0, 2]$. (b) The volume of revolution obtained by revolving R about the y-axis.

Then the volume of the solid is given by

$$\begin{aligned} V &= \int_a^b (2\pi x f(x))dx \\ &= \int_0^2 \left(2\pi x\left(2x - x^2\right)\right)dx = 2\pi \int_0^2 \left(2x^2 - x^3\right)dx \\ &= 2\pi \left[\frac{2x^3}{3} - \frac{x^4}{4}\right]\Bigg|_0^2 = \frac{8\pi}{3} \text{ units}^3. \end{aligned}$$

6.13 Define R as the region bounded above by the graph of $f(x) = 3x - x^2$ and below by the x-axis over the interval $[0, 2]$. Find the volume of the solid of revolution formed by revolving R around the y-axis.

As with the disk method and the washer method, we can use the method of cylindrical shells with solids of revolution, revolved around the x-axis, when we want to integrate with respect to y. The analogous rule for this type of solid is given here.

Rule: The Method of Cylindrical Shells for Solids of Revolution around the x-axis

Let $g(y)$ be continuous and nonnegative. Define Q as the region bounded on the right by the graph of $g(y)$, on the left by the y-axis, below by the line $y = c$, and above by the line $y = d$. Then, the volume of the solid of revolution formed by revolving Q around the x-axis is given by

$$V = \int_c^d (2\pi y g(y))dy.$$

Example 6.14

The Method of Cylindrical Shells for a Solid Revolved around the x-axis

Define Q as the region bounded on the right by the graph of $g(y) = 2\sqrt{y}$ and on the left by the y-axis for $y \in [0, 4]$. Find the volume of the solid of revolution formed by revolving Q around the x-axis.

Solution

First, we need to graph the region Q and the associated solid of revolution, as shown in the following figure.

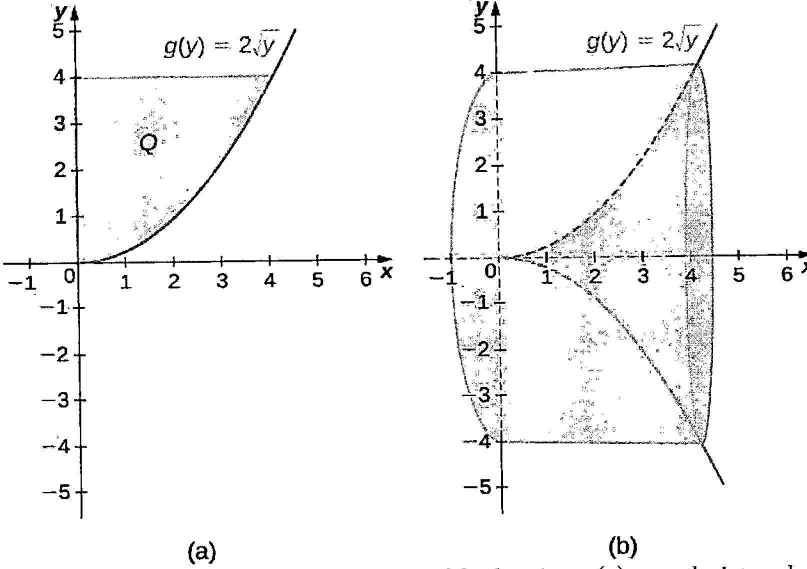

Figure 6.31 (a) The region Q to the left of the function $g(y)$ over the interval $[0, 4]$. (b) The solid of revolution generated by revolving Q around the x-axis.

Label the shaded region Q. Then the volume of the solid is given by

$$\begin{aligned} V &= \int_c^d (2\pi y g(y))dy \\ &= \int_0^4 (2\pi y(2\sqrt{y}))dy = 4\pi \int_0^4 y^{3/2}dy \\ &= 4\pi\left[\frac{2y^{5/2}}{5}\right]\Bigg|_0^4 = \frac{256\pi}{5} \text{ units}^3. \end{aligned}$$

6.14 Define Q as the region bounded on the right by the graph of $g(y) = 3/y$ and on the left by the y-axis for $y \in [1, 3]$. Find the volume of the solid of revolution formed by revolving Q around the x-axis.

For the next example, we look at a solid of revolution for which the graph of a function is revolved around a line other than one of the two coordinate axes. To set this up, we need to revisit the development of the method of cylindrical shells. Recall that we found the volume of one of the shells to be given by

$$\begin{aligned} V_{\text{shell}} &= f(x_i^*)(\pi x_i^2 - \pi x_{i-1}^2) \\ &= \pi f(x_i^*)\left(x_i^2 - x_{i-1}^2\right) \\ &= \pi f(x_i^*)(x_i + x_{i-1})(x_i - x_{i-1}) \\ &= 2\pi f(x_i^*)\left(\frac{x_i + x_{i-1}}{2}\right)(x_i - x_{i-1}). \end{aligned}$$

This was based on a shell with an outer radius of x_i and an inner radius of x_{i-1}. If, however, we rotate the region around a line other than the y-axis, we have a different outer and inner radius. Suppose, for example, that we rotate the region around the line $x = -k$, where k is some positive constant. Then, the outer radius of the shell is $x_i + k$ and the inner radius of the shell is $x_{i-1} + k$. Substituting these terms into the expression for volume, we see that when a plane region is rotated around the line $x = -k$, the volume of a shell is given by

$$\begin{aligned} V_{\text{shell}} &= 2\pi f(x_i^*)\left(\frac{(x_i + k) + (x_{i-1} + k)}{2}\right)((x_i + k) - (x_{i-1} + k)) \\ &= 2\pi f(x_i^*)\left(\left(\frac{x_i + x_{i-2}}{2}\right) + k\right)\Delta x. \end{aligned}$$

As before, we notice that $\frac{x_i + x_{i-1}}{2}$ is the midpoint of the interval $[x_{i-1}, x_i]$ and can be approximated by x_i^*. Then, the approximate volume of the shell is

$$V_{\text{shell}} \approx 2\pi\left(x_i^* + k\right)f(x_i^*)\Delta x.$$

The remainder of the development proceeds as before, and we see that

$$V = \int_a^b (2\pi(x + k)f(x))dx.$$

We could also rotate the region around other horizontal or vertical lines, such as a vertical line in the right half plane. In each case, the volume formula must be adjusted accordingly. Specifically, the x-term in the integral must be replaced with an expression representing the radius of a shell. To see how this works, consider the following example.

Example 6.15

A Region of Revolution Revolved around a Line

Define R as the region bounded above by the graph of $f(x) = x$ and below by the x-axis over the interval $[1, 2]$. Find the volume of the solid of revolution formed by revolving R around the line $x = -1$.

Solution

First, graph the region R and the associated solid of revolution, as shown in the following figure.

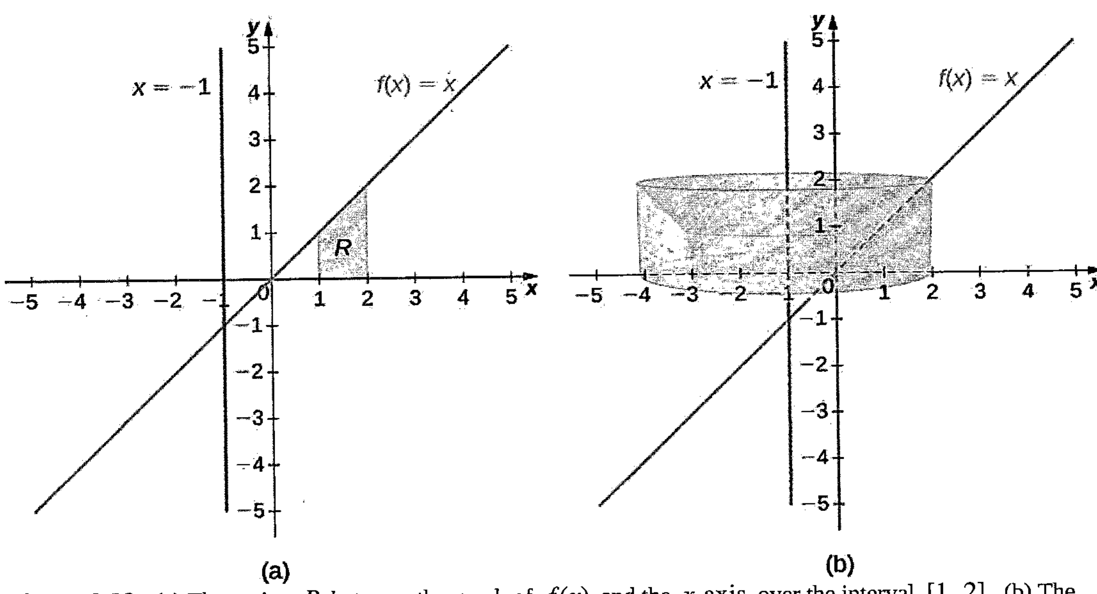

Figure 6.32 (a) The region R between the graph of $f(x)$ and the x-axis over the interval $[1, 2]$. (b) The solid of revolution generated by revolving R around the line $x = -1$.

Note that the radius of a shell is given by $x + 1$. Then the volume of the solid is given by

$$\begin{aligned} V &= \int_1^2 (2\pi(x+1)f(x))dx \\ &= \int_1^2 (2\pi(x+1)x)dx = 2\pi\int_1^2 \left(x^2 + x\right)dx \\ &= 2\pi\left[\frac{x^3}{3} + \frac{x^2}{2}\right]\Big|_1^2 = \frac{23\pi}{3}\text{ units}^3. \end{aligned}$$

6.15 Define R as the region bounded above by the graph of $f(x) = x^2$ and below by the x-axis over the interval $[0, 1]$. Find the volume of the solid of revolution formed by revolving R around the line $x = -2$.

For our final example in this section, let's look at the volume of a solid of revolution for which the region of revolution is bounded by the graphs of two functions.

Example 6.16

A Region of Revolution Bounded by the Graphs of Two Functions

Define R as the region bounded above by the graph of the function $f(x) = \sqrt{x}$ and below by the graph of the function $g(x) = 1/x$ over the interval $[1, 4]$. Find the volume of the solid of revolution generated by revolving R around the y-axis.

Solution

First, graph the region R and the associated solid of revolution, as shown in the following figure.

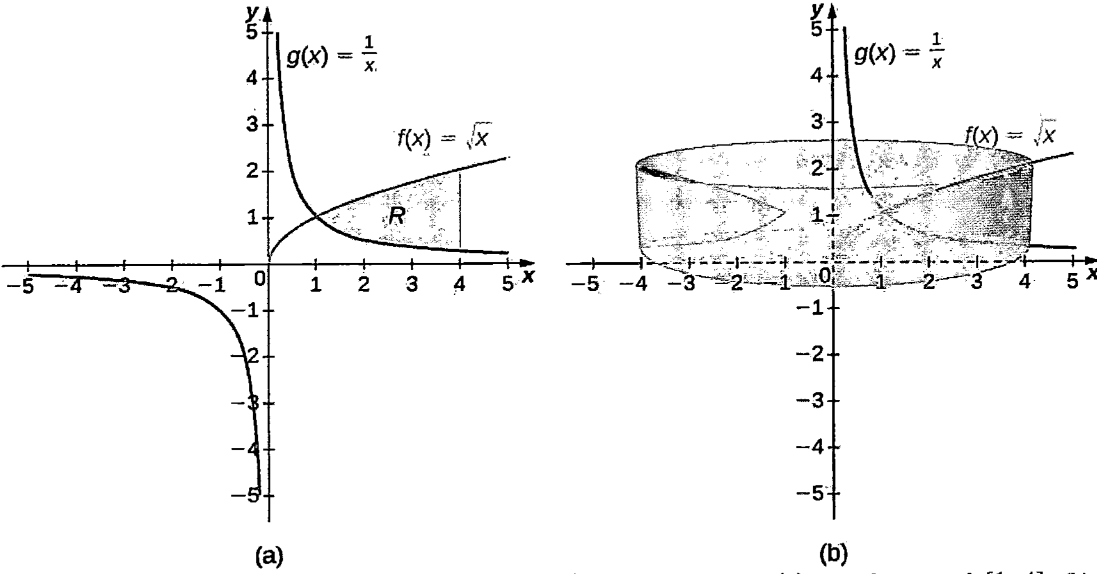

Figure 6.33 (a) The region R between the graph of $f(x)$ and the graph of $g(x)$ over the interval $[1, 4]$. (b) The solid of revolution generated by revolving R around the y-axis.

Note that the axis of revolution is the y-axis, so the radius of a shell is given simply by x. We don't need to make any adjustments to the x-term of our integrand. The height of a shell, though, is given by $f(x) - g(x)$, so in this case we need to adjust the $f(x)$ term of the integrand. Then the volume of the solid is given by

$$\begin{aligned} V &= \int_1^4 (2\pi x(f(x) - g(x)))dx \\ &= \int_1^4 \left(2\pi x\left(\sqrt{x} - \frac{1}{x}\right)\right)dx = 2\pi \int_1^4 \left(x^{3/2} - 1\right)dx \\ &= 2\pi\left[\frac{2x^{5/2}}{5} - x\right]\Bigg|_1^4 = \frac{94\pi}{5} \text{ units}^3. \end{aligned}$$

6.16 Define R as the region bounded above by the graph of $f(x) = x$ and below by the graph of $g(x) = x^2$ over the interval $[0, 1]$. Find the volume of the solid of revolution formed by revolving R around the y-axis.

Which Method Should We Use?

We have studied several methods for finding the volume of a solid of revolution, but how do we know which method to use? It often comes down to a choice of which integral is easiest to evaluate. **Figure 6.34** describes the different approaches for solids of revolution around the x-axis. It's up to you to develop the analogous table for solids of revolution around the y-axis.

Comparing the Methods for Finding the Volume of a Solid Revolution around the x-axis

Compare	Disk Method	Washer Method	Shell Method
Volume formula	$V = \int_a^b \pi[f(x)]^2\,dx$	$V = \int_a^b \pi[(f(x))^2 - (g(x))^2]\,dx$	$V = \int_c^d 2\pi y\, g(y)\,dy$
Solid	No cavity in the center	Cavity in the center	With or without a cavity in the center
Interval to partition	$[a, b]$ on x-axis	$[a, b]$ on x-axis	$[c, d]$ on y-axis
Rectangle	Vertical	Vertical	Horizontal
Typical region	y, f(x), a, b, x	y, f(x), g(x), a, b, x	y, d, c, g(y), x
Typical element	y, f(x), a b, x	y, f(x), g(x), a b, x	y, g(y), x

Figure 6.34

Let's take a look at a couple of additional problems and decide on the best approach to take for solving them.

Example 6.17

Selecting the Best Method

For each of the following problems, select the best method to find the volume of a solid of revolution generated by revolving the given region around the x-axis, and set up the integral to find the volume (do not evaluate the integral).

a. The region bounded by the graphs of $y = x$, $y = 2 - x$, and the x-axis.

b. The region bounded by the graphs of $y = 4x - x^2$ and the x-axis.

Solution

a. First, sketch the region and the solid of revolution as shown.

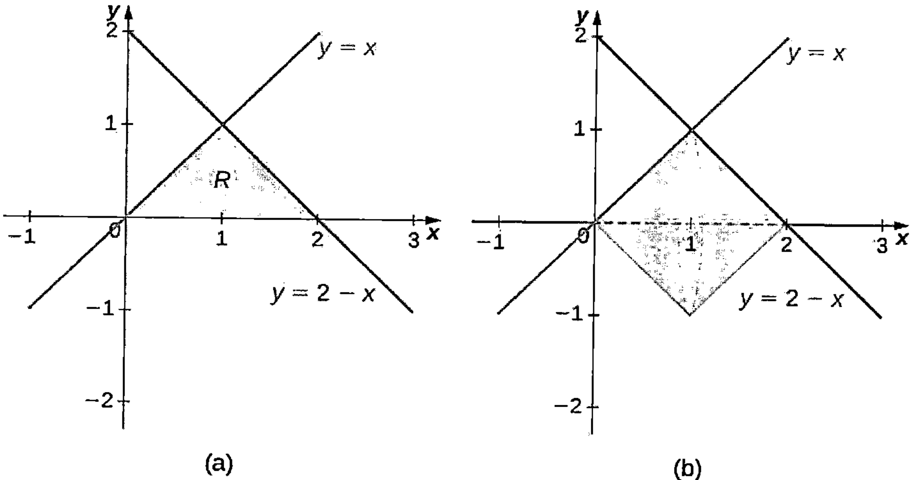

Figure 6.35 (a) The region R bounded by two lines and the x-axis. (b) The solid of revolution generated by revolving R about the x-axis.

Looking at the region, if we want to integrate with respect to $x,$ we would have to break the integral into two pieces, because we have different functions bounding the region over $[0, 1]$ and $[1, 2]$. In this case, using the disk method, we would have

$$V = \int_0^1 \left(\pi x^2\right)dx + \int_1^2 \left(\pi(2 - x)^2\right)dx.$$

If we used the shell method instead, we would use functions of y to represent the curves, producing

$$\begin{aligned} V &= \int_0^1 (2\pi y[(2 - y) - y])dy \\ &= \int_0^1 (2\pi y[2 - 2y])dy. \end{aligned}$$

Neither of these integrals is particularly onerous, but since the shell method requires only one integral, and the integrand requires less simplification, we should probably go with the shell method in this case.

b. First, sketch the region and the solid of revolution as shown.

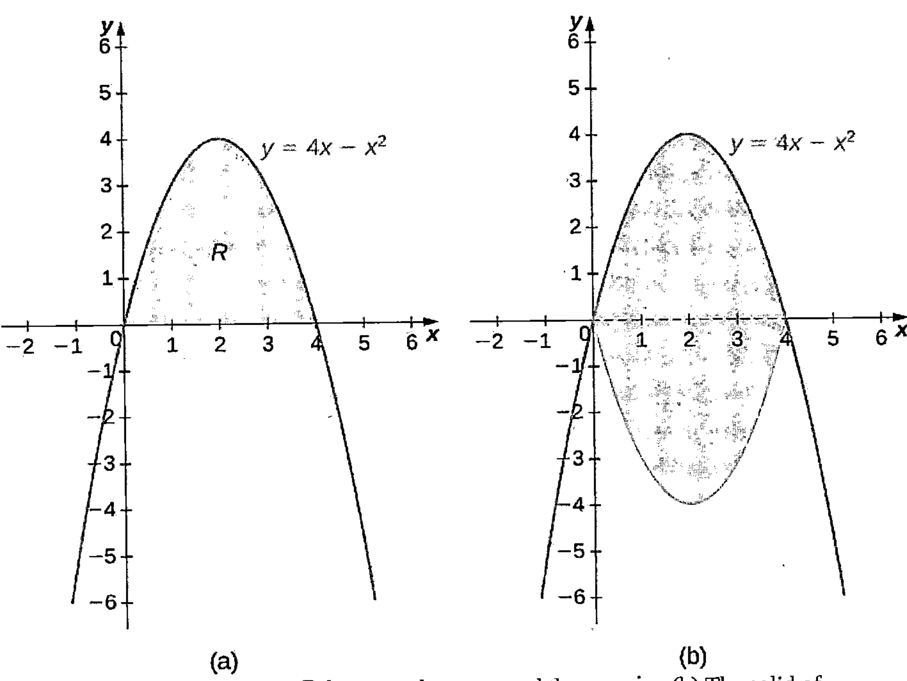

Figure 6.36 (a) The region R between the curve and the x-axis. (b) The solid of revolution generated by revolving R about the x-axis.

Looking at the region, it would be problematic to define a horizontal rectangle; the region is bounded on the left and right by the same function. Therefore, we can dismiss the method of shells. The solid has no cavity in the middle, so we can use the method of disks. Then

$$V = \int_0^4 \pi \left(4x - x^2\right)^2 dx.$$

6.17 Select the best method to find the volume of a solid of revolution generated by revolving the given region around the x-axis, and set up the integral to find the volume (do not evaluate the integral): the region bounded by the graphs of $y = 2 - x^2$ and $y = x^2$.

6.3 EXERCISES

For the following exercise, find the volume generated when the region between the two curves is rotated around the given axis. Use both the shell method and the washer method. Use technology to graph the functions and draw a typical slice by hand.

114. **[T]** Over the curve of $y = 3x$, $x = 0$, and $y = 3$ rotated around the y-axis.

115. **[T]** Under the curve of $y = 3x$, $x = 0$, and $x = 3$ rotated around the y-axis.

116. **[T]** Over the curve of $y = 3x$, $x = 0$, and $y = 3$ rotated around the x-axis.

117. **[T]** Under the curve of $y = 3x$, $x = 0$, and $x = 3$ rotated around the x-axis.

118. **[T]** Under the curve of $y = 2x^3$, $x = 0$, and $x = 2$ rotated around the y-axis.

119. **[T]** Under the curve of $y = 2x^3$, $x = 0$, and $x = 2$ rotated around the x-axis.

For the following exercises, use shells to find the volumes of the given solids. Note that the rotated regions lie between the curve and the x-axis and are rotated around the y-axis.

120. $y = 1 - x^2$, $x = 0$, and $x = 1$

121. $y = 5x^3$, $x = 0$, and $x = 1$

122. $y = \frac{1}{x}$, $x = 1$, and $x = 100$

123. $y = \sqrt{1 - x^2}$, $x = 0$, and $x = 1$

124. $y = \frac{1}{1 + x^2}$, $x = 0$, and $x = 3$

125. $y = \sin x^2$, $x = 0$, and $x = \sqrt{\pi}$

126. $y = \frac{1}{\sqrt{1 - x^2}}$, $x = 0$, and $x = \frac{1}{2}$

127. $y = \sqrt{x}$, $x = 0$, and $x = 1$

128. $y = \left(1 + x^2\right)^3$, $x = 0$, and $x = 1$

129. $y = 5x^3 - 2x^4$, $x = 0$, and $x = 2$

For the following exercises, use shells to find the volume generated by rotating the regions between the given curve and $y = 0$ around the x-axis.

130. $y = \sqrt{1 - x^2}$, $x = 0$, and $x = 1$

131. $y = x^2$, $x = 0$, and $x = 2$

132. $y = e^x$, $x = 0$, and $x = 1$

133. $y = \ln(x)$, $x = 1$, and $x = e$

134. $x = \frac{1}{1 + y^2}$, $y = 1$, and $y = 4$

135. $x = \frac{1 + y^2}{y}$, $y = 0$, and $y = 2$

136. $x = \cos y$, $y = 0$, and $y = \pi$

137. $x = y^3 - 4y^2$, $x = -1$, and $x = 2$

138. $x = ye^y$, $x = -1$, and $x = 2$

139. $x = \cos ye^y$, $x = 0$, and $x = \pi$

For the following exercises, find the volume generated when the region between the curves is rotated around the given axis.

140. $y = 3 - x$, $y = 0$, $x = 0$, and $x = 2$ rotated around the y-axis.

141. $y = x^3$, $y = 0$, and $y = 8$ rotated around the y-axis.

142. $y = x^2$, $y = x$, rotated around the y-axis.

143. $y = \sqrt{x}$, $x = 0$, and $x = 1$ rotated around the line $x = 2$.

144. $y = \frac{1}{4 - x}$, $x = 1$, and $x = 2$ rotated around the line $x = 4$.

145. $y = \sqrt{x}$ and $y = x^2$ rotated around the y-axis.

146. $y = \sqrt{x}$ and $y = x^2$ rotated around the line $x = 2$.

147. $x = y^3$, $y = \frac{1}{x}$, $x = 1$, and $y = 2$ rotated around the x-axis.

148. $x = y^2$ and $y = x$ rotated around the line $y = 2$.

149. **[T]** Left of $x = \sin(\pi y)$, right of $y = x$, around the y-axis.

For the following exercises, use technology to graph the region. Determine which method you think would be easiest to use to calculate the volume generated when the function is rotated around the specified axis. Then, use your chosen method to find the volume.

150. **[T]** $y = x^2$ and $y = 4x$ rotated around the y-axis.

151. **[T]** $y = \cos(\pi x)$, $y = \sin(\pi x)$, $x = \frac{1}{4}$, and $x = \frac{5}{4}$ rotated around the y-axis.

152. **[T]** $y = x^2 - 2x$, $x = 2$, and $x = 4$ rotated around the y-axis.

153. **[T]** $y = x^2 - 2x$, $x = 2$, and $x = 4$ rotated around the x-axis.

154. **[T]** $y = 3x^3 - 2$, $y = x$, and $x = 2$ rotated around the x-axis.

155. **[T]** $y = 3x^3 - 2$, $y = x$, and $x = 2$ rotated around the y-axis.

156. **[T]** $x = \sin\left(\pi y^2\right)$ and $x = \sqrt{2}y$ rotated around the x-axis.

157. **[T]** $x = y^2$, $x = y^2 - 2y + 1$, and $x = 2$ rotated around the y-axis.

For the following exercises, use the method of shells to approximate the volumes of some common objects, which are pictured in accompanying figures.

158. Use the method of shells to find the volume of a sphere of radius r.

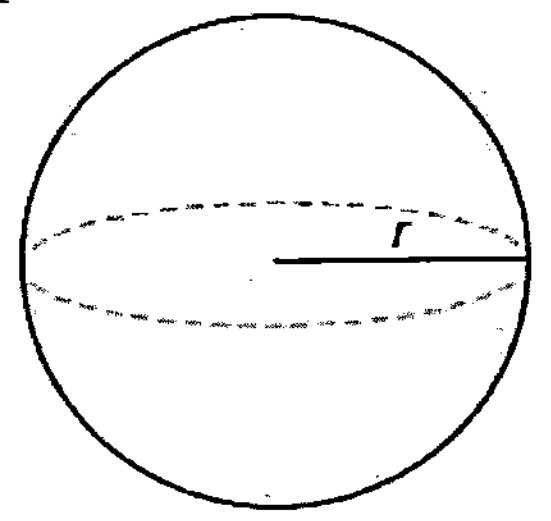

159. Use the method of shells to find the volume of a cone with radius r and height h.

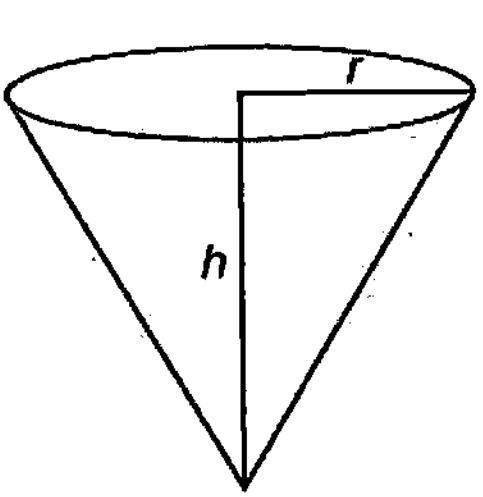

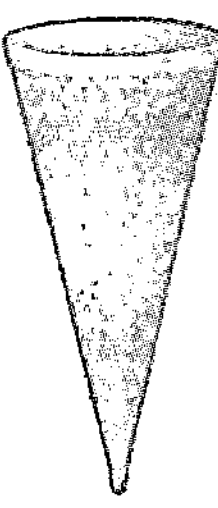

160. Use the method of shells to find the volume of an ellipse $\left(x^2/a^2\right) + \left(y^2/b^2\right) = 1$ rotated around the x-axis.

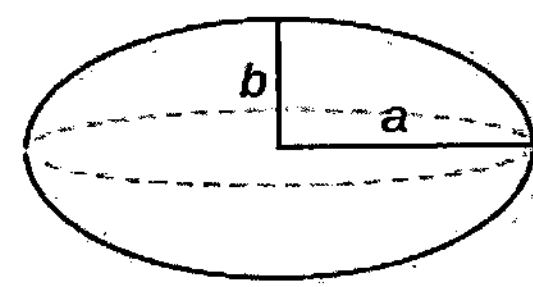

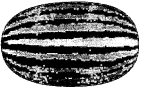

161. Use the method of shells to find the volume of a cylinder with radius r and height h.

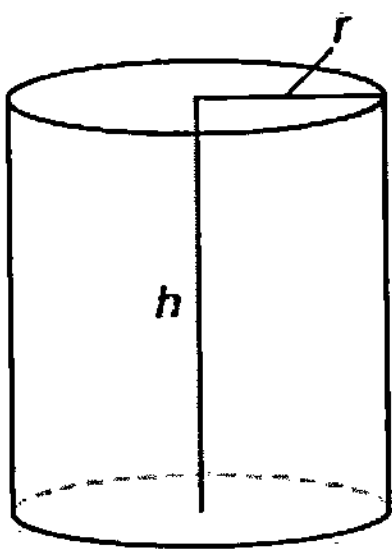

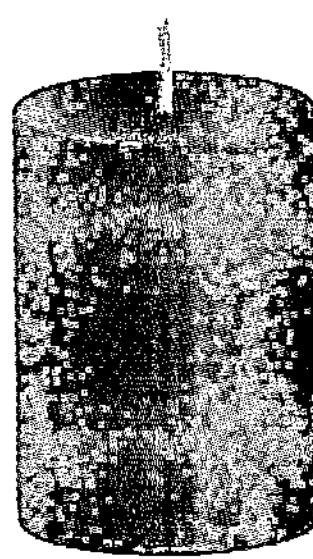

162. Use the method of shells to find the volume of the donut created when the circle $x^2 + y^2 = 4$ is rotated around the line $x = 4$.

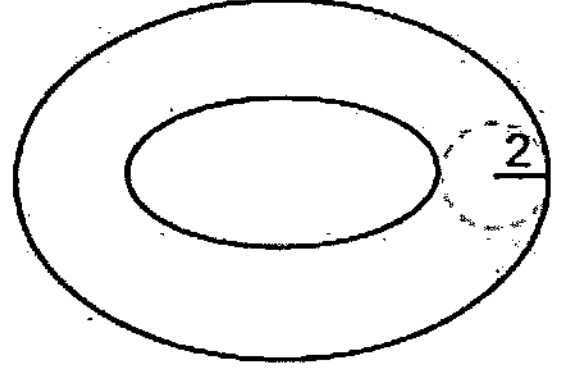

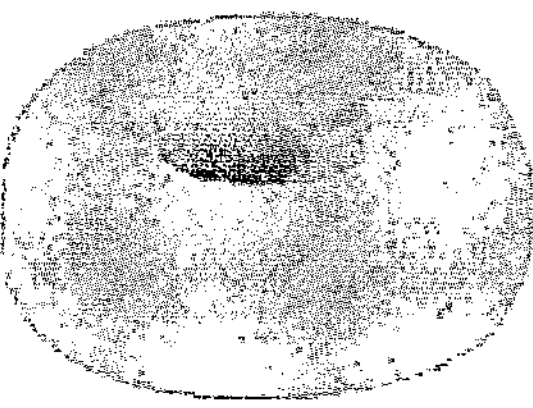

163. Consider the region enclosed by the graphs of $y = f(x)$, $y = 1 + f(x)$, $x = 0$, $y = 0$, and $x = a > 0$. What is the volume of the solid generated when this region is rotated around the y-axis? Assume that the function is defined over the interval $[0, a]$.

164. Consider the function $y = f(x)$, which decreases from $f(0) = b$ to $f(1) = 0$. Set up the integrals for determining the volume, using both the shell method and the disk method, of the solid generated when this region, with $x = 0$ and $y = 0$, is rotated around the y-axis. Prove that both methods approximate the same volume. Which method is easier to apply? (*Hint:* Since $f(x)$ is one-to-one, there exists an inverse $f^{-1}(y)$.)

6.4 | Arc Length of a Curve and Surface Area

Learning Objectives

6.4.1 Determine the length of a curve, $y = f(x)$, between two points.

6.4.2 Determine the length of a curve, $x = g(y)$, between two points.

6.4.3 Find the surface area of a solid of revolution.

In this section, we use definite integrals to find the arc length of a curve. We can think of **arc length** as the distance you would travel if you were walking along the path of the curve. Many real-world applications involve arc length. If a rocket is launched along a parabolic path, we might want to know how far the rocket travels. Or, if a curve on a map represents a road, we might want to know how far we have to drive to reach our destination.

We begin by calculating the arc length of curves defined as functions of x, then we examine the same process for curves defined as functions of y. (The process is identical, with the roles of x and y reversed.) The techniques we use to find arc length can be extended to find the surface area of a surface of revolution, and we close the section with an examination of this concept.

Arc Length of the Curve $y = f(x)$

In previous applications of integration, we required the function $f(x)$ to be integrable, or at most continuous. However, for calculating arc length we have a more stringent requirement for $f(x)$. Here, we require $f(x)$ to be differentiable, and furthermore we require its derivative, $f'(x)$, to be continuous. Functions like this, which have continuous derivatives, are called *smooth*. (This property comes up again in later chapters.)

Let $f(x)$ be a smooth function defined over $[a, b]$. We want to calculate the length of the curve from the point $(a, f(a))$ to the point $(b, f(b))$. We start by using line segments to approximate the length of the curve. For $i = 0, 1, 2,\ldots, n$, let $P = \{x_i\}$ be a regular partition of $[a, b]$. Then, for $i = 1, 2,\ldots, n$, construct a line segment from the point $(x_{i-1}, f(x_{i-1}))$ to the point $(x_i, f(x_i))$. Although it might seem logical to use either horizontal or vertical line segments, we want our line segments to approximate the curve as closely as possible. **Figure 6.37** depicts this construct for $n = 5$.

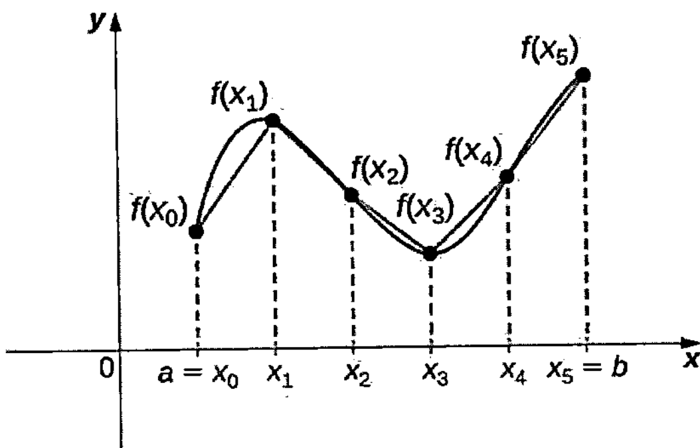

Figure 6.37 We can approximate the length of a curve by adding line segments.

To help us find the length of each line segment, we look at the change in vertical distance as well as the change in horizontal distance over each interval. Because we have used a regular partition, the change in horizontal distance over each interval is given by Δx. The change in vertical distance varies from interval to interval, though, so we use $\Delta y_i = f(x_i) - f(x_{i-1})$ to represent the change in vertical distance over the interval $[x_{i-1}, x_i]$, as shown in **Figure 6.38**. Note that some (or all) Δy_i may be negative.

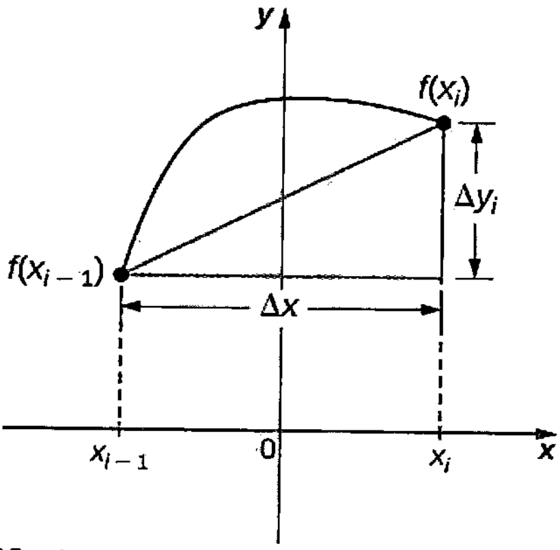

Figure 6.38 A representative line segment approximates the curve over the interval $[x_{i-1}, x_i]$.

By the Pythagorean theorem, the length of the line segment is $\sqrt{(\Delta x)^2 + (\Delta y_i)^2}$. We can also write this as $\Delta x\sqrt{1 + ((\Delta y_i)/(\Delta x))^2}$. Now, by the Mean Value Theorem, there is a point $x_i^* \in [x_{i-1}, x_i]$ such that $f'(x_i^*) = (\Delta y_i)/(\Delta x)$. Then the length of the line segment is given by $\Delta x\sqrt{1 + [f'(x_i^*)]^2}$. Adding up the lengths of all the line segments, we get

$$\text{Arc Length} \approx \sum_{i=1}^{n} \sqrt{1 + [f'(x_i^*)]^2}\,\Delta x.$$

This is a Riemann sum. Taking the limit as $n \to \infty$, we have

$$\text{Arc Length} = \lim_{n \to \infty} \sum_{i=1}^{n} \sqrt{1 + [f'(x_i^*)]^2}\,\Delta x = \int_a^b \sqrt{1 + [f'(x)]^2}\,dx.$$

We summarize these findings in the following theorem.

Theorem 6.4: Arc Length for $y = f(x)$

Let $f(x)$ be a smooth function over the interval $[a, b]$. Then the arc length of the portion of the graph of $f(x)$ from the point $(a, f(a))$ to the point $(b, f(b))$ is given by

$$\text{Arc Length} = \int_a^b \sqrt{1 + [f'(x)]^2}\,dx. \qquad \textbf{(6.7)}$$

Note that we are integrating an expression involving $f'(x)$, so we need to be sure $f'(x)$ is integrable. This is why we require $f(x)$ to be smooth. The following example shows how to apply the theorem.

Example 6.18

Calculating the Arc Length of a Function of *x*

Let $f(x) = 2x^{3/2}$. Calculate the arc length of the graph of $f(x)$ over the interval $[0, 1]$. Round the answer to three decimal places.

Solution

We have $f'(x) = 3x^{1/2}$, so $[f'(x)]^2 = 9x$. Then, the arc length is

$$\begin{aligned}\text{Arc Length} &= \int_a^b \sqrt{1 + [f'(x)]^2}\, dx \\ &= \int_0^1 \sqrt{1 + 9x}\, dx.\end{aligned}$$

Substitute $u = 1 + 9x$. Then, $du = 9\, dx$. When $x = 0$, then $u = 1$, and when $x = 1$, then $u = 10$. Thus,

$$\begin{aligned}\text{Arc Length} &= \int_0^1 \sqrt{1 + 9x}\, dx \\ &= \frac{1}{9}\int_0^1 \sqrt{1 + 9x} 9dx = \frac{1}{9}\int_1^{10} \sqrt{u}\, du \\ &= \frac{1}{9} \cdot \frac{2}{3} u^{3/2}\Big|_1^{10} = \frac{2}{27}[10\sqrt{10} - 1] \approx 2.268 \text{ units.}\end{aligned}$$

6.18 Let $f(x) = (4/3)x^{3/2}$. Calculate the arc length of the graph of $f(x)$ over the interval $[0, 1]$. Round the answer to three decimal places.

Although it is nice to have a formula for calculating arc length, this particular theorem can generate expressions that are difficult to integrate. We study some techniques for integration in **Introduction to Techniques of Integration (http://cnx.org/content/m53654/latest/)** . In some cases, we may have to use a computer or calculator to approximate the value of the integral.

Example 6.19

Using a Computer or Calculator to Determine the Arc Length of a Function of *x*

Let $f(x) = x^2$. Calculate the arc length of the graph of $f(x)$ over the interval $[1, 3]$.

Solution

We have $f'(x) = 2x$, so $[f'(x)]^2 = 4x^2$. Then the arc length is given by

$$\text{Arc Length} = \int_a^b \sqrt{1 + [f'(x)]^2}\, dx = \int_1^3 \sqrt{1 + 4x^2}\, dx.$$

Using a computer to approximate the value of this integral, we get

$$\int_1^3 \sqrt{1 + 4x^2}\, dx \approx 8.26815.$$

6.19 Let $f(x) = \sin x$. Calculate the arc length of the graph of $f(x)$ over the interval $[0, \pi]$. Use a computer or calculator to approximate the value of the integral.

Arc Length of the Curve $x = g(y)$

We have just seen how to approximate the length of a curve with line segments. If we want to find the arc length of the graph of a function of y, we can repeat the same process, except we partition the y-axis instead of the x-axis. **Figure 6.39** shows a representative line segment.

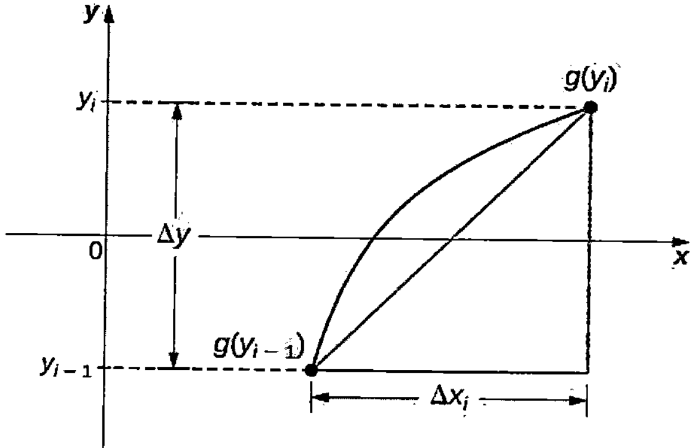

Figure 6.39 A representative line segment over the interval $[y_{i-1}, y_i]$.

Then the length of the line segment is $\sqrt{(\Delta y)^2 + (\Delta x_i)^2}$, which can also be written as $\Delta y\sqrt{1 + ((\Delta x_i)/(\Delta y))^2}$. If we now follow the same development we did earlier, we get a formula for arc length of a function $x = g(y)$.

Theorem 6.5: Arc Length for $x = g(y)$

Let $g(y)$ be a smooth function over an interval $[c, d]$. Then, the arc length of the graph of $g(y)$ from the point $(c, g(c))$ to the point $(d, g(d))$ is given by

$$\text{Arc Length} = \int_c^d \sqrt{1 + [g'(y)]^2}\, dy. \tag{6.8}$$

Example 6.20

Calculating the Arc Length of a Function of y

Let $g(y) = 3y^3$. Calculate the arc length of the graph of $g(y)$ over the interval $[1, 2]$.

Solution

We have $g'(y) = 9y^2$, so $[g'(y)]^2 = 81y^4$. Then the arc length is

$$\text{Arc Length} = \int_c^d \sqrt{1 + [g'(y)]^2}\, dy = \int_1^2 \sqrt{1 + 81y^4}\, dy.$$

Using a computer to approximate the value of this integral, we obtain

$$\int_1^2 \sqrt{1 + 81y^4}\, dy \approx 21.0277.$$

6.20 Let $g(y) = 1/y$. Calculate the arc length of the graph of $g(y)$ over the interval $[1, 4]$. Use a computer or calculator to approximate the value of the integral.

Area of a Surface of Revolution

The concepts we used to find the arc length of a curve can be extended to find the surface area of a surface of revolution. **Surface area** is the total area of the outer layer of an object. For objects such as cubes or bricks, the surface area of the object is the sum of the areas of all of its faces. For curved surfaces, the situation is a little more complex. Let $f(x)$ be a nonnegative smooth function over the interval $[a, b]$. We wish to find the surface area of the surface of revolution created by revolving the graph of $y = f(x)$ around the x-axis as shown in the following figure.

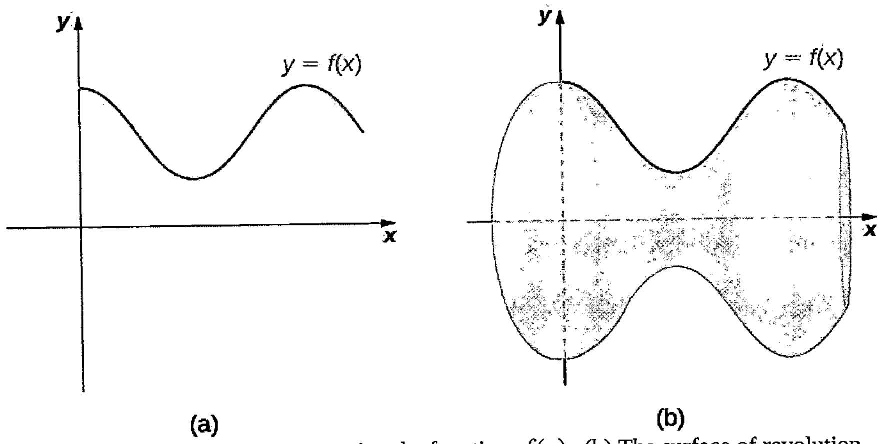

Figure 6.40 (a) A curve representing the function $f(x)$. (b) The surface of revolution formed by revolving the graph of $f(x)$ around the x-axis.

As we have done many times before, we are going to partition the interval $[a, b]$ and approximate the surface area by calculating the surface area of simpler shapes. We start by using line segments to approximate the curve, as we did earlier in this section. For $i = 0, 1, 2,\ldots, n,$ let $P = \{x_i\}$ be a regular partition of $[a, b]$. Then, for $i = 1, 2,\ldots, n,$ construct a line segment from the point $(x_{i-1}, f(x_{i-1}))$ to the point $(x_i, f(x_i))$. Now, revolve these line segments around the x-axis to generate an approximation of the surface of revolution as shown in the following figure.

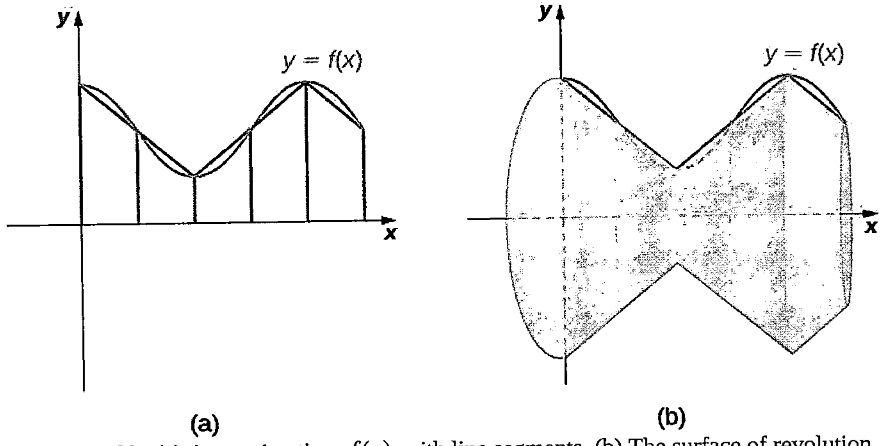

Figure 6.41 (a) Approximating $f(x)$ with line segments. (b) The surface of revolution formed by revolving the line segments around the x-axis.

Notice that when each line segment is revolved around the axis, it produces a band. These bands are actually pieces of cones (think of an ice cream cone with the pointy end cut off). A piece of a cone like this is called a **frustum** of a cone.

To find the surface area of the band, we need to find the lateral surface area, $S,$ of the frustum (the area of just the slanted outside surface of the frustum, not including the areas of the top or bottom faces). Let r_1 and r_2 be the radii of the wide end and the narrow end of the frustum, respectively, and let l be the slant height of the frustum as shown in the following figure.

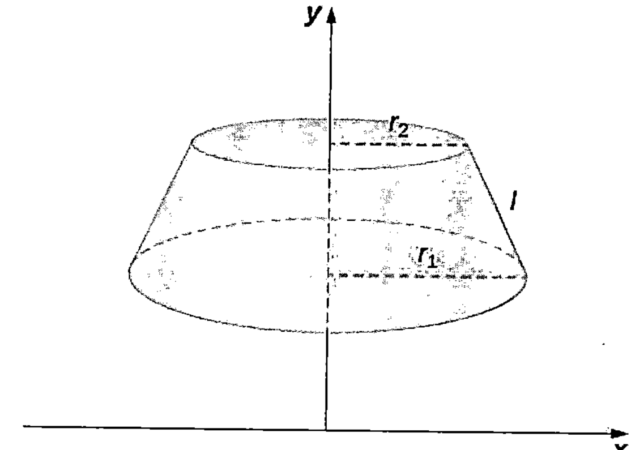

Figure 6.42 A frustum of a cone can approximate a small part of surface area.

We know the lateral surface area of a cone is given by

$$\text{Lateral Surface Area} = \pi rs,$$

where r is the radius of the base of the cone and s is the slant height (see the following figure).

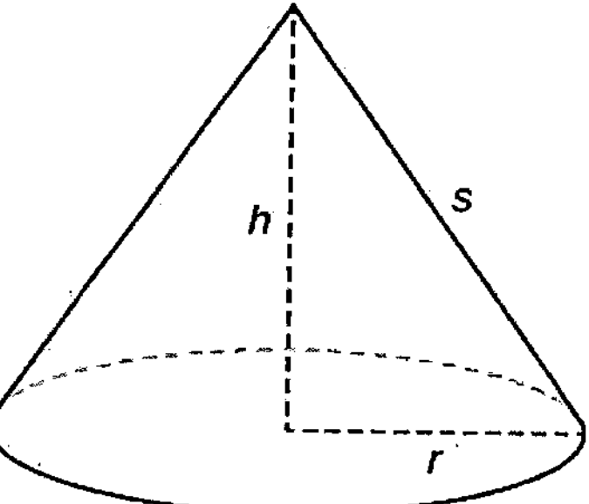

Figure 6.43 The lateral surface area of the cone is given by $\pi rs.$

Since a frustum can be thought of as a piece of a cone, the lateral surface area of the frustum is given by the lateral surface area of the whole cone less the lateral surface area of the smaller cone (the pointy tip) that was cut off (see the following figure).

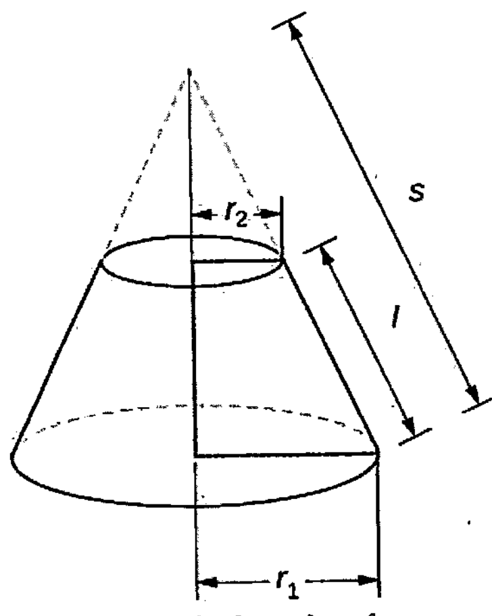

Figure 6.44 Calculating the lateral surface area of a frustum of a cone.

The cross-sections of the small cone and the large cone are similar triangles, so we see that

$$\frac{r_2}{r_1} = \frac{s-l}{s}.$$

Solving for s, we get

$$\begin{aligned}
\frac{r_2}{r_1} &= \frac{s-l}{s} \\
r_2 s &= r_1(s-l) \\
r_2 s &= r_1 s - r_1 l \\
r_1 l &= r_1 s - r_2 s \\
r_1 l &= (r_1 - r_2)s \\
\frac{r_1 l}{r_1 - r_2} &= s.
\end{aligned}$$

Then the lateral surface area (SA) of the frustum is

$$\begin{aligned}
S &= \text{(Lateral SA of large cone)} - \text{(Lateral SA of small cone)} \\
&= \pi r_1 s - \pi r_2(s-l) \\
&= \pi r_1\left(\frac{r_1 l}{r_1 - r_2}\right) - \pi r_2\left(\frac{r_1 l}{r_1 - r_2} - l\right) \\
&= \frac{\pi r_1^2 l}{r_1 - r_2} - \frac{\pi r_1 r_2 l}{r_1 - r_2} + \pi r_2 l \\
&= \frac{\pi r_1^2 l}{r_1 - r_2} - \frac{\pi r_1 r_2 l}{r_1 - r_2} + \frac{\pi r_2 l(r_1 - r_2)}{r_1 - r_2} \\
&= \frac{\pi r_1^2 l}{r_1 - r_2} - \frac{\pi r_1 r_2 l}{r_1 - r_2} + \frac{\pi r_1 r_2 l}{r_1 - r_2} - \frac{\pi r_2{}^2 l}{r_1 - r_2} \\
&= \frac{\pi\left(r_1^2 - r_2^2\right)l}{r_1 - r_2} = \frac{\pi(r_1 - r_2)(r_1 + r_2)l}{r_1 - r_2} = \pi(r_1 + r_2)l.
\end{aligned}$$

Let's now use this formula to calculate the surface area of each of the bands formed by revolving the line segments around the x-axis. A representative band is shown in the following figure.

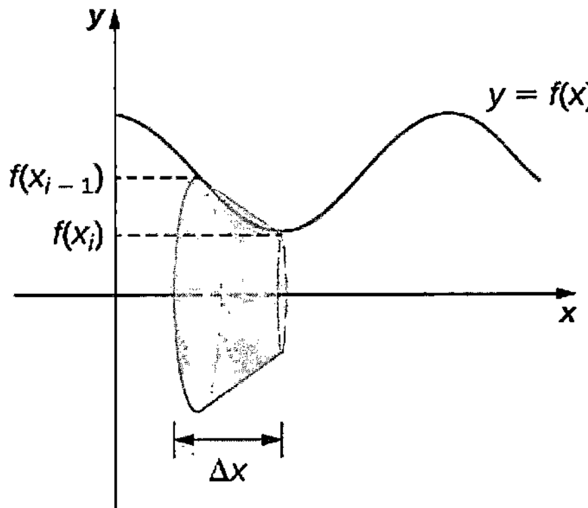

Figure 6.45 A representative band used for determining surface area.

Note that the slant height of this frustum is just the length of the line segment used to generate it. So, applying the surface area formula, we have

$$\begin{aligned} S &= \pi(r_1 + r_2)l \\ &= \pi\left(f(x_{i-1}) + f(x_i)\right)\sqrt{\Delta x^2 + (\Delta y_i)^2} \\ &= \pi\left(f(x_{i-1}) + f(x_i)\right)\Delta x\sqrt{1 + \left(\frac{\Delta y_i}{\Delta x}\right)^2}. \end{aligned}$$

Now, as we did in the development of the arc length formula, we apply the Mean Value Theorem to select $x_i^* \in [x_{i-1}, x_i]$ such that $f'(x_i^*) = (\Delta y_i)/\Delta x$. This gives us

$$S = \pi\left(f(x_{i-1}) + f(x_i)\right)\Delta x\sqrt{1 + \left(f'(x_i^*)\right)^2}.$$

Furthermore, since $f(x)$ is continuous, by the Intermediate Value Theorem, there is a point $x_i^{**} \in [x_{i-1}, x_i]$ such that $f(x_i^{**}) = (1/2)\left[f(x_{i-1}) + f(x_i)\right]$, so we get

$$S = 2\pi f(x_i^{**})\Delta x\sqrt{1 + \left(f'(x_i^*)\right)^2}.$$

Then the approximate surface area of the whole surface of revolution is given by

$$\text{Surface Area} \approx \sum_{i=1}^{n} 2\pi f(x_i^{**})\Delta x\sqrt{1 + \left(f'(x_i^*)\right)^2}.$$

This *almost* looks like a Riemann sum, except we have functions evaluated at two different points, x_i^* and x_i^{**}, over the interval $[x_{i-1}, x_i]$. Although we do not examine the details here, it turns out that because $f(x)$ is smooth, if we let $n \to \infty$, the limit works the same as a Riemann sum even with the two different evaluation points. This makes sense intuitively. Both x_i^* and x_i^{**} are in the interval $[x_{i-1}, x_i]$, so it makes sense that as $n \to \infty$, both x_i^* and x_i^{**} approach x. Those of you who are interested in the details should consult an advanced calculus text.

Taking the limit as $n \to \infty$, we get

$$\text{Surface Area} = \lim_{n \to \infty} \sum_{i=1}^{n} 2\pi f(x_i^{**})\Delta x\sqrt{1 + \left(f'(x_i^*)\right)^2} = \int_a^b \left(2\pi f(x)\sqrt{1 + \left(f'(x)\right)^2}\right)dx.$$

As with arc length, we can conduct a similar development for functions of y to get a formula for the surface area of surfaces of revolution about the y-axis. These findings are summarized in the following theorem.

Theorem 6.6: Surface Area of a Surface of Revolution

Let $f(x)$ be a nonnegative smooth function over the interval $[a, b]$. Then, the surface area of the surface of revolution formed by revolving the graph of $f(x)$ around the x-axis is given by

$$\text{Surface Area} = \int_a^b \left(2\pi f(x)\sqrt{1 + (f'(x))^2}\right)dx. \tag{6.9}$$

Similarly, let $g(y)$ be a nonnegative smooth function over the interval $[c, d]$. Then, the surface area of the surface of revolution formed by revolving the graph of $g(y)$ around the y-axis is given by

$$\text{Surface Area} = \int_c^d \left(2\pi g(y)\sqrt{1 + (g'(y))^2}\right)dy.$$

Example 6.21

Calculating the Surface Area of a Surface of Revolution 1

Let $f(x) = \sqrt{x}$ over the interval $[1, 4]$. Find the surface area of the surface generated by revolving the graph of $f(x)$ around the x-axis. Round the answer to three decimal places.

Solution

The graph of $f(x)$ and the surface of rotation are shown in the following figure.

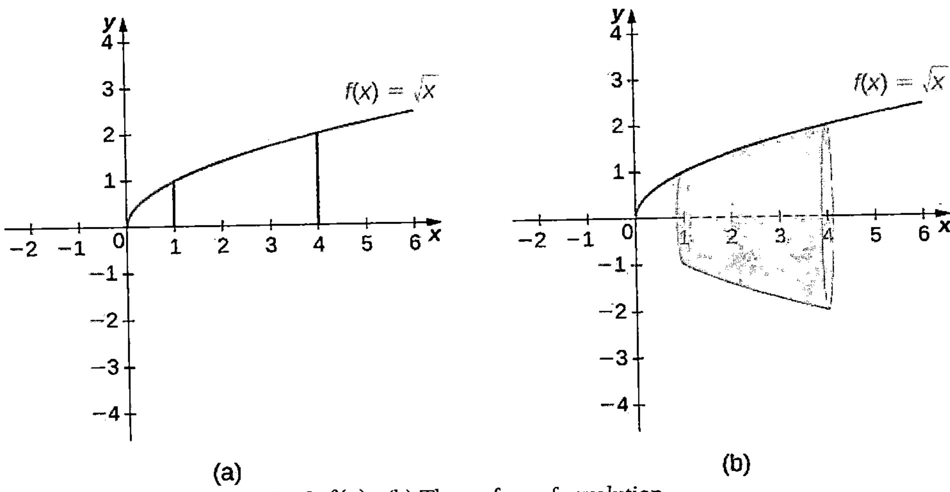

Figure 6.46 (a) The graph of $f(x)$. (b) The surface of revolution.

We have $f(x) = \sqrt{x}$. Then, $f'(x) = 1/(2\sqrt{x})$ and $(f'(x))^2 = 1/(4x)$. Then,

$$\begin{aligned}\text{Surface Area} &= \int_a^b \left(2\pi f(x)\sqrt{1+(f'(x))^2}\right)dx \\ &= \int_1^4 \left(2\pi\sqrt{x}\sqrt{1+\frac{1}{4x}}\right)dx \\ &= \int_1^4 \left(2\pi\sqrt{x+\frac{1}{4}}\right)dx.\end{aligned}$$

Let $u = x + 1/4.$ Then, $du = dx.$ When $x = 1,$ $u = 5/4,$ and when $x = 4,$ $u = 17/4.$ This gives us

$$\begin{aligned}\int_0^1 \left(2\pi\sqrt{x+\frac{1}{4}}\right)dx &= \int_{5/4}^{17/4} 2\pi\sqrt{u}\,du \\ &= 2\pi\left[\frac{2}{3}u^{3/2}\right]\Big|_{5/4}^{17/4} = \frac{\pi}{6}\left[17\sqrt{17} - 5\sqrt{5}\right] \approx 30.846.\end{aligned}$$

6.21 Let $f(x) = \sqrt{1-x}$ over the interval $[0, 1/2]$. Find the surface area of the surface generated by revolving the graph of $f(x)$ around the x-axis. Round the answer to three decimal places.

Example 6.22

Calculating the Surface Area of a Surface of Revolution 2

Let $f(x) = y = \sqrt[3]{3x}.$ Consider the portion of the curve where $0 \le y \le 2.$ Find the surface area of the surface generated by revolving the graph of $f(x)$ around the y-axis.

Solution

Notice that we are revolving the curve around the y-axis, and the interval is in terms of $y,$ so we want to rewrite the function as a function of y. We get $x = g(y) = (1/3)y^3.$ The graph of $g(y)$ and the surface of rotation are shown in the following figure.

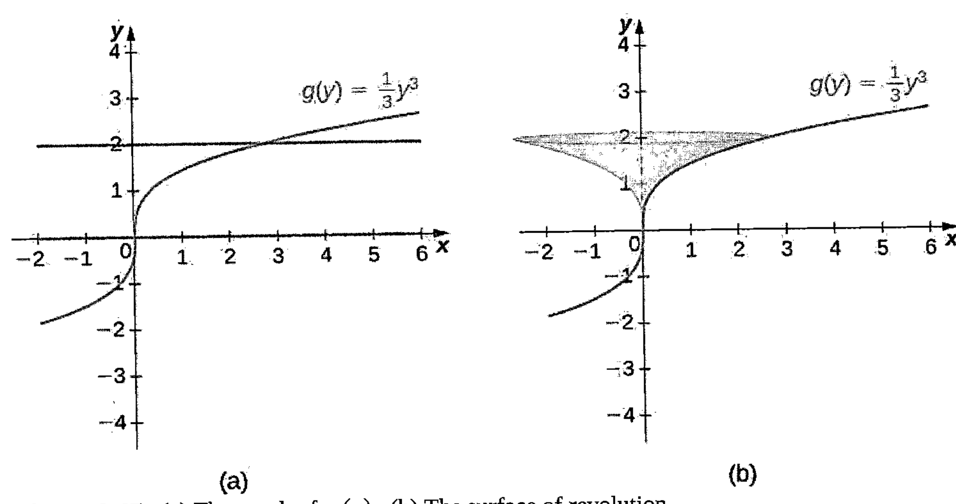

Figure 6.47 (a) The graph of $g(y)$. (b) The surface of revolution.

We have $g(y) = (1/3)y^3$, so $g'(y) = y^2$ and $(g'(y))^2 = y^4$. Then

$$\begin{aligned}\text{Surface Area} &= \int_c^d \left(2\pi g(y)\sqrt{1 + (g'(y))^2}\right)dy \\ &= \int_0^2 \left(2\pi\left(\tfrac{1}{3}y^3\right)\sqrt{1 + y^4}\right)dy \\ &= \frac{2\pi}{3}\int_0^2 \left(y^3\sqrt{1 + y^4}\right)dy.\end{aligned}$$

Let $u = y^4 + 1$. Then $du = 4y^3\,dy$. When $y = 0$, $u = 1$, and when $y = 2$, $u = 17$. Then

$$\begin{aligned}\frac{2\pi}{3}\int_0^2 \left(y^3\sqrt{1 + y^4}\right)dy &= \frac{2\pi}{3}\int_1^{17} \frac{1}{4}\sqrt{u}\,du \\ &= \frac{\pi}{6}\left[\frac{2}{3}u^{3/2}\right]\Big|_1^{17} = \frac{\pi}{9}\left[(17)^{3/2} - 1\right] \approx 24.118.\end{aligned}$$

6.22 Let $g(y) = \sqrt{9 - y^2}$ over the interval $y \in [0, 2]$. Find the surface area of the surface generated by revolving the graph of $g(y)$ around the y-axis.

6.4 EXERCISES

For the following exercises, find the length of the functions over the given interval.

165. $y = 5x$ from $x = 0$ to $x = 2$

166. $y = -\frac{1}{2}x + 25$ from $x = 1$ to $x = 4$

167. $x = 4y$ from $y = -1$ to $y = 1$

168. Pick an arbitrary linear function $x = g(y)$ over any interval of your choice (y_1, y_2). Determine the length of the function and then prove the length is correct by using geometry.

169. Find the surface area of the volume generated when the curve $y = \sqrt{x}$ revolves around the x-axis from $(1, 1)$ to $(4, 2)$, as seen here.

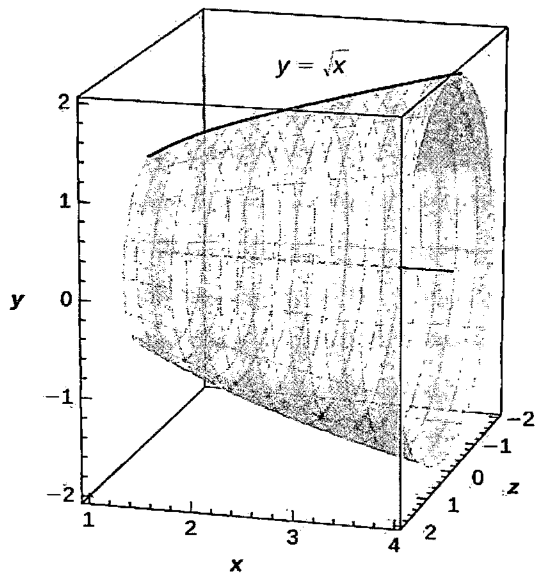

170. Find the surface area of the volume generated when the curve $y = x^2$ revolves around the y-axis from $(1, 1)$ to $(3, 9)$.

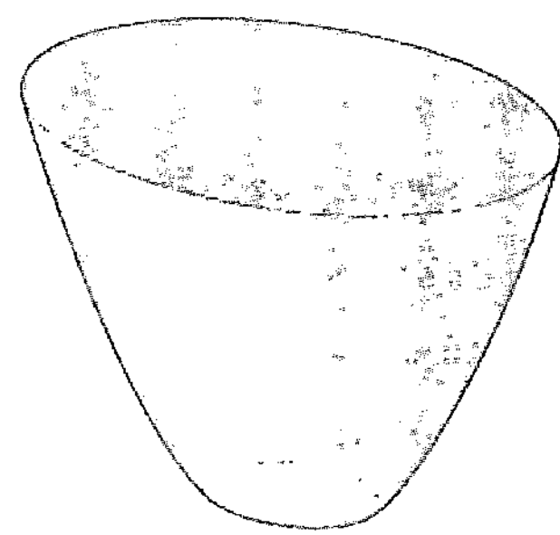

For the following exercises, find the lengths of the functions of x over the given interval. If you cannot evaluate the integral exactly, use technology to approximate it.

171. $y = x^{3/2}$ from $(0, 0)$ to $(1, 1)$

172. $y = x^{2/3}$ from $(1, 1)$ to $(8, 4)$

173. $y = \frac{1}{3}\left(x^2 + 2\right)^{3/2}$ from $x = 0$ to $x = 1$

174. $y = \frac{1}{3}\left(x^2 - 2\right)^{3/2}$ from $x = 2$ to $x = 4$

175. **[T]** $y = e^x$ on $x = 0$ to $x = 1$

176. $y = \frac{x^3}{3} + \frac{1}{4x}$ from $x = 1$ to $x = 3$

177. $y = \frac{x^4}{4} + \frac{1}{8x^2}$ from $x = 1$ to $x = 2$

178. $y = \frac{2x^{3/2}}{3} - \frac{x^{1/2}}{2}$ from $x = 1$ to $x = 4$

179. $y = \frac{1}{27}\left(9x^2 + 6\right)^{3/2}$ from $x = 0$ to $x = 2$

180. **[T]** $y = \sin x$ on $x = 0$ to $x = \pi$

For the following exercises, find the lengths of the functions of y over the given interval. If you cannot evaluate the integral exactly, use technology to approximate it.

181. $y = \frac{5 - 3x}{4}$ from $y = 0$ to $y = 4$

182. $x = \frac{1}{2}\left(e^y + e^{-y}\right)$ from $y = -1$ to $y = 1$

183. $x = 5y^{3/2}$ from $y = 0$ to $y = 1$

184. **[T]** $x = y^2$ from $y = 0$ to $y = 1$

185. $x = \sqrt{y}$ from $y = 0$ to $y = 1$

186. $x = \frac{2}{3}\left(y^2 + 1\right)^{3/2}$ from $y = 1$ to $y = 3$

187. **[T]** $x = \tan y$ from $y = 0$ to $y = \frac{3}{4}$

188. **[T]** $x = \cos^2 y$ from $y = -\frac{\pi}{2}$ to $y = \frac{\pi}{2}$

189. **[T]** $x = 4^y$ from $y = 0$ to $y = 2$

190. **[T]** $x = \ln(y)$ on $y = \frac{1}{e}$ to $y = e$

For the following exercises, find the surface area of the volume generated when the following curves revolve around the x-axis. If you cannot evaluate the integral exactly, use your calculator to approximate it.

191. $y = \sqrt{x}$ from $x = 2$ to $x = 6$

192. $y = x^3$ from $x = 0$ to $x = 1$

193. $y = 7x$ from $x = -1$ to $x = 1$

194. **[T]** $y = \frac{1}{x^2}$ from $x = 1$ to $x = 3$

195. $y = \sqrt{4 - x^2}$ from $x = 0$ to $x = 2$

196. $y = \sqrt{4 - x^2}$ from $x = -1$ to $x = 1$

197. $y = 5x$ from $x = 1$ to $x = 5$

198. **[T]** $y = \tan x$ from $x = -\frac{\pi}{4}$ to $x = \frac{\pi}{4}$

For the following exercises, find the surface area of the volume generated when the following curves revolve around the y-axis. If you cannot evaluate the integral exactly, use your calculator to approximate it.

199. $y = x^2$ from $x = 0$ to $x = 2$

200. $y = \frac{1}{2}x^2 + \frac{1}{2}$ from $x = 0$ to $x = 1$

201. $y = x + 1$ from $x = 0$ to $x = 3$

202. **[T]** $y = \frac{1}{x}$ from $x = \frac{1}{2}$ to $x = 1$

203. $y = \sqrt[3]{x}$ from $x = 1$ to $x = 27$

204. **[T]** $y = 3x^4$ from $x = 0$ to $x = 1$

205. **[T]** $y = \frac{1}{\sqrt{x}}$ from $x = 1$ to $x = 3$

206. **[T]** $y = \cos x$ from $x = 0$ to $x = \frac{\pi}{2}$

207. The base of a lamp is constructed by revolving a quarter circle $y = \sqrt{2x - x^2}$ around the y-axis from $x = 1$ to $x = 2$, as seen here. Create an integral for the surface area of this curve and compute it.

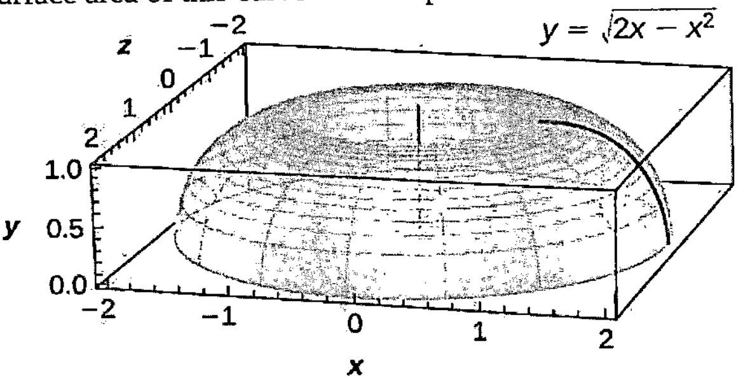

208. A light bulb is a sphere with radius $1/2$ in. with the bottom sliced off to fit exactly onto a cylinder of radius $1/4$ in. and length $1/3$ in., as seen here. The sphere is cut off at the bottom to fit exactly onto the cylinder, so the radius of the cut is $1/4$ in. Find the surface area (not including the top or bottom of the cylinder).

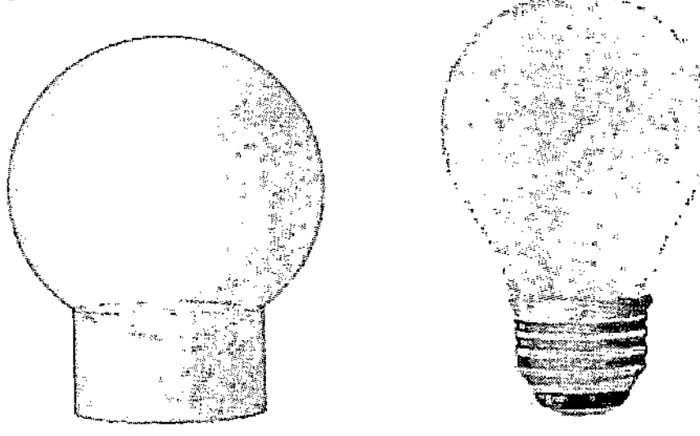

209. **[T]** A lampshade is constructed by rotating $y = 1/x$ around the x-axis from $y = 1$ to $y = 2$, as seen here. Determine how much material you would need to construct this lampshade—that is, the surface area—accurate to four decimal places.

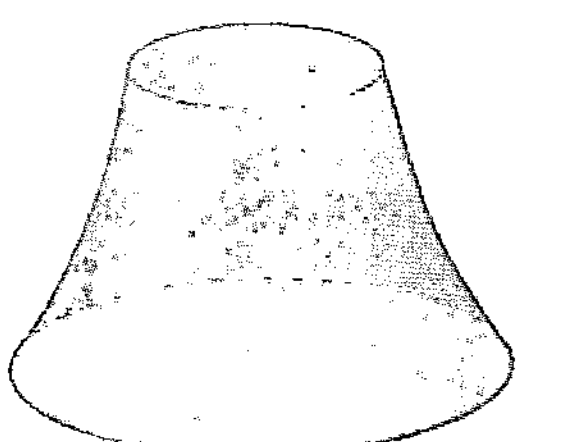
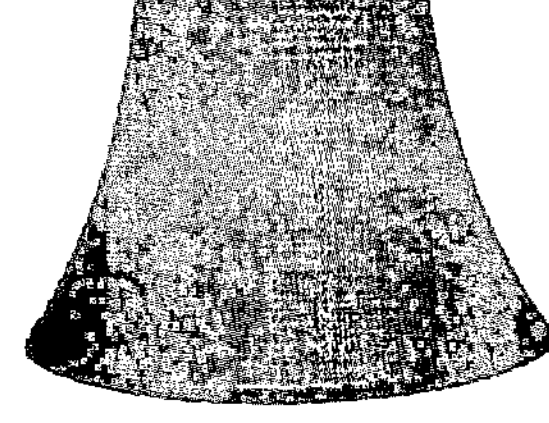

210. **[T]** An anchor drags behind a boat according to the function $y = 24e^{-x/2} - 24$, where y represents the depth beneath the boat and x is the horizontal distance of the anchor from the back of the boat. If the anchor is 23 ft below the boat, how much rope do you have to pull to reach the anchor? Round your answer to three decimal places.

211. **[T]** You are building a bridge that will span 10 ft. You intend to add decorative rope in the shape of $y = 5|\sin((x\pi)/5)|$, where x is the distance in feet from one end of the bridge. Find out how much rope you need to buy, rounded to the nearest foot.

For the following exercises, find the exact arc length for the following problems over the given interval.

212. $y = \ln(\sin x)$ from $x = \pi/4$ to $x = (3\pi)/4$. (*Hint:* Recall trigonometric identities.)

213. Draw graphs of $y = x^2$, $y = x^6$, and $y = x^{10}$. For $y = x^n$, as n increases, formulate a prediction on the arc length from $(0, 0)$ to $(1, 1)$. Now, compute the lengths of these three functions and determine whether your prediction is correct.

214. Compare the lengths of the parabola $x = y^2$ and the line $x = by$ from (0, 0) to $\left(b^2, b\right)$ as b increases. What do you notice?

215. Solve for the length of $x = y^2$ from (0, 0) to (1, 1). Show that $x = (1/2)y^2$ from $(0, 0)$ to $(2, 2)$ is twice as long. Graph both functions and explain why this is so.

216. **[T]** Which is longer between $(1, 1)$ and $(2, 1/2)$: the hyperbola $y = 1/x$ or the graph of $x + 2y = 3$?

217. Explain why the surface area is infinite when $y = 1/x$ is rotated around the x-axis for $1 \le x < \infty$, but the volume is finite.

6.5 | Physical Applications

Learning Objectives

- **6.5.1** Determine the mass of a one-dimensional object from its linear density function.
- **6.5.2** Determine the mass of a two-dimensional circular object from its radial density function.
- **6.5.3** Calculate the work done by a variable force acting along a line.
- **6.5.4** Calculate the work done in pumping a liquid from one height to another.
- **6.5.5** Find the hydrostatic force against a submerged vertical plate.

In this section, we examine some physical applications of integration. Let's begin with a look at calculating mass from a density function. We then turn our attention to work, and close the section with a study of hydrostatic force.

Mass and Density

We can use integration to develop a formula for calculating mass based on a density function. First we consider a thin rod or wire. Orient the rod so it aligns with the x-axis, with the left end of the rod at $x = a$ and the right end of the rod at $x = b$ (**Figure 6.48**). Note that although we depict the rod with some thickness in the figures, for mathematical purposes we assume the rod is thin enough to be treated as a one-dimensional object.

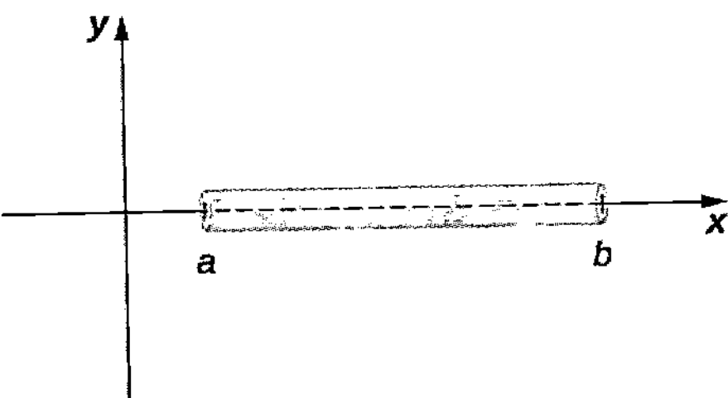

Figure 6.48 We can calculate the mass of a thin rod oriented along the x-axis by integrating its density function.

If the rod has constant density $\rho,$ given in terms of mass per unit length, then the mass of the rod is just the product of the density and the length of the rod: $(b - a)\rho.$ If the density of the rod is not constant, however, the problem becomes a little more challenging. When the density of the rod varies from point to point, we use a linear **density function**, $\rho(x),$ to denote the density of the rod at any point, $x.$ Let $\rho(x)$ be an integrable linear density function. Now, for $i = 0, 1, 2,\ldots, n$ let $P = \{x_i\}$ be a regular partition of the interval $[a, b],$ and for $i = 1, 2,\ldots, n$ choose an arbitrary point $x_i^* \in [x_{i-1}, x_i].$ **Figure 6.49** shows a representative segment of the rod.

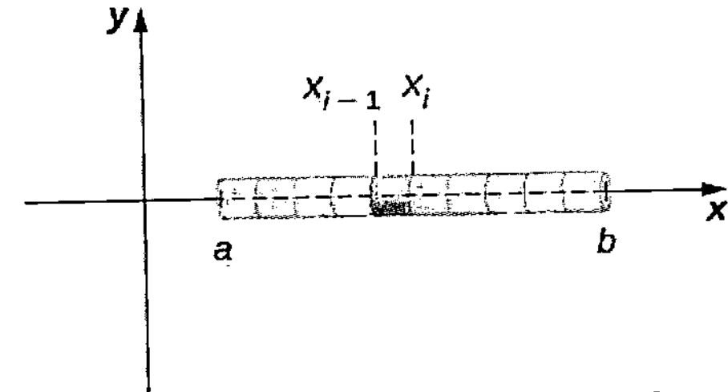

Figure 6.49 A representative segment of the rod.

The mass m_i of the segment of the rod from x_{i-1} to x_i is approximated by

$$m_i \approx \rho(x_i^*)(x_i - x_{i-1}) = \rho(x_i^*)\Delta x.$$

Adding the masses of all the segments gives us an approximation for the mass of the entire rod:

$$m = \sum_{i=1}^{n} m_i \approx \sum_{i=1}^{n} \rho(x_i^*)\Delta x.$$

This is a Riemann sum. Taking the limit as $n \to \infty$, we get an expression for the exact mass of the rod:

$$m = \lim_{n \to \infty} \sum_{i=1}^{n} \rho(x_i^*)\Delta x = \int_a^b \rho(x)dx.$$

We state this result in the following theorem.

Theorem 6.7: Mass–Density Formula of a One-Dimensional Object

Given a thin rod oriented along the x-axis over the interval $[a, b]$, let $\rho(x)$ denote a linear density function giving the density of the rod at a point x in the interval. Then the mass of the rod is given by

$$m = \int_a^b \rho(x)dx. \quad \textbf{(6.10)}$$

We apply this theorem in the next example.

Example 6.23

Calculating Mass from Linear Density

Consider a thin rod oriented on the x-axis over the interval $[\pi/2, \pi]$. If the density of the rod is given by $\rho(x) = \sin x$, what is the mass of the rod?

Solution

Applying **Equation 6.10** directly, we have

$$m = \int_a^b \rho(x)dx = \int_{\pi/2}^{\pi} \sin x\, dx = -\cos x|_{\pi/2}^{\pi} = 1.$$

6.23 Consider a thin rod oriented on the x-axis over the interval $[1, 3]$. If the density of the rod is given by $\rho(x) = 2x^2 + 3$, what is the mass of the rod?

We now extend this concept to find the mass of a two-dimensional disk of radius r. As with the rod we looked at in the one-dimensional case, here we assume the disk is thin enough that, for mathematical purposes, we can treat it as a two-dimensional object. We assume the density is given in terms of mass per unit area (called *area density*), and further assume the density varies only along the disk's radius (called *radial density*). We orient the disk in the xy-plane, with the center at the origin. Then, the density of the disk can be treated as a function of x, denoted $\rho(x)$. We assume $\rho(x)$ is integrable. Because density is a function of x, we partition the interval from $[0, r]$ along the x-axis. For $i = 0, 1, 2,\ldots, n$, let $P = \{x_i\}$ be a regular partition of the interval $[0, r]$, and for $i = 1, 2,\ldots, n$, choose an arbitrary point $x_i^* \in [x_{i-1}, x_i]$. Now, use the partition to break up the disk into thin (two-dimensional) washers. A disk and a representative washer are depicted in the following figure.

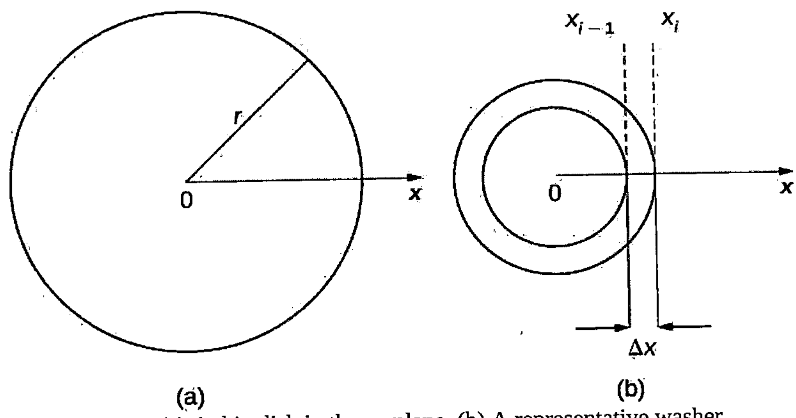

Figure 6.50 (a) A thin disk in the *xy*-plane. (b) A representative washer.

We now approximate the density and area of the washer to calculate an approximate mass, m_i. Note that the area of the washer is given by

$$\begin{aligned} A_i &= \pi(x_i)^2 - \pi(x_{i-1})^2 \\ &= \pi\left[x_i^2 - x_{i-1}^2\right] \\ &= \pi(x_i + x_{i-1})(x_i - x_{i-1}) \\ &= \pi(x_i + x_{i-1})\Delta x. \end{aligned}$$

You may recall that we had an expression similar to this when we were computing volumes by shells. As we did there, we use $x_i^* \approx (x_i + x_{i-1})/2$ to approximate the average radius of the washer. We obtain

$$A_i = \pi(x_i + x_{i-1})\Delta x \approx 2\pi x_i^* \Delta x.$$

Using $\rho(x_i^*)$ to approximate the density of the washer, we approximate the mass of the washer by

$$m_i \approx 2\pi x_i^* \rho(x_i^*)\Delta x.$$

Adding up the masses of the washers, we see the mass m of the entire disk is approximated by

$$m = \sum_{i=1}^{n} m_i \approx \sum_{i=1}^{n} 2\pi x_i^* \rho(x_i^*)\Delta x.$$

We again recognize this as a Riemann sum, and take the limit as $n \to \infty$. This gives us

$$m = \lim_{n \to \infty} \sum_{i=1}^{n} 2\pi x_i^* \rho(x_i^*)\Delta x = \int_0^r 2\pi x \rho(x)dx.$$

We summarize these findings in the following theorem.

Theorem 6.8: Mass–Density Formula of a Circular Object

Let $\rho(x)$ be an integrable function representing the radial density of a disk of radius r. Then the mass of the disk is given by

$$m = \int_0^r 2\pi x \rho(x)dx. \tag{6.11}$$

Example 6.24

Calculating Mass from Radial Density

Let $\rho(x) = \sqrt{x}$ represent the radial density of a disk. Calculate the mass of a disk of radius 4.

Solution

Applying the formula, we find

$$\begin{aligned} m &= \int_0^r 2\pi x\rho(x)dx \\ &= \int_0^4 2\pi x\sqrt{x}dx = 2\pi\int_0^4 x^{3/2}dx \\ &= 2\pi\frac{2}{5}x^{5/2}\Big|_0^4 = \frac{4\pi}{5}[32] = \frac{128\pi}{5}. \end{aligned}$$

6.24 Let $\rho(x) = 3x + 2$ represent the radial density of a disk. Calculate the mass of a disk of radius 2.

Work Done by a Force

We now consider work. In physics, work is related to force, which is often intuitively defined as a push or pull on an object. When a force moves an object, we say the force does work on the object. In other words, work can be thought of as the amount of energy it takes to move an object. According to physics, when we have a constant force, work can be expressed as the product of force and distance.

In the English system, the unit of force is the pound and the unit of distance is the foot, so work is given in foot-pounds. In the metric system, kilograms and meters are used. One newton is the force needed to accelerate 1 kilogram of mass at the rate of 1 m/sec^2. Thus, the most common unit of work is the newton-meter. This same unit is also called the *joule*. Both are defined as kilograms times meters squared over seconds squared $\left(\text{kg} \cdot \text{m}^2/\text{s}^2\right)$.

When we have a constant force, things are pretty easy. It is rare, however, for a force to be constant. The work done to compress (or elongate) a spring, for example, varies depending on how far the spring has already been compressed (or stretched). We look at springs in more detail later in this section.

Suppose we have a variable force $F(x)$ that moves an object in a positive direction along the x-axis from point a to point b. To calculate the work done, we partition the interval $[a, b]$ and estimate the work done over each subinterval. So, for $i = 0, 1, 2,\ldots, n,$ let $P = \{x_i\}$ be a regular partition of the interval $[a, b]$, and for $i = 1, 2,\ldots, n,$ choose an arbitrary point $x_i^* \in [x_{i-1}, x_i]$. To calculate the work done to move an object from point x_{i-1} to point x_i, we assume the force is roughly constant over the interval, and use $F(x_i^*)$ to approximate the force. The work done over the interval $[x_{i-1}, x_i]$, then, is given by

$$W_i \approx F(x_i^*)(x_i - x_{i-1}) = F(x_i^*)\Delta x.$$

Therefore, the work done over the interval $[a, b]$ is approximately

$$W = \sum_{i=1}^{n} W_i \approx \sum_{i=1}^{n} F(x_i^*)\Delta x.$$

Taking the limit of this expression as $n \to \infty$ gives us the exact value for work:

$$W = \lim_{n \to \infty} \sum_{i=1}^{n} F(x_i^*)\Delta x = \int_a^b F(x)dx.$$

Thus, we can define work as follows.

Definition

If a variable force $F(x)$ moves an object in a positive direction along the x-axis from point a to point b, then the **work** done on the object is

$$W = \int_a^b F(x)dx. \tag{6.12}$$

Note that if F is constant, the integral evaluates to $F \cdot (b-a) = F \cdot d$, which is the formula we stated at the beginning of this section.

Now let's look at the specific example of the work done to compress or elongate a spring. Consider a block attached to a horizontal spring. The block moves back and forth as the spring stretches and compresses. Although in the real world we would have to account for the force of friction between the block and the surface on which it is resting, we ignore friction here and assume the block is resting on a frictionless surface. When the spring is at its natural length (at rest), the system is said to be at equilibrium. In this state, the spring is neither elongated nor compressed, and in this equilibrium position the block does not move until some force is introduced. We orient the system such that $x = 0$ corresponds to the equilibrium position (see the following figure).

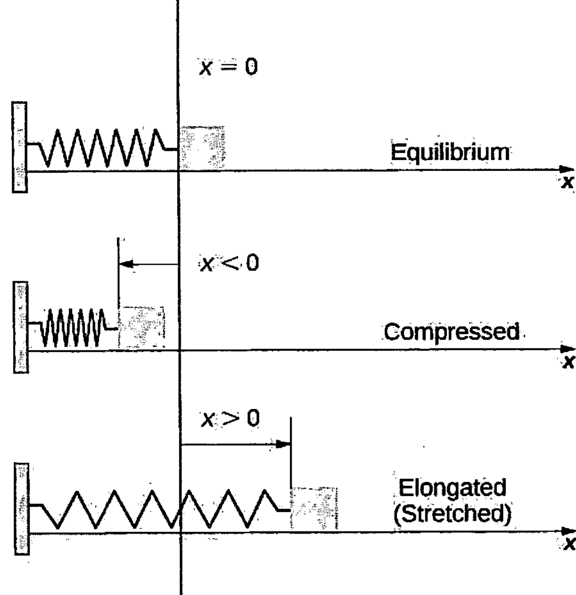

Figure 6.51 A block attached to a horizontal spring at equilibrium, compressed, and elongated.

According to **Hooke's law**, the force required to compress or stretch a spring from an equilibrium position is given by $F(x) = kx$, for some constant k. The value of k depends on the physical characteristics of the spring. The constant k is called the *spring constant* and is always positive. We can use this information to calculate the work done to compress or elongate a spring, as shown in the following example.

Example 6.25

The Work Required to Stretch or Compress a Spring

Suppose it takes a force of 10 N (in the negative direction) to compress a spring 0.2 m from the equilibrium position. How much work is done to stretch the spring 0.5 m from the equilibrium position?

Solution

First find the spring constant, k. When $x = -0.2$, we know $F(x) = -10$, so

$$\begin{aligned} F(x) &= kx \\ -10 &= k(-0.2) \\ k &= 50 \end{aligned}$$

and $F(x) = 50x$. Then, to calculate work, we integrate the force function, obtaining

$$W = \int_a^b F(x)dx = \int_0^{0.5} 50x\,dx = 25x^2\Big|_0^{0.5} = 6.25.$$

The work done to stretch the spring is 6.25 J.

6.25 Suppose it takes a force of 8 lb to stretch a spring 6 in. from the equilibrium position. How much work is done to stretch the spring 1 ft from the equilibrium position?

Work Done in Pumping

Consider the work done to pump water (or some other liquid) out of a tank. Pumping problems are a little more complicated than spring problems because many of the calculations depend on the shape and size of the tank. In addition, instead of being concerned about the work done to move a single mass, we are looking at the work done to move a volume of water, and it takes more work to move the water from the bottom of the tank than it does to move the water from the top of the tank.

We examine the process in the context of a cylindrical tank, then look at a couple of examples using tanks of different shapes. Assume a cylindrical tank of radius 4 m and height 10 m is filled to a depth of 8 m. How much work does it take to pump all the water over the top edge of the tank?

The first thing we need to do is define a frame of reference. We let x represent the vertical distance below the top of the tank. That is, we orient the x-axis vertically, with the origin at the top of the tank and the downward direction being positive (see the following figure).

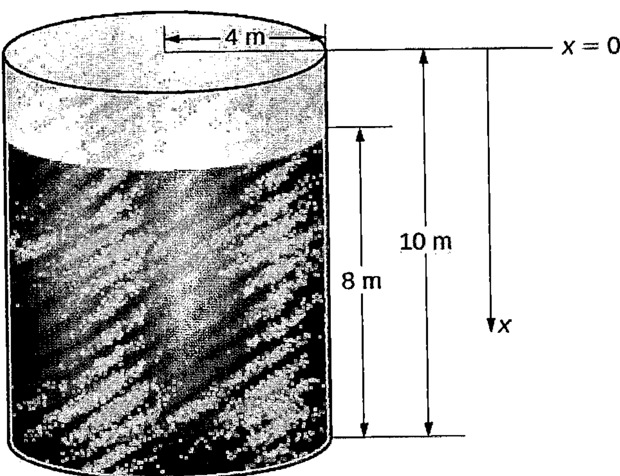

Figure 6.52 How much work is needed to empty a tank partially filled with water?

Using this coordinate system, the water extends from $x = 2$ to $x = 10$. Therefore, we partition the interval $[2, 10]$ and look at the work required to lift each individual "layer" of water. So, for $i = 0, 1, 2, \ldots, n,$ let $P = \{x_i\}$ be a regular partition of the interval $[2, 10],$ and for $i = 1, 2, \ldots, n,$ choose an arbitrary point $x_i^* \in [x_{i-1}, x_i]$. **Figure 6.53** shows a representative layer.

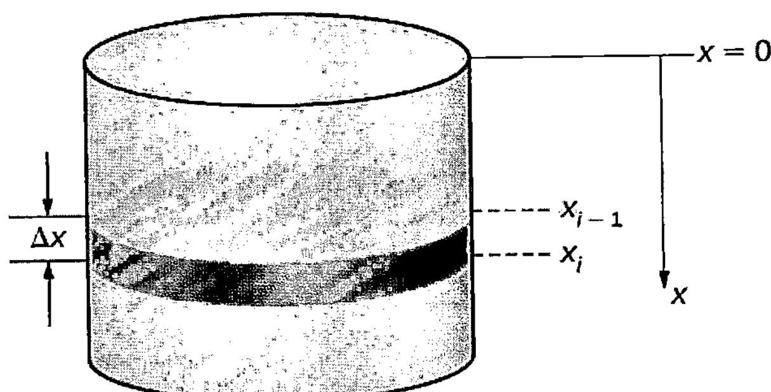

Figure 6.53 A representative layer of water.

In pumping problems, the force required to lift the water to the top of the tank is the force required to overcome gravity, so it is equal to the weight of the water. Given that the weight-density of water is 9800 N/m^3, or 62.4 lb/ft^3, calculating the volume of each layer gives us the weight. In this case, we have

$$V = \pi(4)^2 \Delta x = 16\pi \Delta x.$$

Then, the force needed to lift each layer is

$$F = 9800 \cdot 16\pi \Delta x = 156{,}800\pi \Delta x.$$

Note that this step becomes a little more difficult if we have a noncylindrical tank. We look at a noncylindrical tank in the next example.

We also need to know the distance the water must be lifted. Based on our choice of coordinate systems, we can use x_i^* as an approximation of the distance the layer must be lifted. Then the work to lift the ith layer of water W_i is approximately

$$W_i \approx 156{,}800\pi x_i^* \Delta x.$$

Adding the work for each layer, we see the approximate work to empty the tank is given by

$$W = \sum_{i=1}^{n} W_i \approx \sum_{i=1}^{n} 156{,}800\pi x_i^* \ \Delta x.$$

This is a Riemann sum, so taking the limit as $n \to \infty$, we get

$$\begin{aligned} W &= \lim_{n \to \infty} \sum_{i=1}^{n} 156{,}800\pi x_i^* \ \Delta x \\ &= 156{,}800\pi \int_2^{10} x dx \\ &= 156{,}800\pi \left[\frac{x^2}{2} \right] \Big|_2^{10} = 7{,}526{,}400\pi \approx 23{,}644{,}883. \end{aligned}$$

The work required to empty the tank is approximately 23,650,000 J.

For pumping problems, the calculations vary depending on the shape of the tank or container. The following problem-solving strategy lays out a step-by-step process for solving pumping problems.

Problem-Solving Strategy: Solving Pumping Problems

1. Sketch a picture of the tank and select an appropriate frame of reference.
2. Calculate the volume of a representative layer of water.
3. Multiply the volume by the weight-density of water to get the force.
4. Calculate the distance the layer of water must be lifted.
5. Multiply the force and distance to get an estimate of the work needed to lift the layer of water.
6. Sum the work required to lift all the layers. This expression is an estimate of the work required to pump out the desired amount of water, and it is in the form of a Riemann sum.
7. Take the limit as $n \to \infty$ and evaluate the resulting integral to get the exact work required to pump out the desired amount of water.

We now apply this problem-solving strategy in an example with a noncylindrical tank.

Example 6.26

A Pumping Problem with a Noncylindrical Tank

Assume a tank in the shape of an inverted cone, with height 12 ft and base radius 4 ft. The tank is full to start with, and water is pumped over the upper edge of the tank until the height of the water remaining in the tank is 4 ft. How much work is required to pump out that amount of water?

Solution

The tank is depicted in **Figure 6.54**. As we did in the example with the cylindrical tank, we orient the x-axis vertically, with the origin at the top of the tank and the downward direction being positive (step 1).

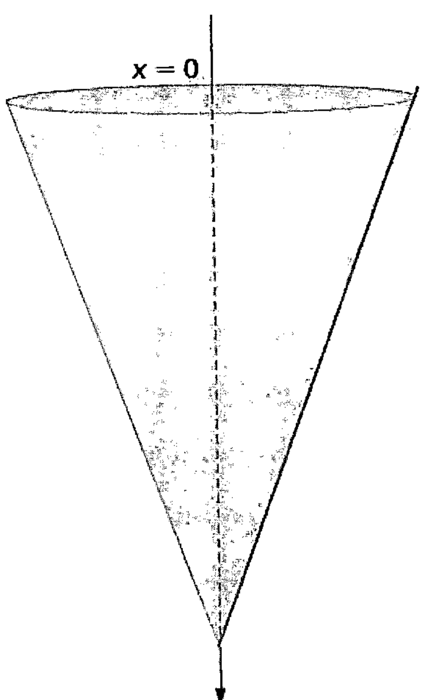

Figure 6.54 A water tank in the shape of an inverted cone.

The tank starts out full and ends with 4 ft of water left, so, based on our chosen frame of reference, we need to partition the interval $[0, 8]$. Then, for $i = 0, 1, 2,\ldots, n,$ let $P = \{x_i\}$ be a regular partition of the interval $[0, 8],$ and for $i = 1, 2,\ldots, n,$ choose an arbitrary point $x_i^* \in [x_{i-1}, x_i]$. We can approximate the volume of a layer by using a disk, then use similar triangles to find the radius of the disk (see the following figure).

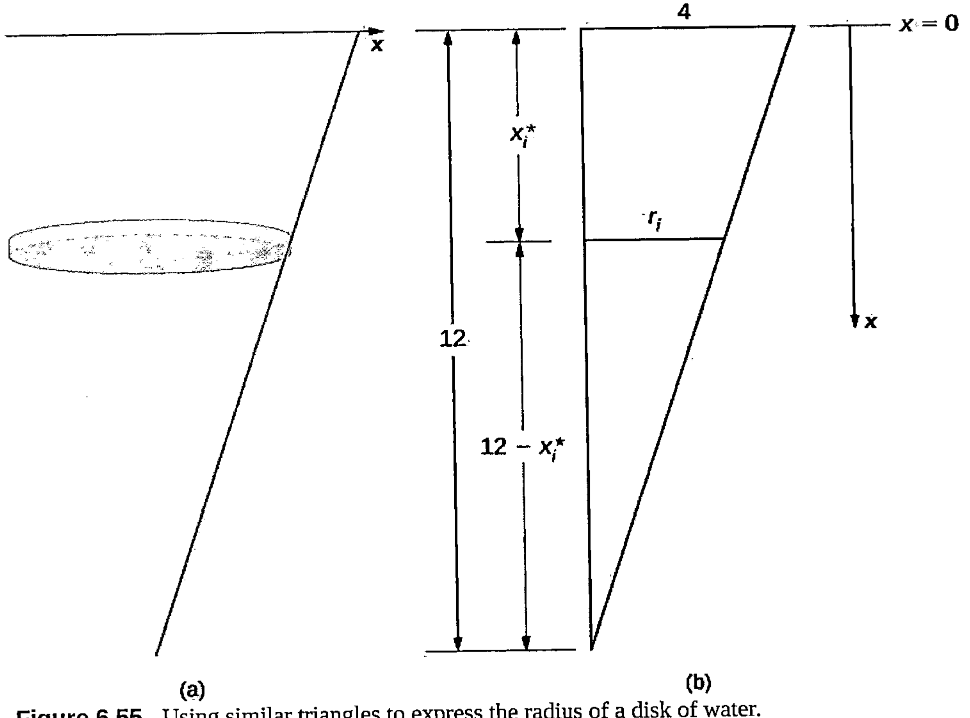

Figure 6.55 Using similar triangles to express the radius of a disk of water.

From properties of similar triangles, we have

$$\begin{aligned}\frac{r_i}{12-x_i^*} &= \frac{4}{12}=\frac{1}{3}\\ 3r_i &= 12-x_i^*\\ r_i &= \frac{12-x_i^*}{3}\\ &= 4-\frac{x_i^*}{3}.\end{aligned}$$

Then the volume of the disk is

$$V_i=\pi\left(4-\frac{x_i^*}{3}\right)^2\Delta x\text{ (step 2).}$$

The weight-density of water is $62.4\ \text{lb/ft}^3$, so the force needed to lift each layer is approximately

$$F_i\approx 62.4\pi\left(4-\frac{x_i^*}{3}\right)^2\Delta x\text{ (step 3).}$$

Based on the diagram, the distance the water must be lifted is approximately x_i^* feet (step 4), so the approximate work needed to lift the layer is

$$W_i\approx 62.4\pi x_i^*\left(4-\frac{x_i^*}{3}\right)^2\Delta x\text{ (step 5).}$$

Summing the work required to lift all the layers, we get an approximate value of the total work:

$$W=\sum_{i=1}^{n}W_i\approx\sum_{i=1}^{n}62.4\pi x_i^*\left(4-\frac{x_i^*}{3}\right)^2\Delta x\text{ (step 6).}$$

Taking the limit as $n\to\infty$, we obtain

$$\begin{aligned}W &= \lim_{n\to\infty}\sum_{i=1}^{n}62.4\pi x_i^*\left(4-\frac{x_i^*}{3}\right)^2\Delta x\\ &= \int_0^8 62.4\pi x\left(4-\frac{x}{3}\right)^2 dx\\ &= 62.4\pi\int_0^8 x\left(16-\frac{8x}{3}+\frac{x^2}{9}\right)dx = 62.4\pi\int_0^8\left(16x-\frac{8x^2}{3}+\frac{x^3}{9}\right)dx\\ &= 62.4\pi\left[8x^2-\frac{8x^3}{9}+\frac{x^4}{36}\right]\Bigg|_0^8 = 10{,}649.6\pi\approx 33{,}456.7.\end{aligned}$$

It takes approximately 33,450 ft-lb of work to empty the tank to the desired level.

6.26 A tank is in the shape of an inverted cone, with height 10 ft and base radius 6 ft. The tank is filled to a depth of 8 ft to start with, and water is pumped over the upper edge of the tank until 3 ft of water remain in the tank. How much work is required to pump out that amount of water?

Hydrostatic Force and Pressure

In this last section, we look at the force and pressure exerted on an object submerged in a liquid. In the English system, force is measured in pounds. In the metric system, it is measured in newtons. Pressure is force per unit area, so in the English system we have pounds per square foot (or, perhaps more commonly, pounds per square inch, denoted psi). In the metric system we have newtons per square meter, also called *pascals*.

Let's begin with the simple case of a plate of area A submerged horizontally in water at a depth s (**Figure 6.56**). Then, the force exerted on the plate is simply the weight of the water above it, which is given by $F = \rho As,$ where ρ is the weight density of water (weight per unit volume). To find the **hydrostatic pressure**—that is, the pressure exerted by water on a submerged object—we divide the force by the area. So the pressure is $p = F/A = \rho s.$

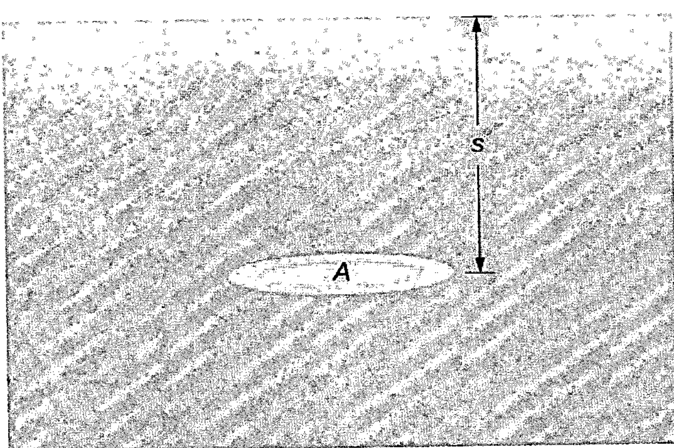

Figure 6.56 A plate submerged horizontally in water.

By Pascal's principle, the pressure at a given depth is the same in all directions, so it does not matter if the plate is submerged horizontally or vertically. So, as long as we know the depth, we know the pressure. We can apply Pascal's principle to find the force exerted on surfaces, such as dams, that are oriented vertically. We cannot apply the formula $F = \rho As$ directly, because the depth varies from point to point on a vertically oriented surface. So, as we have done many times before, we form a partition, a Riemann sum, and, ultimately, a definite integral to calculate the force.

Suppose a thin plate is submerged in water. We choose our frame of reference such that the x-axis is oriented vertically, with the downward direction being positive, and point $x = 0$ corresponding to a logical reference point. Let $s(x)$ denote the depth at point x. Note we often let $x = 0$ correspond to the surface of the water. In this case, depth at any point is simply given by $s(x) = x.$ However, in some cases we may want to select a different reference point for $x = 0,$ so we proceed with the development in the more general case. Last, let $w(x)$ denote the width of the plate at the point $x.$

Assume the top edge of the plate is at point $x = a$ and the bottom edge of the plate is at point $x = b.$ Then, for $i = 0, 1, 2,\ldots, n,$ let $P = \{x_i\}$ be a regular partition of the interval $[a, b],$ and for $i = 1, 2,\ldots, n,$ choose an arbitrary point $x_i^* \in [x_{i-1}, x_i].$ The partition divides the plate into several thin, rectangular strips (see the following figure).

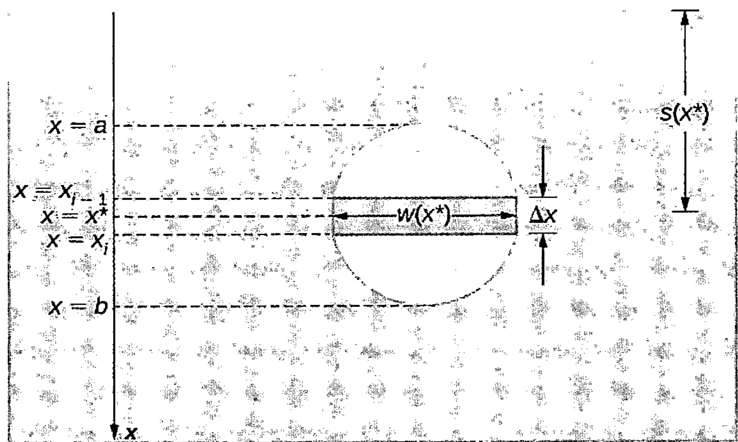

Figure 6.57 A thin plate submerged vertically in water.

Let's now estimate the force on a representative strip. If the strip is thin enough, we can treat it as if it is at a constant depth, $s(x_i^*)$. We then have

$$F_i = \rho A s = \rho\left[w(x_i^*)\Delta x\right]s(x_i^*).$$

Adding the forces, we get an estimate for the force on the plate:

$$F \approx \sum_{i=1}^{n} F_i = \sum_{i=1}^{n} \rho\left[w(x_i^*)\Delta x\right]s(x_i^*).$$

This is a Riemann sum, so taking the limit gives us the exact force. We obtain

$$F = \lim_{n \to \infty} \sum_{i=1}^{n} \rho\left[w(x_i^*)\Delta x\right]s(x_i^*) = \int_a^b \rho w(x)s(x)dx. \quad \textbf{(6.13)}$$

Evaluating this integral gives us the force on the plate. We summarize this in the following problem-solving strategy.

Problem-Solving Strategy: Finding Hydrostatic Force

1. Sketch a picture and select an appropriate frame of reference. (Note that if we select a frame of reference other than the one used earlier, we may have to adjust **Equation 6.13** accordingly.)
2. Determine the depth and width functions, $s(x)$ and $w(x)$.
3. Determine the weight-density of whatever liquid with which you are working. The weight-density of water is 62.4 lb/ft^3, or 9800 N/m^3.
4. Use the equation to calculate the total force.

Example 6.27

Finding Hydrostatic Force

A water trough 15 ft long has ends shaped like inverted isosceles triangles, with base 8 ft and height 3 ft. Find the force on one end of the trough if the trough is full of water.

Solution

Figure 6.58 shows the trough and a more detailed view of one end.

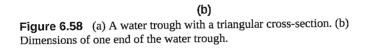

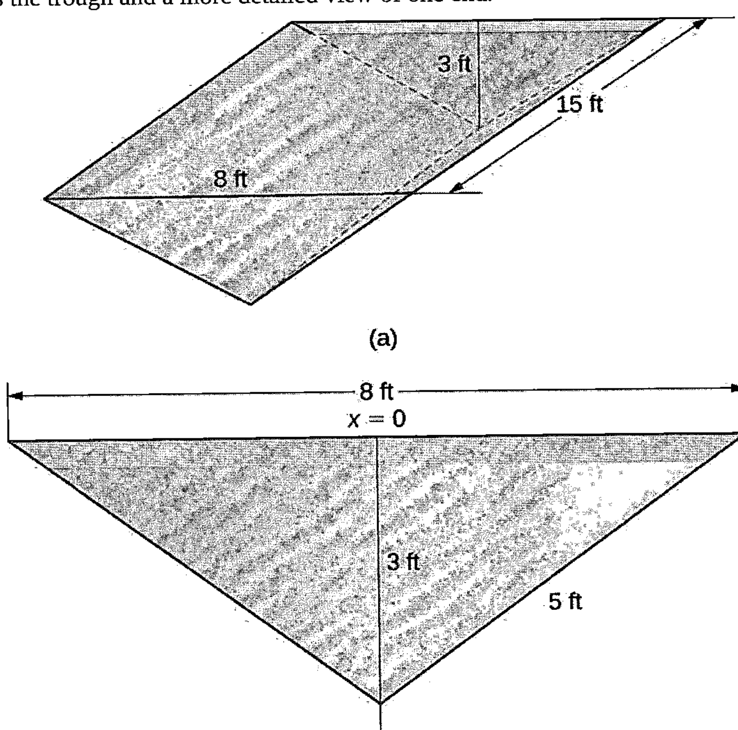

(b)

Figure 6.58 (a) A water trough with a triangular cross-section. (b) Dimensions of one end of the water trough.

Select a frame of reference with the x-axis oriented vertically and the downward direction being positive. Select the top of the trough as the point corresponding to $x = 0$ (step 1). The depth function, then, is $s(x) = x$. Using similar triangles, we see that $w(x) = 8 - (8/3)x$ (step 2). Now, the weight density of water is 62.4 lb/ft^3 (step 3), so applying **Equation 6.13**, we obtain

$$\begin{aligned} F &= \int_a^b \rho w(x) s(x) dx \\ &= \int_0^3 62.4\left(8 - \frac{8}{3}x\right)x\, dx = 62.4 \int_0^3 \left(8x - \frac{8}{3}x^2\right) dx \\ &= 62.4\left[4x^2 - \frac{8}{9}x^3\right]\Big|_0^3 = 748.8. \end{aligned}$$

The water exerts a force of 748.8 lb on the end of the trough (step 4).

6.27 A water trough 12 m long has ends shaped like inverted isosceles triangles, with base 6 m and height 4 m. Find the force on one end of the trough if the trough is full of water.

Example 6.28

Chapter Opener: Finding Hydrostatic Force

We now return our attention to the Hoover Dam, mentioned at the beginning of this chapter. The actual dam is arched, rather than flat, but we are going to make some simplifying assumptions to help us with the calculations. Assume the face of the Hoover Dam is shaped like an isosceles trapezoid with lower base 750 ft, upper base 1250 ft, and height 750 ft (see the following figure).

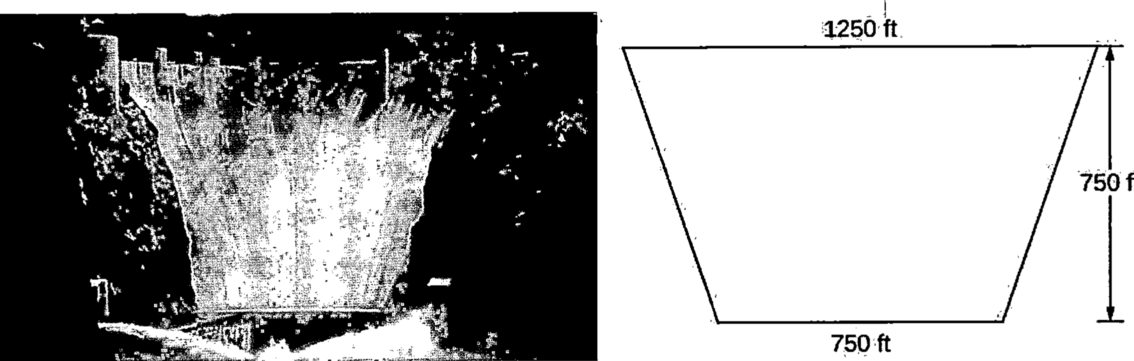

When the reservoir is full, Lake Mead's maximum depth is about 530 ft, and the surface of the lake is about 10 ft below the top of the dam (see the following figure).

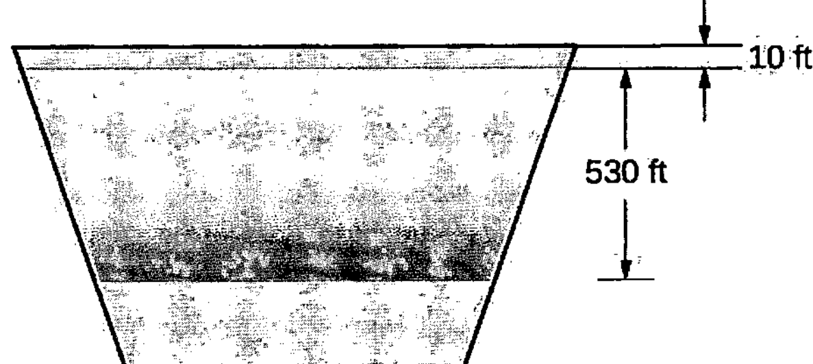

Figure 6.59 A simplified model of the Hoover Dam with assumed dimensions.

a. Find the force on the face of the dam when the reservoir is full.
b. The southwest United States has been experiencing a drought, and the surface of Lake Mead is about 125 ft below where it would be if the reservoir were full. What is the force on the face of the dam under these circumstances?

Solution

a. We begin by establishing a frame of reference. As usual, we choose to orient the x-axis vertically, with the downward direction being positive. This time, however, we are going to let $x = 0$ represent the top of the dam, rather than the surface of the water. When the reservoir is full, the surface of the water is 10 ft below the top of the dam, so $s(x) = x - 10$ (see the following figure).

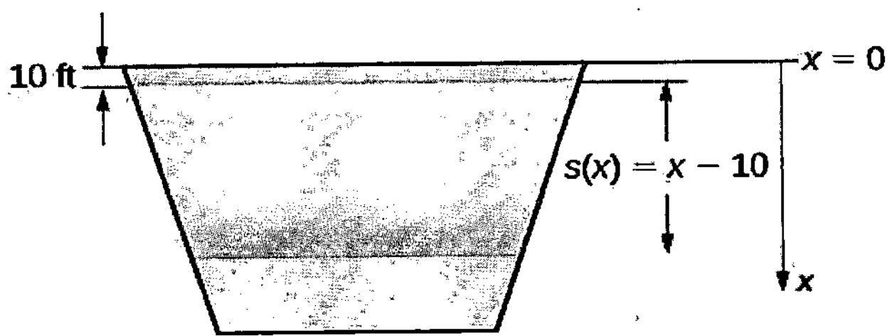

Figure 6.60 We first choose a frame of reference.

To find the width function, we again turn to similar triangles as shown in the figure below.

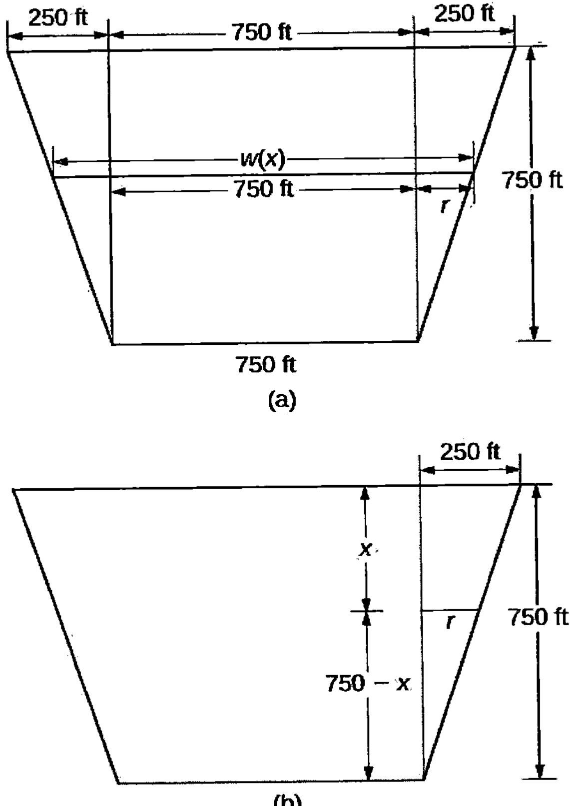

Figure 6.61 We use similar triangles to determine a function for the width of the dam. (a) Assumed dimensions of the dam; (b) highlighting the similar triangles.

From the figure, we see that $w(x) = 750 + 2r$. Using properties of similar triangles, we get $r = 250 - (1/3)x$. Thus,

$$w(x) = 1250 - \frac{2}{3}x \text{ (step 2)}.$$

Using a weight-density of 62.4 lb/ft^3 (step 3) and applying **Equation 6.13**, we get

$$\begin{aligned} F &= \int_a^b \rho w(x)s(x)dx \\ &= \int_{10}^{540} 62.4\left(1250 - \frac{2}{3}x\right)(x-10)dx = 62.4\int_{10}^{540} -\frac{2}{3}\left[x^2 - 1885x + 18750\right]dx \\ &= -62.4\left(\frac{2}{3}\right)\left[\frac{x^3}{3} - \frac{1885x^2}{2} + 18750x\right]\Bigg|_{10}^{540} \approx 8{,}832{,}245{,}000 \text{ lb} = 4{,}416{,}122.5 \text{ t.} \end{aligned}$$

Note the change from pounds to tons $(2000 \text{ lb} = 1 \text{ ton})$ (step 4). This changes our depth function, $s(x)$, and our limits of integration. We have $s(x) = x - 135.$ The lower limit of integration is $135.$ The upper limit remains $540.$ Evaluating the integral, we get

$$\begin{aligned} F &= \int_a^b \rho w(x)s(x)dx \\ &= \int_{135}^{540} 62.4\left(1250 - \frac{2}{3}x\right)(x-135)dx \\ &= -62.4\left(\frac{2}{3}\right)\int_{135}^{540} (x-1875)(x-135)dx = -62.4\left(\frac{2}{3}\right)\int_{135}^{540}\left(x^2 - 2010x + 253125\right)dx \\ &= -62.4\left(\frac{2}{3}\right)\left[\frac{x^3}{3} - 1005x^2 + 253125x\right]\Bigg|_{135}^{540} \approx 5{,}015{,}230{,}000 \text{ lb} = 2{,}507{,}615 \text{ t.} \end{aligned}$$

6.28 When the reservoir is at its average level, the surface of the water is about 50 ft below where it would be if the reservoir were full. What is the force on the face of the dam under these circumstances?

To learn more about Hoover Dam, see this **article (http://www.openstaxcollege.org/l/20_HooverDam)** published by the History Channel.

6.5 EXERCISES

For the following exercises, find the work done.

218. Find the work done when a constant force $F = 12$ lb moves a chair from $x = 0.9$ to $x = 1.1$ ft.

219. How much work is done when a person lifts a 50 lb box of comics onto a truck that is 3 ft off the ground?

220. What is the work done lifting a 20 kg child from the floor to a height of 2 m? (Note that 1 kg equates to 9.8 N)

221. Find the work done when you push a box along the floor 2 m, when you apply a constant force of $F = 100\,\text{N}$.

222. Compute the work done for a force $F = 12/x^2$ N from $x = 1$ to $x = 2$ m.

223. What is the work done moving a particle from $x = 0$ to $x = 1$ m if the force acting on it is $F = 3x^2$ N?

For the following exercises, find the mass of the one-dimensional object.

224. A wire that is 2 ft long (starting at $x = 0$) and has a density function of $\rho(x) = x^2 + 2x$ lb/ft

225. A car antenna that is 3 ft long (starting at $x = 0$) and has a density function of $\rho(x) = 3x + 2$ lb/ft

226. A metal rod that is 8 in. long (starting at $x = 0$) and has a density function of $\rho(x) = e^{1/2x}$ lb/in.

227. A pencil that is 4 in. long (starting at $x = 2$) and has a density function of $\rho(x) = 5/x$ oz/in.

228. A ruler that is 12 in. long (starting at $x = 5$) and has a density function of $\rho(x) = \ln(x) + (1/2)x^2$ oz/in.

For the following exercises, find the mass of the two-dimensional object that is centered at the origin.

229. An oversized hockey puck of radius 2 in. with density function $\rho(x) = x^3 - 2x + 5$

230. A frisbee of radius 6 in. with density function $\rho(x) = e^{-x}$

231. A plate of radius 10 in. with density function $\rho(x) = 1 + \cos(\pi x)$

232. A jar lid of radius 3 in. with density function $\rho(x) = \ln(x + 1)$

233. A disk of radius 5 cm with density function $\rho(x) = \sqrt{3x}$

234. A 12-in. spring is stretched to 15 in. by a force of 75 lb. What is the spring constant?

235. A spring has a natural length of 10 cm. It takes 2 J to stretch the spring to 15 cm. How much work would it take to stretch the spring from 15 cm to 20 cm?

236. A 1-m spring requires 10 J to stretch the spring to 1.1 m. How much work would it take to stretch the spring from 1 m to 1.2 m?

237. A spring requires 5 J to stretch the spring from 8 cm to 12 cm, and an additional 4 J to stretch the spring from 12 cm to 14 cm. What is the natural length of the spring?

238. A shock absorber is compressed 1 in. by a weight of 1 t. What is the spring constant?

239. A force of $F = 20x - x^3$ N stretches a nonlinear spring by x meters. What work is required to stretch the spring from $x = 0$ to $x = 2$ m?

240. Find the work done by winding up a hanging cable of length 100 ft and weight-density 5 lb/ft.

241. For the cable in the preceding exercise, how much work is done to lift the cable 50 ft?

242. For the cable in the preceding exercise, how much additional work is done by hanging a 200 lb weight at the end of the cable?

243. **[T]** A pyramid of height 500 ft has a square base 800 ft by 800 ft. Find the area A at height h. If the rock used to build the pyramid weighs approximately $w = 100\,\text{lb/ft}^3$, how much work did it take to lift all the rock?

244. **[T]** For the pyramid in the preceding exercise, assume there were 1000 workers each working 10 hours a day, 5 days a week, 50 weeks a year. If the workers, on average, lifted 10 100 lb rocks 2 ft/hr, how long did it take to build the pyramid?

245. **[T]** The force of gravity on a mass m is $F = -\left((GMm)/x^2\right)$ newtons. For a rocket of mass $m = 1000\,\text{kg},$ compute the work to lift the rocket from $x = 6400$ to $x = 6500$ km. (*Note:* $G = 6 \times 10^{-17}\text{ N m}^2/\text{kg}^2$ and $M = 6 \times 10^{24}$ kg.)

246. **[T]** For the rocket in the preceding exercise, find the work to lift the rocket from $x = 6400$ to $x = \infty.$

247. **[T]** A rectangular dam is 40 ft high and 60 ft wide. Compute the total force F on the dam when

a. the surface of the water is at the top of the dam and
b. the surface of the water is halfway down the dam.

248. **[T]** Find the work required to pump all the water out of a cylinder that has a circular base of radius 5 ft and height 200 ft. Use the fact that the density of water is 62 lb/ft^3.

249. **[T]** Find the work required to pump all the water out of the cylinder in the preceding exercise if the cylinder is only half full.

250. **[T]** How much work is required to pump out a swimming pool if the area of the base is 800 ft^2, the water is 4 ft deep, and the top is 1 ft above the water level? Assume that the density of water is 62 lb/ft^3.

251. A cylinder of depth H and cross-sectional area A stands full of water at density $\rho.$ Compute the work to pump all the water to the top.

252. For the cylinder in the preceding exercise, compute the work to pump all the water to the top if the cylinder is only half full.

253. A cone-shaped tank has a cross-sectional area that increases with its depth: $A = \left(\pi r^2 h^2\right)/H^3.$ Show that the work to empty it is half the work for a cylinder with the same height and base.

6.6 | Moments and Centers of Mass

Learning Objectives

6.6.1 Find the center of mass of objects distributed along a line.
6.6.2 Locate the center of mass of a thin plate.
6.6.3 Use symmetry to help locate the centroid of a thin plate.
6.6.4 Apply the theorem of Pappus for volume.

In this section, we consider centers of mass (also called *centroids*, under certain conditions) and moments. The basic idea of the center of mass is the notion of a balancing point. Many of us have seen performers who spin plates on the ends of sticks. The performers try to keep several of them spinning without allowing any of them to drop. If we look at a single plate (without spinning it), there is a sweet spot on the plate where it balances perfectly on the stick. If we put the stick anywhere other than that sweet spot, the plate does not balance and it falls to the ground. (That is why performers spin the plates; the spin helps keep the plates from falling even if the stick is not exactly in the right place.) Mathematically, that sweet spot is called the *center of mass of the plate*.

In this section, we first examine these concepts in a one-dimensional context, then expand our development to consider centers of mass of two-dimensional regions and symmetry. Last, we use centroids to find the volume of certain solids by applying the theorem of Pappus.

Center of Mass and Moments

Let's begin by looking at the center of mass in a one-dimensional context. Consider a long, thin wire or rod of negligible mass resting on a fulcrum, as shown in **Figure 6.62**(a). Now suppose we place objects having masses m_1 and m_2 at distances d_1 and d_2 from the fulcrum, respectively, as shown in **Figure 6.62**(b).

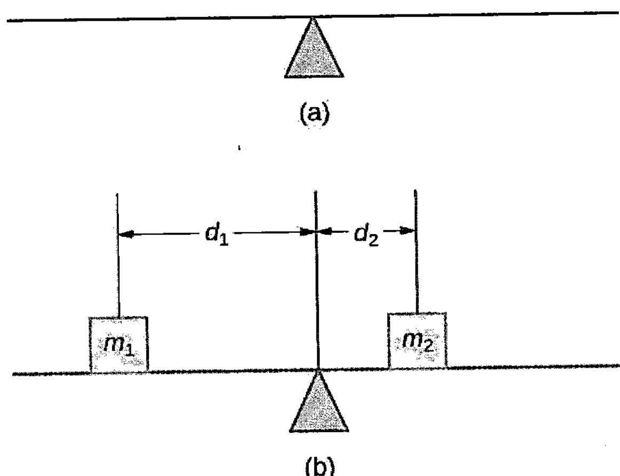

Figure 6.62 (a) A thin rod rests on a fulcrum. (b) Masses are placed on the rod.

The most common real-life example of a system like this is a playground seesaw, or teeter-totter, with children of different weights sitting at different distances from the center. On a seesaw, if one child sits at each end, the heavier child sinks down and the lighter child is lifted into the air. If the heavier child slides in toward the center, though, the seesaw balances. Applying this concept to the masses on the rod, we note that the masses balance each other if and only if $m_1 d_1 = m_2 d_2$.

In the seesaw example, we balanced the system by moving the masses (children) with respect to the fulcrum. However, we are really interested in systems in which the masses are not allowed to move, and instead we balance the system by moving the fulcrum. Suppose we have two point masses, m_1 and m_2, located on a number line at points x_1 and x_2, respectively (**Figure 6.63**). The center of mass, $\bar{x}$, is the point where the fulcrum should be placed to make the system balance.

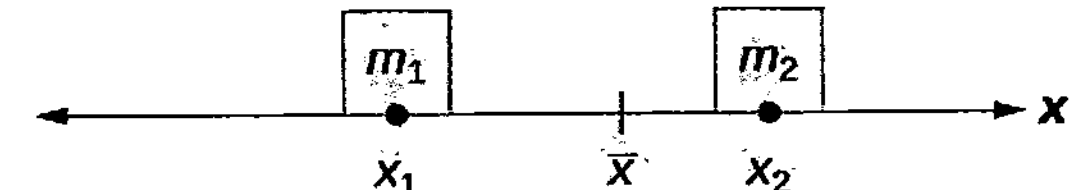

Figure 6.63 The center of mass $\bar{x}$ is the balance point of the system.

Thus, we have

$$\begin{aligned} m_1 |x_1 - \bar{x}| &= m_2 |x_2 - \bar{x}| \\ m_1(\bar{x} - x_1) &= m_2(x_2 - \bar{x}) \\ m_1\bar{x} - m_1 x_1 &= m_2 x_2 - m_2\bar{x} \\ \bar{x}(m_1 + m_2) &= m_1 x_1 + m_2 x_2 \\ \bar{x} &= \frac{m_1 x_1 + m_2 x_2}{m_1 + m_2}. \end{aligned}$$

The expression in the numerator, $m_1 x_1 + m_2 x_2,$ is called the *first moment of the system with respect to the origin.* If the context is clear, we often drop the word *first* and just refer to this expression as the **moment** of the system. The expression in the denominator, $m_1 + m_2,$ is the total mass of the system. Thus, the **center of mass** of the system is the point at which the total mass of the system could be concentrated without changing the moment.

This idea is not limited just to two point masses. In general, if *n* masses, $m_1, m_2, \ldots, m_n,$ are placed on a number line at points $x_1, x_2, \ldots, x_n,$ respectively, then the center of mass of the system is given by

$$\bar{x} = \frac{\sum_{i=1}^{n} m_i x_i}{\sum_{i=1}^{n} m_i}.$$

Theorem 6.9: Center of Mass of Objects on a Line

Let $m_1, m_2, \ldots, m_n$ be point masses placed on a number line at points $x_1, x_2, \ldots, x_n,$ respectively, and let $m = \sum_{i=1}^{n} m_i$ denote the total mass of the system. Then, the moment of the system with respect to the origin is given by

$$M = \sum_{i=1}^{n} m_i x_i \tag{6.14}$$

and the center of mass of the system is given by

$$\bar{x} = \frac{M}{m}. \tag{6.15}$$

We apply this theorem in the following example.

Example 6.29

Finding the Center of Mass of Objects along a Line

Suppose four point masses are placed on a number line as follows:

$m_1 = 30\text{ kg, placed at } x_1 = -2\text{ m} \qquad m_2 = 5\text{ kg, placed at } x_2 = 3\text{ m}$

$m_3 = 10\text{ kg, placed at } x_3 = 6\text{ m} \qquad m_4 = 15\text{ kg, placed at } x_4 = -3\text{ m.}$

Find the moment of the system with respect to the origin and find the center of mass of the system.

Solution

First, we need to calculate the moment of the system:

$$\begin{aligned} M &= \sum_{i=1}^{4} m_i x_i \\ &= -60 + 15 + 60 - 45 = -30. \end{aligned}$$

Now, to find the center of mass, we need the total mass of the system:

$$\begin{aligned} m &= \sum_{i=1}^{4} m_i \\ &= 30 + 5 + 10 + 15 = 60\text{ kg.} \end{aligned}$$

Then we have

$$\bar{x} = \frac{M}{m} = \frac{-30}{60} = -\frac{1}{2}.$$

The center of mass is located 1/2 m to the left of the origin.

6.29 Suppose four point masses are placed on a number line as follows:

$m_1 = 12\text{ kg, placed at } x_1 = -4\text{ m} \qquad m_2 = 12\text{ kg, placed at } x_2 = 4\text{ m}$

$m_3 = 30\text{ kg, placed at } x_3 = 2\text{ m} \qquad m_4 = 6\text{ kg, placed at } x_4 = -6\text{ m.}$

Find the moment of the system with respect to the origin and find the center of mass of the system.

We can generalize this concept to find the center of mass of a system of point masses in a plane. Let m_1 be a point mass located at point (x_1, y_1) in the plane. Then the moment M_x of the mass with respect to the *x*-axis is given by $M_x = m_1 y_1$. Similarly, the moment M_y with respect to the *y*-axis is given by $M_y = m_1 x_1$. Notice that the *x*-coordinate of the point is used to calculate the moment with respect to the *y*-axis, and vice versa. The reason is that the *x*-coordinate gives the distance from the point mass to the *y*-axis, and the *y*-coordinate gives the distance to the *x*-axis (see the following figure).

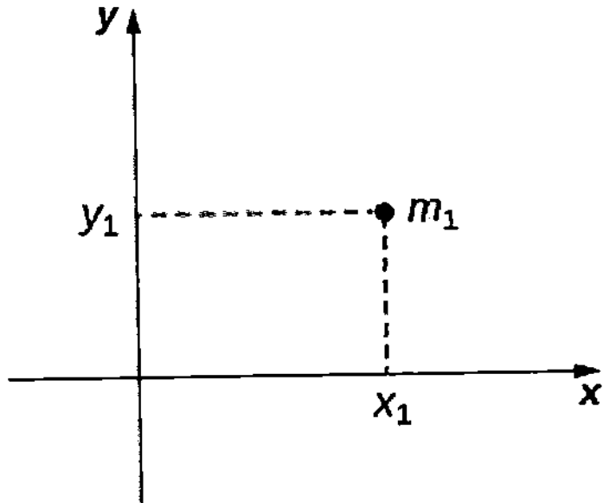

Figure 6.64 Point mass m_1 is located at point (x_1, y_1) in the plane.

If we have several point masses in the *xy*-plane, we can use the moments with respect to the *x*- and *y*-axes to calculate the

x- and y-coordinates of the center of mass of the system.

Theorem 6.10: Center of Mass of Objects in a Plane

Let $m_1, m_2, \ldots, m_n$ be point masses located in the xy-plane at points $(x_1, y_1), (x_2, y_2), \ldots, (x_n, y_n)$, respectively, and let $m = \sum_{i=1}^{n} m_i$ denote the total mass of the system. Then the moments M_x and M_y of the system with respect to the x- and y-axes, respectively, are given by

$$M_x = \sum_{i=1}^{n} m_i y_i \quad \text{and} \quad M_y = \sum_{i=1}^{n} m_i x_i. \tag{6.16}$$

Also, the coordinates of the center of mass $(\bar{x}, \bar{y})$ of the system are

$$\bar{x} = \frac{M_y}{m} \quad \text{and} \quad \bar{y} = \frac{M_x}{m}. \tag{6.17}$$

The next example demonstrates how to apply this theorem.

Example 6.30

Finding the Center of Mass of Objects in a Plane

Suppose three point masses are placed in the xy-plane as follows (assume coordinates are given in meters):

$$\begin{aligned} m_1 &= 2\text{ kg, placed at } (-1, 3), \\ m_2 &= 6\text{ kg, placed at } (1, 1), \\ m_3 &= 4\text{ kg, placed at } (2, -2). \end{aligned}$$

Find the center of mass of the system.

Solution

First we calculate the total mass of the system:

$$m = \sum_{i=1}^{3} m_i = 2 + 6 + 4 = 12\text{ kg}.$$

Next we find the moments with respect to the x- and y-axes:

$$\begin{aligned} M_y &= \sum_{i=1}^{3} m_i x_i = -2 + 6 + 8 = 12, \\ M_x &= \sum_{i=1}^{3} m_i y_i = 6 + 6 - 8 = 4. \end{aligned}$$

Then we have

$$\bar{x} = \frac{M_y}{m} = \frac{12}{12} = 1 \text{ and } \bar{y} = \frac{M_x}{m} = \frac{4}{12} = \frac{1}{3}.$$

The center of mass of the system is $(1, 1/3)$, in meters.

6.30 Suppose three point masses are placed on a number line as follows (assume coordinates are given in meters):

$$m_1 = 5\text{ kg, placed at } (-2, -3),$$
$$m_2 = 3\text{ kg, placed at } (2, 3),$$
$$m_3 = 2\text{ kg, placed at } (-3, -2).$$

Find the center of mass of the system.

Center of Mass of Thin Plates

So far we have looked at systems of point masses on a line and in a plane. Now, instead of having the mass of a system concentrated at discrete points, we want to look at systems in which the mass of the system is distributed continuously across a thin sheet of material. For our purposes, we assume the sheet is thin enough that it can be treated as if it is two-dimensional. Such a sheet is called a **lamina**. Next we develop techniques to find the center of mass of a lamina. In this section, we also assume the density of the lamina is constant.

Laminas are often represented by a two-dimensional region in a plane. The geometric center of such a region is called its **centroid**. Since we have assumed the density of the lamina is constant, the center of mass of the lamina depends only on the shape of the corresponding region in the plane; it does not depend on the density. In this case, the center of mass of the lamina corresponds to the centroid of the delineated region in the plane. As with systems of point masses, we need to find the total mass of the lamina, as well as the moments of the lamina with respect to the x- and y-axes.

We first consider a lamina in the shape of a rectangle. Recall that the center of mass of a lamina is the point where the lamina balances. For a rectangle, that point is both the horizontal and vertical center of the rectangle. Based on this understanding, it is clear that the center of mass of a rectangular lamina is the point where the diagonals intersect, which is a result of the **symmetry principle**, and it is stated here without proof.

Theorem 6.11: The Symmetry Principle

If a region R is symmetric about a line l, then the centroid of R lies on l.

Let's turn to more general laminas. Suppose we have a lamina bounded above by the graph of a continuous function $f(x)$, below by the x-axis, and on the left and right by the lines $x = a$ and $x = b$, respectively, as shown in the following figure.

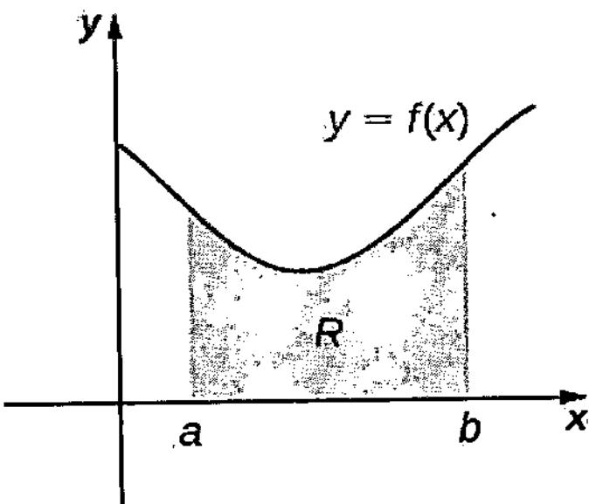

Figure 6.65 A region in the plane representing a lamina.

As with systems of point masses, to find the center of mass of the lamina, we need to find the total mass of the lamina, as well as the moments of the lamina with respect to the x- and y-axes. As we have done many times before, we approximate these quantities by partitioning the interval $[a, b]$ and constructing rectangles.

For $i = 0, 1, 2,\ldots, n,$ let $P = \{x_i\}$ be a regular partition of $[a, b]$. Recall that we can choose any point within the interval $[x_{i-1}, x_i]$ as our x_i^*. In this case, we want x_i^* to be the x-coordinate of the centroid of our rectangles. Thus, for $i = 1, 2,\ldots, n,$ we select $x_i^* \in [x_{i-1}, x_i]$ such that x_i^* is the midpoint of the interval. That is, $x_i^* = (x_{i-1} + x_i)/2.$ Now, for $i = 1, 2,\ldots, n,$ construct a rectangle of height $f(x_i^*)$ on $[x_{i-1}, x_i]$. The center of mass of this rectangle is

$\left(x_i^*, (f(x_i^*))/2\right)$, as shown in the following figure.

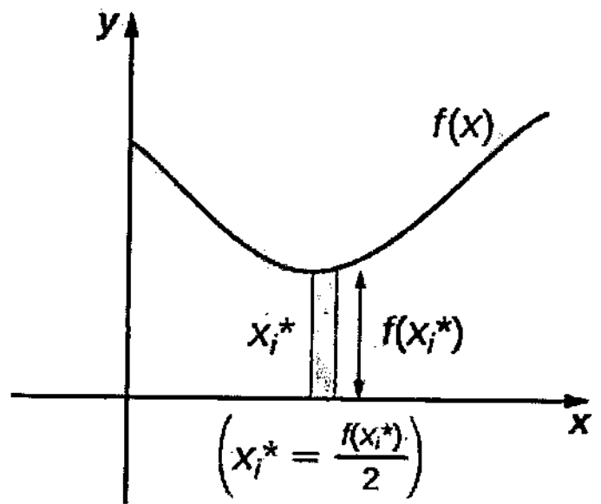

Figure 6.66 A representative rectangle of the lamina.

Next, we need to find the total mass of the rectangle. Let ρ represent the density of the lamina (note that ρ is a constant). In this case, ρ is expressed in terms of mass per unit area. Thus, to find the total mass of the rectangle, we multiply the area of the rectangle by ρ. Then, the mass of the rectangle is given by $\rho f(x_i^*)\Delta x$.

To get the approximate mass of the lamina, we add the masses of all the rectangles to get

$$m \approx \sum_{i=1}^{n} \rho f(x_i^*)\Delta x.$$

This is a Riemann sum. Taking the limit as $n \to \infty$ gives the exact mass of the lamina:

$$m = \lim_{n \to \infty} \sum_{i=1}^{n} \rho f(x_i^*)\Delta x = \rho \int_a^b f(x)dx.$$

Next, we calculate the moment of the lamina with respect to the x-axis. Returning to the representative rectangle, recall its center of mass is $\left(x_i^*, (f(x_i^*))/2\right)$. Recall also that treating the rectangle as if it is a point mass located at the center of mass does not change the moment. Thus, the moment of the rectangle with respect to the x-axis is given by the mass of the rectangle, $\rho f(x_i^*)\Delta x$, multiplied by the distance from the center of mass to the x-axis: $(f(x_i^*))/2$. Therefore, the moment with respect to the x-axis of the rectangle is $\rho\left([f(x_i^*)]^2/2\right)\Delta x$. Adding the moments of the rectangles and taking the limit of the resulting Riemann sum, we see that the moment of the lamina with respect to the x-axis is

$$M_x = \lim_{n \to \infty} \sum_{i=1}^{n} \rho \frac{[f(x_i^*)]^2}{2}\Delta x = \rho \int_a^b \frac{[f(x)]^2}{2}dx.$$

We derive the moment with respect to the y-axis similarly, noting that the distance from the center of mass of the rectangle to the y-axis is x_i^*. Then the moment of the lamina with respect to the y-axis is given by

$$M_y = \lim_{n \to \infty} \sum_{i=1}^{n} \rho x_i^* f(x_i^*)\Delta x = \rho \int_a^b x f(x)dx.$$

We find the coordinates of the center of mass by dividing the moments by the total mass to give $\bar{x} = M_y/m$ and $\bar{y} = M_x/m$. If we look closely at the expressions for M_x, M_y, and m, we notice that the constant ρ cancels out when $\bar{x}$ and $\bar{y}$ are calculated.

We summarize these findings in the following theorem.

Theorem 6.12: Center of Mass of a Thin Plate in the xy-Plane

Let R denote a region bounded above by the graph of a continuous function $f(x)$, below by the x-axis, and on the left and right by the lines $x = a$ and $x = b$, respectively. Let ρ denote the density of the associated lamina. Then we can make the following statements:

i. The mass of the lamina is

$$m = \rho \int_a^b f(x)dx. \tag{6.18}$$

ii. The moments M_x and M_y of the lamina with respect to the x- and y-axes, respectively, are

$$M_x = \rho \int_a^b \frac{[f(x)]^2}{2} dx \text{ and } M_y = \rho \int_a^b x f(x) dx. \tag{6.19}$$

iii. The coordinates of the center of mass $(\overline{x}, \overline{y})$ are

$$\overline{x} = \frac{M_y}{m} \text{ and } \overline{y} = \frac{M_x}{m}. \tag{6.20}$$

In the next example, we use this theorem to find the center of mass of a lamina.

Example 6.31

Finding the Center of Mass of a Lamina

Let R be the region bounded above by the graph of the function $f(x) = \sqrt{x}$ and below by the x-axis over the interval $[0, 4]$. Find the centroid of the region.

Solution

The region is depicted in the following figure.

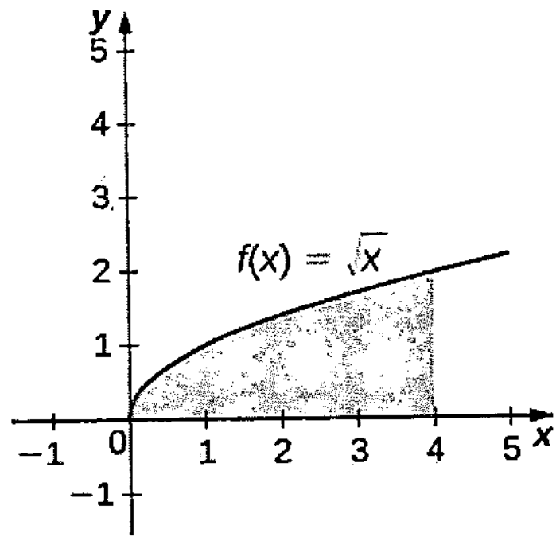

Figure 6.67 Finding the center of mass of a lamina.

Since we are only asked for the centroid of the region, rather than the mass or moments of the associated lamina, we know the density constant ρ cancels out of the calculations eventually. Therefore, for the sake of convenience, let's assume $\rho = 1$.

First, we need to calculate the total mass:

$$\begin{aligned} m &= \rho \int_a^b f(x)dx = \int_0^4 \sqrt{x}\, dx \\ &= \frac{2}{3} x^{3/2} \Big|_0^4 = \frac{2}{3}[8 - 0] = \frac{16}{3}. \end{aligned}$$

Next, we compute the moments:

$$\begin{aligned} M_x &= \rho \int_a^b \frac{[f(x)]^2}{2} dx \\ &= \int_0^4 \frac{x}{2} dx = \frac{1}{4} x^2 \Big|_0^4 = 4 \end{aligned}$$

and

$$\begin{aligned} M_y &= \rho \int_a^b x f(x) dx \\ &= \int_0^4 x\sqrt{x} dx = \int_0^4 x^{3/2} dx \\ &= \frac{2}{5} x^{5/2} \Big|_0^4 = \frac{2}{5}[32 - 0] = \frac{64}{5}. \end{aligned}$$

Thus, we have

$$\bar{x} = \frac{M_y}{m} = \frac{64/5}{16/3} = \frac{64}{5} \cdot \frac{3}{16} = \frac{12}{5} \text{ and } \bar{y} = \frac{M_x}{y} = \frac{4}{16/3} = 4 \cdot \frac{3}{16} = \frac{3}{4}.$$

The centroid of the region is $(12/5, 3/4)$.

6.31 Let R be the region bounded above by the graph of the function $f(x) = x^2$ and below by the x-axis over the interval $[0, 2]$. Find the centroid of the region.

We can adapt this approach to find centroids of more complex regions as well. Suppose our region is bounded above by the graph of a continuous function $f(x)$, as before, but now, instead of having the lower bound for the region be the x-axis, suppose the region is bounded below by the graph of a second continuous function, $g(x)$, as shown in the following figure.

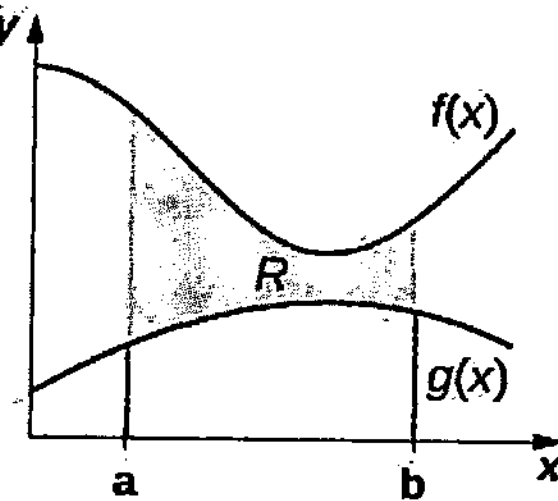

Figure 6.68 A region between two functions.

Again, we partition the interval $[a, b]$ and construct rectangles. A representative rectangle is shown in the following figure.

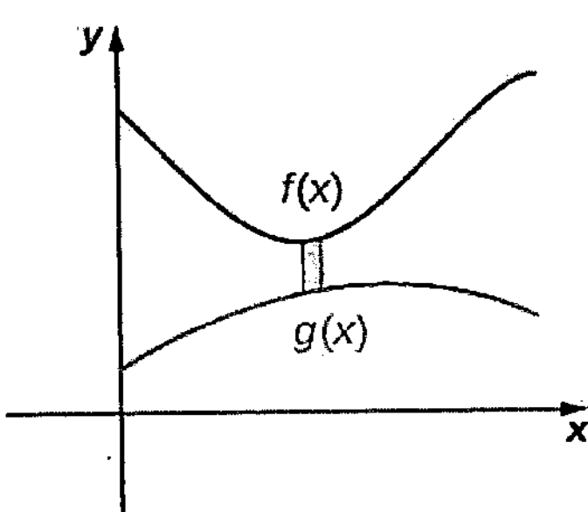

Figure 6.69 A representative rectangle of the region between two functions.

Note that the centroid of this rectangle is $\left(x_i^*, \left(f(x_i^*) + g(x_i^*)\right)/2\right)$. We won't go through all the details of the Riemann sum development, but let's look at some of the key steps. In the development of the formulas for the mass of the lamina and the moment with respect to the y-axis, the height of each rectangle is given by $f(x_i^*) - g(x_i^*)$, which leads to the expression $f(x) - g(x)$ in the integrands.

In the development of the formula for the moment with respect to the x-axis, the moment of each rectangle is found by multiplying the area of the rectangle, $\rho\left[f(x_i^*) - g(x_i^*)\right]\Delta x$, by the distance of the centroid from the x-axis, $\left(f(x_i^*) + g(x_i^*)\right)/2$, which gives $\rho(1/2)\left\{\left[f(x_i^*)\right]^2 - \left[g(x_i^*)\right]^2\right\}\Delta x$. Summarizing these findings, we arrive at the following theorem.

Theorem 6.13: Center of Mass of a Lamina Bounded by Two Functions

Let R denote a region bounded above by the graph of a continuous function $f(x)$, below by the graph of the continuous function $g(x)$, and on the left and right by the lines $x = a$ and $x = b$, respectively. Let ρ denote the density of the associated lamina. Then we can make the following statements:

i. The mass of the lamina is

$$m = \rho\int_a^b \left[f(x) - g(x)\right]dx. \tag{6.21}$$

ii. The moments M_x and M_y of the lamina with respect to the x- and y-axes, respectively, are

$$M_x = \rho\int_a^b \frac{1}{2}\left(\left[f(x)\right]^2 - \left[g(x)\right]^2\right)dx \text{ and } M_y = \rho\int_a^b x\left[f(x) - g(x)\right]dx. \tag{6.22}$$

iii. The coordinates of the center of mass $(\bar{x}, \bar{y})$ are

$$\bar{x} = \frac{M_y}{m} \text{ and } \bar{y} = \frac{M_x}{m}. \tag{6.23}$$

We illustrate this theorem in the following example.

Example 6.32

Finding the Centroid of a Region Bounded by Two Functions

Let R be the region bounded above by the graph of the function $f(x) = 1 - x^2$ and below by the graph of the function $g(x) = x - 1$. Find the centroid of the region.

Solution

The region is depicted in the following figure.

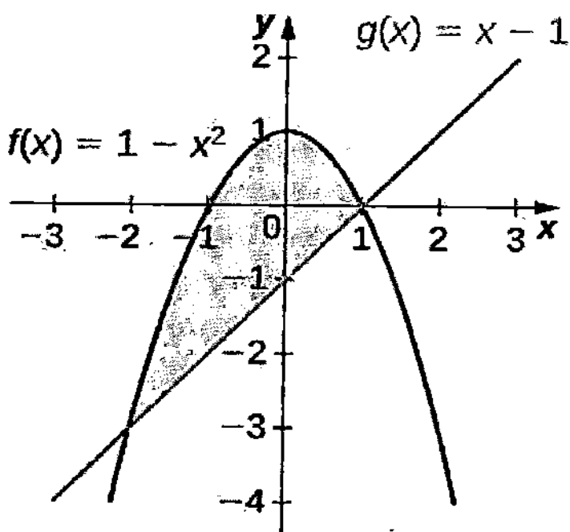

Figure 6.70 Finding the centroid of a region between two curves.

The graphs of the functions intersect at $(-2,\ -3)$ and $(1,\ 0)$, so we integrate from −2 to 1. Once again, for the sake of convenience, assume $\rho = 1$.

First, we need to calculate the total mass:

$$\begin{aligned} m &= \rho\int_a^b [f(x) - g(x)]dx \\ &= \int_{-2}^1 [1 - x^2 - (x-1)]dx = \int_{-2}^1 (2 - x^2 - x)dx \\ &= \left[2x - \tfrac{1}{3}x^3 - \tfrac{1}{2}x^2\right]\Big|_{-2}^1 = \left[2 - \tfrac{1}{3} - \tfrac{1}{2}\right] - \left[-4 + \tfrac{8}{3} - 2\right] = \tfrac{9}{2}. \end{aligned}$$

Next, we compute the moments:

$$\begin{aligned} M_x &= \rho\int_a^b \tfrac{1}{2}\left([f(x)]^2 - [g(x)]^2\right)dx \\ &= \tfrac{1}{2}\int_{-2}^1 \left(\left(1 - x^2\right)^2 - (x-1)^2\right)dx = \tfrac{1}{2}\int_{-2}^1 \left(x^4 - 3x^2 + 2x\right)dx \\ &= \tfrac{1}{2}\left[\tfrac{x^5}{5} - x^3 + x^2\right]\Big|_{-2}^1 = -\tfrac{27}{10} \end{aligned}$$

and

$$\begin{aligned} M_y &= \rho\int_a^b x[f(x) - g(x)]dx \\ &= \int_{-2}^1 x\left[(1 - x^2) - (x-1)\right]dx = \int_{-2}^1 x\left[2 - x^2 - x\right]dx = \int_{-2}^1 \left(2x - x^4 - x^2\right)dx \\ &= \left[x^2 - \tfrac{x^5}{5} - \tfrac{x^3}{3}\right]\Big|_{-2}^1 = -\tfrac{9}{4}. \end{aligned}$$

Therefore, we have

$$\bar{x} = \frac{M_y}{m} = -\frac{9}{4}\cdot\frac{2}{9} = -\frac{1}{2} \text{ and } \bar{y} = \frac{M_x}{y} = -\frac{27}{10}\cdot\frac{2}{9} = -\frac{3}{5}.$$

The centroid of the region is $(-(1/2), -(3/5))$.

6.32 Let R be the region bounded above by the graph of the function $f(x) = 6 - x^2$ and below by the graph of the function $g(x) = 3 - 2x$. Find the centroid of the region.

The Symmetry Principle

We stated the symmetry principle earlier, when we were looking at the centroid of a rectangle. The symmetry principle can be a great help when finding centroids of regions that are symmetric. Consider the following example.

Example 6.33

Finding the Centroid of a Symmetric Region

Let R be the region bounded above by the graph of the function $f(x) = 4 - x^2$ and below by the x-axis. Find the centroid of the region.

Solution

The region is depicted in the following figure.

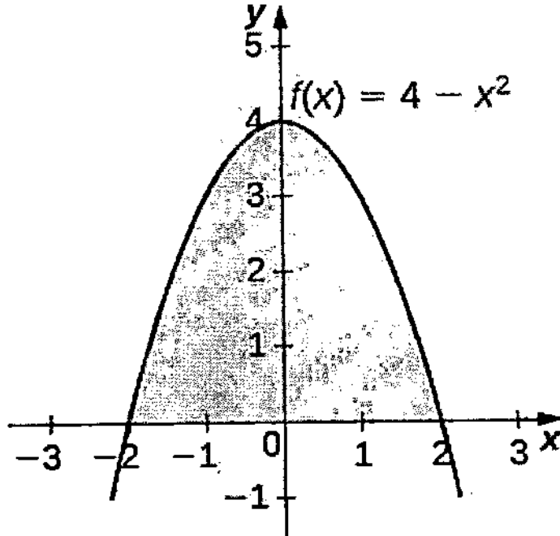

Figure 6.71 We can use the symmetry principle to help find the centroid of a symmetric region.

The region is symmetric with respect to the y-axis. Therefore, the x-coordinate of the centroid is zero. We need only calculate $\bar{y}$. Once again, for the sake of convenience, assume $\rho = 1$.

First, we calculate the total mass:

$$\begin{aligned} m &= \rho \int_a^b f(x)dx \\ &= \int_{-2}^{2} (4 - x^2)dx \\ &= \left[4x - \frac{x^3}{3}\right]\Big|_{-2}^{2} = \frac{32}{3}. \end{aligned}$$

Next, we calculate the moments. We only need M_x:

$$\begin{aligned} M_x &= \rho\int_a^b \frac{[f(x)]^2}{2}dx \\ &= \frac{1}{2}\int_{-2}^{2}\left[4 - x^2\right]^2 dx = \frac{1}{2}\int_{-2}^{2}\left(16 - 8x^2 + x^4\right)dx \\ &= \frac{1}{2}\left[\frac{x^5}{5} - \frac{8x^3}{3} + 16x\right]\Bigg|_{-2}^{2} = \frac{256}{15}. \end{aligned}$$

Then we have

$$\bar{y} = \frac{M_x}{y} = \frac{256}{15} \cdot \frac{3}{32} = \frac{8}{5}.$$

The centroid of the region is $(0,\ 8/5)$.

6.33 Let R be the region bounded above by the graph of the function $f(x) = 1 - x^2$ and below by x-axis. Find the centroid of the region.

Student PROJECT

The Grand Canyon Skywalk

The Grand Canyon Skywalk opened to the public on March 28, 2007. This engineering marvel is a horseshoe-shaped observation platform suspended 4000 ft above the Colorado River on the West Rim of the Grand Canyon. Its crystal-clear glass floor allows stunning views of the canyon below (see the following figure).

Figure 6.72 The Grand Canyon Skywalk offers magnificent views of the canyon. (credit: 10da_ralta, Wikimedia Commons)

The Skywalk is a cantilever design, meaning that the observation platform extends over the rim of the canyon, with no visible means of support below it. Despite the lack of visible support posts or struts, cantilever structures are engineered to be very stable and the Skywalk is no exception. The observation platform is attached firmly to support posts that extend 46 ft down into bedrock. The structure was built to withstand 100-mph winds and an 8.0-magnitude earthquake within 50 mi, and is capable of supporting more than 70,000,000 lb.

One factor affecting the stability of the Skywalk is the center of gravity of the structure. We are going to calculate the center of gravity of the Skywalk, and examine how the center of gravity changes when tourists walk out onto the observation platform.

The observation platform is U-shaped. The legs of the U are 10 ft wide and begin on land, under the visitors' center, 48 ft from the edge of the canyon. The platform extends 70 ft over the edge of the canyon.

To calculate the center of mass of the structure, we treat it as a lamina and use a two-dimensional region in the xy-plane to represent the platform. We begin by dividing the region into three subregions so we can consider each subregion separately. The first region, denoted R_1, consists of the curved part of the U. We model R_1 as a semicircular annulus, with inner radius 25 ft and outer radius 35 ft, centered at the origin (see the following figure).

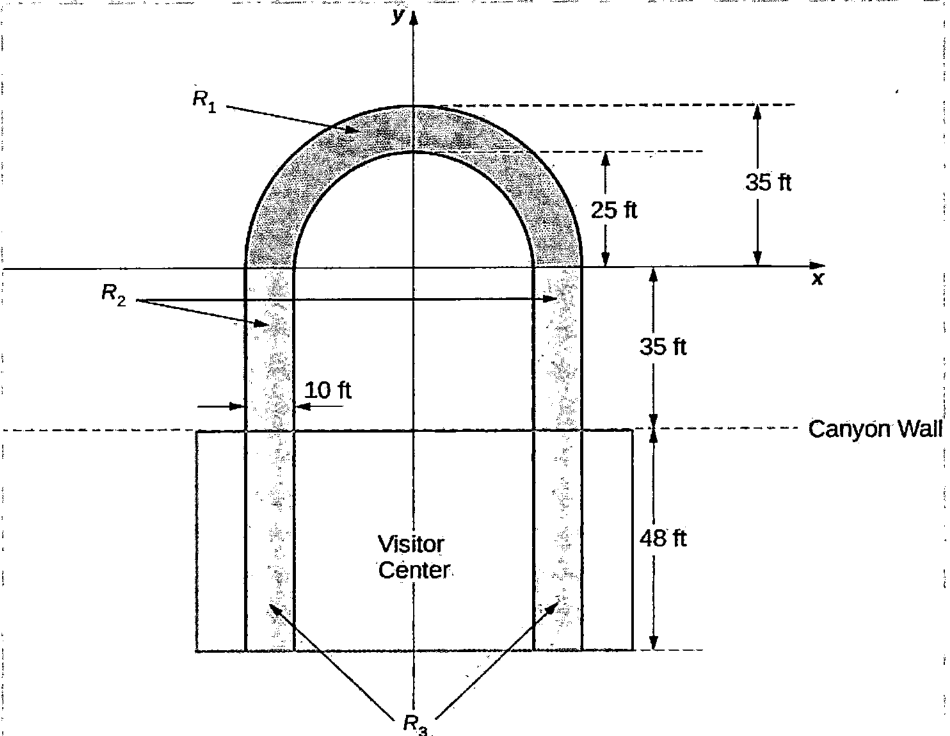

Figure 6.73 We model the Skywalk with three sub-regions.

The legs of the platform, extending 35 ft between R_1 and the canyon wall, comprise the second sub-region, R_2. Last, the ends of the legs, which extend 48 ft under the visitor center, comprise the third sub-region, R_3. Assume the density of the lamina is constant and assume the total weight of the platform is 1,200,000 lb (not including the weight of the visitor center; we will consider that later). Use $g = 32$ ft/sec^2.

1. Compute the area of each of the three sub-regions. Note that the areas of regions R_2 and R_3 should include the areas of the legs only, not the open space between them. Round answers to the nearest square foot.
2. Determine the mass associated with each of the three sub-regions.
3. Calculate the center of mass of each of the three sub-regions.
4. Now, treat each of the three sub-regions as a point mass located at the center of mass of the corresponding sub-region. Using this representation, calculate the center of mass of the entire platform.
5. Assume the visitor center weighs 2,200,000 lb, with a center of mass corresponding to the center of mass of R_3. Treating the visitor center as a point mass, recalculate the center of mass of the system. How does the center of mass change?
6. Although the Skywalk was built to limit the number of people on the observation platform to 120, the platform is capable of supporting up to 800 people weighing 200 lb each. If all 800 people were allowed on the platform, and all of them went to the farthest end of the platform, how would the center of gravity of the system be affected? (Include the visitor center in the calculations and represent the people by a point mass located at the farthest edge of the platform, 70 ft from the canyon wall.)

Theorem of Pappus

This section ends with a discussion of the **theorem of Pappus for volume**, which allows us to find the volume of particular kinds of solids by using the centroid. (There is also a theorem of Pappus for surface area, but it is much less useful than the theorem for volume.)

Theorem 6.14: Theorem of Pappus for Volume

Let R be a region in the plane and let l be a line in the plane that does not intersect R. Then the volume of the solid of revolution formed by revolving R around l is equal to the area of R multiplied by the distance d traveled by the centroid of R.

Proof

We can prove the case when the region is bounded above by the graph of a function $f(x)$ and below by the graph of a function $g(x)$ over an interval $[a, b]$, and for which the axis of revolution is the y-axis. In this case, the area of the region is $A = \int_a^b [f(x) - g(x)]dx.$ Since the axis of rotation is the y-axis, the distance traveled by the centroid of the region depends only on the x-coordinate of the centroid, $\bar{x}$, which is

$$\bar{x} = \frac{M_y}{m},$$

where

$$m = \rho \int_a^b [f(x) - g(x)]dx \text{ and } M_y = \rho \int_a^b x[f(x) - g(x)]dx.$$

Then,

$$d = 2\pi \frac{\rho \int_a^b x[f(x) - g(x)]dx}{\rho \int_a^b [f(x) - g(x)]dx}$$

and thus

$$d \cdot A = 2\pi \int_a^b x[f(x) - g(x)]dx.$$

However, using the method of cylindrical shells, we have

$$V = 2\pi \int_a^b x[f(x) - g(x)]dx.$$

So,

$$V = d \cdot A$$

and the proof is complete.

□

Example 6.34

Using the Theorem of Pappus for Volume

Let R be a circle of radius 2 centered at $(4, 0)$. Use the theorem of Pappus for volume to find the volume of the torus generated by revolving R around the y-axis.

Solution

The region and torus are depicted in the following figure.

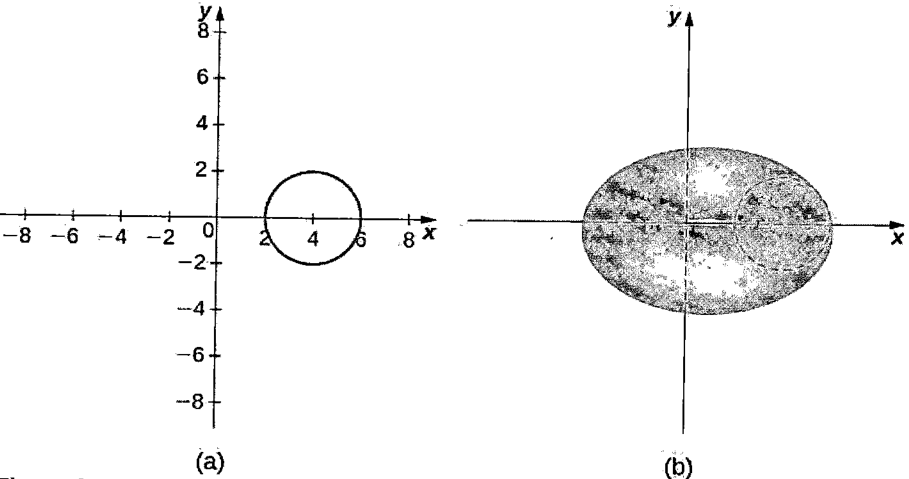

Figure 6.74 Determining the volume of a torus by using the theorem of Pappus. (a) A circular region R in the plane; (b) the torus generated by revolving R about the y-axis.

The region R is a circle of radius 2, so the area of R is $A = 4\pi$ units^2. By the symmetry principle, the centroid of R is the center of the circle. The centroid travels around the y-axis in a circular path of radius 4, so the centroid travels $d = 8\pi$ units. Then, the volume of the torus is $A \cdot d = 32\pi^2$ units^3.

6.34 Let R be a circle of radius 1 centered at $(3, 0)$. Use the theorem of Pappus for volume to find the volume of the torus generated by revolving R around the y-axis.

6.6 EXERCISES

For the following exercises, calculate the center of mass for the collection of masses given.

254. $m_1 = 2$ at $x_1 = 1$ and $m_2 = 4$ at $x_2 = 2$

255. $m_1 = 1$ at $x_1 = -1$ and $m_2 = 3$ at $x_2 = 2$

256. $m = 3$ at $x = 0, 1, 2, 6$

257. Unit masses at $(x, y) = (1, 0), (0, 1), (1, 1)$

258. $m_1 = 1$ at $(1, 0)$ and $m_2 = 4$ at $(0, 1)$

259. $m_1 = 1$ at $(1, 0)$ and $m_2 = 3$ at $(2, 2)$

For the following exercises, compute the center of mass $\bar{x}$.

260. $\rho = 1$ for $x \in (-1, 3)$

261. $\rho = x^2$ for $x \in (0, L)$

262. $\rho = 1$ for $x \in (0, 1)$ and $\rho = 2$ for $x \in (1, 2)$

263. $\rho = \sin x$ for $x \in (0, \pi)$

264. $\rho = \cos x$ for $x \in \left(0, \frac{\pi}{2}\right)$

265. $\rho = e^x$ for $x \in (0, 2)$

266. $\rho = x^3 + xe^{-x}$ for $x \in (0, 1)$

267. $\rho = x \sin x$ for $x \in (0, \pi)$

268. $\rho = \sqrt{x}$ for $x \in (1, 4)$

269. $\rho = \ln x$ for $x \in (1, e)$

For the following exercises, compute the center of mass $(\bar{x}, \bar{y})$. Use symmetry to help locate the center of mass whenever possible.

270. $\rho = 7$ in the square $0 \le x \le 1, \quad 0 \le y \le 1$

271. $\rho = 3$ in the triangle with vertices $(0, 0)$, $(a, 0)$, and $(0, b)$

272. $\rho = 2$ for the region bounded by $y = \cos(x)$, $y = -\cos(x)$, $x = -\frac{\pi}{2}$, and $x = \frac{\pi}{2}$

For the following exercises, use a calculator to draw the region, then compute the center of mass $(\bar{x}, \bar{y})$. Use symmetry to help locate the center of mass whenever possible.

273. **[T]** The region bounded by $y = \cos(2x)$, $x = -\frac{\pi}{4}$, and $x = \frac{\pi}{4}$

274. **[T]** The region between $y = 2x^2$, $y = 0$, $x = 0$, and $x = 1$

275. **[T]** The region between $y = \frac{5}{4}x^2$ and $y = 5$

276. **[T]** Region between $y = \sqrt{x}$, $y = \ln(x)$, $x = 1$, and $x = 4$

277. **[T]** The region bounded by $y = 0$, $\frac{x^2}{4} + \frac{y^2}{9} = 1$

278. **[T]** The region bounded by $y = 0$, $x = 0$, and $\frac{x^2}{4} + \frac{y^2}{9} = 1$

279. **[T]** The region bounded by $y = x^2$ and $y = x^4$ in the first quadrant

For the following exercises, use the theorem of Pappus to determine the volume of the shape.

280. Rotating $y = mx$ around the x-axis between $x = 0$ and $x = 1$

281. Rotating $y = mx$ around the y-axis between $x = 0$ and $x = 1$

282. A general cone created by rotating a triangle with vertices $(0, 0)$, $(a, 0)$, and $(0, b)$ around the y-axis. Does your answer agree with the volume of a cone?

283. A general cylinder created by rotating a rectangle with vertices $(0, 0)$, $(a, 0)$, $(0, b)$, and (a, b) around the y-axis. Does your answer agree with the volume of a cylinder?

284. A sphere created by rotating a semicircle with radius a around the y-axis. Does your answer agree with the volume of a sphere?

For the following exercises, use a calculator to draw the region enclosed by the curve. Find the area M and the centroid $(\overline{x}, \overline{y})$ for the given shapes. Use symmetry to help locate the center of mass whenever possible.

285. **[T]** Quarter-circle: $y = \sqrt{1-x^2}$, $y = 0$, and $x = 0$

286. **[T]** Triangle: $y = x$, $y = 2 - x$, and $y = 0$

287. **[T]** Lens: $y = x^2$ and $y = x$

288. **[T]** Ring: $y^2 + x^2 = 1$ and $y^2 + x^2 = 4$

289. **[T]** Half-ring: $y^2 + x^2 = 1$, $y^2 + x^2 = 4$, and $y = 0$

290. Find the generalized center of mass in the sliver between $y = x^a$ and $y = x^b$ with $a > b$. Then, use the Pappus theorem to find the volume of the solid generated when revolving around the *y*-axis.

291. Find the generalized center of mass between $y = a^2 - x^2$, $x = 0$, and $y = 0$. Then, use the Pappus theorem to find the volume of the solid generated when revolving around the *y*-axis.

292. Find the generalized center of mass between $y = b\sin(ax)$, $x = 0$, and $x = \frac{\pi}{a}$. Then, use the Pappus theorem to find the volume of the solid generated when revolving around the *y*-axis.

293. Use the theorem of Pappus to find the volume of a torus (pictured here). Assume that a disk of radius a is positioned with the left end of the circle at $x = b$, $b > 0$, and is rotated around the *y*-axis.

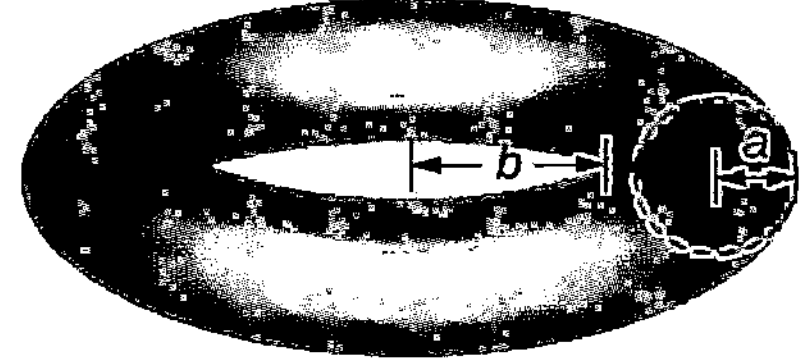

294. Find the center of mass $(\overline{x}, \overline{y})$ for a thin wire along the semicircle $y = \sqrt{1-x^2}$ with unit mass. (*Hint:* Use the theorem of Pappus.)

6.7 | Integrals, Exponential Functions, and Logarithms

Learning Objectives

- **6.7.1** Write the definition of the natural logarithm as an integral.
- **6.7.2** Recognize the derivative of the natural logarithm.
- **6.7.3** Integrate functions involving the natural logarithmic function.
- **6.7.4** Define the number e through an integral.
- **6.7.5** Recognize the derivative and integral of the exponential function.
- **6.7.6** Prove properties of logarithms and exponential functions using integrals.
- **6.7.7** Express general logarithmic and exponential functions in terms of natural logarithms and exponentials.

We already examined exponential functions and logarithms in earlier chapters. However, we glossed over some key details in the previous discussions. For example, we did not study how to treat exponential functions with exponents that are irrational. The definition of the number e is another area where the previous development was somewhat incomplete. We now have the tools to deal with these concepts in a more mathematically rigorous way, and we do so in this section.

For purposes of this section, assume we have not yet defined the natural logarithm, the number e, or any of the integration and differentiation formulas associated with these functions. By the end of the section, we will have studied these concepts in a mathematically rigorous way (and we will see they are consistent with the concepts we learned earlier).

We begin the section by defining the natural logarithm in terms of an integral. This definition forms the foundation for the section. From this definition, we derive differentiation formulas, define the number e, and expand these concepts to logarithms and exponential functions of any base.

The Natural Logarithm as an Integral

Recall the power rule for integrals:

$$\int x^n\,dx = \frac{x^{n+1}}{n+1} + C,\ n \neq -1.$$

Clearly, this does not work when $n = -1$, as it would force us to divide by zero. So, what do we do with $\int \frac{1}{x}dx$? Recall from the Fundamental Theorem of Calculus that $\int_1^x \frac{1}{t}dt$ is an antiderivative of $1/x$. Therefore, we can make the following definition.

Definition

For $x > 0$, define the natural logarithm function by

$$\ln x = \int_1^x \frac{1}{t}dt. \tag{6.24}$$

For $x > 1$, this is just the area under the curve $y = 1/t$ from 1 to x. For $x < 1$, we have $\int_1^x \frac{1}{t}dt = -\int_x^1 \frac{1}{t}dt$, so in this case it is the negative of the area under the curve from x to 1 (see the following figure).

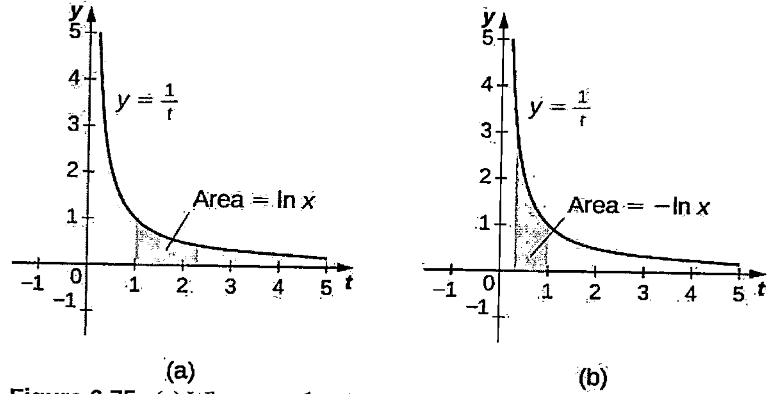

Figure 6.75 (a) When $x > 1$, the natural logarithm is the area under the curve $y = 1/t$ from 1 to x. (b) When $x < 1$, the natural logarithm is the negative of the area under the curve from x to 1.

Notice that $\ln 1 = 0$. Furthermore, the function $y = 1/t > 0$ for $x > 0$. Therefore, by the properties of integrals, it is clear that $\ln x$ is increasing for $x > 0$.

Properties of the Natural Logarithm

Because of the way we defined the natural logarithm, the following differentiation formula falls out immediately as a result of to the Fundamental Theorem of Calculus.

Theorem 6.15: Derivative of the Natural Logarithm

For $x > 0$, the derivative of the natural logarithm is given by

$$\frac{d}{dx}\ln x = \frac{1}{x}.$$

Theorem 6.16: Corollary to the Derivative of the Natural Logarithm

The function $\ln x$ is differentiable; therefore, it is continuous.

A graph of $\ln x$ is shown in **Figure 6.76**. Notice that it is continuous throughout its domain of $(0, \infty)$.

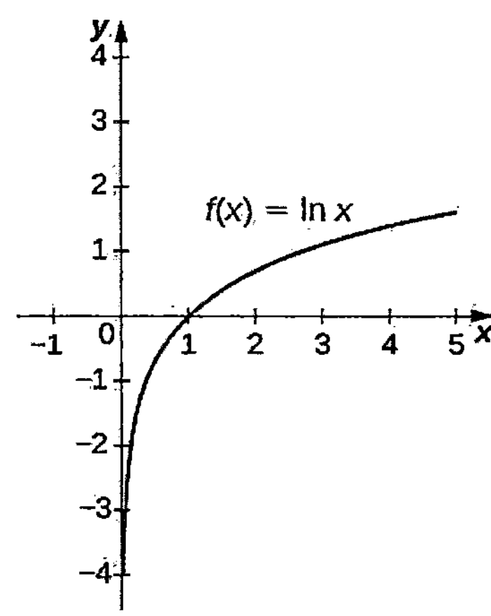

Figure 6.76 The graph of $f(x) = \ln x$ shows that it is a continuous function.

Example 6.35

Calculating Derivatives of Natural Logarithms

Calculate the following derivatives:

a. $\frac{d}{dx}\ln\left(5x^3 - 2\right)$

b. $\frac{d}{dx}(\ln(3x))^2$

Solution

We need to apply the chain rule in both cases.

a. $\frac{d}{dx}\ln\left(5x^3 - 2\right) = \frac{15x^2}{5x^3 - 2}$

b. $\frac{d}{dx}(\ln(3x))^2 = \frac{2(\ln(3x)) \cdot 3}{3x} = \frac{2(\ln(3x))}{x}$

 **6.35** Calculate the following derivatives:

a. $\frac{d}{dx}\ln\left(2x^2 + x\right)$

b. $\frac{d}{dx}\left(\ln\left(x^3\right)\right)^2$

Note that if we use the absolute value function and create a new function $\ln |x|,$ we can extend the domain of the natural logarithm to include $x < 0.$ Then $(d/(dx))\ln |x| = 1/x.$ This gives rise to the familiar integration formula.

Theorem 6.17: Integral of (1/u) du

The natural logarithm is the antiderivative of the function $f(u) = 1/u$:

$$\int \frac{1}{u}du = \ln|u| + C.$$

Example 6.36

Calculating Integrals Involving Natural Logarithms

Calculate the integral $\int \frac{x}{x^2+4}dx.$

Solution

Using u-substitution, let $u = x^2 + 4$. Then $du = 2x\,dx$ and we have

$$\int \frac{x}{x^2+4}dx = \frac{1}{2}\int \frac{1}{u}du\frac{1}{2}\ln|u| + C = \frac{1}{2}\ln\left|x^2+4\right| + C = \frac{1}{2}\ln\left(x^2+4\right) + C.$$

6.36 Calculate the integral $\int \frac{x^2}{x^3+6}dx.$

Although we have called our function a "logarithm," we have not actually proved that any of the properties of logarithms hold for this function. We do so here.

Theorem 6.18: Properties of the Natural Logarithm

If $a, b > 0$ and r is a rational number, then

i. $\ln 1 = 0$

ii. $\ln(ab) = \ln a + \ln b$

iii. $\ln\left(\frac{a}{b}\right) = \ln a - \ln b$

iv. $\ln(a^r) = r\ln a$

Proof

i. By definition, $\ln 1 = \int_1^1 \frac{1}{t}dt = 0.$

ii. We have

$$\ln(ab) = \int_1^{ab}\frac{1}{t}dt = \int_1^a \frac{1}{t}dt + \int_a^{ab}\frac{1}{t}dt.$$

Use u-substitution on the last integral in this expression. Let $u = t/a$. Then $du = (1/a)dt$. Furthermore, when $t = a,\ u = 1,$ and when $t = ab,\ u = b.$ So we get

$$\ln(ab) = \int_1^a \frac{1}{t}dt + \int_a^{ab}\frac{1}{t}dt = \int_1^a \frac{1}{t}dt + \int_1^{ab}\frac{a}{t}\cdot\frac{1}{a}dt = \int_1^a \frac{1}{t}dt + \int_1^b \frac{1}{u}du = \ln a + \ln b.$$

iii. Note that

$$\frac{d}{dx}\ln(x^r) = \frac{rx^{r-1}}{x^r} = \frac{r}{x}.$$

Furthermore,

$$\frac{d}{dx}(r\ln x) = \frac{r}{x}.$$

Since the derivatives of these two functions are the same, by the Fundamental Theorem of Calculus, they must differ by a constant. So we have

$$\ln(x^r) = r\ln x + C$$

for some constant C. Taking $x = 1$, we get

$$\begin{aligned} \ln(1^r) &= r\ln(1) + C \\ 0 &= r(0) + C \\ C &= 0. \end{aligned}$$

Thus $\ln(x^r) = r\ln x$ and the proof is complete. Note that we can extend this property to irrational values of r later in this section.

Part iii. follows from parts ii. and iv. and the proof is left to you.

□

Example 6.37

Using Properties of Logarithms

Use properties of logarithms to simplify the following expression into a single logarithm:

$$\ln 9 - 2\ln 3 + \ln\left(\frac{1}{3}\right).$$

Solution

We have

$$\ln 9 - 2\ln 3 + \ln\left(\frac{1}{3}\right) = \ln\left(3^2\right) - 2\ln 3 + \ln\left(3^{-1}\right) = 2\ln 3 - 2\ln 3 - \ln 3 = -\ln 3.$$

6.37 Use properties of logarithms to simplify the following expression into a single logarithm:

$$\ln 8 - \ln 2 - \ln\left(\frac{1}{4}\right).$$

Defining the Number e

Now that we have the natural logarithm defined, we can use that function to define the number e.

Definition

The number e is defined to be the real number such that

$$\ln e = 1.$$

To put it another way, the area under the curve $y = 1/t$ between $t = 1$ and $t = e$ is 1 (**Figure 6.77**). The proof that such a number exists and is unique is left to you. (*Hint*: Use the Intermediate Value Theorem to prove existence and the fact that

$\ln x$ is increasing to prove uniqueness.)

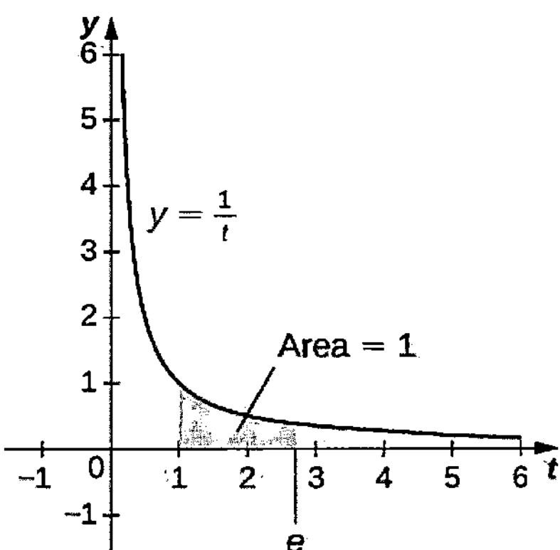

Figure 6.77 The area under the curve from 1 to e is equal to one.

The number e can be shown to be irrational, although we won't do so here (see the Student Project in **Taylor and Maclaurin Series (http://cnx.org/content/m53817/latest/)**). Its approximate value is given by

$$e \approx 2.71828182846.$$

The Exponential Function

We now turn our attention to the function e^x. Note that the natural logarithm is one-to-one and therefore has an inverse function. For now, we denote this inverse function by $\exp x$. Then,

$$\exp(\ln x) = x \text{ for } x > 0 \text{ and } \ln(\exp x) = x \text{ for all } x.$$

The following figure shows the graphs of $\exp x$ and $\ln x$.

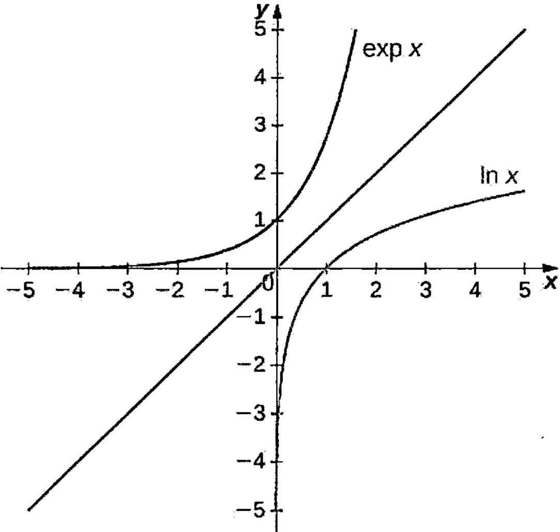

Figure 6.78 The graphs of $\ln x$ and $\exp x$.

We hypothesize that $\exp x = e^x$. For rational values of x, this is easy to show. If x is rational, then we have $\ln(e^x) = x \ln e = x$. Thus, when x is rational, $e^x = \exp x$. For irrational values of x, we simply define e^x as the inverse function of $\ln x$.

Definition

For any real number x, define $y = e^x$ to be the number for which

$$\ln y = \ln(e^x) = x. \tag{6.25}$$

Then we have $e^x = \exp(x)$ for all x, and thus

$$e^{\ln x} = x \text{ for } x > 0 \text{ and } \ln(e^x) = x \tag{6.26}$$

for all x.

Properties of the Exponential Function

Since the exponential function was defined in terms of an inverse function, and not in terms of a power of e, we must verify that the usual laws of exponents hold for the function e^x.

Theorem 6.19: Properties of the Exponential Function

If p and q are any real numbers and r is a rational number, then

i. $e^p e^q = e^{p+q}$

ii. $\dfrac{e^p}{e^q} = e^{p-q}$

iii. $(e^p)^r = e^{pr}$

Proof

Note that if p and q are rational, the properties hold. However, if p or q are irrational, we must apply the inverse function definition of e^x and verify the properties. Only the first property is verified here; the other two are left to you. We have

$$\ln(e^p e^q) = \ln(e^p) + \ln(e^q) = p + q = \ln\left(e^{p+q}\right).$$

Since $\ln x$ is one-to-one, then

$$e^p e^q = e^{p+q}.$$

□

As with part iv. of the logarithm properties, we can extend property iii. to irrational values of r, and we do so by the end of the section.

We also want to verify the differentiation formula for the function $y = e^x$. To do this, we need to use implicit differentiation. Let $y = e^x$. Then

$$\begin{aligned} \ln y &= x \\ \frac{d}{dx}\ln y &= \frac{d}{dx}x \\ \frac{1}{y}\frac{dy}{dx} &= 1 \\ \frac{dy}{dx} &= y. \end{aligned}$$

Thus, we see

$$\frac{d}{dx}e^x = e^x$$

as desired, which leads immediately to the integration formula

$$\int e^x \, dx = e^x + C.$$

We apply these formulas in the following examples.

Example 6.38

Using Properties of Exponential Functions

Evaluate the following derivatives:

a. $\frac{d}{dt}e^{3t}e^{t^2}$

b. $\frac{d}{dx}e^{3x^2}$

Solution

We apply the chain rule as necessary.

a. $\frac{d}{dt}e^{3t}e^{t^2} = \frac{d}{dt}e^{3t+t^2} = e^{3t+t^2}(3+2t)$

b. $\frac{d}{dx}e^{3x^2} = e^{3x^2}6x$

6.38 Evaluate the following derivatives:

a. $\frac{d}{dx}\left(\frac{e^{x^2}}{e^{5x}}\right)$

b. $\frac{d}{dt}\left(e^{2t}\right)^3$

Example 6.39

Using Properties of Exponential Functions

Evaluate the following integral: $\int 2xe^{-x^2}dx.$

Solution

Using u -substitution, let $u = -x^2$. Then $du = -2x\,dx,$ and we have

$$\int 2xe^{-x^2}dx = -\int e^u\,du = -e^u + C = -e^{-x^2} + C.$$

6.39 Evaluate the following integral: $\int \frac{4}{e^{3x}}dx$.

General Logarithmic and Exponential Functions

We close this section by looking at exponential functions and logarithms with bases other than e. Exponential functions are functions of the form $f(x) = a^x$. Note that unless $a = e$, we still do not have a mathematically rigorous definition of these functions for irrational exponents. Let's rectify that here by defining the function $f(x) = a^x$ in terms of the exponential function e^x. We then examine logarithms with bases other than e as inverse functions of exponential functions.

Definition

For any $a > 0$, and for any real number x, define $y = a^x$ as follows:

$$y = a^x = e^{x \ln a}.$$

Now a^x is defined rigorously for all values of x. This definition also allows us to generalize property iv. of logarithms and property iii. of exponential functions to apply to both rational and irrational values of r. It is straightforward to show that properties of exponents hold for general exponential functions defined in this way.

Let's now apply this definition to calculate a differentiation formula for a^x. We have

$$\frac{d}{dx}a^x = \frac{d}{dx}e^{x \ln a} = e^{x \ln a} \ln a = a^x \ln a.$$

The corresponding integration formula follows immediately.

Theorem 6.20: Derivatives and Integrals Involving General Exponential Functions

Let $a > 0$. Then,

$$\frac{d}{dx}a^x = a^x \ln a$$

and

$$\int a^x \, dx = \frac{1}{\ln a}a^x + C.$$

If $a \neq 1$, then the function a^x is one-to-one and has a well-defined inverse. Its inverse is denoted by $\log_a x$. Then,

$$y = \log_a x \text{ if and only if } x = a^y.$$

Note that general logarithm functions can be written in terms of the natural logarithm. Let $y = \log_a x$. Then, $x = a^y$. Taking the natural logarithm of both sides of this second equation, we get

$$\begin{aligned} \ln x &= \ln(a^y) \\ \ln x &= y \ln a \\ y &= \frac{\ln x}{\ln a} \\ \log x &= \frac{\ln x}{\ln a}. \end{aligned}$$

Thus, we see that all logarithmic functions are constant multiples of one another. Next, we use this formula to find a differentiation formula for a logarithm with base a. Again, let $y = \log_a x$. Then,

$$\begin{aligned}\frac{dy}{dx} &= \frac{d}{dx}(\log_a x)\\ &= \frac{d}{dx}\left(\frac{\ln x}{\ln a}\right)\\ &= \left(\frac{1}{\ln a}\right)\frac{d}{dx}(\ln x)\\ &= \frac{1}{\ln a}\cdot\frac{1}{x}\\ &= \frac{1}{x\ln a}.\end{aligned}$$

Theorem 6.21: Derivatives of General Logarithm Functions

Let $a > 0$. Then,

$$\frac{d}{dx}\log_a x = \frac{1}{x\ln a}.$$

Example 6.40

Calculating Derivatives of General Exponential and Logarithm Functions

Evaluate the following derivatives:

a. $\frac{d}{dt}\left(4^t \cdot 2^{t^2}\right)$

b. $\frac{d}{dx}\log_8\left(7x^2+4\right)$

Solution

We need to apply the chain rule as necessary.

a. $\frac{d}{dt}\left(4^t \cdot 2^{t^2}\right) = \frac{d}{dt}\left(2^{2t} \cdot 2^{t^2}\right) = \frac{d}{dt}\left(2^{2t+t^2}\right) = 2^{2t+t^2}\ln(2)(2+2t)$

b. $\frac{d}{dx}\log_8\left(7x^2+4\right) = \frac{1}{\left(7x^2+4\right)(\ln 8)}(14x)$

6.40 Evaluate the following derivatives:

a. $\frac{d}{dt}4^{t^4}$

b. $\frac{d}{dx}\log_3\left(\sqrt{x^2+1}\right)$

Example 6.41

Integrating General Exponential Functions

Evaluate the following integral: $\int \frac{3}{2^{3x}} dx.$

Solution

Use u-substitution and let $u = -3x$. Then $du = -3dx$ and we have

$$\int \frac{3}{2^{3x}} dx = \int 3 \cdot 2^{-3x} dx = -\int 2^u \, du = -\frac{1}{\ln 2} 2^u + C = -\frac{1}{\ln 2} 2^{-3x} + C.$$

6.41 Evaluate the following integral: $\int x^2 2^{x^3} \, dx.$

6.7 EXERCISES

For the following exercises, find the derivative $\frac{dy}{dx}$.

295. $y = \ln(2x)$

296. $y = \ln(2x + 1)$

297. $y = \frac{1}{\ln x}$

For the following exercises, find the indefinite integral.

298. $\int \frac{dt}{3t}$

299. $\int \frac{dx}{1 + x}$

For the following exercises, find the derivative dy/dx. (You can use a calculator to plot the function and the derivative to confirm that it is correct.)

300. **[T]** $y = \frac{\ln(x)}{x}$

301. **[T]** $y = x\ln(x)$

302. **[T]** $y = \log_{10} x$

303. **[T]** $y = \ln(\sin x)$

304. **[T]** $y = \ln(\ln x)$

305. **[T]** $y = 7\ln(4x)$

306. **[T]** $y = \ln\left((4x)^7\right)$

307. **[T]** $y = \ln(\tan x)$

308. **[T]** $y = \ln(\tan(3x))$

309. **[T]** $y = \ln\left(\cos^2 x\right)$

For the following exercises, find the definite or indefinite integral.

310. $\int_0^1 \frac{dx}{3 + x}$

311. $\int_0^1 \frac{dt}{3 + 2t}$

312. $\int_0^2 \frac{x\,dx}{x^2 + 1}$

313. $\int_0^2 \frac{x^3\,dx}{x^2 + 1}$

314. $\int_2^e \frac{dx}{x\ln x}$

315. $\int_2^e \frac{dx}{(x\ln(x))^2}$

316. $\int \frac{\cos x\,dx}{\sin x}$

317. $\int_0^{\pi/4} \tan x\,dx$

318. $\int \cot(3x)dx$

319. $\int \frac{(\ln x)^2\,dx}{x}$

For the following exercises, compute dy/dx by differentiating $\ln y$.

320. $y = \sqrt{x^2 + 1}$

321. $y = \sqrt{x^2 + 1}\sqrt{x^2 - 1}$

322. $y = e^{\sin x}$

323. $y = x^{-1/x}$

324. $y = e^{(ex)}$

325. $y = x^e$

326. $y = x^{(ex)}$

327. $y = \sqrt{x}\sqrt[3]{x}\sqrt[6]{x}$

328. $y = x^{-1/\ln x}$

329. $y = e^{-\ln x}$

For the following exercises, evaluate by any method.

330. $\int_5^{10} \frac{dt}{t} - \int_{5x}^{10x} \frac{dt}{t}$

331. $\int_1^{e^{\pi}} \frac{dx}{x} + \int_{-2}^{-1} \frac{dx}{x}$

332. $\frac{d}{dx}\int_x^1 \frac{dt}{t}$

333. $\frac{d}{dx}\int_x^{x^2} \frac{dt}{t}$

334. $\frac{d}{dx}\ln(\sec x + \tan x)$

For the following exercises, use the function $\ln x$. If you are unable to find intersection points analytically, use a calculator.

335. Find the area of the region enclosed by $x = 1$ and $y = 5$ above $y = \ln x$.

336. **[T]** Find the arc length of $\ln x$ from $x = 1$ to $x = 2$.

337. Find the area between $\ln x$ and the x-axis from $x = 1$ to $x = 2$.

338. Find the volume of the shape created when rotating this curve from $x = 1$ to $x = 2$ around the x-axis, as pictured here.

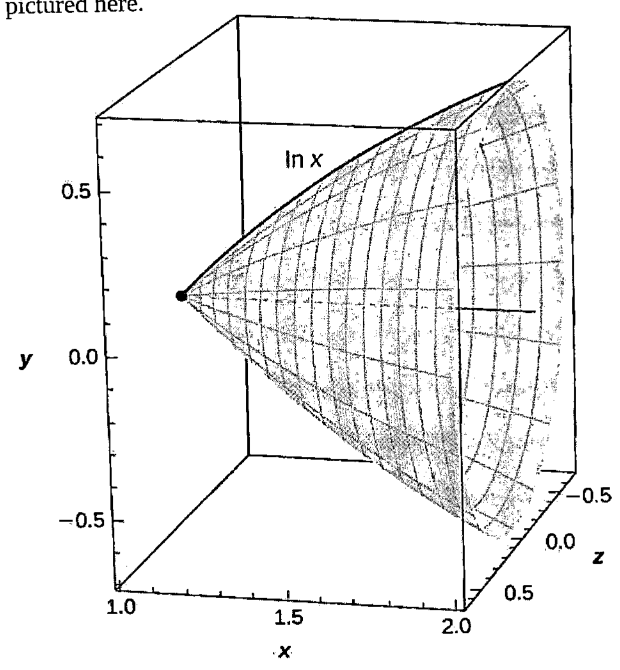

339. **[T]** Find the surface area of the shape created when rotating the curve in the previous exercise from $x = 1$ to $x = 2$ around the x-axis.

If you are unable to find intersection points analytically in the following exercises, use a calculator.

340. Find the area of the hyperbolic quarter-circle enclosed by $x = 2$ and $y = 2$ above $y = 1/x$.

341. **[T]** Find the arc length of $y = 1/x$ from $x = 1$ to $x = 4$.

342. Find the area under $y = 1/x$ and above the x-axis from $x = 1$ to $x = 4$.

For the following exercises, verify the derivatives and antiderivatives.

343. $\frac{d}{dx}\ln\left(x + \sqrt{x^2 + 1}\right) = \frac{1}{\sqrt{1 + x^2}}$

344. $\frac{d}{dx}\ln\left(\frac{x - a}{x + a}\right) = \frac{2a}{\left(x^2 - a^2\right)}$

345. $\frac{d}{dx}\ln\left(\frac{1 + \sqrt{1 - x^2}}{x}\right) = -\frac{1}{x\sqrt{1 - x^2}}$

346. $\frac{d}{dx}\ln\left(x + \sqrt{x^2 - a^2}\right) = \frac{1}{\sqrt{x^2 - a^2}}$

347. $\int \frac{dx}{x\ln(x)\ln(\ln x)} = \ln(\ln(\ln x)) + C$

6.8 | Exponential Growth and Decay

Learning Objectives

6.8.1 Use the exponential growth model in applications, including population growth and compound interest.

6.8.2 Explain the concept of doubling time.

6.8.3 Use the exponential decay model in applications, including radioactive decay and Newton's law of cooling.

6.8.4 Explain the concept of half-life.

One of the most prevalent applications of exponential functions involves growth and decay models. Exponential growth and decay show up in a host of natural applications. From population growth and continuously compounded interest to radioactive decay and Newton's law of cooling, exponential functions are ubiquitous in nature. In this section, we examine exponential growth and decay in the context of some of these applications.

Exponential Growth Model

Many systems exhibit exponential growth. These systems follow a model of the form $y = y_0 e^{kt}$, where y_0 represents the initial state of the system and k is a positive constant, called the *growth constant*. Notice that in an exponential growth model, we have

$$y' = ky_0 e^{kt} = ky. \tag{6.27}$$

That is, the rate of growth is proportional to the current function value. This is a key feature of exponential growth. **Equation 6.27** involves derivatives and is called a *differential equation*. We learn more about differential equations in **Introduction to Differential Equations (http://cnx.org/content/m53696/latest/)** .

Rule: Exponential Growth Model

Systems that exhibit **exponential growth** increase according to the mathematical model

$$y = y_0 e^{kt},$$

where y_0 represents the initial state of the system and $k > 0$ is a constant, called the *growth constant*.

Population growth is a common example of exponential growth. Consider a population of bacteria, for instance. It seems plausible that the rate of population growth would be proportional to the size of the population. After all, the more bacteria there are to reproduce, the faster the population grows. **Figure 6.79** and **Table 6.1** represent the growth of a population of bacteria with an initial population of 200 bacteria and a growth constant of 0.02. Notice that after only 2 hours $(120$ minutes), the population is 10 times its original size!

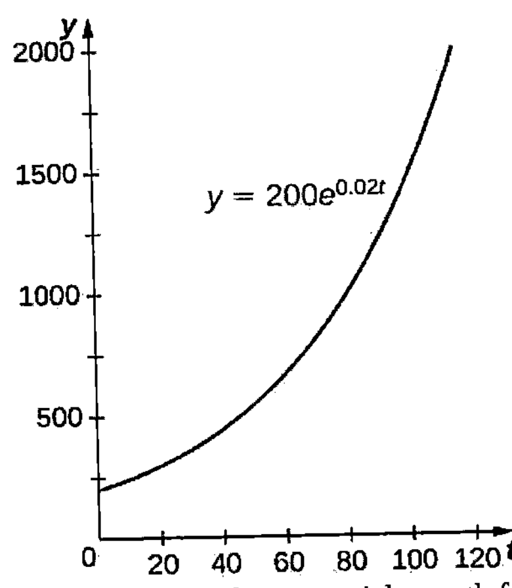

Figure 6.79 An example of exponential growth for bacteria.

Time (min)	Population Size (no. of bacteria)
10	244
20	298
30	364
40	445
50	544
60	664
70	811
80	991
90	1210
100	1478
110	1805
120	2205

Table 6.1 Exponential Growth of a Bacterial Population

Note that we are using a continuous function to model what is inherently discrete behavior. At any given time, the real-world population contains a whole number of bacteria, although the model takes on noninteger values. When using exponential growth models, we must always be careful to interpret the function values in the context of the phenomenon we are modeling.

Example 6.42

Population Growth

Consider the population of bacteria described earlier. This population grows according to the function $f(t) = 200e^{0.02t},$ where t is measured in minutes. How many bacteria are present in the population after 5 hours (300 minutes)? When does the population reach 100,000 bacteria?

Solution

We have $f(t) = 200e^{0.02t}$. Then

$$f(300) = 200e^{0.02(300)} \approx 80{,}686.$$

There are 80,686 bacteria in the population after 5 hours.

To find when the population reaches 100,000 bacteria, we solve the equation

$$\begin{aligned} 100{,}000 &= 200e^{0.02t} \\ 500 &= e^{0.02t} \\ \ln 500 &= 0.02t \\ t &= \frac{\ln 500}{0.02} \approx 310.73. \end{aligned}$$

The population reaches 100,000 bacteria after 310.73 minutes.

6.42 Consider a population of bacteria that grows according to the function $f(t) = 500e^{0.05t},$ where t is measured in minutes. How many bacteria are present in the population after 4 hours? When does the population reach 100 million bacteria?

Let's now turn our attention to a financial application: compound interest. Interest that is not compounded is called *simple interest*. Simple interest is paid once, at the end of the specified time period (usually 1 year). So, if we put \$1000 in a savings account earning 2% simple interest per year, then at the end of the year we have

$$1000(1 + 0.02) = \$1020.$$

Compound interest is paid multiple times per year, depending on the compounding period. Therefore, if the bank compounds the interest every 6 months, it credits half of the year's interest to the account after 6 months. During the second half of the year, the account earns interest not only on the initial \$1000, but also on the interest earned during the first half of the year. Mathematically speaking, at the end of the year, we have

$$1000\left(1 + \frac{0.02}{2}\right)^2 = \$1020.10.$$

Similarly, if the interest is compounded every 4 months, we have

$$1000\left(1 + \frac{0.02}{3}\right)^3 = \$1020.13,$$

and if the interest is compounded daily (365 times per year), we have \$1020.20. If we extend this concept, so that the interest is compounded continuously, after t years we have

$$1000 \lim_{n \to \infty} \left(1 + \frac{0.02}{n}\right)^{nt}.$$

Now let's manipulate this expression so that we have an exponential growth function. Recall that the number e can be expressed as a limit:

$$e = \lim_{m \to \infty} \left(1 + \frac{1}{m}\right)^{m}.$$

Based on this, we want the expression inside the parentheses to have the form $(1 + 1/m)$. Let $n = 0.02m$. Note that as $n \to \infty$, $m \to \infty$ as well. Then we get

$$1000 \lim_{n \to \infty} \left(1 + \frac{0.02}{n}\right)^{nt} = 1000 \lim_{m \to \infty} \left(1 + \frac{0.02}{0.02m}\right)^{0.02mt} = 1000 \left[\lim_{m \to \infty} \left(1 + \frac{1}{m}\right)^{m}\right]^{0.02t}.$$

We recognize the limit inside the brackets as the number e. So, the balance in our bank account after t years is given by $1000e^{0.02t}$. Generalizing this concept, we see that if a bank account with an initial balance of $\$P$ earns interest at a rate of $r\%$, compounded continuously, then the balance of the account after t years is

$$\text{Balance} = Pe^{rt}.$$

Example 6.43

Compound Interest

A 25-year-old student is offered an opportunity to invest some money in a retirement account that pays 5% annual interest compounded continuously. How much does the student need to invest today to have $\$1$ million when she retires at age 65? What if she could earn 6% annual interest compounded continuously instead?

Solution

We have

$$\begin{aligned} 1{,}000{,}000 &= Pe^{0.05(40)} \\ P &= 135{,}335.28. \end{aligned}$$

She must invest $\$135{,}335.28$ at 5% interest.

If, instead, she is able to earn 6%, then the equation becomes

$$\begin{aligned} 1{,}000{,}000 &= Pe^{0.06(40)} \\ P &= 90{,}717.95. \end{aligned}$$

In this case, she needs to invest only $\$90{,}717.95$. This is roughly two-thirds the amount she needs to invest at 5%. The fact that the interest is compounded continuously greatly magnifies the effect of the 1% increase in interest rate.

6.43 Suppose instead of investing at age $25\sqrt{b^2 - 4ac}$, the student waits until age 35. How much would she have to invest at 5%? At 6%?

If a quantity grows exponentially, the time it takes for the quantity to double remains constant. In other words, it takes the same amount of time for a population of bacteria to grow from 100 to 200 bacteria as it does to grow from $10{,}000$ to $20{,}000$ bacteria. This time is called the doubling time. To calculate the doubling time, we want to know when the quantity reaches twice its original size. So we have

$$\begin{aligned} 2y_0 &= y_0 e^{kt} \\ 2 &= e^{kt} \\ \ln 2 &= kt \\ t &= \frac{\ln 2}{k}. \end{aligned}$$

Definition

If a quantity grows exponentially, the **doubling time** is the amount of time it takes the quantity to double. It is given by

$$\text{Doubling time} = \frac{\ln 2}{k}.$$

Example 6.44

Using the Doubling Time

Assume a population of fish grows exponentially. A pond is stocked initially with 500 fish. After 6 months, there are 1000 fish in the pond. The owner will allow his friends and neighbors to fish on his pond after the fish population reaches 10,000. When will the owner's friends be allowed to fish?

Solution

We know it takes the population of fish 6 months to double in size. So, if t represents time in months, by the doubling-time formula, we have $6 = (\ln 2)/k$. Then, $k = (\ln 2)/6$. Thus, the population is given by $y = 500e^{((\ln 2)/6)t}$. To figure out when the population reaches 10,000 fish, we must solve the following equation:

$$\begin{aligned} 10{,}000 &= 500e^{(\ln 2/6)t} \\ 20 &= e^{(\ln 2/6)t} \\ \ln 20 &= \left(\frac{\ln 2}{6}\right)t \\ t &= \frac{6(\ln 20)}{\ln 2} \approx 25.93. \end{aligned}$$

The owner's friends have to wait 25.93 months (a little more than 2 years) to fish in the pond.

6.44 Suppose it takes 9 months for the fish population in **Example 6.44** to reach 1000 fish. Under these circumstances, how long do the owner's friends have to wait?

Exponential Decay Model

Exponential functions can also be used to model populations that shrink (from disease, for example), or chemical compounds that break down over time. We say that such systems exhibit exponential decay, rather than exponential growth. The model is nearly the same, except there is a negative sign in the exponent. Thus, for some positive constant k, we have $y = y_0 e^{-kt}$.

As with exponential growth, there is a differential equation associated with exponential decay. We have

$$y' = -ky_0 e^{-kt} = -ky.$$

Rule: Exponential Decay Model

Systems that exhibit **exponential decay** behave according to the model

$$y = y_0 e^{-kt},$$

where y_0 represents the initial state of the system and $k > 0$ is a constant, called the *decay constant.*

The following figure shows a graph of a representative exponential decay function.

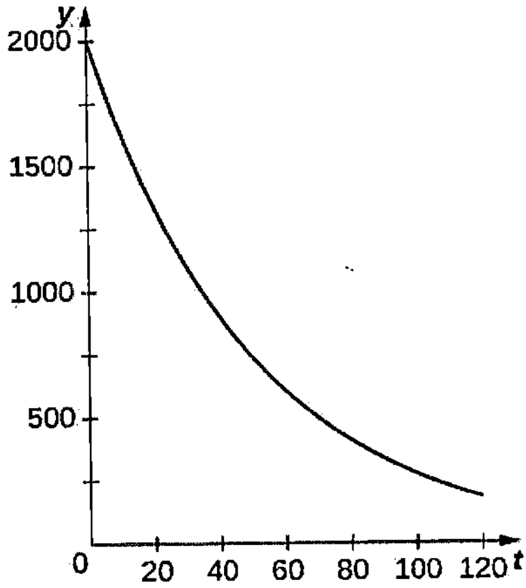

Figure 6.80 An example of exponential decay.

Let's look at a physical application of exponential decay. Newton's law of cooling says that an object cools at a rate proportional to the difference between the temperature of the object and the temperature of the surroundings. In other words, if T represents the temperature of the object and T_a represents the ambient temperature in a room, then

$$T' = -k(T - T_a).$$

Note that this is not quite the right model for exponential decay. We want the derivative to be proportional to the function, and this expression has the additional T_a term. Fortunately, we can make a change of variables that resolves this issue. Let $y(t) = T(t) - T_a$. Then $y'(t) = T'(t) - 0 = T'(t),$ and our equation becomes

$$y' = -ky.$$

From our previous work, we know this relationship between y and its derivative leads to exponential decay. Thus,

$$y = y_0 e^{-kt},$$

and we see that

$$\begin{aligned} T - T_a &= (T_0 - T_a)e^{-kt} \\ T &= (T_0 - T_a)e^{-kt} + T_a \end{aligned}$$

where T_0 represents the initial temperature. Let's apply this formula in the following example.

Example 6.45

Newton's Law of Cooling

According to experienced baristas, the optimal temperature to serve coffee is between 155°F and 175°F. Suppose coffee is poured at a temperature of 200°F, and after 2 minutes in a 70°F room it has cooled to 180°F. When is the coffee first cool enough to serve? When is the coffee too cold to serve? Round answers to the nearest half minute.

Solution

We have

$$\begin{aligned} T &= (T_0 - T_a)e^{-kt} + T_a \\ 180 &= (200 - 70)e^{-k(2)} + 70 \\ 110 &= 130e^{-2k} \\ \frac{11}{13} &= e^{-2k} \\ \ln\frac{11}{13} &= -2k \\ \ln 11 - \ln 13 &= -2k \\ k &= \frac{\ln 13 - \ln 11}{2}. \end{aligned}$$

Then, the model is

$$T = 130e^{(\ln 11 - \ln 13/2)t} + 70.$$

The coffee reaches 175°F when

$$\begin{aligned} 175 &= 130e^{(\ln 11 - \ln 13/2)t} + 70 \\ 105 &= 130e^{(\ln 11 - \ln 13/2)t} \\ \frac{21}{26} &= e^{(\ln 11 - \ln 13/2)t} \\ \ln\frac{21}{26} &= \frac{\ln 11 - \ln 13}{2}t \\ \ln 21 - \ln 26 &= \frac{\ln 11 - \ln 13}{2}t \\ t &= \frac{2(\ln 21 - \ln 26)}{\ln 11 - \ln 13} \approx 2.56. \end{aligned}$$

The coffee can be served about 2.5 minutes after it is poured. The coffee reaches 155°F at

$$\begin{aligned} 155 &= 130e^{(\ln 11 - \ln 13/2)t} + 70 \\ 85 &= 130e^{(\ln 11 - \ln 13)t} \\ \frac{17}{26} &= e^{(\ln 11 - \ln 13)t} \\ \ln 17 - \ln 26 &= \left(\frac{\ln 11 - \ln 13}{2}\right)t \\ t &= \frac{2(\ln 17 - \ln 26)}{\ln 11 - \ln 13} \approx 5.09. \end{aligned}$$

The coffee is too cold to be served about 5 minutes after it is poured.

6.45 Suppose the room is warmer (75°F) and, after 2 minutes, the coffee has cooled only to 185°F. When is the coffee first cool enough to serve? When is the coffee be too cold to serve? Round answers to the nearest half minute.

Just as systems exhibiting exponential growth have a constant doubling time, systems exhibiting exponential decay have a constant half-life. To calculate the half-life, we want to know when the quantity reaches half its original size. Therefore, we have

$$\begin{aligned} \frac{y_0}{2} &= y_0 e^{-kt} \\ \frac{1}{2} &= e^{-kt} \\ -\ln 2 &= -kt \\ t &= \frac{\ln 2}{k}. \end{aligned}$$

Note: This is the same expression we came up with for doubling time.

Definition

If a quantity decays exponentially, the **half-life** is the amount of time it takes the quantity to be reduced by half. It is given by

$$\text{Half-life} = \frac{\ln 2}{k}.$$

Example 6.46

Radiocarbon Dating

One of the most common applications of an exponential decay model is carbon dating. Carbon-14 decays (emits a radioactive particle) at a regular and consistent exponential rate. Therefore, if we know how much carbon was originally present in an object and how much carbon remains, we can determine the age of the object. The half-life of carbon-14 is approximately 5730 years—meaning, after that many years, half the material has converted from the original carbon-14 to the new nonradioactive nitrogen-14. If we have 100 g carbon-14 today, how much is left in 50 years? If an artifact that originally contained 100 g of carbon now contains 10 g of carbon, how old is it? Round the answer to the nearest hundred years.

Solution

We have

$$\begin{aligned} 5730 &= \frac{\ln 2}{k} \\ k &= \frac{\ln 2}{5730}. \end{aligned}$$

So, the model says

$$y = 100e^{-(\ln 2/5730)t}.$$

In 50 years, we have

$$\begin{aligned} y &= 100e^{-(\ln 2/5730)(50)} \\ &\approx 99.40. \end{aligned}$$

Therefore, in 50 years, 99.40 g of carbon-14 remains.

To determine the age of the artifact, we must solve

$$\begin{aligned} 10 &= 100e^{-(\ln 2/5730)t} \\ \frac{1}{10} &= e^{-(\ln 2/5730)t} \\ t &\approx 19035. \end{aligned}$$

The artifact is about $19,000$ years old.

6.46 If we have 100 g of carbon-14, how much is left after. years? If an artifact that originally contained 100 g of carbon now contains $20g$ of carbon, how old is it? Round the answer to the nearest hundred years.

6.8 EXERCISES

True or False? If true, prove it. If false, find the true answer.

348. The doubling time for $y = e^{ct}$ is (ln (2))/(ln (*c*)).

349. If you invest $500, an annual rate of interest of 3% yields more money in the first year than a 2.5% continuous rate of interest.

350. If you leave a 100°C pot of tea at room temperature (25°C) and an identical pot in the refrigerator (5°C), with $k = 0.02$, the tea in the refrigerator reaches a drinkable temperature (70°C) more than 5 minutes before the tea at room temperature.

351. If given a half-life of *t* years, the constant *k* for $y = e^{kt}$ is calculated by $k = \ln(1/2)/t$.

For the following exercises, use $y = y_0 e^{kt}$.

352. If a culture of bacteria doubles in 3 hours, how many hours does it take to multiply by 10?

353. If bacteria increase by a factor of 10 in 10 hours, how many hours does it take to increase by 100?

354. How old is a skull that contains one-fifth as much radiocarbon as a modern skull? Note that the half-life of radiocarbon is 5730 years.

355. If a relic contains 90% as much radiocarbon as new material, can it have come from the time of Christ (approximately 2000 years ago)? Note that the half-life of radiocarbon is 5730 years.

356. The population of Cairo grew from 5 million to 10 million in 20 years. Use an exponential model to find when the population was 8 million.

357. The populations of New York and Los Angeles are growing at 1% and 1.4% a year, respectively. Starting from 8 million (New York) and 6 million (Los Angeles), when are the populations equal?

358. Suppose the value of $1 in Japanese yen decreases at 2% per year. Starting from $1 = ¥250, when will $1 = ¥1?

359. The effect of advertising decays exponentially. If 40% of the population remembers a new product after 3 days, how long will 20% remember it?

360. If $y = 1000$ at $t = 3$ and $y = 3000$ at $t = 4$, what was y_0 at $t = 0$?

361. If $y = 100$ at $t = 4$ and $y = 10$ at $t = 8$, when does $y = 1$?

362. If a bank offers annual interest of 7.5% or continuous interest of 7.25%, which has a better annual yield?

363. What continuous interest rate has the same yield as an annual rate of 9%?

364. If you deposit $5000 at 8% annual interest, how many years can you withdraw $500 (starting after the first year) without running out of money?

365. You are trying to save $50,000 in 20 years for college tuition for your child. If interest is a continuous 10%, how much do you need to invest initially?

366. You are cooling a turkey that was taken out of the oven with an internal temperature of 165°F. After 10 minutes of resting the turkey in a 70°F apartment, the temperature has reached 155°F. What is the temperature of the turkey 20 minutes after taking it out of the oven?

367. You are trying to thaw some vegetables that are at a temperature of 1°F. To thaw vegetables safely, you must put them in the refrigerator, which has an ambient temperature of 44°F. You check on your vegetables 2 hours after putting them in the refrigerator to find that they are now 12°F. Plot the resulting temperature curve and use it to determine when the vegetables reach 33°F.

368. You are an archaeologist and are given a bone that is claimed to be from a Tyrannosaurus Rex. You know these dinosaurs lived during the Cretaceous Era (146 million years to 65 million years ago), and you find by radiocarbon dating that there is 0.000001% the amount of radiocarbon. Is this bone from the Cretaceous?

369. The spent fuel of a nuclear reactor contains plutonium-239, which has a half-life of 24,000 years. If 1 barrel containing 10 kg of plutonium-239 is sealed, how many years must pass until only 10*g* of plutonium-239 is left?

For the next set of exercises, use the following table, which features the world population by decade.

Years since 1950	Population (millions)
0	2,556
10	3,039
20	3,706
30	4,453
40	5,279
50	6,083
60	6,849

Source: http://www.factmonster.com/ipka/A0762181.html.

370. **[T]** The best-fit exponential curve to the data of the form $P(t) = ae^{bt}$ is given by $P(t) = 2686e^{0.01604t}$. Use a graphing calculator to graph the data and the exponential curve together.

371. **[T]** Find and graph the derivative y' of your equation. Where is it increasing and what is the meaning of this increase?

372. **[T]** Find and graph the second derivative of your equation. Where is it increasing and what is the meaning of this increase?

373. **[T]** Find the predicted date when the population reaches 10 billion. Using your previous answers about the first and second derivatives, explain why exponential growth is unsuccessful in predicting the future.

For the next set of exercises, use the following table, which shows the population of San Francisco during the 19th century.

Years since 1850	Population (thousands)
0	21.00
10	56.80
20	149.5
30	234.0

Source: http://www.sfgenealogy.com/sf/history/hgpop.htm.

374. **[T]** The best-fit exponential curve to the data of the form $P(t) = ae^{bt}$ is given by $P(t) = 35.26e^{0.06407t}$. Use a graphing calculator to graph the data and the exponential curve together.

375. **[T]** Find and graph the derivative y' of your equation. Where is it increasing? What is the meaning of this increase? Is there a value where the increase is maximal?

376. **[T]** Find and graph the second derivative of your equation. Where is it increasing? What is the meaning of this increase?

6.9 | Calculus of the Hyperbolic Functions

Learning Objectives

6.9.1 Apply the formulas for derivatives and integrals of the hyperbolic functions.

6.9.2 Apply the formulas for the derivatives of the inverse hyperbolic functions and their associated integrals.

6.9.3 Describe the common applied conditions of a catenary curve.

We were introduced to hyperbolic functions in **Introduction to Functions and Graphs**, along with some of their basic properties. In this section, we look at differentiation and integration formulas for the hyperbolic functions and their inverses.

Derivatives and Integrals of the Hyperbolic Functions

Recall that the hyperbolic sine and hyperbolic cosine are defined as

$$\sinh x = \frac{e^x - e^{-x}}{2} \text{ and } \cosh x = \frac{e^x + e^{-x}}{2}.$$

The other hyperbolic functions are then defined in terms of $\sinh x$ and $\cosh x$. The graphs of the hyperbolic functions are shown in the following figure.

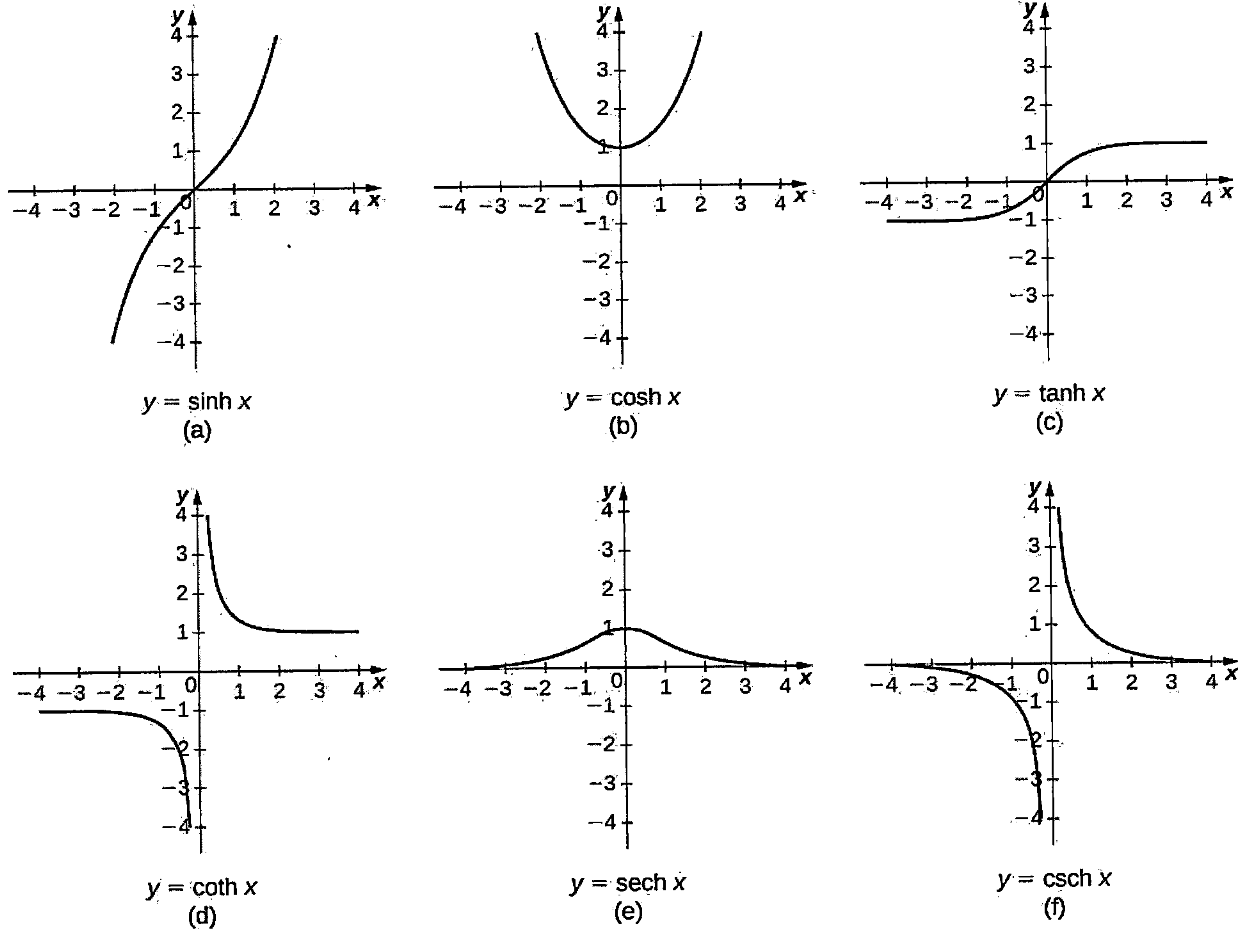

Figure 6.81 Graphs of the hyperbolic functions.

It is easy to develop differentiation formulas for the hyperbolic functions. For example, looking at $\sinh x$ we have

$$\begin{aligned}\frac{d}{dx}(\sinh x) &= \frac{d}{dx}\left(\frac{e^x - e^{-x}}{2}\right) \\ &= \frac{1}{2}\left[\frac{d}{dx}(e^x) - \frac{d}{dx}(e^{-x})\right] \\ &= \frac{1}{2}[e^x + e^{-x}] = \cosh x.\end{aligned}$$

Similarly, $(d/dx)\cosh x = \sinh x$. We summarize the differentiation formulas for the hyperbolic functions in the following table.

$f(x)$	$\frac{d}{dx}f(x)$
$\sinh x$	$\cosh x$
$\cosh x$	$\sinh x$
$\tanh x$	$\text{sech}^2\, x$
$\coth x$	$-\text{csch}^2\, x$
$\text{sech}\, x$	$-\text{sech}\, x \tanh x$
$\text{csch}\, x$	$-\text{csch}\, x \coth x$

Table 6.2 Derivatives of the Hyperbolic Functions

Let's take a moment to compare the derivatives of the hyperbolic functions with the derivatives of the standard trigonometric functions. There are a lot of similarities, but differences as well. For example, the derivatives of the sine functions match: $(d/dx)\sin x = \cos x$ and $(d/dx)\sinh x = \cosh x$. The derivatives of the cosine functions, however, differ in sign: $(d/dx)\cos x = -\sin x$, but $(d/dx)\cosh x = \sinh x$. As we continue our examination of the hyperbolic functions, we must be mindful of their similarities and differences to the standard trigonometric functions.

These differentiation formulas for the hyperbolic functions lead directly to the following integral formulas.

$$\begin{aligned}\int \sinh u\,du &= \cosh u + C & \int \text{csch}^2\, u\,du &= -\coth u + C \\ \int \cosh u\,du &= \sinh u + C & \int \text{sech}\, u \tanh u\,du &= -\text{sech}\, u + C \\ \int \text{sech}^2 u\,du &= \tanh u + C & \int \text{csch}\, u \coth u\,du &= -\text{csch}\, u + C\end{aligned}$$

Example 6.47

Differentiating Hyperbolic Functions

Evaluate the following derivatives:

a. $\frac{d}{dx}\left(\sinh\left(x^2\right)\right)$

b. $\frac{d}{dx}(\cosh x)^2$

Solution

Using the formulas in **Table 6.2** and the chain rule, we get

a. $\frac{d}{dx}\left(\sinh\left(x^2\right)\right) = \cosh\left(x^2\right) \cdot 2x$

b. $\frac{d}{dx}(\cosh x)^2 = 2\cosh x \sinh x$

6.47 Evaluate the following derivatives:

a. $\frac{d}{dx}\left(\tanh\left(x^2 + 3x\right)\right)$

b. $\frac{d}{dx}\left(\frac{1}{(\sinh x)^2}\right)$

Example 6.48

Integrals Involving Hyperbolic Functions

Evaluate the following integrals:

a. $\int x\cosh\left(x^2\right)dx$

b. $\int \tanh x\, dx$

Solution

We can use u-substitution in both cases.

a. Let $u = x^2$. Then, $du = 2x\, dx$ and

$$\int x\cosh\left(x^2\right)dx = \int \frac{1}{2}\cosh u\, du = \frac{1}{2}\sinh u + C = \frac{1}{2}\sinh\left(x^2\right) + C.$$

b. Let $u = \cosh x$. Then, $du = \sinh x\, dx$ and

$$\int \tanh x\, dx = \int \frac{\sinh x}{\cosh x}dx = \int \frac{1}{u}du = \ln|u| + C = \ln|\cosh x| + C.$$

Note that $\cosh x > 0$ for all x, so we can eliminate the absolute value signs and obtain

$$\int \tanh x\, dx = \ln(\cosh x) + C.$$

6.48 Evaluate the following integrals:

a. $\int \sinh^3 x \cosh x \, dx$

b. $\int \operatorname{sech}^2 (3x) dx$

Calculus of Inverse Hyperbolic Functions

Looking at the graphs of the hyperbolic functions, we see that with appropriate range restrictions, they all have inverses. Most of the necessary range restrictions can be discerned by close examination of the graphs. The domains and ranges of the inverse hyperbolic functions are summarized in the following table.

Function	Domain	Range
$\sinh^{-1} x$	$(-\infty, \infty)$	$(-\infty, \infty)$
$\cosh^{-1} x$	$(1, \infty)$	$[0, \infty)$
$\tanh^{-1} x$	$(-1, 1)$	$(-\infty, \infty)$
$\coth^{-1} x$	$(-\infty, -1) \cup (1, \infty)$	$(-\infty, 0) \cup (0, \infty)$
$\operatorname{sech}^{-1} x$	$(0, 1)$	$[0, \infty)$
$\operatorname{csch}^{-1} x$	$(-\infty, 0) \cup (0, \infty)$	$(-\infty, 0) \cup (0, \infty)$

Table 6.3 Domains and Ranges of the Inverse Hyperbolic Functions

The graphs of the inverse hyperbolic functions are shown in the following figure.

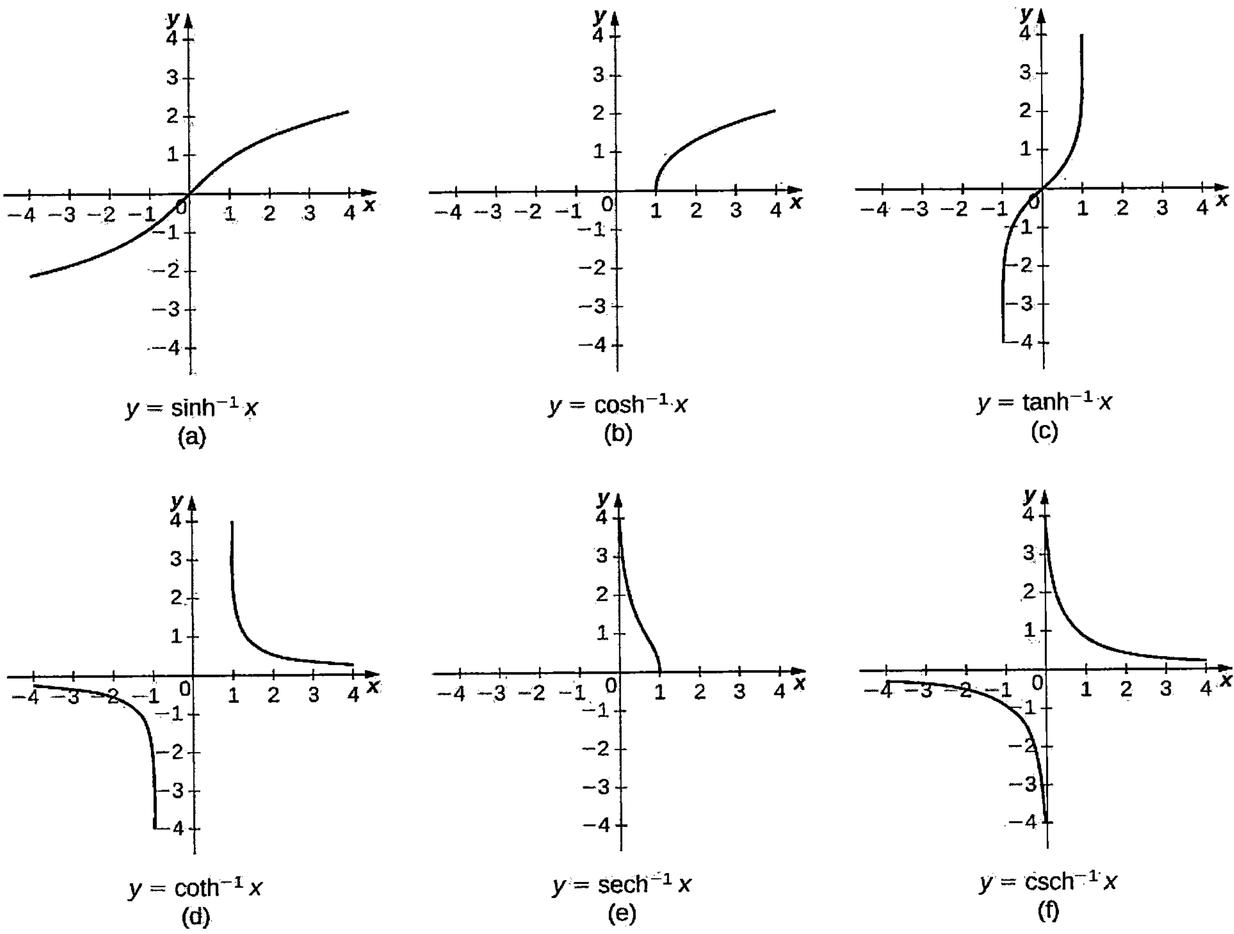

Figure 6.82 Graphs of the inverse hyperbolic functions.

To find the derivatives of the inverse functions, we use implicit differentiation. We have

$$\begin{aligned} y &= \sinh^{-1} x \\ \sinh y &= x \\ \frac{d}{dx}\sinh y &= \frac{d}{dx}x \\ \cosh y\frac{dy}{dx} &= 1. \end{aligned}$$

Recall that $\cosh^2 y - \sinh^2 y = 1$, so $\cosh y = \sqrt{1 + \sinh^2 y}$. Then,

$$\frac{dy}{dx} = \frac{1}{\cosh y} = \frac{1}{\sqrt{1 + \sinh^2 y}} = \frac{1}{\sqrt{1 + x^2}}.$$

We can derive differentiation formulas for the other inverse hyperbolic functions in a similar fashion. These differentiation formulas are summarized in the following table.

$f(x)$	$\frac{d}{dx}f(x)$
$\sinh^{-1}x$	$\frac{1}{\sqrt{1+x^2}}$
$\cosh^{-1}x$	$\frac{1}{\sqrt{x^2-1}}$
$\tanh^{-1}x$	$\frac{1}{1-x^2}$
$\coth^{-1}x$	$\frac{1}{1-x^2}$
$\operatorname{sech}^{-1}x$	$\frac{-1}{x\sqrt{1-x^2}}$
$\operatorname{csch}^{-1}x$	$\frac{-1}{\lvert x\rvert\sqrt{1+x^2}}$

Table 6.4 Derivatives of the Inverse Hyperbolic Functions

Note that the derivatives of $\tanh^{-1}x$ and $\coth^{-1}x$ are the same. Thus, when we integrate $1/\left(1-x^2\right)$, we need to select the proper antiderivative based on the domain of the functions and the values of x. Integration formulas involving the inverse hyperbolic functions are summarized as follows.

$$\int \frac{1}{\sqrt{1+u^2}}du = \sinh^{-1}u + C \qquad \int \frac{1}{u\sqrt{1-u^2}}du = -\operatorname{sech}^{-1}|u| + C$$

$$\int \frac{1}{\sqrt{u^2-1}}du = \cosh^{-1}u + C \qquad \int \frac{1}{u\sqrt{1+u^2}}du = -\operatorname{csch}^{-1}|u| + C$$

$$\int \frac{1}{1-u^2}du = \begin{cases} \tanh^{-1}u + C \text{ if } |u| < 1 \\ \coth^{-1}u + C \text{ if } |u| > 1 \end{cases}$$

Example 6.49

Differentiating Inverse Hyperbolic Functions

Evaluate the following derivatives:

a. $\frac{d}{dx}\left(\sinh^{-1}\left(\frac{x}{3}\right)\right)$

b. $\frac{d}{dx}\left(\tanh^{-1}x\right)^2$

Solution

Using the formulas in **Table 6.4** and the chain rule, we obtain the following results:

a. $\frac{d}{dx}\left(\sinh^{-1}\left(\frac{x}{3}\right)\right) = \frac{1}{3\sqrt{1 + \frac{x^2}{9}}} = \frac{1}{\sqrt{9 + x^2}}$

b. $\frac{d}{dx}\left(\tanh^{-1} x\right)^2 = \frac{2\left(\tanh^{-1} x\right)}{1 - x^2}$

6.49 Evaluate the following derivatives:

a. $\frac{d}{dx}\left(\cosh^{-1}(3x)\right)$

b. $\frac{d}{dx}\left(\coth^{-1} x\right)^3$

Example 6.50

Integrals Involving Inverse Hyperbolic Functions

Evaluate the following integrals:

a. $\displaystyle\int \frac{1}{\sqrt{4x^2 - 1}} dx$

b. $\displaystyle\int \frac{1}{2x\sqrt{1 - 9x^2}} dx$

Solution

We can use u-substitution in both cases.

a. Let $u = 2x.$ Then, $du = 2dx$ and we have

$$\int \frac{1}{\sqrt{4x^2 - 1}} dx = \int \frac{1}{2\sqrt{u^2 - 1}} du = \frac{1}{2}\cosh^{-1} u + C = \frac{1}{2}\cosh^{-1}(2x) + C.$$

b. Let $u = 3x.$ Then, $du = 3dx$ and we obtain

$$\int \frac{1}{2x\sqrt{1 - 9x^2}} dx = \frac{1}{2}\int \frac{1}{u\sqrt{1 - u^2}} du = -\frac{1}{2}\operatorname{sech}^{-1}|u| + C = -\frac{1}{2}\operatorname{sech}^{-1}|3x| + C.$$

6.50 Evaluate the following integrals:

a. $\displaystyle\int \frac{1}{\sqrt{x^2 - 4}} dx, \quad x > 2$

b. $\displaystyle\int \frac{1}{\sqrt{1 - e^{2x}}} dx$

Applications

One physical application of hyperbolic functions involves hanging cables. If a cable of uniform density is suspended between two supports without any load other than its own weight, the cable forms a curve called a **catenary**. High-voltage power lines, chains hanging between two posts, and strands of a spider's web all form catenaries. The following figure shows chains hanging from a row of posts.

Figure 6.83 Chains between these posts take the shape of a catenary. (credit: modification of work by OKFoundryCompany, Flickr)

Hyperbolic functions can be used to model catenaries. Specifically, functions of the form $y = a\cosh(x/a)$ are catenaries. **Figure 6.84** shows the graph of $y = 2\cosh(x/2)$.

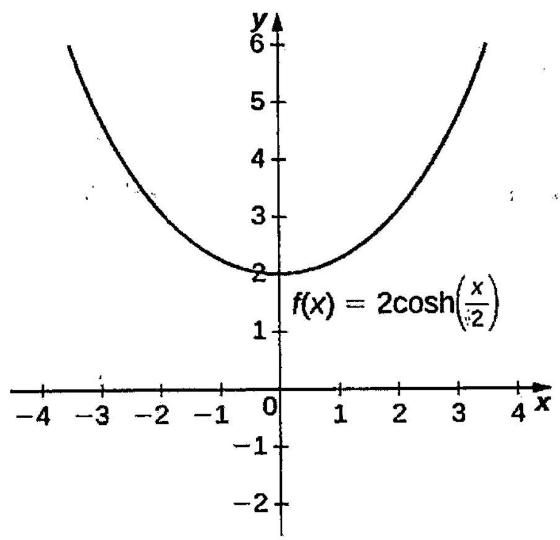

Figure 6.84 A hyperbolic cosine function forms the shape of a catenary.

Example 6.51

Using a Catenary to Find the Length of a Cable

Assume a hanging cable has the shape $10\cosh(x/10)$ for $-15 \le x \le 15,$ where x is measured in feet. Determine the length of the cable (in feet).

Solution

Recall from Section 6.4 that the formula for arc length is

$$\text{Arc Length} = \int_a^b \sqrt{1 + [f'(x)]^2}\,dx.$$

We have $f(x) = 10\cosh(x/10),$ so $f'(x) = \sinh(x/10).$ Then

$$\begin{aligned}\text{Arc Length} &= \int_a^b \sqrt{1 + [f'(x)]^2}\,dx \\ &= \int_{-15}^{15} \sqrt{1 + \sinh^2\left(\frac{x}{10}\right)}\,dx.\end{aligned}$$

Now recall that $1 + \sinh^2 x = \cosh^2 x,$ so we have

$$\begin{aligned}\text{Arc Length} &= \int_{-15}^{15} \sqrt{1 + \sinh^2\left(\frac{x}{10}\right)}\,dx \\ &= \int_{-15}^{15} \cosh\left(\frac{x}{10}\right)dx \\ &= 10\sinh\left(\frac{x}{10}\right)\Big|_{-15}^{15} = 10\left[\sinh\left(\frac{3}{2}\right) - \sinh\left(-\frac{3}{2}\right)\right] = 20\sinh\left(\frac{3}{2}\right) \\ &\approx 42.586 \text{ ft.}\end{aligned}$$

6.51 Assume a hanging cable has the shape $15\cosh(x/15)$ for $-20 \le x \le 20.$ Determine the length of the cable (in feet).

6.9 EXERCISES

377. **[T]** Find expressions for $\cosh x + \sinh x$ and $\cosh x - \sinh x$. Use a calculator to graph these functions and ensure your expression is correct.

378. From the definitions of $\cosh(x)$ and $\sinh(x)$, find their antiderivatives.

379. Show that $\cosh(x)$ and $\sinh(x)$ satisfy $y'' = y$.

380. Use the quotient rule to verify that $\tanh(x)' = \text{sech}^2(x)$.

381. Derive $\cosh^2(x) + \sinh^2(x) = \cosh(2x)$ from the definition.

382. Take the derivative of the previous expression to find an expression for $\sinh(2x)$.

383. Prove $\sinh(x+y) = \sinh(x)\cosh(y) + \cosh(x)\sinh(y)$ by changing the expression to exponentials.

384. Take the derivative of the previous expression to find an expression for $\cosh(x+y)$.

For the following exercises, find the derivatives of the given functions and graph along with the function to ensure your answer is correct.

385. **[T]** $\cosh(3x+1)$

386. **[T]** $\sinh(x^2)$

387. **[T]** $\dfrac{1}{\cosh(x)}$

388. **[T]** $\sinh(\ln(x))$

389. **[T]** $\cosh^2(x) + \sinh^2(x)$

390. **[T]** $\cosh^2(x) - \sinh^2(x)$

391. **[T]** $\tanh\left(\sqrt{x^2+1}\right)$

392. **[T]** $\dfrac{1+\tanh(x)}{1-\tanh(x)}$

393. **[T]** $\sinh^6(x)$

394. **[T]** $\ln(\text{sech}(x) + \tanh(x))$

For the following exercises, find the antiderivatives for the given functions.

395. $\cosh(2x+1)$

396. $\tanh(3x+2)$

397. $x\cosh(x^2)$

398. $3x^3\tanh(x^4)$

399. $\cosh^2(x)\sinh(x)$

400. $\tanh^2(x)\text{sech}^2(x)$

401. $\dfrac{\sinh(x)}{1+\cosh(x)}$

402. $\coth(x)$

403. $\cosh(x) + \sinh(x)$

404. $(\cosh(x) + \sinh(x))^n$

For the following exercises, find the derivatives for the functions.

405. $\tanh^{-1}(4x)$

406. $\sinh^{-1}(x^2)$

407. $\sinh^{-1}(\cosh(x))$

408. $\cosh^{-1}(x^3)$

409. $\tanh^{-1}(\cos(x))$

410. $e^{\sinh^{-1}(x)}$

411. $\ln\left(\tanh^{-1}(x)\right)$

For the following exercises, find the antiderivatives for the functions.

412. $\displaystyle\int \frac{dx}{4-x^2}$

413. $\displaystyle\int \frac{dx}{a^2-x^2}$

414. $\int \frac{dx}{\sqrt{x^2+1}}$

415. $\int \frac{x\,dx}{\sqrt{x^2+1}}$

416. $\int -\frac{dx}{x\sqrt{1-x^2}}$

417. $\int \frac{e^x}{\sqrt{e^{2x}-1}}$

418. $\int -\frac{2x}{x^4-1}$

For the following exercises, use the fact that a falling body with friction equal to velocity squared obeys the equation $dv/dt = g - v^2$.

419. Show that $v(t) = \sqrt{g}\tanh(\sqrt{g}t)$ satisfies this equation.

420. Derive the previous expression for $v(t)$ by integrating $\frac{dv}{g - v^2} = dt$.

421. **[T]** Estimate how far a body has fallen in 12 seconds by finding the area underneath the curve of $v(t)$.

For the following exercises, use this scenario: A cable hanging under its own weight has a slope $S = dy/dx$ that satisfies $dS/dx = c\sqrt{1+S^2}$. The constant c is the ratio of cable density to tension.

422. Show that $S = \sinh(cx)$ satisfies this equation.

423. Integrate $dy/dx = \sinh(cx)$ to find the cable height $y(x)$ if $y(0) = 1/c$.

424. Sketch the cable and determine how far down it sags at $x = 0$.

For the following exercises, solve each problem.

425. **[T]** A chain hangs from two posts 2 m apart to form a catenary described by the equation $y = 2\cosh(x/2) - 1$. Find the slope of the catenary at the left fence post.

426. **[T]** A chain hangs from two posts four meters apart to form a catenary described by the equation $y = 4\cosh(x/4) - 3$. Find the total length of the catenary (arc length).

427. **[T]** A high-voltage power line is a catenary described by $y = 10\cosh(x/10)$. Find the ratio of the area under the catenary to its arc length. What do you notice?

428. A telephone line is a catenary described by $y = a\cosh(x/a)$. Find the ratio of the area under the catenary to its arc length. Does this confirm your answer for the previous question?

429. Prove the formula for the derivative of $y = \sinh^{-1}(x)$ by differentiating $x = \sinh(y)$. (*Hint:* Use hyperbolic trigonometric identities.)

430. Prove the formula for the derivative of $y = \cosh^{-1}(x)$ by differentiating $x = \cosh(y)$. (*Hint:* Use hyperbolic trigonometric identities.)

431. Prove the formula for the derivative of $y = \text{sech}^{-1}(x)$ by differentiating $x = \text{sech}(y)$. (*Hint:* Use hyperbolic trigonometric identities.)

432. Prove that $(\cosh(x) + \sinh(x))^n = \cosh(nx) + \sinh(nx)$.

433. Prove the expression for $\sinh^{-1}(x)$. Multiply $x = \sinh(y) = (1/2)(e^y - e^{-y})$ by $2e^y$ and solve for y. Does your expression match the textbook?

434. Prove the expression for $\cosh^{-1}(x)$. Multiply $x = \cosh(y) = (1/2)(e^y - e^{-y})$ by $2e^y$ and solve for y. Does your expression match the textbook?

CHAPTER 6 REVIEW

KEY TERMS

arc length the arc length of a curve can be thought of as the distance a person would travel along the path of the curve

catenary a curve in the shape of the function $y = a\cosh(x/a)$ is a catenary; a cable of uniform density suspended between two supports assumes the shape of a catenary

center of mass the point at which the total mass of the system could be concentrated without changing the moment

centroid the centroid of a region is the geometric center of the region; laminas are often represented by regions in the plane; if the lamina has a constant density, the center of mass of the lamina depends only on the shape of the corresponding planar region; in this case, the center of mass of the lamina corresponds to the centroid of the representative region

cross-section the intersection of a plane and a solid object

density function a density function describes how mass is distributed throughout an object; it can be a linear density, expressed in terms of mass per unit length; an area density, expressed in terms of mass per unit area; or a volume density, expressed in terms of mass per unit volume; weight-density is also used to describe weight (rather than mass) per unit volume

disk method a special case of the slicing method used with solids of revolution when the slices are disks

doubling time if a quantity grows exponentially, the doubling time is the amount of time it takes the quantity to double, and is given by $(\ln 2)/k$

exponential decay systems that exhibit exponential decay follow a model of the form $y = y_0 e^{-kt}$

exponential growth systems that exhibit exponential growth follow a model of the form $y = y_0 e^{kt}$

frustum a portion of a cone; a frustum is constructed by cutting the cone with a plane parallel to the base

half-life if a quantity decays exponentially, the half-life is the amount of time it takes the quantity to be reduced by half. It is given by $(\ln 2)/k$

Hooke's law this law states that the force required to compress (or elongate) a spring is proportional to the distance the spring has been compressed (or stretched) from equilibrium; in other words, $F = kx$, where k is a constant

hydrostatic pressure the pressure exerted by water on a submerged object

lamina a thin sheet of material; laminas are thin enough that, for mathematical purposes, they can be treated as if they are two-dimensional

method of cylindrical shells a method of calculating the volume of a solid of revolution by dividing the solid into nested cylindrical shells; this method is different from the methods of disks or washers in that we integrate with respect to the opposite variable

moment if n masses are arranged on a number line, the moment of the system with respect to the origin is given by $M = \sum_{i=1}^{n} m_i x_i$; if, instead, we consider a region in the plane, bounded above by a function $f(x)$ over an interval $[a, b]$, then the moments of the region with respect to the x- and y-axes are given by $M_x = \rho\int_a^b \frac{[f(x)]^2}{2}dx$ and $M_y = \rho\int_a^b xf(x)dx$, respectively

slicing method a method of calculating the volume of a solid that involves cutting the solid into pieces, estimating the volume of each piece, then adding these estimates to arrive at an estimate of the total volume; as the number of slices goes to infinity, this estimate becomes an integral that gives the exact value of the volume

solid of revolution a solid generated by revolving a region in a plane around a line in that plane

surface area the surface area of a solid is the total area of the outer layer of the object; for objects such as cubes or bricks, the surface area of the object is the sum of the areas of all of its faces

symmetry principle the symmetry principle states that if a region R is symmetric about a line l, then the centroid of R lies on l

theorem of Pappus for volume this theorem states that the volume of a solid of revolution formed by revolving a region around an external axis is equal to the area of the region multiplied by the distance traveled by the centroid of the region

washer method a special case of the slicing method used with solids of revolution when the slices are washers

work the amount of energy it takes to move an object; in physics, when a force is constant, work is expressed as the product of force and distance

KEY EQUATIONS

- **Area between two curves, integrating on the x-axis**
  $$A = \int_a^b [f(x) - g(x)]dx$$
- **Area between two curves, integrating on the y-axis**
  $$A = \int_c^d [u(y) - v(y)]dy$$
- **Disk Method along the x-axis**
  $$V = \int_a^b \pi[f(x)]^2 \, dx$$
- **Disk Method along the y-axis**
  $$V = \int_c^d \pi[g(y)]^2 \, dy$$
- **Washer Method**
  $$V = \int_a^b \pi\left[(f(x))^2 - (g(x))^2\right]dx$$
- **Method of Cylindrical Shells**
  $$V = \int_a^b (2\pi x f(x))dx$$
- **Arc Length of a Function of x**
  $$\text{Arc Length} = \int_a^b \sqrt{1 + [f'(x)]^2} \, dx$$
- **Arc Length of a Function of y**
  $$\text{Arc Length} = \int_c^d \sqrt{1 + [g'(y)]^2} \, dy$$
- **Surface Area of a Function of x**
  $$\text{Surface Area} = \int_a^b \left(2\pi f(x)\sqrt{1 + (f'(x))^2}\right)dx$$
- **Mass of a one-dimensional object**
  $$m = \int_a^b \rho(x)dx$$
- **Mass of a circular object**
  $$m = \int_0^r 2\pi x \rho(x)dx$$

- **Work done on an object**
  $W = \int_a^b F(x)dx$
- **Hydrostatic force on a plate**
  $F = \int_a^b \rho w(x)s(x)dx$
- **Mass of a lamina**
  $m = \rho \int_a^b f(x)dx$
- **Moments of a lamina**
  $M_x = \rho \int_a^b \frac{[f(x)]^2}{2} dx$ and $M_y = \rho \int_a^b x f(x)dx$
- **Center of mass of a lamina**
  $\bar{x} = \frac{M_y}{m}$ and $\bar{y} = \frac{M_x}{m}$
- **Natural logarithm function**
- $\ln x = \int_1^x \frac{1}{t} dt$ Z
- **Exponential function** $y = e^x$
- $\ln y = \ln(e^x) = x$ Z

KEY CONCEPTS

6.1 Areas between Curves

- Just as definite integrals can be used to find the area under a curve, they can also be used to find the area between two curves.
- To find the area between two curves defined by functions, integrate the difference of the functions.
- If the graphs of the functions cross, or if the region is complex, use the absolute value of the difference of the functions. In this case, it may be necessary to evaluate two or more integrals and add the results to find the area of the region.
- Sometimes it can be easier to integrate with respect to y to find the area. The principles are the same regardless of which variable is used as the variable of integration.

6.2 Determining Volumes by Slicing

- Definite integrals can be used to find the volumes of solids. Using the slicing method, we can find a volume by integrating the cross-sectional area.
- For solids of revolution, the volume slices are often disks and the cross-sections are circles. The method of disks involves applying the method of slicing in the particular case in which the cross-sections are circles, and using the formula for the area of a circle.
- If a solid of revolution has a cavity in the center, the volume slices are washers. With the method of washers, the area of the inner circle is subtracted from the area of the outer circle before integrating.

6.3 Volumes of Revolution: Cylindrical Shells

- The method of cylindrical shells is another method for using a definite integral to calculate the volume of a solid of revolution. This method is sometimes preferable to either the method of disks or the method of washers because we integrate with respect to the other variable. In some cases, one integral is substantially more complicated than the other.

- The geometry of the functions and the difficulty of the integration are the main factors in deciding which integration method to use.

6.4 Arc Length of a Curve and Surface Area

- The arc length of a curve can be calculated using a definite integral.
- The arc length is first approximated using line segments, which generates a Riemann sum. Taking a limit then gives us the definite integral formula. The same process can be applied to functions of y.
- The concepts used to calculate the arc length can be generalized to find the surface area of a surface of revolution.
- The integrals generated by both the arc length and surface area formulas are often difficult to evaluate. It may be necessary to use a computer or calculator to approximate the values of the integrals.

6.5 Physical Applications

- Several physical applications of the definite integral are common in engineering and physics.
- Definite integrals can be used to determine the mass of an object if its density function is known.
- Work can also be calculated from integrating a force function, or when counteracting the force of gravity, as in a pumping problem.
- Definite integrals can also be used to calculate the force exerted on an object submerged in a liquid.

6.6 Moments and Centers of Mass

- Mathematically, the center of mass of a system is the point at which the total mass of the system could be concentrated without changing the moment. Loosely speaking, the center of mass can be thought of as the balancing point of the system.
- For point masses distributed along a number line, the moment of the system with respect to the origin is $M = \sum_{i=1}^{n} m_i x_i$. For point masses distributed in a plane, the moments of the system with respect to the x- and y-axes, respectively, are $M_x = \sum_{i=1}^{n} m_i y_i$ and $M_y = \sum_{i=1}^{n} m_i x_i$, respectively.
- For a lamina bounded above by a function $f(x)$, the moments of the system with respect to the x- and y-axes, respectively, are $M_x = \rho \int_a^b \frac{[f(x)]^2}{2} dx$ and $M_y = \rho \int_a^b x f(x) dx$.
- The x- and y-coordinates of the center of mass can be found by dividing the moments around the y-axis and around the x-axis, respectively, by the total mass. The symmetry principle says that if a region is symmetric with respect to a line, then the centroid of the region lies on the line.
- The theorem of Pappus for volume says that if a region is revolved around an external axis, the volume of the resulting solid is equal to the area of the region multiplied by the distance traveled by the centroid of the region.

6.7 Integrals, Exponential Functions, and Logarithms

- The earlier treatment of logarithms and exponential functions did not define the functions precisely and formally. This section develops the concepts in a mathematically rigorous way.
- The cornerstone of the development is the definition of the natural logarithm in terms of an integral.
- The function e^x is then defined as the inverse of the natural logarithm.
- General exponential functions are defined in terms of e^x, and the corresponding inverse functions are general logarithms.

- Familiar properties of logarithms and exponents still hold in this more rigorous context.

6.8 Exponential Growth and Decay

- Exponential growth and exponential decay are two of the most common applications of exponential functions.
- Systems that exhibit exponential growth follow a model of the form $y = y_0 e^{kt}$.
- In exponential growth, the rate of growth is proportional to the quantity present. In other words, $y' = ky$.
- Systems that exhibit exponential growth have a constant doubling time, which is given by $(\ln 2)/k$.
- Systems that exhibit exponential decay follow a model of the form $y = y_0 e^{-kt}$.
- Systems that exhibit exponential decay have a constant half-life, which is given by $(\ln 2)/k$.

6.9 Calculus of the Hyperbolic Functions

- Hyperbolic functions are defined in terms of exponential functions.
- Term-by-term differentiation yields differentiation formulas for the hyperbolic functions. These differentiation formulas give rise, in turn, to integration formulas.
- With appropriate range restrictions, the hyperbolic functions all have inverses.
- Implicit differentiation yields differentiation formulas for the inverse hyperbolic functions, which in turn give rise to integration formulas.
- The most common physical applications of hyperbolic functions are calculations involving catenaries.

CHAPTER 6 REVIEW EXERCISES

True or False? Justify your answer with a proof or a counterexample.

435. The amount of work to pump the water out of a half-full cylinder is half the amount of work to pump the water out of the full cylinder.

436. If the force is constant, the amount of work to move an object from $x = a$ to $x = b$ is $F(b - a)$.

437. The disk method can be used in any situation in which the washer method is successful at finding the volume of a solid of revolution.

438. If the half-life of seaborgium-266 is 360 ms, then $k = (\ln(2))/360$.

For the following exercises, use the requested method to determine the volume of the solid.

439. The volume that has a base of the ellipse $x^2/4 + y^2/9 = 1$ and cross-sections of an equilateral triangle perpendicular to the y-axis. Use the method of slicing.

440. $y = x^2 - x$, from $x = 1$ to $x = 4$, rotated around the$y$-axis using the washer method

441. $x = y^2$ and $x = 3y$ rotated around the y-axis using the washer method

442. $x = 2y^2 - y^3$, $x = 0$, and $y = 0$ rotated around the x-axis using cylindrical shells

For the following exercises, find

a. the area of the region,

b. the volume of the solid when rotated around the x-axis, and

c. the volume of the solid when rotated around the y-axis. Use whichever method seems most appropriate to you.

443. $y = x^3$, $x = 0$, $y = 0$, and $x = 2$

444. $y = x^2 - x$ and $x = 0$

445. **[T]** $y = \ln(x) + 2$ and $y = x$

446. $y = x^2$ and $y = \sqrt{x}$

447. $y = 5 + x$, $y = x^2$, $x = 0$, and $x = 1$

448. Below $x^2 + y^2 = 1$ and above $y = 1 - x$

449. Find the mass of $\rho = e^{-x}$ on a disk centered at the origin with radius 4.

450. Find the center of mass for $\rho = \tan^2 x$ on $x \in \left(-\frac{\pi}{4}, \frac{\pi}{4}\right)$.

451. Find the mass and the center of mass of $\rho = 1$ on the region bounded by $y = x^5$ and $y = \sqrt{x}$.

For the following exercises, find the requested arc lengths.

452. The length of x for $y = \cosh(x)$ from $x = 0$ to $x = 2$.

453. The length of y for $x = 3 - \sqrt{y}$ from $y = 0$ to $y = 4$

For the following exercises, find the surface area and volume when the given curves are revolved around the specified axis.

454. The shape created by revolving the region between $y = 4 + x$, $y = 3 - x$, $x = 0$, and $x = 2$ rotated around the y-axis.

455. The loudspeaker created by revolving $y = 1/x$ from $x = 1$ to $x = 4$ around the x-axis.

For the following exercises, consider the Karun-3 dam in Iran. Its shape can be approximated as an isosceles triangle with height 205 m and width 388 m. Assume the current depth of the water is 180 m. The density of water is 1000 kg/m ^{3}.

456. Find the total force on the wall of the dam.

457. You are a crime scene investigator attempting to determine the time of death of a victim. It is noon and 45°F outside and the temperature of the body is 78°F. You know the cooling constant is $k = 0.00824$°F/min. When did the victim die, assuming that a human's temperature is 98°F ?

For the following exercise, consider the stock market crash in 1929 in the United States. The table lists the Dow Jones industrial average per year leading up to the crash.

Years after 1920	Value ($)
1	63.90
3	100
5	110
7	160
9	381.17

Source: http://stockcharts.com/freecharts/historical/djia19201940.html

458. **[T]** The best-fit exponential curve to these data is given by $y = 40.71 + 1.224^x$. Why do you think the gains of the market were unsustainable? Use first and second derivatives to help justify your answer. What would this model predict the Dow Jones industrial average to be in 2014 ?

For the following exercises, consider the catenoid, the only solid of revolution that has a minimal surface, or zero mean curvature. A catenoid in nature can be found when stretching soap between two rings.

459. Find the volume of the catenoid $y = \cosh(x)$ from $x = -1$ to $x = 1$ that is created by rotating this curve around the x-axis, as shown here.

460. Find surface area of the catenoid $y = \cosh(x)$ from $x = -1$ to $x = 1$ that is created by rotating this curve around the x-axis.

APPENDIX A | TABLE OF INTEGRALS

Basic Integrals

1. $\int u^n \, du = \frac{u^{n+1}}{n+1} + C, \; n \neq -1$

2. $\int \frac{du}{u} = \ln|u| + C$

3. $\int e^u \, du = e^u + C$

4. $\int a^u \, du = \frac{a^u}{\ln a} + C$

5. $\int \sin u \, du = -\cos u + C$

6. $\int \cos u \, du = \sin u + C$

7. $\int \sec^2 u \, du = \tan u + C$

8. $\int \csc^2 u \, du = -\cot u + C$

9. $\int \sec u \tan u \, du = \sec u + C$

10. $\int \csc u \cot u \, du = -\csc u + C$

11. $\int \tan u \, du = \ln|\sec u| + C$

12. $\int \cot u \, du = \ln|\sin u| + C$

13. $\int \sec u \, du = \ln|\sec u + \tan u| + C$

14. $\int \csc u \, du = \ln|\csc u - \cot u| + C$

15. $\int \frac{du}{\sqrt{a^2 - u^2}} = \sin^{-1} \frac{u}{a} + C$

16. $\int \frac{du}{a^2 + u^2} = \frac{1}{a} \tan^{-1} \frac{u}{a} + C$

17. $\int \frac{du}{u\sqrt{u^2 - a^2}} = \frac{1}{a} \sec^{-1} \frac{u}{a} + C$

Trigonometric Integrals

18. $\int \sin^2 u \, du = \frac{1}{2}u - \frac{1}{4}\sin 2u + C$

19. $\int \cos^2 u\, du = \frac{1}{2}u + \frac{1}{4}\sin 2u + C$

20. $\int \tan^2 u\, du = \tan u - u + C$

21. $\int \cot^2 u\, du = -\cot u - u + C$

22. $\int \sin^3 u\, du = -\frac{1}{3}(2 + \sin^2 u)\cos u + C$

23. $\int \cos^3 u\, du = \frac{1}{3}(2 + \cos^2 u)\sin u + C$

24. $\int \tan^3 u\, du = \frac{1}{2}\tan^2 u + \ln|\cos u| + C$

25. $\int \cot^3 u\, du = -\frac{1}{2}\cot^2 u - \ln|\sin u| + C$

26. $\int \sec^3 u\, du = \frac{1}{2}\sec u \tan u + \frac{1}{2}\ln|\sec u + \tan u| + C$

27. $\int \csc^3 u\, du = -\frac{1}{2}\csc u \cot u + \frac{1}{2}\ln|\csc u - \cot u| + C$

28. $\int \sin^n u\, du = -\frac{1}{n}\sin^{n-1} u \cos u + \frac{n-1}{n}\int \sin^{n-2} u\, du$

29. $\int \cos^n u\, du = \frac{1}{n}\cos^{n-1} u \sin u + \frac{n-1}{n}\int \cos^{n-2} u\, du$

30. $\int \tan^n u\, du = \frac{1}{n-1}\tan^{n-1} u - \int \tan^{n-2} u\, du$

31. $\int \cot^n u\, du = \frac{-1}{n-1}\cot^{n-1} u - \int \cot^{n-2} u\, du$

32. $\int \sec^n u\, du = \frac{1}{n-1}\tan u \sec^{n-2} u + \frac{n-2}{n-1}\int \sec^{n-2} u\, du$

33. $\int \csc^n u\, du = \frac{-1}{n-1}\cot u \csc^{n-2} u + \frac{n-2}{n-1}\int \csc^{n-2} u\, du$

34. $\int \sin au \sin bu\, du = \frac{\sin(a-b)u}{2(a-b)} - \frac{\sin(a+b)u}{2(a+b)} + C$

35. $\int \cos au \cos bu\, du = \frac{\sin(a-b)u}{2(a-b)} + \frac{\sin(a+b)u}{2(a+b)} + C$

36. $\int \sin au \cos bu\, du = -\frac{\cos(a-b)u}{2(a-b)} - \frac{\cos(a+b)u}{2(a+b)} + C$

37. $\int u \sin u\, du = \sin u - u \cos u + C$

38. $\int u \cos u\, du = \cos u + u \sin u + C$

39. $\int u^n \sin u\, du = -u^n \cos u + n\int u^{n-1} \cos u\, du$

40. $\int u^n \cos u\, du = u^n \sin u - n\int u^{n-1} \sin u\, du$

41.
$$\begin{aligned}\int \sin^n u \cos^m u\, du &= -\frac{\sin^{n-1} u \cos^{m+1} u}{n+m} + \frac{n-1}{n+m}\int \sin^{n-2} u \cos^m u\, du \\ &= \frac{\sin^{n+1} u \cos^{m-1} u}{n+m} + \frac{m-1}{n+m}\int \sin^n u \cos^{m-2} u\, du\end{aligned}$$

Exponential and Logarithmic Integrals

42. $\int ue^{au}\,du = \frac{1}{a^2}(au - 1)e^{au} + C$

43. $\int u^n e^{au}\,du = \frac{1}{a}u^n e^{au} - \frac{n}{a}\int u^{n-1} e^{au}\,du$

44. $\int e^{au}\sin bu\,du = \frac{e^{au}}{a^2 + b^2}(a\sin bu - b\cos bu) + C$

45. $\int e^{au}\cos bu\,du = \frac{e^{au}}{a^2 + b^2}(a\cos bu + b\sin bu) + C$

46. $\int \ln u\,du = u\ln u - u + C$

47. $\int u^n \ln u\,du = \frac{u^{n+1}}{(n+1)^2}[(n+1)\ln u - 1] + C$

48. $\int \frac{1}{u\ln u}\,du = \ln|\ln u| + C$

Hyperbolic Integrals

49. $\int \sinh u\,du = \cosh u + C$

50. $\int \cosh u\,du = \sinh u + C$

51. $\int \tanh u\,du = \ln\cosh u + C$

52. $\int \coth u\,du = \ln|\sinh u| + C$

53. $\int \operatorname{sech} u\,du = \tan^{-1}|\sinh u| + C$

54. $\int \operatorname{csch} u\,du = \ln\left|\tanh\frac{1}{2}u\right| + C$

55. $\int \operatorname{sech}^2 u\,du = \tanh u + C$

56. $\int \operatorname{csch}^2 u\,du = -\coth u + C$

57. $\int \operatorname{sech} u \tanh u\,du = -\operatorname{sech} u + C$

58. $\int \operatorname{csch} u \coth u\,du = -\operatorname{csch} u + C$

Inverse Trigonometric Integrals

59. $\int \sin^{-1} u\,du = u\sin^{-1} u + \sqrt{1 - u^2} + C$

60. $\int \cos^{-1} u\,du = u\cos^{-1} u - \sqrt{1 - u^2} + C$

61. $\int \tan^{-1} u\,du = u\tan^{-1} u - \frac{1}{2}\ln\left(1 + u^2\right) + C$

62. $\int u\sin^{-1} u\,du = \frac{2u^2 - 1}{4}\sin^{-1} u + \frac{u\sqrt{1 - u^2}}{4} + C$

63. $\int u\cos^{-1}u\,du = \frac{2u^2-1}{4}\cos^{-1}u - \frac{u\sqrt{1-u^2}}{4} + C$

64. $\int u\tan^{-1}u\,du = \frac{u^2+1}{2}\tan^{-1}u - \frac{u}{2} + C$

65. $\int u^n\sin^{-1}u\,du = \frac{1}{n+1}\left[u^{n+1}\sin^{-1}u - \int\frac{u^{n+1}\,du}{\sqrt{1-u^2}}\right],\ n \neq -1$

66. $\int u^n\cos^{-1}u\,du = \frac{1}{n+1}\left[u^{n+1}\cos^{-1}u + \int\frac{u^{n+1}\,du}{\sqrt{1-u^2}}\right],\ n \neq -1$

67. $\int u^n\tan^{-1}u\,du = \frac{1}{n+1}\left[u^{n+1}\tan^{-1}u - \int\frac{u^{n+1}\,du}{1+u^2}\right],\ n \neq -1$

Integrals Involving $a^2 + u^2$, $a > 0$

68. $\int\sqrt{a^2+u^2}\,du = \frac{u}{2}\sqrt{a^2+u^2} + \frac{a^2}{2}\ln\left(u+\sqrt{a^2+u^2}\right) + C$

69. $\int u^2\sqrt{a^2+u^2}\,du = \frac{u}{8}(a^2+2u^2)\sqrt{a^2+u^2} - \frac{a^4}{8}\ln\left(u+\sqrt{a^2+u^2}\right) + C$

70. $\int\frac{\sqrt{a^2+u^2}}{u}\,du = \sqrt{a^2+u^2} - a\ln\left|\frac{a+\sqrt{a^2+u^2}}{u}\right| + C$

71. $\int\frac{\sqrt{a^2+u^2}}{u^2}\,du = -\frac{\sqrt{a^2+u^2}}{u} + \ln\left(u+\sqrt{a^2+u^2}\right) + C$

72. $\int\frac{du}{\sqrt{a^2+u^2}} = \ln\left(u+\sqrt{a^2+u^2}\right) + C$

73. $\int\frac{u^2\,du}{\sqrt{a^2+u^2}} = \frac{u}{2}\left(\sqrt{a^2+u^2}\right) - \frac{a^2}{2}\ln\left(u+\sqrt{a^2+u^2}\right) + C$

74. $\int\frac{du}{u\sqrt{a^2+u^2}} = -\frac{1}{a}\ln\left|\frac{\sqrt{a^2+u^2}+a}{u}\right| + C$

75. $\int\frac{du}{u^2\sqrt{a^2+u^2}} = -\frac{\sqrt{a^2+u^2}}{a^2u} + C$

76. $\int\frac{du}{\left(a^2+u^2\right)^{3/2}} = \frac{u}{a^2\sqrt{a^2+u^2}} + C$

Integrals Involving $u^2 - a^2$, $a > 0$

77. $\int\sqrt{u^2-a^2}\,du = \frac{u}{2}\sqrt{u^2-a^2} - \frac{a^2}{2}\ln\left|u+\sqrt{u^2-a^2}\right| + C$

78. $\int u^2\sqrt{u^2-a^2}\,du = \frac{u}{8}(2u^2-a^2)\sqrt{u^2-a^2} - \frac{a^4}{8}\ln\left|u+\sqrt{u^2-a^2}\right| + C$

79. $\int\frac{\sqrt{u^2-a^2}}{u}\,du = \sqrt{u^2-a^2} - a\cos^{-1}\frac{a}{|u|} + C$

80. $\int\frac{\sqrt{u^2-a^2}}{u^2}\,du = -\frac{\sqrt{u^2-a^2}}{u} + \ln\left|u+\sqrt{u^2-a^2}\right| + C$

81. $\int \frac{du}{\sqrt{u^2 - a^2}} = \ln\left|u + \sqrt{u^2 - a^2}\right| + C$

82. $\int \frac{u^2\,du}{\sqrt{u^2 - a^2}} = \frac{u}{2}\sqrt{u^2 - a^2} + \frac{a^2}{2}\ln\left|u + \sqrt{u^2 - a^2}\right| + C$

83. $\int \frac{du}{u^2\sqrt{u^2 - a^2}} = \frac{\sqrt{u^2 - a^2}}{a^2 u} + C$

84. $\int \frac{du}{\left(u^2 - a^2\right)^{3/2}} = -\frac{u}{a^2\sqrt{u^2 - a^2}} + C$

Integrals Involving $a^2 - u^2$, $a > 0$

85. $\int \sqrt{a^2 - u^2}\,du = \frac{u}{2}\sqrt{a^2 - u^2} + \frac{a^2}{2}\sin^{-1}\frac{u}{a} + C$

86. $\int u^2\sqrt{a^2 - u^2}\,du = \frac{u}{8}\left(2u^2 - a^2\right)\sqrt{a^2 - u^2} + \frac{a^4}{8}\sin^{-1}\frac{u}{a} + C$

87. $\int \frac{\sqrt{a^2 - u^2}}{u}\,du = \sqrt{a^2 - u^2} - a\ln\left|\frac{a + \sqrt{a^2 - u^2}}{u}\right| + C$

88. $\int \frac{\sqrt{a^2 - u^2}}{u^2}\,du = -\frac{1}{u}\sqrt{a^2 - u^2} - \sin^{-1}\frac{u}{a} + C$

89. $\int \frac{u^2\,du}{\sqrt{a^2 - u^2}} = -\frac{u}{u}\sqrt{a^2 - u^2} + \frac{a^2}{2}\sin^{-1}\frac{u}{a} + C$

90. $\int \frac{du}{u\sqrt{a^2 - u^2}} = -\frac{1}{a}\ln\left|\frac{a + \sqrt{a^2 - u^2}}{u}\right| + C$

91. $\int \frac{du}{u^2\sqrt{a^2 - u^2}} = -\frac{1}{a^2 u}\sqrt{a^2 - u^2} + C$

92. $\int \left(a^2 - u^2\right)^{3/2}\,du = -\frac{u}{8}\left(2u^2 - 5a^2\right)\sqrt{a^2 - u^2} + \frac{3a^4}{8}\sin^{-1}\frac{u}{a} + C$

93. $\int \frac{du}{\left(a^2 - u^2\right)^{3/2}} = -\frac{u}{a^2\sqrt{a^2 - u^2}} + C$

Integrals Involving $2au - u^2$, $a > 0$

94. $\int \sqrt{2au - u^2}\,du = \frac{u - a}{2}\sqrt{2au - u^2} + \frac{a^2}{2}\cos^{-1}\left(\frac{a - u}{a}\right) + C$

95. $\int \frac{du}{\sqrt{2au - u^2}} = \cos^{-1}\left(\frac{a - u}{a}\right) + C$

96. $\int u\sqrt{2au - u^2}\,du = \frac{2u^2 - au - 3a^2}{6}\sqrt{2au - u^2} + \frac{a^3}{2}\cos^{-1}\left(\frac{a - u}{a}\right) + C$

97. $\int \frac{du}{u\sqrt{2au - u^2}} = -\frac{\sqrt{2au - u^2}}{au} + C$

Integrals Involving $a + bu$, $a \neq 0$

98. $\int \frac{u\,du}{a+bu} = \frac{1}{b^2}(a + bu - a\ln|a + bu|) + C$

99. $\int \frac{u^2\,du}{a+bu} = \frac{1}{2b^3}\left[(a+bu)^2 - 4a(a+bu) + 2a^2\ln|a+bu|\right] + C$

100. $\int \frac{du}{u(a+bu)} = \frac{1}{a}\ln\left|\frac{u}{a+bu}\right| + C$

101. $\int \frac{du}{u^2(a+bu)} = -\frac{1}{au} + \frac{b}{a^2}\ln\left|\frac{a+bu}{u}\right| + C$

102. $\int \frac{u\,du}{(a+bu)^2} = \frac{a}{b^2(a+bu)} + \frac{1}{b^2}\ln|a+bu| + C$

103. $\int \frac{u\,du}{u\,(a+bu)^2} = \frac{1}{a(a+bu)} - \frac{1}{a^2}\ln\left|\frac{a+bu}{u}\right| + C$

104. $\int \frac{u^2\,du}{(a+bu)^2} = \frac{1}{b^3}\left(a + bu - \frac{a^2}{a+bu} - 2a\ln|a+bu|\right) + C$

105. $\int u\sqrt{a+bu}\,du = \frac{2}{15b^2}(3bu - 2a)(a+bu)^{3/2} + C$

106. $\int \frac{u\,du}{\sqrt{a+bu}} = \frac{2}{3b^2}(bu - 2a)\sqrt{a+bu} + C$

107. $\int \frac{u^2\,du}{\sqrt{a+bu}} = \frac{2}{15b^3}\left(8a^2 + 3b^2u^2 - 4abu\right)\sqrt{a+bu} + C$

108. $$\begin{aligned}\int \frac{du}{u\sqrt{a+bu}} &= \frac{1}{\sqrt{a}}\ln\left|\frac{\sqrt{a+bu}-\sqrt{a}}{\sqrt{a+bu}+\sqrt{a}}\right| + C, \quad \text{if } a > 0 \\ &= \frac{2}{\sqrt{-a}}\tan - 1\sqrt{\frac{a+bu}{-a}} + C, \quad \text{if } a < 0\end{aligned}$$

109. $\int \frac{\sqrt{a+bu}}{u}\,du = 2\sqrt{a+bu} + a\int \frac{du}{u\sqrt{a+bu}}$

110. $\int \frac{\sqrt{a+bu}}{u^2}\,du = -\frac{\sqrt{a+bu}}{u} + \frac{b}{2}\int \frac{du}{u\sqrt{a+bu}}$

111. $\int u^n\sqrt{a+bu}\,du = \frac{2}{b(2n+3)}\left[u^n(a+bu)^{3/2} - na\int u^{n-1}\sqrt{a+bu}\,du\right]$

112. $\int \frac{u^n\,du}{\sqrt{a+bu}} = \frac{2u^n\sqrt{a+bu}}{b(2n+1)} - \frac{2na}{b(2n+1)}\int \frac{u^{n-1}\,du}{\sqrt{a+bu}}$

113. $\int \frac{du}{u^n\sqrt{a+bu}} = -\frac{\sqrt{a+bu}}{a(n-1)u^{n-1}} - \frac{b(2n-3)}{2a(n-1)}\int \frac{du}{u^{n-1}\sqrt{a+bu}}$

APPENDIX B | TABLE OF DERIVATIVES

General Formulas

1. $\frac{d}{dx}(c) = 0$

2. $\frac{d}{dx}(f(x) + g(x)) = f'(x) + g'(x)$

3. $\frac{d}{dx}(f(x)g(x)) = f'(x)g(x) + f(x)g'(x)$

4. $\frac{d}{dx}(x^n) = nx^{n-1}$, for real numbers n

5. $\frac{d}{dx}(cf(x)) = cf'(x)$

6. $\frac{d}{dx}(f(x) - g(x)) = f'(x) - g'(x)$

7. $\frac{d}{dx}\left(\frac{f(x)}{g(x)}\right) = \frac{g(x)f'(x) - f(x)g'(x)}{(g(x))^2}$

8. $\frac{d}{dx}[f(g(x))] = f'(g(x)) \cdot g'(x)$

Trigonometric Functions

9. $\frac{d}{dx}(\sin x) = \cos x$

10. $\frac{d}{dx}(\tan x) = \sec^2 x$

11. $\frac{d}{dx}(\sec x) = \sec x \tan x$

12. $\frac{d}{dx}(\cos x) = -\sin x$

13. $\frac{d}{dx}(\cot x) = -\csc^2 x$

14. $\frac{d}{dx}(\csc x) = -\csc x \cot x$

Inverse Trigonometric Functions

15. $\frac{d}{dx}\left(\sin^{-1} x\right) = \frac{1}{\sqrt{1 - x^2}}$

16. $\frac{d}{dx}\left(\tan^{-1} x\right) = \frac{1}{1 + x^2}$

17. $\frac{d}{dx}\left(\sec^{-1} x\right) = \frac{1}{|x|\sqrt{x^2 - 1}}$

18. $\frac{d}{dx}\left(\cos^{-1} x\right) = -\frac{1}{\sqrt{1 - x^2}}$

19. $\frac{d}{dx}\left(\cot^{-1} x\right) = -\frac{1}{1 + x^2}$

20. $\frac{d}{dx}\left(\csc^{-1} x\right) = -\frac{1}{|x|\sqrt{x^2 - 1}}$

Exponential and Logarithmic Functions

21. $\frac{d}{dx}(e^x) = e^x$

22. $\frac{d}{dx}(\ln|x|) = \frac{1}{x}$

23. $\frac{d}{dx}(b^x) = b^x \ln b$

24. $\frac{d}{dx}(\log_b x) = \frac{1}{x \ln b}$

Hyperbolic Functions

25. $\frac{d}{dx}(\sinh x) = \cosh x$

26. $\frac{d}{dx}(\tanh x) = \operatorname{sech}^2 x$

27. $\frac{d}{dx}(\operatorname{sech} x) = -\operatorname{sech} x \tanh x$

28. $\frac{d}{dx}(\cosh x) = \sinh x$

29. $\frac{d}{dx}(\coth x) = -\operatorname{csch}^2 x$

30. $\frac{d}{dx}(\operatorname{csch} x) = -\operatorname{csch} x \coth x$

Inverse Hyperbolic Functions

31. $\frac{d}{dx}\left(\sinh^{-1} x\right) = \frac{1}{\sqrt{x^2 + 1}}$

32. $\frac{d}{dx}\left(\tanh^{-1} x\right) = \frac{1}{1 - x^2}(|x| < 1)$

33. $\frac{d}{dx}\left(\operatorname{sech}^{-1} x\right) = -\frac{1}{x\sqrt{1 - x^2}} \quad (0 < x < 1)$

34. $\frac{d}{dx}\left(\cosh^{-1} x\right) = \frac{1}{\sqrt{x^2 - 1}} \quad (x > 1)$

35. $\frac{d}{dx}\left(\coth^{-1} x\right) = \frac{1}{1 - x^2} \quad (|x| > 1)$

36. $\frac{d}{dx}\left(\operatorname{csch}^{-1} x\right) = -\frac{1}{|x|\sqrt{1 + x^2}} (x \neq 0)$

APPENDIX C | REVIEW OF PRE-CALCULUS

Formulas from Geometry

$A =$ area, $V =$ Volume, and $S =$ lateral surface area

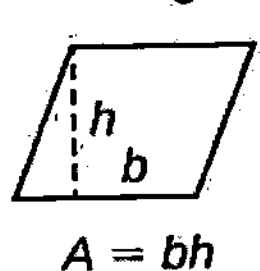

$A = bh$

Triangle

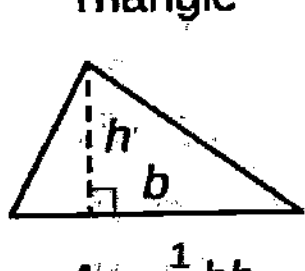

$A = \frac{1}{2}bh$

Trapezoid

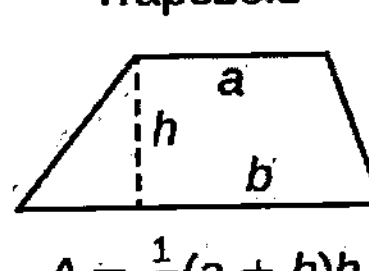

$A = \frac{1}{2}(a + b)h$

Circle

$A = \pi r^2$
$C = 2\pi r$

Sector

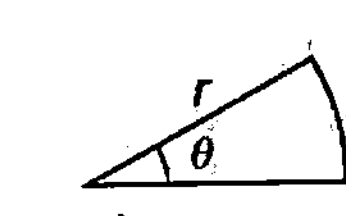

$A = \frac{1}{2}r^2\theta$
$s = r\theta$ (θ in radians)

Cylinder

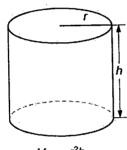

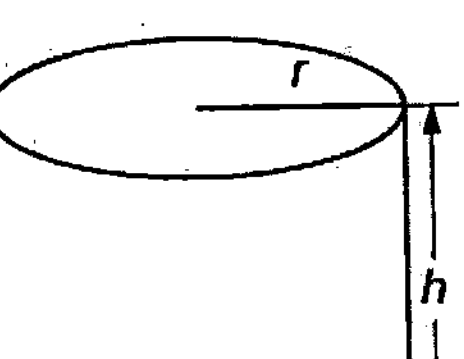

$V = \pi r^2 h$
$S = 2\pi rh$

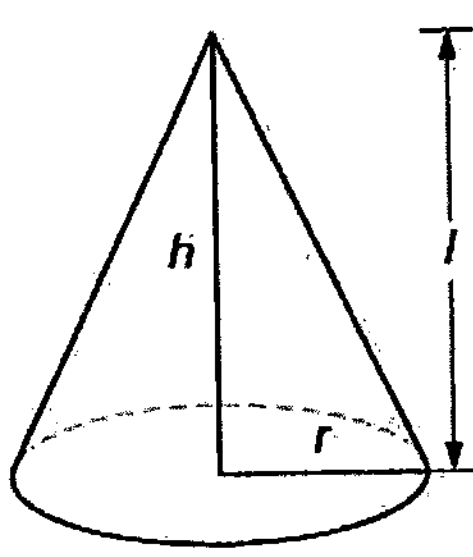

$V = \frac{1}{3}\pi r^2 h$
$S = \pi rl$

Sphere

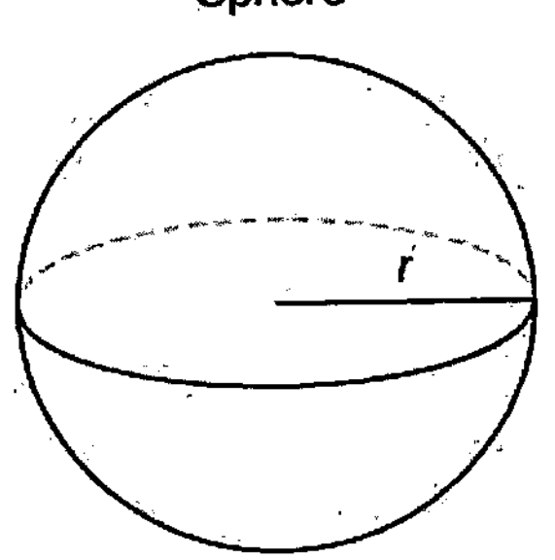

$V = \frac{4}{3}\pi r^3$
$S = 4\pi r^2$

Formulas from Algebra

Laws of Exponents

$$x^m x^n = x^{m+n} \qquad \frac{x^m}{x^n} = x^{m-n} \qquad (x^m)^n = x^{mn}$$

$$x^{-n} = \frac{1}{x^n} \qquad (xy)^n = x^n y^n \qquad \left(\frac{x}{y}\right)^n = \frac{x^n}{y^n}$$

$$x^{1/n} = \sqrt[n]{x} \qquad \sqrt[n]{xy} = \sqrt[n]{x}\sqrt[n]{y} \qquad \sqrt[n]{\frac{x}{y}} = \frac{\sqrt[n]{x}}{\sqrt[n]{y}}$$

$$x^{m/n} = \sqrt[n]{x^m} = (\sqrt[n]{x})^m$$

Special Factorizations

$$x^2 - y^2 = (x + y)(x - y)$$
$$x^3 + y^3 = (x + y)\left(x^2 - xy + y^2\right)$$
$$x^3 - y^3 = (x - y)\left(x^2 + xy + y^2\right)$$

Quadratic Formula

If $ax^2 + bx + c = 0$, then $x = \dfrac{-b \pm \sqrt{b^2 - 4ca}}{2a}$.

Binomial Theorem

$$(a+b)^n = a^n + \binom{n}{1}a^{n-1}b + \binom{n}{2}a^{n-2}b^2 + \cdots + \binom{n}{n-1}ab^{n-1} + b^n,$$

where $\binom{n}{k} = \dfrac{n(n-1)(n-2)\cdots(n-k+1)}{k(k-1)(k-2)\cdots 3\cdot 2\cdot 1} = \dfrac{n!}{k!(n-k)!}$

Formulas from Trigonometry

Right-Angle Trigonometry

$\sin\theta = \dfrac{\text{opp}}{\text{hyp}}$ $\quad \csc\theta = \dfrac{\text{hyp}}{\text{opp}}$

$\cos\theta = \dfrac{\text{adj}}{\text{hyp}}$ $\quad \sec\theta = \dfrac{\text{hyp}}{\text{adj}}$

$\tan\theta = \dfrac{\text{opp}}{\text{adj}}$ $\quad \cot\theta = \dfrac{\text{adj}}{\text{opp}}$

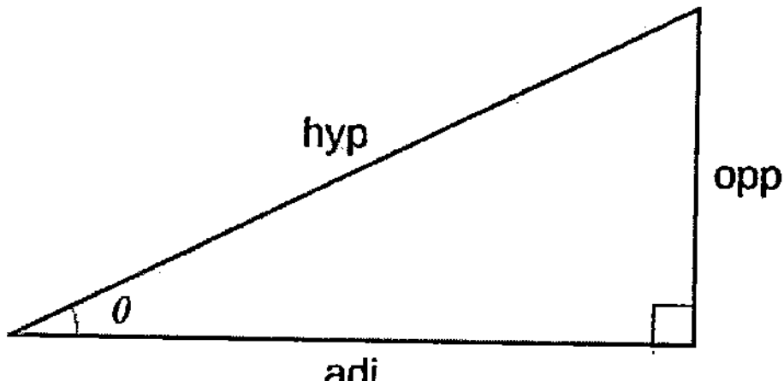

Trigonometric Functions of Important Angles

θ	Radians	$\sin\theta$	$\cos\theta$	$\tan\theta$
0°	0	0	1	0
30°	$\pi/6$	1/2	$\sqrt{3}/2$	$\sqrt{3}/3$
45°	$\pi/4$	$\sqrt{2}/2$	$\sqrt{2}/2$	1
60°	$\pi/3$	$\sqrt{3}/2$	1/2	$\sqrt{3}$
90°	$\pi/2$	1	0	—

Fundamental Identities

$$\sin^2\theta + \cos^2\theta = 1 \qquad \sin(-\theta) = -\sin\theta$$
$$1 + \tan^2\theta = \sec^2\theta \qquad \cos(-\theta) = \cos\theta$$
$$1 + \cot^2\theta = \csc^2\theta \qquad \tan(-\theta) = -\tan\theta$$
$$\sin\left(\frac{\pi}{2} - \theta\right) = \cos\theta \qquad \sin(\theta + 2\pi) = \sin\theta$$
$$\cos\left(\frac{\pi}{2} - \theta\right) = \sin\theta \qquad \cos(\theta + 2\pi) = \cos\theta$$
$$\tan\left(\frac{\pi}{2} - \theta\right) = \cot\theta \qquad \tan(\theta + \pi) = \tan\theta$$

Law of Sines

$$\frac{\sin A}{a} = \frac{\sin B}{b} = \frac{\sin C}{c}$$

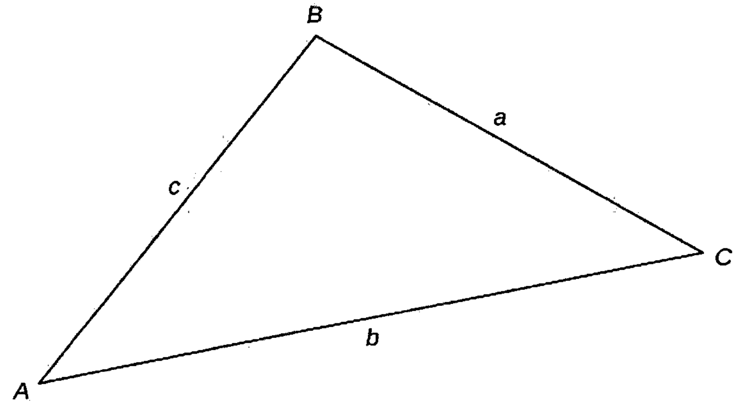

Law of Cosines

$$a^2 = b^2 + c^2 - 2bc\cos A$$
$$b^2 = a^2 + c^2 - 2ac\cos B$$
$$c^2 = a^2 + b^2 - 2ab\cos C$$

Addition and Subtraction Formulas

$$\sin(x + y) = \sin x\cos y + \cos x\sin y$$
$$\sin(x - y) = \sin x\cos y - \cos x\sin y$$
$$\cos(x + y) = \cos x\cos y - \sin x\sin y$$
$$\cos(x - y) = \cos x\cos y + \sin x\sin y$$
$$\tan(x + y) = \frac{\tan x + \tan y}{1 - \tan x\tan y}$$
$$\tan(x - y) = \frac{\tan x - \tan y}{1 + \tan x\tan y}$$

Double-Angle Formulas

$$\sin 2x = 2\sin x\cos x$$
$$\cos 2x = \cos^2 x - \sin^2 x = 2\cos^2 x - 1 = 1 - 2\sin^2 x$$
$$\tan 2x = \frac{2\tan x}{1 - \tan^2 x}$$

Half-Angle Formulas

$$\begin{aligned}\sin^2 x &= \frac{1-\cos 2x}{2}\\ \cos^2 x &= \frac{1+\cos 2x}{2}\end{aligned}$$

ANSWER KEY

Chapter 1

Checkpoint

1.1. $f(1) = 3$ and $f(a+h) = a^2 + 2ah + h^2 - 3a - 3h + 5$

1.2. Domain = $\{x|x \le 2\}$, range = $\{y|y \ge 5\}$

1.3. $x = 0, 2, 3$

1.4. $\left(\frac{f}{g}\right)(x) = \frac{x^2+3}{2x-5}$. The domain is $\left\{x|x \ne \frac{5}{2}\right\}$.

1.5. $(f \circ g)(x) = 2 - 5\sqrt{x}$.

1.6. $(g \circ f)(x) = 0.63x$

1.7. $f(x)$ is odd.

1.8. Domain = $(-\infty, \infty)$, range = $\{y|y \ge -4\}$.

1.9. $m = 1/2$. The point-slope form is $y - 4 = \frac{1}{2}(x-1)$. The slope-intercept form is $y = \frac{1}{2}x + \frac{7}{2}$.

1.10. The zeros are $x = 1 \pm \sqrt{3}/3$. The parabola opens upward.

1.11. The domain is the set of real numbers x such that $x \ne 1/2$. The range is the set $\{y|y \ne 5/2\}$.

1.12. The domain of f is $(-\infty, \infty)$. The domain of g is $\{x|x \ge 1/5\}$.

1.13. Algebraic

1.14.

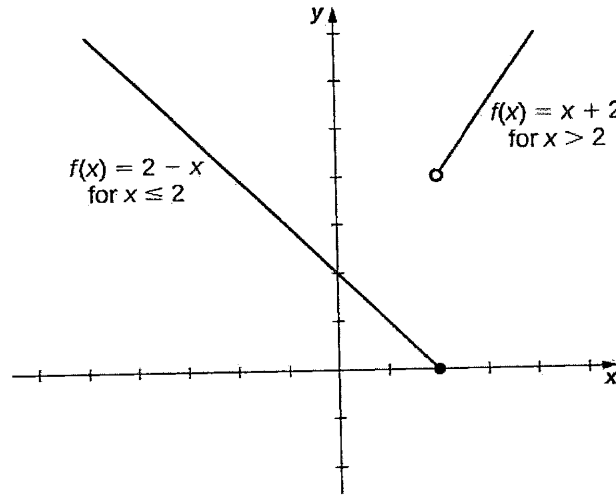

1.15. $C(x) = \begin{cases} 49, & 0 < x \le 1 \\ 70, & 1 < x \le 2 \\ 91, & 2 < x \le 3 \end{cases}$

1.16. Shift the graph $y = x^2$ to the left 1 unit, reflect about the x-axis, then shift down 4 units.

1.17. $7\pi/6$; $330°$

1.18. $\cos(3\pi/4) = -\sqrt{2}/2$; $\sin(-\pi/6) = -1/2$

1.19. 10 ft

1.20. $\theta = \frac{3\pi}{2} + 2n\pi, \frac{\pi}{6} + 2n\pi, \frac{5\pi}{6} + 2n\pi$ for $n = 0, \pm 1, \pm 2, \ldots$

1.22. To graph $f(x) = 3\sin(4x) - 5$, the graph of $y = \sin(x)$ needs to be compressed horizontally by a factor of 4, then stretched vertically by a factor of 3, then shifted down 5 units. The function f will have a period of $\pi/2$ and an amplitude of 3.

1.23. No.

1.24. $f^{-1}(x) = \frac{2x}{x-3}$. The domain of f^{-1} is $\{x|x \neq 3\}$. The range of f^{-1} is $\{y|y \neq 2\}$.

1.25.

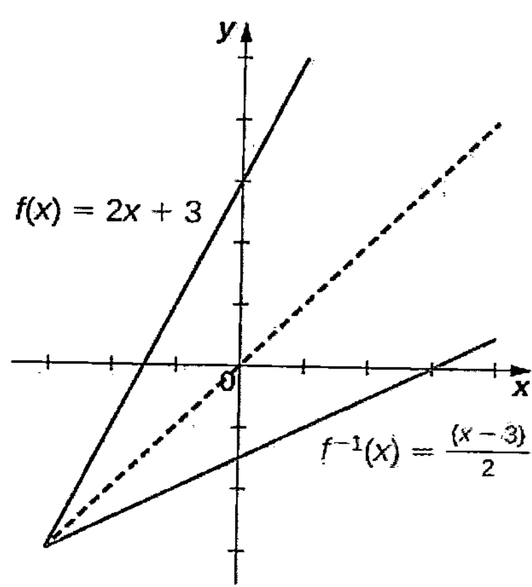

1.26. The domain of f^{-1} is $(0, \infty)$. The range of f^{-1} is $(-\infty, 0)$. The inverse function is given by the formula $f^{-1}(x) = -1/\sqrt{x}$.

1.27. $f(4) = 900$; $f(10) = 24,300$.

1.28. $x/(2y^3)$

1.29. $A(t) = 750e^{0.04t}$. After 30 years, there will be approximately $\$2,490.09$.

1.30. $x = \frac{\ln 3}{2}$

1.31. $x = \frac{1}{e}$

1.32. 1.29248

1.33. The magnitude 8.4 earthquake is roughly 10 times as severe as the magnitude 7.4 earthquake.

1.34. $(x^2 + x^{-2})/2$

1.35. $\frac{1}{2}\ln(3) \approx 0.5493$.

Section Exercises

1. a. Domain = $\{-3, -2, -1, 0, 1, 2, 3\}$, range = $\{0, 1, 4, 9\}$ b. Yes, a function

3. a. Domain = $\{0, 1, 2, 3\}$, range = $\{-3, -2, -1, 0, 1, 2, 3\}$ b. No, not a function

5. a. Domain = $\{3, 5, 8, 10, 15, 21, 33\}$, range = $\{0, 1, 2, 3\}$ b. Yes, a function

7. a. -2 b. 3 c. 13 d. $-5x - 2$ e. $5a - 2$ f. $5a + 5h - 2$

9. a. Undefined b. 2 c. $\frac{2}{3}$ d. $-\frac{2}{x}$ e $\frac{2}{a}$ f. $\frac{2}{a+h}$

11. a. $\sqrt{5}$ b. $\sqrt{11}$ c. $\sqrt{23}$ d. $\sqrt{-6x+5}$ e. $\sqrt{6a+5}$ f. $\sqrt{6a+6h+5}$

13. a. 9 b. 9 c. 9 d. 9 e. 9 f. 9

15. $x \geq \frac{1}{8}$; $y \geq 0$; $x = \frac{1}{8}$; no y-intercept

17. $x \geq -2$; $y \geq -1$; $x = -1$; $y = -1 + \sqrt{2}$

19. $x \neq 4$; $y \neq 0$; no x-intercept; $y = -\frac{3}{4}$

21. $x > 5$; $y > 0$; no intercepts

23.

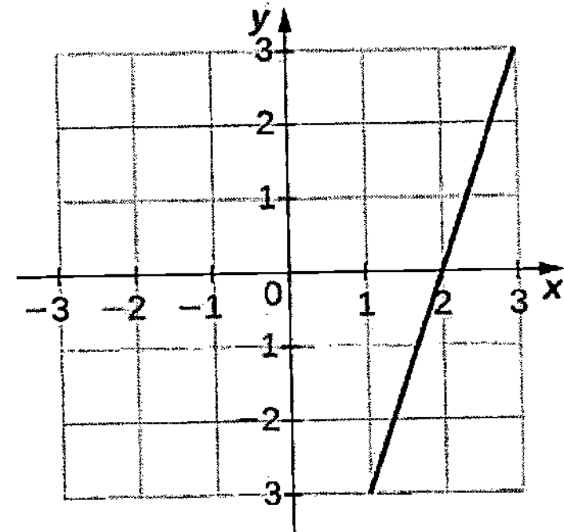

25.

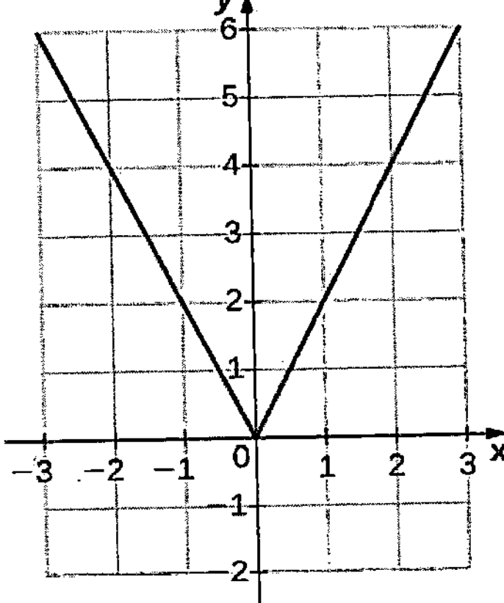

27.

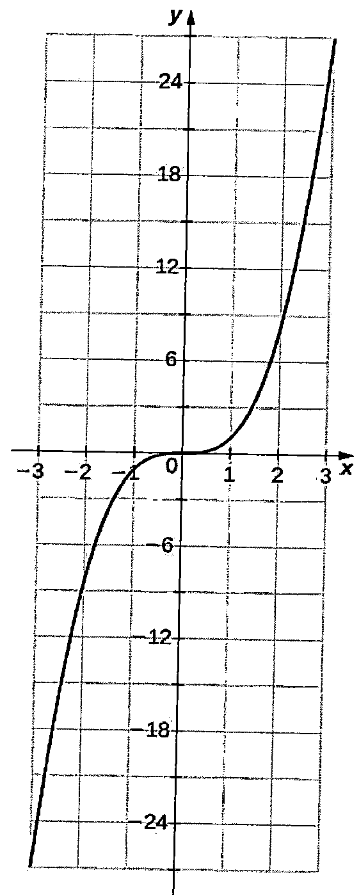

29. Function; a. Domain: all real numbers, range: $y \geq 0$ b. $x = \pm 1$ c. $y = 1$ d. $-1 < x < 0$ and $1 < x < \infty$ e. $-\infty < x < -1$ and $0 < x < 1$ f. Not constant g. y-axis h. Even

31. Function; a. Domain: all real numbers, range: $-1.5 \leq y \leq 1.5$ b. $x = 0$ c. $y = 0$ d. all real numbers e. None f. Not constant g. Origin h. Odd

33. Function; a. Domain: $-\infty < x < \infty$, range: $-2 \leq y \leq 2$ b. $x = 0$ c. $y = 0$ d. $-2 < x < 2$ e. Not decreasing f. $-\infty < x < -2$ and $2 < x < \infty$ g. Origin h. Odd

35. Function; a. Domain: $-4 \leq x \leq 4$, range: $-4 \leq y \leq 4$ b. $x = 1.2$ c. $y = 4$ d. Not increasing e. $0 < x < 4$ f. $-4 < x < 0$ g. No Symmetry h. Neither

37. a. $5x^2 + x - 8;$ all real numbers b. $-5x^2 + x - 8;$ all real numbers c. $5x^3 - 40x^2;$ all real numbers d. $\frac{x-8}{5x^2};\ x \neq 0$

39. a. $-2x + 6;$ all real numbers b. $-2x^2 + 2x + 12;$ all real numbers c. $-x^4 + 2x^3 + 12x^2 - 18x - 27;$ all real numbers d. $-\frac{x+3}{x+1};\ x \neq -1, 3$

41. a. $6 + \frac{2}{x};\ x \neq 0$ b. 6; $x \neq 0$ c. $\frac{6}{x} + \frac{1}{x^2};\ x \neq 0$ d. $6x + 1;\ x \neq 0$

43. a. $4x + 3;$ all real numbers b. $4x + 15;$ all real numbers

45. a. $x^4 - 6x^2 + 16;$ all real numbers b. $x^4 + 14x^2 + 46;$ all real numbers

47. a. $\frac{3x}{4+x};\ x \neq 0, -4$ b. $\frac{4x+2}{3};\ x \neq -\frac{1}{2}$

49. a. Yes, because there is only one winner for each year. b. No, because there are three teams that won more than once during the years 2001 to 2012.

51. a. $V(s) = s^3$ b. $V(11.8) \approx 1643;$ a cube of side length 11.8 each has a volume of approximately 1643 cubic units.

53. a. $N(x) = 15x$ b. i. $N(20) = 15(20) = 300;$ therefore, the vehicle can travel 300 mi on a full tank of gas. Ii. $N(15) = 225;$ therefore, the vehicle can travel 225 mi on 3/4 of a tank of gas. c. Domain: $0 \leq x \leq 20;$ range: $[0, 300]$ d. The driver had to stop at least once, given that it takes approximately 39 gal of gas to drive a total of 578 mi.

55. a. $A(t) = A(r(t)) = \pi \cdot \left(6 - \frac{5}{t^2 + 1}\right)^2$ b. Exact: $\frac{121\pi}{4};$ approximately 95 cm^2 c. $C(t) = C(r(t)) = 2\pi\left(6 - \frac{5}{t^2 + 1}\right)$ d. Exact: $11\pi;$ approximately 35 cm

57. a. $S(x) = 8.5x + 750$ b. \$962.50, \$1090, \$1217.50 c. 77 skateboards

59. a. −1 b. Decreasing

61. a. 3/4 b. Increasing

63. a. 4/3 b. Increasing

65. a. 0 b. Horizontal

67. $y = -6x + 9$

69. $y = \frac{1}{3}x + 4$

71. $y = \frac{1}{2}x$

73. $y = \frac{3}{5}x - 3$

75. a. $(m = 2,\ b = -3)$ b.

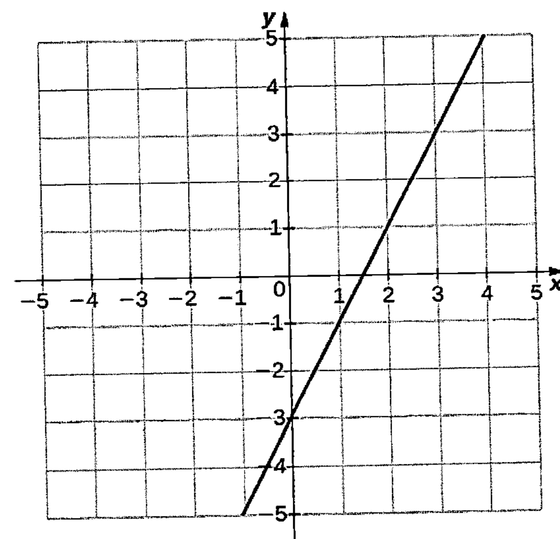

77. a. $(m = -6,\ b = 0)$ b.

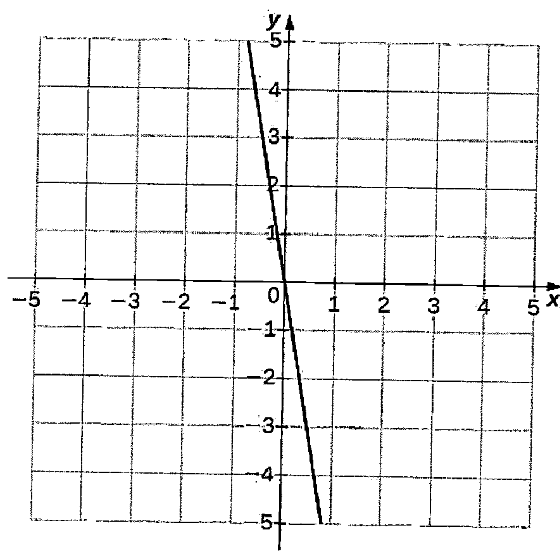

79. a. $(m = 0,\ b = -6)$ b.

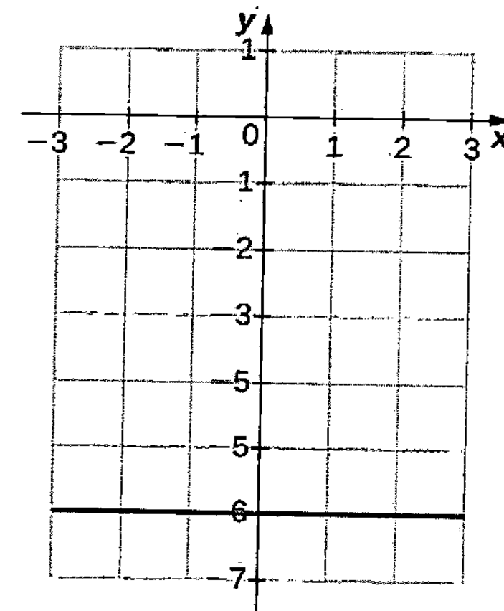

81. a. $\left(m = -\frac{2}{3},\ b = 2\right)$ b.

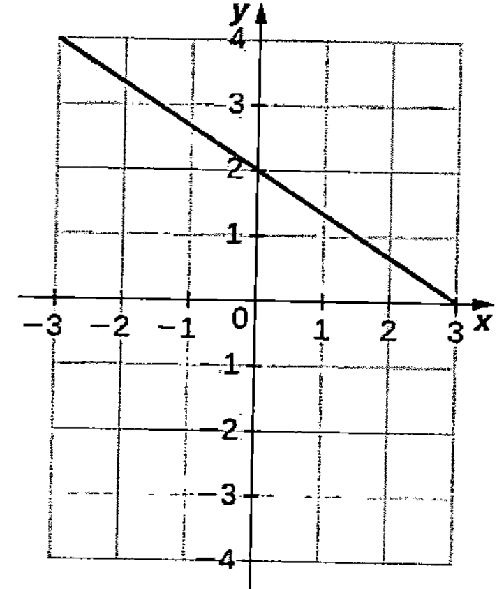

83. a. 2 b. $\frac{5}{2}, -1;$ c. −5 d. Both ends rise e. Neither

85. a. 2 b. $\pm\sqrt{2}$ c. −1 d. Both ends rise e. Even

87. a. 3 b. 0, $\pm\sqrt{3}$ c. 0 d. Left end rises, right end falls e. Odd

89.

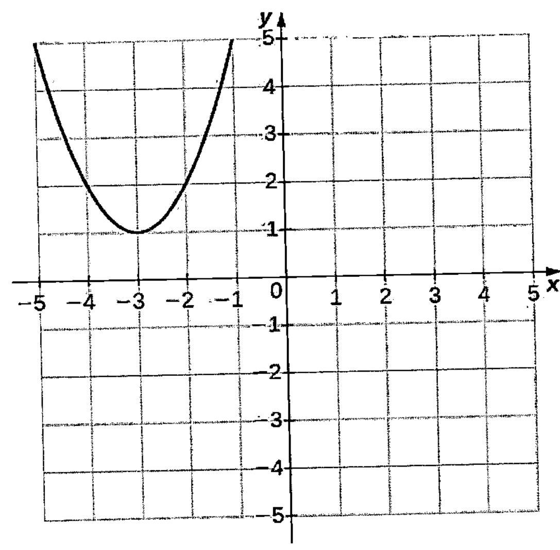

91.

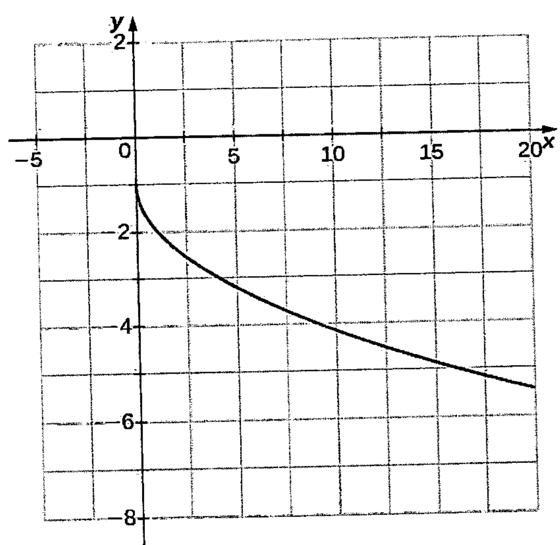

93.

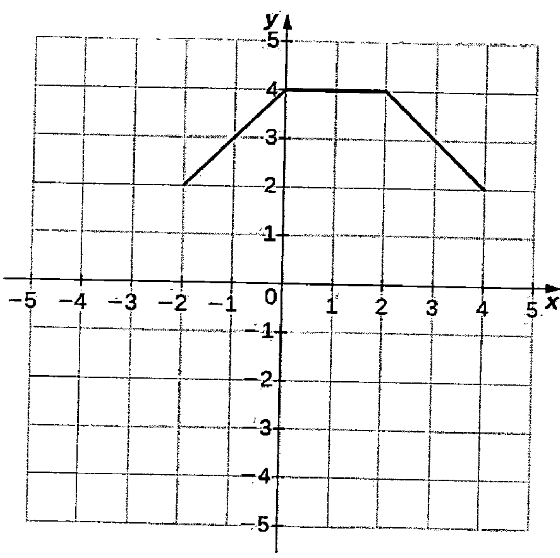

95. a. $13, -3, 5$ b.

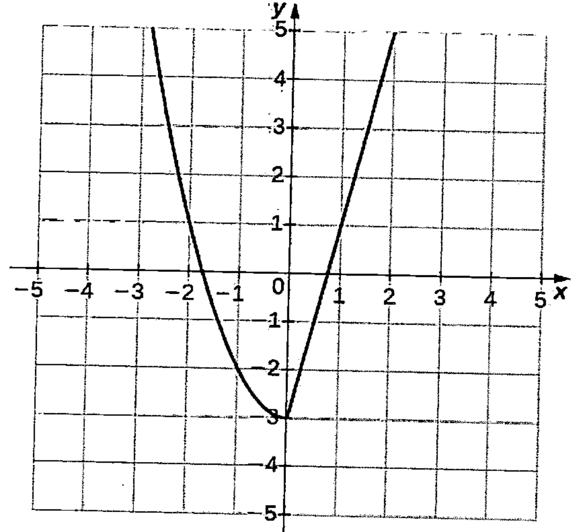

97. a. $\frac{-3}{2}, \frac{-1}{2}, 4$ b.

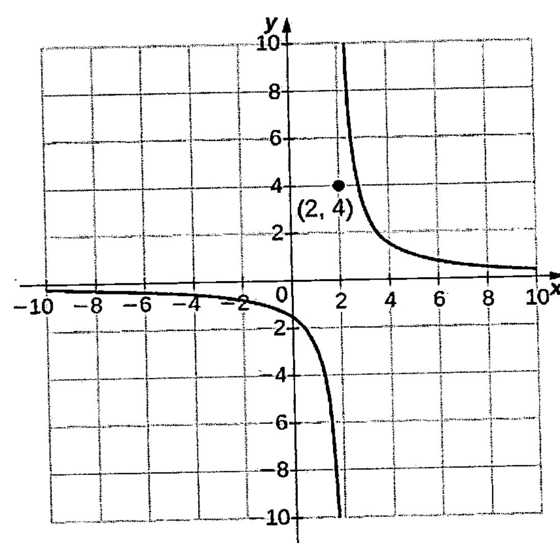

99. True; $n = 3$

101. False; $f(x) = x^b$, where b is a real-valued constant, is a power function

103. a. $V(t) = -2733t + 20500$ b. $(0,\ 20,\ 500)$ means that the initial purchase price of the equipment is \$20,500; $(7.5,\ 0)$ means that in 7.5 years the computer equipment has no value. c. \$6835 d. In approximately 6.4 years

105. a. $C = 0.75x + 125$ b. \$245 c. 167 cupcakes

107. a. $V(t) = -1500t + 26{,}000$ b. In 4 years, the value of the car is \$20,000.

109. \$30,337.50

111. 96% of the total capacity

113. $\frac{4\pi}{3}$ rad

115. $\frac{-\pi}{3}$

117. $\frac{11\pi}{6}$ rad

119. $210°$

121. $-540°$

123. -0.5

125. $-\frac{\sqrt{2}}{2}$

127. $\frac{\sqrt{3}-1}{2\sqrt{2}}$

129. a. $b = 5.7$ b. $\sin A = \frac{4}{7}$, $\cos A = \frac{5.7}{7}$, $\tan A = \frac{4}{5.7}$, $\csc A = \frac{7}{4}$, $\sec A = \frac{7}{5.7}$, $\cot A = \frac{5.7}{4}$

131. a. $c = 151.7$ b. $\sin A = 0.5623$, $\cos A = 0.8273$, $\tan A = 0.6797$, $\csc A = 1.778$, $\sec A = 1.209$, $\cot A = 1.471$

133. a. $c = 85$ b. $\sin A = \frac{84}{85}$, $\cos A = \frac{13}{85}$, $\tan A = \frac{84}{13}$, $\csc A = \frac{85}{84}$, $\sec A = \frac{85}{13}$, $\cot A = \frac{13}{84}$

135. a. $y = \frac{24}{25}$ b. $\sin\theta = \frac{24}{25}$, $\cos\theta = \frac{7}{25}$, $\tan\theta = \frac{24}{7}$, $\csc\theta = \frac{25}{24}$, $\sec\theta = \frac{25}{7}$, $\cot\theta = \frac{7}{24}$

137. a. $x = \frac{-\sqrt{2}}{3}$ b. $\sin\theta = \frac{\sqrt{7}}{3}$, $\cos\theta = \frac{-\sqrt{2}}{3}$, $\tan\theta = \frac{-\sqrt{14}}{2}$, $\csc\theta = \frac{3\sqrt{7}}{7}$, $\sec\theta = \frac{-3\sqrt{2}}{2}$, $\cot\theta = \frac{-\sqrt{14}}{7}$

139. $\sec^2 x$

141. $\sin^2 x$

143. $\sec^2\theta$

145. $\frac{1}{\sin t} = \csc t$

155. $\left\{\frac{\pi}{6}, \frac{5\pi}{6}\right\}$

157. $\left\{\frac{\pi}{4}, \frac{3\pi}{4}, \frac{5\pi}{4}, \frac{7\pi}{4}\right\}$

159. $\left\{\frac{2\pi}{3}, \frac{5\pi}{3}\right\}$

161. $\left\{0, \pi, \frac{\pi}{3}, \frac{5\pi}{3}\right\}$

163. $y = 4\sin\left(\frac{\pi}{4}x\right)$

165. $y = \cos(2\pi x)$

167. a. 1 b. 2π c. $\frac{\pi}{4}$ units to the right

169. a. $\frac{1}{2}$ b. 8π c. No phase shift

171. a. 3 b. 2 c. $\frac{2}{\pi}$ units to the left

173. Approximately 42 in.

175. a. 0.550 rad/sec b. 0.236 rad/sec c. 0.698 rad/min d. 1.697 rad/min

177. $\approx 30.9 \text{ in}^2$

179. a. π/184; the voltage repeats every π/184 sec b. Approximately 59 periods

181. a. Amplitude = 10; period = 24 b. $47.4\ °F$ c. 14 hours later, or 2 p.m. d.

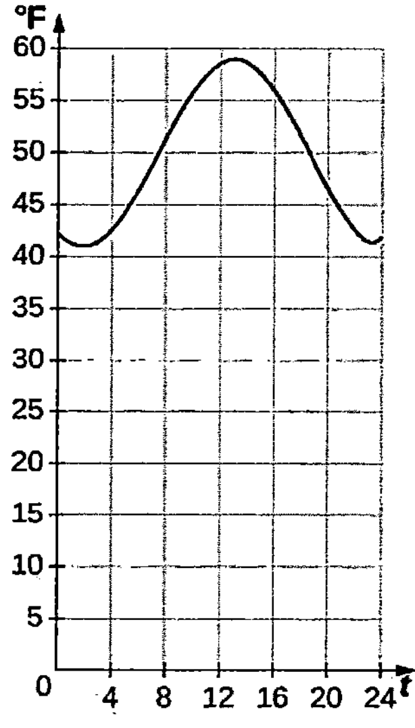

183. Not one-to-one

185. Not one-to-one

187. One-to-one

189. a. $f^{-1}(x) = \sqrt{x+4}$ b. Domain $: x \geq -4$, range: $y \geq 0$

191. a. $f^{-1}(x) = \sqrt[3]{x-1}$ b. Domain: all real numbers, range: all real numbers

193. a. $f^{-1}(x) = x^2 + 1,$ b. Domain: $x \geq 0,$ range: $y \geq 1$

195.

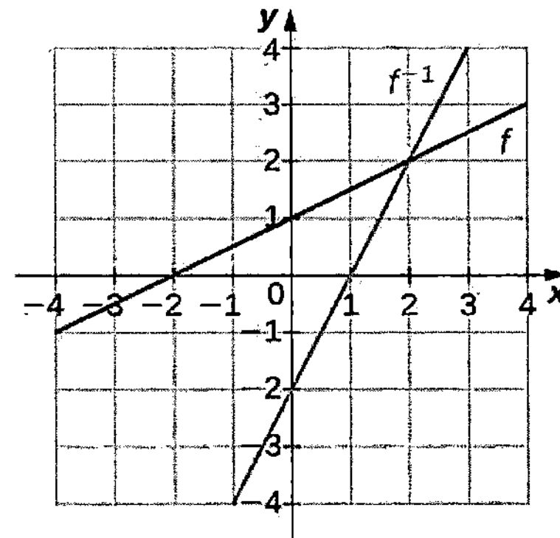

197.

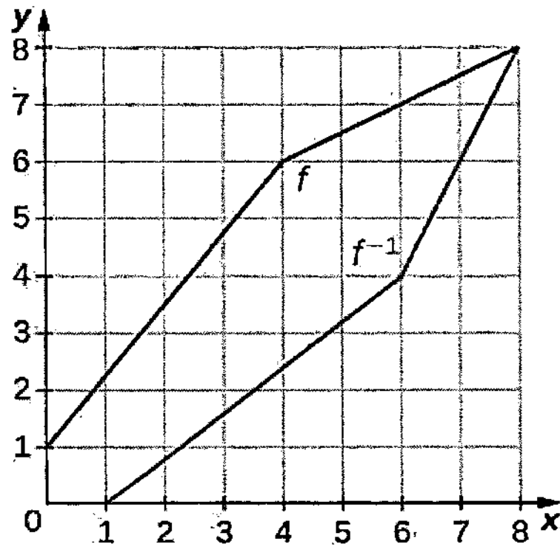

199. These are inverses.
201. These are not inverses.
203. These are inverses.
205. These are inverses.
207. $\frac{\pi}{6}$
209. $\frac{\pi}{4}$
211. $\frac{\pi}{6}$
213. $\frac{\sqrt{2}}{2}$
215. $-\frac{\pi}{6}$
217. a. $x = f^{-1}(V) = \sqrt{0.04 - \frac{V}{500}}$ b. The inverse function determines the distance from the center of the artery at which blood is flowing with velocity V. c. 0.1 cm; 0.14 cm; 0.17 cm
219. a. \$31,250, \$66,667, \$107,143 b. $\left(p = \frac{85C}{C+75}\right)$ c. 34 ppb
221. a. $\sim 92°$ b. $\sim 42°$ c. $\sim 27°$
223. $x \approx 6.69,\ 8.51;$ so, the temperature occurs on June 21 and August 15
225. ~ 1.5 sec
227. $\tan^{-1}(\tan(2.1)) \approx -1.0416;$ the expression does not equal 2.1 since $2.1 > 1.57 = \frac{\pi}{2}$—in other words, it is not in the restricted domain of $\tan x$. $\cos^{-1}(\cos(2.1)) = 2.1,$ since 2.1 is in the restricted domain of $\cos x$.
229. a. 125 b. 2.24 c. 9.74
231. a. 0.01 b. 10,000 c. 46.42
233. d
235. b

237. e

239. Domain: all real numbers, range: $(2, \infty)$, $y = 2$

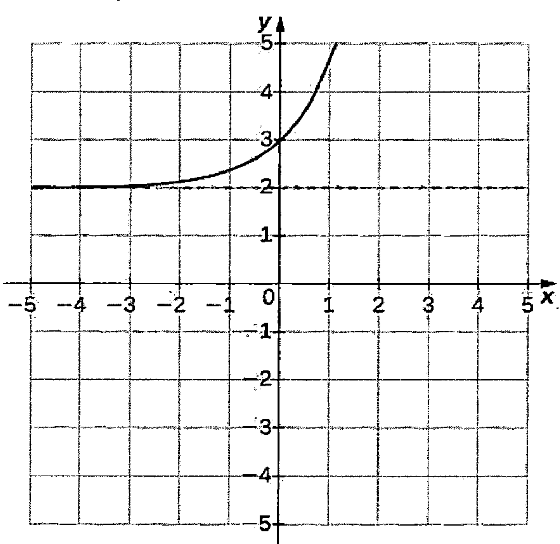

241. Domain: all real numbers, range: $(0, \infty)$, $y = 0$

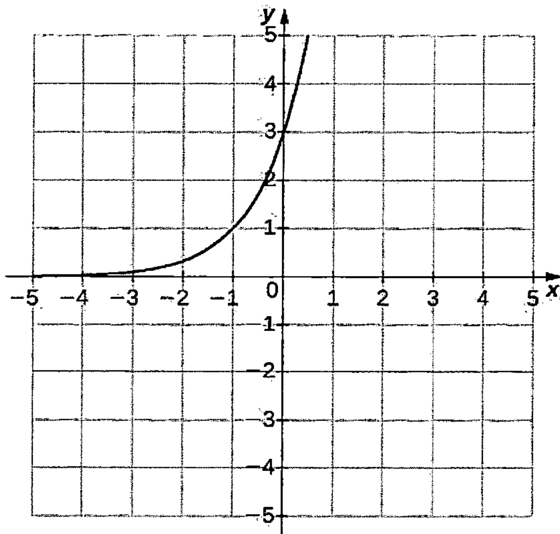

243. Domain: all real numbers, range: $(-\infty, 1)$, $y = 1$

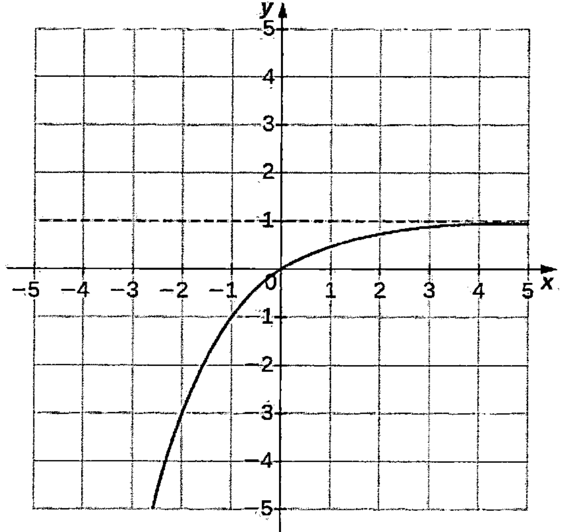

245. Domain: all real numbers, range: $(-1, \infty)$, $y = -1$

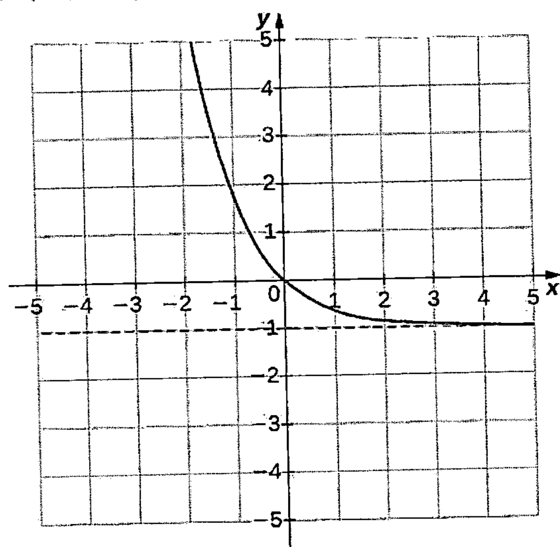

247. $8^{1/3} = 2$

249. $5^2 = 25$

251. $e^{-3} = \frac{1}{e^3}$

253. $e^0 = 1$

255. $\log_4\left(\frac{1}{16}\right) = -2$

257. $\log_9 1 = 0$

259. $\log_{64} 4 = \frac{1}{3}$

261. $\log_9 150 = y$

263. $\log_4 0.125 = -\frac{3}{2}$

265. Domain: $(1, \infty)$, range: $(-\infty, \infty)$, $x = 1$

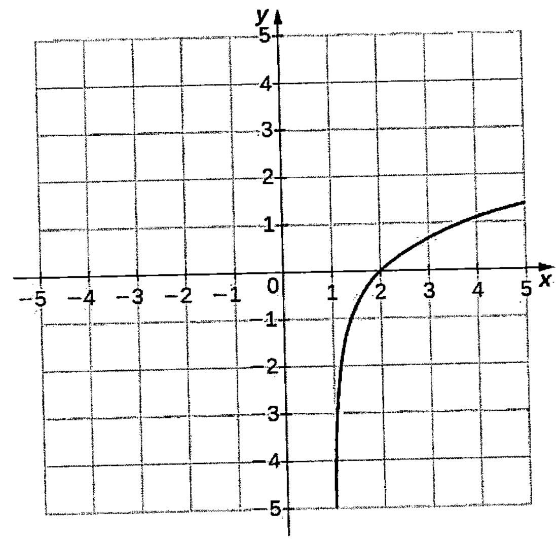

267. Domain: $(0, \infty)$, range: $(-\infty, \infty)$, $x = 0$

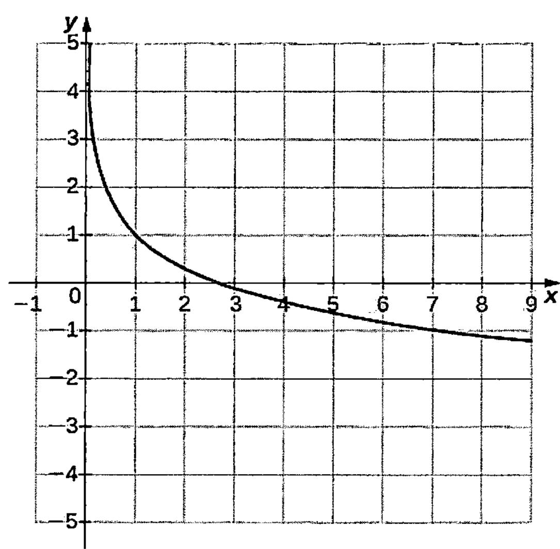

269. Domain: $(-1,\ \infty)$, range: $(-\infty,\ \infty)$, $x=-1$

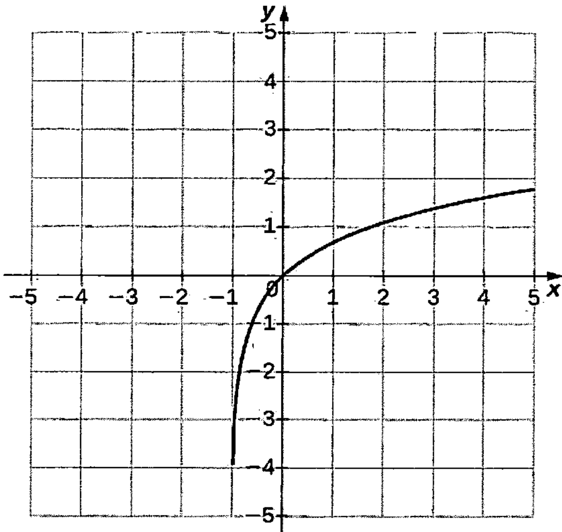

271. $2+3\log_3 a-\log_3 b$

273. $\frac{3}{2}+\frac{1}{2}\log_5 x+\frac{3}{2}\log_5 y$

275. $-\frac{3}{2}+\ln 6$

277. $\frac{\ln 15}{3}$

279. $\frac{3}{2}$

281. $\log 7.21$

283. $\frac{2}{3}+\frac{\log 11}{3\log 7}$

285. $x=\frac{1}{25}$

287. $x=4$

289. $x=3$

291. $1+\sqrt{5}$

293. $\left(\frac{\log 82}{\log 7}\approx 2.2646\right)$

295. $\left(\frac{\log 211}{\log 0.5} \approx -7.7211\right)$

297. $\left(\frac{\log 0.452}{\log 0.2} \approx 0.4934\right)$

299. $\sim 17, 491$

301. Approximately $131,653 is accumulated in 5 years.

303. i. a. pH = 8 b. Base ii. a. pH = 3 b. Acid iii. a. pH = 4 b. Acid

305. a. ~ 333 million b. 94 years from 2013, or in 2107

307. a. $k \approx 0.0578$ b. ≈ 92 hours

309. The San Francisco earthquake had $10^{3.4}$ or ~ 2512 times more energy than the Japan earthquake.

Review Exercises

311. False

313. False

315. Domain: $x > 5,$ range: all real numbers

317. Domain: $x > 2$ and $x < -4,$ range: all real numbers

319. Degree of 3, y -intercept: 0, zeros: 0, $\sqrt{3} - 1, -1 - \sqrt{3}$

321. $\cos(2x)$ or $\frac{1}{2}(\cos(2x) + 1)$

323. $0, \ \pm 2\pi$

325. 4

327. One-to-one; yes, the function has an inverse; inverse: $f^{-1}(x) = \frac{1}{y}$

329. $x \geq -\frac{3}{2}, f^{-1}(x) = -\frac{3}{2} + \frac{1}{2}\sqrt{4y - 7}$

331. a. $C(x) = 300 + 7x$ b. 100 shirts

333. The population is less than 20,000 from December 8 through January 23 and more than 140,000 from May 29 through August 2

335. 78.51%

Chapter 2

Checkpoint

2.1. 2.25

2.2. 12.006001

2.3. 16 unit^2

2.4. $\lim\limits_{x \to 1} \frac{\frac{1}{x} - 1}{x - 1} = -1$

2.5. $\lim\limits_{x \to 2} h(x) = -1.$

2.6. $\lim\limits_{x \to 2} \frac{|x^2 - 4|}{x - 2}$ does not exist.

2.7. a. $\lim\limits_{x \to 2^-} \frac{|x^2 - 4|}{x - 2} = -4;$ b. $\lim\limits_{x \to 2^+} \frac{|x^2 - 4|}{x - 2} = 4$

2.8. a. $\lim\limits_{x \to 0^-} \frac{1}{x^2} = +\infty;$ b. $\lim\limits_{x \to 0^+} \frac{1}{x^2} = +\infty;$ c. $\lim\limits_{x \to 0} \frac{1}{x^2} = +\infty$

2.9. a. $\lim\limits_{x \to 2^-} \frac{1}{(x - 2)^3} = -\infty;$ b. $\lim\limits_{x \to 2^+} \frac{1}{(x - 2)^3} = +\infty;$ c. $\lim\limits_{x \to 2} \frac{1}{(x - 2)^3}$ DNE. The line $x = 2$ is the vertical asymptote of $f(x) = 1/(x - 2)^3$.

2.10. Does not exist.

2.11. $11\sqrt{10}$

2.12. −13;

2.13. $\frac{1}{3}$

2.14. $\frac{1}{4}$

2.15. −1;

2.16. $\frac{1}{4}$

2.17.

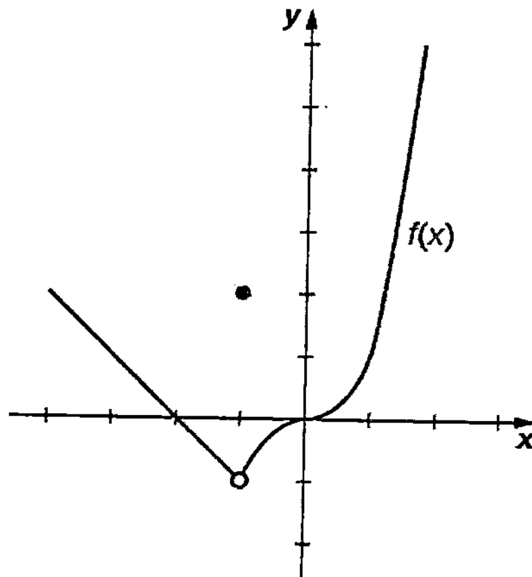

$\lim_{x \to -1^-} f(x) = -1$.

2.18. +∞

2.19. 0

2.20. 0

2.21. *f* is not continuous at 1 because $f(1) = 2 \neq 3 = \lim_{x \to 1} f(x)$.

2.22. $f(x)$ is continuous at every real number.

2.23. Discontinuous at 1; removable

2.24. $[-3, +\infty)$

2.25. 0

2.26. $f(0) = 1 > 0,\ f(1) = -2 < 0$; $f(x)$ is continuous over $[0, 1]$. It must have a zero on this interval.

2.27. Let $\varepsilon > 0$; choose $\delta = \frac{\varepsilon}{3}$; assume $0 < |x - 2| < \delta$. Thus, $|(3x - 2) - 4| = |3x - 6| = |3| \cdot |x - 2| < 3 \cdot \delta = 3 \cdot (\varepsilon/3) = \varepsilon$. Therefore, $\lim_{x \to 2} 3x - 2 = 4$.

2.28. Choose $\delta = \min\{9 - (3 - \varepsilon)^2,\ (3 + \varepsilon)^2 - 9\}$.

2.29. $\left|x^2 - 1\right| = |x - 1| \cdot |x + 1| < \varepsilon/3 \cdot 3 = \varepsilon$

2.30. $\delta = \varepsilon^2$

Section Exercises

1. a. 2.2100000; b. 2.0201000; c. 2.0020010; d. 2.0002000; e. (1.1000000, 2.2100000); f. (1.0100000, 2.0201000); g. (1.0010000, 2.0020010); h. (1.0001000, 2.0002000); i. 2.1000000; j. 2.0100000; k. 2.0010000; l. 2.0001000

3. $y = 2x$

5. 3

7. a. 2.0248457; b. 2.0024984; c. 2.0002500; d. 2.0000250; e. (4.1000000,2.0248457); f. (4.0100000,2.0024984); g. (4.0010000,2.0002500); h. (4.00010000,2.0000250); i. 0.24845673; j. 0.24984395; k. 0.24998438; l. 0.24999844

9. $y = \frac{x}{4} + 1$

11. π

13. a. −0.95238095; b. −0.99009901; c. −0.99502488; d. −0.99900100; e. (−1;.0500000,−0;.95238095); f. (−1;.0100000,−0;.9909901); g. (−1;.0050000,−0;.99502488); h. (1.0010000,−0;.99900100); i. −0.95238095; j. −0.99009901; k. −0.99502488; l. −0.99900100

15. $y = -x - 2$

17. −49 m/sec (velocity of the ball is 49 m/sec downward)

19. 5.2 m/sec
21. −9.8 m/sec
23. 6 m/sec
25. Under, 1 unit^2; over: 4 unit^2. The exact area of the two triangles is $\frac{1}{2}(1)(1) + \frac{1}{2}(2)(2) = 2.5$ units^2.

27. Under, 0.96 unit^2; over, 1.92 unit^2. The exact area of the semicircle with radius 1 is $\frac{\pi(1)^2}{2} = \frac{\pi}{2}$ unit^2.

29. Approximately 1.3333333 unit^2

31. $\lim_{x \to 1} f(x)$ does not exist because $\lim_{x \to 1^-} f(x) = -2 \neq \lim_{x \to 1^+} f(x) = 2$.

33. $\lim_{x \to 0} (1 + x)^{1/x} = 2.7183$

35. a. 1.98669331; b. 1.99986667; c. 1.99999867; d. 1.99999999; e. 1.98669331; f. 1.99986667; g. 1.99999867; h. 1.99999999; $\lim_{x \to 0} \frac{\sin 2x}{x} = 2$

37. $\lim_{x \to 0} \frac{\sin ax}{x} = a$

39. a. −0.80000000; b. −0.98000000; c. −0.99800000; d. −0.99980000; e. −1.2000000; f. −1.0200000; g. −1.0020000; h. −1.0002000; $\lim_{x \to 1} (1 - 2x) = -1$

41. a. −37.931934; b. −3377.9264; c. −333,777.93; d. −33,337,778; e. −29.032258; f. −3289.0365; g. −332,889.04; h. −33,328,889 $\lim_{x \to 0} \frac{z - 1}{z^2 (z + 3)} = -\infty$

43. a. 0.13495277; b. 0.12594300; c. 0.12509381; d. 0.12500938; e. 0.11614402; f. 0.12406794; g. 0.12490631; h. 0.12499063; $\therefore \lim_{x \to 2} \frac{1 - \frac{2}{x}}{x^2 - 4} = 0.1250 = \frac{1}{8}$

45. a. −10.00000; b. −100.00000; c. −1000.0000; d. −10,000.000; Guess: $\lim_{\alpha \to 0^+} \frac{1}{\alpha} \cos\left(\frac{\pi}{\alpha}\right) = \infty$, actual: DNE

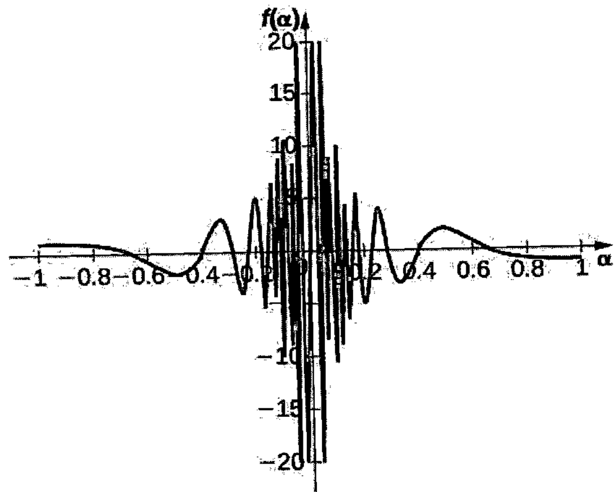

47. False; $\lim_{x \to -2^+} f(x) = +\infty$

49. False; $\lim_{x \to 6} f(x)$ DNE since $\lim_{x \to 6^-} f(x) = 2$ and $\lim_{x \to 6^+} f(x) = 5$.

51. 2
53. 1
55. 1
57. DNE
59. 0
61. DNE
63. 2
65. 3
67. DNE
69. 0

71. −2
73. DNE
75. 0
77. Answers may vary.

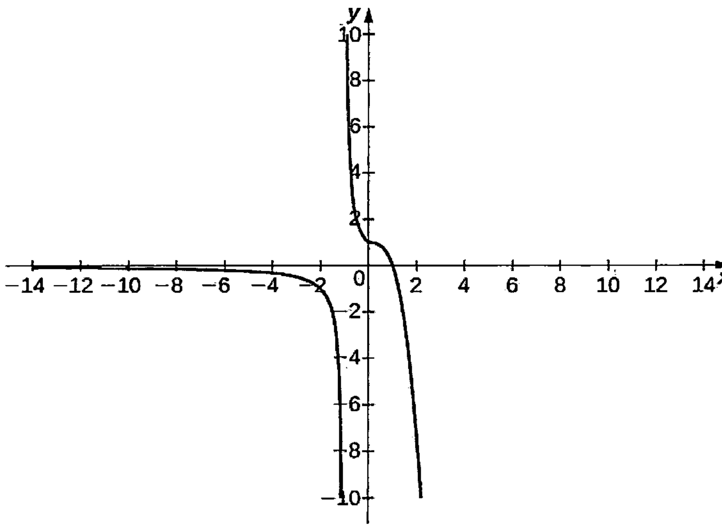

79. Answers may vary.

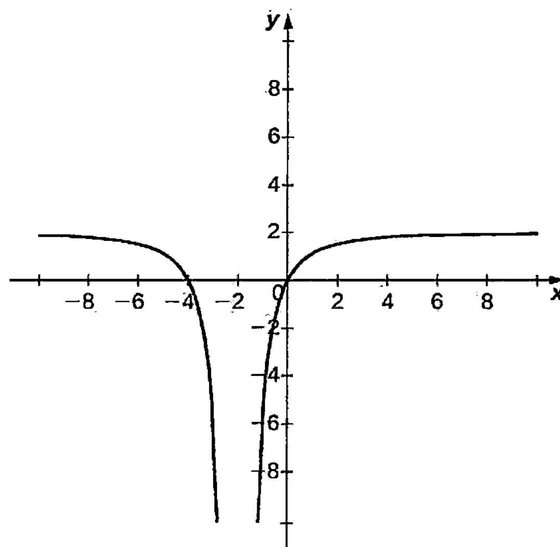

81. a. ρ_2 b. ρ_1 c. DNE unless $\rho_1 = \rho_2$. As you approach x_{SF} from the right, you are in the high-density area of the shock. When you approach from the left, you have not experienced the "shock" yet and are at a lower density.

83. Use constant multiple law and difference law: $\lim_{x \to 0}\left(4x^2 - 2x + 3\right) = 4\lim_{x \to 0} x^2 - 2\lim_{x \to 0} x + \lim_{x \to 0} 3 = 3$

85. Use root law: $\lim_{x \to -2} \sqrt{x^2 - 6x + 3} = \sqrt{\lim_{x \to -2}\left(x^2 - 6x + 3\right)} = \sqrt{19}$

87. 49
89. 1
91. $-\frac{5}{7}$

93. $\lim_{x \to 4} \frac{x^2 - 16}{x - 4} = \frac{16 - 16}{4 - 4} = \frac{0}{0}$; then, $\lim_{x \to 4} \frac{x^2 - 16}{x - 4} = \lim_{x \to 4} \frac{(x + 4)(x - 4)}{x - 4} = 8$

95. $\lim_{x \to 6} \frac{3x - 18}{2x - 12} = \frac{18 - 18}{12 - 12} = \frac{0}{0}$; then, $\lim_{x \to 6} \frac{3x - 18}{2x - 12} = \lim_{x \to 6} \frac{3(x - 6)}{2(x - 6)} = \frac{3}{2}$

97. $\lim\limits_{x \to 9} \frac{t-9}{\sqrt{t}-3} = \frac{9-9}{3-3} = \frac{0}{0}$; then, $\lim\limits_{t \to 9} \frac{t-9}{\sqrt{t}-3} = \lim\limits_{t \to 9} \frac{t-9}{\sqrt{t}-3} \frac{\sqrt{t}+3}{\sqrt{t}+3} = \lim\limits_{t \to 9}(\sqrt{t}+3) = 6$

99. $\lim\limits_{\theta \to \pi} \frac{\sin\theta}{\tan\theta} = \frac{\sin\pi}{\tan\pi} = \frac{0}{0}$; then, $\lim\limits_{\theta \to \pi} \frac{\sin\theta}{\tan\theta} = \lim\limits_{\theta \to \pi} \frac{\sin\theta}{\frac{\sin\theta}{\cos\theta}} = \lim\limits_{\theta \to \pi} \cos\theta = -1$

101. $\lim\limits_{x \to 1/2} \frac{2x^2+3x-2}{2x-1} = \frac{\frac{1}{2}+\frac{3}{2}-2}{1-1} = \frac{0}{0}$; then, $\lim\limits_{x \to 1/2} \frac{2x^2+3x-2}{2x-1} = \lim\limits_{x \to 1/2} \frac{(2x-1)(x+2)}{2x-1} = \frac{5}{2}$

103. $-\infty$

105. $-\infty$

107. $\lim\limits_{x \to 6} 2f(x)g(x) = 2\lim\limits_{x \to 6} f(x) \lim\limits_{x \to 6} g(x) = 72$

109. $\lim\limits_{x \to 6}\left(f(x) + \frac{1}{3}g(x)\right) = \lim\limits_{x \to 6} f(x) + \frac{1}{3}\lim\limits_{x \to 6} g(x) = 7$

111. $\lim\limits_{x \to 6}\sqrt{g(x) - f(x)} = \sqrt{\lim\limits_{x \to 6} g(x) - \lim\limits_{x \to 6} f(x)} = \sqrt{5}$

113. $\lim\limits_{x \to 6}[(x+1)f(x)] = \left(\lim\limits_{x \to 6}(x+1)\right)\left(\lim\limits_{x \to 6} f(x)\right) = 28$

115.

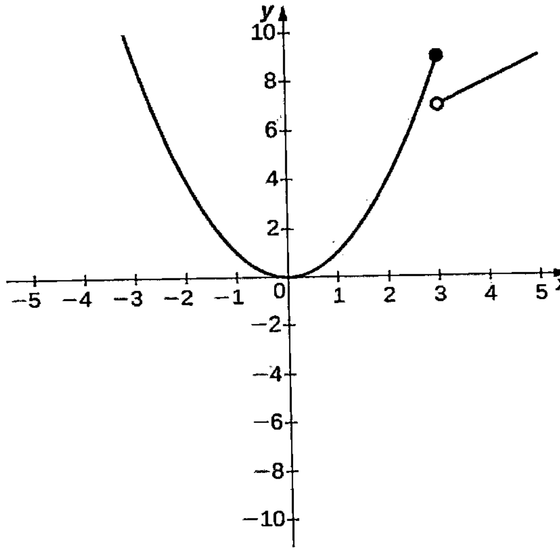

a. 9; b. 7

117.

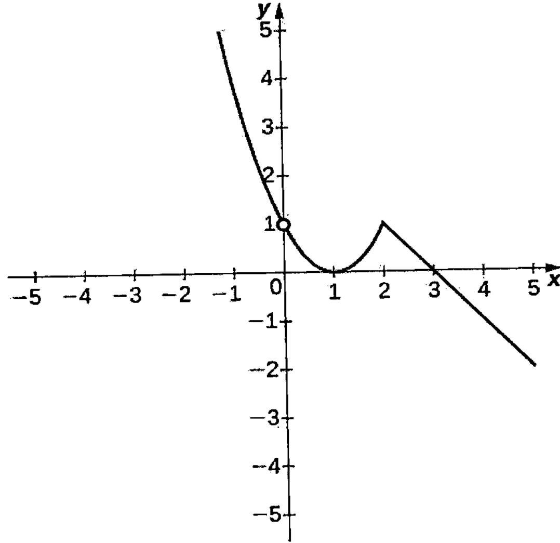

a. 1; b. 1

119. $\lim\limits_{x \to -3^-}(f(x) - 3g(x)) = \lim\limits_{x \to -3^-} f(x) - 3\lim\limits_{x \to -3^-} g(x) = 0 + 6 = 6$

121. $\lim\limits_{x \to -5} \frac{2 + g(x)}{f(x)} = \frac{2 + \left(\lim\limits_{x \to -5} g(x)\right)}{\lim\limits_{x \to -5} f(x)} = \frac{2 + 0}{2} = 1$

123. $\lim\limits_{x \to 1} \sqrt[3]{f(x) - g(x)} = \sqrt[3]{\lim\limits_{x \to 1} f(x) - \lim\limits_{x \to 1} g(x)} = \sqrt[3]{2 + 5} = \sqrt[3]{7}$

125. $\lim\limits_{x \to -9}(xf(x) + 2g(x)) = \left(\lim\limits_{x \to -9} x\right)\left(\lim\limits_{x \to -9} f(x)\right) + 2\lim\limits_{x \to -9}(g(x)) = (-9)(6) + 2(4) = -46$

127. The limit is zero.

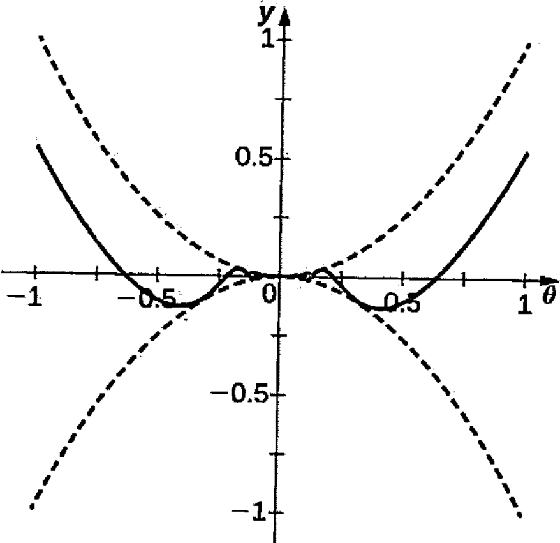

129. a.

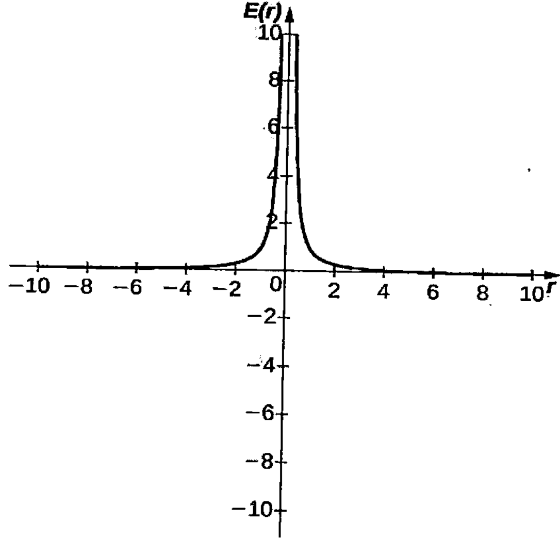

b. ∞. The magnitude of the electric field as you approach the particle q becomes infinite. It does not make physical sense to evaluate negative distance.

131. The function is defined for all x in the interval $(0, \infty)$.

133. Removable discontinuity at $x = 0$; infinite discontinuity at $x = 1$

135. Infinite discontinuity at $x = \ln 2$

137. Infinite discontinuities at $x = \frac{(2k+1)\pi}{4}$, for $k = 0, \pm 1, \pm 2, \pm 3, \ldots$

139. No. It is a removable discontinuity.

141. Yes. It is continuous.

143. Yes. It is continuous.

145. $k = -5$

147. $k = -1$

149. $k = \frac{16}{3}$

151. Since both s and $y = t$ are continuous everywhere, then $h(t) = s(t) - t$ is continuous everywhere and, in particular, it is continuous over the closed interval $[2, 5]$. Also, $h(2) = 3 > 0$ and $h(5) = -3 < 0$. Therefore, by the IVT, there is a value $x = c$ such that $h(c) = 0$.

153. The function $f(x) = 2^x - x^3$ is continuous over the interval $[1.25, 1.375]$ and has opposite signs at the endpoints.

155. a.

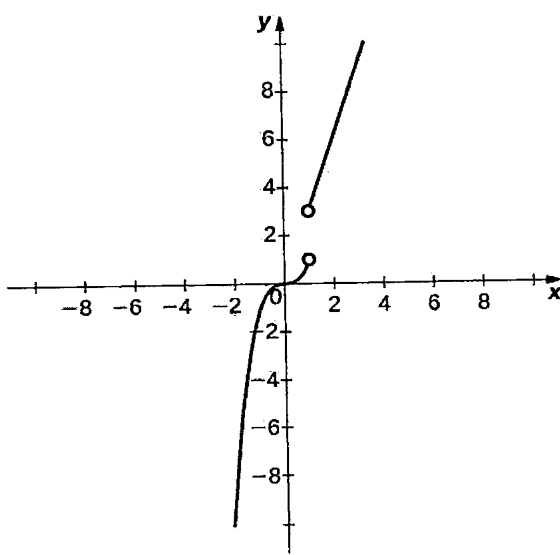

b. It is not possible to redefine $f(1)$ since the discontinuity is a jump discontinuity.

157. Answers may vary; see the following example:

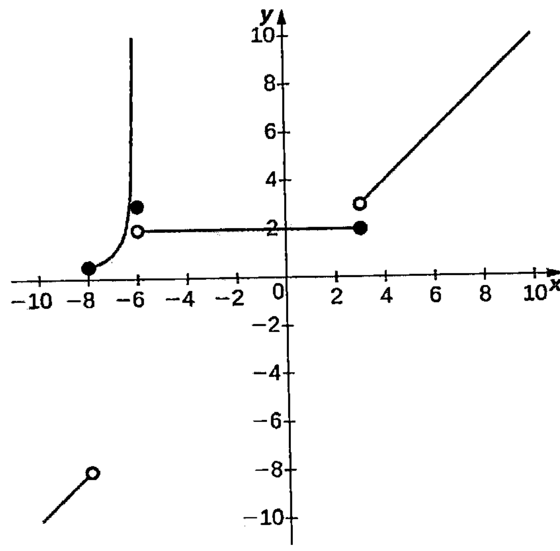

159. Answers may vary; see the following example:

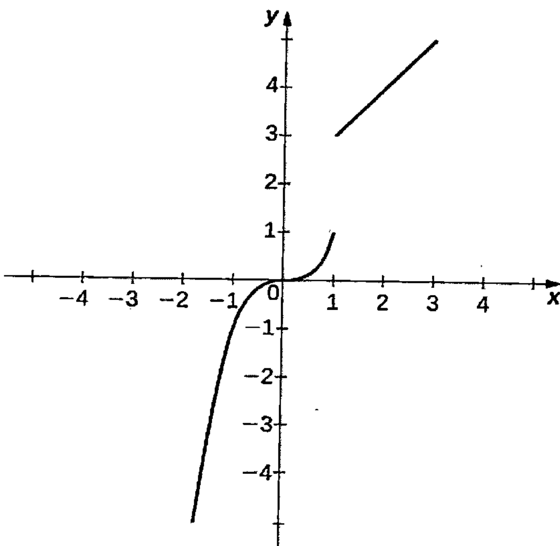

161. False. It is continuous over $(-\infty,\ 0) \cup (0,\ \infty)$.

163. False. Consider $f(x) = \begin{cases} x \text{ if } x \neq 0 \\ 4 \text{ if } x = 0 \end{cases}$.

165. False. Consider $f(x) = \cos(x)$ on $[-\pi,\ 2\pi]$.

167. False. The IVT does *not* work in reverse! Consider $(x-1)^2$ over the interval $[-2,\ 2]$.

169. $R = 0.0001519\text{ m}$

171. $D = 63.78\text{ km}$

173. For all values of a, $f(a)$ is defined, $\lim_{\theta \to a} f(\theta)$ exists, and $\lim_{\theta \to a} f(\theta) = f(a)$. Therefore, $f(\theta)$ is continuous everywhere.

175. Nowhere

177. For every $\varepsilon > 0$, there exists a $\delta > 0$, so that if $0 < |t - b| < \delta$, then $|g(t) - M| < \varepsilon$

179. For every $\varepsilon > 0$, there exists a $\delta > 0$, so that if $0 < |x - a| < \delta$, then $|\varphi(x) - A| < \varepsilon$

181. $\delta \leq 0.25$

183. $\delta \leq 2$

185. $\delta \leq 1$

187. $\delta < 0.3900$

189. Let $\delta = \varepsilon$. If $0 < |x - 3| < \varepsilon$, then $|x + 3 - 6| = |x - 3| < \varepsilon$.

191. Let $\delta = \sqrt[4]{\varepsilon}$. If $0 < |x| < \sqrt[4]{\varepsilon}$, then $\left|x^4\right| = x^4 < \varepsilon$.

193. Let $\delta = \varepsilon^2$. If $5 - \varepsilon^2 < x < 5$, then $\left|\sqrt{5 - x}\right| = \sqrt{5 - x} < \varepsilon$.

195. Let $\delta = \varepsilon/5$. If $1 - \varepsilon/5 < x < 1$, then $|f(x) - 3| = 5x - 5 < \varepsilon$.

197. Let $\delta = \sqrt{\frac{3}{N}}$. If $0 < |x + 1| < \sqrt{\frac{3}{N}}$, then $f(x) = \frac{3}{(x+1)^2} > N$.

199. 0.033 cm, $\varepsilon = 8$, $\delta = 0.33$, $a = 12$, $L = 144$

201. Answers may vary.

203. 0

205. $f(x) - g(x) = f(x) + (-1)g(x)$

207. Answers may vary.

Review Exercises

209. False

211. False. A removable discontinuity is possible.

213. 5

215. 8/7

217. DNE

219. 2/3

221. −4;

223. Since $-1 \le \cos(2\pi x) \le 1$, then $-x^2 \le x^2 \cos(2\pi x) \le x^2$. Since $\lim_{x \to 0} x^2 = 0 = \lim_{x \to 0} -x^2$, it follows that $\lim_{x \to 0} x^2 \cos(2\pi x) = 0$.

225. $[2, \infty]$

227. $c = -1$

229. $\delta = \sqrt[3]{\varepsilon}$

231. 0 m/sec

Chapter 3

Checkpoint

3.1. $\frac{1}{4}$

3.2. 6

3.3. $f'(1) = 5$

3.4. −32 ft/s

3.5. $P'(3.25) = 20 > 0$; raise prices

3.6. $f'(x) = 2x$

3.7. $(0, +\infty)$

3.8. $a = 6$ and $b = -9$

3.9. $f''(x) = 2$

3.10. $a(t) = 6t$

3.11. 0

3.12. $4x^3$

3.13. $f'(x) = 7x^6$

3.14. $f'(x) = 6x^2 - 12x$.

3.15. $y = 12x - 23$

3.16. $j'(x) = 10x^4\left(4x^2 + x\right) + (8x + 1)\left(2x^5\right) = 56x^6 + 12x^5$.

3.17. $k'(x) = -\frac{13}{(4x - 3)^2}$.

3.18. $g'(x) = -7x^{-8}$.

3.19. $3f'(x) - 2g'(x)$.

3.20. $\frac{5}{8}$

3.21. −4.4

3.22. left to right

3.23. 3,300

3.24. $2

3.25. $f'(x) = \cos^2 x - \sin^2 x$

3.26. $\frac{\cos x + x \sin x}{\cos^2 x}$

3.27. $t = \frac{\pi}{3}$, $t = \frac{2\pi}{3}$

3.28. $f'(x) = -\csc^2 x$

3.29. $f'(x) = 2\sec^2 x + 3\csc^2 x$

3.30. $\frac{4}{3}$

3.31. $\cos x$

3.32. $-\cos x$

3.33. $v\left(\frac{5\pi}{6}\right) = -\sqrt{3} < 0$ and $a\left(\frac{5\pi}{6}\right) = -1 < 0.$ The block is speeding up.

3.34. $h'(x) = 4\left(2x^3 + 2x - 1\right)^3 (6x + 2) = 8(3x + 1)\left(2x^3 + 2x - 1\right)^3$

3.35. $y = -48x - 88$

3.36. $h'(x) = 7\cos(7x + 2)$

3.37. $h'(x) = \frac{3 - 4x}{(2x + 3)^4}$

3.38. $h'(x) = 18x^2 \sin^5\left(x^3\right)\cos\left(x^3\right)$

3.39. $a(t) = -16\sin(4t)$

3.40. 28

3.41. $\frac{dy}{dx} = -3x^2 \sin\left(x^3\right)$

3.42. $g'(x) = -\frac{1}{(x + 2)^2}$

3.43. $g(x) = \frac{1}{5}x^{-4/5}$

3.44. $s'(t) = (2t + 1)^{-1/2}$

3.45. $g'(x) = \frac{1}{1 + x^2}$

3.46. $h'(x) = \frac{-3}{\sqrt{6x - 9x^2}}$

3.47. $y = x$

3.48. $\frac{dy}{dx} = \frac{5 - 20x^4}{\sec^2 y - 2y}$

3.49. $y = \frac{5}{3}x - \frac{16}{3}$

3.50. $h'(x) = e^{2x} + 2xe^{2x}$

3.51. 996

3.52. $f'(x) = \frac{15}{3x + 2}$

3.53. $9\ln(3)$

3.54. $\frac{dy}{dx} = x^x(1 + \ln x)$

3.55. $y' = \pi(\tan x)^{\pi - 1} \sec^2 x$

Section Exercises

1. 4

3. 8.5

5. $-\frac{3}{4}$

7. 0.2

9. 0.25

11. a. -4 b. $y = 3 - 4x$

13. a. 3 b. $y = 3x - 1$

15. a. $\frac{-7}{9}$ b. $y = \frac{-7}{9}x + \frac{14}{3}$

17. a. 12 b. $y=12x+14$

19. a. -2 b. $y=-2x-10$

21. 5

23. 13

25. $\frac{1}{4}$

27. $-\frac{1}{4}$

29. -3

31. a. (i) 5.100000, (ii) 5.010000, (iii) 5.001000, (iv) 5.000100, (v) 5.000010, (vi) 5.000001, (vii) 4.900000, (viii) 4.990000, (ix) 4.999000, (x) 4.999900, (xi) 4.999990, (x) 4.999999 b. $m_{\text{tan}}=5$ c. $y=5x+3$

33. a. (i) 4.8771, (ii) 4.9875 (iii) 4.9988, (iv) 4.9999, (v) 4.9999, (vi) 4.9999 b. $m_{\text{tan}}=5$ c. $y=5x+10$

35. a. $\frac{1}{3}$; b. (i) $0.\overline{3}$ m/s, (ii) $0.\overline{3}$ m/s, (iii) $0.\overline{3}$ m/s, (iv) $0.\overline{3}$ m/s; c. $0.\overline{3}=\frac{1}{3}$ m/s

37. a. $2(h^2+6h+12)$; b. (i) 25.22 m/s, (ii) 24.12 m/s, (iii) 24.01 m/s, (iv) 24 m/s; c. 24 m/s

39. a. 1.25; b. 0.5

41. $\lim\limits_{x\to 0^-}\frac{x^{1/3}-0}{x-0}=\lim\limits_{x\to 0^-}\frac{1}{x^{2/3}}=\infty$

43. $\lim\limits_{x\to 1^-}\frac{1-1}{x-1}=0\neq 1=\lim\limits_{x\to 1^+}\frac{x-1}{x-1}$

45. a. (i) 61.7244 ft/s, (ii) 61.0725 ft/s (iii) 61.0072 ft/s (iv) 61.0007 ft/s b. At 4 seconds the race car is traveling at a rate/velocity of 61 ft/s.

47. a. The vehicle represented by $f(t)$, because it has traveled 2 feet, whereas $g(t)$ has traveled 1 foot. b. The velocity of $f(t)$ is constant at 1 ft/s, while the velocity of $g(t)$ is approximately 2 ft/s. c. The vehicle represented by $g(t)$, with a velocity of approximately 4 ft/s. d. Both have traveled 4 feet in 4 seconds.

49. a.

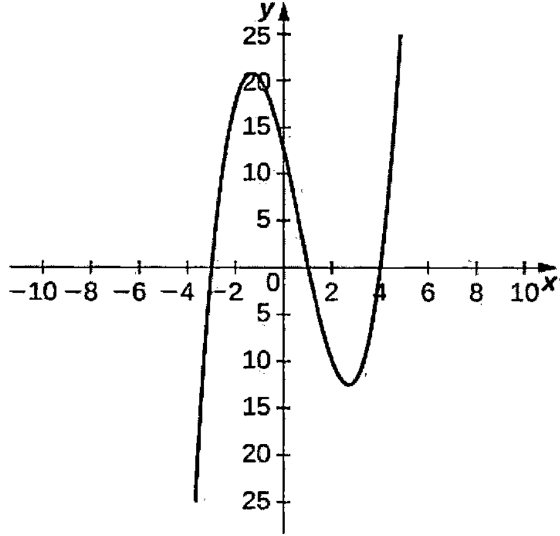

b. $a\approx -1.361, 2.694$

51. a. $N(x)=\frac{x}{30}$ b. ~ 3.3 gallons. When the vehicle travels 100 miles, it has used 3.3 gallons of gas. c. $\frac{1}{30}$. The rate of gas consumption in gallons per mile that the vehicle is achieving after having traveled 100 miles.

53. a.

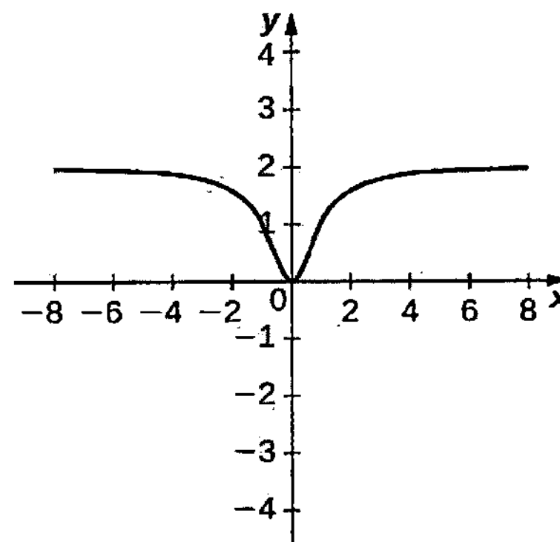

b. $-0.028, -0.16, 0.16, 0.028$

55. -3

57. $8x$

59. $\frac{1}{\sqrt{2x}}$

61. $\frac{-9}{x^2}$

63. $\frac{-1}{2x^{3/2}}$

65.

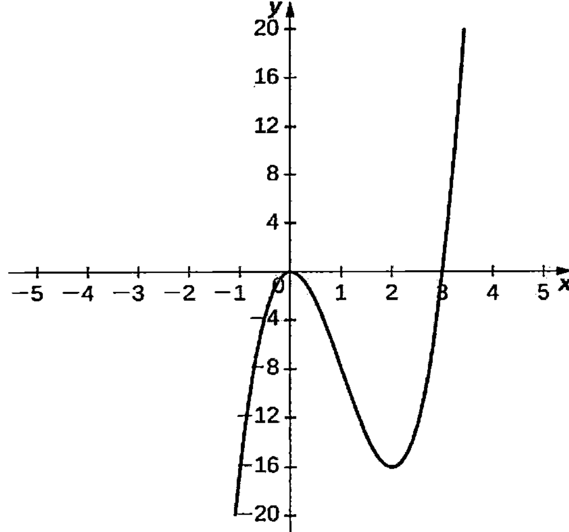

67.

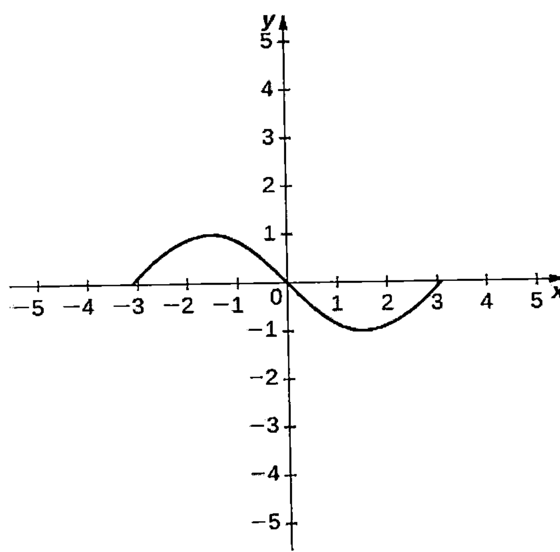

69. $f(x) = 3x^2 + 2,\ a = 2$

71. $f(x) = x^4,\ a = 2$

73. $f(x) = e^x,\ a = 0$

75. a.

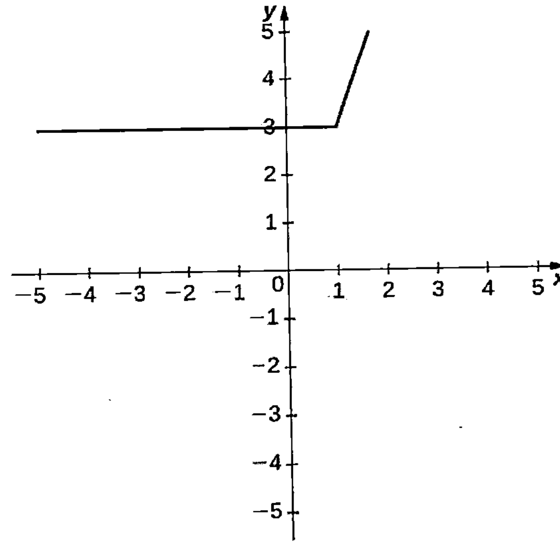

b. $\lim\limits_{h \to 1^-} \frac{3-3}{h} \neq \lim\limits_{h \to 1^+} \frac{3h}{h}$

77. a.

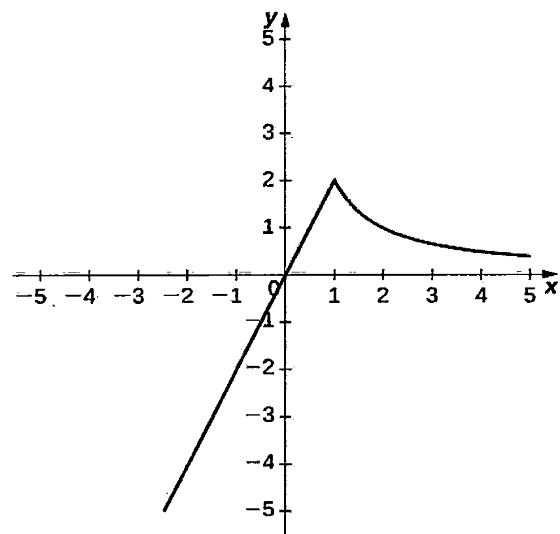

b. $\lim_{h \to 1^-} \frac{2h}{h} \neq \lim_{h \to 1^+} \frac{\frac{2}{x+h} - \frac{2}{x}}{h}.$

79. a. $x = 1$, b. $x = 2$

81. 0

83. $\frac{2}{x^3}$

85. $f'(x) = 6x + 2$

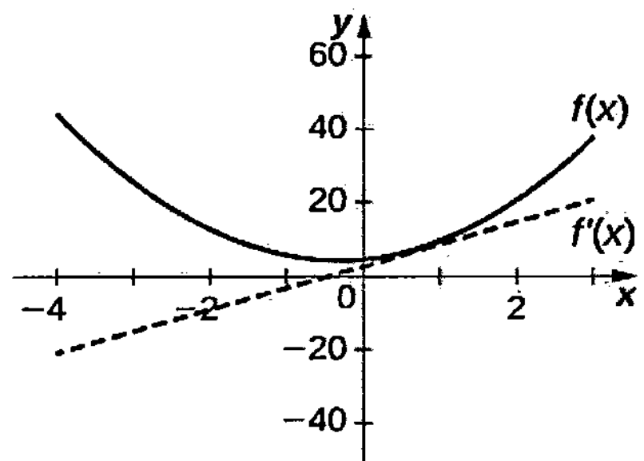

87. $f'(x) = -\frac{1}{(2x)^{3/2}}$

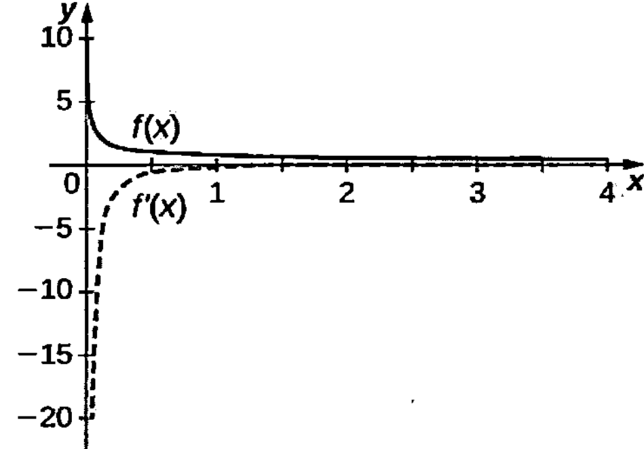

89. $f'(x) = 3x^2$

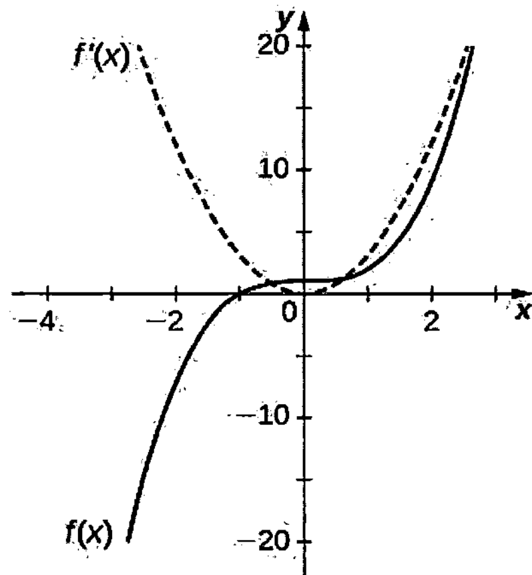

91. a. Average rate at which customers spent on concessions in thousands per customer. b. Rate (in thousands per customer) at which x customers spent money on concessions in thousands per customer.

93. a. Average grade received on the test with an average study time between two values. b. Rate (in percentage points per hour) at which the grade on the test increased or decreased for a given average study time of x hours.

95. a. Average change of atmospheric pressure between two different altitudes. b. Rate (torr per foot) at which atmospheric pressure is increasing or decreasing at x feet.

97. a. The rate (in degrees per foot) at which temperature is increasing or decreasing for a given height x. b. The rate of change of temperature as altitude changes at 1000 feet is -0.1 degrees per foot.

99. a. The rate at which the number of people who have come down with the flu is changing t weeks after the initial outbreak. b. The rate is increasing sharply up to the third week, at which point it slows down and then becomes constant.

101.

Time (seconds)	$h'(t)$ (m/s)
0	2
1	2
2	5.5
3	10.5
4	9.5
5	7

103. $G'(t) = 2.858t + 0.0857$

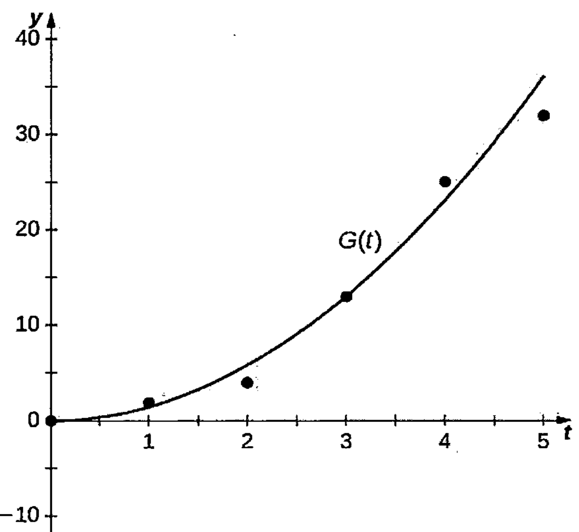

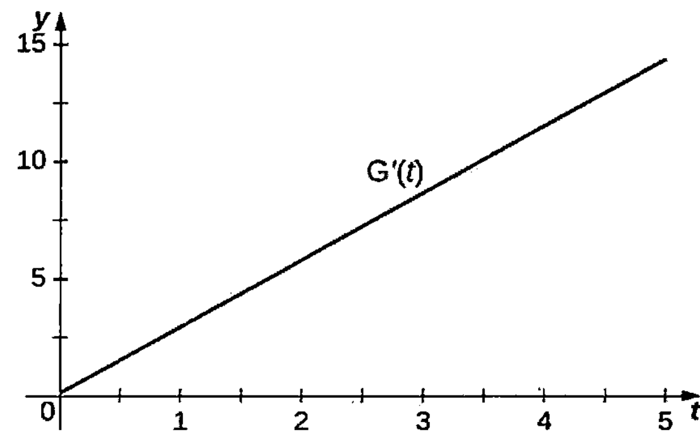

105. $H''(t) = 0,\ G''(t) = 2.858$ and $f''(t) = 1.222t + 5.912$ represent the acceleration of the rocket, with units of meters per second squared $\left(\text{m/s}^2\right)$.

107. $f'(x) = 15x^2 - 1$

109. $f'(x) = 32x^3 + 18x$

111. $f'(x) = 270x^4 + \dfrac{39}{(x+1)^2}$

113. $f'(x) = \dfrac{-5}{x^2}$

115. $f'(x) = \dfrac{4x^4 + 2x^2 - 2x}{x^4}$

117. $f'(x) = \dfrac{-x^2 - 18x + 64}{\left(x^2 - 7x + 1\right)^2}$

119.

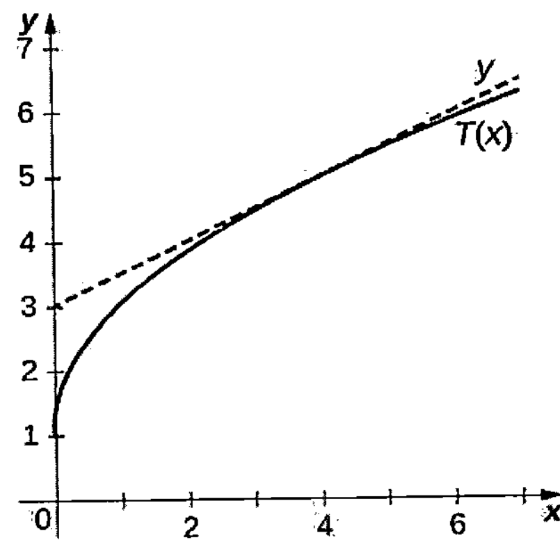

$T(x) = \frac{1}{2}x + 3$

121.

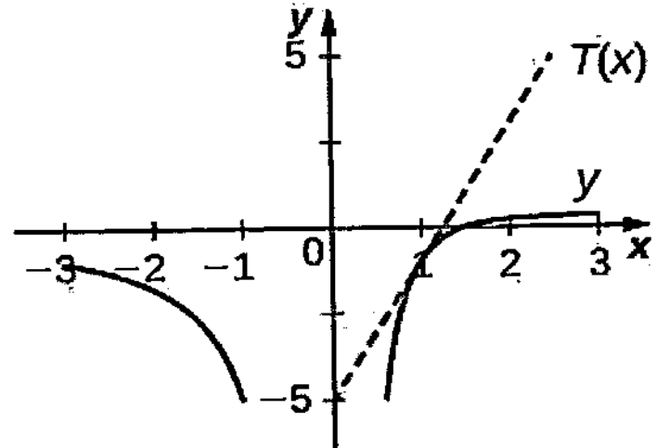

$T(x) = 4x - 5$

123. $h'(x) = 3x^2 f(x) + x^3 f'(x)$

125. $h'(x) = \frac{3f'(x)(g(x)+2) - 3f(x)g'(x)}{(g(x)+2)^2}$

127. $\frac{16}{9}$

129. Undefined

131. a. $2,$ b. does not exist, c. 2.5

133. a. 23, b. $y = 23x - 28$

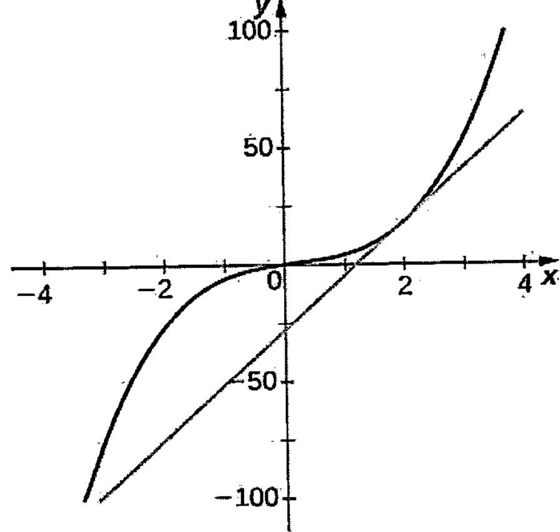

135. a. 3, b. $y = 3x + 2$

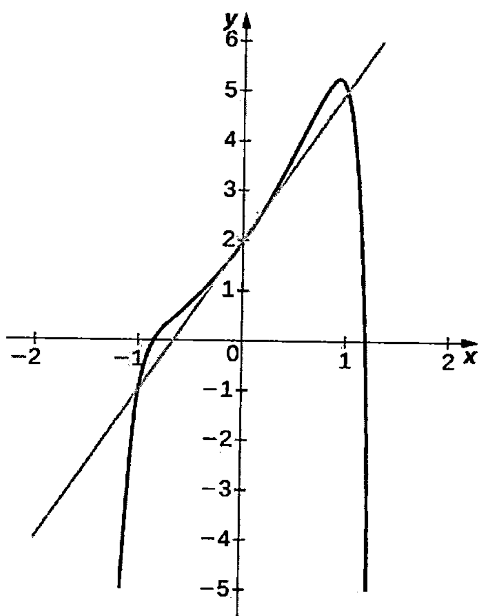

137. $y = -7x - 3$

139. $y = -5x + 7$

141. $y = -\frac{3}{2}x + \frac{15}{2}$

143. $y = -3x^2 + 9x - 1$

145. $\frac{12}{121}$ or 0.0992 ft/s

147. a. $\frac{-2t^4 - 2t^3 + 200t + 50}{\left(t^3 + 50\right)^2}$ b. -0.02395 mg/L-hr, -0.01344 mg/L-hr, -0.003566 mg/L-hr, -0.001579 mg/L-hr c. The rate at which the concentration of drug in the bloodstream decreases is slowing to 0 as time increases.

149. a. $F'(d) = \frac{-2Gm_1 m_2}{d^3}$ b. -1.33×10^{-7} N/m

151. a. $v(t) = 6t^2 - 30t + 36,\ a(t) = 12t - 30;$ b. speeds up $(2, 2.5) \cup (3, \infty)$, slows down $(0, 2) \cup (2.5, 3)$

153. a. $464\ \text{ft/s}^2$ b. $-32\ \text{ft/s}^2$

155. a. 5 ft/s b. 9 ft/s

157. a. 84 ft/s, −84 ft/s b. 84 ft/s c. $\frac{25}{8}$ s d. $-32\ \text{ft/s}^2$ in both cases e. $\frac{1}{8}\left(25 + \sqrt{965}\right)$ s f. $-4\sqrt{965}$ ft/s

159. a. Velocity is positive on $(0, 1.5) \cup (6, 7)$, negative on $(1.5, 2) \cup (5, 6)$, and zero on $(2, 5)$. b.

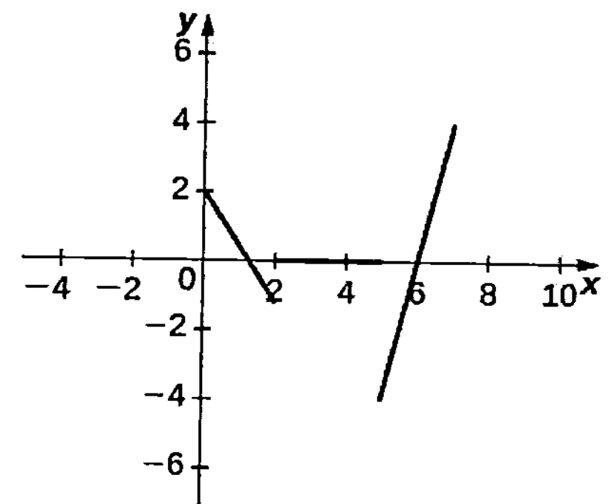

c. Acceleration is positive on $(5, 7)$, negative on $(0, 2)$, and zero on $(2, 5)$. d. The object is speeding up on $(6, 7) \cup (1.5, 2)$ and slowing down on $(0, 1.5) \cup (5, 6)$.

161. a. $R(x) = 10x - 0.001x^2$ b. $R'(x) = 10 - 0.002x$ c. \$6 per item, \$0 per item

163. a. $C'(x) = 65$ b. $R(x) = 143x - 0.03x^2$, $R'(x) = 143 - 0.06x$ c. $83, -97$. At a production level of 1000 cordless drills, revenue is increasing at a rate of \$83 per drill; at a production level of 4000 cordless drills, revenue is decreasing at a rate of \$97 per drill. d. $P(x) = -0.03x^2 + 78x - 75000$, $P'(x) = -0.06x + 78$ e. $18, -162$. At a production level of 1000 cordless drills, profit is increasing at a rate of \$18 per drill; at a production level of 4000 cordless drills, profit is decreasing at a rate of \$162 per drill.

165. a. $N'(t) = 3000\left(\dfrac{-4t^2 + 400}{\left(t^2 + 100\right)^2}\right)$ b. $120, 0, -14.4, -9.6$ c. The bacteria population increases from time 0 to 10 hours; afterwards, the bacteria population decreases. d. $0, -6, 0.384, 0.432$. The rate at which the bacteria is increasing is decreasing during the first 10 hours. Afterwards, the bacteria population is decreasing at a decreasing rate.

167. a. $P(t) = 0.03983 + 0.4280$ b. $P'(t) = 0.03983$. The population is increasing. c. $P''(t) = 0$. The rate at which the population is increasing is constant.

169. a. $p(t) = -0.6071x^2 + 0.4357x - 0.3571$ b. $p'(t) = -1.214x + 0.4357$. This is the velocity of the sensor. c. $p''(t) = -1.214$. This is the acceleration of the sensor; it is a constant acceleration downward.

171. a.

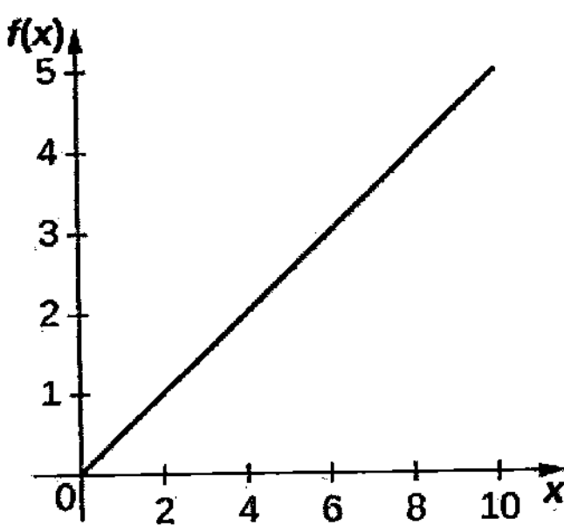

b. $f'(x) = a$. The more increase in prey, the more growth for predators. c. $f''(x) = 0$. As the amount of prey increases, the rate at which the predator population growth increases is constant. d. This equation assumes that if there is more prey, the predator is able to increase consumption linearly. This assumption is unphysical because we would expect there to be some saturation point at which there is too much prey for the predator to consume adequately.

173. a.

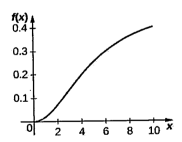

b. $f'(x) = \dfrac{2axn^2}{\left(n^2 + x^2\right)^2}$. When the amount of prey increases, the predator growth increases. c. $f''(x) = \dfrac{2an^2\left(n^2 - 3x^2\right)}{\left(n^2 + x^2\right)^3}$. When the amount of prey is extremely small, the rate at which predator growth is increasing is increasing, but when the amount of prey reaches above a certain threshold, the rate at which predator growth is increasing begins to decrease. d. At lower levels of prey, the prey is more easily able to avoid detection by the predator, so fewer prey individuals are consumed, resulting in less predator growth.

175. $\dfrac{dy}{dx} = 2x - \sec x \tan x$

177. $\dfrac{dy}{dx} = 2x\cot x - x^2 \csc^2 x$

179. $\frac{dy}{dx} = \frac{x\sec x\tan x - \sec x}{x^2}$

181. $\frac{dy}{dx} = (1 - \sin x)(1 - \sin x) - \cos x(x + \cos x)$

183. $\frac{dy}{dx} = \frac{2\csc^2 x}{(1 + \cot x)^2}$

185. $y = -x$

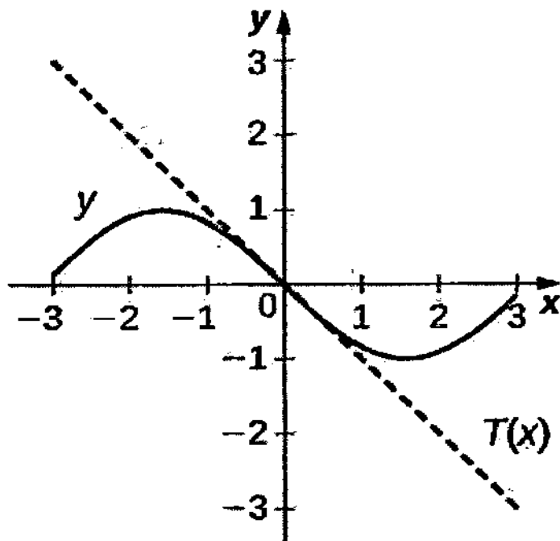

187. $y = x + \frac{2 - 3\pi}{2}$

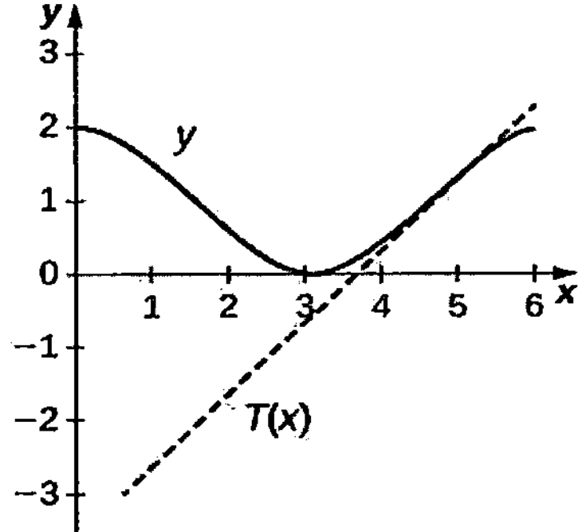

189. $y = -x$

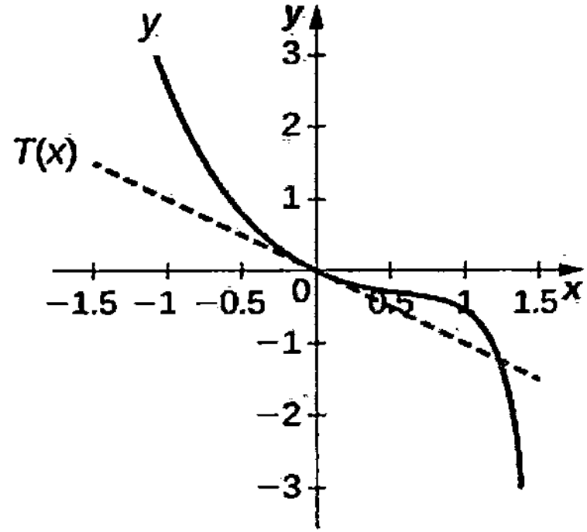

191. $3\cos x - x\sin x$

193. $\frac{1}{2}\sin x$

195. $\csc(x)\left(3\csc^2(x) - 1 + \cot^2(x)\right)$

197. $\frac{(2n+1)\pi}{4}$, where n is an integer

199. $\left(\frac{\pi}{4}, 1\right), \left(\frac{3\pi}{4}, -1\right)$

201. $a = 0,\ b = 3$

203. $y' = 5\cos(x)$, increasing on $\left(0, \frac{\pi}{2}\right), \left(\frac{3\pi}{2}, \frac{5\pi}{2}\right)$, and $\left(\frac{7\pi}{2}, 12\right)$

209. $3\sin x$

211. $5\cos x$

213. $720x^7 - 5\tan(x)\sec^3(x) - \tan^3(x)\sec(x)$

215. $18u^2 \cdot 7 = 18(7x-4)^2 \cdot 7$

217. $-\sin u \cdot \frac{-1}{8} = -\sin\left(\frac{-x}{8}\right) \cdot \frac{-1}{8}$

219. $\frac{8x-24}{2\sqrt{4u+3}} = \frac{4x-12}{\sqrt{4x^2-24x+3}}$

221. a. $u = 3x^2 + 1$; b. $18x\left(3x^2+1\right)^2$

223. a. $f(u) = u^7,\ u = \frac{x}{7} + \frac{7}{x}$; b. $7\left(\frac{x}{7} + \frac{7}{x}\right)^6 \cdot \left(\frac{1}{7} - \frac{7}{x^2}\right)$

225. a. $f(u) = \csc u,\ u = \pi x + 1$; b. $-\pi\csc(\pi x + 1) \cdot \cot(\pi x + 1)$

227. a. $f(u) = -6u^{-3},\ u = \sin x$, b. $18\sin^{-4} x \cdot \cos x$

229. $\frac{4}{(5-2x)^3}$

231. $6\left(2x^3 - x^2 + 6x + 1\right)^2\left(3x^2 - x + 3\right)$

233. $-3(\tan x + \sin x)^{-4} \cdot \left(\sec^2 x + \cos x\right)$

235. $-7\cos(\cos 7x) \cdot \sin 7x$

237. $-12\cot^2(4x+1) \cdot \csc^2(4x+1)$

239. $10\frac{3}{4}$

241. $y = \frac{-1}{2}x$

243. $x = \pm\sqrt{6}$

245. 10

247. $-\frac{1}{8}$

249. -4

251. -12

253. a. $-\frac{200}{343}$ m/s, b. $\frac{600}{2401}$ m/s^2, c. The train is slowing down since velocity and acceleration have opposite signs.

255. a. $C'(x) = 0.0003x^2 - 0.04x + 3$ b. $\frac{dC}{dt} = 100 \cdot \left(0.0003x^2 - 0.04x + 3\right)$ c. Approximately $90,300 per week

257. a. $\frac{dS}{dt} = -\frac{8\pi r^2}{(t+1)^3}$ b. The volume is decreasing at a rate of $-\frac{\pi}{36}$ ft^3/min.

259. ~2.3 ft/hr

261. a.

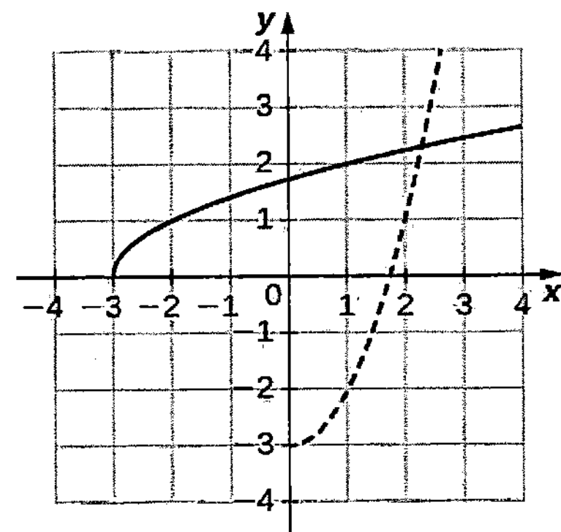

b. $(f^{-1})'(1) \sim 2$

263. a.

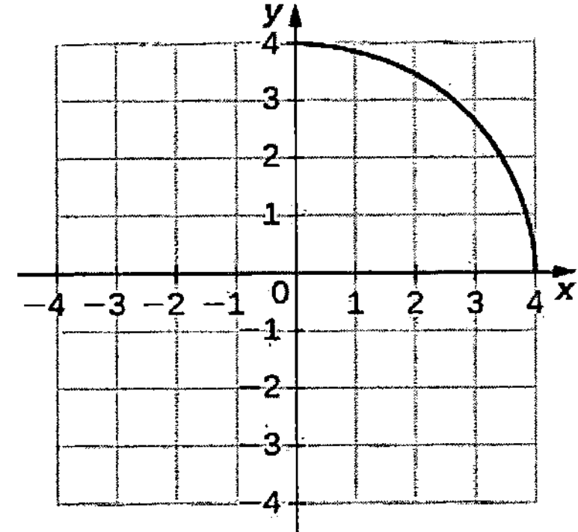

b. $(f^{-1})'(1) \sim -1/\sqrt{3}$

265. a. 6, b. $x = f^{-1}(y) = \left(\frac{y+3}{2}\right)^{1/3}$, c. $\frac{1}{6}$

267. a. 1, b. $x = f^{-1}(y) = \sin^{-1} y$, c. 1

269. $\frac{1}{5}$

271. $\frac{1}{3}$

273. 1

275. a. 4, b. $y = 4x$

277. a. $-\frac{1}{96}$, b. $y = -\frac{1}{13}x + \frac{18}{13}$

279. $\frac{2x}{\sqrt{1-x^4}}$

281. $\frac{-1}{\sqrt{1-x^2}}$

283. $\frac{3\left(1+\tan^{-1} x\right)^2}{1+x^2}$

285. $\frac{-1}{\left(1+x^2\right)\left(\tan^{-1} x\right)^2}$

287. $\frac{x}{\left(5-x^2\right)\sqrt{4-x^2}}$

289. -1

291. $\frac{1}{2}$

293. $\frac{1}{10}$

295. a. $v(t) = \frac{1}{1+t^2}$ b. $a(t) = \frac{-2t}{\left(1+t^2\right)^2}$ c. $(a)0.2,\ 0.06,\ 0.03;\ (b)-0.16,\ -0.028,\ -0.0088$ d. The hockey puck is decelerating/slowing down at 2, 4, and 6 seconds.

297. -0.0168 radians per foot

299. a. $\frac{d\theta}{dx} = \frac{10}{100+x^2} - \frac{40}{1600+x^2}$ b. $\frac{18}{325}, \frac{9}{340}, \frac{42}{4745}, 0$ c. As a person moves farther away from the screen, the viewing angle is increasing, which implies that as he or she moves farther away, his or her screen vision is widening. d. $-\frac{54}{12905}, -\frac{3}{500}, -\frac{198}{29945}, -\frac{9}{1360}$ e. As the person moves beyond 20 feet from the screen, the viewing angle is decreasing. The optimal distance the person should stand for maximizing the viewing angle is 20 feet.

301. $\frac{dy}{dx} = \frac{-2x}{y}$

303. $\frac{dy}{dx} = \frac{x}{3y} - \frac{y}{2x}$

305. $\frac{dy}{dx} = \frac{y - \frac{y}{2\sqrt{x+4}}}{\sqrt{x+4} - x}$

307. $\frac{dy}{dx} = \frac{y^2 \cos(xy)}{2y - \sin(xy) - xy\cos xy}$

309. $\frac{dy}{dx} = \frac{-3x^2y - y^3}{x^3 + 3xy^2}$

311.

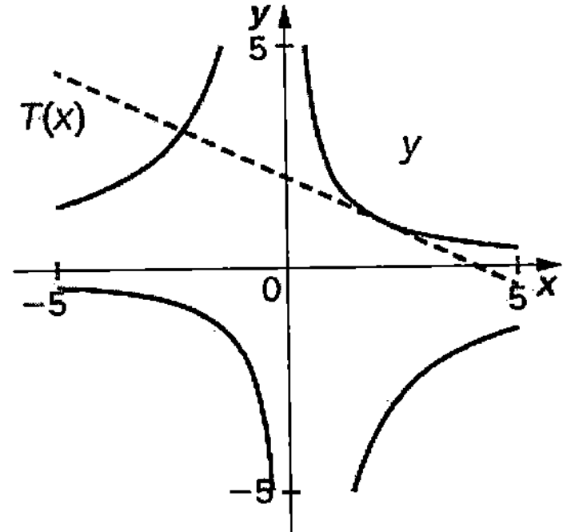

$y = \frac{-1}{2}x + 2$

313.

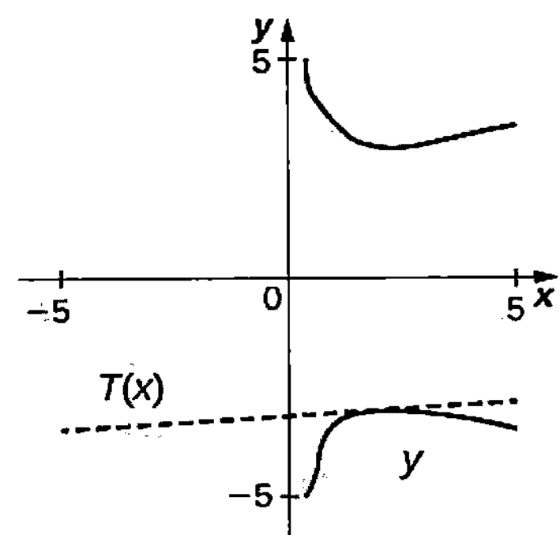

$y = \frac{1}{\pi + 12}x - \frac{3\pi + 38}{\pi + 12}$

315.

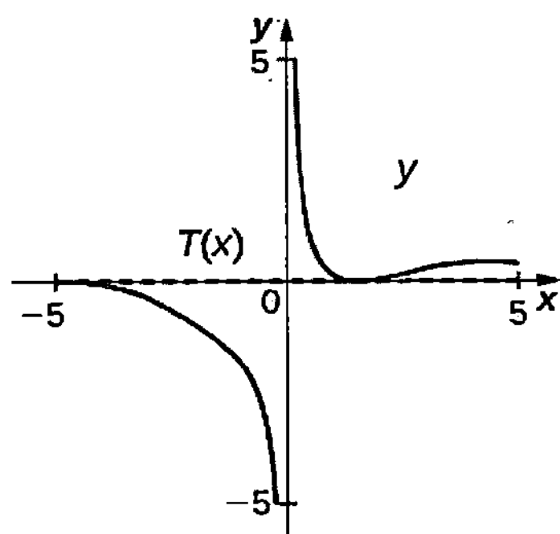

$y = 0$

317. a. $y = -x + 2$ b. $(3, -1)$

319. a. $\left(\pm\sqrt{7}, 0\right)$ b. -2 c. They are parallel since the slope is the same at both intercepts.

321. $y = -x + 1$

323. a. -0.5926 b. When \$81 is spent on labor and \$16 is spent on capital, the amount spent on capital is decreasing by \$0.5926 per \$1 spent on labor.

325. -8

327. -2.67

329. $y' = -\frac{1}{\sqrt{1 - x^2}}$

331. $2xe^x + x^2 e^x$

333. $e^{x^3 \ln x}\left(3x^2 \ln x + x^2\right)$

335. $\frac{4}{(e^x + e^{-x})^2}$

337. $2^{4x + 2} \cdot \ln 2 + 8x$

339. $\pi x^{\pi - 1} \cdot \pi^x + x^{\pi} \cdot \pi^x \ln \pi$

341. $\frac{5}{2(5x - 7)}$

343. $\frac{\tan x}{\ln 10}$

345. $2^x \cdot \ln 2 \cdot \log_3 7^{x^2 - 4} + 2^x \cdot \frac{2x \ln 7}{\ln 3}$

347. $(\sin 2x)^{4x}[4 \cdot \ln(\sin 2x) + 8x \cdot \cot 2x]$

349. $x^{\log_2 x} \cdot \frac{2\ln x}{x\ln 2}$

351. $x^{\cot x} \cdot \left[-\csc^2 x \cdot \ln x + \frac{\cot x}{x}\right]$

353. $x^{-1/2}\left(x^2+3\right)^{2/3}(3x-4)^4 \cdot \left[\frac{-1}{2x} + \frac{4x}{3\left(x^2+3\right)} + \frac{12}{3x-4}\right]$

355.

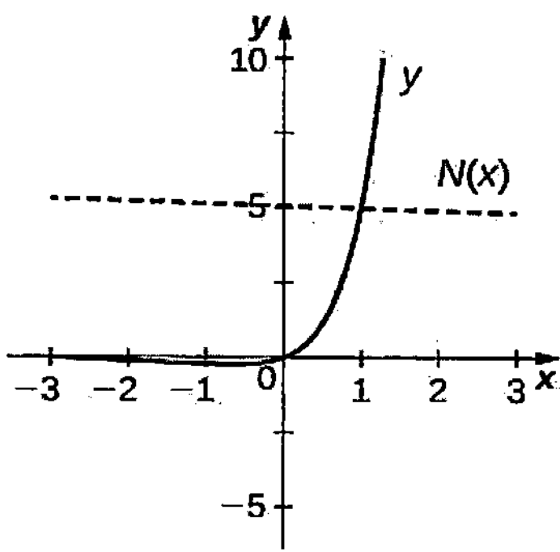

$y = \frac{-1}{5+5\ln 5}x + \left(5 + \frac{1}{5+5\ln 5}\right)$

357. a. $x = e \sim 2.718$ b. (e, ∞), $(0, e)$

359. a. $P = 500{,}000(1.05)^t$ individuals b. $P'(t) = 24395 \cdot (1.05)^t$ individuals per year c. $39{,}737$ individuals per year

361. a. At the beginning of 1960 there were 5.3 thousand cases of the disease in New York City. At the beginning of 1963 there were approximately 723 cases of the disease in the United States. b. At the beginning of 1960 the number of cases of the disease was decreasing at rate of -4.611 thousand per year; at the beginning of 1963, the number of cases of the disease was decreasing at a rate of -0.2808 thousand per year.

363. $p = 35741(1.045)^t$

365.

Years since 1790	P''
0	69.25
10	107.5
20	167.0
30	259.4
40	402.8
50	625.5
60	971.4
70	1508.5

Review Exercises

367. False.

369. False

371. $\frac{1}{2\sqrt{x+4}}$

373. $9x^2 + \frac{8}{x^3}$

375. $e^{\sin x} \cos x$

377. $x\sec^2(x) + 2x\cos(x) + \tan(x) - x^2 \sin(x)$

379. $\frac{1}{4}\left(\frac{x}{\sqrt{1-x^2}} + \sin^{-1}(x)\right)$

381. $\cos x \cdot (\ln x + 1) - x\ln(x)\sin x$

383. $4^x(\ln 4)^2 + 2\sin x + 4x\cos x - x^2 \sin x$

385. $T = (2+e)x - 2$

387.

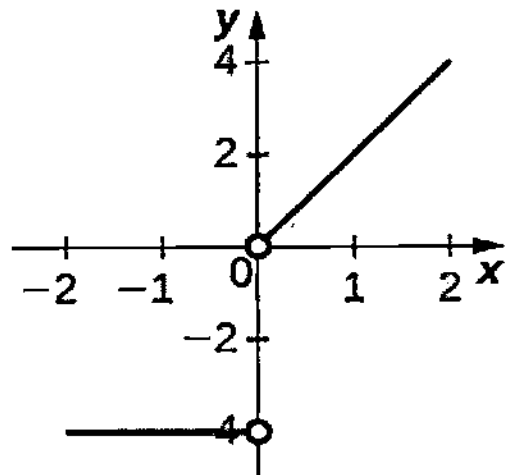

389. $w'(3) = -\frac{2.9\pi}{6}$. At 3 a.m. the tide is decreasing at a rate of 1.514 ft/hr.

391. -7.5. The wind speed is decreasing at a rate of 7.5 mph/hr

Chapter 4

Checkpoint

4.1. $\frac{1}{72\pi}$ cm/sec, or approximately 0.0044 cm/sec

4.2. 500 ft/sec

4.3. $\frac{1}{10}$ rad/sec

4.4. -0.61 ft/sec

4.5. $L(x) = 2 + \frac{1}{12}(x-8)$; 2.00833

4.6. $L(x) = -x + \frac{\pi}{2}$

4.7. $L(x) = 1 + 4x$

4.8. $dy = 2xe^{x^2}dx$

4.9. $dy = 1.6, \quad \Delta y = 1.64$

4.10. The volume measurement is accurate to within $21.6\ \text{cm}^3$.

4.11. 7.6%

4.12. $x = -\frac{2}{3}, \quad x = 1$

4.13. The absolute maximum is 3 and it occurs at $x = 4$. The absolute minimum is -1 and it occurs at $x = 2$.

4.14. $c = 2$

4.15. $\frac{5}{2\sqrt{2}}$ sec

4.16. f has a local minimum at -2 and a local maximum at $3.$

4.17. f has no local extrema because f' does not change sign at $x = 1.$

4.18. f is concave up over the interval $\left(-\infty, \frac{1}{2}\right)$ and concave down over the interval $\left(\frac{1}{2}, \infty\right)$

4.19. f has a local maximum at -2 and a local minimum at $3.$

4.20. Both limits are $3.$ The line $y = 3$ is a horizontal asymptote.

4.21. Let $\varepsilon > 0.$ Let $N = \frac{1}{\sqrt{\varepsilon}}.$ Therefore, for all $x > N,$ we have $\left|3 - \frac{1}{x^2} - 3\right| = \frac{1}{x^2} < \frac{1}{N^2} = \varepsilon$ Therefore, $\lim_{x \to \infty}\left(3 - 1/x^2\right) = 3.$

4.22. Let $M > 0.$ Let $N = \sqrt{\frac{M}{3}}.$ Then, for all $x > N,$ we have $3x^2 > 3N^2 = 3\left(\sqrt{\frac{M}{3}}\right)^2 2 = \frac{3M}{3} = M$

4.23. $-\infty$

4.24. $\frac{3}{5}$

4.25. $\pm\sqrt{3}$

4.26. $\lim_{x \to \infty} f(x) = \frac{3}{5}, \quad \lim_{x \to -\infty} f(x) = -2$

4.27.

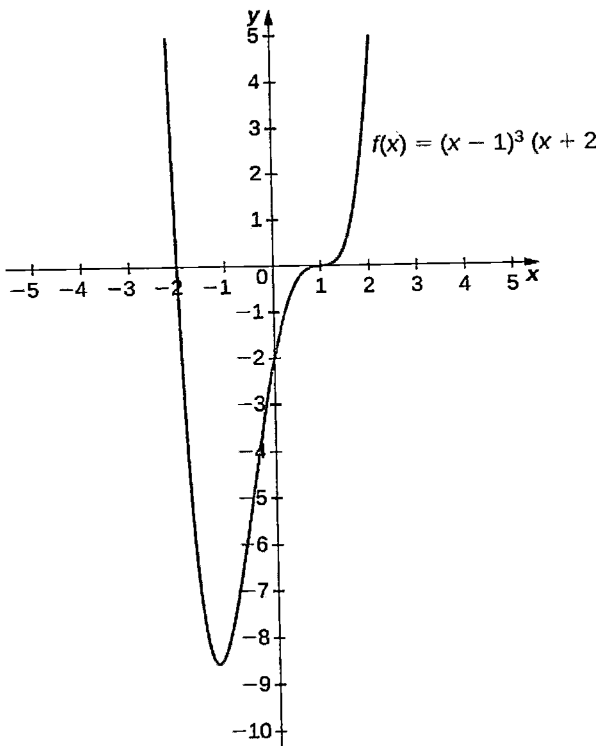

4.28.

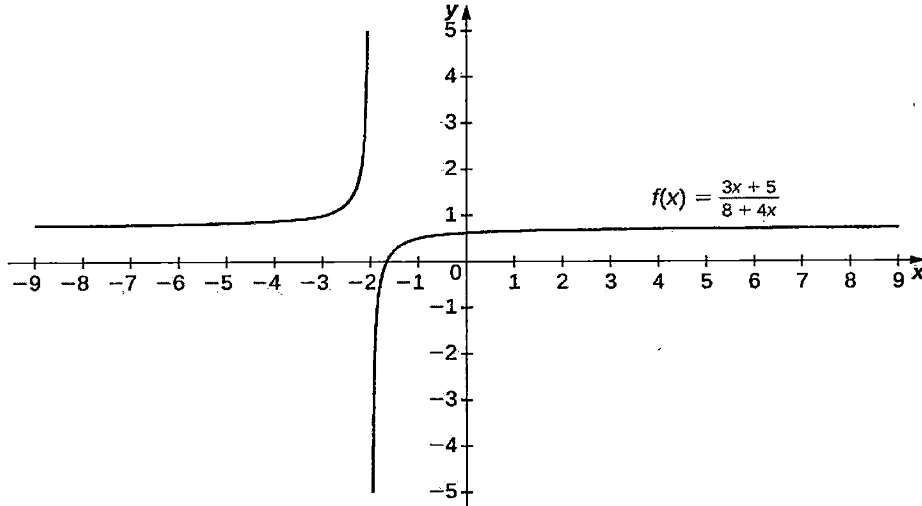

4.29. $y = \frac{3}{2}x$

4.30. The function f has a cusp at $(0, 5)$ $\lim_{x \to 0^-} f'(x) = \infty$, $\lim_{x \to 0^+} f'(x) = -\infty$. For end behavior, $\lim_{x \to \pm\infty} f(x) = -\infty$.

4.31. The maximum area is 5000 ft^2.

4.32. $V(x) = x(20 - 2x)(30 - 2x)$. The domain is $[0, 10]$.

4.33. $T(x) = \frac{x}{6} + \frac{\sqrt{(15 - x)^2 + 1}}{2.5}$

4.34. The company should charge $\$75$ per car per day.

4.35. $A(x) = 4x\sqrt{1 - x^2}$. The domain of consideration is $[0, 1]$.

4.36. $c(x) = \frac{259.2}{x} + 0.2x^2$ dollars

4.37. 1

4.38. 0

4.39. $\lim_{x \to 0^+} \cos x = 1$. Therefore, we cannot apply L'Hôpital's rule. The limit of the quotient is ∞

4.40. 1

4.41. 0

4.42. e

4.43. 1

4.44. The function 2^x grows faster than x^{100}.

4.45. $x_1 \approx 0.33333333$, $x_2 \approx 0.347222222$

4.46. $x_1 = 2$, $x_2 = 1.75$

4.47. $x_1 \approx -1.842105263$, $x_2 \approx -1.772826920$

4.48. $x_1 = 6$, $x_2 = 8$, $x_3 = \frac{26}{3}$, $x_4 = \frac{80}{9}$, $x_5 = \frac{242}{27}$; $x^* = 9$

4.49. $-\cos x + C$

4.50. $\frac{d}{dx}(x \sin x + \cos x + C) = \sin x + x \cos x - \sin x = x \cos x$

4.51. $x^4 - \frac{5}{3}x^3 + \frac{1}{2}x^2 - 7x + C$

4.52. $y = -\frac{3}{x} + 5$

4.53. 2.93 sec, 64.5 ft

Section Exercises

1. 8

3. $\frac{13}{\sqrt{10}}$

5. $2\sqrt{3}$ ft/sec

7. The distance is decreasing at 390 mi/h.

9. The distance between them shrinks at a rate of $\frac{1320}{13} \approx 101.5$ mph.

11. $\frac{9}{2}$ ft/sec

13. It grows at a rate $\frac{4}{9}$ ft/sec

15. The distance is increasing at $\frac{(135\sqrt{26})}{26}$ ft/sec

17. $-\frac{5}{6}$ m/sec

19. 240π m^2/sec

21. $\frac{1}{2\sqrt{\pi}}$ cm

23. The area is increasing at a rate $\frac{(3\sqrt{3})}{8}$ft /sec.

25. The depth of the water decreases at $\frac{128}{125\pi}$ ft/min.

27. The volume is decreasing at a rate of $\frac{(25\pi)}{16}$ft^3 /min.

29. The water flows out at rate $\frac{(2\pi)}{5}$m /min.

31. $\frac{3}{2}$ m/sec

33. $\frac{25}{19\pi}$ ft/min

35. $\frac{2}{45\pi}$ ft/min

37. The angle decreases at $\frac{400}{1681}$ rad/sec.

39. 100π/min

41. The angle is changing at a rate of $\frac{21}{25}$ rad/sec.

43. The distance is increasing at a rate of 62.50 ft/sec.

45. The distance is decreasing at a rate of 11.99 ft/sec.

47. $f'(a) = 0$

49. The linear approximation exact when $y = f(x)$ is linear or constant.

51. $L(x) = \frac{1}{2} - \frac{1}{4}(x - 2)$

53. $L(x) = 1$

55. $L(x) = 0$

57. 0.02

59. 1.9996875

61. 0.001593

63. 1; error, ~0.00005

65. 0.97; error, ~0.0006

67. $3 - \frac{1}{600}$; error, $\sim 4.632 \times 10^{-7}$
69. $dy = (\cos x - x \sin x)dx$
71. $dy = \left(\frac{x^2 - 2x - 2}{(x-1)^2}\right)dx$
73. $dy = -\frac{1}{(x+1)^2}dx, \quad -\frac{1}{16}$
75. $dy = \frac{9x^2 + 12x - 2}{2(x+1)^{3/2}}dx, \quad -0.1$
77. $dy = \left(3x^2 + 2 - \frac{1}{x^2}\right)dx, \quad 0.2$
79. $12x\,dx$
81. $4\pi r^2\,dr$
83. $-1.2\pi\ \text{cm}^3$
85. $-100\ \text{ft}^3$
91. Answers may vary
93. Answers will vary
95. No; answers will vary
97. Since the absolute maximum is the function (output) value rather than the x value, the answer is no; answers will vary
99. When $a = 0$
101. Absolute minimum at 3; Absolute maximum at −2.2; local minima at −2, 1; local maxima at −1, 2
103. Absolute minima at −2, 2; absolute maxima at −2.5, 2.5; local minimum at 0; local maxima at −1, 1
105. Answers may vary.
107. Answers may vary.
109. $x = 1$
111. None
113. $x = 0$
115. None
117. $x = -1, 1$
119. Absolute maximum: $x = 4, \quad y = \frac{33}{2}$; absolute minimum: $x = 1, \quad y = 3$
121. Absolute minimum: $x = \frac{1}{2}, \quad y = 4$
123. Absolute maximum: $x = 2\pi, \quad y = 2\pi$; absolute minimum: $x = 0, \quad y = 0$
125. Absolute maximum: $x = -3$; absolute minimum: $-1 \le x \le 1, \quad y = 2$
127. Absolute maximum: $x = \frac{\pi}{4}, \quad y = \sqrt{2}$; absolute minimum: $x = \frac{5\pi}{4}, \quad y = -\sqrt{2}$
129. Absolute minimum: $x = -2, \quad y = 1$
131. Absolute minimum: $x = -3, \quad y = -135$; local maximum: $x = 0, \quad y = 0$; local minimum: $x = 1, \quad y = -7$
133. Local maximum: $x = 1 - 2\sqrt{2}, \quad y = 3 - 4\sqrt{2}$; local minimum: $x = 1 + 2\sqrt{2}, \quad y = 3 + 4\sqrt{2}$
135. Absolute maximum: $x = \frac{\sqrt{2}}{2}, \quad y = \frac{3}{2}$; absolute minimum: $x = -\frac{\sqrt{2}}{2}, \quad y = -\frac{3}{2}$
137. Local maximum: $x = -2, \quad y = 59$; local minimum: $x = 1, \quad y = -130$
139. Absolute maximum: $x = 0, \quad y = 1$; absolute minimum: $x = -2, 2, \quad y = 0$
141. $h = \frac{9245}{49}\ \text{m}, \ t = \frac{300}{49}\ \text{s}$
143. The global minimum was in 1848, when no gold was produced.
145. Absolute minima: $x = 0, \quad x = 2, \quad y = 1$; local maximum at $x = 1, \quad y = 2$
147. No maxima/minima if a is odd, minimum at $x = 1$ if a is even
149. One example is $f(x) = |x| + 3, \ -2 \le x \le 2$
151. Yes, but the Mean Value Theorem still does not apply

153. $(-\infty, 0), (0, \infty)$

155. $(-\infty, -2), (2, \infty)$

157. 2 points

159. 5 points

161. $c = \frac{2\sqrt{3}}{3}$

163. $c = \frac{1}{2}, 1, \frac{3}{2}$

165. $c = 1$

167. Not differentiable

169. Not differentiable

171. Yes

173. The Mean Value Theorem does not apply since the function is discontinuous at $x = \frac{1}{4}, \frac{3}{4}, \frac{5}{4}, \frac{7}{4}$.

175. Yes

177. The Mean Value Theorem does not apply; discontinuous at $x = 0$.

179. Yes

181. The Mean Value Theorem does not apply; not differentiable at $x = 0$.

183. $b = \pm 2\sqrt{c}$

185. $c = \pm\frac{1}{\pi}\cos^{-1}\left(\frac{\sqrt{\pi}}{2}\right), \quad c = \pm 0.1533$

187. The Mean Value Theorem does not apply.

189. $\frac{1}{2\sqrt{c+1}} - \frac{2}{c^3} = \frac{521}{2880}; \; c = 3.133, 5.867$

191. Yes

193. It is constant.

195. It is not a local maximum/minimum because f' does not change sign

197. No

199. False; for example, $y = \sqrt{x}$.

201. Increasing for $-2 < x < -1$ and $x > 2$; decreasing for $x < -2$ and $-1 < x < 2$

203. Decreasing for $x < 1$, increasing for $x > 1$

205. Decreasing for $-2 < x < -1$ and $1 < x < 2$; increasing for $-1 < x < 1$ and $x < -2$ and $x > 2$

207. a. Increasing over $-2 < x < -1, 0 < x < 1, x > 2$, decreasing over $x < -2$, $-1 < x < 0, 1 < x < 2$; b. maxima at $x = -1$ and $x = 1$, minima at $x = -2$ and $x = 0$ and $x = 2$

209. a. Increasing over $x > 0$, decreasing over $x < 0$; b. Minimum at $x = 0$

211. Concave up on all x, no inflection points

213. Concave up on all x, no inflection points

215. Concave up for $x < 0$ and $x > 1$, concave down for $0 < x < 1$, inflection points at $x = 0$ and $x = 1$

217. Answers will vary

219. Answers will vary

221. a. Increasing over $-\frac{\pi}{2} < x < \frac{\pi}{2}$, decreasing over $x < -\frac{\pi}{2}, x > \frac{\pi}{2}$ b. Local maximum at $x = \frac{\pi}{2}$; local minimum at $x = -\frac{\pi}{2}$

223. a. Concave up for $x > \frac{4}{3}$, concave down for $x < \frac{4}{3}$ b. Inflection point at $x = \frac{4}{3}$

225. a. Increasing over $x < 0$ and $x > 4$, decreasing over $0 < x < 4$ b. Maximum at $x = 0$, minimum at $x = 4$ c. Concave up for $x > 2$, concave down for $x < 2$ d. Infection point at $x = 2$

227. a. Increasing over $x < 0$ and $x > \frac{60}{11}$, decreasing over $0 < x < \frac{60}{11}$ b. Minimum at $x = \frac{60}{11}$ c. Concave down for $x < \frac{54}{11}$, concave up for $x > \frac{54}{11}$ d. Inflection point at $x = \frac{54}{11}$

229. a. Increasing over $x > -\frac{1}{2}$, decreasing over $x < -\frac{1}{2}$ b. Minimum at $x = -\frac{1}{2}$ c. Concave up for all x d. No inflection points

231. a. Increases over $-\frac{1}{4} < x < \frac{3}{4}$, decreases over $x > \frac{3}{4}$ and $x < -\frac{1}{4}$ b. Minimum at $x = -\frac{1}{4}$, maximum at $x = \frac{3}{4}$ c. Concave up for $-\frac{3}{4} < x < \frac{1}{4}$, concave down for $x < -\frac{3}{4}$ and $x > \frac{1}{4}$ d. Inflection points at $x = -\frac{3}{4}, x = \frac{1}{4}$

233. a. Increasing for all x b. No local minimum or maximum c. Concave up for $x > 0$, concave down for $x < 0$ d. Inflection point at $x = 0$

235. a. Increasing for all x where defined b. No local minima or maxima c. Concave up for $x < 1$; concave down for $x > 1$ d. No inflection points in domain

237. a. Increasing over $-\frac{\pi}{4} < x < \frac{3\pi}{4}$, decreasing over $x > \frac{3\pi}{4}, x < -\frac{\pi}{4}$ b. Minimum at $x = -\frac{\pi}{4}$, maximum at $x = \frac{3\pi}{4}$ c. Concave up for $-\frac{\pi}{2} < x < \frac{\pi}{2}$, concave down for $x < -\frac{\pi}{2}, x > \frac{\pi}{2}$ d. Infection points at $x = \pm\frac{\pi}{2}$

239. a. Increasing over $x > 4$, decreasing over $0 < x < 4$ b. Minimum at $x = 4$ c. Concave up for $0 < x < 8\sqrt[3]{2}$, concave down for $x > 8\sqrt[3]{2}$ d. Inflection point at $x = 8\sqrt[3]{2}$

241. $f > 0, f' > 0, f'' < 0$

243. $f > 0, f' < 0, f'' < 0$

245. $f > 0, f' > 0, f'' > 0$

247. True, by the Mean Value Theorem

249. True, examine derivative

251. $x = 1$

253. $x = -1, x = 2$

255. $x = 0$

257. Yes, there is a vertical asymptote

259. Yes, there is vertical asymptote

261. 0

263. ∞

265. $-\frac{1}{7}$

267. -2

269. -4

271. Horizontal: none, vertical: $x = 0$

273. Horizontal: none, vertical: $x = \pm 2$

275. Horizontal: none, vertical: none

277. Horizontal: $y = 0$, vertical: $x = \pm 1$

279. Horizontal: $y = 0$, vertical: $x = 0$ and $x = -1$

281. Horizontal: $y = 1$, vertical: $x = 1$

283. Horizontal: none, vertical: none

285. Answers will vary, for example: $y = \frac{2x}{x-1}$

287. Answers will vary, for example: $y = \frac{4x}{x+1}$

289. $y = 0$

291. ∞

293. $y = 3$

295.

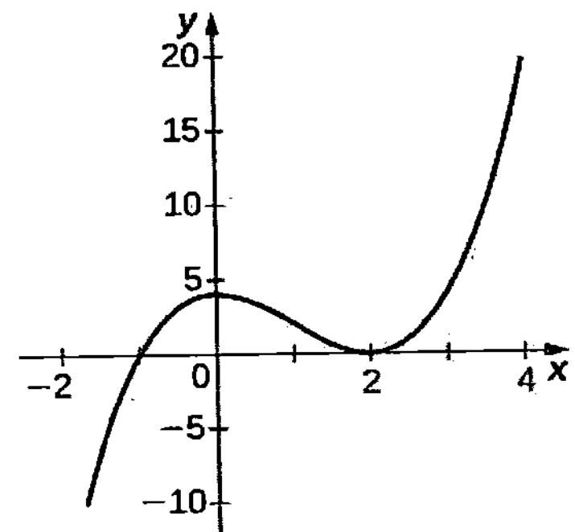

297.

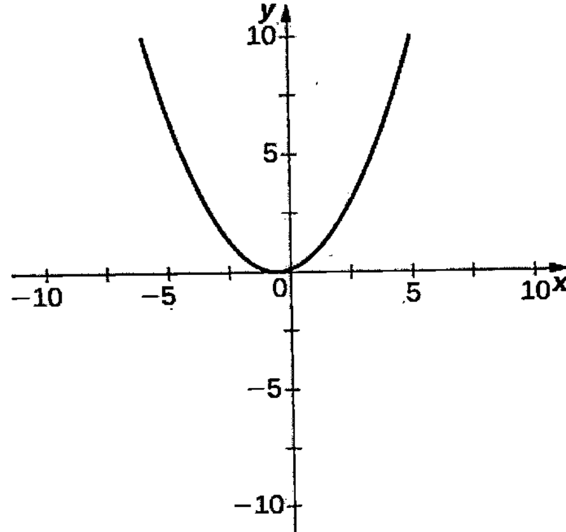

299.

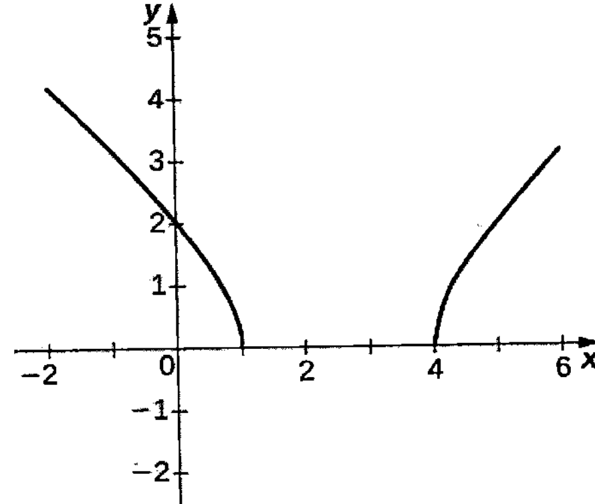

301.

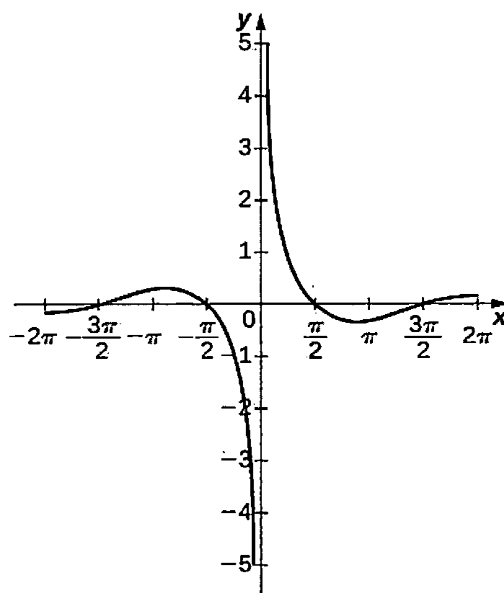
y
5
4
3
2
1
0
−1
−2
−3
−4
−5
x
−2π
−3π/2
−π
−π/2
π/2
π
3π/2
2π

303.

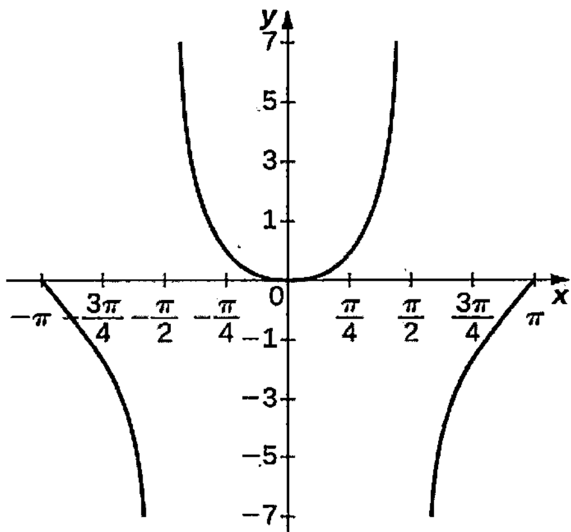
y
7
5
3
1
0
−1
−3
−5
−7
x
−π
−3π/4
−π/2
−π/4
π/4
π/2
3π/4
π

305.

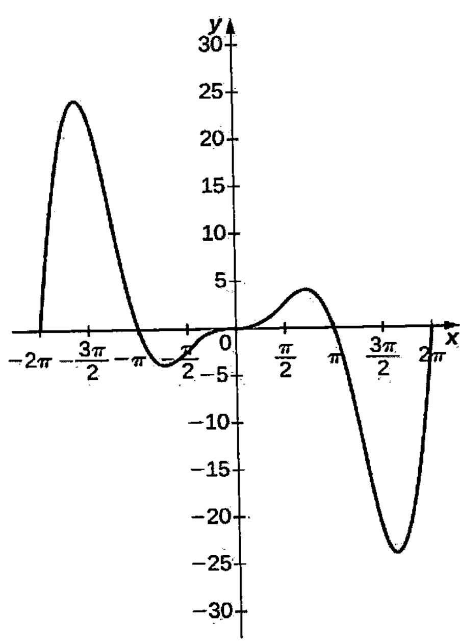

307. The degree of $Q(x)$ must be greater than the degree of $P(x)$.

309. $\lim_{x \to 1^-} f(x) = -\infty$ and $\lim_{x \to 1^-} g(x) = \infty$

311. The critical points can be the minima, maxima, or neither.

313. False; $y = -x^2$ has a minimum only

315. $h = \frac{62}{3}$ in.

317. 1

319. 100 ft by 100 ft

321. 40 ft by 40 ft

323. 19.73 ft.

325. 84 bpm

327. $T(\theta) = \frac{40\theta}{3v} + \frac{40\cos\theta}{v}$

329. $v = \sqrt{\frac{b}{a}}$

331. approximately 34.02 mph

333. 4

335. 0

337. Maximal: $x = 5, y = 5$; minimal: $x = 0, y = 10$ and $y = 0, x = 10$

339. Maximal: $x = 1, y = 9$; minimal: none

341. $\frac{4\pi}{3\sqrt{3}}$

343. 6

345. $r = 2, h = 4$

347. (2, 1)

349. (0.8351, 0.6974)

351. $A = 20r - 2r^2 - \frac{1}{2}\pi r^2$

353. $C(x) = 5x^2 + \frac{32}{x}$

355. $P(x) = (50 - x)(800 + 25x - 50)$

357. ∞

359. $\frac{1}{2a}$

361. $\frac{1}{na^{n-1}}$

363. Cannot apply directly; use logarithms

365. Cannot apply directly; rewrite as $\lim_{x \to 0} x^3$

367. 6

369. -2

371. -1

373. n

375. $-\frac{1}{2}$

377. $\frac{1}{2}$

379. 1

381. $\frac{1}{6}$

383. 1

385. 0

387. 0

389. -1

391. ∞

393. 1

395. $\frac{1}{e}$

397. 0

399. 1

401. 0

403. $\tan(1)$

405. 2

407. $F(x_n) = x_n - \frac{x_n{}^3 + 2x_n + 1}{3x_n{}^2 + 2}$

409. $F(x_n) = x_n - \frac{e^{x_n}}{e^{x_n}}$

411. $|c| > 0.5$ fails, $|c| \leq 0.5$ works

413. $c = \frac{1}{f'(x_n)}$

415. a. $x_1 = \frac{12}{25}, x_2 = \frac{312}{625}$; b. $x_1 = -4, x_2 = -40$

417. a. $x_1 = 1.291, x_2 = 0.8801$; b. $x_1 = 0.7071, x_2 = 1.189$

419. a. $x_1 = -\frac{26}{25}, x_2 = -\frac{1224}{625}$; b. $x_1 = 4, x_2 = 18$

421. a. $x_1 = \frac{6}{10}, x_2 = \frac{6}{10}$; b. $x_1 = 2, x_2 = 2$

423. 3.1623 or -3.1623

425. 0, -1 or 1

427. 0

429. 0.5188 or -1.2906

431. 0

433. 4.493

435. 0.159, 3.146

437. We need f to be twice continuously differentiable.

439. $x = 0$

441. $x = -1$

443. $x = 5.619$

445. $x = -1.326$

447. There is no solution to the equation.

449. It enters a cycle.

451. 0

453. -0.3513

455. Newton: 11 iterations, secant: 16 iterations

457. Newton: three iterations, secant: six iterations

459. Newton: five iterations, secant: eight iterations

461. $E = 4.071$

463. 4.394%

465. $F'(x) = 15x^2 + 4x + 3$

467. $F'(x) = 2xe^x + x^2 e^x$

469. $F'(x) = e^x$

471. $F(x) = e^x - x^3 - \cos(x) + C$

473. $F(x) = \frac{x^2}{2} - x - 2\cos(2x) + C$

475. $F(x) = \frac{1}{2}x^2 + 4x^3 + C$

477. $F(x) = \frac{2}{5}(\sqrt{x})^5 + C$

479. $F(x) = \frac{3}{2}x^{2/3} + C$

481. $F(x) = x + \tan(x) + C$

483. $F(x) = \frac{1}{3}\sin^3(x) + C$

485. $F(x) = -\frac{1}{2}\cot(x) - \frac{1}{x} + C$

487. $F(x) = -\sec x - 4\csc x + C$

489. $F(x) = -\frac{1}{8}e^{-4x} - \cos x + C$

491. $-\cos x + C$

493. $3x - \frac{2}{x} + C$

495. $\frac{8}{3}x^{3/2} + \frac{4}{5}x^{5/4} + C$

497. $14x - \frac{2}{x} - \frac{1}{2x^2} + C$

499. $f(x) = -\frac{1}{2x^2} + \frac{3}{2}$

501. $f(x) = \sin x + \tan x + 1$

503. $f(x) = -\frac{1}{6}x^3 - \frac{2}{x} + \frac{13}{6}$

505. Answers may vary; one possible answer is $f(x) = e^{-x}$

507. Answers may vary; one possible answer is $f(x) = -\sin x$

509. 5.867 sec

511. 7.333 sec

513. 13.75 ft/sec^2

515. $F(x) = \frac{1}{3}x^3 + 2x$

517. $F(x) = x^2 - \cos x + 1$

519. $F(x) = -\frac{1}{(x+1)} + 1$

521. True
523. False

Review Exercises

525. True, by Mean Value Theorem
527. True
529. Increasing: $(-2, 0) \cup (4, \infty)$, decreasing: $(-\infty, -2) \cup (0, 4)$

531. $L(x) = \frac{17}{16} + \frac{1}{2}(1 + 4\pi)\left(x - \frac{1}{4}\right)$

533. Critical point: $x = \frac{3\pi}{4}$, absolute minimum: $x = 0$, absolute maximum: $x = \pi$

535. Increasing: $(-1, 0) \cup (3, \infty)$, decreasing: $(-\infty, -1) \cup (0, 3)$, concave up: $\left(-\infty, \frac{1}{3}\left(2 - \sqrt{13}\right)\right) \cup \left(\frac{1}{3}\left(2 + \sqrt{13}\right), \infty\right)$, concave down: $\left(\frac{1}{3}\left(2 - \sqrt{13}\right), \frac{1}{3}\left(2 + \sqrt{13}\right)\right)$

537. Increasing: $\left(\frac{1}{4}, \infty\right)$, decreasing: $\left(0, \frac{1}{4}\right)$, concave up: $(0, \infty)$, concave down: nowhere

539. 3

541. $-\frac{1}{\pi}$

543. $x_1 = -1, x_2 = -1$

545. $F(x) = \frac{2x^{3/2}}{3} + \frac{1}{x} + C$

547.

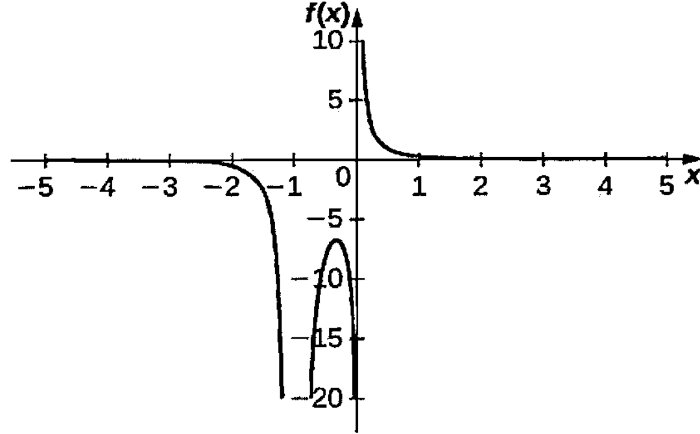

Inflection points: none; critical points: $x = -\frac{1}{3}$; zeros: none; vertical asymptotes: $x = -1$, $x = 0$; horizontal asymptote: $y = 0$

549. The height is decreasing at a rate of 0.125 m/sec

551. $x = \sqrt{ab}$ feet

Chapter 5

Checkpoint

5.1. $\sum_{i=3}^{6} 2^i = 2^3 + 2^4 + 2^5 + 2^6 = 120$

5.2. 15,550
5.3. 440
5.4. The left-endpoint approximation is 0.7595. The right-endpoint approximation is 0.6345. See the below **image**.

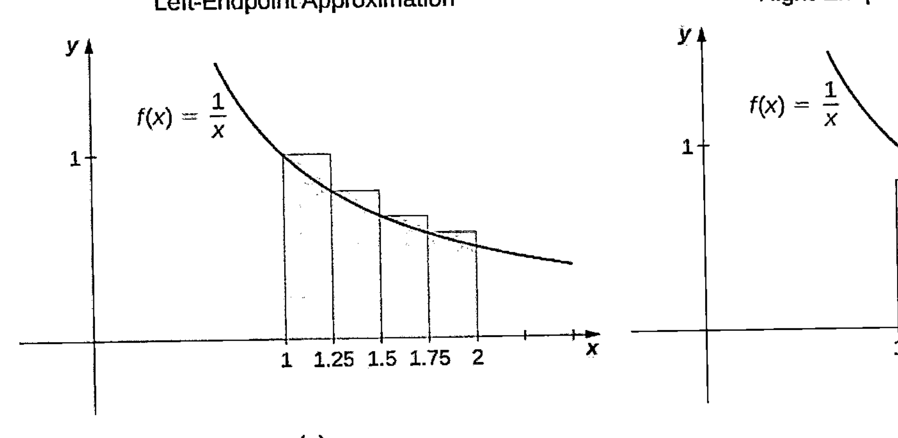

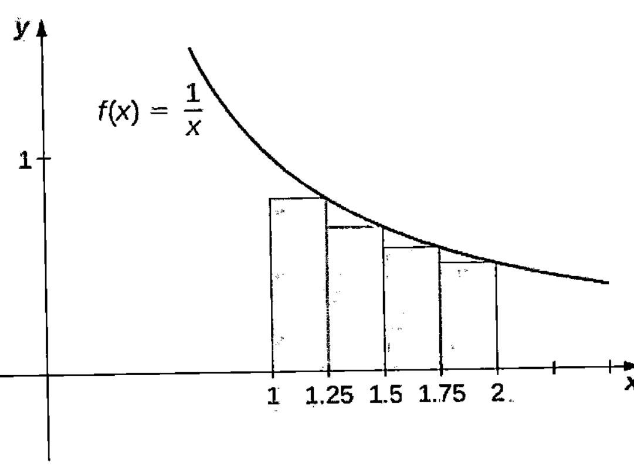

5.5.

a. Upper sum $= 8.0313$.

b.

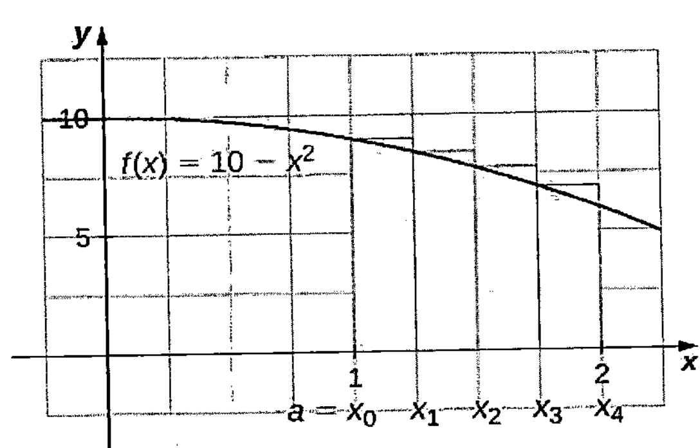

5.6. $A \approx 1.125$

5.7. 6

5.8. 18 square units

5.9. 6

5.10. 18

5.11. $6\int_1^3 x^3\,dx - 4\int_1^3 x^2\,dx + 2\int_1^3 x\,dx - \int_1^3 3\,dx$

5.12. −7

5.13. 3

5.14. Average value $= 1.5$; $c = 3$

5.15. $c = \sqrt{3}$

5.16. $g'(r) = \sqrt{r^2 + 4}$

5.17. $F'(x) = 3x^2 \cos x^3$

5.18. $F'(x) = 2x \cos x^2 - \cos x$

5.19. $\frac{7}{24}$

5.20. Kathy still wins, but by a much larger margin: James skates 24 ft in 3 sec, but Kathy skates 29.3634 ft in 3 sec.

5.21. $-\frac{10}{3}$

5.22. Net displacement: $\frac{e^2-9}{2} \approx -0.8055$ m; total distance traveled: $4\ln 4 - 7.5 + \frac{e^2}{2} \approx 1.740$ m

5.23. 17.5 mi

5.24. $\frac{64}{5}$

5.25. $\int 3x^2\left(x^3-3\right)^2 dx = \frac{1}{3}\left(x^3-3\right)^3 + C$

5.26. $\frac{\left(x^3+5\right)^{10}}{30} + C$

5.27. $-\frac{1}{\sin t} + C$

5.28. $-\frac{\cos^4 t}{4} + C$

5.29. $\frac{91}{3}$

5.30. $\frac{2}{3\pi} \approx 0.2122$

5.31. $\int x^2 e^{-2x^3} dx = -\frac{1}{6}e^{-2x^3} + C$

5.32. $\int e^x(3e^x-2)^2 dx = \frac{1}{9}(3e^x-2)^3$

5.33. $\int 2x^3 e^{x^4} dx = \frac{1}{2}e^{x^4}$

5.34. $\frac{1}{2}\int_0^4 e^u du = \frac{1}{2}\left(e^4-1\right)$

5.35. $Q(t) = \frac{2^t}{\ln 2} + 8.557$. There are 20,099 bacteria in the dish after 3 hours.

5.36. There are 116 flies.

5.37. $\int_1^2 \frac{1}{x^3}e^{4x^{-2}} dx = \frac{1}{8}\left[e^4 - e\right]$

5.38. $\ln|x+2| + C$

5.39. $\frac{x}{\ln 3}(\ln x - 1) + C$

5.40. $\frac{1}{4}\sin^{-1}(4x) + C$

5.41. $\sin^{-1}\left(\frac{x}{3}\right) + C$

5.42. $\frac{1}{10}\tan^{-1}\left(\frac{2x}{5}\right) + C$

5.43. $\frac{1}{4}\tan^{-1}\left(\frac{x}{4}\right) + C$

5.44. $\frac{\pi}{8}$

Section Exercises

1. a. They are equal; both represent the sum of the first 10 whole numbers. b. They are equal; both represent the sum of the first 10 whole numbers. c. They are equal by substituting $j = i - 1$. d. They are equal; the first sum factors the terms of the second.

3. $385 - 30 = 355$

5. $15 - (-12) = 27$

7. $5(15) + 4(-12) = 27$

9. $\sum_{j=1}^{50} j^2 - 2\sum_{j=1}^{50} j = \frac{(50)(51)(101)}{6} - \frac{2(50)(51)}{2} = 40,375$

11. $4\sum_{k=1}^{25} k^2 - 100\sum_{k=1}^{25} k = \frac{4(25)(26)(51)}{9} - 50(25)(26) = -10,400$

13. $R_4 = 0.25$

15. $R_6 = 0.372$

17. $L_4 = 2.20$

19. $L_8 = 0.6875$

21. $L_6 = 9.000 = R_6$. The graph of f is a triangle with area 9.

23. $L_6 = 13.12899 = R_6$. They are equal.

25. $L_{10} = \frac{4}{10}\sum_{i=1}^{10} \sqrt{4 - \left(-2 + 4\frac{(i-1)}{10}\right)}$

27. $R_{100} = \frac{e-1}{100}\sum_{i=1}^{100} \ln\left(1 + (e-1)\frac{i}{100}\right)$

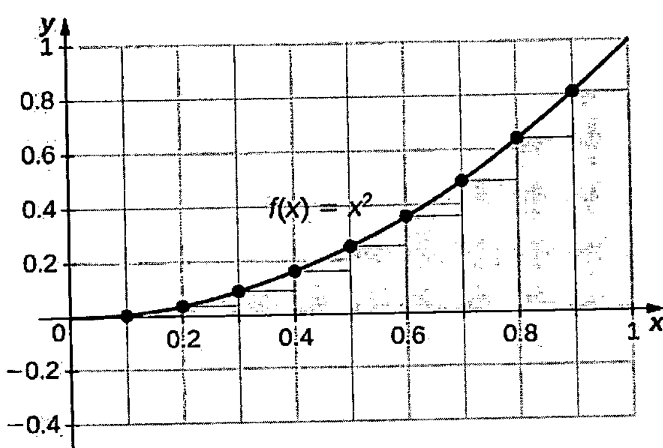

29.
$R_{100} = 0.33835,\ L_{100} = 0.32835$. The plot shows that the left Riemann sum is an underestimate because the function is increasing. Similarly, the right Riemann sum is an overestimate. The area lies between the left and right Riemann sums. Ten rectangles are shown for visual clarity. This behavior persists for more rectangles.

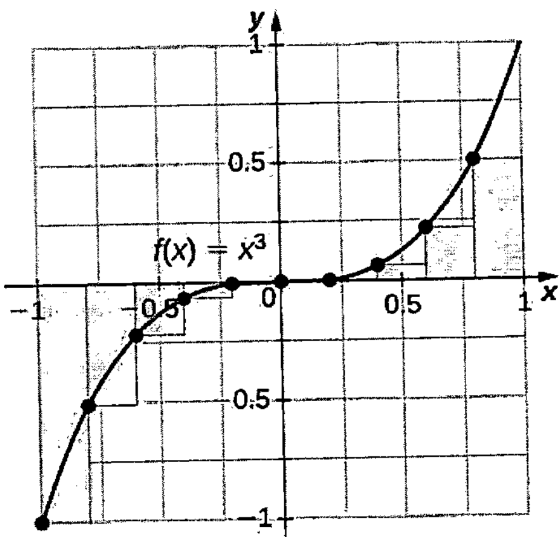

31.
$L_{100} = -0.02,\ R_{100} = 0.02$. The left endpoint sum is an underestimate because the function is increasing. Similarly, a right endpoint approximation is an overestimate. The area lies between the left and right endpoint estimates.

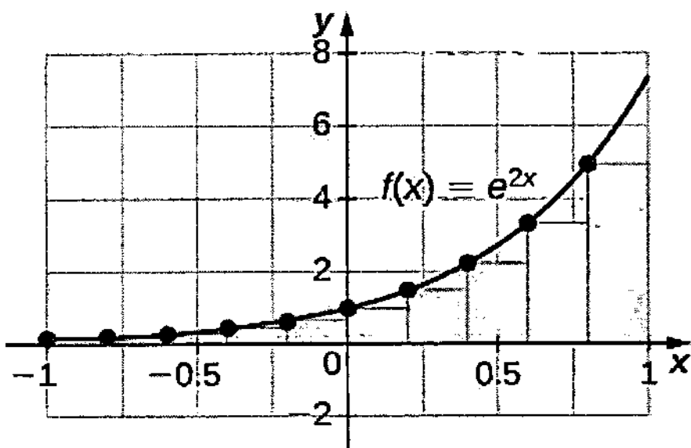

33. $L_{100} = 3.555,\ R_{100} = 3.670.$ The plot shows that the left Riemann sum is an underestimate because the function is increasing. Ten rectangles are shown for visual clarity. This behavior persists for more rectangles.
35. The sum represents the cumulative rainfall in January 2009.
37. The total mileage is $7 \times \sum_{i=1}^{25} \left(1 + \frac{(i-1)}{10}\right) = 7 \times 25 + \frac{7}{10} \times 12 \times 25 = 385 \text{ mi}.$
39. Add the numbers to get 8.1-in. net increase.
41. 309,389,957
43. $L_8 = 3 + 2 + 1 + 2 + 3 + 4 + 5 + 4 = 24$
45. $L_8 = 3 + 5 + 7 + 6 + 8 + 6 + 5 + 4 = 44$
47. $L_{10} \approx 1.7604,\ L_{30} \approx 1.7625,\ L_{50} \approx 1.76265$
49. $R_1 = -1,\ L_1 = 1,\ R_{10} = -0.1,\ L_{10} = 0.1,\ L_{100} = 0.01,$ and $R_{100} = -0.1.$ By symmetry of the graph, the exact area is zero.
51. $R_1 = 0,\ L_1 = 0,\ R_{10} = 2.4499,\ L_{10} = 2.4499,\ R_{100} = 2.1365,\ L_{100} = 2.1365$
53. If $[c,\ d]$ is a subinterval of $[a,\ b]$ under one of the left-endpoint sum rectangles, then the area of the rectangle contributing to the left-endpoint estimate is $f(c)(d-c).$ But, $f(c) \le f(x)$ for $c \le x \le d,$ so the area under the graph of f between c and d is $f(c)(d-c)$ plus the area below the graph of f but above the horizontal line segment at height $f(c),$ which is positive. As this is true for each left-endpoint sum interval, it follows that the left Riemann sum is less than or equal to the area below the graph of f on $[a,\ b]$.
55. $L_N = \frac{b-a}{N} \sum_{i=1}^{N} f\left(a + (b-a)\frac{i-1}{N}\right) = \frac{b-a}{N} \sum_{i=0}^{N-1} f\left(a + (b-a)\frac{i}{N}\right)$ and $R_N = \frac{b-a}{N} \sum_{i=1}^{N} f\left(a + (b-a)\frac{i}{N}\right).$ The left sum has a term corresponding to $i = 0$ and the right sum has a term corresponding to $i = N.$ In $R_N - L_N,$ any term corresponding to $i = 1, 2, \ldots, N-1$ occurs once with a plus sign and once with a minus sign, so each such term cancels and one is left with $R_N - L_N = \frac{b-a}{N}\left(f(a + (b-a))\frac{N}{N}\right) - \left(f(a) + (b-a)\frac{0}{N}\right) = \frac{b-a}{N}(f(b) - f(a)).$
57. Graph 1: a. $L(A) = 0,\ B(A) = 20;$ b. $U(A) = 20.$ Graph 2: a. $L(A) = 9;$ b. $B(A) = 11,\ U(A) = 20.$ Graph 3: a. $L(A) = 11.0;$ b. $B(A) = 4.5,\ U(A) = 15.5.$
59. Let A be the area of the unit circle. The circle encloses n congruent triangles each of area $\frac{\sin\left(\frac{2\pi}{n}\right)}{2},$ so $\frac{n}{2}\sin\left(\frac{2\pi}{n}\right) \le A.$ Similarly, the circle is contained inside n congruent triangles each of area $\frac{BH}{2} = \frac{1}{2}\left(\cos\left(\frac{\pi}{n}\right) + \sin\left(\frac{\pi}{n}\right)\tan\left(\frac{\pi}{n}\right)\right)\sin\left(\frac{2\pi}{n}\right),$ so $A \le \frac{n}{2}\sin\left(\frac{2\pi}{n}\right)\left(\cos\left(\frac{\pi}{n}\right)\right) + \sin\left(\frac{\pi}{n}\right)\tan\left(\frac{\pi}{n}\right).$ As $n \to \infty,\ \frac{n}{2}\sin\left(\frac{2\pi}{n}\right) = \frac{\pi\sin\left(\frac{2\pi}{n}\right)}{\left(\frac{2\pi}{n}\right)} \to \pi,$ so we conclude $\pi \le A.$ Also, as $n \to \infty,\ \cos\left(\frac{\pi}{n}\right) + \sin\left(\frac{\pi}{n}\right)\tan\left(\frac{\pi}{n}\right) \to 1,$ so we also have $A \le \pi.$ By the squeeze theorem for limits, we conclude that $A = \pi.$
61. $\int_0^2 \left(5x^2 - 3x^3\right)dx$
63. $\int_0^1 \cos^2(2\pi x)dx$

65. $\int_0^1 x dx$

67. $\int_3^6 x dx$

69. $\int_1^2 x \log(x^2) dx$

71. $1 + 2 \cdot 2 + 3 \cdot 3 = 14$

73. $1 - 4 + 9 = 6$

75. $1 - 2\pi + 9 = 10 - 2\pi$

77. The integral is the area of the triangle, $\frac{1}{2}$

79. The integral is the area of the triangle, 9.

81. The integral is the area $\frac{1}{2}\pi r^2 = 2\pi$.

83. The integral is the area of the "big" triangle less the "missing" triangle, $9 - \frac{1}{2}$.

85. $L = 2 + 0 + 10 + 5 + 4 = 21$, $R = 0 + 10 + 10 + 2 + 0 = 22$, $\frac{L + R}{2} = 21.5$

87. $L = 0 + 4 + 0 + 4 + 2 = 10$, $R = 4 + 0 + 2 + 4 + 0 = 10$, $\frac{L + R}{2} = 10$

89. $\int_2^4 f(x)dx + \int_2^4 g(x)dx = 8 - 3 = 5$

91. $\int_2^4 f(x)dx - \int_2^4 g(x)dx = 8 + 3 = 11$

93. $4\int_2^4 f(x)dx - 3\int_2^4 g(x)dx = 32 + 9 = 41$

95. The integrand is odd; the integral is zero.

97. The integrand is antisymmetric with respect to $x = 3$. The integral is zero.

99. $1 - \frac{1}{2} + \frac{1}{3} - \frac{1}{4} = \frac{7}{12}$

101. $\int_0^1 \left(1 - 6x + 12x^2 - 8x^3\right)dx = \left(x - 3x^2 + 4x^3 - 2x^4\right) = \left(1 - 3 + 4 - 2\right)\left(0 - 0 + 0 - 0\right) = 0$

103. $7 - \frac{5}{4} = \frac{23}{4}$

105. The integrand is negative over $[-2, 3]$.

107. $x \le x^2$ over $[1, 2]$, so $\sqrt{1 + x} \le \sqrt{1 + x^2}$ over $[1, 2]$.

109. $\cos(t) \ge \frac{\sqrt{2}}{2}$. Multiply by the length of the interval to get the inequality.

111. $f_{\text{ave}} = 0$; $c = 0$

113. $\frac{3}{2}$ when $c = \pm\frac{3}{2}$

115. $f_{\text{ave}} = 0$; $c = \frac{\pi}{2}, \frac{3\pi}{2}$

117. $L_{100} = 1.294$, $R_{100} = 1.301$; the exact average is between these values.

119. $L_{100} \times \left(\frac{1}{2}\right) = 0.5178$, $R_{100} \times \left(\frac{1}{2}\right) = 0.5294$

121. $L_1 = 0$, $L_{10} \times \left(\frac{1}{2}\right) = 8.743493$, $L_{100} \times \left(\frac{1}{2}\right) = 12.861728$. The exact answer ≈ 26.799, so L_{100} is not accurate.

123. $L_1 \times \left(\frac{1}{\pi}\right) = 1.352$, $L_{10} \times \left(\frac{1}{\pi}\right) = -0.1837$, $L_{100} \times \left(\frac{1}{\pi}\right) = -0.2956$. The exact answer ≈ -0.303, so L_{100} is not accurate to first decimal.

125. Use $\tan^2\theta + 1 = \sec^2\theta$. Then, $B - A = \int_{-\pi/4}^{\pi/4} 1dx = \frac{\pi}{2}$.

127. $\int_0^{2\pi} \cos^2 tdt = \pi$, so divide by the length 2π of the interval. $\cos^2 t$ has period π, so yes, it is true.

129. The integral is maximized when one uses the largest interval on which p is nonnegative. Thus, $A = \frac{-b - \sqrt{b^2 - 4ac}}{2a}$ and $B = \frac{-b + \sqrt{b^2 - 4ac}}{2a}$.

131. If $f(t_0) > g(t_0)$ for some $t_0 \in [a, b]$, then since $f - g$ is continuous, there is an interval containing t_0 such that $f(t) > g(t)$ over the interval $[c, d]$, and then $\int_d^d f(t)dt > \int_c^d g(t)dt$ over this interval.

133. The integral of f over an interval is the same as the integral of the average of f over that interval. Thus, $\int_a^b f(t)dt = \int_{a_0}^{a_1} f(t)dt + \int_{a_1}^{a_2} f(t)dt + \cdots + \int_{a_{N+1}}^{a_N} f(t)dt = \int_{a_0}^{a_1} 1dt + \int_{a_1}^{a_2} 1dt + \cdots + \int_{a_{N+1}}^{a_N} 1dt$ $= (a_1 - a_0) + (a_2 - a_1) + \cdots + (a_N - a_{N-1}) = a_N - a_0 = b - a.$ Dividing through by $b - a$ gives the desired identity.

135. $\int_0^N f(t)dt = \sum_{i=1}^N \int_{i-1}^i f(t)dt = \sum_{i=1}^N i^2 = \frac{N(N+1)(2N+1)}{6}$

137. $L_{10} = 1.815,\ R_{10} = 1.515,\ \frac{L_{10} + R_{10}}{2} = 1.665,$ so the estimate is accurate to two decimal places.

139. The average is $1/2$, which is equal to the integral in this case.

141. a. The graph is antisymmetric with respect to $t = \frac{1}{2}$ over $[0, 1]$, so the average value is zero. b. For any value of a, the graph between $[a, a+1]$ is a shift of the graph over $[0, 1]$, so the net areas above and below the axis do not change and the average remains zero.

143. Yes, the integral over any interval of length 1 is the same.

145. Yes. It is implied by the Mean Value Theorem for Integrals.

147. $F'(2) = -1$; average value of F' over $[1, 2]$ is $-1/2$.

149. $e^{\cos t}$

151. $\frac{1}{\sqrt{16 - x^2}}$

153. $\sqrt{x}\frac{d}{dx}\sqrt{x} = \frac{1}{2}$

155. $-\sqrt{1 - \cos^2 x}\frac{d}{dx}\cos x = |\sin x|\sin x$

157. $2x\frac{|x|}{1 + x^2}$

159. $\ln(e^{2x})\frac{d}{dx}e^x = 2xe^x$

161. a. f is positive over $[1, 2]$ and $[5, 6]$, negative over $[0, 1]$ and $[3, 4]$, and zero over $[2, 3]$ and $[4, 5]$. b. The maximum value is 2 and the minimum is −3. c. The average value is 0.

163. a. ℓ is positive over $[0, 1]$ and $[3, 6]$, and negative over $[1, 3]$. b. It is increasing over $[0, 1]$ and $[3, 5]$, and it is constant over $[1, 3]$ and $[5, 6]$. c. Its average value is $\frac{1}{3}$.

165. $T_{10} = 49.08,\ \int_{-2}^3 x^3 + 6x^2 + x - 5dx = 48$

167. $T_{10} = 260.836,\ \int_1^9 \left(\sqrt{x} + x^2\right)dx = 260$

169. $T_{10} = 3.058,\ \int_1^4 \frac{4}{x^2} dx = 3$

171. $F(x) = \frac{x^3}{3} + \frac{3x^2}{2} - 5x,\ F(3) - F(-2) = -\frac{35}{6}$

173. $F(x) = -\frac{t^5}{5} + \frac{13t^3}{3} - 36t,\ F(3) - F(2) = \frac{62}{15}$

175. $F(x) = \frac{x^{100}}{100},\ F(1) - F(0) = \frac{1}{100}$

177. $F(x) = \frac{x^3}{3} + \frac{1}{x},\ F(4) - F\left(\frac{1}{4}\right) = \frac{1125}{64}$

179. $F(x) = \sqrt{x},\ F(4) - F(1) = 1$

181. $F(x) = \frac{4}{3}t^{3/4},\ F(16) - F(1) = \frac{28}{3}$

183. $F(x) = -\cos x,\ F\left(\frac{\pi}{2}\right) - F(0) = 1$

185. $F(x) = \sec x,\ F\left(\frac{\pi}{4}\right) - F(0) = \sqrt{2} - 1$

187. $F(x) = -\cot(x),\ F\left(\frac{\pi}{2}\right) - F\left(\frac{\pi}{4}\right) = 1$

189. $F(x) = -\frac{1}{x} + \frac{1}{2x^2},\ F(-1) - F(-2) = \frac{7}{8}$

191. $F(x) = e^x - e$

193. $F(x) = 0$

195. $\int_{-2}^{-1}\left(t^2 - 2t - 3\right)dt - \int_{-1}^{3}\left(t^2 - 2t - 3\right)dt + \int_{3}^{4}\left(t^2 - 2t - 3\right)dt = \frac{46}{3}$

197. $-\int_{-\pi/2}^{0} \sin t dt + \int_0^{\pi/2} \sin t dt = 2$

199. a. The average is 11.21×10^9 since $\cos\left(\frac{\pi t}{6}\right)$ has period 12 and integral 0 over any period. Consumption is equal to the average when $\cos\left(\frac{\pi t}{6}\right) = 0$, when $t = 3$, and when $t = 9$. b. Total consumption is the average rate times duration: $11.21 \times 12 \times 10^9 = 1.35 \times 10^{11}$ c. $10^9\left(11.21 - \frac{1}{6}\int_3^9 \cos\left(\frac{\pi t}{6}\right)dt\right) = 10^9\left(11.21 + \frac{2}{\pi}\right) = 11.84x10^9$

201. If f is not constant, then its average is strictly smaller than the maximum and larger than the minimum, which are attained over $[a, b]$ by the extreme value theorem.

203. a. $d^2\theta = (a\cos\theta + c)^2 + b^2\sin^2\theta = a^2 + c^2\cos^2\theta + 2ac\cos\theta = (a + c\cos\theta)^2$; b. $\bar{d} = \frac{1}{2\pi}\int_0^{2\pi}(a + 2c\cos\theta)d\theta = a$

205. Mean gravitational force = $\frac{GmM}{2}\int_0^{2\pi} \frac{1}{\left(a + 2\sqrt{a^2 - b^2}\cos\theta\right)^2} d\theta.$

207. $\int\left(\sqrt{x} - \frac{1}{\sqrt{x}}\right)dx = \int x^{1/2}dx - \int x^{-1/2}dx = \frac{2}{3}x^{3/2} + C_1 - 2x^{1/2} + C_2 = \frac{2}{3}x^{3/2} - 2x^{1/2} + C$

209. $\int\frac{dx}{2x} = \frac{1}{2}\ln|x| + C$

211. $\int_0^{\pi} \sin x dx - \int_0^{\pi} \cos x dx = -\cos x|_0^{\pi} - (\sin x)|_0^{\pi} = (-(-1) + 1) - (0 - 0) = 2$

213. $P(s) = 4s,$ so $\frac{dP}{ds} = 4$ and $\int_2^4 4ds = 8.$

215. $\int_1^2 Nds = N$

217. With p as in the previous exercise, each of the 12 pentagons increases in area from $2p$ to $4p$ units so the net increase in the area of the dodecahedron is $36p$ units.

219. $18s^2 = 6\int_s^{2s} 2xdx$

221. $12\pi R^2 = 8\pi\int_R^{2R} rdr$

223. $d(t) = \int_0^t v(s)ds = 4t - t^2.$ The total distance is $d(2) = 4$ m.

225. $d(t) = \int_0^t v(s)ds.$ For $t < 3,\ d(t) = \int_0^t (6 - 2t)dt = 6t - t^2.$ For $t > 3,\ d(t) = d(3) + \int_3^t (2t - 6)dt = 9 + (t^2 - 6t).$ The total distance is $d(6) = 9$ m.

227. $v(t) = 40 - 9.8t;\ h(t) = 1.5 + 40t - 4.9t^2$ m/s

229. The net increase is 1 unit.

231. At $t = 5,$ the height of water is $x = \left(\frac{15}{\pi}\right)^{1/3}$ m.. The net change in height from $t = 5$ to $t = 10$ is $\left(\frac{30}{\pi}\right)^{1/3} - \left(\frac{15}{\pi}\right)^{1/3}$ m.

233. The total daily power consumption is estimated as the sum of the hourly power rates, or 911 gW-h.

235. 17 kJ

237. a. 54.3%; b. 27.00%; c. The curve in the following plot is $2.35(t + 3)e^{-0.15(t + 3)}$.

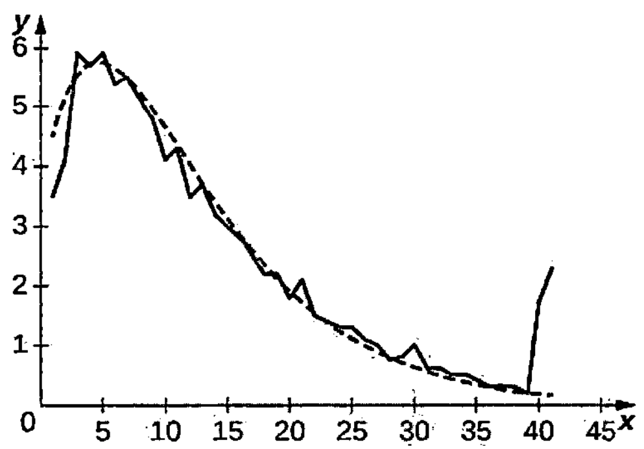

239. In dry conditions, with initial velocity $v_0 = 30$ m/s, $D = 64.3$ and, if $v_0 = 25,\ D = 44.64.$ In wet conditions, if $v_0 = 30,$ and $D = 180$ and if $v_0 = 25,\ D = 125.$

241. 225 cal

243. $E(150) = 28,\ E(300) = 22,\ E(450) = 16$

245. a.

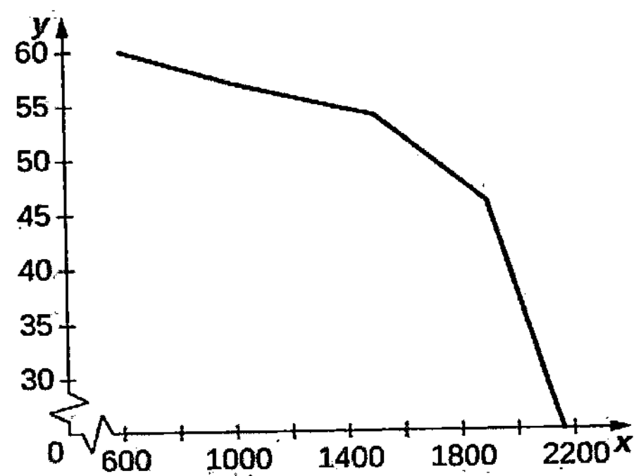

b. Between 600 and 1000 the average decrease in vehicles per hour per lane is −0.0075. Between 1000 and 1500 it is −0.006 per vehicles per hour per lane, and between 1500 and 2100 it is −0.04 vehicles per hour per lane. c.

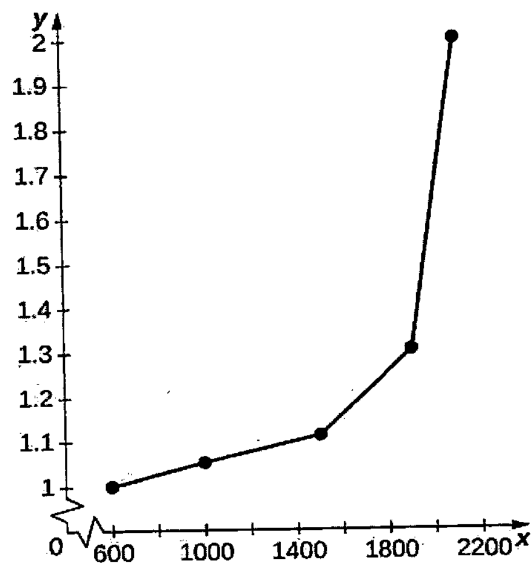

The graph is nonlinear, with minutes per mile increasing dramatically as vehicles per hour per lane reach 2000.

247. $\frac{1}{37}\int_0^{37} p(t)dt = \frac{0.07(37)^3}{4} + \frac{2.42(37)^2}{3} - \frac{25.63(37)}{2} + 521.23 \approx 2037$

249. Average acceleration is $A = \frac{1}{5}\int_0^5 a(t)dt = -\frac{0.7(5^2)}{3} + \frac{1.44(5)}{2} + 10.44 \approx 8.2$ mph/s

251. $d(t) = \int_0^1 |v(t)|dt = \int_0^t \left(\frac{7}{30}t^3 - 0.72t^2 - 10.44t + 41.033\right)dt = \frac{7}{120}t^4 - 0.24t^3 - 5.22t^3 + 41.033t.$ Then, $d(5) \approx 81.12$ mph $\times$ sec ≈ 119 feet.

253. $\frac{1}{40}\int_0^{40}(-0.068t + 5.14)dt = -\frac{0.068(40)}{2} + 5.14 = 3.78$

255. $u = h(x)$

257. $f(u) = \frac{(u+1)^2}{\sqrt{u}}$

259. $du = 8xdx;\ f(u) = \frac{1}{8\sqrt{u}}$

261. $\frac{1}{5}(x+1)^5 + C$

263. $-\frac{1}{12(3-2x)^6} + C$

265. $\sqrt{x^2+1} + C$

267. $\frac{1}{8}\left(x^2 - 2x\right)^4 + C$

269. $\sin\theta - \frac{\sin^3\theta}{3} + C$

271. $\frac{(1-x)^{101}}{101} - \frac{(1-x)^{100}}{100} + C$

273. $-\frac{1}{22\left(7 - 11x^2\right)} + C$

275. $-\frac{\cos^4\theta}{4} + C$

277. $-\frac{\cos^3(\pi t)}{3\pi} + C$

279. $-\frac{1}{4}\cos^2\left(t^2\right) + C$

281. $-\frac{1}{3(x^3 - 3)} + C$

283. $-\frac{2\left(y^3 - 2\right)}{3\sqrt{1 - y^3}}$

285. $\frac{1}{33}\left(1 - \cos^3\theta\right)^{11} + C$

287. $\frac{1}{12}\left(\sin^3\theta - 3\sin^2\theta\right)^4 + C$

289. $L_{50} = -8.5779$. The exact area is $\frac{-81}{8}$

291. $L_{50} = -0.006399$ … The exact area is 0.

293. $u = 1 + x^2,\ du = 2xdx,\ \frac{1}{2}\int_1^2 u^{-1/2}\,du = \sqrt{2} - 1$

295. $u = 1 + t^3,\ du = 3t^2,\ \frac{1}{3}\int_1^2 u^{-1/2}\,du = \frac{2}{3}(\sqrt{2} - 1)$

297. $u = \cos\theta,\ du = -\sin\theta d\theta,\ \int_{1/\sqrt{2}}^1 u^{-4}\,du = \frac{1}{3}(2\sqrt{2} - 1)$

299.

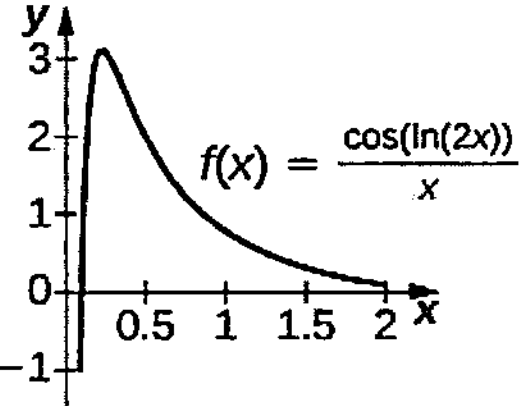

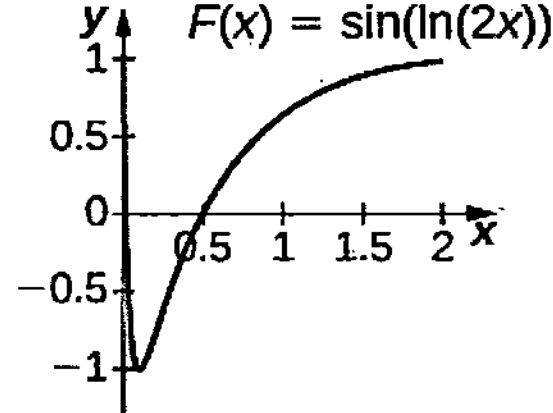

The antiderivative is $y = \sin(\ln(2x))$. Since the antiderivative is not continuous at $x = 0$, one cannot find a value of C that would make $y = \sin(\ln(2x)) - C$ work as a definite integral.

301.

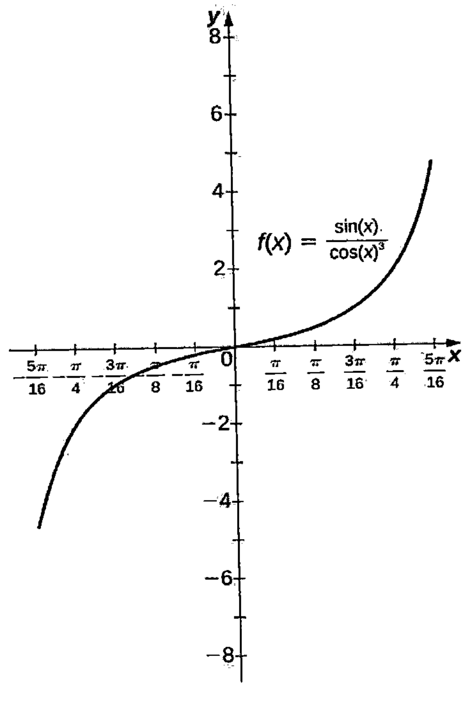

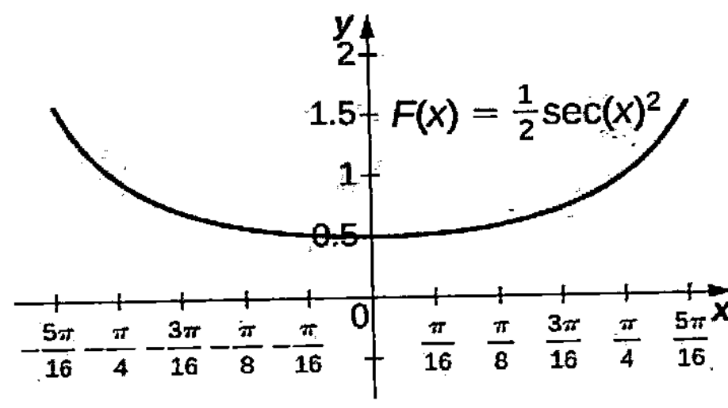

The antiderivative is $y = \frac{1}{2}\sec^2 x$. You should take $C = -2$ so that $F\left(-\frac{\pi}{3}\right) = 0$.

303.

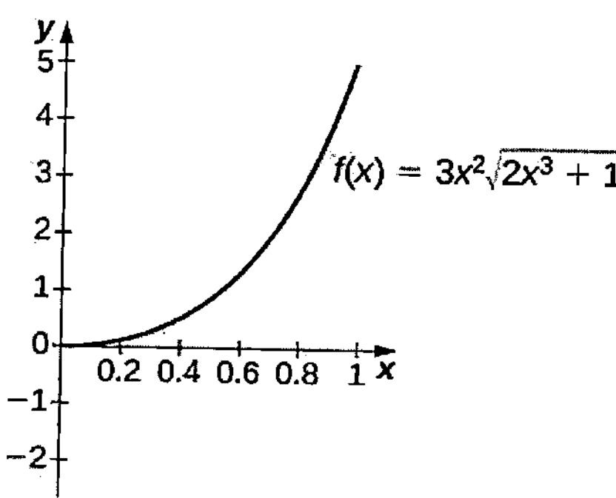

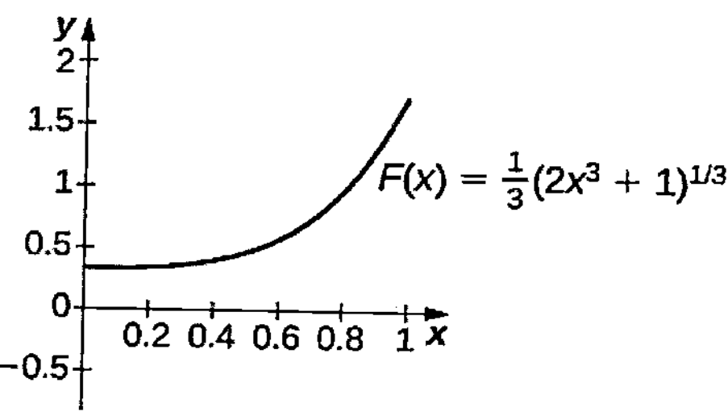

The antiderivative is $y = \frac{1}{3}\left(2x^3 + 1\right)^{3/2}$. One should take $C = -\frac{1}{3}$.

305. No, because the integrand is discontinuous at $x = 1$.

307. $u = \sin\left(t^2\right)$; the integral becomes $\frac{1}{2}\int_0^0 u\,du$.

309. $u = \left(1 + \left(t - \frac{1}{2}\right)^2\right)$; the integral becomes $-\int_{5/4}^{5/4} \frac{1}{u}du$.

311. $u = 1 - t$; the integral becomes

$$\int_1^{-1} u\cos(\pi(1-u))du$$
$$= \int_1^{-1} u[\cos\pi\cos u - \sin\pi\sin u]du$$
$$= -\int_1^{-1} u\cos u\,du$$
$$= \int_{-1}^{1} u\cos u\,du = 0$$

since the integrand is odd.

313. Setting $u = cx$ and $du = c\,dx$ gets you $\frac{1}{\frac{b}{c} - \frac{a}{c}}\int_{a/c}^{b/c} f(cx)dx = \frac{c}{b-a}\int_{u=a}^{u=b} f(u)\frac{du}{c} = \frac{1}{b-a}\int_a^b f(u)du.$

315. $\int_0^x g(t)dt = \frac{1}{2}\int_{u=1-x^2}^{1} \frac{du}{u^a} = \frac{1}{2(1-a)}u^{1-a}\Big|_{u=1-x^2}^{1} = \frac{1}{2(1-a)}\left(1 - \left(1 - x^2\right)^{1-a}\right)$. As $x \to 1$ the limit is $\frac{1}{2(1-a)}$ if $a < 1$, and the limit diverges to $+\infty$ if $a > 1$.

317. $\int_{t=\pi}^{0} b\sqrt{1 - \cos^2 t} \times (-a\sin t)dt = \int_{t=0}^{\pi} ab\sin^2 t\,dt$

319. $f(t) = 2\cos(3t) - \cos(2t)$; $\int_0^{\pi/2} (2\cos(3t) - \cos(2t)) = -\frac{2}{3}$

321. $\frac{-1}{3}e^{-3x} + C$

323. $-\frac{3^{-x}}{\ln 3} + C$

325. $\ln(x^2) + C$

327. $2\sqrt{x} + C$

329. $-\frac{1}{\ln x} + C$

331. $\ln(\ln(\ln x)) + C$

333. $\ln(x\cos x) + C$

335. $-\frac{1}{2}(\ln(\cos(x)))^2 + C$

337. $\frac{-e^{-x^3}}{3} + C$

339. $e^{\tan x} + C$

341. $t + C$

343. $\frac{1}{9}x^3\left(\ln(x^3) - 1\right) + C$

345. $2\sqrt{x}(\ln x - 2) + C$

347. $\int_0^{\ln x} e^t\,dt = e^t\Big|_0^{\ln x} = e^{\ln x} - e^0 = x - 1$

349. $-\frac{1}{3}\ln(\sin(3x) + \cos(3x))$

351. $-\frac{1}{2}\ln\left|\csc(x^2) + \cot(x^2)\right| + C$

353. $-\frac{1}{2}(\ln(\csc x))^2 + C$

355. $\frac{1}{3}\ln\left(\frac{26}{7}\right)$

357. $\ln\left(\sqrt{3} - 1\right)$

359. $\frac{1}{2}\ln\frac{3}{2}$

361. $y - 2\ln|y + 1| + C$

363. $\ln|\sin x - \cos x| + C$

365. $-\frac{1}{3}\left(1 - \left(\ln x^2\right)\right)^{3/2} + C$

367. Exact solution: $\frac{e-1}{e}$, $R_{50} = 0.6258$. Since f is decreasing, the right endpoint estimate underestimates the area.

369. Exact solution: $\frac{2\ln(3) - \ln(6)}{2}$, $R_{50} = 0.2033$. Since f is increasing, the right endpoint estimate overestimates the area.

371. Exact solution: $-\frac{1}{\ln(4)}$, $R_{50} = -0.7164$. Since f is increasing, the right endpoint estimate overestimates the area (the actual area is a larger negative number).

373. $\frac{11}{2}\ln 2$

375. $\frac{1}{\ln(65, 536)}$

377. $\int_N^{N+1} xe^{-x^2}\,dx = \frac{1}{2}\left(e^{-N^2} - e^{-(N+1)^2}\right)$. The quantity is less than 0.01 when $N = 2$.

379. $\int_a^b \frac{dx}{x} = \ln(b) - \ln(a) = \ln\left(\frac{1}{a}\right) - \ln\left(\frac{1}{b}\right) = \int_{1/b}^{1/a} \frac{dx}{x}$

381. 23

383. We may assume that $x > 1$, so $\frac{1}{x} < 1$. Then, $\int_1^{1/x} \frac{dt}{t}$. Now make the substitution $u = \frac{1}{t}$, so $du = -\frac{dt}{t^2}$ and $\frac{du}{u} = -\frac{dt}{t}$, and change endpoints: $\int_1^{1/x} \frac{dt}{t} = -\int_1^x \frac{du}{u} = -\ln x$.

387. $x = E(\ln(x))$. Then, $1 = \frac{E'(\ln x)}{x}$ or $x = E'(\ln x)$. Since any number t can be written $t = \ln x$ for some x, and for such t we have $x = E(t)$, it follows that for any t, $E'(t) = E(t)$.

389. $R_{10} = 0.6811$, $R_{100} = 0.6827$

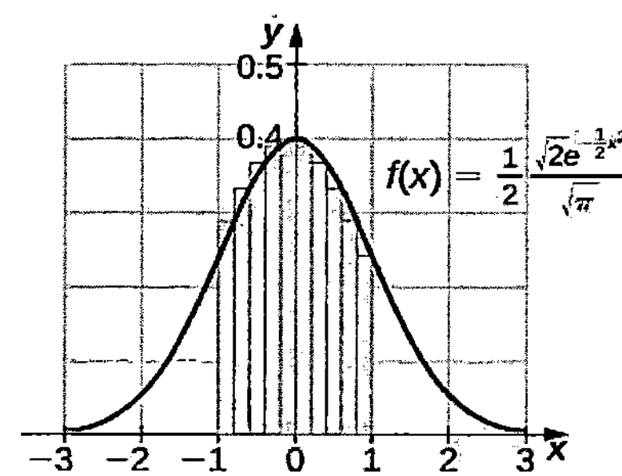

391. $\sin^{-1} x \Big|_0^{\sqrt{3}/2} = \frac{\pi}{3}$

393. $\tan^{-1} x \Big|_{\sqrt{3}}^{1} = -\frac{\pi}{12}$

395. $\sec^{-1} x \Big|_1^{\sqrt{2}} = \frac{\pi}{4}$

397. $\sin^{-1}\left(\frac{x}{3}\right) + C$

399. $\frac{1}{3}\tan^{-1}\left(\frac{x}{3}\right) + C$

401. $\frac{1}{3}\sec^{-1}\left(\frac{x}{3}\right) + C$

403. $\cos\left(\frac{\pi}{2} - \theta\right) = \sin\theta$. So, $\sin^{-1} t = \frac{\pi}{2} - \cos^{-1} t$. They differ by a constant.

405. $\sqrt{1 - t^2}$ is not defined as a real number when $t > 1$.

407.

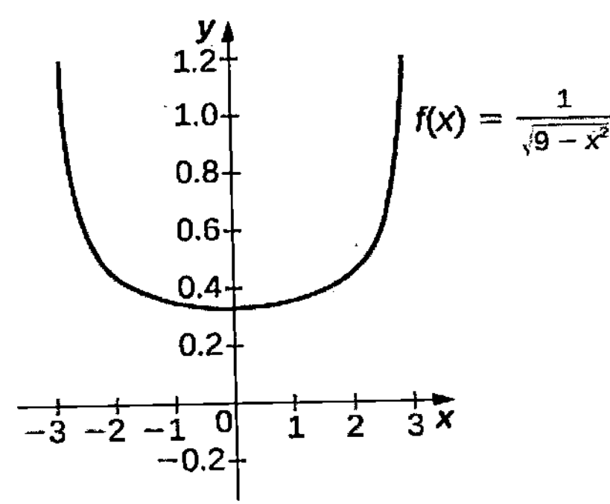

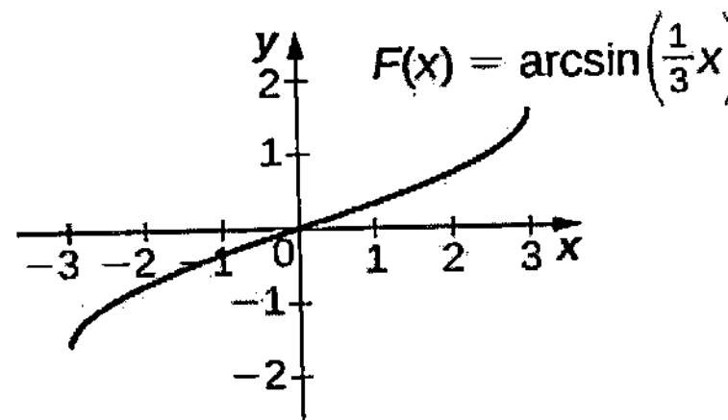

The antiderivative is $\sin^{-1}\left(\frac{x}{3}\right) + C$. Taking $C = \frac{\pi}{2}$ recovers the definite integral.

409.

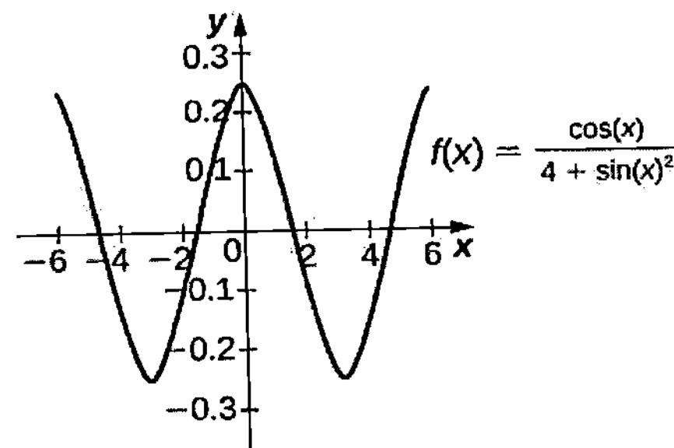

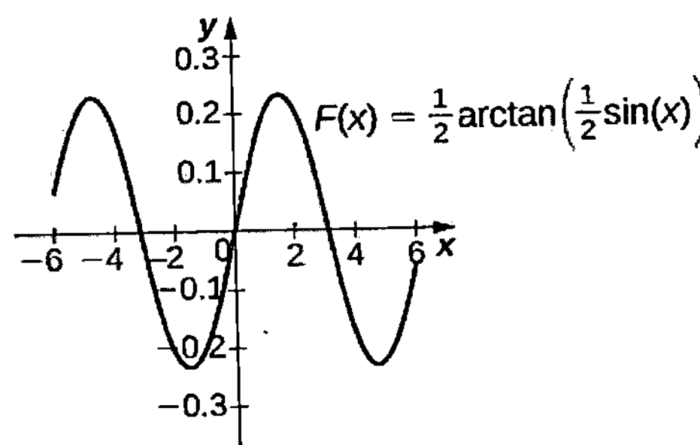

The antiderivative is $\frac{1}{2}\tan^{-1}\left(\frac{\sin x}{2}\right) + C$. Taking $C = \frac{1}{2}\tan^{-1}\left(\frac{\sin(6)}{2}\right)$ recovers the definite integral.

411. $\frac{1}{2}\left(\sin^{-1} t\right)^2 + C$

413. $\frac{1}{4}\left(\tan^{-1}(2t)\right)^2$

415. $\frac{1}{4}\left(\sec^{-1}\left(\frac{t}{2}\right)^2\right) + C$

417.

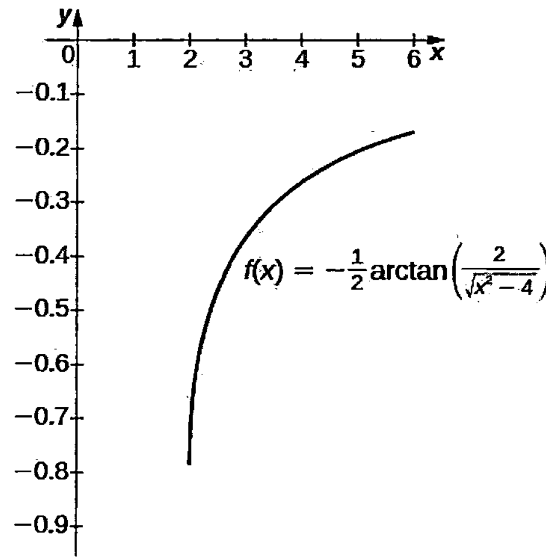

The antiderivative is $\frac{1}{2}\sec^{-1}\left(\frac{x}{2}\right) + C.$ Taking $C = 0$ recovers the definite integral over $[2, 6]$.

419.

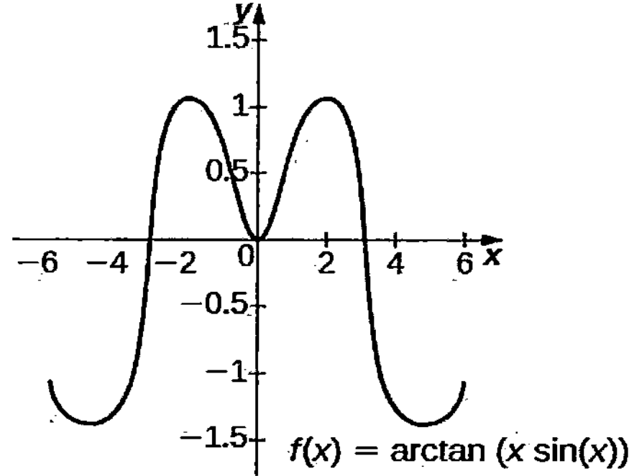

The general antiderivative is $\tan^{-1}(x\sin x) + C.$ Taking $C = -\tan^{-1}(6\sin(6))$ recovers the definite integral.

421.

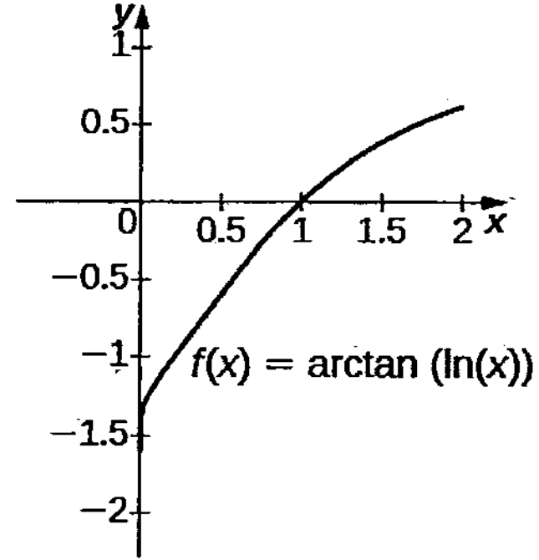

The general antiderivative is $\tan^{-1}(\ln x) + C.$ Taking $C = \frac{\pi}{2} = \tan^{-1}\infty$ recovers the definite integral.

423. $\sin^{-1}(e^t) + C$

425. $\sin^{-1}(\ln t) + C$

427. $-\frac{1}{2}\left(\cos^{-1}(2t)\right)^2 + C$

429. $\frac{1}{2}\ln\left(\frac{4}{3}\right)$

431. $1 - \frac{2}{\sqrt{5}}$

433. $2\tan^{-1}(A) \to \pi$ as $A \to \infty$

435. Using the hint, one has $\int \frac{\csc^2 x}{\csc^2 x + \cot^2 x} dx = \int \frac{\csc^2 x}{1 + 2\cot^2 x} dx$. Set $u = \sqrt{2}\cot x$. Then, $du = -\sqrt{2}\csc^2 x$ and the integral is $-\frac{1}{\sqrt{2}}\int \frac{du}{1 + u^2} = -\frac{1}{\sqrt{2}}\tan^{-1} u + C = \frac{1}{\sqrt{2}}\tan^{-1}(\sqrt{2}\cot x) + C$. If one uses the identity $\tan^{-1} s + \tan^{-1}\left(\frac{1}{s}\right) = \frac{\pi}{2}$, then this can also be written $\frac{1}{\sqrt{2}}\tan^{-1}\left(\frac{\tan x}{\sqrt{2}}\right) + C$.

437. $x \approx \pm 1.13525$. The left endpoint estimate with $N = 100$ is 2.796 and these decimals persist for $N = 500$.

Review Exercises

439. False

441. True

443. $L_4 = 5.25$, $R_4 = 3.25$, exact answer: 4

445. $L_4 = 5.364$, $R_4 = 5.364$, exact answer: 5.870

447. $-\frac{4}{3}$

449. 1

451. $-\frac{1}{2(x+4)^2} + C$

453. $\frac{4}{3}\sin^{-1}\left(x^3\right) + C$

455. $\frac{\sin t}{\sqrt{1 + t^2}}$

457. $4\frac{\ln x}{x} + 1$

459. $6,328,113

461. $73.36

463. $\frac{19117}{12}$ft/sec, or 1593 ft/sec

Chapter 6

Checkpoint

6.1. 12 units^2

6.2. $\frac{3}{10}$ unit^2

6.3. $2 + 2\sqrt{2}$ units^2

6.4. $\frac{5}{3}$ units^2

6.5. $\frac{5}{3}$ units^2

6.7. $\frac{\pi}{2}$

6.8. 8π units^3

6.9. 21π units^3

6.10. $\frac{10\pi}{3}$ units^3

6.11. 60π units^3

6.12. $\frac{15\pi}{2}$ units^3

6.13. 8π units^3

6.14. 12π units^3

6.15. $\frac{11\pi}{6}$ units^3

6.16. $\frac{\pi}{6}$ units^3

6.17. Use the method of washers; $V = \int_{-1}^{1} \pi\left[\left(2 - x^2\right)^2 - \left(x^2\right)^2\right]dx$

6.18. $\frac{1}{6}\left(5\sqrt{5} - 1\right) \approx 1.697$

6.19. Arc Length ≈ 3.8202

6.20. Arc Length $= 3.15018$

6.21. $\frac{\pi}{6}\left(5\sqrt{5} - 3\sqrt{3}\right) \approx 3.133$

6.22. 12π

6.23. 70/3

6.24. 24π

6.25. 8 ft-lb

6.26. Approximately 43,255.2 ft-lb

6.27. 156,800 N

6.28. Approximately 7,164,520,000 lb or 3,582,260 t

6.29. $M = 24,\ \bar{x} = \frac{2}{5}$ m

6.30. $(-1, -1)$ m

6.31. The centroid of the region is $(3/2,\ 6/5)$.

6.32. The centroid of the region is $(1,\ 13/5)$.

6.33. The centroid of the region is $(0,\ 2/5)$.

6.34. $6\pi^2$ units^3

6.35.

a. $\frac{d}{dx}\ln\left(2x^2 + x\right) = \frac{4x + 1}{2x^2 + x}$

b. $\frac{d}{dx}\left(\ln\left(x^3\right)\right)^2 = \frac{6\ln\left(x^3\right)}{x}$

6.36. $\int \frac{x^2}{x^3 + 6}dx = \frac{1}{3}\ln\left|x^3 + 6\right| + C$

6.37. $4\ln 2$

6.38.

a. $\frac{d}{dx}\left(\frac{e^{x^2}}{e^{5x}}\right) = e^{x^2 - 5x}(2x - 5)$

b. $\frac{d}{dt}\left(e^{2t}\right)^3 = 6e^{6t}$

6.39. $\int \frac{4}{e^{3x}}dx = -\frac{4}{3}e^{-3x} + C$

6.40.

a. $\frac{d}{dt}4^{t^4} = 4^{t^4}(\ln 4)\left(4t^3\right)$

b. $\frac{d}{dx}\log_3\left(\sqrt{x^2 + 1}\right) = \frac{x}{(\ln 3)\left(x^2 + 1\right)}$

6.41. $\int x^2 2^{x^3}\,dx = \frac{1}{3\ln 2}2^{x^3} + C$

6.42. There are 81,377,396 bacteria in the population after 4 hours. The population reaches 100 million bacteria after

244.12 minutes.

6.43. At 5% interest, she must invest \$223,130.16. At 6% interest, she must invest \$165,298.89.

6.44. 38.90 months

6.45. The coffee is first cool enough to serve about 3.5 minutes after it is poured. The coffee is too cold to serve about 7 minutes after it is poured.

6.46. A total of 94.13 g of carbon remains. The artifact is approximately 13,300 years old.

6.47.

a. $\frac{d}{dx}\left(\tanh\left(x^2+3x\right)\right) = \left(\text{sech}^2\left(x^2+3x\right)\right)(2x+3)$

b. $\frac{d}{dx}\left(\frac{1}{(\sinh x)^2}\right) = \frac{d}{dx}(\sinh x)^{-2} = -2(\sinh x)^{-3}\cosh x$

6.48.

a. $\int \sinh^3 x \cosh x\,dx = \frac{\sinh^4 x}{4} + C$

b. $\int \text{sech}^2(3x)dx = \frac{\tanh(3x)}{3} + C$

6.49.

a. $\frac{d}{dx}\left(\cosh^{-1}(3x)\right) = \frac{3}{\sqrt{9x^2-1}}$

b. $\frac{d}{dx}\left(\coth^{-1} x\right)^3 = \frac{3\left(\coth^{-1} x\right)^2}{1-x^2}$

6.50.

a. $\int \frac{1}{\sqrt{x^2-4}}dx = \cosh^{-1}\left(\frac{x}{2}\right) + C$

b. $\int \frac{1}{\sqrt{1-e^{2x}}}dx = -\text{sech}^{-1}\left(e^x\right) + C$

6.51. 52.95 ft

Section Exercises

1. $\frac{32}{3}$

3. $\frac{13}{12}$

5. 36

7.

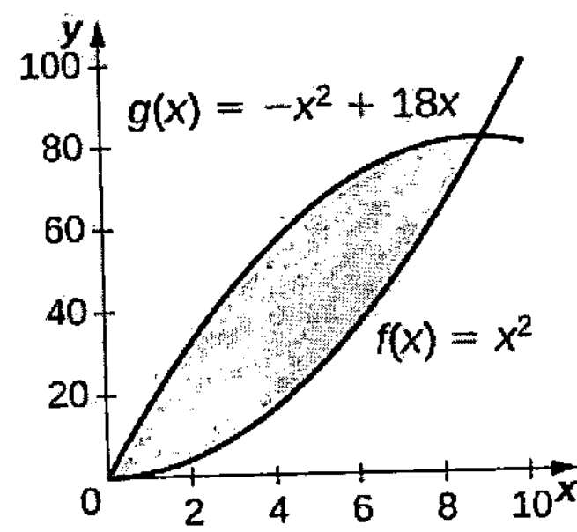

243 square units

9.

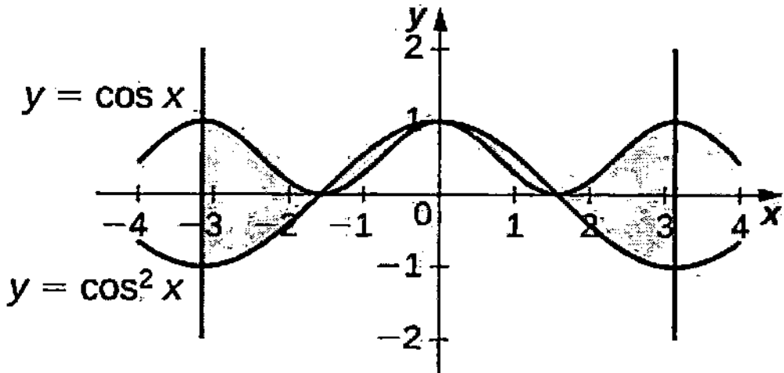

4

11.

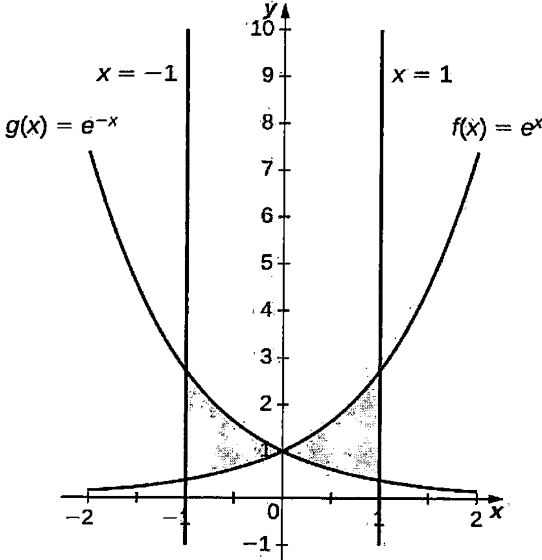

$\frac{2(e-1)^2}{e}$

13.

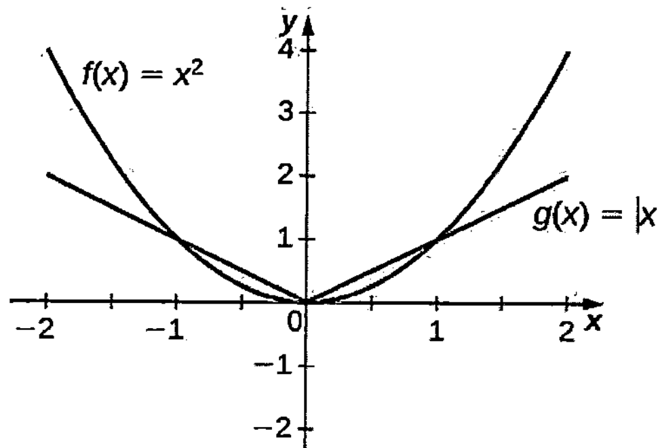

$\frac{1}{3}$

15.

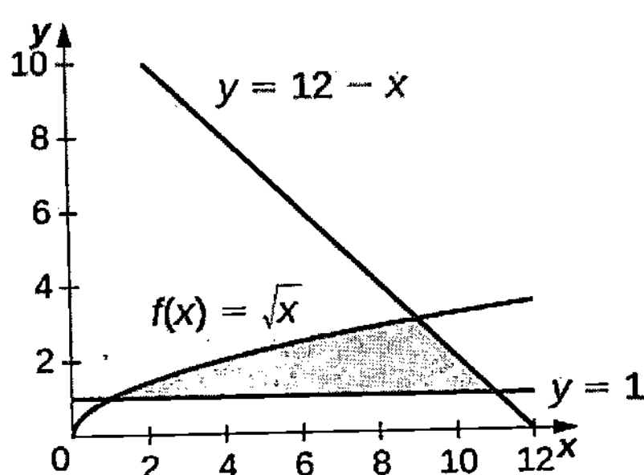

$\frac{34}{3}$

17.

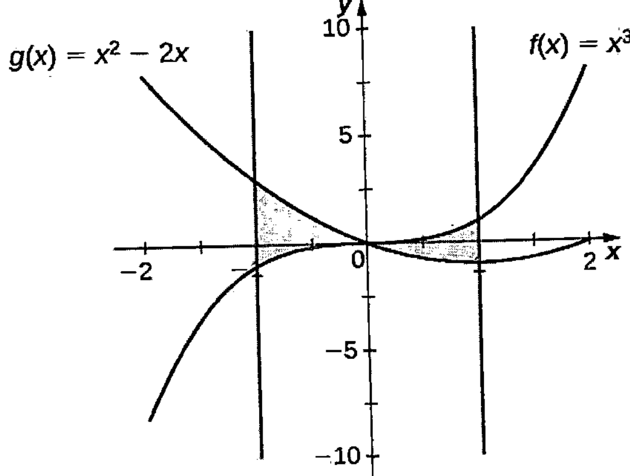

$\frac{5}{2}$

19.

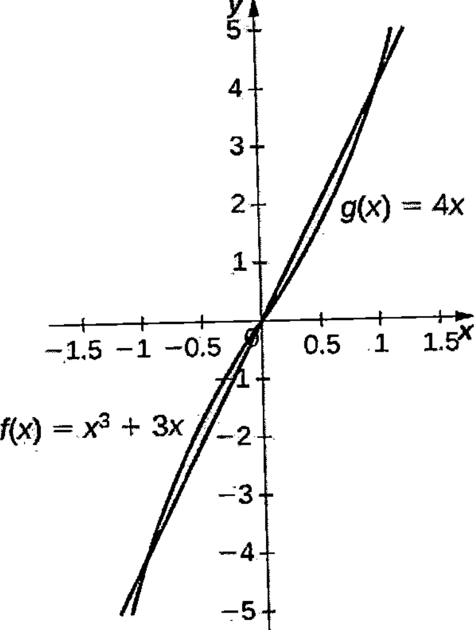

$\frac{1}{2}$

21.

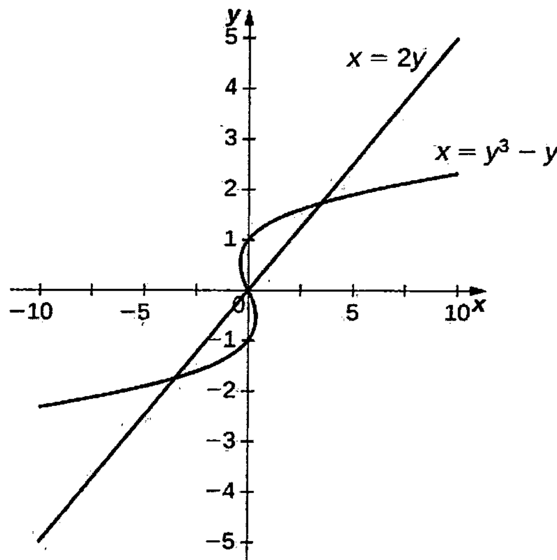

$\frac{9}{2}$

23.

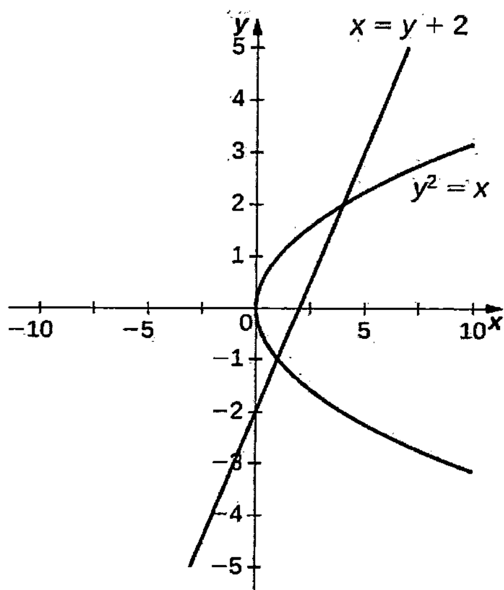

$\frac{9}{2}$

25.

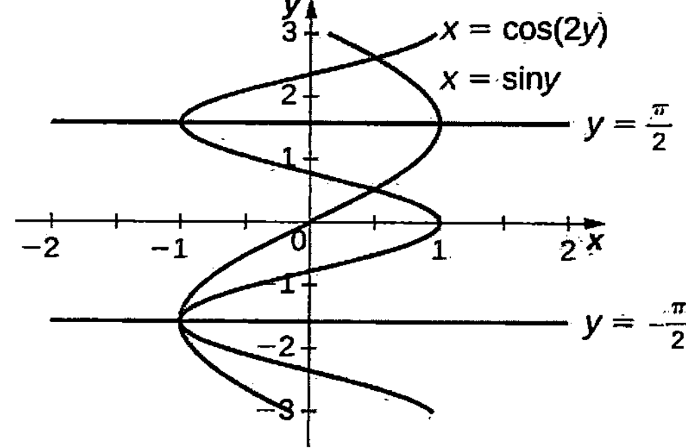

$\frac{3\sqrt{3}}{2}$

27.

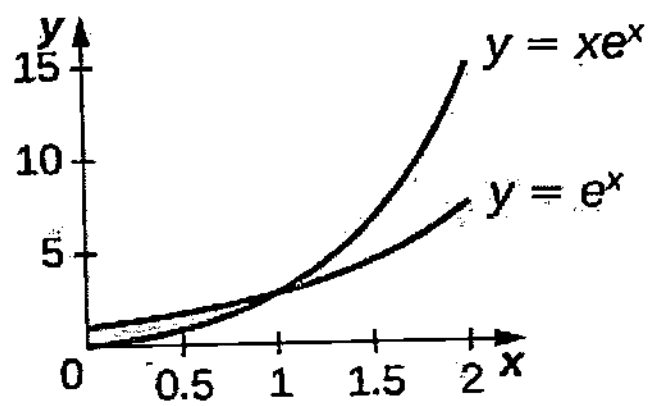

e^{-2}

29.

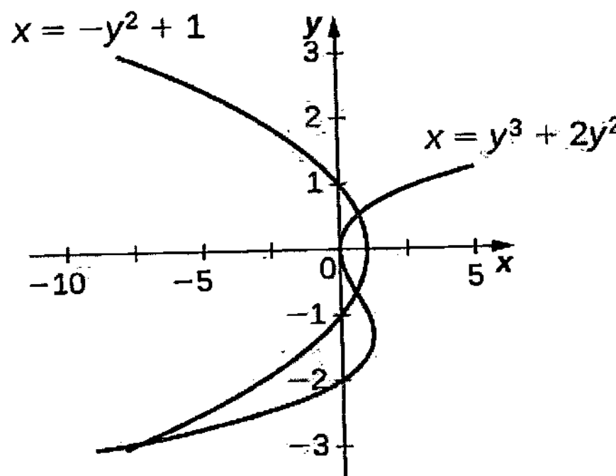

$\frac{27}{4}$

31.

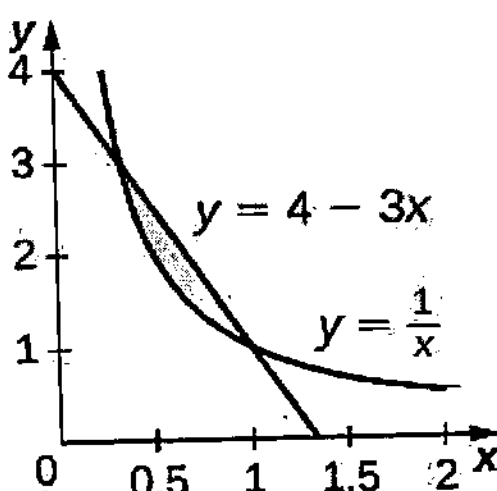

$\frac{4}{3} - \ln(3)$

33.

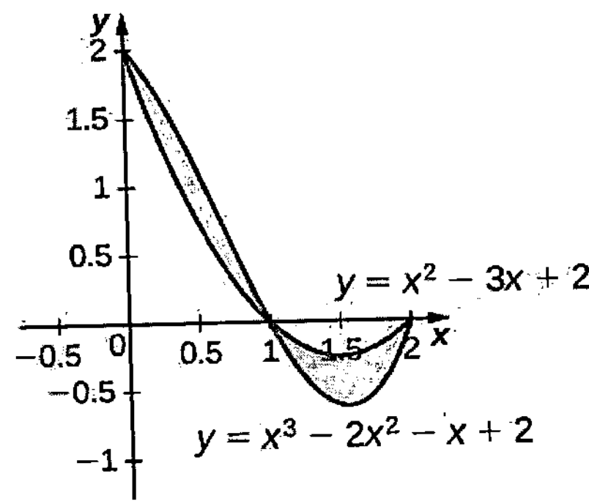

$\frac{1}{2}$

35.

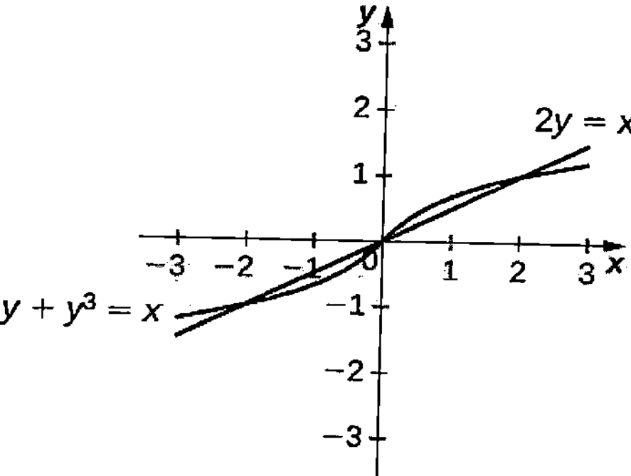

$\frac{1}{2}$

37.

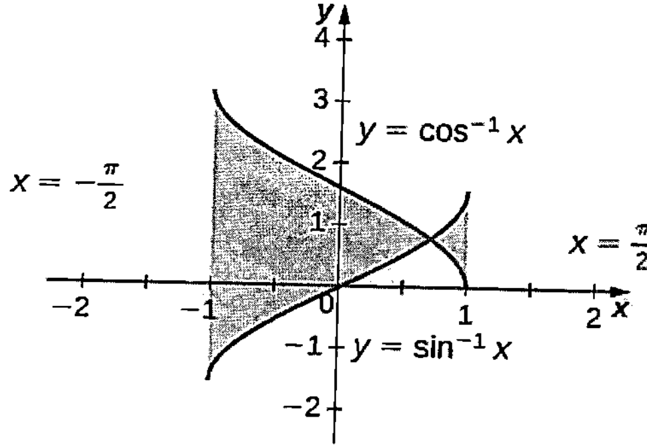

$-2\left(\sqrt{2}-\pi\right)$

39. 1.067

41. 0.852

43. 7.523

45. $\frac{3\pi-4}{12}$

47. 1.429

49. $\$33,333.33$ total profit for 200 cell phones sold

51. 3.263 mi represents how far ahead the hare is from the tortoise

53. $\frac{343}{24}$

55. $4\sqrt{3}$

57. $\pi-\frac{32}{25}$

63. 8 units^3

65. $\frac{32}{3\sqrt{2}}$ units^3

67. $\frac{7\pi}{12}hr^2$ units^3

69.

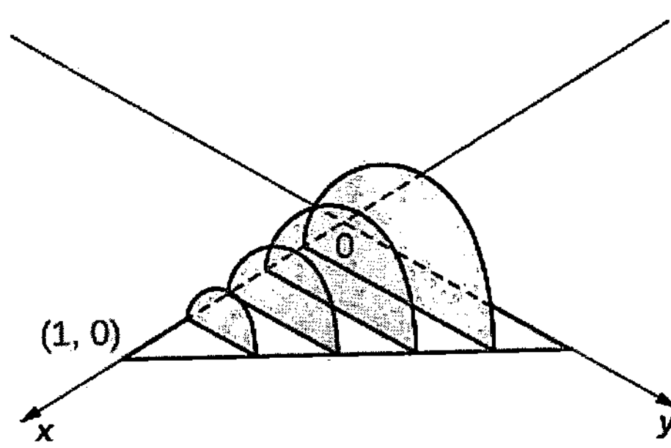

$\frac{\pi}{24}$ units^3

71.

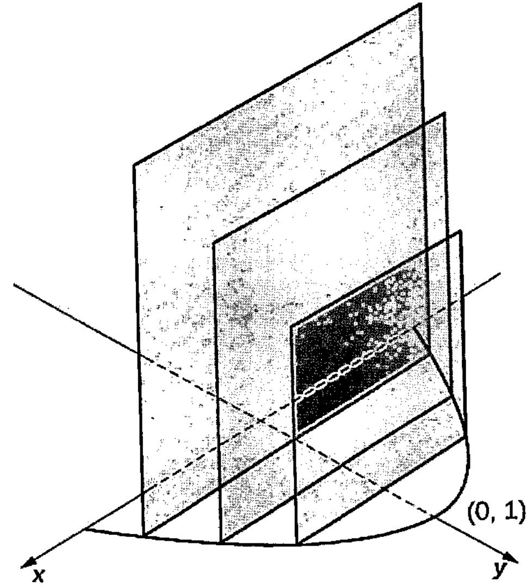

2 units^3

73.

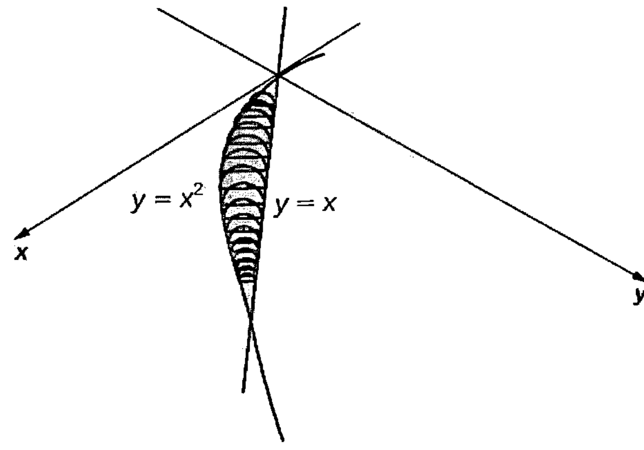

$\frac{\pi}{240}$ units^3

75.

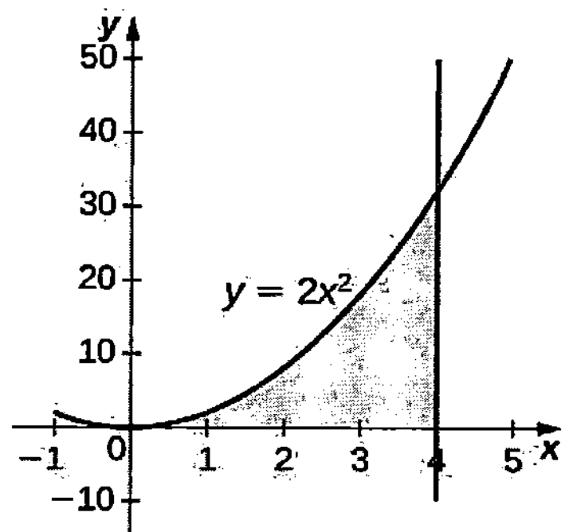

$\frac{4096\pi}{5}$ units^3

77.

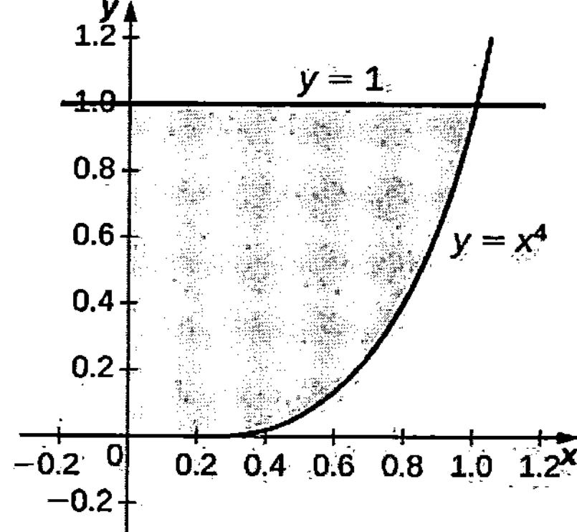

$\frac{8\pi}{9}$ units^3

79.

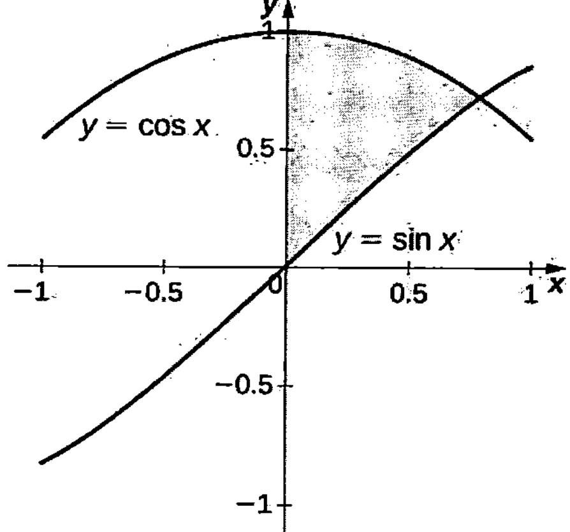

$\frac{\pi}{2}$ units^3

81.

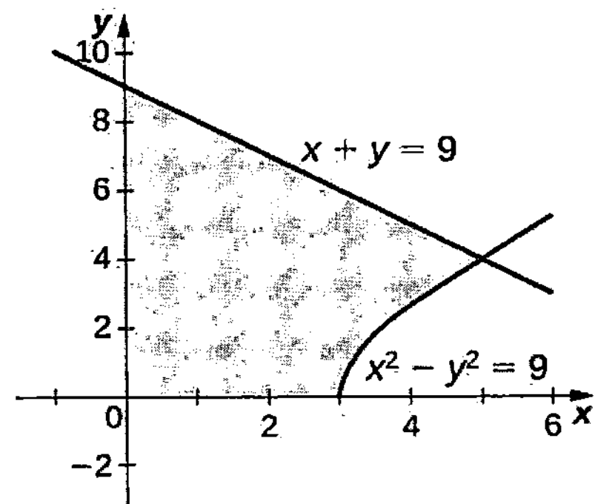

207π units^3

83.

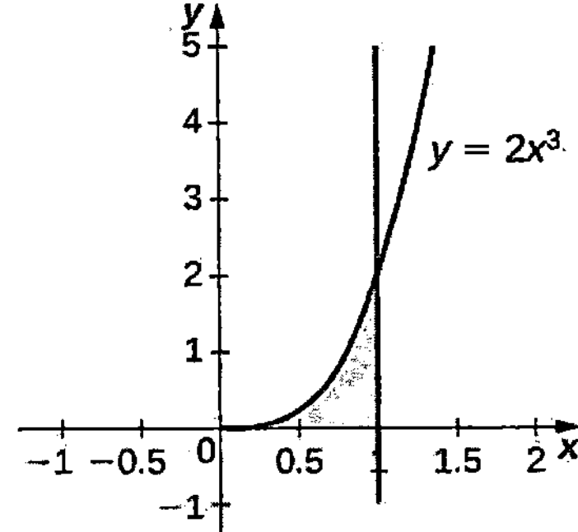

$\frac{4\pi}{5}$ units^3

85.

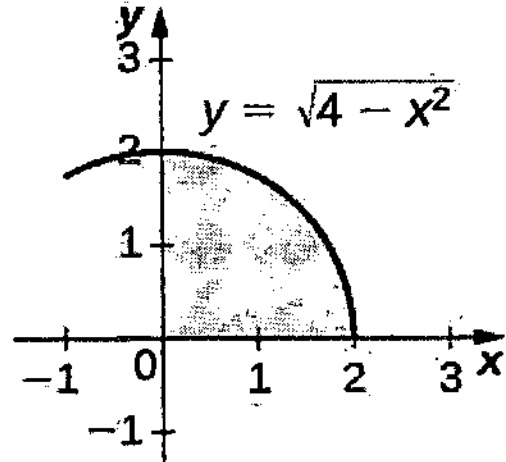

$\frac{16\pi}{3}$ units^3

87.

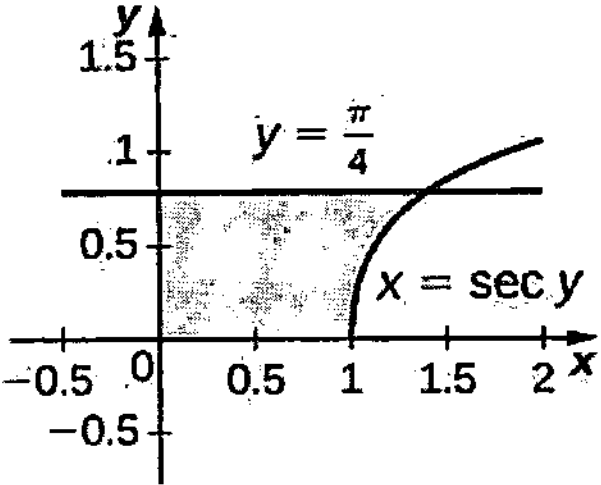

π units^3

89.

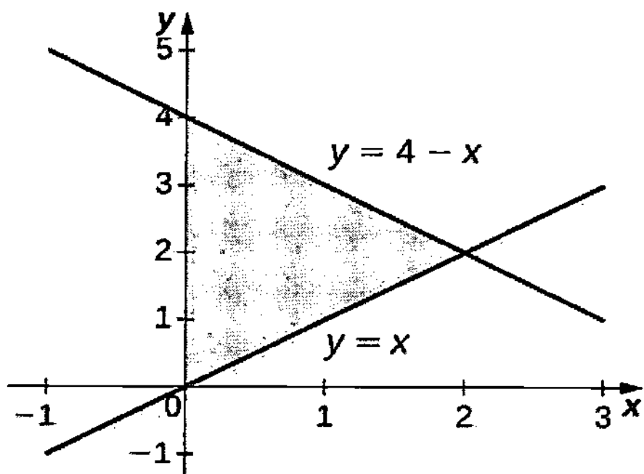

$\frac{16\pi}{3}$ units^3

91.

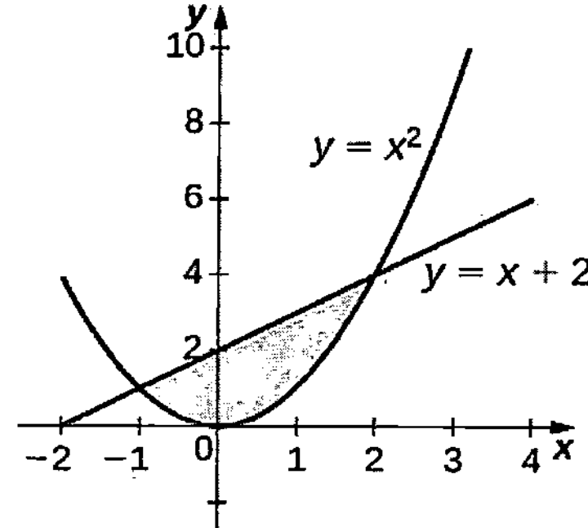

$\frac{72\pi}{5}$ units^3

93.

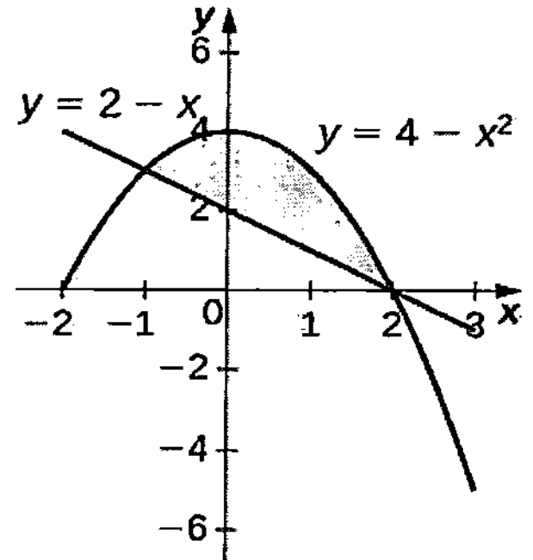

$\frac{108\pi}{5}$ units^3

95.

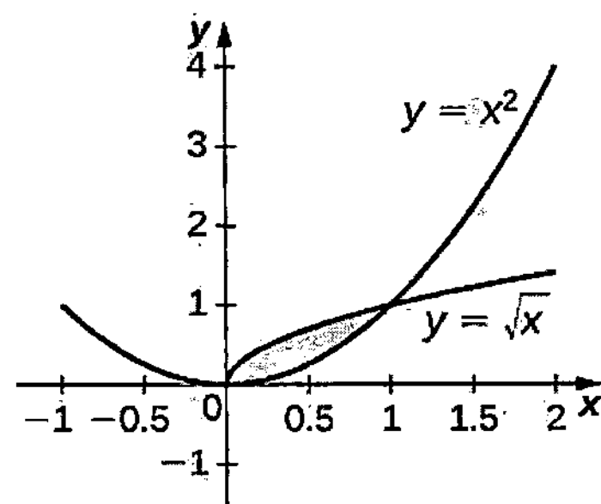

$\frac{3\pi}{10}$ units^3

97.

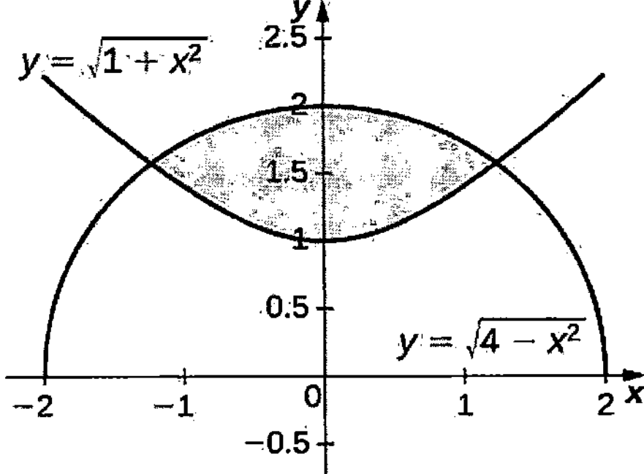

$2\sqrt{6}\pi$ units^3

99.

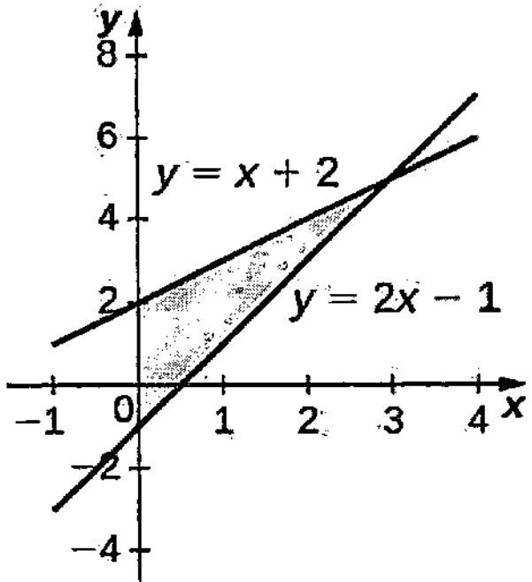

9π units^3

101.

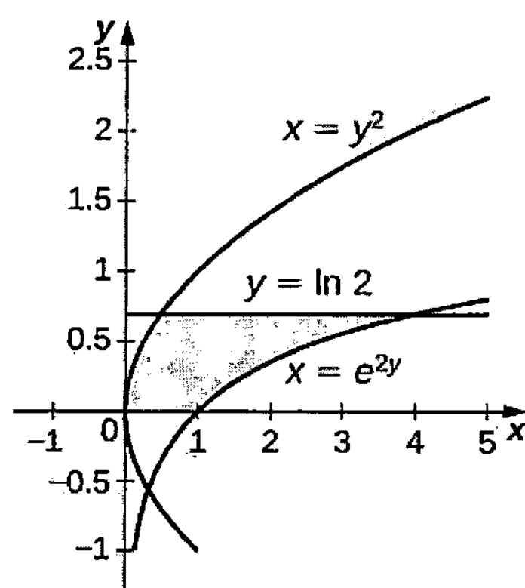

$\frac{\pi}{20}\left(75-4\ln^5(2)\right)$ units^3

103. $\frac{m^2\pi}{3}\left(b^3-a^3\right)$ units^3

105. $\frac{4a^2b\pi}{3}$ units^3

107. $2\pi^2$ units^3

109. $\frac{2ab^2\pi}{3}$ units^3

111. $\frac{\pi}{12}(r+h)^2(6r-h)$ units^3

113. $\frac{\pi}{3}(h+R)(h-2R)^2$ units^3

115.

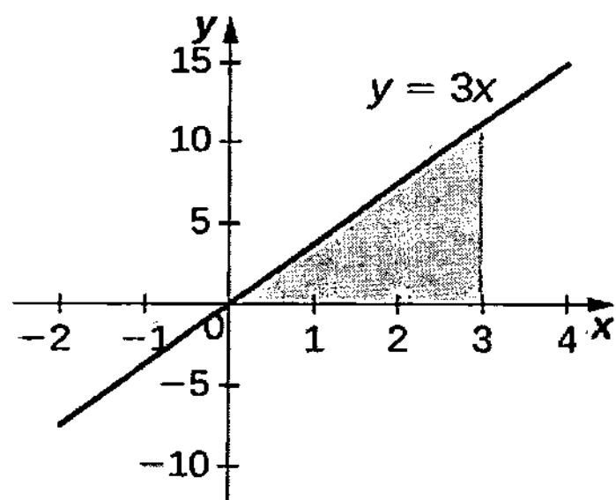

54π units^3

117.

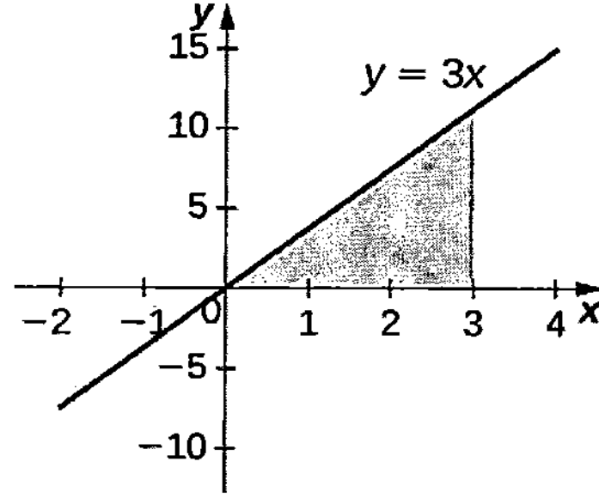

81π units^3

119.

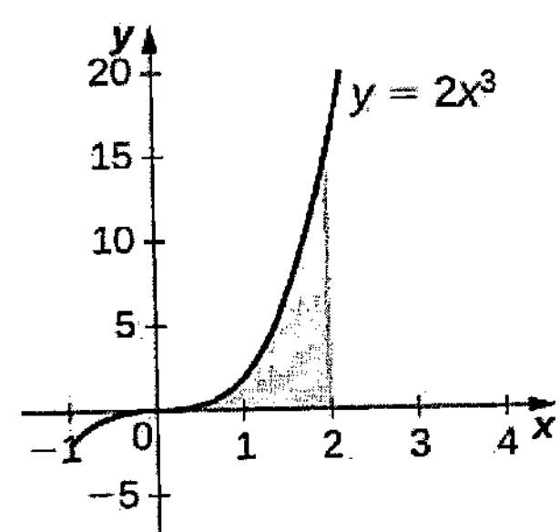

$\frac{512\pi}{7}$ units^3

121. 2π units^3

123. $\frac{2\pi}{3}$ units^3

125. 2π units^3

127. $\frac{4\pi}{5}$ units^3

129. $\frac{64\pi}{3}$ units^3

131. $\frac{32\pi}{5}$ units^3

133. $\pi(e-2)$ units^3

135. $\frac{28\pi}{3}$ units^3

137. $\frac{-84\pi}{5}$ units^3

139. $-e^{\pi}\pi^2$ units^3

141. $\frac{64\pi}{5}$ units^3

143. $\frac{28\pi}{15}$ units^3

145. $\frac{3\pi}{10}$ units^3

147. $\frac{52\pi}{5}$ units^3

149. 0.9876 units^3

151.

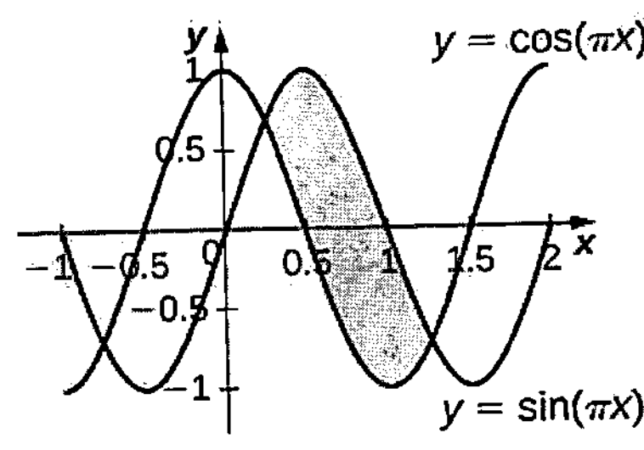

$3\sqrt{2}$ units^3

153.

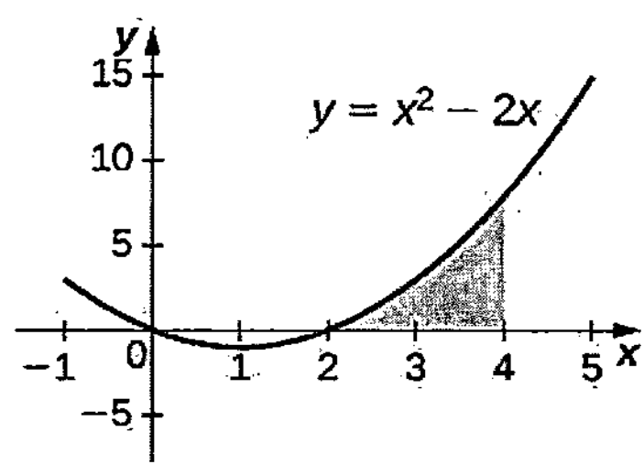

$\frac{496\pi}{15}$ units^3

155.

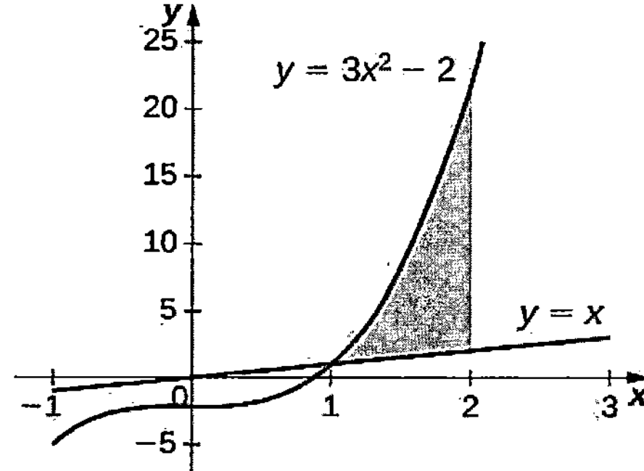

$\frac{398\pi}{15}$ units^3

157.

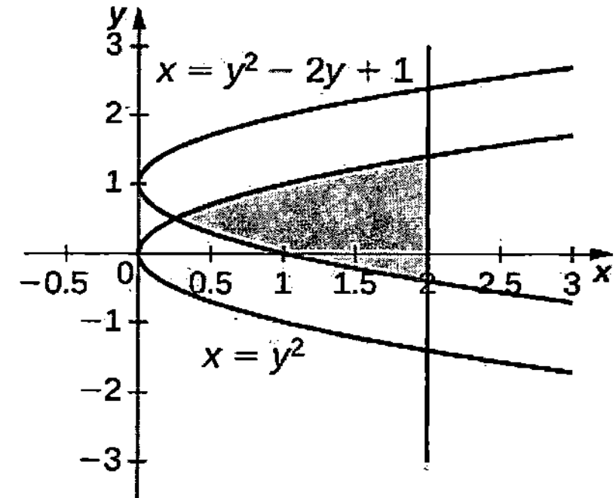

15.9074 units^3

159. $\frac{1}{3}\pi r^2 h$ units^3

161. $\pi r^2 h$ units^3

163. πa^2 units^3

165. $2\sqrt{26}$

167. $2\sqrt{17}$

169. $\frac{\pi}{6}\left(17\sqrt{17} - 5\sqrt{5}\right)$

171. $\frac{13\sqrt{13} - 8}{27}$

173. $\frac{4}{3}$

175. 2.0035

177. $\frac{123}{32}$

179. 10

181. $\frac{20}{3}$

183. $\frac{1}{675}\left(229\sqrt{229} - 8\right)$

185. $\frac{1}{8}\left(4\sqrt{5} + \ln\left(9 + 4\sqrt{5}\right)\right)$

187. 1.201

189. 15.2341

191. $\frac{49\pi}{3}$

193. $70\pi\sqrt{2}$

195. 8π

197. $120\pi\sqrt{26}$

199. $\frac{\pi}{6}(17\sqrt{17} - 1)$

201. $9\sqrt{2}\pi$

203. $\frac{10\sqrt{10}\pi}{27}\left(73\sqrt{73} - 1\right)$

205. 25.645

207. 2π

209. 10.5017

211. 23 ft

213. 2

215. Answers may vary

217. For more information, look up Gabriel's Horn.

219. 150 ft-lb

221. 200 J

223. 1 J

225. $\frac{39}{2}$

227. $\ln(243)$

229. $\frac{332\pi}{15}$

231. 100π

233. $20\pi\sqrt{15}$

235. 6 J

237. 5 cm

239. 36 J

241. 18,750 ft-lb

243. $\frac{32}{3} \times 10^9$ ft-lb

245. 8.65×10^5 J

247. a. 3,000,000 lb, b. 749,000 lb

249. 23.25π million ft-lb

251. $\frac{A\rho H^2}{2}$

253. Answers may vary

255. $\frac{5}{4}$

257. $\left(\frac{2}{3}, \frac{2}{3}\right)$

259. $\left(\frac{7}{4}, \frac{3}{2}\right)$

261. $\frac{3L}{4}$

263. $\frac{\pi}{2}$

265. $\frac{e^2+1}{e^2-1}$

267. $\frac{\pi^2-4}{\pi}$

269. $\frac{1}{4}\left(1+e^2\right)$

271. $\left(\frac{a}{3}, \frac{b}{3}\right)$

273. $\left(0, \frac{\pi}{8}\right)$

275. $(0, 3)$

277. $\left(0, \frac{4}{\pi}\right)$

279. $\left(\frac{5}{8}, \frac{1}{3}\right)$

281. $\frac{m\pi}{3}$

283. $\pi a^2 b$

285. $\left(\frac{4}{3\pi}, \frac{4}{3\pi}\right)$

287. $\left(\frac{1}{2}, \frac{2}{5}\right)$

289. $\left(0, \frac{28}{9\pi}\right)$

291. Center of mass: $\left(\frac{a}{6}, \frac{4a^2}{5}\right)$, volume: $\frac{2\pi a^4}{9}$

293. Volume: $2\pi^2 a^2 (b+a)$

295. $\frac{1}{x}$

297. $-\frac{1}{x(\ln x)^2}$

299. $\ln(x+1)+C$

301. $\ln(x)+1$

303. $\cot(x)$

305. $\frac{7}{x}$

307. $\csc(x)\sec x$

309. $-2\tan x$

311. $\frac{1}{2}\ln\left(\frac{5}{3}\right)$

313. $2-\frac{1}{2}\ln(5)$

315. $\frac{1}{\ln(2)}-1$

317. $\frac{1}{2}\ln(2)$

319. $\frac{1}{3}(\ln x)^3$

321. $\frac{2x^3}{\sqrt{x^2+1}\sqrt{x^2-1}}$

323. $x^{-2-(1/x)}(\ln x - 1)$

325. ex^{e-1}

327. 1

329. $-\frac{1}{x^2}$

331. $\pi - \ln(2)$

333. $\frac{1}{x}$

335. $e^5 - 6\text{ units}^2$

337. $\ln(4) - 1\text{ units}^2$

339. 2.8656

341. 3.1502

349. True

351. False; $k = \frac{\ln(2)}{t}$

353. 20 hours

355. No. The relic is approximately 871 years old.

357. 71.92 years

359. 5 days 6 hours 27 minutes

361. 12

363. 8.618%

365. $6766.76

367. 9 hours 13 minutes

369. 239,179 years

371. $P'(t) = 43e^{0.01604t}$. The population is always increasing.

373. The population reaches 10 billion people in 2027.

375. $P'(t) = 2.259e^{0.06407t}$. The population is always increasing.

377. e^x and e^{-x}

379. Answers may vary

381. Answers may vary

383. Answers may vary

385. $3\sinh(3x+1)$

387. $-\tanh(x)\text{sech}(x)$

389. $4\cosh(x)\sinh(x)$

391. $\frac{x\,\text{sech}^2\left(\sqrt{x^2+1}\right)}{\sqrt{x^2+1}}$

393. $6\sinh^5(x)\cosh(x)$

395. $\frac{1}{2}\sinh(2x+1)+C$

397. $\frac{1}{2}\sinh^2\left(x^2\right)+C$

399. $\frac{1}{3}\cosh^3(x)+C$

401. $\ln(1+\cosh(x))+C$

403. $\cosh(x)+\sinh(x)+C$

405. $\frac{4}{1-16x^2}$

407. $\frac{\sinh(x)}{\sqrt{\cosh^2(x)+1}}$

409. $-\csc(x)$

411. $-\frac{1}{\left(x^2-1\right)\tanh^{-1}(x)}$

413. $\frac{1}{a}\tanh^{-1}\left(\frac{x}{a}\right)+C$

415. $\sqrt{x^2+1}+C$

417. $\cosh^{-1}(e^x)+C$

419. Answers may vary

421. 37.30

423. $y=\frac{1}{c}\cosh(cx)$

425. -0.521095

427. 10

Review Exercises

435. False

437. False

439. $32\sqrt{3}$

441. $\frac{162\pi}{5}$

443. a. 4, b. $\frac{128\pi}{7}$, c. $\frac{64\pi}{5}$

445. a. 1.949, b. 21.952, c. 17.099

447. a. $\frac{31}{6}$, b. $\frac{452\pi}{15}$, c. $\frac{31\pi}{6}$

449. 245.282

451. Mass: $\frac{1}{2}$, center of mass: $\left(\frac{18}{35},\frac{9}{11}\right)$

453. $\sqrt{17}+\frac{1}{8}\ln(33+8\sqrt{17})$

455. Volume: $\frac{3\pi}{4}$, surface area: $\pi\left(\sqrt{2}-\sinh^{-1}(1)+\sinh^{-1}(16)-\frac{\sqrt{257}}{16}\right)$

457. 11:02 a.m.

459. $\pi(1+\sinh(1)\cosh(1))$

INDEX